锲而不舍

脊柱侧凸矫形内固定奠基者哈灵顿

【美】马克·A. 阿舍 **著**

杨惠林　郑召民　海　涌　仉建国 **主译**

季甜甜 **主译助理**

王金熙　邱　勇　吕国华 **主审**

苏州大学出版社

著作权合同登记号　图字:10-2023-306 号
Dogged Persistence: Harrington, Post- polio Scoliosis, and the Origin of Spine Instrumentation by Marc A. Asher

图书在版编目(CIP)数据

锲而不舍 : 脊柱侧凸矫形内固定奠基者哈灵顿 : 英汉对照 / (美) 马克·A.阿舍 (Marc A. Asher) 著 ; 杨惠林等主译. -- 苏州 : 苏州大学出版社, 2023.9
书名原文: Dogged Persistence:Harrington,Post-polio Scoliosis,and the Origin of Spine Instrumentation
ISBN 978-7-5672-4508-2

Ⅰ. ①锲… Ⅱ. ①马… ②杨… Ⅲ. ①哈灵顿-传记-英、汉 Ⅳ. ①K837.126.2

中国国家版本馆 CIP 数据核字(2023)第 157812 号

书　　名　锲而不舍——脊柱侧凸矫形内固定奠基者哈灵顿
　　　　　QIE'ERBUSHE—JIZHU CETU JIAOXING NEIGUDING DIANJIZHE HALINGDUN
著　　者　马克·A. 阿舍
主　　译　杨惠林　郑召民　海　涌　仉建国
责任编辑　倪　青
助理编辑　闫莹莹
出版发行　苏州大学出版社
　　　　　(地址:苏州市十梓街 1 号　邮编:215006)
印　　刷　苏州工业园区美柯乐制版印务有限责任公司
开　　本　787 mm×1 092 mm　1/16
印　　张　50
字　　数　952 千
版　　次　2023 年 9 月第 1 版
　　　　　2023 年 9 月第 1 次印刷
书　　号　ISBN 978-7-5672-4508-2
定　　价　210.00 元

苏州大学出版社营销部　电话:0512-67481020
苏州大学出版社网址　http://www.sudapress.com
苏州大学出版社邮箱　sdcbs@suda.edu.cn

译者名单

陈凡	陈建	陈亮	陈其昕	初同伟
董健	范顺武	方向前	冯世庆	葛隽
顾勇	郭辰	海涌	郗定均	何达
黄宇明	季甜甜	姜横	姜建元	姜为民
金大地	邝冠明	邝磊	李明	李危石
李泽民	李章富	梁裕	刘海鹰	刘宏建
刘辉	刘立岷	刘瑞端	刘滔	刘晓光
刘新宇	刘亚军	刘义灏	柳善睿	卢旭华
罗卓荆	马文政	毛克亚	孟斌	钱邦平
桑宏勋	申才良	沈怀霜	史建刚	宋跃明
宋智博	孙端	陶惠人	王华	王建强
王建儒	王连雷	王挽涛	王迎松	王征
徐宝山	杨操	杨惠林	殷国勇	于滨生
原所茂	袁文	曾建成	张劲	张卿义
张一健	张忠民	仉建国	赵杰	赵钇伟
郑鲁豫	郑召民	钟锦涛	钟培言	周许辉
朱剑	朱悦	朱泽章	邹俊	

Figure 1 *Paul R. Harrington in the mid-1960s.* (*Harrington Archives*)
图 1　保罗 · R. 哈灵顿。20 世纪 60 年代中期(哈灵顿档案馆)

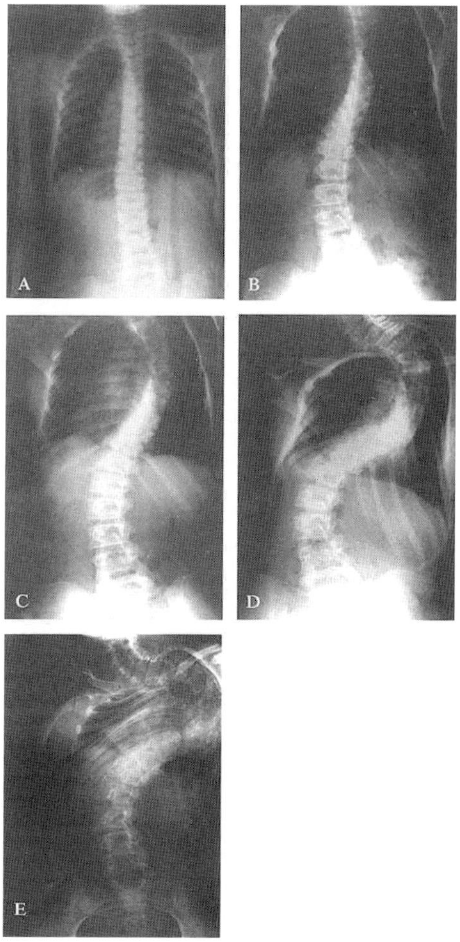

Figure 2 *Radiographic sequence documenting the progressive scoliosis of a patient who suffered paralytic poliomyelitis at age five years*: (*A*) *at seven years*, (*B*) *eleven years*, (*C*) *twelve years*, (*D*) *thirteen years*, *and* (*E*) *at fifteen years in 1959.* (*Harrington Archives*)
图 2　这组 X 光片记录了一例五岁时患麻痹性脊髓灰质炎病人出现的进展性脊柱侧凸: (A) 7 岁, (B) 11 岁,(C) 12 岁,(D) 13 岁,(E) 15 岁(1959 年)(哈灵顿档案馆)

(季甜甜 译　郑召民　杨惠林 审校)

中文版序一

时光流逝，一转眼我已经成了一名“90后”。原不想再做什么，然而得知原我院毕业的三位博士生杨惠林、郑召民、王金熙，准备翻译一本美国编写的《锲而不舍——脊柱侧凸矫形内固定奠基者哈灵顿》，邀我为本书撰写一篇序文，我应允了，这给我重新注入了生命的活力，让我感到无比荣幸。这一切都要感谢我学生的邀请和信任。

本书出版的目的，在于记载哈灵顿的业绩，使其智慧的宝库代代相传。医学史是一门科学，德国医学史家苏德霍夫（Kail Sudhoff）曾写道，历史的回顾是预告未来最好的借鉴。书中生动地展示了要成功研制哈灵顿内固定并对其进行创新所需的坚持不懈的决心。哈灵顿最初的思路，表现出许多不确定性，因此成为被质疑的对象。人的生命是有限的，他将有限的生命投入到无限的医疗事业中，这是他的人生价值，真正做到了人性的美和仁术的美。

1916年脊髓灰质炎开始在北美流行，导致大量病人出现严重的功能损害和残疾，有些甚至造成脊柱侧凸。在这万般无奈的情况下，究竟该何去何从？应该说受脊髓灰质炎流行影响，自1949年起，哈灵顿一直在考虑、推敲和研究，不断激发灵感，增强创意思维。他有独特的魅力，把医生这个职业，视为人生的使命，固执追求。

20世纪50年代中后期，随着疫苗的研发成功，脊髓灰质炎在美国的患病人数逐渐减少，从而使哈灵顿棒手术应用的范围扩大到了特发性脊柱侧凸、脊柱创伤、退行性疾病和滑脱等。

1955年后，在进行脊柱侧凸矫治的过程中，他深感必须将生物力学方面的知识融入，他是第一个将生物力学与脊柱内植物设计结合起来的人。最终在1959年，他推出了自行设计的钩棒系统。他又认为基础科学是脊柱侧凸的病因学和发病学，特别是分子医学研究的最终解决之道。

早在1959年，他建立了一个病案资料数据库。1960年，他每周会做5~7例手术，并向世界各地演示他的手术。1966年，他积极参与，与同道共同创建了脊柱侧凸研究学会（Scoliosis Research Society，SRS），并在他生命的最后15年，不断支持和关爱该学会的运作。1973年，他担任脊柱侧凸研究学会第四届主席，并确立了学会的宗旨和目标。

1968 年秋，他心脏病发作，至此他已做了 1 500 多例手术。20 世纪 70 年代初，他因身体原因，委托他的学生迪克森，继承他的工作，希望迪克森不忘初心，继续前行。

这本巨著的完成，要归功于马克・阿舍博士。他呕心沥血，花了四年多时间来撰写这本书。书中叙述了脊柱畸形外科治疗的演变历史和一个将概念变为现实的大师背后鲜为人知并充满传奇的故事。他收集和保存了与本书相关的核心材料，并使之成为堪萨斯大学医学中心哈灵顿档案馆的文物。

哈灵顿器械是一个平面、两维矫正技术，80—90 年代中期，国内大多还是应用哈灵顿-卢克技术。20 世纪 80 年代，北京协和医院吴之康教授率先将脊柱畸形手术治疗引入中国。在加拿大阿姆斯特朗教授的支持下，开展了哈灵顿-卢克技术，并推广全国。传统的脊柱侧凸矫形技术，如凹侧撑开凸侧加压技术等可获得较好的矫形。

20 世纪 60 年代中期，哈灵顿首次尝试置入椎弓根螺钉治疗腰椎滑脱症，近年来开展的全椎弓根钉技术，矫形效果更是大大提升。但应该认识到，哈灵顿器械是脊柱侧凸矫正治疗史上的一个里程碑。应用哈灵顿器械的钩棒进行凹侧撑开凸侧加压的方法，25 年来久盛不衰。哈灵顿技术就是脊柱侧凸矫正治疗从原始方法到现代技术的基础和转折点。

哈灵顿于 1980 年逝世，但他的精神为世人所钦佩、所颂扬。因为他敢于维护自己的信念，敢于坚持创新。他成为我们这一代医务界的楷模。哈灵顿的人生的意义与价值，就在于对人类健康发展承上启下、承前启后的责任感。

本书的出版首先要感谢哈灵顿将其所有专业资料赠给他的母校堪萨斯大学医学中心档案馆存档和管理。在撰写这本书的这些年，马克・阿舍博士曾向许多人寻求帮助和指导，包括他的夫人和女儿也为此付出了很多。

在此，我很荣幸地向国内读者推荐本书。得知中英文双语版即将在中国出版发行，我心中十分高兴。由于翻译必会有分歧和争论，特别译者们都是在繁忙的医疗、教学和科研工作任务之外完成的，译文必然会有谬误不妥之处。衷心希望读者们给予指正。

本书的出版承蒙苏州大学苏州医学院和苏州大学附属第一医院领导大力支持和美国堪萨斯大学医学中心骨科哈灵顿杰出教授兼哈灵顿分子骨科实验室主任王金熙博士的帮助。谨在此致以衷心的谢忱。

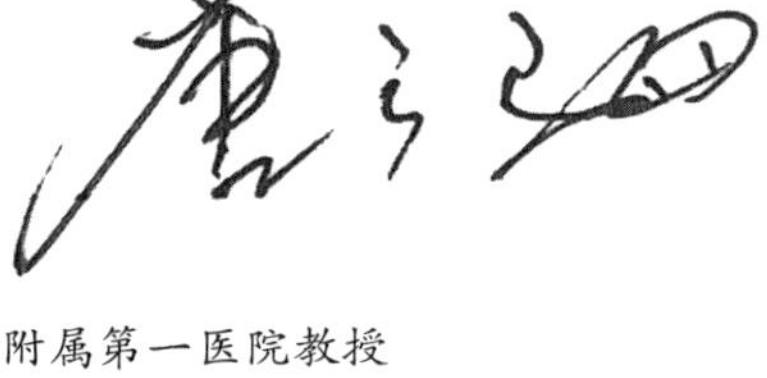

苏州大学附属第一医院教授
中华医学会骨科学分会副主任委员（第五届）
中华医学会骨科学分会脊柱外科学组组长（第三、四届）

中文版序二

在医学辉煌的发展历程中，有着许多杰出的学者和研究者，他们的贡献不仅推动了学科的发展，还为人类社会带来了巨大的变化。保罗·兰德尔·哈灵顿教授无疑是其中的耀眼之星。作为一位卓越的脊柱外科医学科学家，他在自己的领域取得了非凡的成就，为现代脊柱外科的临床治疗与基础研究树立了崭新的标杆。

哈灵顿教授的学术生涯充满了无数的辉煌时刻和里程碑式的成就。他以深厚的学术造诣和卓越的创新能力，为人类对脊柱外科的理解和应用做出了重大贡献。他的杰出成就和追求卓越的精神，不仅深刻影响了他所从事的学科领域，也对全球科学界产生了广泛而深远的影响。

哈灵顿教授具备着卓越的智慧和博大的胸怀，他始终将科学的进步和社会的发展紧密相连。他的研究不仅解开了脊柱生物力学中的许多谜团，还为脊柱外科的临床治疗提供了创新思路。他始终坚持以实证为基础，推动科学研究与应用相结合，为人类健康福祉不懈努力。

在本传记中，我们将深入探索哈灵顿教授的人生经历和学术成就，追溯他在科学界的辉煌历程。他的故事将鼓舞并激励那些追求知识和追求卓越的年轻学者，同时也将向广大读者展示一个充满希望和机遇的科学时代。

作为世界脊柱外科领域的先驱，哈灵顿教授用他的智慧、勇气和坚持，书写着属于自己的传奇。他的学术成就和人格魅力将使这个传记成为一本真正意义上的启迪之书，引领读者走向更加辉煌的未来。

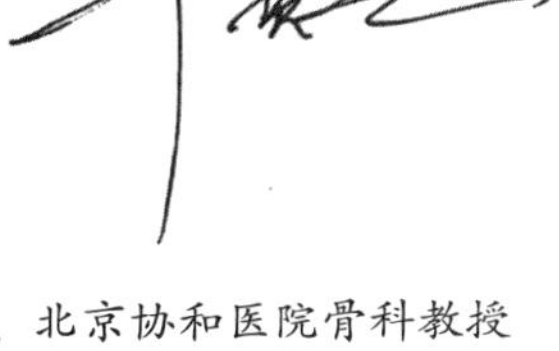

中国工程院院士，北京协和医院骨科教授
中华医学会骨科学分会主任委员（第六、七、八届）
中华医学会骨科学分会脊柱外科学组组长（第七、八届）

中文版序三

在科学和医学领域，一些杰出的个人通过他们的贡献和奉献，成为推动人类医学进步的力量。他们的工作不仅改变了我们对世界的理解，还为未来的研究和创新铺平了道路。在这个群体中，保罗·兰德尔·哈灵顿教授是一位备受尊敬的科学家，他的工作对骨科和脊柱疾病的治疗产生了深远的影响。

本书的目的是向读者介绍哈灵顿教授的职业生涯，以及他在骨科领域的突出贡献。通过详细的研究和调查，我们将探索他的科学成就和对医学界的影响。此外，我们还将深入了解他的早年生活、教育背景和对于骨科学的热爱。

哈灵顿教授的传奇之旅始于他对医学的热情。在他的职业生涯早期，他专注于骨科疾病的治疗，特别是针对脊柱的疾病和畸形的治疗。通过不懈的努力和卓越的才能，他开发了一种创新的脊柱内固定器械——“哈灵顿棒”。这一系统主要用于矫正脊柱的畸形和脊柱不稳。这一系统结合了医学和工程学的原理，通过植入金属棒和钩来稳定脊柱，使其保持正确的姿势和正常的功能。这项创新在骨科手术中引起了革命性的变革，极大地提高了脊柱矫形的手术成功率和患者的生活质量。

哈灵顿教授的工作对生物医学工程领域产生了广泛的影响。他的创新激发了更多生物工程领域专家和研究人员对于改进脊柱矫正技术的兴趣，推动了医疗器械的发展和创新。他的成果也激发了更多跨学科合作，使医学专业人员和工程师之间的合作变得更加紧密，以共同解决医疗挑战和改善患者治疗效果。

本书还将深入探讨哈灵顿教授的影响力和领导力。他通过多年的教学和指导，培养了无数骨科医生和研究人员，为下一代医学专业人员的发展奠定了坚实的基础。他不仅对学术界有重大贡献，还在世界各地的医疗机构和骨科手术中发挥了重要作用。

本书还将结合时代背景详细讲述哈灵顿教授的个人故事，让读者更好地了解这位杰出医学家的品格。他的职业生涯充满了挑战、奉献和成就，他的热情、智慧和勇气在医学界留下了深刻的印记，激励着无数人追求卓越和创新。

通过本书，我们希望向读者展示哈灵顿教授作为一位杰出的医学家的非凡人生。他的成就和贡献不仅对骨科学产生了深远影响，而且为整个医学领域树立了榜样。我们相信，通过深入了解哈灵顿教授的故事，读者们将从中汲取灵感和启示，不仅为自己的职业生涯而努力，也为人类健康的未来做出积极的贡献。

中国工程院院士，北京积水潭医院教授
中华医学会骨科学分会主任委员（第十届）
中华医学会骨科学分会脊柱外科学组组长（第十一届）

中文版序四

Dogged Persistence by Marc Asher is an important chronicle of one of the icons and innovators of spine surgery, Paul Harrington. Having his story translated to Mandarin Chinese, so that it can be read and understood by such a large proportion of the world's population and surgeons will allow a deeper understanding of the challenges and persistence that Harrington faced as he designed one of the earliest spine implants for the treatment of scoliosis. While many Chinese doctors understand English, I expect that having the personal story in their native tongue will allow them to better appreciate the more subtle details of his struggles. It is not till we appreciate and learn from our history as spine surgeons that we can truly build on and advance our field.

马克·阿舍的《锲而不舍——脊柱侧凸矫形内固定奠基者哈灵顿》是一本关于脊柱外科的代表人物和创新者之一保罗·哈灵顿的传记。将他的故事翻译成中文，以便让占世界人口如此大比例的中国人，特别是中国的外科医生们能够阅读和了解哈灵顿的故事，从而使人们更深入地理解哈灵顿在设计最早用于治疗脊柱侧凸的矫形器械时所面临的挑战和他的坚持不懈的精神，有极其重大的价值。虽然许多中国医生都懂英语，但我还是希望能用他们的母语讲述这个故事，这样能让他们更好地了解哈灵顿当年奋斗时更加微妙的细节。只有从脊柱外科医生的角度去欣赏和学习这段历史，我们才能真正在此基础上建立并推进脊柱外科发展。

Drs. Yang Huilin and Zheng Zhaomin are to be commended for their foresight in recognizing the need for this translation. *Dogged Persistence* is a particularly memorable book because of the inclusion of so many of Harrington's original drawings. The evolution of his thoughts and understanding of biomechanics of metal, bone and scoliosis reminds us of how far we have come but yet how we still have to go in the understanding and treatment of spine deformities. Marc Asher's writing of this book was completed only a few years before he passed away and was a true labor of love, respecting and honoring one of the pillars of spine deformity surgery as well as the early formative years of the Scoliosis Research Society. His own dogged persistence in the writing of this book as well as his own design of the Isola instrumentation system for scoliosis treatment reminds of the dedication that our predecessors brought to the goal of improving the lives of our spine and scoliosis patients.

杨惠林和郑召民医生很有远见，认识到翻译本书的必要性，值得赞扬。这是一本特别令人难忘的书，因为它包含了哈灵顿的许多原始绘图。哈灵顿对金属、骨骼和脊柱侧凸的生物力学的思想和理解的演变提醒我们，在理解和治疗脊柱畸形方面，我们已经走了多远，以及我们仍然需要走多远。这本书是马克·阿舍在去世前几年完成的，是一份真正的凝聚爱意的劳动成果，是对脊柱侧凸研究学会建立早期脊柱畸形外科支柱技术之一的尊重和纪念。他对写作这本书的坚持，以及他自己设计的 Isola 脊柱侧凸治疗器械系统，都是在提醒我们：前辈们为改善脊柱和脊柱侧凸患者的生活质量而做出的奉献。

Serena Shaw Hu, MD
胡莎盈

Professor and Vice Chair
Department of Orthopedic Surgery
And, by courtesy, Professor of Neurological Surgery
Stanford University
斯坦福大学骨科教授和副主任，神经外科教授

President, Scoliosis Research Society 2023
3rd Chinese President of the SRS
after Donald P.K. Chan (1998), Kenneth M.C. Cheung (2017)
2023 年度脊柱侧凸研究学会主席
曾炳权（1998）和 张文智（2017）之后的第 3 位华人主席

中文版前言

脊柱外科一直是骨科领域发展最快的学科之一，有关脊柱的专著众多，但专门聚焦人文与学术的书籍甚少，多年来仅有马克·阿舍教授撰写的《锲而不舍》一书。本书是作者历时四年，利用堪萨斯大学医学中心哈灵顿档案馆的第一手资料书写的哈灵顿传记以及脊柱侧凸的学术研究内容。

《锲而不舍》一书以哈灵顿成功研发脊柱外科第一个矫形内固定系统的艰辛过程为主线，叙述了脊柱畸形外科治疗的演变历史，涉及脊柱侧凸研究学会成立的过程及成立后最初15年间学术年会的主要内容。该书不仅有丰富的学术内容，还介绍了一位将概念变为现实的脊柱外科大师背后许多鲜为人知的生活和工作轶事。此外为帮助读者更好地了解哈灵顿其人，本书开篇讲述了哈灵顿的故乡堪萨斯城在世纪之交的情况，他中小学时代的成长和发展，从考入医学院到成为一名专科医生及二战时的军医生涯。书中还简要介绍了脊髓灰质炎疾病的诊疗史，以引出哈灵顿对脊髓灰质炎后所导致的脊柱侧凸的反应和研发内固定棒的想法。最后介绍了他成功获得的各种业内荣誉及对母校的回馈。本书也介绍了他如何对脊柱侧凸开展临床研究，如何收集资料、建立数据库，以及他是如何对自己终生痴迷的特发性脊柱侧凸进行病因学研究的。

哈灵顿矫形内固定系统的研发经历了1949到1959年十年的酝酿期，1960年开始临床推广应用，随后，直到1984年科特雷尔–杜布塞特器械（CD）在北美推出才逐渐淡出市场。改革开放后，我国于1981年开始引进哈灵顿矫形内固定系统并持续应用了十余年，到20世纪90年代才为椎弓根钉棒所取代。哈灵顿不仅研发了第一个成功的脊柱内固定钩棒器械系统，本书中专门有一章还介绍了他在1966年应用设计的椎弓根螺钉治疗重度脊柱滑脱症，这促使了1995年美国食品药品监督管理局批准椎弓根螺钉用于脊柱滑脱等疾病的治疗。过去几十年里，脊柱外科两大内固定系统：哈灵顿矫形内固定系统和椎弓根螺钉系统的成功研发和应用，堪称脊柱外科的两大里程碑。

今天阅读本书，具有非常重要的现实意义。虽然脊柱外科临床上已不再使用哈灵顿棒，但哈灵顿在研发创新中锲而不舍的精神，以及团队合作的模式，仍是一个成功医工结合的典范，值得今天的临床医生学习。此外，国际脊柱研究学会成立后最初15年间讨论的一些学术问题，如早期的撑开性截瘫，矢状面失衡，特发性脊柱侧凸病因学，后期对早发性侧凸和退变性侧凸的治疗难题，尽管过去了四十多年，仍然是我们今天研究的热点和面临的挑战。可惜一代伟人哈灵顿在1968年一场大病后，此后十余年虽仍投身于脊柱侧凸事业，但在1980年过早去世，享年69岁，否则今日，说不定他仍能与我们一起探讨和分享脊柱侧凸的学术问题。

四位主要译者通读原著，一致认为本书既有一定的学术价值，又有很好的趣味性，遂决定组织国内著名脊柱和脊柱侧凸领域的专家翻译为中文，呈现给我国同道。所有译校者都是临床一线医生，在完成繁重的脊柱外科临床工作的同时，利用业余时间，结合自身经验，忠实于原文，使此书中文版得以面世。考虑到诸多英语术语在中文中难以找到确切的词句表达，决定以中英文双语的形式出版，这样既可以弥补上述不足，读者阅读中文时也可以同时浏览英语原著，潜移默化地学习英语专业词汇，尤其对于年轻医生来说，可谓“一举两得”。

这本书是一部学术和人文的专著，我们已尽可能把原文呈现给各位读者，但正如本书原作者在前言中所言：“本书是从北美人的视角来撰写的”，因此希望我们的读者可以用批判的眼光和审慎的态度来阅读、鉴赏本书的内容。

本书翻译出版过程中，尽管译者做了最大努力，由于时间紧迫，水平有限，错误之处在所难免，敬希各位同道批评指正。感谢为本书出版付出辛勤劳动的所有同道，正是大家的共同努力，才使本书得以顺利面世。

杨惠林
苏州大学附属第一医院骨科主任，大外科主任
苏州大学骨科研究所所长，教授，主任医师，博士生导师

郑召民
中山大学附属第一医院脊柱外科副主任
教授，主任医师，博士生导师

海涌
首都医科大学附属北京朝阳医院骨科主任
教授，主任医师，博士生导师

仉建国
中国医学科学院北京协和医院骨科主任
教授，主任医师，博士生导师

FOREWORD
序 言

by Jesse H. Dickson

杰西·H. 迪克森

I first met Paul Harrington in the spring of 1962. I was a first-year orthopedic resident rotating through his service. I had heard of Dr. Harrington and what he had developed in regard to the surgical treatment of scoliosis, as well as some of the negative comments other physicians had made. My duty was to assist him in surgery of which he would do five to seven cases per week when he was in Houston. This was probably the most active time of his life for he had numerous visitors, traveled extensively, and demonstrated his operation in various cities and countries throughout the world.

1962 年春天，我作为第一年的骨科住院医生，第一次见到保罗·哈灵顿，当时我正在参加轮转。我听说过哈灵顿医生在脊柱侧凸手术方面的成就，也听说过其他医生对他的一些负面评价。在休斯敦时，他每周会主刀 5~7 例手术，而我则在手术中充当助手。这可能是他一生中最活跃的时期，因为他有着众多访客，同时周游世界，在不同城市和国家演示他的手术。

As I helped him in surgery, it became very apparent to me he had an excellent procedure. I also observed he was an extremely skilled surgeon, as well as courteous to those who worked with him. Above all else he had empathy for his patients and what they were going through.

在协助他进行手术的过程中，我发现他拥有出色且熟练的手术技巧，并且对和他一起工作的人非常有礼貌。最重要的是，他非常体恤他的病人，同情他们的遭遇。

Paul was meticulous about everything he did: from the design of a 54-foot aluminum catamaran, its structure based on the design of bone, to his mastery of musical instruments, both the trumpet and organ. Any subject he became interested in he studied to the point where he became an expert, such as when high fidelity first came on the scene and photography.

保罗在他所做的一切事情上都极致认真，他既能从骨架开始设计一艘 54 英尺①长的铝制双体船，也能纯熟地演奏小号和管风琴等乐器。他对任何感兴趣的事都会学习到专业的程度，比如高保真电影技术和摄影技术。

He seemed never to let those who made derogatory remarks about his procedure bother him. I never heard him say an unkind word about his fellow orthopedists or acquaintances.

他似乎从不在意那些对他手术指指点点的人。我从未听他说过一句对骨科同行或熟人的不友善的话。

When he had his heart attack in the fall of 1968, he sent word for me to see him when I came into work. In an ICU bed, he was his usual upbeat self. He said, "I don't know what is going to happen to me, but I want you to take over my practice. All I ask of you is to keep it going." I knew he was referring to the care of his patients. I told myself that it also meant to collect his work and present it to the orthopedic community. Up to that point, Paul had not published up-to-date case series although he had performed 1,500–2,000 surgeries.

1968 年秋天，他心脏病发作时，他让我在上班的时候去见他。当时他在重症监护室的病床上，还像平常一样乐观。他说："我不知道我能不能好，但我想让你接管我的工作。我希望你能继续前行。"我知道他指的是处理好他的病人，同时也清楚这也意味着收集他做的病例资料，并将其展示给骨科学界的同行。在那之前，尽管保罗已经做了 1 500~2 000 例手术，但他新的系列病例资料尚未公开发表。

Paul was an unusual thinker. He approached scoliosis as a structural abnormality of a segmented column, not as a disease. Therefore, it had to be managed in a mechanical

① 1 英尺 = 30.48 厘米，编者注。后无特殊说明，均为编者注。

way. As such, he taught himself structural engineering principles, as well as metallurgical properties of stainless steel to such a degree he could converse easily with any bio-mechanical engineer. He also anticipated that his instruments would be used in treating fractured spines, spondylolisthesis and degenerative arthritis of the vertebra, and he first inserted pedicle screws in the mid-1960s.

保罗的思维非常独特。他认为脊柱侧凸是脊柱的节段性结构异常，而非疾病。因此，它必须以机械矫形的方法进行治疗。为此，他自学了结构工程原理和不锈钢的冶金特性，以至于他可以轻松地与任何生物力学工程师交流。他还预期他的器械将用于治疗脊柱骨折、滑脱和退行性脊柱疾病。在 20 世纪 60 年代中期，他首次使用了椎弓根螺钉。

Paul returned to his practice part-time in the early 1970s. In surgical cases I would expose the spine, he would do the instrumentation, and I would do the fusion and closure. One day after finishing a case, he and I walked down to the coffee shop. He commented that he could still do his operation better than anyone in the world, but not as good as before his heart attack. He then said, “I quit.”

保罗在 20 世纪 70 年代初重返岗位，但不再担任全职工作。在手术过程中，我负责完成脊柱的显露，然后由他完成内固定，我最后进行融合和缝合切口。有一天，在完成一例手术后，他和我步行去了一家咖啡馆。他说，虽然他的手术仍然可以做得比世界上任何人都好，但已经不如心脏病发作前的自己了。他接着说：“我不干了。”

During the years after his retirement, he and I would talk about whatever subject he was interested in at the time. It was fascinating to hear his thoughts on topics, which varied from diets to politicians and almost any subject you could name.

He was a dynamic individual and a great mentor.

在他退休后的几年里，任何只要他感兴趣的话题我们都会畅谈不拘。从饮食，到政客，任何你能想到的话题，他都能提出独特的见解，简直太有趣了。

他是一个充满活力的人，一位伟大的导师。

Jesse H. Dickson, MD

杰西 · H. 迪克森，医学博士

Professor Emeritus, Orthopedic Surgery
骨科荣休教授
Baylor College of Medicine
贝勒医学院

（黄宇明 译　郑召民 邝磊 王建儒 审校）

FOREWORD
序 言

by Behrooz A. Akbarnia and Nathan Lebwohl

贝鲁兹·A. 阿克巴尼亚、内森·莱布沃尔

Many of us may not remember those days when we treated scoliosis with Risser or localizer casts, opening the wedges in the plaster and applying a tumbuckle with the hope that correction would not cause any skin sores. The patients endured months of bedrest and multiple surgeries with mediocre correction of deformity and frequent failure to maintain that correction. In comparison, today's surgical techniques for correction of scoliosis are nothing short of miraculous. Paul Harrington's operation was the turning point from primitive methods to the modern era of scoliosis care.

我们当中许多人可能已经忘记当初用里泽石膏或局部矫形石膏治疗脊柱侧凸的苦日子了。当时要在石膏中锯开一个楔形的口，然后用铰链拉紧开口对脊柱侧凸进行矫形，同时希望石膏不要压伤皮肤。患者除需要忍受卧床数月之久外，还需要接受多次效果平平的矫形手术，最糟糕的是矫形效果通常无法维持。相比之下，今天的脊柱侧凸矫形手术技术简直就是奇迹，而保罗·哈灵顿的手术方法就是脊柱侧凸治疗从原始方法到现代技术的转折点。

Tasked with the care of thousands of children suffering from the devastating effects of polio, Harrington recognized that existing techniques were inadequate and probably detrimental for treating the spinal deformities that so often followed after recovery from viral infection. He began to search for a way to prevent small curves from worsening. Harrington believed that internal mechanical support was needed to solve this problem and courageously persisted to find a solution in spite of many early failures and criticism. His courage and his commitment to excellence created the foundation on which we have built the modern surgical treatment of scoliosis, as it is known today.

那个年代，成千上万的儿童遭受了脊髓灰质炎的灾难性打击。即使感染康复后，仍有很多患者出现脊柱畸形。哈灵顿意识到当时的技术不仅不能有效治疗这些脊柱畸形，而且可能起到反作用。于是，他开始寻找一种新方法阻止一些轻度脊柱侧凸进一步恶化。哈灵顿认为，内部的机械性支撑才是解决这个问题的根本方法。尽管早期经历了许多的失败，受到了许多的批判，他还是勇敢地在这个方向上坚持寻找解决方案。正如我们今天所知道的那样，他的勇气与对卓越的追求奠定了现代脊柱侧凸手术治疗的基础。

Harrington's contributions to the modern care of scoliosis and to the practice of spinal surgery extend well beyond the invention of a hook and rod instrumentation system. He showed us by example how to collect data and share results for the purpose of research and audit, so that we could continue what we have done correctly and avoid repeating our mistakes. He openly and honestly presented his early failed results and continued to share his outcomes through regular communication with other surgeons by presentations, publications, and travel.

哈灵顿对现代脊柱侧凸治疗与脊柱外科的贡献远远不止钩棒内固定系统的发明。他通过病例教会我们如何收集数据和分享成果，以达到进行研究和探索的目的，让我们得以在正确的道路上继续前进，避免重蹈覆辙。他坦诚地向我们展示了他早期失败的教训，并通过会议演讲、发表文章和游学的方式与其他外科医生进行定期交流，分享他的成果。

Harrington's greatest contribution to teaching and research may have been his role in helping to create the Scoliosis Research Society and through his support and participation in that Society in the last 15 years of his life. When, with the encouragement of Vernon Nickel, David Levine proposed the formation of a scoliosis club in 1964, Harrington immediately pledged a donation of $1,000 for this purpose, the first contribution on record to the SRS. He played a key role in the early evolution of that society, in defining its purpose and goals, and emphasizing its role in education and research. He remained active, served as SRS president, and with his leadership elevated the Society to the next level and improved scoliosis care, not only for patients who suffered from poliomyelitis, but for all deformities of the spine.

哈灵顿对教学和研究的最大贡献可能是他帮助创建了脊柱侧凸研究学会，并在他生命的最后15年中支持和参与该学会的运作。1964年，在弗农·尼克尔的鼓励下，大卫·列维因提议成立一个脊柱侧凸研究学会，哈灵顿立即承诺为此捐赠1 000美元，成为自有记录以来脊柱侧凸研究学会收到的第一笔捐赠。他在该学会的早期发展中发挥了关键作用，确立了学会的宗旨和目标，并强调了它在教育和研究中的作用。他积极参与学会活动并曾担任脊柱侧凸研究学会主席。在他的带领下，学会水平大幅提升，脊柱侧凸的治疗也得到了改善，不仅仅是拯救了脊髓灰质炎患者，更是造福了所有脊柱畸形患者。

In this book, Marc Asher weaves the personal story of Paul Harrington into the larger story of scoliosis treatment beginning at its infancy with the operations of Hibbs, Albee, and Galloway. The book is also a documentary of the first 15 years of the Scoliosis Research Society, and the evolution and development of spine surgery during those years. Along with all that. Dr Asher takes us into turn-of-the century Kansas City, into school and onto the playing field with a young Paul Harrington and teaches us about the history of vaccines and drugs for the treatment and prevention of polio, the impetus for the founding of the FDA, the development of the halo device for cervical immobilization, and even the details surrounding the design and construction of Harrington's cruising catamaran motor sailboat. That this book is also a great read is a credit to Marc Asher, who devoted four years of his life to writing it and who has proven to have as much "dogged persistence" as Paul Harrington.

在这本书里，马克·阿舍从最早的希伯斯、阿尔比和加洛韦等人的手术方法开始，将保罗·哈灵顿的个人事迹汇入脊柱侧凸治疗史的大潮中。本书也记录了脊柱侧凸研究学会成立最初15年间脊柱外科的演变和发展历程。阿舍医生会带领我们穿越时光，回到世纪之交的堪萨斯城，走进学校和球场，认识年轻的保罗·哈灵顿，并向我们讲述疫苗和药物用于治疗和预防脊髓灰质炎的历史，以及建立美国食品药品监督管理局的原因，还有颈部制动的halo头环的研制，甚至是哈灵顿设计和建造巡航双体帆船的细节。这真的是一本巨作，也是马克·阿舍的荣誉之作，他花了四年时间来撰写这本书。事实证明，他和保罗·哈灵顿一样具有“锲而不舍”的精神。

As "Frenchy" Chuinard (chief surgeon at Shriners Hospital for Crippled Children in Portland, Oregon) wrote in thanking Harrington for his visit to lecture and operate: "There is no surgical contribution without the man—and knowing him adds to the great value." No one could have summed up more clearly the reason to read this book and learn not just about Harrington's hooks and rods, but about Paul Harrington the man, and about the circumstances that helped make him who he was. This book not only recounts the history of evolution of spine deformity surgery, it also introduces the untold stories behind the man who brought a concept to reality. It is a must read for students of medical history, and for anyone involved in the care of patients of all ages with spinal deformity.

正如乔伊纳德（俄勒冈州波特兰市施莱纳斯残疾儿童医院的首席外科医师）在感谢哈灵顿的访问演讲和手术时写道："没有他，就没有今天外科手术的成就，而了解他能够带来更多的收获。"通过阅读此书，不但可以了解哈灵顿的钩棒内固定系统，更能深入了解他的为人，以及造就他的生活环境。此书不仅叙述了脊柱畸形外科治疗的演变历史，还讲述了一位将概念变为现实的大师背后鲜为人知的故事。本书应为研读医学史的学生以及致力于治疗各年龄段脊柱畸形患者的医师的必读之作。

Behrooz A. Akbarnia, MD
贝鲁兹 · A. 阿克巴尼亚，医学博士
Historian and Past President, *Scoliosis Research Society*
脊柱侧凸研究学会前任主席及史学工作者
Nathan Lebwohl, MD
内森 · 莱布沃尔，医学博士
Historian, *Scoliosis Research Society* (2005-11)
脊柱侧凸研究学会史学工作者(2005—2011)

（黄宇明 译　郑召民　邝磊　王建儒 审校）

FOREWORD
序　言

by Christopher Crenner
克里斯托弗·克伦纳

You hold in your hands an unusual and valuable volume. This book tells the story of the development of Harrington Rods, the first successful spine instrumentation system for the connection of abnormal spinal curvature—or scoliosis. In explaining this revolution in spinal surgery, *Dogged Persistence* examines in humane detail the life and work of the inventor of the rods, Dr. Paul R. Harrington, a pioneering orthopedic surgeon whose work began in the 1950s.

您现在手中捧着的是一本特别珍贵的书籍，它讲述了哈灵顿棒的诞生和发展。哈灵顿棒是世界上第一个成功用于治疗脊柱异常弯曲或侧凸的脊柱内固定器械系统。为记载脊柱外科手术的这场革命，《锲而不舍》一书回顾了哈灵顿棒的发明者保罗·哈灵顿医生生活与工作中的点滴细节。他在 20 世纪 50 年代开始从事骨科工作，是骨科手术领域的先驱。

How do new surgical techniques come into being? We may tend to think of surgical innovation as occurring in a single, defining leap or, more comfortingly, as a product taken ready made into effective use. But no longer.

新的外科技术是如何产生的？我们倾向于认为手术的创新来自偶尔一次的决定性突破，或者更简单地说，是使用了一种投入生产且有效的手术器械。但这在现实中并不是一蹴而就的。

Dogged Persistence provides an unprecedented, close examination of the step-by-step process that brought Harrington Rods gradually into satisfactory use, then into professional acceptance, and finally into widespread adoption by surgeons nationally and internationally. It was not a simple process. *Dogged Persistence* leads us into the metal shop, the hotel meeting rooms, and the surgical suites where Harrington painstakingly worked out and definitively established the use of metal rods for spinal stabilization. *Dogged Persistence* is unrivaled in its resolute attention literally to the "nuts and bolts" of surgical innovation. The book brings into vivid focus the hard work and determination that was required, and it brings due recognition to Paul Harrington, who strove to find a solution to a worldwide form of human suffering. There is comparable reason as well to celebrate the author of this book, Dr. Marc Asher, who took great pains to give us a full and honest account of an often hidden and critically important process in surgery.

《锲而不舍》前所未有地回顾了哈灵顿棒从提出设计理念到临床应用满意，再到后来被同行专家认可，最终在全国和全球广泛使用的发展历程。这并不是一个简单的过程。此书还将带领我们游历五金店、酒店会议室和手术室，当年哈灵顿曾在这些地方精心设计、研发并最终确定使用金属棒来稳定脊柱。《锲而不舍》对脊柱外科内固定器械"螺母和螺栓"的创新进行了非常详尽的描述，同时也向我们生动地展示了成功和创新所需的艰苦努力和决心。保罗·哈灵顿也因努力寻找解决全世界人类疾苦的策略而得到了广泛的认可。在这里，我们也感谢本书的作者马克·阿舍医生，他呕心沥血地向我们全面真实地介绍了手术过程中经常容易被人忽略但又至关重要的细节。

It is worth noting that this book is one branch of a larger undertaking, which promises to bear fruit in the future. Before setting a single line to paper, Dr. Asher provided the inspiration and support to gather, organize, and preserve the mass of materials that provided the evidentiary core of this study. The resulting collection of laboratory note-books, correspondence, diaries, patient letters, instruments, and publications has become the Harrington Archives, established in the Department of History and Philosophy of Medicine at the University of Kansas School of Medicine. The Harrington Archives, in turn, has provided a rationale and basis for the continued expansion and preservation of archival materials relating to the development of surgery in the late twentieth century. My hope is these growing archival collections in the Department of History and Philosophy of Medicine will offer the opportunity for tomorrow's scholars to explore the expansive and influential enterprise of orthopedic and spinal surgery in the latter half of the twentieth century—though I am sure that the book you hold in your hands will long remain unique and valuable.

值得注意的是，本书是一项伟大事业的一个分支，有望在未来结出硕果。在下笔之前，阿舍医生收集、组织和保存的大量材料为其写作提供了灵感，同时也是本研究的证据核心。他收集整理的材料包括当时的实验笔记、通讯录、日记、患者信件、器械和发表的文章等，现在都已经成为堪萨斯大学医学院的医学历史与哲学系哈灵顿档案馆的馆藏文物。这些馆藏资料也为20世纪末与外科手术发展相关的档案材料的保存和扩展提供了基本原理和操作基础。我希望医学历史与哲学系这些日益增长的档案材料将为未来学者探索20世纪后期骨科和脊柱外科这一广阔而有影响力的行业创造条件，因此我确信您手中的这本书将永远独一无二而又无比珍贵。

Christopher Crenner, MD, PhD
克里斯托弗·克伦纳，医学和哲学博士
Robert Hudson and Ralph Major Professor and Chair
罗伯特·赫德森和拉尔夫·梅杰教授兼系主任
Department of History and Philosophy of Medicine
医学历史与哲学系
University of Kansas School of Medicine
堪萨斯大学医学院

（黄宇明 译　郑召民 王华 钟培言 审校）

PREFACE
前　言

The introduction of Harrington Spine Instrumentation in 1960 forever changed spine surgery by providing the surgeon for the first time with some measure of direct control over spine position and stability. Its development was stimulated by the post-World-War-II North American poliomyelitis epidemics and scoliosis, which is a lateral curve predominant, three-dimensional, and often progressive spine collapse that sometimes developed in the post-polio child or adolescent. Its development was sustained by the more common idiopathic scoliosis. Harrington Instrumentation marked the beginning of the end for months of enforced postoperative bed rest in a body cast, loss of much scoliosis correction, and the likelihood of additional surgery. With its usage, the instrumentation was found to be helpful in the treatment of many patients with other categories of scoliosis or spine deformities of both known and unknown causes. It was the most widely used spine instrumentation for the next twenty-five years. This is a story of its origin and early evolution.

1960 年，哈灵顿脊柱内固定器械的诞生让当时的脊柱外科发生了翻天覆地的变化。它第一次为外科医生提供了一种直接调节脊柱位置和稳定性的新方法。它的研发动力来自第二次世界大战后北美脊髓灰质炎疫情所致的脊柱侧凸，多发于感染脊髓灰质炎后的儿童或青少年群体，主要表现为脊柱向侧方弯曲的三维结构畸形，具有进行性加重并导致脊柱塌陷的特点。但是，哈灵顿脊柱内固定器械获得进一步发展和应用则归功于它在特发性脊柱侧凸治疗上取得的成功，因为这种脊柱畸形更加常见。该器械的诞生也标志着当时的一些传统、落后的治疗方法走向终结。之前患者在手术后需要用石膏固定脊柱并卧床数月，而且因为由于术后极易复发，患者还需要面临额外手术的折磨。随着哈灵顿器械的应用，专家们发现该器械对许多其他类型的，无论病因是否明确的脊柱侧凸或脊柱畸形均有效果。在随后的 25 年里，它是使用最广泛的脊柱内固定器械。这本书讲述的就是一个关于它的起源和早期演变的故事。

My involvement with this story began while a first-year faculty member at the University of Texas San Antonio. On a beautiful spring Saturday in 1971 Albert L. Sanders, knowing that Harrington and I shared Kansas roots, asked me to take his mentor, who had been consulting in San Antonio, to the airport for his short fight to Houston. Several missed fights and hours of conversation later Harrington boarded the plane. By 1974 I had returned to the University of Kansas Medical Center and had a growing spine deformity practice. That spring I visited Harrington in Houston, and there after we met with some regularity. His older sister Verna and her family still lived in the Kansas City area, and he and Mary Alice, his wife, paid them an annual visit. From that summer on and continuing to just a few months before his death in November 1980, Harrington utilized this opportunity to visit his alma mater where he spent many hours discussing scoliosis and research with me, leading bone scientist H. Clarke Anderson, and Robert P. Hudson, Chair of the Department of History and Philosophy of Medicine. During this time two recurring questions formed: why had Harrington succeeded where others had failed and why hadn't there been more research into the possibility of spine instrumentation, which by the 1970s seemed so intuitive?

故事始于我加入得克萨斯大学圣安东尼奥分校工作的第一年，当时哈灵顿也刚好在这个学校当顾问。在1971年春天的一个美丽的周六，哈灵顿的学生阿尔伯特·L. 桑德斯，知道我与他导师是堪萨斯老乡，于是就让我送他的导师去机场乘坐飞往休斯敦的短途航班。由于航班延误，我和哈灵顿有了一次长达几个小时的交谈。1974年，我回到了堪萨斯大学医学中心，并开展了越来越多脊柱畸形的治疗。同年春天，我在休斯敦拜访了哈灵顿，从那之后我们定期见面。由于他的姐姐韦尔娜和她家人仍住在堪萨斯城，哈灵顿和他的妻子玛丽·艾丽斯每年都会去探望他们一次。从那年夏天开始，一直到1980年11月他去世前的几个月，哈灵顿利用探亲的机会多次访问了他的母校，在那里他花了很多时间与我，还有权威的骨骼研究员H. 克拉克·安德森和医学历史与哲学系主任罗伯特·P. 赫德森，一起探讨脊柱侧凸的研究。在这段时间里，我们反复思考两个问题：为什么哈灵顿在其他人失败的地方取得了成功？当时为什么没有对脊柱内固定器械的可行性进行更多的研究，而到了20世纪70年代时，这些器械却看起来如此直观易懂？

Harrington willed his professional materials to the University of Kansas Medical

Center Archives, raising the question of why he chose this institution instead of the Baylor College of Medicine or the Texas Institute for Rehabilitation and Research. Following Harrington's death, Hudson went to Houston and confirmed that the material was worthy of archiving. A bit later our department archivist, a seasoned professional, went to help finish preparing the material for shipping, and I went along to assist her. She told me it would be more helpful if I were to become acquainted with the leaders of the Texas Institute for Rehabilitation and Research. That was an insightful suggestion that resulted in solidifying my desire to understand, as much as possible, Harrington's creative process. As the archiving progressed, it seemed that enough material had survived to allow me to achieve this goal, a possibility increased by the acquisition of additional materials during the following years. Distilling all of this into a coherent story and writing a book detailing the evolution of his work seemed to be tasks that I was best positioned to attempt. One reason was that I was a spine deformity surgeon using Harrington and subsequent spine instrumentation systems on a weekly basis. Perhaps most importantly, I was at the institution where his archives were housed. But before embarking on this project, I had to finish my own career: that included regular contributions to the scientific programs of the Scoliosis Research Society and participation in its leadership, including its presidency in 1997, I also had the opportunity to experience incremental spine instrumentation innovation firsthand. And through it all I had to manage my fears about my ability to adequately explore and describe his groundbreaking accomplishment.

遵照哈灵顿的遗嘱，他的专业资料交由堪萨斯大学医学中心档案馆保存。为什么他选择这个机构而不是贝勒医学院或得克萨斯康复与研究中心（TIRR）给大家留下了疑问。哈灵顿去世后，赫德森前往休斯敦并确认这些资料值得存档。后来，我们部门一位经验丰富的专业档案管理员和我一起完成了资料的运送。她告诉我，如果我能结识得克萨斯康复与研究中心的领导，那对我的研究会更有帮助。这是一个很有见地的建议，也更加坚定了我深入和全面地研究哈灵顿富有创造性的研发过程的信念。随着归档工作的开展，似乎有足够的材料让我实现这一目标。在接下来的几年里，我获得了更多的材料，进一步提高了实现这一目标的可能性。将所有内容汇总成一个连贯的故事，并编写一本详细描述他工作演进的书籍，这对我来说是最适合的一项工作。其中一个原因是，我是一名脊柱畸形外科医生，每周都会使用哈灵顿棒和脊柱内固定器械开展手术。最重要的一个原因是，我在存放他档案的地方工作。但在开始写作前，我必须完成自己的本职工作，包括定期参加脊柱侧凸研究学会的学术会议并参与其领导工作（1997 年我担任主席一职），亲自体验脊柱器械的创新产品。在这一系列经历中，我需要克服内心的恐惧，相信自己有能力全面探索和描述哈灵顿开创性的成就。

The purpose of *Dogged Persistence* is to document the details of the development of Harrington Spine Instrumentation in order to better understand why and how this creative process occurred. I followed the principle that knowing exactly when something occurred will usually explain why it occurred, and for this reason the narrative closely mirrors the chronology of events.[1] Harrington himself recognized this principle when late in life he wrote, "Over the last twenty years, many people have asked me 'How did you come up with the idea of spine instrumentation?' That question mystifies me, because I've never considered the instrumentation as a result of a single idea, or one creative thought, but rather a result of a life-long process that was triggered by circumstances—the 1950's polio epidemic."[2]

《锲而不舍》一书旨在记录哈灵顿脊柱内固定器械的研发细节，以便更好地了解这个创新过程发生的缘由和方式。我遵循的原则是，确切地知道某件事发生的时机通常可以解释它发生的原因，因此，故事的叙述与事件发生的时间顺序密切相关。[1] 哈灵顿本人在晚年时也认识到这一原则，他写道："在过去的二十多年里，很多人问我，'你是如何提出脊柱内固定器械这个想法的？'那个问题使我感到困惑。因为我从不认为脊柱器械是单一想法或头脑风暴的结果，而是由环境——20 世纪 50 年代脊髓灰质炎流行——所触发的让我努力终生的结果。"[2]

The story is structured as a dual biography with the principal focus on Paul Randall Harrington (1911–1980) and his research and development leading to the first successful spine instrumentation system. The secondary focus is on the early evolution of spine instrumentation through 1980, as documented by the Scoliosis Research Society beginning with its first meeting in 1966. *Dogged Persistence* is based in large part on original materials preserved in the Harrington Archives, which were weighed heavily in the reconstruction of the events. The early evolution of spine instrumentation is based on the abstracts and committee reports of the annual meetings of the Scoliosis Research Society, whose archives were deeded to the University of Kansas Medical Center Archives for safekeeping in 2009. In following the philosophy of why and when, abstracts were chosen over full-length publications because they were closer to real time developments. Of course, full-length publications, related literature, and other sources were considered.

本书的故事结构为双重叙事，首先重点关注保罗·兰德尔·哈灵顿（1911—1980）以及他研发成功的第一个脊柱内固定器械系统。其次是到20世纪80年代脊柱内固定器械的早期演变的历史，正如脊柱侧凸研究学会在1966年第一次会议记录的那样。《锲而不舍》在很大程度上基于哈灵顿档案馆保存的原始材料写成，这些材料在事件的复原中至关重要。脊柱内固定器械早期演变的书写则基于脊柱侧凸研究学会年会的摘要和委员会报告，其档案于2009年交由堪萨斯大学医学中心档案馆保管。在遵循“何因”和“何时”的哲学理念时，选择摘要而不是长篇出版物，是因为它们更接近实时发展。当然，也参考了长篇出版物、相关文献和其他来源的资料。

The jumping off point in the story is the post-World-War-Ⅱ polio epidemics, which in Houston began in 1948. To get to that point, Chapters 1, 2, and 3 are devoted to Harrington's development as a physician and surgeon entering private practice. Chapter 4 presents a brief history of the disease poliomyelitis and traces the development of spine stabilization by spine fusion. Chapter 5 details his response to the polio epidemics, leading to the research and development of Harrington Instrumentation. Chapters 6 and 7 cover the instrumentation's acceptance and the valid action of its safely and effectiveness. Chapter 8 is devoted to the formation of the Scoliosis Research Society. Chapter 9 shows Harrington at his peak, and Chapters 10 through 12 portray his declining, though still productive, years and the rise of the Scoliosis Research Society to the preeminent international society it has become. In the Epilogue the essential ingredients of innovation as encountered in this story are presented and an answer proposed for the reason why the development of a successful spine instrumentation system took so long.

故事发生在1948年正暴发疫情的休斯敦，源于第二次世界大战后的脊髓灰质炎流行。为了契合这个时间节点，第1、2和3章专门讲述了哈灵顿作为一名内外全科医生进入私人执业的成长过程。第4章介绍了脊髓灰质炎疾病的简史，并追溯了脊柱融合术稳定脊柱的发展历程。第5章详细介绍了哈灵顿对脊髓灰质炎流行的反应，引发了哈灵顿器械的研究与发展。第6章和第7章介绍了器械被接受的过程及对其安全有效性的验证。第8章是关于脊柱侧凸研究学会的成立。第9章介绍了哈灵顿的巅峰时期，第10章到第12章描绘了他的衰落（尽管他仍然产出颇丰），以及脊柱侧凸研究学会成长为一个卓越的国际组织的过程。在后记中，本书介绍了使这个故事完美呈现的基本创新要素，并对“为什么研发出一个成功的脊柱内固定器械系统需要花这么长时间”的问题给出了答案。

Two words are used seemingly interchangeably throughout this book that may require definition for some readers. Arthrodesis is an operation intended to cause *fusion* of or across joints, thereby eliminating motion. Two other words, *orthopaedic* and *orthopedic*, have the same meaning but different spellings. The latter is used unless the source specifies *orthopaedic*. When in doubt, *orthopedic* is used. The reader is encouraged to briefly review the Notes that follow the Epilogue to gain an idea about the endnote content and citation conventions.

本书中有两个单词可以互换使用，可能需要向某些读者解释其定义。Arthrodesis 是一种旨在引起融合或跨关节融合，从而消除活动的手术。另外两个单词 orthopaedic 和 orthopedic，虽然拼写不同，但意思均为“骨科”。除非来源指定了 orthopaedic，否则使用后者。如有疑问，请使用 orthopedic。在此，我鼓励读者简要复习后记之后的注释，以了解注释内容和引文规范。

At its heart *Dogged Persistence* is the nitty gritty case study of a trial and error (perhaps better described as trial and observation) surgical research effort that opened a new surgical era. An attempt has been made to present it in a manner that will interest both the medical and non-medical reader. If at times it is too abbreviated or detailed for either, I apologize. Because it is written from the vantage point of a North American, it is possible that important overseas developments have been missed or shortchanged.

《锲而不舍》的核心主题是一个关于外科研究工作的试验和错误（或许更准确的描述应为试验和观察）的具体案例研究，它开辟了外科手术新纪元。本书尝试以医学和非医学读者都感兴趣的方式撰写。如有太过简略或过于详细之处，我深表歉意。因为这本书是从北美人的视角来撰写的，很有可能会遗漏或缺失一些重要的海外进展信息。

（黄宇明 译　郑召民 邝冠明 李泽民 审校）

ACKNOWLEDGEMENTS
致　谢

Paul Randall Harrington willed his professional materials to his alma mater, the University of Kansas, for preservation by the Department of History and Philosophy of Medicine, Clendening Library, and the University of Kansas Medical Center Archives. The wealth of information in the Harrington Archives made *Dogged Persistence* possible. Many people have lent their support as I researched and wrote this story. Topping the list are members of his immediate family: Randall and Jane Harrington, Sue (Harrington) and Ned Price, and Richard Harrington. Information they provided allowed me to piece together the family genealogy, tell touching family stories, and document young Paul Harrington's athletic accomplishments. Jesse H. Dickson, Harrington's associate, who fully supported his mentor in life and in death, has been very helpful to me.

保罗·兰德尔·哈灵顿将他的专业资料遗赠给了他的母校堪萨斯大学，由堪萨斯大学医学历史与哲学系、克伦丁图书馆和堪萨斯大学医学中心档案馆共同保存。哈灵顿档案馆中丰富的资料使撰写《锲而不舍》一书成为可能。当我调查、研究并撰写这个故事时，许多人给了我支持，排在首位的是哈灵顿的直系亲属：兰德尔·哈灵顿、简·哈灵顿、苏·哈灵顿 和内德·普赖斯，以及理查德·哈灵顿。他们提供的信息使我得以拼凑出族谱，讲述感人的家庭故事，记录哈灵顿小时候的运动成就。哈灵顿的助手杰西·H. 迪克森竭尽全力地支持哈灵顿，他提供的资料对我的写作帮助很大。

Many members of the Department of History and Philosophy of Medicine have helped the Harrington Archives find a scholarly home. Robert P. Hudson, chairman of the department at the time Harrington's gift was made, offered his total commitment. At that same time Bea Jackson, rare books librarian, was a source of wisdom during the packing transfer, and handling of the materials. Although arriving about eighteen months after the

Harrington Archives was launched, D. Kay Clawson, executive vice-chancellor and orthopaedic surgeon, fully supported it. Hudson's two successors, Robert L. Martenson and current chair Christopher Crenner, maintained a strong commitment to the Hanington Archives. In addition, Crenner has provided invaluable help at every step of the way, from helping visualize the overall structure of the book to editing every chapter, sometimes several times. Eugene W. J. Pearce obtained many important oral histories that otherwise would have been lost. Archivist Nancy Hulston and assistant Jerry Motsinger catalogued, boxed, and filed the material so that it was accessible for research. Nancy also read every chapter and offered helpful comments. Rare books librarian Dawn McInnis has contributed to the preservation of the historically valuable books in Harrington's collection and supplied her fact-finding skills as I worked on the manuscript.

当时医学历史与哲学系的许多职员帮助哈灵顿档案馆找到了一个学术之家。哈灵顿捐赠档案资料时，罗伯特·P. 赫德森担任该系的系主任并全力支持。与此同时，贝亚·杰克森，一位珍本图书管理员，在包装转移和资料处理过程中展现出其过人的智慧。在档案馆启动大约 18 个月后，新到任的执行副校长兼骨科医生 D. 凯·克劳森也给予了大力支持。赫德森的两位继任者，罗伯特·L. 马滕森和现任主任克里斯托弗·克伦纳对哈灵顿档案馆始终保持着不懈的支持。此外，从对本书整体结构的构建，到具体每一章的编辑，克伦纳在每一步都提供了很多帮助，有些甚至需要反复多次的修改才能完成。若非从尤金·W. J. 皮尔斯那里获得了许多重要的口述资料，这些历史就会丢失。档案管理员南希·赫尔斯顿和助理杰瑞·莫辛格对这些资料进行了分类、装箱和归档，以便于进行研究。南希阅读了每一章并提供了宝贵的意见。珍本图书管理员唐·麦金尼斯为保存哈灵顿馆藏中具有历史价值的书籍做出了贡献，并在我撰写手稿时展现了她的实况调查技能。

My home department, orthopedic surgery, supported both the Harrington Archives and *Dogged Persistence* projects. Three chairmen. Frederick W. Reckling, Bradford W. Olney, and E. Bruce Toby as well as early associates, Rae R. Jacobs and James R. Neff, were a few of those aiding my effort. Our department's present-day spine team, Douglas C. Burton, his associate R. Sean Jackson, and laboratory scientists Terence E. McIff and Jinxi Wang, have helped keep me somewhat current. Our office and laboratory staff, (listed alphabetically) Jan Brunks, Dick Lark, Barbara Manna, Janice Orrick, and Terry Orrick, provided much-needed general support.

我所在的部门——骨科对哈灵顿档案馆和《锲而不舍》这部著作均给予了支持。弗雷德里克·W. 雷克林、布拉德福德·W. 奥尔尼和E. 布鲁斯·托比，这三位主任以及早期的同事瑞伊·R. 雅各布斯和詹姆斯·R. 内夫均给予了帮助。我们科室现在的脊柱团队，道格拉斯·C. 伯顿和他的同事R. 肖恩·杰克逊以及实验室科学家特伦斯·E. 麦基夫和王金熙帮助我了解最新进展。我们办公室和实验室的工作人员（按姓氏字母顺序排列）简·布伦克斯、迪克·拉克、芭芭拉·曼纳、贾尼丝·奥里克和特里·奥里克提供了许多必要的支持。

I have had the opportunity to learn from a number of outstanding adopted mentors, including Robert B. Winter, instrument maker Walter E. Strippgen, Charles F. Heinig, engineer William L. Carson, and Arthur D. Steffee. Although they did not contribute directly to the book, I never could have written it without the benefit of the wisdom they shared with me over many years.

我有机会向许多杰出的老师学习，包括罗伯特·B. 温特、器械制造商瓦尔特·E. 施特里普根、查尔斯·F. 海尼希、工程师威廉·L. 卡森和阿瑟·D. 斯菲特。尽管他们对这本书没有做出直接贡献，但如果没有他们多年来将自己的智慧与我分享，我可能永远写不出这本书。

In 2009, during the presidency of Oheneba Boachie-Adjei, the Scoliosis Research Society deeded its archives to the University of Kansas Medical Center for deposit in the KUMC Archives, where they are available to SRS members and for approved researchers. A succession of SRS historians has worked diligently to preserve the record. Through 1980 when Harrington died and this story ends, John H. Moe, Sidney L. Wallace, and Rober B. Keler served in that office.

奥赫贝巴·鲍彻-阿德杰在2009年担任脊柱侧凸研究学会主席期间，将学会的档案转交给堪萨斯大学医学中心并存放在堪萨斯大学医学中心档案馆，让脊柱侧凸研究学会会员和经批准的研究人员得以使用这些档案。多位从事脊柱侧凸研究学会的历史学工作的继任者一直在努力保存这些记录。到1980年哈灵顿逝世，这个故事结束时，约翰·H. 莫、西德尼·L. 华莱士和罗伯特·B. 凯勒都曾担任过史学工作者。

Dogged Persistence's excellent production team included Barbara Funk, editor of most of my writing since 1983 and without Whom the book could not have been completed, Anne Huffman, librarian and EndNote specialist who has worked with me the longest on this project, and book designer Pat Eschbacher.

《锲而不舍》的优秀编辑团队包括芭芭拉·芬克，自 1983 年以来她一直担任我大部分文章的编辑，没有她这本书就不可能完成；还有在这个项目上与我合作时间最长的图书管理员和注释专家安妮·赫夫曼以及书籍设计师帕特·埃希巴赫。

Having been through this, my only book writing experience, I'm convinced that the largest price has been paid by the author's family. Through its long gestation my wife Elinor (Ellie) and my daughter Janet Asher Vreeland never gave up believing in the *Dogged Persistence* story for both its historical and inspirational value. It would not exist without their unqualified love and encouragement, for which I am eternally grateful.

经历了这唯一一次编书经历，我深信我的家人付出了最大的代价。在漫长的酝酿过程中，我的妻子埃莉诺和我的女儿珍妮特·阿舍·弗里兰一致坚信《锲而不舍》一书的历史价值和精神价值。如果没有他们无条件的爱和鼓励，这本书就不会和读者见面了，对此我永远心存感激。

Over the years of researching and writing *Dogged Persistence* I asked many, many people for help and guidance, and I can't remember anyone who hasn't willingly helped. My sincerest thank-you to those not specifically cited.

在研究和编写《锲而不舍》的这些年里，我曾经向许许多多的人寻求过帮助和指导，在我的记忆里，似乎没有人拒绝向我提供帮助。我对那些没有特别提及的人表示最诚挚的感谢。

Marc A. Asher, MD
马克·A. 阿舍,医学博士
Kansas City, Kansas
堪萨斯城,堪萨斯州
August 2015
2015 年 8 月

(黄宇明 译　郑召民 李泽民 刘瑞端 审校)

Dedicated to the ordinary North Americans who were asked to donate dimes to combat poliomyelitis after World War Ⅱ.

They responded and gave millions of dollars to the National Foundation for Infantile Paralysis through its March of Dimes campaign.

In doing so, thousands of families were spared bankruptcy, the first successful polio vaccine was developed, and the research and development of the first successful spine instrumentation system were assisted.

谨以此书献给那些普通的北美人，在第二次世界大战后，他们被要求捐款以对抗脊髓灰质炎。

他们响应号召，通过“爱婴三月运动”向全国小儿麻痹症基金会捐赠了数百万美元。正是此举让成千上万的家庭免于破产，从而成功研发了第一个脊髓灰质炎疫苗和第一套脊柱内固定器械。

（季甜甜 译　郑召民 审校）

CONTENTS
目　录

1 ROOTS

To return home is always a joy.[1]

故乡

回家总是充满乐趣。[1]

Paul Harrington was always proud of his roots. A visitor to Kansas City, Kansas, in the latter decades of the twentieth century might have wondered if his pride had been a bit misplaced. But in 1885 when Grandfather Edgar Harrington moved his family to the town, it was rapidly becoming a major industrial city, eventually ranking seventeenth in the country. This, of course, meant jobs, jobs that paid about 20% more than the national average.[2]

保罗·哈灵顿一直为自己的故乡感到自豪。若是在20世纪末期，来到位于堪萨斯州的堪萨斯城的游客可能会质疑他的自豪是从何而来的。但是在1885年，当保罗的祖父埃德加·哈灵顿举家搬到这个地方的时候，这座城市正在快速工业化，成为当时全国排名第17名的大型工业城市。当然，发达的工业也意味着能找到更好的工作——当地的工资比全国平均水平高出约20%。[2]

The future Kansas City, Kansas, and Kansas City, Missouri, owed their good fortune to location. Near what was to become the geographic center of the contiguous United States, the overriding geologic feature was the Missouri River, both in its presence and configuration. From its origin in Montana its twisting course angled about 40° southeast until reaching the Kansas Cities where it turned and flowed almost straight east. A little over 350 river miles later this longest river in North America emptied into the Mississippi River.[3] The

Kansas River, also called the Kaw River, pursued a generally direct west to east course except near its end where it made two sharp turns, the first to the northwest and the second back to the east. Here the Kansas emptied into the apex of the Missouri River's big bend to the east. The confluence became known as the Kaw's mouth, and the northern point of land was called Kaw Point.[4]

堪萨斯州和密苏里州的堪萨斯城未来的发展机遇均得益于它们良好的地理位置。毗邻美国本土的地理中心，无论是从位置还是从地形轮廓来看，堪萨斯城最重要的地理优势都是密苏里河。密苏里河发源于蒙大拿州，向东南约 40°方向蜿蜒流动，到达堪萨斯城后几乎完全向东奔流。大约 350 多英里①后，这条北美最长的河流汇入密西西比河。[3]堪萨斯河，也被称为“考河”，除了末端的两个急转弯外，河道总体从西到东流动。其中第一个急转弯转向西北，而第二个则折返回东方。在这里，堪萨斯河汇入密苏里河的东向大弯道的顶端。而这个汇流处就是著名的“考口”，北边的登陆点则被称为“考点”。[4]

The Missouri River and its tributaries were well populated by fur-bearing animals. While the increasing presence of French trappers and fur traders from the late seventeenth century on was enough to validate French claims to the area, it was not enough to explore and populate this vast space. The Louisiana Purchase in 1803 changed this. President Thomas Jefferson initiated an exploration of the uncharted territory, and the Lewis and Clark Expedition (1804-1806) provided the first detailed information about the purchase.[5] This heightened the interest in scouting and settling of what was "by far the largest single territorial gain in the history of the United States", including the country's later purchase of Alaska.[6] The Missouri River was navigable and provided an obvious east-west transportation route from St. Louis to the frontier, which was defined as the land west of the meeting of the two rivers. However, the Missouri was fast, treacherous, and muddy with limited suitable landing sites. It frequently changed course, hiding submerged obstacles, such as tree remains that ripped open the bottom of many steamboats, usually causing them to sink within minutes.[7] Although it remained navigable for several hundred miles north of the Kaw's mouth, the hazards and course changes rapidly diminished its usefulness for transportation.

密苏里河流域栖息着很多毛皮动物。虽然从 17 世纪晚期开始，法国猎人和毛

① 1 英里=1.609 344 千米。

皮商人的不断出现足以证实法国对这片广袤土地的所有权，但这片土地上的探索者以及定居者很少。1803 年的路易斯安那购地案改变了这一切。托马斯·杰弗逊总统开始了对这片未知领土的探索，“刘易斯和克拉克探险”（1804—1806）第一次提供了这片土地的详细信息。[5] 这极大提高了人们对“当时美国历史上最大一笔土地交易”的兴趣，促使人们去探索和定居这片土地。这也影响到了美国后来和阿拉斯加的土地交易。[6] 密苏里河是可通航的，并明确提供了一条从圣路易斯到边陲地区的东西方向运输路线。当时的边陲地区是两条河流交汇处以西的土地。然而，密苏里河水流湍急、凶险且泥泞，适合登陆的地方非常有限。它的流向曲折多变，水下隐藏着障碍物，比如树的残干。这些障碍物可以撕开蒸汽船的底部，通常导致船只在几分钟内沉没。[7] 尽管密苏里河在考口以北几百英里处仍可航行，但潜在的危险和多变的流向极大降低了它的运输价值。

The Kansas River was not reliably navigable, but the surrounding terrain, which it and its tributaries partially shaped, provided a relatively easy overland route west. The location around the Kaw's mouth was destined to become a major transportation hub since it was the end of the line for river transportation for most travelers and the beginning of the overland route that became the"great highway to the Pacific."[8] However, the location around the Kaw's mouth also had a profound social liability: the issue of slavery. Missouri was admitted as a slave state in 1821, following the Missouri Compromise of 1820 that excluded slavery north of latitude 36°30', which was the southern border of Missouri. This evened the slave-free state balance at fifteen. All other land of the Louisiana Purchase that was north of this line prohibited slavery, and this included the area west of the Kaw's mouth.

尽管堪萨斯河通航不是很可靠，但它及其支流周围形成的平整土地，提供了一条相对便捷的西向陆路交通路线。考口周围注定会成为一个大型交通枢纽。因为它不仅是运输大多数旅客的水路交通的终点，还是“通往太平洋的大公路”的陆路交通的起点。[8] 然而，考口周围也有一个深远的社会问题：奴隶制。1820 年通过的《密苏里妥协案》规定：废除北纬 36°30' 以北的奴隶制，这刚好是密苏里州的南部边界。1821 年，密苏里州被认定为蓄奴州。但为平衡 15 个自由州的数量，路易斯安那购地案中该线以北的其他土地（包括考口以西的地区）都禁止奴隶制。

The State of Missouri's western boundary was originally based on the mouth of the

Kansas River. The longitudinal meridian was 94°36’ west. In 1836 Missouri purchased the land north of the Kaw’s mouth lying between this meridian and the Missouri River.[9] The land west of Missouri, which included the sites of the municipalities that would come together to form Kansas City, Kansas, was variously referred to as the Frontier or Indian Territory. The year Missouri became a state the first small commercial trip to Santa Fe, Mexico, was made, confirming the feasibility of this trade. As it grew, the point of embarkation to the southwest moved up the Missouri River to Independence and finally to Westport Landing, about a mile downriver from the Kaw’s mouth and about three miles north of the Town of Westport, located on the road to Independence. A town began forming on the bluffs above Westport Landing, but languished until stimulated by the supply needs of the Mexican-American War(1846–1848). By 1850 the town had grown to 2,500 and received its formal charter as the Town of Kansas, the forerunner of Kansas City, Missouri(1889).[10]

密苏里州的西部边界最初在考口附近，大致在西经94°36’。1836年，密苏里州买下了西经94°36’和密苏里河之间考口以北的土地。[9] 密苏里州西部的土地，其中包括未来将合并形成堪萨斯城的市政当局所在地，被重新命名为“边境”或“印第安人领地”。密苏里州建州的那一年，通往墨西哥圣达菲小镇的小商品贸易之旅的成功，证实了这项交易的可行性。随着它的发展，向西南的登陆点沿密苏里河上游挪到独立城，最后到达韦斯特波特登陆点。韦斯特波特登陆点大约在考口下游一英里和韦斯特波特镇以北约三英里处，位于通往独立城的路上。在韦斯特波特登陆点上方的陡岸上开始形成了一个萧条的小镇，直到受到美墨战争（1846—1848）的供应需求的刺激小镇才繁荣起来。到1850年，该镇人口已经增长到2 500人，并被正式特许成立堪萨斯镇，即密苏里州堪萨斯城的前身（1889年）。[10]

The history of the area that would become Kansas City, Kansas, in 1886 could not have been more different. The United States government used the Indian Territory for resettling Indian tribes from the east, moving them west to make room for settlers. The last and by far the most consequential migration into the region of the Kaw’s mouth was the resettlement of the Wyandot tribe of about 700 persons from Upper Sandusky, Ohio, in 1843. The United States government had agreed to buy land for the Wyandots and provide a cash settlement for their land in Ohio. The transition was not smooth, and the hardships associated with the relocation resulted in 60 deaths. But eventually the Wyandots were able to obtain 39 sections of valuable land rising from the west bank of the

Kansas River immediately upriver from the Kaw's mouth.[11] In Ohio they had lived in towns, and most had adopted the Christian faith, spoke English, translated their tribal names into English, and intermarried with whites. Many were cultured, read books, farmed, and were acquainted with business and trades.[12] In their new home they assumed a leadership role by establishing a government based on representative democracy, the first free school, a Sunday school, and a public utility in what was to become the State of Kansas. For years that public utility, the National Ferry that provided a crossing over the Kansas River near the Kaw's mouth, was the only entrance into Indian Territory.[13] The increasing westward traffic associated with the California gold rush in 1849 did not go unnoticed by the Wyandots. Most of them concluded that the best way to both avoid being relocated again and to participate in the growth was to gain severalty, or individual ownership, of their land and to help develop a market for it. The admission of California as the 31st state the following year was fortuitous for them. By tipping the balance in the United States Senate to the free states, the way was opened for the negotiations leading to the passage of the Kansas-Nebraska Act on May 30, 1854.[14] Events then moved swiftly.

1886 年成立的堪萨斯州堪萨斯城的历史与其他地区大同小异。美国政府设置印第安人领地重新安置东部的印第安部落，再将他们向西迁移，为后来的定居者腾出空间。最后也是到目前为止最重要的一次对考口地区的移民安置是 1843 年对来自俄亥俄州上桑达斯基怀恩多特部落约 700 人的重新安置。美国政府同意为怀恩多特购买土地，并为他们俄亥俄州的土地提供现金补偿。这个过渡时期并不顺利，迁移过程中的艰辛困苦造成了 60 人死亡。但最终，怀恩多特人获得了来自考口上游堪萨斯河西岸的 39 块宝贵的土地。[11]在俄亥俄州，他们住在城镇里，大多数人都皈依了基督教，说英语，用英文名字替代部落名字，并与白人通婚。许多人是有教养的，他们读书，耕种，熟悉商业和贸易。[12]在他们的新家——未来的堪萨斯州，他们成立了一个代议制民主政府，建立了第一所自由学校和主日学校，成立了公共事业公司。多年来，公共事业公司，即在考口附近提供横跨堪萨斯河服务的国家渡轮公司，是进入印第安人领地的唯一途径。[13]1849 年加利福尼亚州淘金热导致的西部交通运输业大发展并没有被怀恩多特人所忽视。他们中的大多数人认为，兼顾避免再次搬迁和保持发展的最好方法是将土地按份分配或获得土地的个人所有权，并为此开发一个市场。非常巧合的是，第二年加利福尼亚州以自由州身份加入联邦，成为美国第 31 个州。美国参议院的平衡被打破，天平倾向于自由州。这件事引起了南北双方的谈判，在 1854 年 5 月 30 日通过了《堪萨斯-内布拉斯加法案》。[14]随后，事态迅速发展。

The Kansas-Nebraska Act included the concept of popular sovereignty, which reserved for the territorial legislatures the right to decide their free or slave status. This was directly contrary to the Missouri Compromise, and the competition between free and slave forces to gain a voting advantage in the Kansas Territory began almost immediately, as did the bloody and divisive Kansas-Missouri Border War, which was a preamble to the Civil War.[15] In 1855 the Wyandots concluded a treaty with the United States government that accomplished their goals of US citizenship and individual ownership of their land. This also stopped most of their annuity payments from the government.[16] Later that year the first Wyandotte post office was established, and the following year the first building for business was constructed. Three Wyandot leaders joined with four white developers to form the Wyandotte City Town Company, and in early 1857 the town site of Wyandotte was platted. By January 1859 the City of Wyandotte had been incorporated, Wyandotte County had been created (from parts of Leavenworth and Johnson counties), and the City of Wyandotte with a population of 1,259 had been named the temporary county seat.[17,18] In July the fourth Kansas Constitutional Convention was held on the fourth floor of a new but unimposing building bordering on the levee. The draft was finished in twenty-four days and approved on July 29, 1859. It prohibited slavery, gave women suffrage in school elections, left other suffrage issues to the legislature, and did not prohibit African-American immigration. In the fall Kansans approved the draft by a vote of two to one. Hostilities on the border decreased, but the violence moved east.[19]

《堪萨斯-内布拉斯加法案》采取“人民主权原则”，即当地的立法机关有权自行决定其为自由州还是蓄奴州。这与《密苏里妥协案》直接相悖。蓄奴和废奴双方为了在投票时获得优势，均大肆涌往堪萨斯州。随即出现了血腥分裂的“堪萨斯-密苏里边境战争”，这是内战的先声。[15]1855年，怀恩多特人与美国政府签订了一项条约，取得了美国公民身份和个人土地所有权。他们中的大部分人也停止向政府缴纳年金。[16]同年晚些时候，第一家怀恩多特邮局成立了。第二年，第一家商务大楼也建成了。三位怀恩多特政府领导与四名白人开发商一起成立了怀恩多特市镇开发公司。1857年年初，怀恩多特镇建成。到1859年1月，怀恩多特市与莱文沃思县和约翰逊县的部分地区合并成立怀恩多特县。人口为1 259人的怀恩多特市被指定为临时县政府所在地。[17,18]同年7月，第四届堪萨斯州制宪会议在与河堤临近的一个崭新但平平无奇的建筑的四楼内举行。草案在24天后完成，并于1859年7月29日获得了批准。它禁止奴隶制，在学校选举中给予妇女选举权，把其他选举权问题划拨给立法机构处理，允许非裔美国人移民。到了秋天，堪萨斯州以 2 比 1 的票数通过了该草案。边境上的敌对行为有所减少，但暴力活动向东蔓延。[19]

By the time Kansas gained statehood on January 29,1861, Minnesota (1858) and Oregon (1859) had been admitted, bringing the count to nineteen free and fifteen slave states. The tipping point in north-south, free-slave differences had been passed, and the Civil War began a few months later at Fort Sumter, South Carolina, on April 12,1861.[20] Missouri did not secede, but its policy of neutrality did not prevent the renewal of the Kansas-Missouri border skirmishes during the war.[21] By the end of the Civil War at Appomattox Court House, Virginia, on April 9, 1865, commercial life in the area surrounding the Missour-Kansas rivers' confluence was economically depressed. Trade from the trails west had all but stopped, ending a $10 million-plus yearly income stream. Westport's population had fallen by one-fourth. The US government was failing to pay the annuities still due to many of the Indians, and banks had closed.[22] Then there came deliverance in the form of railroads and cattle.

1861 年 1 月 29 日，堪萨斯州获得州地位成为自由州，自此，加上 1858 年建州的明尼苏达州和 1859 年建州的俄勒冈州，美国自由州和蓄奴州数量比变为 19：15。北方和南方、自由和蓄奴的矛盾达到顶点。几个月后，1861 年 4 月 12 日，在南卡罗来纳爆发的萨姆特堡战役揭开了南北战争的序幕。[20]密苏里州没有退出联邦，但在战争期间它的中立政策并没有使堪萨斯−密苏里边境避免冲突。[21] 1865 年 4 月 9 日，在弗吉尼亚州阿波马托克斯法院的罗伯特·李投降，内战结束，但密苏里−堪萨斯河汇合处的周围地区经济萧条，西边的圣达菲之路上的贸易几乎完全停止，每年损失 1 000 多万美元的收入。韦斯特波特的人口减少了四分之一。由于大量的印第安人，美国政府支付不起年金，银行也已经倒闭。[22]不过铁路业和畜牧业倒是得到了解脱。

The Civil War had demonstrated the strategic importance of railroads and railroad centers that were the scenes of many battles. During the war while free of Southern pressure, the United States Congress had authorized construction of three rail lines through the west, beginning at Omaha, Atchison, and Wyandotte. The Wyandotte to Lawrence segment was opened in 1864. That same year the Kansas legislature passed a law declaring Kansas rivers not navigable and subject to bridging and damming. But, the crowning achievement for the area was winning the first railroad bridge across the

Missouri. Awarded in 1867 over competitor Leavenworth (a city which was twice as large) and opened in 1869, the Hannibal Bridge was located about three-quarters of a mile downstream from the Kaw's mouth and connected the United States' land in the southwest to Chicago and beyond.[23] While overland trails sought high ground, rivers and their flood plains were the natural routes for railroads. The flood plain extending several miles up the Kansas River from the Kaw's mouth was contiguous with the shorter flood plain, or west bottoms, along the south side of the Missouri River below the Kaw's mouth. These flood plains also provided extensive flat space to build the industries needed to support the railroads and the commerce they brought with them. The problem, of course, was flooding. However, it occurred infrequently enough to forget, downplay, or postpone preventive measures.[24]

内战中很多战斗都发生在铁路和铁路中心，这证明了铁路的战略重要性。在战争期间，由于没有南方压力，美国国会授权在奥马哈、艾奇逊、怀恩多特各修建一条穿过西部的铁路。怀恩多特到劳伦斯区的部分于1864年开通。同年，堪萨斯州立法机关通过了一项法律，宣布堪萨斯州的河流不能直接通航，而要修建桥梁和堤坝。然而，该地区最耀眼的成就是成功建造了第一座横跨密苏里州的铁路桥——汉尼拔大桥。堪萨斯州在1867年打败竞争对手莱文沃思（一个面积是堪萨斯城两倍大的城市）获取了建桥资格。位于考口下游约0.75英里处的汉尼拔大桥于1869年开通，将美国西南部的土地与芝加哥乃至更远的地方相连。[23]当陆路交通一味寻求高地时，河流和冲积平原这些洼地成为修建铁路的最佳选择。从考口向堪萨斯河上游延伸几英里的冲积平原与考口下密苏里河南侧狭小的冲积平原相连。这些冲积平原区也提供了广阔的平坦空间来建造工业所需的铁路和发展随之而来的商业。当然，也存在洪水泛滥的问题。然而，这种情况很少发生，少到足以让人们慢慢淡忘这一点，并最终推迟预防措施的实施。[24]

For many reasons the livestock industry was poised for growth at the end of the Civil War. The flow of livestock eastward had been interrupted by the war, leaving an unfulfilled market. In turn this led to a buildup of excess stock on the ranges of the west where the imported Spanish cattle thrived. During the war, railroads matured as a new and better way of bringing supply and demand closer together. Ranchers and farmers were rapidly settling the west, providing a steady flow of livestock after the open range closed. The two future Kansas Cities were ideally located to serve the livestock industry. The first Livestock Exchange in Kansas City opened in 1871 and was initially located on the

Kansas side of the state line.[25] The area of the Kansas City Stockyards grew from 5 to over 200 acres, two-thirds of which were found on the Kansas side.[26] Development of successful refrigerated railcars from the early 1880s on helped move meatpacking west, increasingly saving the long-distance shipment of livestock.[27] By 1905 the Kansas City Stockyards was receiving 7,000,000 animals a year and at its peak was second only to the Union Stock Yards in Chicago.[28] There were twenty-three meatpacking plants nearby, and sixteen railroads had direct connections to the stockyards.[29] The need for manpower for the cattle industry resulted in a flood of workers. The first to heed the call, settlers largely of English and Irish descent, were soon followed by immigrants from Mexico and central Europe. From 1878 through 1882 there was a mass migration of African-Americans from the southern states to Kansas. They were known as the Exodusters, and most came through Kansas City, Kansas, with some settling in the city and others moving farther west into Kansas.[30]

由于各种各样的原因，在内战结束时畜牧业的发展已经蓄势待发。稳定供应的东部畜牧业被战争中断，留下了一个未饱和的市场。反过来，这导致此前大量进口西班牙牛的西部发展繁荣起来。在战争期间，新发展成熟的铁路更好地促进了市场的供需平衡。西进运动结束后，牧场主和农民迅速在西部定居下来，他们提供了稳定而又持续供应的牲畜。未来的两个堪萨斯城均是发展畜牧业的理想地点。堪萨斯城的第一家牲畜交易所于 1871 年开业，最初位于堪萨斯州的州线一侧。[25]堪萨斯城的畜牧场面积从 5 英亩①增加到超过 200 英亩，其中三分之二在堪萨斯州一侧。[26]从 19 世纪 80 年代初开始，冷藏火车的发明和普及推动了西部的肉类加工业的发展，大量节省了牲畜长途运输所需的运力。[27]到 1905 年，堪萨斯城的“牲畜围栏公司”每年接收 7 000 000 只动物，在其鼎盛时期仅次于芝加哥的“联合牲畜饲养场”。[28]“牲畜围栏公司”附近有 23 家肉类加工厂，而且有 16 条铁路直接通向“联合牲畜饲养场”。[29]畜牧业对人力的需求产生了大量工人。第一批闻召而来的主要是英裔和爱尔兰裔，很快紧接着的是来自墨西哥和中欧的移民。从 1878 年到 1882 年，有一大批被称为“逃离者”的非裔美国人从南部各州迁移到堪萨斯州。他们大多数都要经过堪萨斯州的堪萨斯城，有一些人在这里定居，而有一些人则继续向西。[30]

In 1886 Kansas City, Kansas, incorporated, consolidating the cities of Wyandotte

① 1 英亩约等于 0.004 047 平方千米。

(12,086 residents), old Kansas City, Kansas (3,802 residents), and Armourdale (1,582 residents). Riverside had already been annexed by Wyandotte, and Armstrong, an unincorporated area between Wyandotte and Armourdale, was included in the consolidation. The combined population was well over the 15,000 required for a first-class city. Bankers and speculators had convinced the governor that debt would sell better with the name of Kansas City, Kansas, than Wyandotte, Kansas. As could be expected, Wyandotte's residents were not happy with this decision.[31] Meanwhile, on the other side of the state line the City of Kansas had passed 100,000 and would become Kansas City, Missouri, in 1889, boasting a population of 130,000.[32]

1886 年，怀恩多特（12 086 名居民）、堪萨斯州的老堪萨斯城（3 802 名居民）和阿默代尔（1 582 名居民）合并建制形成了堪萨斯州的堪萨斯城。河滨地区被怀恩多特合并；怀恩多特和阿默代尔之间的非建制地区阿姆斯特朗，也被怀恩多特吞并。怀恩多特总人口远远超过了一个一流城市所需的 1.5 万人。银行家和投机商已经说服州长，用堪萨斯城而不是怀恩多特作为名字，债券会卖得更好。正如所料，怀恩多特的居民并不满意这个决定。[31]与此同时，在州线的另一边的堪萨斯城已经超过了 10 万人口，并在 1889 年成为拥有 13 万人口、隶属于密苏里州的堪萨斯城。[32]

It was into this dynamic environment that Paul Harrington's ancestors moved.

正是在此时，保罗·哈灵顿的祖先刚好走进了这种多变的环境中。

Thanks largely to Laura Harrington, Paul's mother, and to family genealogy notes, we know something of the early history of his family.[33,34] With the exception of his maternal grandfather, his ancestors were English and came to the United States by way of Canada. Parental family lore included several stories of interactions with royalty. Paul's paternal great-grandfather, Charles Harrington, was born in Millbrook, Southampton, England, and died when he was 35 years old. His brother Alfred, Paul's great-great-uncle, was said to have been knighted by Queen Victoria. Paul's grandparents were Edgar and Harriet Randall Harrington. Edgar was born in Southampton, England, in 1832, and his family worked in the shipbuilding industry. Harriet Randall, born in 1835 in Warrington, England, appears to have been reared in a prosperous family. Her father manufactured broadcloth and was reported to have sold about 500 guineas' worth each Saturday.[35] Two of her brothers, John and James, did hand carving in the House of Lords for seven years. John married Edgar Harington's sister, Clara, and the couple remembered all of Harriet's children in their wills. The wife of one of Harriet's brothers was a guest at the wedding of Princess Eugénie and Napoleon Ⅲ,[36] and one of Harriet's brothers was in the British navy, attained the rank of corporal, and served a tour of duty on Queen Victoria's yacht, the Prince Albert. A favorite family story was about the time that the queen was disciplining her son, the future King Edward VI, by locking him in a closet. She stationed Corporal Randall on guard, instructing him to liberate her son at the end of a given time. The child forcefully kicked the door and threatened to behead Corporal Randall when he became king if he was not liberated at once. The story had another twist as the captain of the *Prince Albert* at that time was engaged to a sister of Corporal Randall.[37]

我们能够对哈灵顿家族早期的历史有所了解，在很大程度上得益于保罗的母亲劳拉和他们家族家谱的记录。[33,34]除了他的外公，他的祖先都是英国人，经由加拿大来到美国。家族传说中甚至有几个与皇室成员互动的故事。保罗的曾祖父查尔斯·哈灵顿出生在英格兰南安普敦的米尔布鲁克，并在35岁时去世。他的兄弟阿尔弗雷德，保罗的叔公，据说被维多利亚女王封为爵士。保罗的祖父母是埃德加·哈灵顿和哈丽特·兰德尔·哈灵顿。埃德加于1832年出生在英国的南安普敦，他的家人在造船厂工作。哈丽特·兰德尔于1835年出生在英国的沃灵顿，她似乎是在一个富裕的家庭中长大的。她的父亲生产阔幅布，据说每个周六能卖出约500几尼①。[35]她的两个兄弟，约翰和詹姆斯，在上议院大楼做了七年的手工雕刻。约翰娶了埃德加·哈灵顿的妹妹克拉拉。这一对夫妇在遗嘱中记下了哈丽特所有的孩子。哈丽特其中一个兄弟的妻子出席了尤金妮公主和拿破仑三世的婚礼，[36]另一个兄弟在英国海军当兵，获得了下士军衔，甚至在维多利亚女王的游艇“阿尔伯特亲王”号上服役。最让人喜欢的一个家庭故事是关于女王惩罚她的儿子，即未来的国王爱德华七世的。女王把他锁在一个壁橱里，并让兰德尔下士站岗，指示在一段时间后再放她儿子出来。这孩子拼命踢门，威胁说如果兰德尔下士不立即放他出去，当他成为国王时，就砍了他的头。这个故事还有一个转折在于，当时“阿尔伯特亲王”号的船长和兰德尔下士的一个妹妹订婚了。[37]

Although when Edgar Harrington and Harriet Randall were married is not documented, we know that around 1871 they immigrated to Canada. They had eight

① 英国旧时金币或货币单位，1几尼价值21先令，现值1.05镑。译者注。

children, the first born in 1857 and the last in 1880. Four were born in England and four in Canada. Paul's father, Joseph Alfred, the seventh child, was born in 1877 in London, Ontario, Canada.[38] When Joseph was eight, his parents moved to Kansas City, Kansas. At that time Edgar would have been 53 and Harriett 50. Edgar declared his intent to become a citizen of the United States in 1888 and achieved the goal in 1896.[39]

虽然埃德加·哈灵顿和哈里特·兰德尔结婚的时间没有记录，但我们知道他们在 1871 年左右移民到了加拿大。他们有八个孩子，第一个出生于 1857 年，最后一个出生于 1880 年。其中四个出生在英格兰，四个出生在加拿大。保罗的父亲，约瑟夫·阿尔弗雷德，作为第七个孩子于 1877 年出生在加拿大安大略省的伦敦。[38]当约瑟夫八岁时，他的父母搬到了堪萨斯州的堪萨斯城。那时埃德加是 53 岁，哈丽特是 50 岁。埃德加在 1888 年宣布他打算成为一名美国公民，并在 1896 年实现了这个目标。[39]

Paul's maternal great-grandfather, James Newberry, was a Canadian pioneer, and his father, Paul's great-great-grandfather, was a pensioned British soldier. Paul's maternal grandparents were Frank and Matilda (Newberry) Billinsky. Born in Paris, Frank had run away to the gold fields. Matilda was born in Canada. Paul's mother was Laura Bilinsky, the fifth of Frank and Matilda's six children. Born in Webberville, Michigan, in 1879, Laura was two years old when her father died. Neither his age nor the cause of death is documented.[40,41] When she was five years old and still living in Webberville, her mother took her to visit London, Ontario, Canada. Matilda and her late husband had once lived there and been friends of Edgar and Harriet Harrington before Paul's parents, Joseph and Laura, were born. A common bond between the families was their active participation in church activities.[42] On a side note, the temperature during their visit in London must have been really cold since the brittle snow crunching underfoot as they went to Christmas entertainment left a lasting impression on little Laura.[43]

保罗的外曾祖父詹姆斯·纽伯里是加拿大的拓荒者，他的父亲，保罗的外曾曾祖父是一名领取养老金的英国士兵。保罗的外祖父母是弗兰克和玛蒂尔达（纽伯里）·比林斯基。弗兰克出生在巴黎，后来淘金去了。玛蒂尔达出生在加拿大。保罗的母亲是劳拉·比林斯基，是弗兰克和玛蒂尔达六个孩子中的第五个，1879 年出生在密歇根州的韦伯维尔，她两岁时弗兰克去世了。他的年龄和死亡原因都没有被记录下来。[40,41]她在韦伯维尔待到五岁，她的母亲带她去了加拿大安大略省的伦敦。在保罗的父母约瑟夫和劳拉出生之前，玛蒂尔达和她已故的丈夫曾住在那里，他们是埃德加和哈里特·哈灵顿的朋友。这两个家庭之间的一个共同纽带是他们都积极参与教会活动。[42]另外，他们访问伦敦期间的温度一定很低，因为他们去参加圣诞娱乐活动时，脚踩着雪发出的嘎吱嘎吱声给小劳拉留下了难忘的印象。[43]

Life was undoubtedly difficult for the widowed Matilda and her six children. Laura remembered that her mother owned a four-room house with enough outdoor space for a garden to supplement their diet and sometimes to provide family presents. One Christmas all Santa left Laura was a small piece of kindling, a potato, a turnip, and a gingerbread boy in her small stocking. She saved the gingerbread boy all day long, but by evening her sister, Lydia, had managed to break its head off. "How I cried," she wrote. At times her mother kept the children in bed with the blinds drawn because of the intense cold and the fact there was nothing in the house to eat or wood for a fire. Breakfast usually consisted of stale bread and hot water. Sometimes they had sugar and occasionally a little jelly, but Laura did not remember feeling discomfort. Later she understood they "were very poor, but we were happy."[44] At five years old Laura had "brain fever," which was probably meningitis. She recalled a terrible pain in the back of her head and that her eight-year-old sister, Lydia, was her nurse during the day. One evening when their mother had not returned from work, Lydia became afraid and called a neighbor. When the neighbor picked Laura up, she screamed terribly because the back of her head hurt so much. Laura remembered being fat before then but after that illness being thin and sallow until she was fourteen.[45,46]

寡居的玛蒂尔达和她的六个孩子的生活无疑是非常困难的。劳拉记得她的母亲住在一个四室的房子里，这栋房子有足够的户外空间用来种菜以补充他们的食物，那些菜有时还可以充当家庭礼物。有次圣诞节，圣诞老人在劳拉的小长筒袜里留下了一包引火柴、一个土豆、一个萝卜和一个姜饼男孩。她一整天都不舍得吃那个姜饼男孩。但到了晚上，她的姐姐莉迪亚已经掰断了它的头，"我当时难过极了，"她写道。有时，她的母亲让孩子们躺在床上，拉上了百叶窗。因为天寒地冻，而房子里既没有东西可以吃，也没有东西可以生火。早餐通常是不新鲜的面包和热水。有时他们吃点糖或一点点果冻。但劳拉并不觉得生活很苦。后来她明白了"尽管我们很穷，但我们很幸福。"[44]五岁时，劳拉患上了"脑热病"，很可能是脑膜炎。她回忆起自己后脑勺的剧烈疼痛，她八岁的姐姐莉迪亚负责在白天照顾她。一天晚上，他们的母亲还没有下班，莉迪亚很害怕，叫来了一个邻居。当邻居把劳拉抱起来时，她大声尖叫起来，因为她的后脑勺疼得很厉害。劳拉记得在那之前她很胖，但生了那次病后她一直面黄肌瘦的，一直到 14 岁才好起来。[45,46]

Margaret, Matilda's eldest child, had moved to Kansas City, Kansas, and established a family. Lydia joined her about six months before Matilda and Laura, then about eight and a half years old, also came. At that point Laura had never had an orange or a banana but had had lemonade. Lydia wrote Laura that they had buckets full of lemonade in her new home, so after arriving in Kansas City the first thing Laura did was to go to the water bucket, expecting to find it filled with lemonade. She was so disappointed to find water. But little setbacks aside, life seemed to be getting somewhat easier. Soon after moving, Matilda remarried, and she took the job of providing postpartum care for the church architect's wife. Laura remembered "being everywhere."[47] It certainly seemed that Matilda's move had agreed with her and her family.

玛蒂尔达的长女玛格丽特搬到了堪萨斯州的堪萨斯城成了家。莉迪亚投奔了她。大约六个月后，玛蒂尔达和约八岁半的劳拉也来了。那时，劳拉从来没有吃过橘子和香蕉，只喝过柠檬水。莉迪亚写信告诉劳拉，她的新家有整桶整桶的柠檬水。所以劳拉一到堪萨斯城，做的第一件事就是去找水桶，希望水桶里面装满了柠檬水。但她很失望地发现里面全是水。撇开这些小小的不足，生活确实变得轻松了很多。搬家后不久，玛蒂尔达再婚了，她开始为教堂建筑师的妻子提供产后护理。劳拉回忆"她无处不在"。[47]玛蒂尔达的举动获得了她和她家人的认可。

Laura attended Riverview School in Kansas City, Kansas, at South Seventh Street and Pacific Avenue, and it was there that her romance with Joseph Harrington began. She remembered that Joe delighted in tormenting her by dipping her braids in the inkwells, untying her hair ribbons, and planting caterpillars on her shoulders.[48] Both of them had memories of their city, too. Joe remembered when the first part of nearby St. Margaret's Hospital was built. It had just a few rooms, and only extreme surgical cases went to the hospital in those days. The city limits were only three blocks away at Tenth and Minnesota, and there were no paved streets or streetcars. Boats on the Kansas River could be seen loading at Armour's dock.[49]

劳拉就读于位于堪萨斯州堪萨斯城南第七街和太平洋大道之间的河景学校。她和约瑟夫·哈灵顿的爱情就是在那里开始的。她记得乔（约瑟夫的小名）非常喜欢捉弄她：把她的辫子浸在墨水瓶里，偷偷解开她的发带，在她的肩上放毛毛虫。[48]他们俩都对这座城市有着难忘的记忆。乔还记得附近的圣玛格丽特医院的第一部分刚完工的时候，只有几个房间。当时只有非常严重的急需手术治疗的病人才被送去医院。市区距离第十区和明尼苏达州虽然只有三个街区远，却没有铺好的街道或有轨电车。在市区，可以看到堪萨斯河上的船只在阿默码头上装货。[49]

In thought and action Laura led a life of faith. She recalled, "I was born with the gift of faith, the kind that can open the heavens."[50] She was baptized in the Kansas River when she was nine years old. It is unclear how long she stayed in school, but she made steady progress in her Christian schooling. At age fifteen she began teaching Sunday school classes and at age seventeen was elected assistant superintendent. She later did the superintendent's work for four years.[51] It is apparent that religion played an important role in the lives of Joe and Laura. He would later become a pastor, and Laura was acknowledged for her devotion to the gospel.[52]" What effect the headquartering of the Church in Independence, Missouri, had on their parents' decisions to move to Kansas City, Kansas, is not known. Laura recalled many incidents that tested her faith. One occurred when she was sixteen and had been out of work for months. She found a job doing housework for $3 a week, a sum that she owed to someone so her first paycheck was spoken for. At the same time she was dismayed to see that one of her only pair of shoes was cracking across the toe. "I told Him I couldn't get new shoes for two weeks. Please make that crack stop." It did so she decided to buy a new dress with her second paycheck. But when she headed for the store with money in hand, she saw that her shoe was now cracked from sole to sole. She bought new shoes that week just as she had promised Him that she would do.[53]

在思想和行动上，劳拉都过着充满信仰的生活。她回忆说："我生下来就有信仰，那种能叩开天堂之门的信仰。"[50]她 9 岁时在堪萨斯河受洗。虽然不清楚她在学校里面待了多久，但她在课堂里有很多收获。15 岁时她开始在主日学校当老师，17 岁时她被选为助理督学。这份工作她干了四年。[51]很明显，宗教信仰在乔和劳拉的生活中扮演了重要的角色。乔后来成了一名牧师，而劳拉对福音的虔诚也得到了广泛认可。[52]教会总部设在密苏里州独立城，这对他们的父母决定搬到堪萨斯州的堪萨斯城有什么影响，我们不清楚。劳拉回忆起了许多考验她信仰的事，其中有一次发生在她 16 岁。她当时已经失业好几个月了，最终找到了一份做家务的工作，每周 3 美元。因为劳拉刚好欠了别人 3 美元，所以她的第一份工资就用来还钱了。但她同时沮丧地发现她唯一的一双鞋子在脚趾处开裂了。“我告诉上帝我两周内没钱买新鞋，希望鞋子不再开裂。”鞋子如愿没再开裂。于是她决定用第二份薪水买一件新衣服。但当她拿着钱到商店时，发现鞋底已经裂开了。她按照许诺上帝的那样在周末买了一双新鞋。[53]

Figure 1.1 ***Parents' wedding picture, December 25, 1899.*** (***Harrington Archives***)
图 1.1 **父母的婚纱照，1899 年 12 月 25 日（哈灵顿档案馆）**

Joe and Laura were married on Christmas Day of 1899. *See figure 1.1.* He was twenty-two, and she was twenty. Even though Kansas City, Kansas, consolidation, which included the Armstrong neighborhood, had taken place in 1886, Joe and Laura still identified Armstrong as their residence. Their wedding certificate was signed by Joe's older brother George, who apparently performed the ceremony, and the witnesses were his younger brother Ed and Laura's sister, Lydia,[54] "I paid $20 for my wedding dinner served only to the Harrington family and my family."[55] Before marriage Laura was spending $2 a week for her room, and both she and Joe had "tithed all they had." After their marriage they were able to buy a three-room house at 298 South Harrison (later Coy) within sight of St. Margaret's Hospital. *See figure 1.2.* The price was $600, putting $100 down with $10 and interest due each month. For $10 they had a cellar dug under two rooms and a toilet added. Taxes on the property were about $30 a year. This remained their home for twenty-two years.[56]

乔和劳拉于 1899 年的圣诞节结婚。（图 1.1）当时他 22 岁，她 20 岁。尽管堪萨斯州的堪萨斯城已经在 1886 年合并了阿姆斯特朗社区，但乔和劳拉仍然只认为阿姆斯特朗是他们的家乡。他们的结婚证书上有乔的哥哥乔治的签名，显然是乔治主持了婚礼。而乔的弟弟埃德和劳拉的姐姐莉迪亚是见证人。[54]“婚礼晚宴我只花了 20 美元，只邀请了哈灵顿的家人和我的家人。”[55]结婚前，劳拉要为她的房间支付每周 2 美元的租金，她和乔都要“为所有的东西缴纳什一税”。婚后，他们在南哈里森（后来的科伊）298 号买了一套三室的房子，就在圣玛格丽特医院附近。（图 1.2）房子总价是 600 美元，先交 100 美元首付，然后每个月支付 10 美元外加利息。他们又花了 10 美元在两个房间和卫生间下面挖了一个地窖。该房产的税收约为每年 30 美元。他们在这里住了 22 年。[56]

Figure 1.2 ***Harrington family home at 298 South Harrison.*** (***Harrington Anchives***)
图 1.2　哈灵顿一家位于南哈里森 298 号的住宅（哈灵顿档案馆）

Joe found a job in the meatpacking industry to support his family. For about three years he missed some work every fall because of sickness. His earnings increased from $572 in 1900 to $1,103 in 1903, despite losing two weeks of work because of the flood that year. In 1904 there was a meatpackers' strike, and, needing a steady income, he went to work for the railroad at $1.60 a day, far less than he had been bringing home. The next year that Laura kept records was 1912 when Joe's annual earnings were $845. About midway through 1913 Laura commented that she "lost heart and quit keeping accounts."[57]

乔找了一份在肉类加工厂上班的工作来养家。这三年来每到秋天，他都会请病假。他的收入从 1900 年的 572 美元增加到 1903 年的 1 103 美元，尽管他 1903 年因洪水两周没上班。1904 年发生了一次肉类加工厂工人罢工。由于需要稳定的收入，他以每天 1.60 美元的报酬去铁路工作，远低于他之前的工资。劳拉从 1911 年开始记账，1912 年，记账显示乔的年收入是 845 美元。大约到了 1913 年年中，劳拉说她“灰心丧气，不再记账”。[57]

Joe and Laura were blessed with children, four in all. Verna was born in 1901, Edgar in 1904, Myrtle in 1906, and Paul in 1911.[58] *See figure 1.3.* The doctor's charge for Vema's delivery was $10 and increased to $12 for Edgar and Myrtle. A sister stayed with Laura for $8 after Verna's birth, while her mother and sister Margaret each earned $3 a week after Edgar's birth. There was no mention of the costs associated with Paul's birth.[59] *See figure 1.4.*

乔和劳拉蒙上帝赐福，共生了四个孩子。韦尔娜生于 1901 年，埃德加生于 1904 年，默特尔生于 1906 年，保罗生于 1911 年。[58]（图 1.3）医生接生韦尔娜的费用是 10 美元，接生埃德加和默特尔的费用增加到了 12 美元。韦尔娜出生后，一个女教徒因照顾劳拉收了 8 美元，而她的母亲和姐姐玛格丽特在埃德加出生后每周只挣 3 美元。保罗的出生费用没有相关的记录。[59]（图 1.4）

Figure 1.3 ***Paul's three elder siblings, ca.1911.***
(***Harrington Archives***)
图 1.3　保罗的三个哥哥姐姐，1911 年
（哈灵顿档案馆）

Figure 1.4 ***Pau Harrington.***
(***Harrington Archives***)
图 1.4　保罗・哈灵顿
（哈灵顿档案馆）

Laura possessed an inventive imagination that Paul also would come to exhibit. She wrote to him much later in his life, recounting this episode. "Once, before you were born, I had to have a hat, folks do. Lydia had paid five dollars for one, I didn't have five cents. I had a box full of junk in the hat line. I put it on the table, knelt down and told Him that was all I had and I had to have a hat. Would He give me an idea how I could make a hat out of that. I got up and started. I got the top done but had only one row of braid for the facing on the brim. When I got that far, I remembered that a sofa pillow gift from Aunt Josie had a ribbon ruffle.I ripped it off and sewed it on the facing but didn't think to measure it. When it was finished I cut a half inch off, it was just enough!" Her brother-in-law, Dave Hepworth, said of Lydia's hat, "Why didn't you get a pretty hat, like Laura's?"[60]

劳拉拥有想象力，极富创造性，保罗经常这样赞扬自己的母亲。劳拉在保罗之后的人生中多次给他写信，并和他讲述了这样一件事："在你出生之前，有一次所有人都要戴帽子，我也不例外。莉迪亚花了 5 美元买了一个，而我连 5 美分都没有。我有一个装满毛线的盒子。我把它放在桌子上，跪下来，告诉上帝这就是我所拥有的一切，而我必须有一顶帽子。不知道他会不会告诉我如何利用这些毛线做出一顶帽子。我起身开始自己的制作。我完成了顶部，但帽檐下只有一条辫子光秃秃垂下来。当我到那一步的时候，我突然想起乔西阿姨送的沙发枕头礼物上有缎花边。我把它撕了下来，缝在了帽檐上，甚至都没有想到去量它。当它完成时，我剪掉了半英寸①。刚刚好！"她的姐夫戴夫・赫普沃斯谈到莉迪亚的帽子时说："你为什么没有一顶像劳拉一样漂亮的帽子呢？"[60]

Considering Paul's subsequent profound gratitude for the quality of his public school education, some understanding of how these educational opportunities developed is necessary. When the consolidated city of Kansas City, Kansas, was formed in 1886, it was a time of "reform and optimism." President Grover Cleveland was in the second year of his first term fighting corruption, promoting integrity, and supporting education. At the local level, one of the goals of the new city's organizers was to establish a "free" high school to make the opportunity for higher education available to all. A six-member board of education was formed, and in November 1886 the new Kansas City, Kansas High School opened in two rooms borrowed from the Riverview Grade School.[61] The physical conditions were challenging. The school was not well situated and reaching it required walking through deep mud and clay, which the students cleared from their clothes with corncobs and from the floor with shovels. Nevertheless, the standards were high. To qualify for enrollment, the students were required to pass a general entrance examination with a score of 75% and had to maintain above a 50% average in all their classes. Out-of-city students paid a tuition of $2 per month. There were four courses of study: English or Latin and science to prepare for college or university for four years, normal to prepare for teaching for three years, and commercial for accounting and business for two

---

① 1 英寸约等于 2.54 厘米。

years.[62]

考虑到保罗日后非常感激他早年所在的公立学校提供的优质教育，因此有必要了解这些教育机会是如何发展起来的。1886 年，当堪萨斯州的堪萨斯城建立时，那是一个“改革和乐观”的时代。格罗弗·克利夫兰总统在他第一个任期的第二年，打击腐败，促进诚信和发展教育。在地方层面，这座新兴城市的目标之一是建立一所“免费的”高中，为所有人提供接受高等教育的机会。1886 年 11 月，一个由六人组成的教育委员会成立了，新的堪萨斯高中从河景小学借来了两个教室，在物质条件非常艰苦的情况下宣布了开学。[61]学校的位置不佳，上学需要走过深深的泥潭和黏土，学生们只能用玉米芯拍打来清理衣服，用铲子打扫地板。然而，入学标准还是很高的。为了达到入学资格，学生必须参加入学考试，成绩必须不低于 75 分且需要超过 50%的班级同学。城外的学生每月支付 2 美元的学费。学校一共开设了四门课程：四年语言（英语或拉丁语）和科学课程，为上大学打好基础；三年师范类课程；两年与会计、贸易相关的商业课程。[62]

The Kansas City, Kansas High School was a success from the beginning. Initially, there were two teachers, Professor Wherrel, a seasoned teacher, and John Rust, a recent Yale graduate. The first graduating class consisted of eleven girls, all from the normal course. By 1892 when compulsory education laws, requiring a minimum of 12 weeks of school each year for children 8 to 14 years old, were passed in Kansas, 154 students were enrolled, and 16 boys and 3 girls graduated. In 1899 when Joe and Laura were married, a new “hundred-thousand-dollar high school” building was occupied by 16 teachers and 535 students. By 1910, the year before Paul was born, enrollment was over 1,000, and the number of teachers had increased to 40.[63]

堪萨斯高中一开始就取得了不错的成绩。起初，学校有两位老师，经验丰富的韦雷尔教授和耶鲁大学刚毕业的约翰·鲁斯特老师。第一个毕业班由 11 名女孩组成，她们学习的都是通识课程。到 1892 年，堪萨斯州通过了要求 8 至 14 岁儿童每年至少上学 12 周的义务教育法，共有 154 名学生入学。当年有 16 名男孩和 3 名女孩毕业。1899 年，当乔和劳拉结婚时，一座新的“造价 10 万美元的学校”大楼容纳了 16 名教师和 535 名学生。到 1910 年，也就是保罗出生的前一年，入学人数已经超过了 1 000 人，教师的人数已经增加到 40 人。[63]

Segregation was an important, if not the most important, issue facing public education as the twentieth century dawned. The United States Supreme Court in its 1896

Plessy v.Ferguson ruling had upheld by a vote of seven to one the constitutionality of state laws requiring racial segregation in public facilities under the doctrine of "separate but equal."[64] Although many areas of the country had become fully segregated, it was not universal in Kansas. The state legislature had struggled with this issue for years and passed school laws allowing, but not requiring, racial segregation. This culminated in an 1879 statute permitting elementary level segregation only in cities with populations of greater than 15,000. Enforcement of the law was spotty, and cities such as Emporia and Hutchinson that grew to over 15,000 residents still refused to segregate. By 1890 Kansas City, Kansas, grammar schools were fully segregated. At the high school level, segregation was prohibited by state law.[65] This was the status on April 12, 1904, when Louis Gregory, an eighteen-year-old African-American employee of the Swift meatpacking plant, shot dead Roy Martin, a popular white student at the Kansas City, Kansas High School. Gregory, who carried a revolver for protection between home and work, and a crowd of fifteen to twenty young African-Americans had taunted Martin and his white teammates as they practiced track at Kerr Park. Finally, Martin started an altercation. The ensuing furor that followed this incident revealed the conflicted state of Kansans' minds on the race issue and resulted in legislation signed by a reluctant Governor Edward W. Hoch on February 22,1905, which allowed segregation of Kansas City, Kansas High School.[66]

20世纪初，种族隔离是公共教育面临的一个重要问题。美国最高法院在其1896年的普莱西诉弗格森案的裁决中以7票对1票的结果支持了“隔离但平等”原则，确认在公共场所中进行种族隔离的州法律的合宪性。虽然这个国家的许多地区已经完全实行种族隔离，但在堪萨斯州并不如此。州立法机构多年来一直在努力解决这个问题，并通过了允许但不强制实行种族隔离的学校法律。1879年颁布了一项法令，允许只在人口超过15 000人的城市进行基本的种族隔离。这项法律的执行情况很不稳定，恩波里亚和哈钦森等城市已经增长到超过15 000名居民，但仍然拒绝隔离。到1890年，堪萨斯州堪萨斯城的文法学校完全实行种族隔离。而在高中，州法律禁止种族隔离。[65]这是1904年4月12日的情形：18岁的斯威夫肉加工厂的非裔工人路易斯·格雷戈里枪杀了堪萨斯城高中受欢迎的白人学生罗伊·马丁。带着左轮手枪的格雷戈里和15到20名年轻的非裔美国人嘲笑在克尔公园进行田径训练的马丁和他的白人队友。最后，马丁与他们发生冲突。这一事件随后引发的公愤反映出了堪萨斯州人在种族问题上的矛盾态度，并导致州长爱德华·W. 霍奇在1905年2月22日不情愿地签署了法案，让堪萨斯城的高中也实施种族隔离。[66]

By 1911 the frontier of medical science and the tools of therapeutic methodology where Paul Harrington's future lay had advanced considerably. Pathology, physiology, epidemiology, microbiology, and radiology had been added to anatomy as major disciplines and contributors to making sense of disease. The pathologic lesion and causative organism of polio had been identified. Plaster of paris, anesthesia, and antisepsis had expanded therapeutic options. However, these developments had yet to make any difference in the management of scoliosis. With the exception of anesthesia these developments had all originated in Europe. The Kansas City, Kansas, world Harrington was born into was rapidly emerging from a hardscrabble collection of frontier towns into a vibrant, working-class city with a dedication to quality public education. And the medical school he would be forever grateful to was now six years old.[67]

到 1911 年，医学领域的前沿技术和治疗设备都取得了长足发展，这也是保罗·哈灵顿未来的发展方向。病理学、生理学、流行病学、微生物学和放射学已和解剖学一样成为研究疾病的主要方法。当时脊髓灰质炎的病理病变和病原体已被确定。熟石膏、麻醉术和消毒术增加了可选择的治疗方案。然而，这些发展对脊柱侧凸的治疗没有什么影响。除了麻醉术，这些技术发展都起源于欧洲。虽然哈灵顿居住的堪萨斯城已经从贫瘠的边缘小镇发展为生机勃勃的拥有高质量的公共教育的工业城市，但那个他将会永怀感恩之情的堪萨斯大学医学院当时才建院 6 年。[67]

（郑鲁豫 译　方向前 卢旭华 审校）

2 GROWTH AND DEVELOPMENT (1911-34)

Without him there isn't any team.[1]

成长与发展(1911—1934)

团队里的主心骨。[1]

A childhood friend had this recollection: "We didn't get to see too much of Paul in his early days. He always had projects he was working on. I remember one time they had a contest for boys, I think he was ten or eleven, and they had to make an automobile out of boards and whatever they could salvage. And I'm going to tell you, Paul was a genius! I could not believe what he made! He won the contest. All these kids, they had some nice cars there, but none of them matched. But everything was perfect on his. Paul, you know, was a stickler for perfection. I never will forget that. I told Paul, and I said, 'Paul, how did you do this? 'And he said, 'Well, you just have to work at it and by hit and miss.'"[2]

一位儿时的朋友回忆道："保罗小的时候，我们很少见到他。他总有自己的事要忙。我记得在他十岁还是十一岁的时候，有次男孩们举办了一场比赛，他们要用木板和任何能回收到的东西制作一辆汽车。我要告诉你，保罗真是个天才！我简直不敢相信那是他自己做出来的汽车！他赢得了比赛。参赛的孩子中也有人做出了很漂亮的车，但没有一辆能和保罗的相媲美，保罗的车无可挑剔。当然，保罗是一个追求完美的人，这一点我永远也不会忘记。我有一次问他，'保罗，你是怎么做到的？'他回答'你只需要尽全力去做，总会有成功的时候。'"[2]

This perfectionist, Paul Randall Harrington, was born on September 27, 1911, in Kansas City, Kansas. It is fortunate that his mother Laura wrote down many recollections of her youngest child.[3] These and other records portray a person of immense natural ability and many admirable personal traits, although in infancy the state of his health did cause some concern. At age two he had what Laura believed was an intestinal illness with passage of blood and slime. She felt he almost died.[4] After that he appeared to have been healthy. Because Laura' s religious faith was so important to her, Paul was joined to the Sunday School Cradle Roll of Armstrong "his first Sunday on earth" and started attending Sunday school when he was two years old, rarely missing more than once a year until he went to college.[5] His mother remembered in detail the following particularly revealing story about him.

这位完美主义者保罗·哈灵顿在1911年9月27日出生于堪萨斯州的堪萨斯城。幸运的是，他的母亲劳拉写下了关于她最小孩子的许多回忆。[3]这些回忆记录了他的杰出天赋和许多令人钦佩的个人品质。然而在他还是个婴儿的时候，他的健康状况确实引起了大家的一些担忧。两岁时，他患上了一种伴有血液和黏液排出的肠道疾病，这让劳拉都觉得他奄奄一息。[4]但在那之后，他似乎一直都很健康。由于劳拉有着虔诚的宗教信仰，所以保罗加入了阿姆斯特朗的主日学校摇篮名册"降临到世界上的第一个星期日"，并在他两岁时开始上主日学校，每年都未曾缺席超过一次，一直到他上大学。[5]他母亲清楚地记得下面这个关于他的令人深省的故事。

"Our beginner's class used a little room over the baptismal font. I took him to the room and left him. In a few minutes he came to me crying. I quieted him and took him back. I told him he must stay and he said he would. Soon he came to me again, crying. He was only two years old. I quieted him and asked him a half dozen questions about why he didn't want to stay, he only shook his head. I thought him stubborn. I took him outdoors and spanked him. When he was quiet I took him to the room again and left him. He came to me crying in a few minutes. I felt sure he must have some reason he could not explain. After church I took him to the little room and sat down, holding him in my arms to see what he would do. I said nothing. Soon he crept down to the floor, cautiously raised a corner of the rug and peeked under, raised it higher and said, 'Water mama, water? Water? ' I removed the benches and rug, raised the trap door, showed him the hole in the corner of the font where the water ran out and said, 'Water all gone.' That was the end of the trouble. He must have seen the font full and children being baptized a few months before and was terrified. He was too young to reason he was safe if the other children were. He only knew he was safe as long as mama was there."[6] The episode also suggests an unusually observant, curious, inquisitive, and persistent two-year-old, and these characteristics stayed with him throughout his life.

"我们初学者的班级在圣洗池上方有一个小房间。我把他带到房间后便离开了。几分钟后他哭着向我走来，我让他安静下来，便带他回去。我告诉他必须留下来，他答应了。不久后他又哭着跑到我身边。他当时只有两岁，我让他安静下来，问了他半天为什么不想留下来，他只摇了摇头。我以为他在耍赖不听话，便把他带到房间外，打了他屁股。等他安静下来，我又把他带回房间里，让他待在那。几分钟后他再次哭着来找我，我确信他一定有什么难言之隐。做完礼拜后，我把他带到小房间里坐下来，把他抱在怀里，看他会怎么做。我什么也没说，不一会儿他蹑手蹑脚地走到地板上，小心翼翼地掀起地毯的一角往下偷看，而后把它举高，说：'水？妈妈，有水？'我移开凳子和地毯，拉开活板门，指给他看圣洗池角落里出水的洞，对他说：'水都没了。'麻烦就此解决。他一定是几个月前看到孩子们正在蓄满水的圣洗池中洗礼时被吓到了。他太小了，并不觉得别的孩子没事自己就没事，只有妈妈在的时候他才觉得自己是安全的。"[6]这段插曲也表明他是一个善于观察、探究，充满好奇心且坚持不懈的两岁孩子，这些特点后来都伴随着他的一生。

From an early age Paul's manual dexterity was apparent and extraordinary. As a small child he enjoyed playing in the yard and digging many holes about the size of a quart can. He also liked to make tunnels. When Paul was three, he would often spend three hours at a time driving fine shingle nails into pieces of scrap 2×4s. He would sit on the floor with the board between his knees and drive nail after nail into it without ever hitting a finger, or if he did, he chose not to mention it. As early as he was able to handle a knife, he whittled boats—and only boats. With time some splendid carvings emerged.[7] He was very respectful of adult conversation and would often refuse to go out and play, preferring to sit on a stool and listen.[8] When he was about eight, he started tooting his dad's old trumpet, and when boys asked him to come outside and play, he refused because he wanted to practice.[9] He was described as always being an obedient child at home and school.[10] In summation he was persistent, talented, and disciplined.

从小，保罗的手就非常灵巧。小时候他喜欢在院子里玩，挖很多大约有一夸脱①罐子那样大小的洞，他还喜欢挖隧道。3 岁时，他经常每次花 3 个小时将细小的木瓦钉钉在 2×4② 大小的废料碎片上。他坐在地板上，用膝盖夹着木板，把钉子一颗又一颗地钉进去，却从未钉到过手指，或者即便钉到了，他也从不提此事。早在他会用刀的时候，他便开始削小船，且只削小船。随着时间的推移，他能做出一些精美的雕刻作品。[7]他在大人们聊天时非常谦恭，经常宁愿坐在凳子上听也不愿出去玩。[8]大约 8 岁大时，他开始吹他父亲的老式小号，他拒绝男孩们叫他出去玩的邀请，因为他想练习吹奏。[9]家里和学校的人都说他是一个听话的孩子。[10]总之，他有毅力，有才华，有纪律。

Paul attended the Kansas City, Kansas, public schools throughout his primary and secondary education years. He entered first grade at the Riverview School, where his parents had attended, on September 10, 1917. He was nearly six years old. During the first three years of school the basics of study were arithmetic, reading, language, and writing, and grades were reported as numbers. Paul's average was 80, surpassing the 75 needed for promotion. The third year a qualitative grade was given for each area of study, and his were either good or medium. At the age of eight years, Paul was promoted to the fourth grade on May 20, 1920.[11] Three months before this, tragedy struck the Harrington family. On February 3, 1920, older brother Edgar, then just a few days from his seventeenth birthday, developed encephalitis from which he never fully recovered.[12] Although able to walk, he was left physically and mentally handicapped the rest of his life. Edgar had been talented with a bright future ahead so his condition continually tested Laura Harrington's faith.[13]

保罗在堪萨斯城的公立学校度过了他的小学和中学。1917 年 9 月 10 日，快 6 岁的他去了父母曾就读的河景小学上一年级。在学校的前三年里，学习的是算术、阅读、语言和写作等基础知识，成绩均以数字表示。保罗的平均成绩是 80 分，超过了升学所需的 75 分。第三年，每个学习领域都有一个定性的成绩，他的成绩是好或中等。1920 年 5 月 20 日，8 岁的保罗升为四年级学生。[11]而在此之前的三个月里，哈灵顿家族一直被厄运笼罩着。1920 年 2 月 3 日，他的哥哥埃德加在他 17 岁生日的前几天得了脑炎，从此再也没能完全康复。[12]虽然能够走路，但他

---

① 依美制．若为干量单位，1 夸脱约等于 1. 10 升；若为湿量单位，1 夸脱等于 0. 946 升。

② 原著未标明单位，依上下文，应为 2 英寸×4 英寸。

的余生都将身心残疾。埃德加一直很有天赋，本来前途光明，因此他的病情不断地考验着母亲劳拉的信念。[13]

Paul's fourth grade has proved to be a mystery. He should have enrolled in September 1920, and after graduation from that grade in May of the next year he should have begun the fifth grade in September 1921. However, his school records show that he enrolled in the fifth grade on September 11, 1922, indicating the delay of a full year. Perhaps this was related to Edgar's illness. Over the years Laura felt that Paul "had made thousands of sacrifices because of his brother's sickness,"[14] and disruption of Paul's school progression may have been one of the first. Another possibility is that because he was one of the youngest in his class, the decision was made to give him more time to develop. Perhaps it was a combination of the two or some unknown factor. One thing is clear though, the year's delay was not because of academic or disciplinary reasons.

保罗的四年级是个谜。他在 1920 年 9 月入学，第二年 5 月从这个年级毕业后，他本该在 1921 年 9 月就开始读五年级。然而，学校记录却显示他在 1922 年 9 月 11 日才进入五年级，这意味着他推迟了整整一年。这也许和埃德加的病有关。这些年来，劳拉觉得保罗“为了他哥哥的疾病做出了不计其数的牺牲”，[14]而保罗在学校的学业进展中断可能是首当其冲的牺牲之一。另一种可能是，因为他是班上最年轻的学生之一，所以学校决定给他更多的时间来成长。也许是这两者的结合，或是某种未知的因素，但保罗绝不是因为学业或纪律问题延迟这一年。

From 1922 to 1930 the Harringtons made three moves with the first in an effort to increase their income and the following two to decrease expenses. In 1922 they moved to a larger, ten-room house at 229 North Seventeenth Street so that they could rent out rooms to raise extra funds. Netting $1,400 from the sale of their first house, they invested $1,000 in this new one, which cost $6,500. With roomers and boarders Laura cleared $10 a week, which was enough to feed the family of six. However, Edgar began having seizures that were worsened by the commotion produced by all the people in the house. It was clear that roomers could no longer be taken in so in 1925 they sold the house for $3,500 cash, which was their equity. The Harringtons built a five-room bungalow at 2004 Orville for $5,600, reducing their property tax to $170 per year. In 1930 they traded houses, still owing $1,800, which the trading owner assumed. Their new house, located at 11 South Twentieth Street, was clear of debt, and the annual property tax was much less at just $90 per year.[15]

1922 年到 1930 年间，哈灵顿家族搬了三次家，第一次是为了增加收入，后两次是为了减少开支。1922 年他们搬到了位于北十七街 229 号一栋包含十个房间的更大的房子，这样他们就可以出租多余的房间来筹集额外的资金。卖掉第一套房子净赚 1 400 美元后，他们又投资了 1 000 美元买了套价值 6 500 美元的新房。有了房客和寄宿生，劳拉每周能赚到 10 美元，这足以养活他们一家六口。然而，埃德加的癫痫却开始发作，屋子里的人所引起的任何骚动都会使他病情恶化。很显然，他们无法再收留房客了，因此在 1925 年，他们以 3 500 美元的价格卖掉了房子，这是他们的净资产。哈灵顿夫妇在奥维尔 2004 号花了 5 600 美元建造了一座有五个房间的平房，并将他们的房产税降低到每年 170 美元。1930 年，他们向银行借贷 1 800 美元，换了新房子。他们的新房位于南二十街 11 号，因为没有了其他债务，每年的房产税也少了很多，只有 90 美元。[15]

Of all the family members, his mother remembered Paul as the only one who never forgot to keep the noise level down.[16] When Paul was ten, one morning he was pumping water. The cog slipped, and to avoid wakening his sick brother, he grabbed the handle and in the process tore off the end of his finger, nail and all. His mother looked up and saw him holding his hand, blood streaming from the finger.[17] Paul's humanism was being regularly tested and proving strong.

保罗的母亲记得，他是家里唯一一个牢记尽量不发出噪声的人。[16]保罗 10 岁时，有天早上他正在抽水，但齿轮滑落了，为了不吵醒他生病的哥哥，他抓住了把手，但在这个过程中他的手指指尖、指甲都被撕掉了。劳拉抬起头，看到他握住自己的手，鲜血沿手指直往下流。[17]保罗善良的秉性经常受到考验，但事实证明他的内心非常强大。

His abilities were being recognized by others. Paul was eleven the month he enrolled in fifth grade at Prescott School in September 1922, and he remained there for sixth grade. His scores in arithmetic, geography, language, and spelling ranged from 80 to 90. His attitude to school was consistently noted as being "very commendable." In the category of recitations his teachers checked the "capable of doing much better work" option. He was a member of the school's basketball team that won the city championship.[18] It was becoming apparent that Paul had many talents, including academics, music, and theater. It didn't seem there was anything he couldn't do well, but where he really excelled was in athletics and leadership. His mother remembered that "he has a high standard of morals and no amount of meanness on the part of the other fellow moves him an inch. He is very modest. Never brags. Never feels exalted, because he compares his successes to perfection and of course they always measure down."[19] In short, Paul was a natural in every sense of the word. The qualities his mother described remained with him for the rest of his life.

他的能力得到了别人的认可。1922 年 9 月，11 岁的保罗开始在普雷斯科特学校上五年级，并在那里接着读了六年级。他在算术、地理、语言和拼写方面的成绩在 80 至 90 分之间。他在学校的表现一直是"非常值得赞扬"的。在朗诵方面，他的老师在"能够做得很好"的选项上打钩。他是学校篮球队成员，他们得过市级冠军。[18]显然保罗有很多才能，包括学术、音乐和戏剧。似乎没有什么是他做不好的，但他真正擅长的是体育运动和领导他人。他母亲回忆道："他有很高的道德标准，其他同学的卑鄙行径丝毫不能动摇他。他非常谦虚，从不骄傲自大，因为他把自己的成功与完美相比较，总觉得自己仍有待完善。[19]简而言之，他在各个方面都极具天赋，他母亲所描述的这些品质伴随了他的一生。

In September 1924 Paul enrolled in the seventh grade at Kansas City, Kansas Central Junior High School, and his popularity and leadership qualities flourished during his three years there. *See figure 2.1.* His mother had the following recollection. "When he was elected president of the seventh grade, a class of over 300, also president of the student council—out of 900 students, he did not mention it at home. Our nephew told us. Paul's father Joe, not knowing classes have sponsors to direct their affairs, gave him a half hour instruction in parliamentary usages etc. without interruption. At its close Paul quietly said, 'We did all of that today.' He seemed amazed when we laughed." Laura's recollections continued. "When he was president of his class at junior high, he had been asking for some overalls. One day I got a pair in the morning, put them on the table and went on an errand. Paul came home, saw the overalls and into them he went. When he came home

Figure 2.1 ***Paul, president of his seventh grade class. (Harrington Archives)***
图 2.1 保罗，七年级年级长
（哈灵顿档案馆）

he was delighted because he had dipped the ice cream. I said, 'Did you have your class party today?' He said, 'It wasn't a party, we just had ice cream and wafers.' I said who was there? He said, 'Oh! Just Mr. Shaw (principal), the teachers and the class of 300.' I chuckle when I think of that picture. The class party, the principal and fifteen to twenty teachers and the class president, all dressed up in his new overalls, dipping ice cream. He got two dips because there was some left. I wanted him to be free of a care for what the other fellow thought. But it seemed too good to be true."[20]

1924 年 9 月，保罗进入堪萨斯州堪萨斯城中心初级中学就读七年级，在那的三年里，他的知名度和领导才能都得到了长足的提升。(图 2.1) 他的母亲回忆如下，"当他在有 300 多名学生的七年级担任年级长时，同时还是 900 名学生的学生会主席时，他在家里只字不提，后来还是侄子告诉了我们。保罗的父亲乔不知道其实每个班级都有负责人来指导他们的班级事务，就不间断地给保罗上了半个小时的关于学校议会管理等方面的课。结束时，保罗悄悄地说'其实今天我们都学了'。当我们笑的时候，他显得很惊讶"。劳拉继续回忆道："当他在初中担任班长时，他一直想要一些工作服。有天早上我买了一套放在桌上，然后出门办事了。保罗回到家，看到工作服就穿上了。当他回到家时很高兴，因为他穿工作服参与了冰激凌的制作。我说：'你们今天有班级派对吗？'他说：'那不是派对，我们只是吃了冰激凌和华夫饼'。我问在那儿都有谁？他说：'哦！有肖校长、老师和全班同学，共 300 人'。我一想到那张照片就笑了。班级聚会，校长，15 到 20 位老师，还有班长都看着他穿着那套新工作服做冰激凌。因为还剩了一些材料，他便制作了两轮。我希望他不去在意别人的想法。但（别人对他的评价）似乎好得令人难以置信。"[20]

He did well in his classes, achieving a B+ average. His courses of study included geography, mathematics, science, English, Latin, civics, and history.[21] His ninth grade general science class required an individual project, and he appeared to have known exactly what he wanted to do since he had had years of practice leading up to that moment. The local newspaper reported as follows: "The history of yachts was told by a boy who made a typical yacht to explain the many points of construction that differentiate a yacht from other boats. The model is thirty inches long and is valued at $40." A tattered and faded surviving picture shows a very handsome sloop-rigged model with an aggressive display of sail.[22]

他在课堂上表现良好，平均成绩为 B+。他学习的课程包括地理、数学、科学、英语、拉丁语、公民学和历史。[21]九年级的普通科学课中要求他做一个单独的项目，他似乎很清楚自己想做什么，因为在这之前他已经有很多年的实践经验。当地报纸报道如下，"一个制作了一艘典型游艇的男孩讲述游艇的历史，他解释了游艇与其他船只许多不同的构造要点。这个模型长30英寸，价值40美元"。一张破旧褪色的保存照片展示了一艘非常漂亮的拥有醒目船帆的单桅帆船模型。[22]

Paul excelled in athletics even though football does not appear to have been offered and basketball was not emphasized. In the one surviving basketball box score we learn that his team lost to Olathe 13 to 8 with Paul scoring 6 points. He participated in other non-school-related games: a team sponsored by the Sterling Chemical Company won lopsided victories with Paul the leading scorer with 19 and 20 points. Junior high track was offered, and Paul broke two state records. At one meet he easily won the high jump with a 5' 5" leap and the 100-yard low hurdles with a time of 13. 5 seconds.[23] *See figure 2.2.* His coach, Mr. Cogswell, told Laura that "Paul is a leader of a group of 40 boys and gets better discipline with less friction than any other group head. He is a gentleman in the fullest sense of the word."[24] His mother remembered the following interesting episode illustrating the tensions between academics and athletics. "When he attended junior high he had a teacher who was opposed to athletics. If a boy's work wasn't satisfactory the teacher could refuse to let him go to a meet. One time Paul had to hand in a theme on a certain kind of paper. He worked late on lessons, but then when the theme was about finished he ran out of that kind of paper, finished on another kind, intending to copy it before he handed it in. On the grounds of unsatisfactory work she refused to OK him. The coach went to the principal and said, 'There is no use of us entering the meet if Paul can't go, without him there isn't any team.' The principal called the teacher to find how bad Paul's work was. She contended he should have gone to a drugstore at 11 o'clock and gotten more paper. The principal ruled since his work was

Figure 2.2 ***Paul in the midst of a competitive high jump.*** (***Harrington Archives***)
图 2.2 保罗在竞技跳高比赛中(哈灵顿档案馆)

done, even on other paper, he could go. The whole school held their breath, in a way."[25]

保罗在体育方面表现出色，尽管似乎没有提到足球，也没有强调篮球，但在现存的一份篮球比赛记录中，我们了解到他所在的球队以 8 比 13 输给了奥拉西队时，保罗个人得到了 6 分。他还参加了其他的校外比赛：他帮助由斯特林化学公司赞助的球队赢得了压倒性的胜利，且他是主要得分手，两场比赛分别得到 19 分和 20 分。在初中田径比赛中，保罗打破了两项州纪录。在一次运动会上，他以 5 英尺 5 英寸的成绩轻松赢得了跳高比赛，并以 13.5 秒的成绩赢得了 100 码①低栏比赛。[23]（图 2.2）他的教练科格斯韦尔对劳拉说："保罗作为领队带领一个由 40 名男孩组成的团队，与其他领队相比，他更加遵守纪律，较少与他人发生冲突，他是一位真正意义上的绅士。"[24]他的母亲还记得一段反映了学业和体育之间矛盾关系的对话。"他上初中时遇到了一位反对体育运动的老师。这位老师如果对班里某位男生的表现不满意，便会拒绝他参加运动会。有一次，老师要求保罗必须要用特定纸张书写作文。他在课堂上写到很晚，快要完成时，那种特定纸用完了，于是他用另一种纸完成作文，并打算在交作业前用特定纸张誊写一份。老师以作业完成得不理想为由拒绝他进入球队。教练对校长说：'如果保罗不能去，我们没法参加比赛，因为球队不能没有他。'后来校长打电话给老师了解保罗的作业有多差。老师坚持认为他应该在 11 点的时候去店里买更多的纸。校长则认为，虽然使用了其他的纸，但他的工作已经完成了，因此可以去参加运动会。在某种程度上，似乎全校师生都在这件事情的结果出来之前，替保罗捏了一把汗。"[25]

Mrs. Harrington played an active role as a parent. About 1927 a firestorm arose when the Kansas City, Kansas school board did not renew the contracts of 30 teachers and executives and refused to give the reason. The action targeted the teachers and administrators that had been working to unionize the teachers. When criticized, board chair John E. Wilson said that the board had been willing to talk, but that instead of consulting with them, the teachers' organization had contacted the newspapers, bringing propaganda into the picture. At one of the meetings Mrs. Harrington spoke up. "I am only interested in my children. It isn't just a question of a courteous hearing, which you have given us, but a matter of justice and truth. No matter what has happened or how the board

① 1 码 = 0.914 4 米。

feels about this thing, if this action is allowed to go unchallenged and perhaps repeated, it will be impossible to obtain a high class teaching body in Kansas City, Kansas, ten years from now. The whole city is distressed. There is a feeling of distrust and instability about our schools."[26]

哈灵顿夫人是一位尽责的母亲。大约在1927年，堪萨斯城的堪萨斯学校董事会没有与30名教师和高管续签合同并拒绝给出理由，这引发了一场针对教师和一直在为教师工会工作的服务人员的风波。面对批评，董事会主席约翰·E. 威尔逊说，董事会始终愿同教师组织对话，但他们未经协商就联系了报社，并通过照片传播了这件事情。在一次会议上，哈灵顿夫人发言："我只关心我的孩子。问题不在于你为我们安排的友好听证会，而在于正义和真理。不管发生了什么，也不管董事会对这件事有什么看法，如果这种做法不受公众质疑，甚至在未来重复出现，那么十年后在堪萨斯州的堪萨斯城将不可能存在高水平的教学机构。整个城市将会陷入困境，人们会对我们的学校产生一种不信任感和不安稳感"。[26]

In September 1927 Paul enrolled in the tenth grade, spending the next three years at Kansas City, Kansas High School where his athleticism became evident. The school prided itself on being the first free public high school in the city, opening its doors in 1886, which was the same year this unified city was founded.[27] In January 1928 the school's name was formally changed to Wyandotte High School, in recognition that recent Kansas City, Kansas annexations had included two fully accredited high schools: Argentine and Rosedale.[28] As a sophomore his course work included geometry 1 and 2, English 3 and 4, typewriting, and biology. His average grade was B−.[29] Wyandotte High School was in the Northeast (Kansas) League that included eight other high schools: Atchison, Topeka, Lawrence, Ottawa, Olathe, Leavenworth, Argentine, and Rosedale.[30] The latter two, along with Wyandotte and Catholic High School, formed the unofficial intracity league. At the beginning of the 1927−28 school year basketball coach Percy Parks was recruited from Olathe where his team had won the Northeast League championship. In his first year at Wyandotte High his basketball team broke a four-year losing streak to Olathe. The team did lose one regular season game by three points to Southwest, the premier high school in Kansas City, Missouri. But, Wyandotte was the intracity champion, nearly won the Northeast League, and advanced through the first two games in the state championship playoffs before losing in the semifinals to Winfield, the 1926−27 state champion. Paul started the season as a frequent substitute and ended as a starter playing guard. He was emerging as a playmaker.[31] The Wyandotte High School 1928 track team had a good year. Their best event was the mile relay, in which they set a new state interscholastic record of 3 minutes, 33 seconds. *See figure 2.3.* This time was as good as any other in the country. Believing it would be a good form of promotion for the city, the milers entered the National Interscholastic Track Meet held in June at the University of Chicago. The cost of the trip for the team, including Paul, Clerin Zumwalt, Earl "Jiggers" Harrison, team captain Steve Hawkins, and Coach Fred R. Powers, was $200, which was raised from supporters. Team members were disappointed to finish fifth.[32] When he was fourteen, he ranked third in the in the city's men's tennis tournament. And, one of his senior high coaches said that Paul was one of his best swimmers and his best diver. Time did not allow further development of these skills.[33]

Figure 2.3 ***Nineteen twenty-eight Kansas state champion mile relay team: left to right, Clerin Zumwalt, Harrington, Coach Fred R. Powers, Earl "Jiggers" Harrison, and captain Steve Hawkins. (Harrington Archives)***

图 2.3　1928 年堪萨斯州一英里接力赛冠军队伍:从左至右,克莱林·朱姆沃尔特,哈灵顿,弗雷德·R. 鲍尔斯教练,"跳蚤"哈里森伯爵和史蒂夫·霍金斯队长(哈灵顿档案馆)

1927 年 9 月，保罗进入了十年级，在堪萨斯城堪萨斯高中度过了接下来的三年，在那里他的运动天赋逐渐彰显。这所学校以成为该市第一所免费公立高中为荣，它建立于 1886 年，与这座城市同龄。[27] 1928 年 1 月，学校正式更名为怀恩多特高中，以便同堪萨斯州堪萨斯城最近合并的两所有资质的高中，阿根廷高中和罗斯代尔高中[28]区分开。第二学年，他的课程包括几何 1 和 2，英语 3 和 4，打字和生物。他的平均成绩是 B-。[29]怀恩多特高中属于东北（堪萨斯）联盟，该联盟包括其他八所高中：艾奇逊、托皮卡、劳伦斯、渥太华、奥拉西、莱文沃思、阿根廷和罗斯代尔高中。[30]后两所学校，与怀恩多特和天主教高中，组成了非官方的内部联盟。在 1927—1928 学年开始时，校方从奥拉西请来篮球教练珀西·帕克斯，他指导的球队在那里赢得了东北联盟冠军。保罗在怀恩多特高中的第一年，他带领的篮球队打破了连续四年输给奥拉西的局面。怀恩多特高中篮球队确实以三分之差输给了密苏里州堪萨斯城的最好的高中西南高中，但是几乎赢得了东北联盟的内部冠军，并在州锦标赛季后赛的前两场比赛中晋级，最后在半决赛中输给了 1926—1927 年的州冠军温菲尔德高中。本赛季开始时保罗经常作为替补出场，在结束时又作为首发后卫出场。后来他逐渐成为一名组织进攻者。[31] 1928 年一整年，怀恩多特高中田径队都表现不错。田径队擅长一英里接力赛，在该项目中创造了 3 分 33 秒的州际纪录。（图 2.3）他们参加了 6 月份在芝加哥大学举行的全国校际田径运动会，他们相信这次运动会同国内的其他运动会一样，将成为一个很好的推广城市的机会。团队成员包括保罗，克莱林 · 朱姆沃尔特，“跳蚤”哈里森伯爵，队长史蒂夫 · 霍金斯和教练弗雷德 · R. 鲍尔斯，支持者为他们的出行募集了 200 美元。但第五名的成绩令团队感到失望。[32] 14 岁时，保罗在全市男子网球锦标赛中排名第三。此外，他的一位高中教练说，保罗是他带过的最好的游泳运动员和潜水员之一。然而，他没有足够的时间去进一步提升这些技能。[33]

In addition to these athletic pursuits, Paul had many other talents. Even though he entered the junior high orchestra having had only four cornet lessons, he was chosen first cornetist. When he entered the 75-member senior high band that included 10 or 12 cornets, he was made a soloist. The band was skilled, winning the conference in three out of five years. He played in it for two years, but his athletics interfered too much so he quit even though he loved music. He was a natural leader and actor. Less obvious was his talent for making do with limited resources. His mother was an excellent teacher in this course and recorded several examples from this time. “When he was a sophomore he wanted a loose-leaf notebook. He took some leather that had been a chair bottom for years; made holes for rings and has used it every day for two years.”[34] She remembered, “When he went to a club dinner at the Baltimore Hotel, he had me cut his vest low, semiformal, dark blue, got new trousers, the sleeves were short as it was two years old. He was careful not to stretch his arms.” Whether she knew it or not, Laura time and again reinforced the adage that necessity was the mother of invention. Laura recalled the time he needed a sweater, and together they worked through the innovative process. “The school colors were red and white; he wanted a sweater. There was an eight year old one that had been his brother’s. I had some soft leather from an old pillow top. I cut a square for the elbow and ran a two and a half inch strip down to and over the cuff as the underside of the sleeve was gone. He wanted a doodad. Their emblem was a bulldog. They cost seventy-five cents. I took another piece of said pillow, lined it with a scrap of red silk, cut a K in the leather and stitched it in red silk like a football lace and all. We put it over a mended hole in the sweater and he used it as a pocket. The above was his idea, I did the work. It was so unusual some of the boys thought he picked it up at some sports shoppe."[35]

除了这些运动爱好，保罗还有许多其他才能。尽管他只上了四节短号课就进入了初中管弦乐队，但他还是第一个被选为短号演奏者。当他进入有75人的高中乐队（包括10或12个短号手）时，他成了独奏者。这支乐队技术精湛，五年中有三年赢得了大会冠军。他参加了两年的乐队，但体育运动占了他太多时间，即便他很热爱音乐，最终也只能选择退出。他天生就是一位领导者和演员，另一个隐藏天赋就是他善于利用有限的资源完成各种事情。他的母亲在这方面是一位出色的老师，并记录了当时的一些事迹。“高二的时候，他想要一本活页笔记本。他拿了一些贴在陈年旧椅底上的皮革，用戒指在上面打洞，自制了活页笔记本，并且两年来每天都用它。”[34]她回忆道，“当他去巴尔的摩酒店参加一个俱乐部晚宴时，他让我把他的半正式深蓝色背心的领口剪得很低，袖子短得像他两年前穿的那样，还准备了条新裤子。穿上衣时他格外小心，且没有伸展手臂”。不管她是否明白它的含义，劳拉一次又一次地强调这句格言：需要是发明之母。劳拉回想起有次他需要一件毛衣，他们便一起完成了这个创新的过程。“他想要一件毛衣，学校要求红色和白色。我有一件他哥哥8岁大时穿过的毛衣，还有一些旧枕头套上的软皮革。我在毛衣肘部剪了一个正方形，然后去掉袖子的下面，在袖口上剪了一条2.5英寸长的长条。他还想要个小玩意：一只标志着他们学校的斗牛犬，商场售价75美分。我又拿了一个枕头，用一块红色的丝绸做衬里，在皮革上剪了一个K字，然后像足球蕾丝一样用红色的丝绸缝制起来，把它盖在毛衣上一个补好的洞上当口袋用。这些是他的主意，由我来完成。这些想法都太不同寻常了，有些男孩甚至以为他毛衣上的斗牛犬是在体育用品店里买的。”[35]

In addition to his many pursuits, work began to intrude into his schedule. The summer after his sophomore year the only work he could find was on the construction gang at Cudahy Packing House. His mother described it as "the hardest, dirtiest manual labor," and of fifteen men hired he was the only one who stayed with the job. The first part of the summer after his junior year he worked at Sheffield Steel handling hot iron rods, the latter part for Perry Motor Company.[36] He also added new activities to his calendar. The summer after his sophomore year he was initiated into a social fraternity, Delta Omicron Omicron, on July 25, 1928, and attended its 31st annual convention held in Wichita from August 30 to September 1. The following year the annual meeting was held in Kansas City, Kansas, and he was listed as historian for his chapter.[37]

除这些爱好之外，工作也开始进入了他的日程当中。高二结束的夏天，他唯一能找到的工作是在卡达希包装厂当建筑工。他的母亲形容这是“最艰苦、最恶劣的体力劳动”，在 15 名雇用男工人中，他是唯一一位留到最后的人。高三后的第一个暑假，前面一半时间他在谢菲尔德钢铁公司工作，处理热铁棒，接下来又在佩里汽车公司工作了半个暑假。[36]他还在日程表上增加了新的活动：高二后的夏天，他于 1928 年 7 月 25 日加入了一个社会兄弟会，并参加了 8 月 30 日至 9 月 1 日在威奇托举行的第三十一届年度大会。第二年的年会在堪萨斯州的堪萨斯城举行，因为履历，他被列入往届老会员名单中。[37]

His junior year began in September 1928, and he was promptly elected president of his class of just over 400 students. Course work for the year included English 5 and 6, physics 1, drama, and band. He made straight A's and in the spring was one of ten juniors elected to the National Honor Society. To be eligible, a student had to be in the top 25% of the class academically and be outstanding in scholarship, character, leadership, and service.[38] He was a member of the cast of the junior class play and also had the lead role in a play put on by the K Club, whose members were athletic letter holders.[39] He lettered in football, basketball, and track, which was and is a remarkable achievement. Paul played end on the football team that lost only one game and tied for the Northeast League championship. He was chosen for the city all-star team.[40] The basketball team had another winning season, and Paul was selected a second team forward on the intracity team. The track team won the Northeast League championship and was second to Wichita in the state meet. Paul amassed high point individual honors at the regional meet, winning the 120-yard high hurdles (in 16.5 seconds) while placing second in the low hurdles and third in javelin. He ran on the winning mile relay team (in 3 minutes, 37 seconds).[41]

1928 年 9 月，他进入高二后很快当选了有着 400 多名学生的班长。这一年的课程包括英语 5 和 6、物理 1、戏剧和乐队。这些课程他全都拿到了 A 的成绩，次年春天，包括他在内的十位高中生被选入国家荣誉协会。要获得这一资格，学生必须在学业上处于班上前 25%，并在奖学金、性格、领导力和服务方面表现突出。[38]他是少年班戏剧演员，也在 K 俱乐部演出的一部戏剧中担任主角，该俱乐部的成员也都加入了校运动队。[39]他在足球、篮球和田径方面都有出类拔萃的表现，这无论在过去还是现在都是了不起的成就。保罗在足球队中发挥了作用，该球队历史上只输了一场比赛，曾并列东北联赛冠军。他还入选了城市全明星队。[40]篮球队取得胜利的另一个赛季，保罗担任市队的第二队前锋。田径队赢得了东北联赛冠军，在州际比赛中仅次于威奇托。保罗在地区运动会上收获了个人最高荣誉，他赢得了120码高栏比赛冠军（成绩16.5秒），同时在低栏比赛中获得第二名，标枪项目获得第三名。他加入英里接力队并获得了州团体冠军（成绩3分37秒）。[41]

In September 1929 Paul began his senior year at Wyandotte High. His course work for the year included constitution, geometry III, algebra III, American history, English 7-8, and art. His average grade was A-.[42] He was again elected class president and was also elected to Quill and Scroll, the national honorary society for high school journalists.[43] The qualifications for membership included junior or senior class status, scholastic standing in the upper one-third of the class, and superior work in writing, editing, or business management. Paul was the boys' athletic editor of the school paper, the *Quiverian*, a position described as "requiring tactfulness and keenness of insight."[44]

1929年9月，保罗在怀恩多特高中开始了他最后一学年的学习。他这一年的课程包括宪法、几何3、代数3、美国历史、英语7-8和艺术。他的平均成绩是A-。[42]他再次当选班长，同时也加入美国国际高中传媒荣誉协会。[43]该协会会员包括学业成绩位列班级前三分之一，以及在写作、编辑或社交活动方面有出色表现的初中或者高中生。保罗是校报《奎维里安》的男士运动栏目编辑，大家普遍认为担任这一职位"需要机智和敏锐的洞察力"。[44]

Basketball and track were his major sports during his senior year, and he excelled at both. However, football told a different story. A news item at the completion of the one-win football season under the headline of "Harrington is Unfortunate" said a lot about his character. "Harrington was a sacrifice to the best interests of his team. Of all-star ability beyond a doubt as an end, he had to be shifted to the Wyandotte backfield as signal caller this year, where he was somewhat miscast, even if he was the best quarter Coach Parks could find. He played a great defensive game there, but fell down on offensive play. We couldn't work him in anywhere on the first team because of this, but we are really sorry."[45] The year before, as a junior, he had played end and been selected for the city all-star team.[46] Paul's height and weight were listed as 6'1" and 170 pounds.[47] The 1929-30 Wyandotte High School basketball team won the state championship tournament, beat-

Figure 2.4 ***Nineteen thirty state champion Wyandotte High School basketball team. Captain Harrington front row, far right. (Harrington Archives)***
图 2.4 1930 年州锦标赛冠军怀恩多特高中篮球队。队长哈灵顿在前排的最右边(哈灵顿档案馆)

ing Augusta 36-13, Quinter 38-17, Hutchinson 23-14, and for the championship, Newton 17-9. *See figure 2.4*. Wyandotte had last won the state basketball championship in 1923. Part of Coach Parks' genius in this sport was a devotion to zone defense. Schools from the southeastern part of Kansas, most of them playing in the Arkansas Valley League, had dominated basketball in Kansas for years and played one-on-one defense. They found it very hard to penetrate the Parks-coached zone defense.[48] Coach Parks did not substitute in the championship game, during which Paul gave it his all.[49] Laura recalled that he lost fifteen pounds during the tourmament.[50] His teacher, Bess Helwig, characterized her pupil as a dependable and consistent player noted for his stamina and endurances.[51]

高三时他的主要运动项目是篮球和田径，在这两方面他都很擅长。然而，他在橄榄球方面的成绩却不尽如人意。在单淘汰赛的橄榄球赛季结束时，一则标题为“哈灵顿很不幸”的新闻充分地体现了他的性格。“哈灵顿为了球队的最大利益而做出了牺牲。英雄也有气短时，他今年不得不被调到怀恩多特后场当发球员，尽管他是帕克斯教练所能找到的最好的四分卫，但他在那里的表现还是有些不尽如人意。在那里他打了一场很出色的防守比赛，但在进攻上失败了。鉴于此，我们无法把他安排在一线队的任何位置上，但我们真的很抱歉。”[45]一年前，他参加了青少年组的比赛并被挑选为市级全明星球员。[46]保罗的身高和体重分别为 6 英尺 1 英寸和 170 磅①。[47] 1929—1930 年间，怀恩多特高中篮球队以 36 比 13 击败奥古斯塔，38 比 17 击败昆特，23 比 14 击败哈钦森，并以 17 比 9 击败牛顿，赢得了州锦标赛冠军。（图 2.4）怀恩多特上一次赢得州篮球锦标赛冠军是在 1923 年。帕克斯教练在这项运动中的天赋之一就是区域防守。位于堪萨斯州东南

① 1 磅约等于 453.59 克。

部的学校里，大多数人都在阿肯色山谷联盟中打球，多年来一直统治着堪萨斯州的篮球赛场，并且擅长打一对一的防守，但他们发现很难突破帕克斯执教的区域联防。[48]帕克斯教练没有在冠军赛中派替补上场，因此在这场比赛中保罗必须全力以赴。[49]劳拉回忆说，他在锦标赛期间体重掉了 15 磅。[50]他的老师贝丝·赫尔维格将她的学生描述为一个可靠而稳定的球员，尤以他的体力和耐力而令人瞩目。[51]

Paul was a first-team selection for the Northeast League all-star team. One sportsreporter wrote about him: "There was plenty of potency in that fast breaking offense, functioning around Harrington. This boy Harrington is our nominee for the Northeast League hall of fame. He can shoot, pass, dribble when necessary, and how he does handle the ball. In other words, his play was sensational."[52] Paul played in all 27 regular season games, scored the most points for his team for the season (176 compared to 134 for the next most points), and had the fewest total fouls of all starters (10 compared to 25 fouls for the next closest starter).[53] At the postseason banquet his teammates chose him as honorary captain.[54]

保罗入选为东北联盟全明星队的一线队球员。一位体育记者这样评价他："在哈灵顿身上，那种快速突破的进攻充满了潜力。这个叫哈灵顿的男孩是我们东北联盟名人堂的候选人。他可以在必要时进行投篮、传球、运球，以及控球。换句话说，他表现得非常棒。"[52]保罗参加了本赛季的所有 27 场常规赛，为球队中得分最高（176 分，其次是 134 分）、犯规次数最少（10 次，其次是 25 次）的球员。[53]在季后赛的宴会上，他的队友纷纷推举他为荣誉队长。[54]

In April 1930 nearly one thousand athletes from 110 Kansas high schools competed at the 27th annual Interscholastic Track and Field Meet, which was held at the Universityof Kansas. Wyandotte High School won the meet with 33 points compared to runner-up Wichita's 17. Paul won the javelin event with a 162' 2.5" throw. Glenn Cunningham of Elkhart, soon to be Paul's teammate on some of the best track teams in the history of the University of Kansas, won the high school mile run with a track record time of 4 minutes, 31.4 seconds.[55]

1930 年 4 月，来自堪萨斯州 110 所高中的近千名运动员参加了在堪萨斯大学举行的第二十七届校际田径运动会。怀恩多特高中以 33 分的成绩取得比赛冠军，而亚军威奇塔学校的成绩为 17 分。其中，保罗以 162 英尺 2.5 英寸的投掷成绩赢得了标枪项目的冠军。来自埃尔克哈特学校的格伦·坎宁安则以 4 分 31.4 秒的成绩赢得了高中一英里跑的冠军，并很快成了保罗在堪萨斯大学田径队中最好的队友。[55]

It is hard to imagine that Paul was able to accomplish so much during his primary and secondary school years. Fortunately, his mother recorded some observations about his habits when he was a senior that give some insight into her son's daily life. "He gets up at seven, school starts at eight-ten. We live about two miles from school. He walks in fair weather, rides the streetcar in bad weather. School closes at two fifteen; he spends near an hour with the *Quiverian Staff* (yearbook). Practices athletics till five-thirty, eats at home about six, gets lessons or plays a game and goes to bed. He has neither money nor time for many dates. During holidays he goes to three or four parties, but nearly always stag so he can leave earlier. Parties are usually from nine to twelve o'clock. If he had a date he could not get to bed till one-thirty or two. He leaves by eleven and gets to bed by eleven-thirty. He had two real healthy crushes, one in sophomore and one in junior year. Both died a natural death, as such things usually do if not magnified."[56] One of these must have been with Bernice. On her 1929 basketball banquet program Paul wrote, " To the sweetest date I ever had or ever will have to such a banquet." On his she wrote, "You know there is a difference between a friend and a love. Well you're not exactly just a friend."[57]

很难想象保罗在小学和中学时代能够取得如此大的成就。但幸运的是，他的母亲在他高中时记录了他的一些习惯，这让我们能够对保罗的日常生活有一些了解。“他 7 点起床，8:10 开始上学。我们住的地方离学校大约两英里。他在天气好时走路上学，天气不好时就乘坐有轨电车。学校 2:15 放学；他在《奎维里安学人》（年鉴）的编辑部消磨了将近一个小时的时间。练习田径直到 5 点半，大约 6 点到家吃饭，然后做功课或玩游戏，最后上床睡觉。他既没太多钱也没太多时间去约会。在假期里他会去参加三四次聚会，但几乎总是去没有异性的聚会，这样他就可以早点离开。聚会通常从 9 点持续到 12 点。而如果他有约会，他要到一点半或两点才能上床睡觉。平时他 11 点离开，11 点半上床睡觉。他有过两次很棒的恋爱，一次在高二，一次在高三。两次都自然结束，就像这种事情通常的结局那样。”[56]其中一次是和伯尼斯在一起。在她 1929 年的篮球宴会节目中，保罗写道：“给我拥有过的最甜蜜的约会，再也不会有超过这样的宴会了。”她在回信中写道：“你知道朋友和爱情是有区别的，而你，不仅仅是朋友。”[57]

Laura Harrington continued, "He doesn't smoke, may have tried it as most boys do while small. He diligently refrained from breaking what he then thought were training rules. All year he ate no candy. Honey and raisins furnished his sweets. Occasionally he ate a piece of pie or unfrosted cake after the weekend games. No fried food. He ate vegetables and fruits. He drank no coffee. During his senior year he drank two quarts of milk a day. He works about home what time he has; cuts grass, helped paint the house and screens, wash woodwork, clean windows, and press trousers. He can do anything and does each task well. He has very little (extra) time."[58] His mother also recorded some observations that give an idea of what others thought of him: "Dozens of times, when out with Paul, I have seen a worshipful look in the eyes of boys, saying, 'Hello Paul.' While arranging, over the phone, for the delivery of our coal last fall Mr. Worth said, 'Mrs. Harrington have you a son attending Wyandotte High named Paul? ' I said, yes. He said, 'I told my wife I was going to tell you our son said, "If I could just be like Paul H. I would sure be happy." We think our son is a mighty fine chap. We are proud of him. We consider that a huge compliment coming from him."[59] Paul was indeed popular, underscored when his class elected him to represent Wyandotte High School in a high school senior popularity contest sponsored by the University of Kansas.[60]

他的母亲劳拉·哈灵顿继续说道，“他不抽烟，最多可能像大多数男孩小时候那样尝试抽过。他努力避免违反当时他认为的训练规则。他一整年都不吃糖果，而用蜂蜜和葡萄干充当他的甜食。在周末比赛后他偶尔会吃一块派或不加糖霜的蛋糕。他不吃油炸食品，但吃蔬菜和水果，他也不喝咖啡。在他高三的时候，他每天喝两夸脱牛奶。他有空就在家里工作：修剪草坪、帮忙粉刷房子和屏风、洗木制品、擦窗户、熨裤子。他什么都能做，并且每项任务都能做得很好。他的（空余）时间很少。”[58]他的母亲还记录了一些观察到的结果，这些结果反映了别人对他的看法：“很多次，当我和保罗一起出去的时候，我看到男孩们眼中充满着崇拜的神情，他们会说，‘你好，保罗。’去年秋天，沃思先生通过电话安排我们的煤炭运送时说，‘哈灵顿夫人，你有一个儿子在怀恩多特念高中，名叫保罗？’我说，是的。他说，‘我和我妻子说，我要告诉你，我们的儿子说，“如果我能像保罗·哈灵顿一样，我一定会很开心。”我们认为我们的儿子是一个非常好的小伙子。我们为他感到骄傲。我们认为这是来自他的一个巨大的赞美。’”[59]保罗确实很受欢迎，当他所在的班级选他代表怀恩多特高中参加由堪萨斯大学主办的高中生人气竞赛时，这一点就更加突出了。[60]

Attending the University of Kansas (KU) in Lawrence on a basketball and trackscholarship was Paul's next logical step after high school graduation. Consistent with his boatbuilding heritage and passion, in September 1929 he inquired about admission to the US Naval Academy at Annapolis, but did not appear to pursue an appointment since he was too young to be considered for admission until 1931.[61] So in September 1930 Paul enrolled at the University of Kansas and began a course of study in the College of Liberal Arts and Sciences. As a freshman his classes included algebra, trigonometry, continental America, principles of geology, English literature, elementary Spanish, physiology, and rhetoric. His grade point average for the year was 2.2 on a four-point scale, which was a little above C. His sophomore classes included Spanish, zoology, economics, physics, comparative anatomy, and economic history. His grade point average was 2.[62]

保罗高中毕业后的下一个合乎逻辑的步骤本该是进入位于劳伦斯的堪萨斯大学（KU），并获得篮球和田径奖学金。但由于他对造船传统的酷爱，在 1929 年 9 月他询问了是否可以进入位于安纳波利斯的美国海军学院，但因为他太年轻，除非到 1931 年才会被考虑录取，[61]但他似乎没有执着于去读。1930 年 9 月，保罗进入了堪萨斯大学并开始在文理学院学习。他大一的课程包括代数、三角学、美洲大陆、地质学原理、英国文学、西班牙语基础、生理学和修辞学。他当年的平均绩点是 2. 2 分（四分制），略高于 C。他大二的课程则包括西班牙语、动物学、经济学、物理学、比较解剖学和经济史。此阶段他的平均绩点是 2 分。[62]

The University of Kansas had excellent basketball and track programs. This was especially true for basketball as the inventor of the game, Dr. James A. Naismith, was a member of the physical education faculty as was Forrest C. "Phog" Allen, the athletic director and head basketball coach. Allen was a proven winner. As head basketball coach for the 1909 and 1910 seasons, his University of Kansas teams won the Missouri Valley Conference. He then moved to Warrensburg Teachers College for the 1911–27 seasons where his teams won six consecutive Missouri Valley Conference championships (1922–27), including a 34 consecutive conference game-winning streak.[63] Coach Allen returned to KU in 1928, the year the Big Six, consisting of Kansas, Kansas State, Missouri, Oklahoma, Nebraska, and Iowa State, was formed. His team first won the conference title in 1931, Paul's freshman year. In the varsity versus freshman exhibition game at the end of the season, the freshmen won, and Paul was the high scorer with 13 points. Coach Allen and Dr. Naismith refereed and introduced two experimental rules changes for the game. The goal was raised to twelve feet from the floor and a ten-foot diameter circle was added at midcourt to prevent players from interfering with the center jump. In the critique after the game Dr. Naismith was concerned that raising the basket would not be desirable for high school teams. Apparently the tip-off circle was accepted, and this marked its beginning. This also could have either marked or heightened Paul's appreciation of the research process that he would later characterize as trial, error, and observation.

堪萨斯大学拥有出色的篮球和田径项目，尤以篮球运动为甚，因为这项运动的发明者詹姆斯·A. 内史密斯博士和体育总监兼篮球主教练福里斯特·C.“福格”·艾伦都是资深体育教师。艾伦是个公认的赢家。作为1909年和1910年两个赛季的篮球主教练，他带领堪萨斯大学篮球队赢了密苏里山谷联盟赛。后来他到沃伦斯堡州立师范学院执教，并在1911—1927年赛季带领球队连续六次获得密苏里山谷联盟冠军（1922—1927），其中包括34场连胜。[63]艾伦教练于1928年回到了堪萨斯大学，那一年恰逢六大联盟成立，包括堪萨斯大学、堪萨斯州立大学、密苏里大学、俄克拉何马大学、内布拉斯加大学和艾奥瓦州立大学。他带领的堪萨斯大学篮球队首次赢得冠军是在1931年，那时保罗还是大一新生。在本赛季末的校队对阵新生的表演赛中，新生队获胜，保罗以13分的高分位居榜首。艾伦教练和内史密斯博士担任裁判，并为比赛引入了两个实验性的规则变化。即篮筐被提高到离地面12英尺，并且在中场增加了一个直径10英尺的中圈，以防止球员干扰中锋的跳球。在赛后的点评中，内史密斯博士担心高中球队不希望提高篮筐。但显然，这个提议被接受了，这标志着它的开始，也可能标志着或增加了保罗对他后来将其描述为试验、错误和观察的研究过程的欣赏。

In his sophomore year of 1931-32 Paul made the starting team at forward, a position Coach Allen had switched him to from guard.[64] Before the regular season began, the Jayhawks played some intersectional teams, including the University of Pittsburgh. For these games, box seats sold for $1.50 and unreserved upper-balcony seats for 35 cents.[65] The Jayhawks repeated as Big Six champions. The team's other forward, Ted O'Leary, was conference high scorer, averaging 11 points a game, while Paul was tenth with 5.2 points per game.[66]

在1931—1932年赛季，保罗在大二的时候成了首发前锋，艾伦教练将他从后卫调到了这个位置。[64]在常规赛开始之前，堪萨斯大学松鸦鹰队与一些地区间的球队交手，包括匹兹堡大学。在这些比赛中，包厢座位售价1.50美元，未被预订的上层包厢座位售价35美分。[65]松鸦鹰队再次成为六大联盟冠军。球队的另一名前锋泰德·奥利里是联盟得分王，场均11分，保罗以场均5.2分位列第十。[66]

With the basketball season over, Paul refocused on other activities. The track team was having a good season, and fellow sophomore Glenn Cunningham was well on the way to becoming a famous middle distance runner.[67] Paul won or placed at several meets with javelin throws up to 186'.[68] In May 1932 as the spring semester was ending, Paul was chosen as one of twenty-four men in the entire class to join the Owl Society, a junior men's honorary organization.[69] In July he attended the national convention of his fraternity, Sigma Alpha Epsilon, held at the Ambassador Hotel in Los Angeles and in August the 10th Olympiad held in Los Angeles. His college teammate, Cunningham, placed fourth in the mile run. In between these two dates Paul was a lifeguard at the Hotel Antero in Buena Vista, Colorado, the same job he had held the previous summer.[70]

随着篮球赛季的结束，保罗重新专注于其他活动。田径队本赛季表现不错，大二的格伦·坎宁安正朝着成为著名的中长跑运动员的目标迈进。[67]保罗参加了也赢得了几次标枪比赛，最高投出了186英尺。[68] 1932年5月春季学期即将结束时，保罗被从全班24人中选出，加入了青年男子荣誉组织猫头鹰协会。[69]同年7月，他参加了在洛杉矶大使酒店举行的SAE兄弟会全国大会，并在8月出席参加了在洛杉矶举行的第十届奥林匹克运动会。他的大学队友坎宁安在一英里跑中位列第四。在这两个赛季之间，保罗在科罗拉多州比尤纳维斯塔的安特罗酒店担任救生员，这与他去年夏天从事的工作相同。[70]

Paul had entered KU intending on a career in physical education. At some point he began to dream of a medical career, and he later credited his track coach, Brutus Hamilton, with encouraging him to pursue his dream.[71] In his junior year (1932-33) Paul's academic work showed a focus on pre-medicine, making it likely that he had decided to make this switch between his sophomore and junior years. His classes included inorganic chemistry 2, pre-medical physics, general psychology, elementary sociology, inorganic chemistry 3, vertebral embryology, vertebral paleontology, and parasitology. His grade point average was 2.69, which was a high C and an improvement.[72] Paul was one of five KU students chosen to compete for a 1934 Rhodes Scholarship.[73] This proved to be one of the few competitions he failed to win.

保罗进入堪萨斯大学本打算从事体育教育工作。但在某个时候，他开始梦想从事医学事业，后来他认为是他的田径教练布鲁特斯·汉密尔顿鼓励他去追求自己的梦想。[71]保罗在大三时（1932—1933）的课程反映出了他对医学预科的关注，因此他很可能在大二到大三之间已决定进行转变。他的课程包括无机化学 2、医用物理学、普通心理学、基础社会学、无机化学 3、脊椎胚胎学、脊椎古生物学和寄生虫学。他的平均绩点为 2.69，属 C+等级，有所进步。[72]保罗是被选中参评 1934 年罗兹奖学金的五名堪萨斯大学生之一。[73]这也被证明是他少数几次失败的竞争之一。

As a junior Paul again made the starting basketball team. In the preseason it won all three games from the visiting Stanford team, a match-up that came about because of the KU connections with Stanford's coaching staff.[74] But, KU lost both preseason games to Kansas State, whose star senior, Andrew Skradski, had played with Paul at Wyandotte High School. In the first game two new rules were tried. One required the offensive team to cross the center line in ten seconds, and the other prohibited the offensive team from passing back into their defensive territory after the ball entered the offensive zone. The penalty was loss of possession. The rules, designed to put "pep and speed into the game," had been voted for by 160 coaches and athletic directors. However, Naismith offered a dissenting view. He held that the ten-second rule violated a fundamental of basketball, which was to "play the ball."[75] Both rules were adopted and used to this day. Paul had participated in this experiment and perhaps realized that inventions were either eventually modified or replaced. Hopefully, Naismith was satisfied with modification. The day following the second exhibition game loss to Kansas State, Coach Allen made some dramatic changes in his lineup. Paul was moved to guard to make room for a promising sophomore at forward, and a letterman guard was benched to make room for Harrington.[76] This worked, and in league competition the Jayhawks repeated as Big Six champions, finishing with eight wins and two losses. Their center, 6' 3-1/2" Bill Johnson, was the league's second high scorer, averaging 10.9 points per game, was chosen for the All-Big Six first team, and was elected honorary captain by his team. Paul was chosen for an All-Big Six second team and was the conference's ninth-ranked high scorer, averaging 6.5 points per game.

保罗大三时，他再一次进入了球队首发阵容。在季前赛中，他们赢得了与斯坦福大学球队的全部三场比赛，这些赛事是由堪萨斯大学和斯坦福大学教练组共同组织的。[74]但是，堪萨斯大学在两场季前赛中都输给了堪萨斯州立大学，堪萨斯州立大学的明星球员，即大四学生安德鲁·斯克拉德斯基，曾在怀恩多特高中与保罗一起打过球。在第一场比赛中试行了两项新规则，一项是要求进攻方在10秒内越过中线，另一项则是禁止进攻方在篮球进入进攻区域后再传回防守区域，否则将会失去球权。这项旨在“让比赛充满活力和速度”的规则由160名教练和体育主管投票通过。然而，内史密斯则提出了不同的观点。他认为10秒的规则违反了篮球的一个基本原则，即“打球”。[75]不过这两条规则均被采纳并沿用至今。保罗参与了这个试验，他可能也意识到新规则最终要么被修改，要么被取代。他希望内史密斯能对此修改感到满意。在第二场表演赛输给堪萨斯州立大学后的第二天，教练艾伦对阵容做了极其大的改变。保罗被调到后卫位置，给一个前途无量的大二学生腾出前锋位置，而另一名优秀的后卫被调到替补席上，为哈灵顿腾出位置。[76]这一做法奏效了，在联赛中，松鸦鹰队再次夺得了六大联盟的冠军，最终以八胜两负的成绩收官。他们的中锋，身高6英尺3.5英寸的比尔·约翰森是联盟排名第二的得分手，场均10.9分，入选全六大联盟首发阵容，并被他的球队选为荣誉队长。保罗则入选全六大联盟的第二阵容，他是联盟排名第九的得分手，场均6.5分。

For all of its success and prominence then and especially now, it is informative to note that the net profit from the 1932-33 basketball season for the University of Kansas was \$2,668.31. The highest single game attendance was 3,359 and the smallest 745.[77] Imagine! Nowadays KU games regularly draw capacity crowds of 16,300.

尽管它在当时甚至是现在都取得了巨大的成功和成就，但值得注意的是，在1932—1933年的赛季中，堪萨斯大学的净利润为2 668.31美元。单场比赛的最高上座是3 359人，最低是745人。[77]这难以想象！而如今，堪萨斯大学的比赛通常能吸引16 300名观众。

Paul was involved in many activities other than basketball while at the University of Kansas, and it would be possible to conclude that he was a golden boy. In April at a dual track meet with Haskell Institute, the Indian college also located in Lawrence, he placed third in the high jump with the winning jump being 5’11” and won the javelin with a throw of 186’.[78] In January 1933 KU coeds picked Paul as the most fascinating man on campus.[79] In the spring he was elected president of Sigma Alpha Epsilon for the fall semester and was reelected for the 1934 spring semester.[80] That summer he was a lifeguard at the Jayhawk Plunge, a swimming pool in Lawrence.[81]

保罗在堪萨斯大学期间还参加了篮球以外的许多活动，可以说他是一个“金童”①。1932 年 4 月，在与同样位于劳伦斯的印度哈斯克尔学院的双轨制比赛中，他以 5 英尺 11 英寸的成绩获得跳高比赛第三名，并以 186 英尺的成绩赢得了标枪比赛。[78] 1933 年 1 月，堪萨斯大学的女生们选择了保罗作为校园里最迷人的男生。[79] 1933 年春，他被选为秋季学期的兄弟会主席，并再次当选为 1934 年春季学期的主席。[80]那年夏天，他在劳伦斯的一个松鸦鹰跳水游泳池担任救生员。[81]

As the 1933-34 basketball season was getting underway, Paul was briefly sidelined with a sprained ankle. The team repeated as Big Six champions with nine wins and one loss. KU sophomore Ray Ebling set a conference individual scoring record for the season with an average of 12.4 points per game. Harrington was second highest Jayhawk scorer behind Ebling, averaging 6.8 points per game. At season's end Harrington was elected honorary team captain.[82] See figure 2.5. Three newspapers selected Paul for their All-Big Six first teams, one as forward, one as guard, and one as center! The Lawrence Daily Kansan explained selecting the 6'0" Harrington for center as follows: "The first team selection would be agreeable to any close follower of the sport, with the possible exception of Harrington at center. Harrington, however, seems deserving of a place on the all-star first team. The only three-year man on the team, he exhibited coolness under fire and leadership that made him one of the reasons why the Jayhawkers were able to win their fourth successive Big Six title in the most decisive manner of all. Harrington was listed at forward and guard in starting lineups, but in every game this season he shifted to center after the tip-off and

Figure 2.5 ***Nineteen thirty-four Big Six basketball champions with honorary captain Harrington third from left, second row, and Coach Phog Allen second from left, back row. (Harrington Archives)***
图 2.5　1934 年六大联盟篮球冠军，荣誉队长哈灵顿在第二排左起第三位，教练福格·爱伦在后排左起第二位(哈灵顿档案馆)

① 一个男子在早期就取得了很大的成就，被称为“金童”。

played that position. His was essentially the center post. Wenger (Iowa State) was a capable man who kept his team in the running, but his leadership was not as great as Harrington's."[83] The writer choosing him for a guard position had this to say: "I consider Harrington the coolest player and the best defensive guard in the Big Six."[84] The writer who chose him for a forward position commended him "for his three years of all-around dependable play."[85]

1933—1934 年赛季开始时，保罗因脚踝扭伤暂时缺席比赛。这支球队以九胜一负的成绩再次夺得了六大联盟的冠军。堪萨斯大学二年级学生雷·伊布林以场均 12.4 分的成绩刷新了本赛季个人得分纪录。哈灵顿是松鸦鹰队仅次于伊布林的第二高得分手，场均 6.8 分。赛季结束时，哈灵顿被选为荣誉队长。[82]（图 2.5）三家报纸各自选择保罗作为六大联盟首发阵容的位置，分别是前锋、后卫和中锋！堪萨斯的《劳伦斯日报》对选择身高 6 英尺的哈灵顿作为中锋这件事解释道："对于任何密切关注这项运动的人来说首发阵容位置的选择都是合适的，但哈灵顿在中锋的位置可能是个例外。然而，哈灵顿似乎值得在全明星首发阵容中占有一席之地。作为球队中唯一一个打了三年球的球员，他在激烈的比赛中表现出的冷静和领导力，是他能带领松鸦鹰队以最果断的方式连续四次赢得六大联盟冠军的原因之一。首发阵容中哈灵顿在前锋和后卫位置上，但在本赛季的每场比赛中，他都在跳球后转移到中锋位置并担任该位。他的位置基本上是中心职位。来自艾奥瓦州立大学的温格是一个有能力的人，他能让球队保持运转，但他的领导能力不如哈灵顿。"[83]选择哈灵顿担任后卫位置的作者是这样说的："我认为哈灵顿是六大联盟中最冷静的球员，也是最好的防守后卫。"[84]选择他担任前锋位置的作家称赞他"三年以来一直有全面可靠的发挥"。[85]

The KU track team won both the indoor and outdoor Big Six track championships. At the outdoor meet Kansas won nine firsts with two of his teammates winning three events each. Glenn Cunningham came in first in the 880-yard run in 1 minute 58 seconds, the mile run in 4 minutes 23.3 seconds, and the 2-mile run in 10 minutes 2.1 seconds. Ed Hall won the 100-yard dash in 9.7 seconds, the 220-yard dash in 21.4 seconds, and the broad jump with 23′ 11 - 1/2″.[86] Cunningham became one of the most celebrated University of Kansas athletes of all time. And he did it on legs severely damaged in the schoolhouse fire that killed his brother and with teeth abscessed after being hit by a baseball his senior year in high school. At the 1936 Olympics he won the silver medal in the 1,500 meter run, and in 1938 he set the world record for the fastest mile at 4 minutes

4.4 seconds. He devoted his life to working with troubled youth and self-funded this to his own financial detriment. At age 70 Cunningham was still fit and pursuing his humanitarian dreams.[87] *See figure 2.6.*

Figure 2.6 ***Nineteen thirty-four University of Kansas track stars. Harrington third from the left, Glen Cunningham far right. (Harrington Archives)***

图 2.6　1934 年堪萨斯大学田径明星运动员，哈灵顿在左起第三个，格伦·坎宁安在最右边（哈灵顿档案馆）

堪萨斯大学田径队赢得了室内外六大联盟田径锦标赛冠军。在户外比赛中，堪萨斯大学运动员共获得了 9 个第一，其中两个队员各赢得了 3 个项目。格伦·坎宁安以 1 分 58 秒的成绩获得了 880 码赛跑第一，一英里赛跑用时 4 分 23.3 秒，两英里赛跑用时 10 分 2.1 秒。埃德·霍尔以 9.7 秒的成绩赢得了 100 码短跑，220 码短跑用时 21.4 秒，并在跳远比赛中获得了 23 英尺 11.5 英寸的成绩。[86]坎宁安成为堪萨斯大学有史以来最著名的运动员之一。他用自己在校舍火灾中严重受伤的双腿交出了这份成绩，难以想象的是，他的哥哥因火灾而丧生。此外，在高中最后一年他的牙齿还被棒球击中后化脓。在 1936 年的奥运会上，他获得了 1 500 米跑的银牌，并在 1938 年以 4 分 4.4 秒的成绩刷新了一英里赛跑的最高世界纪录。他毕生致力于帮助问题青年，并自筹资金以至于自己的经济受到了影响。坎宁安在 70 岁时仍很健康，并继续追求着他的人道主义梦想。[87]（图 2.6）

Paul won the javelin event with a throw of 208'11-3/4". One newspaper reported the event as follows. "Harrington's amazing throw, which bettered the Kansas Relays record by more than two feet, was not witnessed by most of the crowd. Judges called the javelin participants back on the field after the crowd had left when it was discovered that only three trials had been given to each man instead of four as the new regulations call for."[88] June was a big month as he was one of seven KU track stars awarded an expense-paid trip to participate in the National Collegiate Athletic Association track meet in Los Angeles.[89] A week later on June 28 he received notification of his acceptance to the University of Kansas School of Medicine.[90]

保罗以 208 英尺 11.75 英寸的成绩赢得了标枪比赛。一家报纸对这件事作了如下报道："哈灵顿惊人的投掷比堪萨斯接力队的纪录高出两英尺多，但大多数观众都没有看到。当观众离开后，裁判们重新召集标枪运动员回到场上，因为他们发现每个人只进行了三次投掷，而不是新规则要求的四次。"[88] 6 月对于保罗来说是一个重要的月份，因为他是 7 名堪萨斯大学田径明星运动员之一，获得了去参加在洛杉矶举行的全国大学体育协会田径运动会的自费旅行机会。[89]一周后的 6 月 28 日，他收到了堪萨斯大学医学院的录取通知书。[90]

Rev. and Mrs. Harrington, as they were now referred to, must have been proud of their youngest child. Mrs. Harrington attended Sigma Alpha Epsilon's annual mother-son weekends, and the group photos show a proud pair. His senior year they were front and center as Paul was president.[91] Although it was his father who became the minister, it was his mother who continued to fortify him with words of wisdom. For instance, when Paul was competing in a spring track meet in Lincoln, Nebraska, in 1933, she took up the subjects of morals and character. She commented, "Making one's self do right, do right, do right, year after year, builds such an iron muscle of moral fiber that no amount of inner or outer temptation can overcome it; the only way it can be destroyed is within itself, lack of exercise. If you quit trying to do right for one year can you guess how much moral fiber you would lose?"[92] On the sect of responsibility she wrote, "I think our obligation in this world is to carry our responsibilities. The small child learns to go to the bathroom, later washes its face, feeds itself, dresses itself and years afterward ties its shoe-laces. When it learns all the tasks that concern itself, it should learn to do tasks about the house that compensates for the sewing, laundry and cooking the mother does for it. Later it does more tasks and bigger ones as part of the structure of the home. When the child earns money it should start to keep itself financially by paying its board, amount in' proportion to salary. Then buy needed garments. Its board should be paid first. No child should be permitted to spend all its earnings on a good time, a car or fine clothes. You are not fair to your child if you do not teach it to always observe the rules of life. You teach it. Don't just think maybe it will learn somewhere or somehow. Don't ever be too busy to know your child."[93]

正如大家现在所说的那样，牧师和哈灵顿夫人一定会为他们最小的孩子而感到骄傲。哈灵顿夫人参加了兄弟会一年一度的母子周末活动，从合影中可以看出，这对母子非常自豪。保罗在高中担任班长时，哈灵顿夫妇是兄弟会最重要的人物。[91]虽然他的父亲成了牧师，但继续用智慧的语言来鼓励他的是他的母亲。例如，1933 年，当保罗参加内布拉斯加州林肯市的春季田径比赛时，她开始谈论道德和性格的问题。她说："年复一年，让自己做正确的事，做正确的事，做正确的事，这无疑会建立起铮铮铁骨般的道德品质，任何内在或外在的诱惑都无法战胜它；唯一能摧毁它的是缺乏锻炼的自身品质。如果你一年不做正确的事，你能猜到你会失去多少的道德品质吗?"[92]关于责任，她写道："我认为我们在这个世界上的义务就是承担责任。小孩学会去洗手间，自己洗脸，自己吃饭，自己穿衣，几年后自己系鞋带。当他学会了做所有与自己相关的任务以后，就应该开始学会做家务，以补偿母亲为他做的缝纫、洗衣和做饭等工作。之后作为家庭中的一员，他会做更多的和更大的任务。当孩子挣到了钱，就应该开始通过支付与工资成比例的伙食费来维持自己的生活，然后购买所需的衣服。他也应首先支付膳宿费用。不能允许孩子把所有的收入都花在玩乐、买汽车或买漂亮衣服上。如果你不教导你的孩子永远遵守生活规则，那么这对他而言是不公平的。你得教导他，不要单纯地以为他可能会在某个地方或以某种方式自学。永远不要因为太忙而不去了解你的孩子。"[93]

(张劲 柳善睿 钟锦涛 译　桑宏勋 徐宝山 审校)

3 BECOMING A PRACTICING PHYSICIAN AND SURGEON(1934-46)

resourcefulness, the ability to recognize a problem for what it was, throw away the book and improvise, and do a good job regardless of situation or supply[1]

成为一名执业医师和外科医生(1934—1946)

足智多谋,能够认识到问题的本质,扔掉书本,随机应变,无论情况或条件如何,都能做好工作[1]

In September 1934 Paul again became a freshman at the University of Kansas, but this time in its school of medicine. Given both Paul's lifelong gratitude for the public education that had shaped him and the somewhat unique origins of the University of Kansas School of Medicine, a brief history is in order. The university first offered a one year preparatory course in medicine in 1879 and expanded it to two years in 1899. But its location in the small university town of Lawrence, 35 miles west of Kansas City, Kansas, made addition of the two clinical years problematic since it could not provide adequate clinical material for teaching or attracting qualified clinical faculty. But, relocating the two clinical years to the more urban center near Kansas City would have split the campus and left behind the basic science faculty.

1934 年 9 月，保罗再次成为堪萨斯大学的新生，但这次是在医学院。鉴于保罗对塑造他的公共教育怀着终身感激，以及堪萨斯大学医学院独特的起源，需要简单介绍一下堪萨斯大学医学院的历史。该大学于1879年首次开设一年制医学预科课程，并于1899年将其扩展为两年制。但它位于堪萨斯州堪萨斯城以西35英里的劳伦斯小型大学城，不能提供足够的临床资源和吸引取得执业资格的临床教师，这使得延长成两年的临床教学成为问题。但是，如果将这两年临床实习转移到堪萨斯城附近的城市中心，则会把校园分割成两个校区，并使基础学科的教学员工滞留在原校区。

The University of Kansas and its leaders faced this dilemma at a time of medical education reform in the United States. Medical education in nineteenth-century America increasingly came to be dominated by proprietary schools that proliferated until they were no longer profitable, even after lowering their admission and graduation standards. Courses of study, staffing, and regulations were almost universally deficient so it was not surprising that with just a few exceptions medical and surgical advances originated in Europe. The reaction to this distressful state was the formation of university-affiliated medical schools and the closing of proprietary schools in the United States.[2] The organization of the newly created centers for medical education depended upon a complex mixture of factors, including university location, university governance and interest in the school, state government interest, and funding possibilities. The resulting institutions were consequently just as varied as the circumstances that led to their creation.

堪萨斯大学及其领导恰逢美国医学教育改革时期面临这一困境。19世纪，美国的医学教育越来越多地由营利性质的专科学校主导，直到它们不再盈利，这类学校的数量才不再增加，即使在降低了入学和毕业标准之后，这种情况也没有得到好转。专科学校的课程设置、人员配备和规章制度几乎普遍存在着缺陷，因此，除了极少数个例，医学和外科技术的进步起源于欧洲也就不足为奇了。为了应对这种情况，美国大学附属的医学院逐渐形成，专科学校开始逐渐关闭。[2] 新成立的医学教育中心取决于一系列复杂的因素，包括大学的选址、大学的管理、学校的利益、州政府的利益以及资金的来源。由此产生的机构就像导致它们产生的环境条件一样多种多样。

Philanthropy was probably the deciding factor in where to locate the medical center that would support the clinical teaching required for the University of Kansas to award the MD degree. Philanthropist Simeon Bishop Bell, MD, whose foresight and funding were key to the decision, had been born in New Jersey in 1820, went with his family to Ohio in 1832, and worked at farming and small mill construction.[3] At the age of twenty-one he began his formal education. He soon graduated from Norwalk Seminary and briefly taught while beginning to read medicine. Bell and Eleanor Taylor married when he was twenty-six, and they relocated to Columbus, Ohio, where he could formally study medicine. Leasing a large house allowed Eleanor to rent rooms to twelve other medical students, whose room and board charges covered the Bells' living expenses. When he was 33, Bell graduated in a class of 39 from Starling Medical College, which is now the College of Medicine of Ohio State University. Since his first practice location had a surplus of doctors, four years later in 1857 they moved by covered wagon to Johnson County, Kansas. Here they thrived-for a time.

慈善事业（捐助）可能是建立医疗中心的决定因素，以支持堪萨斯大学授予医学博士学位所需的临床教学。慈善家西米恩·毕晓普·贝尔1820年出生于新泽西州，他同时也是一名医学博士。1832年，他随家人来到俄亥俄州，从事农业和小型工厂建设工作，[3]他的远见对这一决定起到关键的作用。21岁时，他才开始接受正规教育并很快从诺沃克神学院毕业，并在开始学医的同时短暂地教过书。26岁时贝尔和埃莉诺·泰勒结婚并搬到俄亥俄州的哥伦布市，在那里他正式开始学习医学。他们租了一所大房子，并把房间租给了另外12名医学生，靠着他们的食宿费用，贝尔夫妇解决了自身的生活费用。33岁时，贝尔从斯塔林医学院，也就是现在的俄亥俄州立大学医学院的一个包含39名学生的班级毕业。由于他的第一个执业地点医生人数严重超编，1857年，他们用遮篷马车把家搬到了堪萨斯州的约翰逊县，并在这里生活了一段时间。

Located south of Wyandotte County and Kansas City, Kansas, adjacent to the Missouri-Kansas state line, they found themselves in the path of the border war between Quantrill's Raiders and the Jayhawkers. In the turmoil Bell suffered two skull fractures, and he and Eleanor lost all their possessions except ownership of 1,100 acres of land. Their lives were spared probably because of the medical services they provided and their past association with Quantrill, who had once lived nearby. Finally, in 1865 the Bells took refuge with a brother-in-law farther north and west in the county, which removed them from the eye of the storm. The following year Eleanor Taylor Bell died seven weeks after the birth of their tenth child. Bell relocated his family to Rosedale, Kansas, so named because of its many wild roses. Found in the southeast corner of Wyandotte County, it was bound on the east by the state line, the south by Johnson County, and the north by the Kansas River. Turkey Creek flowed through Rosedale from the southwest to the northeast and crossed and recrossed the state line before emptying into the Kansas River. The creek's flood plain was a natural pathway, over which Interstate Highway 35 now runs.[4]

约翰逊县位于堪萨斯州怀恩多特县和堪萨斯市的南部，毗邻密苏里–堪萨斯州界，正处于匡特里尔突击队和拥护废奴的游击队之间的边境战争范围内。在混乱中，贝尔两次颅骨骨折，他和埃莉诺失去了除1 100英亩土地之外的所有财产。可能是因为他们在战争中提供过医疗服务以及过去曾与住在附近的匡特里尔游击队员保持联系，他们最终幸免于难。1865年，贝尔一家投靠了住在该县西北部的姐夫家，这使他们远离了风暴中心。第二年，埃莉诺·泰勒在他们第十个孩子出生七周后去世。贝尔把他的家搬到了堪萨斯州的罗斯代尔，这样命名是因为那里有许多野玫瑰。它位于怀恩多特县的东南角，东临州界，南接约翰逊县，北接堪萨斯河。火鸡溪从西南向东北流经罗斯代尔，在注入堪萨斯河之前穿过州界。小溪形成的冲积平原是一条天然的通道，现在35号州际公路就在这条通道上。[4]

After his wife's death Bell no longer practiced medicine but set about to accumulate a fortune in real estate. Having succeeded in that pursuit, around 1886 he decided that he wanted to establish an institution of higher learning as a living monument to his late wife, Eleanor Taylor Bell.[5] His ultimate goal was for every young man and woman in the country to have college opportunities at the least possible expense. To accomplish this in his environs, he offered about five acres of land, a "magnificent piece of property... on a prominent eminence." Bell originally envisioned a college that would be managed by a board of trustees of men drawn equally from Kansas and Missouri. Gradually, he changed his focus to the creation of a medical school and hospital. In 1894 he made an offer of land and salable property valued at $100,000 to the University of Kansas. After the university's governing board accepted the offer, Bell deeded the site, which had expanded from 5 to 7 acres and 101 residential lots. Sale proceeds of this land were to fund construction of the hospital, but the Kansas legislature took no action.

妻子去世后，贝尔不再行医，而是开始进入房地产行业积累财富。在房地产行业取得成功后，1886年前后，他决定建立一所高等教育机构，以此纪念他已故的妻子埃莉诺·泰勒·贝尔。[5] 他的最终目的是让这个国家的每个年轻人都有机会花尽可能少的钱上大学。为了实现这一目标，他提供了大约5英亩的土地，这相当于一笔"巨款"。贝尔最初设想的大学是由董事会管理，董事会成员分别来自堪萨斯州和密苏里州。渐渐地，他将注意力转移到创建一所医学院校和一所医院上。1894 年，他向堪萨斯大学提供了价值 10 万美元的资助。大学董事会接受这个提议后，贝尔签订了场地合同，场地当时已经从 5 英亩扩大到 7 英亩，有 101 个住宅区。这块土地的销售收入被用来资助医院的建设，但是堪萨斯州议会没有对此采取任何行动。

Legislators were confused by the conflicting claims of those involved in medicine, be they the regular and the irregular physicians, the town fathers, or the citizenry. The struggle to improve this sorry state of affairs was taken on by Bob Schauffler when he returned to the area in 1898. Having graduated from the New York College of Physicians and Surgeons and completed a two-year internship, he began his orthopedic surgery practice at the Kansas City Medical College, a proprietary institution in Missouri. His father was its president and Franklin E. Murphy its secretary. (Murphy's son, Franklin D., at the age of 32 later became the youngest dean of the University of Kansas School of Medicine and the author of the acclaimed Murphy Plan to improve health care in rural Kansas.) Since Schauffler and others at the school held the view that proprietary medical colleges would soon be on the way out, they made a concerted effort to have the two-year preparatory curriculum at the University of Missouri School of Medicine in Columbia moved to Kansas City and expanded to four years while taking over three proprietary schools. This effort failed.[6] The group next turned to the University of Kansas, and negotiations with Chancellor Strong were more successful. In 1903 Bell deeded additional land in Cass and Jackson counties in Missouri valued at $25,000. In 1905 the Kansas legislature approved the plan, and the following year the university's Eleanor Taylor Bell Memorial Hospital was completed at a cost of $75,000. The first class of medical students was also admitted.[7] A lingering problem was created: a split campus with the basic science years in Lawrence and the clinical years in Rosedale. It was a compromise as there was no one best location at that time. In 1909 the Carnegie Foundation hired educator Abraham Flexner to inspect and report on medical education in North America, which he did the following year. The split campus was a major criticism of the University of Kansas School of Medicine, probably preventing it from receiving the Rockefeller financial assistance that was received by several favored schools.[8]

立法者被那些涉及医学的相互矛盾的主张弄糊涂了，不管这些想法是来自正规的还是非正规的医生，是来自镇上孩子们的父亲们，还是来自其他的普通市民。鲍勃·肖夫勒于 1898 年回到这个地区，开始改善这种糟糕的状况。他毕业于纽约内外科学院，并在那完成了两年的实习，然后开始在密苏里州的一所专科机构——喀纳斯市医学院进行骨科手术。他的父亲是院长，富兰克林·E. 墨菲是秘书长。（墨菲 32 岁的儿子富兰克林·D. 后来成为堪萨斯大学医学院最年轻的院长，也是广受赞誉的改善堪萨斯农村医疗保健的“墨菲计划”的倡导者。）由于肖夫勒和学校的其他人认为专科医学院很快就会过时，他们齐心协力将密苏里大学医学院的两年制预科课程从哥伦比亚转移到堪萨斯城，并在接管三所专科学校的同时将课程延长到四年制，但是这一努力失败了。[6] 该小组随后转向堪萨斯大学，与斯特朗校长的谈判相对来说比较成功。1903 年，贝尔在密苏里州的卡斯县和杰克逊县签订了价值 25 000 美元的附加土地契约。1905 年，堪萨斯州议会批准了该计划，次年，该大学附属的埃莉诺·泰勒·贝尔纪念医院竣工，耗资 75 000 美元，第一届医学生也成功入学了。[7] 一个不可避免的问题产生了：校园被分割成两部分，基础学科在劳伦斯，临床实践则在罗斯代尔。这是一种妥协，因为当时没有一个更合适的位置。1909 年，卡内基基金会聘请教育家亚伯拉罕·弗莱克斯纳对北美的医学教育进行了考察和报告，次年报告得到了落实。对堪萨斯大学医学院的批评主要集中在“分割的校园”这一点上，也可能是这个原因使它错失了洛克菲勒财团的援助，而另外几个受青睐的学校都已获得资助。[8]

The original "magnificent piece of property" in Rosedale had had two additional buildings added to it, but because it was too hilly for further development, it had acquired the derisive nickname of Goat Hill. More land was needed. By 1912 the hospital, medical school, and the five-year-old nursing school were prospering, and several Kansas towns, especially Topeka, sought to become their home. Just six days before his death on January 16, 1913, Simeon Bell wrote to the Kansas legislature reminding it that his was the original gift that enabled the state to build the hospital and school in Rosedale and asking that the Eleanor Taylor Bell Hospital remain there.[9] In 1919 the legislature voted $200,000 for new hospital and left the choice for its site to the governor. To prove their support for the new building, the citizens of Rosedale voted on a bond issue of $35,000 and launched campaign to raise that amount. Both were successful. The University of Kansas Medical Center (KUMC) moved upland, almost a mile south to a beautiful flat site where it could grow. The new hospital opened in 1924, two years after Rosedale had been annexed by Kansas City.

罗斯代尔最初的“宏伟地产版图”增加了两栋建筑，但因为它有太多山地，不适合做进一步开发，所以被命名为山羊山，这样就需要更多的土地来兴建学校。到1912年，医院、医学院和诞生五年的护士学校都兴建起来，几个堪萨斯城的城镇，尤其是托皮卡是比较合适的选址。1913年6月16日，就在他去世的前六天，西米恩·贝尔写信给堪萨斯州议会并提醒他们，他是该州罗斯代尔医院和学校的创始人，并要求保留埃莉诺·泰勒·贝尔医院。[9] 1919年，议会投票拨款20万美元修建新医院，由州长决定医院的选址。为了证明他们对新医院的支持，罗斯代尔的市民投票发行了35 000美元的债券，并发起了募资活动，均取得了成功。堪萨斯大学医学中心搬离了山地，来到向南近一英里的美丽平原上，在那里继续发展。罗斯代尔被堪萨斯城兼并的两年后，1924年，新医院开业。

It should never be thought that the growth of KUMC and its school of medicine had been accomplished smoothly or easily.[10] Professional jealousies in part aggravated by the easy access of specialists with private practices just across State Line Road, various relocation attempts, state financial support that was vacillating and inadequate at and best, partisan politics, and capricious administrative decisions had to be weathered and overcome. A particularly important transition took in 1924 when, without cause, Governor Jonathan M. Davis fired Mervin T. Sudler, a respected de facto dean of eighteen years.[11] The fallout included ending any Flexner/Carnegie Foundation/Rockefeller interest in the school, but it precipitated the hiring of the new dean, Johns Hopkins graduate and pathologist Harry R. Wahl, who successfully led the medical center for the next quarter century.

堪萨斯大学医学中心及其医学院的发展并不是一帆风顺的。[10]因为穿过州际公路就能方便地接触到私人诊所，在某种程度上加剧了专业人士对医学院的嫉妒，此外，各种搬迁的尝试，国家财政支持的摇摆不定和资金的不足，党派政治，以及反复无常的行政决定，都是医学中心及其医学院必须经受和克服的问题。1924年，一个重大转变发生了，州长乔纳森·M. 戴维斯无缘无故地解雇了受人尊敬、担任了18年院长的默文·T. 撒德勒。[11]该决定终止了弗莱克斯纳/卡耐基基金会/洛克菲勒财团对该中心的任何资助，但它促成了新院长的诞生——约翰霍普金斯大学毕业生和病理学家哈利·R. 沃尔，他在接下来的25年里成功领导了该医学中心。

It was during this period of stability and expansion that Paul Harrington received his medical education. His first two years spent in Lawrence must have seemed like an extension of his undergraduate years. For instance, he was elected president of his medical school class and completed the few hours of academic work necessary to complete the requirements for a bachelor of arts degree in June 1935.[12] *See figure 3.1*. He trained with his javelin in hopes of participating in the 1936 Olympics in Berlin. After winning the regional tryout competition, he thought he had a good chance to make the squad, but was unable to finance the trip to Chicago for the finals.[13] When Paul came to the KUMC campus in the fall of 1936 for his clinical years, the north-south running Seventh Street Trafficway had been completed four years before. This was important because it provided a direct route between KUMC and St.Margaret's Hospital, which was the medical school's major affiliated teaching hospital and was located a few blocks from where Paul was born and reared. Although he could have lived at his family's home just a few miles from the medical center during his two years of study, the recollections of his roommate, Harold Patterson from Larned, Kansas, made that unlikely. After Paul's death, Patterson wrote to his widow, Mary Alice Harrington, that "Paul and I were roommates in college and for three years in medical school. We were also partners in many of our medical classes. I can truthfully say we never had a disagreement during that time, even when we were night desk clerks at the Melbourne apartment hotel on the Plaza."[14]

正是在医学院发展稳定且逐步扩张的这段时期，保罗·哈灵顿开始接受医学教育。他在劳伦斯度过的头两年像是大学生活的延续。1935 年 6 月，他被选为医学院的年级学生会主席，并完成了文学学士学位所需的数小时学术工作。[12]（图 3.1）为了参加 1936 年的柏林奥运会，他开始进行标枪训练。在赢得了地区选拔赛后，他认为自己有很大的机会进入总决赛，但他无法支付前往芝加哥参加总决赛的费用。[13]当保罗在 1936 年秋天来到堪萨斯大学医学中心开始他的临床实习生涯时，南北贯通的第七街道路建设已经在 4 年前完工。这是很重要的一点，因为它提供了一条从医学中心到圣玛格丽特医院的直接路线，圣玛格丽特医院是医学院的主要附属教学医院，距离保罗出生和长大的地方只有几个街区。在这两年的学习期间，他本可以住在离医疗中心只有几英里远的家里，但据他室友，来自堪萨斯州拉尼德的哈罗德·帕特森的回忆，认为这不太可能。保罗死后，帕特森给他的遗孀玛丽·艾丽斯·哈灵顿写信说："保罗和我在大学时是室友，在医学院也做了三年室友。我们在许多医学课上是搭档。我可以诚实地说，在那段时间我们从未有过分歧，包括我们在墨尔本广场公寓酒店做夜班服务员的那段时间。"[14]

Figure 3.1 ***President of the 1934 University of Kansas freshman medical school class, front row, fifth from left.* (*Harringron Archives*)**

图 3.1　1934 年堪萨斯大学医学院新生班主席，前排左数第五名(哈灵顿档案馆)

Paul credited the financing of his education to his basketball ability. During his medical school years this meant playing semiprofessional basketball, which was flourishing in those pre-NBA years. His senior year he played for the Phillips 66 Refiners of Kansas City Kansas, who won the six-team Naismith Conference but lost in the early rounds of the Amateur Athlétic Union National Championship tournament in Denver.[15] How much Harrington earned is unknown, but it must have paid his bills as there is no record that he received any other funding. Harrington recalled that in the 1930s nobody had a nickel, but if you did, you could go through college on it.[16] He also appeared to have played the sport for fun, such as when he was on a team comprised of students from the chiropractic school in Kansas City, Missouri. He was a member, that is, until the day Dean Wahl called him in and "suggested it would be a good idea if didn't play with them."[17]

保罗的学费来源归功于他的球技。他在医学院学习期间，参加半职业篮球赛，这在 NBA 出现之前非常流行。大四那年，他效力于堪萨斯城的菲利普斯-66 精锐队，赢了 6 支奈史密斯联盟的冠军队，但在丹佛举行的业余体育联盟全国锦标赛的前几轮中失利。[15]哈灵顿挣了多少钱不得而知，但这些钱肯定是用来支付学费了，因为没有记录表明他接受过任何其他资助。哈灵顿回忆说，在 20 世纪 30 年代，没有人有钱，但是如果你有，你可以靠它读完大学。[16]他似乎也把这项运动当作乐趣，比如他曾经也加入了密苏里州堪萨斯城一所脊柱按摩学校学生组成的球队。直到有一天，沃尔院长把他叫了进来，并"暗示我不和他们一起打篮球是个好主意"。[17]

His medical education was solid. A major factor in the medical center's survival and growth was an unusually strong faculty that replenished itself as it grew.[18] In Paul's time four members were Johns Hopkins School of Medicine graduates: Harry Wahl, chair of pathology and dean; Ralph Major, chair of medicine; Thomas G. Orr, chair of surgery; and Russell Haden, renowned hematologist. Others who left a lasting impression on Paul Harrington included Logan Clendening, medical historian and the most popular syndicated lay medical writer of the day, and Peter T. Bohan, a superb clinical teacher, who practiced at St. Margaret's Hospital. Paul appeared to have been an average medical student, mostly earning C's and occasionally B's. The exercises that seemed to have remained with him and left the best insights into his thought processes were the researching and writing of the required junior and senior theses. The subjects he chose were "The Adrenal Cortex"[19] and "The Therapeutic Value of Cevitamic Acid."[20] These related topics were both biological rather than mechanical, which supported his later contention that he always tried to think fundamentally.

他的医学教育基础十分扎实。医疗中心得以生存和发展的一个主要因素是师资力量异常强大，并在发展中不断补充。[18]在保罗时代，有四名成员是约翰斯·霍普金斯大学医学院毕业生：院长兼病理学主任哈利·沃尔；内科学主任拉尔夫·梅杰；外科主任托马斯·G. 奥尔；以及著名血液学家拉塞尔·哈登。其他给保罗·哈灵顿留下深刻印象的人包括医学历史学家洛根·克兰德宁，他是当时最受欢迎的非专业医学作家，以及在圣玛格丽特医院工作的优秀临床教师彼得·T. 博安，一位出色的临床教师。保罗似乎是一个普通的医科学生，大部分成绩是C，偶尔是B。在校期间，医学研究和论文撰写成为他的日常，并对他的医学思维过程做了最好的见证和记录。他选择的主题是“肾上腺皮质”[19]和“抗坏血酸（维生素C）的治疗价值”。[20]这些主题都是与生物学相关的而不是与机械相关的，这为他后来的论点提供了支持，即他总是试图从根本上思考问题。

In the introductory paragraphs of "The Adrenal Cortex" he used words and phrases that suggested an iconoclastic thought process. For instance, he commented that the chemical similarity of many biological substances "is quite intriguing to anyone who has any challenging spirit." He opined that the many puzzles the new and rapidly expanding field of endocrinology was presenting "threatens to be the system that plays a major role in the regulation of birth, development, propagation, and death in man as he struggles for perfection." He used phrases like "the great process of evolution-better adapted to its environment is found by trial and error-untiring, ever experimenting efforts of nature in its progress, to we know not where, we suspect, perfection." The following comments about research were representative of his views. "It is unfortunate indeed that an indicator is not available to tell investigators they are laboring under biased opinion, erring in chemical analysis, substituting without justification or indication, accepting erroneous controls or observations, or wandering down the many by-ways of error that are always present in dealing with obscure functions of complex organisms, for if this were true our problems would be simple." He wrote, "The few minds of genius accept very few facts as proof but weigh the evidence, follow the indicating trend of evidence cautiously and produce the factors of progress in the world."

在有关"肾上腺皮质"的论文的引言中，他使用了一些特殊的词语和短语，暗示了一种打破传统的思维过程。例如，他评论说，许多生物物质的化学相似性"对任何有挑战精神的人来说都是很有趣的"。他认为，迅速发展的内分泌学领域提出了许多谜题，"在人类为追求完美而奋斗的过程中，这个系统可能会在人类的出生、成长、繁殖和死亡的调控中发挥重要作用"。他使用了这样的语句："更好地适应环境的进化过程是通过不断尝试和犯错，不断实验的自然努力来发现的，我们提出疑问，然后尽力完善"。以下关于研究的评论代表了他的观点，"不幸的是，一个指标不足以告诉研究者，他们会在偏见下工作，在化学分析中犯错，在没有理由或指示的情况下进行置换反应，接受错误的控制或观察，甚至在处理复杂生物的模糊功能时会一直存在许多间接错误，如果一个指标就可以实现这些，我们的问题就简单了。"他写道，"少数天才的头脑接受很少的事实作为证据，但会通过权衡证据，谨慎地遵循证据的指示趋势，产生让世界进步的因素。"

He surveyed the embryology, anatomy, and current state of knowledge about the function of the adrenal glands. He puzzled at the different origins of the adrenal cortex and the adrenal medulla, just as he did about the exclusion of medullary secretions from the cortex and the portal circulation of the left adrenal. What he couldn't explain, he attributed to nature, "which does some queer things, according to man, but there is always a reason." Following a list of physical and biochemical changes leading up to death after either adrenalectomy or adrenal failure from disease (Addison's), he reviewed some known and possible interactions of the glands with the other endocrine organs. The most obvious was with the hypophysis where removal of either one led to atrophy of the other. Cushing's syndrome with its hyperactivity of the hypophysis causing adrenal hyperactivity was only briefly mentioned, and he opined that overactivity of the adrenal cortex proper had not been recognized. Interaction with the gonads, resulting in the adrenogenital syndrome, was mentioned but incompletely described. Any interaction with the thyroid was thought to be indirect. There appeared to be no direct interaction with the parathyroid gland. He mentioned hemorrhages into the adrenals as a cause of acute adrenal insufficiency often associated with general infections, intoxications, burns, and diseases with a hemorrhagic diathesis.

他调查了关于胚胎学、解剖学和肾上腺功能的认知现状。就像他对肾上腺皮质和门静脉循环中髓质分泌物被排除在外的困惑一样，他对肾上腺皮质和肾上腺髓质的不同起源也感到困惑。对于无法解释的，他将其归因于自然，“根据人类的说法，世间万物，总有原委”。他根据一系列导致肾上腺切除或因疾病导致肾上腺衰竭（艾迪生病）后死亡的物理和生化变化，回顾了一些已知的和可能的腺体与其他内分泌器官的相互作用。最明显的是垂体，切除其中一个会导致另一个萎缩。库欣综合征是垂体功能亢进引起的肾上腺功能亢进，对此，他只简要地提到肾上腺皮质本身的功能亢进尚未被认识到。他曾提到肾上腺皮质与性腺相互作用，会导致肾上腺生殖综合征，但描述并不完全。与甲状腺的相互作用也被认为是间接的。他提到肾上腺出血是由于急性肾上腺皮质功能不全，通常与全身感染、中毒、烧伤和出血性疾病有关。

When Paul wrote his senior thesis, cevitamic acid (vitamin C. ascorbic acid) was in the scientific spotlight since two 1937 Nobel Prizes had been awarded to its investigators.[21] Paul began philosophically, "Nature arrayed with all its defense mechanisms against the invasion of destructive agents is the greatest one factor a physician is able to utilize in his struggle to aid mankind as he gropes about for better health and a longer and happier life." After presenting the highlights of eleven publications, he summarized their findings of the signs, symptoms, and diagnosis of deficiency and listed the uses, including the doubtful ones, of the vitamin, all of which were related to deficiency. The doubtful utilizations that he cataloged were rheumatic fever, wound healing, cataracts, hemorrhagic diseases, gastroenteritis, and dry sockets. Inclusion of wound healing in the doubtful use list was surprising, but there it was. His conclusion was that "the therapeutic value of cevitamic acid is mainly prophylactic." He hastened to add that, in part, "it is one essential in the maintenance of a healthy body and its importance cannot be taken lightly." Harrington remained interested in cevitamic acid the rest of his life.

当保罗写他的毕业论文时，抗坏血酸（维生素 C）是当时科学界的焦点，因为它的研究者获得了 1937 年的两项诺贝尔奖。[21]保罗从哲学的角度开始了他的论文，“大自然拥有各种防御机制来抵御破坏性因素的入侵，这是一个医生在努力帮助人类获得更健康、更长寿和更幸福的生活时所能利用的最伟大的机制。”在介绍了 11 篇论文的要点后，他总结了关于维生素缺乏的体征、症状和诊断，并列出了维生素的用途，包括可疑的用途，所有这些都与维生素缺乏有关。他列出的可疑用途有风湿热、伤口愈合、白内障、出血性疾病、肠胃炎和干燥症。将伤口愈合列入可疑用途清单令人惊讶，但事实就是如此。他的结论是“抗坏血酸的治疗价值主要是预防”。他同时补充道，“在某种程度上，这是保持健康身体的一个基本要素，其重要性不容忽视。”在他的余生，哈灵顿一直对抗坏血酸充满兴趣。

Graduation from medical school on June 6, 1938, marked the end of Paul's life as a student in the Kansas public school system.[22] He was proud and thankful for what the State of Kansas had made possible, and for the rest of his life he was never bashful about spreading the good word about his education.

1938 年 6 月 6 日保罗从医学院毕业，标志着他在堪萨斯公立教育系统的学生生活结束了。[22]他为堪萨斯州所做的一切感到骄傲并充满感激，在他的余生中，他从不羞于宣扬他所受教育的好处。

In July 1938 Harrington began his internship at Roper General Hospital in Charleston, South Carolina, which was owned and operated by the Medical Society of South Carolina that had been formed in 1789 and was the sixth oldest in the country.[23] He must have been popular with his new colleagues. Known as the White Wave, the team of interns and residents at Roper took on the AKK medical fraternity of the Medical College of South Carolina in a touch football game and won 24 to 2. “Harrington cinched the game in the early minutes when he intercepted a pass on the two yard line and waltzed ninety-eight yards to score standing up. He didn't even get his white uniform dirty, it was reported.”[24]

1938 年 7 月，哈灵顿开始在南卡罗来纳州查尔斯顿的罗珀综合医院实习，该医院由成立于 1789 年的南卡罗来纳州医学会所有并经营，是美国历史最悠久的六所医院之一。[23]他很受新同事们的欢迎，这支由罗珀大学的实习生和住院医生组成的团队被称为“白浪”，他们在一场触体橄榄球比赛中与南卡罗来纳医学院的

AKK医学兄弟会进行了较量，并以24比2获胜。“哈灵顿在比赛刚开始的几分钟就锁定了比分，他在两码线上拦截了一个传球，然后站着跳了98码的华尔兹得分。据报道，他甚至没有弄脏他的白色制服。”[24]

The main reason Harrington chose Roper General Hospital was almost certainly its location near open water. Harrington intended to build a boat and selected plans from *Rudder*; a leading nautical magazine. It was to be an 18'-long knockabout sailboat of the seagull type with a 7' beam designed to carry 194 feet of sail on a marconi rig and genoa jib. Work began on September 27, his twenty-seventh birthday. Where it began isn't in dispute. Roper General Hospital had been deeded a house, the Grover Thomas Bennett House, and the upper three stories were used for intern and resident housing. Harrington shared the largest room with an assistant surgery resident, Eldon B. Fine, who was crowded into one corner of the room. Fine apparently tolerated without complaint the inconvenience of living with the noise, dirt, and turmoil as the boat took shape in their room. It is also not in dispute that the boat was too large to carry downstairs. What is in dispute is the method of extraction from their room. By one account the boat had to be disassembled.[25] Another account stated three windows were removed, and the whole boat lowered by block and tackle.[26] At any rate, once removed, work was continued in an old shed on hospital property. *See figure 3.2.* On May 27, 1939, the boat was christened on dry land.[27] This was of such importance that Harrington's oldest sibling, Verna Tate, travelled halfway across the country to attend the celebration. She joined twenty four others, including his tolerant roommate, who signed the christening document. The boat's name was *MAWH*, short for Mary Alice Wade (and soon-to-be) Harrington, his fiancée. The foam from the champagne bottle used in the ceremony was produced by a chemical solution because the real stuff had been imbibed during the preceding luncheon.

Figure 3.2 ***Building his boat in Charleston. (Harrington Archives)***

图3.2 在查尔斯顿建造船（哈灵顿档案馆）

哈灵顿选择罗珀综合医院的主要原因是它靠近开放水域。哈灵顿打算建造一艘船，并从一本先进的航海杂志《方向舵计划》那里选择了一些方案。这是一艘18英尺长的海鸥型帆船，7英尺的横梁，能够装载194英尺的帆，采用马可尼帆架和热那亚三角帆。造船工作开始于他27岁生日那天，也就是9月27日。造船工作并没有引起争议。罗珀综合医院已经签约了一套房子，格罗弗·托马斯·班内特之家。房子的上面三层用作实习生和住院医生的住所。哈灵顿和外科住院医师助理埃尔登·B. 法恩共用一个最大的房间，法恩挤在房间的一个角落里。法恩毫无怨言地忍受了噪声、泥土和脏乱给生活带来的不便，直到船修建完成。这艘船毫无疑问太大了，不能抬下楼。该如何将船从房间里弄出来就成了争议点。一种说法是这条船不得不被拆解。[25]另一种说法是他们拆掉了三扇窗户后用滑车把整条船放下来。[26]无论如何，从房间内搬离之后，造船工作就在医院的一个旧棚子里继续进行。(图3.2) 1939年5月27日，这艘船在陆地上被命名。[27]这是如此重要的事情，以至于哈灵顿的长姐韦尔娜·泰特横跨半个国家，赶来和其他24人一起参加了庆祝活动，其中包括和保罗一起签署命名文件的宽容室友。这艘船的名字是MAWH，是他的未婚妻玛丽·艾丽斯·韦德·哈灵顿的缩写。仪式上使用的香槟泡沫其实是用一种化学溶液制成的，因为真正的香槟在之前的午餐时已经被喝掉了。

In the spring of 1939 a profoundly moving event in Harrington's life was playing out. His mother was dying.[28] The alarm began to sound in November when Verna wrote that Laura was having increasing difficulty with dyspnea. He pleaded with his mother to lighten her physical burdens, which included not keeping Edgar, her disabled son, dressed in shirts and ties. Efforts to control her symptoms at home failed, and she was admitted Bell Memorial Hospital for medication regulation. Paul tried to to cheer her up from afar with news of the day, sharing memories and best wishes. The turmoil in Europe received attention as he asked his mother's thoughts about enlisting in the Reserve Naval Medical Corps, which would give him seniority and a greater likelihood of being assigned to a base hospital. Laura sent him a poem she had written to comfort herself and $20 to help with his boat.[29] Laura Harrington died on June 27, 1939. On June 3 Paul had written that he would be seeing her in about twenty days along with Mary Alice and her mother.[30] He commented on how much thinner she had appeared in recent snapshots, but fewer pounds were a lot better for her heart. But whether Paul was able to see her for the last time before her death in her sixtieth year, almost certainly of heart failure, is unknown.

1939年春天，哈灵顿生活中发生了一件意义深远的事情；他的母亲即将不久于人世。[28] 1938年11月，当韦尔娜写到劳拉的呼吸困难越来越严重时，警报开始响起。他恳求母亲减轻身体负担，包括不要帮残疾的儿子埃德加穿衬衫和打领带。因劳拉病情严重，已不再允许居家疗养，于是她住进了贝尔纪念医院接受药物治疗。保罗试图通过从远方告诉她当天的新闻、分享回忆和美好的祝福，让她高兴起来。欧洲的动荡引起了关注，他询问母亲，对他加入海军后备军有什么想法，因为加入后备军会让他获得相应资历，更有可能被分配到基地医院。劳拉寄给他一首她写的安慰自己的诗，并给他20美元帮他修船。[29]劳拉·哈灵顿于1939年6月27日去世。6月3日，保罗写信说，他将在大约20天后与玛丽·艾丽斯以及她的母亲一起去看劳拉。[30]他说她最近的照片看起来瘦了很多，但体重减少几磅对她的心脏反而有利。但保罗是否在劳拉60岁去世前见了她最后一面，目前不得而知。几乎可以肯定的是她死于心脏衰竭。

In July Harrington began his second year of postgraduate training at Roper General Hospital as an assistant resident in surgery. Sometime during the first year there he had decided to train in orthopedic surgery, for which a year as an assistant resident in surgery was a prerequisite. His choice of specialty fit well with his family and personal history of craftsmanship and was reportedly fostered by a Roper General Hospital orthopedic surgeon.[31]

7月，哈灵顿作为外科住院医师助理在罗珀综合医院开始了他毕业后培训的第二年。在第一年的某个时候，他决定接受骨科的培训。在那里，一年的外科助理住院医师经验是做骨科医师的先决条件。他选择的专业与他的家庭和个人的手工经历非常吻合；此外，他的专业选择也得益于罗珀综合医院对骨科医生的培养。[31]

Germany invaded Poland on September 1, 1939, marking the first day of World War II. This probably delayed his grief over his mother's death, but in November he began recording his feelings."In a frenzy and a half daze I have spent the past sixteen months treading where only fools have dared to place a wandering foot. Finding that only one trend of thought, one frame of mind and one state of being is satisfactory to Him and (me). There is not harmony in my soul, my physical mind, or my physical being when pass these ways. When read these notes written by my mother, who has claimed her crown of richness in the great beyond, I am brought to myself. To realize my heritage is not of receiving but of giving, not of laziness but zest, not of following but of leading ."[32] He must have rediscovered a copy of July 1933 "Dear Lad" letter from his mother that included the following passage: "Life will test your goodness under all kinds of circumstances. You will learn mostly by meditation and communion with Him, because you will be a leader or teacher, ahead of the crowd. You will acquire many beautiful characteristics that come only as one passes thru experiences. You have done well and feel you will always do well."[33] He closed his ledger entry with this pledge: "With intelligence for learning and faith in my heritage, I hope to serve man as she would have me."[34]

1939 年 9 月 1 日，德国入侵波兰，标志着第二次世界大战开始。这可能延缓了他对母亲去世的悲痛。但在 11 月，他开始记录自己的感受。"在过去的 16 个月里，我在疯狂和半迷糊的状态下，走在只有傻瓜才敢走的地方。我发现只有一种思潮、一种心境和一种存在状态，才能使上帝和我满意。当我走过这些道路时，我的灵魂、我的身心都不和谐。当我读到我母亲留下来的这些笔记时，我开始审视自己的内心深处。认识到母亲留给我的遗产不是接受而是给予，不是懒惰而是热情，不是跟随而是领导。"[32]他重新发现了一封 1933 年 7 月母亲写给他的名为"亲爱的孩子"的信，信中有这样一段话："生活将在各种情况下考验你的善良。你可以通过冥想、和它交流来学习，因为你将走在人群的前面，成为一个领导者或老师。你将获得许多只有通过历练才能获得的美好特性。你已经做得很好，而且我觉得你会一直做得很好。"[33]他以这样的誓言结束了自己的记录："凭借学习得来的智慧和遗传的信念，我希望像她那样为人类服务。"[34]

A month later he wrote that he would soon leave for Kansas City where he would be married to his life's partner. "I believe I am passing from my past state of [a blank space] to a new world."[35] Paul Harrington and Mary Alice Wade were married in Kansas City, Kansas, on December 18, 1939, he at the age of 28 and she 24.[36] Officiating was Minister of the Gospel Joseph A. Harrington, Paul's father. His new bride's family traced their roots to antebellum Kentucky. Mary Alice had been born in LeTour, Missouri, the second of Louis and Ethel (Baxter) Wade's three children.[37] Raised in Hoxie, Kansas, a western Kansas farming community where her parents raised wheat, she was described as a dark-haired beauty. She and Paul likely met at the University of Kansas, and it probably wasn't merely coincidental that Paul spent an out-state externship late in his medical school years in Sherman County, where Hoxie was the county seat.

一个月后，他写信说他很快要动身去堪萨斯城，在那里他将和他的终身伴侣举办婚礼。“我相信我正在从过去的空白状态进入一个新的世界。”[35]保罗·哈灵顿和玛丽·艾丽斯·沃德于1939年12月18日在堪萨斯州的堪萨斯城结婚，当时他28岁，她24岁。[36]主礼人是福音牧师约瑟夫·A. 哈灵顿，保罗的父亲。玛丽来自南北战争前的肯塔基州，出生在密苏里州的勒图尔，是路易斯和埃塞尔（巴克斯特）·沃德三个孩子中的老二。[37]她在堪萨斯州西部的霍克西县长大，她的父母在那里种植小麦，她被描述成一个黑发美人。她和保罗很可能是在堪萨斯大学相识的，保罗在医学院学习的后期在谢尔曼县（霍克西县的所在地）进行了一次州外实习，这可能不仅仅是巧合。

Shortly after his marriage while waiting for news about his application for an orthopedic surgery residency, Paul waxed philosophically. He remarked that work was long and tiring and the "up road is a hard path to beat."[38] He wondered if mortals didn't depend too much on the Lord. He reasoned that science was the expression of human intelligence, religion of the human soul, and that soul was often poorly interpreted because of a lack of intelligence. He reckoned that the combination of intelligence and soul should be successful. He further reflected on childrearing, which mirrored his mother's thoughts, and concluded with the importance of responsibility.

婚后不久，在他申请成为骨科住院医师期间，保罗变得富有哲理。他说，工作是漫长而疲惫的，“前方的路是一条艰难的道路”[38]。他想知道人类是不是太依赖上帝了。他的理由是，科学是人类智慧的表达，宗教是人类灵魂的表达，而灵魂往往因为缺乏智慧而得不到很好的诠释。他认为智慧和灵魂的结合应该是成功的。他进一步思考了育儿的问题，这反映了他母亲的想法。此外，他还总结了责任的重要性。

In February 1940 his appointment to the Dickson-Diveley orthopaedic residency in Kansas City, Missouri, arrived.[39] It was a choice position, and he was obviously ecstatic. He wrote, "This move almost establishes my future work. My ultimate aim from now on must be the top in orthopedic surgery." He commented that "specialization of orthopedic surgery is actually in its infancy" and outlined his aims:

"1. Simplified, universal treatment of fractures

2. Ambulatory correction of deformities

3. Early recognition or preventative measures of acute infections available to public

a. Osteomyelitis

b. Polio

c. Arthritis: Infectious, rheumatoid, or hypertrophic

4. Reach as many, who need good care, as possible regardless of remuneration; Comfortable existence and rendering of service

5. My health is imperative, therefore rest-frequent short vacations."[40]

(In 1974 he added these words beside the last aim:" I did not do -.")

1940 年 2 月，他收到了在密苏里州堪萨斯城迪克森-戴夫利医院担任骨科住院医师的任命。[39]这对于他来说显然是一件让人欣喜若狂的事。他写道："这几乎奠定了我未来的工作。从现在开始，我的最终目标必须是成为骨科领域的佼佼者。"他评论说，"骨外科的专业化实际上还处于起步阶段"，并概述了他的目标：

"1. 骨折通用治疗方法的简化

2. 肢体畸形的可活动矫正

3. 公众可获得急性感染的早期识别或预防措施

a. 骨髓炎

b. 脊髓灰质炎

c. 关节炎：感染性、类风湿性或肥大性

4. 不论报酬如何，尽可能为更多需要良好医疗的人提供服务；提供舒适的生活和服务

5. 我的健康状况很重要，所以要休息——经常休短假。"[40]

（1974 年，他在最后一个目标旁边加上了这些话："我没有这样做——"）

Harrington had entered a period of introspection and creativity that continued the rest of his life. His views on family were integral parts of his beliefs. In a letter from Webberville, Michigan, relatives that he had not met before a visit in 1934 reminded him of that time and the strong connection of family."Our stay was only a few days, however when we departed our attachment was so great that tears could not be held back."[41] Harrington concluded that family love and friendship were more valuable than anything money could buy. He longed to have the stellar traits of his mother. "How many times have called her a fool for enduring, for bearing her cross and its added loads? As I see her now her cross was tremendous, her stamina gigantic, her effort sincere, her love for humanity and hers as deep as the Master's for his people. If she would have done as said she would have failed: which all means must change-to her way or I shall fail."[42]

哈灵顿进入了一个延续其余生的自省和创造的时期。他对家庭的看法是他信仰的组成部分。一封来自密歇根州韦伯维尔的亲戚的信让他想起了那段时期，以及家人之间的紧密联系。他直到 1934 年才和亲戚相会。“我们只待了几天，但当我们离开时，我们的感情是如此强烈，以至于眼泪止不住地流了下来。”[41]哈灵顿得出了结论，亲情和友谊比金钱能买到的任何东西都更有价值。他渴望拥有母亲的卓越品质。“有多少次我说她是傻瓜，因为她忍受着，承受着她的苦难和额外的负担。当我现在看到她的时候，她背负的十字架是巨大的，她的耐力是强大的，她的努力是真诚的，她对人类的爱和上帝对他的人民的爱一样深。如果她照我说的去做，她就失败了。这就意味着我必须改变——按她的方式去做，否则我就失败了。”[42]

Harrington's acceptance for an orthopaedic residency had certainly given his spirits a boost, but he still had four months of a surgical residency to complete at Roper. He commented that work had been very hard, his 60-bed ward had 100 patients, and his coresident was on a two-week vacation! But he commented, "I am coming into my own in surgery. It was quite distasteful at first."[43] He expressed concern for Mary Alice with his long working hours, hoping she "will be able to do something to fill her time," especially with the added time commitment that orthopaedic residency would bring. In March 1940 peace and its lack were on everyone's mind. He asked rhetorically if Europe would be in so much trouble if those responsible for the situation had peace of mind. Harrington concluded that the nation's educational system was wanting, and ignorance was the greatest barrier to peace of mind.[44] He found in his mother's handwritten notes a litany of how she lived her life. Included were self-admonitions to never seek excuses for her weakness, to always be charitable in her judgments, to try to always be teachable, to live life as He would have her, to not complain of circumstances, and to find out and obey the laws of nature.[45] Leaving moral qualities aside, he pondered the qualities necessary for success. He concluded there were two prerequisites: first to "offer the public something they need and make it within their reach, and second to cause the least inconvenience to the public."[46] Using fractures as an example, the broad goals were to reduce both hospitalization and inactivity. He posed three areas for investigation: first, the cause of the amount, both quality and extent, of new bone formation; second, effect of movement after callus; and third, the effect of endocrinology on healing fractures. Years later in 1975 he noted his conclusions: "time, regulated activity, and little."

哈灵顿获得了骨科住院医师的职位，这无疑给了他带来了很大的精神上的鼓舞，但他还需要在罗珀完成四个月的外科住院医师培训。他说工作非常辛苦，60张床位的病房有100个病人，而他的室友正在进行为期两周的度假！但他说："在外科手术中，尽管一开始并不愉快，但是我逐渐有了自己的风格。"[43]由于工作时间过长，他特别考虑到骨科住院医师需要投入额外的时间，因此对玛丽·艾丽斯表示了担忧，希望她"能做点什么来使她的生活变得充实"。1940年3月，对和平的渴望和战争的阴影笼罩在每个人的心头。面对时局，哈灵顿反诘道，如果那些对当前局势负责的人能够心平气和，欧洲是否还会陷入如此大的麻烦？后来，他得出了结论，国家的教育体系存在缺陷，无知是心灵平静的最大障碍。[44]他在母亲的手写笔记中发现了她是如何生活的，其中包括告诫自己不要为自己的软弱找借口，对自己的判断要总是宽厚，要总是受教，要像上帝希望的那样生活，不要抱怨环境，要发现并遵守自然的法则。[45]抛开道德品质不谈，他思考成功所必需的品质。他总结了两个先决条件：第一，"为公众提供他们需要的东西……并使其触手可及，其次是尽量减少对公众造成的不便"[46]。以骨折为例，总体目标是减少住院和制动。他提出了三个研究领域：第一，新骨形成数量、质量和程度的原因；第二，骨痂形成后对运动的影响；第三，内分泌学对骨折愈合的影响。多年后的1975年，他提出了自己对上述三个问题的答案："时间，有节制的活动，很少。"

In April his workload lightened in Charleston, leaving more time for him to be creative and explore new possibilities. Medically, he had been trying to get some investigations of sulfonamides going, but commented that this had proved to be difficult. He also recorded his first attempts at surgical innovation with sketches and supportive narrative for two instruments. One was a three-nail guide to aid in the internal fixation of hip fractures. The second was a "drill eye", a drill bit with a hole near the tip to "simplify threading holes with wire."[47] *See figure 3.3*. During the month he also met several leading South

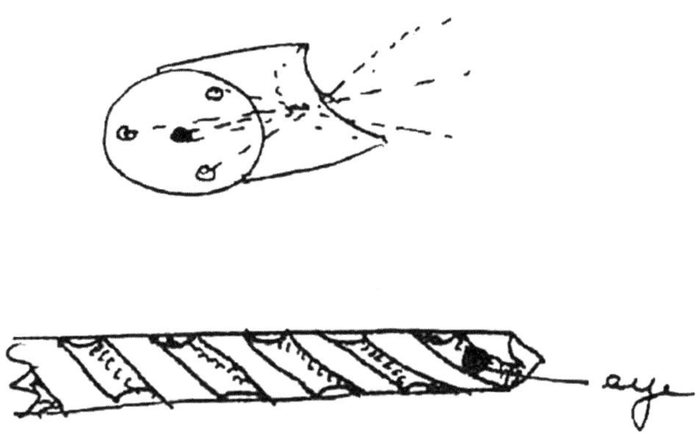

Figure 3.3 ***Hip pin guie and drill eye, surgical instrument sketches, spring 1940.*** **(*Harrington Archives*)**

图3.3 髋销导向和钻眼，手术器械草图，1940年春季(哈灵顿档案馆)

Carolina orthopaedic surgeons, who congratulated him on his Dickson Diveley residency, noting that Dickson was president of the American Board of Orthopaedic Surgery. His lightened workload also allowed more time for his personal life and recreation. He and Mary Alice visited Cypress Gardens, described as "a truly beautiful sight."[48] They also toured the Magnolia Gardens and Middleton Gardens, keeping their notations of the layout for future reference. Not surprisingly, their major project involved a boat. He wrote, "This spring and the sail boats in the harbor have stimulated my soul, I am planning another sail boat."[49] The previous summer he had competed in several regattas with *MAWH*, always finishing in the lower tier in his class. As he sketched the design of his new boat, he kept speed and safety in mind, and what emerged was a catamaran hull design with lateral steps on the pontoons to prevent side slipping. *See figure 3.4*. In the next two months he assembled an eighteen-foot prototype, and Mary Alice helped make the sails. He described the experience as "hard work but loads of fun. and will never forget this experience as long as I live. Which may not be too long, for the destiny of youth is very unstable because of the present world affairs."[50] This was spring 1940 when Hitler's Nazi Germany conquered Norway, invaded the Netherlands, Belgium, and France, and between May 26 and June 4 over 300,000 Allied troops were evacuated at Dunkirk.[51]

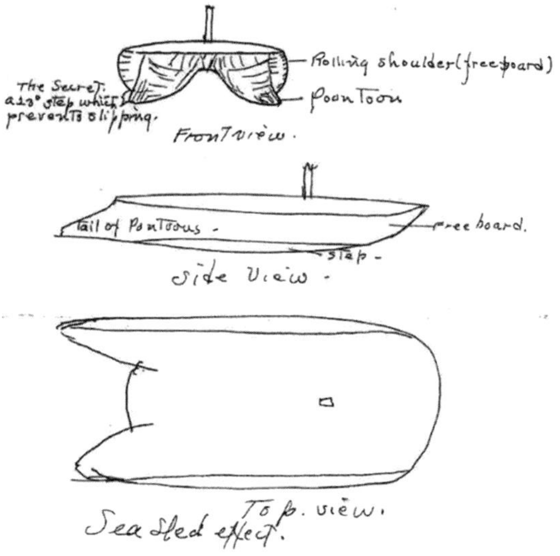

Figure 3.4 ***Sketches of first catamaran design spring 1940.*** **(*Harrington Archives*)**
图 3.4 第一艘双体船设计草图,1940 年春季
(哈灵顿档案馆)

4月，他在查尔斯顿的工作量减轻了，这让他有更多的时间发挥创造力，探索新的可能性。在医学上，他一直试图开展一些对磺胺类药物的研究，但他评论说，事实证明这很困难。他还记录了他在外科手术创新方面的第一次尝试，并绘制了两种器械草图，进行了相关叙述。一种是三钉导板，用于帮助髋部骨折的内固定。第二个是“钻眼”，一种靠近钻头尖端有孔的钻头，目的是“用金属丝简化穿线孔”。[47]（图 3.3）在这个月，他还会见了几位南卡罗来纳州的顶级骨科医生，他们祝贺他在迪克森-戴夫利医院获得职位，并指出迪克森是美国骨外科委

员会主席。工作量的减轻也让他有更多的时间来安排个人生活和娱乐。他和玛丽·艾丽斯参观了被称为“真正美丽的风景”的柏树花园。[48]他们还参观了木兰花园和米德尔顿花园，记录了它们的布局特征，以备将来参考。不出所料，他们的主要项目是一艘船。他写道：“这个春天和港湾里的帆船刺激了我的灵魂，我正在计划制造另一艘帆船。”[49]去年夏天，他驾驶 MAWH 参加了几场帆船赛，排名靠后。在勾画新船的设计草图时，他把速度和安全牢记于心，于是出现了一种双体船身设计，浮筒上有侧向台阶以防止船身侧滑。（图 3.4）在接下来的两个月里，他组装了一个 18 英尺的原型，玛丽·艾丽斯帮忙制作了帆。他将这段经历描述为虽辛苦但充满乐趣，“我这辈子都不会忘记这段经历。而且由于当前的世界形势所导致的年轻人的不稳定命运，这可能不会持续太久。”[50]那是 1940 年春天，希特勒的纳粹德国占领了挪威，入侵了荷兰、比利时和法国，5 月 26 日至 6 月 4 日期间，超过 30 万盟军从敦刻尔克撤离。[51]

Harrington reported sailing his prototype on June 20 and 22 and described the experiment as follows: “The boat is the fastest thing in the harbor in light winds—cannot take heavy weather but that is a matter of construction which can be worked... Its essential features are a flat bottom for planning, straight free board for side slipping and balance, and more beam and more sail.”[52]

哈灵顿记录了他的原型船在 6 月 20 日和 22 日的航行情况，并这样描述了实验：“在微风中，船是港口中速度最快的东西——不能承受恶劣的天气，但这是一个可以解决的结构问题……它的基本构造是平整的船底，用于侧滑和平衡的直自由板，更多的横梁和更多的帆。”[52]

On July 1, 1940, after his successful completion of a year of internship and a year of assistant surgery residency, the Harringtons departed for Kansas City. “Charleston will hold numerous experiences in my memories. Our marriage will be grand one—we are very happy—even under the circumstances.”[53] He was not charitable in his assessment of Roper Hospital when he observed that “pathology is unlimited but the hands in which this pathology lies is most inadequate to cope with the situation.”[54] Ropers administrator apparently responded in some unknown manner.

1940 年 7 月 1 日，在他顺利完成一年的实习和一年的外科助理住院医生的工作后，哈灵顿一家启程前往堪萨斯城。“在查尔斯顿的诸多经历将留存在我的记忆中。即使在这种情况下，我们的婚姻也会很美满——我们很幸福。”[53]他对罗珀综合医院的评价并不宽容，他观察到，“病理学能解决很多问题，但掌握这种病理方法的人手却不足以应对这种情况。”[54]罗珀的管理层显然以某种不为人知的方式做出了回应。

They arrived July 3, and Harrington immediately began the Dickson-Diveley orthopaedic residency. The first year was at St. Luke's Hospital in Kansas City, Missouri. After just eleven days he wrote, "St. Luke's is a fine modern hospital with a grand staff. My chiefs are among the top notches in orthopedic surgery and as men. My opportunities will be many, as will my chastisements be. It should be a grand year... I've assisted on more real major orthopedic surgery here than saw in Charleston."[55]

他们于 7 月 3 日抵达，哈灵顿立即在迪克森–戴夫利骨科开始住院医师实习。第一年是在密苏里州堪萨斯市的圣卢克医院。仅仅过了 11 天，他就写道：“圣卢克医院是一所优秀的现代医院，拥有优秀的员工。我的上司们都是骨外科的顶尖人物。我的机会会很多，我的惩罚也会很多。这将是有重大意义的一年……我在这里作为助手参与过的真正的大型骨科手术比在查尔斯顿见过的还多。”[55]

Frank D. Dickson and Rex L. Diveley came from comfortable but differing backgrounds, forged an unusually productive professional team, and importantly influenced the evolution of the young specialty of orthopaedic surgery. Franklin Drake Dickson (1882–1964) was born and raised in Pittsburgh, Pennsylvania.[56] His paternal grandfather opened the first soft coal mine in western Pennsylvania and was a cofounder of the Pennsylvania Railroad.[57] Dickson received his BA (1902) and MD (1905) from the University of Pennsylvania. Following eighteen months' study abroad, he returned for an internship in Philadelphia. In 1908 he began practice and became associated with Gwilym Davis, a leading general surgeon very interested in orthopaedic surgery. Dickson later recalled that "previously very little surgery was being done by orthopaedic surgeons, who were called strap-and-buckle specialists, since their main reliance had been manipulation, braces and supports."[58] In 1912 Davis succeeded DeForest Willard as professor of orthopaedic surgery at the University of Pennsylvania and made Dickson chief of the outpatient clinic and instructor in orthopaedic surgery. Soon after that Sir Harry Platt, a prominent English surgeon, visited and a lasting friendship was formed. Dickson believed, "This was one of the early steps in establishing a firm cooperation between British and American orthopaedic surgeons." In 1916 orthopaedic care in the Midwest was said to be limited to one or two practitioners between Chicago and Denver, and Dickson was recruited to come to Kansas City to establish crippled children's clinics in Kansas and an orthopaedic clinic at the new Christian Church Hospital in Kansas City, Missouri.[59] After arrival Dickson also joined the teaching faculty at the University of Kansas School of Medicine.[60] His intent was to return to Philadelphia. But World War intervened, and in 1917 he joined the orthopaedic surgeons gathered by Dr. Joel Goldthwait of Boston to augment the serious medical service shortages in Britain. After four months in the Royal Army Medical Corps he returned to the United States Army as an orthopaedic divisional consultant where he helped introduce emergency splinting, including traction splinting. Dickson was a lieutenant colonel when he left the service.

弗兰克·D. 迪克森和雷克斯·L. 戴夫利拥有不同的良好背景，他们组建了一支异常高效的专业团队，并对骨科这一年轻专业的发展产生了重要影响。富兰克林·德雷克·迪克森（1882—1964）在宾夕法尼亚州的匹兹堡出生并长大。[56]他的祖父在宾夕法尼亚州西部开发了第一个软煤矿，也是宾夕法尼亚铁路公司的创始人之一。[57]迪克森在宾夕法尼亚大学获得学士学位（1902 年）和医学博士学位（1905 年）。在国外学习了 18 个月后，他回到了费城实习。1908 年，他开始行医，并与格威利姆·戴维斯合作，后者是一位对骨科手术非常感兴趣的著名普外科医生。迪克森后来回忆说，“以前很少有骨科医生做手术，他们被称为‘皮带扣’专家，因为他们主要依靠的是（手法）、支具和支架。”[58] 1912 年，戴维斯接替德福雷斯特·威拉德成为宾夕法尼亚大学的骨外科教授，并任命迪克森为门诊主任和骨外科讲师。此后不久，一位著名的英国外科医生哈利·普拉特爵士来访，和他们建立了长久的友谊。迪克森认为，“这是英美两国骨科医生建立牢固的合作关系的早期阶段。”1916 年，中西部的骨科学部在芝加哥和丹佛之间据说只有一两个医生，迪克森被招募到堪萨斯城，在堪萨斯建立了残疾儿童诊所，并在密苏里州堪萨斯城的新基督教会医院建立了骨科门诊，[59]迪克森还加入了堪萨斯大学医学院的教学团队。[60]他的意图是回到费城。但是第一次世界大战爆发了，1917 年他加入了波士顿的乔尔·戈德思韦特医生组织的骨科医生团队，以解决英国严重的医疗服务短缺问题。在皇家陆军医疗队待了四个月后，他回到美国陆军担任骨科医师顾问，在那里他协助引进了急救夹板疗法，包括牵引夹板疗法。迪克森最终以中校军衔退役。

Rexford Leon Diveley (1892–1980) was born in Bazine, Kansas, a town of less than 500 in western Kansas.[61,62] His grandfather was an early settler, and his father was the owner of a large variety store in Indian Territory. Diveley graduated from the University of Kansas with a BA in 1915 and an MD in 1917, after which he enlisted in the Army, serving from April 1917 to April 1919. His first assignment was to the radiological training school in Kansas City, Missouri. After that he was sent as an instructor to the Army X-ray school at Bellevue Hospital in New York City. From there he was assigned as a ward surgeon in the Army's base hospital #28, located at Limoges, France. At discharge he held the rank of captain. After a year's residency in medicine at Johns Hopkins, returned to Kansas City to establish a radiology department at Mercy Hospital.

雷克斯福德·利昂·戴夫利（1892—1980）出生于堪萨斯州的巴赞，这是州西部一个人口不足500人的小镇。[61,62]他的祖父是早期的定居者，他的父亲是印第安人领地上一家大型杂货店的老板。1915年，戴夫利毕业于堪萨斯大学，获得了文学学士学位，1917年获得了医学博士学位，之后他应征入伍，从1917年4月至1919年4月在军队服役。他的第一个任务是在密苏里州堪萨斯城的放射培训学校教学。之后，他被派往纽约市贝尔维尤医院的陆军放射学校担任讲师。在那里，他被分配到位于法国利摩日的陆军第28基地医院担任病房外科医生。退伍时，他的军衔是上尉。在约翰·霍普金斯医院实习一年后，他回到了堪萨斯城，在广慈医院建立了放射科。

Diveley, a student of poliomyelitis, from about 1923 to 1927 performed epidemiological, treatment, and laboratory experimental studies, publishing his observations in 1929.[63] From 1913 through 1924 he reported that cases in Kansas averaged 57 per year (+40: range, 16 to 149) and in Minnesota 204 per year (+275: range, 22 to 912). There was no definite trend over time, especially when population increases were considered. The death rate for 1914 through 1924 averaged 36% (+17.6%: range, 22% to 86%) in Kansas and 21% (+8.2%: range, 11% to 36%) in Minnesota, a significant difference.[64] During the 1923 epidemic 185 (72 female, 113 male) cases were seen in Kansas and the bordering states, but only 46% (85 of 185) were able to be followed two years. Diveley's opinion was that earlier diagnosis and better care provided better recovery. He believed repeated lumbar puncture resulted in better neurologic outcome. The treatment arm of the study was interpreted as showing better recovery when Rosenow's antistreptococcus serum was administered, but the numbers were too small (ten treated and four not treated) to allow any conclusions. The laboratory studies involved thirteen

Macacus rhesus monkeys. Convalescent serum seemed to neutralize the virus, provide passive immunization of no more than six months' duration, and render some treatment effect. Diveley ascribed some benefit from Rosenow's serum, but when compared to the controls, it seemed ineffective. His overall conclusions were that early diagnosis, absolute bed rest, fever control, early and frequent spinal taps to keep the spinal pressure down, and intravenous or intramuscular specific serum therapy offered the best chance of recovery. He did not specify convalescent serum therapy.

戴夫利的研究方向是脊髓灰质炎。从 1923 年到 1927 年，他进行了流行病学、治疗和实验室相关研究，并于 1929 年出版了他的研究结果。[63]从 1913 年到 1924 年，他注意到堪萨斯州的病例数平均每年 57 例（±40，范围：16～149），明尼苏达州病例数平均每年 204 例（±275，范围：22～912）。随着时间的推移，考虑到人口增长的因素，发病数并无明确的增长趋势。从 1914 年到 1924 年，堪萨斯州的平均死亡率为 36%（±17.6%，区间：22%～86%），明尼苏达州平均死亡率 21%（±8.2%，区间：11%～36%），具有显著的统计学差异。[64] 1923 年脊髓灰质炎流行期间，在堪萨斯州和与其接壤的州发现了 185 例（72 例女性，113 例男性）病例，但只有 46%（85/185）的病人能够被随访两年。戴夫利认为，早期诊断和良好的治疗是康复的关键。他认为重复腰椎穿刺会得到更准确的神经病学诊断结果。该研究的治疗组在应用罗斯诺的抗链球菌血清治疗后，恢复较好，但病例数太少（10 人接受治疗，4 人未接受治疗），所以无法得出任何结论。实验室研究需要 13 只猕猴。恢复期血清可能可以中和病毒，提供不超过六个月的被动免疫，并有一些治疗效果。戴夫利认为罗斯诺的血清有一定作用，但与对照组相比，效果并不是特别明显。他得出了最终结论，早期诊断、绝对卧床休息、控制发热、早期多次的脊椎穿刺以保持脊椎压力下降，以及静脉内或肌肉注射特异性血清的治疗办法可以提供最好的康复机会。他对恢复期血清疗法没有进行具体说明。

In 1922 Dickson and Diveley became acquainted, and five years later they opened the Dickson-Diveley Clinic. The following year they were invited to move to the new St. Luke's Hospital where they began residency-training program. In 1938 the board requirement was changed to three years, and the Dickson-Diveley residency increased accordingly. Also at that time Kansas City General Hospital's orthopaedic department was integrated into the St. Luke's orthopaedic department.[65]

1922 年，迪克森和戴夫利相识，五年后，他们开办了迪克森-戴夫利诊所。

第二年，他们被邀请去圣卢克医院新院区，在那里他们开始了住院医师培训。1938 年，住院医师培训改为三年，迪克森-戴夫利住院医师培训的时间也相应增加。也是在那个时候，堪萨斯城综合医院的骨科被并入圣卢克骨科。[65]

A result of the World War I experience with large numbers of bone and joint injuries was the realization of the need for many well-educated and more highly trained orthopaedic surgeons. The American Orthopaedic Association (AOA) had formed in 1887 and maintained a restricted membership, which inhibited growth of the specialty. But when guests far outnumbered members at its annual meeting, the time had come for action. On October 11, 1931, during a meeting of eight leaders, including Dickson, held during the meeting of another restrictive society's (Clinical Orthopaedic Society) meeting, the way was opened for the formation of what was to become the American Academy of Orthopaedic Surgeons (AAOS).[66] From its beginning the AAOS was merit based and dedicated to high standards of preparation, practice, and skill maintenance. Its first meeting in 1933, Dickson became the fourth president in 1936.[67] He was also one was and of the leaders in forming the American Board of Orthopaedic Surgery, one of the oldest medical specialty boards in the United States, in 1934. President of the AOA in 1940, he was one of the few to serve in that office both in the AOA and the AAOS.[68] Diveley also had a distinguished orthopaedic career. A member of the AAOS and AOA, he served as the fifteenth president of the AAOS in 1948 and later established its central office. Rising to the rank of colonel during World War II, he was the chief consultant of orthopaedic surgery on the headquarters staff in the chief surgeon's office in the European Theater of Operations.[69]

第一次世界大战导致产生了大量的骨、关节损伤的患者，他们意识到急需更多受过良好教育和高水平训练的骨科医生。美国骨科学会（AOA）成立于 1887 年，由于会员人数有限，阻碍了该专业的发展。在年会上，当来宾人数远远超过会员人数时，大家意识到是时候采取行动了。1931 年 10 月 11 日，在另一个有入会限制的学会（临床骨科学会）会议举行期间，包括迪克森在内的 8 位领导人，为后来的美国骨科医师学会（AAOS）的创立铺平了道路。[66]从一开始，美国骨科医师学会就以自己的优势为基础，致力于保持高标准的准备工作、业务练习和技能掌握。1933 年召开第一次会议，迪克森在 1936 年成为第四任主席。[67]他也是 1934 年成立的美国骨科委员会（ABOS）的领导人之一，这是美国最古老的医学专业委员会之一。作为美国骨科学会的主席，在 1940 年，他是少数几个在美国骨科学会和美国骨科医师学会都任职的医生之一。[68]戴夫利的骨科职业生涯也足够辉煌。作为美国骨科医师学会和美国骨科学会的会员，他在 1948 年担任美国骨科医师学会的第十五任主席，后来建立了它的中心办事处。第二次世界大战期间，他晋升为上校，是欧洲战区首席外科医生办公室原总参谋部骨科首席顾问。[69]

Indeed, Harrington was trained by two leaders of orthopaedic surgery. He acknowledged this in a November 1940 diary entry. "Four months have passed since my arrival. The work is long and hard but, darn it, I like it; a grand place for training. I often get down in the dumps but it is my own choosing, in trying to live two or three years ahead." [70] Still he was clearly unsettled and working to understand why. After reading H. G. Wells' *The Outline of History*, he recorded these thoughts. "It seems a pity that civilization after reaching its present status must plunder itself into self-destruction as it is today. After the long years of progress thru the ages, surely man is capable of reaching the acme of perfection. In times like these one would think it hopeless however." [71] He wondered, "Is religion behind or in front of the times? I wonder. Is our social order behind or in front? I wonder! Is our diplomacy behind or in front? I wonder! Is our education in front or behind? I wonder! Is the human race in front or behind? Is mankind on the uphill or downhill grade? I wonder. What is ***time***?" He continued, "If we must and we shall believe that the human being is capable of reaching the pinnacle, the acme of perfection, what must he know before he shall begin the upward climb?" Again and again perfection and the pursuit of it were themes in Harrington's life. A week later he commented, "Today is Sunday—a dreary day far as environment and weather goes." [72] He had chanced on is as an article in the *Reader's Digest* titled "Why Don't Go to Church," indicating he was still wrestling with his religious beliefs. Whatever the origins of his discontent, if there were any beyond that of the imminent war, he seemed to work through them, and writing seemed to have helped.

事实上，哈灵顿是由两位骨科的领导者培养出来的。他在 1940 年 11 月的日记中承认了这一点。"我到这里已经四个月了。这项工作冗长又辛苦，但是，该死的，我喜欢它；这是锻炼的绝佳地方。我经常感到沮丧，但这是我自己的选择，我会努力坚持两三年。"[70]显然，他还是很不安，并在努力寻找原因。在读完 H. G. 韦尔的《历史大纲》后，他记录了这些想法。"似乎很遗憾，文明在达到目前的水平后，必须像今天这样掠夺自己，走向自我毁灭。经过漫长岁月的进步，人类肯定能够达到完美的极致。然而，在这种时候，人们会认为这是没有希望的。”[71]他疑惑道，“宗教是落后于时代还是领先于时代？我想知道。我们的社会秩序是在后退还是在前进？我想知道！我们的外交是在后退还是在前进？我想知道！我们的教育是在后退还是在前进？我想知道！人类是在后退还是在前进？人类是在上坡还是下坡？我想知道。**时间**是什么？”他继续说，“如果我们必须并且应该相信人类能够到达顶峰，完美的极致，那么在他开始向上攀登之前，他必须知道什么呢？”完美和追求完美是哈灵顿一生的主题。一周后，他说：“今天是星期天——就环境和天气而言，这是可怕的一天。”[72]他偶然在《读者文摘》上看到一篇题为《为什么不去教堂》的文章，这表明他仍在与自己的宗教信仰作斗争。不管他不满的来源是什么，如果除了迫在眉睫的战争还有其他什么，他似乎都解决了，写作似乎有所帮助。

Figure 3.5 ***As a Dickson-Diveley orthopaedic surgery resident in a shirt made by Mary Alice.*** (***Harrington Archives***)
图3.5 哈灵顿做迪克森-戴夫利骨科住院医生时的照片，穿着玛丽·艾丽斯制作的衬衫(哈灵顿档案馆)

It is also possible that salvation from his worries may have also been related at least in part to a new opportunity for orthopaedic creativity. *See figure 3.5*. His residency and his persistence combined to enable him to study sulfonamides, the first antibiotics, in the fight against infection, which was one of the major scourges of bone and joint surgery. Harrington was already attuned to the drug's development and had been unsuccessful in initiating a clinical study while at Roper General Hospital.[73] But it was about to become a reality. Sulfonamides were the outcome of laborious trial-and-error research based on the observation that coal-tar dyes could attach to and attack bacteria and parasites.[74] The research had begun in 1932, and success was announced in 1935 after researchers at Germany's Bayer AG laboratories had patented the drug under the trade name Prontosil. As efforts were made to commercialize the finding, French researchers discovered why the drug was only effective in the body and not in the test tube. The drug was metabolized into two pieces, releasing the smaller, colorless, active molecule sulfanilamide from the inactive dye portion. This discovery was important in establishing the concept of bioactivation and ended prospects of large profits since sulfanilamide had been synthesized in 1906 and its patent had long since expired. However, it opened the floodgates for hundreds of manufacturers unconstrained by testing requirements. This led to the Elixir Sulfanilamide disaster in 1937, which resulted in over 100 deaths from the ethylene glycol in the medication and hastened the passage of the Federal Food, Drug, and Cosmetic Act in 1938 in the United States. This expanded the authority of the FDA, assuring the evolution of safe sulfa drugs.[75]

骨科创造性发展的新契机可能在一定程度上将他从忧虑中解脱出来。（图3.5）住院医师的经历和坚持不懈的努力使他能够研究磺胺类药物，这是对抗感染的第一种抗生素，而感染是骨和关节外科疾病的主要病因之一。哈灵顿已经熟悉了这种药物的研发，虽然在罗珀综合医院启动临床研究时他的研发没有成功，[73]但也离成功不远了。磺胺类药物是经过艰苦试验和错误研究的结果，其试验基础是观察到煤焦油染料可以附着并攻击细菌和寄生虫。[74]这项研究始于1932年。1935年，德国拜耳公司实验室的研究人员以商品名百浪多息为该药物申请了专利，并宣布成功。随着将这一药物投向市场，法国研究人员发现了为什么这种药物只在体内有效而在体外无效。药物代谢分解成两部分，从无活性染料部分释放出较小的无色活性分子磺胺。这一发现对建立生物活性的概念非常重要，并终结了磺胺产生巨大利润的可能，因为磺胺在1906年就已经合成，其专利早已过期。然而，它为数百家不受测试要求约束的制造商打开了大门。这导致了1937年的磺胺药物灾难：100多人死于药物中的乙二醇中毒，并加速了1938年《联邦食品、药品和化妆品法案》的通过。这扩大了美国食品药品监督管理局的权力，确保了磺胺药物的安全发展。[75]

Development of these first-ever antimicrobial drugs suggested a new approach to the treatment of previously intractable problems, such as chronic osteomyelitis, and for the prevention of infection in vulnerable situations, such as open fractures. On May 9, 1940, two related papers were presented in Kansas City, Missouri, at the annual meeting of the AOA. One was an opinion paper about the local effects of sulfanilamide; it was based on experience, laboratory animal experiments, and an incomplete review of the literature.[76] Five conclusions were drawn: sulfanilamide needed to be sterilized before placement in clean wounds, joints tolerated the drug very well, primary wound healing was slightly inhibited, repeated use did not interfere with healing of open infected wounds, and use was advocated for both contaminated wounds and clean, operative wounds where there was increased risk of infection. The second presentation reported on 54 patients with compound fractures treated with internal fixation with vitallium implants and locally placed sulfanilamide.[77] The authors concluded that locally applied sulfanilamide wasn't helpful in preventing infection in fresh compound fractures, but was helpful in reconstructing existing compound fractures with previous or active infection. These two publications appeared just five months later.

首个抗微生物药物的开发为之前治疗困难的疾病（如慢性骨髓炎）和预防虚弱情况下的感染（如开放性骨折）提供了一种新的方法。1940 年 5 月 9 日，在密苏里州堪萨斯城举行的美国骨科学会年会上，研究人员发表了两篇相关论文。第一篇是关于磺胺局部作用的研究报告，它是基于经验、实验室动物实验和不完全的文献综述。[76]这篇报告最终得出了五个结论：磺胺在应用于干净的伤口之前需要灭菌，关节对药物的耐受性很好，伤口初次愈合时受到轻微抑制，重复使用不会干扰开放性感染伤口的愈合，并且提倡在感染风险增加的情况下可用于被污染的伤口和干净的手术伤口。第二篇文章报道了 54 名复合骨折患者，采用钴铬钼合金内固定物和局部放置磺胺类药物进行内固定治疗。[77]作者得出了结论，局部应用磺胺对预防新鲜复合骨折感染没有帮助，但有助于先前或活动性感染的现有复合骨折重建。这两份研究报告在五个月后出版。

On August 1, 1940, just three months later and one month after Harrington began his residency, Dickson and Diveley began treatment of a series of patients with subacute or chronic osteomyelitis using sulfathiazole in the local treatment regime.[78] This drug was chosen because they said it was more effective against staphylococcus, the most common infecting organism. The local dose was based on Key's report. Treatment included oral sulfathiazole (5 g per 100-pound body weight for at least 3 days preoperative and postoperative, which achieved a blood level of 4.7 mg%, near their goal of 5 mg%), thorough debridement, 1–2 g of sulfathiazole applied with nasal insufflators to the exposed tissues, closure of dead spaces, a voluminous firm dressing and cast, and continuation of oral medication postoperative (an average of 15 days). Only five months later in January 1941 they were able to present their preliminary results at the annual meeting of the AAOS. The results published in July 1941 showed success in 18 of 22 patients treated, an 82% success rate.[79] Although not included as a co-author in this study, he had done a lot of the work, and his efforts were soon to be rewarded.

1940 年 8 月 1 日，在哈灵顿开始住院实习的一个月后，迪克森和戴夫利开始在局部治疗研究中应用磺胺噻唑治疗一系列亚急性或慢性骨髓炎患者。[78]选择这种药物是因为他们说这种药物对最常见的感染微生物葡萄球菌更为有效。使用的剂量是根据基的研究确定的，治疗包括口服磺胺噻唑（术前和术后至少 3 天，每 100 磅体重 5g，达到 4.7mg%的血药浓度，接近 5mg%的目标），彻底清创，用鼻吸器将 1~2g 磺胺噻唑喷于暴露的组织，封闭无效腔，用大量的敷料和石膏固定，术后继续口服药物进行治疗（平均 15 天）。仅仅五个月后，即 1941 年 1 月，他们在美国骨科医师学会年会上提交了初步的研究结果。1941 年 7 月发表的结果显示，22 名接受治疗的患者中有 18 人成功恢复了健康，成功率为 82%。[79]虽然没有作为共同作者参与这项研究，但哈灵顿做了大量的工作，他的努力很快得到了回报。

Harrington received his due recognition and his first published paper on their second study presented at the annual meeting of the AMA on June 6, 1941, and published in the November 29, 1941, issue of the *Journal of the American Medical Association*.[80] Authored by Diveley and Harrington, "Chemotherapy in Infections of the Bones and Soft Tissues" was a sequel to the paper published five months earlier by Dickson, Diveley, and Kiene. The initial 22 patients in the study had increased to 56. Thirty-eight had subacute or chronic osteomyelitis, sixteen had compound fractures, and two had miscellaneous infected wounds (one infected sinus in the thigh of about eight years' duration and one infected ulcer of the foot). Patients with established infections had sulfathiazole administered by mouth at an average dosage of 6. 6 g per day to obtain a blood concentration of 5 mg% several days before operation. One hour after dosage the average blood level was 4. 2 mg% and at eight hours was 4. 7 mg%. For compound fractures where delay was not permissible, sodium sulfathiazole was administered intravenously at 0. 06 g per kg of body weight (the average daily dose was 4. 1 g). The average blood level was 47. 5 mg% at five minutes, 10. 75 mg% at two hours, and 5.25 mg% at four hours after administration.

1941 年 6 月 6 日，哈灵顿在美国医学会（AMA）年会上发表了他的第二项研究，并在 1941 年 11 月 29 日的《美国医学会杂志》上发表了他的第一篇论文。[80]由戴夫利和哈灵顿合作撰写的《骨骼和软组织感染的药物治疗》，是迪克森、戴夫利和基内五个月前发表的论文的续篇。研究由最初的 22 名患者增加到 56 名。38 人患有亚急性或慢性骨髓炎，16 人有复合骨折，2 人有各种感染的伤口（一名患者因大腿感染形成约 8 年的窦道，一名患者因感染导致足部溃疡）。在手术前几天，已确诊感染的患者口服平均剂量为6.6 g/天的磺胺噻唑，以获得5 mg%的血药浓度。给药后1小时，平均血药浓度为4.2 mg%，8小时后为4.7 mg%。对于不允许延迟的复合骨折，以每千克体重0.06 g的剂量静脉注射磺胺噻唑钠（平均每日剂量为4.1 g）。给药后5分钟，平均血药浓度为47.5 mg%，2小时后为10.75 mg%，4小时后为5.25 mg%。

The local treatment of compound fractures was thorough debridement, alignment of the bone ends, and internal fixation using a silent metal such as vitallium. The wound was cleansed with a warm saline solution and thoroughly dried. One to 3 g of powdered sulfathiazole were applied to the bone surfaces and into the minutest crevices with nasal insufflators. Closure without tension was done, but if not possible, it was left open and tamponed. A plaster dressing was applied to adequately immobilize the extremity. Of the sixteen patients with compound fractures eleven were acute and five were old with persistent infection. Based on their protocol, all sixteen would have received internal fixation. The results for the compound fracture group were as follows: "The mean average healing time for this series was 24.8 days. (Two cases of the series are of too recent occurrence to be reported, but both seem destined to satisfactory healing. Three other cases are to be reported later.)" With results in five of the sixteen incomplete, the usefulness of the protocol was still pending. The results for all 56 patients in the series were reported as follows: "In 53 cases [95%] healing was by primary intention with an average healing period of 21.6 days. Two cases should be termed successful but with greatly prolonged healing time as compared to the others. One case we consider a failure as regards this method, but the case is still under treatment." There is an unaddressed discrepancy between the subgroup of compound fractures with results in five pending and the full series with one failure and no report of pending results.

复合性骨折的局部治疗是彻底清创，骨端对齐，使用惰性金属如钴铬钼合金进行内固定。用温盐水清洗伤口，并彻底擦干。用鼻吹入器将1~3 g粉状磺胺噻唑喷于骨表面和微小的缝隙中。做无张力闭合，如果不可能，就开放并填塞。用石膏敷料来充分固定四肢。在16例复合骨折病例中，11例为急性骨折，5例为老年慢性感染。根据他们的方案，16名患者都将接受内固定。复合骨折组的结果如下："该组的平均愈合时间为24.8天。（这一系列的两个病例都是最近才报道的病例，但两者似乎取得了令人满意的疗效。稍后将报告其他三例病例。）"由于16名患者中有5名患者的结果不完整，该治疗方案对患者康复的有效性仍然悬而未决。该研究中所有56名患者的结果报告如下:"在53例一期愈合的病例中[95%],平均愈合期为21.6天。其中有两个案例应该被认为是成功的,但与其他案例相比,愈合时间大大延长。有一个我们认为是失败的案例,但这个案例中的患者仍在治疗中。复合骨折亚组中有5例暂无结果,有1例失败,且与无结果报告之间存在未解决的差异。

The sulfonamide clinical research projects were important milestones in Harrington's development, and they illustrated the importance of his Dickson-Diveley residency. Theirs was a big practice, making it possible to readily develop patient series. The two men, his mentors, were actively expanding the capabilities of orthopedic practice and communicating their findings. Harrington was receiving early and apparently favorable exposure to the use of metallic implants in orthopedic surgery, years before such practice was widely accepted. Internal fixation of fracture with plates and screws had waxed and waned for several decades because of the corrosive effect of the implants used. Acting on a dentist's information that vitallium (a new chrome-cobalt alloy formulated in 1929) implants were inert to the mouth's saliva, San Antonio surgeon innovators, Venable and Stuck, had conducted experiments that showed vitallium plates and screws did not cause electrolysis and thus corrosion when applied to long bones.[81] After successful clinical use in 1936, they asked that the vitallium plates and screws be made available for use by a select group: Willis Campbell in Memphis, Frank Dickson, and Melvin S. Henderson at the Mayo Clinic.

磺胺类药物临床研究项目是哈灵顿事业发展过程中的重要里程碑，这说明了他担任迪克森-戴夫利住院医师这段经历的重要性。这是一项重大实践，让随时准备制订治疗方案成为可能。他的导师，迪克森和戴夫利这两个人，正在积极提高骨科实践的能力，并就他们的发现进行交流。在骨科手术中使用金属内植物，哈灵顿早在这种做法被广泛接受之前的几年就预感到它可以带来明显有利的效果。由于所用内植物的腐蚀作用，骨折的钢板和螺钉内固定几十年来时好时坏。根据牙医的经验，钴铬钼合金（1929年研制的一种新的铬钴合金）内植物对口腔唾液呈惰性。圣安东尼奥外科医生创始者维纳布尔和斯塔克进行了实验，表明钴铬钼合金板和螺钉在应用于长骨时不会引起电解和腐蚀。[81] 1936年临床成功使用后，他们将钴铬钼合金钢板和螺钉提供给一个精选的小组使用：孟菲斯的威利斯·坎贝尔，梅奥诊所的弗兰克·迪克森和梅尔文·S. 亨德森。

The extra time and intellectual demands of the sulfathiazole studies could be credited with giving Harrington the focus he needed. On April 19, 1941, as he was nearing the end of his year at St. Luke's Hospital, he made a lengthy diary entry summarizing his progress to date and laying out his aspirations for the future. "I have been pondering over a subject for some time, i.e., the problem of orthopedics. I believe I have reached a decision. It must be all or none. I am starting to compile a potential book, My Orthopedic Bible. In it all possible subjects of this phase of medicine shall be considered too, interesting and timely suggestions with fundamental background will be included. Being associated with one of the masters of the art I believe his frequent words of wisdom should be written, preserved and profited by. Offhand the following:

The proof of the pudding is not in the eating thereof,

All fractures in or about or affecting the joint should be started in passive motion early,

Judgment is the result of well-directed experience,

I believe the lurching gait in postoperative Smith-Peterson arthroplasties is due to shortened gluteals,

Abdominal transplants in polios should be done early,

All fascial transplants, in flail hips, from trochanter to lumbar muscles should have a check—fascial transplant to anterior superior [iliac] spine,

Polios should not be allowed to develop contracted capsules about joints even in the neutral position,

In correcting flexion deformities of knees always use compound or Russell's type of traction, and

In stubborn varus deformities of club feet tenotomy of the adductor pollicis and mesial fascia is indicated."[82]

哈灵顿花费了更多的时间和精力研究磺胺噻唑。1941年4月19日，他在圣卢克医院的培训即将结束时，他写了一篇长长的日记，总结了他迄今为止的进步，并提出了对未来的期望。"我已经思考一个课题有一段时间了，即骨科的课题。我相信我已经做出了决定。我打算开始编写一本有潜力的书《我的骨科圣经》。在这本书里，所有可能的医学主题也将被考虑，包括有趣的和及时的建议与基本背景。这些内容和艺术大师中的一位有关联，我相信他的智慧之言应该被书写、保存并让读者从中受益。随口说出以下内容：

布丁的好坏不在于吃不吃，

所有在关节内或关节周围骨折或关节感染都应该在早期开始制动，

判断是经验的结果，

我认为史密斯-彼得森关节成形术后步态蹒跚是臀肌挛缩导致的，

脊髓灰质炎患者应尽早进行腹部肌肉移植，

在连枷式髋关节中，所有从大转子到腰肌的筋膜移植都应在髂前上棘进行检查，

即使在中立位，脊髓灰质炎症患者也不应该在关节周围形成关节囊挛缩，

在纠正膝关节屈曲畸形时，需要使用复合式或罗素式牵引，

对于顽固的内翻畸形，拇内收肌和内侧筋膜切开术是必要的。[82]

Even though Harrington did not follow-up with additional references to My Orthopedic Bible, his renewed focus and interest in creativity were apparent.

尽管哈灵顿没有给《我的骨科圣经》添加新的内容，但他对创造力的重新关注和兴趣是显而易见的。

The day-to-day life of medical trainees and their spouses has always been built around work, hope, and a tight budget. The income and expenditure ledgers that Paul and Mary Alice periodically kept affirmed this. As an example, for the two-week period beginning March 15, 1941, their income was $53.89, with $25 from Paul and $28.89 from Mary Alice.[83] Their expenses were $57.54, the largest being $21.25 for rent and $10 for food. Also budgeted were $4.50 for savings. This left a shortfall of $3.65 that was covered by a $4.35 surplus they had carried forward. These tight finances would not have changed as his year of training at St. Luke's ended and his year at Kansas City General Hospital began on July 1, 1941. The residents' long work hours left little time for life outside of medicine, but those who were married followed the lead of their spouses. Since Mary Alice and the wife of a resident in urology had become friends, they included their husbands in social events. Mary Alice was remembered as being beautiful and being a lady in every sense of the word.[84] On December 26, 1941, Paul and Mary Alice's first child was born. A boy, his parents named him Randall Wade. Years later he would graduate from the University of Kansas with a B.S. in mechanical engineering.[85]

医学实习生及其爱人的日常生活总是围绕着工作、希望和紧张的预算展开。保罗和玛丽·艾丽斯定期记录的收支账目证实了这一点。例如，从 1941 年 3 月 15 日开始，两周内，他们的收入是 53.89 美元，其中 25 美元来自保罗，28.89 美元来

自玛丽·艾丽斯。[83]他们的花费是57.54美元，最大的一笔是21.25美元的房租和10美元的伙食费。预算中还包括4.50美元的储蓄。这留下了3.65美元的差额，由他们此前结转的4.35美元盈余补齐。1941年7月1日，他在圣卢克医院的培训结束，在堪萨斯综合医院的一年开始，这种紧张的财政状况并没有改变。住院医生长时间的工作使得他们除了医疗工作，几乎没有时间享受生活。自从玛丽·艾丽斯和一位泌尿科住院医生的妻子成为朋友后，她们就和自己的丈夫一起参加社交活动。人们记得玛丽·艾丽斯是一位美丽的、名副其实的淑女。[84] 1941年12月26日，保罗和玛丽·艾丽斯的第一个孩子出生了。一个男孩，他的父母给他取名兰德尔·沃德。多年后，他从堪萨斯大学毕业，获得了机械工程学士学位。[85]

The Japanese attack on Pearl arbor just nineteen days before the birth cast the die for the lives of Paul, Mary Alice, and their baby.[86] Actually, it had come in the early summer of 1940 when the Surgeon General of the United States Army proposed that Dean Wahl organize an affiliated evacuation unit comprised of doctors from KUMC's teaching staff and nurses from the Kansas City area. The proposal was accepted, and orthopedic surgeon James B. Weaver was chosen to head the surgical team and internist Edward J. Hashinger the medical team. Lt Col. Hashinger was the acting commanding officer. The unit became the 77th Evacuation Hospital.[87] During 1941 and early 1942, group of 144 enlisted men, who had received the thirteen-week basic medical training, were assembled at Fort Leonard Wood in south central Missouri for further training in the many skills needed to activate and operate evacuation hospitals. Harrington prepared for the inevitable and was appointed to the University of Kansas as an assistant in orthopedic surgery on January 1, 1942. He continued his Dickson-Diveley orthopaedic surgery residency until mid-May when the order came to activate the 77th Evacuation Hospital with the enlisted men, medical staff, and nurses assembled at Fort Leonard Wood. *See figure 3.6.*

就在孩子出生前19天，日本对珍珠港的袭击给保罗、玛丽·艾丽斯以及他们的孩子的生命带来了威胁。[86]事实上，1940年初夏，当时美国陆军医务官建议沃尔院长组织一个附属的后送小组，由堪萨斯大学医学院教师中的医生和堪萨斯地区的护士组成。这个提议被采纳后，骨科医生詹姆斯·B. 韦弗被选为外科组组长，内科医生爱德华·J. 哈辛格被选为内科组组长。哈辛格中校是代理指挥官。该小组成为第77后送医院。[87]在1941年和1942年初，144名接受了13周基本医疗训练的应征者在密苏里州中南部的伦纳德·伍德堡集合，接受启动和运营后送医院所需技能的进一步训练。哈灵顿为此做好了准备，并于1942年1月1日被任命为堪萨斯大学骨科助理。他继续在迪克森-戴夫利骨科外科医院实习，直到5月中旬，当启动第77后送医院的命令下达时，应征者、医务人员和护士都聚集在伦纳德·伍德堡。(图3.6)

Figure 3.6 ***Medical Officers of the 77th US Anny Evacuation Hospital, 1942. Left to right, front row: James B. Weaver surgical section head, and Edward J. Hashinger medical sectioin head and temporary direction Harrington third row. fourth front left. Max S. Alfen, fourth row, second front right, who subsequently compiled and edited Medicine under Canvas, the unit's war journal. (Unversiny of Kansas Medical Center Archives)***

图3.6 1942年，美国陆军第77后送医院的医务人员，前排从左到右，外科主任詹姆斯·B.韦弗和医务科长兼临时主任爱德华·J.哈辛格。哈辛格在第三排、左四，马克斯·艾伦在第四排、右二，他后来创立该部队的战地杂志《帆布下的医学》(堪萨斯大学医学中心档案馆)

"The mission of the Medical Department of the United States Army in World War II was to keep the soldier well and able to fight, or if he is wounded or sick to evacuate him and restore him to well-being as soon as possible."[88] The facilities to accomplish this were organized into three zones: combat, communications, and interior, which were linked by a transportation network of litter bearers, ambulances, and specialized trains, planes, and ships. Evacuation hospitals were the last medical facilities in the combat zone and the most forward capable of providing all types of definitive medical and surgical care. "The purposes of an evacuation hospital, as set forth in the *Military Medical Manual*, are: one, to provide facilities for major medical and surgical procedures in treatment of casualties as near the front as practicable; two, to provide definitive treatment as early as practicable; three, to relieve combat troops of the burden of casualties; four, to provide facilities for concentration of evacuees so that mass evacuation by rail, motor, airplane, or water transport can be undertaken economically; five, to prepare serious cases for further evacuation; six, to remove from the chain of evacuation those casualties which fit for duty or soon will be."[89] The evacuation hospitals were likened to the neck of a are funnel through which all casualties had to pass on their way out of the combat zone. On the combat side of the funnel there were four tiers of care, listed by increasing distance from the line of battle: 1) battalion aid stations, about 500 yards; 2) collecting companies, about 1 mile; 3) division clearing stations and mobile surgical hospitals (also called field hospitals), about 5 miles; and 4) evacuation hospitals, 5 to 15 miles, which was usually out of the range of artillery. Also in tier 4 were convalescent hospitals for lightly out wounded or recovering ill personnel, who were expected to soon return to duty. On the communication zone side of the funnel were base hospitals, referred to as station if for civilians or general if for military personnel. Base hospitals were located up to hundreds of miles from combat.[90] The US military had 34 field hospitals, 63 evacuation hospitals, 47 station hospitals, and 146 general hospitals in Europe.[91]

第二次世界大战中，美国陆军医疗部门的任务是使士兵保持健康并能参与战斗，如果有人受伤或生病，则要将他送到后方的后送医院并使他尽快恢复健康。[88]这一过程的完成分散在三个区域：作战区、通信区和内部区，由担架车、救护车、专用火车、飞机和轮船组成的运输网络连接起来。后送医院是战区后方的医疗机构，也是最有能力提供各种类型最终医疗和先进外科护理技术的医疗机构。按照《军事医疗手册》的规定："后送医院的职责如下：一、在尽可能靠近前线的地方为伤员提供治疗所需的主要医疗和外科手术设施；二、在可行的情况下尽早提供明确的治疗方案；三、减少作战部队的伤亡；四、提供集中后送人员的设施，以便更高效地通过铁路、汽车、飞机或水路进行大规模后送；五、为进一步疏散严重病例做准备；第六，从后送链中剔除那些适合执行任务或即将执行任务的伤员。"[89]后送医院被比作一个漏斗的颈部，所有伤员在离开战区时都必须通过这个漏斗。在漏斗的战斗一侧，有四个级别的医疗机构，按照离战线的距离远近排列分别是：(1) 营救护所，大约500码；(2) 团救护所，1英里左右；(3) 师救护所和流动外科医院（也叫野战医院），约5英里；(4) 后送医院，约5到15英里，通常在火炮射程之外。第四级医疗机构中还有为轻伤或康复中的病人提供治疗的康复医院，预计病人将很快返回战斗岗位。在漏斗的通信区一侧是基地医院，如果是平民，则称为驻地医院，对军事人员来说则是综合医院。基地医院距离战斗地点最远，可达数百英里。[90]美军在欧洲有34个野战医院、63个后送医院、47个驻地医院和146个综合医院。[91]

Evacuation hospitals, ranging in size from 400 to 750 beds/cots, were usually housed in tents although occasionally in available buildings, were mobile, and were selfcontained except for transportation. Patient stays lasted from one to twelve days. The 77th had 750 beds/cots with an authorized strength of 318 enlisted men, 52 nurses, 1 dietitian, and 47 officers. Lt. Col. Hashinger was the acting commanding officer until June 15 when Col. Burgh S. Burnet arrived to take command. Although organized into a number of departments, their functions were to be closely integrated and coordinated.[92] The logistics were daunting, and building the 77th into the cohesive and effective unit it became was the experience of a lifetime for many of its members. After slightly more than two months of basic training, the 77th passed inspection by representatives of the Second Army and made an uneventful troop ship passage through the German U-boat infested North Atlantic to a staging area in England. Their ship, *H. M. S. Orcades*, was sunk by enemy action two months later.[93] On November 8, 1942, while back at sea, they learned they were to join Operation Torch, the Allied invasion of North Africa under the command of Major General Dwight Eisenhower.[94,95]

后送医院的规模从400到750张床不等，通常被安置在帐篷里，尽管偶尔也会被安置在现有的建筑物里，但是他们是可移动的。病人住院时间从1天到12天不等。第77后送医院有750张床，核定兵力为318名应征者、52名护士、1名营养师和47名军官。哈辛格中校是代理指挥官，直到6月15日伯格·S. 伯内特上校来到这里接管指挥权。虽然被划分成若干部门，但他们的职能是紧密结合和保持协调的[92]。后勤工作令人望而生畏，将第77后送医院建设成一支团结、高效的部队对许多成员来说是一生中宝贵的经历。经过两个多月的基本训练后，第77后送医院通过了第二集团军代表的检查，并平安地通过了德国U型潜艇出没的北大西洋，到达了位于英格兰的集结地。运送他们的船，英国皇家海军“奥卡德斯”号，在两个月后被敌军击沉。[93] 1942年11月8日，在回到海上时，他们得知自己

将参加火炬行动，即由德怀特·艾森豪威尔少将指挥的盟军入侵北非行动。[94,95]

North Africa had been brought into the war in June 1940, when France fell and Italy declared war on Britain and France. The prize there was control of the Suez Canal, key to the Mediterranean shipping lanes. Italy's army of nearly 300,000 men in Cyrenaica (Libya) promptly advanced eastward into Egypt toward the canal. But by February 1941 they had been outmaneuvered and driven well back into Cyrenaica with heavy losses of men and materiel. They surrendered to the smaller British Eighth Army stationed in Cairo. That month German General Erwin Rommel arrived with two mechanized divisions. In Northwest Africa the French military assets in their colonies, Algeria and Morocco, were now under the command of the French puppet government led by Petain and provided some military assistance to Germany.[96]

1940 年 6 月，法国沦陷，意大利向英法宣战，北非被卷入了战争。胜利者的战利品是苏伊士运河的控制权，这是掌控地中海航道的关键。意大利在昔兰尼加（利比亚）近 30 万人的军队迅速向东进入埃及，向运河推进。但到了 1941 年 2 月，他们被打败了，并被远远地赶回了昔兰尼加，人员和物资损失惨重。他们向驻扎在开罗的规模较小的英国第八军投降了。当月，德国将军埃尔温·隆美尔带着两个机械师来到这里。在非洲西北部，法国在其殖民地阿尔及利亚和摩洛哥的军事资产现在由佩塔因领导的法国傀儡政府所有，并向德国提供一些军事援助。[96]

The Allied invasion of North Africa, involving approximately 110,000 mostly American and some British troops, began on November 8 with landings near Casablanca, Oran, and Algiers. Farther east on November 11 were landings near Bougie and a day later near Bone. Resistance varied, but was stiffest at Oran where the harbor was blocked by sunken British and French warships, delaying the landing of the 77th until November 12 at the nearby port of Mers el Kebir. The nurses were taken to the civil hospital in trucks with armed guards. "The sight that greeted the nurses as they entered the building was appalling. There were only a few beds in the building, and the patients were lying about the rooms and halls on litters, filthy blankets, or piles of discarded clothing. Cases of pneumonia, dysentery, and contagious disease were lying beside seriously wounded soldiers, some of whom had undergone amputations. Dressings and bandages had been covered with paper. A few wounded French and Arab soldiers were scattered among the Americans."[97] The men arrived later after a twelve-mile march passing through a tunnel in

Santa Cruz Mountain that separated Mers el Kebir and Oran. By the time they arrived, the nurses had begun to make some order out of chaos. However, their supplies had not yet arrived, and they had to do with the equipment they had been able to carry with them or find (e.g., an amputation had to be done with an ordinary hacksaw).[98]

大约有11万名盟军参与对北非的战争，主要是美国和一些英国的军队。他们于11月8日开始在卡萨布兰卡、奥兰和阿尔及尔附近登陆。11月11日，在更东边的布日伊登陆，一天后在波尼附近进行了登陆。遭遇的抵抗程度各不相同，但在港口被封锁的奥兰最为激烈。第77后送医院的登陆行动推迟到11月12日在附近的默斯港进行。12日在附近的凯比尔港港口登陆。护士们被送入有武装警卫的卡车中，送往民用医院。“护士们进入医院时看到的景象令人震惊。大楼里只有几张床，病人躺在房间和大厅里的担架上、肮脏的毯子上或者堆积着的丢弃衣服上。肺炎、痢疾和传染病病例躺在受伤严重的士兵旁边，其中一些人已经被截肢了。敷料和绷带都被用纸覆盖。一些受伤的法国和阿拉伯士兵散落在美国人中间。”[97]这些人经过12英里的行军，穿过圣克鲁斯山的一个隧道到达这里，这条隧道将凯比尔港和奥兰分开。当他们到达时，护士们已经开始从混乱中恢复秩序。然而，他们的供应品还没有到达，他们不得不使用他们随身携带的现有设备来工作（例如，截肢只能用普通钢锯完成）。[98]

It was soon learned that another hundred or more Allied casualties were located at the military hospital in another part of the city. Conditions there were described "as so chaotic as almost to defy description... A few French nuns and two hospital orderlies were attempting to cope with the situation, but had little with which to work. The Germans had taken most of the instruments and much older equipment... One of the first dressings changed was that of a British sailor. His shoulders, arms, and chest were swathed in bandages which were sticky with blood and covered with dirt. As no anesthetic was available, his screams of pain as the dressings were pulled from the stumps of both arms were terrifying. Some of the 77th men who had little previous experience found this too much as a beginning of their medical career. Both arms had been amputated above the elbows; an incision ran up the stump of the right arm and down over the right side of the chest... On the second day Brig. Gen. Teddy Roosevelt came to the hospital with a captain and master sergeant. As he limped through the wards, his combat suit still showing the dirt of battle, he called many of the patients by name and several by their first names. With 'H' yadoin' Joe? ' the gruff-voiced sergeant passed out cigarettes, matches, razors and blades to the First Division soldiers. Frequently, the General stopped to chat with one of his ‘boys,’ and they exchanged information about just what had happened when the machine gun had cut loose on the platoon. Seeing a general in grimy combat clothes walking along in muddy GI shoes was an entirely new experience for the 77th. After he had gone, one patient pointed a bandaged arm after him, and with a lump in his throat, vowed, ‘There's a man I'd follow through hell.’”[99]

人们很快得知，另有一百多名盟军伤员被安置在该市另一地区的军队医院。那里的情况被描述为“混乱得几乎无法形容……几名法国修女和两名医护人员正试图应对这种情况，但他们几乎没有什么可做的。德国人拿走了大部分的仪器和一些陈旧的设备……第一批更换敷料的伤员中有一位是一名英国水手。他的肩膀、手臂和胸部都缠着绷带，上面沾满了血迹和污垢。由于没有麻醉剂，当敷料从两只手臂的残肢上被扯下来时，他痛苦的尖叫声令人恐惧。一些以前没有什么经验的医生发现，将第77后送医院作为他们医疗生涯的开始，实在是令人难以招架。有的士兵两只手臂肘部以上的都被截去；有的则一个切口从右臂残端向上延伸到右胸上方……第二天，西奥多·罗斯福准将带着一位上尉和军士长来到医院。当他一瘸一拐地走过病房时，他的作战服上还留有战斗的痕迹，他叫着许多伤员的姓名，还只以名称呼另外几个人。“你好吗，乔？”这位声音粗哑的军士长给第一师的士兵们分发了香烟、火柴、剃刀和刀片。将军经常停下来和一个“男孩”聊天，他们交换了信息，了解机枪在排里失控时发生了什么。看到一个穿着脏兮兮作训服、穿着沾满泥巴的鞋子走来走去的将军，对第77后送医院来说是一种全新的体验。在他走后，一个病人用绷带指着他的手臂，喉咙里发出一声叹息，发誓说：‘我愿意誓死效忠这个人。’”[99]

The civil hospital had more potential than the military so the 77th concentrated on developing it and transferred patients from the military as soon as possible. On November 21, after eleven days of hard work making the civil hospital functional, the 77th received orders to erect and move into their tent hospital. That evening the Luftwaffe attacked the harbor area and city creating “quite a spectacle” but leaving little additional damage. The transition was complete on December 1, and the civil hospital was taken over by the 7th Station Hospital.[100] From November 13-28, Harrington treated a total of 89 patients, of whom 19 were wounded in action, 10 injured in action, and 60 injured in accidents. Major operations were performed in nine, who all received sulfonamides in the wound and by mouth. Minor operations or fracture reductions with cast applications were performed in 47.[101]

民用医院比军用医院更有收治潜力，因此第 77 后送医院集中精力发展它，并尽快从军用医院转移病人。11 月 21 日，经过 11 天的艰苦工作，民用医院发挥了作用，第 77 后送医院接到了命令，建立并搬进他们的帐篷医院。当天晚上，德国空军袭击了港口地区和城市，造成了“相当壮观的场面”，但没有造成什么额外的损失。[100]从 11 月 13 日至 28 日，哈灵顿共治疗了 89 名病人，其中 19 人受了火器伤，10 人在战斗中受伤，60 人在事故中受伤。9 名患者进行了大手术，他们都口服和外用了磺胺类药物。有 47 人进行了小手术或用石膏进行了骨折复位。[101]

The site chosen for the 77th's first tent city hospital had been a vineyard that was just visible from the top of the civil hospital where they were working. Between the setup begun about November 21 and the mover into on December 1, the fall rains began, turning the site into a soupy mass of red mud, a "Mud Flats".[102] It clung to clothes, bedding, cots, tents, everything. Too soft to hold its stakes, tents were constantly collapsing, but the earth below this quagmire was so hard that engineers had to dig latrines with pneumatic drills. It was in this spot that the 77th acted as a station hospital and took in 233 patients from a hospital ship and 151 from a torpedoed British troop ship. About twenty of the troop ship patients were mental casualties of the war, the staff's first experience with the disorder. [103]

第 77 后送医院的第一个城市帐篷医院位于一个葡萄园，从他们工作的民用医院顶部就可以看到。从 11 月 21 日开始搭建，到 12 月 1 日搬运工人进入期间，秋雨开始下了，把工地变成了一片红色的泥浆，一片“泥滩”。[102]红色的泥浆附着在衣服、被褥、小床、帐篷等所有东西上。由于太软，无法固定木桩，帐篷不断倒塌，但泥滩下面的土地非常坚硬，工程师们不得不使用风钻挖厕所。就是在这个地方，第 77 后送医院成了一个驻地医院，从一艘医疗船上接收了 233 名病人，从一艘被鱼雷击中的英国军舰上接收了 151 名病人。有大约 20 名是因战争引起精神异常的伤员，这是工作人员第一次经手这种伤员。[103]

The Allied western front in North Africa was firmly established with relatively few casualties. Helpful in limiting the casualties were negotiations between the United States and the French Vichy government that had helped limit French military resistance to Allied landings. In retaliation, German and Italian troops invaded southern France, trapping the main French fleet in the harbor of Toulon. The Germans blocked the harbor, and the French sailors scuttled their ships to prevent them from being used by the Germans.[104]

盟军在北非的西部建立了稳固的战线，所以伤亡相对较少。美国和法国维希政府之间的谈判牵制了法国军队对盟军登陆的军事抵抗，也有助于减少伤亡。作为报复，德国和意大利军队入侵法国南部，将法国主要舰队困在了土伦港。德国人封锁了港口，法国水手将己方的船只炸毁，以防止被德国人利用。[104]

December 1942 brought with it the first Christmas away from home for many and the first out of the United States for most. For the Harringtons it was special as Mary Alice gave birth to the couple's second child, daughter Sue, born on the eighth.[105] Brother Randy, just twelve months older, was presented with an in-house playmate and competitor. Far removed from this happy family event, Harrington was experiencing a general slowdown in work in Algeria. From December 15, 1942, to January 4, 1943, he recorded officially seeing only 41 patients, 13 of whom were consultations.[106] Six of the nineteen with lower extremity injuries had been wounded in action and were major cases, and thirteen were minor. Casts were applied to twelve patients, and eight were operated on under general anesthesia. Of these eight, two with lower extremity fractures had open reduction and internal fixation with stainless molybdenum steel plates. An orally administered sulfa drug was given as prophylaxis. A patient with fulminating forearm infection responded well to incision and drainage (I & D), continuous moist heat, and oral sulfa. Three successful secondary closures and two I & D's, one of a palmar and forearm infection, accounted for the other five operated on under general anesthesia. Harrington's impression was that time lag from injury to treatment, adequate surgery, immobilization, and the anatomical location of the injury were the important factors in war injuries. In addition to caring for the relatively few patients, staff used their time to inventory their equipment, much of which they hadn't seen and which required repair and/or ingenuity to make functional. Using the limited supplies available, the crates for shipment were either repaired or rebuilt to better withstand the rigors of relocation moves. During their off-duty hours some personnel volunteered to help sort mail that had stacked up in piles as high as 30' covering hundreds of feet of floor space, a job that had completely overwhelmed the postal workers.

1942 年 12 月，对许多人来说是第一个远离家乡的圣诞节，对大多数人来说是第一个离开美国的圣诞节。对哈灵顿夫妇来说，这是一个特别的日子，因为玛丽·艾丽斯在8号生下了他们的第二个女儿，苏。与这一家庭幸福相反的是，哈灵顿在阿尔及利亚的工作节奏普遍放缓。从1942年12月15日到1943年1月4日，根据他的正式记录，他只看了41个病人，其中13个是会诊病人。[106]在19个下肢受伤的病人中，有6个是在战斗中受伤的重伤员，13个是轻伤员。12名伤员被打上了石膏，8名伤员在全身麻醉的情况下进行了手术。在这8名伤员中，有2名下肢骨折的患者进行了切开复位、不锈钢钼钢板内固定术，同时给予口服磺胺类药物作为预防措施。一名前臂感染的患者经切开引流、持续湿敷和口服磺胺类药物后恢复良好，另一名患者在全麻状态下进行了三次成功的二次闭合和两次切开引流术，其中一次是手掌和前臂感染。哈灵顿的经验是，受伤到治疗的时间间隔、手术、充分的制动和受伤部位的解剖位置是影响战争中伤员救治的重要因素。除了照顾相对较少的病人，工作人员还利用时间清点设备，其中许多设备他们都没有见过，需要修理和/或另辟蹊径才能使之发挥作用。此外，还要利用有限的物资，对装运的箱子进行修理或改造，以更好地承受搬迁时的严酷考验。在下班时间，一些人员自愿帮助分拣占地数百英尺、堆积30英尺高的邮件，这项分拣工作让邮政工人不堪重负。

In general, time hung heavily on the 77th's hands, and they were ready for action. Relief came on January 7, 1943, when they received orders to move, and in the following days the tent hospital was crated for shipment by boat.[107] At 3 a.m. on January 15, 1943, the 77th boarded an old, dilapidated, six-hours-late train for the approximately 750-mile trip to Constantine, located in the Atlas Mountains at an elevation of 3,000 feet and approximately 75 miles from Tunisia. Many colorful descriptions were provided of the three-day, two-night, culturally enlightening and miserable trip. The train cars, filled with seething masses of humanity, were cold and at night nearly pitch-black. Floor sleepers could count on frequent tramplings by toilet visitors. During daytime they were treated to scenery and unusual sights, including "the Arab quarters and market, the camels plodding by with awkward yet graceful deliberation, the women with huge water pots carried on a shoulder, and the milling, screaming begging hordes of children." From Constantine the 77th moved to bivouac about 75 miles southeast, south of the ancient city of Tebessa but north of the disputed Kasserine Pass into Tunisia. Several medical units were bivouacked in this same area that was known as Pine Ridge.[108]

总的来说,第77后送医院的时间非常紧迫,他们已经做好了行动的准备。1943年1月7日,他们接到了转移的命令,在接下来的几天里,帐篷医院被装箱,准备用船运走。[107] 1943 年 1 月 15 日凌晨 3 点，第 77 后送医院登上了一列破旧的、晚点 6 小时的火车，前往位于海拔 3 000 英尺、距离突尼斯大约 75 英里的阿特拉斯山脉。人们对这三天两夜、具有文化启蒙意义的悲惨旅程作了许多丰富多彩的描述。火车车厢里挤满了沸腾的人群，车厢里很冷，晚上几乎漆黑一片。睡在地板上的人可能会被去厕所的人频繁踩踏。白天，他们可以欣赏到美丽的风景和不寻常的景象，包括“阿拉伯人聚居区和市场，骆驼笨拙而优雅地走过，妇女肩上扛着巨大的水壶，还有成群结队、尖叫着乞讨的儿童”。从君士坦丁出发，第 77 后送医院转移到东南方向约 75 英里处的宿营地，从特贝萨古城以南，有争议的卡塞林山口以北进入突尼斯。几支医疗队也在这个被称为松树岭的地方扎营。[108]

On February 14, 1943, they were ordered to set up the hospital, but two days later with about 150 patients they were ordered to close it and move back 60 miles toward Constantine because the German Army was breaking through at Kasserine Pass. Artillery fire was getting louder and the constant stream of vehicles to the rear heavier. Within 48 hours, the 77th had taken down, moved, and set-up over 100 tons of equipment, relocated 400 personnel and 150 patients, received 480 new patients, and accumulated a new census of 628. Their new location was near La Meskiana, just off the highway between Constantine and Tebessa.[109] This was the 77th's first experience with receiving 150 to 200 patients at a time.[110] Many organizational and procedural problems thus emerged, such as too few clerks to admit patients, too few litter bearers, too small operating tents, lack of a central location for the receiving ward and the X-ray department, too little electrical power output, insufficient fresh water and firewood, and inadequate laundry capacity. Many efficiency improvements were needed: among others, integration of the shock, preoperative, and postoperative wards as well as provision of a mess for ambulatory patients. Possibly the biggest improvement was the initiation of an evacuation form that specified the needs of every patient, which considerably reduced recordkeeping. For instance, litter patients did not need shoes while ambulatory patients did. The 77th also used this experience to work out a well-organized moving plan. An advance detachment was deployed to select an appropriate, well-drained site and stake out the roadways and locations the tents. After packing and loading the unit on trucks at the old site, the unit's personnel along with their personal belongings rode to the new site on the top of the trucks.

1943 年 2 月 14 日，他们奉命建立医院，但两天后，他们带着大约 150 名病人，奉命关闭医院，向康斯坦丁方向后撤60英里，因为德军正在向卡塞林山口聚集火力。炮火声越来越大，后方川流不息的车辆也越来越多。在48小时内，第77后送医院拆除、搬走并装配了100多吨设备，转移了400名人员和150名病人，接收了480名新病人，并积累了628人的新普查数据。他们的新地点在拉梅斯基纳附近，就在君士坦丁和特贝萨之间的高速公路旁。[109]这是第77后送医院首次一次性接收150到200名病人。[110]因此出现了许多组织和程序上的问题，如接收病人的人员太少，担架员太少，手术帐篷太小，接收病房和放射科缺乏一个中心位置，电力输出太少，淡水和木柴缺乏，以及洗衣能力不足。很多地方需要得到改善，其中包括整合休克的病人、术前和术后病房，以及为流动病人提供食堂。最大的改进可能是使用疏散表，明确每个病人的需求，这大大减少了记录工作。例如，躺着的病人不需要鞋子，而流动的病人则需要。第77后送医院还利用这一经验制订了一个组织良好的转移计划，部署了一支先遣部队，以选择一个合适的、排水良好的地点，并在道路上打桩，安置好帐篷。在旧址将这些装备打包并装上卡车后，部队人员和他们的个人物品一起乘上卡车前往新址。

From February 19 through March 24, while at the La Meskiana location, Harrington reported that 104 patients had been received and evacuated by his Ward S-9.[111] Eighty percent were combat personnel. The most common diagnoses were flat feet (29), fractures (22), lumbosacral strain (16), and gunshot or high-energy wounds (14). Only one operation was performed, a debridement and reduction of a compound, comminuted fracture of the lower extremity caused by an accidentally discharged weapon. He wrote that in "0.9% of the cases it was necessary to have the surgical facilities that are present in the unit." Twenty-four patients were returned to duty, and 80 evacuated to a station hospital.

从2月19日到3月24日，在拉梅斯基亚纳医院的时候，哈灵顿报告他的S-9病房接收和疏散了104名病人，[111]其中80%是战斗人员。最常见的诊断是扁平足（29），骨折（22），腰骶部劳损（16），枪伤或高能量伤（14）。只进行了一次手术，是对意外发射的武器造成的下肢复合粉碎性骨折进行清创和复位。他写道："在0.9%的病例中，有必要在病房中配备手术设施。"经过治疗后，24名病人被送回了工作岗位，80名病人被疏散到了驻地医院。

On the German side, February and March were critical. After having broken through at Kasserine Pass, Rommel's next goal was Tebessa. However, he was ordered by Hitler to attack Thala to the northeast of Tebessa, where the Allies repelled him. By the time Rommel turned east, the British had been reinforced and stopped his attack. Sick and disappointed, Rommel was relieved of his command and returned to Germany.[112]

对德国而言，2月和3月至关重要。通过卡塞林山口，隆美尔的下一个目标是特贝萨。然而，当他奉希特勒之命进攻泰贝萨东北部的塔莱时，盟军在那里击退了他。当隆美尔转向东方时，英军已经得到了增援，并阻止了他的进攻。病痛和失望之下，隆美尔被解除了指挥权，回到了德国。[112]

On March 27, 1943, the 77th closed and moved from La Meskiana to its fourth location, Tebessa II. The hospital reopened within 24 hours with 157 new patients, which grew to 629 admissions in 48 hours.[113] The new organizational plan had worked well, and Lt. Col. Hashinger was credited with creating the plan. The fighting was intense as the Americans from the west and British from the east linked up and drove the Germans into the north of Tunisia where their escape by sea had been blocked. Fifty-six percent of the 77th's patients were cases of psychoneurosis due to the long periods of heavy shelling, bombing, and strafing, for which four or five days of nearly constant sleep under sedation seemed to be the most effective treatment. Occasionally, one of these patients was found to have a severe case of organic disease. The patient load was so heavy that many of the 77th's personnel worked for as long as 72 hours with only brief catnaps; this contributed to the development of 12-hour shifts.

1943年3月27日，第77后送医院关闭，并从拉梅斯基纳转移到了第四个驻地——特贝萨二号。医院在24小时内重新开张，一开始有157名新病人，48小时内增加到629人。[113]新的组织计划运作良好，哈辛格中校是创建该计划的功臣。战斗非常激烈，来自西部的美国人和来自东部的英国人联起手来，将德军赶到了突尼斯北部，并堵死了他们从海上逃跑的路。在第77后送医院的病人中，有56%由于长期的猛烈的炮击、轰炸和扫射导致神经衰弱，对于这些病人来说，在镇静剂的作用下持续四五天的睡眠似乎是最有效的治疗。偶尔，会有个别伤员被发现患有严重的器质性疾病。救治的负担非常沉重，医务人员持续工作长达72个小时，只有短暂的午睡，这促进了12小时轮班制的发展。

From March 28 to April 10, 1943, at the Tebessa II location, Harrington's wards received and evacuated 224 patients. The most common injuries were the 110 high-energy and gunshot wounds. Eighty-four of the 224 had fractures, 55 open and 29 closed. Thirty-two operations were performed. See figure 3.7. One patient with an L2 fracture without cord injury developed respiratory embarrassment 12 hours after injury and was successfully operated on 23 hours after injury for a ruptured diaphragm. Another patient arrived with rigor mortis of the left forearm and at 36 hours after injury was successfully operated on with arm amputation and ligation of an ipsilateral aneurysm at the junction of the second and third part of the left axillary artery.[114] To facilitate placement of casts to immobilize arms, shoulders, backs, hips, and thighs, Harrington and Sgt. Robert Block constructed a portable frame, using materials from an ordnance salvage department, which could be placed on any litter.[115] As the final stages of the Tunisian campaign moved north, the 77th received fewer patients, giving them a little time for extracurricular activities. One of the feudal chieftains hosted a dinner for them, and staff members took trips to the Roman city of Timgad, whose ruins rivaled those of Pompeii.[116]

Figure 3.7 ***Harrington operating at one of the 77th locations.*** **(*University of Kansas Medical Center Archives*)**
图 3.7　哈灵顿在第 77 后送医院的一个驻点进行手术（堪萨斯大学医学中心档案馆）

从 1943 年 3 月 28 日至 4 月 10 日，在特贝萨二号驻地，哈灵顿的病房接收并疏散了 224 名病人。最常见的是高能量损伤和枪伤，有 110 人。224 人中有 84 人骨折，55 人是开放性骨折，29 人是闭合性骨折。（图 3.7）一名第 2 腰椎骨折但没有脊髓损伤的病人在受伤 12 小时后出现呼吸窘迫，在受伤 23 小时后成功进行了横膈膜破裂修补手术。另一个病人入院时有左前臂僵硬，伤后 36 小时，成功地进行了手臂截肢和结扎同侧左腋动脉第二和第三部分交界处动脉瘤手术。[114] 为了方便放置石膏，以固定手臂、肩膀、背部、臀部和大腿，哈灵顿和罗伯特·布洛克军士利用军械抢救部门的材料建造了一个可移动的框架，可以放在任何类型的担架上。[115] 随着突尼斯战役向北推进的最后阶段，第 77 后送医院接收的病人越来越少，他们有了一些属于自己的自由活动时间。一位联邦头领为他们举办了一次晚宴，而工作人员则前往罗马城市提姆加德旅行，那里的古城遗址可以与庞贝古城相媲美。[116]

On April 12, 1943, the 77th closed the Tebessa II site, moved nearly 100 miles north out of the mountains to the outskirts of Bone, Algeria, and reopened 4 days later. Since fighting was heavy in the final weeks of the Tunisian campaign, the 77th treated a total of 4,577 patients in their first 45 days there.[117] Harrington and his team reported managing 419 patients, much of the work recasting fractures and redressing wounds, including 140 strains, 103 compound fractures, and 70 simple fractures. Although little major surgery was done, in three wounds with large amounts of tissue loss and destruction he set up topical antiseptic (azochloramide) drip irrigations. Since these patients were evacuated, he did not have any follow-up.[118] The 77th had to cope with public health challenges that came with the near sea level location. Mosquitoes and flies were abundant. Despite netting, treatment of standing water, and prophylactic quinacrine hydrochloride (Atabrine ©), several people developed malaria. In that event, the Atabrine © dosage was increased, which usually resulted in mild cases. Bacillary dysentery flared up, caused by poor sanitation in a nearby prisoner of war camp. Better control of flies and a reliable supply of hot water helped limit the number and severity of the cases.[119]

1943 年 4 月 12 日，第 77 后送医院关闭了特贝萨二号基地，向北移动了近 100 英里，离开了山区，来到了阿尔及利亚的波尼郊区，并在 4 天后重新开张。由于突尼斯战役的最后几周战事激烈，第 77 后送医院在那里的头 45 天共治疗了 4 577 名病人。[117]哈灵顿和他的团队报告说处理了 419 名病人，大部分的工作是骨折复位和处理伤口，包括 140 例拉伤、103 例复合骨折和 70 例简单骨折。虽然很少做大的手术，但在三个有大量组织缺失和破坏的伤口的临床实践中，他建立了局部消毒（偶氮氯胺）冲洗系统。由于这些病人已经疏散，他没法进行任何随访。[118]蚊子和苍蝇很多，第 77 后送医院不得不应对因接近海平面而带来的公共卫生问题的挑战。尽管使用了蚊帐，处理了积水，预防性地使用了人造奎宁，还是有几个人患上了疟疾。在这种情况下，增加人造奎宁的剂量，通常只作用于症状较轻的病人。附近的战俘营卫生条件差导致了细菌性痢疾的爆发。有效地控制苍蝇和可靠的热水供应有助于限制病例的数量、控制病情的严重程度。[119]

The Allies captured Tunis on May 7, and on May 13, 1943, the Germans surrendered, thus ending the war in North Africa. In addition to General Von Arnim and most of his staff, the Allies eventually took about 250,000 prisoners of war.

盟军于5月7日占领突尼斯，1943年5月13日，德军投降，北非战争结束。除了冯·阿尼姆将军和他的大部分下属，盟军最终还带走了大约25万名战俘。

The 77th's participation in the successful invasion of Sicily beginning on July 10 was limited to a 65-man detachment to the United States Navy. Assigned to the naval hospital at Bizerte, Tunisia, Harrington was not one of the 42 who landed in Sicily. There were no 77th casualties, but their contribution's importance was evidenced by Captain Cornelius Mahoney of the medical corps being awarded a Silver Star for gallantry, which read in part "Captain Mahoney steadfastly stayed on board with utter disregard for his own personal safety to assist in transferring all wounded to another ship, leaving the stricken vessel only when his task had been accomplished."[120] On July 25 Mussolini was forced to resign and was arrested. On August 17, 1943, the liberation of Sicily was complete.[121]

第77后送医院从7月10日开始成功进入西西里岛，但规模仅限于一支65人的美国海军分队。哈灵顿被分配到突尼斯比塞大的海军医院，他不是在西西里岛登陆的42人之一。第77后送医院没有伤亡，医疗队科尔内留斯·马奥尼上尉因英勇表现被授予银星勋章，其中部分内容写道："马奥尼上尉完全不顾自己的人身安全，坚定地留在船上，协助将所有伤员转移到另一艘船上，直到完成任务后才离开遇难船只。"[120] 1943年7月25日，墨索里尼被迫辞职并被捕。8月17日，西西里岛完全解放。[121]

Days were not spent exclusively in the hospital. "During the remainder of the stay at Morris [near Bone], there was little to do in the way of operating a hospital, and the majority of effort was spent in recreation. A training program consisting of close order drill and road marches several mornings each week was instituted in order to comply with the directives of higher headquarters, but otherwise there were few duties."[122] Sightseeing, unusual native meals, and softball games, complete with league play, were popular. Entertainment that included occasional movies, local talent shows, and boxing matches reached its pinnacle in a Bob Hope show featuring Tony Romero and Francis Langford. Staying as cool as possible was a popular pastime with shade preferred by many and swimming in the Mediterranean and beachcombing by others. One day when Harrington was in charge of the swimmers, several had not returned at the appointed time of departyre. He found them in a cove on an anchored trawler enjoying an afternoon of libation. All were able to safely swim back to shore.[123] The Luftwaffe's periodic raids on the nearby Bone harbor were both showy and dangerous, and a stark reminder of the war. One killed twenty-one and burned many others when a flaming German plane crashed into a bivouacked African-American quartermaster company and another killed several when an antiaircraft shell fell into the British 5th General Hospital.[124] On August 28 the 77th was ordered to pack the hospital and move to Sicily. At some point during August and September, its commander changed when Col. Burnet became the Atlantic base surgeon and Lt. Col. Weaver became interim commander until Col. Samuel B. Cooke arrived to become their second commander.[125]

这些日子并不是完全在医院里度过的。“在莫里斯（波尼附近）停留的剩余时间里，医院的运转方面几乎没有什么可做的，大家大部分的精力都花在了娱乐上。为了遵守上级指挥部的指示，每周有几个早晨都有训练计划，包括严密的操练和公路行军，但除此之外，几乎没有什么任务。”[122]风景、当地美食和垒球比赛，以及联赛都很受欢迎。娱乐活动包括不定期的电影、当地的才艺表演以及在托尼·罗梅罗和弗朗西斯·兰福德担纲嘉宾的鲍勃·霍普秀中最受欢迎的拳击比赛。尽可能地保持凉爽是一种流行的消遣方式，许多人喜欢在阴凉处，而其他人则喜欢在地中海游泳和在海滩上玩耍。有一天，哈灵顿负责管理去游泳的一批人，有几个人到指定的出发时间还没有回来。哈灵顿发现他们正在一艘停泊的拖网渔船上饮酒作乐，整个下午都在享受。最终，所有的人都安全地回到了岸上。[123]德国空军对附近的波尼港的定期袭击既引人注目又充满危险，同时也清楚地提醒着战争的来临。一次是一架燃烧着的德国飞机撞上了一个在此宿营的非裔美军军需连，造成了21人死亡，许多人被烧伤；另一次是一枚高射炮弹落入了英国第五总医院，造成了数人死亡。[124]在8月和9月的某个时候，其指挥官发生了变化，贝内特上校成为大西洋基地的外科医生，韦弗中校成为临时指挥官，直到塞缪尔·B. 库克上校抵达，成为他们的第二任指挥官。[125]

On September 2 the three-day sea trip to Palermo, Sicily, began. Upon arrival their first assignment was to the University of Palermo Hospital and medical school where the 59th Evacuation was already stationed. The invasion of Italy had begun on September 3. To accommodate the large numbers of casualties, tents were set up in the courtyards of the medical center.[126] Since the initial invasion of Italy on its southern tip offered limited possibilities for rapid advancement, on September 9 a second invasion at the Gulf of Salerno was begun by a mixed British and American Fifth Army commanded by General Mark Clark. This was a day after the announcement of Italy's surrender, but in reality six days after the actual surrender, a delay designed to prevent Germans from occupying the Italians' defensive positions. Still, resistance was stiff, and the landing's success wasn't secure for days.[127] The 77th's much needed equipment arrived fifteen days later on September 20. As witnessed by those who accompanied and received it, the journey on a dirty ship had been rough. Before loading the equipment, thieves had to be scared off, and during unloading the stevedores deliberately dropped crates on the dock to break them open so that they could be pilfered.[128] The 77th and its now compromised equipment were transported by antiquated and poorly maintained trains that were barely able to climb and over the up the central mountains of Sicily to Licata on southern shore, which was about 60 miles from Palermo. The hospital became operational on September 27 when 211 patients were admitted. The United States First Division was bivouacked in the area and supplied most of the patients. Admissions were mostly medical, involving malaria, acute infectious hepatitis with jaundice, amoebic and bacillary dysentery, and skin infections. Surgical cases were most commonly from traffic accidents and explosive injuries.

9 月 2 日，前往西西里岛巴勒莫的三天海上旅行开始了。抵达后，他们的第一个任务是去巴勒莫大学医院和医学院，第 59 后送医院已经在那里驻扎。和意大利的战争于 9 月 3 日开始。为了容纳大量的伤员，在医疗中心的院子里搭起了帐篷。[126]对意大利南端的初次进攻因为没有找到很好的快速推进机会而失败，9 月 9 日，由马克·克拉克将军指挥的英美混合第五军在萨莱诺湾开始第二次入侵。这是意大利宣布投降后的一天，实际上是投降后的第六天，这种延迟是为了防止德国人占领意大利人的防御阵地。不过，抵抗还是很激烈的。[127]第 77 后送医院急需的装备在 15 天后，即 9 月 20 日抵达。正如那些陪同和接收装备的人所见的那样，在一艘重油船上的旅程是异常艰难的。在装载设备之前，必须把小偷吓跑，在卸货过程中，装卸工人故意把板条箱丢在码头上，并将其砸开，便于其被盗。[128]第 77 后送医院及其已损坏的设备由陈旧且维护不良的火车运送，这些火车几乎难以爬上并越过西西里岛的中央山脉，到达南岸的利卡塔，那里距离巴勒莫约 60 英里。医院于 9 月 27 日开始运作，当时接收了 211 名病人。美国第一师在该地区扎营，为大多数患者提供了补给。入院病人大多是内科患者，所患病症包括疟疾、急性传染性肝炎和黄疸、阿米巴痢疾和杆菌痢疾以及皮肤感染。外科病例中，最常见的则是因交通事故和爆炸受的伤。

The initially appealing site chosen for the tent hospital turned out to have been a lake bed as they discovered when heavy rains came in October and the whole area turned into a nearly impassable quagmire. Soon after the First Division began moving out, the 77th was ordered to return to England. The return to the staging area at Palermo was completed on October 29, but departure was delayed for a variety of reasons, including an enemy torpedo plane attack on their approaching convoy that sank at least one ship. While waiting, several nurses went on detached duty to help care for the large number of Italian campaign casualties being received by the 59th Evacuation Hospital.[129]

最初帐篷医院的选址是一个湖床，但是当 10 月大雨来临，整个地区变成了一个几乎无法通行的泥潭。在第一师开始撤离后不久，第 77 后送医院就奉命返回英国。返回巴勒莫集结地的工作于 10 月 29 日完成，但由于各种原因，包括敌人的鱼雷飞机对他们邻近的护航船队的攻击，至少击沉了一艘船，所以出发时间被推迟。在等待期间，几名护士分头去帮助照顾第 59 后送医院接收的大量意大利伤员。[129]

On November 11, 1943, exactly one year from the day they went ashore in Oran and 67 days after going ashore at Palermo, they departed for England. The general feeling seemed to be "one of anticipation of better things to come."[130] On November 25 they arrived in Liverpool, beginning a nearly seven-month period of preparing and waiting for the invasion of Europe. They were first stationed at Everleigh Manor near London. Their mud-caked equipment with its entrapped mummified lizards, dead centipedes, live mice, and moisture drew the ire of the inspecting officers, and for a time it seemed that all the 77th received was criticism. Their assignments were to prepare a never-opened semipermanent hospital, built under Lend-Lease, for opening as a station hospital and to set up a model tent hospital. Their worn equipment was left behind. The station hospital opened on December 27, and the 77th admitted 646 patients, mostly for medical diseases or traffic accidents.[131] From January 24 to April 1, 1944, they were stationed at Gloucester, 114 miles west of London, where they were billeted in private homes. Time was spent in physical training and continuing education. A few of their nurses were sent for special training in the treatment of burns and others for neuropsychiatric nursing. Their commanding officer changed as Col. Cook was moved to the 58th General Hospital, and Col. Dean M. Walker assumed command. Lt. Col. Hashinger, who had played an important leadership role for the 77th, was rotated back to the United States.[132]

1943 年 11 月 11 日，距离登陆奥兰整整一年，距离登陆巴勒莫 67 天，他们启程前往英格兰。众人普遍觉得"一件充满期待的事情终于到来了。"[130] 11 月 25 日，他们抵达了利物浦，为了回到欧洲，开始了近七个月的准备和等待。他们最初驻扎在伦敦附近的埃弗利庄园。装备上沾满了泥，里面夹杂着木乃伊蜥蜴、死蜈蚣、活老鼠和湿气，这引起了安检人员的愤怒，因此有一段时间，第77后送医院似乎饱受批评。他们的任务是筹建一所半永久性医院，该医院是在租借协议下建造的，准备作为驻地医院，并建立成一个示范性帐篷医院。他们破旧的设备被留了下来。医院于12月27日开业，收治了646名病人，大部分是由于内科疾病或交通事故受伤。[131] 1944年1月24日至4月1日，他们驻扎在伦敦以西114英里的格洛斯特，在那里医务人员被安置在私人住宅内。他们花了大量时间进行体能训练和继续教育。其中一些护士被派去接受治疗烧伤的特殊培训，另一些则被派去接受神经和精神护理工作的培训。同样，指挥官也发生了变化，库克上校被调到第58总医院，由迪恩·M. 沃克上校担任指挥官。曾在第77后送医院发挥重要领导作用的哈辛格中校被轮调回美国。[132]

Harrington was invited to present "Orthopedic Surgery in an Evacuation Hospital" to incoming American orthopedic surgeons. His presentation follows.

哈灵顿应邀向即将到来的美国骨科医生介绍"后送医院的骨科手术"。他的演讲内容如下。

The function of an orthopedic surgeon in an evacuation hospital as I see it today is a far cry from the glorified position that I had pictured it in 1942, just years ago. The learning has been difficult for obvious reasons. There is no two comparison between military and civilian practice other than the requirements of professional knowledge. The evolution that is required to change one is the most difficult individual transition that can be asked for. The principles that follow apply, I believe, to every phase of military medicine.

正如我们今天所看到的那样，骨科医生现在在后送医院发挥的作用，与我在1942年，也就是仅仅两年前所想象的那种荣耀的地位相去甚远。由于某些显而易见的原因，在这里学习是非常困难的。除了对专业知识的要求，军事医学和普通医学之间没有什么可比性。改变一个人是极其困难的。我相信，下面的原则适用于军事医学的每个阶段。

Our job in an evacuation hospital is three fold: One, Orientation; Two, Return as many soldiers to the front in the shortest time that we can; and

Three, To save lives. It is eminent that we realize the importance of evacuation and the part we play in its chain. In this process the soldier is under the direct observation of doctors. If I may be permitted to coin a term, he receives lifesaving treatment "on the fly."

我们在后送医院的工作有三个方面。第一，定位；第二，在最短的时间内让尽可能多的士兵返回前线；第三，拯救生命。认识到后送的重要性以及我们在后送链中所扮演的角色是非常迫切的。在这个过程中，医生直接对士兵的伤情进行监测。如果允许我创造一个术语，士兵将“在飞行中”接受拯救生命的治疗。

The first long step that the patient makes is the evacuation hospital. This is the first breathing spell of too many stops in the shuttle system. This is the first place that the patient eats more than one meal or sleeps one night with a fair assurance of saying "Good morning" to the same doctor, when he wakes up. It is here that the segregation of patients must start, and it is important that it does start here. So it is necessary to have facilities to take care of all types of casualties, to handle a large number and treat them adequately. From an orthopedic standpoint definitive treatment must always be in our minds but not our aim. The virtue of restraint must be well developed. Our job is only to return the patient to his proper destination in the best possible condition. With this point constantly in view, there are many situations in which the treatment can be carried out more fully to assure a quicker and more successful recovery at another point in the chain of evacuation. Our greatest fault lies in the time consuming, nerve racking abominable practice of piddling. We must see the picture as it with relation to this moving chain of treatment and evacuation that goes on is constantly. In other words our first responsibility is to realize the part we play to this moving chain known as evacuation, an orientation of ourselves.

伤员迈出康复的第一步是进入后送医院。这里是病人吃了不止一顿饭或睡了不止一个晚上的地方，每次醒来，对同一个医生说“早上好”。很重要的一点是，伤员的隔离必须从这里开始。因此，必须有相应设施来照顾所有类型的伤员，处理大批量的伤员，并对他们进行适当的治疗。从骨科的角度来看确切的治疗必须始终保持在我们的头脑中，但这并不是我们的目标。必须充分发扬保持克制这一美德。我们的工作就是让病人能以最好的状态恢复健康。考虑到这一点，在许多情况下，需要对患者进行更充分的治疗，来确保在后送链另一端的患者能够更快、更好地恢复。我们最大的错误是将时间浪费在那些伤脑筋的琐碎小事上。必须意识到这一点，因为它与持续性的治疗，也就是这条后送链的顺利运转有关。换句话说，我们的首要责任是意识到我们在这个所谓的后送链中所扮演的角色，对自我进行准确定位。

To fulfill the second part of our function, that of returning as many to the front as possible and as quickly as possible, the attention of the orthopedic surgeon is demanded and into his care are shunted, gladly, all the odd sprains, strains of the joints and vague complaints of the back that are admitted to the hospital. Why all physicians have closed their minds to these complaints and insist that it is the orthopedists responsibility amazes me. But such is our lot in fighting a war, and an important one. We must not only be an orthopod but a psychiatrist too. This situation can either be a hoax or an interesting study for us. It demands of us to know what we see when we see it and likewise the negative, i.e. have faith in our negative findings. It compels us to judge the conditions, the complaints and the findings into a coordinated whole. Otherwise we will lose the one thing we can retain in military medicine, self-confidence, for it is easy to revert to the"old army game" of passing the buck without chastisement. Along this same line I have insisted that all casualties regardless of their injury do some kind of exercise, the basics are breathing and extremity exercises. This can be done in all cases to a certain extent. well remember the statement of one boy "but Doc" he says, "I just had my hand shot off day before yesterday, I have been bounced around in an ambulance for one day, and you want me to exercise. Can't I just lay around and think for a few days?" now Need say any more to illustrate my point? The good, sincere soldier wants to get well and will do what you tell him if for no other reason than to spend his time. I know of no other more useful way of spending time than in exercise, even though one is restricted to the confined of a bed, tent, or camp.

为了完成我们的第二部分任务，即尽可能快地将更多的人送回前线，我们需要骨科医生们集中精力，对那些被送进医院的患者根据病因进行分类，包括各种挫伤、关节扭伤和背部不适，并进行适当治疗。为什么所有的医生都对这些抱怨置若罔闻，并坚持认为这是骨科医生的责任？这让我感到惊讶。但这就是我们在战争中，而且是一场重要的战争中的命运。我们不仅要做一名骨科医生，还要做一名精神科医生。对我们来说，这种情况既可能是一个骗局，也可能成为一项有趣的研究。它需要我们不仅要看到现实所呈现的景象，还要看到这里面存在的消极内容，更要在消极情绪中寻找信心。它迫使我们把当时的情况、抱怨和调查结果综合起来进行判断。否则，我们将失去在军事医学中一直保留的美德——自信，因为它很容易消失，从而变成不加惩罚地推卸责任的“旧军队游戏”。本着同样的原则，我坚持所有的伤员无论受伤与否都要做一些锻炼，最基本的是呼吸和肢体锻炼。在一定程度上，这些锻炼是所有情况下都能做到的。我清楚地记得一个男孩的陈述——“但是，医生，”他说，“我的手在前天刚刚打了针，我在救护车里颠簸了一天，现在你就要我锻炼。我就不能躺着好好歇一歇吗？”还需要说什么来证明我的观点吗？一个善良、真诚的士兵想要康复，他会按照你说的去做，不为别的，只是为了消磨时间。我知道没有比锻炼更有效的消磨时间的方法，即便是他被勒令待在床上、帐篷或营地里。

Minor wounds and injuries of the ambulatory or semi-ambulatory patients are of the utmost importance. Herein lies our task. The best care and consideration is well spent in the direction in our hospital. It is through this channel that we serve our second course well. These patients require more of our time and energy than the others. This situation makes us feel, from a specialist's standpoint as though our lot is a poor one in an evacuation hospital. But there are two viewpoints on this one issue. I think our place is a hard one but a good one.

对能够自主行走或辅助下行走的病人来说，解决他们的轻伤是我们的首要任务。我们医院的指导方针，就是让他们得到最好的照顾。正是通过这种方式，我们才能更好地提供第二步治疗。这些病人与其他病人相比，需要我们付出更多的时间和精力。从一个专家的角度来看，这种情况让我们觉得我们就像是一个身处后送医院里的可怜人。但在这个问题上有两种观点，我觉得我们的处境很艰难，但也可以说是很好。

The saving of lives in an evacuation hospital is a rare occasion. However, if life is to be saved after it leaves the forward echelon, then it is our responsibility. Because of the hustle, bustle, drive them thru the gauntlet method, that is employed at times when the chain of evacuation is being strained; slighting of the patient is the result. It is at this time that our function in the evacuation hospital becomes of utmost importance. Longer hours are worked, the strain tells, but we cannot let down or be lax for if we slight them, they don't live to be slighted any more. By the time they have reached us their time of good grace and the powers of nature have been spent.

在后送医院里抢救生命是很罕见的。然而，如果一条生命要在它离开前线后才能得到拯救，那么这就是我们的责任。如果由于拥挤、喧嚣而迫使他们在紧张的后送过程中受到影响，造成的后果就是对病人的轻视。在这个时候，我们后送医院的作用变得至关重要。随着工作时间变长，压力告诉我们，绝不能感到失望或有一丝松懈，因为如果我们怠慢他们，他们就会失去生命。当他们被送到我们这里的时候，上帝赐予他们的恩典和力量即将消耗殆尽。

Surprisingly enough, the complications of hemorrhage and infections rarely occur in our limited time of care of the patient under our present military chain method of treatment. To us they only compromise the minority of cases. This has been our experience. This astounding fact can be explained adequately, believe. The patients are not under our care long enough to develop hemorrhages of any note. This danger period is seen to be from 8 to 21 days, post injury. The majority of cases being at or over 14 days. Why injured large vessels hold for this duration of time, then suddenly break, is explained in the pathogenesis of contused arteries. This deadly span of time falls in the chain of evacuation at about the base hospital level. Here a bit of good information might be obtained. As a warning you who are in these hospitals during a run of casualties, eat and sleep on a keg of dynamite. It is most disconcerting to watch a patient die from hemorrhage under your very eyes.

令人惊讶的是，在我们目前实行的军事链式治疗方法下，在有限的处理时间内很少发生出血和感染等并发症。根据我们的经验，这些并发症只在极少数情况下出现。我相信，这个令人震惊的事实有充分的理由来解释。病人接受治疗的时间还不够长，不会出现明显的出血。危险期一般是伤后 8 到 21 天，大多数病例的危险期是在发病 14 天或 14 天后。为什么受伤的大血管能够在维持这么长的时间后才突然断裂，这要从动脉挫伤的发病机制中寻找原因。这段危险期范围大约就是后送链所需的时间，那时候患者应该在一级基地医院，在那里可以获得一些有用的信息。在基地医院里的人仿佛吃饭和睡觉都在炸药上，要随时保持警惕。这时候，眼睁睁看着一个病人在你眼前出血死去是最令人不安的。

Fulminating infections are prone to be the result of one of two things: (1) Unfortunate contamination, I refer to gas bacillus, or (2) poor debridement. This latter category is based upon circulatory basis completely. Devitalized tissue (tissue without blood supply) must be removed. When in doubt, be conservative but establish a safety valve thru adequate drainage. The front line operator is not asked to be superhuman in his ability to eradicate all devitalized tissue, but there is no excuse for violation of all the rules of surgery.[133]

暴发性感染的发生往往由以下两种情况导致：(1) 不幸感染，我指的是气体杆菌，或 (2) 清创不彻底。后一类完全以循环为基础。失活组织（没有血液供应的组织）必须切除。如果有疑虑，需要保守治疗，要通过充分的引流建立一个安全通道。前线的术者并不具有超人的能力能够去除所有失活的组织，但也不会违反所有的手术原则。[133]

Harrington reviewed the facets of immobilization. He decried sloppy plasterwork, quoting the phrase so familiar to surgeons: "Success of operation does not end with operation." He advised that casts should have the following: "Adequate padding and small dressings, splints at the top and bottom of the cast, adequate length, molded, split (protecting the underlying skin with a removable tin strip), and marked and labeled, including fracture outline and important dates." He described thirteen different splints or casts, their alteration of the hip spica table and cast spreaders. In summary, he emphasized that practically no surgery was done at evacuation hospitals and the importance of rehabilitation centers should not be diminished. He closed by reiterating the three functions of the evacuation hospital: "Orientation of doctors and patients, return as many to the front as possible, and be constantly on the watch for complications including hemorrhage, infection, and overlooked diagnosis." Two days after this presentation Col. Rex Diveley, MD. Senior Consultant in Orthopaedic Surgery, European Theater of Operations and Harrington's recent residency mentor, wrote thanking Harrington for his excellent presentation.[134]

哈灵顿回顾了关于制动的各方面内容。他引用了外科医生们最熟悉的一句话："手术的成功不以手术结束而结束。"他建议包括以下内容："足够的填充物包括小的敷料，顶部使用石膏，底部使用夹板，要有足够的长度，固定形态，可以打开（用可移动的锡条保护下层皮肤），并做标记，包括骨折的形态和重要日期。"他描述了 13 种不同的夹板和石膏，以及对髋臼盘和石膏支架进行改造。总而言之，他强调说，虽然后送医院实际上并没有做任何手术，但是康复中心的重要性不应被削弱。最后，他重申了后送医院的三个功能："引导医生和病人的自我准确定位，让尽可能多的患者回到前线，并时刻关注并发症，包括出血、感染和被忽视的诊断。"演讲两天后，欧洲战区骨科外科高级顾问、哈灵顿当时的住院医生导师、医学博士雷克斯·戴夫利上校写信感谢哈灵顿精彩的演讲。[134]

Harrington responded expressing his appreciation for the opportunity, explaining his experience with the Tobruk splint that had apparently come in for considerable discussion at the time of his presentation.[135] This splint was a British Army Medical Corps innovation used during their rapid evacuation of Tobruk, Libya, in June 1942.[136] It was an adaptation of the Thomas splint, a ring for the upper thigh resting on the ischium and groin attached to longitudinal medial and lateral rods that were connected as a stirrup below the foot to provide quick method to immobilize the thigh and thus the underlying fractured femur during transport. The adaptation had longitudinal traction applied through adhesive straps placed down each side of the thigh and leg and secured under tension to the stirrup. Initially, a long leg cast was applied before placing the extremity in the splint. In its modified form the splint was placed before the cast and plaster rolls an extension of the work Lt. John Charnley was doing. Charnley, like Harrington born in 1911, had enlisted in the Royal Medical Army Medical Corps on May 1, 1940. He was an experienced surgeon with over 600 laparotomies performed before joining the Army. His initial postings were near the English Channel, and he made five or six trips across it to help bring the wounded back during the Dunkirk evacuation. His talent recognized, Sir Harry Platt steered Charnley's postings toward orthopaedics. A step along the way to this conversion was assignment to the No. 2 Orthopaedic Centre in the 63rd General Hospital in Cairo, where he arrived on May 14, 1941, after a two-month trip around the Cape of Good Hope.[137] Later Maj. Charnley published the experience with the traction treatment of 130 femur fractures from November 1941 to May 1943 based on the mechanics of reduction and fixation. He concluded that weight traction and fixed traction were interchangeable and the only absolute indication for weight traction was a "closed transverse fracture with gross swelling of the thigh."[138] He described several helpful small appliances, foreshadewing the innovative genius that would create the first successful total joint replacement in response to hip arthritis of epidemic proportions.

哈灵顿对此表示感谢，并分享了他使用图卜鲁格夹板的经验，他的演讲引起了相当多的讨论。[135]这种夹板是英国陆军医疗队在 1942 年 6 月快速撤离利比亚图卜鲁格时发明的。[136]这是对托马斯夹板的一种改造，托马斯夹板是一种用于大腿上部且放置在坐骨和腹股沟的环，与纵向的内侧和外侧杆连接，并连接至脚部下方的镫带，以便在运输过程中快速固定大腿，即下方骨折的股骨。通过调节放置在大腿两侧的黏着带施加纵向牵引，并在保持黏着带紧张的条件下将其固定在镫带上。最初，在将肢体置入夹板之前，必须先使用长腿石膏。改良后，先放夹板，再放置石膏和石膏卷来连接肢体与夹板。图卜鲁格夹板应该是对约翰·查恩利中尉工作的改进。查恩利和哈灵顿一样，出生于 1911 年，于 1940 年 5 月 1 日应征入伍。他是一名经验丰富的外科医生，在参军前做过 600 多例剖腹手术。他最初驻扎在英吉利海峡附近，敦刻尔克大撤退期间，他曾五六次横渡英吉利海峡，帮助把伤员运送回来。因此，他的才华得到了认可，哈利·普拉特爵士将查恩利调到了骨科。接下来，查恩利被分配到开罗第 63 总医院的第二骨科中心，在结束了两个月的好望角旅行后，于 1941 年 5 月 14 日到达了开罗。[137]后来，查恩利少校从 1941 年 11 月至 1943 年 5 月期间，根据复位和固定的力学原理，发表牵引治疗 130 例股骨骨折的经验。他的结论是，负重牵引和固定牵引是可以互换的，负重牵引的唯一绝对指征是"伴有大腿明显肿胀的闭合性横形骨折"。[138]他描述了几个有用的小器械，极具创新性，并完成了第一个成功的全关节置换术，为流行性髋关节炎的治疗奠定了基础。

The United States Army's surgeons were introduced to the Tobruk splint during the Battle of Tunisia (November 1942-May 1943) where they joined forces with the British Army.[139] Harrington's objections to the Tobruk splint as expressed to Diveley were many: patients were not comfortable; some had circulatory disturbances; the majority had pressure sites of varying severity on the ischium, gluteal fold, or dorsum of the foot;

traction was not maintained; and they looked "abominable." He acknowledged the added manpower, material, and time necessary to apply the alternative, a spica cast, but believed this was not problem for the US Army Medical Corps. Harrington closed with, "I would advise the discontinuance of the Tobruk splint and stop all this false ballyhoo it is receiving," conceding that "it is grand thing to know if the U.S.A.M.C. ever gets into a spot where the scarcity of doctors and the numbers of femoral immobilizations are large enough and the material for immobilization is scarce."[140] The balanced view that emerged during World War II seemed to be that the Tobruk splint was quicker and easier to apply than a spica cast, was satisfactory for lower femur fractures and knee injuries, and was needed in patients with abdominal wounds and colostomies that required access to the abdomen. For upper femur fractures the spica cast was better.[141]

美国陆军的外科医生在突尼斯战役（1942 年 11 月至 1943 年 5 月）期间和英国军队联合，开始接触并使用图卜鲁格夹板。[139]哈灵顿向戴夫利表达了很多针对图卜鲁格夹板的反对意见：患者感觉不舒服；部分患者有循环障碍；对坐骨、臀部、足背有不同程度的压迫；没有维持牵引；他们看起来“非常糟糕”。他也承认选择使用替代方法“髋人字形绷带”需要额外的人力、物力和时间，但他相信这对美国陆军医疗队来说并不是问题。哈灵顿最后说：“我建议停止使用图卜鲁格夹板，停止所有虚假的宣传。”他承认，“如果美国医学会陷入这样一种境地：医生稀缺，大量需要股骨固定的病人，固定术材料稀缺，这是一种值得仔细考虑的情况。”[140]第二次世界大战期间出现了平衡点，相比髋人字形石膏，图卜鲁格夹板因使用更加简便而得到了广泛的应用，对于股骨下端骨折和膝关节损伤取得了令人满意的治疗结果，也适用于有腹部伤口和结肠造口的患者。而对于股骨上段骨折，石膏的固定效果更好。[141]

On April 1, 1944, the 77th completed a move to Tunbridge Wells, which was south of London and near the English Channel, where they found a nearly complete tent hospital. All equipment was new, and packing had to be built. The crates were designed so that they could be used as furniture when the hospital was set up. On April 26 the hospital opened and admitted 419 patients. A few were seriously wounded casualties of the air war, who had been moved either from emergency landing strips in the area or British hospitals on the coast near Canterbury. The usual patient load was relatively light, consisting of those with respiratory diseases, non-traumatic surgical diseases, or minor injuries. The hospital was operated with a skeleton crew. The personnel's time was spent in conditioning through close order drill and road marches, preparing for defense against the various types of chemical warfare, and readying equipment for the coming invasion, including waterproofing the motorized equipment so it could be driven underwater. This still left ample time for recreation and sightseeing in this picturesque resort town.[142] On May 27, 1944, the hospital was closed and packed, and two days later put on 48-hour alert. Walker had pushed their chief supply officer, Lt. Earl Hoard, to be aggressively acquisitive, and so the 77th was well equipped for their venture. The prize was a large diesel electric generator. Personnel were urged to minimize their personal belongings in anticipation of long marches, which were reminiscent of the 77th's first landing.[143]

1944年4月1日，第77后送医院完成了向伦敦南部英吉利海峡附近坦布里奇韦尔斯的迁移，在那里他们发现了一个几乎完整的帐篷医院。所有的设备都是新的，必须好好打包以免损坏，打包所用的箱子设计巧妙，可以在医院开放时当作家具。4月26日，该医院开放并收治了419名患者。一些人是从该地区的紧急降落跑道或坎特伯雷附近海岸的英国医院转移过来的，他们在空战中受伤严重。相比较而言，医院收治的普通患者症状较轻，主要为呼吸系统疾病、非创伤性外科疾病和轻伤。这家医院靠精干人员维持运行，他们的时间都花在了紧密有序的演习和道路行军准备工作上，为防御各种类型的化学袭击做准备，并为即将到来的入侵准备设备，包括为机动化设备增加防水保护措施，以便它可以在水下行驶。此外，还给自己留出了在这个风景如画的度假小镇娱乐和观光的时间。[142] 1944年5月27日，由于人满为患，医院不得不关闭，两天后进入48小时警戒状态。沃克敦促他们的首席供应官厄尔·霍尔德中尉积极收购物资，自此第77后送医院为他们的冒险做好了充分的准备。奖品是一台大型柴油发电机。工作人员必须尽量减少个人物品，因为他们要进行长时间的行军，这让人想起了第77后送医院专机的首次着陆时长时间行军的情形。[143]

D-Day, the long awaited European invasion, occurred on June 6 on Normandy beaches about 150 miles west of Paris. Beginning on June 15, the unit witnessed German V-1 rockets barraging London and the British efforts to defend against them with a fence of barrage balloons, antiaircraft fire, and stripped-down, latest-model Spitfire (XVI) interceptors.[144] On July 7, D-Day+31 days, the 77th went ashore at Normandy, marched miles, and bivouacked field near Ste. Germaine de Ville. The following morning 3 surgical teams were sent on detached service to the 400 bed/cot 67th Evacuation Hospital that had arrived at D+17 days and despite constant work still had an operative backlog of

200 patients. Soon most of their nurses were sent on detached service to the 67th, 128th, 96th, or 44th evacuation hospitals. These detachments were sent because supply officer Hoard had encountered a number of understandable transportation delays in moving the 77th with approximately 120 2-1/2 ton trucks or 75 10-ton trucks.[145]

6 月 6 日，人们期待已久的欧洲登陆在巴黎以西约 150 英里的诺曼底海滩上举行。从 6 月 15 日开始，该部队见证了德国 V-1 火箭弹袭击伦敦，以及英国用弹幕气球、防空火力和最新型号的喷火拦截弹组成的防线进行防御。[144] 7 月 7 日，诺曼底登陆的第 31 天，第 77 后送医院在诺曼底登陆，行军 7 英里，在圣・杰曼・德・维尔扎营。次日上午，3 个外科医疗队被派往第 67 后送医院，该医院已于诺曼底登陆后第 17 天抵达，拥有 400 张床位。尽管不间断地工作，但仍有 200 名病人未得到救治。由于供应官霍尔德在运送第 77 军 120 辆 2-1/2 吨卡车和 75 辆 10 吨卡车时遇到了一些问题导致延误，很快，医院大部分护士被派往第 67、128、96 或 44 后送医院。[145]

The 77th's first location was near Ste. Mere-Eglise, the first town in France to be liberated. After their equipment finally arrived on July 16, it took 36 hours to clear a recent battlefield site and set up their 189 tents. Four operating tables and two fracture tables were immediately put in continuous use, while three tables for minor surgery were used eighteen to twenty-four hours day. The personnel were organized into two twelve-hour shifts, each with one triage and one liaison officer, and a medical or surgical team that made rounds on their patients at the beginning and end of each shift. In 20 days of active operation 3,234 patients were admitted and 1,775 operations performed. On one day alone 319 were performed.[146] This location tested the hospital's principles of one doctor for one group of patients and its succinct evacuation record system. The unit most strained at the peak of the patient load was the shock section, which had patients in many wards. Shock section personnel were required to prepare each intravenous medication and carry it to the appropriate ward and administer it. However, the team was able to keep up, and the evacuation record system worked well.

第 77 后送医院的第一站是法国第一个被解放的城镇，圣母教堂。装备于 7 月 16 日抵达，之后他们花了 36 个小时清理了最近的一个战场，并搭建了 189 顶帐篷。4 台手术床和 2 台骨折床立即投入使用，其中 3 台小手术床每天使用 18—24 小时。医护人员每 12 小时一个班，每个班次有一名分诊和一名联络官，以及一个医疗或外科小组，每天交接班时进行查房。经历了 20 天的积极救治，共收治患者

3 234 例，实施手术 1 775 例，其中仅一天就有 319 例。[146]这个情况也是对医院的检验，包括一名医生对应一组患者的原则和简洁的疏散记录系统。在病人载荷达到峰值时，最紧张的单元是抗休克区，该病区有很多病人。抗休克区医护人员需要准备各种静脉用药给不同的患者进行治疗。然而即使在这种情况下，医疗团队的工作仍能够有条不紊地进行，后送记录系统运行良好。

On August 9 the hospital was set up near St. Lo, about thirty miles east and the site of the worst destruction the 77th had seen. Here, their eighth war zone location, they served as both a hospital and triage station. A backlog of patients for possible evacuation had built up, and an efficient system was sorely needed. The 77th was assigned the task of funneling all these patients. Patients were divided into four groups: those not transportable in which case they were admitted, those both seriously and less seriously wounded who could be moved without danger or discomfort, those who could be transported at will, and those who would be ready for duty in a few days. Special hospitals were set up to receive patients with venereal disease or self-inflicted wounds. At St. Lo they received 6,903 patients, a rate of 48 per hour for 6 days. Five hundred ninety-nine of them were admitted.[147] The experience here emphasized two points. First was the importance of concise, clearly written records to quickly convey the diagnosis and treatment summary. Longer typewritten notes, even if conforming to the medical manual, were less helpful. Second, the condition of the patient at the end of a long ambulance ride could not always be predicted.

8 月 9 日，医院在圣洛附近大约 30 英里以东的位置安营扎寨，这里也是第 77 后送医院所经历的破坏最严重的地方。这是他们在战区的第八个根据点，他们同时扮演了医院和分诊站的角色。由于已经积压了大量需要疏散的病人，因此迫切需要一个有效的系统。第 77 后送医院接到的任务是收拢这些患者，并将患者分为四组：入院时无法转运的患者，无危险无不适可转运的重型和轻重型患者，可随意转运的患者，几天后可以重返前线的患者。同时还设立了专门收治性病患者和自杀患者的专门医院。在圣洛，他们 6 天接收了 6 903 名患者，平均每小时收治 48 名患者，其中 599 人被收入院。[147]通过这段经历得出了两点经验，首先是简洁、清晰的书面记录，能够快速传达诊断和治疗意见。即使符合医疗手册的要求，太长的文字记录也并没有太多帮助。其次，在救护车长途运送的过程中，患者的病情是随时变化着的。

From August 16 when they left St. Lo to October 8 when they set up at Verviers, Belgium, the 77th made three stops while following the front as it rapidly moved east and north. At Le Mans they were ordered to bivouac as the smaller 400-bed evacuation hospitals were better able to keep up by leapfrogging each other.[148] This was a welcome respite, coming at the end of six weeks of almost continuous work. On August 24 they opened at Chartres and for a few days were nearly as busy as they had been at St. Mere-Eglise.[149] But on August 25 the source of their patients changed considerably after Paris was liberated. Admission of Allied soldiers slowed, but they were quickly replaced with large numbers of wounded British and American airmen found in German hospitals, wounded prisoner-of-war soldiers, and a few French civilians. The 77th was next ordered to the Ste. Menehould area. The advance party had chosen a site near Clermont-Sur-Argonne about 15 miles south of Verdun, a distance of about 200 miles on a route skirting the southern edge of Paris. By September 14 the 77th was set up and opened. In the 23 days they were open, 1,155 patients were received.[150] As most had received care at forward hospitals, little was required. Malnourished prisoners of war, both from the front and those taken locally, were admitted. The most pathetic were the Polish, Russian, and French used by the Germans as slave laborers. Many had been worked and starved to the point of death, which ultimately claimed several. But, in general the 77th's work was light, leaving plenty of time to become acquainted with the area and its people.

8 月 16 日从圣洛出发至 10 月 8 日到达比利时韦尔维耶，第 77 后送医院在快速向东北方向移动的过程中经过了 3 次停留。在勒芒，为了让拥有 400 张床位的小型后送医院可以及时跟上，他们按照命令就地扎营。[148]对于连续工作了六个星期的他们来说，这是一个难得的喘息机会。8 月 24 日，医院在沙特尔开放，有几天时间几乎和在圣母教堂时一样忙碌。[149]但 8 月 25 日，巴黎解放后，他们的病人的来源发生了巨大变化。那些在德国医院发现的大量受伤的英美空军士兵、战俘和一些法国平民很快取代了盟军士兵。第 77 后送医院随后接到命令到达圣默努。先遣部队在阿尔贡河畔克莱蒙特附近选择了一个地点，位于凡尔登以南约 15 英里，距离巴黎南部边缘大约 200 英里。9 月 14 日，第 77 后送医院成立并开放。在接下来的 23 天里，收治了 1 155 名患者。[150]由于大多数人在前线医院已经接受了治疗，因此需要治疗的患者很少。其中也包括了营养不良的战俘以及来自前线和当地的战俘。最可怜的是那些被德国人当作奴工的波兰人、俄国人和法国人。许多人被迫挨着饿工作，最终饥饿夺去了一部分人的生命。但是总的来说，第 77 后送医院的工作是轻松的，有大量的时间来熟悉这个地区和当地的居民。

On October 6 the hospital was closed and moved approximately 140 miles northeast to Verviers, Belgium, very close to the front and about 10 miles from the border with Germany. It was to be set up in school building, the Ecole Normale de 1'Etat, possibly because of the absence of large fields in the area. Making the four-story, semi-abandoned building a functional hospital required imagination and work. On October 11, the day it was scheduled to open, the Luftwaffe conducted an air attack against Verviers, strafing the hospital, which suffered bomb damage. It was the first time it had come under direct fire. There were no fatalities, although three received bomb fragment injuries requiring surgery and ten had minor injuries from bomb fragments and flying glass. The hospital opening was postponed two days.[151] Initially, the 77th served as the funnel through which all patients from the field and evacuation hospitals of the First Army triaged for evacuation were gathered. Continued treatment and surgery were provided as patients were further triaged by destination: return to duty for a few, general hospital in nearby Liege if soon ready for duty, general hospital in France or England for the more severely injured, or an interior zone hospital in the United States for those needing special care, such as reconstructive surgery. This was their first experience with large numbers of admissions with trench foot that was caused by enforced standing in cold water for long periods. As the front intensified, this meant a large turnover of patients, and some days as many as three evacuation trains of 300 patients each were loaded out. One day the hospital had over 1,400 patients, a number double its capacity.[152] The evacuation documentation that had been worked out so many locations ago in La Meskiana and continually perfected since then continued to function well. Other units sent observers to learn their method.

10 月 6 日，医院关闭，转移到了比利时东北部约 140 英里的韦尔维耶，这里非常接近前线，距离德国边境约 10 英里。由于该地区没有大面积的农田，医院设立在巴黎高等师范的学校大楼里。将这座四层的几乎废弃的建筑建为功能性医院，不仅需要想象力，还需要大量的工作。医院原本定 10 月 11 日开放，但是当天德国空军对韦尔维耶进行了空袭，扫射医院，医院遭到了炸弹的破坏。这是医院第一次受到直接攻击，所幸没有人员死亡，3 人因炸弹碎片受伤需要手术，10 人因炸弹碎片和飞溅的玻璃受到了轻伤。因此，医院推迟两天开放。[151]最初，第 77 后送医院充当漏斗的角色，患者从第 1 集团军的野战医院和后送医院进行分诊后，由第 77 后送医院将所有患者集合。在根据目的地对患者进行进一步分类的同时，继续提供治疗和手术；少数患者返回岗位，如果能够很快返岗的患者就近收治在位于列日的综合医院，严重的伤者收至法国或英国的综合医院接受治疗，需要特殊护理（如重建手术）的患者在美国内陆地区的医院接受治疗。这是他们第一次遇到大量因长时间被迫站在冷水中而导致战壕足的病例。随着战线的拉长，大量的患者需要周转，有时需要多达三辆满载300名患者的后送列车。有一天，这家医院接待了1 400多名病人，这个数字是其容量的两倍还多。[152]他们在拉梅斯基亚纳的很多地方都制订过疏散方案，并不断完善，使其持续发挥了良好的作用。其他单位也派观察员去学习他们的方法。

On December 16 the Germans launched a major offensive through the Ardennes toward Liege where the Allies had a large supply center with food and fuel badly needed by the Germans. Beyond Liege were Brussels and Antwerp that were also well stocked with supplies. Here began the Battle of the Bulge.[153] Verviers, located in the center of the northern edge of this German offensive, was an important bottleneck through which Allied forces entered the war front.[154] The 77th quickly became the focal point for battle casualties because the smaller 9th Field Hospital located in a nearby school building had limited capacity, the 76th General Hospital in Liege had been hit by bomb, and the 67th Evacuation Hospital had been pulled back to bivouac. To help the 77th cope, 66 medics, including 6 surgeons and 20 nurses, were attached from other Army hospitals. Some operating personnel worked eighteen-hour shifts at the eight operating tables and two fracture tables that were in use day and night. To add to the tension, bombs and V-weapons frequently landed near the hospital, accompanied by strafing. Early in the morning of the fifth day a shell hit the south side of the 77th, and severely injured Red Cross worker, who was a patient, was found under the wreckage. In spite of prompt treatment she expired. On the eleventh day an even bigger tragedy struck the medical community when a 500-pound German bomb directly hit the 9th Field Hospital killing 14 and injuring nearly 50.[155]

12月16日，德国人通过阿登向列日发起了一场大规模进攻，在那里，盟军有一个大型的补给中心可提供德国人急需的食物和燃料。列日之外的布鲁塞尔和安特卫普也有充足的物资储备。突出部战役由此开始。[153]韦尔维耶位于这次德军攻势的北部边缘中心，是盟军进入前线的一个重要瓶颈。[154]由于位于学校大楼附近的第9野战医院很小，能力有限，第77后送医院很快成为收治战斗伤亡士兵的关键点。列日的第76总医院遭到了炸弹袭击，第67后送医院被撤回了营地。为了帮助第77后送医院应对大量伤员，其他军队医院派出了66名医护人员，其中包括6名外科医生和20名护士。一些医护人员日夜不停地在8台外科手术和2台骨折手术台上奋斗了 18 个小时。炸弹和 V 型武器不断地落在医院附近，伴随着扫射，大大增加了紧张的氛围。第 5 天凌晨，一枚炮弹击中了第 77 后送医院的南面，在残骸下发现了受伤严重的红十字会工作人员，尽管治疗及时，她还是死去了。在第 11 天，一枚重 500 磅的德国炸弹直接击中了第 9 野战医院，造成了 14 人死亡，近 50 人受伤。[155]

The wounded soldiers brought back harrowing stories of "narrow escapes, foolhardy bravery, desperate chances," Germans impersonating Allies, and at least one welldocumented massacre. The machine gunning of several tightly packed prisoner groups by a German combat unit on December 14 and the following days became reported as the Malmedy Massacre.[156,157] In general, the attitude of the wounded American soldier was how quickly can you get me back to the front. This was exemplified in the defiant "Nuts" response to the German commander who demanded the surrender of Bastogne. The Battle of the Bulge had begun under cover of inclement weather, neutralizing the Allied air superiority. Beginning on December 24, the weather was clear much of the time, allowing the Allied air forces to work. By December 30 the bulge had begun to shrink with Liege never taken by the Germans.[158]

受伤的士兵带回了"死里逃生、勇猛无畏、险象环生"，德国人冒充盟军，以及不完全记录的大屠杀等悲惨故事。12 月 14 日，一支德国战斗部队用机枪扫射了几个拥挤的俘虏群，随后被报道为"马尔默迪大屠杀"[156,157]。在德国指挥官要求巴斯托涅投降时，受伤的美国士兵会用挑衅的态度反问：你能多快把我送回前线？突击战在恶劣天气的掩护下开始，抵消了盟军的空中优势。12 月 24 日开始，大部分时间天气晴朗，盟军空军得以开展战斗。12 月 30 日，由于德军一直未能占领列日，冲突地区的范围已开始缩小。[158]

On January 4, 1945, the 77th moved to La Louviere, Belgium, about 80 miles west of Verviers and well away from the front. The stay here was described by some as an extended furlough. The hospital, set up in three schools, opened on January 9 with the admission of 392 patients. Its mission was to care for convalescent patients, those who were able to return to the front within 30 days. There was ample time to get to know and spend off-duty hours in the town. The 77th had earned the respite: between going ashore on July 7 and December 31, 1944, it had admitted 35,086 patients. Verviers saw the most admissions with 20,925 and the largest number of in-patients at any one time with

1,454. At St Lo 1,400 patients were seen in the first 12 hours after opening.[159]

1945 年 1 月 4 日，第 77 后送医院撤离了前线，迁至位于韦尔维耶以西约 80 英里处的比利时拉卢维耶尔。一些人将这次逗留描述为漫长的无薪假期。医院建立在 3 所学校的校区，于 1 月 9 日开放，收治了 392 名患者。医院的任务是处理那些能够在 30 天内返回前线的康复期病人。由于任务比之前轻松，医护人员下班后有足够的时间去了解镇上的生活。第 77 后送医院获得了喘息的机会，在 1944 年 7 月 7 日上岸到 12 月 31 日之间，已经收治了 35 086 名病人。在韦尔维耶收治的人数最多，前后总计达到了 20 925 人，住院人数达到了 1 454 人。在圣洛，1 400 名病人在开放后的 12 小时内接受了治疗。[159]

While at the La Louviere site Harrington was promoted to major.[160] A Bronze Star and the Croix de Guerre with Silver Star were received by Col. Dean M. Walker for overall command and the Legion of Merit by Lt. Col. James B. Weaver for his professional skill and foresight in organizing the surgical service. T/3 Robert J. Gerlach, who had been assigned to another unit, received the Bronze Star for developing "an exceptionally efficient system of evacuation" allowing approximately 14,000 patients to be evacuated during the Tunisian Campaign with "not a single error in the final records submitted."[161]

在拉卢维耶尔的时候，哈灵顿被提升为少校。[160]迪恩·M. 沃克上校因出色的指挥能力得到了表彰，获得了一枚铜星勋章和一枚银星十字勋章，詹姆士·B. 韦弗中校因其在组织外科服务方面的专业技能和远见卓识而获得了荣誉军团勋章。罗伯特·J. 格拉克被分配到另一个单位，因其在突尼斯战役期间开发了"高效的后送系统"，该系统因使约 14 000 名患者在"提交的最终记录中没有出现一个错误"而获得了铜星勋章。[161]

On March 14 the 77th was ordered to Munchen-Gladbach, Germany, and an advance party, including Harrington, was sent to select the site. *See figure 3. 8*. Having located a

Figure 3. 8 ***The 7th's last full setup at Munchen-Gladbach, Germany. (Harrington Archives)***
图 3. 8　第 77 后送医院在德国慕尼黑-格拉德巴赫的最后一次整装（哈灵顿档案馆）

suitable flat field about 150 by 500 yards, the move was made on March 22, and the first patients arrived three days later. At first they were quite busy, regularly receiving 400 patients a day. In early April the German defense began to unravel, and the number of American patients decreased while that of German prisoners of war increased. Many of them had neglected medical conditions, and some recent conscripts were not really fit for combat.[162]

3 月 14 日，第 77 后送医院奉命前往德国的慕尼黑–格拉德巴赫，包括哈灵顿在内的先遣队被派去选择根据地。(图 3.8) 在选好一块大约 150 码乘 500 码的平地后，他们于 3 月 22 日开始行动，第一批患者于 3 天后抵达。一开始他们非常忙碌，每天定期接诊 400 个病人。4 月初，德国的防线开始崩溃，美军伤员减少，而德国战俘增加。其中有许多人有被忽略的健康状况，一些新近应征入伍的士兵实际上并不适合参加战斗。[162]

Attention to prisoners of war was the last major assignment for the 77th. The unit had been ordered to prepare for 2,000 such patients, but they had only 500 beds. The basement and first floor of an adjacent, partially demolished factory was salvageable, using the floor of the destroyed second story as the roof. With hard physical and equipment procurement work, a 1,200-bed unit was quickly developed. As soon as it was functioning, it was turned over to a complete German staff. In the month it functioned, the unit admitted 6,083 and had 72 deaths. Soon after this opening the 77th was ordered to prepare to receive 1,500 additional prisoners of war. This time they found a relatively new and lightly damaged, sturdy six-story community theater in a town about two miles and staffing processes were repeated. Known as the 77th Annex, away. The development this unit admitted 3,049 patients with 21 deaths during the 27 days it operated under the 77th's supervision.[163]

照顾战俘是第 77 后送医院的最后一项主要任务。医院接到命令，准备接纳 2 000 名战俘，但医院只有 500 张床位。附近一个已拆除工厂的地下室和一楼可以使用，二楼已被摧毁，剩余的地板作为屋顶。经过艰苦的装备采购，很快就建立了一个拥有 1 200 个床位的病区。病区刚开始运作，就被全部移交给了德国工作人员。在它运作的一个月里，接收了 6 083 人，其中有 72 人死亡。开放后不久，第 77 后送医院又接到了准备接收 1 500 名战俘的命令。这一次，他们在两英里外的一个小镇上发现了一个相对较新、受损较轻、坚固的六层社区剧院。他们又重复着建造和人员配置过程。该病区被称为第 77 后送医院附属医院，在第 77 后送医院监督下运作，27 天内收治了 3 049 名患者，其中 21 人死亡。[163]

Victory in Europe Day, officially May 8, 1945, witnessed quiet, respectful celebrations by the 77th. Virtually all original members of the 77th had enough points for discharge. But working through the logistics required time, and the Information and Education Program, of which Harrington was a staff member, was intended to ease the transition. Orientation lectures, news updates, and information about discharge and redistribution were provided. Social, recreational, cultural, and travel opportunities were offered, and an athletic program was created with Harrington in charge. Softball and hardball diamonds, a basketball court, volleyball courts, a badminton court, and horseshoe pitching ranges were set up and leagues developed. The tennis courts and swimming pool of a local club were made available for their use. A field day between the 77th and the 610th Ordnance was set up, which the 610 won with a score of 145 to 133. "The competition was keen throughout and no contestant was an easy winner, except in the diving where Maj. Paul Harrington of the 77th far outclassed the field with his near perfect execution of beautiful dives."[164] In June those with the most accumulated points, many of whom were the remaining original members, began going home. On June 19 the 77th was ordered to turn their remaining prisoner of war patients over to a British hospital unit, close, and move to Mailly-le-Camp, France, near Chalons, about hundred miles east of Paris.[165] There the hospital was set up and presumably operated by the low point replacements coming in. The original 77th Evacuation Hospital was in its last days as a unit. Harrington left with a group in July, and the last original members left in September. The original 77th was no more.

1945 年 5 月 8 日的“欧洲胜利日”见证了第 77 后送医院安静而又充满敬意的庆祝活动。实际上，第 77 后送医院的所有初始成员都有足够的资历退伍。但完成后勤工作需要时间，作为“信息与教育项目”的一员，哈灵顿提供了入职讲座、最新资讯、出院及重新分配的资讯，努力让这段过渡时期变得较为轻松。学校提供了社交、娱乐、文化和旅行的机会，并创建了体育项目，由哈灵顿负责。垒球和硬球、篮球场、排球场、羽毛球场和马蹄形投球场也建立起来，并成立了联盟。当地一家俱乐部的网球场和游泳池也提供了相应服务。第 77 后送医院和第 610 军械署设定了比赛日，610 军械署以 145 比 133 的分数获胜。“比赛自始至终都很激烈，除了跳水项目，没有选手能轻易获胜，因为第 77 后送医院的保罗·哈灵顿少校以近乎完美的跳水动作远超赛场其他选手。”[164] 6 月，资历最高的人开始回家，其中许多是剩余的初始成员。6 月 19 日，第 77 后送医院接到命令，将他们剩下的战俘病人移交给英国的一所医院，并转移到法国位于巴黎以东约 100 英里的沙隆附近的马伊勒康。[165]那是第 77 后送医院最后“战斗”的日子。7 月，哈灵顿和团队一起离开；9 月，最后一名初始成员离开了。第 77 后送医院自此不复存在。

Despite the fact that the 77th Evacuation Hospital had been involved in three of the four amphibious invasions and six of seven battles in the European Theater of Operations,[166] there was a delay in recognition. In April 1945 it had been recommended for the Meritorious Service Unit Plaque, but in August the award was denied because the "VD rate set forth in basic communication is considered excessive for this unit."[167] This negative report was explained: "The VD (venereal in the 77th was always zero tive report disease) rate or near zero. The group of litter bearers attached to the 77th at Verviers, however, had a rather high rate which was included in the reports of the 77th at that time. Apparently this fact resulted in disapproval of the recommendation by Gen. Lee."[168] On April 22, 1948, the 77th received the Meritorious Unit Commendation which read in part: "The 77th Evacuation Hospital is commended for exceptionally meritorious conduct in performance of outstanding services in the European Theater from 29 March 1944 to 30 April 1945. This unit rendered medical care of exceptional quality to the sick and wounded during Normandy, Northern France, Rhineland, Ardennes offensive, and Central Europe Campaigns. Personnel of this hospital worked long and untiringly to care for and treat anunusually large number of patients during its operation in Europe. The consistent high standards of efficiency, military discipline, and esprit de corps exemplified a superior degree of leadership and teamwork in the performance of duty and reflect great credit on the 77th Evacuation Hospital, the Medical Department, and the Army of the United States. By Order Of The Secretary of the Army. Omar N. Bradley, Chief of Staff, United States Army. Official: Edward R. Witsell, Major General, The Adjutant General."[169]

尽管第 77 后送医院参与了欧洲战区四次两栖入侵中的三次战争和七次战役中的六次战役,[166]但迟迟没有得到认可。1945 年 4 月，它才被授予功勋部队的牌匾，但在 8 月因为“该部队性病患病率过高”被撤销。[167]这份负面报告的解释是：“第 77 后送医院的性病患病率总是为零或接近零。然而，隶属于韦尔维耶的第 77 团的性病携带者群体的比例相当高，这在当时的第 77 后送医院的报告中也体现了出来。显然，这一事实导致了李将军的误解。”[168] 1948 年 4 月 22 日，第 77 后送医院获得了功勋单位表彰，其中部分内容是：“第 77 后送医院因 1944 年 3 月 29 日至 1945 年 4 月 30 日在欧洲战区的杰出表现而受到表彰。这支部队在诺曼底、法国北部、莱茵兰、阿登战役和中欧战役中为伤病员提供了优质的医疗服务。这家医院的工作人员长期不懈地工作，在手术期间处理和治疗了非常多的患者，并保持一贯的高效率、军事纪律和团队精神，体现了履行职责中卓越的领导能力和团队合作精神，为第 77 后送医院、美国医疗部门和美国陆军带来了巨大的荣誉。奥马尔·N. 布拉德利，美国陆军参谋长。爱德华·R. 威特塞尔少将、副官。”[169]

In 1949 Max Allen, MD and a twelve-person editorial board published Medicine Under Canvas: A War Journal of the 77th Evacuation Hospital. After briefly reviewing the hospital's origin, they cited its traits as revealed when first tested at Oran. Algeria. "Within a matter of hours after landing, the 77th demonstrated the resourcefulness, speed and hard work which were to characterize the unit during the following three years. The ability to recognize a problem for what it was, to throw away the book and improvise, to do a good job regardless of situation or supply—all these were manifested during those first trying days at Oran." They closed by paying homage to the "hardships and sacrifices of the valiant men of the combat troops."[170]

1949 年，医学博士马克斯·艾伦和一个拥有 12 名编辑的委员会共同出版了《帆布下的医学：第 77 后送医院的战争杂志》。在简要回顾了医院的起源后，他们列举了在阿尔及利亚奥兰市首次建立时表现出的特征。“在着陆后的几个小时内，第 77 后送医院表现出了智谋、速度和勤奋，这是该部队在接下来的三年里一直保持的特质。意识到问题本质的能力，抛开书本随机应变的能力，不管环境或条件如何都能做好工作——所有这些都在奥兰医院建立初期艰难的日子里得到了体现。”最后，他们向“战斗部队中英勇的战士们所付出的艰辛和牺牲致敬”。[170]

Harrington and the 77th Evacuation Hospital appear to have had no wartime experience with polio as it is not mentioned in his notes or in their war journal. This is not too surprising given their mission. US troops were, however, acquiring polio during World War II, though at the very low annual rate of less than per 10,000 in the countries the 77th had been deployed to. For US troops as a whole, this began to change at the end of the war and soon after when the annual rate of new polio cases skyrocketed to nearly 10 per 10,000 in 1947 in Korea.[171] Polio was stirring and would soon meet Harrington in Houston.

哈灵顿和第77后送医院没有战时治疗脊髓灰质炎的经历，因为在他的笔记和他们的战争日记中都没有提到。结合他们的使命，想来这并不奇怪。美军在第二次世界大战期间脊髓灰质炎每年发病率非常低，不到万分之一。对于整个美国军队来说，这种情况在战争结束后的不久开始改变。1947年，朝鲜脊髓灰质炎年发病率暴涨到接近万分之十。[171]脊髓灰质炎肆虐，很快就传播到了哈灵顿所在的休斯敦。

Maj. Harrington separated from the United States Army on November 13, His separation record indicated he was an orthopedic surgeon, who had served as chief of orthopedics at an evacuation hospital. While on active duty he had supervised a total of 8 orthopedic surgeons and 65 nurses in the examination, treatment, and care of patients suffering from disorders of bones and joints. He had supervised application of splints, interpreted X-rays of orthopedic cases, and immobilized fractures by open or closed methods. He also was responsible for the maintenance of records on orthopedic cases and the maintenance of orthopedic appliances.[172] Once home, Harrington took some time reacclimating to civilian life and selecting his practice site. Living near open water had always been his dream, and Houston fit that criterion. Another factor was the immense potential he saw in the Texas Medical Center that had just been chartered. Ground had been broken for its first occupant, the Baylor University College of Medicine, which was moving from Dallas. Sometime in late 1945 or early 1946 he entered into a one-year practice charter with Duncan McKeever, a member of the Dickson-Diveley Clinic from 1932 to 1938, who had moved his practice to Houston.[173] From the beginning Harrington was an active participant and contributor to the academic life of the Texas Medical Center. During the summer of 1946 he took a postgraduate course in pathology at the Baylor College of Medicine.[174] And, he joined the clinical staff of the orthopedic department that was led by Fred Bloom at the Jefferson Davis Hospital, which served the city and county and Baylor as a teaching hospital.[175]

1945年11月13日，哈灵顿少校离开了美国陆军部队。他的离职记录显示，他是一名骨科医生，曾在一家后送医院担任骨科主任。在服役期间，他曾指导8名骨科医生和65名护士检查、治疗和护理患有骨关节疾病的患者。他曾指导夹板的应用，解读骨科病例的X光片，并通过开放或闭合方法固定骨折。他还负责骨科病历记录和骨科器械维护。[172]回到家后，哈灵顿花了一段时间重新适应平民生活，并建立了自己的诊所。他一直以来的梦想是住在开阔的水域附近，休斯敦是绝佳选择。另一个原因是他看到了刚刚被特许的德州医疗中心具有巨大潜力。贝勒大学医学院作为第一家进驻的医院，已经破土动工，将从达拉斯搬来。1945 年年末或 1946 年年初的某个时候，哈灵顿与邓肯·麦基弗签订了为期一年的执业合同，麦基弗从 1932 年到 1938 年在迪克森–戴夫利医院工作，后来他的诊所搬到了休斯敦。[173]从一开始，哈灵顿就积极参与，并为得克萨斯医疗中心的学术做出了贡献。1946 年夏天，他在贝勒大学医学院攻读病理学研究生课程。[174]他加入由弗雷德·布鲁姆领导的杰斐逊·戴维斯医院并成为骨科的临床医师，该医院是一所教学型医院，为城市、乡村和贝勒大学服务。[175]

（刘义灏 译　毛克亚 史建刚 审校）

4 POLIO AND POST-POLIO SCOLIOSIS (1789–1946)

What is not explained is the fact of summer prevalence; for all other nose and throat diseases are winter diseases.[1]

脊髓灰质炎和脊髓灰质炎后脊柱侧凸(1789—1946)

鼻部和咽喉部的疾病多发于冬季,但脊髓灰质炎流行于夏季,其中的原因仍然未知。[1]

All of them have been given a much better posture, much more stability and, it is believed, protection from a progressive increase of deformity.[2]

所有的病例均得到了姿势改善,稳定性加强,并确切地被保护免于畸形进展。[2]

The human vertebrate spine functions mechanically to provide the stability needed to maintain trunk position, trunk mobility, and spinal cord and nerve protection. Trunk position includes both balance and alignment. Whether standing, sitting, or walking, the normal spine is balanced with the head vertically positioned over the pelvis. Between the head and the pelvis, the normal spine alignment is straight in the coronal plane (viewed back to front or front to back) and curved, for stability, in the sagittal plane with mild posterior rounding (kyphosis) of the thoracic spine and anterior rounding (lordosis) of the cervical spine and lumbar spine. These functions are readily appreciated by an awareness of oneself and others.

人类脊柱提供了维持躯干姿势、躯干活动并保护脊髓和神经功能所必需的机械稳定性。躯体的姿势包括平衡和协调。不论站、坐或行走，正常的脊柱需要维持头部垂直于骨盆上方的平衡。脊柱在冠状面的排列呈直线（前后位或后前位观察），在矢状面呈曲线。为了维持矢状面的稳定，胸椎有一轻微向后的弯曲（后凸），颈椎和腰椎有一向前的弯曲（前凸）。稍微留意自己或别人的身体就会很容易理解这些表象的意义。

At the beginning of the twentieth century, two diseases in particular threatened spine stability—one directly and the other indirectly. Tuberculosis, a bacterial infection most commonly involving the lungs, sometimes entered the bloodstream, seeded, and gradually destroyed one or more vertebral bodies. Poliomyelitis, or infantile paralysis, a viral infection with an affinity for the motor neurons in the anterior horn of the spinal cord, sometimes left trunk muscles weakened, and in the growing child's spine collapse into the lateral curve predominant, three-dimensional spine deformity called scoliosis could occur. Treatment was aimed at providing spine stability using the only available techniques of exercise, manipulation, prolonged bed rest, traction, or external support with braces, corsets, or casts. These treatments lasted several years, their effectiveness was questionable, and there was no doubt about the need for improvement.[3,4] Tuberculosis, which has been recognized since the beginning of recorded history, has been responsible for hundreds of thousands of deaths over the centuries.[5] In contrast, poliomyelitis' tie to antiquity is tenuous, connected by inference that a leg deformity on an ancient Egyptian art object was caused by the disease. It was not even recognized as a distinct clinical entity until relatively recently in 1789. Its first clear description was made by London pediatrician and midwife Michael Underwood, who connected the characteristic febrile episode and the paralysis that followed a few days later, most commonly appearing in children from one to four or five years old. He termed it "Debility of the Lower Extremities" in the second edition of A Treatise on Diseases of Children.[6] In later editions of his widely popular book he more clearly described the disease and its effect on the upper as well as the lower extremities. However, he didn't appear to make the connection between scoliosis and the debility.[7]

20 世纪初，有两种疾病直接或间接地威胁着脊柱的稳定性。一种是最常累及肺部的细菌感染——肺结核，结核菌从肺通过血液播散到脊柱，并逐渐破坏一个或多个椎体。另一种是脊髓灰质炎，或称小儿麻痹症，是一种累及脊髓前角运动神经元的病毒感染。后遗躯干肌肉力量的减弱，导致生长期儿童脊柱的塌陷并向侧方弯曲，进而造成脊柱三维畸形，称为脊柱侧凸。当时，对该病的治疗方法很有限，仅能通过运动、手法、长期卧床休息、牵引或佩戴支具、紧身衣及石膏等外部支撑维持脊柱稳定。这些疗法应用了数年，其疗效值得怀疑，需要改进。[3,4]自有记录以来，结核是很早就被认识的疾病，在几个世纪内造成了数十万人的死亡。[5]相反，脊髓灰质炎却鲜有描述，一种可溯的来源是人们推断一件古埃及艺术品的腿部畸形是此病导致的。直到1789年，脊髓灰质炎才被认定为一种独立的临床疾病。来自伦敦的儿科医生兼助产士迈克尔·安德伍德首次对其进行了明确描述，他认为这种病表现为一次典型的发热伴随之后几天内出现的瘫痪，最常见于一岁到四五岁的儿童。在《儿童疾病论》第二版中他将其称为“下肢无力症”。[6]在广受欢迎的再版中，他更清楚地描述了此病对上肢和下肢的影响。然而，他似乎并没有发现脊柱侧凸与该病的联系。[7]

The relationship between “Debility of the Lower Extremities, and “distortion of the spine” was made in 1823 by London surgeon John Shaw. It is curious that he did not use the term scoliosis, and he may not have been the first to connect polio and post-polio scoliosis. But his chapter titled “Enquiry into the causes of the partial paralysis and wasting of one of the limbs during infancy, which frequently produce distortion of the spine” left no doubt he recognized the connection.[8] The following year he published an atlas that included elegant engravings by a T. Landseer of distortions of the spine, including lateral distortions (e. g., scoliosis).[9] *See figure 4.1.*

1823年，伦敦的外科医生约翰·肖阐述了“下肢无力症”和“脊柱扭曲”之间的关系。奇怪的是，他并未使用脊柱侧凸这一术

Figure 4.1 ***John Shaw's 1824 illustration of a “distortion of the spine,” or scoliosis, without the “osseous system being specifically affected.” so it was not rickets, but the cause was not otherwise specified. (Clendening Library Spine and Orthopedic Historical Collections)***

图4.1　1824年约翰·肖著作所展示的“脊柱扭曲”（或脊柱侧凸）插图。并没有典型的骨骼系统病变，这不是佝偻病，但具体病因并不清楚（科伦德宁图书馆脊柱和骨科史）

语，也可能他不是第一个将脊髓灰质炎与脊髓灰质炎后脊柱侧凸建立联系的人。但是，他的著作的其中一个章节名为“一种婴儿期一侧肢体部分瘫痪和萎缩的疾病常导致脊柱扭曲的原因探究”，这无疑证实了他关注到了两者之间的联系。[8]第二年，他出版了一本画册，其中包括T. 兰西尔对脊柱扭曲（诸如侧凸）的优雅刻画。[9]（图4.1）

Unlike most neurological diseases, the anatomical location of the lesion causing Underwood's "Debility of the Lower Extremities" spared sensory function. Aided by the neurophysiological research of Charles Bell of London and Francois Magendie of Paris revealing sensory function to be located in the posterior grey matter of the spinal cord and motor function in the anterior grey matter, Scottish neurologist J. Abercrombie was able to name the probable location of the offending lesion[10]. This 1828 observation was decades ahead of its time as it wasn't until his 1860 book that the German orthopedic surgeon and disease expert Jacob von Heine expressed the view that the spinal cord was the seat of the pathology[11]. However, the pathological lesions were not visible on autopsy specimens, and it wasn't until the development of histology that the site of the lesion was confirmed by several French scientists, most notably Jean-Martin Charcot in 1870.[12] This provided the information that was used in the early years of the twentieth century to provide a descriptive name for the disease: acute anterior *polio-* (grey) *-myelo-* (marrow of the spinal cord) *-itis* (inflammation), poliomyelitis or polio for short. In between it had at least ten other names, including infantile paralysis. Polio or poliomyelitis is our name of choice although infantile paralysis is used as historical context requires.

安德伍德注意到，与大多数神经疾病不同，“下肢无力症”的解剖学病变位置处并没有感觉功能异常。伦敦的查尔斯·贝尔和巴黎的弗朗西斯·马金迪的神经生理学研究发现，感觉功能区位于脊髓灰质后部，运动功能区位于灰质前部。在此基础上，1828年，苏格兰神经学家J. 阿伯克龙比指出，该病的可能病变位置在脊髓。[10]但这项研究过于超前，直到1860年的出版著作中，德国矫形外科医生和疾病专家雅各布·凡·海涅才发表了脊髓是病理根基的观点。[11]然而，病理损害在尸检标本上无法找到，随着组织学的蓬勃发展，几位法国科学家才得以确认病变的位置，这其中，以让–马丁·沙尔科在1870年的报道最为著名。[12]这项研究首次将该病命名为“急性脊髓前角灰质炎症”，或简称“脊髓灰质炎”，这一名称在20世纪早期被广泛应用。在此之前有包括“小儿麻痹症”在内的数十个其他的名称。尽管小儿麻痹症的命名有其历史背景，我们还是选择了脊髓灰质炎的命名。

From approximately the end of the eighteenth century some surgeons increasingly focused their practices on the diagnosis and treatment of disorders of the musculoskeletal system, becoming orthopaedic ("straight child") surgeons. Giovanni Monteggia in Italy and later Jacob Heine in Germany were two of the most prominent. Heine's 1840 book on detailing management of the acute illness and residual paralysis was so well received that for a time he was included in a name of the ailment: Heine Medin disease.[13] Among its characteristics he listed age of onset as 6 to 36 months, good general health and "blooming" bodily constitution, fever and irritation before paralysis, pain, and involvement of the lower extremities in most cases. He shunned the treatments of the time, including purges, emetics, blisters, and bleeding. Instead he recommended exercises, baths, simple surgical procedures (e.g., tenotomy for contractures or muscle imbalance), bracing, and adaptive apparatus. It was through the literature and an 1840 aiticle on tenotomy that polio's existence in America was traced back to at least 1810.[14] But unlike Heine, the focus in America was more on the treatment of rather than the disease itself, with the remedies often based on the false assumption that the cause was pressure on the nerves from inflammation. In an 1872 lecture, prominent Philadelphia surgeon Samuel D. Gross recommended counterirritants, bleeding, and establishment of an ulcerous lesion with a red-hot iron over the affected spot.[15] Such barbaric forms of treatment persisted for years, finally prompting William Osler in the 1892 edition of his *Principles and Practice of Medicine* to urge discarding irrational treatments until the day when ones based on scientific principles could be developed.[16] Such principles were being supplied by the new disciplines of epidemiology and bacteriology, with epidemiology taking the lead.

18 世纪末，一些外科医生专注于骨骼肌肉系统疾病的诊断和治疗，成为矫形外科的雏形。意大利的乔瓦尼·蒙特基亚和后来德国的雅各布·海涅是其中的佼佼者。海涅 1840 年出版的著作详细介绍了本病在急性起病期及后遗瘫痪期的治疗策略，并广为流传，之后有人将该病称为：海涅-梅丁病。[13]他将疾病特征描述如下：发病年龄在 6 个月到 3 岁，总体健康状况良好，在疼痛和瘫痪之前往往出现发热和易受刺激，大多数累及下肢。他并未采用包括通便、催吐、热疗以及放血等当时推荐的疗法。相反，他推崇锻炼、热水浴、外科小手术（如肌腱松解术以改善肌挛缩和肌力失衡）、支具及适应性固定等方法。通过回顾一篇 1840 年关于肌腱松解术的文章，我们发现脊髓灰质炎的治疗在美国的历史至少可追溯到 1810 年。[14]与海涅不同，当时很多美国医生将治疗重点放到“对症”而非疾病本身，其治疗方法往往基于错误的假设，即病因是炎症对神经的压迫。在 1872 年的一次讲课中，费城的著名外科医生塞缪尔 · D. 格罗斯建议使用抗刺激剂及放血疗法，并通过在受累部位局部加热形成溃疡病变进行治疗。[15]这些野蛮的治疗方式持续了很久，以至于威廉 · 奥斯勒在 1892 年版的《医学原理与实践》中敦促在基于科学原理的治疗方法出现前要摒弃这些不合理疗法。[16]流行病学和细菌学等新学科提供了证据，其中流行病学研究尤为重要。

In the early nineteenth century contagion from interpersonal contact was apparently not even considered as a cause of poliomyelitis.[17] Soon after that, the earliest reported epidemics occurred in England (1835), St. Helena (circa 1835), and Louisiana (1841). Each involved a few (four to ten) cases, all with paralysis. The outbreaks in England and Louisiana had occurred in the summer or early fall.[18] Candidate epidemics, or at least the reporting of them, then seemed to recede. As the new science of bacteriology was developed by Louis Pasteur (1822–95) and Robert Koch (1843–1910), a rational explanation of contagion was born: infection. By 1879 infection had been suggested as an etiology,[19,20] but the likelihood of continuity of human contact wasn't clear until 1887 when pediatrician Karl Oskar Medin observed that the generalized, systemic illness characterized by the minor symptoms of slight fever and malaise was not always followed by paralysis. Medin had studied the first big Swedish epidemic that involved 44 cases.[21,22] He also noted a higher incidence in rural areas. His work complimented the pathological work of fellow Scandinavian J. Rissler, who had the unusual opportunity to study material from five fresh cases who had died in a Norwegian epidemic, three of them after their first week of illness. "He was the first to note enlargement of the spleen and of the lymphoid follicles in the intestines and adjacent lymph nodes. These findings indicated the widespread nature of the infection during the early phases and led Rissler to suggest that poliomyelitis was primarily an acute systemic infection with lesions not necessarily limited to the central nervous system, although the latter were obviously the most serious and indeed the only serious lesions."[23]

19 世纪初，人们还不认为接触传播是脊髓灰质炎的发病原因。[17]之后，最早的流行病学报告出现在英格兰（1835 年）、圣赫勒拿（约 1835 年）和路易斯安那（1841 年）。每次都涉及数个病例（4 到 10 个），均伴有瘫痪。英格兰和路易斯安那的病例发生于夏季或初秋。[18]之后，这种流行病的报道逐渐减少，随着路易斯 · 巴斯德（1822—1895）和罗伯特 · 科赫（1843—1910）细菌学学科框架的建立，一种合理的解释诞生了：感染。到 1879 年，感染已被认为是脊髓灰质炎的病因之一，[19,20]但直到 1887 年儿科医生卡尔·奥斯卡·梅丁观察到有轻微发热和不适等症状的全身系统性疾病并不总伴随瘫痪时，人们才意识到脊髓灰质炎可能通过接触传播。梅丁研究了瑞典 44 例感染病例的第一次大流行，[21,22]发现农村的发病率更高。他的研究为斯堪的纳维亚同胞 J. 里斯勒的病理学工作提供了支持，使他有机会研究五个死于挪威脊髓灰质炎疫情的病理切片，其中 3 份样本来源于患病一周内的病患。因此他成为发现脊髓灰质炎伴有脾肿大及肠系膜淋巴结滤泡增大的第一人，该发现表明早期感染具有广泛性。同时里斯勒提出，尽管脊髓灰质炎可伴有严重的神经系统损害，但它是一种急性全身性感染，病理损害不仅仅局限于中枢神经系统。[23]

The next large epidemic began about mid-June 1894 in Vermont, involving 132 patients.[24] When comparing the sporadic case series with the epidemic case series, three points became clear.[25] First, comparison of the Vermont epidemic with five pooled sporadic series revealed that the epidemic series had older patients; the percent in the 15 years or older category was 9.8% (12 of 122) compared to 0% (0 of 619). This suggested that the sporadic cases were occurring in areas where the disease was endemic, was present all the time, and acquired immunity was high. On the other hand, epidemic areas did not have uniform levels of acquired immunity, which consequently exposed a wider age spectrum of the populace. Second, the risk of death from this usually nonfatal disease was greater among older patients. The death rate of the 1894 Vermont epidemic that had 34.3% of patients age six years or older was considered to be high at 13.5%. Third, epidemics were more likely to occur away from city centers. These observations suggested a shift from endemic to epidemic poliomyelitis. The Vermont epidemic included six cases without paralysis, thus confirming the presence of abortive or nonparalytic cases, which was an important finding of the 1887 Swedish epidemic. However, the importance of contagion was completely discounted, an incorrect conclusion that seems remarkable when considering all the correct observations made during the 1894 epidemic.

大约在 1894 年 6 月中旬，佛蒙特州发生了一次感染 132 例病例的大规模疫情。[24]通过与散发病例的比较，可以发现 3 个特点。[25]第一，佛蒙特州的疫情中大于 15 岁的占 9.8%（12/122），而散发病例中则为 0（0/619）。这表明散发病例发生在获得性免疫力较高的地区，疫区则没有获得群体免疫，因此疾病波及的年龄范围更广。第二，大龄患者死于这种通常不致命疾病的风险更大，1894 年佛蒙特州疫情死亡率高达13.5%，有34.3%的患者年龄在6岁以上。第三，疫情更容易发生在远离市中心的地方。这些证据表明，脊髓灰质炎从地方病转向了流行病。佛蒙特州的疫情还出现了6例未瘫痪病例，这是自1887年瑞典疫情以来的一个重大发现。然而，传染的重要性被完全忽视了，让后人深省的是1894年疫情期间所有准确的观察结果竟然未能得出一个正确的结论。

The significance of nonparalytic cases was finally fully appreciated by a 33-year-old medical doctor, Ivar Wickman.[26,27] His subject was the 1905 Swedish epidemic, which spiked in August and was the first to involve more than 1,000 cases. He estimated that 15% of cases were nonparalytic and emphasized their role in the spread of the disease. Rural areas were hard-hit, cities were relatively spared, and there was no doubt that the disease was contagious. In addition, he established an incubation period of three to four days for the minor illness (nonparalytic cases) rather than the generally accepted eight to ten days based on the onset of the major illness (paralytic phase). This fact was not proven until the advent of live attenuated vaccines a half century later.

33岁的医生伊瓦尔·威克曼最终发现了非瘫痪病例的重要性。[26,27]他对1905年瑞典疫情展开研究，第一波疫情在8月份达到顶峰，有超过1 000例感染病例。他发现15%的病例是非瘫痪性的，并强调他们在疾病传播中的作用。农村地区受灾严重，而城市地区传染性一般，至此疾病的传染性再无疑问。另外，他提出了轻症（非瘫痪病例）的潜伏期是3到4天，这与被普遍接受的重症（瘫痪病例）8到10天的潜伏期完全不同。这一事实直到半个世纪后减毒活疫苗的出现才得到了证实。

The cause of polio was discovered in 1908. Viennese pathologist Karl Landsteiner and Erwin Popper, his assistant, reported producing poliomyelitis in two old world monkeys by means of intraperitoneal injection of a sterile suspension of spinal cord from the fatal case of a nine-year-old boy who died on the third day of his illness.[28,29] To produce the sterile suspension, the spinal cord of the deceased was ground up and filtered through pores too small to transmit bacteria. The *Cynocephalus hamadryas* died in eight days and the *Macaca rhesus* was paralyzed in seventeen days. Following autopsy, histological study of their spinal cords showed the characteristic death and dissolution of the motor cells of the anterior horn of the grey matter of the spinal cord. Similar injections into rabbits, guinea pigs, and mice produced no disease. Even though the second and third of Koch's postulates of proof of infection (isolation in pure culture and reproduction by inoculation) were only partially satisfied and the first (always present) was not at all, the results were irrefutable. Whether by choice or chance, use of old world monkeys was fortunate because new world monkeys would be found to be relatively insusceptible to experimental polio. Landsteiner documented in at least a dozen papers published by 1911 the presence of the virus in nonnervous tissues from fatal human cases. These tissues included the tonsils, salivary glands, and intestinal (mesenteric) lymph nodes. However, because he recognized that further progress was going to be time-consuming and costly, he voluntarily returned to his efforts to further understand the immunological differences among human blood. This was the science that led to safe blood transfusions during World War I and to the understanding of the hereditary transmission of blood groups. For this he received the 1930 Nobel Prize in medicine.[30]

脊髓灰质炎的病因直到 1908 年才确定。维也纳的病理学家卡尔·兰德施泰纳和他的助手欧文·波佩尔将一位发病 3 天后死亡的 9 岁男孩的脊髓组织碎片化，经过滤提取无菌上清液。把它注射到两只旧大陆猴的腹腔后成功使它们感染了脊髓灰质炎。[28,29] 8 天后一只金丝猴死亡，而另一只猕猴在 17 天后瘫痪。尸检表明脊髓灰质前角的运动细胞出现了典型的死亡和溶解。相同的操作在兔子、豚鼠及小鼠动物模型中并未诱发疾病。尽管这次试验仅部分满足于科赫法则的第二和第三条（从单一组织中分离以获得纯培养物，接种到健康个体产生相同的症状），且完全不满足第一条（从个体中发现上次分离的同一致病微生物），但其结果依然无可辩驳。无论是偶然还是必然，很幸运的是实验选择了旧大陆猴，因为后来发现新大陆猴不容易在实验中受到脊髓灰质炎的影响。1911 年，兰德施泰纳发表的一系列论文中记录了在死亡的人类病例的非神经组织中发现了致命病毒的存在，包括扁桃体、唾液腺和肠系膜淋巴结。然而，考虑到在这些方向上继续突破的时间和经济因素，他将研究的方向转到明确人类血液中是否存在免疫差异。正是这些研究使人们更进一步提高了对血型的遗传学认识，并在第一次世界大战中推动了安全输血的实践，他也因此获得了 1930 年的诺贝尔医学奖。[30]

Discovery of the causative virus was most ardently followed up by Simon Flexner, head of the Rockefeller Institute for Medical Research.[31] Pathologist Flexner had field experience with infectious diseases: tropical ailments of all kinds in the Philippines, the plague in San Francisco, and meningococcal meningitis. In addition, the Rockefeller Institute had the laboratory facilities and financing Landsteiner lacked. Following up on

Landsteiner's breakthrough, the next year Flexner and Martha Wollstein successfully reproduced the disease in passage from monkey to monkey, fulfilling Koch's second postulate. In 1910 the team of Flexner and Lewis demonstrated simultaneously with Landsteiner that the serum of monkeys convalescing from polio had antibodies that inactivated the virus. Later that year similar findings in humans were reported from France.

洛克菲勒医学研究所所长西蒙·弗莱克斯纳密切关注了这种新发现的致命病毒。[31]作为病理学家，他也有许多传染病学经验：菲律宾的各种热带疾病，圣弗朗西斯科的鼠疫以及双球菌脑膜炎。此外，洛克菲勒研究所拥有兰德施泰纳所缺少的实验室设备和资金。在他发表报道后的第二年，弗莱克斯纳和玛莎·沃尔斯坦在猴子间成功地复制了这种疾病，满足了科赫法则第二条。1910 年，弗莱克斯纳、李维斯团队与兰德施泰纳同期证实了在脊髓灰质炎康复的猴子血清中存在可灭活病毒的抗体。同年，法国科学家在人身上发现了同样的抗体。

The Swedish polio epidemic of 1911 was a landmark event because of its size of over 3,800 cases, the use of the new tool of monkey infection, and the thorough study by the well-qualified team of epidemiologists Carl Kling, Alfred Pettersson, and Wilhelm Wernstedt.[32] Utilizing what must have been a large number of monkeys to experimentally infect, the investigators found the filterable agent from a wide variety of sites in fatal cases. In addition, they found that washings obtained from the mouth, nose, pharynx, and intestine of patients with paralysis, those without paralysis, and even those from healthy carriers also contained the infecting filterable agent/virus. Finally, the virus was found in intestinal and throat washings for as long as six months or more. Utilizing the knowledge gained from this epidemic, Kling, Pettersson, and Wernstedt proved four important points with the first being that patients with mild or even no apparent infection were important in spreading the disease. This had been suggested from studies of earlier Swedish epidemics by Medin in 1887 and Wickman in 1905. Second, since the virus was shed from the body for long periods, isolation was useless. Third, because older persons had longer periods to become infected and thus acquire natural immunity, the predilection of the disease for younger persons was explained. This natural immunity also explained why the principal centers of the 1905 epidemic were not involved in that of 1911. Finally, the likely route of infection was enteric with entry through the mouth and exit in the feces. Unfortunately, the veracity of these findings was not universally accepted until the late 1930s because of two reasons. First, Kling and his team had suggested that the virus weakened after the acute stage, a finding that was later proved wrong. The other reason was that some investigators were unable to reproduce their results, and this was at least partially due to the lack of major epidemics to study and the resources needed to conduct a study.

1911 年瑞典的脊髓灰质炎疫情是一次里程碑事件，疫情规模超过 3 800 例。在此次疫情中，卡尔·克林、艾尔弗雷德·彼得松和威廉·韦恩斯泰特使用猴子作为感染动物模型，组成专业的流行病学研究团队。[32]研究者先让大量的猴子感染了脊髓灰质炎，从致死性病例的各个部位获取冲洗液提取物。此外，他们还发现从瘫痪病例、非瘫痪病例甚至一些无症状感染者的口、鼻、咽部及肠道获取的冲洗液中也含有可感染的物质/病毒。最后，在感染后的六个月及更长时间内，均能从肠道或咽喉部冲洗液中发现这种病毒。通过这次疫情，克林、彼得松和韦恩斯泰特证明了以下四个观点：第一，轻微症状或无症状感染者在疾病传播过程中扮演重要角色，这一点在 1887 年梅丁和 1905 年威克曼对早期瑞典疫情的研究中也被提及。第二，由于病毒在体内存在的时间很长，隔离是无效的。第三，年长患者因为暴露时间相对较长并获得了自然免疫，故年幼者更易患病。自然免疫也解释了为什么 1905 年的疫情流行地区在 1911 年并未发生疫情。第四，可能的感染途径是通过口腔进入消化道，然后从粪便中排出。遗憾的是这些推论的真实性直到 20 世纪 30 年代才被证实，原因有两个：第一，克林和他的团队曾提出，病毒在急性期后复制减弱，而这一推论后来被证明是错误的；第二，一些研究者无法复制他们的研究成果，部分原因是此后未爆发可供研究的脊髓灰质炎疫情，并且缺乏研究所需的其他资源。

After approximately 1912, progress in understanding the disease slowed for about twenty or more years. The principal reason seemed to be the ascendancy of experimental polio. This research supported the hypothesis that the pathogenesis of the disease was a nasal portal of entry with passage up the olfactory nerves to the brain and on to the spinal cord.[33] One of the two main problems was that experimental poliomyelitis was based on work with rhesus monkeys that could not be infected by the alimentary route. The second problem was active resistance to the findings of Kling, Pettersson, and Wernstedt supporting the idea that poliomyelitis was an enteric infection.[34]

1912 年后的 20 年以至更长时间里，人们对该病的认识进展逐渐放缓，主要原因是实验性脊髓灰质炎的盛行。此类研究做出了这样的假设：疾病是通过鼻部进入体内，沿着嗅神经向上进入大脑和脊髓。[33]其中存在的一个问题是实验性脊髓灰质炎的动物模型是恒河猴，而它不会通过食物途径感染；另一问题是对克林、彼得松和韦恩斯泰特所提出的肠道感染观点的消极抵制。[34]

The July to October epidemic of 1916 in New York and the Northeast was the worst yet, eclipsing the 1914 record of 87 cases per 100,000 residents in Vermont. In New York City there were 185 cases per 100,000, The death rate in the Northeastern states was 22% (5,000 of 23,000), and in New York City it was 24%.[35] The epidemic was addressed with strict quarantine and travel restrictions, sometimes enforced by court actions. A committee of scientific investigators and leaders, formed to develop a research agenda, came up with six projects, all of which were said to be influenced by Flexner. Apparently none were carried out.[36] When the epidemic was over, four previous interpretations of the Public Health Service seemed upheld. Polio was exclusively a human disease, infection was more prevalent than apparent, unrecognized carriers were more important than frank paralytic cases in the spread of infection, and an epidemic of one to three recognized cases per thousand or even less, immunizes the general population to such an extent that the epidemic declines spontaneously, due to exhaustion or thinning out of infectable material.[37] Overall, it was believed that a prime opportunity to advance the clinical virology of polio had been missed.

迄今为止，1916 年 7 月至 10 月间发生于纽约和东北各州的疫情是最严重的，发病率超过了 1914 年佛蒙特州每十万人检出 87 例的纪录。在纽约，每 10 万人中有 185 名患者，东北部各州的死亡率为 22%（5 000/23 000），纽约的死亡率为 24%。[35]为了应对此次疫情采取了严格的检测手段和旅行限制，有时甚至向法院申请强制执行。据说在弗莱克斯纳的授意下，由研究者和领导者组成的委员会提出了六项研究议程，然而似乎并没有一项得以落实。当疫情结束后，既往提出的四项公共卫生体系的研究推论似乎得到了印证。[36]脊髓灰质炎完全是一种人类传染病，感染率远大于发病率；在传播中，未发现的病毒携带者比瘫痪病例更为重要。每千人中有一到三个甚至更少的显性病例，其会对普通人群进行群体免疫，从而使疾病的流行由于可感染对象的耗尽或减少而自动下降。[37]不论如何，脊髓灰质炎临床病毒学研究的最好机会已经错过了。

Possibly the most unusual polio epidemic began in the spring of 1934 in Los Angeles. It was a relatively small epidemic, in which more adults than children were affected, most cases were mild, paralysis was uncommon, and nearly half of the cases were considered to be other unrecognized neurological conditions. During the epidemic "an atmosphere of stark dread prevailed among hospital personnel who had the task of caring for the patients."[38] Even though polio transmission from clinical cases seldom occurred, this epidemic was different as 10.7% of nurses and 5.4% of physicians became sick; whether this was due to polio or a coincidental disease was never clear. The whole work, social, political, and media atmosphere became toxic. Flexner's help was sought early in the epidemic, and he sent a team of three scientists along with the equipment and laboratory animals needed to isolate the virus.[39] It had been decided to look for the virus in oropharyngeal washings as well as central nervous system material from fatal cases by inoculation of monkeys, as well as bacteria- and virus-susceptible mice recently developed by team leader and Flexner associate Leslie Webster. Intestinal washings were not collected because the group had prior unsuccessful experience with them. Poliovirus was recovered from the central nervous system material of a few fatal cases by inoculation of monkeys, but not the virus-susceptible mice. Poliovirus was recovered by monkey inoculation from the oropharyngeal washings of just one patient, who had a minor illness only. When typing later became available, this frozen specimen was found to be type II poliovirus, an uncommon cause of epidemics. There were 2,499 suspected cases in the Los Angeles epidemic, of which only slightly more than half were actually diagnosed and reported as polio. Other neurological conditions and hysteria made meaningful analysis and definitive conclusions impossible, even to later analysis. If nothing else, this epidemic illustrated just how complex polio epidemiology could be.

1934年春，洛杉矶发生了一次极不寻常的疫情。这是一次小流行，但成年患者多于儿童，且大多数病例为轻症，瘫痪的病例较少，近一半的病例被诊断为某种未知的神经疾病。“疫情期间，医务工作者陷入了十足的恐惧中”。[38]尽管很少发生脊髓灰质炎的医源性传播，但这次不同，有10.7%的护士和5.4%的医生患病。由于未能明确感染的是脊髓灰质炎还是其他疾病，整个工作、社会、政治和媒体氛围都变得“有毒”。弗莱克斯纳在疫情早期就派出了一个由三名科学家组成的团队，并资助分离病毒所需的设备和实验动物。[39]他们在猴子、细菌和病毒易感小鼠（由团队带头人，弗莱克斯纳的助手莱斯利·韦伯斯特培育）体内接种病毒，并通过在实验动物的口咽冲洗液和死亡动物的中枢神经系统组织中寻找病毒以研究疾病的发病机制。受限于前期实验的失败，此次研究未能收集到肠道冲洗液。最终，从死亡猴子的中枢神经系统组织中分离出脊髓灰质炎病毒，但并未在死亡的小鼠中找到。同时，仅在一例轻症猴子的口咽冲洗液中发现脊髓灰质炎病毒。直到后来能够对病毒进行分型，才从冷冻标本中发现Ⅱ型脊髓灰质炎病毒，这是此次疫情不同寻常的原因。洛杉矶疫情出现 2 499 例疑似病例，其中只有略超过半数的患者最终确诊为脊髓灰质炎。尽管后期仍在关注此次疫情中诊断为其他神经系统疾病和癔症的患者，但已无法获得有价值的分析和结论。至少，这场疫情说明脊髓灰质炎的流行病学研究非常复杂。

The meager scientific return from study of the 1916 and 1934 polio epidemics reflected the slow progress being made in understanding the fundamentals of polio and managing its consequences. Passive immunization with convalescent serum was tried and failed, not because the concept was fundamentally wrong, but because the logistics were insurmountable.[40] In 1935 active immunization with either weakened (attenuated) live virus or killed virus preparations was tried. Several thousand persons had been injected, a few developed polio, and at least one in each group died. One scientist survived the criticism and completed a successful career, but the other suffered disgrace and death at age 36. Many at the time and since have speculated that he killed himself.[41] In a cruel twist of fate the agent he used to kill the virus, formaldehyde, was the same one used by Salk two decades later. Missing knowledge about the disease stood in the way of developing a successful vaccine.

从 1916 年到 1934 年，脊髓灰质炎流行病学研究成果的匮乏，意味着在认识其发病原理和治疗疾病方面进展缓慢。尽管概念上并无根本性错误，但受限于运输和储存条件限制，恢复期血清被动免疫治疗的尝试失败了。[40] 1935 年，科学家们尝试用减毒或灭活病毒制剂进行主动免疫，但数千人的注射试验使得一部分人感染脊髓灰质炎，同时每组均有受试者死亡。其中一位科学家在批判的浪潮中艰难前行，并成功地完成了自己的历程；但另一位科学家在 36 岁时不堪蒙受羞辱去世，很多人猜测他死于自杀。[41]命运的残酷和戏谑之处在于，被他用来杀死病毒的物质——甲醛，就是 20 年后索尔克成功研发脊髓灰质炎疫苗时用以灭活病毒并保持抗原活性的物质。对疾病认识的不充分性阻碍了疫苗的成功研制。

These setbacks, unfortunate as some were, were offset by four developments that would have far-reaching consequences for the history of polio. These were Franklin Roosevelt's poliomyelitis leading to formation of the National Foundation for Infantile Paralysis (NFIP), the iron lung, discovery of more than one polio type, and new findings lending support to the likelihood of an intestinal-vascular pathogenesis. Although usually affecting children, it was an afflicted adult who had the single most influence on the disease. Thirty-nine-year-old Franklin Delano Roosevelt was the picture of health when he became ill with acute polio on August 10, 1921,[42] but he was determined to recover and help others do the same.[43] This led to a series of events that culminated in the founding of an organization with the capacity to confront the polio menace. It began in 1922 with a chance encounter on the polished marble floor of a Manhattan office building where Roosevelt had fallen and fellow New York attorney Basil O'Connor was among those who helped him to his feet. The men became acquainted, and two years later formed the Roosevelt and O'Connor partnership, to which Roosevelt contributed his connections and legal advice. O'Connor had emerged from a working-class background, graduated from Dartmouth College and Harvard Law, and at only 32 was already successful, specializing in oil business law that required bringing business people together. He proved to be an outstanding leader and administrator, especially adept at making difficult decisions, likely sometimes at the cost of a little broken china.[44,45] In 1926 Roosevelt was sold Warm Springs, a broken-down mineral springs spa in western Georgia, where he had found hope for himself and where he gave hope to other polio victims. As Roosevelt became reengaged in politics and won the New York governorship in 1928 and the presidency in 1932, he increasingly relied on O'Connor to manage his efforts to combat polio. One step was establishing the Georgia Warm Springs Foundation that had the dual purposes of providing direct aid to patients and communicating helpful observations or special methods to hospitals and the medical profession. It also included fund-raising, but it soon became apparent that more money was needed for the foundation and the fight against polio. The plan settled on was an annual President's Birthday Ball held each year in January from 1934 to 1938 with proceeds managed by the President's Birthday Ball Commission (PBBC). The funding saved the Georgia Warm Springs Foundation and provided research grants totaling several hundred thousand dollars. But as the balls decreased in popularity, the dollars raised became inadequate for the task. A new plan was needed. Thus, the NFIP was formed, becoming operational in January 1938. Its purposes were to provide care for those with polio and prevent others from contracting the disease.[46] Roosevelt asked his law partner to lead the NFIP and O'Connor brought to the organization the skills needed to build it into the driving force behind the quest to understand, manage and eventually prevent poliomyelitis. It has been written that O'Connor was "the person most responsible for eliminating polio from the United States and later most of the world," not Jonas Salk.[47].

对脊髓灰质炎历史产生深远影响的四个事件弥补了上述略显不幸的结局。富兰克林·罗斯福患上了脊髓灰质炎，从而成立了国家小儿麻痹基金会（NFIP）；铁肺（呼吸机）在脊髓灰质炎中的应用；科学家发现不止有一种脊髓灰质炎类型；支持脊髓灰质炎是一种肠道–血管疾病的新发现。尽管儿童是易感染群体，但对脊髓灰质炎影响最大的是一位成人患者。1921 年 8 月 10 日，39 岁的富兰克林·德拉诺·罗斯福患上了急性脊髓灰质炎，[42]尽管照片上看还算健康，但他决心要完全康复并帮助和他有相同遭遇的人。[43]由此产生了一系列有影响的措施并最终建立起一个同脊髓灰质炎抗争的组织。这一切始于 1922 年，罗斯福在曼哈顿一座光鲜的办公楼内不慎摔倒，许多人将他扶起，来自纽约的律师同僚巴兹尔·奥康纳便是其中之一。两人结识后的第三年建立了合作关系，罗斯福提供自己的人脉和法律建议。奥康纳是工人阶级出身，毕业于达特茅斯学院和哈佛法学院，才 32 岁就取得了成功。他专注于石油商业法，需要将商界人士聚拢到一起。事实证明，他是一位杰出的领导者和管理者，尤其擅长于权衡利弊后做出正确而艰难的决定。[44,45]1926 年罗斯福买下了位于佐治亚州西部的沃姆斯普林斯市一处废弃的矿物质温泉，在那儿寻求自己和其他脊髓灰质炎患者的康复希望。随着罗斯福重新投身政坛，并在 1928 年赢得了纽约州州长，1932 年赢得了总统宝座后，他越来越信赖奥康纳来辅佐他应对脊髓灰质炎的事业。其中之一便是建立佐治亚温泉基金会，其职能包括向患者提供直接援助和向医疗机构宣讲有效的观察结果和特殊疗法，同时兼有募集资金的义务。但很快他们就发现现有资金对于基金会和抗击脊髓灰质炎远远不够。最终他们确定了在 1934 年到 1938 年每年 1 月举行的总统生日舞会上的募资计划，收益由总统生日舞会委员会（PBBC）管理。这项资金挽救了佐治亚州温泉基金会，并为脊髓灰质炎的研究提供了数十万美元资助。之后，随着舞会受欢迎程度减退，募集的资金再次捉襟见肘，不得不考虑新的方案。国家小儿麻痹基金会应运而生，并于 1938 年 1 月开始运行。它的宗旨是为脊髓灰质炎患者提供治疗并阻断疾病的传播。[46]罗斯福邀请他的法律合伙人来领导国家小儿麻痹基金会，奥康纳的到来，为国家小儿麻痹基金会实现从认识疾病、治疗疾病并最终预防疾病提供了所需的一切技能和实力。有人写道，奥康纳是“美国乃至后来世界的大部分地区消除脊髓灰质炎最重要的人”，而非乔纳斯·索尔克。[47]

The work of the NFIP was funded by the March of Dimes campaign, which far outraised competing disease-specific charities. The campaign included year-round fund-raising involving a network of several thousand local chapters staffed by volunteers. Celebrities also lent their endorsements and gave their time. In result, over $600 million were raised from 1938 to 1962. The funds were primarily used to provide care for afflicted patients, saving many families from financial ruin. And, the NFIP was also able to make available money for basic polio research that far exceeded the sums provided by the National Institutes of Health.[48] At its founding, O'Connor recruited Thomas M. Rivers, a leading virologist at the Rockefeller Institute, to develop and run the research effort. Rivers developed a list of eleven research priorities, the last being development of a vaccine.[49] This set the direction of the NFIP during the war years.

国家小儿麻痹基金会的工作得到了美国出生缺陷基金会运动的资助，资助规模远超其他疾病。这项活动还包括由数千名志愿者组成的地方分会的全年资助，名人们也付诸行动，为它代言。结果，从 1938 年到 1962 年，募集到 6 亿多美元。资金主要用于患者治疗，使许多家庭免于破产。国家小儿麻痹基金会还为脊髓灰质炎的基础研究提供远超美国国家卫生研究院的资金。[48]在成立之初，奥康纳招募了洛克菲勒研究院的首席病毒学家托马斯 · M. 里弗斯来开发和管理这项研究工作。里弗斯列出了 11 项研究的优先事项，最后一项是开发疫苗。[49]这为国家小儿麻痹基金会在战争年代的工作确定了方向。

The second major development in the fight against this disease was the invention of the iron lung in 1929 by Philip Drinker and Louis Shaw at the Harvard School of Public Health.[50] This imposing apparatus that provided mechanical breathing when the muscles of respiration could not became one of the most iconic images of the clinical struggle with polio. *See figure 4. 2*. The iron lung was an airtight tube enclosing the patient's body except for the head, into which intermittent negative (inspiration) and positive (expiration) pressures were introduced at short regular intervals.[51] The higher the paralysis, the more the muscles

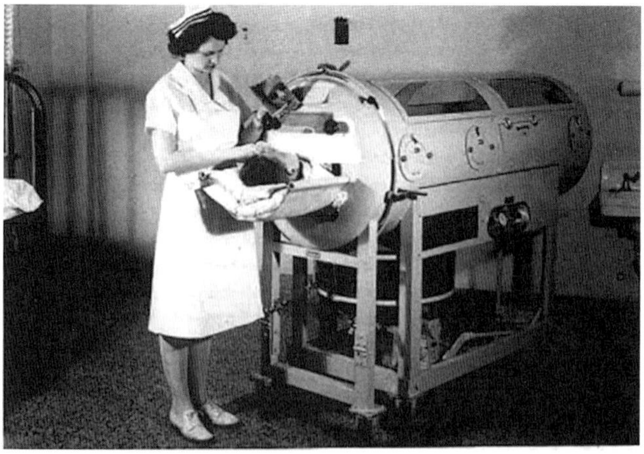

Figure 4. 2 ***Iron lung. ca. 1950.*** (***University of Kansas Medical Center Archives***)
图 4. 2　铁肺，1950 年（堪萨斯大学医学中心档案馆）

of respiration, the intercostal muscles and diaphragm, were affected. Infection in the base of the brain, referred to as bulbar polio because of the bulb shape of the base of the brain, resulted in paralysis involving the muscles of the pharynx, the area between the mouth and the entries to the trachea and esophagus, with loss of swallowing control. The mortality rate for bulbar paralysis was 90%.[52] Those motor neuron cells in which the infection did not cause the irreversible change of nucleus destruction did experience functional recovery.[53] Thus, as the acute paralytic phase of the infection passed, most patients experienced varying amounts of nerve function recovery over a period of approximately four to six weeks. This hope for meaningful paralysis resolution stimulated development of acute management methods to provide pulmonary support. Tracheostomy, the surgical creation of an opening into the trachea through the neck, secured an opening for air passage and suctioning of secretions. But tracheostomy did not provide the inspiration and expiration necessary for respiration. The iron lung did and it worked! From 1920 through 1929, the ten years before the iron lung came into existence, the death rate from polio was 31%. From 1930 through 1939 the death rate decreased to 16%. Antibiotics, effective in treating pulmonary infections, began to become available, and from 1940 through 1949 the death rate dropped to 8%.[54] *See figure 4.3.* Unfortunately, paralysis resolution did not always occur, and some patients who did not die were confined to an iron lung full- or part-time for the rest of their shortened lives, leaving behind stories of heroism and heartbreak.[55-59] For the caregivers the iron lung presented a series of challenges best faced in a group atmosphere—and this form of response became the forerunner of today's intensive care units.

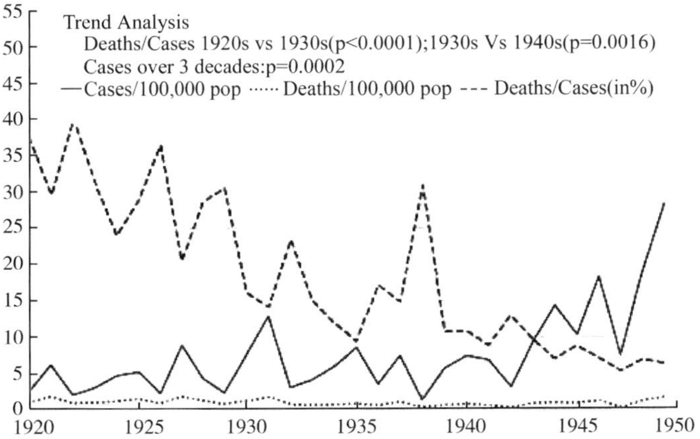

Figure 4.3 ***Graph of the significant decrease in death rate from polio over three ten-year intervals: before iron lung, after iron lung, and as antibiotics first began to become available.***
图 4.3 脊髓灰质炎死亡率在 30 年间显著下降:铁肺出现之前的十年、应用铁肺后十年和开始应用抗生素的十年

1929 年哈佛大学公共卫生学院的菲利浦·德林克和路易斯·肖发明了铁肺，这是与脊髓灰质炎抗争中的第二个重大突破。[50] 这个硕大无比的设备为呼吸肌无力的患者提供机械性的呼吸辅助，成为临床

上与脊髓灰质炎抗争中最具标志性的图景。(图 4.2) 铁肺是包裹患者身体的密闭管腔，仅留患者头部在外。在短暂规律的间隔期内，间歇性地注入、排出空气以形成正压（呼气)、负压（吸气）的交替循环。[51]瘫痪的节段越高，呼吸肌、肋间肌和膈肌受累越多。脑基底部的感染又称延髓脊髓灰质炎，会导致咽部肌肉（口腔与气管和食管区域之间的肌肉）瘫痪，并失去吞咽控制。延髓麻痹的死亡率达到 90%。[52]病毒感染后，未出现不可逆细胞核破坏的运动神经元细胞依然能恢复功能。[53]因此，度过急性感染期后，大多数患者在 4 到 6 周内神经功能均会有不同程度的恢复。对瘫痪恢复的期望加速了急性期呼吸支持技术和策略的发展。气管切开术通过在颈部的气管上切开一个口子，给呼吸和气管分泌物提供了进出通道，但它对气体交换并没有辅助功能。此时，铁肺发挥了重要作用！在 1920 年至 1929 年铁肺出现前的十年间，脊髓灰质炎的死亡率为 31%。而到了 1930 至 1939 年，死亡率下降到 16%。之后有了治疗肺部感染的抗生素，从 1940 至 1949 年，死亡率下降到 8%。[54]（图 4.3）不幸的是，并不是所有的瘫痪者均会获得恢复，部分幸存者在其短暂的余生中无法脱离铁肺，留下了许多充满英雄主义色彩的心碎故事。[55-59]在铁肺的应用过程中，迫切需要多学科密切合作辅助治疗的开展，其解决方案即为当今重症监护病房的雏形。

The third major development was the 1931 finding of Frank M. Burnett and Jean Macnamara that there were at least two different serotypes of the poliovirus. Acceptance of their discovery was somewhat slowed because they worked in the far-off location of Melbourne, Australia. Verification came three years later from France and six years later from the Yale Poliomyelitis Study Unit. The latter invested two and a half years of work and hundreds of monkeys, and their findings were clear that there were at least two types of poliovirus. With this established, it was obvious that the differences between strains and types would have to be identified before vaccines and serological tests to study immunity could be developed. To accomplish this would require intense labor and vast resources, but the world was on the verge of another war, and poliovirus typing would have to wait.

第三个重大进展是 1931 年弗兰克·M. 伯内特和让·麦克纳马拉的新发现，他们认为至少有两种不同的脊髓灰质炎病毒血清。由于他们远在澳大利亚墨尔本，很长时间后主流科学界才认可了他们的研究成果。法国和耶鲁大学的学者分别于 3 年和 6 年后验证了他们的结论。后者更是花了 2 年半的时间，耗费数百只猴子，确定至少有两种不同类型的脊髓灰质炎病毒。这些证据意味着，在开发研究疫苗和血清学试验之前，需要确定不同类型毒株之间的差异。然而，此时的世界正处于一场大战的边缘，难以保障研究所需的大量人力和资源，因此脊髓灰质炎病毒分型的研究只能延后了。

The fourth major development was the reawakening of interest in polio's pathogenesis, in other words the determination of how the virus entered the human body and spread to invade the central nervous system.[60] This began in 1937 when orthopedic surgeon and bacteriology PhD Paul H. Harmon briefly reported isolating the poliovirus from five rectal washings in four of twenty convalescent patients from the 1936 Chicago epidemic in whom they had been unable to isolate virus from the nasopharynx. He listed ten reasons the nasopharynx was the unlikely portal of entry.[61] The Yale polio unit reacted immediately and soon confirmed and enlarged on this finding.[62] They had injected their lab's pet cercopithecus, an old world monkey, intraperitoneally rather than intracerebrally, thinking they were protecting it from the unpredictable effect of intracerebral injection of the fecal extracts, but he became quadriplegic and died. At first their report was met with skepticism. The Swedish epidemiological studies, which had been sidelined for about twenty-five years at least partially due to scientific prejudice, were given new credence. Additional support came in experiments begun in 1939 by Howard Howe and David Bodian at Johns Hopkins. They investigated the chance observation of spontaneous polio in two chimpanzees in a children's zoo and found chimpanzees susceptible to polio by feeding, even more so than their cynomolgus, an old world monkey.[63]

第四个重大进展重新唤起了人们对脊髓灰质炎发病机制的研究兴趣，即确定病毒如何进入人体并播散到中枢神经系统。[60]这始于 1937 年，骨科医生兼细菌学博士保罗·H. 哈蒙的研究。他从 1936 年芝加哥疫情中处于康复期的 4 位患者身上获取到 5 份直肠冲洗液，并成功分离出脊髓灰质炎病毒，然而，这些患者的鼻咽部却无法分离出毒株。他还提出了 10 个原因以反驳从鼻咽部感染病毒的假设。[61]耶鲁大学脊髓灰质炎研究小组立即跟进，很快就证实并拓展了这一发现。[62]他们为了消除脑内注射带来的不可预测因素的影响，将感染者粪便中的提取物注射到实验室长尾猴（旧世界猴）的腹腔内，之后它四肢瘫痪，最终死亡。刚开始，他们的报道受到了质疑，但后来发现，25 年前由于科学偏见搁置了的瑞典流行病学研究竟然佐证了这次实验结果。约翰·霍普金斯大学的霍华德·豪和戴维·博迪恩于 1939 年的研究给这一结论提供了额外的支持。他们从一次偶然的观察研究中发现了两只在儿童动物园里无症状感染的黑猩猩，进一步研究表明，黑猩猩通过进食感染脊髓灰质炎病毒，且比食蟹猴（旧世界猴）更易染病。[63]

Flexner's work with experimental polio, infecting rhesus monkeys by intracerebral injection, had led him to support inhalation and passage along the olfactory nerves to the brain and on to the spinal cord as polio's likely pathogenesis. But these latest studies increasingly supported ingestion and passage through the bloodstream as the likely route. An opening statement at a roundtable discussion held in 1916 was coming back to haunt polio research. After acceding to Flexner's theories, Yale Professor Winslow added, what is not explained is the fact of summertime prevalence; for all other nose and throat diseases are winter diseases."[64] This basic oversight could at least be attributed to the strict separation of laboratory research from clinical research espoused by Flexner.

弗莱克斯纳通过脑内注射的实验让恒河猴患上脊髓灰质炎，从而促使他更支持病毒被吸入后沿着嗅神经进入大脑和脊髓的发病机制这一假设。但最新的研究更加支持经口腔和血液传播的感染途径。1916 年举行的一次圆桌论坛的开幕式上，耶鲁大学教授温斯洛在认可了弗莱克斯纳的理论后，再次补充道，“鼻部和咽喉部的疾病多发于冬季，但脊髓灰质炎流行于夏季，其中的原因仍然未知。”这给脊髓灰质炎研究带来了新的问题。[64]对基础性问题的忽视反映出弗莱克斯纳所提倡的实验室研究与临床研究之间缺乏紧密联系。

World War II soon took precedence over both spine deformity advancement and to a lesser extent polio research. Perhaps the polio researchers could have or did predict the postwar North American polio epidemics, but the vast majority of citizens had no way of anticipating this future. But, thanks to the farsightedness of Roosevelt, O'Connor, Rivers, and others, the President's Birthday Ball Commission experience had been put to good use in forming the organizational structure that would prove necessary to address the epidemics that came.

第二次世界大战很快影响了脊柱畸形和脊髓灰质炎研究的发展。也许研究者能够预测到战后北美地区的脊髓灰质炎疫情，但普通民众没有这项能力。幸亏罗斯福、奥康纳和里弗斯等人的远见卓识，总统生日舞会委员会的经验在形成应对即将到来疫情所必需的组织架构上得到了很好的利用。

At the beginning of the twentieth century three powerful forces for change were building in the management of scoliosis and spine deformity. First, the diseases contributing most of the deformities, tuberculosis and poliomyelitis, were not controllable. Antibiotics for tuberculosis and vaccination for poliomyelitis lay decades in the future. Although a relatively small minority of these affected patients developed spine deformity, the accumulative effect was problematic. Second, existing methods of scoliosis and spine deformity management were so ineffective that "scoliosis was considered incurable and termed by many the cancer of orthopedics.[65] And third, recent medical advances, including aseptic surgery, anesthesia, and radiology, made the development of spine surgery possible.

在20世纪初，有三股强大的力量推动着脊柱侧凸和脊柱畸形治疗发生变革。第一，结核和脊髓灰质炎等造成脊柱畸形的主要疾病缺乏有效疗法，而抗结核药物和脊髓灰质炎疫苗的应用是几十年后的事。尽管这些病患中发生脊柱畸形的比例并不高，但巨大人口基数的累积效应不可忽视。第二，已有的脊柱畸形治疗措施几乎无效，许多人认为脊柱侧凸无法治愈，甚至被称为"骨科的癌症"。[65]第三，包括无菌术、麻醉和影像学在内的医学技术的发展给脊柱外科手术变革奠定了坚实的基础。

Tuberculosis of the spine (Pott's disease) was the initial stimulus to develop a surgical method of spine stabilization. As the result of the vertebral body destruction, the vertebra's strength was progressively compromised, and fragmentation and collapse of the spine anteriorly into kyphosis occurred, sometimes progressing to the point of causing spinal cord compression and paralysis (Pott's paraplegia).[66,67] Motion seemed to accelerate the destruction of the diseased vertebrae. It had been observed that ankylosis (the complete immobility of a joint by bony union) of other joints infected by tuberculosis, either as part of the disease process or by surgical arthrodesis, resulted in "rapid disappearance of the tuberculous process."[68] The natural extension of the observation was "perfection of a method which will absolutely immobilize the spine throughout the diseased area and make the development of deformity impossible."[69] On this principle Russell Hibbs[70] and Fred Albee,[71] working separately in New York City in 1911, successfully performed the first posterior spine arthrodesis operations, procedures intended to eliminate joint motion by causing adjacent bones to grow solidly together and become a fusion. Posterior fusion indirectly immobilized the spine anteriorly. Both techniques used a midline approach, but they differed. Hibbs emphasized developing and closing the periosteal layer over cut and reorganized spinous process bone. No additional bone graft was added. Albee's method was based on the incorporation of a prism-shaped tibial autograft with the spinous processes to provide leverage to counteract anterior collapse. Just a few years earlier Fritz Lange of Munich had tried to accomplish the same goal with bars or rods fixed to the spinous processes at either end with silk or steel wire.[72,73] This was before biocompatible implant materials were available, so his attempts failed because of bone liquefaction at the bone implant contact sites.

脊柱结核（波特病）促使医生们开发出一种稳定脊柱的外科术式。随着椎体破坏和椎体强度降低，受累区域的脊柱发生塌陷进而形成后凸，逐渐进展的后凸压迫到脊髓，有时甚至导致瘫痪（波特瘫痪）。[66,67]而活动加速了椎体的损坏。有人观察到，无论是疾病的自然进展或是外科关节融合术的干预，结核感染后一旦出现关节强直（骨融合后关节完全不动），“结核病程也随之迅速结束”。[68]因此衍生出一种治疗想法，“通过完善一种技术，将脊柱受累区域完全固定并阻止脊柱畸形的发生和进展”[69]。根据这一设想，1911 年拉塞尔·希伯斯[70]和弗雷德·阿尔比[71]于纽约分别完成了首次脊柱后路关节融合术，通过让邻近骨骼长到一起形成牢固的融合来消除关节活动，后路融合也间接地稳定了前方椎体。两种手术均采用后正中入路，不同之处在于，希伯斯更强调棘突的切割与重排，以及骨膜闭合，而不是额外植骨；阿尔比则通过条块状的自体胫骨移植来实现棘突间的牢固结合。在这之前的几年，慕尼黑的弗里茨·朗格曾试图实现相同的目标，他用丝线或钢丝将固定棒连接到棘突的两端。[72,73]但因缺乏具有可靠生物相容性的植入材料，植骨区接触部位发生了骨溶解，尝试失败了。

In the years that followed, posterior spinal arthrodesis became an accepted treatment for spinal tuberculosis. Hibbs and Albee never wavered in their support and recommended the operation for all patients well enough for the surgery. In 1918 Hibbs reported that 75% of 210 patients were cured, 10% were doubtful cures, and 15% were dead. Patients with disease durations of six months or less had an 82% cure rate, which was better than the general average of 75%.[74] A 1923 study of ten autopsy specimens obtained five weeks to eleven months post-Hibbs arthrodesis reported progressing arthrodesis healing in nine.[75] In 1928 Hibbs reported on 286 patients operated on from 1915 to 1920 with 71% cured, 3% not cured, and 26% deceased.[76] Albee did not report his cure rate, but in 1930 wrote that 90% of 865 patients had excellent or good results.[77] Many case series were published with most reporting favorable results. However, direct comparison of non-operated and operated on patients raised doubts about the effectiveness of posterior spine arthrodesis for treating tuberculous spondylitis. In a 1937 study comparing 100 non-operated to 50 comparable operated on patients, the percent good clinical results were 70% versus 32%, good radiological results 62% versus 38%, and late abscess formation 4% versus 40%.[78] In a 1940 radiographic study of anterior healing to fusion, 36% of cases not operated versus 34% of those operated on healed.[79] Soon after that, continuing public health measures and antimicrobial therapy that began with streptomycin provided prevention and cure for most tuberculosis in the United States[80] and the developed world. This did not hold true in developing nations so tuberculous spondylitis later made a comeback.

之后的数年，脊柱后路融合术被逐渐认可，成为脊柱结核公认的治疗方法。希伯斯和阿尔比也极力向患者推荐这项疗法。1918 年，希伯斯对 210 名患者进行了研究，治愈率为 75%，好转率为 10%，死亡率为 15%。病程小于 6 月的患者治愈率高达 82%，优于平均水平 75%。[74]1923 年，希伯斯对其关节融合术后 5 周到 11 个月的 10 个尸检标本的研究发现，其中 9 个均已实现关节融合。[75]1928 年，希伯斯观察了从 1915 年到 1920 年间接受手术的 286 名患者情况，其中 71%治愈，3%未治愈，26%死亡。[76]阿尔比没有提到其治愈率，但在 1930 年他提到 865 名患者中，90%的术后效果良好。[77]许多回顾性病例研究均显示了这种手术的良好疗效，然而，由于缺少手术组与非手术组的队列研究，也有人对脊柱融合术治疗结核性脊椎炎的疗效提出了质疑。1937 年的一项研究比较了 100 名未手术患者和 50 名手术患者，临床疗效良好的比例分别是 70%和 32%，影像学疗效良好的比例分别为 62%和 38%，晚期脓肿形成的比例分别为 4%和 40%。[78]1940 年的一项影像学比较研究中，36%的未手术患者和 34%的手术患者椎体前方损害均已愈合。[79]后来，公共卫生措施的推行和以链霉素为代表的抗生素治疗法使美国和其他发达国家的结核病得以预防和治疗。[80]但发展中国家的情况并非如此，之后结核性脊椎炎卷土重来。

Around 1911 in the United States the incidenceof tuberculosis was falling while that of poliomyelitis was rising.[81,82] By then the potential for scoliosis to develop and often progress to severe scoliosis after paralytic polio in childhood was well recognized. So, in 1914 Hibbs began using a slightly modified version of his posterior spinal arthrodesis procedure that he used to treat tuberculous spondylitis to stabilize post-polio scoliosis. Eleven months earlier Herbert Galloway had used the Albee technique to treat a six-year-old boy with post-polio scoliosis and gained the distinction of performing the first published case.[83] However, further experience soured him on the operation.[84] Recognizing that scoliosis was a more complex deformity than kyphosis, Hibbs extended the arthrodesis laterally to include "the articulation between the lateral processes, thus giving a cantilever effect." All eight (one female, seven male) patients in his initial report had either a positive history of infantile paralysis or "evidence of having the disease previously."[85] The same was true of his next publication in 1924 based on 59 (30 female, 29 male) consecutive patients operated on from 1914 to 1919 by him and three other surgeons at New York Orthopaedic Dispensary and Hospital.[86] From 1924 until his death in 1932 Hibbs and his colleagues, most notably radiologist Albert Ferguson and Joseph Risser from 1924 on, worked to improve the arthrodesis operation for treatment of scoliosis.[87] The indications for the operation, selection of arthrodesis levels, and arthrodesis technique matured early in their experience. The principal needs were better scoliosis correction and arthrodesis healing, both dependent on external correction and stabilization. This led to a series of improvements in casting technique that resulted in traction turnbuckle casts. From 1920 to 1927 there was a single hinge on the side, but after that an anterior and a posterior hinge were used, which improved the lateral bending effect.[88] This final version of the "wedging jacket, devised by Risser"[89] became generally known as either the Risser or traction turnbuckle cast, or just turnbuckle cast.[90] *See figure 4.4.*

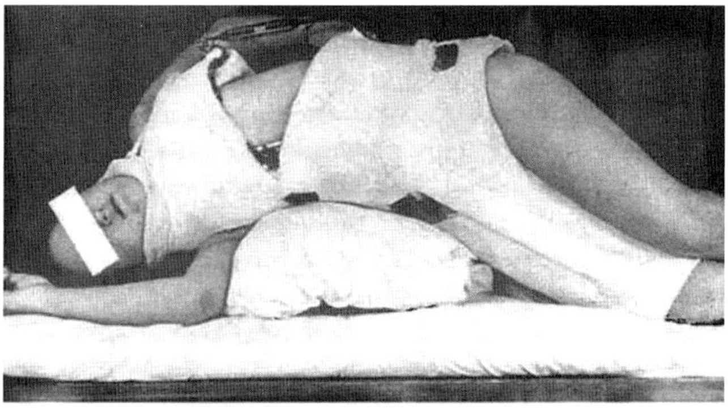

Figure 4.4 ***Risser turnbuckle cast designed to provide correction of scoliosis by oblique traction. Reprinted wih permission from Risser JC, Lunder CH. Norquist DM, Craig WA: Three Types of Body Casts in Pese CN (ed): Instructinnadl Course Lectures 10. Rosemont, IL, American Academy of Orthopaedic Strgeons, 1953, pp 131–142.***

图 4.4 为了通过侧方牵引来矫正脊柱侧凸所设计的里泽铰链石膏。授权后转载于 Risser JC, Lander CH, Norquist DM, Craig WA: Three Types of Body Casts in Pease CN (ed): Instructional Course Lectures 10. Rosemont, IL, American Academy of Orthopaedic Surgeons, 1953, pp 131–142

1911 年前后，美国结核病的发病率在下降，但脊髓灰质炎的发病率在上升。[81,82] 那时人们已经充分认识到，儿童期患脊髓灰质炎瘫痪之后，脊柱侧凸会不断发展，最终成为重度脊柱侧凸。因此，1914 年，希伯斯改进了他用来治疗结核性脊椎炎的脊柱后路融合术用，以阻止脊髓灰质炎后脊柱侧凸的进一步发展。在此之前的 11 个月，赫伯特·加洛韦首次采用阿尔比的方法治疗了一位患有脊髓灰质炎后脊柱侧凸的6岁男孩。[83]但是，更多的手术实践后，他对这种方法表示失望。[84]人们认识到脊柱侧凸要比脊柱后凸复杂得多，希伯斯将关节融合范围扩大到侧方，"通过横突间融合后的悬臂效应来阻止畸形进一步发展"。在他的初步报告中，共8例病例（1女7男）有婴儿期瘫痪的病史或患有脊髓灰质炎的其他证据。[85]1924年，他研究了从1914年到1919年的59名（30女29男）患者，得出了与此前相似的结果。这些患者都在纽约骨科医院接受了由他和其他三位外科医生主刀的脊髓灰质炎后脊柱侧凸手术。[86]从1924年到1932年去世，希伯斯和他的同事们，包括著名的放射科医生阿尔伯特·弗格森和约瑟夫·里泽始终致力于改进脊柱侧凸的脊柱关节融合术。[87]手术适应证的把握，关节融合范围的选择和手术技术早已是他们团队成员驾轻就熟的技能，但主要的问题在于如何更好地矫正脊柱侧凸，同时提高骨融合率，两者都依赖于外部的矫形和稳定方法。这促使石膏技术的一系列改进，最终牵引铰链石膏诞生了。从1920年到1927年，石膏的侧面仅有一个铰链，但之后采用前后双铰链的结构增加侧方屈曲的效果。[88]"由里泽设计的楔形石膏"[89]成为最终版本，称为里泽铰链石膏或牵引铰链石膏，或仅称为铰链石膏，并广泛为人所知。[90]（图4.4）

Hibbs' last publication was in 1931, and it reported a series of 360 patients, who were operated on from June 1914 to June 1927. The series included the first patient Hibbs had operated on for scoliosis and did not include any patients treated with Risser turnbuckle casts. One hundred sixty (76 females, 84 males) of them had prior poliomyelitis, and 184 (141 females, 43 males) had no demonstrable cause. The authors believed the majority of these "may have been due to an intrinsic muscle imbalance" from infantile paralysis and did not comment on the striking difference in sex distribution between the post-polio and the "no demonstrable cause" groups. Fourteen of the remaining sixteen had congenital scoliosis, and two had scoliosis secondary to empyema, a chest cavity abscess. Two percent (7 of 360) died of perioperative complications. At least a two-year follow-up was available for 79% (285 of 360). Lasting scoliosis correction of 5° or more was found in only 27% (76 of 285), although lasting correction of 5° to 15° had improved from 4% to 42% midway through the series. Pseudarthrosis, the failure of arthrodesis to result in fusion, was documented or suspected in 5.3% (15 of 285). One of the authors' conclusions was that "constant cast support of the correction should be applied for from six to twelve months after correction."[91] No patient-based end-result studies were reported.

1931年希伯斯发表的最后一篇文章提到了360名患者，这些患者于1914年6

月至 1927 年 6 月间接受了手术。研究排除了接受里泽铰链石膏治疗的患者。其中 160 人（76 女 84 男）有脊髓灰质炎病史，184 人（141 女 43 男）无明确病因。作者认为大部分脊柱侧凸是脊髓灰质炎后躯干肌力失衡所致，但并没有描述脊髓灰质炎后脊柱侧凸患者与未明确病因的患者出现显著性别差异的原因。其余 16 人中有 14 例先天性脊柱侧凸，2 例继发于脓胸的脊柱侧凸。2%（7/360）死于围手术期并发症。79%的患者（285/360）至少进行了为期两年的随访。尽管中期随访时经过持续矫正，获得 5°到 15°侧凸矫正的比例从 4%提高到 42%，但末次随访时依然维持 5°以上侧凸矫正的患者仅为 27%（76/285）。假关节，即关节融合术失败的发生率约为 5.3%（15/285）。作者的其中一条结论是“矫形术后 6 到 12 月内应持续应用石膏辅助固定”[91]，但并没有基于此项结论的最终研究成果。

Hibbs' successors at the New York Orthopaedic Dispensary and Hospital continued publishing in the 1930s. Risser and Ferguson documented the relationship between scoliosis curvature increase and rapidity of growth regardless of etiology, adding that curvature ceased when vertebral growth stopped, which was at or before age sixteen years in girls and seventeen in boys.[92] Butte described this hospital's method of determining fusion end vertebrae.[93] Allan DeForest Smith reported on the 301 (213 female, 88 male) patients operated on from 1928 through 1935. The diagnosis was "idiopathic or unknown" in 197, post-polio in 86, and other in 18. Sex distribution was not provided for the diagnostic categories. Treatment included curve correction and immobilization with the Risser turnbuckle cast in 265 patients.[94] Three to four weeks were spent obtaining curve correction. The Hibbs arthrodesis, including facet curetting and local bone graft only, was then done in cast. An average of two operations per patient was performed. The patients were maintained in plaster for a total of nine months, three months of which were spent in the preoperatively placed turnbuckle cast, three months in an ambulatory semi-bent cast, and three months in a straight body cast. There were 2 (0.66%, 2 of 301) deaths related to the operation. Pseudarthrosis occurred in 23% (61 of 265). Follow-up details at an average of 4 years, 4 months (range, 1 to 10 years) were available for 97% (257 of 265) of the turnbuckle cast treated patients. Curve correction of 50% to 90% was obtained and 30% to 80% maintained. A composite estimate of result was reported for 257 patients with 51% excellent, 28% good, 16% fair, and 5% poor. These results were better than those at the beginning of the twentieth century, but they had come from one center, revealed a disturbing increase in pseudarthrosis as correction was improved, and were based on a very time-consuming regimen for the patient and caregivers. Furthermore, the reproducibility of these results was unknown. There was plenty of room for improvement.

20 世纪 30 年代，纽约骨科医院希伯斯的继任者们依然不断地发表研究成果。里泽和弗格森描述了脊柱侧凸进展程度与脊柱生长速度之间的关系（不考虑病因）。同时指出当女孩 16 岁、男孩 17 岁左右脊柱停止生长时，侧凸也不再加剧。[92]比特介绍了医院确定融合端椎的方法。[93]艾伦·德弗雷斯特·史密斯研究了从 1928 年到 1935 年进行手术的 301 名患者（女 213 男 88），197 例为特发性或病因未知的脊柱侧凸，86 例为脊髓灰质炎后脊柱侧凸，18 例为其他类型的脊柱侧凸，但此研究未提供不同诊断类别的性别分布情况。其中 265 名患者的治疗方法包括以里泽铰链石膏行矫形和制动。[94]患者在 3 到 4 周内获得侧凸矫正，通过小关节刮除和局部骨移植进行希伯斯融合，并用石膏维持。每名患者平均要接受两次手术，石膏固定 9 个月，其中术前 3 个月采用铰链石膏，3 个月采用活动的半屈曲石膏，3 个月采用直的躯体石膏。2 例死亡与手术相关（0.66%，2/301），假关节发生率为 23%（61/265），97%的患者（257/265）获得了平均 4.4 年（1～10 年）的随访。不同病因的矫正率在 50%～90%，而随访期的矫正率在 30%～80%。对 257 名患者的综合疗效评估，优秀占比 51%，良好占比 28%，变化不大占比 16%，疗效不佳占比 5%。这些结果显然比 20 世纪初要好得多，但这只是来源于单中心的研究成果。随着畸形矫正率的提升，假关节发生率也不断增加，且这套治疗措施无论对患者或医生来说都是极其耗时的方案。此外，这些结果的可重复性未被证实，且依然有很大的改进空间。

The reproducibility of results question would be answered in 1941 with publication of a landmark study conducted by the research committee of the American Orthopaedic Association (AOA) that was titled "End-Result Study of the Treatment of Idiopathic Scoliosis."[95] When and why did the shift in focus from post-polio scoliosis to idiopathic scoliosis occur? Slowly, as Reginald H. Sayre in 1892 mentioned idiopathic lateral curvature,[96] and before him Henry Reeves had declared that scoliosis was the most common idiopathic deviation of the spine.[97] There were probably others who touched on this topic, but at least in the United States the term idiopathic scoliosis is usually attributed to Samuel Kleinberg, who used it in 1922 and again in 1929 to explain the fact that in the majority of scoliosis patients he treated no cause could be found.[98,99] This observation apparently resonated with the experience of his colleagues, and his terminology stuck. The AOA "End-Result Study" was well focused on the most common scoliosis category, avoiding a common pitfall of analyzing data on the basis of deformity rather than the underlying disease, even a disease of exclusion (e. g., idiopathic scoliosis). It included 425 patients treated at 16 major North American centers. Females predominated four to one. The average age at which scoliosis was noted, considered the age of onset, was twelve years (range, two to nineteen years), and 55% presented for treatment within a year of onset. The presenting complaint was cosmetic in 92% spine curvature, a high or prominent shoulder, or a prominent hip. Curve severity was measured on a radiograph taken standing using what became known as the Cobb method of measurement.100,101 *See figure 4.5*. Scoliosis curves were rated as mild (0°–20°), moderate (25°–40°), and severe (>45°). Initially, 185 patients were treated with exercise, usually in conjunction with some type of brace, 180 had surgery (arthrodesis and cast), and the remaining 60 patients apparently had no treatment. Thirty-four patients in the two non-surgery groups eventually had surgery. All 425 patients were followed for 1 to 10 years and 76% of them for 2 to 10 years. All were at least fifteen years old at follow-up, and 84% were sixteen years or older, making it likely that most patients were fully grown. For the 185 patients treated with exercise, the curve on X-ray was unchanged or improved in 39% and was increased in 61%. For those who had surgery, additional bone grafts were used in 60%, and the average curve correction was 65% postoperative and 27% at follow-up. Pseudarthrosis occurred in 28%, and other complications were reported in 10.2%.

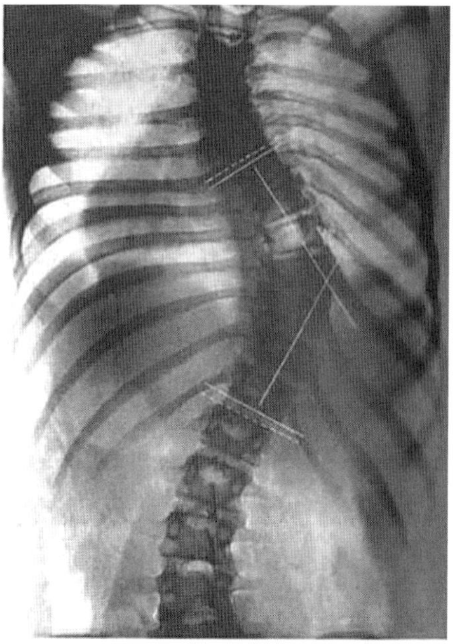

Figure 4. 5 ***Trunk radiograph viwed posteroanterior with markings illustrating a 60° scoliosis using the measurement technique suggested by Robert Linppman to John Cobb in 1935 and subsequently widely adopted as the Cobb measurement, It was used in the AOA "End-Result Study" and is in universal use today Reprinted with permission from Alfred R. Shands, Jr. Joseph S. Barr; Paul C. Golonna, Lawrence Noall, "End-Result Study of the Treatment of ldiopathic Scoliosis," J Bone Joint Surg 23(1941):968. figure 3.***

图 4.5 采用 1935 年罗伯特 · 利普曼和约翰 · 柯布提出的方法测量躯干后前位 X 片上的侧弯角度为 60°,之后泛称柯布测量法。此法在美国骨科学会的"最终结果研究"中被采用并沿用至今。授权后转载于:Alfred R. Shands, Jr. Joseph S. Barr, Paul C. Colonna, Lawrence Noall, "End-Result Study of the Treatment of Idiopathic Scoliosis," JBJS 23(1941): 968, figure 3

1941 年，美国骨科学会研究委员会发表了一项具有里程碑意义的研究，题为“特发性脊柱侧凸治疗的最终结果研究”，回答了结果的可重复性问题。[95]什么时候、什么原因导致了研究焦点从脊髓灰质炎后脊柱侧凸转移到特发性脊柱侧凸？这一过程其实很久。1892 年雷金纳德 · H. 塞尔就提到特发性脊柱侧方弯曲，[96]甚至在此之前，亨利 · 里夫斯就已指出脊柱侧凸是最常见的脊柱特发性偏斜。[97]也许还有其他人谈论过这个话题，但至少在美国，人们认为特发性脊柱侧凸是塞缪尔 · 克莱因伯格最先提出的，他在 1922 年和 1929 年均使用这一术语来描述大多数找不到原因的脊柱弯曲情况。[98,99]这一术语在很多有相同经历的同道中产生共鸣，因此沿用下来。美国骨科学会的“最终结局研究”敏锐地聚焦于最常见的脊柱侧凸的分类，提出不能仅限于畸形的形态去分析数据，而更应该结合其病因进行研究，包括排除性诊断（如特发性脊柱侧凸），也应该是侧凸分类的一种。该研究分析了在 16 个北美医疗中心接受治疗的 425 名患者，男女比例为 1∶4。发现脊柱侧凸时即为发病年龄，平均年龄为 12 岁（2~19 岁），55%的患者在确诊后一年内接受治疗。92%的主诉是脊柱偏斜，高低肩或髋部突出影响美观。通过站立位 X 光片测量角度（柯布测量法）以确定侧凸严重程度。[100,101]（图 4.5）脊柱侧凸分为轻度（0~20°），中度（25°~40°），重度（>45°）。最初，185 名患者接受支具结合运动治疗，180 名患者接受手术（关节融合术联合石膏固定），其余 60 名患者未接受任何治疗，最终两个非手术组中有 34 名患者还是接受了手术。425 名患者平均被随访了 1 至 10 年，其中 76%的患者被随访 2 至 10 年。所有患者在末次随访时均在 15 岁或以上，其中 84%患者在 16 岁以上，这时大多数患者骨骼均已发育成熟。运动治疗组中的 185 名患者有 39%角度不变或改善，61%发生角度增大。而对于手术组，60%的患者接受了取骨植骨，术后平均矫正率为 65%，随访时为 27%。假关节发生率为 28%，其他并发症发生率为 10.2%。

The authors developed a qualitative outcome rating scale based on clinical appearance and X-ray measurement. Considering all 425 patients, 31% were rated excellent or good and 69% fair or poor. Children aged two to ten years fared the worst as none had excellent or good results. The 149 in the Risser turnbuckle cast and arthrodesis subgroup fared the best of all the patients: 35% were rated excellent or good and 63% fair or poor. The authors also developed a qualitative outcome rating scale based on the clinical appearance of the back at the end of follow-up as compared to when first seen. Patients managed by observation were considered to have unchanged or better back appearance in 88% and worse in 12%. Patients treated with exercise augmented by bracing were rated as unchanged or better in 64% and worse in 36%. No patients treated by cast correction without arthrodesis were improved. The Risser turnbuckle cast and arthrodesis group did the best with 89% unchanged or improved and 11% worse.

作者基于临床表现和X光片测量结果开发了一种定性评价量表。在所有425名患者中，31%获评优秀或良好，69%为一般或不佳。两岁到十岁年龄段的孩子结果最差，没有一个优秀或良好。里泽铰链石膏联合关节融合术治疗组的149名患者表现最好，其中35%为优秀或良好，63%为一般或不佳。作者还根据末次随访和首次就诊时的背部外观比较情况制订了一份定性评价量表。发现88%的患者认为背部外观有改善或无明显变化，12%的患者背部外观变差。接受支具结合运动疗法的患者中，64%的患者认为背部外观有改善或无明显变化，36%的患者认为外观变差。未行关节融合术仅接受石膏治疗的患者无一例获得改善。里泽铰链石膏结合关节融合术的患者对疗效最为满意，89%的患者背部外观有改善或无明显变化，仅11%的患者认为外观变差。

The answers for idiopathic scoliosis were clear. Results in patients with scoliosis appearing before the age of ten years were poor even with early treatment. About 14%(34 of 245 patients) initially treated nonoperatively with either no treatment or exercise augmented by bracing progressed to the point of requiring surgery. Exercise accompanied by bracing was not successful for moderate curves. The Risser turnbuckle cast and arthrodesis yielded better results than other types of treatment, but this success was hardly convincing as there were more fair or poor results (63%) than good or excellent (35%) when the qualitative scale considering both clinical appearance and X-ray measurement was used. In addition, achieving even these results came with a heavy price of prolonged cast immobilization and considerable curve correction loss. On the basis of their study the authors recommended three months of recumbence in a cast followed by support for an additional seven to nine months after ambulation was begun. AOA "End-Result Study" results were generally extrapolated to apply to the more severe post-polio scoliosis. Although the results left much to be desired, the Risser turnbuckle cast and arthrodesis did offer a means of stabilizing progressive curves. But there was obviously considerable room for improvement. At this point the start of World War II appeared to cast a pall over further advances in scoliosis treatment.

特发性脊柱侧凸的治疗效果是明显的。10岁前出现的脊柱侧凸，即使接受早期治疗，其最终结局也不尽如人意。约14%（34/254）早期接受非手术治疗（支具结合运动疗法）或未接受治疗的患者，最终发展到需要手术的程度。对于中度的脊柱侧凸，支具结合运动疗法是无效的。里泽铰链石膏结合关节融合术显示出最优的疗效，但这种成功并不值得称道，因为通过 X 线测量比较，疗效一般或不佳的患者比例为 63%，依然高于疗效优秀或良好的患者（35%）。此外，为了达到理想疗效，患者要付出长期接受石膏固定的巨大代价，而且矫正后还会有很大程度的复发。基于这项研究，作者们建议术后石膏保护卧床三个月，下床活动后继续佩戴石膏保护 7 到 9 个月。美国骨科学会的“最终结局研究”结论被推广应用到更加严重的脊髓灰质炎后脊柱侧凸。尽管结果还是不尽如人意，但里泽铰链石膏结合关节融合术确实提供了一种控制畸形加剧的方法。这当然还有很大的改进余地。然而，此时爆发的第二次世界大战给脊柱侧凸治疗的发展蒙上了阴影。

（宋智博 译　王迎松 于滨生 审校）

5 RESPONDING TO THE POLIO EPIDEMIC (1947–59)

Climate of tragedy accepted[1]

He was right on the nip and tuck of being totally washed out of the system[2]

应对脊髓灰质炎流行（1947—1959）

接受这种悲剧性社会氛围[1]

他正处于被体制彻底淘汰的边缘[2]

Soon after his agreement with McKeever ended, Harrington accepted the invitation of Joseph B. Foster, MD to assume responsibility for the patients of the National Foundation for Infantile Paralysis (NFIP) in Houston. Foster, a native Texan, as a graduate of the University of Texas Medical Branch in Galveston and received his orthopedic training at Massachusetts General Hospital and Boston Children's Hospital. He was a leader in the Houston orthopedic community and served as chairman of the advisory committee for the Harris County Chapter of the NFIP, the Texas Society for Crippled Children, and the Crippled Children's Division of the State Department of Health. In 1943 he became professor of orthopedic surgery and chairman of the Department of Orthopedics at the Baylor University College of Medicine when it moved to Houston. Although he died in 1949 at the age of 54, the usefulness of the Foster reversible orthopedic bed he devised for patients requiring frequent turning outlived him by decades.[3,4]

在与麦基弗合约到期后不久，哈灵顿接受了约瑟夫·B. 福斯特博士的邀请，负责位于休斯敦的国家小儿麻痹基金会的病人。福斯特是得克萨斯州本地人，毕业于得克萨斯大学加尔维斯顿医学分部，并在麻省总医院和波士顿儿童医院接受了骨科专科培训。他是休斯敦骨科学界的领军人物，并担任国家小儿麻痹基金会哈里斯县分会咨询委员会、得克萨斯州残疾儿童协会以及得克萨斯州卫生部残疾儿童部门主席。1943 年当贝勒大学医学院迁至休斯敦后，他成为骨科教授并出任贝勒大学医学院骨科主任。福斯特于 1949 年逝世，时年 54 岁，他为那些需要频繁翻身的病人设计的可翻转骨科治疗床，在他去世后仍沿用多年。[3,4]

At the time Harrington accepted responsibility for these patients, the NFIP had for years been leasing the ninth floor of the old Jefferson Davis Hospital where they provided treatment for polio cases. He recalled going to survey the situation and being shown around by Miss Prudence, the nurse in charge. “There were nine chronically ill patients who had been there for some time, and most of their families lived there as well, which was the usual thing. They had a dining room in which they fed each other. They had stoves, boxes had been brought into the hospital, they had laundry facilities. The nine patients were cared for by the mother and father and sisters and it was almost a big family unit.... [This] seemed to be a well-run organization on the basis just described, with one P.T. showing up daily taking care of the patients with Miss Prudence in charge of the nurses and having some help from some other shifts, one or two maids and that was the course of the whole event.... This was all paid for by the NFIP.... This was in 1947 late and early 1948. I had been told there had been very little polio, acute, certainly no epidemic.... Yet within six months we started having an epidemic.”[5] Although Harrington’s writings and recollections leave some doubt about when the polio epidemic began in Houston, the documentation available supports 1948 as the first epidemic year in Houston.[6]

在哈灵顿承担起照顾这些病人的职责时，国家小儿麻痹基金会多年来一直租用老旧的杰斐逊·戴维斯医院的九楼，为脊髓灰质炎患者提供治疗。他回忆起主管护士普鲁登丝小姐带领自己去视察时的情况。“有 9 名慢性患者在那里住了一段时间，他们的大多数家人也住在那里，这在当时是很常见的事情。有一个餐厅供他们解决伙食。他们还把炉子、箱子和洗衣机带进了医院。9 名病人由父母和姐妹们照顾，几乎是一大家子……这似乎是一个运作良好的机构，每天都有一名理疗师来照顾病人，普鲁登丝小姐领导护士，还有一两个女佣帮忙，基本就是这样的情况……这些费用都是由国家小儿麻痹基金会支付的……那是在1947年年底和1948年年初。他们告诉我那里几乎没有脊髓灰质炎，肯定没有流行……然而，不到6个月，这里就开始出现流行。”[5]虽然在哈灵顿的著作和回忆中脊髓灰质炎在休斯敦的流行时间留有疑问，但现有文献表明脊髓灰质炎流行始于1948年。[6]

During the lull before this storm hit, on October 12, 1947, Mary Alice gave birth to the couple's third and last child, Richard Eugene. The Harrington children have this memory of their mother. "Our Mother, Mary Alice, was Daddy's partner, as he himself said. She made all he did possible. She was beautiful inside and out, smart, a talented seamstress and gardener, and a wonderful cook. She was in charge at home—she created a refuge for Daddy to come home to. Daddy left the house for work at 6:30 every day. They had an agreement that work did not come home. This did not, however, include the fact that we had a spine hanging from the doorknob in their bedroom. Daddy was home for our family dinner every night-6:30 and no excuses."[7]

1947年10月12日，在这场风暴来临之前的宁静中，玛丽·艾丽斯生下了他们的第三个也是最后一个孩子理查德·尤金。哈灵顿家的孩子们对他们的母亲有这样的记忆。“我们的母亲，玛丽·艾丽斯，就像父亲自己说的那样，是他的合伙人。她使他所做的一切都成为可能。她秀外慧中，是一个有才华的裁缝和园丁，还是一个很棒的厨师。她是家里的主人，她为爸爸创造了一个避难所。爸爸每天六点半出门上班。他们有一个协议，不将工作带回家。然而，这并不包括他们卧室门把手上挂着一串脊柱的事实。爸爸每天晚上六点半回家，和家人一起吃晚饭，从不找借口不回家。”[7]

In the spring of 1948, three years after the end of World War II, Houston experienced a major polio epidemic. It returned every spring and summer until the Salk attenuated virus vaccine was introduced in 1955.[8] Epidemics occurred in other locations, but Houston was especially hard hit; Harrington's recollections were that approximately 300 to 400 new polio patients were treated and more than 30 iron lungs acquired the first year.[9,10] By 1957 approximately 4,000 post-polio patients had been managed.[11] (The number of patients varied between 3,000 and 4,000 in different estimations.) In the acute phase of polio, diagnosis and management were usually provided by a pediatrician or internist, but since none was available, Harrington set up the emergency room protocol. Every patient admitted to the ER was to be seen by the doctor on call to obtain the following: a history of progressive headache, documented fever, presence of a meningeal irritation as evidenced by neck stiffness or positive straight leg raising, positive findings of paralysis or weakness, and a breathing capacity with anything below 1,200 cc as abnormal. Paralysis did not automatically mean polio until a spinal tap was done and a high cellular count found. Patients with positive findings as well as those with paralysis and a positive spinal tap were admitted to the ninth floor where they were reexamined by Harrington.[12] He had estimated that the polio floor would hold at least 100 patients, especially if many were in cribs. All families living on the floor and their excess baggage had to be moved out, and the staff necessary to care for ill, sometimes critically ill patients moved in. The NFIP provided extensive help in providing nursing and physical therapy staff. After consulting Wallace Cole, a Minneapolis orthopedic surgeon, the Sister Kinney approach to therapy was adopted, which included hot pack treatment, bed splitting and rolling, and periodic checks of the patient's physiology.[13]

1948 年春天，也就是第二次世界大战结束三年后，休斯敦经历了严重的脊髓灰质炎流行。它在每年的春夏时爆发，直到 1955 年脊髓灰质炎病毒疫苗的出现。[8]脊髓灰质炎在其他地方也流行过，但在休斯敦尤其严重。据哈灵顿回忆，在第一年就有大约 300 到 400 名新发脊髓灰质炎患者接受治疗，其中 30 多名患者需要用到铁肺。[9,10]到 1957 年，大约有 4 000 名脊髓灰质炎患者得到了治疗。[11]（根据不同的估计，患者人数在 3 000 至 4 000 人之间）。在脊髓灰质炎急性期，通常由儿科医生或内科医生诊治，但由于缺少人手，哈灵顿建立了急诊室流程。每一个被送进急诊室的病人都由值班医生接诊，筛查是否有以下异常：持续性头痛，发热史，存在颈项强直或直腿抬高实验阳性等脑膜刺激症状，瘫痪或无力，肺活量低于 1 200 cc。瘫痪并不意味着脊髓灰质炎，还需要腰穿结果证实细胞计数升高。检查结果呈阳性以及有瘫痪且腰穿结果呈阳性的患者都被送入九楼，由哈灵顿再次检查。[12]他估计脊髓灰质炎楼层至少能容纳 100 名患者，特别是多数病人可能需要使用婴儿床。所有住在这层楼里的家庭和他们多余的行李都要搬出，把位置留给照顾患者（包括危重症患者）的工作人员。国家小儿麻痹基金会在提供护理和理疗人员方面提供了很多的帮助。在咨询了明尼阿波利斯骨科医生华莱士·科尔之后，金尼修女的治疗方法被采用，她的治疗方法包括热敷疗法、翻身以及定期检查患者的生理状况。[13]

After a few months Harrington was buried in an avalanche of work, spending eight to ten hours in the polio unit and making periodic trips to handle an emergency or examine one or two patients in his private office, after which he often returned to the ninth floor and stayed until midnight. Soon the Department of Pediatrics at Baylor sent a resident, Helen Pratt, to help. Harrington remembered her doing a beautiful job and taking a lot of work off his shoulders. In addition, ears, nose, and throat residents were assigned to do tracheostomies and assist with their care as needed. To complement the emergency and inpatient care necessary to manage the 1arge patient volume, Harrington established and personally staffed the clinics necessary for outpatient follow-up.[14]

几个月后，哈灵顿在繁忙的工作中连轴转，他在脊髓灰质炎中心要工作8~10个小时，还需要定期出差处理紧急情况或在私人办公室检查一两个病人，之后他经常返回九楼的病房并直到午夜才离开。很快，贝勒医学院儿科派了一位住院医生海伦·普拉特前来支援。哈灵顿回忆，普拉特干得很棒并替他分担了很多工作。此外，耳鼻喉科住院医生也被派来负责气管切开术，并在需要时协助他们的治疗。为了更好地管理急诊和住院治疗，以能够服务更多的患者，哈灵顿组织人力建立了门诊随访所必需的诊所。[14]

An antiviral medication would have been agodsend for these patients and their physicians. Since Harrington had clinically researched the use of sulfa drugs at an earlier time, he endorsed the work of Murray Sanders in nearby Galveston whose team had just reported that a brand of phenosulfazole (Darvisul©, Lederle) was an effective antiviral against experimental murine SK poliomyelitis virus. Their work later appeared in print.[15] In the summer of 1948 Harrington developed an uncontrolled series in which the outcomes in 79 treated patients were compared to 207 untreated. At Sanders' suggestion he started with a dose of 200 mg which, based on lack of toxic reaction, was gradually increased to 900 mg per kg of body weight per 24 hours. Harrington was encouraged as only 1 of the 79 (1%) treated patients died whereas 13 of the 207 (6%) untreated did. When he presented his study at the annual section on pediatrics of the State Medical Association of Texas in San Antonio on May 3, 1949, his discussant cited three negative findings. First, in the previous summer in Galveston, using doses up to 450 mg per kg of body weight, no clinical benefit had been found. Second, the same results had been reported in a carefully controlled series in North Carolina. Third, a later study of phenosulfazole effect on murine SK poliomyelitis had been negative, thus not confirming Sanders' report.[16] This ended Harrington's attempts to modify clinical poliomyelitis with sulfa medication, but not before he had presented his study to the NFIP, which turned it down. This was a major disappointment for him because he felt that had patients with bulbar polio received sulfa, they would not have died.[17]

抗病毒药物的问世对患者和医生来说是场及时雨。由于哈灵顿早些时候曾对磺胺类药物的使用进行过临床研究，他认同加尔维斯顿附近的默里·桑德斯团队近期的研究工作，该研究发现酚磺胺噻唑（Darvisul ©，Lederle）可作为有效对抗实验小鼠 SK 脊髓灰质炎病毒的药物，该研究随后得以发表。[15] 1948 年夏天，哈灵顿用一个非对照队列研究比较了 79 名接受治疗的患者和 207 名未接受治疗的患者的预后情况。在桑德斯的建议下，哈灵顿从 200 mg 的剂量开始给药，并在没有毒性反应的基础上，逐渐增加到每天每千克体重 900 mg 的剂量。让哈灵顿备受鼓舞的是，相比于未接受治疗的 207 名患者中有 13 人（6%）死亡，接受治疗的 79 名患者中只有 1 人（1%）死亡。1949 年 5 月 3 日，当他在圣安东尼奥举行的德州医学会儿科年度会议上报告他的研究时，与会的讨论嘉宾引用了三个反证。首先，既往夏季在加尔维斯顿地区使用每公斤体重 450 mg 的剂量，未发现有临床疗效。其次，同样的结果也曾在北卡罗来纳州的一个严格对照的系列中报道过。第三，后来的一项关于酚磺胺噻唑对小鼠 SK 脊髓灰质炎影响的研究呈阴性结果，因此并未证实桑德斯的报告。[16]国家小儿麻痹基金会其实在此之前就拒绝了哈灵顿提交的研究计划，但实际上是这次事件终止了他试图用磺胺类药物治疗临床脊髓灰质炎的尝试。哈灵顿非常失望，因为他觉得如果脊髓灰质炎患者接受了磺胺药物的治疗，他们就不会死亡。[17]

When Basil O'Connor returned to the NFIP from his full-time job as head of the American Red Cross during World War Ⅱ, he was disappointed that very little polio research progress had been achieved in the interim.[18] Accordingly, he tried to refocus the NFIP's scientific program. To do this, he established a director of research position and filled it with an anatomist based on his leadership skills rather than his curriculum vitae. The man he chose, Harry Weaver, was probably an iconoclast. From 1946 through 1953 his work was guided by the principle that a safe and effective vaccine was the best, indeed the only, method of controlling polio. To accomplish this goal, three obstacles had to be overcome. The number of poliovirus types had to be determined, a safe and reliable source of each of the viruses had to be developed, and the pathogenesis or pathway through which disease developed had to be discovered.[19] Central to Weaver's leadership was management of the funds needed to support these projects.[20] He had to find the right investigators, many at universities, and then adequately fund them long-term. The typing program research was tiring work that created substantial overhead expenses. To assure participation of the most qualified investigators, Weaver worked out formulas to compensate their institutions for overhead.

当巴兹尔·奥康纳结束了在第二次世界大战期间担任的美国红十字会主席的全职工作，回到国家小儿麻痹基金会时，他对在此期间脊髓灰质炎的研究几乎没有进展感到失望。[18]因此，他尝试重新聚焦国家小儿麻痹基金会的科学项目。为此，他设立了一个研究主任的职位，并根据其领导能力而不是履历聘请了一位解剖学家来担任这个职务。他的人选，哈利·韦弗，或许是个离经叛道的人。从1946年到1953年，他的工作原则是：安全、有效的疫苗是控制脊髓灰质炎最好的，甚至是唯一的方法。要实现这一目标，必须克服三个障碍。必须确定脊髓灰质炎病毒类型的数量，需要明确每一种病毒安全、可靠的来源，以及发现相应的发病机制。[19]韦弗领导的核心是管理支持这些项目所需的资金。[20]他必须找到合适的研究人员，然后为他们提供充足的长期资金，这些研究人员许多来自大学。分型研究是一项艰辛的工作，且花费巨大。为了保证最有资质的科研人员的参与，韦弗制订了一些方案来补偿他们机构的开销。

To guarantee the required supply of healthy research monkeys, the NFIP established a conditioning farm. The typing project, which alone used over 17,000 monkeys, was in full operation by 1949 and achieved an answer in 1951. The 196 tested strains fit into three types, which made production of a vaccine achievable. Maintaining a safe and steady supply of virus using monkeys was very expensive and complicated by the presence of monkey neural tissue. Tissue culture was a promising alternative, but it had been tried in 1936 with the finding that nerve tissue was necessary for the virus to survive. The experiment, done at the Rockefeller Institute by Sabin and Olitsky, seemed to have forever put the possibility of tissue culture to rest.[21] However, in 1948 it occurred to John Enders that since the virus grew in the body in nonneural tissue it should do the same in tissue culture, and it did![22] Sabin and Olitsky ***had*** been blindsided by the virus they used, Simon Flexner's highly neurotrophic "MV" virus that would only grow in nervous tissue.[23] Enders and his two resident colleagues, Tom Weller and Fred Robbins, received a Nobel Prize for this breakthrough, which opened the way to the safe and secure viral source necessary for vaccine production.

为了保证研究所需的健康猴子的供应，国家小儿麻痹基金会建立了一个培育农场。光是分型项目就用了17 000多只猴子，于1949年全面运行并在1951年便取得了进展。196株被测试的毒株被分为三种类型，使得疫苗的生产成为可能。利用猴子来维持安全、稳定的病毒供应是非常昂贵的，而且还因猴子神经组织的存在而变得复杂。组织培养是一种极具潜力的替代方案，但 1936 年的研究发现神经组织是病毒存活所必需的。这个由萨宾和奥利茨基在洛克菲勒研究所完成的实验，似乎永远终结了组织培养的可能性。[21]然而，1948 年约翰·恩德斯突然想到，既然病毒是在人体的非神经组织中生长的，它应该在组织培养中也能做到这一点，它的确做到了！[22]萨宾和奥利茨基被他们使用的病毒限制了，这种病毒是由西蒙·弗莱克斯纳提纯的高度亲神经的"MV"病毒，只能在神经组织中生长。[23]恩德斯和他的两位住院医师同事汤姆·韦勒和弗雷德·罗宾斯因为这一突破而获得了诺贝尔奖，这为疫苗生产开辟了安全、可靠的病毒来源。

The third obstacle to developing a vaccine was uncertainty about the pathogenesis by which the virus reached the central nervous system. The two possibilities seemed to be either direct passage from the nose along the olfactory nerves or viremia, circulation through the bloodstream. The direct passage possibility had been researched and championed by Simon Flexner, where laboratory studies supported this theory. By the early 1940s, however, several studies refuted the olfactory nerve pathway.[24] But evidence for polio viremia was lacking until 1943[25] when Dorothy Horstmann, a Yale researcher, deduced and proved in monkeys and chimpanzees (1951)[26] and latcr in humans during the incubation stage (1952)[27] that the viremia occurred very early in the infection. This finding meant that the virus was being killed by the relatively small amounts of antibody produced from the earliest occurrence of viremia.

研制疫苗的第三个障碍是病毒到达中枢神经系统的发病机制尚不明确。有两种可能，一种是从鼻子直接通过嗅神经进入中枢，另一种是通过病毒血症经血液循环进入中枢。西蒙·弗莱克斯纳以实验研究结果支持前者。然而，到 20 世纪 40 年代初，几项研究结果反对嗅神经通路这一设想。[24]直到 1943 年[25]，耶鲁大学的研究人员多萝西·霍斯特曼在猴子实验中推断并证明了病毒血症发生在感染早期，并于 1951 年[26]和 1952 年[27]分别在黑猩猩和人体中证明了潜伏期内存在病毒血症。这一发现意味着仅有少量病毒在早期病毒血症中被相应抗体所杀灭。

The science was now in place to support vaccine research. Although success was achieved in 1954 and reported the following year, the road to a commercially available vaccine was still fraught with hazard.[28]

尽管 1954 年已经有了支持疫苗研究的科学依据并于次年报道，但通往可获得的疫苗商业化的道路仍然充满艰险。[28]

Harrington was involved in all aspects of managing polio epidemics and from 1949 to 1959 served as chairman of the Polio Committee of the Harris County Medical Society.[29] As the epidemic progressed, his attention was drawn to rehabilitation. This led to his development of a standing bed as a means of preventing the damaging effects of recumbence, which included bone demineralization, muscle atrophy, vasomotor instability, and proprioception (information about the movements and position of the body) loss.[30] In 1949–50 he participated in a failed effort to establish what was to have been named the Barr Foundation as a patient memorial. Its goals were lofty; the initial projects were envisioned to be a combination bed to accommodate standing and a portable respirator as well as extensive stool studies.[31] This never-activated dream illustrated his desire to do something constructive.

哈灵顿参与了处理脊髓灰质炎流行的各个方面的工作，并于1949年至1959年担任哈里斯县医学会脊髓灰质炎委员会主席。[29]随着疫情的发展，他更关注于疫情后的康复方面。因此他开发了一种站立床，用于减轻卧床的并发症，包括骨矿流失、肌肉萎缩、血管舒缩不稳定和本体感觉（关于身体的动作和位置的信息）丧失。[30] 1949年至1950年他参与了巴尔基金会（为纪念一位患者而命名）的成立，但最终以失败告终。巴尔基金会的目标是崇高的，最初的项目设想是发明一种可容纳便携式呼吸机以及便于开展广泛粪便研究的立式组合床。[31]这个从未付诸实践的梦想表明哈灵顿非常渴望做一些开创性工作。

With time Harrington's focus progressively shifted to the evaluation and management of post-polio musculoskeletal deformities, the traditional focus of orthopedics. Some muscle imbalances, especially the milder ones involving an adult's foot and ankle, could be managed with an orthosis (brace)[32]. However, the operative volume was steadily increasing as extremity muscle imbalances in children often caused flexible or fixed deformity that required tendon transfer, osteotomy, arthrodesis alone, or a combination of them. These operations had become reliable, but as the patients were followed, it became apparent that many were developing scoliosis.[33] Harrington recalled that he had seen only one scoliotic patient during his time with Dickson and Diveley[34]. But it was clear to him that lives saved by using a respirator were likely to have residual respiratory weakness or imbalance that would result in more children that would develop scoliosis. The nonoperative methods of corsets, casts, and traction were tried, but they failed to prevent progression of post-polio scoliosis in the growing child. The turnbuckle cast further decreased pulmonary function, an intuitive yet anecdotal observation at the time.[35] This impression was subsequently confirmed.[36, 37] The prospect of several hundred patients with progressive scoliosis was his stimulus, the motivation for his work.[38, 39] *See figure 5.1.*

随着时间的推移，哈灵顿的工作重心逐渐转移到传统骨科的重点，即对脊髓灰质炎后肌肉骨骼畸形的评估和处理。一些肌肉失衡，尤其是成年人足部和脚踝较轻微的肌肉不平衡，可以用矫形器（支具）治疗。[32]然而，由于儿童的四肢肌肉不平衡经常导致软性或僵硬畸形，需要肌腱转位、截骨、关节融合或三者结合，手术量大大增加。这些手术虽然疗效可靠，但随访发现许多患者出现脊柱侧凸。[33]哈灵顿回忆，在他与迪克森和戴夫利工作期间，他只见过一位脊柱侧凸患者。[34]但他很清楚，使用呼吸机挽救回来的患者很可能存在残留的呼吸功能虚弱或不平衡，这将导致更多的孩子患上脊柱侧凸。束身衣、石膏和牵引等非手术方法均被尝试过，但这些方法都未能防止儿童脊髓灰质炎后脊柱侧凸的发展。铰链石膏进一步降低了肺功能，这在当时是一种直观但有趣的现象，[35]并在随后得以证实。[36,37]几百名进展性脊柱侧凸患者的未来成为哈灵顿工作的动力。[38,39]（图 5.1）

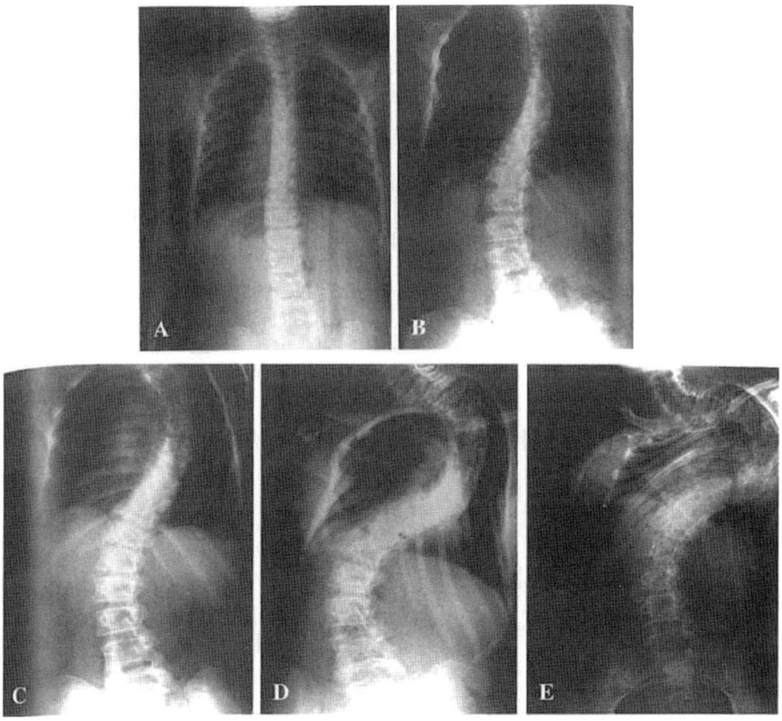

Figure 5.1 ***Radiographic sequence documenting the progressive scoliosis of a patient who suffered paralytic poliomyelitis at age five years:（A）at seven years,（B）eleven years,（C）twelve years,（D）thirteen years, and（E）at fifteen years in 1959.（Harrington Archives）***

图 5.1　影像序列记录了一名五岁时患有麻痹性脊髓灰质炎的患者的进行性脊柱侧凸：(A)7 岁，(B)11 岁，(C)12 岁，(D)13 岁，(E)15 岁(1959 年)(哈灵顿档案馆)

Harrington began to think of surgical ways to prevent small curves from progressing in young patients. His attention had been drawn to the spine's tripod structure (the intervertebral disc and two facet joints) of transverse plane intervertebral load transfer and motion.[40] He reasoned that not treating the curves until they got to be "100° was stupid" and treatment "in an age range and a deformity range that was tolerable to the patient's physiology" was preferable.[41] This led him to the idea of internally stabilizing the convex facet joint of small 20° to 30° curves with transfacet screws placed with the spine in the corrected position during a twenty-minute operation, a procedure that he first did in 1949.[42] He made no mention of arthrodesis or planned sequential operations. The curves were initially improved, but by three to five months they had returned to the same magnitude. He next fixed more convex facets and finally both convex and concave facets, but always with the same result: initial curve correction followed by curve recurrence in a few months.[43] Based on his research notes, sixteen patients were operated on probably in 1949 and 1950 with facet fixation.[44] He concluded that this was "not the answer."[45] Whether these patients were included in the first experimental group (Group 1) of nineteen patients he later reported on is not recorded, but they almost certainly were.[46] Harrington never commented on where he got the idea of placing screws across the facet joint. Perhaps it was his alone, although it seems possible that it was from Don King's 1948 article titled "Internal Fixation for Lumbosacral Fusion" and is believed to be the first reference to the use of facet screws.[47] Although both men shared the same goal of internal fixation to stabilize the spine, all else was dissimilar. King's work has focused on treating low back pain, believed to be due to L5-S1 degeneration, with arthrodesis.

哈灵顿开始考虑用外科手术的方法来阻止年轻患者的轻度侧凸。脊柱横截面的三关节结构（椎间盘及两侧关节突关节）及椎间载荷的转移与运动引起了他的注意。[40]他推断直到侧凸达到100°才进行治疗是愚蠢的，而在患者可耐受的年龄和畸形范围内进行治疗才是更可取的。[41]这使他产生了一个想法：通过20分钟的手术，在脊柱处于矫正位置的情况下，使用经关节突螺钉对20°~30°侧凸范围内的凸侧关节突关节进行内固定。这个想法在1949年首次实施，[42]但哈灵顿没有提及关节融合或计划内的多次手术。侧凸最初得到了改善，但3到5个月后，它们又回到了初始水平。接着他又固定了更多的凸侧关节突，最后又固定了凸侧和凹侧关节突，但结果总是一样的：最初的侧凸得以矫正，几个月后侧凸再次复发。[43]根据他的研究记录，大约在1949年和1950年对16名患者进行了关节突关节内固定手术。[44]他的结论是“这并非解决方案”[45]。虽然没有记录，但几乎可以肯定这些患者被包括在他后来报告的第一个试验组（第 1 组）的 19 名患者中。[46]哈灵顿从来没有提及他是怎么想到在小关节突上安装螺钉的。也许这是他的个人想法，尽管这似乎可能受唐·金在 1948 年发表的文章《腰骶融合内固定》的启发，该文章被认为是使用关节突螺钉的第一篇文献。[47]尽管二人的目标都是使用内固定来稳定脊柱，但其他方面并不相同。金关注的是通过关节融合术治疗由 L5-S1 退变引起的腰痛。

Harrington recognized from the beginning of the polio epidemics that a patient's treatment program badly needed coordination and reorganization. Thus, he was one of the first to spearhead the drive that resulted in the 1950 decision by the Baylor College of Medicine and the NFIP to develop a regional care center for polio victims with both acute and chronic respiratoly compromise.[48] To address the problem of respiratory polio, O'Connor had chosen Ken Landauer, a pediatrician and medical director of the New York State Rehabilitation Hospital, who formed the Houston care center following the "concept of treating respiratory polio as a categorical disease and organizing a group of specialists to develop new approaches for improved care and reduced costs."[49] Landauer consulted with James Wilson, who earlier had developed the concept of a respiratory center.[50] Initially called the Southwestern Poliomyelitis Respiratory Center, it was the first of its kind and a model for several additional centers around the country.[51] William A. Spencer, a twenty-eight-year-old United States Army captain and assistant chief of medical services at Fort Riley, Kansas, was recruited to head to new center. He began his employment in June at the end of his military obligation.[52] *See figure 5.2.* Stanley Olson, former dean of the Baylor College of Medicine, later described the situation into which Spencer had

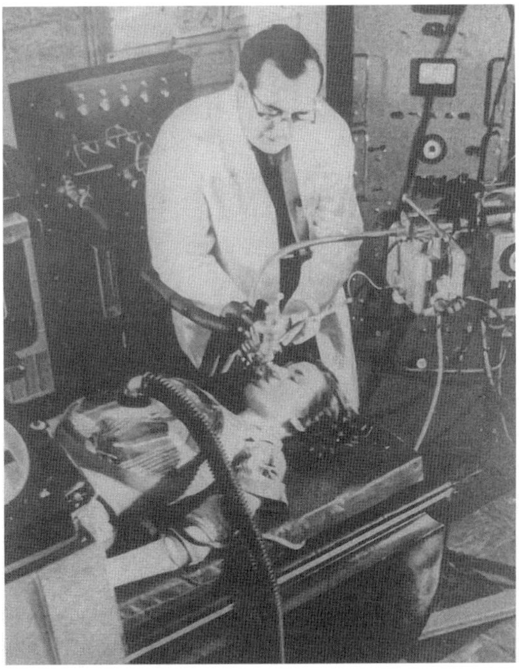

Figure 5.2 ***William A. Spencer, MD in his early years at the Southwestern Poliomyelitis Respiratory Center (Harrington Archives)***
图 5.2 威廉·A.斯宾塞医学博士早年在西南脊髓灰质炎呼吸中心工作(哈灵顿档案馆)

stepped: "It is hard to recreate now the mood prevailing then that severe disability was a fateful judgment to be borne-bravely, if possible, but in quiet desperation in any event.... Into this climate of tragedy accepted, Spencer brought special abilities and convictions fired by the fuel of incredible energy and buoyant optimism.... he reached out to anticipate the disability in the acute state instead of waiting to receive the patient when disability had fastened itself upon its victim.... critical evaluation of the entire rehabilitation effort, and innovative adaptation to remedy deficiencies have characterized the services that he and his associates have placed at the disposal of the patients."

哈灵顿从脊髓灰质炎流行之初就认识到，患者的治疗方案急需协调和重组。因此，他是促使贝勒医学院和国家小儿麻痹基金会在1950年决定为伴随急性和慢性呼吸系统疾病的脊髓灰质炎患者建立一个区域治疗中心的先驱者之一。[48]为了解决脊髓灰质炎呼吸系统受累的问题，奥康纳选择了纽约州康复医院的儿科医生和医疗主任肯·兰道尔。他秉承将呼吸系统受累及的脊髓灰质炎作为一种疾病分类来治疗的观念开办了休斯敦治疗中心，并组织了一组专家开发了新的治疗方法并降低了成本。[49]兰道尔咨询了詹姆斯·威尔逊，他早前提出了呼吸中心的概念。[50]最初被称为西南脊髓灰质炎呼吸中心，是同类中心中的第一家，也是全国其他几个中心的典范。[51]威廉·A. 斯宾塞是一名28岁的美国陆军上尉，也是堪萨斯州莱利堡的医疗服务助理主任，被聘请来管理这个新中心。他在六月份结束了军旅生涯并开始工作。[52]（图5.2）贝勒医学院的前任院长斯坦利·奥尔森后来这样描述斯宾塞的处境："现在很难再重现当时流行的那种情景，即认为严重的残疾是一种命运的审判，如果可能重现（当时的情景），患者注定要独自勇敢承担这种审判，然而无论如何都是默默地绝望……斯宾塞带着特殊的能力和信念让人们接受这种悲剧性社会氛围，这种能力和信念是由令人难以置信的能量和乐观的情绪点燃的……他主动在急性状态下预判残疾的发生，而不是等待接收已经残疾的患者，并且对整个康复工作进行关键评估，对缺陷进行创新性调整，这是他和他的同事为病人提供的服务的特点。"[53]

Spencer had grown up in Oklahoma City, where his teachers and family "taught him to aspire."[54] He was drawn to science, with becoming a doctor his dream. Self-described as both idealistic and naive, he had worked his way through Georgetown University and received his medical degree and training at Johns Hopkins School of Medicine. As a pediatrician trained in respiratory physiology, he had the background for the task ahead. But, just being in his twenties, he was admittedly "scared to death" when he arrived to find he had twenty-five patients in iron lungs.

斯宾塞在俄克拉何马城长大，在老师和家人的教育下立志成才。[54]他被科学所吸引，梦想成为一名医生。他评价自己既理想又天真，他曾先后在乔治敦大学学习，并在约翰·霍普金斯医学院获得医学学位并完成培训。作为一名接受过呼吸生理学训练的儿科医生，他有胜任这项工作的能力。但是，当他20多岁的时候发现有25个病人在使用铁肺时，他承认自己“快吓死了”。

Due to the leadership of Houston philanthropists Ben Taub and Mrs. Lamar Fleming, the Southwestern Poliomyelitis Respiratory Center with its total staff of eight was able to move into a new building adjacent to the hospital in 1951, just a year after its founding.[55] Harrington became chief of orthopedic services.[56] Spencer appreciated Harrington's "tremendous clinical experience and wisdom" in helping establish the center and credited him with continued "assistance in the development of clinical procedures and in the generation and pursuit of important research ideas. There have helped formulate a new approach in the anticipatory management of severe disabling conditions such as severe polio."[57] For instance, Harrington had developed a two-stage muscle test form in 1950 that was utilized for at least the next decade.[58]

在休斯敦慈善家本·陶布和拉马尔·弗莱明夫人的领导下，共有8名工作人员的西南脊髓灰质炎呼吸中心在成立仅一年之后，于1951年搬进了医院隔壁的新大楼。[55]哈灵顿担任骨科主任。[56]对于哈灵顿在筹建该中心时提供的丰富的临床经验和智慧，以及在制订临床流程和对重要研究思路的产生和探索方面给予的持续帮助，斯宾塞表示由衷的感谢。在这些帮助下，一种全新的对类似重症脊髓灰质炎的严重致残疾病的前瞻性处理新方法得以制订。[57]例如，哈灵顿在1950年开发的一份两步肌肉测试表，在接下来的至少十年里一直被使用。[58]

Freed from overall responsibility for the polio unit and faced with the failure of facet joint fixation of passively corrected scoliosis, Harrington began his pursuit of a surgical solution to scoliosis in earnest. Because few of his early research notes were dated and some that were appear to have been misdated, a definitive timeline is hard to establish, but there are enough time-anchoring events to determine a reasonably accurate one. He recalled that he began to "experiment with rods and hooks" to place a "clamp" on the convex side of the curve. The threaded rod was initially introduced through two small incisions and attached to the posterior elements of the spine through two hooks, one above and one below. He did not make clear exactly which posterior elements the hooks were attached to. Based on surviving photos of X-rays, the hooks were placed on the spine, not the ribs, presumably under the transverse process at the top and in the facet at the bottom. *See figure 5.3*. He soon observed that the thread-nut mechanism "walked" and loosened so he learned to crimp the threads to stop the walking of the nuts. Then the rods broke. "We applied two or three clamps above and below with a large shank, hoping to increase the metal bulk that would reduce the stress on the flexibility and elasticity of the rod and lower its breaking potential but this was not true, it broke anyway. Then a concave distraction force was applied by reversing the hooks on the rod. This lasted two or three months longer before it broke."[59] *See figure 5.4*. Three facts were becoming apparent to him: "the instrument was not strong enough to take the stresses placed on it,… the thread-nut principle had much to be desired," and there was very little tissue reaction to the stainless steel metal. It is clear that Harrington knew he was experimenting and made certain to mentally prepare both patients and their parents for what was being done and why. He did not feel he was creating any hazard to their lives. Although he was venturing into unknown territory, his patients and their parents were willing to go there with him. By this time the operation had grown to 30 to 40 minutes and included an "attempt to make fusion."

从脊髓灰质炎病房的重压中解脱出来后，哈灵顿开始致力于将脊柱侧凸的外科治疗策略作为关节突关节固定失败的替代方案。因为他早期的研究笔记很少标注日期，而且有些似乎标注了错误的日期，所以很难确定一个明确的时间轴，但有足够多确定时间点的事件来帮助建立一个相对准确的时间轴。他回忆自己开始“棒和钩的实验”，在凸侧放置一个“夹子”。螺纹棒最初通过两个小切口插入，并借由一上一下的两个钩固定到脊柱后侧的附件上。他并没有确切说明这些钩连

Figure 5.3 ***Hooks designed to anchor the threaded rods to the posterior elements of the spine: early 1950s models on the left, mid-1950s models on the right. (Harrington Archives)***
图 5.3　用于将螺纹棒固定在脊柱后侧附件的钩：左侧两个为 20 世纪 50 年代早期模型，右侧两个为 20 世纪 50 年代中期模型（哈灵顿档案馆）

接在后方哪些位置。根据遗留下的 X 光片，钩被放置在脊柱上，而不是肋骨上，大概是头端放在横突下而尾端置于关节突。（图 5.3）不久后哈灵顿发现螺纹-螺母装置出现滑移和松动，所以他学会折弯螺纹来阻止螺母滑动。然后是断棒的问题。“我们在上方和下方分别放置两个或三个带有一个长柄的钩，希望增加金属体积，以减少对棒的弯曲和弹性应力来降低它断裂的可能性，但这并不奏效，最终还是断了。后来通过反转棒上的钩对凹侧进行撑开，这样可以多维持 2~3 个月。”[59]（图 5.4）三个事实提醒哈灵顿，“这个装置不足以承受施加在它身上的应力，螺纹螺母结构还有待改进”，以及组织对不锈钢几乎没有反应。显然哈灵顿知道他在做实验，并确保让患者和他们的父母对实验内容和做这个实验的原因做好心理准备。他并不觉得自己对他们的生命造成了任何危害。尽管他在一个未知的领域冒险，但他的病人和他们的父母都愿意和他同行。这时，手术时间已经增加到 30~40 分钟，还包括对融合的尝试。

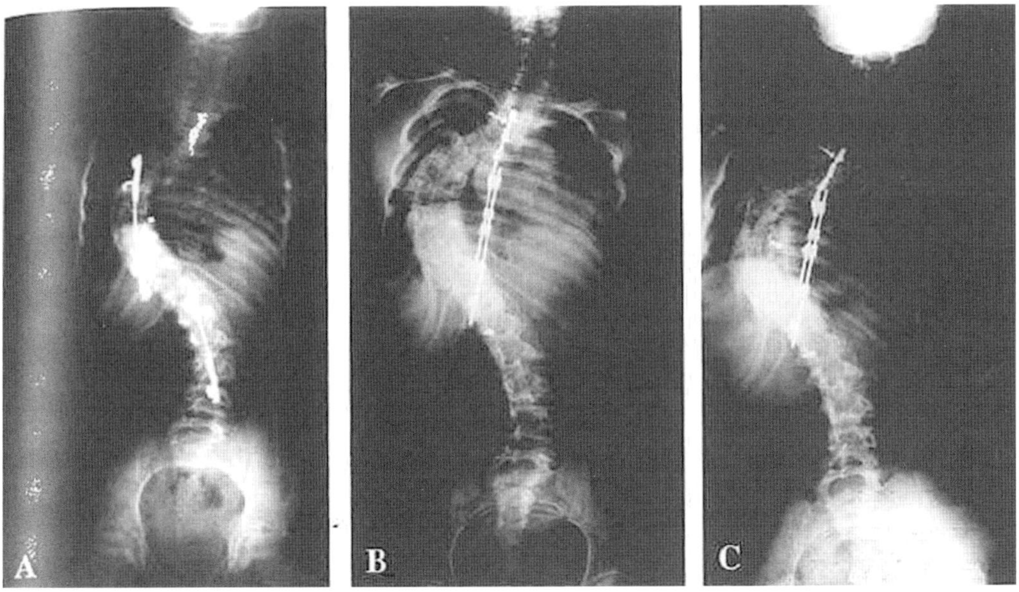

Figure 5.4 ***Sequence of coronal plane radiographs viewed anteroposterior showing implant evolution from 1952 to 1955. A. Facet screws from earlier surgery and small convex threaded rods. B. After revision to paired threaded distraction rods. C. After breakage near upper end of threaded rod used in distraction.*** **(*Harrington Archives*)**

图 5.4 冠状面前后位 X 光片序列显示的内植物从 1952 年到 1955 年的演变。A. 早期手术的关节突螺钉和小凸侧螺纹棒。B. 修改后为成对的螺纹撑开棒。C. 用于撑开的螺纹棒上端断裂后（哈灵顿档案馆）

This evolution could be characterized as his clamp-and-strut era. Implant design remained centered on the original 1/8"-diameter threaded rod and accommodating hooks. In this period he began to envision extending the instrumentation to the pelvis, either with what appears to have been the forerunners of the transiliac rod or with intrasacral rods.[60] However, the observation that instrumentation of the major curve resulted in proportionate correction of the secondary curves probably delayed the pelvic fixation effort.[61] Doubling the rods to strengthen them at the apex and developing a crimping mechanism to effect hook-rod connection and prevent nut migration were two of the many instrument modifications Harrington worked on.[62]

这种演变可以被描述为他的“钩和棒”时代。内植物的设计仍然集中于原先的直径 1/8 英寸的螺纹棒和钩。在此期间，他开始设想借用经髂骨棒的前身装置或骶骨内棒，将固定范围扩展到骨盆。[60]然而，主弯内固定导致相应的继发弯矫正的现象，可能推迟了骨盆固定的应用。[61]使用双棒增强顶椎区域的强度，以及开发一种皱褶机制以增强钩棒连接并防止螺母移位，是哈灵顿众多器械优化方案的其中两项。[62]

By 1953 despite broken implants and an average of 3.1 operations per patient, Harrington recalled six encouraging observations. He wrote that "progression of terrible deformities had been held to a minimum but not controlled."[63] He also noted that based on photographs and pathological specimens, there was very little soft-tissue reaction to the implants, which were made of 306 or 316 stainless steel. His third observation was that mixing of the steels did not seem to increase tissue reaction to the implants. Additionally, he saw that the bone under the hooks was not undergoing erosion, necrosis, or sequestration, and there was no sign of infection. His fifth finding was that the bone under the hooks sometimes showed increased trabeculation, suggesting strengthening under load. Finally, he commented that a fibrocartilaginous interface was always present between the hook and bone. Harrington's research notes began to sound a note of optimism: "hook and strut idea has definite possibilities." He lamented that hook placement was poor because of a lack of knowledge and inaccessibility, which would be solved by observation and instruments, respectively. He counted on developing better tools to shorten operative time, and he marveled at the frequency of minor asymmetries in children's spines. New design concepts flowed, which included reducing the size of the hook tail, cross strutting for stability, and adding a sacral strut. He considered strutting every level, but had second thoughts, commenting "maybe/maybe not." Even though rod breakage was still a problem, his goal was to reduce the amount of metal to that adequate for the job.[64]

到 1953 年，尽管内植物存在断裂问题，且每个病人平均需要 3.1 次手术，哈灵顿还是回忆了 6 个令人鼓舞的观察结果。他这样写道："严重畸形的进展没有得到控制，但被限制在最低限度。"[63]他还指出，根据照片和病理标本，机体对 306 或 316 不锈钢制成的内植物几乎没有软组织反应。他的第三个观察结果是，钢的混合似乎并没有增加组织对内植物的反应。此外，他看到钩下的骨头没有发生侵蚀、坏死或形成死骨，也没有感染的迹象。他的第五个发现是，钩下的骨小梁有时会增加，这表明在载荷作用下会进一步加强骨结构。最后，哈灵顿做出评论，在钩和骨之间总是存在纤维软骨界面。哈灵顿的研究笔记开始听起来有些乐观："钩棒结构的思路具有明确的可行性。"遗憾的是，由于缺乏背景知识和置钩困难，钩的放置很差，这将分别通过观察和工具来解决。哈灵顿希望能开发更好的工具来缩短手术时间，同时他也对儿童脊柱轻微不对称的发生率感到惊讶。新的设计概念不断涌现，其中包括减小钩尾的尺寸，增加交叉支柱来提升稳定性，以及增加骶骨支柱。他考虑撑开每一个节段，但转念一想，又觉得"或许可以/或许不该"。尽管断棒仍是一个问题，但他的目标是在满足任务的前提下尽可能降低金属含量。[64]

During this time, roughly 1951-54, Harrington worked to articulate the biological theory of his operation. The concept he was developing was that the "whole theory of this treatment is based on eliminating stress in critical points and allowing the characteristics of bone growth to restore the dynamic stability of the individual vertebrae by an operation which I call Dynamic Internal Strut Traction." He equated dynamic stability and dynamic balance, and he also attributed maintenance of dynamic balance to reciprocal motion.[65] His dedication to this concept may have served as a compass for him as he stuck with and elaborated on it throughout the remainder of his career, even as it became increasingly clear that arthrodesis was an essential part of the operation he was developing. Reconciling arthrodesis, thus eliminating motion, with his theory of restoring dynamic balance through reciprocal motion was and would continue to be like reconciling the irreconcilable.

大约在 1951—1954 年间，哈灵顿致力于阐明他的手术的生物学理论。他提出"这种治疗的整个理论是基于通过一种他称之为动态内部棒牵引的手术消除临界点应力，让骨生长的特性来恢复每个椎体的动态稳定性。”他把动态稳定等同于动态平衡，并把保持动态平衡归因于相互运动。[65]即使愈发清晰地认识到关节融合术是他正在开发的手术中的必要部分，他在之后的职业生涯中仍坚持和详细阐述该理论，对这份概念的执着可能是他的指南针。消除活动的融合术，与他通过相互运动恢复动态平衡的理论是持续不可调和的。

In 1954 he took stock of the problems of all the post-polio musculoskeletal deformities and in the process confirmed his belief that management possibilities for post-polio upper and lower extremity deformities were at least adequate. But that was not the case for post-polio scoliosis patients, some of whom were at risk of death, pain, or crippling. He and the Southwestern Poliomyelitis Respiratory Center had accumulated several hundred patients at risk for developing post-polio scoliosis, and this large prospective caseload reinforced his belief that spine instrumentation to control scoliosis “was one of necessity.”[66] But he held fast to a dynamic theory and a static practice with experimental implants too weak for the loads experienced and rod-hook connections dependent on the problematic threaded rod-nut mechanism. Two developments in 1954 brought deliverance from his approaching dead end: research grants and a collaborator.

1954 年，他对所有脊髓灰质炎后肌肉骨骼畸形的问题进行了评估，并在此过程中证实了他的观点，即对脊髓灰质炎后四肢畸形的治疗有足够的可行性。但对脊髓灰质炎后脊柱侧凸患者来说，情况并非如此，其中一些患者面临死亡、疼痛或残疾的风险。他和西南脊髓灰质炎呼吸中心已经积累了几百名有可能发展为脊髓灰质炎后脊柱侧凸的患者，这个大型的前瞻性队列研究增强了他的理念，即脊柱内固定器械是控制脊柱侧凸所必需的手段之一。[66] 但他仍坚持动态理论和静态实践，因为实验内植物太脆弱而无法承受所经受的载荷，而且棒-钩连接依赖于有问题的螺纹棒-螺母结构。1954 年的两项进展使他免于在死胡同中继续挣扎：获得研究经费资助和拥有一位合作者。

When at a professional crossroad, it is not unusual to turn to one’s mento. Thus after speaking with Frank Dickson, Harrington recorded the following: “Need research grants: 1-answer growth response to pressure, 2-electronic model to reproduce pressure & record.”[67] By the first notation he had written $18,000 and by the second one $150,000. Based on the research notebook pages that followed, this phone call seems to have reenergized him. Immediately, he began envisioning a bipedal mouse experiment.[68]

Although impractical, it started the thought process leading to an experimental animal model of scoliosis that he eventually saw to a finish. For the first time he addressed the issue of needed implant strength since the rod was clearly the weak point. It was estimated that it should be able to withstand a compression load of 150 pounds, but the bending strength of the 1/8"-diameter threaded rod that had been used exclusively was only 2 pounds with a 10" length exposed and 90 pounds with a 2-1/2" length exposed. For a 1/8"-diameter unthreaded rod the comparable bending strengths were 30 pounds and greater than 200 pounds.[69] The 1/8"-diameter threaded rods were hopelessly inadequate for the load they experienced. Who did the testing isn't clear, but recollections and later reports suggest it likely was Professor James R. Sims at Rice University.[70, 71]

在职业发展的十字路口，向导师寻求帮助是很正常的。因此，在同弗兰克·迪克森交谈后，哈灵顿记录了以下内容："需要研究资助：1. 阐明压力作用下的生长反应；2. 电子模型再现压力并记录。"[67]在第一项和第二项那里，他分别写下了 18 000 美元和 150 000 美元。根据他的研究笔记，这次通话似乎让他恢复了活力。很快，他开始设想一个双足小鼠实验。[68]虽然不切实际，但他开始思考如何建立一个脊柱侧凸的动物模型，并最终完成了实验。这是他第一次提出内植物强度的问题，因为棒的载荷强度显然是薄弱环节。据估计，所用的棒应能够承受 150 磅的压缩载荷，但对于广泛应用的直径 1/8 英寸的螺纹棒，在 10 英寸长时抗弯强度只有 2 磅，2.5 英寸长时抗弯强度达 90 磅。对于一个直径 1/8 英寸的无螺纹棒来说，相应的抗弯强度分别为 30 磅和大于 200 磅。[69]直径 1/8 英寸的螺纹棒完全无法承受其所面对的载荷。测试者的身份尚不清楚，但回忆和后来的报告显示，可能是莱斯大学的詹姆斯·R. 西姆斯教授。[70, 71]

Sometime during 1954 Harrington did apply for research grants from the NFIP "for a two-phase investigation, the first ever to be made a purely surgical project. The first phase proposed to develop instrumentation on approximately 50 poliomyelitis scoliotic patients over a period of five years. The second was a proposal to produce experimental scoliosis in mice and observe microscopically both the changes taking place in the growth centers and the reversible potential of the growth centers when the scoliotic deformity was released."[72] The exact amounts requested are believed to have been $150,000 for the clinical study and $18,000 for the laboratory study. The clinical proposal drew "a great deal of opposition... by a large number of distinguished orthopedic surgeons that were active as medical advisors to the National Foundation." This opposition was remembered as reaching rage level.[73] Spencer's success in establishing and operating the Southwestern Poliomyelitis Respiratory Center and Harrington's active contribution to his efforts resulted in Spencer's appeal to Landauer, who in turn appealed to O'Connor. Consequently, the grants were awarded, and funding began in 1955.[74]

在 1954 年，哈灵顿确实向国家小儿麻痹基金会申请了研究资助进行一项分为两个阶段的研究，这是有史以来第一个纯外科研究项目。第一阶段是计划在五年内为大约 50 名脊髓灰质炎后脊柱侧凸患者开发器械。第二阶段研究提出在小鼠体内进行实验性脊柱侧凸造模，并在显微镜下观察生长中心发生的变化和脊柱侧凸畸形解除时生长中心的可逆潜力。[72]据信所要求的确切数额为 150 000 美元用于临床研究及 18 000 美元用于实验研究。这一临床建议招致了由大量著名骨科医生组成的国家基金会顾问团的反对。反对力度之大，足可见他们的愤怒程度。[73]由于哈灵顿对斯宾塞成功地建立并运营了西南脊髓灰质炎呼吸中心做出了积极贡献，这使得斯宾塞向兰道尔发出了呼吁，而后者又向奥康纳发出了呼吁。最后申请得以批准，并于 1955 年开始资助。[74]

The other major development in 1954 was Bill Spencer's recruitment of Thorkild J. Engen, who would become a good friend of Harrington and an important contributor tor to Harrington's research. *See figure 5.5*. Spencer named Engen as head of the Department of Orthotics where he became an international leader in the making of braces that supported, aligned, prevented, or corrected deformities or improved the function of moveable parts of the body.[75] Engen was born in Randers, Denmark, on July 6, 1924, the son of a successful tailor. As was the practice in Europe, he took qualifying examinations that included technical skill evaluation. Although meeting the qualifications, he did not have the required financial background

Figure 5.5 ***Thorkild J. Engen with Mary Alice and Paul Harrington, ca. 1959. (Harrington Archives)***
图 5.5 托基尔·J. 恩金、玛丽·艾丽斯和保罗·哈灵顿，加利福尼亚州，1959 年(哈灵顿档案馆)

for medical training and was channeled into orthotics. Starting in 1939, he began five years of apprenticeship and schooling at the W. A. Kaiser Institute in Arhus, which was 50 miles from home. The daily commute, daytime work, and evening schooling meant arising at 5:00 a.m. and retiring sometime after 10:00 p.m. Because his country was occupied by the Germans during World War Ⅱ, he occasionally served as a sort of Danish courier, resulting in a few tense moments for him.[76]

1954 年的另一项重大进展是比尔·斯宾塞聘请了托基尔·J. 恩金，他后来成为哈灵顿的好朋友，也是哈灵顿研究的重要贡献者。(图 5.5) 斯宾塞任命恩金为矫形器科主任，在那里他成为制造支撑、对齐、预防或矫正畸形或改善身体可活动部位功能的支具的国际领导者。[75]恩金于 1924 年 7 月 6 日出生在丹麦的兰德斯，父亲是一个成功的裁缝。和欧洲的模式一样，他参加了包括技术技能评估在内的资格考试。虽然符合资格，但他无法承担医学培训所需的费用，因此被安排从事矫形器工作。从 1939 年开始，他在离家 50 英里，位于奥尔胡斯的 W. A. 凯泽研究所开始了五年的学徒生涯和学校教育。每天的通勤、白天的工作和晚上的学习意味着早上 5 点起床，晚上 10 点以后才能休息。由于丹麦在第二次世界大战期间被德国人占领，他偶尔充当丹麦人的信使，这给他带来了一些危险。[76]

The Kaiser Institute employed 30 to 40 people and created and produced surgical instruments, prosthetics (artificial limbs), and orthotics. The foreman was a "very, very highly skilled German... named Slattlau."[77] Years later Engen remembered Slattlau showing him to his well-worn workbench and instructing him to make a piece of steel, square all the way around using hand instruments. One day turned into five, the pile of filings got larger and larger, and the steel piece smaller and smaller. Still he could not get it perfectly square on all sides. Finally, he took it to the foreman, who said, "'Okay Tork, you got it?' I said, No sir, no. 'What do you mean no?' Well, here it is. 'Okay, that's all right. Small, but I can still see air. You don't have it square yet.' At that time when he said that, I said, what am I going to tell my Dad? So he said, 'don't worry about it. If anything is worth doing at all, do it right and I want this as an indelible lesson for the rest of your life; that these things, tools, are instruments that must be respected and used in the proper manner. Then you can do things.' That was powerful. From then on everything went beautiful."[78] His final examination included making a leg brace, an artificial leg, and a surgical instrument. He was assigned a mouth spacer to hold the mouth open during work in the oral cavity. He received an excellent grade on each and passed the other tests with "good acceptance and so on." In 1945 Engen graduated with a certificate in orthotics.[79]

凯泽研究所有30到40名人员致力于研发和生产手术器械、假肢和矫形器。领导是一个"非常非常熟练的德国人，名叫斯莱特劳"。[77]多年后，恩金还记得斯莱特劳带他去看他那破旧的工作台，并指导他用手持工具制作一个方形钢材的情景。一晃眼五天过去了，钢屑堆得越来越大，钢块却越来越小。但他仍然无法在所有方面都做到完美。最后，他把它拿给工头，工头说："'好了，托基尔，你搞定了吗？'我说没有，先生，并没有。'没有是什么意思？''好吧，给。''没关系。很小，但我仍能看见空隙，你还没把它做成方形。'当他说完时，我问他我应该怎么告诉我父亲。他说，'别担心，如果有什么事情值得去做，那就去做好，我希望这能成为你一生中不可磨灭的教训；这些工具必须被尊重并恰当使用。'懂得这些之后，任何人都可以做好东西了。"[78]这些话很有力量。从那以后，一切都变得美好起来。他的最终测试包括做一个腿支架，一条假肢和一个手术器械。最终，他被分配去制作用于在口腔作业时保持口腔张开的口腔撑开器。他在每项测试中都取得了优异的成绩，并以"良好的接受度"通过了其他测试。1945年，恩金毕业并获得矫形学证书。[79]

Engen went to work at the Nyrop oq Maag Institute in Copenhagen and was asked to prepare and present an exhibit at the First International Poliomyelitis Congress held in the city in 1950. He had a "lot of fun" doing it and tended the exhibit faithfully from 9:00 a.m. to 6:00 p.m. Next to his small exhibit was a huge exhibit from the Warm Springs, Georgia, NFIP unit manned by its medical director, Robert Bennett. Through a multilingual Norwegian, the two had a "tremendous professional discussion, even arguments, so on, pro's and con's."[80] At the conclusion of the congress Bennett gave Tork Engen his card and said "if you care to come to the United States, my door will be open for you. I'll have a job for you." Engen, a decisive and adventurous person, told his girlfriend that she was going to marry him and go to the United States! Bennett was true to his word, and the Engens moved to Ame1ica in November 1952. They came on a freighter, awakened after their arrival to the spectacle of New York City's Macy's Thanksgiving Day Parade, and traveled to Warm Springs by bus, experiencing racial segregation for the first time.[81] At Warm Springs the practical application of his thorough educational background quickly propelled him to prominence among his colleagues.[82]

恩金前往哥本哈根的尼罗普·奥克·马格研究所工作，并被邀请在1950年在哥本哈根举行的第一届国际脊髓灰质炎大会上做展示。从早上9点到下午6点，他一直尽兴地做展示。在他的小展位旁边是由医疗主任罗伯特·班尼特负责的来自乔治亚州沃姆斯普林的国家小儿麻痹基金会的巨大的展位。通过一位会说多种语言的挪威人，两人进行了“大量的专业讨论，甚至争论，交流了彼此赞成和反对的观点。”[80]在会议结束时，班尼特把自己的名片交给了托基尔·恩金，并告诉他：“如果你愿意来美国，我的大门将为你敞开，并为你提供一份工作。”恩金是一个果断又爱冒险的人，把这个消息告诉了他的女朋友让她嫁给他然后一起去美国！班尼特信守了诺言，恩金一家于1952年11月搬到了美国。他们乘坐货轮来到纽约市，被梅西百货的感恩节大游行的壮观场面所震撼，然后乘公共汽车前往沃姆斯普林斯，并第一次体验到种族隔离。[81]在沃姆斯普林斯，他丰富的教育背景使他在同事中迅速脱颖而出。[82]

How or when they met or even if they had met isn't recorded, but Spencer was obviously impressed with Engen's reputed skill and invited him to visit Houston. Engen told Spencer he wasn't interested four times, but Spencer persisted. Finally, Engen gave in, and he and his wife went for a visit, which began when he was escorted into the front of a large lecture hall where Spencer was teaching a class of about 200. After a "hi, Tork" greeting, Spencer completed his lecture, after which he turned to him and said, "Hey, I'm so glad you're here. I have just a little time. You and I are going to spend a half an hour together." After a brief tour of the facilities Spencer made his pitch. "This is what we need. I know that you have the background to do it. We'll get some money for your equipment, and so on. You'll have a free hand. You will get an academic appointment once we get settled; Blah, blah, blah. It's your choice. You are completely in charge."[83] On the way back to the hotel Engen's thought was "you're not going to," but in the early evening Harrington interviewed and in the process impressed him. "He was a very, very genuine type of person. I liked him instantly." Engen met others and gradually came around to the idea that this was something he would do. He saw it as going the academic route with his career so he signed on and joined Spencer's team at the Southwestern Poliomyelitis Respiratory Center on August 26, 1954.[84] Engen would later say, "whole new world opened up to me in Houston. I was young and enthusiastic, and I jumped into it."[85]

他们是如何、何时见面的，甚至他们是否见过面都没有记录，但斯宾塞显然对恩金出色的技术印象深刻，并邀请他访问休斯敦。恩金前后四次告诉斯宾塞他不感兴趣，但斯宾塞依然坚持。最后，恩金让步了，他和妻子去参观了一番。一开始，他被带到一个大讲堂的前面，斯宾塞正在那里给大约 200 人上课。在“你好，托基尔”的招呼之后，斯宾塞结束了他的授课，之后他转向托基尔说：“嘿，我很高兴你在这里。我只有一点时间，大约一个半小时。”简单参观了一下设施后，斯宾塞开始了游说。“像你这样的人就是我们需要的人才，我们会为你筹集设备资金，你可以在这里自由发挥。一旦我们安顿下来，你就会得到一个学术任职。这件事完全由你自己决定。”[83]在回酒店的路上，恩金的想法仍是“我不会这样做。”但在傍晚的时候，哈灵顿来访并给他留下了深刻的印象。“他是一个非常非常真诚的人。我立刻就喜欢上了他。”遇到了其他一些人后，恩金逐渐意识到他愿意过来。他认为这是在他的职业生涯中的学术路线，所以他签约并于 1954 年 8 月 26 日加入了斯宾塞在西南脊髓灰质炎呼吸中心的团队。[84]恩金后来说：“在休斯敦，一个全新的世界向我敞开了大门。当时我年轻，充满热情，投身其中。”[85]

Apparently nothing had been said about Harrington's project during the visit. Perhaps as early as a week after their arrival in Houston, the Engens were invited to the Harringtons' house. There Harrington shared his "dream" for management of "scoliosis, kyphosis, and lordosis," showing some of his prototypes and explaining his dream. "If we could go in surgically to mechanically support the spine, then we can help these patients live longer because the internal organs are freed up, and so on." Engen asked why he didn't go to a surgical instrument maker and was told that he had tried numerous times and had been told their business was to sell instruments, not to research them. None would work with him because his idea was in its "very, very infancy." He did have a machinist he was working with who created the very first instruments and hooks. "Well as he talked, I could feel more and more enthusiastic about it. I thought he had a marvelous idea."[86] Harrington began visiting Engen's laboratory almost daily, and they became closer personally and professionally. Until the NFIP grants were awarded and funded, Harrington had no money to pursue his vision. To address this problem, Engen suggested that discarded surgical instruments be collected, restored, and converted into new forms and uses. The two men also shared the mutual hobby of sailing. Harrington took each Thursday off and occasionally would invite his friend to join him on the water. Leaving midmorning, they would pick up a bucket of fried chicken at Youngblood's and spend the rest of the day sailing the small boat Harrington had made, presumably the *MAWH*, which he had built as an intern in South Carolina. Engen described the time as delightful because they discussed instruments and future exhibits to sell them to physician.[87] Soon Engen was spending evenings and weekends on the instrumentation. Their wives often joined them for dinner at one of their homes.

显然在这次访问期间，他们对哈灵顿的项目只字未提。也许早在他们到达休斯敦一个星期后，恩金一家就被邀请到哈灵顿家做客。在那里，哈灵顿分享了他对脊柱侧凸、后凸和前凸处理的“梦想”，展示了他的一些原型并作解释。“如果我们可以通过外科手术机械地支撑脊柱，从而解放患者的内脏，这些患者将活得更久。”恩金问他为什么不去找外科器械制造商，得知哈灵顿已经尝试无数次但被告知他们的业务是销售工具，而不是研究工具。没有人愿意和他合作，因为他的想法还“非常非常初级”。他确实同一个机械师合作过，并创造了最早的器械和钩。“当他讲述的时候，我可以感到我对此越来越富有激情。我认为他有一个了不起的主意”。[86]哈灵顿开始几乎每天都去恩金的实验室，他们在私下和工作上都变得更加亲密。在接受国家小儿麻痹基金会的拨款资助之前，哈灵顿一直没有钱去追求他的愿景。为了解决这个问题，恩金建议收集、修复废弃的手术器械，并将其转化为新的形式和用途。两人还有共同的航海爱好。哈灵顿偶尔会在每周四休息时邀请他的朋友和他一起出海。上午出发后，他们会在青年餐厅买一桶炸鸡，然后在剩下的时间里驾驶哈灵顿造的小船，大概是他在南卡罗来纳州实习时造的 MAWH。恩金说这段时间很愉快，因为他们讨论了器械和将来的展品，以便把它们卖给医生。[87]很快，恩金就把晚上和周末都花在了器械上。他们两对夫妇经常共进晚餐，有时在哈灵顿家，有时在恩金家。

Engen's recollection was that early in their relationship Harrington said, “Tork, I know you're spending a lot of time. I don't have any money, but you are showing me the confidence that you are doing this for me, and you have the rights, once this is developed and proven, to commercialize these instruments. This is all yours.”[88] Lending credence to Engen's recollections is a sketch in Harrington's personal research notebook of a monogram linking E and H by Inc. Although not precisely dated, it appears to have been done in March 1955 or soon after.[89] Harrington did not address this issue specifically in his recollections, although he frequently recognized Engen's work.[90,91] This appears to be where the seed of future discontent was sown.

他们初识时哈灵顿说：“托基尔，我知道你花了很多时间。我没有经费，但你向我展示了你为我做这件事的决心。一旦它被开发和证明，你有权利将这些工具商业化。这都是你的。”[88]在哈灵顿的个人研究笔记本上有一幅草图，上面有一个用 Inc 连接 E 和 H 组成的字母组合。虽然没有确切的日期，但似乎是在 1955 年 3 月或之后不久完成的。[89] 哈灵顿在他的回忆中没有特别提到这个问题，尽管他经常认可恩金的工作。[90,91] 这似乎就是未来他们不和的起因。

Harrington later considered 1949 through 1954 as the first phase of implant development. During this time he operated on 19 patients, the youngest aged 9 years and the oldest 33 years. Fifty-eight percent (eleven of nineteen) were fifteen years old or younger. Fourteen of the nineteen had post-polio scoliosis. Fifty-three operations were performed, averaging 2.8 per patient. None were cast postoperative, and "fusion was used in nearly all cases eventually to acquire reasonable results."[92] The principal complications encountered were bone erosion, instrument fracture, and pseudarthrosis, which seldom resulted in anything more than temporary pain or correction loss. He was very grateful to these first nineteen patients. His associate, Jesse Dickson, remembered that on the occasion of Harrington's receipt of the Cora and Webb Mading Medal in 1973 his only comment was to express his gratitude to this group.[93] During these 5 years, he cited 35 design modifications although they were not chronicled.

哈灵顿后来认为 1949 年到 1954 年是植入物发展的第一阶段。在此期间，他为 19 名患者做了手术，其中最小的 9 岁，最大的 33 岁。58%（19 人中的 11 人）的年龄在 15 岁或以下。19 人中有 14 人患有脊髓灰质炎后脊柱侧凸。共进行了 53 次手术，平均每位患者 2.8 次。术后无一名患者打石膏，"几乎所有病例都采用了融合术，最终获得了合理的结果。"[92] 除了短期疼痛和矫正丢失，主要的并发症是骨侵蚀、内植物断裂和假关节形成。他非常感谢这最早的 19 名患者。他的助手杰西·迪克森回忆，1973 年哈灵顿获得科拉和韦布·马丁奖章时，他唯一的评论就是表达了他对这组病人的感激之情。[93] 在这 5 年里，他引用了 35 个设计修改，尽管它们没有被记录在案。

The dawn of 1955 found Harrington hard at work preparing a progress report planned for presentation to the clinical section of the Texas Orthopedic Association later in the year. His detailed notes covering most of sixteen pages in his research notebook included a developmental timeline, concept, design principles, the rudimentary axial compression test results, and patient examples. Most notes were devoted to his ideas about the normal function of the spine and the pathogenesis of scoliosis. These ideas kept returning to the concept of a normal condition of symmetrical growth and dynamic stability with its kinetic (muscles) and static (bone and joint) elements produced by reciprocal motion turned pathological by the stress of asymmetrical reciprocal motion such as that produced by asymmetrical trunk muscle paralysis from polio. Less than a page was devoted to the design principles of the instruments. They were described as an "adjustable rod and hook... unit for the application of power with variability to meet multi position and still seat (swivel), be adjustable, and [have] rotation adjustments." His last draft summation statement reflected the reality that many problems with the development of this operation still existed. "This field of approach offers merit but answers must be had thru research and time with intelligent observations [that] will light the way for a sound, reliable procedure." The date at the end of this draft was February 25, 1955.[94] No further reference to this presentation exists in his archives. It is believed Harrington presented this at the annual meeting of the Southern Medical Society in Houston later that year and that guest speaker John Moe was justifiably not impressed.[95]

1955 年伊始，哈灵顿正在努力准备一份进展报告，计划在这一年晚些时候在得克萨斯州骨科学会的临床分会上进行汇报。他整整用了 16 页来详细记录他的笔记内容，包括发展时间表、概念、设计原则、初步轴压测试结果以及病例。大部分笔记都是关于脊柱的正常功能和脊柱侧凸的发病机理的。这些想法不断回归到对称生长和动态稳定的正常状态的概念，其运动（肌肉）和静态（骨骼和关节）元素由相互运动产生，而不对称相互运动的压力将导致病态，例如，由脊髓灰质炎引起的不对称躯干肌肉瘫痪。关于内固定装置设计原则的篇幅不到一页。它们被描述为“可调节的棒和钩……用于应用具有可变性的动力，以满足多位置和静止座椅（旋转），可调节和旋转调节”。他的最后一份总结性发言草案反映了这一项目的发展仍然存在许多问题的现实。“这类方法具有优点，但必须通过研究和时间，以及明智的观察验证，这将为一个健全、可靠的程序指明道路。”这份草稿的最后日期是 1955 年 2 月 25 日，在他的档案中没有进一步提及这份报告。[94]据说，哈灵顿在当年晚些时候在休斯敦举行的南方医学会年会上提出了这一观点，而特邀演讲者约翰·莫对此不以为意。[95]

On the next page of his research notebook, not dated but almost certainly before any presentation, Harrington listed five problems. The first was "**weak point... rod.**" Probably the rigor of preparing this presentation had forced him to face the reality that his results to date were not competitive with the current standard of surgical treatment for scoliosis, arthrodesis, and Risser localizer cast correction and immobilization. About halfway down the page after several blank lines were the words of deliverance: "rod answer is without threads."[96] The other four problems listed were "metal still too bulky, stretch system too complicated, how to adjust length, and determine when to use." A non-threaded rod immediately presented the problem of connection mechanism, and the innovation that followed was almost immediate. From a starting point of lock rings, the ratchet concept was born between February 25 and March 21, 1955.[97] *See figure 5.6.* He later recalled his thinking. "How are you going to put in the rods, how are you going to correct it? Well I knew that pulling on it was a disadvantage, we couldn't get a maximum correction so one Sunday morning about 9 o'clock, thinking, sitting in my room, about it, I thought of the ratchet mechanism and made a copy of it out of pasteboard from a shirt laundry and designed a hook, ratchet mechanism on a rod and presented it to Zimmer and they made one for me and we put it in and that is the creation of it."[98] Although the pasteboard artifact has not survived, two detailed original drawings have. Harrington called them Walking Lock Rod for Strut Fixation of Spine and Self Locking Spinal Hook, both of which he dated and signed in March 1955.[99] *See figure 5.7.* He specified that they were to be made of "S.M.O. 1808 stainless steel."

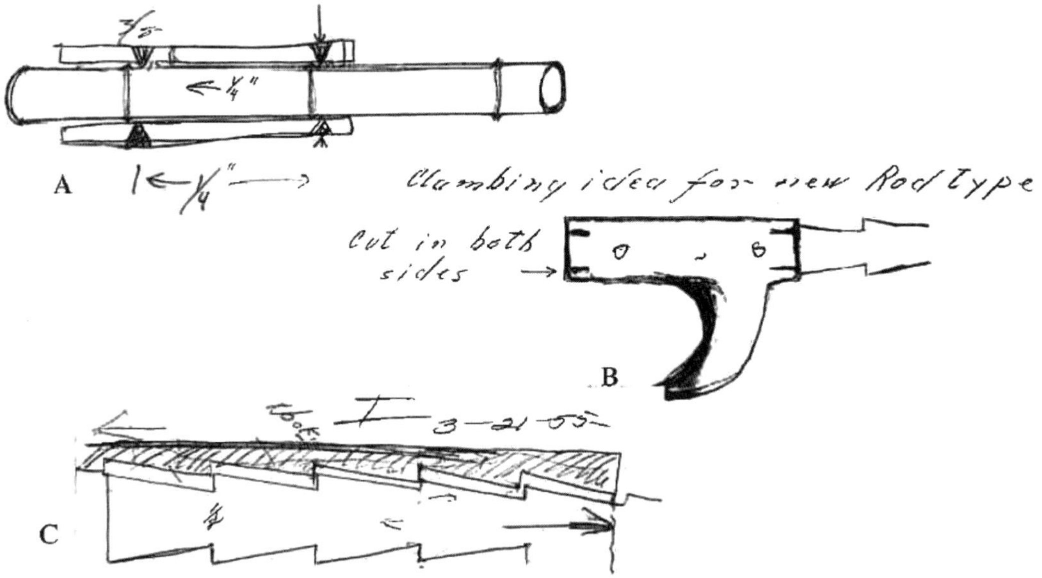

Figure 5.6 ***Sequence of Harrington's original sketches showing the birth of the ratchet connection. A. Rod ratchet. B. Hook crimp. C. Hook and rod ratchets. There is nothing in these drawings to suggest the toggle locking mechanism. (Harrington Archives)***

图 5.6　哈灵顿的原始草图序列显示了棘齿连接的诞生。A. 棒棘齿。B. 钩卷曲。C. 钩和棒棘齿。在这些图纸中没有任何东西表明切换锁定机制(哈灵顿档案馆)

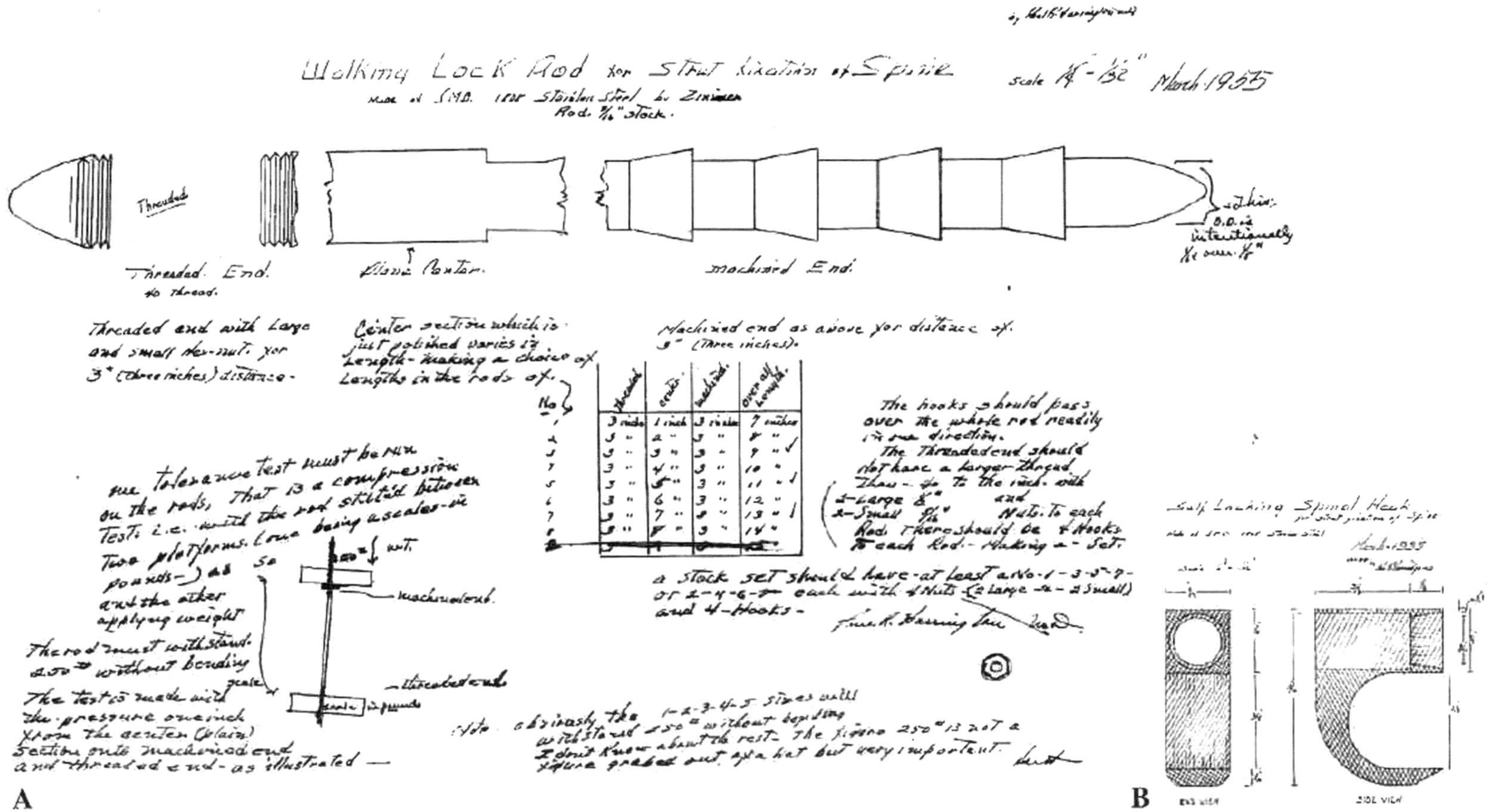

Figure 5.7 *Images of Harrington's original March 1955 drawings. A. Walking Lock Rod for Strut Fixation of Spine showing the ratchet rod design that became the hallmark of Harrington Spine Instrumentation. B. Drawing of the companion Self-locking Spinal Hook for strut fixation of the spine design to be used with the walking lock rod. The drawings were based on 3/16"-diameter rods.* (*Harrington Archives*)

图 5.7 哈灵顿在 1955 年 3 月的原始图纸。A. 用于脊柱支撑固定的滑动锁定棒中的棘齿棒设计，成为哈灵顿脊柱器械的标志。B. 与滑动锁棒一起使用的配套自锁脊柱钩设计图纸。图纸基于 3/16 英寸直径的棒绘制（哈灵顿档案馆）

在他的研究笔记本的下一页上，虽然没有注明日期，但几乎可以肯定是在任何演讲之前，哈灵顿列出了五个问题。第一个是“弱点……棒”。可能是准备这个报告的严格要求迫使他面对现实，他的结果到目前为止还不能与脊柱侧凸标准术式、融合术以及里泽局部石膏矫正和固定方法相媲美。在这一页的中间，在几行空白之后，出现了解决方案：“棒的解决办法是取消螺纹。”[96]列出的另外四个问题是“金属仍然太笨重，撑开系统太复杂，如何调整长度，以及确定何时使用”。无螺纹棒立即引出了连接方式的问题，随之而来的创新也是迅速的。从锁环开始，棘齿概念诞生于 1955 年 2 月 25 日至 3 月 21 日之间。[97]（图 5.6）他稍后回忆这个想法：“如何把棒放进去，如何纠正它？我知道拉它是一个劣势，我们无法得到最大矫正。一个星期天的上午 9 点，我坐在自己的房间里思考。我想到棘齿结构，用洗衣店的纸板做出一个模型。在这个模型上设计了一个钩，并在棒上添加棘齿结构，随后把它拿到捷迈公司，他们为我做了一个，这就是它诞生的过程。”[98]虽然纸板模型没有保存下来，但两张详细的原始图纸保存了下来。哈灵顿称它们为脊柱支撑固定滑动锁棒和自锁脊柱钩系统，均签名并记录为 1955 年 3 月。[99]（图 5.7）他明确指出，它们要用“S. M. O. 1808 不锈钢”制造。

The original ratchet rod and hook were designed for a 3/16”-diameter rod, and the essential feature was the mechanism allowing elongation and its maintenance. The machined or ratchet end of the rod was 3” long and incorporated the dimensions necessary to achieve 1/8” incremental lengthenings, a key feature that would survive throughout the long life of the instrumentation. There were a series of twelve notches or ratchets spaced 1/4” apart. The 1/8” incremental lengthening distance was achieved by this inter-ratchet spacing of 1/4”, a 1/2”-long hook body that spanned two ratchets when the hook was toggled (seated) on its trailing edge, and a raised ridge in the hook body through-hole located 1/8” from the hook’ leading edge so that hook advancement to the next toggling was 1/8”, which was half the inter-ratchet distance. The next advancement stop was 1/8”, where the hook would again toggle onto its trailing edge. The rod minimum diameter at the notches was 9/64” for the 1/8” of rod just above the beginning of the notch and then tapered over the next 1/8” to the full 3/16”-diameter rod just before the next notch. The opposite end of the rod was threaded for 3”, and the option of a large or small nut was provided. The rod between the ratchet and threaded ends, the shank, was smooth and used to provide a 7” to 14” range of overall rod lengths. On the rod drawing Harrington described and illustrated the mechanical test set-up to determine if the rod could withstand a 250-pound vertical load without bending. He specified that the load be placed at an offset of 1” to the vertical rod. He added that “the figure 250 pounds is not a figure grabbed out of a hat but very important.” This, coupled with his earlier request that the rod withstand a 100-pound vertical load for several million cycles, further supports his later recollection that he was receiving guidance from someone at Rice University.[100]

最初的棘齿棒和钩是为直径 3/16 英寸的棒设计的，其基本特点是允许撑开和维持。该棒末端 3 英寸被加工成棘齿，并包含了实现 1/8 英寸增量延长所需的尺寸，是保证该器械长寿命的一个关键特征。共有间隔 1/4 英寸的 12 个缺口或棘齿。1/8 英寸的增量延长距离是通过 1/4 英寸的棘齿间距来实现的，当钩在其尾缘上切换（固定）时，1/2 英寸长的钩主体跨越两个棘齿，钩体通孔中的隆起脊位于距钩前缘 1/8 英寸处，因此钩前进到下一个翻转的距离为 1/8 英寸，这是棘齿间距离的一半。下一个前进点是 1/8 英寸，此时钩将再次切换到后缘。缺口处的棒最小直径为 9/64 英寸，棒的 1/8 英寸处正好位于缺口的开始处，然后在下一个 1/8 英寸处逐渐变细，直到下一个缺口之前的整个直径 3/16 英寸的棒。棒的另一端螺纹为 3 英寸，提供了大螺母或小螺母的选择。棘齿和螺纹两端之间的棒是光滑的，用于提供 7 英寸到 14 英寸的整体棒长范围。在棒的图纸上，哈灵顿描述和说明了机械测试设置，以确定棒是否可以承受 250 磅的垂直载荷而不弯曲。他指定载荷与垂直棒的位移量为 1 英寸。他补充说：“250 镑这个数字不是凭空捏造的，而是非常重要的。”这一点，再加上他早些时候要求棒承受几百万次循环的 100 磅垂直载荷，进一步证实了他后来的回忆，即他是从莱斯大学的某个人那里得到的指导。[100]

The hook blade provided the anchorage site to the posterior bony elements of the spine. The sagittal plane opening between the hook blade and hook body was a half circle having a diameter of 3/8”（0. 375”）, which was only 0. 028” larger than what the latest 1/8”-diameter threaded pre-ratchet hooks had evolved to. At the ends of the half circle, the hook opening was completed by parallel extensions of approximately 7/32” that coincided with the sagittal plane length of the hook body. The end of the hook blade was finished with a chisel edge, coming to a point on the side leading into the hook radius. The width of the hook blade was the same as that of the hook body.

钩刃在脊柱后方附件上提供了锚定点。钩刃和钩体之间的矢状面开口是一个直径为 3/8 英寸的半圆，只比最新的直径为 1/8 英寸的螺纹预棘齿钩大 0. 028 英寸。在半圆的末端，钩开口由大约 7/32 英寸的平行延伸完成，与钩体矢状面长度一致。钩刃的末端有一个凿形的边缘，在一端的一个点上延伸到钩的半径。钩刃的宽度与钩身的宽度相同。

Apparently Harrington sent his drawings to Zimmer, and he recalled that he went there and presented a conference where the attendees were surprised by his detailed explanation of the mechanical specifications he envisioned.[101] In his research notebook, sandwiched between musings about the method of producing experimental scoliosis, he noted in April 1955 that "strut bar to be made by Zimmer."[102] About two months later a nineteen-yearlong blizzard of correspondence with Zimmer began.

显然，哈灵顿把他的图纸寄给了捷迈公司。捷迈公司回忆说，他去了那里并在一个会议上发表了演讲，与会者对他对自己所设想的机械规格的详细解释感到惊讶。[101] 1955 年 4 月，在他的研究笔记本中，在沉思产生实验性脊柱侧凸的方法时，他写道："由捷迈公司制造支撑棒。"[102]大约两个月后，一场与捷迈长达 19 年的通信风暴开始了。

（张卿义 译　刘立岷 刘新宇 陶惠人 审校）

In early 1955 he was also actively engaged in the development of the experimental scoliosis animal model needed for "An Experimental Study of Scoliosis," his second NFIP-funded study. He had begun his work with scoliosis envisioning a dynamic system, but his inability to devise one had increasingly moved him to add arthrodesis to his procedure. However, he remained committed to developing a dynamic approach, and the experimental scoliosis project served to keep this dream alive. In March 1955 while he was making tremendous progress with the design of the human implants, he wrote in his research notebook that "dynamic strut fixation has tremendous possibilities."[103] But years later he recalled that it was then that he was "discontinuing the thought of having a dynamic system that wou1d correct the spine, hold it for a while until the Volkmann's principle... reversed asymmetrical growth."[104] He was conflicted. The purpose of his experimental scoliosis study was "to investigate the feasibility of producing experimental scoliosis in the newborn mouse during growth and development; and, if possible to determine whether or not scoliosis produces bony changes of the vertebrae and its elements, gross or histological."[105] His hypothesis was that "the presence of unequal forces and movements may affect the rate of vertebral bone growth and development so that growth of these tissues may be unequal and lead to progressive curvature of the spine." The corollary was that removal of unequal forces would lead to resolution of the scoliosis. Whereas previous studies had focused on the vertebral body, Harrington's was focused on the paired, posterior face joints.

1955年年初，他也积极参与了以“脊柱侧凸的实验研究”为导向的实验性脊柱侧凸动物模型的构建，这是他由国家小儿麻痹基金会资助的第二项研究。他开始设想在治疗脊柱侧凸时置入一种动态系统，但由于未能设计出这个动态系统，这促使他在手术中进行脊柱融合。然而，他仍然致力于开发一种动态的方法，而脊柱侧凸实验项目一直保持他这一设想。1955年3月，当他在人体内植物的设计上取得巨大进展时，他在研究记录本中写道：“动态支撑固定系统具有巨大的可行性。”[103]但几年后，他回忆说，正是在那时，他“放弃了制造一种可以矫正脊柱的动态系统的想法，这种想法在他脑海中维持了很长时间，直到福尔克曼原理……反向不对称生长”。[104]这让他非常矛盾。他进行实验性脊柱侧凸研究的目的是“研究在新生小鼠的生长和发育过程中产生实验性脊柱侧凸的可行性；如果可能的话，确定脊柱侧凸是否会导致椎体及附件大体形态或组织学上的骨质改变”。[105]他的假设是：“脊柱不平衡的力量和运动可能会影响椎体的生长和发育速度，因此这些椎体组织的生长可能是不平衡的，由此导致脊柱的逐渐弯曲。他推断消除脊柱不平衡的受力可能解决脊柱侧凸。既往研究集中在脊柱椎体上，而哈灵顿的研究则集中于脊柱后方两侧关节突关节的的应力改变。

He spent all of 1955 and part of 1956 doing pilot experiments to work out the details of the experimental study. The animal he chose was a Swiss mouse strain, the albino-C mouse that had been developed by Arthur Kirschbaum, professor and chair of the Department of Anatomy at the Baylor University College of Medicine, for experimental cancer studies. This strain was so highly inbred that different generations were as similar as identical twin littermates. A 44-day-old mouse was equivalent to a 12-year, 5-month-old human. A 45-day survival period was chosen with study intervals of 5 days. Harrington initially envisioned producing scoliosis by suturing the tail of a two-week-old mouse to its left ilium or left ilium and right shoulder to produce a compensatory curve. Apparently neither method was satisfactory; he didn't record why they failed. His research notebook doesn't reveal the satisfactory alternative he arrived at, which was securing/tethering the right hind- and forequarters together with a suture through the knee and elbow joints.

Three experimental groups were formed: control/normal (N), pathological tethered (PT), and pathological tethered and released (PTR). Both pathological groups received the tethering operation at the age of five days. Animals from the N and PT groups were sacrificed at 5-day intervals up to age 45 days. Animals from the PTR group had the tether released at 5-day intervals and were either sacrificed 10 days later or at the age of 45 days. The study methods were radiology, morphology, and quantitative histology using 7-micron thick transverse plane sections for study of the facet joints and growth measurement.[106,107] This was not a small project, and it extended in to 1957. For at least two years the clinical and experimental studies were both in progress, and trying to reconcile the emerging findings was important to the evolution of Harrington Spine Instrumentation.

他花了1955年整整一年和1956年的部分时间进行初步实验，以确定实验研究的细节。他选择的动物是一种瑞士小鼠品系，由贝勒大学医学院解剖学系主任阿瑟·基施鲍姆教授培育的、用于实验性癌症研究的白化小鼠。这种品系是高度近亲繁殖的，不同的世代就像同卵双胞胎一样。一只44天大的老鼠相当于一个12岁零5个月大的人。老鼠的存活期为45天，研究间隔为5天。哈灵顿最初设想通过将一只两周大的小鼠的尾巴缝合到它的左髂骨或将左髂骨和右肩缝合，以产生一个代偿来制作脊柱侧凸模型。这两种方法都不能令人满意，但他没有记录它们失败的原因。他的研究笔记本没有揭示出他得出的令人满意的替代方案，即固定/拴住右后腿和前大腿，并通过膝关节和肘关节缝合。实验分为：对照组/正常组（N）、病理性拴系组（PT）和病理性拴系松解组（PTR）三个小组。两个病理组均在老鼠5日龄时进行拴系手术。正常组和病理性栓系组每隔5天或10天处死动物。病理性拴系松解组的动物每隔5天释放一次系绳，10天后或在45天龄时处死。研究方法包括放射学、形态学和采用7微米厚的切片定量组织学，进行关节突关节和生长测量。[106,107]这不是一个小项目，该研究一直持续到1957年。在至少两年的时间里临床和实验研究都在进行中，重复调整新出现的研究发现对哈灵顿脊柱内固定系统的发展非常重要。

The first surviving correspondence with Zimmer began in June 1955, and the communication was to continue until December 1974. Despite the presence of more than 350 letters in the Harrington Archives, the record is incomplete, primarily because of the absence of blueprints that Harrington edited and returned to Zimmer. To help bridge the gaps and communicate the record as clearly as possible, the measurement, nomenclature, and Zimmer parts number practices used in their communications were closely followed Measurements are given in English units (inches) because metric was in limited use in the United States at that time. The instrumentation dimensions eventually coalesced around three rod diameters and the compatibility with them; the three expressed as a fraction and decimal form were 1/8" (0.125"), 3/16" (0.188"), and 1/4" (0.250").[108] Availability, clinical adequacy, and manufacturing efficiency appear to be the main reasons they were chosen. Dimensions are usually presented in fractions of inches only although the decimal equivalent will sometimes be added for clarity and will usually be added with off-sizes. When indicating tolerances, decimals are used (e.g., 0.252"-0.255"). Because nomenclature for spine instrumentation was being created and was sometimes confusing (e.g., bar, strut, and rod all used for the same item and universal, which was the name of two quite different hooks), extra descriptions that are necessary to make it clear what is being referred to are included. Zimmer parts numbers during the developmental stage were usually preceded by experimental, exp., Exp., or EXP, and this has been deleted. Zimmer part numbers are always preceded by the number sign # and are shown in parentheses.

现存的第一封与捷迈的通信始于 1955 年 6 月，通信交流一直持续到 1974 年 12 月。尽管哈灵顿档案馆存有 350 多封信件，但记录并不完整，主要是因为没有哈灵顿编辑并返还给捷迈的设计蓝图。为了帮助弥合差距，尽可能清晰地传达记录，他们的交流中所使用的测量、命名和捷迈的零件编号都严格一致。因当时公制单位在美国使用有限，所以测量使用英制单位（英寸），器械尺寸最终围绕三个杆径及其兼容性确定；这三个直径以分数和十进制小数形式表示为 1/8 英寸（0.125 英寸）、3/16 英寸（0.188 英寸）和 1/4 英寸（0.250 英寸）。[108]可用性、临床实用性和生产效率是选择他们的主要原因。尺寸通常只以英寸的分数表示，但为了清晰起见，有时会添加相当于十进制的数字，并且通常会添加小数尺寸。当表示公差范围时，使用小数（例如，0.252 英寸~0.255 英寸）。由于当时脊柱器械的术语正在形成阶段，有时会引起混淆（例如，杆、支杆和棒都用于同一个物品，而通用钩是两个完全不同钩子的名称），因此包括了必要的额外描述，使其明确所指的是什么。在开始研发阶段，捷迈零件编号前通常会有 experimental、exp.、Exp.或 EXP，但这些已被删除。后期捷迈零件编号总是以数字符号#为前导，并在括号中显示。

With his June 16, 1955, letter to Harrington, Zimmer's Forrest Perkins transmitted four drawings (strut bar, hook, nuts, and composite) prepared from Harrington's strut bar and hook drawings.[109] *See figure 5.8*. Perkins defended changing the threaded end from 40 to 32 threads per inch because the difference in minor diameter, and therefore strength, was minimal at 0.008". Zimmer had labeled the strut bar (rod) overall length as dimension (a), subdivided into a threaded end (b), central solid portion (c), and ratchet end (d). Harrington responded by acknowledging that the letter and plans "are good and appear to be satisfactory."[110] He noted the only major difference in their drafts, that being the slightly bigger inner diameter of the hole in the hook at the raised inner ridge (0.191" - 0.195") than the outer diameter of the rod ratchet (d) (0.185" - 0.190") and rod thread (b) (0.185" - 0.189"). "I assume that we have a few thousandths of an inch clearance so the hook will pass freely over all parts of the strut bar in extension, only locking itself on section (d) of Plate 50 (#3019-50) when eccentric pressure is applied in compression. He asked, "Will the lip of the hook or strut roll wear excessively, or lock the freedom of extension motion by rolling or lipping after pressure is applied?" Although he sai1 "one answer is IMPERATIVE," it was a question that couldn't be answered at this point. He asked that the 250-pound pressure test on the strut bar be made end-to-end and also through a hook attached to the ratchet (d) end. Harrington also asked that the original drawings or photostatic copies of them be returned to his home address.

在 1955 年 6 月 16 日写给哈灵顿的信中，捷迈团队的福里斯特·珀金斯邮寄了四张图纸（支撑杆、钩、螺母和复合体），这些图纸是从哈灵顿的支撑杆和钩的图中准备的。[109]（图 5.8）珀金斯对将螺纹端从每英寸 40 个螺纹改为 32 个螺纹进行了解释，因为较小直径和强度的差异很小，最小为 0.008 英寸。捷迈将支撑杆（棒）的总长度标记为总长（a），细分为螺纹棒（b）端、中间实心部分（c）和棘齿棒（d）端。哈灵顿回应说他对信和计划非常满意。[110]他注意到在他们的草稿中唯一的主要区别，是在凸起的内脊处的钩子孔的内径（0.191 英寸~0.195 英寸）比棘齿棒（d）（0.185 英寸~0.190 英寸）和螺纹棒（b）（0.185 英寸~0.189 英寸）的外径略大。“我假设我们有千分之几英寸的间隙，这样钩子将在延伸时自由通过支撑杆的所有部分，只有在偏心压力作用于压缩时才会将自身锁定在板 50（#3019-50）的（d）部分上。”他问道，“钩子或杆的边缘是否会过度滚动磨损，或在施加压力后通过滚动或击打边缘来锁定伸展运动的自由?”虽然他说：“一定会有一个答案”，但这是一个当时无法回答的问题。他要求对支撑杆进行 250 磅的压力测试，并通过连接在棘齿端（d）的钩子进行测试。哈灵顿还要求将图纸原件或复印件寄回他的家庭住址。

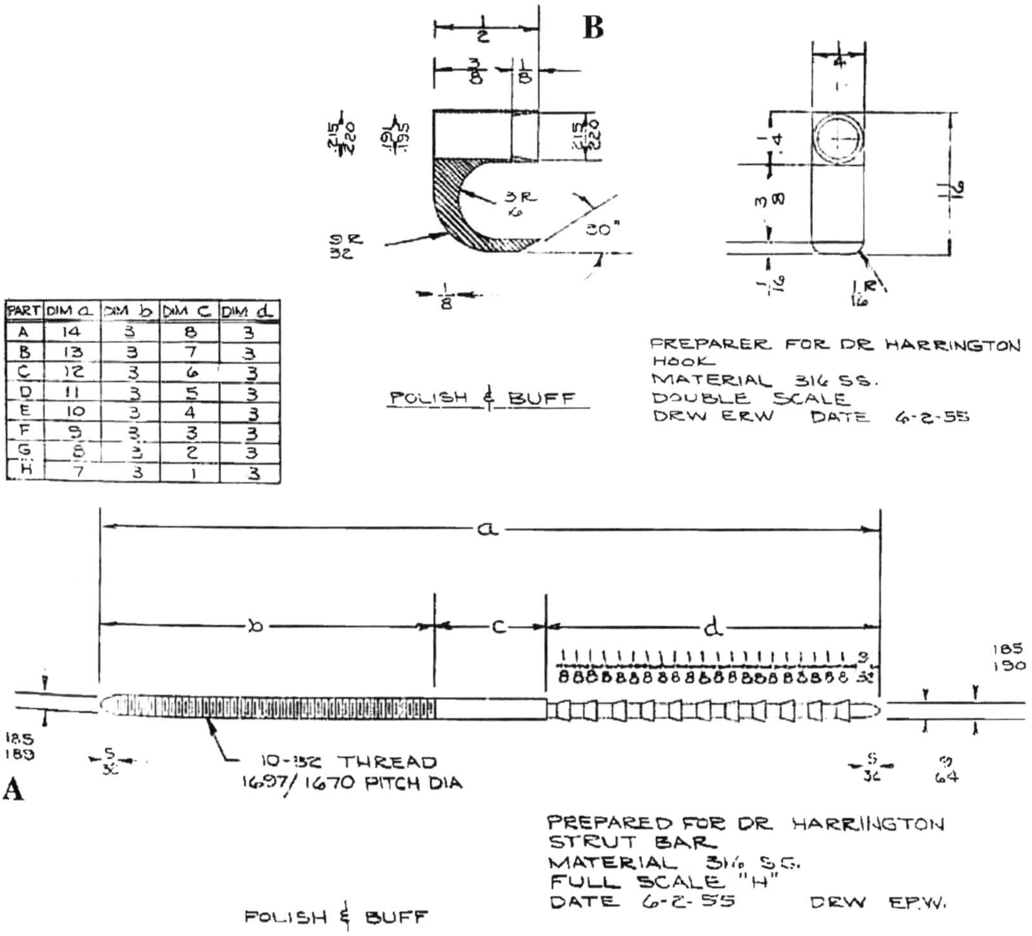

PART	DIM a	DIM b	DIM c	DIM d
A	14	3	8	3
B	13	3	7	3
C	12	3	6	3
D	11	3	5	3
E	10	3	4	3
F	9	3	3	3
G	8	3	2	3
H	7	3	1	3

Figure 5.8 ***First Zimmer drawings prepared from Harrington's original drawings. A Strut bar. B strut bar hook. Not shown are the small and large buts and the assembly. (Harrington Archives)***

图 5.8 根据哈灵顿的原始图纸绘制的捷迈第一张设计图。A. 支撑杆。B. 支撑杆的钩。图中未显示的是小的和大的螺母和装配(哈灵顿档案馆)

Based on his original drawings, he had envisioned the outer diameter of the ratchet and the inner diameter at the hook inner ridge as being the same, 3/16". Considering the small machining tolerance inherent in manufacture, reliable rod passage through the hook hole would have been impossible from a practical standpoint. His drawings didn't make clear how he envisioned the interconnection stop would work, and neither did Zimmer's. While his didn't suggest toggling of the hook on the rod as the locking mechanism, his mention of eccentric pressure did. This sleeve interconnection with toggle locking made manipulation of the distraction load relatively easy. But, it would be several years before Harrington's concern about wear at the rod-hook ratchet interface was relieved. A better mechanism than the thread and nut to complete the rod-sleeve interconnection had been needed for some time. The major alternative considered before the ratchet interconnection appeared to have been a crimping mechanism.[111] It was an idea that would resurface later in the form of a safety C-ring. But the ratchet interconnection concept proved to be the critical step in the development of Harrington Spine Instrumentation. In his research notes he had repeatedly admonished himself to keep the instrumentation design and operation as simple as possible.[112] The ratchet connection was to prove to be quick, precise, and dependable, meeting the simplicity criterion. With this barrier broken, instrumentation refinement, development of tools for implantation, and understanding of the principles of clinical usage could happen. But it would not be an easy or quick trip.

根据他最初的图纸，他设想棘齿的外径和钩内脊的内径是相同的，都为 3/16 英寸。考虑到制造中固有的微小的加工公差，从实用的角度来看，性能可靠的棒穿过钩孔是不可能的。他的图纸没有清楚地说明他设想的互连停止时整个系统将如何工作，捷迈的也没有。虽然他没有建议将棒上的钩切换成锁定机制，但他提到的偏心压力确实如此。这种套筒与拔动锁定的相互连接使得操纵撑开载荷相对容易。但是，哈灵顿在几年后才消除对棒钩棘齿端面磨损的担忧。一段时间以来，哈灵顿需要一种比螺纹和螺母更好的结构来完成棒-套筒的互连。[111]在棘齿互连之前考虑的主要替代方案似乎是卷曲机制，这是一个后来以安全 C 形环的形式重新出现的想法。但棘齿互连的概念被证明是哈灵顿脊柱器械发展的关键一步。在他的研究笔记中，他一再告诫自己，要让器械的设计和操作尽可能简单。[112]棘齿连接被证明是快速、准确和可靠的，符合简化标准。随着这一障碍被打破，器械的完善、内植物植入器械的研发以及对临床使用原则的理解都可能进步，但这不会是一个简单或快速的过程。

A ten-month gap in their correspondence ended with an April 9, 1956, letter from Harrington to Zimmer.[113] Nearly two pages in length and quite detailed, it was apparent that he had gained clinical experience. He first addressed the strut bar (also called bar, distraction rod, or rod, #3019-50). "The bar is not strong enough yet and I would like to increase the size of the weakest points which are the stair steps from 9/64" (0.141") to the present overall size of 3/16" (0.188")." This was a major, 30% increase in diameter. Harrington estimated the outer diameter of the ratchet ridge would have to be increased by 1/32" (0.031"), making the outer diameter 7/32" (0.219"), approaching the commonly available 1/4"-diameter rod stock. He asked that the threaded portion (b) of the rod be completely removed and replaced by a collar placed 1" from the end of the bar (rod). He requested that the smooth section (c) remain the same and be used to provide the range of rod lengths needed, and that the ratchet section (d) remain 3" in length. He addressed the hook (#3019-51) by writing that it "is to be made proportionately larger to work on the strut bar and I would like to have all edges rounded, including the top of the hook as we discussed in our last order, which was quite satisfactory." The nuts (#3019-52 A and B) would be eliminated. He asked that this original Zimmer hook (#3019-51) be kept as the small hook and the new hook designed for the enlarged ratchet would be the large hook.

1956年4月9日，哈灵顿给捷迈的一封信结束了他们中断了长达10个月的通信。[113]这封信将近两页的篇幅，内容相当详细，很明显，哈灵顿已经获得了临床经验。他首先谈到了支撑杆（也叫杆、撑开杆或棒，#3019-50）。“撑杆还不够结实，我想把最薄弱的地方，也就是台阶部分的尺寸从9/64英寸（0.141英寸）增加到现在的整体尺寸3/16英寸（0.188英寸），这是一个比较大的提升，直径增加了30%。哈灵顿估计棘齿脊的外径必须增加1/32英寸（0.031英寸），使外径达到7/32英寸（0.219英寸），接近常用的直径1/4英寸的棒。他要求将杆的螺纹部分（b）完全去除，代之以距杆端1英寸的套环。他要求光滑部分（c）保持不变，用于提供所需的棒长范围，而棘齿部分（d）保持3英寸。他在谈到钩(#3019-51)时写道：“要按比例做得更大，以便在支撑杆上工作，我想把所有的边缘都打磨圆，包括钩的顶部，正如我们在上一份订单中讨论的那样，这很令人满意。”螺母（#3019-52 A和B）将被去除。他要求保留这个原来的捷迈钩(#3019-51)作为小钩，为加大的棘齿设计的新钩是大钩。

"I am sending, under separate cover, instruments to accomplish the surgical procedure. These were made by hand. Would like to have you duplicate these... and will discuss as follows: The spreader is to fit the new enlarged bar. Please note that the saddle effect of the spreader fits snugly the narrowest shoulder of Section d (ratchet end of the rod). The other saddle is large enough to pass over the widest portion of Section dstrutting force is applied by this." Harrington later recalled that he got the inspiration for the spreader from a rib spreader he had brought home from a French storehouse bunker during World War II.[114] In the same letter he wrote, "The hemostats that have been converted are to act as clamping mechanisms on which we can use the regular above described spreader. I would like to have you construct a hook similar to the one sent to you. The holders for the wire and the hook are enclosed in this same package. These I want made." These two requests were the first mention in the surviving Harrington-Zimmer correspondence of instruments and tools based on a 1/8"-diameter rod that he had been using since 1951. He concluded with the following: "Dr. S. Ben Fowler, 1921 Broadway, Nashville, Tennessee would like a set of instruments and material. The following composes a set: 1) Rods or bars, the new enlarged type ranging from 4" to 16"-12 in all; 2) Hooks, the 1arge new type-24 in all; 3) 1/8" threaded rod 6 inches long with 12 nuts to fit 6 threaded rods; 4) Small hooks—12 in all (note design); 5) 6 saddle washers (see accompanying drawing #2); 6) Instruments: 1 spreader, 1 threaded clamp, and 1 hook clamp. Dr.Fowler is very desirous of receiving this equipment as soon as possible. Can you give me some estimate as to when this may be accomplished?"

"我另外寄来了完成手术过程的工具，是单独密封的。这些是手工制作的。希望您能复制这些……并讨论如下：请注意，撑开钳的鞍座与 d 部分（杆的棘齿端）的最窄的肩部紧密配合，另一个撑开钳的鞍座足够大，足以通过 d 部分，支撑力由它施加。"哈灵顿后来回忆说，他从第二次世界大战期间从法国仓库和地堡带回来的一个肋骨吊具中得到了撑开钳的灵感。[114]在同一封信中，他写道："已经改造好的止血器钳将作为夹持机制，我们可以在上面使用上述的常规撑开钳。我想让您制造一个类似于寄给您的那个钩子。支持钢丝和钩子的工具也在附件里。我想做这些。"这两个要求是在现存的哈灵顿-捷迈的通信中第一次提到基于他自 1951 年以来一直使用的直径 1/8 英寸的棒和工具。他最后写道："位于田纳西州纳什维尔市百老汇大街 1921 号的 S. 本·福勒博士希望得到一套器械和工具。包括以下内容：(1) 棒或杆，新的加大型，范围从 4 英寸到 16 英寸——共 12 根；(2) 钩，新的大型钩——共 24 个；(3) 1/8 英寸的螺纹棒，6 英寸，有 12 个螺母，适合 6 根螺纹棒；(4) 小钩——共 12 个（注意设计）；(5) 6 个鞍形垫圈（附图#2）；(6) 器械。1 个撑开钳，1 个螺纹钳，1 个钩子钳。福勒博士非常希望能尽快收到这些器械。你能否估计一下什么时候可以完成?"

Some parts of the letter require commentary. First, this was the beginning of the evolution of the strut bar with the increase of the inner and outer diameters of the ratchet section (d) and removal of the threaded end (b). Second, it would lead to the 1/4"-diameter rod compatible hook. Third, it left unclear the status of the original 3/16"-diamete1 rod compatible hook. Fourth, it marked the beginning of Zimmer's involvement with the manufacturing of the 1/8"-diameter threaded rod compatible implants, which

Engen apparently had been providing. Fifth, a drawing of the saddle washer referred to has not been found, and whether this was the forerunner of the safety ring isn't known. While it seems likely that it was, the safety ring doesn't come up again in the Harrington-Zimmer correspondence for many months.

这封信的某些部分是需要讨论的。第一，这是支撑杆变化的开始，棘齿部分（d）的内径和外径增大，并取消了螺纹端（b）。第二，它将导致直径 1/4 英寸的棒兼容钩。第三，它不清楚原来的直径 3/16 英寸棒兼容钩的状态。第四，它标志着捷迈开始参与制造直径为 1/8 英寸的螺纹棒兼容内植物，恩金显然一直在提供这种产品。第五，没有找到提到的鞍座垫圈的图纸，这是否是安全环的前身也不得而知。虽然看起来很可能是，但安全环在哈灵顿-捷迈的通信中几个月都没有再出现。

Zimmer's response was limited to a drawing prepared April 17, 1956, of the large 1/4"-diameter rod compatible strut bar (distraction) hook, for which they used the original hook identification number, with the addition of a 99-prefix (#99-3019-51). *See figure 5.9*. The inner diameter of the hole had been increased to 0.252"-0.255", large enough for the passage of a 1/4"-diameter rod, 14% more than the 7/32" (0.219") Harrington had recommended. It had taken only two steps to arrive at an outer rod dimension that would accommodate the new ratchet mechanism and ultimately allow the rod-hook interconnection to withstand the required loads. The design of the ratchet hook was essentially complete, requiring only minor refinements over time. It became the first "mature" instrumentation/implant component. There is no extant drawing of the updated rod, which was referred to in later correspondence. However, a now lost artifact from that iteration was remembered as showing a smaller diameter smooth shaft in relation to the ratchet end.

捷迈的答复仅在 1956 年 4 月 17 日的一张大的直径 1/4 英寸的棒兼容支撑杆（牵张）钩的图纸，他们使用了原来的钩识别号，并加上了#99 前缀（#99-3019-51)。(图 5.9) 孔的内径已经增加到 0.252 英寸~0.255 英寸，足以通过 1/4 英寸直径的棒，比哈灵顿建议的 7/32 英寸（0.219 英寸）多 14%。只用了两个步骤，就得到能容纳新的棘齿机制的外杆尺寸，并最终使棒-钩连接处能承受所需的载荷。棘齿钩的设计基本上已经完成，只需要随着时间的推移进行小的改进。它成为第一个“成熟”的器械/植入物。在后来的通信中提到的更新升级的棒没有现存的图纸。然而，人们认为那次更新迭代中的一件、现已遗失的器械与棘齿末端相比，光滑轴的直径更小。

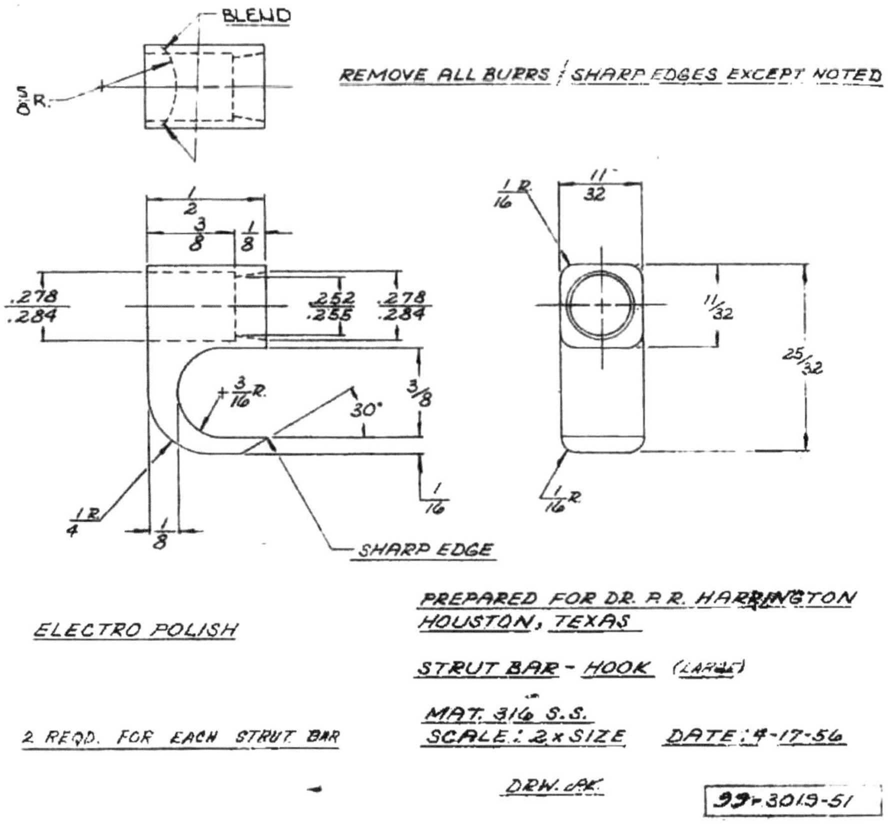

Figure 5.9 ***Zimmer drawing of the enlarged 1/4" out diameter ratchet compatible strut bar hook (#99-3091-51), April 17, 1956. (Harrington Archives)***

图 5.9　**扩大的** 1/4 **英寸外径棘齿兼容支撑杆钩**(#99-3091-51)**的捷迈设计图。**1956 **年** 4 **月** 17 **日(哈灵顿档案馆)**

Harrington's offering of the instrumentation to Fowler, who had requested the instruments, at such an early stage of its development requires some explanation. Harrington's NFIP counterpart in Nashville was Don L. Eyler. He and Harrington were both deeply involved in the treatment of poliomyelitis and developed a strong and lasting professional and personal friendship. Fowler and Eyler were associates, with Fowler doing the spinal surgery. Eyler later characterized Fowler as "probably the finest orthopedist I ever saw or worked with."[115] Fowler became president of the AAOS in 1969. In short, Harrington wasn't offering it to just anyone. His request that instrumentation be sent to Fowler suggests that he was experiencing increasing clinical success. It also suggests that his work was beginning to draw at least some favorable attention. Unfortunately, it is unknown whether Fowler received the instruments and used them.

哈灵顿在器械设计发展的早期阶段就向福勒提供了这些器械并做出解释说明。哈灵顿在纳什维尔的国家小儿麻痹基金会的共事伙伴是唐·L. 艾勒。他和哈灵顿都深耕于脊髓灰质炎的治疗工作，并建立了牢固而持久的同事关系和个人友谊。福勒和艾勒是同事，艾勒负责做脊柱手术。艾勒后来称福勒为“可能是我见过的并合作过的最好的骨科医生”。[115]福勒在1969年成为美国骨科医师学会的主席。简而言之，哈灵顿并不是要把它提供给任何人。他要求将器械寄给福勒表明他在临床方面越来越成功。这也表明，他的工作至少开始引起学界大师的关注。不幸的是，我们不知道福勒是否收到了这些器械并使用了它们。

Probably about midyear 1956 the NFIP held a symposium on poliomyelitis in Houston.[116,117] The orthopedists known to be present were Harrington, Eyler, and Vernon Nickel from Rancho Los Amigos Medical Center in Downey, California. Eyler recalled that "one evening after a long session, we were sitting in the lounge having a few and, of course, talking shop. We discussed the problem of postoperative immobilization of dorsocervical fusions in poliomyelitis patients with essentially flail necks. We had tried the usual modalities of tongs, braces, and casts, and usually the complications outweighed the benefits. Paul suddenly said he thought he had an answer to that problem. He said there was an orthopedist in Houston named Freddy Bloom who was also a tool and die maker. He had his own machine shop and even made his own hip prostheses. Harrington said that Freddy had devised a stainless steel horseshoe that fastened to the skull with ingenious screws that penetrated only the outer table of the skull. It was nearly midnight, but nothing would do but that we go over and talk with Freddy. Freddy came to the door in his bathrobe and Paul explained his mission. And he [Freddy] said sure, just come around to the garage door entrance and I'll admit you to the shop. There he showed us the stainless steel horseshoe that Paul had described. Freddy had devised it for use by maxillofacial surgeons to treat craniofacial dis-associations with wires and outriggers."[118] Eyler later photographed Bloom and Nickel modeling his device. *See figure 5.10.* Bloom had served in the South Pacific during World War Ⅱ and had seen a common injury, a depressed facial fracture, which resulted from the sudden deceleration of a P-40 fighter during landing when its front landing wheel hit one of the pockmarks on the uneven runways.[119]

Figure 5.10 ***Freddy Bloom, left, and Vernon Nickel demonstrating Bloom's halo, 1956.*** **(*Harrington Archives*)**
图 5.10　**弗雷迪·布卢姆(左)和弗农·尼克尔展示布卢姆的 halo 支架,1956 年(哈灵顿档案馆)**

大概在 1956 年年中，国家小儿麻痹基金会在休斯敦举行了一次关于脊髓灰质炎的研讨会。[116,117]已知出席会议的骨科医生有哈灵顿、艾勒和来自加利福尼亚州唐尼市洛杉矶兰乔医疗中心的弗农·尼克尔。艾勒回忆说："在漫长的会议结束后的一个晚上，我们坐在休息室里喝了几杯，当然，也谈了很多。我们讨论了脊髓灰质炎患者的颈背部融合术后固定问题，这些患者的颈部基本上是连枷样的。我们已经尝试了钳子、支具和石膏等常规方式，但通常情况下，患者的并发症都大于临床获益。保罗突然说他认为他有办法解决这个问题。他说在休斯敦有一位名叫弗雷迪·布卢姆的骨科医生，同时他也擅长工具和模具制造。他有自己的机械车间，甚至自己制作髋关节假体。哈灵顿说，弗雷迪设计了一个不锈钢马蹄形固定器，用巧妙的螺丝钉固定在颅骨上，只穿透颅骨的外皮质。当时已近午夜，但我们还是去找弗雷迪谈谈。弗雷迪穿着浴袍来到门口，保罗解释了他的来意。弗雷迪说当然可以，我带你们到车间去参观。在那里，他向我们展示了保罗描述的不锈钢马蹄形内固定器。弗雷迪设计了它，供颌面外科医生使用，用钢丝和外撑开器来治疗颅面分离。"[118]艾勒后来拍下了布卢姆和尼克尔为他的装置建模的照片。(图 5.10) 布卢姆在第二次世界大战期间曾在南太平洋服役，看到过一种常见的面部凹陷性骨折，这是由于飞行员在 P-40 战斗机着陆时突然减速，其前轮撞到不平整的跑道上的坑而造成的。[119]

Nickel talked Bloom out of one of the horseshoes and took it back to Rancho where he, Jacquelin Perry, and their orthotist modified it by closing the ring. They renamed it the halo and used it to provide secure, skeletal fixation to the skull using four transfixing skull pins designed to prevent excessive skull penetration. Through attachments to the halo, corrective and/or stabilizing loads could be applied to facilitate treatment of the deformed, unstable, or diseased cervical spine. Perry and Nickel, citing their inspiration from Bloom, introduced the halo as a skeletal fixation device as part of a large experience with "Total Cervical-Spine Fusion for Neck Paralysis" presented at the annual meeting of the AAOS in New York on February 4, 1958. It was subsequently published.[120] In their next publication of a series of 204 patients whose treatment included the halo device, the authors left doubt about the original inspiration year of 1956 by stating that the patients were treated from June 1955 to January 1967.[121] In yet another publication of a different mix of patients, the halo series was listed as running from 1957 to 1961.[122] What was not in doubt were the stimulus of severely involved post-polio survivors and the contributions of Frederick A. Bloom to the origin of halo-skeletal fixation and Nickel, Perry, and their associates to its clinically useful development.[123] What has not been well recognized was that the connection was Harrington's idea, although "Paul had no desire to get any credit."[124]

尼克尔说服布卢姆赠予了一个马蹄形固定器，并把它带回了兰乔，在那里他和杰奎琳·佩里以及矫形器技师把它修改成环形。他们将其重新命名为halo，并使用四个转轴式颅骨针提供安全的骨骼固定，以防止颅骨过度穿透。通过与halo的连接，可以进行矫正和/或稳定载荷，以促进对畸形、不稳定或退变的颈椎的治疗。佩里和尼克尔从布卢姆那里得到了灵感，在1958年2月4日纽约美国骨科医师学会年会上介绍了作为固定装置的halo是“颈部瘫痪的全颈椎融合”大型经验的重要组成部分。该报告随后被发表。[120]在之后的接受halo装置治疗的204名患者的系列文章中，作者对1956年这一原始灵感年留下了疑问，称这些患者从1955年6月到1967年1月接受了治疗。[121]在另一篇纳入不同患者的文献中，halo装置的使用从1957年到1961年。[122]毫无疑问的是，严重受累的脊髓灰质炎后遗症患者，以及halo骨骼固定的设计者弗雷德里克·A. 布卢姆和尼克尔、佩里和他们的同事一起推动了halo装置应用于临床的研发。[123]没有被充分认识到的是，这种联系是哈灵顿的想法，尽管“保罗对荣誉没有任何兴趣”。[124]

The Harrington-Zimmer correspondence began again in October 1956, leaving six months undocumented. This pattern of intermittent bursts of correspondence was consistent with clinical practice since patients with the indications for surgery presented at varying rates. This was true even when the indications were clear-cut, which they certainly were not at this developmental stage of a new technique. After implantation, time was required to study their performance. Harrington and his patients had always been and continued to be in precarious ethical territory. Years later his associate Jesse Dickson said that as far as he knew, none of Harrington's patient or their families had ever sued him, partly because he made it a point to include the patient and family as part of the care team.[125] Pure intentions, talent, and mutual trust bridged the ethical divide.

哈灵顿–捷迈从1956年10月开始再次通信，有6个月没有记录。这种断断续续的通信模式与临床实践是一致的，因为具有手术指征的病人出现的频率是不同的。即使在适应证明确的情况下也是如此，而在新技术的发展阶段肯定不是这样。植入后需要时间来验证其性能。哈灵顿和他的病人一直处于并将继续处于不稳定的伦理领域。后来，他的助手杰西·迪克森说，据他所知，哈灵顿的病人或他们的家人没有一个起诉过他，部分原因是他把病人作为治疗团队的一部分。[125]纯粹的医患关系、卓越的医学才能和医患之间的相互信任弥合了伦理的鸿沟。

The correspondence burst between the surgeon and Zimmer that began on October 10, 1956, lasted four months; eleven letters are in the archives. The first was by R. E Delp, works manager, responding to an unavailable letter from Harrington, who had requested that a concave junction or fillet be left at the junction of 90° cut to form the stop, or ratchet, thereby strengthening this weak point. *See figure 5.11*. Delp responded that "there is no doubt in our minds but that it will make a much stronger fixation. The one question that has been brought to our attention is, if we put a fillet on the stops, there may be a tendency for the hooks to slip off. Mr. Hite suggested we make up one model and send it to you for your approval before we make this change."[126] Harrington had also inquired about the inspection for quality that the rods received. He

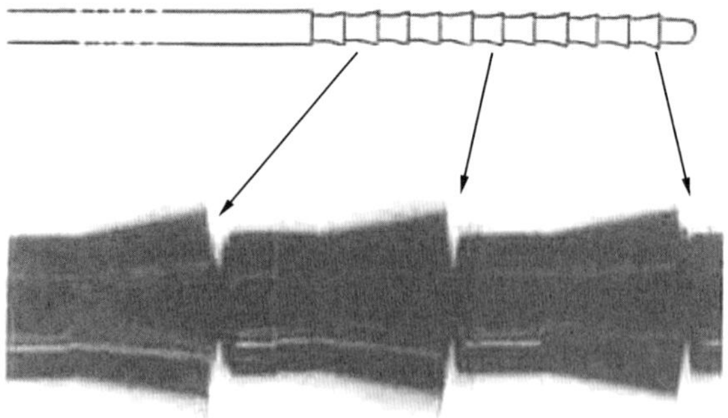

Figure 5.11 ***Fillets, concave junctions where two surfaces meet, to strengthen the weak point of the ratchet.*** **(*Harrington Archives*)**
图5.11 凹角，在两面相接处的凹陷处，加强棘齿的薄弱处（哈灵顿档案馆）

was advised "that all of them are given zyglo inspection which has proven to be more accurate in finding defect than X-ray." He had also indicated that he "was returning all threaded rods of the smaller design plus hook." Delp commented that these had not been received and asked to be advised when they would be sent so they could be on the lookout for them. Although not identified by size, these were probably the original 3/16"-diameter distraction rods with one end threaded, although it is impossible to be sure they weren't the 1/8"-diameter threaded rods and hooks to go with them.

从 1956 年 10 月 10 日开始，哈灵顿和捷迈之间的通信变得频繁，持续了四个月；档案中共有 11 封信。第一封是由工厂经理 R. E. 德尔普写的，他对哈灵顿的一封信作出了回应，哈灵顿要求在 90°切口的交界处留下一个凹形的连接点或圆角，以形成停止点或棘齿，从而加强这个薄弱点。（图 5. 11）德尔普回答说："在我们看来，毫无疑问，这将使固定更加牢固。有一个问题引起了我们的注意，如果我们在挡板上加一个圆角，可能会造成钩出现滑落的趋势。海特先生建议我们制作一个模型，并在我们进行此更改之前将其发送给您以供批准。"[126] 哈灵顿还询问了棒的质量检查情况。他被告知"所有的棒都通过荧光探伤法（探测是否有缺陷），荧光探伤器已被证明能比 X 射线更准确地发现缺陷"。他还表示，他正在退回所有较小规格的螺纹棒和钩子。德尔普说，这些材料还没有收到，并要求告知何时发送，以便他们能够及时关注。虽然没有通过尺寸来识别，尽管无法确定它们不是直径 1/8 英寸的螺纹棒和钩，但这些一端是螺纹的棒可能是最初的直径 3/16 英寸的撑开棒。

Harrington's response was prompt. He discounted Zimmer's concern that the fillet might destabilize the ratchet interconnection unless, of course, the bevels were large.[127] He backed up his request with the observation that "strength is lost if a straight cut is made into the outer diameter of the bar at its smallest point." He did not directly respond to their offer to make and send a model. Rod strength was clearly becoming an issue as he reported that, since writing and changing the rod design in the spring of 1956, by removing the threaded (b) portion another earlier rod had broken at the junction of the threads and the "main body of the bar." Harrington's focus next turned to a critique of the clamping instrument copies Zimmer was making of the threaded wire holder and small hook clamp that he had returned. He criticized the small hook clamp, describing it as "no good." The opening "to receive the hook is too deep and too large." The tit for engaging the side hole in the hook, which had been fitted into a hole in the clamp jaw, "has fallen out already. You can see if the clamp is closed on the hook without perfect centering of the hole that the plug would be forced out... Under separate cover I will send you the clamp I am referring to above for your inspection with a clamp that we have made." Changing course, he placed an order for two dozen small hooks, and it is impossible to know if they were the original Zimmer-made 3/16"-diameter rod compatible #3019-51 hooks or the 1/8"-diameter threaded rod compatible hooks. These October 10 and 19 letters between Harrington and Delp were their last.

哈灵顿的反应很迅速。他打消了捷迈的担忧，认为除非斜角很大，不然凹角不会破坏棘齿互连的稳定性。[127]为了支持自己的请求，他观察到"如果在最小点处对棒材的外径进行直切，强度就会丧失"。他没有直接回应他们制作和发送模型的提议。棒强度显然成为一个问题，因为他报告说，自从1956年春天更改棒设计以来，通过去除螺纹（b）部分，另一个早期的棒在螺纹和"主体的连接处断裂"。哈灵顿接下来的注意力转向了对捷迈正在制作的夹具复制品的批评，这些夹具复制品是他归还的螺纹线架和小钩夹。他批评小钩夹，称其"不好"。接钩的开口"太深太大了"。用在夹具侧孔上并已经安装在孔里的钩"已经掉了。可以看到如果没有完美的中心孔让夹具紧钩在钩上，插头将被逼出……我将另函寄上上述夹具，供您用我们制作的夹具检查"。他改变了策略，订购了24个小钩，现在已不可能知道它们是捷迈公司制造的直径3/16英寸棒兼容的#3019-51钩还是直径1/8英寸螺纹棒的兼容钩。哈灵顿和德尔普10月10日和19日的这些信件是他们最后的通信。

On December 5, 1956, James P. Keeton of the engineering department picked up the correspondence for the first time with a letter of inquiry about a strut bar blueprint sent October 29.[128] Harrington promptly responded that after going through their files completely, they had no record of receiving the blueprint.[129] He commented that "in my letter of October 19, most of the desired information was given on the rods and instruments. The last design you have on the strut rod is good. However, I suggest that the whole middle section of the rod be left the same size as your stock, leaving it full overall 1/4" diameter. The rod would be, therefore, the same on the step [ratchet] end and on the lower end." Obviously, this would both strengthen the smooth portion of the rod and decrease the machining time. He did not address the interconnection changes at the lower end of the rod that would have resulted. Harrington requested three each of the last design in 6", 8", and 10" lengths. Keeton promptly responded on December 19, 1956, sending three strut bar blueprints. The original version that was then obsolete was made from about June 1955 to April 1956 and had a 3/16" diameter all the way and one end was threaded (b). The second style that was then in use had no threaded end, a 3/16"-diameter center shaft (c), and a 1/4"-diameter ratchet end (d). The third style, which Harrington had recently recommended, had a 1/4" diameter for its full length.[130] There are no copies of the blueprints, which is Unfortunately as it makes it difficult to confirm these details and follow the evolution of the connection at the non-ratchet end of the rod (originally 3/16"-diameter threaded, then 3/16" unthreaded, and then presumably 1/4" unthreaded with a stop collar to block the 1/4"-diameter rod compatible distraction hook, #99-3019-51).

1956 年 12 月 5 日，工程部的简斯·P. 基顿第一次收到了一封 10 月 29 日寄出的关于支撑杆设计蓝图的询问信。[128]哈灵顿立即回应说，在彻底检查了他们的文件后，他们没有收到设计蓝图的记录。[129]他评论说，“在我 10 月 19 日的信中，大部分想要的信息都是关于棒和器械的。您在支撑棒上的最后的一个设计很好。但是，我建议整个棒中间部分保持与卡住的尺寸相同，使其整体直径为 1/4 英寸，因此，棒在台阶（棘齿）端和下端相同。”显然，这既可以加强杆的光滑度，又可以减少加工时间。他没有解决可能导致的棒下端的互连变化。哈灵顿要求最后一种设计中的三个长度分别为 6 英寸、8 英寸和 10 英寸。基顿于 1956 年 12 月 19 日迅速做出了回应，发送了三张支撑杆蓝图。当时过时的原始版本大约在 1955 年 6 月至 1956 年 4 月期间制造，直径为 3/16 英寸，一端是螺纹的（b）。当时使用的第二种样式没有螺纹端，一个直径 3/16 英寸的中心轴（c）和一个直径 1/4 英寸的棘齿端（d）。哈灵顿最后推荐的第三种款式是全长直径为 1/4 英寸的棒。[130]不幸的是设计图纸没有副本，因为这使得确认这些细节和追踪连接的所有非棘齿端都变得困难（最初是直径 3/16 英寸有螺纹，然后是 3/16 英寸无螺纹，然后大概是 1/4 英寸无螺纹，带有止动环以阻挡 1/4 英寸直径棒兼容的撑开钩，#99-3019-51）。

Harrington had returned some original style strut bars to be altered, and Keeton asked how they should proceed. "Do you want them duplicated or do you want them made in the later style?" This was a strange inquiry as the only way they could have been altered was to remove the lower threaded connection since an increase in the diameter of the ratchet or of the smooth central portion of the rod was not feasible. The obvious question was why Harrington would even want these components modified. There was a probable answer rooted in the funding. It is important to remember that the implants

Zimmer was making were being paid for from Harrington's NFIP grant, and he was merely trying to conserve the funds.

哈灵顿已经退回了一些原始风格的支撑杆让捷迈进行修改，基顿问他们应该如何进行。“你想复制它们还是想让它们变为后来的风格?”这是一个奇怪的问题，因为他们可以改变的唯一方法是移除下螺纹连接，因为增加棘齿的直径或棒的平滑中心部分是不可行的。显而易见的问题是，为什么哈灵顿甚至希望修改这些组件。有一个可能的答案是资金原因。重要的是捷迈正在研发的内植物是由哈灵顿所在的国家小儿麻痹基金会拨款支付的，他只是想节省资金。

Their 1957 correspondence began with a January 10 letter from Keeton announcing, "Under separate cover I am sending your strut bars, hook clamp, and threaded wires."[131] Two sets of drawings also were included, one for checking and the other for his files. It is regrettable that they are not in the archives because without them it is impossible to know the diameter of the smooth portion of the strut bar. However, the tone and content of Harrington's quick response suggested that Keeton's mailing included only the latest versions of the instruments.[132] Harrington had several minor suggestions, including a more rounding of the distraction hook (#3019-51) surface. The 99-prefix was not used so #3019-51 appeared to be solely associated with the 1/4"-diameter rod compatible distraction hook. He requested that the small 1/8"-diameter threaded compression rod (#3517) have six nuts and that the strut bar (distraction rod, #3019-50) have a 0.025"-diameter hole drilled as was illustrated. Presumably, this was near the end of the rod opposite the ratchet end and intended to provide for placement of a safety wire to prevent disengagement of the lower end of the rod from the hook. The diameter of the distraction rod shaft was not mentioned. Most of his comments were made about the spreader (#3515), and he enclosed a drawing of his wishes. In short, he criticized the reverse grip as annoying and painful to the operator, drew a better spring, and asked that the tips be squared rather than rounded so that they would not slip off. Harrington closed with the information that "another threaded rod broke last week after six months, at precisely the same spot as the others did that I sent you." This would have been at the threaded, smooth rod junction of the original strut bar/rod.

他们 1957 年的通信始于 1 月 10 日基顿的一封信，信中宣称：“在另一个信件中有我寄给您的支撑杆、钩夹和螺纹线。”[131]还包括两套图纸，一套用于检查，另一套用于存档。遗憾的是，它们不在档案中，因为没有它们，就不可能知道支撑杆光滑部分的直径。然而，哈灵顿快速回应的语气和内容表明，基顿的邮件只包括最新版本的器械。[132]哈灵顿有几个小建议，包括一个更圆的撑开钩（#3019-51）表面。没有使用99前缀，因此#3019-51似乎仅与直径1/4英寸的棒兼容撑开钩相关联。他要求直径为1/8英寸的小型螺纹压缩棒（#3517）有六个螺母，支撑杆（撑开棒，#3019-50）如图所示，钻孔直径为0.025英寸。据推测，这是靠近棘齿端对面的棒末端，旨在提供安全线的位置，以防止棒的末端与钩脱离。哈灵顿没有提到牵引杆轴的直径。他的大部分意见都是关于撑开钳（#3515）的，他还附上了一张符合他期望的图纸。简而言之，他对让病人反向握把持批评态度，因为这对操作者来说是令人讨厌和痛苦的，他画了一个更好的弹簧，并要求尖端是方形的而不是圆形的，这样它们就不会滑落。哈灵顿最后说："另一根螺纹杆在六个月后于上周断裂，断裂的位置与我寄给你的其他杆子的位置完全相同。"断裂点应该是在原支撑杆/棒的螺纹和光滑杆的连接处。

Keeton's response contains a very curious comment. "Sorry to hear that the strut bars are breaking. I hope that the new 5/16" inch diameter bar will prove out much better than the old style did."[133] A strut bar bigger than 1/4" diameter had never been mentioned and would never be mentioned again so this was possibly a mistake, albeit a glaring one. Otherwise, the letter was accompanied by a complete set of new drawings (that have been lost) and, for the first but not the last time, a request for information about the technique for using the strut bars, hooks, and instruments. Harrington closed his response with, "Before long, I will send some explanations about application of this strut to the spine." But this was not before focusing on prototype #3518, the small 1/8"-diameter threaded rod compatible hook clamp: "as you see, it fell apart." Harrington explained, "This clamp is used with the resistance against the spreader. The jaw of the clamp, therefore, must be left beefed as much as possible."[134] A few days later Harrington offered detailed advice about modifying a needle holder (e.g., using a file rather than a drill to fashion the tunnel and rounding the locking it so that it didn't bind on the rod passing through).[135] He requested two important changes in the design of the 1/8"-diameter threaded rod compatible hook (#3519): removal of the heel of the hook and reversal of the hook's sharp leading edge. Keeton closed out this communication sequence by sending a new beefier type of small hook clamp.[136]

基顿回信道，"很遗憾听到支撑杆断裂的消息，我希望新式的直径5/16英寸的杆会比之前的更好。"[133]直径大于1/4英寸的支撑杆在信中未被提及，也不会再被提及，这可能本身就是一个明显的错误。除此之外，信中还附有一套完整的新图纸（已经丢失），并且第一次但不是最后一次要求提供关于支撑杆、钩和工具的使用技术资料。哈灵顿在信的最后写道："在不久之后，我会发给你一些关于在脊柱上应用这种杆的说明。"但这之前，他关注的是#3518 原型，即直径为 1/8 英寸的小螺纹棒，与兼容的钩夹。"如你所见，它失败了。"哈灵顿解释说，"这个夹子是用于放置撑开钳进行撑开的，因此，夹具的钳口必须尽可能加强。"[134] 几天后，哈灵顿提供了关于修改持针器的详细建议（例如，用锉刀而不是钻头来打磨通道，并将锁扣磨圆，这样它就不会在穿过棒时卡住）。[135] 他要求对直径为 1/8 英寸的螺纹杆兼容钩（#3519）的设计进行两项重要修改：去除钩的后跟和扭转钩的尖锐前缘。这次联系以基顿向哈灵顿邮寄了一个新的更坚固的小钩夹告一段落。[136]

In the spring of 1957 Harrington had a mission other than spinal instrumentation to complete. In addition to his intense involvement with the secondary effects of polio, he had always maintained an interest in the disease itself. That spring he was the director of the Harris County, Texas, Polio-Salk vaccination program or Polio V-Day, sponsored by the Harris County Medical Society and the Harris County Chapter of the NFIP, which was financially underwriting the program. Tens of thousands were vaccinated, and since over 70% of the vaccinated paid, the program paid for itself.[137,138] From this Polio V-Day involvement came a favorite family story that was told many years later by his daughter, Sue Harrington Price. "With the development of the Salk vaccine, Houston and Harris County planned an immunization program for the elementary school children. Daddy was in charge of the program. Of course Mother signed the parental permission slip for us to receive our shots. Richard was in the second grade and did not like shots, so he threw the slip out of the school bus on the way to school. Since he was one of only two children at the school not to sign up, his teacher asked the reason. Richard said his parents didn't believe in shots. When Daddy found out he marched him down to the front of the line at Hermann Hospital to get his shot."[139]

1957 年春天，除要研究脊柱内固定之外，哈灵顿还有另一项任务。一直以来，他密切关注着脊髓灰质炎的并发症，同时还对脊髓灰质炎疾病本身感兴趣。那年春天，他成为得克萨斯州哈里斯县脊髓灰质炎–索尔克疫苗接种计划（"脊髓灰质炎日"活动）的负责人，该计划由哈里斯县医学会和国家小儿麻痹基金会哈里斯县分会主办，并由国家小儿麻痹基金会哈里斯县分会提供资金支持。数以万计的人接种了疫苗，而且由于超过70%的接种者支付了费用，该计划收回了成本。[137,138]他的女儿苏·哈灵顿·普赖斯多年后讲述了“脊髓灰质炎日”开展时发生在她家的故事，“随着索尔克疫苗的开发，休斯敦和哈里斯县计划为小学生实施免疫接种计划，由爸爸负责该计划。当然，妈妈也在家长知情同意书上签了字，让我们接种疫苗。理查德当时上二年级，不喜欢打针，所以他在去学校的路上把单子扔出了校车。由于他是学校里仅有的两个没有签字的孩子之一，他的老师问其原因，理查德说他的父母不相信打针，当爸爸知道后，立即带着他到赫尔曼医院排队打针。”[139]

After a three-month gap in communication with Zimmer, Harrington wrote Keeton on May 14, 1957, with a number of observations and requests.[140] "On December 28, 1956, you sent me a set of strut bars, #3019 – 50. These have proved unsatisfactory. Please discontinue all references to this model." Since nothing that verifies the specifications of this model has been found and the different strut bar models shared the same Zimmer identification number, what was unsatisfactory is unknown. Harrington continued, "The one that is satisfactory is the strut bar you did on a drawing dated April 17, 1956, #3019–50. I would like to have a consistent way to order these and use only the (b) dimensions, the measurement from the stop sleeve to the walking steps." This had originally been the (c) dimension before eliminating the thread portion. There is no drawing of this in the archives, but the correspondence strongly suggests this had a smooth shaft of 3/16"-diameter, as Harrington hadn't requested increasing the smooth middle section of the rod to 1/4" until December 13, 1956.[141] After inquiring about the progress correcting the small hook #3519 that he had requested three months earlier, Harrington placed a 1arge order. This included six strut bars (#3019 – 50 as drawn on April 17, 1956) of each of the (b) dimensions: 4", 5", 6", 7", and 8". Of the 1/8"-diameter instruments and implants, he ordered three dozen small hooks (#3519), two small rod clamps (#3516 as drawn on April 15, 1956), and two small hook clamps (#3518 as drawn on April 16, 1956).[142] Obviously, he was rapidly gaining clinical experience with the instrumentation.

在与捷迈的联系中断了三个月后，哈灵顿于1957年5月14日写信给基顿，叙述了发现的问题和需求。[140]“1956年12月28日，你给我寄了一套支撑杆(#3019–50)，它用起来不太令人满意，请停止对这一型号的所有参考。”由于没有任何可以确认该型号规格的东西，而且不同的支撑杆使用同一个捷迈识别号，所以令人不满意的地方不得而知。哈灵顿继续说道："你按1956年4月17日图纸做的支撑杆#3019-50是很令人满意的。我希望有一个统一的方式来订购这些产品，只使用（b）尺寸，即从止动套到齿槽的测量。"在取消螺纹部分之前，这原本是（c）的尺寸。尽管档案中没有这方面的图纸，但通信中明确提到有一个直径为3/16英寸的光滑轴，因为哈灵顿直到1956年12月13日才要求将棒的光滑中间部分增加到1/4英寸。[141]在询问了他三个月前要求的#3519小钩的修正进度后，哈灵顿下了一个大订单。包括六套支撑杆（#3019-50，如1956年4月17日图纸），每套支撑杆的（b）尺寸为4英寸、5英寸、6英寸、7英寸、8英寸。在直径为1/8英寸的器械和内植物中，他订购了三打小钩（#3519），两个小棒夹（#3516，1956年4月15日图纸），和两个小钩夹（#3518，1956年4月16日图纸）。[142]很明显，他正在将这些内固定器械应用于临床并获取了相关经验。

In closing, he made the following unusual request. "I am presenting these instruments to the Fourth International Poliomyelitis Congress which meets in Geneva, Switzerland on July 8-12, 1957, and I would appreciate your sending me at your earliest date similar drawings that are presentable, together with a full set of instruments and gadgets with your company name on them, and boxed attractively." He asked that this order be charged to his NFIP grant at the Baylor University College of Medicine. This makes it likely that at least some of the instrumentation being used clinically was then being paid for by the hospital. Keeton responded promptly and positively.[143] In the follow-up exchanges solidifying some details, further insight was gained into the dimension of strut bar #3019-50. Harrington wrote, "Remember that Section One of the #3019-50, I wish brought back to the smaller O.D."[144] Section one appeared to be a new way of referring to the smooth section of the rod, which initially was section (c) and became (b) when the threaded portion was removed. This clearly suggested that the increase in smooth portion diameter, as requested by Harrington on December 13, 1956, had been done. We do not know whether the increase in diameter was to 1/4" as he had requested on that date or to 5/16" as mentioned only once in Keeton's January 22, 1957, letter. Either approach would have required some attention to the lower connection, which was never discussed. The correspondence seems to lack precision here. Based on patient X-rays from the summer of 1957, the increase in diameter of the smooth portion of the distraction must have been to 5/16".[145] *See figure 5.12.*

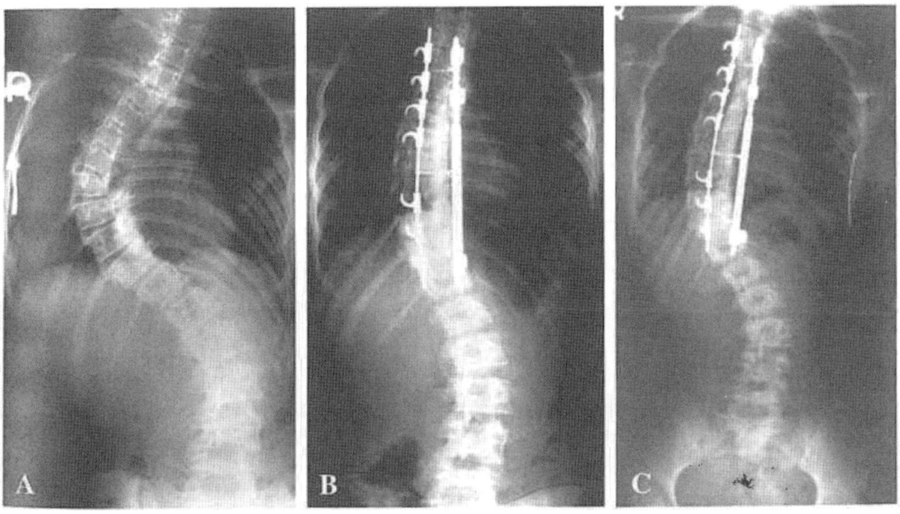

Figure 5. 12 ***Anteroposterior radiographs of a patient with right thoracic apex scoliosis operated in 1957 utilizing a distraction rod with a diameter of 5/16" smooth portion diameter. A. Preoperative. B. Postoperative. C. About six months follow-up. In addition to the "oversize" distraction rod, the sequence shows transverse connection of the distraction and compression rods and lower add-on from instrumenting too short.*** **(*Harrington Archives*)**

图 5. 12　一名右胸弯脊柱侧凸患者术前、术后前后位 X 光片。该患者在 1957 年使用光滑部分直径 5/16 英寸的撑开棒进行了矫形手术。A. 术前。B. 术后。C. 术后大约 6 个月时的随访。除了"大号"的撑开棒,图中显示了撑开棒和压缩棒间的横联,以及因为内固定过短导致的远端附加现象(哈灵顿档案馆)

最后，他提出了以下不同寻常的请求："我将在 1957 年 7 月 8 日至 12 日在日内瓦召开的第四届国际脊髓灰质炎大会上介绍这些器械，如果您能尽早将漂亮的图纸、一整套器械和工具寄来，我将不胜感激。上面最好有贵公司的名称，如果包装精致一些就更好了。"他要求将这笔订单算入他在贝勒大学医学院的国家小儿麻痹基金会账上。这使得当时至少有一部分临床上使用的器械能够由医院进行支付。基顿迅速作出了积极的回应。[143]在后续的交流中，对细节做了进一步巩固，对#3019-50 支撑杆的尺寸做了进一步的沟通。哈灵顿写道："记住#3019-50 的第一部分，我希望有更小的外径"。[144]第一部分是指杆的光滑部分，最初是（c）部分，当螺纹部分被移除后，变成了（b）部分。这清楚地表明，按照哈灵顿在 1956 年 12 月 13 日的要求，增加光滑部分直径的工作已经完成。我们不确定直径是按照他在哪一天的要求增加到 1/4 英寸，还是像基顿在 1957 年 1 月 22 日的信中仅提到的一次那样增加到 5/16 英寸。无论哪种方法都需要对下端连接进行关注，而这一点从未被讨论过。信件在这里似乎缺乏精确性。根据 1957 年夏天的病人的 X 光片，撑开的光滑部分的直径已经增加到了 5/16 英寸。[145]（图 5. 12）

From June 1955 to May 1957, Harrington and Zimmer had made excellent progress with the design of Harrington Spine Instrumentation, but on May 30, 1957, Harrington wrote Keeton essentially a change of direction letter. It was a real bombshell.[146] He listed the problems with the current design of the strut rod as protrusion of the strut rod end and the need to reoperate to "walk the hook up the rod for more correction and to take up the slack brought on by growth and by seating of the instrument." The latter was probably due to "erosion of the hooks on their bony purchase. We have no erosion when more than one hook of the strut bar is applied. I believe it is possible to design a self-walking strut of distraction bar. I am sending this to you and wish you to work it out from a practical standpoint." He imagined a self-locking device consisting of a "rod working inside of a tube" and the "self-locking device is made possible by a cylinder of Silastic©" used "as a sleeve over the locking device." He envisioned that the "the upper end will purchase on three small hooks which will be one unit and purchase on the middle hook by fitting into a sleeve. Enclosed are photographs of X-rays showing the use of the rod in the back." The photos and drawings cannot be found. Whoa, this represented a major change of direction in the instrumentation design! It happened just as the ratchet strut bar design they had spent the last two years developing was nearly mature. Why now? To understand this change of direction, it is necessary to remember Harrington's devotion to the dynamic treatment of scoliosis, his aversion to arthrodesis, and his NFTP grant to develop "An Experimental Model of Scoliosis."

从1955年6月到1957年5月，哈灵顿和捷迈在哈灵顿脊柱器械的设计方面取得了卓越的进展。但在1957年5月30日，哈灵顿给基顿写了一封从本质上改变设计方向的信，可谓一个关键的转折点。[146]他列举了目前支撑棒设计的问题，即支撑棒顶部的突出，以及需要重新"将钩子往上移以获得更多的力的反馈，并弥补因生长和坐姿改变而带来内植物的松动。"后者可能是由于"钩在其骨质上的侵蚀造成的。当支撑杆的一个以上的钩子被应用时，我们没有发现侵蚀现象。我相信有可能设计出一种自移式撑开杆支撑。我把这个寄给你，希望你能从实际出发来解决这个问题"。他设想了一个由"套管+支撑棒"组成的自锁装置，而"自锁装置是由一个硅橡胶的圆筒来实现的"，用来"作为锁紧装置的套管"。他设想，"棒的上端与三个钩子相连接，中间部分通过钩子与套管相固定。随函附上X光片，显示了后面的棒的使用情况"，照片和图纸已经无法找到了。但这代表了器械设计方向的一个重大改变！它发生在他们花了两年时间开发的棘齿支撑杆设计接近成熟的时候。为什么是这个时候？为了理解这一方向的改变，有必要记住哈灵顿对脊柱侧凸的动态治疗的奉献，他对融合的厌恶，以及他为开发“脊柱侧凸的实验模型”而获得的国家小儿麻痹基金会资助。

The mouse experiment appeared to have been largely performed in 1956. The normal group (N) was used to quantify the normal symmetrical growth and development of the vertebral column. The two pathological groups, pathological tethered (PT) and pathological tethered and released (PTR), were designed to study the course of scoliosis experimentally induced without operation on the spinal column. The PT group was formed to determine the effect of unremitting scoliosis and the PTR group to study the capacity of the scoliotic spine to self-correct. The results showed that the PT group developed progressive scoliosis, but that it did not become severe (more than 80° to 90°) until the tether had been in place for 35 or 40 days. *See figure 5.13.* Vertebral asymmetry was first observed in the facets and was not present until the tether had been in place "for at least 40 days." In the PTR group all the specimens had spines that were restored to prescoliotic appearance, or nearly so, within ten days. *See figure 5. 14.* Microscopic examination revealed that compared to normal the restricted facets had loss of the normal architecture of the cartilaginous cells and the appearance of a visible facet joint space. The pathologic changes in the facet joints resolved following tether release. *See figure 5.15.* Concave (right) facet joints and convex (left) facet joints were considered to be asymmetrical. The vertebral body endochondral zone of ossification "evealed no marked pathology in the coronal plane." Harrington concluded, "This study provides further evidence for inherent form potential of vertebral bone. It has been shown in this investigation that this is controlled by the endochondral ossifying centers which are the major factors in control of vertebral form. Extrinsic factors can therefore affect form in the presence of functional disturbances and consequent alterations of physical forces acting upon growing bony tissues of the vertebra. Pathogenesis of scoliosis should include appreciation of the role of facet changes as well as changes in the body of the vertebra." He reported his preliminary results in an unpublished bound volume in 1957.[147] Twenty-one years he published them in peer-reviewed literature.[148] Now that's dogged persistence!

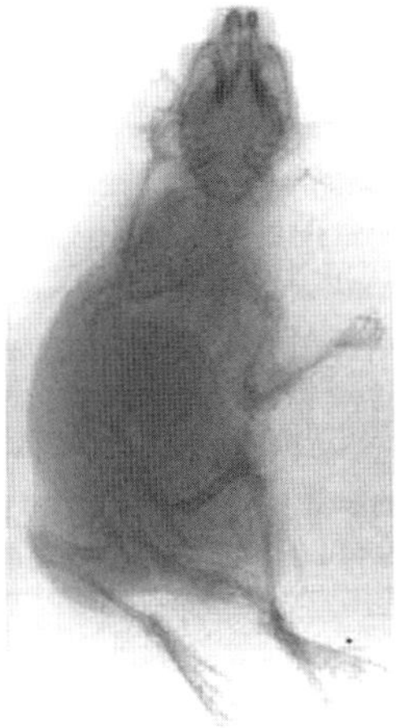

Figure 5.13 *Posteroanterior radiograph of a mouse from the pathological tethered (PT) group at age 45 days, 40 days after tethering, showing a large thoracolumbar scoliosis (Harrington Archives)*

图 5.13 来自病理拴系(PH)组的小鼠在 45 日龄,拴系 40 天后的后前位 X 光片,显示较大的胸腰弯侧凸(哈灵顿档案馆)

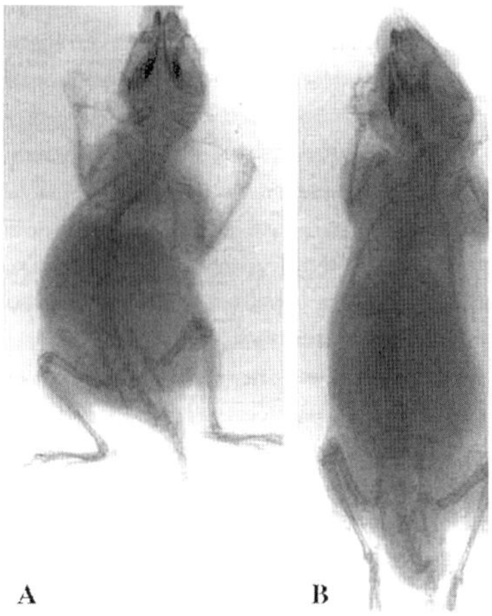

Figure 5.14 *Posteroanterior radiograph of a mouse from the pathological tethered and released (PTR) group. A. At age 35 days. B. At age 45 days, 10 days after tether release. (Harrington Archives)*

图 5.14 病理拴系松解(PHR)组的一只小鼠的后前位 X 光片。A. 35 日龄时。B. 45 日龄时,拴系松解后 10 天(哈灵顿档案馆)

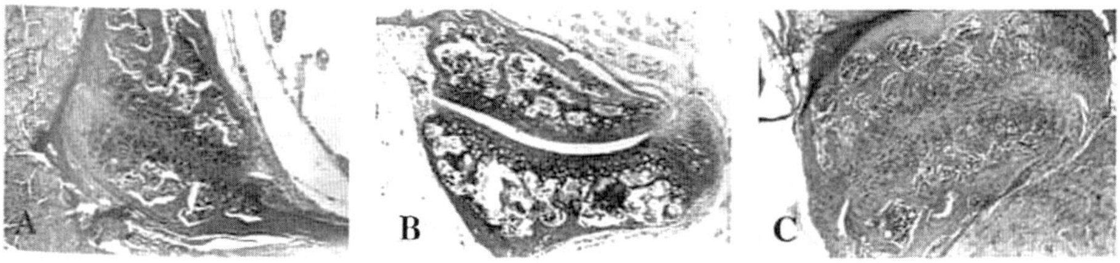

Figure 5.15 *Transverse plane histological sections (magnification 100x and 150x) of a thoracic vertebra facet joint. A. From a normal (N) 45-day-old mouse. B. From a 35-day-old pathological tethered (PT) series mouse. C. From a 45-day-old pathological tethered and released (PTR) series mouse, 10 days after tether release. The visible joint space had disappeared and the endochondral bone-forming zone returned toward normal (Harrington Archives)*

图 5.15 胸椎关节突关节面的横断面组织学切片(放大倍数 100 倍和 150 倍)。A. 来自正常(N)45 日龄的小鼠。B. 来自 35 日龄的病理拴系组(PT)小鼠。C. 来自 45 日龄的病理拴系松解组(PTR)小鼠。拴系解除后 10 天,关节突间隙已经消失,软骨内成骨的骨形成区也恢复了(哈灵顿档案馆)

大部分的小鼠实验似乎是在 1956 年进行的。正常组 (N) 用于观察并量化椎体的正常对称性生长和发育。两个病理组,即病理栓系组 (PT) 和病理栓系松解组 (PTR),旨在研究经实验诱发而没有接受手术的脊柱侧凸的病理进程。病理栓系组是为了确定持续脊柱侧凸的影像,病理栓系松解组是为了研究脊柱侧凸的自我矫正能力。结果显示,病理栓系组脊柱侧凸进行性加重,但直到栓系放置了 35 或 40 天后才变得严重 (超过 80°至 90°) (图 5.13) 椎体不对称首先出现在关节面上，但直到栓系放置“至少40天”才会出现。在病理栓系松解组中，所有标本的脊柱几乎都在10天内恢复到脊柱弯曲前的外观。(图5.14) 显微镜检查发现，与正常情况相比，受限的关节面表现为软骨细胞的正常结构丧失并出现异常的关节突关节间隙。而在松解栓系后，关节突关节的病理变化得到了改善（图5.15)。凹侧（右侧）和凸侧（左侧）关节突关节是不对称的。椎体内软骨化区“在冠状面没有发现明显的病变”。哈灵顿总结说：“这项研究为椎体骨的固有形态潜力提供了进一步的证据。在这项调查中显示，软骨内层骨化中心是控制椎体形态的主要因素。因此，在存在功能紊乱和随之而来的作用于椎体生长的骨组织的物理力改变的情况下，外在因素可以影响椎体形态。脊柱侧凸的发病机制应包括对椎体关节面变化以及椎体内变化的作用的认识。”1957年，他在一本未出版的合订本中报告了他的初步结果。[147] 21年后，他在同行评议的文献中发表了这些结果。[148]这就是锲而不舍！

In short, Harrington interpreted the results as supporting his hypothesis that the growing scoliotic spine had the capacity, through Volkmann's principle of return of growth after release of growth-retarding growth plate pressure, to straighten after removal of unequal forces and movements. He would later recall that “these mouse experiments, the dramatic restoration to normal seen when the scoliotic deformity was released, guided the next years of instrument development into an unsuccessful channel.”[149] Although this study has been largely overlooked in the Harrington Spine Instrumentation story, it may best illustrate the man's uniqueness. As he later expressed it, “I was always striving to think fundamentally and I feel that because of this I was able to meet my objective.”[150]

简而言之，哈灵顿认为这些结果支持他的假设，即通过福尔克曼的生长板压力释放后恢复生长的原则，生长中的侧凸脊柱有能力在消除不对等的力量和运动后变直。他后来回忆说：“这些小鼠动物实验体的脊柱侧凸畸形在松解后戏剧性地恢复到正常，使得接下来的器械研发进入一个未成功的轨道。”[149]尽管这项研究在哈灵顿脊柱器械研发的故事中基本上被忽略了，但它可能最能说明这个人的独特性。正如他后来所表达的那样，“我一直努力从根本上思考问题，我觉得正因为如此，我才能达到我的目标。”[150]

It is doubtful that Zimmer knew or even really cared about the mouse experiment, but it certainly did inform the instrumentation design effort for the twenty-five months from May 30, 1957, until June 11, 1959.[151,152] All documentation suggests that Zimmer had been and remained very responsive in their collaboration with Harrington throughout what was probably a difficult time for them. For instance, a Harrington complaint about some hook modifications drew an apology from the company president with the assurance that the problem would be addressed.[153] Responding a day later, Keeton apologized, but then was blunt. He wrote, "So that this incident will not happen again will you please double check your drawings before placing an order to us in the future. You are the judge of what you need. We know nothing about your process of using these fixations so all we have to go by is our blueprints."[154] Two missing Harrington letters dated June 7 and 18 make it impossible to know the exact issues. But the abrupt change in design course had to be stressful. The size of the new and incomplete design submitted would have been very difficult to control and part of the mechanism involved Silastic©, a synthetic rubberlike product that Zimmer had no experience with. And the prospect of redesigning the #3019-50 strut bar (later referred to as a distraction rod) after spending so much time refining it must have been distressing.

捷迈公司是否知道甚至是否关心这个小鼠实验，是值得怀疑的，但他们确实为 1957 年 5 月 30 日至 1959 年 6 月 11 日之间为期 25 个月的器械设计工作提供了帮助。[151,152]所有的文件都表明，在他们最为困难的时期，捷迈一直和哈灵顿保持着非常积极的合作。例如，哈灵顿对一些钩的修改表达了不满，公司总裁向他道歉并保证会解决这个问题。[153]一天后，基顿也作出了道歉回应，但随后直言不讳地写道："为了使这一事件不再发生，请你在今后向我们下订单之前仔细检查你的图纸，你的临床应用需求只有你自己了解，我们对你使用这些器械的过程一无所知，所以我们只能依据图纸。"[154] 6 月 7 日和 18 日的两封失踪的信件使我们无法获得具体细节。但设计路线的突然改变不得不让人感到压力，提交的新的和不完整的设计方案的尺寸将很难控制，而且部分机制涉及硅橡胶（一种类似合成橡胶的产品），捷迈对此没有经验。而且，在花了这么多时间对#3019-50 支撑杆（后来被称为撑开杆）进行改进后，再重新设计一定是令人痛苦的。

On July 8-12, 1957, Harrington attended the Fourth International Poliomyelitis Congress in Geneva, Switzerland, where he participated on the program as the discussant of a paper by Carlos E. Ottolenghi titled "Surgical Methods of Improving Scoliosis in Poliomyelitis Patients."[155] His instrumentation exhibit must have been well received as he received a Presidential Award for it.[156] On the second day he received the ultimate backhanded compliment when the whole exhibit, including blueprints, was stolen. About two months later Harrington reported the incident to Zimmer; this delay was due to touring in Europe. He and Mary Alice had traveled by themselves some of the time and at other times either with Vernon Nickel and his wife or Don Eyler and his daughter Kate. In Rome, Eyler rented a small car, and Harrington recorded their trip over rough roads to the toe of Italy with a new Bolex movie camera. Watching the film was said to have required Dramamine![157,158] Life was not all work for the orthopedic surgeon and innovator.

1957 年 7 月 8 日至 12 日，哈灵顿出席了在瑞士日内瓦举行的第四届国际脊髓灰质炎大会，他作为卡洛斯·E. 奥托伦吉一篇题为“改善脊髓灰质炎患者脊柱侧凸的手术方法”的论文的讨论者参加了会议。[155]他的器械展品很受欢迎，因此获得了主席奖。[156]在第二天因为整个展品包括图纸，都被偷走了，他受到了嘲讽。由于在欧洲旅行，直到两个月后哈灵顿才向捷迈报告了这一意外情况。他和玛丽·艾丽斯有些时候是单独旅行，其他时候则是与弗农·尼克尔和他的妻子或者唐·艾勒和他的女儿凯特一起旅行。在罗马，艾勒租了一辆小车，哈灵顿用一台新的宝莱克斯录像机记录了他们在崎岖的道路上前往意大利最南部的旅程。据说看这个视频需要服用镇静剂![157,158]对于这位骨科医生和创新者来说，生活并不全是工作。

When Harrington did report his exhibit's theft to Zimmer, he wrote, “I am suspicious of the Russians. There was considerable inquiry as to where to purchase a set of these instruments and the sample set you furnished me will pay off. However, I am not recommending anyone do this procedure at this time.” He continued, shifting the focus of his letter with the question, “Will you kindly send me another copy of the self-adjusting strut? I think we should get to work on this for it is sorely needed. It is my intention to have its upper end and lower purchase transferred through three hooks which will be united by a common bar. I am sending a requisition for an order on the threaded rods with hex nuts. I would like to have eight hex nuts instead of six with each threaded rod. These are, of course, the 1/8” diameter threaded rods which should pass freely through the small hooks. For the future, it is my intention to enlarge the small hooks a small amount and do away with the large hooks and the present strut rods. I would like to have you make up a small hook, enlarging it to take a 5/32” [0.156”] diameter threaded rod with hex nuts, about six or eight hooks to a 10” threaded rod. This will be included with the requisition. Thank you for your kind cooperation.”[159] Keeton promptly responded by sending a new blueprint of the self-adjusting strut bar. He commented that they were having trouble working with the Silastic© cover of the tube and believed that a groove in the tube would be necessary to prevent the Silastic© from slipping. Because such a groove would considerably weaken the tube, they were "trying to get a spring lock built into the tube." However, this had increased the cylinder "to about 3/8" diameter which is getting rather large for your purposes. If you have any ideas on the above, please submit them to me."[160] Keeton registered his frustration in his closing line. "If you have any suggestions as to how long the tube and strut bar should be please inform me because you have a better overall view of the situation than I do."

当哈灵顿向捷迈报告他的展品被盗时，他写道："我对俄罗斯人很怀疑，有很多人询问在哪里可以买到一套这样的器械，你提供给我的样品套装会有回报的，但我不建议任何人现在做这个手术。"他继续说，用问题转移了信的重点，"你能不能再给我寄一份自我调节支撑杆的副本？我想我们应该着手这件事，因为我们非常需要它，我打算让它的上端和下端通过三个钩转移，这三个钩将由一个共同的杆连接起来。我正在发送一份关于带六角螺母的螺纹棒的订单申请书。我希望每个螺纹杆能有 8 个六角螺母，而不是 6 个。当然，这些是直径为 1/8 英寸的螺纹棒，应该可以自由通过小钩。在未来，我打算将小钩放大一点，并取消大钩和现在的支撑杆。我想让你制作一个小钩，把它放大到可以使用直径为 5/32 英寸［0.156 英寸］的带六角螺母的螺纹棒，需要大约 6 个或 8 个钩子与 10 英寸的螺纹棒相配。这将包括在请购单中，谢谢你的友好合作。"[159] 基顿迅速作出回应，发送了一份新的自我调节支撑杆的图纸。他评论说，他们在使用套管的硅橡胶盖子时遇到了麻烦，并认为有必要在套管上开一个槽，以防止硅橡胶滑落。因为这样的凹槽会大大削弱管子，所以他们"试图在套管里安装一个弹簧锁"。然而，这使圆柱体的直径增加到"大约 3/8 英寸，为了达到你的目的，这已经相当大啦。如果你对上述问题有任何想法，请转给我"[160]。基顿在他的结束语中记录了他的挫败感，"如果你对套管和支撑杆的长度有任何建议，请告知我，因为你比我对情况有更好的了解。"

It was two months before Harrington responded, and he began with a fresh request for a double action bolt cutter suitable for both the 1/8"-diameter threaded rod and the large strut bar. He emphasized the need for a slender nose unlike the unworkable blunt noses of available cutters.[161] He turned to his pet topic, the self-adjusting strut. He suggested a ridge in the casing, which had previously been referred to as a tube, to keep the Silastic© ring in place rather than a strength-reducing groove. "Now as to the purchase of the strut bar, in the hook system my present intention is to place 3 individual hooks together at the upper portion of the curve and 3 below and use the new strut bar as you have designed it to distract the upper hook system from the lower hook system. My dilemma at the present is how to make this connection strong enough with a moderate amount of mobility and still make it detachable as far as pulling out is concerned. In other words, once it is applied the distraction force will keep it intact. However, in growing children this distraction force is lost with growth and there must be a security to keep the bar intact so that the pull on the distraction force will lengthen it or walk it to maintain a continuous distraction force."[162] Harrington's goal of maintaining continuous distraction force during growth without further direct or indirect intervention was the essential need. Further, his hope was to further simplify the system by having one size hook for distraction and compression, and the "larger small hook you just sent me should fill the bill." Keeton promptly responded with a drawing of a proposed pin cutter, indicating it would cost $75 and be ready for shipping in four to five weeks. Regarding the self-adjusting strut, Keeton wrote that "I would like to devise some sort of spring mechanism rather than use the Silastic©. It is not that I don't like the Silastic© but I don't think we are in any position to do this type of work in our department. It would be rather difficult for our machinists to apply this type of coating and keep it as clean as it should be."[163]

两个月后，哈灵顿才作出回应，他首先提出了一个新的要求，即需要一种既适用于直径为 1/8 英寸的螺纹杆，又适用于大支撑杆的双动螺栓切割器。他强调需要一个细长的刀头，而不是像现有刀具那样无法使用的钝刀头。[161]紧接着对于他最喜欢的自我调节支撑杆，他建议在外壳（以前被称为套管）上开一个脊，而不是一个降低强度的槽，以保持硅橡胶环的位置。“现在关于抓牢支撑杆的问题，在钩系统中，我目前的打算是将 3 个单独的钩放在一起，放在弯曲的上部，下面有 3 个，并按照你的设计使用新的支撑杆来分散上部钩系统和下部钩系统的力。我目前遇到的难题是，如何使这种连接足够坚固，具有合适的活动度，并且就拉出而言，仍然使其可分离。换句话说，一旦它被应用，分散的力量将使它保持完整。然而，在儿童的成长过程中，这种撑开力会随着成长而丧失，必须有一种安全的方式来保持杆的完整，以便在撑开力的拉动下逐渐延长，以保持持续的撑开力。”[162]哈灵顿的目标是使杆在儿童的成长过程中保持持续的撑开力，而不需要进一步的直接或间接干预，这是基本需求。此外，他希望通过使用一种尺寸的钩进行撑开和压缩来进一步简化系统，“你刚寄给我的较大的小钩应该可以满足这个要求”。基顿迅速回复了一份讨论针切割器的图纸，表示它将花费 75 美元，并在

4~5 周内准备好发货。关于自我调节支撑杆，基顿写道：“我想设计某种弹簧机制，而不是使用硅橡胶。这并不是说我不喜欢硅橡胶，而是我认为我们的部门没有能力做这种工作。对我们的机械师来说，应用这种类型的涂层并保持其应有的清洁是相当困难的。”[163]

A five-month lull in the Harrington-Zimmer correspondence occurred during which time the 1958 annual meeting of the AAOS was held in New York on February 1-6. There is no mention of this meeting in their correspondence or anywhere else in the Harrington Archives, and Harrington is not listed in the proceedings of the meeting.[164] However, Cobb and Hall independently recalled Harrington having presented there.[165,166] In his recollection to Cotrel, Cobb completely dismissed Harrington's work as a "weird idea" and "completely crazy." But which of his ideas, the strut bar or the self-adjusting strut, might they have seen? If the latter, Cobb's view is more understandable.

哈灵顿-捷迈的通信有 5 个月的空白期，在此期间，1958 年的美国骨科医师学会年会于 2 月 1 日至 6 日在纽约举行。在他们的通信中或哈灵顿档案中的其他记录中都没有提到这次会议，而且哈灵顿也没有在会议记录中出现。[164]然而，柯布和霍尔分别回忆说，哈灵顿在那里做了报告。[165,166]在他对科特雷尔的回忆中，柯布完全将哈灵顿的工作视为“奇怪又完全疯狂的想法”。但是，不确定他们指的是哪个想法，支撑杆还是自我调节支撑杆？如果是后者，柯布的观点就更容易理解了。

The next design-related letter came five months later in April 1958. Harrington began by reporting that the bolt cutter was working nicely and reminding Keeton that his November 1957 comments and recommendations about the adjustable strut bar had never been answered.[167] Actually, that was not true since Keeton had signaled that his department was unable to proceed with the Silastic® design.[168] However, Harrington was still offering advice based on Silastic® use.[169] He then dropped another, albeit smaller, bombshell. In two months he was planning to operate on two or three patients with the self-adjusting strut bar. He had concluded that the threaded rod connecting three hooks at either end would have to be increased from 1/8" to 3/16" diameter. He envisioned this as changing the 1/8"-diameter threaded rod (#3517), compatible hook (#3519), and hook clamp (#3518). This implied that the 1/8"-diameter items would be taken out of the system. The following month Keeton responded that the threaded rod had been increased to 3/16" and the necessary changes made to the accompanying hook and hook clamp.[170] He enclosed a new working print of the self-adjusting strut bar, which isn't in the archives. In his letter Keeton commented he that had noted on the drawing why the plug could not be pressed into the tube. The description is too abbreviated to gain a picture of the fine points. A few days later Harrington ordered 36 hooks (#3019-51) for the rod with the 1/4"-diameter ratchets (#3019-50). He added the comment, "We have an excess of rods and no hooks, although we anticipate changing the whole system, we might as well use up what we have."[171] This suggested that the 1/4"-diameter ratchet rod was showing promise in actual clinical use.

下一封与设计有关的信是在五个月后的 1958 年 4 月。哈灵顿首先提到螺栓切割器很好用，并提醒基顿他 1957 年 11 月提出的关于可调节支撑杆的建议还未得到答复。[167]事实上，这不是真的，因为基顿已经表示他的部门无法继续进行硅橡胶的设计。[168]然而，哈灵顿仍然在提供基于硅橡胶使用的建议。[169]然后，他又抛出了另一个重要议题，在两个月内，他计划使用自我调节支撑杆为两到三名患者进行手术。他认为连接两端 3 个钩的螺纹棒的直径必须从 1/8 英寸增加到 3/16 英寸。他设想应该改变直径为 1/8 英寸的螺纹棒（#3517）、兼容钩（#3519）和钩夹（#3518）。这意味着直径 1/8 英寸的器械将被移除。接下来的一个月，基顿回应说，螺纹棒的直径已经增加到 3/16 英寸，并对配套的钩和钩夹进行了必要的修改。[170]他还附上了一份新的自我调节支撑杆的工作图纸，该图纸并不在档案里。基顿在信中评论说，他已经从图纸上注意到为什么塞子不能被压入套管里。由于这段描述过于简略，我们无法了解其中的细节。几天后，哈灵顿为带有直径 1/4 英寸棘齿的棒（#3019-50）订购了 36 个钩（#3019-51）。他补充说："我们有多余的棒，没有钩，虽然我们预计要改变整套系统，但我们不妨用完我们的东西。"[171]这表明 1/4 英寸直径的棘齿棒在实际的临床使用中显示出了前景。

Beginning on May 16 and extending through October 21, five letters passed between Harrington and Keeton, all regarding the self-adjusting strut bar design. Harrington acknowledged receipt of the self-adjusting strut bar blueprint, said it looked fine, and shifted the focus to the junction of the self-adjusting strut bar with the 3/16"-threaded rod connecting the end hooks, planned as three levels.[172] At the junction there would be a coronal plane angle between the end assembly rods and the vertical self-adjusting strut bar. This angle between the upper and lower assemblies was estimated to be as much as 30° to 40°, and thus 15° to 20° at each end. A two-hole, over-under hook was designed to be used in the middle of the upper and lower assemblies with the outer hole sized to accommodate this angle. A week later Keeton wrote enclosing "a new set of detail drawings on the new self-adjusting strut bar. These drawings are what we will make the actual strut bar from. Provisions have been made on the hooks so that they will have distraction range of about 40°."[173] Whether drawings of the hooks were included is not known. Keeton called attention to the two self-adjusting strut bar drawings (#3925-50 and #3925-51) where he had left the length dimensions blank and asked Harrington to "please mark on these two prints about what lengths you prefer." A full two months later Harrington responded with 3" and 6".[174] On August 5 a sales order with the notation "no charge" was written for the two experimental self-adjusting strut bars that were 3-7/8" and 5-7/8" long.[175] A few days later Keeton wrote that the order had been placed, but due to vacations and a heavy list of specials, shipment would be the latter part of September.[176]

从5月16日开始，一直到10月21日，哈灵顿和基顿之间互通了五封信，都是关于自我调节支撑杆的设计。哈灵顿表示收到了自我调节支撑杆的图纸，说它看起来很好，并将重点转移到自我调节支撑杆与连接端部挂钩的3/16英寸螺纹杆的交界处，计划为三层。[172]在交界处，端部装配杆和垂直的自我调节支撑杆之间会有一个冠状面的角度。上部和下部组件之间的这个角度估计高达30°到40°，因此每端有15°到20°。设计了一个两孔的上下钩，用于上下组件的中间，外孔的大小是为了适应这个角度。一周后，基顿来信，附上“一套新的关于自我调节支撑杆的详细图纸。这些图纸是我们制作实际支撑杆的依据。钩上已经做了规定，所以它们将有大约40°的撑开范围”。[173]钩的图纸是否包括在内，不得而知。基顿要求注意两张自我调节支撑杆的图纸（#3925-50和#3925-51），他在图纸上留下了长度尺寸的空白，并要求哈灵顿：“请在这两张图纸上标注你喜欢的长度。”整整两个月后，哈灵顿回信说3英寸和6英寸。[174] 8月5日，一份写有“免费”字样的销售订单，用于购买两根长为（3+7/8）英寸和（5+7/8）英寸的试验性自我调节支撑杆。[175]几天后，基顿写道，订单已经下达，但由于休假和订单积压，发货时间将在9月下旬。[176]

Harrington received the materials in October, and his assessment was both good and bad.[177] Considering the former, this could be regarded as the birth of the 3/16"-diameter implants even though he did not use that dimension in describing them, but referred to them as the larger "small-type" size. He accepted the 36 hooks and the 4 clamps to hold them, asked that a compatible "threaded wire" be made and furnished with 8 hex nuts, and recommended that these new instruments be given a number. He did not mention a use for them beyond that for the self-adjusting strut bar, though it was a small step to use them as an alternative, stronger compression system. It is at least interesting to remember that the first self-locking spinal hook was designed to accept a 3/16"-diameter rod, and the only required alteration was removal of the inner locking ridge. Considering the latter, the 20° slots in the double hooks were in the wrong plane. "They are not to be in the vertical plane but in the horizontal plane." He also remarked that the "Silastic© holding tube is too thick" and inquired about the possibility of a steel spring. Keeton responded that they would proceed immediately with the threaded wires and nuts without referring to the 3/16"-diameter dimension.[178] He acknowledged that the slot of the new style strut bar hook would have to be in the horizontal plane, repeating Harrington's error as it seems it should have been in the coronal plane. Keeton pointed out that this would increase the hook width to about 1/2", which would require a little longer clamp, and he was working on it. He also agreed with Harrington that the wall of the Silastic© tubing was too thick, and he had ordered some smaller tubing, which would be sent under separate cover. If still too thick, he promised to get more samples. He did not respond to Harrington's steel spring inquiry.

哈灵顿在 10 月份收到了这些材料，他的评价有好有坏。[177]好的方面是直径 3/16 英寸的内植物的诞生，尽管他在描述它们时没有使用这个尺寸，而是将其称为较大的“小尺寸”。他同意用 36 个钩和 4 个夹来固定它们，要求制作一个兼容的“螺纹棒”，并提供 8 个六角螺母，并建议给这些新器械一个编号。他没有提到它们在自我调节支撑杆之外的用途，尽管把它们作为一个替代的、更强大的压缩系统使用是一个小步骤。至少值得一提的是，第一个自锁脊柱钩的设计是为了适应直径为 3/16 英寸的杆，唯一需要改动的是去除内锁脊。考虑到后者，双钩中的 20°槽处于错误的平面。“它们不应该在垂直面上，而应该在水平面上。”他还说，“硅橡胶固定套管太厚了”，并询问了使用钢制弹簧的可能性。基顿回答说，他们将尽快进行螺纹棒和螺母的工作，而没有提及直径 3/16 英寸的尺寸。[178]他承认哈灵顿说的是对的，新式支撑杆钩的槽位于冠状面上是错误的，应该位于水平面上。基顿指出，这将使钩的宽度增加到大约 1/2 英寸，这就需要一个稍长的夹子，他正在努力。关于哈灵顿提出的硅橡胶套管的管壁太厚的问题，他也表示赞同，他已经订购了一些较小的套管，这些套管将被单独送去。如果还是太厚，他承诺会准备更多样品。他没有对哈灵顿的钢制弹簧询问作出回应。

Keeton's October 21, 1958, letter to Harrington was to be his last. On December 12 Jim Hite, the company's chief engineer, notified Harrington that draftsman James P. Keeton had enlisted in the US Army Air Corps.[179] It cannot be determined what the role of Harrington's effort to develop the self-adjusting strut bar had on this decision. It seems impossible not to imagine some effect because the back-and-forth correspondence often seemed to lack optimism, and it would soon become obvious that the concept of a self-adjusting, really self-lengthening, strut bar was doomed. Hite, who took over the correspondence for Zimmer, becoming Harrington's fourth primary contact, reassured him they would "try to get the strut bar assembly to his liking." The fact that the company's chief engineer was taking the lead correspondent role was promising and could be interpreted as a show of confidence in Harrington's work. Even if the self-adjusting strut bar project seemed stuck, Harrington's probably increasing use of the 1/4"-diameter ratchet rod and 1/8"-diameter threaded rod and hooks must have given Zimmer the hope for brighter days ahead.

1958 年 10 月 21 日，基顿和哈灵顿通了最后一封信。12 月 12 日，公司的总工程师吉姆·海特通知哈灵顿，绘图员詹姆斯·R. 基顿已经加入了美国陆军航空队。[179]我们无法确定哈灵顿开发自我调节支撑杆的努力对这一变动有没有影响。似乎无法想象会有什么影响，因为来回的通信似乎经常缺乏乐观的态度，而且很快就会发现，自我调节（真正的自动加长）支撑杆的概念是注定要失败的。海特接管了捷迈的通信，成为哈灵顿的第四个主要联系人，他向哈灵顿保证，他们将"努力使支撑杆组件符合他的要求"。公司的首席工程师担任首席通讯员的角色足以昭示出公司对哈灵顿工作的信任。即使自我调节支撑杆项目似乎遇到了瓶颈，哈灵顿可能会越来越多地使用直径为 1/4 英寸的棘齿棒、直径为 1/8 英寸的螺纹棒和钩，这给捷迈带来了希望，让他们看到了光明的未来。

Harrington promptly responded, expressing sorrow about Keeton's departure but predicting he would enjoy his move.[180] By separate mail Harrington returned the new self-adjusting spine strut and included a detailed composite drawing he had made of the components with an accompanying description of their assembly.[181] *See figure 5.16*. He was still committed to this concept: "eventually I believe that developing this design will replace all that has gone heretofore." He announced his intention "to exhibit the clinical study of this type of metallic instrumentation of the spine at the annual meeting of the American Academy of Orthopaedic Surgeons in Chicago, January 24-29, 1959."[182] A list of tasks that he hoped Zimmer could accomplish by that time was included. The items identified by capital letters can be seen in figure 5.16. The main items requested were six strut hooks ("L"), a spring ("C") to close the lock wedge ("B"), a new spreader so that forceful distraction could be applied between the ratchets and the strut cylinder ("A"), and hook holders for the universal hook ("K"). At that point the only hook holder that had been developed was for the small hooks accommodating the 1/8"-diameter threaded rod that he and Engen had developed beginning in 1954. Harrington commented that "the tit which purchased on the hole was left square, and bound on the threaded rods that passed through this hook. I have designed at the foot of the drawing what I mean." Harrington left no clues as to why he felt the need to rush the public display of this as yet unmade and untried experimental design.

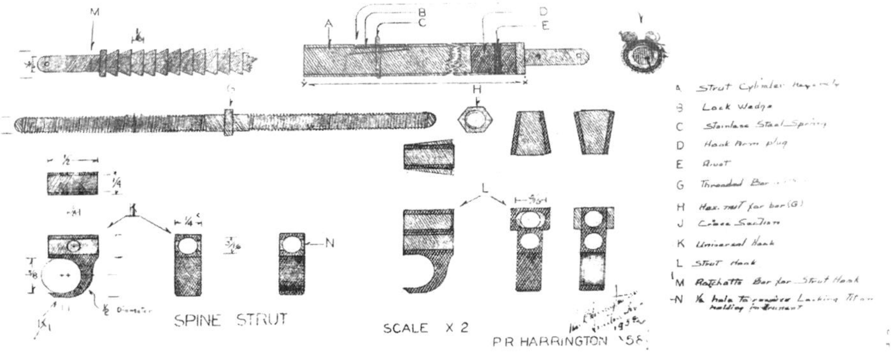

Figure 5.16 ***Harrington's December 1958 composite drawing of the components of the (ill-fated) new self-adjusting spine strut. The strut cylinder assembly (A) lengths (x to y) requested were 4", 6", and 8". In this version the Silastic© sleeve over the cylinder to control the lock wedge (B) had been abandoned in favor of a stainless steel spring (C) The hook arm plug (D) was secured in the strut cylinder assembly with a rivet (E). The ratchet bar for strut hook (M) completed the self-adjusting spine strut. Lengthening occurred as the ratchet bar (m) emerged from the strut cylinder assembly (A). The protruding ends of self-adjusting spine strut were 3/16" in diameter, designed to engage the conical upper hole of the strut hook (L), The end subassemblies of three hooks and one rod were to be constructed using a universal hook (K) on either side of a strut hook (L) all connected and stabilized by the threaded bar with machine ring (G) and nut (H). The ends of the self-adjusting spine strut were to engage the conical hole in the strut hook (L). (Harrington Archives)***

图 5.16 哈灵顿在 1958 年 12 月绘制的(命运多舛的)新的自我调节脊柱支撑杆的组件的综合图。要求的支撑杆套筒组件(A)的长度(X 到 Y)分别是 4、6、8 英寸。在这个版本中,锁定楔(B)的圆柱体上的硅树脂套筒已被放弃,转而使用不锈钢弹簧(C)。钩臂塞(D)用一个铆钉(E)固定在支柱套筒组件上。用于支柱钩的杆齿槽端(M)完成了脊柱支撑杆长度的自我调整。当杆齿槽端(m)在支撑杆套筒组件(A)中被拉出时,就实现了支撑杆长度的延长。自我调节支撑杆的突出端直径为 3/16 英寸,旨在与支撑钩(L)的锥形上的孔相啮合。由三个钩子和一个杆子组成的端部组件将在支撑钩(L)的两侧使用一个万向钩(K),所有这些都由带有机环(G)和螺母(H)的螺纹杆连接和稳定。自调脊柱支杆的两端与支撑钩(L)上的圆锥孔啮合(哈灵顿档案馆)

哈灵顿迅速回信，对基顿的离开表示惋惜，并相信他在未来会有更好的发展。[180]特另寄去了新的自我调节支撑杆，并附上了他制作的部件的详细合成图，以及对其装配的附带说明。[181]（图 5.16）他仍然致力于这个概念："最终我相信，这个设计将取代迄今为止的所有设计。"哈灵顿宣布要在 1959 年 1 月 24 日至 29 日芝加哥举行的美国骨科医师学会年会上展示关于此类脊柱金属内固定器械的临床研究。[182]回信中还提及了他希望捷迈届时能完成的任务清单。清单中的项目用大写字母标识。（图 5.16）主要包括 6 个支撑钩（"L"），一个用以关闭锁定楔（"B"）的弹簧（"C"），一个新的撑开器以便在棘齿和支撑杆套筒组件（"A"）之间施加力量撑开，以及万向钩（"K"）的持钩钳。当时，唯一的持钩钳是用来持夹一种小钩，这个小钩是他和恩金在 1954 年开始开发的用于容纳直径 1/8 英寸的螺纹棒。哈灵顿评论道："这个紧紧环绕洞的结构是正方形的，绑在穿过钩的螺纹棒上。我已经把我的想法画在末尾了。"哈灵顿没有留下任何理由来解释他为什么觉得有必要立刻向公众展示这个尚未完成、未经试验的实验设计。

The 1959 New Year's celebrations were hardly over when Hite's detailed response arrived, assuring that his requests could almost entirely be met.[183] Harrington answered quickly with their exchange reflecting an easy style of communication.[184] As a postscript he suggested that "you might furnish a sign saying that the material for this product was furnished by Zimmer Manufacturing Company." This was a good afterthought as his scientific exhibit was recognized with an AAOS certificate at its meeting.[185] Exactly what he showed was not documented. Harrington and Hite must have had a very productive meeting in Chicago, but their correspondence didn't restart for three months. Harrington announced that he was going to set up a clinic in June for "various doctors inquiring to see the program."[186] Interestingly, he did not intend to promote the self-adjusting strut rod. He recommended a list of instruments that would be necessary to perform the operation, which included the spreader (#3515), large hooks (#99-3019-51), large rods in various lengths, small hooks, threaded wires with hex nuts, two wire holders, and six small hook holders. The wires were the 1/8"-diameter threaded rods, which Harrington often referred to as wires. Hite responded immediately with an update on the projects he had been working on since the AAOS meeting.[187] He mentioned that they were still having trouble finding a suitable item to modify into a hook holder for the universal K-hook. This hook, compatible with a 3/16"-diameter threaded rod, was the direct descendant of the Self Locking Spinal Hook design Harrington had sent to Zimmer in March 1955.

1959年的新年庆祝活动刚刚结束，海特的详细答复就到了，确定他的要求基本上可以全部得到满足。[183]哈灵顿回复得很快，他们交流得十分轻松。[184]在附言中他建议“你可以提一句，说明该产品的材料是由捷迈制造公司提供的”。这是一个很好的补救办法，随着他的科学展示在会议上得到了美国骨科医师学会的认可，该建议也被认为是明智的。[185]他究竟展示了什么并没有记录在案。哈灵顿和海特在芝加哥一定参加了一次富有成效的会议，但他们的通信中断了三个月之久。哈灵顿宣布，他将在6月成立一个诊所，因为众多医生对该项目感兴趣。[186]有趣的是，他并没有打算推广自我调节支撑棒。他推荐了一系列对于做手术所必需的器械，其中包括撑开钳（#3515）、大钩（#99-3019-51）、各种长度的大号固定棒、小钩、带六角螺母的螺纹丝、两个持棒钳和六个小持钩器。这些线是直径1/8英寸的螺纹棒，哈灵顿经常把它们称为线。海特立即作出回应，介绍了自美国骨科医师学会会议以来他一直在从事的项目的最新情况。[187]他提到，他们仍然难以找到一个合适的物品用以改装成持钩钳，以适应K型万向钩。K型万向钩与直径3/16英寸的螺纹棒兼容，是哈灵顿在1955年3月发送给捷迈的自锁脊柱钩设计的衍生物。

In his June 11, 1959, letter to Hite he asked that the self-adjusting strut bar system development be halted. “It is experimental and will not work. I will write you later as to why.[188] Further explanation didn’t follow, probably because it had become obvious that self-adjusting really meant self-lengthening and without some added power wasn’t possible. The self-adjusting strut had occupied the majority of his design thought from May 1957 to June 1959! It seems very unlikely that all of Zimmer’s expenses would have been defrayed by his NFIP grant, and this must have increased the company’s vested interest in Harrington Spine Instrumentation development. His promotional activities, including “barnstorming”, as he called his travels, and the June clinic in Houston, had heightened notice of his work. Consequently, he was beginning to accumulate followers, who were impatient to use the instrumentation. He communicated to Zimmer that the only doctors oriented to use this equipment were Garret Pipkin, Kansas City; Vernon Nickel, Downey; and William Stewart, Columbia, Missouri.[189]

在他1959年6月11日给海特的信中，他要求停止自我调节支撑杆系统的开发。“这是实验性的，不会奏效，我稍后会写信告诉你原因。”[188]哈灵顿并没有做进一步解释，这可能是因为自我调节实际上仅仅意味着自我延长，不施加额外的力是不可能的。从 1957 年 5 月到 1959 年 6 月，自我调节支撑杆占据了他设计思想的大部分！捷迈公司的花费不可能完全由国家小儿麻痹基金会的资金来支付，而且这肯定增加了公司在哈灵顿脊柱器械开发中的既得利益。他的推广活动，包括他称为旅行的巡回演讲，以及 6 月在休斯敦开办的诊所，提高了人们对他的工作的关注度。因此，迫不及待要使用他的器械的追随者们越来越多。他告诉捷迈公司，只有堪萨斯城的加勒特·皮普金、唐尼市的弗农·尼克尔以及密苏里州哥伦比亚的威廉·斯图尔特医生可以使用这种器械。[189]

In 1959 and extending into 1960 Harrington and Zimmer increasingly pushed and were being pushed by some surgeons wishing to use it to complete the Harrington Spine Instrumentation design. For many reasons this was a difficult task, but the construct of a patient operated on in the spring of 1959 illustrated the still incomplete status of the design. *See figure 5.17.* One of the biggest hurdles was Harrington's own ambivalence about the need for and type of accompanying arthrodesis and the need for, extent, and duration of postoperative immobilization. This left an uncertainty in the mind of the prospective user, and too much doubt is not the surgeon's or the teacher's friend. Another difficulty was the delay inherent in the trial-and-error method of research and development where actual use was the only method of implant and technique testing. Sometimes implant and/or technique problems were immediately apparent, but often two or more years were required to uncover them. Yet another hurdle was the surgeons themselves because all of them at some level were innovators so new input was to be expected. Technique modification or improvement provided solutions for many of the problems, but some suggestions were sure to be helpful and sorting them out was time-consuming. Underlying all of this was incomplete knowledge of spine deformity and disease, surgical anatomy, and biomechanics. These were truly vast, incompletely charted knowledge universes. Sometimes their frustration showed through, as in this Hite to Harrington correspondence: "Please advise at your earliest convenience your thoughts on all this rambling so that we might get underway with the finalized design."[190] But they got through it with openness and honesty in their communications.

1959 年到 1960 年间，由于内在或外在因素如外科医生希望尽快使用哈灵顿内固定器械等，哈灵顿和捷迈不断完善哈灵顿内固定器械。由于众多因素，这是一项艰巨的任务。在 1959 年春天，一个病人的手术显示了该设计仍然存在缺陷。

(图 5.17) 最大的障碍之一是哈灵顿内固定器械本身具有的矛盾性，即对于融合的需要以及融合类型的不同，与术后固定的需要、程度及持续时间之间的矛盾。这给未来潜在的使用者留下了一种不确定的心理，而且很多疑问并不是来自外科医生或医学院的老师、朋友。另一个困难是对于研究和发展的试错法所具有的固有延迟性。而实际使用过程才是对于植入和技术测试的唯一方法。有时内植物和/或技术问题能立即显现，但更多的需要两年或更长时间才能发现。还有一个障碍在于外科医生本身，因为他们在某种程度上都是创新者，所以新的发现或技术是被寄予厚望的。技术的改进或提升为许多问题提供了解决办法，有些建议肯定是有帮助的，需要费时分清它们。这是由于对脊柱畸形和疾病、外科解剖学和生物力学的了解不够全面。这些都是真正广阔的、难以穷尽的知识宇宙。有时他们会感到挫败，就像海特写给哈灵顿的这封信："请在您方便的时候尽早告知您对所有这些杂乱无章的东西的想法，以便我们可以着手完成最终的设计。"[190] 但是他们靠着开明和诚实的沟通渡过了难关。

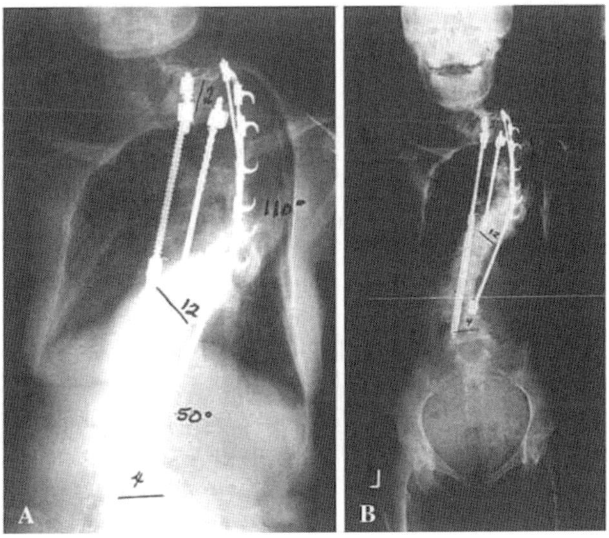

Figure 5.17 ***Standing posteroanterior radiographs of the patient shown in figure 5.1. who was operated on in the spring of 1959 at age of 15 years. These X-rays taken 6 (A) and 12 (B) years postoperative, show the unsettled instrumentation design at the time of operation. On the upper right are two 1/8"-diameter threaded compression rods dating back to before 1955. The two distraction rods have 3/16" diameter smooth portions. The distraction construct on the left appears to be a self-adjusting spine strut with a two-hook foundation at the top (Harrington Archives)***

图 5.17　在图 5.1 中，患者站立后前位 X 光片，该患者于 1959 年春天进行手术治疗，当时患者 15 岁。这些 X 光片分别拍摄于术后 6 年(A)和 12 年(B)，可以看出手术时内固定器械设计并不完善。右上方所示是两个 1/8 英寸直径的螺纹压缩棒，可追溯到 1955 年以前。两个撑开棒有直径 3/16 英寸的光滑部分。左边的撑开装置似乎是一个顶部有双钩基座的自我调节支撑杆(哈灵顿档案馆)

Seven specific examples of implant design problems that he and Hite faced in finalizing the Harrington Spine Instrumentation design for wider use deserve discussion. Strut bar (distraction rod) breakage, which initially occurred at the threaded end-smooth shank junction, had been eliminated by replacing the threaded end with a sleeve interconnection completed with a stop collar to accept distraction load. However, on June 1, 1959, Harrington sent a broken strut to Zimmer for analysis.[191] The site of the break was not documented either by Harrington or the Zimmer quality control report of June 23. The report confirmed the material to be type 316 stainless steel of Rockwell C 32 hardness. The conclusions were that "there was no evidence that defective material contributed to the failure of the strut. The bent condition of the broken sections indicates the strut was loaded beyond the yield strength of the metal. Failure was probably due to cyclic overloading."[192] Rod dimensions, such as diameter, were not documented. Some additional light was shed on the rod breakage issue in Harrington's letter of June 22, 1959, to Hite, in which he commented, "As I told you, several of these rods have broken in the main shaft, so let's beef it up."[193] So, the breakage was in the shank or smooth part of the strut bar shaft. In response, Hite commented that "we have scheduled those items requested m your letter of June 22, so you should receive them by July 10."[194]

哈灵顿和海特在最终完成哈灵顿脊柱内固定器械设计用以推广使用时所面临的七个与内植物设计问题相关的具体例子值得讨论。第一个问题是支撑杆（撑开棒）的断裂最初发生在螺纹末端与棒的连接处，后来通过将螺纹替换为套筒加止动环，进而承受撑开载荷，撑开棒断裂的问题得到解决。然而，在 1959 年 6 月 1 日，哈灵顿将一根断裂的撑开棒拿给捷迈分析。[191]哈灵顿和捷迈在 6 月 23 日的质控报告中都没有记录断裂的位置。报告确认材料为洛氏 C32 硬度的 316 型不锈钢。结论如下："尚无证据显示撑开棒的断裂是由材料缺陷问题所导致的。撑开棒断裂部分的弯曲情况表明支撑棒的载荷已经超过了金属本身的强度，断裂可能是由于反复过载导致。"[192] 棒的尺寸，例如直径，没有被记录。1959 年 6 月 22 日，哈灵顿在给海特的信中对棒发生断裂的问题提出了一些补充意见，他在信中说道："正如我告诉过你的，有几根棒在主长柄处断了，所以需要增强棒的强度。"[193]因此，断裂常发生在撑开棒的长柄部或者轴的光滑部分。在回复中，海特提到："我们已经准备了你 6 月 22 日来信中要求的那些物品，你应该能在 7 月 10 日之前收到。"[194]

Thirty-one months earlier in a December 13, 1956, letter Harrington had asked that the whole middle section of the rod be left the same size as the stock, leaving it a full 1/4" indiameter.[195] Keeton responded, expressing the hope that the new 5/16"-diameter (0.313") bar would be better.[196] This seems to be the only mention of a rod of this diameter in their correspondence, although at least two cases in the Harrington Archives had what appear to be 5/16" shafts. Harrington's letter of May 14, 1957, stated that strut bars (#3019-50) sent December 28, 1956, fifteen days after he had requested a full 1/4"-diameter, were unsatisfactory and asked for a return to the strut bar #3019-50 drawing dated April 17, 1956, which had a 3/16" smooth portion (b). Harrington was sending contradictory instructions, first increasing and soon decreasing the smooth portion of the strut bar. The confusion was worsened by identifying the three different rods with the same experimental number, leaving the date drawn as the only differentiating identification. At any rate the diameter of the smooth central portion of the strut bar was apparently not permanently increased from 3/16" to 1/4" until July 1959. This conclusion is supported by Hite's query at the end of his July 9, 1959, letter to Harrington. "We do have a rather good stock of the old type strut bars with the reduced diameter shaft which we would like to use up providing there is no danger of their breakage. Possibly these could be worked in to some of your selected cases, if not we will just discard them and make the beefed model from here on out."[197] A Zimmer blueprint dated September 9, 1959, shows the outer diameter of the strut bar shank to be 1/4"[198] Why it had taken 31 months (December 1956 to June 1959) to permanently increase the diameter of the smooth portion of the strut bar (distraction rod) isn't clear. However, plausible explanations may be Harrington's desire to limit implant bulk as much as possible and the change in focus to the self-adjusting strut bar design, which began five months later in May 1957.

早在 31 个月前，即 1956 年 12 月 13 日，哈灵顿曾在一封信中要求棒的整个中间部分保持与主棒相同的尺寸，即整个棒的直径均达到 1/4 英寸。[195]基顿在回复中提到，新的 5/16 英寸（0.313 英寸）直径的棒会更好。[196]尽管在哈灵顿档案中至少有两个案例好像是直径 5/16 英寸的棒，但这似乎是他们在通信中唯一一次提到这种直径的棒。哈灵顿在 1957 年 5 月 14 日的信中说，在他要求直径 1/4 英寸棒的 15 天之后，即 1956 年 12 月 28 日发送的支撑杆（#3019-50）并不令人满意，哈灵顿要求退还标注日期为 1956 年 4 月 17 日型号为#3019-50 的支撑杆，该杆有直径 3/16 英寸的光滑部分（b）。哈灵顿发出了自相矛盾的指令，先是增加支撑杆的光滑部分，然后再次减少。此外，三种不同的杆使用了相同的实验编号，只有标注日期可以用来识别，这也加剧了混淆。无论如何，直到 1959 年 7 月，支撑杆光滑部分的直径并没有从 3/16 英寸持续增加到 1/4 英寸。海特在 1959 年 7 月 9 日写给哈灵顿的信的末尾对该结论表示支持："我们确实认为主棒直径较小的老式支撑杆更好，我们想将这些用完，因为它们没有断棒的危险。也许这些可以用在你选择的一些案例中，如果不可以，我们就丢弃它们，从现在开始做增强的样品。"[197]一份日期为 1959 年 9 月 9 日的捷迈图纸中显示支撑杆长柄的外径为 1/4 英寸。[198]为什么要花费 31 个月的时间（1956 年 12 月至 1959 年 6 月）来持续增加支撑杆（撑开棒）光滑部分的直径尚不清楚。然而，合理的解释可能是哈灵顿希望尽可能地限制内植物的体积，并从 5 个月后的 1957 年 5 月开始将重点转移到自我调节支撑杆的设计上。

The second specific implant design problem could be remembered as the reverse ratchet detour. In a June 22, 1959, letter Harrington introduced a new design when he requested a smaller strut rod with the ratchet end reversed. "I wish to use this as a compression force and eliminate the threaded rod and hex nut, for this system is always working loose and very difficult to take up on secondary operations."[199] This new reverse ratchet rod was to be compatible with the universal hook and thus with a 3/16"-diameter smooth rod. "This will necessitate putting a ridge (locking) inside the universal hook." A few days later Hite responded and suggested that the stop collar end of the rod be replaced with two or three reverse ratchets. He added, "Actually it seems this approach of having notches on both ends of the rods would be highly desirable in both cases, that is in the strut bar and also in the smaller compression bar. This of course would simplify manufacturing procedures and I see no reason why it would not work as effectively as the bars with the solid stop collar, however if I am missing an important point here let us know as we plan to proceed with at least the small compression rods on this basis."[200] Harrington responded in the positive: "I see no reason why the strutting mechanism cannot be used on both ends of the rods and reverse for compression as well. If anything shows up that would make this design inferior I will let you know right away."[201] Just twelve days later he wrote reporting that ratchets on both ends were definitely undesirable as they made application very difficult.[202] After a month he wrote, "Also am sending back all compression rods you sent with reverse ratchet. They are just no good."[203]

第二个特定的内植物设计问题可以被视为反向棘齿走弯路。在 1959 年 6 月 22 日的一封信中，哈灵顿提出了一种新的设计，即带有反向末端棘齿的更小的支撑棒。“我希望使用这个设计可作为压缩力，代替螺纹棒和六角螺母，因为之前的设计常发生松动，难以在二次手术过程中取出。[199]这种新的反向棘齿棒与万向钩相吻合，因此能与直径3/16英寸的光滑棒兼容。这就需要在万向钩里面放一个脊(锁)。”几天后，海特回复并建议用两个或三个反向棘齿替换棒两端的止动环。他补充说：“实际上，在棒的两端设计凹槽似乎适用于支撑杆和较小的压缩杆。这当然会简化制造程序，并且我认为它会像具有坚固的止动环的杆一样有效。然而，如果我的想法仍有欠缺之处，请告诉我们，因为我们计划在此基础上着手设计小型的压缩棒。[200]哈灵顿的回答是肯定的：“我认为这种支撑设计可以用在棒的两端和反向压缩。如果有证据显示该设计有不足之处，我会立即告诉你。”[201]仅仅12天后，他写了一份报告说棒两端的棘齿设计肯定是不可取的，因为这种设计使棒的应用变得非常困难。[202]一个月后，他写道：“我也将你们寄来的带反向棘齿的压缩棒全部退回，它们并不是非常好。”[203]

But Harrington was not yet quite ready to give up on the reverse ratchet compression rod. In fact, on August 26 he requested on an experimental basis reverse ratchet compression rods to fit a big hook (i.e., 1/4"-diameter reverse ratchet rod)![204] One reason he was trying this was his and Hite's shared aspiration to make the hooks uniform. A month later Harrington gave a negative report on the 1/4"-diameter compression ratchet rod, remarking that it would not work for severe curves.[205] Two months later he requested one of the large compression ratchet rods, and Hite promptly reminded him that he had returned an earlier one since it was too stiff.[206, 207] In December Harrington responded. "As far as I am concerned the compression rod to the same specifications as the large hook is out. Bill Stewart of Columbia, Mo. almost talked me into this."[208] This would be the last of the reverse ratchet developmental effort until after Harrington's death.

但哈灵顿还没有完全打算放弃反向棘齿压缩棒。事实上，在8月26日，他在实验基础上要求反向棘齿压缩棒匹配一个大钩（直径1/4英寸的反向棘齿棒)![204]他这么做的原因是他和海特都希望能够统一钩的大小，使其标准化。一个月后，哈灵顿给出了针对直径1/4英寸压缩棘齿棒的负面报告，指出它不适用于严重的脊柱弯曲的情况。[205]两个月后，他要了一根大型压缩棘齿棒，海特立即提醒他，他已经退回了以前的一根，因为它太硬了。[206,207] 12月哈灵顿回应道：“就我所知，与大型钩相匹配的压缩棒已经过时了。密苏里州哥伦比亚的比尔·斯图尔特差点说服我。”[208]这将是哈灵顿生前最后一次为反向棘齿的发展而努力。

As the component parts of Harrington Spine Instrumentation vied for survival, they sometimes acquired confusing names, such as universal, universal swivel, and strut hooks, which illustrates a third design problem that arose. The 3/16"-diameter rod compatible hook was the one emerging with the first ratchet distraction rod. Almost immediately the ratchet portion of the rod was increased to a 1/4" outer diameter displacing the smaller original hook. Although the smaller hook still fit the opposite end of the rod, it was not developed as the toggle allowed by the larger hook was considered desirable to decrease the strain on the bone-metal and metal-metal interfaces.[209] Three years later this original 3/16"-diameter rod compatible hook reemerged as part of the ill-fated self-adjusting strut rod endeavor. It was used on either side of a double opening hook designed to provide connection of the vertical strut rod with the end foundations of three hooks connected by a 3/16"-diameter threaded rod, which were at an angle to vertical. The central double opening hook was named the strut hook, and the ones on either side were called universal hooks. Even though Harrington had come to realize that the self-adjusting strut rod was unworkable, he felt the strut (#99-4132-53) and universal (#99-4132-52) hooks were good.[210] Soon Zimmer produced a drawing of the universal swivel hook, which Harrington apparently envisioned as a means of allowing loads from either direction to the same hook.[211] In spite of repeated attempts at use and design modification, a purpose was never found for it because the opposing rod forces interfered with the toggle locking mechanism. The only new design to survive the self-adjusting strut bar detour was the 3/16"-diameter threaded rod, which helped secure a lasting place for the original hook submitted to Zimmer.

作为哈灵顿脊柱器械的部件，它们有时会有一些令人混淆的名称，如万向、万向旋转和支撑钩，这就产生了第三个设计问题。直径3/16英寸的棒及其兼容钩是首次出现的棘齿撑开棒。随即棒的棘齿部分的直径马上增加到1/4英寸并取代了较小的原始钩。虽然小型钩仍然适用于棒的另一端，但它并没有得到发展，因为大型钩可以更好地减小骨-金属和金属-金属交界面的应力。[209]三年后，最初的直径3/16英寸的棒及兼容钩，作为倒霉的自我调节支撑棒的尝试的一部分重新出现。它被用于双开口钩的一侧，用于连接垂直支撑棒和三个钩的末端基座，三个钩的基座由直径3/16英寸的螺纹棒连接，它们与垂直方向成一定角度。中间的双开口钩称为支撑钩，两侧的称为万向钩。尽管哈灵顿已经意识到自我调节支撑棒是不可行的，但他觉得撑开钩（#99-4132-53）和万向钩（#99-4132-52）还不错。[210]很快，捷迈就画出了一幅万向旋转钩的图。哈灵顿显然把它设想成一种可以使压力或载荷从一个方向连接到同一个钩上的方法。[211]尽管反复尝试使用和修改，但效果并不算好，因为相反的棒的压力干扰了开关锁定机制。唯一能有利于自我调节支撑杆的新设计是直径为3/16英寸的螺纹棒，这有助于确保提交给捷迈的原始钩有固定的位置。

A fourth specific implant design problem was the threaded compression rod dimension and survival saga. The 1/8"-diameter threaded rod predated the ratchet rod, and the 3/16"-diameter threaded rod was a residual of the failed self-adjusting rod detour. Both were used to apply compression, and the hope was that the reverse ratchet compression rods would make it possible to render the threaded compression rods obsolete, as the threaded nut connection was time-consuming and prone to load loss. Even before the reverse ratchet rod failure was complete, Hite had written, "In a previous correspondence we had agreed the threaded rods, 1/8" and 3/16" diameter, along with the hexagon nuts and their accompanying hooks would be obsoleted. However, we frequently get calls from those surgeons who saw your earlier technique and insist upon continuing with the threaded rods. I'm just wondering if we will be in a position to obsolete these threaded rods or will we be required to catalogue them as part of the complete Harrington set. If we do this, of course, it will become necessary to supply all of the instruments that we have made, such as the threaded rod clamps, the various hook clamps, etc."[212] Harrington promptly responded, "It will be necessary to furnish both threaded rods and I think we should stay to 3/16" diameter and forget the 1/8 inch."[213] Confusing, yes? But his next sentence made it probable that he meant unnecessary, rather than necessary. "This will eliminate the 1/8" in the rod and the real small hook, as well as the small hook holder." And his next sentence reflected their concern about controlling the number of components as much as possible. "Using the 3/16" diameter threaded rod... will necessitate making the middle sized hook part of the whole system." Two months later Harrington returned all the 1/8"-diameter threaded rods that he had and asked that they be discontinued. "They break 100%... In the future, this [3/16"-diameter] is the only size threaded rod to be used with this instrumentation."[214] But, as he began to expand his teaching activities, he realized that the difficulties imposed on the surgeon by the stiffer 3/16" compression rod were defeating his efforts to convince surgeons to use it. Also, cast immobilization time had been increased, and these two developments caused him to recommend that the 1/8"-diameter compression rod be made available again.[215]

第四个内植物的设计问题是螺纹压缩棒的尺寸和去留的传奇故事。直径 1/8 英寸的螺纹棒比棘齿棒问世早，直径 3/16 英寸的螺纹棒是在自我调节棒失败的过程中残留下来的。这两种棒都用于加压，并希望反向棘齿压缩棒可以代替螺纹压缩棒，因为螺纹螺母连接费时且容易产生载荷丢失。甚至在反向棘齿棒被证实彻底失败之前，海特就曾写道：“在之前的通信中，我们已经同意淘汰直径为 1/8 英寸和 3/16 英寸的螺纹棒，以及六角螺母和相应的钩。然而，我们经常接到那些看过你早期手术的外科医生的电话，他们坚持要继续使用螺纹棒。我只是想知道，我们是要淘汰这些螺纹棒，还是需要将它们作为完整的哈灵顿内固定系统的一部分。当然，如果我们这样做，就必须提供我们所制造的所有器械，如螺纹棒夹、各种钩夹等。”[212] 哈灵顿立即回答说：“我认为有必要提供直径为 3/16 英寸的螺纹棒以及，不再关注 1/8 英寸。”这很令人困惑，不是吗？[213] 但他的下一句话又让人认为，他的意思是不必要的，而不是必要的。“这将去除 1/8 英寸直径的棒和小型钩，以及小型持钩钳。”此外，下面这句话反映了他们尽可能地控制组件数量。“使用 3/16 英寸直径的螺纹棒……也就等于将中等大小的钩作为整个系统的一部分。”两个月后，哈灵顿归还了他拥有的所有直径 1/8 英寸的螺纹棒，并要求停止使用。“他们 100% 断棒……在未来，这个［3/16 英寸直径］是唯一用于该器械的螺纹棒尺寸。”[214]但是，当他开始扩大他的教学活动时，他意识到，硬度更强的直径为 3/16 英寸压缩棒给外科医生带来的困难使他无法说服外科医生使用它。此外，铸造固定时间增加了，这两个问题使他建议再次使用直径 1/8 英寸的压缩棒。[215]

The interconnections between the rod and hooks left little extra space, and very occasionally they didn't work. Overlapping manufacturing tolerances were a fifth implant design concern. Here are just two examples. “The instruments are received. I hate to tell you this, but none of the small [3/16”-diameter compatible] universal hooks will pass over the compression rod. Our orthotist will re-drill all of the hooks and I hope he doesn't ruin them. There isn't time to return them to you for this correction.”[216] Also, when a strut rod was received that did not pass through the large hook (#3019-51), Harrington sent it back and signaled that it was very important that this type of error not occur.[217]

棒和钩之间的连接处几乎没有留下多余的空间，它们偶尔也不匹配。重叠的制造允差是内植物设计的第五个问题。这里仅举两个例子。“器械已经收到了。我不想告诉你这一点，但所有的小型万向钩［3/16 英寸直径兼容］都无法通过压缩棒。我们的器械矫形技师会重新把所有的钩钻孔，我希望他不会把它们弄坏，因为没有时间退回给你做修正。”[216]此外，当收到一根没有穿过大型钩（#3019-51）的支撑棒时，哈灵顿也将其退回，并表示这种错误坚决不能再发生。[217]

Hook dimensions were a surprisingly small design problem at this stage, but are included as the sixth design problem because of their centrality in the spine instrumentation bone connection. The evolution of the hook dimensions had taken place from 1951 to 1954, were incorporated into the self-locking spinal hook drawing Harrington had authored in March 1955, and required minimal design attention during the finalization of the original design. The half-circle hook opening diameter of 3/8" had been arrived at incrementally beginning with less than half circles of about 1/4" diameter. Hook body length had been both shorter and longer than the 1/2" arrived at as part of the ratchet design. The 1/8"-and 3/16"-diameter rod compatible hooks had the same body length, opening diameter, hook length, and blade shape as the 1/4"-diameter rod compatible hooks. The only major outer dimension difference in the three hooks was the width of the body. Of course, the 1/4"-diameter rod compatible hook had the inner ratchet ridge. Zimmer occasionally had to be reminded of the proper orientation of the chisel shoe end, which was sharp toward radius.[218] The manufacturers also had their memory refreshed that the length of the shoe end should be even with hook body end.[219]

钩的尺寸在这个阶段是一个令人惊讶的小的设计问题，但被列入第六个设计问题，因为它们位于脊柱器械与骨连接的中心位置。钩的尺寸从 1951 年到 1954 年发生了变化，并被纳入哈灵顿在 1955 年 3 月撰写的自锁脊柱钩图纸中，从最初设计到最后定稿只得到了很少的关注。半圆钩从半圆直径约为 1/4 英寸增加到开口直径为 3/8 英寸，作为棘齿设计的一部分，钩体长度与棘齿设计的1/2 英寸相比，有短的也有长的。与直径 1/8 英寸和 3/16 英寸的棒相兼容的钩具有与直径 1/4 英寸的棒相兼容的钩相同的体长、开口直径、钩长和叶片形状。三种钩唯一主要的外部尺寸差异是主体的宽度。当然，直径 1/4 英寸棒兼容的钩有内部棘齿脊。捷迈偶尔需要注意一下凿端正确的方向，它向半径方向变得锋利。[218]厂家也重新记了一下，尖的长度要和钩身的长度一样。[219]

Hook holders, a seventh and last design problem to be considered, were, of course, not implants but instruments to facilitate hook placement. Counterintuitively, their evolution required more attention than the hooks. Harrington and Engen had worked out holders for the 1/8"-diameter threaded rod compatible hooks. The most difficult parts of the design were the security of the posts in the jaws and the provision for rod clearance by a semicircular longitudinally oriented relief on the protruding tip. The 3/16"-diamete1 rod compatible hook that Harrington initially submitted to Zimmer did not have side holes to accommodate a hook holder. As part of the unsuccessful self-adjusting strut bar detour, a 3/16"-diameter rod compatible hook holder was developed.[220] Looking to the future, Hite questioned the need to continue these side holes to accommodate a hook holder if the reverse ratchet compression rod was to replace the threaded rod. He justified his question by pointing out that a hook holder had never been part of the 1/4"-diameter ratchet rod compatible hook.[221] Harrington responded that, on the contrary, addition of the hook-holding feature to the 1/4"-diameter rod compatible distraction hooks "would be desirable." To that point he had made do with pliers, which worked well for him. However, the "forces used to put in the compression instrumentation necessitate holding the hook firmly."[222] In this way a hook holder for the 1/4"-diameter ratchet hook came about somewhat obliquely, because of its perceived need to better hold the 1/4"-diameter rod compatible hook applied in compression. This perceived need was a real one and was quickly satisfied.

持钩器是第七个也是最后一个设计问题。当然，它不是内植物，而是用来放置钩的工具。出乎意料的是它们的发展比钩需要更多的关注。哈灵顿和恩金已经为与直径 1/8 英寸的螺纹棒兼容的钩制作了持钩器。设计中最困难的部分是持钩器的钳口部支撑点的确认，以及通过对突出的器械尖端半圆形纵向的减弱对于棒的间隙进行保留。哈灵顿最初提交给捷迈的与直径 3/16 英寸棒所兼容的钩没有侧孔，无法适应持钩器。作为失败的自我调节支撑棒的一部分，一种与直径 3/16 英寸的棒兼容的持钩器得到了发展。[220]考虑到之后的发展，海特质疑，如果反向棘齿压缩棒要取代螺纹棒，是否需要继续使用这些侧孔来适应持钩器。他为自己的问题辩解，指出持钩器从来没有为与直径 1/4 英寸的棘齿棒兼容而设计。[221]哈灵顿回应说，相反，在与直径 1/4 英寸的棒兼容的撑开钩上增加持钩功能“是可取的”。到那时，他还凑合着用钳子，钳子对于他来说很管用。然而，用于安装压缩棒的力需要牢牢地握住钩。[222]在这种情况下，用于直径 1/4 英寸棘齿钩的持钩器间接地产生了，因为人们认为它需要在压缩过程中更好地钳夹住与直径 1/4 英寸的棒兼容的钩。这种可感知到的需求很真实，因而很快就得到了满足。

The design of Harrington Spine Instrumentation had made immense progress.

Harrington and Hite worked well together, which was important because their collaboration was still a two steps forward, one step backward process. Patients with scoliosis, for which surgical treatment was warranted, did not present on schedule, and Harrington couldn't go any faster than his ethical clinical practice would allow. What seemed right for one case wasn't for another. For instance, the 3/16"-diameter compression rod worked well for small curves, but was unworkable for large curves. It also took time for many of the problems to become apparent, such as rod fatigue breakage. Zimmer worked with no firsthand knowledge of the overall problem and had to rely on Harrington for direction. But together they had brought the design and technique to the point that it could be shared, and by the second half of 1959 Harrington was ready for exposure to and honest feedback from scoliosis experts.

哈灵顿脊柱器械的设计取得了巨大的进步。哈灵顿和海特合作得很好这一点很重要，因为他们的合作仍然效率较低。有些脊柱侧凸患者，先前告知他们要接受手术治疗，最终并没有及时治疗，因为哈灵顿无法在临床伦理允许之前进行手术。而且一种器械并非适用于所有的患者。例如，直径3/16英寸的压缩棒适用于弯曲较小的患者，但并不适用于弯曲较大的患者。许多问题也需要经过一段时间才能显现出来，如棒的疲劳性断裂。对于全部的问题，捷迈无法得到第一手资料，不得不依赖哈灵顿的指导。但如果能很好地合作，对于设计和技术问题则能切中要害并能得到共享，到1959年下半年，哈灵顿已经准备好接受脊柱侧凸专家的真实反馈。

This is a good time to update other scoliosis management development after World War Ⅱ. Quite apart from Harrington's work, substantial progress in the treatment of scoliosis had been made, and much of this was due to the untiring efforts of John H. Moe in Minneapolis-St. Paul. Six years older than Harrington, he had spent the war years in practice and was acquainted firsthand with the shortcomings of scoliosis treatment. In 1947 he was invited to join the Contemporary Orthopaedic Society, a small travel club of several leading orthopaedic surgeons. At its annual meeting in Milwaukee, Moe was inspired by John Cobb's arthrodesis and modified turnbuckle corrective work as well as the Milwaukee brace work of meeting host Walter Blount. Subsequently, Moe sought and received permission to establish a scoliosis service at the Gillette State Hospital for Crippled Children in St. Paul.[223] His entire practice was dedicated to providing better care for patients with scoliosis and other spine deformities. In particular he focused on improving selection of arthrodesis levels and techniques. He also adopted two improved methods of postoperative correction and immobilization, both having origins in the late 1940s and entering mainstream practice in the early 1950s: the Risser localizer cast and the Milwaukee brace.[224, 225] Both included the neck, although the main corrective forces were transverse rather than longitudinal. They allowed earlier mobilization, and the Milwaukee brace morphed into a mainstay of nonoperative treatment.[226] By 1958 Moe was able to report pseudarthrosis in fewer than 15% of his operated patients.[227]

第二次世界大战后是脊柱侧凸诊疗飞速发展的好时机。哈灵顿的工作暂且不说，脊柱侧凸的治疗也取得了实质性的进展，这在很大程度上要归功于明尼阿波利斯的约翰·H. 莫的不懈努力。他比哈灵顿大 6 岁，战争期间一直在实践，对脊柱侧凸治疗的不足有第一手的了解。1947 年，现代骨科学会邀请他加入，这是一个由顶尖骨外科医生组成的小型宣讲团性质的学会。在密尔沃基举行的年度会议上，莫受到了约翰·柯布的融合术和改良的铰链矫形工作以及会议主持人沃尔特·布朗特的密尔沃基支具相关工作的激励。随后，莫在圣保罗的吉列州立残疾儿童医院寻求资助并获得了许可，成立了脊柱侧凸专科。[223]他致力于为脊柱侧凸和其他脊柱畸形的患者提供更好的治疗。他特别关注改善融合节段和技术选择策略。他还采用了两种改进的术后矫正和固定方法——里泽局部定位矫形石膏和密尔沃基支具，这两种方法都起源于 20 世纪 40 年代末，并在 50 年代初被广泛应用。[224,225]这两种技术都包括对颈部的矫正，允许早期活动，尽管主要的矫正力是横向的而不是纵向的。密尔沃基支具演变成非手术治疗的主要手段。[226]到 1958 年，莫的手术患者中出现假关节的比例不到 15%。[227]

During this period of time three concerted efforts were made to develop instrumentation to improve the treatment of scoliosis. The first was that of Adam Gruca in Warsaw, Poland, who in 1958 reported his experience with a series of 172 adolescent idiopathic scoliosis patients begun in 1945. Based on electrodiagnostic and histological studies and observations of a mobile spine model with muscles represented by rubber bands, he developed the view that idiopathic scoliosis was initially a functional deformity caused by hyperactivity of the concave muscles, becoming structural only after failure of the convex muscles to compensate. For curves up to 30° he recommended that muscle equilibrium be reestablished by either muscle transfer or spring alloplasty, the implantation of a flattened spring hooked to the end vertebrae transverse processes on the convex side of the curve. The spring strength necessary was estimated considering superimposed body weight and patient age. Apparently arthrodesis was not included. Treatment of curves 30° to 60° and greater than 60° included a screw-spring distractor with bifid ends inserted between the concave transverse processes of the end vertebrae and arthrodesis. No follow-up results were included, and no further series were reported.

在此期间，内固定器械的发展取得了三项成就，这些均改善了脊柱侧凸的治疗。第一项成就来自波兰华沙的亚当·格鲁卡，他在1958年报告了他从1945年开始对172名青少年特发性脊柱侧凸患者的治疗经验。基于电诊断学、组织学研究和对以橡皮筋代替肌肉的活动脊柱模型的观察，他提出特发性脊柱侧凸最初是由凹侧肌肉过度活动引起的功能性畸形，只有在凸侧肌肉失去代偿后才变为结构性畸形。对于小于等于30°的弯曲，他建议通过肌肉转移或弹簧异体成形术来重建肌肉平衡，即将弹性装置挂于侧弯凸侧椎体的横突处。依据附加的体重和患者年龄估计所需的弹簧强度。显然融合术不包括在内。弯曲的度数在30°~60°及大于60°时，治疗包括在凹侧上、下端椎的横突打入尾端分叉的螺钉-弹簧撑开器以及融合术。该术式没有相关随访结果，也没有进一步的报道。

Another effort was by Francis G. Allan of Birmingham, England, who used his turnbuckle distractor in eleven patients from January 1951 to December 1954 and published his preliminary report in 1955.[228] The innovative instrumentation was a turnbuckle distractor with forked or Y-ends to gage "the base of the transverse process at its junction with the vertebral body." The age of the patients ranged from twelve to twenty-four years and included patients with idiopathic, paralytic, and congenital curves. The nine primary curves averaged 100° before and 72° after operation. Arthrodesis was performed, and no external immobilization was used. Allan recommended that "the jack should be left in for at least six months-in fact it might be better left indefinitely." He further recommended that curves less than 70° should be treated by other methods because the jack became less efficient for smaller curves. No follow-up results were included. Allan presented a pre-publication report in late 1954 at a meeting of the International Society of Orthopaedic Surgery and Traumatology (SICOT) where brief mention was made of two other scoliosis instrumentation efforts, about which nothing more was to be heard.[229]

第二项成就是由英国伯明翰的弗朗西斯·G. 艾伦做出的，他在1951年1月至1954年12月期间对11名患者使用了他的铰链撑开器，并在1955年发表了他的初步报告。[228]这项新型器械是一种带有叉形或Y形末端的铰链撑开器，用在

"横突与椎体交界处的根部"。患者的年龄从12到24岁不等，包括特发性、麻痹性和先天性脊柱侧凸的患者。9个术前平均100°的原始曲度，术后平均72°。这些患者进行了融合术，未使用其他外固定。艾伦建议："该撑开器应该至少放置六个月——事实上，最好是无限期地放置。"他进一步建议小于70°的侧凸应该用其他方法处理，因为该撑开器对于度数较小的侧凸作用较小，并未发现相关随访结果。1954年底，艾伦在国际矫形与创伤外科学会（SICOT）的一次会议上做了一份预出版的报告，该报告简单提到了另外两种脊柱侧凸器械的相关工作，但没有其他更多的消息。[229]

The third approach was that of H. Leslie Wenger of New York, whose instrumentation series began in January 1953. This had been preceded by several years with concave costotransversectomy alone as a treatment for thoracic scoliosis. From there the author added a method to provide distraction between the end vertebral bodies. To do this, he devised a turnbuckle spine jack device anchored to the two end vertebrae with a single screw placed obliquely through the intervertebral disc and anchored in the next vertebra. Usually the medial 2" of seven ribs and their transverse processes were excised, and the intercostal bundles were divided and clamped. The extrapleural plane was developed, and exposure of the vertebrae usually required ligation of the intercostal vessels as they arose from the aorta. The end vertebrae were exposed to the point that about two-thirds of their mass could be palpated. The end vertebra screws were placed, the spanning jack inserted, and distraction applied. A chest tube was usually required. No fusion was done, and no external support was used. In 1957 he self-published a booklet of his work, and at that point he had 3 deaths in 49 patients, 19 having the spine jack procedure and 30 costotransversectomy alone.[230] In 1961 the author reported that in 36 patients having the spine jack operation, one patient died of hemorrhage on the sixteenth postoperative day, and one had become paraplegic. The average curves were 63° preoperative and 42° postoperative, an initial correction of 33%. Follow-up information was not provided.[231] The author described the operation as "formidable." These procedures were never reported on again, although an attempt to utilize Gruca's springs in the treatment of spine fracture was later made. This recalls two other efforts to develop spine instrumentation, these using plates bolted to the spinous processes to stabilize thoracolumbar fractures[232] and lumbosacral fusions.[233] Neither became accepted practice.

第三项工作来自纽约的H. 莱斯利·温格，他的器械系列研究开始于1953年

1 月。这之前的几年他以单纯凹侧的肋骨椎骨横突切除术治疗胸椎侧凸。从那以后，温格发明了一种办法，即在端椎椎体之间进行撑开。为此，他设计了一种铰链脊柱撑开装置，该装置通过一个螺钉固定在上、下端椎上，螺钉斜行穿过椎间盘进而固定在下一椎体上。通常切除 7 根肋骨的内侧 2 英寸及其横突，将肋间束分开并夹紧。胸膜外平面暴露出来，暴露椎体通常需要结扎从主动脉发出的肋间血管。端椎应当暴露至大约三分之二以使椎体可以触及。于端椎放置螺钉，植入撑开装置，进而进行撑开。通常需要放置胸管。没有进行融合，也没有使用外部支撑。1957 年，他自己出版了一本关于他的工作的小册子，当时，在 49 个病人中有 3 人死亡，19 人进行了脊柱撑开装置植入术，30 人只接受了肋骨横突切除手术。[230] 1961 年，作者报道了在 36 名脊柱撑开手术患者中，1 名患者在术后第 16 天因出血死亡，1 名患者截瘫。术前平均弯曲为 63°，术后平均弯曲为 42°，初始矫正率为 33%。没有提供随访资料。[231]作者将这种手术描述为“可怕的”。这些手术再也没有被报道过，尽管后来有人尝试利用格鲁卡弹簧治疗脊柱骨折。这让人想起了另外两个有助于研发脊柱内固定器械的例子，它们使用固定在棘突上的钢板来稳定胸腰椎骨折[232]和腰骶融合，[233]然而两者都没有得到认可。

In this interval between the end of World War II and the introduction of Harrington Spine Instrumentation a major contribution to spine deformity surgery was made with Professor Arthur Hodgson's introduction of anterior spine surgery for the treatment of Pott's disease and Pott's paraplegia. The logic was clearly spelled out in his 1956 report: direct access to allow thorough "decompression of the abscess with its pus, caseous material, granulation material, intervetebral discs, and sequestra" followed by manual correction of abnormal kyphosis and structural grafting.[234] At the time of the preliminary report 50 patients had been treated, and 82% (14 of 17) of the first patients had fused rapidly. Hodgson acknowledged that Hiromu Ito of Kyoto, Japan, had reported in 1934 on ten patients using a similar approach, but Hodgson stated he was unaware of Ito's work at the beginning of his studies.[235] Hodgson and Ito both credited W. Muller who reported similar surgery in 1906. Ito had studied a translation of Muller's paper in which he reported that his first case was successful, but subsequent cases were so unsuccessful he had to give up the operation. Ito had the advantage of operating after the advent of aseptic surgery, and Hodgson had the added advantage of operating after effective chemotherapy was available. Hodgson's work set the course that would lead to the development of the first successful anterior spine instrumentation, that of Alan Dwyer.

在第二次世界大战结束和哈灵顿脊柱器械推行之间的这段时间里，阿瑟·霍奇森教授为治疗波特病和波特瘫痪引入了脊柱前路手术，对脊柱畸形手术做出了重大贡献。他在 1956 年的报告中清楚地阐述了其逻辑：直接“通过去除脓肿与脓液、干酪样物质、肉芽组织、椎间盘和死骨进行彻底的减压”，然后手法矫正异常脊柱后凸和进行结构性骨移植。[234]在初步报告时，50 名患者接受了治疗，第一批患者中的 82%（17 例中的 14 例）实现了迅速融合。霍奇森承认日本京都的伊藤博文 1934 年曾对接受类似手术的 10 名患者进行了报道，但霍奇森指出他在研究之初并不了解伊藤的工作。[235]霍奇森和伊藤博文都称赞了 W. 米勒在 1906 年报告了类似的手术。伊藤曾研究过米勒一篇论文的译文，在这篇论文中，他声称他的第一个病例成功了，但随后的病例都很不成功，他不得不放弃此类手术。伊藤的优势是此前无菌手术技术已经出现，霍奇森的优势是在有效的化疗后进行手术。霍奇森的工作为艾伦·德怀尔第一个完善的脊柱前路固定器械的成功研发奠定了基础。

Figure 5.18 ***The persuaders, Paul Harrington and Basil O'Connor, meeting and greeting, ca. 1959 (Harrington Archives)***
图 5.18 说服者，保罗·哈灵顿 和 巴兹尔·奥康纳，会面和问候，约 1959 年（哈灵顿档案馆）

Aside from Harrington, no person or group had more interest in seeing him succeed than the NFIP. Its president, Basil O'Connor, had probably first met Harrington in 1959. *See figure 5. 18.* Vernon Nickel, Harrington's counterpart at the NFIP unit at Rancho Los Amigos Medical Center, was asked to take the lead and organize a program for Harrington to present his work. Nickel was acquainted with all the leading scoliosis, and his recollection of Harrington's position was sobering: "Well, he was right on the nip and tuck of being totally washed out of the system. I mean, just within a hair."[236] Nickel turned to his mentor and predecessor, the well-respected Vernon Thompson, who although ill with cancer and in a wheelchair was asked to chair the program. Harrington's presentation apparently was well received.[237] Nickel was impressed to the point that he urged Moe to visit Harrington, which is believed to have occurred although primary documentation in the Harrington Archives is lacking.[238] Harrington did have two well-documented high profile visitors in 1959, John Hall and Jack Kennedy.[239] Further increasing exposure to and knowledge of his instrumentation system were four trips to perform six demonstration operations. The host surgeons were well-established orthopedic surgeons, but were not scoliosis thought leaders.[240, 241]

除了哈灵顿，没有人或组织比国家小儿麻痹基金更希望看到他成功。主席巴兹尔·奥康纳第一次见到哈灵顿大概是在 1959 年。(图 5.18) 弗农·尼克尔是在兰乔洛杉米戈斯医疗中心国家小儿麻痹基金会分部与哈灵顿职位相当的人，他被要求牵头组织一个项目，让哈灵顿展示他的工作。尼克尔认识所有顶尖的脊柱侧凸外科医生，他非常清楚地回忆起哈灵顿当时的处境："嗯，他正处于被体制彻底淘汰的边缘。我是说，就差那么一点点。"[236]尼克尔求助于他备受尊敬的导师和前任弗农·汤普森。汤普森虽然身患癌症，坐着轮椅，但还是被请来主持这个项目。哈灵顿的报告显然很受欢迎。[237]尼克尔清楚地记得他让莫去拜访哈灵顿，而且认为莫去拜访了哈灵顿，尽管哈灵顿的档案中并没有记录。[238] 1959 年，哈灵顿确实有两位备受关注的访客，约翰·霍尔和杰克·肯尼迪。[239]使他的内固定器械进一步亮相的是四次巡回演讲和六次手术演示，演示邀请的外科医生是知名的骨科医生，但不是专注于脊柱侧凸专业的思想领袖。[240, 241]

As 1959 drew to a close and the 1960 AAOS annual meeting that would be held in Chicago approached, Zimmer's chief engineer, Jim Hite, became concerned. In October he wrote Harrington, "Interest is steadily growing in this technique and I'm sure we will be flooded with inquiries at the coming meeting. We are also wondering if you intend to have any type of display or exhibit at the above meeting. If so, is there anything we can do to assist you in preparing for such an exhibit? If you do not intend to exhibit, we are wondering if you would be willing to let Zimmer Mfg. Co. show this in our booth."[242] Harrington responded, "I think it would be wiser to exhibit at the Academy not as major issue, but have it available. I will present spine instrumentation as a formal article in June 1960 at the annual meeting of the American Orthopaedic Association. From then on it is 'Katie bar the door.'"[243]

随着 1959 年接近尾声，1960 年美国骨科医师学会年会即将在芝加哥举行，捷迈的总工程师吉姆·海特开始担心起来。10 月，他在给哈灵顿的信中写道："人们对这项技术的兴趣正在稳步增长，我相信在即将到来的会议上，将有很多问题等着我们。我们还想知道您是否打算在上述会议上进行任何形式的展示或展览。如果有的话，我们能为您做些什么来帮助您准备这样的展览？如果您不打算展出，我们想知道您是否愿意让捷迈制造公司在我们的展位上展出一下。”[242] 哈灵顿回答说：“我认为更明智的做法是在学会上展出，但不把它作为一个重点。我将在 1960 年 6 月美国骨科学会年会上以正式文章的形式介绍脊柱内固定器械。那之后的事，让我们向上帝祈祷吧。”[243]

（王连雷 原所茂 译　刘新宇 刘立岷 张忠民 审校）

6

ACCEPTANCE (1960-62)

The interest has been almost overpowering.[1]

接纳和认可 (1960—1962)

吾辈兴致勃勃[1]

The lengthy process of research and development through trial and error moved Harrington gradually from his iconoclastic begging toward established practice. As a result he was now performing arthrodesis at the initial surgery, using casts more frequently, and prolonging immobilization.[2] And some scoliosis physician and surgeon thought leaders were beginning to appreciate the possibilities of improved long-term scoliosis correction and less cumbersome postoperative care offered by Harrington Spine Instrumentation. He would very soon begin to feel the pressure to standardize his techniques and develop educational materials in cooperation with Zimmer.

哈灵顿在漫长的探索和不断试错中一步步打破传统，走向成熟，提出初次手术时通过佩戴石膏并延长制动时间促进融合。[2]一些脊柱侧凸内科及骨科医生中有远见卓识的领导者已经认识到哈灵顿脊柱器械有可能对侧凸矫正有长期效果，还能减少冗长、复杂的术后处理负担。因此哈灵顿迫切感受到需要与捷迈公司合作，将自己的技术标准化并编写教材。

There was a subtle indication of both Harrington's former ostracism and his coming acceptance at the 1960 annual meeting of the American Academy of Orthopaedics Surgeons (AAOS) held in Chicago. On January 25 Harrington received his Certificate of Fellowship.[3] But, it should be noted that he had passed the American Board of Orthopedist earlier![4] In the normal course of events a surgeon was eligible to apply for fellowship in the AAOS after three years of practice limited to orthopedic surgery.[5] Each application, accompanied by letters of recommendation from two fellows, was investigated by the admissions committee and the regional admissions committee, which arranged an interview. The application and the recommendations were sent to the board of directors where a two-thirds favorable vote was required. The large majority of applicants were accepted on their first application.

哈灵顿也曾遭受同行的反对，直至1960年于芝加哥举办的美国骨科医师学会年会上，人们的态度才有了微妙的变化。1月25日，哈灵顿收到了他的会员资格证书，[3]其实他早已经通过了美国骨科医师（ABO）执业考试。[4]正常情况下，经过三年骨科培训的外科医生有资格申请美国骨科医师学会的会员。[5]每个申请都需要附有两名会员的推荐信，由遴选委员会和地区遴选招生委员会考察并安排面试。申请和考察结果提交至委员会，得到三分之二的委员同意即可。大多数申请人都是一次成功。

On a day-to-day basis Harrington found that it was necessary to evaluate the needs, both real and perceived, and ideas for new or existing instruments. The first new need addressed in 1960 was that for pelvic fixation, and exactly how it was realized is unclear. The day after a February 3 phone conversation Zimmer sent Harrington "four stainless steel threaded rods 8" overall length with 1/4-20 threads. The pins are equipped with a diamond point for self-threading."[6] On Monday, February 8, at the annual meeting of the AAOS, Jim Hite had a discussion with William Fisher of Chicago, who apparently had a case requiring a method of supporting strut bars across the pelvis. Hite mentioned the larger threaded pins he had just sent Harrington, and Fisher thought "that perhaps these might be used to bridge the pelvic bone." Earlier in the meeting Fisher had discussed his needs with Harrington, who offered a major criticism that Fisher was unable to recall.[7]

基于日复一日的临床工作，哈灵顿发现有必要平衡客观和主观的需求、新器械研发与旧器械改良之间的关系。1960年，第一个解决的问题是骨盆固定，到底如何具体实现尚不清楚。2月3日电话交流后，捷迈公司向哈灵顿提供了如下一些东西："四根不锈钢螺纹棒，总长度为8英寸，螺纹为1/4-20①。这些锚定钉

① 英制螺丝大小表示法，1/4-20表示螺丝外径为1/4英寸，螺丝牙数为20。

配有可用于自锁定的菱形顶端。”[6] 2月8日的星期一，在美国骨科医师学会年会上，吉姆·海特与芝加哥的威廉·费希尔讨论到支撑骨盆的方法。费希尔认为海特刚刚提供给哈灵顿的更大型号的螺纹钉“也许可以用来连接和固定骨盆”。在会议的早些时候，费希尔向哈灵顿提出了他的需求，哈灵顿便提出了费希尔无法回忆起的重大批评。[7]

Zimmer provided Harrington three sizes of threaded rods/pins/bars (1/4”, 5/16”, and 3/8” in diameter) to bridge the ilia and sacrum or, more precisely, to transfix the ilia and bridge the sacrum. To connect the strut bar to the sacral bar at a 90° (+10°) angle, Harrington had provided drawings of two options, a hook and a closed eyelet. Zimmer fabricated the eyelet version and sent it for his approval. Remarkably, surgeons had somehow become aware of this development, and orders for the sacral bar and connector were already coming in just two months after the sacral bar development began and before it was even finished![8] There was obviously a real need for fixing to the pelvis. The process for selecting the final sacral pin diameter illustrated the time lag in trial and error research. In April Harrington signaled acceptance of the 5/16” threaded sacral pin.[9] However, by July two practical problems helped guide the development to the smallest diameter, the 1/4” threaded pin. One was that the maximum diameter drill bit accommodated by the universally available operating room drills was 1/4. This obstacle could be overcome by machining one end of the rod to fit a 1/4” chuck. The bigger obstacle to using the larger pins was the unavailability of a suitable pin cutter to remove the excess length of a pin that size after insertion. The sacral bar was subsequently strengthened by reducing the depth of the threads. When Harrington became convinced that the 1/4”-diameter, shallow-threaded rod was strong enough, it was chosen.[10] “Zimmer took back the unused larger pins, apparently without cost to Harrington.” This patience-testing process played out over and over as each instrument part or component evolved.

捷迈为哈灵顿提供了三种尺寸的螺纹棒/钉/杆（直径为1/4英寸、5/16英寸和3/8英寸），用以连接髂骨和骶骨，准确地说是用于固定髂骨并桥接骶骨。为了以90°（+10°）的角度将支撑棒与骶骨棒连接起来，哈灵顿提供了两种选择，一种是钩，另一种是闭式的孔眼。捷迈制作了孔眼版本，并送交他批准。此时，外科医生们也意识到了这一发展，因此，开发后仅两个月，甚至在完成前，订单就接踵而至！[8]显然，医生们急需这种骨盆固定器械。骶骨棒直径的最终确立过程说明了试验与临床实际的差距。4 月，哈灵顿表示决定使用 5/16 英寸螺纹骶骨棒,[9]但到了 7 月，两个临床实际问题迫使哈灵顿开发出了最小直径为 1/4 英寸的螺纹棒。一是手术室通用钻头的最大直径是 1/4 英寸，这个问题可以通过加工棒的一端来解决。二是没有合适的裁棒器来裁剪粗棒。后来，通过减少螺纹深度，骶骨棒也得到了加强。最终，哈灵顿确信直径 1/4 英寸的浅螺纹棒足够坚固，并选择它作为最终产品。[10]由于捷迈回收了（未使用的）粗螺纹棒，没有给哈灵顿造成损失。随着器械部件或组件的不断改进，费时费力的测试过程也持续进行。

As the process of developing the sacral bar progressed, Hite expressed concern about the lever moment caused by the off-center designs Harrington had offered and suggested an alternative in which the force of the distraction rod was direct toward the axis of the sacral rod.[12] Harrington's response is confusing as he opened with "this should be of no concern", and closed with "your idea is very good and I would like to try a few."[13] The evolution of the sacral bar connector may have also caused a cooling of the Harrington-Engen collaboration. Harrington had invited Engen into an operating room to view the first-time use of a sacral bar hook prototype that Engen had made. It broke during loading and Engen, who was not scrubbed, recalled that he "pushed him (Harrington) aside... and went with my fingers up into the wound" to retrieve the prototype. Tempers flared, words were said, and feelings were hurt causing lasting memories. Harrington later apologized to Engen for not having properly introduced him to operating room etiquette.[14]

随着骶骨棒的开发，海特对哈灵顿提供的偏心设计表示担忧，并提出了一种替代方案，即把撑开棒的应力直接导向骶骨棒的中轴线。[12] 对此哈灵顿的回答自相矛盾，他一开始说“这不值得关注”，最后又说，“你的想法非常好，可以一试。”[13]骶骨棒连接器的发明过程差点引起哈灵顿和恩金的决裂。哈灵顿曾邀请恩金进入他的手术室，观看第一例（恩金制作的）骶骨钩原型的手术。棒在装载过程中断裂了，没有刷手消毒的恩金回忆说：“我把他（哈灵顿）推到一边……想把手指伸进刀口”去取回原型。双方自然发生了冲突，言辞激烈。哈灵顿后来向恩金道歉，因为他没有提前向恩金介绍手术室的无菌原则。[14]

While letter exchanges about pelvic fixation were going on, another communication occurred that illustrated how protective Harrington was of the NFIP grant funds. On May 27 he responded to a shipment he had just received as follows: "I was not aware that we were going to be charged for these items. The three universal hooks were right and left type and purely experimental. The three threaded (compression) rod assemblies were your idea and made in three different lengths, and the threaded rod holder was to replace the one I have with a better design." The bill was for $52.55.[15] A few days later Hite responded. "This was in error and a credit memo for the same amount will be issued. These items should not have been billed since they were experimental."[16]

在关于骨盆固定的信件往来中，有一件事说明了哈灵顿对国家小儿麻痹基金会提供的基金的重视程度。5 月 27 日，他对刚刚收到的一批器械作出如下答复。"我不知道这需要收取费用。三个通用钩是分左右的，纯粹是实验性的。三个螺纹（压缩）棒是你们的主意，且制备了三种不同的长度，螺纹棒持棒器是更好的设计，可以取代我原有的。"账单上的金额是 52.55 美元。[15]几天后，海特回复说："是我们的工作失误，我将开具相同金额的信用备忘录。这些项目不应该计费，它们是实验性的。"[16]

As these research and design exchanges continued, a major landmark was passed in the origin and evolution of Harrington Spine Instrumentation. On June 2, 1960, which was the last day of the annual meeting of the American Orthopaedic Association (AOA), Harrington made the first major podium presentation of his work. This was an important step up from the exhibits he had presented at AAOS annual meetings. Just being on the program was promising because the AOA, founded in 1887, was older and more prestigious than the AAOS. All but 6 of the 36 AOA charter members practiced on the East Coast, and membership was limited to leaders of the specialty. The membership process was initiated by invitation, and one of the rites of passage was the submission of a thesis, which was to be presented orally and in manuscript form. Election was not a foregone conclusion. For example, Russell Hibbs was first proposed for membership in 1904. Earlier he had replaced Newton M. Shaffer at the New York Orthopaedics Hospital, and a group of influential members of the AOA expressed the view that "Hibbs course in achieving the position had been unfair to his colleague and not altogether honorable." After multiple attempts Hibbs was finally elected to membership in 1921, seventeen years later![17]

随着器械研究和设计交流的不断进行，哈灵顿脊柱器械出现了里程碑事件。1960 年 6 月 2 日，在美国骨科学会年会的最后一天，哈灵顿在讲台上首次正式地介绍了他的工作。与他在美国骨科医师学会上的演讲相比，这次有了重要的进步。因为成立于1887年的美国骨科学会比美国骨科医师学会更古老、更有名望。美国骨科学会的36个创始会员中，有6人在东海岸执业，而且成员只限于本专业的带头人。学会采用邀请制，收到邀请后需要提交论文，论文以口头和稿件形式提交。不需要投票表决。例如，拉塞尔·希伯斯在1904年首次被提名为会员。此前，他曾在纽约骨科医院取代了牛顿·M. 谢弗的位置，美国骨科学会的一些有影响力的会员表示，“希伯斯获得这个职位的过程对他的同事不公平，他自己也不光荣。”多次努力后，希伯斯终于在1921年，即17年后当选为会员！[17]

Harrington was the sole author of his presentation, "Surgical Instrumentation for Management of Scoliosis." Four men were asked to critique his work: John H. Moe of Minneapolis, Minnesota; William J. Stewart of Columbia, Missouri; Joseph C. Risser of Pasadena, California; and William H. Bickel of Rochester, Minnesota.[18] Unfortunately, their comments were not included in the published proceedings of the meeting,[19] but they could not have helped being impressed.[20] *See figure 6.1.* While Moe and Stewart were almost certainly supportive, Risser was known to be very opposed to Harrington's work.[21] Study of the June AOA program abstract and the December *Journal of Bone & Joint Sugery* American volume (*JBJS Am.*) proceedings, both of which were similar in length but typically were submitted several months apart, revealed his still rapidly evolving technique. In both abstracts Harrington depicted distraction and compression loads as being applied by a ratchet mechanism, when in fact he had abandoned this mechanism for applying compression in August 1959: "Also am sending back all compression rods you sent with reverse ratchet. They are just no good."[22] He was returning to the thread-nut connecting mechanism for compression loading, favoring at that time the larger 3/16" over the 1/8" diameter rod.[23] Both abstracts contained the following sentence suggesting frequent use of instrumentation without arthrodesis: "By surgical intervention at one or two year intervals, progressive correction can be accomplished to adjust for growth changes." Arthrodesis/fusion was not mentioned in the AOA program abstract whereas in the *JBJS Am.* proceedings there were two related statements: "Experience derived from 103 cases in which instrumentation was used with and without fusion is the basis of this paper." Further on he stated that, "When the patient is ten years of age or older, spine fusion of the major curve is recommended with the initial corrective surgery." These discrepancies probably reflected Harrington's steep learning curve involved with developing this new, quickly evolving treatment for the still incompletely understood condition of scoliosis.[24] *See figure 6.2.*

哈灵顿是《应用内固定手术器械治疗脊柱侧凸》的唯一作者。有四位专家受邀评论他的工作：明尼苏达州明尼阿波利斯的约翰·H. 莫，密苏里州哥伦比亚的威廉·J. 斯图尔特，加利福尼亚州帕萨迪纳的约瑟夫·C. 里泽，以及明尼苏达州罗切斯特的威廉·H. 比克尔。[18]尽管他们的评论没有被收录到会议记录中，[19]但他们都大为震撼。[20]（图 6.1）四人中莫和斯图尔特表示绝对支持，但里泽非常反对哈灵顿的工作。[21]在 6 月份的美国骨科学会会议摘要和 12 月份的《骨与关节外科杂志》（美国卷）的论文都揭示了他的技术仍在飞速发展，这两篇论文的篇幅相似，但提交时间相隔数月。在这两份摘要中，哈灵顿描述了通过棘齿施加的撑开和压缩应力。而事实上，他在 1959 年 8 月就已经放弃了这种压缩机制：“同时，我还将寄回你采用反向棘齿的压缩棒。他们不太好用。”[22]他重新使用螺纹螺母连接压缩机制，当时倾向于较大的 3/16 英寸而不是 1/8 英寸直径的棒。[23]两份摘要都建议首选器械矫形而不进行融合：“通过每隔一到两年的手术干预，可以逐渐完成矫形以适应生长变化。”美国骨科学会项目摘要中没有提到融合，而在《骨与关节外科杂志》（美国卷）的论文中，有两个相关的声明：“在 103 个病例中，无论是否进行融合术，均进行了器械矫形。”此外，他还表示：“当病人年龄在 10 岁以上时，建议在初次矫正手术中进行主弯的融合。”这些差异可能反映了哈灵顿早期仍在摸索脊柱侧凸治疗方案。[24]（图 6.2）

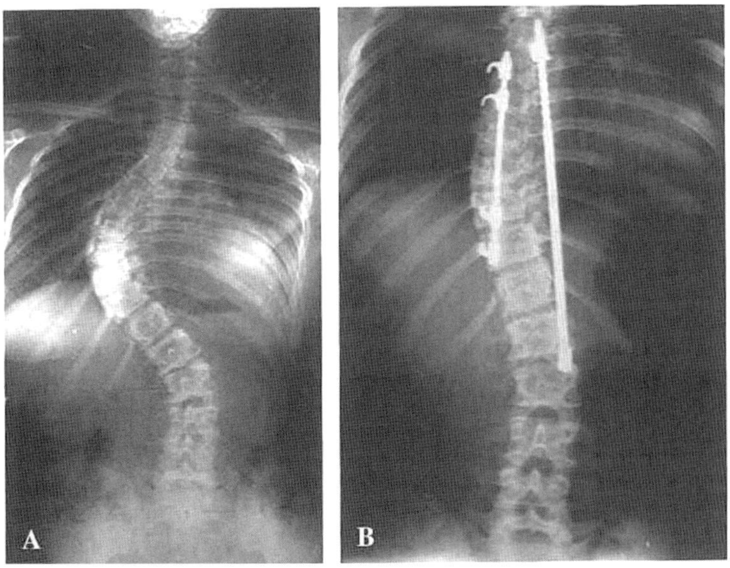

Figure 6.1 ***Spine radiographs viewed anteroposterior of a fifteen-year-old girl with idiopathic scoliosis. A. Standing preoperative; B. Supine postoperative.*** **(*Harrington Archives*)**

图 6.1　一个 15 岁的特发性脊柱侧凸女孩的脊柱 X 光片的前后图片。A. 术前站立位；B. 术后仰卧位（哈灵顿档案馆）

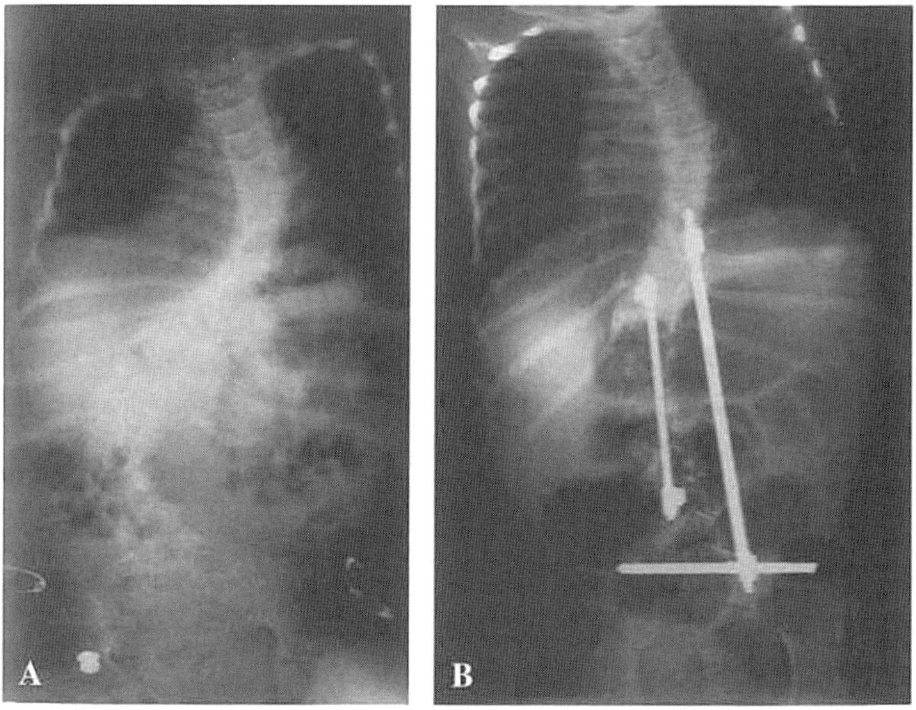

Figure 6.2 ***Use of the sacral bar and nonfusion instrumentation is illustrated in this six-year-old male with extreme trunk and leg paralysis from polio at age eighteen months. A. Preoperative. B. Postoperative. Fusion was not done and distraction force adjustment was planned annually. (Harrington Archives)***

图6.2 这名6岁的男性在18个月时因小儿麻痹症导致躯干和腿部严重瘫痪,说明了骶骨棒和非融合性器械的使用情况。A. 术前。B. 术后。没有进行融合,每年计划进行牵引力调整(哈灵顿档案馆)

Harrington had been immediately preceded on the program by John Cobb's presentation on "The Problem of the Primary Curve." This could have been a little intimidating as Cobb was one of the leading scoliosis experts and very well established, having been elected to the AOA in 1948.[25] Published just six months later, his thesis was that the commonly used descriptors *primary* and *secondary* were less helpful in describing scoliosis curves than *maior structural* and *minor structural*.[26] That Harrington had been up to the challenge was reflected in the letter Hite wrote twenty-eight days later: "The interest has been almost overpowering."[27] Hite's concerns were the urgent need for educational materials and guidance about release of the instrumentation for sale. Zimmer had been "swamped with requests for technique, movies, slides, and all other sorts of information." Hite suggested that a copy of his AOA presentation would be helpful and reminded Harrington that he had "mentioned that by the time of the formal presentation you would have the technique completed and also movies available." The educational material requested would be "distributed to interested people." Regarding availability, Harrington was reminded that he "had suggested that this would be ready to release following the AOA meeting." Hite added, "I assume that you are still of the same opinion and am wondering if we are in order in supplying this equipment to anyone who orders it?" The answer to the last question is not documented in the surviving correspondence. In Harrington's recollections the answer was "no one was permitted to purchase instruments or to use them without first having observed a demonstration of the procedure, a prerequisite that was carried out for approximately two years."[28]

在哈灵顿之前，约翰·柯布发表了"关于主弯的相关问题"的演讲，与哈灵顿针锋相对，因为柯布是最出色的脊柱侧凸专家之一，而且地位稳固，于1948年入选美国骨科学会。[25]仅仅6个月后，他的论文就发表了，在描述脊柱侧凸弯曲时，常用的描述词原发弯和继发弯不如主弯和次弯更有帮助。[26]海特在28天后写的信中反映了哈灵顿已经接受了挑战："吾辈兴致勃勃。"[27]海特所关注的是教材和器械销售应用指南。捷迈"沉浸在人们对于技术、视频、幻灯片和其他各种信息的需求中"。海特提到他在美国骨科学会的演讲稿可以用来教学，并提醒哈灵顿："你可以在正式演讲时提供视频。"所需求的教材将被"分发给感兴趣的人"。关于时间点，哈灵顿回忆他"曾被建议在美国骨科学会大会后发布"。海特补充说："我想你也应该有相似的疑问，即我们是否能向任何订购者提供器械?"最后一个问题的答案没有记录在现存的信件中。在哈灵顿的回忆中，答案是"在现场学习观摩之前，不允许购买或使用该器械，这个规定被执行了大约两年"[28]。

Harrington responded by phone five days later, and, as events unfolded, he had clearly listened and began a prodigious long-lasting effort to codify and illustrate his techniques. He was focused on recognizing and responding to design shortcomings being uncovered with wider usage. For instance, twelve days after his presentation he wrote Hite, "I hate to tell you this, but I believe I am going back to using (in some cases) the small hook set up."[29] So the original 1/8"-diameter threaded rod and hook similar to those he had worked out before the NFIP grant and Zimmer collaboration were finding a place after all. The 3/16"-diameter threaded rod that had grown out of the misguided self-walking strut design was proving difficult to apply to the convex side of the curves.[30] As a result, surgeons were leaving off the compression element of the instrumentation which was not how Harrington intended for his instrumentation to be used.

5天后，哈灵顿作出了电话回应，随着事件的发展，他耳听心受，付出了惊人的长期的努力来阐明他的技术。他专注于发现和改进那些临床中暴露出的设计缺陷。诸如在他的演讲结束12天后，他写信给海特，“我想我们不得不回到钩时代。”[29] 因此，作为原型的1/8英寸直径的螺纹棒和钩结构（和他在国家小儿麻痹基金和捷迈合作之前制订的那些类似）最终获得了一席之地。事实证明，从被误导的自我调节支撑杆设计中发展出来的3/16英寸直径的螺纹棒难以应用于弯曲的凸侧。[30]因此，外科医生们不再使用该器械来加压，这违背了哈灵顿的初衷。

In July, Hite and LaMack spent a day with Harrington in Houston, described by Hite as a “most enlightening day for me.”[31] The issues addressed included clarifying the terms *small* and *large compression hooks* and *rods*, 1/8”- and 3/16”-diameter, respectively; developing a shallow thread version of the 1/8”-diameter threaded rod; reinforcing the dimensions of the sacral bar; and last but not least, agreeing on the importance of educational materials. Also, the requested movie had been completed.[32] In early August Harrington sent a series of intraoperative slides and photographic reprints of two patients operated on along with four pages of captions for the images. Harrington used the slides to explain the placement of the hooks. The upper concave distraction hook was placed under the inferior facet of the thoracic vertebra. Placement of the lower distraction hook was more complicated. A notch was prepared on the lateral aspect of the inferior facet process and laminar ridge of the lowest vertebra to be instrumented. The hook was introduced into the notch at an angle to the mid line and driven home perpendicular to the spine with the shoe of the hook placed below the articular surface of the inferior facet. Later Harrington would identify the lower distraction hook as “the weakest feature of the whole procedure.”[33]

7月，海特和拉马克在休斯敦与哈灵顿度过了一天，海特声称“这是对我最有启发性的一天。”[31]解决的问题包括澄清术语，例如小型和大型加压钩和棒；直径1/8英寸和3/16英寸；开发直径1/8英寸螺纹棒的浅螺纹版本；加强骶骨棒的尺寸；最后则是一致同意教材的重要性。此外，所要求的视频材料已经完成。[32] 8月初，哈灵顿发送了一系列与手术相关的幻灯片和两名患者的术后照片以及四页图片说明。哈灵顿使用幻灯片来解释钩的位置。上部凹侧撑开钩放置在胸椎下关节突。下部凸侧加钩的放置更加复杂，在下关节突外侧面和最低器械椎体的椎板缘上准备一个凹口，将钩以与中线成一定角度的方式插入凹口，并垂直于脊柱将钩的底部放置在下关节面的关节面下方。后来，哈灵顿将下部撑开钩称为“整个过程中最薄弱的点”。[33]

From July 12 through August 29, 1960, Harrington operated on twenty-three patients in five states, including four in Los Angeles with Vernon Nickel, three in Boston with Paul Norton, six in New Jersey with Charles Nadel, and six in Minneapolis with John Moe.[34] Out of this came a number of small but user-friendly refinements, some of which had been in the making for a period of time. Among these were fitting all the large strut bar hooks with side holes to accommodate a hook holder, providing a large hook driver suggested by Moe, creating a threaded rod holder that fit either the 3/16"- or 1/8"-diameter threaded rod, shortening the compression rod hook shoes by 1/16", and shortening the short end of the 1/4"-diameter strut bar to just accommodate the suture wire on the end. The custom pin cutter with cutting edges on one side was cost prohibitive, so the cutter with the jaws cutting in the midline made do. Because Harrington was still unsettled about the best size for the compression rod, with the 3/16"-diameter one being too stiff and the 1/8"-diarneter too weak, he was provided an intermediate size, a 5/32"-diameter threaded rod, for experimental use. The possibility of using this slightly increased diameter threaded rod with 3/16"-diameter threaded rod compatible compression hooks was being considered to assist compression hook placement by toggling, as the hooks were placed when already mounted on the rod.[35,36]

从 1960 年 7 月 12 日到 8 月 29 日，哈灵顿为五个州的 23 名患者进行了手术，其中在洛杉矶与弗农·尼克尔合作治疗了 4 名患者，在波士顿与保罗·诺顿合作治疗了 3 名患者。在新泽西州与查尔斯·纳德尔合作治疗了 6 名患者，在明尼阿波利斯与约翰·莫合作治疗了 6 名患者。[34]由此改进了许多细节。其中包括莫建议的给所有撑棒钩增加侧孔以容纳持钩器，为钩提供更大的推进力；制作新的持棒器，以适合 3/16 英寸或 1/8 英寸直径的螺纹棒；将压缩棒钩靴部缩短为 1/16 英寸，并缩短 1/4 英寸直径支撑棒的短端，以刚好容纳末端的缝合钢丝；一侧带有裁棒的定制裁棒器成本过高，因此采用中线切割的裁棒器就可以了。因为哈灵顿仍然不确定加压棒的最佳尺寸，3/16 英寸直径的太硬而 1/8 英寸直径的太软，因此他得到了一个中间尺寸，5/32 英寸直径的螺纹棒，以供实验。他考虑了能兼容比 3/16 英寸直径稍大的螺纹棒的压缩钩的可能性，来辅助放置压缩钩，因为钩是安装在棒上的。[35,36]

To this point in late summer 1960 the Harrington and Zimmer collaboration had been based on a buyer-seller relationship. Harrington provided the specifications of the product he wanted, which Zimmer produced and sold to him. Payment came from Harrington's NFIP clinical grant. The products resulting from this collaboration were being sold on a progressively wider scale. In retrospect, it seems remarkable, if not incredible, that Harrington and Zimmer could have had such a stable and productive relationship for so long without a contract. But, the time had come for a formal agreement. Negotiations for a licensing agreement were apparently formally opened by a July 27 proposal letter from Zimmer President J. F. Hartle to Harrington. A copy of that letter has not been found. On September & Spencer sent Hartle's letter to Baylor University College of Medicine Dean Stanley W. Olson with a memorandum that began, "Does the attached proposal meet with your approval or do you prefer to have it handled through the Department of Rehabilitation?" Spencer continued, "What we propose to do is set up a royalty fund whose disbursal will be under Dr. Harrington's direction with my approval. I have no idea of the amount of money that will come from royalties but guess it will not be more than $1,500 a year. This will be used for educational purposes in scoliosis research, uraveling funds, the development of new devices or instruments, exhibits, etc., and definitely not accrue to the personal income of Dr. Harrington although its use should be under his guidance since he has developed this spine instrumentation."[37] Olson responded with an undated handwritten note on the bottom of the memo that read, "I have no great preference except that if the royalties are to be used for academic purposes then it might better be handled under the Dept. of Rehab." He commented that the usual royalty rate was 5% of gross retail sales, but if the suggested agreement were better, he'd take it.

直到1960年夏末，哈灵顿和捷迈一直是买卖关系：哈灵顿提供产品规格，捷迈生产并出售。资金来自哈灵顿获得的国家小儿麻痹基金会的基金。基于这种合作方式所生产出的器械正逐步扩大销售规模。现在回想起来，哈灵顿和捷迈能在没有明确合同的情况下维持如此牢靠、稳固和富有成效的关系长达数年，实在不可思议。但是，达成正式协议的时机已经到来。7月27日，捷迈公司总裁J. F. 哈特尔给哈灵顿写了一封建议信，标志着正式的授权协议的达成。那封信的副本没有找到。9月，斯宾塞将哈特尔的信发送给斯坦利·W. 奥尔森（贝勒大学医学院的院长）并附上了一份备忘录，开头写道："您是直接批准所附提案，还是希望让康复科处理?"斯宾塞继续说，"我们建议设立一个特许使用（版税）基金，资金由我来批准，由哈灵顿医生指导使用。我不知道特许权使用费的具体金额，但我猜测每年不会超过1 500美元。这笔资金将用于脊柱侧凸的研究教育、交通费用以及新器械的开发、展示等，并且不能计入哈灵顿医生的个人收入，尽管他是发明者。”[37]奥尔森在备忘录的底部写了一个没有日期的手写说明，内容是“我对此没有很大的兴趣，如果特许使用基金是用于学术目的，那么最好由康复科来处理”。他评论说，通常的版税是零售总额的5%，但如果协议更优惠，他则会考虑接受。

On September 21 Harrington responded to Hartle that Zimmer's proposition had been "duly processed through Baylor University College of Medicine." It was Harrington's instruction that "monies derived from this agreement will be sent to Baylor University College of Medicine, Texas Medical Center, Houston, Texas, and to be assigned the Paul R. Harrington Surgical Research Fund, the Department of Rehabilitation." Harrington did not address the royalty rates.[38] On October 27 Hartle responded with a one-page letter that appears to have been the only license/royalty agreement that ever existed between Zimmer and Harrington.[39]

9月21日，哈灵顿回复哈特尔说，捷迈的提议已经“由贝勒大学医学院正式处理”。哈灵顿指示说，“从该协议中的获利将被送到得克萨斯休斯敦贝勒大学医学院得克萨斯医学中心，并被指定为保罗·R. 哈灵顿康复科的外科研究基金。”哈灵顿没有提到版税率。[38] 10月27日，哈特尔回复了一封一页的信件，这似乎是捷迈和哈灵顿之间唯一的特许权协议。[39]

The agreement appears to have favored Zimmer in several ways. By specifying part numbers, no allowance was made for changing usage and ongoing innovation. The only part numbers listed for the compression rod and compression hook in the agreement were 1257 and 1256, respectively. These were 3/16"-diameter compatible implants.[40] Although they were Harrington's favored size at the time, this would soon permanently change to the easier to use 1/8"-diameter compatible implants.[41] Their parts numbers were 1258 and 1259, which were not mentioned in the agreement. One part listed, the Universal Swivel Hook 1260, was already nearly obsolete and would be discontinued in 1962.[42] No allowance was made for the sacral rod 1261 or sacral rod eyelet 1263, both of which were listed on the earliest Zimmer product information sheets.[43] Not addressed was the whole array of instruments for insertion, including the spreader, hook and rod clamps, and the distraction hook driver. All these instruments had emerged from laborious trial and error development. In addition, promising new parts soon appeared, such as the flat type storage rack that Harrington would never be compensated for.[44] There is no indication that either Harrington or Baylor sought legal counsel or negotiated the offer.

该协议似乎在几个方面都对捷迈有利。由于指定了零件编号，阻绝了用法的变化和持续性创新。协议中列出的压缩棒和加压钩的唯一零件号分别是 1257 和 1256，它们均兼容直径 3/16 英寸的内植物。[40]虽然它们是哈灵顿当时偏好的尺寸，但很快就永久改变为更容易使用的兼容直径 1/8 英寸的内植物。[41]它们的零件号是 1258 和 1259，在协议中没有提到。[42]骶骨棒 1261 或骶骨棒孔 1263 这两个部件也被排除在外，而它们在早期的捷迈产品信息表上都有被列出。[43]用于安装的全部工具都没有涉及，包括撑开器、钩和持棒器，以及撑开钩推进器。所有这些工具都来源于艰苦的试验和失败的经验。此外，新的部件很快就出现了，比如，哈灵顿从没拿到报酬的扁平式的器械盒。[44]没有迹象表明哈灵顿或贝勒大学医学院寻求过法律顾问或协商报价。

The royalty amounts documented in the agreement appear to have been based on the sales price at that time, and a typical distraction-compression, eight-hook construct used in the treatment of a typical right thoracic scoliosis would sell for $59.75. Harrington's royalty was $3.00 and thus 5%. However, the fixed payment rate per component left no room for adjustment for inflation. Even in 1960 a future price increase would have seemed more likely than a price decrease, which would result in an erosion of the royalty rate over time. Finally, in turn for providing Zimmer with exclusive rights to manufacture and market the instrumentation, Harrington and Baylor were saddled with the responsibility for policing Zimmer's exclusive use of the Harrington and Baylor University Department of Rehabilitation names. That this would be tested seems almost a foregone conclusion. In the accompanying cover letter, Hartle explained the payout mechanism as follows: "A report will be made quarterly between the first and fifteenth of January, April, July, and October and will be mailed to the Department of Rehabilitation, Baylor University College of Medicine with a check for the royalties which have accumulated during the preceding quarter year."[45] There is no indication that Engen was aware of these negotiations, let alone involved with them. This resulted in a long-term unhappiness on his part that was apparently not severe enough that he ever confronted Harrington about it. From Harrington's vantage point the advantages of an established manufacturer with whom he worked well must have been obvious.

协议中记录的版税数额似乎是基于当时的售价，用于治疗典型的右胸脊柱侧凸的撑开–压缩系统、八个钩结构，售价为59.75美元。哈灵顿的版税是3美元，因此版税率是5%。然而，每个部件的固定支付率没有为通货膨胀留下空间。即使在1960年，未来价格上涨的可能性仍很大，这将导致版税率随着时间的推移而削弱价值。最后，由于向捷迈提供了制造和独家销售权，哈灵顿和贝勒大学医学院承担了监督捷迈独家使用哈灵顿和贝勒大学康复系名称的责任。毫无疑问，这些都是需要面临的挑战。在附信中，哈特尔对支付机制作了如下解释："将在1月、4月、7月和10月的第1天至第15天之间进行一次报告，并将报告邮寄给贝勒大学医学院康复系，同时附上上一季度积累的版税支票。"[45]恩金并不知道这些谈判，也没有参与其中。这引起了他的不满，但显然还没有严重到与哈灵顿对峙的程度。从哈灵顿的角度来看，一个与他合作良好的成熟制造商的重要性是显而易见的。

It might be asked why Harrington was so aligned with rehabilitation medicine rather than orthopedic surgery. The answer undoubtedly related to the strong leadership of William Spencer, who arrived to take charge of the polio unit in June 1950. Freed from his administrative responsibilities, Harrington could concentrate on the many and varied orthopedic challenges presented by paralytic polio survivors. At that time Houston was in its third straight summer of epidemic polio. Dean Olson later characterized Spencer as having brought "into this climate of tragedy accepted... special abilities and convictions fired by the fuel of incredible energy and buoyant optimism."[46] Spencer and Harrington were compatible visionaries sharing similar purposes, and it was apparent they helped each other achieve their mutual goals of restoring ability and limiting disability. Harrington's lesser alignment with orthopedic surgery was probably also influenced by that community's concern about his departure from established scoliosis management and the failures he was experiencing.[47] One manifestation of this was that "the (orthopedic) residents from the Baylor program were not allowed to work with him, because he was considered to be a madman."[48]

也许有人会问，为什么哈灵顿会如此重视康复医学而不是骨科手术。答案无疑是与威廉·斯宾塞的有力领导有关，他于1950年6月来到这里负责处理脊髓灰质炎。卸下行政职位之后，哈灵顿可以集中精力解决瘫痪的脊髓灰质炎患者所面临的许多骨科问题。当时休斯敦正处于连续爆发流行性脊髓灰质炎的第三个夏天。校长奥尔森后来称斯宾塞使人们"接受这种悲剧性社会氛围……这些特殊的能力和信念是由令人难以置信的能量和乐观的情绪点燃的”[46]。斯宾塞和哈灵顿志同道合，显然，他们彼此帮助，以实现病人运动能力的恢复。可能是受到了学界对他偏离传统脊柱侧凸治疗的担忧以及其所经历的失败的影响，哈灵顿与传统骨科界的步调不太一致。[47]一个典型表现是来自贝勒大学医学院的骨科住院医师竟不被允许同他一起工作，因为他被认为是个疯子。[48]

At no time in the negotiations was there mention of a patent on any aspect of the instrumentation. Subsequent research has not revealed any patents or patent application activity, and later Harrington-Zimmer communication confirmed this. The explanation may be related to the "National Foundation's stated position that a vaccine developed with money from public donations should not be privately held." This NFIP policy became well known when the results of the Salk vaccine trial were reported on April 12, 1955, at the University of Michigan, leading to this famous exchange during Edward R. Murrow's interview of Jonas Salk on *See It Now*. Murrow: "Who owns the patent on this vaccine?" Salk: "Well, the people I would say. There is no patent. Could you patent the sun?"[49] In the instance of the Salk polio vaccine the truth was not quite so simple or altruistic, as the NFIP's lawyers had researched the patent possibilities and concluded that it included no new processes. Formaldehyde for inactivation, adjuvants to increase vaccine potency, and tissue culture to grow the virus were all well-established processes.[50] Regarding Harrington Instrumentation, it may have been decided that the ratchet mechanism on the distraction rod was not patentable, but barring some new revelation, we'll never know. Harrington was always quick to credit the NFIP's grant support of his spine instrumentation project, and actively deciding not to seek patent status would have been consistent with NFIP policy.

在谈判中，有关内固定的专利均未被提及。随后哈灵顿和捷迈的通信也证实了后续的研究并未透露出专利或专利申请的相关活动。这可能与国家基金会的声明有关，即“用公募基金开发的疫苗不应该被私有化”。1955 年密歇根大学的索尔克疫苗的临床试验公布后，国家小儿麻痹基金会的政策变得广为人知。同时也促成了爱德华·R. 墨罗在《现在请看》节目上对乔纳斯·索尔克的访谈。墨罗问道：“谁拥有这种疫苗的专利?”索尔克说：“疫苗没有专利，就像你没法给太阳申请专利。”[49]事实上，在索尔克脊髓灰质炎的案例中，事实并不是那么简单无私。国家小儿麻痹基金会的律师其实研究了申请专利的可能性，但发现其中并没有新的工艺。用于灭活的甲醛、用于提高疫苗效力的佐剂以及用于培养病毒的组织培养都是已证实行之有效的工艺。[50]关于哈灵顿的内固定器械，可能已经自知撑开棒上的棘齿结构不可能申请专利，具体情况我们无从得知。哈灵顿总是毫不犹豫地将他的脊柱器械项目归功于国家小儿麻痹基金会的资助支持，并且根据国家小儿麻痹基金会的政策，主动放弃专利申请。

Harrington's first request for funds came in a May 9, 1962, letter from Harrington to A. O. Johnson, business manager at the Baylor University College of Medicine. Harrington began, "$3,762.50 has now accrued in the Paul R. Harrington Surgical Research Fund #934 and the time has come that I would like to draw against it for several research projects I am carrying on." This amount seems to have been the accumulation of five quarters' royalties, which averaged $752.50 per quarter.[51] On May 15 a royalty check for $866.50 arrived covering the first quarter of 1962.[52] Spencer's original guess of $1,500 per year had obviously been a little low.

1962 年 5 月 9 日，哈灵顿的第一个资金请求来自哈灵顿写给 A. O. 约翰森的一封信，A. O. 约翰森是贝勒大学医学院的业务经理。哈灵顿说道："保罗 · R. 哈灵顿外科研究基金#934 已经累计了 3 762. 50 美元，现在我想用它来开展几个研究项目。"这个数额似乎是五个季度的累计收入，平均每季度 752. 50 美元。[51] 5 月 15 日，支付给 1962 年第一季度的 866. 50 美元版税支票到账。[52]斯宾塞最初估计的每年 1 500 美元显然有点低。

A facet of Harrington's relationship with Zimmer that he often spoke of was his commitment to teaching proper use of the instrumentation. Later he recalled the commitment as follows: "Although the instruments had been simplified and standardized by Zimmer Manufacturing Co. of Warsaw, Indiana, no one was permitted to purchase instruments or to use them without first having observed a demonstration of the procedure, a prerequisite that was carried for approximately 2 years."[53] This was not included in his license/royalty agreement with Zimmer and does not appear in any of the surviving Zimmer correspondence of the time. At this point no further commitments to paying for the expenses associated with this policy, other than the royalties to the PRH (Paul Randall Harrington) Surgical Research Fund, had been made or requested.

在哈灵顿与捷迈的关系中，他经常提到的一个方面是他致力于器械的正确使用方法的教学。后来他回忆起如下承诺：尽管印第安纳州华沙的捷迈制造公司对器械进行了简化和标准化，但任何人都不得在没有学习使用方法的情况下购买或使用它们，这项先决条件进行了大约 2 年。[53]这没有包含在他与捷迈的版税协议中，也没有出现在当时留存下来的任何与捷迈的通信中。此时，除了支付给保罗·兰德尔·哈灵顿外科研究基金的版税外，并没有要求支付与此政策相关的费用。

In October Zimmer asked what now was becoming a perennial question: what type of display they should prepare, this time targeting the upcoming 1961 AAOS annual meeting in Miami Beach.[54] Harrington initially responded that an extensive display would not be necessary as he would have both audiovisual and exhibit booth displays.[55] As the date drew closer, Harrington asked for technical information he could use for his presentation. This included metal composition, engineering specifications, component dimensions, and specifications of the sacral bar (its unique thread structure and results of its three-point bending strength resistance at 1", 2", or 3" of suspension). In addition, he asked for drawings of the instruments pertinent to the operation. He closed with "this thing is going like wildfire."[56] Hite's response included the metal specifications, which Harrington sent to Dr. James R. Sims at the nearby prestigious Rice University.[57] This appears to have been the first documentation of Harrington's collaboration with Rice faculty, almost certainly a reflection of his desire to better understand the science of his work. Further, Hite responded that he did not have sufficient mechanical data and had submitted the sacral bar and strut bar to a commercial laboratory for deflection testing.[58]

10 月，捷迈提出了一个长期存在的问题：他们应该准备什么样的展示，这次是针对即将在迈阿密海滩举行的 1961 年美国骨科医师学会年会。[54]哈灵顿最初回应说，没有必要进行过于宽泛的展示，他将同时拥有视听展示位和展台。[55]随着日期的临近，哈灵顿要求提供用于演讲的技术信息。这包括金属成分、工程规格、部件尺寸和骶骨棒的规格（其独特的螺纹结构和其在 1 英寸、2 英寸或 3 英寸悬挂下的三点抗弯强度数据）。此外，他还需要与手术有关的器械图纸。他以“这件事进展迅速”结束了这封信。[56]海特的回应包括金属规格，哈灵顿将其发送给附近著名莱斯大学的詹姆斯·R. 西姆斯博士。这似乎是哈灵顿与莱斯大学教师合作的第一份文件[57]，显然说明他希望更好地理解其工作的科学性。此外，海特回应说他没有足够的力学数据，并已将骶骨棒和支撑棒提交给商业实验室进行抗扭曲测试。[58]

The mechanical testing was done by Leonard M. Taussig of Taussig Associates in Chicago, which reported results on November 15, 1960. Simple beam deflection tests were performed between 1", 2", and 3" centers on the 1/4"-diameter strut bar ratchet end and on the 3/16"- and 1/8"-diameter threaded compression rods. The yield point was highest for the strut bar and 1" center at 750 pounds and lowest for the 1/8"-diameter threaded rod and 3" center at 10 pounds. The shear strength of the 1/4"-diameter sacral rod with its reduced depth thread was done on three rods, and the results were very similar, ranging from 3,370 to 3,400 pounds. "Three #1250 strut bars were subjected to a compression loading with the bar acting as a column. The load was applied between the flange on one end and the end of the notched teeth on the opposite end. The buckling strength of the strut bars when stressed as a column ranged from 440 lbs. to 460 lbs. before permanent deformation was recorded." The report did not indicate the length of the rod although 8 was later written in. Where the permanent deformation appeared was not reported. The wording of the report also made it difficult to know where the rod was fixed on the ratchet end, the last notch before the rod ended or the last notch before the smooth portion of the rod. And, finally, there port did not make it clear whether the loading was axial or axial offset, as it was in use with the hooks.[59] Later studies would suggest the loading was purely axial. This appears to have been the first time mechanical testing had been done on any of the Harrington Spine Instrumentation Design had preceded engineering, which was the sequence Steve Jobs followed at Apple during more complex development processes a half century later.[60] Early in his quest Harrington had repeatedly reminded himself to keep it simple, a goal he achieved. Again, this foreshadowed another Jobs principle that "simplicity is the ultimate sophistication."

机械测试由芝加哥陶西格事务所的伦纳德·M. 陶西格完成，该公司于 1960 年 11 月 15 日报告了测试结果。在直径为 1/4 英寸的支撑棒棘齿端和直径为 3/16 英寸和 1/8 英寸的螺纹压缩棒上的 1 英寸、2 英寸和 3 英寸中心之间进行了简单的梁抗扭曲试验。在 750 磅时，支撑棒和 1 英寸中心的屈服点最高，而在 10 磅时，直径 1/8 英寸的螺纹棒和 3 英寸中心的屈服点最低。对三根直径为 1/4 英寸的骶骨棒进行了剪切强度测试，测试结果非常相似，从 3 370 磅到 3 400 磅不等。"三个#1250 支撑棒承受加压应力，棒作为支柱。应力施加在一端的轮缘和槽齿另一端之间。支撑棒当作为支柱受力时，使其产生永久形变的压力为 440 磅到 460 磅不等。"报告中没有标明棒的长度，后来标明为 8 英寸。形变情况也未见报道。报告的措辞也让人很难知道棒是在哪里固定了棘齿端，可能是棒末端之前的最后一个槽口的位置或棒的光滑部分之前的最后一个槽口的位置。最后，报告没有明确说明应力是不是为轴向或偏离轴向，因为它与是钩一起使用的。[59]后来的研究表明应力是纯轴向的。这似乎是第一次对所有哈灵顿脊柱器械进行机械测试！设计先于工程，这是半个世纪后史蒂夫·乔布斯在苹果公司更加复杂的开发过程中遵循的顺序。[60]早期，哈灵顿反复提醒自己要让哈灵顿脊柱器械保持简单，他实现了这一目标。这再次预示了乔布斯的另一个原则，即"简洁是终极的复杂"。

Harrington was grateful for the Taussig report and wrote "thanks a million."[61] In his response he returned the instrument silhouettes to Zimmer with several complaints and suggestions. One was that the compression hooks were still being made with the shoe too long, making insertion during surgery difficult. Unlike the distraction hooks, which were placed before the rod, the compression hooks were strung onto the compression rod. Thus, they could not be angled into position. Since this had been a recurring complaint, he pleaded "can't this be corrected?" Other problems were that the threaded rod holders were not strong enough and the spreader yoke was still too deep and the feathering not right. These issues must have been handled by phone as they were not written about again. He asked for some metal stock: a 1/4"-diameter rod 18" long and a 1"×2" rectangle 6" long, indicating he had an idea for a new design. He closed his letter commenting that "the new jaw (presumably the rod cutter) is working very nicely."

哈灵顿对陶西格的报告表示"万分感谢"。[61]作为回应，他将器械原型退还给了捷迈，并提出了一些建议。其一由于钩靴部太长，压缩钩仍在制作中，这使得在手术过程中难以插入。与安棒之前放置的撑开钩不同，压缩钩连接在压缩棒上。因此，它们无法通过倾斜位置来放置到恰当的位置。由于这是一个反复出现的问题，他恳求道"这难道不能纠正吗?"其他问题是螺纹棒持棒器不够坚固，撑开器的轭仍然太深，顺桨也不正确。这些问题应该是通过电话处理的，因为没有记录在册。他要了一些金属库存：一根直径为 1/4 英寸、长 18 英寸的棒和 1 英寸×2 英寸的矩形，长 6 英寸，这表明他想到了一个新设计。他在信的结尾评论道，"新的钳口（大概是裁棒器）很好用"。

By now interest in Harrington Spine Instrumen-tation was increasing in the lay press. This reached a peak when the November 14 issue of *Time* magazine featured a story, "Spine of Steel."[62] The article about his instrumentation ran with a photograph of Harrington. *See figure 6.3*. The full text of the three-paragraph article with comments after each paragraph follows:

Figure 6. 3 **"*Spine of Steel. Okay if you don't play football.*" (Time *Magazine*)**
图 6. 3 "钢铁脊梁——如果你不踢足球的话"(《时代》杂志)

Some ailments seem almost preferable to their cures. A case in point is scoliosis, an abnormal curvature of the spine that occurs in childhood. As seen from behind, the spine should appear straight; in scoliosis. It has a C-shaped or S-shaped curve. Extreme cases of scoliosis often require fusion of the spinal vertebrae. For most cases the standard treatment is forcible straightening of the spine, with the patient encased for four to six months in a massive, immobilizing plaster cast. To some parents of scoliosis victims, this treatment seems so punishing that they cannot be persuaded to permit it even to save their child from permanent deformity.

到目前为止，非专业媒体对哈灵顿脊柱器械的兴趣逐步增加。当《时代》杂志 11 月 14 日刊登了一篇报道"钢铁脊梁"时，[62] 这种关注达到了顶峰。这篇关于他的器械的文章附有一张哈灵顿的照片。(图 6.3) 文章的全文及段后评论如下：

现在，有些疾病似乎存在更有效的治疗方法。一个典型的例子是脊柱侧凸，一种在儿童时期发生的脊柱异常弯曲。正常人的脊柱从后面看起来应该是直的；而在脊柱侧凸患者的后背有一个 C 形或 S 形的弯曲。严重的脊柱侧凸病例通常需要脊柱融合。对于大多数病例，目前的标准治疗方法是强行矫正脊柱，将患者包裹在巨大的石膏中 4~6 个月。对一些患者的父母来说，这种治疗似乎是一种惩罚，因此，即使能让他们的孩子免于永久性畸形，他们也不愿意接受这种治疗。

This was a promising start to the article as it is entirely factual and could easily be related to by scoliosis patients and their families.

Last week Houston Surgeon Paul Harrington was winning converts to a new and happier method. Capable of correcting spinal curvature in people up to age of 40, Dr Harrington's technique frees patients from the confines of a cast, permits them to lead normal lives during treatment. Key to Harrington's method is a slender, stainless-steel rod that resembles a soda straw and serves somewhat like a splint. In a complicated, two-hour operation, the curved spine is straight-ened, then bound into place with two to three rods, which are fastened to the spine with metal hooks.

这是一篇很好的文章,它阐明了事实,并且很容易使脊柱侧凸患者及其家人产生共鸣。

上周,来自休斯敦的外科医生保罗·哈灵顿使用了一种全新的、更先进的方法。哈灵顿医生的技术能够矫正40岁以下人群的脊柱侧凸,使患者摆脱石膏的束缚,在治疗期间就能过上正常的生活。哈灵顿方法的关键是一根细长的不锈钢棒,它类似于吸管,也类似于夹板。在这个复杂的、两个小时的手术中,弯曲的脊柱被拉直,然后用2~3根棒固定,这些棒通过金属钩固定在脊柱上。

This was also all factual except for the second sentence. Harrington had originally hoped to do away with the cast entirely but by 1960 was using a cast in nearly half of his patients.[63] The patients were not confined to bed in their cast. Whether or not they led "normal lives during treatment" at that point in his practice is doubtful but unknown. In his AOA thesis he stated that "casts were used more frequently" and "post-operative management (immobilization) was prolonged" in his patient group Ⅲ-1960.[64]

The rods are readily accepted by the body, says Harrington, and need never be removed. Affixed to the spine just beneath the back muscles, they cause no pain, do not restrict physical activity. After ten days in the hospital and a six week convalescent period, says Surgeon Harrington, youngsters equipped with the rods can run, swim, play tennis. The only restriction: no contact sports such as football.

除了第二句话外,基本讲述的是事实。哈灵顿最初希望完全取代石膏,但到1960年为止,他的近一半患者都使用了石膏。[63]但病人并没有被石膏禁锢在床上动弹不得。在他的临床实践中,患者是否"在治疗期间就能过上正常的生活"是值得怀疑且不得而知的。在他提交给美国骨科学会的论文中,他指出,患者组Ⅲ-1960中"更频繁地使用石膏"和"更长的术后处理(制动)"。[64]

哈灵顿说,这些植入棒有较强的生物相容性,后期不需要去除。它们固定在背部肌肉下方的脊柱上,不会引起疼痛,也不会限制活动。在住院10天和恢复6周后,这些年轻人可以跑步、游泳、打网球。唯一禁止的是接触性运动,例如足球。

Harrington's instructions to his patients, so well documented later on, weren't at this point. However, he had operated on over 100 cases by this time, and it is difficult to imagine that he allowed such patient activity. And if he did, he soon would not. The *Time* article had started off well but ended with overstatement and did not address the role of fusion in his practice. The published abstract of his AOA presentation appeared about the time of the *Time* article, and in Harrington had conceded that "When the patient is ten years of age or older, spine fusion of the major curve is recommended with the initial corrective surgery."[66] Whether or not Harrington had any editorial input into the "Spines of Steel" article isn't known. It would not be difficult to imagine that this article with its exaggerated claims bordering on hyperbole caused some unhappiness among his colleagues and possibly Harrington as well, although there is no documentation of any. What the article did do was gain the interest of the public, an effect magnified by follow up local news media stories that the brief article had stimulated. Several hundred telephone and letter inquiries were received, but tabulating the total is impossible because no record of phone calls was kept and many letters ended up in his patient charts. However, 237 inquiries resulting in several hundred letter exchanges and many long distance phone calls from all over the United States and eleven foreign countries were analyzed and summarized.[67] Since few sent X-rays and less than half provided a diagnosis, the summary stated that "the information given in the letters was disappointing in its adequacy." Nevertheless, some observations were possible. The most common category of inquiry came from people unhappy with current treatment options. The summary added, "Many people were contemplating conventional fusions and wanted his comparison of spine instrumentation with this method. Twenty patients had already been fused by the conventional methods (some more than once). Others (50%) mentioned previous treatment: exercise, physical therapy; casts, braces and traction. Many stated they had refused treatment by turnbuckle casts and two-stage fusion. Their reasons were length of time, finances, pain and discomfort, probability of little or no correction, fear, differences of opinion among physicians as to whether or not surgery was indicated, and other difficulties, such as heart defects. Many were told no treatment was indicated-'Learn to live with it.'"

哈灵顿对他的病人的术后指导此时还鲜有记录。然而，他已经手术了100多例，很难想象他会允许病人做这些活动。即使之前允许过，很快就不会了。[65]《时代》杂志的文章开头不错，但结尾有些夸大其词，并且没有说明融合术在他临床实践中的作用。他在美国骨科学会的演讲摘要也在《时代》的这篇文章中，摘要中哈灵顿写道："当患者年满10岁或以上时，建议在初次矫正手术中对主弯进行融合。"[66]哈灵顿是否对"钢铁脊梁"文章有任何意见不得而知。尽管没有任何文件证实，但不难想象这篇夸大其词的文章引起了哈灵顿和他同事们的不满。这篇文章的目的是引起公众的兴趣，也确实激发了当地新闻媒体的后续报道，这种效果得到了放大。哈灵顿收到了数百个电话和信件咨询，我们无法将总数制表，因为电话记录没有保留，而且许多信件都在他的病历中。然而，对237项电话和信件咨询进行了分析和总结，发现他们来自美国各地和11个国家。[67]由于很少有人发送X光片，而且只有不到一半的人提供了诊断证明，摘要称"信件中能提供的信息非常有限"。然而，仍能观察到一些结果。最常见的询问类别来自对当前治疗方案不满意的人。摘要补充说，"许多人都在考虑传统的融合术，并希望他将脊柱器械与这种方法进行比较。已有20名患者采用传统的融合术（有些不止一次）。其他人（50%）提到之前的治疗：运动、理疗、石膏、支具和撑开。许多人表示他们拒绝铰链石膏和二期融合术。他们考虑的原因是时间长短、财务状况、疼痛和不适、矫形效果、恐惧、医生间的意见分歧，以及其他困难，如心脏缺陷。许多人被告知不需要治疗——'学会与它共同生存'。"

The signs and symptoms that led these adults to seek further help were varied. Again, in the words of the summation: "At least twenty mention recent progression of the curvature (this is years after completion of growth). Forty-one mention pain that is severe enough to interfere with normal daily living, even of reasonable nature. Another outstanding symptom was extreme fatigue with minimal exertion. Twelve women related the onset of symptoms and progression of the curve to pregnancy. The number of pregnancies varied from one to five. Other symptoms were pulmonary, i.e. shortness of breath, dyspnea, frequent upper respiratory infections, cardiopulmonary compromise, reduced vital capacity; psychological, such as personality changes, difficulty with employment, worry about the future, cosmetic effect. Other difficulties were numbness and weakness in extremities, progressive paralysis, muscle spasms and gastrointestinal problems." Finally, there was a group that could be categorized as patients with no scoliosis but serious medical problems "shopping for miracles."

导致这些成年人寻求进一步帮助的体征和症状各不相同。再次，用摘要的话来说："至少有20人提到最近的侧凸进展（在完成生长后的几年）。41人提到严重到影响正常日常生活的疼痛。另一个突出的症状是极易疲劳，运动耐受量低。

12 名女性将症状的发作和侧凸的进展与怀孕联系起来。怀孕的次数从 1 次到 5 次不等。其他症状集中在心肺功能，即呼吸急促、呼吸困难、上呼吸道频繁感染、心肺损害、肺活量下降。也有心理问题，如性格改变、就业困难、对未来的担忧、外观焦虑。其他困难是四肢麻木无力、进行性瘫痪、肌肉痉挛和胃肠道问题。”最后，有一个群体可以归类为没有脊柱侧凸但有严重医学问题的患者，他们“希望奇迹出现”。

Harrington's responses to these inquiries were detailed, patient, and useful. For many he was able to provide reassurance that nothing was needed. For others he was able to recommend that they contact a leading orthopedic spine deformity surgeon near them. This was facilitated because of his many teaching program contacts, a number that was rapidly increasing. From September through the end of the year he did another ten surgeries in four different cities, including four at the Alfred I. DuPont Institute in Wilmington, Delaware, with Alfred Shands Jr. and Dean MacEwen; three in St. Louis with H. Relton McCarroll and a host surgeon whose name wasn't recorded; two in Indianapolis, Indiana, with George Garceau; and, on a return visit to John Moe, one in Minneapolis. Like all of Harrington's host surgeons earlier in the year, these men were prominent thought leaders in orthopedic surgery. This brought the total number of surgeries he performed away from Houston in 1960 to 33![68,69]

哈灵顿对这些询问的回答是详细、耐心和实用的。对许多人，他能够安慰他们无须（医学）干预。对于其他人，他能够为他们推荐附近的脊柱外科医生。这得益于他的许多教学项目，可以进行矫形手术的医生人数迅速增加。从 9 月到年底，他又在四个不同的城市做了十次手术，其中四例在特拉华州威尔明顿的阿尔弗雷德·I. 杜邦研究所，与小阿尔弗雷德·桑兹和迪恩·麦克尤恩一起完成；三例在圣路易斯与 H. 雷尔顿·麦卡罗尔和一位名字未被记录的主治外科医生一起完成；两例在印第安纳州的印第安纳波利斯与乔治·加尔索一起完成；以及在回访明尼阿波利斯的约翰·莫时完成了一例。与今年早些时候哈灵顿邀请的所有外科医生一样，这些人都是矫形领域的杰出带头人。这使他在 1960 年于休斯敦以外的地区进行了多达 33 例手术![68,69]

In December Harrington was a faculty member of Moe's continuation course for orthopedic surgeons and general physicians at the University of Minnesota. The title of his presentation was "Surgical Instrumentation for Management of Scoliosis," the same title he had used for his AOA presentation six months earlier, and the presentations were probably the same.[70] Arthrodesis of the Moe-Hibbs type was being performed with no mention of bone graft usage. A modified Risser cast (meaning no neckpiece) from twelve days to about twelve weeks postoperative was used, and sitting was limited for at least an additional three months. This was a very different postoperative regimen than that described in the *Time* article. A photo of the instrumentation parts as they were at the end of 1960 was included.[71] *See figure 6.4.*

12 月，哈灵顿成为莫在明尼苏达大学为骨科医生和全科医生开设的继续教育课程的教员。他演讲的题目是“应用内固定器械治疗脊柱侧凸”，这与他六个月前在美国骨科学会演讲中使用的标题相同，内容也可能是相同的。[70]莫-希伯斯融合术已经使用，但未提及植骨。术后 12 天至约 12 周使用改良的里泽石膏（没有颈托），并且坐姿限制至少再延长三个月。这是一个与《时代》中描述的完全不同的术后方案。1960 年年底使用的器械组件的照片如下。[71]（图 6.4）

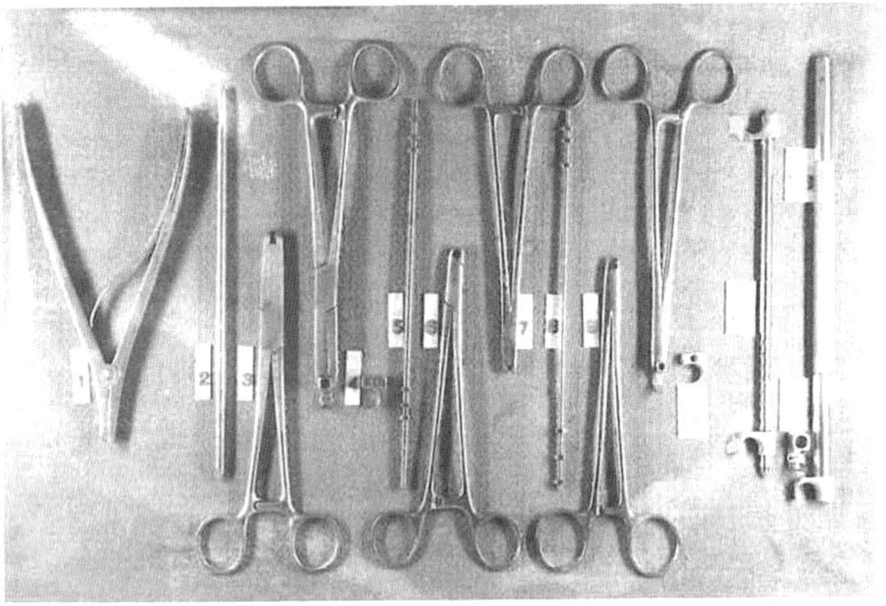

Figure 6.4 ***Instruments for spine insrumentation, December 1960: 1. spreader; 2. sacral bar; 3. hook holder; 4. large compression hook; 5. large compression rod; 6. large threaded rod holder; 7. small threaded rod holder; 8. small compression rod with threaded hex nuts; 9. small holder; 10. smell compression hook; 11. distraction rod; 12. large distraction hook, and 13. hook driver for large distraction hook. (Harrington Archives)***

图 6.4　1960 年 12 月，脊柱内固定器械：1. 撑开器；2. 骶骨棒；3. 持钩器；4. 大压缩钩；5. 大压缩杆；6. 大螺纹棒持棒器；7. 小螺纹棒持棒器；8. 小压缩杆，带螺纹六角螺母；9. 小持棒器；10. 小压缩钩；11. 撑开棒；12. 大撑开钩，以及 13. 大撑开钩推进器（哈灵顿档案馆）

Hite's last letter of 1960 focused on three scheduling possibilities for early 1961, all centered on Chicago.[72] First, he invited Harrington to speak at the Zimmer national sales meeting. Second was an invitation to visit the Zimmer plant in Warsaw, Indiana, located about two hours from Chicago by either train or car. And third, since Harrington had not yet been to Chicago to demonstrate his technique, Hite proposed a meeting with local surgeons. Harrington realized the demands on his time were about to further increase, and beginning in 1961 and continuing through 1967, the travel arrangements and related correspondence were gathered annually and preserved in bound books.[73] His preface to each of the seven volumes read: "In order to fulfill the demands of a post-graduate educational program, numerous trips were made each year. In attempting to synchronize consultations, surgical demonstrations and lectures which were given all over the country, the amount of detail involved in such intricate planning was tremendous." A few days after the arrival of the new year in 1961 Harrington received the metal stock to try his new, unspecified idea. This was a fairly common open-ended exchange between him and Zimmer. He had accepted a speaking engagement with the Chicago Orthopedic Society on March 10 and 11.[74] Whether or not Harrington attended the 1961 Zimmer national sales meeting in February in Chicago, or for that matter ever attended one of their national sales meetings, isn't known. He did visit their factory the following year.

海特 1960 年的最后一封信着重于 1961 年年初的三个计划的可能性，所有这些都以芝加哥为中心。[72]第一，他邀请哈灵顿在捷迈全国销售会议上发言；第二，参观位于印第安纳州华沙的捷迈工厂，该工厂距离芝加哥约有两个小时的火车或汽车车程；第三，由于哈灵顿未曾到芝加哥展示过他的技术，海特提议与当地外科医生会面。哈灵顿意识到外访需要花费他更多的时间。从 1961 年开始一直持续到 1967 年，外访安排和相关信件每年都会收集并保存在装订本中。[73]他在七卷本的序言中写道："为了满足研究生教育的计划，每年需要多次外访。为了使全国各地的会诊、手术演示和讲座同步进行，计划所涉及的细节是极其大量的。"1961 年新年到来后的几天，哈灵顿收到了金属库存用以尝试他未具体说明的新想法。这是他和捷迈之间相当常见的开放式交流。他接受了在 3 月 10 日和 11 日召开的芝加哥骨科学会的演讲邀请。[74]哈灵顿是否参加了 2 月在芝加哥举行的 1961 年捷迈全国销售会议，我们不得而知。但他确实在次年参观了他们的工厂。

The annual meeting of the AAOS in 1961 was held in Miami Beach during the second week of January. Hartle wrote congratulating Harrington on the excellent reception of his scientific exhibit and movie titled Harrington Spine Instrumentation in the Management of Scoliosis.[75] Harrington's movie had a long gestation period. He had always conceived of it as having two separate parts: Part I, the basic concept, and Part I, the surgical procedure. In this regard he may have been influenced by the example of another controversial participant in the treatment of polio, Elizabeth (Sister) Kenney who had produced separate concept and treatment films about her polio management methods.[76] Harrington's Part I had first been scripted with the Texas Industrial Film Company in July 1958 and presented Harrington's theory of the spine's inherent potential form, its dependence on dynamic balance throughout growth, and the role of the endochondral bone forming zones in the paired facets. At that time Harrington was committed to making a self-adjusting strut bar based on the principle of a rod within a sleeve, but this procedure was not scripted. Scripting for Part I occurred sometime later, after June 1959 when he had given up on the rod within a sleeve concept, as the scripted versions were based on distraction and compression instrumentation with arthrodesis.[77] Now that the movies actually existed and were good, *especially Part* I, several questions arose, and the course was set to resolve them. Zimmer asked and was permitted to add a statement at the end of the movies to the effect that Harrington Instrumentation was produced by Zimmer. Zimmer would work with the AAOS to donate a copy of each part to the AAOS for their film library, and Zimmer would obtain a copy (or copies) of Part II to loan to surgeon customers.[78] It was to be understood that further editing would occur from time to time. The movies, produced by the Texas Industrial Film Company, were available through the Methodist Hospital photographic department at the Texas Medical Center in Houston. The prices of the films were $73.46 for Part I and $173.58 for Part II.[79]

1961年的美国骨科医师学会年会于1月的第二周在迈阿密海滩举行。哈特尔写信祝贺哈灵顿的展览和视频《哈灵顿脊柱器械治疗脊柱侧凸》受到了好评。[75]哈灵顿的视频有一段很长的酝酿期。他一直认为它有两个独立的部分：第一部分，基本概念，第二部分，外科手术。在这方面，他可能受到了另一位有争议的脊髓灰质炎治疗参与者修女伊丽莎白·肯尼的影响，她制作了关于她对脊髓灰质炎处理方法的概念介绍和治疗视频。[76]哈灵顿的第一部分于1958年7月首次与得克萨斯工业电影公司合作编写，介绍了哈灵顿关于脊柱固有潜在形态的理论、脊柱在整个生长过程中对动态平衡的依赖性，以及上下关节突中软骨内骨形成区的作用。当时哈灵顿致力于根据套筒内棒的原理制造一种自我调节支撑棒，但没有写进剧本。第二部分的剧本是在1959年6月之后编写的，当时他放弃了套筒的概念，因此该版剧本是基于融合术的撑开和压缩器械所编写的。[77]既然视频已经出版并广受好评，尤其是第一部分，那么就出现了几个问题，并且需要课程去解决这些问题。捷迈被允许在视频结尾添加声明：哈灵顿器械是由捷迈生产的。捷迈将与美国骨科医师学会合作，捐赠两部分视频的副本到美国骨科医师学会的视频库，捷迈将获得第二部分的副本使用权，以借阅给其他外科医生。[78]可以想见，随着版本的迭代，对视频的纠正或编辑会不时发生。这些视频由得克萨斯州工业电影公司制作，可通过休斯敦得克萨斯州医疗中心的卫理公会医院视频部获得。第一部分视频定价为 73.46 美元，第二部分为 173.58 美元。[79]

At the end of a late January Hite-Harrington letter exchange, Harrington mentioned for the first and only documented occasion an issue that probably had been bothering him for some time: travel expenses. Hite wrote first sending three #1261 sacral rods (flattened on one side) and six hex nuts, like the ones supplied to William Stewart for Harrington's input. He also re-requested that Harrington send a model of the flat type instrument storage rack he had designed and was using so it could be duplicated and made available with the rest of the Harrington Instrumentation.[80] Harrington sent the storage rack and requested stress figures on the sacral bar as well as the return of two old spreaders that had fallen apart. He announced that from February 8-13 he would be in Gastonia, North Carolina, with Drs. Roberts and Miller to do surgery and would take his own instruments. He did not explain why. He brought up the issue of travel expenses by asking "Is there a possibility that Zimmer has a fund that could help me on some of these demonstrations?"[81] There is no record of a Zimmer response or of the question being asked again. Harrington did five surgeries in Gastonia, and it is unknown who paid for the implants, whose list price from Zimmer would probably have totaled $300 to $400. He was reimbursed $159.81 for travel expenses from the TIRR Surgical Fund.[82] How this fund was financed is unclear. In 1959 the Southwestern Poliomyelitis Respiratory Center had expanded its mission and become the Texas Institute for Rehabilitation and Research (TIRR). But this could not have been expected to bring new travel funds. It is evident that its source was not implant royalties as the Paul R. Harrington Surgical Research Fund, the Department of Rehabilitation had just been set up at the Baylor University College of Medicine, and it did not receive any request for withdrawal until May 1962.[83]

在 1 月底海特与哈灵顿的书信往来中，哈灵顿第一次也是唯一一次提到了一个困扰他的问题：差旅费。海特首先写了三个#1261骶骨棒（一侧扁平）和六个六角螺母，就像那些根据哈灵顿的要求提供给威廉·斯图尔特的一样。他还要求哈灵顿重新发送一个他设计并正在使用的扁平式的器械盒的模型，这样就可以作为模板与哈灵顿的其他器械一起使用。[80]哈灵顿寄来了器械盒，并要求提供骶骨棒上的应力数据，并归还两个已经散架的旧撑开器。他声称从2月8日到13日，他将与罗伯茨医生以及米勒一起前往北卡罗来纳州的加斯托尼亚进行手术，并将带上自己的器械。他并没有解释原因。他也提出了差旅费的问题，并问道："捷迈有没有可能成立一个基金，资助我进行这些演示？"[81]捷迈没有回应，这个问题也没有再被提起。之后，哈灵顿在加斯托尼亚做了五次手术，不知道是谁支付了内植物的费用，按照捷迈的标价，可能总共是300到400美元。他从得克萨斯州康复与研究中心外科基金报销了159.81美元的差旅费。[82]这个基金的资金来源尚不清楚。1959年，西南脊髓灰质炎呼吸中心扩大了其工作范围，成立了得克萨斯州康复与研究中心。但这并不能带来新的差旅费补助。显然，它的来源不是如同保罗·R. 哈灵顿外科研究基金那样的内植物版税，那时康复科刚刚在贝勒大学医学院成立，直到1962年5月并没有收到任何提款请求。[83]

Harrington had indirectly raised the larger issue of the proper financial relationships beyond royalties between physicians and surgeons and industry. Harrington's professional travels before 1960 weren't documented, but in 1960 TIRR reimbursed him a total of $2,477.82 for travel expenses for seven trips. Five of these were specifically for Harrington Spine Instrumentation teaching, and the other two were for attending professional association meetings, where he was on the program because of his instrumentation. After the Gastonia trip TIRR reimbursed him for only two trips over the next four years.[84] There is no suggestion in the Harrington-Zimmer correspondence that Zimmen ever directly or indirectly paid the expenses of his teaching trips.

哈灵顿间接地提出了一个更大的问题，即医生、外科医生和公司之间除版税交易之外，还存在着适当的财务关系。哈灵顿在1960年之前的出差外访没有记录，但在1960年，得克萨斯州康复与研究中心为他报销了七次差旅费，共计2 477.82美元。其中五次是专门用来进行哈灵顿脊柱器械的教学，另外两次是因为他的器械而参加的学会会议。加斯托尼亚之旅后的四年里，得克萨斯州康复与研究中心只报销了两次差旅费。[84]在哈灵顿和捷迈的通信中，没有任何迹象表明捷迈曾经直接或间接地提供差旅费。

On March 10, 1961, Harrington was invited to present the Fremont A. Chandler Memorial Lecture to the Chicago Orthopaedic Society. The title of his talk listed on the program was "Spine Instrumentation in the Treatment of Scoliosis," but the manuscript left behind is titled "Biomechanics of the Spine."[85] He included a lightly edited version along with the illustrations as the first article in *Scoliosis 1965*.[86] "Biomechanics of the Spine" supported Harrington's later claim that thinking fundamentally helped him achieve his goal of achieving a biological end through the use of mechanical force.[87] From study of load transfer in a full-length specimen spine he concluded that the "critical point of instability is T7 and T8." From study of the lateral bending motion of normal persons he concluded that the lateral bend per vertebra was not more than 5°. He utilized this observation to quantify the point beyond which scoliosis could be expected to be progressive by devising the Harrington factor, which was the Cobb measurement divided by the number of vertebrae in the curve. When a factor of 5 or more was present in the growing child, curve progression "is inevitable without active treatment." He discussed elastic and plastic deformations, elasticity, relaxation, cohesive forces and potential troughs, and primary and secondary bonds. He showed histological specimens that illustrated both the tolerance and response of the underlying bone and surrounding soft tissue to the instrumentation.[88] *See figure 6.5*. Harrington also illustrated the effect of exposing the distraction rod ratchets to the eccentric compression loads they sustained during usage. The 10" distraction rods tested were 13" when the 3" ratchet (notched) section was included. Exposing the ratchets to the loads lowered rod ultimate strength from 211 pounds to 159 pounds and changed the yield point from the smooth portion of the rod to the ratchet section.[89] *See*

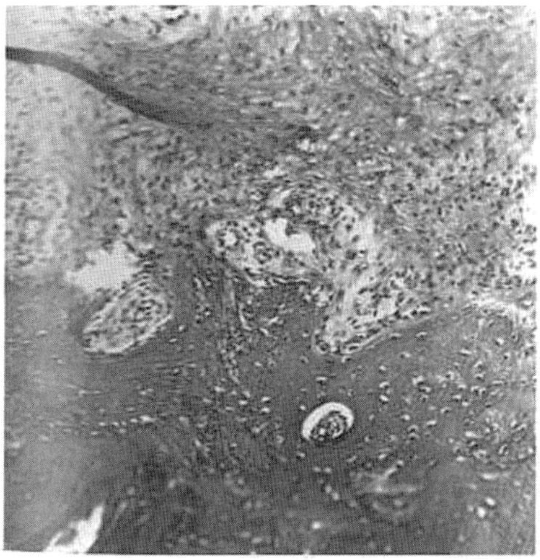

Figure 6.5 ***High power photomicrograph of a section of bone and fibrous tissue removed from under a distracion hook over two years after placement. Of note is the healthy appearance of the fibrous tissue (top) that formed between the metal and the bone, and the dense bone reaction (bottom) adjacent to the fibrous tissue. (Harrington Archives)***

图 6.5　钩子放置两年后,从钩子下取出的一段骨和纤维组织的高倍显微照片。值得注意的是纤维组织的健康外观。(上)在金属和骨头之间形成的纤维组织的健康外观,以及(下)与纤维组织相邻的致密骨反应(哈灵顿档案馆)

figure 6.6. While in Chicago he performed two demonstration surgeries with Claude N. Lambert.[90]

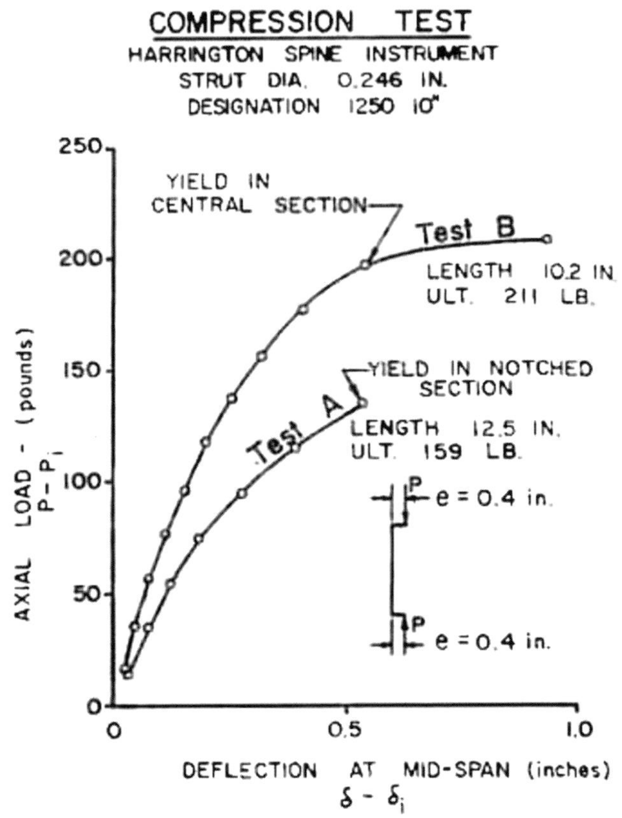

Figure 6.6 ***Stress-strain diagram illustrating the mechanical effect of exposing the rod ratchets to eccentric compression loading.*** **(*Harrington Archives*)**

图 6.6　应力-应变图说明了将棒状棘轮暴露在偏心压缩载荷下的机械效应（哈灵顿档案馆）

1961 年 3 月 10 日，哈灵顿应邀在芝加哥骨科学会做弗里蒙特·A. 钱德勒纪念演讲。他的演讲题目是“脊柱外科器械在脊柱侧凸治疗中的应用”，但留下的手稿题目是“脊柱的生物力学”。[85]在演讲中，他展示了一个简单插图的版本，如同他发表在《脊柱侧凸 1965》的第一篇文章。[86]《脊柱的生物力学》支持了哈灵顿后来的说法，即从根本上帮助他实现了通过使用机械应力达到生物学目的的目标。[87]通过对脊柱全长标本的应力研究，他得出了结论，“不稳定的关键位置是 T7 和 T8。”通过对正常人侧屈运动的研究，他得出了结论，每个椎体的侧方屈曲不超过 5°。他利用这一观察，提出了哈灵顿系数（柯布测量值除以累及的椎体数）来量化脊柱侧凸可能的进展程度。当生长中的儿童出现哈灵顿系数大于或等于 5 时，“如果不积极治疗，脊柱侧凸的进展是不可避免的”。他讨论了弹性变形和塑性变形、柔软度、松弛度、内聚力和潜在的凹槽，以及原发弯和代偿弯。他展示了组织学标本，说明了骨和周围软组织对器械的耐受性和反应。[88]（图 6.5）哈灵顿还说明了撑开棒的棘齿暴露在持续性的偏心加压力中的影响。测试用的 10 英寸撑开棒加上 3 英寸的棘齿（缺口）部分，总长实际为 13 英寸。当棘齿暴露在应力下时，棒的极限强度从 211 磅降低到 159 磅，同时棒的屈服点也从棒的主体部分转为棘齿部分。[89]（图 6.6）在芝加哥期间，他与克劳德·N. 兰伯特进行了两次示范手术。[90]

By now it was becoming clear that Harrington Spine Instrumentation had not only opened a new surgical frontier but also had introduced or at least further defined the role of the surgeon product champion as one who provided education to inform colleagues about the use of a product. In 1961 Harrington would make eight teaching trips, not counting the AAOS annual meeting in Miami Beach. He visited 15 North American cities, performed at least 34 surgeries, and gave several lectures and many consultations. He was away from Houston for at least 50 days.[91,92,93] Harrington was in private practice and not only were there travel expenses but there were also ongoing office overhead charges and lost outpatient and surgical fee income because of his travels to educate others about his instrumentation system. His trip in August to Minneapolis, Calgary, and Salt Lake City probably represented a transition in travel reimbursement. He received payment for travel expenses by TIRR for the last time until 1965 and appeared for the first time to have charged for at least some of the eight surgeries he did with Gordon Townsend in Canada.[94] On that trip his surgical fee was either $1,000 or $350 (the difference was unexplained).[95] There is no record that all or even any of the fees were paid. There also is no suggestion that temporary licensing was obtained or necessary for these demonstration surgeries. From this point on there was increasing documentation of travel reimbursement by hosts, such as orthopaedic societies, honoraria, and charged consultation and surgical fees.[96] But there was no suggestion that he was paid any kind of a consulting fee by Zimmer.

到目前为止，哈灵顿脊柱器械不仅开辟了一个新的外科前沿，而且还进一步定义了外科器械的全新销售方式，即除了产品本身，还向医生同行们提供有关产品的教学培训。1961 年，哈灵顿一共进行了 8 次教学访问，这还不算在迈阿密海滩举行的美国骨科医师学会年会。他访问了 15 个北美城市，进行了至少 34 例手术、数次演讲和多次会诊。他离开休斯敦至少 50 天。[91,92,93]因为他经常外出做培训，他的私人诊所不仅需要承担支出的差旅费，还有持续支出的办公管理费用以及门诊和手术费用收入的损失。8 月份的明尼阿波利斯、卡尔加里和盐湖城之行可能代表了差旅报销单位的转变。1965 年，他最后一次接受得克萨斯州康复与研究中心支付的差旅费。在他与戈登·汤森在加拿大做的八次手术中至少一次是自费差旅。[94]在那次出国访问中，他的手术费为 1 000 美元或 350 美元（差额无法解释）。[95]没有任何记录在案的费用支付，也没有迹象表明这些手术演示需要临时执照。从那时起，主办方报销旅费和其他资金来源的文件记录越来越多，如骨科学会报销的费用，他的酬金、会诊费和手术费。[96]但没有任何证据表明捷迈向他支付了任何形式的顾问费。

Harrington also regularly hosted visiting surgeons, many from overseas, to observe his surgery. The visitors' names and numbers were less well documented than the trips, but easily exceeded 100 between 1953 and 1978. The majority visited from 1959 through 1974.[97] These visits were transformative for some, including James W. Tupper of Seattle, whose recollection follows.[98]

哈灵顿还定期接待来访的外科医生，让他们观摩他的手术，这些医生许多来自海外。访问学者的姓名和人数没有外访记录那么详细，但在 1953 年至 1978 年间，超过 100 人来访。多数人的来访时间主要集中在 1959 年到 1974 年之间。[97]这些访问经历刷新了一些医生的认知，包括西雅图的詹姆斯·W. 塔珀，他的回忆如下。[98]

> As the end of my first year in practice approached, I volunteered to work at Children's Hospital and was assigned to the Flat Foot and Rotation Clinic. The year before, a Seattle orthopedic surgeon from another private office had gone to visit Dr Harrington and on return did the first Harrington instrumentation in Seattle. When it was successful, the patients started "coming out of the woodwork" and the surgeon began to be overwhelmed by non-paying patients with big curves. So he asked me if I would be willing to help and I said "I'll do anything to get out of the flat foot clinic but you'll have to teach me about scoliosis because I don't know anything about it." So the change was made and was assigned to the Scoliosis Clinic. However, before the next meeting of the Scoliosis Clinic the surgeon, because of various personal problems, shipped out on the Hope Ship for a three months' stint in Indonesia

and ultimately did not come back to Seattle. At that point I did one of the smarter things I've done in my life and I called Paul Harrington in Houston and said, "You don't know me but you showed another Seattle surgeon how to do your operation, but he's not here to help me and I need to come to Houston for a crash course in scoliosis, if it's possible." Amazingly he said "Sure, come on down. I'll get a room in the motel for you." Soon I was in Houston engaging in the most fascinating 5 or 6 days I've ever experienced in medicine. That was in early 1961.

实习的第一年即将结束时，我自愿到儿童医院工作，并被分配到扁平足和轮转诊所。在这前一年，西雅图另一家私人诊所的骨科医生拜访了哈灵顿医生，回来后在西雅图做了第一个应用哈灵顿器械的手术，手术很成功，病人突然越来越多。但一些无法支付手术费的重度侧凸患者开始让这位骨科医生感到困扰。所以他问我是否愿意帮忙，我说："我愿意做任何事来摆脱'扁平足诊所'，但你必须教我关于脊柱侧凸的知识，因为我对它一无所知。"之后我被分配到脊柱侧凸门诊。然而，在脊柱侧凸诊所的下次例会前，这位外科医生因为个人问题，乘坐前往印度尼西亚进行了三个月的工作，最终没有返回西雅图。那时，我做了一件我这辈子最聪明的事，我直接打电话给休斯敦的保罗·哈灵顿，说："虽然您不认识我，但您向西雅图的另一位外科医生展示了您的手术，可他目前无法教授我；如果可能的话，我想去休斯敦参加一个脊柱侧凸的速成班。"令人惊讶的是，他说："当然可以，我来为你安排住宿。"很快，我就在休斯敦度过了我从医以来的最精彩的五六天。那是 1961 年年初。

I scrubbed with him several times; saw his follow-up patients with him, read all the pamphlets and literature he gave me, one time had dinner with him and his wife, and in summary, lived scoliosis under the best mentor anyone could ever ask for. And he didn't know me from Adam and no one that I knew had suggested that I try to spend time with him. He did all this on my one phone call.

我和他一起做过好几次手术，和他一起分析病人随访结果，读了他给我的所有小册子和文献，有一次同他们夫妻俩共进晚餐，总之，是跟着脊柱侧凸方面最好的专家学习。他不知道我来自亚当，我认识的人也没有建议我去找他学习。只是一通电话他就愿意为我做这么多。

During the time I was there it was obvious that heads of orthopedic departments were sending down their junior doctors to see what was going on, and why he spent that much time with me. I'll never know. I went back to Seattle filled with scoliosis and my older partner did a Harrington instrumentation that turned out OK, and I was off in a new direction for the rest of my orthopedic career. Soon Dr Ma Mullen, from another private office, joined the clinic and we ran the Scoliosis Clinic at Children's Orthopaedic Hospital for many years.

我在那里的时候，很明显，骨科主任都派他们的医师来观察情况。为什么他花时间陪着我，当然我也不会知道。我带着脊柱侧凸技术回到了西雅图，和我的老搭档做了一个哈灵顿器械手术，结果很好，我的骨科生涯开始有了新的方向。不久，来自另一家私人诊所的马·马伦医生加入了我们的诊所，我们在儿童骨科医院开了脊柱侧凸门诊，并持续多年。

Nineteen sixty-one signaled the first full year of widespread use of Harrington Spine Instrumentation, and although a few design refinements and component additions were made, there were far fewer than in years past. With growing usage the need for an instrument storage rack became apparent. The one designed by Zimmer had drawn this comment from Harrington: "Personally, I think the carrier should be put in the can."[99] Harrington was using a flat storage rack apparently made in Houston most likely at TIRR by Tork Engen. Hite had seen or learned of it and asked for a model, which Harrington sent. Using this as the starting point, Zimmer was able to design a flat rack that stored the strut bars, compression rods, sacral rods, and all hooks. *See figure 6.7*. The base plate was aluminum to keep the weight down while the fixtures holding the stainless steel implants were made of the same stainless steel to avoid electrolysis between dissimilar metals.[100] Harrington's reaction speaks for itself. "The hook holder rack is excellent. Put her in for production. I appreciate the one you sent me and feel it is superior to what we have made. After you sell three or four dozen, I would appreciate another one 'free of charge.'" Harrington did suggest that specific holders for the different hooks would be helpful.[101] These racks were used throughout the long life of the instrumentation.

1961 年是哈灵顿脊柱器械被广泛使用的第一年，尽管做了一些设计改进和部件增添，但比过去的几年少得多。随着使用量的增长，对器械盒的需求变得明显。捷迈设计的那个盒子得到了哈灵顿的评论：“个人而言，我认为器械应该放在金属容器里。”[99]哈灵顿使用的扁平式的器械盒显然出自休斯敦，很可能是托基尔·恩金在得克萨斯州康复与研究中心制造的。海特听说了哈灵顿的想法并要了一个模型。以此为基础，捷迈设计了一个扁平的架子，用来储存撑开棒、压缩棒、骶骨棒和所有的钩。(图 6.7) 底座是铝制的，以减轻重量，而不锈钢的内固定植入物的夹子是由相同的不锈钢制成的，以避免不同金属之间的电解效应。[100]哈灵顿的评价不言自明：“持钩支架非常棒，把它投入生产吧。我很喜欢你寄给我的产品，它比我们做的要好。在你卖了三四十个之后，我想再要一个‘免费的’。”哈灵顿也建议为不同的钩提供特定的支架会更好。[101]而这些支架将会一直保护着这些器械。

Figure 6.7 ***Harrington Spine Instrumentation rack/tray*****, *ca. 1961* (*Harrington Archives*)**
图 6.7　哈灵顿脊柱器械架/盒，约 1961 年(哈灵顿档案馆)

In this same exchange the Moe hook modification was first mentioned. Although not specifically described, it almost certainly was the 1/4"-diameter rod compatible distraction hook (#1252) with the addition of a center keel/rib. The purpose wasn't specified in this correspondence, but as was later described, it was to prevent displacement of the lower distraction hook from its seat into the outer aspect of the inferior facet.[102] Although Harrington hadn't used it, he thought it was a good idea. Harrington also gave his blessing to Moe's request for a strut bar with a threaded end rather than the ratchet end, with the caveat that the threads had fillets at the bottom of each thread. Whether or not the threading was to be at both ends wasn't specified.

在同样的技术交流中，莫氏钩的改进也首次被提到。虽然没有具体描述，但几乎可以肯定是直径 1/4 英寸的棒兼容撑开钩（#1252）且带有中心脊/肋。虽然没有提到具体的目的，但正如后来描述的那样，它是为了防止下方撑开钩从它的底座滑到下关节突的外侧。[102]虽然哈灵顿没有用过，但他认为这确实是个好主意。哈灵顿还赞同莫的想法，他希望棒的一端是螺纹，而不是棘齿，并提醒到，无论两端是否都需要螺纹，每个螺纹的底部都要是圆角。

As might be expected, the orderly growth of instrumentation parts was stressed by suggestions for modifications from less experienced surgeons and by different instrumentation requirements that presented when treating spine deformities other than scoliosis. Hite appears to have been the recipient of most of these ideas and probably shared a good portion of them with Harrington, who offered his thoughts.[103,104] For instance, Hite reported that after only two cases one surgeon requested that the hooks have greater depth to allow for two holes, over-under style, to make the holes easier to line up. Harrington commented that the effect of the increased eccentricity of the loading on the rod would have to be considered. Another surgeon suggested that a flattened side be added to the strut bar so that additional hooks could be added and locked with a set screw against the flat. Hite commented that this would involve increasing the thickness of the top of the hook to allow threading. Harrington thought the set screw would work and then slip. This same surgeon asked for a universal joint at the midsection of the compression rod. Harrington thought the idea "stinks" and suggested using the smaller, more flexible compression rod. Finally, the exchange addressed the ongoing problem with developing the ideal hook holders. There are no extant drawings and prototypes to allow analysis of the fine points of the problems. What followed was a three-month hiatus in communication, a good indication that Hite had been able to handle the special requests. But in September Hite wrote that a surgeon had recently asked if it would be permissible to bend a distraction bar for use on a combined kyphosis and scoliosis deformity.[105] After stating the obvious from an engineer's viewpoint that he never liked to see appliances cold bent. Hite confessed that he did not have a solution to offer. The possible solution that he posed to Harrington was to use a series of their existing #1260 universal (over-under) two-rod receptacle hook and short rods.

正如预期的那样，缺乏经验的外科医生提出的改进建议以及对治疗脊柱侧凸外的脊柱畸形内固定器械的要求都大大推动了器械的发展。海特似乎收集了很多这样的想法，并与哈灵顿分享了其中的大部分。[103,104]例如，海特说，在只做了两个病例后，一位外科医生要求钩有更大的深度以允许适配两个孔，一上一下，使其更容易对齐。哈灵顿评论，对棒上增加的偏心量必须加以考虑。另一位外科医生建议在撑开棒上增加一个平面，这样就可以增加额外的钩，并用固定螺钉将钩固定在有平面的那侧。海特评论，这将增加钩顶部的厚度，会影响螺纹。哈灵顿认为可以安装螺钉但是容易滑脱。还是这位外科医生，他要求在压缩棒的中段安装通用关节。哈灵顿认为这个想法“很糟糕”，并建议使用更小、更灵活的压缩棒。最后，他们的交流解决了理想的持钩器的研发问题。可惜的是没有现存的图纸和原型来分析这些问题的微妙之处。接下来是三个月的断联，这表明海特已经能够独立处理这些特殊的要求。但在 9 月，海特写道，一名外科医生最近询问是否允许折弯撑开棒用于脊柱后凸和脊柱侧凸合并畸形。[105]显而易见，从工程师的角度来看，海特不喜欢看到器械被折弯，但也承认没有解决办法。他向哈灵顿提出的解决方案是将一系列现有的#1260 通用（上下）双棒钩和短棒组合使用。

The other specific issue Hite addressed was the request they received from several sources asking “for some better method of purchase between the distraction rod and the sacral rod (bar). They had supplied both the offset eyelet and the rather bulky centerline oriented version. Based on limited feedback, the latter seemed to be preferred. Hite offered the following observations.” Many special modifications continue to be brough to our attention, most of them we are able to side track, however, occasionally someone insists we produce the unusual. All in all the Harrington equipment seems to be moving quite well and I believe with a minimum amount of critical reports. “It was obvious that Harrington Spine Instrumentation, inspired by post-polio scoliosis, had been found useful in the treatment of scoliosis and other spinal deformities of a wide variety of types and causes.” Hite closed with, “If the above suggestions have their place in the instrumentation we will be glad to include them if you so desire.”

海特解决的另一个具体问题是，他们收到了来自多方的请求，要求“在撑开棒和骶骨棒之间寻求更好的方法”。他们提供了偏移孔和相当笨重的中心线导向两个解决方案。根据有限的反馈，后者似乎更受欢迎。海特提出了以下声明：“许多建议持续地引起了我们的注意，其中大多数我们能够理解，但偶尔有人坚持生产那些不寻常的器械。总的来说，我们的工具运行得很好，我相信我们受到的直接批评是最少的。”很明显，哈灵顿脊柱器械受到继发于脊髓灰质炎的脊柱侧凸的启发，已用于治疗脊柱侧凸和其他各种类型以及由各种原因造成的脊柱畸形。海特最后说：“如果上述关于器械的建议确实有意义，我们会高兴将它们考虑在内。”

Harrington responded that the universal hooks would not perform in the manner described because the compression rods held the hook level, thus preventing the eccentricity (angulation) for the ratchet mechanism to work.[106] He had experienced this mode of failure a year and a half earlier. He did not offer a suggestion to solve the important hyperkyphosis/round back problem that the surgeon had encountered. This was a problem that would not go away. About the method of attachment of the strut bar to the sacra bar, he answered, “Your large heavy sacral bar attachment is no good. The smaller ones can be used.” Then Harrington unloaded on Hite with the following: “My suggestion to everyone who wants to change this instrument is this: remember no one can do as good a job as I and I don't change the instruments. If they learn to use well what they have they can do a good job with it, but now is not the time to change everything. Please don't hook my name to any of the drawings.” Finally, in a more constructive tone he added that the most common mistake he observed was using the large compression rod rather than the small one. After asking if anything had been done about the hook holders, he close with, “Hope this finds you well and in a good mood.” Of course, it is possible and likely that not all of the Harrington-Zimmer correspondence survived, but based on what did, it would be seven months, or well into 1962, before the next communication about design was sent. Thus, in late 1961 the pace of Harrington Spine Instrumentation design leveled off, and the components depicted on Zimmer product listing had found user acceptance.[107] *See figure 6.8.*

哈灵顿回答说，通用钩不会以所想象的方式工作，因为压缩棒保持钩的水平状态，从而防止了棘齿的偏心（成角）。一年半以前他在工作时就遭遇过这种失败。[106]他没有解决外科医生遇到的重度脊柱后凸问题，因为这是一个不会消失的问题。关于撑开棒与骶骨棒的连接方法，他回答说：“又大又重的骶骨棒不好，可以使用小一点的。”然后哈灵顿对海特大吐苦水：“我对所有想改进器械的人说：‘记住，没有人能比我做得更好，我也不会更改我的器械。’如果他们学会使用这套器械后，也许可以做得很好，但现在显然不是改变的时候。请不要把我的名字和任何草图挂钩。”最后，他以一种更具建设性的语气补充，他观察到的最常见的错误是使用大压缩棒而不是小压缩棒。在咨询了一下持钩器的问题后，他最后说："希望你看到这封信时一切都好。"当然，哈灵顿和捷迈之间并不是所有的通信都被保存了下来，他们的下一个关于设计的通信是在 7 个月后，或直到 1962 年。因此，在 1961 年年底，哈灵顿的器械设计趋于稳定，捷迈在产品清单上描述的组件已经获得了用户的认可。[107]（图 6.8）

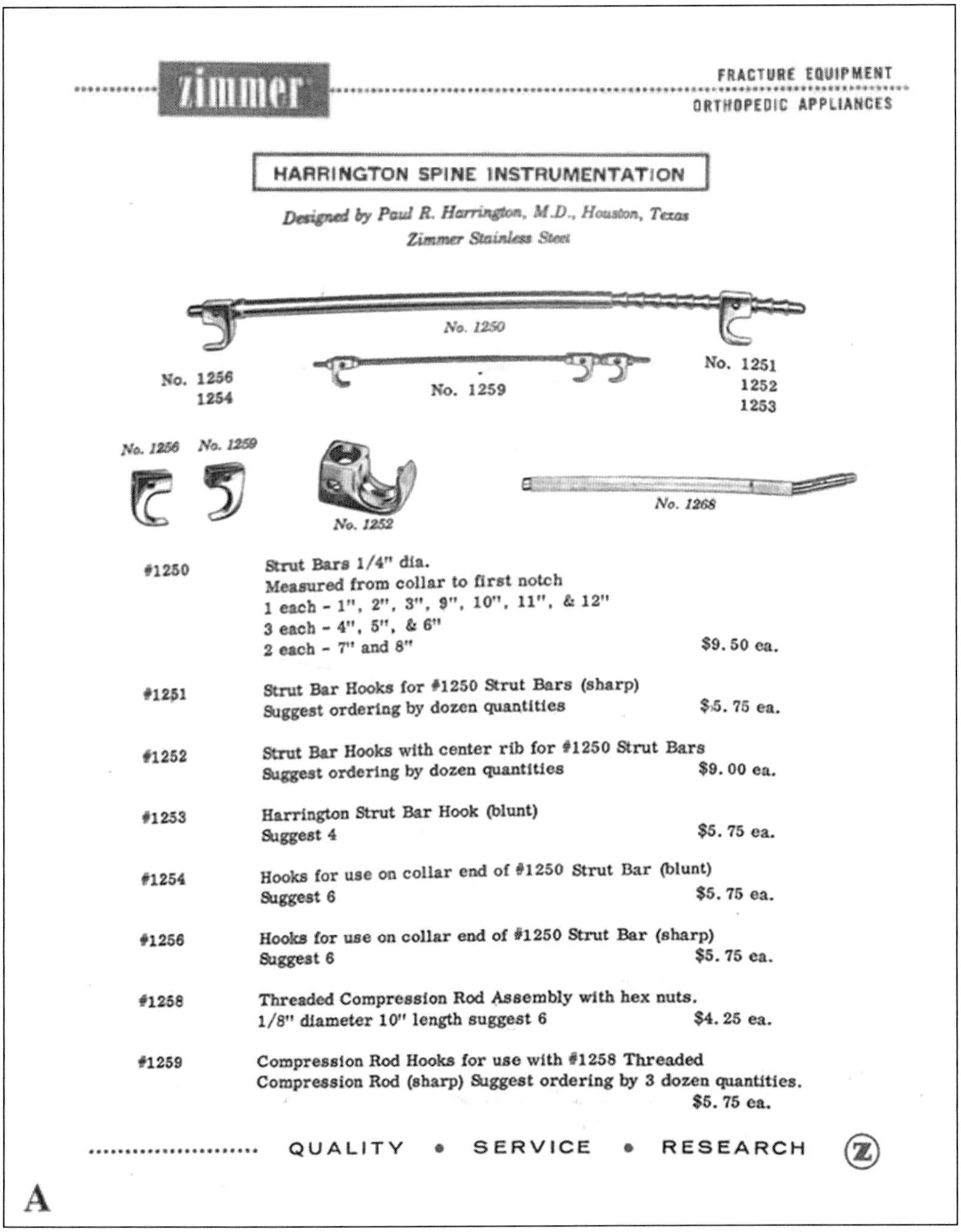
zimmer

FRACTURE EQUIPMENT
ORTHOPEDIC APPLIANCES

HARRINGTON SPINE INSTRUMENTATION

Designed by Paul R. Harrington, M.D., Houston, Texas
Zimmer Stainless Steel

#1250	Strut Bars 1/4" dia. Measured from collar to first notch 1 each - 1", 2", 3", 9", 10", 11", & 12" 3 each - 4", 5", & 6" 2 each - 7" and 8"	$9.50 ea.
#1251	Strut Bar Hooks for #1250 Strut Bars (sharp) Suggest ordering by dozen quantities	$5.75 ea.
#1252	Strut Bar Hooks with center rib for #1250 Strut Bars Suggest ordering by dozen quantities	$9.00 ea.
#1253	Harrington Strut Bar Hook (blunt) Suggest 4	$5.75 ea.
#1254	Hooks for use on collar end of #1250 Strut Bar (blunt) Suggest 6	$5.75 ea.
#1256	Hooks for use on collar end of #1250 Strut Bar (sharp) Suggest 6	$5.75 ea.
#1258	Threaded Compression Rod Assembly with hex nuts. 1/8" diameter 10" length suggest 6	$4.25 ea.
#1259	Compression Rod Hooks for use with #1258 Threaded Compression Rod (sharp) Suggest ordering by 3 dozen quantities.	$5.75 ea.

QUALITY • SERVICE • RESEARCH

A

STANDARD SET OF INSTRUMENTS

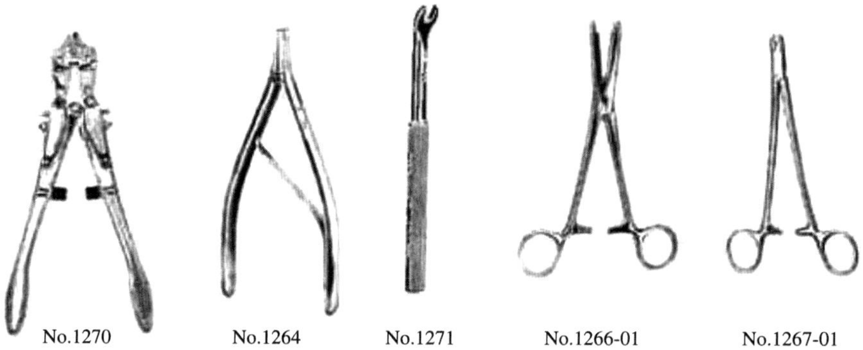

No.1270 No.1264 No.1271 No.1266-01 No.1267-01

2	#1263	Harrington Sacral Rod Eyelet	9.50
1	#1264	Spreader	24.50
2	#1266-01	Hook Clamp	22.50
1	#1267-01	Threaded Rod Clamp for #1258 Threaded Compression Rod	17.50
1	#1268	Driver for #1251, #1252, #1253	9.50
1	#1271	Flat Wrench	5.00
1	#1272	Harrington Spinal Elevator 3/4	35.00
	#1273	Harrington "C" Washer Suggest 6	1.50

ACCESSORY ITEMS FOR
HARRINGTON SPINE INSTRUMENTATION

#1260	Universal Swivel Hook. One only required per rod.	7.25 ea.
#1261	Sacral Rod - fully threaded 1/4" dia. x 8" length, trocar point	4.50 ea.
#1261-50	Harrington Sacral Rod Nut	1.00 ea.
#1270	Pin Cutter	38.50 ea.
#3180	Needle Nose Pliers	3.50 ea.

#1266-02 Hook Clamp - one size fits all hooks with side holes (2 req)-w/2 lugs 17.50 ea.

B

Figure 6.8 ***Harrington Spine Instrumentation as shown on the front (A) and back (B) of a Zimmer product information sheet, ca. late 196t or early 1962. Not shown is the #1257. a 3/16"-diameter threaded rob assembly with hex nuts. The #1251 and #1253 hooks were still being used at the lumbar distraction site. (Harrington Archives)***

图 6.8 哈灵顿脊柱器械的正面(A)和背面(B)。捷迈公司的产品信息表,大约在 1969 年年底或 1962 年年初。没有显示的#1257 是一个直径为 3/16 英寸的带六角螺母的螺纹套筒组件。#1251 和# 1253 钩子当时仍在腰部撑开部位使用(哈灵顿档案馆)

In November 1961 Bill Spencer, Harrington's academic chairman, read a paper entitled "Rehabilitation in Concept and Practice" that helps us understand the special synergy between the two men.[108] Presented to the sections on Physical Medicine and Rehabilitation and Preventive Medicine at the Southern Medical Association's 55th annual meeting in Dallas, Spencer began by quoting from Sir William Osler's *Medicine in the Nineteenth Century*: "There is no one measure which can compare with the decrease of physical suffering in man, woman, and child when stricken by disease or accident. This is the one fact of supreme personal import to every one of us. This is the Promethean gift to the century of man.[109] Promethean, that is being daringly original or creative, relates to Prometheus, the Greek god who was chained and tortured for stealing fire from heaven and giving it to man.[110] Spencer and Harrington were fellow Prometheans. An example Spencer presented was the case of a 42-year-old female. who sustained an L2 fracture from an airplane accident while overseas. *See figure 6.9*. Part of her treatment after transfer to TIRR was spine instrumentation and fusion, which was followed by improvement in her leg function to the point that she could walk with braces. This was just one facet of her multidisciplinary care, but it was highlighted because she probably represented the first time that Harrington used his instrumentation in the treatment of a spine fracture. It was to lead to a resurgence in the possibilities of surgical treatment of unstable spine fractures. Spencer summarized his presentation: "The concept of rehabilitation for the completion of total and adequate medical care has not penetrated the mind of the average doctor as he manages his patient. He is mainly concerned with curative or symptomatic treatment. Much education within the medical profession is needed before rehabilitation as a philosophic concept will make headway."

1961 年 11 月，哈灵顿的系主任比尔·斯宾塞朗读了一篇题为《康复理论和实践》的论文，这篇论文帮助我们理解了两人之间的互助关系。[108]在达拉斯举行的第五十五届南方医学会年会上，斯宾塞在理疗、康复和预防医学部分发言时，引用了威廉·奥斯勒爵士的《19 世纪医学》中的一段话："没有一种行为可以与减少人类的疾苦（的医学）相提并论，无论是男人、女人还是儿童。这是对我们每个人都至关重要的事实，也是普罗米修斯给人类纪元的礼物。[109] "Promethean"，意指巨大的创造，该词来源于"Prometheus"（普罗米修斯），一位希腊神话里的神明，他因偷取天火并将其赐予人类而承受枷锁和折磨。[110]斯宾塞和哈灵顿正是创造性的代表。斯宾塞展示了一个案例，一位 42 岁的女性，在一次飞机事故中造成了 L2 骨折。(图 6.9) 转去得克萨斯州康复与研究中心接受脊柱融合内固定手术治疗后，她的下肢功能得到了改善，可以佩戴支具行走。虽然脊柱融合内固定术只是对该女士所进行的多学科治疗的一方面，但仍值得重视，因为这代表哈灵顿第一次用他的器械治疗脊柱骨折。这也使得手术治疗不稳定性脊柱骨折成为可能。斯宾塞总结道："普通医生由于没有深入理解康复的概念，他们主要针对疾病本身进行治疗或仅仅对症治疗，无法对患者进行全面、充分的医学处理。我们需要在医学教育领域中开展大量的工作，才有可能使康复医学变为一个深入人心的重要概念。"

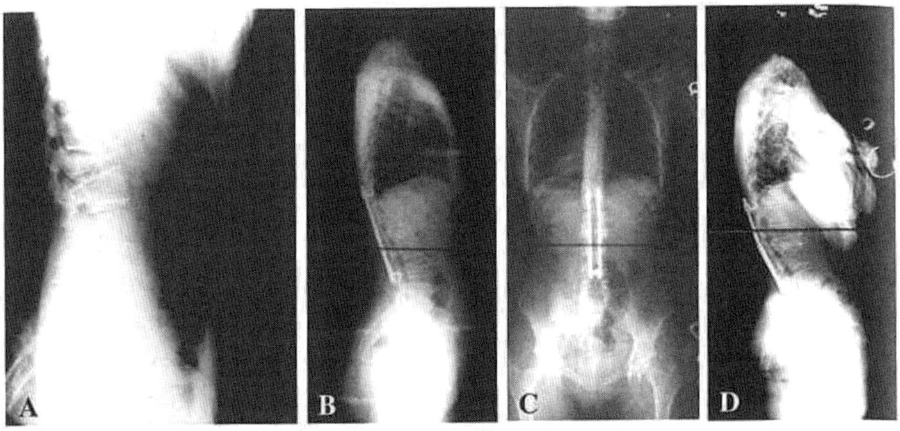

Figure 6.9 ***This 42-year-old woman was paraplegic following an airplane crash. She had been treated with laninectomy making her spine more unstable. A. L2 burst fracture on the preoperative lateral. B. postoperative lateral and (C) posteroanterior following Harrington distraction instrumentation and arthrodesis, the anticipated site. She had had 70% neurological recovery from her paraplegia and could play golf without braces. (Harrington Archives)***

图 6.9 这名 42 岁的妇女在一次飞机失事后高位截瘫。她曾接受过椎板切除术治疗，使她的脊柱更加不稳定。A. 术前侧位的 L2 断裂性骨折。B. 术后侧位和(C) 哈灵顿撑开器械和关节融合术后，预期部位。她的截瘫的神经系统已经恢复了 70%，可以不戴支具打高尔夫(哈灵顿档案馆)

The last Zimmer communication for 1961 was about education. On December 19 Alvin Brallier, their sales manager, wrote that a number of orthopaedic surgeons had contacted the company about arranging a consultation session during the upcoming annual meeting of the AAOS in Chicago in 1962.[111] A Monday evening session beginning at 5:00 p.m. was suggested. All the surgeons were using the instrumentation, and their feeling was "that a joint discussion covering your experiences would be of great benefit to them." Those expressing interest included scoliosis thought leaders: Dean MacEwen, Wilmington, Delaware; Edmond McDonnell and George Eaton, Baltimore, Maryland; Alvin McKelvie, Washington, D.C.; and Charles Nadel, Iryington, New Jersey. This could be interpreted as being another step in the creation of the surgeon product cham pion as well as the foreshadowing of industry's future role in organizing and sponsoring surgeon education. Harrington responded that the time sounded good and requested that Brallier："take the initiative and notify all doctors using the equipment that this meeting will be available to them."[112] He estimated that there would be 30 to 40 doctors. He continued, "Such a meeting would be unofficial as far as the Academy is concerned, but I think your clearing with them would be a wise idea, and particularly if you state as you did in my letter, the doctors wishing such a get-together." He volunteered to have "adequate material available to answer most clinical questions." Harrington requested that Hite be alerted and that he have previously discussed material available.

1961 年哈灵顿和捷迈的最后一次交流是关于教育的。12 月 19 日，携迈的销售经理阿尔文·布莱利尔写道，一些骨科医生已经联系了公司，希望在 1962 年即将在芝加哥举行的美国骨科医师学会年会上安排一个咨询讨论会[111]，并建议该咨询会在星期一晚上 5 点开始。这里的所有外科医生都在应用该器械，并且他们认为"对您的经验进行讨论将对他们大有裨益"。对此表示感兴趣的包括许多脊柱侧凸领域的带头人，比如特拉华州威尔明顿的迪恩·麦克尤恩、马里兰州巴尔的摩的埃德蒙·麦克唐纳和乔治·伊顿、华盛顿特区的阿尔文·麦凯尔维以及新泽西州欧文顿的查尔斯·纳德尔。这既说明了外科器械销售的进一步发展，也预示着器械公司未来在组织和赞助外科医生教育方面的重要作用。哈灵顿回应说，时间听起来不错，他同时要求布莱利尔："主动通知所有使用器械的医生，我们将为他们提供这次咨询会"[112]。哈灵顿估计有三四十个医生参会。他继续说："不同于学术会议，这是非正式会面。我认为你向他们澄清这一点是明智的，尤其是如果这次咨询会真的像你在给我的信中所说的那样——医生们所盼望的一次聚会。"哈灵顿自愿提供"足够的资料来解答大多数临床问题"，他要求通知海特，因为他有之前讨论的资料。

Harrington's presentation at the 1960 AOA annual meeting was based on 103 patients operated on over a 12-year span[113]. But he had yet to publish a full-length description of his work. By the end of 1960 the study group had grown to 129 patients, and it is apparent that Harrington was documenting his work in the detail necessary for a comprehensive presentation. Two similar, very instructive versions emerged, and a comparison of the two is insightful. Sometime in 1961 Harrington submitted his thesis entitled "Spine Instrumentation in the Management of Spine Deformity and Instability" to the AOA, at that time one of the requirements for membership selection process.[114] This unpublished thesis was 28 pages long and supported by 64 figures and illustrations.[115]

哈灵顿在1960年的美国骨科学会年会上的报告的基础是在12年间进行手术的103名患者。[113]但他还没有发表过对于他工作的完整介绍。到1960年年底，他的研究团队分析了多达129名患者。显然，哈灵顿正在详细记录他的工作，以便日后进行全面的介绍。当出现两篇类似的、启发性很强的研究论文时，比较是非常有必要的。1961年的某个时候，哈灵顿向美国骨科学会提交了他的论文《脊柱器械在脊柱畸形和不稳治疗中的应用》，这是当时成为美国骨科学会会员的要求之一。[114]这篇未发表的论文有28页长，共有图片和插图64幅。[115]

At about the same time he submitted the thesis as a manuscript to the *JBJS Am.* for publication. The journal's editorial process was remembered by Harrington as a many-rewrite and costly ordeal.[116,117] But he stuck it out, and his now classic primary paper, "Treatment of Scoliosis: Correction and Internal Fixation by Spine Instrumentation," was published as the lead article in the June 1962 issue.[118] The 21-page article included 31 figures and illustrations, all of which had appeared in the AOA thesis. It differs most from the submitted manuscript in that Harrington's concept of the pathobiology of scoliosis had been edited out. He stated that "The pathogenesis of the growing scoliotic spine is loss of geometrical stability through asymmetrical growth of the endochondral segments at their load transfer areas. In man, the fulfillment of inherent potential skeletal form lies in its dynamic balance." The operative words were *asymmetrical growth and dynamic balance*. This was conjecture, and Harrington would ultimately have the opportunity to test it. However, focus on biology as well as on mechanics was a prominent part of the vision that started and sustained his quest for a better method of treating scoliosis. To miss this may be to miss the roots of his genius. Or, as he later wrote, "I was always striving to think fundamentally and I feel that because of this I was able to meet my objective... Fortunately the instrumentation system used to treat paralytic scoliosis was found to be equally applicable to the treatment of idiopathic scoliosis as well as other pine deformities and instabilities."[119] This would turn out to be a bit of an overreach.

大约在同一时间，哈灵顿向《骨和关节外科杂志》（美国卷）提交了他的手稿。在哈灵顿的记忆中，在杂志的评审和编辑过程中进行了多次重写，这简直是一种折磨。[116,117]但他坚持了下来，现在被奉为经典的论文——《脊柱侧凸的治疗：通过脊柱器械矫形和内固定》，作为1962年6月刊的主要文章发表[118]。这篇21页的论文包括31幅图和插图，所有这些都出现在美国骨科学会的论文中。最终的论文与提交的手稿最大的不同之处在于，哈灵顿关于脊柱侧凸病理生理学的概念被删掉了。哈灵顿指出，“脊柱侧凸进一步恶化的发病机制是软骨内骨在其应力转移区域的不对称生长，进而失去结构稳定性。对于人类而言，潜在的骨骼形态的形成的关键在于其动态平衡。”这其中关键词是不对称生长和动态平衡。虽然这只是猜测，但哈灵顿认为总有机会验证这一想法。对生物学和力学的关注是他寻求更好的治疗脊柱侧凸方法的一个特色。忽视这一点，可能错过他天才的根源。或者，正如哈灵顿后来所写的那样，“我总是努力从根源上思考，正因为如此，我才能够达到我的目标……幸运的是，用于治疗麻痹性脊柱侧凸的内固定系统同样适用于治疗特发性脊柱侧凸以及其他脊柱畸形和不稳定。”[119]但这可能有点夸大其词。

Comparative reading of his AOA thesis and the *JBJS Am.* article shows that in addition to omitting his concept of the pathobiology of scoliosis, his attention to consent detail had been considerably shortened, his inclusion of fusion had increased, and his thoughts about non-fusion rod lengthening were ambiguous. As published, it was primarily a technique paper, and one that has stood the test of time. In a recent study of the 100 most cited articles in orthopaedic surgery, Harrington's article was tied for eighty-seventh overall, eleventh among spine articles, and second among spine surgery articles.[120]

比较哈灵顿的美国骨科学会论文和《骨和关节外科杂志》（美国卷）上的论文，我们可以看出，在《骨和关节外科杂志》（美国卷）的论文中，除了他的脊柱侧凸病理生理学的概念被删除外，他对知情同意书细节的关注也大幅减少，而关于融合的内容则大大增加，此外，他对非融合棒延长的想法变得模糊。它作为一篇技术类论文出版，并且经受住了时间的考验。最近的一项研究发现，在 100 篇被引用最多的骨科手术文章中，哈灵顿的这篇文章位列第 87 位，在脊柱文章中位列第 11 位，在脊柱外科文章中位列第 2 位。[120]

His *JBJS Am.* article begins with a timeline of his work and chronological descriptions of patient groups. The years 1947–49 involved anatomical study of the spine and the problem of post-polio scoliosis. In the years 1949–55 nineteen patients, fourteen (74%) having post-polio scoliosis, underwent surgery, and they formed Group I. During this period a metal fixation system to apply safe forces and stabilize the affected spine was developed, and analysis of the complications of bone erosion, instrument fracture, and pseudarthrosis resulted in 35 instrument modifications. No casts were used, and fusion was eventually used in nearly all patients to acquire reasonable results. In the years 1955–60, 42 patients, 37 (88%) having post-polio scoliosis, underwent surgery, and they composed Group II. During this period twelve instrument modifications along with surgical approach and clinical application modifications resulted in greater force application but increased bone erosion. Fusion was used extensively to accomplish better results, and no casts were used. Research for this group was supported by a grant from the NFIP. In 1960 Group III, comprising 68 patients, 34 (50%) with post-polio scoliosis, underwent surgery. The method perfected to this point, including fusion at the initial surgery and more frequent use of casts and prolonged immobilization, resulted in reduction of instrument fracture and bone erosion. There was no mention of supplemental bone graft being used in this or the earlier patient groups.

哈灵顿发表在《骨和关节外科杂志》（美国卷）的文章是以他的工作的时间顺序和病人群体展开的。1947 年至 1949 年期间，哈灵顿主要研究脊柱的解剖和继发于脊髓灰质炎的脊柱侧凸问题。在 1949—1955 年间，19 名患者接受了手术，其中 14 名（74%）患者患有继发于脊髓灰质炎的脊柱侧凸，他们组成了第Ⅰ组。在此期间，一种可以确保手术安全性并稳定脊柱的金属内固定系统被开发了出来。此外，有关骨质侵蚀、器械断裂和假关节并发症的分析推动了 35 种手术器械的改良。19 名患者均没有使用石膏，全部施行融合术，几乎所有患者都获得了良好的结果。在 1955—1960 年间，42 名患者接受了手术，其中 37 名（88%）患有继发于脊髓灰质炎的脊柱侧凸，他们组成了第Ⅱ组。12 种手术器械和手术入路都有改良，它们的临床应用方式的改进使得术者的发力更加合理，但也导致了骨质侵蚀的增加。42 名患者中，广泛使用融合术，所有患者均未使用石膏。哈灵顿对第Ⅱ组的研究得到了国家小儿麻痹基金会的资金支持。在 1960 年，哈灵顿将第Ⅲ组患者纳入研究。本组包括 68 名患者，其中 34 名（50%）患有继发于脊髓灰质炎的脊柱侧凸。68 名患者全部接受了手术。哈灵顿进一步完善这 68 名患者的手术方法，比如，在初次手术时就施行融合术，更频繁地应用石膏，延长制动时间等。这些措施可减少器械断裂和骨质侵蚀。哈灵顿未在第Ⅲ组或前两组患者中提及额外的植骨。

The component parts, made of stainless steel (SMO 18–8) were described with instructions, including illustrations about their application. The 8" long, 1/4"-diameter distraction rod was described as having a yield point of about 400 pounds on axial loading and over 200 pounds on eccentric loading. The actual force applied was more related to the bone strength into which the hooks were set. The purchase sites on the posterior elements of the thoracic and lumbar spine were illustrated along with the range of compression and distraction forces possible at each. Exactly how these were determined was not explained. The preferred site for thoracic distraction was under the inferior facet process and for lumbar distraction a notch cut into the lateral side of the inferior articular process. The preferred thoracic compression sites were the base of the transverse processes and the inferior edge of the lumbar lamina.

由不锈钢（SMO 18-8）组成的部分，附有使用说明书，包括应用说明。8 英寸长，直径 1/4 英寸的撑开棒可以承载约 400 磅的轴向载荷和超过 200 磅的偏心载荷。实际施加的力与钩处的骨强度相关。绘图展示了胸椎和腰椎后部结构上的置入点，以及各点可能的压缩力和撑开力的范围，但这些数据的确定过程没有解释。胸椎撑开的首选部位是下关节突下方，腰椎撑开的首选部位是下关节突的外侧。首选的胸椎压缩部位是横突基底部和腰椎椎板的下缘。

The next section was about clinical considerations for operation that were not discussed in detail because they were still evolving (and to some extent that continues to be true today). Harrington described the Harrington factor, determined from a standing coronal plane radiography by dividing the Cobb curve size by the number of vertebrae in the curve. His general recommendation for treatment with the "device" was a Harrington factor of 5 or more, "with one or more of the following signs or symptoms: progression of the curve (in children); increasing pain or fatigue (in adults); and progressive cardiopulmonary decompensation." The locations of curve corrective forces were decided before the operation. All curves and their transitional vertebrae were identified as was the major curve. "Distraction is applied to the concave side of the upper transitional vertebra or to the vertebra above this and to one or two vertebrae below the transitional vertebra. Compression is applied on the convex side to multiple vertebrae between the transitional vertebrae."

文章的下一节是关于手术方式的临床实践，由于这些实践仍在发展中，因此没有详细讨论。哈灵顿描述了哈灵顿系数，通过站立冠状面 X 光片判断，将柯布度数除以弯曲中椎体的数目。他建议接受治疗的脊柱的哈灵顿因子是 5 以上，"具有一个或多个迹象或症状：不断进展的脊柱侧凸（儿童）；疼痛或疲劳加重（成人）；和进一步恶化的心肺呼吸困难。"术前确定矫正侧凸的位置。所有侧凸及其移行椎体被确定为主弯。"撑开棒应用于上端椎体的凹侧或其上方的椎体或移行椎体下方的一个或两个椎体。压缩应用于移行椎体之间的多个椎体的侧面。”

The next and longest section was on the surgical technique. The consent statement in the publication read, "The limitations of the operation and the possible complications should be thoroughly discussed with all concerned before operation is undertaken." In his AOA thesis Harrington devoted nearly a full manuscript page to the points of his consent process, beginning with the statement that "orientation of oneself, the patient and guardian is essential. The parties are told there are no miracles." Endotracheal anesthesia and the prone position were used, and a sterile field was maintained. Subperiosteal exposure to the tips of the thoracic transverse processes and of the lumbar articular processes was obtained. Vertebra number was based on "identifying the anatomically unique characteristics of the twelfth thoracic vertebra. By careful subperiosteal dissection, which proceeds beneath the capsule of each right and left posterior articulation, the arteries, veins, and nerves to the paraspinal muscles that emerge through the notch caudad to the inferior articular process of each vertebra can be spared." The distraction rod hook sites were prepared. The most difficult one was the inferior distraction site, always located in the lumbar spine. The preferred site was a notch prepared on the lateral aspect of the inferior articular process. Harrington directed that "the hook attached to the driver is driven in at such an angle that its tip enters the superior articular process and the rest of the hook is lodged between the superior and inferior articular processes." If this wasn't adequate, "a notch can be prepared beginning in the superior border of the lamina just lateral to the base of the spinous process." Harrington cautioned against injury to the dura, but his concern was not realized and history would show that this placement was the solution to "the weakest feature of the whole procedure."

再下一节是关于手术技术的，是最长的一个章节。公开的知情同意书写道："在进行手术之前，应彻底讨论手术的局限性和可能的并发症。”在他的美国骨科学会论文中，哈灵顿几乎用一整页手稿论述他关于知情同意流程的观点，他在开头这样写道："对自己、患者和监护人的定位至关重要。患者应被告知没有奇迹。”麻醉方式为全身麻醉，体位为俯卧位，手术环境要保证无菌。骨膜下剥离到胸椎横突和腰椎关节突。确定椎体节段的基础是“通过解剖学的特征识别第十二胸椎。仔细的骨膜下剥离，在每个关节囊的左右后下方进行操作，可以保留椎体下关节突尾部的动脉、静脉和脊柱旁肌肉的神经。”关于撑开棒钩的部位的准备，最困难的是下方撑开的部位，通常位于腰椎。首选部位是在下关节突外侧所制备的凹槽。哈灵顿指出，“连接到推进器的钩应以这样的角度被驱动，即其尖端进入上关节突，钩的其余部分卡在上下关节突之间。”如果这还不够，“可以在棘突根部外侧的椎板上缘制备凹槽。”哈灵顿警告不要损伤硬膜，但人们此时没有意识到，历史将表明，该位置是“整个过程中最薄弱的环节”。

Compression rod hook sites were prepared. At each of the selected levels an individual compression hook securely attached to a holder was placed around the transverse process "as close to the pedicle as possible." The hook's sharp shoe served to "dissect the costotransverse ligament off the bone as the hook is worked into place." At the caudal end the compression hook was often placed under the lamina, but only "below the level of the second vertebra because of the risk of penetration of the dura in the region of the caudal extremity of the spinal cord." The compression rod was placed first. A small or large compression rod with hooks and nuts at the appropriate levels was assembled. The individual hooks used in preparation were removed and the upper hooks placed first. Placement was aided by the hook and rod holders. The hooks were moved to a tight position by advancing the hexagonal nuts. A distraction rod of the proper length was selected. "If it appears that these (concave) joints will be covered by the rod and spine fusion is thought indicated, a fusion of the facet block type (using spinous process grafts) is performed on this side before the rod is placed." The distraction rod was back entered through the upper hook until the lower hook could be engaged. This maneuver could have been impeded by concave ribs when scoliosis was accompanied by kyphosis. The solutions Harrington offered were depression of the ribs using a three-point bending technique and, if needed, osteotomy of the prominent ribs. "The distraction and compression systems are tightened gradually in orderly sequence until both mechanisms are tight." The hooks were locked into place by crimping the compression hooks and placing a looped wire between the upper distraction hook and the adjacent ratchet below. If fusion was to be performed and the patient's condition permitted, a Hibbs-type fusion (decortication including facets and no supplemental bone) was done. A brief description of supplemental techniques (e. g., sacral balancing forces and overlapping distraction and compression forces) was provided.

压缩棒钩部位的准备。在每个被选择的节段，于横突周围放置装在持钩器上的独特的压缩钩，并“尽可能靠近椎弓根”。钩的钩锋可以“将肋横突韧带从骨上剥离”。在尾端，压缩钩通常放置在椎板下，但仅低于“第二椎体的水平面，高于此水平有穿透脊髓尾端区域硬脊膜的风险”。第一步是放置压缩棒。将不同大小的压缩棒和钩和螺母组装起来。去除用于准备的独特钩，随后先放置上方钩，由持钩和持棒器帮助放置。通过六角螺母旋紧钩，同时，选择适当长度的撑开棒。“如果这些（凹侧）小关节均被棒所覆盖，且有融合指征，那么在放棒之前就应该在侧面进行小关节的融合（使用棘突骨）。”撑开棒通过上方钩进入，直到下钩啮合。但是，当侧凸伴有脊柱后凸时，凹侧肋骨可能会妨碍操作。哈灵顿提供的解决方案是使用三点弯曲技术压低肋骨，或者施行凸起肋骨截骨术，使“撑开和压缩系统按顺序逐步锁紧”。通过卷曲压缩钩，并在上部撑开钩和下方相邻棘齿之间放置一根环形钢丝，共同锁定钩。如果有融合指征且患者状况允许，则进行希伯斯融合术（包括关节面的去皮质，不额外植骨）。文章也提供了对补充技术的简要描述（例如，骶骨平衡力、重叠的干扰和压缩力）。

Postoperative management was described in some detail. The elastic adhesive compression bandage was left on at least five days. At ten to fourteen days the sutures were removed and a molded plaster body cast applied. *See figure 6.10.* After discharge the patient was kept supine allowing logrolling for six to eight weeks. Ambulation was then allowed, and the cast was kept on for a minimum of three to five months. After cast removal, activity was restricted for another three months with no athletics or physical education for another three months.

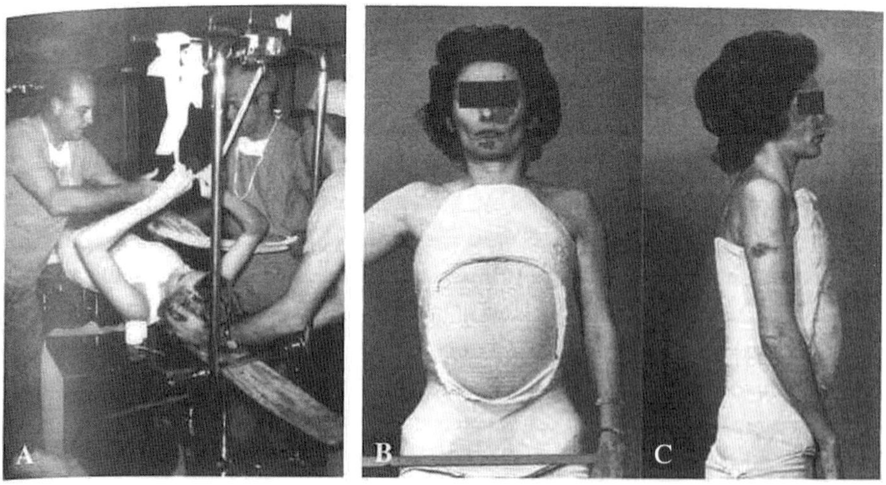

Figure 6.10 ***Molded body cast. A. Application. B. Frontal view showing ample cutout to accommodate breathing. C. Lateral view. (Harrington Archives)***
图 6.10 模制石膏体模 A. 石膏制作;B. 正面,展示了为保持呼吸所预留的切口;C. 侧面(哈灵顿档案馆)

对术后处理进行了详细的描述。弹性绷带至少保留5天。在术后第10~14天时，拆除缝线，并制作石膏支具。(图6.10) 出院后，患者保持持续仰卧位6~8周，之后再下床活动。石膏固定至少3~5个月。石膏拆除后，限制体育活动3个月。

Although individual patient data for each patient group were provided in three detailed tables, there was no documentation of curve size or of follow-up intervals. In Group Ⅰ, thirteen of the nineteen patients operated on had attempted fusion. Four (33%) of the thirteen had pseudarthrosis. No infections were reported. In Group Ⅱ, 30 of the 42 patients had attempted fusion. Three (10%) of 30 had pseudarthrosis. One infection was reported in the 42 patients. In Group Ⅲ, 2 of the 68 patients operated on died, one from obstructive bronchial edema 4 hours after intubation and one 6 days postoperative from cardiac failure and cor pulmonale of 9 months' duration. Of the 66 surviving patients, 2 (3%) developed infection, and of the 56 that had fusion 3 (5%) developed pseudarthrosis. The ages of the ten non-fused patients ranged from nine to nineteen years. Based on a comparison of Groups Ⅰ, Ⅱ, and Ⅲ, Harrington concluded that "spine fusion combined with instrumentation and prolonged immobilization in a plaster jacket (Group Ⅲ) gave better results than those obtained with no cast and no immobilization in Groups Ⅰ and Ⅱ. The results indicate that spine instrumentation is a useful tool in the treatment of spine instability." Harrington's first conclusion was clearly justified. However, his second conclusion could not be inferred from the data, as there was not a comparable group treated without instrumentation. Although the results based on pseudarthrosis would appear to compare favorably to the most recent published studies of Risser[121] and Moe[122] lack of follow-up interval and curve magnitude data limited the usefulness of comparison, and indeed Harrington did not try. Validation of Harrington's second conclusion would require further documentation.

尽管三个表格提供了每个患者组的详细数据，但未记录脊柱侧凸的程度及随访的间隔。在第Ⅰ组中，19名手术患者中有13名尝试融合术。13名中有4名(33%)出现假关节。没有报告感染。在第Ⅱ组中，42名患者中有30名尝试融合术。其中有3名患者(10%)出现假关节。报告了1名患者感染。在第Ⅲ组中，68名手术患者中有2名患者死亡，1名死于插管后4小时出现的阻塞性支气管水肿，1名死于术后6天出现的心力衰竭和持续9个月的肺心病。在66名存活患者中，2名(3%)发生了感染。在56名融合患者中，3名(5%)产生了假关节。

10名未融合患者的年龄范围为9~19岁。基于对第Ⅰ、Ⅱ和Ⅲ组的比较，哈灵顿得出了结论：“首先，脊柱融合内固定联合石膏支具长期固定（第Ⅲ组）的结果优于第Ⅰ和Ⅱ组中无石膏和无固定的结果。其次，结果表明，脊柱内固定是治疗脊柱失稳的有效工具。”第一个结论显然是有道理的。然而，他的第二个结论却无法从现有数据中推断出来，因为没有设置一个未使用器械的对照组。虽然哈灵顿器械减少假关节的结果似乎比里泽[121]和莫[122]最近发表的研究结果更好，但由于缺乏随访时间和侧凸角度而减弱了哈灵顿的结论的说服力，事实上哈灵顿并没有强有力的证据证明第二个结论，仍需要进一步的论证。

The article did not completely address Harrington's then current opinion about the use of instrumentation without fusion. In the discussion he stated, "On the basis of my experience to date, I believe that a progressive scoliosis in a child less than ten years old can be managed with the apparatus alone without fusion, whereas in a child more than ten years old fusion should usually be done at the time of the initial correction. No form of treatment including the method described here with or without spine fusion can be considered definitive in a child whose axial skeleton is still growing." But the article did not make any statement about what should be done as the child grew, and, of course, the rods didn't. This was addressed in his thesis. "By a minor surgical procedure at intervals ranging from six months to eighteen months, a dimensional adjustment can be made in the instrument as required by growth.[123] Harrington seldom mentioned scheduled, periodic lengthening of the rods. Nor did he address what to do when growth was over. These seeming oversights are probably best attributed to his hypothesis that once stabilized and partially corrected the scoliotic spine would grow straighter.

这篇文章并没有完全阐明哈灵顿对非融合手术的看法。在讨论部分，他提出，“根据目前的经验，10岁以下儿童的进展性脊柱侧凸可以单独使用器械进行矫形治疗，无须融合，而10岁以上儿童通常应在初次矫正时进行融合。对于中轴骨仍在生长的儿童，目前仍没有公认的治疗策略。”但这篇文章并没有对儿童成长过程中的治疗方案作出指导，也不涉及治疗的钩棒系统。不过他在文中提到，“每隔6到18个月进行一次小的外科手术，就可以根据生长的需要对器械进行尺寸调整。”[123]哈灵顿很少提及定期延长的生长棒。他也没有提到生长发育结束后该怎么办。这些看似疏忽的部分可能归因于他的假设，即一旦脊柱侧凸部分得到矫正且稳定后，脊柱会自发生长变直。

Data provided in the article allowed an estimation of the likelihood of post-polio. The three operated on groups came from a total group of approximately 3,000 poliomyelitis patients, of whom 400 or 13% developed scoliosis, less than the 30% (150 of 500) already reported.[124] In Harrington's series the prevalence of scoliosis surgery was 3% (85 of 3,000) overall and 21% (85 of 400) in scoliotics. It was possible, even likely, that the percent of patients with post-polio scoliosis who would eventually require surgery was a little low. While the polio epidemics ended in 1955 with the advent of the Salk vaccine, Harrington's series extended to the end of 1960. Even though it was unlikely many or any of the survivors who were going to develop scoliosis hadn't, it was probable that some with scoliosis would progress to the need for surgery. Counterbalancing this was the frequency of post-polio scoliosis in Harrington's three groups, which decreased from 74% (14 of 19) with known diagnosis in Group Ⅰ and 88% (37 of 42) in Group Ⅱ to 50% (34 of 68) in Group Ⅲ. Also, it was likely that some of the patients operated on by Harrington, especially in 1960, lived outside the Houston acute poliomyelitis catchment area. These considerations made it unlikely that large numbers of additional patients from the 3,000 total poliomyelitis survivors or the 400 of them with scoliosis would need surgery for scoliosis. This relative infrequency of post-polio scoliosis requiring surgery underscored the importance of the prolonged polio epidemics in Houston in creating the atmosphere necessary to initiate and sustain Harrington's creative process leading to a dramatic, even radical, departure from accepted surgical practice.

文章中提供的数据可以预估继发于脊髓灰质炎的脊柱侧凸的概率以及其侧凸后需要手术治疗的概率。这三个手术组的数据来自大约 3 000 名脊髓灰质炎患者，其中 400 名（13%）发生了脊柱侧凸，低于之前已经报道的 30%（150/500）。[124] 在哈灵顿的研究中，脊柱手术率为 3%（85/3 000），患有脊柱侧凸的手术率为 21%（85/400）。有很大可能，继发于脊髓灰质炎的脊柱侧凸患者最终需要手术的比例较低。1955 年索尔克疫苗的出现终结了脊髓灰质炎的流行，而哈灵顿的系列研究一直延续到 1960 年年底。尽管大多数幸存者不太可能发生脊柱侧凸，但也有一些患者会发展到需要手术的地步。与此对应，在哈灵顿的三个手术组中，继发于脊髓灰质炎的脊柱侧凸的发生率从Ⅰ组的 74%（14/19）和Ⅱ组的 88%（37/42）下降到Ⅲ组的 50%（34/68）。此外，哈灵顿进行手术的部分患者，特别是 1960 年的患者，很可能住在休斯敦急性脊髓灰质炎覆盖区域之外。这使得 3 000 名脊髓灰质炎幸存者中的大部分人，甚至 400 名存在脊柱侧凸患者中的大多数人都不需要手术治疗。继发于脊髓灰质炎的脊柱侧凸需要手术的情况相对较少，这突出了在休斯敦进行长期流行病调查的重要性，休斯敦成为启发和延续哈灵顿的创新过程的土壤，从而彻底改变了曾被公认的外科处理办法。

Whether or not the late afternoon users' meeting Zimmer had been asked to arrange was held during the 1962 AAOS annual meeting in Chicago isn't documented. What is well documented is that Harrington gave his first AAOS Instructional Course Lecture (Lecture #44) at that January meeting.[125,126] Members applied to present these lectures, and selection was competitive. The previous year John Moe had presented a 90-minute course by himself that must have been well received as not only was he asked to return, but the course time had also been increased to the full 3 hours. His invitation for Harrington to join him was an important indicator of Harrington's growing acceptance. Their course was simply titled "Treatment of Scoliosis," and Harrington's portion was "Spine Instrumentation in the Management of Spine Deformity and Instability." By this time idiopathic scoliosis had emerged as the most common type of scoliosis, and post-polio scoliosis was rapidly receding. Many different causes of scoliosis and other spinal deformities were being identified, some with very challenging problems, so a new subspecialty was emerging.

1962 年的美国骨科医师学会年会在芝加哥举办，捷迈安排的咨询会是否举行并没有记录在案。但有记录在案的是，哈灵顿在 1 月的会议上进行了第一次美国骨科医师学会教学课程讲座（ICL）#44。[125,126]许多会员申请参加这次讲座，入选名额的竞争也非常激烈。前一年，约翰·莫亲自讲授了 90 分钟，之后他不仅被重新邀请返台，而且时间也增加到了 3 个小时，课程的受欢迎程度可见一斑。莫邀请哈灵顿参加讲座是哈灵顿被逐渐认可的一个重要标志。他们的课程标题很简单，即“脊柱侧凸的治疗”，哈灵顿讲授的部分是“脊柱器械在脊柱畸形和失稳中的应用”。此时特发性脊柱侧凸已成为最常见的脊柱侧凸类型，继发于脊髓灰质炎的脊柱侧凸正迅速减少。脊柱侧凸和其他引起脊柱畸形的原因被逐一揭示，其中伴随着一些非常具有挑战性的问题，一个新的亚专业出现了。

But possibly the most important event in Harrington's professional life as 1962 dawned was his change of practice status. In writing to Dean Olson, Spencer recommended that effective January 1, 1962, Harrington be considered fulltime in his appointment as assistant professor in the Department of Rehabilitation.[127] "On that date he is relinquishing his private [non-scoliosis] practice and restricting his activities to consultative work solely in scoliosis. The requirements of his contribution to this important field are occupying his full attention. The scope of the national recognition of his surgery is attested to in the attached schedule of his teaching activities and demonstration visits to other medical centers and visitors to this Center. I was privileged to attend his grand rounds, teaching seminar, and surgical demonstration at Johns Hopkins recently and was proud of his recognition there. On this occasion, Doctor Mark Ravitch complimented him on a major contribution to surgery." In closing, Spencer announced his recommendation to the Administrative and Academic Council that Harrington's academic rank be increased to the unqualified rank of associate professor beginning with the coming academic year.

1962 年，对哈灵顿职业生涯影响最大的事可能是年初他的调职。斯宾塞在给迪恩·奥尔森的信中建议，从 1962 年 1 月 1 日起，任命哈灵顿为康复科全职的助理教授。[127] "从那一天起，他将放弃他的私人（非脊柱侧凸）实践，并将其工作范围限于脊柱侧凸的咨询。他需要全身心地投入在这一重要领域。他的手术得到了全国的认可，体现在他的教学工作和络绎不绝的学术访问中。我有幸参加了他最近在约翰·霍普金斯大学的演讲、教学研讨会和手术演示，并为他感到自豪。在此，马克·拉维奇医生称赞了他对外科手术行业做出的重大贡献。"最后，斯宾塞向行政和学术委员会宣布了他的建议：从下一学年开始，哈灵顿晋升为副教授。

Enclosing a copy of his Olson letter, Spencer also wrote to Michael E. DeBakey, Professor and Chair of the Department of Surgery, suggesting that he make a similar request for Harrington's joint appointment in surgery.[128] He commented that this request "is consistent with the great amount of time he contributes to the College's orthopedic program at the Institute. It will allow him to set up a scoliosis follow-up teaching clinic and devote more time to his research projects and his scoliosis surgery." Harrington's work time was to be divided with two half-day clinics in the new Baylor clinic building when it was completed, TIRR, and Methodist Hospital. If Olson or DeBakey responded, the letters are not in the archives, and Harrington did not detail his academic status in his curriculum vitae. In fact, the surviving correspondence doesn't allow precise documentation of Harrington's academic positions. He joined the Baylor faculty in 1947, or possibly 1946, and was promoted to assistant (probably clinical assistant) professor of rehabilitation on July 1, 1959, at an annual salary of $8,400.[129] At that time he was also a clinical assistant professor of orthopedic surgery. He was promoted to unrestricted associate professor of rehabilitation and probably orthopedic surgery too in 1962 or 1963. The salary level was not mentioned. Sometime later, a July 1969 letter confirmed his appointment as associate professor, Division of Orthopedic Surgery and Department of Rehabilitation, with an annual salary of $19,500.[130]

斯宾塞还附上了一封写给奥尔森的信的副本，写给外科学教授兼主任迈克尔·E. 德贝基，建议他提出类似的请求，邀请哈灵顿与他共同参与手术。[128]他说，这一要求“与他在学院的骨科项目中投入的大量时间是相称的。这将使他能够建立脊柱侧凸随访教学门诊，并将更多的时间用于他的研究项目和脊柱侧凸手术中”。哈灵顿的工作时间被分成两个半天的门诊，分别位于得克萨斯州康复与研究中心的新的贝勒门诊大楼，以及卫理公会医院。即使奥尔森或德贝基做出了回应，档案中也无法查询，哈灵顿在简历中也没有详细说明他的学术职称。事实上，现存的信件并不能准确记录哈灵顿的学术职称。他于 1947 年或可能是 1946 年加入了贝勒大学医学院，1959 年 7 月 1 日被提升为康复医学助理教授（也可能为康复医学临床助理教授），年薪 8 400. 129 美元。[129]当时，他还是骨科的临床助理教授。他在 1962 或是 1963 年被提升为康复医学（或同为骨科学）副教授。工资未知。一段时间后，1969 年 7 月的一封信证实了他被任命为骨科和康复科副教授，年薪 19 500 美元。[130]

The first instrument correspondence of 1962 did not come until April. It included a bending tool for the 1/4"-diameter strut bars (distraction rods), and Hite raised the question of the need for two benders.[131] Harrington responded that there had been a lot of inquiry about bending and that he had put them off until he could see the instrument. Unfortunately, Harrington phoned his comments so his response isn't known.[132] In July Hite sent a print and three samples of a C-washer to replace the loop of wire as a safety stop on the ratchet rod.[133] It had been submitted by their West Coast sales representative, who had encountered "slight dissatisfaction" with the wire method. Harrington said he did this "over eight years ago" and objected to it because it was too small, hard to keep track of, got lost in the wound, was hard to retrieve, and required a special instrument. It was "added gadgetry."[134] He had also tried threaded versions for threaded rods and had the same objections. "I personally do not want it in any part of the present system." In October Hite sent twelve pieces of a round-tippect version of the #1251 strut bar hook (distraction), which became the #1253 hook, and twelve C-washers for use as safety locks.[135] There was no instrument to apply the C-washer. Surprisingly, Harrington approved both for the catalog.[136] He did push back slightly by writing, "I don't feel that it would be wise to introduce too many new gadgets until I have written the indications for their use and reasons changes [are] being made. In lieu of this fact, just use your own judgment as regard the cataloguing."

1962 年，哈灵顿和捷迈有关器械的第一次交流发生在 4 月。它包括直径 1/4 英寸的支撑棒（撑开棒）的弯棒工具，海特提出了需要两个弯棒器的问题。[131]哈灵顿回答说，有很多关于弯棒的问题，他准备先看到器械，然后再去处理这些问题。因为哈灵顿是通过电话给出的意见，所以具体内容不得而知。[132] 7 月，海特从公司寄来了一个 C 形垫圈的设计图纸和三个样品，用来替换棘齿棒上用作安全制动装置的线圈。[133]这是由他们的西海岸销售代表寄出的，他们对线圈方式感到"稍微不满"。哈灵顿说，他"8 年多前"就做过了，但他没有采用，因为它太小，一旦在刀口里丢失，就很难找回，而且安装需要一种特殊的器械。它是一种"附加品"。[134]他也曾尝试过螺纹棒的版本，但也有同样的问题。"我个人不希望它出现在当前的手术器械系统里。" 10 月，海特从公司寄来了 12 个圆形的#1251 支撑棒钩（撑开），后来成为#1253 钩，以及 12 件用作安全锁的 C 形垫圈，[135]但并没有出现 C 形垫圈的安装工具。令人咋舌的是哈灵顿居然批准了这两个产品。[136]他确实稍微反对了一下："我觉得在写明使用说明和改进原因之前，引入太多新的小工具是不明智的。但最终还是由你们自己决定吧。"

Following a phone conversation in December, Harrington was full of ideas and suggestions.[137] One was that Zimmer make a protractor, which he characterized as "an advertising gimmick for scoliosis." Some others were more substantive, including the development of an outrigger distraction force instrument with a pressure gauge. Almost as an aside he mentioned a change in distraction rod design, but offered no details. He again recommended that no more universal hooks (#1260) be made. The blunt and sharp distraction hooks were again discussed. Moe's center keel version of the #1251 distraction hook, which had a chisel leading edge, was assigned catalog #1252.

在 12 月的一次电话交谈后，哈灵顿的脑海里充满了新的想法和建议。[137]其中之一是捷迈制作了一个量角器，哈灵顿将其描述为"脊柱侧凸的广告噱头"。其他一些更具实用性，包括开发了带有测压表的外撑开器。此外，他还提出了一个改进设计的撑开棒，但没有提供细节。他再次建议不再制造通用钩（#1260），并再次讨论了撑开钩钝性和锐性的问题。莫的#1251 撑开钩的另一个版本，它的前缘有一个凹槽，被编号为#1252。

Beginning in 1962 and continuing for eleven years, Harrington prepared a book of selected academic pursuits during the year. A limited number of hardback copies and far more softbound copies were printed, and he mailed them to colleagues using the instrumentation. How they were paid for isn't documented, but presumably it came from the royalty fund. The 1962 edition contains threg manuscripts, one of which is his instructional course lecture.[138] It was largely a restatement of his techniques as described in his *JBJS Am.* paper. He did go into a little more detail about his evolution to a more gradual mobilization of the patients after surgery in an effort to decrease postoperative loss of correction, which he estimated to be 5° to 15°. The lecture contained a large before-and-after radiograph and clinical photo gallery of twelve adolescent idiopathic scoliosis patients, organized into three groups based on curve severity: moderate, moderately severe, and severe curves with four examples for each group, one each of the four basic curve patterns (lumbar, thoracic, double, and thoracolumbar). The five curves of the moderate group averaged 49° pre- and 9° postoperative for a remarkable 82% correction. For the moderately severe group the numbers were 81° pre- and 22° postoperative, a likewise remarkable 73% correction. *See figure 6.11*. For the severe group the numbers were 100° pre- and 61° postoperative, a relatively disappointing 39% correction. However, the average age of the patients with severe curves was considerably older at twenty-four years as compared to fifteen years four months (moderate group) and fifteen years (moderately severe group). In any event, such correction was unheard of without instrumentation.

自 1962 年起，11 年间，哈灵顿编写了一本年度学术精选集。印刷了限量的精装本和更多的软皮普通本，并邮寄给同事。出版费用没有记录，但很可能是来自版税基金。1962 年版包含三篇手稿，其中一篇是他的教学课程讲座的讲稿。[138]这在很大程度上是对他的《骨和关节外科杂志》（美国卷）中描述的技术的重申。他更详细地介绍了他嘱咐患者术后要逐步恢复活动，以增强矫形效果，他估计矫形损失为 5°至 15°。讲座包含了 12 名青少年特发性脊柱侧凸患者手术前后 X 光片和临床照片集锦，根据侧凸的严重程度将其分为三组：中度组、中重度组和重度组。每组有四个案例，四种基本侧凸类型（腰弯、胸弯、双弯和胸腰弯）各一个。中度组的 5 例柯布度数在术前平均 49°，术后平均 9°，矫正率为 82%。中重度组术前 81°，术后 22°，矫正率 73%。（图 6.11）对于重度组，术前和术后角度分别为 100°和 61°，矫正率为相对令人失望的 39%。然而，严重侧凸患者的平均年龄为 24 岁，明显高于 15 岁 4 个月（中度组）和 15 岁（中重度组）。无论如何，在曾经没有矫形器械的时代，这样良好的手术效果是闻所未闻的。

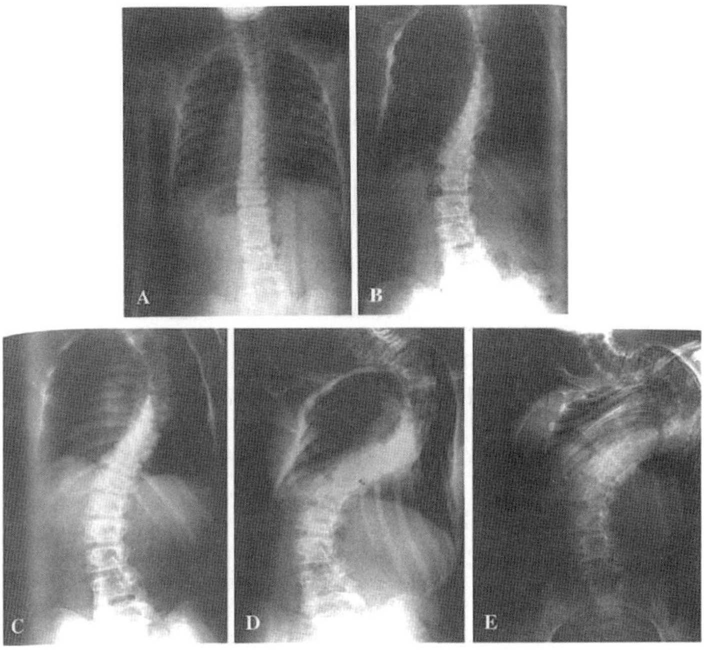

Figure 6.11 *Standing preoperative and recumbent postoperative spine radiographs viewed posteranterior of four patients Harrington considered to have moderately severe idiopathic scoliosis illustrating the four characteristic curve patterns, from left to right, lumbar, thoracic, double, and thoracolumbar. Their average age was 14 years, and the average of their 5 major curves was 81° pre- and 22° postoperative.* (*Harrington Archives*)
图 6.11　哈灵顿认为中重度特发性脊柱侧凸的四名患者术前站立和术后卧位脊柱 X 光片，从左到右分别显示了腰弯、胸弯、双弯和胸腰椎弯曲的四种特征弯曲。他们的平均年龄为 14 岁，5 条主要弯曲的平均值为术前 81°和术后 22°（哈灵顿档案馆）

Fifteen additional patients with a variety of pathologies, including several with complications, were well documented. Three examples, illustrating the variety of issues encountered, were briefly presented. One was a 6-year-old girl with probable infantile idiopathic scoliosis (not congenital idiopathic as captioned), who presented with an 81° right thoracic curve, fatigue, and shortness of breath. The curve was corrected to 31° with instrumentation and no fusion. *See figure 6.12.* Fatigue and shortness of breath were gone, but at one year she had lost 5° of correction. She was being treated in a Milwaukee brace. He closed with "problems still remain for the next seven years, but seem manageable." Harrington included her in a paper being written at that time and stated in a caption, "the instruments will be adjusted ant one-, two- or three year intervals to keep up with her growth."[139] He reported two severe complications. One occurred in a 17-year-old girl with idiopathic scoliosis and a 150° right thoracic major and a 90° left lumbar compensatory curve. The curves were corrected to 93° and 50°, respectively, using two distraction and one compression rod. She awakened with heaviness in her legs that progressed to incomplete paraplegia. Distraction was let down 1/4". This feared complication apparently occurred betwcem patient #129[140] and #200[141]. At the time of the instructional course lecture in 1962 she had partially recovered and was the only patient with paraplegia in over 400 operations. *See figure 6.13*. In a 1976 interview with John P. O'Brien, Harrington recalled that the patient had 90% recovery of use in one leg, 30% recovery in the other, and bowel and bladder function recovery in five years.[142] The other severe complication occurred in a 22-year-old, female with severe idiopathic thoracolumbar scoliosis, who had a right thoracic curve reduced from 170° to 100° using three distraction rods. Three weeks after returning home she developed vomiting and drowsiness and, after severe vomiting, died. Autopsy revealed extensive pyelonephrosis and hydronephrosis with the ureters dilated four times their normal size, apparently from stretching over the pelvic rim. Both of these patients had large curves and had distraction with two and three rods, respectively. The two deaths previously reported in his 1962 *JBJS Am.* article based on his first 129 patients were again described. One, a patient with post-polio scoliosis, developed a bronchial plug in the recovery room, and the second, a twenty-six-year-old with post-polio scoliosis, who had been on digitalis for over nine months, died of pulmonary edema on the sixth postoperative day.

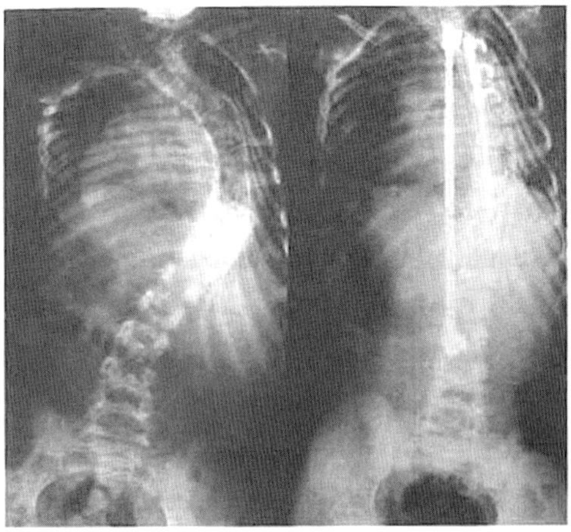

Figure 6. 12 ***Sitting preoperative and postoperative spine radiographs viewed posteroanterior of a six-year-old girl with probable infantile idiopathic scoliosis following instrumentation without arthrodesis.*** (***Harrington Archives***)
图 6. 12 一个 6 岁女孩的术前和术后脊柱 X 光片，该女孩可能患有婴幼儿特发性脊柱侧凸，在进行器械治疗后没有进行关节融合（哈灵顿档案馆）

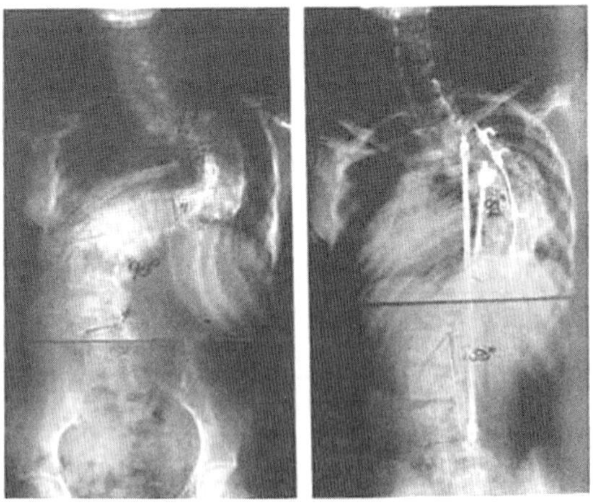

Figure 6. 13 ***Standing preoperative and sitting postoperative spine radiographys viewed posteroanaterior of a seventeen-year-old female with severe idiopathic scoliosis, who developed incomplete paraplegia.*** (***Harrington Archives***)
图 6. 13 一名患有严重特发性脊柱侧凸的 17 岁女性的术前站立和术后坐位脊柱 X 光片，她出现了不完全截瘫（哈灵顿档案馆）

另外还有15名有各种其他疾病的患者，包括几个有并发症的患者，都有很好的记录。他介绍了三个典型案例。其中一个为一名6岁的女童，可能为婴幼儿特发性脊柱侧凸（而非标题中的先天性），胸弯81°，向右侧凸，主诉为易疲劳与呼吸短促。使用内固定和非融合技术矫正至31°。（图6.12）疲劳和呼吸短促症状消失了，但一年后，她的胸弯变成了36°。她正在用密尔沃基支具治疗。哈灵顿的记录以“未来七年可能还会进展，但尚能控制”结尾。哈灵顿在当时撰写的一篇论文中提到了她，并在一个标题中写道，“这些器械将每隔一年、两年或三年进行调整，以跟上她的成长速度。”[139]他报告了两例严重的并发症。其中一例为患有特发性脊柱侧凸的17岁女性，右侧胸弯150°，左侧腰椎代偿弯90°。使用两个撑开棒和一个压缩棒将侧凸角度分别矫正为93°和50°。她醒来时自诉双腿沉重，最终出现不完全瘫痪。撑开棒放松了近1/4英寸。这一严重的并发症也发生在129号[140]患者和200号[141]患者身上。等到1962年的教学课程讲座时，她已经部分康复。她是400多例手术中唯一的截瘫患者。（图6.13）在约翰·P. 奥布赖恩1976年的采访中，哈灵顿回忆说，患者的一条腿恢复了90%，另一条腿恢复了30%，大小便自主功能在五年内得到了恢复。[142]另一例严重并发症发生在一名22岁患有严重的特发性胸腰段脊柱侧凸的女性身上，使用三根撑开棒将右胸弯从170°降至100°。回家三周后，她出现呕吐和嗜睡，在严重的呕吐后死亡。尸检显示重度肾盂肾炎和肾积水，输尿管扩张到正常大小的四倍，显然是由于牵拉超过了骨盆边缘。这两名患者均有较大的侧凸角度，分别采用2根和3根棒撑开。1962年《骨与关节外科杂志》（美国卷）报道了两起死亡事件。文章基于他最初的129名患者进行了再次描述。一个是继发于脊髓灰质炎的脊柱侧凸的患者，在术后恢复室出现支气管堵塞；另一个是26岁的继发于脊髓灰质炎的脊柱侧凸患者，他服用了9个多月的洋地黄，在术后第6天死于肺水肿。

The second presentation in *Scoliosis 1962* was “Principles of Scoliosis: Concept” that had been given at a symposium on scoliosis at the Division of Orthopedic Surgery, University of Florida College of Medicine on March 15, 1962.[143] Apparently his host was William F. Enneking as three days later Harrington did demonstration surgeries on two of Enneking's patients. In the first paragraph of this twenty-one page, twenty-seven figure essay Harrington again stated his hypothesis. “The growing scoliotic spine is vulnerable structural living matter reacting to abnormal physical forces resulting in a deformed functional state. In man, the fulfillment of inherent potential vertebral form lies in dynamic balance. Dynamic balance of the axial skeleton exists only when the bone growth process is sound and structural equilibrium is maintained by musculature adequately coordinated. The pathogenesis of the growing scoliotic spine is loss of mechanical stability through asymmetrical growth of the endochondral segments at their load transfer areas." He discussed the "physical chemistry of structure" and the "mechanics of gross structure." Early in the mechanics section he restated his view of the importance of dynamic balance. "The healthy human spine will grow to an inherent potential form providing dynamic balance prevails throughout its perod of growth. Dynamic balance is present when bone (living) structure is symmetrical and kinetic forces affecting the growing spine are maintained in suitable equilibrium by reciprocal action of adequate musculature coordinated by the central nervous system." Musculature and the central nervous system were not discussed in more detail. Rather, the focus was on his concept of the effects of time and asymmetrical force resulting in asymmetrical growth of the endochondral bone of the facet joints. During his presentation he showed the histology of same level concave and convex inferior facet processes removed at the time of surgery that he interpreted as confirming his hypothesis. The seeds of a valuable collaboration had been sown. Enneking, fifteen years younger, was well on his way to becoming an internationally acclaimed orthopedic pathologist and had the laboratory and skills needed to test Harrington's hypothesis. Soon Harrington was providing same level (apex), concave, and convex inferior facet processes for histological study. But it would be a while before the results were known.

《脊柱侧凸1962》的第二个报告是“脊柱侧凸的原理：概念”，该报告于1962年3月15日在佛罗里达大学医学院骨科脊柱侧凸研讨会上发表。[143]邀请他的是威廉·F. 恩内金，并且三天后哈灵顿在恩内金的两名患者身上演示了手术。在这篇长达21页、内含27幅图的文章的第一段，哈灵顿再次陈述了他的假设。“进展中的脊柱侧凸是脆弱的生物结构，可以对物理应力做出反应，引起功能状态的改变。在人身上，固有潜在椎体形态的实现取决于动态平衡。只有在骨骼生长过程良好、肌肉组织充分协调、维持结构平衡的情况下，中轴骨才存在动态平衡。进展性脊柱侧凸的发病机制是由于软骨内节段在其应力转移区域的不对称生长而导致的失稳。”他讨论了“结构的物理化学”和“大体结构的力学”。在力学部分的开头，他重申了动态平衡的重要性。“健康人的脊柱遵循一种内在的潜在形态，使其在整个生长过程中保持动态平衡。当骨结构是对称的，并在中枢神经系统协调的肌肉组织的作用下，影响脊柱生长的动力保持在适当状态时，即为动态平衡。”肌肉组织和中枢神经系统没有被更详细地讨论。相反，他的重点是时间和不对称力的影响，导致了小关节软骨内骨的不对称生长。在他的演讲中，他展示了在手术时切除的同一节段的凹侧和凸侧的下关节突以证实他的假设。一颗宝贵的协作种子已经播下。比他年轻15岁的恩内金正朝着成为国际知名骨病理学专家的方向迈进，他拥有检验哈灵顿假说所需的设备和技能。不久，哈灵顿提供了相同节段（顶椎）、凹侧和凸侧下关节突来进行组织学研究，但需要一段时间后才知道结果。

The third essay in *Scoliosis 1962* was "Scoliosis in the Growing Spine," an introductory instructional article for pediatricians, which was published in 1963.[144] He wrote that spine fusion always accompanied instrumentation and was always followed by a east, usually for twelve weeks. The case of a four-year-old girl with a severe right thoracic idiopathic scoliosis he had instrumented without fusing was illustrated, possibly confusing the reader. However, he explained this seeming deviation in the caption. "This patient is now being managed in a Milwaukee brace until she reaches nearer to maturity when spine fusion will be done to insure more permanent results. The instruments will be adjusted at one, two or three year intervals to keep up with growth."

《脊柱侧凸1962》中的第三篇文章是《生长中的脊柱侧凸》，这是一篇针对儿科医生的科普文章，发表于1963年。[144]他写道，脊柱融合术通常需要器械固定，并且术后还需要进行12周的石膏支具治疗。一个案例为患有严重的特发性脊柱侧凸的4岁女孩，进行了非融合矫形手术。这个案例很可能会使读者难以理解。但是，他文中也作出了解释："这名患者现在使用密尔沃基支具治疗，待其接近成年时将进行脊柱融合术，以确保更持久的效果。这些内固定将每隔一年、两年或三年进行调整，以跟上生长的步伐。"

Harrington continued his extensive travel and teaching schedule throughout 1962. Excluding the annual meeting of the AAOS, he was away from Houston for 34 days on 7 trips to 14 cities in North America. On these trips he performed at least fifteen demonstration operations, provided numerous consultations, and made several podium presentations. In addition, he hosted a growing number of visiting surgeons from North America and many international visitors.

1962年，哈灵顿继续他的外出访问和教学计划。除去美国骨科医师学会的年度会议，他离开休斯敦34天，外出7次，前往了北美的14个城市。在这些行程中，他进行了至少15次演示手术，提供了多次咨询，并做了几次演讲。此外，他还接待了越来越多的来自北美的外科医生和许多国际访客。

In the years 1960 through 1962 Harrington Spine Instrumentation was introduced and was increasingly being accepted as a reasonable additional option for the treatment of scoliosis. However, not everyone was convinced as he kept modifying his technique. Harrington was doing his best to teach the new technique, even as he was still learning a lot about scoliosis and its treatment. But, he had a "sincere respect for the extent of the surgery required to apply instrumentation" andl commitment to the idea that "good results are the reflection of effort andl understanding applied through a prolonged period of time."[145] For the first two years after his instrumentation was introduced at the AOA annual meeting on June 2, 1960, he arranged with Zimmer to limit sales to surgeons until they had "observed a demonstration of the procedure."[146] Harrington's schedule shows that he worked hard to make himself available for surgical demonstrations and other teaching opportunities assuring an orderly release of Harrington Spine Instrumentation to the surgical community. In retrospect, he could be seen as initiating the role of the surgeon as a champion of his products.

在1960—1962年间，哈灵顿脊柱器械问世，并被越来越多地的外科医生所接受，成为脊柱侧凸的合理治疗方案。然而，并不是所有人都对他的器械表示信服，所以他仍在不断改进自己的技术。哈灵顿尽力传授这项新技术，尽管他自己仍在学习很多关于脊柱侧凸及其治疗的相关知识。但是，他“严格尊重手术器械的手术适应证”，并坚信“良好的结果来源于长时间应用的努力和理解”。[145] 1960年6月2日，即他在美国骨科学会年会上介绍矫形器械的两年后，他与捷迈达成了协议，手术器械必须在外科医生“观摩到手术演示”后才能向他们销售。[146]哈灵顿的日程表显示，他通过努力，获得了参加手术演示和其他教学的机会，确保哈灵顿脊柱器械在外科学界的有序发布。回想起来，他可以被看作是以外科医生的身份，成为该器械的第一个拥护者。

（郭辰 译　刘海鹰 初同伟 刘亚军 审校）

7

VALIDATION (1963-65)

a good man with a good idea[1]

验证 (1963—1965)

智者出高见[1]

For a new medical treatment, it is a long leap from acceptance to validation as safe and effective and further still to reach proof that the new treatment is more effective than the natural course of the condition or the existing methods to treat it. As an example, for centuries therapeutic bleeding was an accepted treatment for almost every serious illness encountered. It had many prominent champions, lacked competition from the few other therapeutic methods available, and was lucrative to the practitioner. But, gradually therapeutic bleeding was discredited as being worse than no treatment at all.[2]

对于一种新的治疗方法而言，从被接受到验证其安全有效，再到进一步证明该方法可干预疾病的自然进程或优于现有治疗方法，是一个漫长的过程。例如，几个世纪以来，放血疗法几乎是所有严重的疾病的公认治疗方法。当时，这种方法拥有许多著名的支持者，几乎没有其他可用的治疗方法与之竞争。并且，这种方法对从业者来说也有利可图。但是，人们之后逐渐认识到放血疗法的效果比完全不采取治疗更糟糕。[2]

When a disease often terminates in death, it is relatively easy to determine if a treatment has been effective. But, when a disease process seldom results in death, it is very difficult to tell if a therapy has changed the natural history of the condition. In these cases surrogate measures are used to determine the safety and efficacy of a particular therapeutic method. These measures may be related to the therapeutic process, including operative time, blood loss, wound infection, unplanned reoperation, and pseudarthrosis (a very important measure when successful fusion is the goal). More recently, these measures may be related directly to objective patient outcome variables, such as physical performance, or subjective measures, such as the patient's perceived quality of life as measured using validated questionnaires. There are two general experimental designs to evaluate medical therapeutic effectiveness: the newer randomized controlled trial and the older observational study. The former is generally considered the better validation method. One of its strongest features is that the patient and often the evaluation personnel can be made unaware of the treatment received, which is called blinding. Though difficult, blinding is usually possible in medication research, but in therapeutic methodology research it is frequently impossible. Other problems associated with the latter include study population recruitment, patient preference, surgeon preference, and expense. For these reasons therapeutic methodology validation is more often sought through observational studies based on the comparison of two case series addressing the same problem.

如果一种疾病通常会导致死亡，那么确定它的一种治疗方法是否有效就相对容易。但是当一种疾病很少导致死亡时，判断相应治疗是否有效干预了疾病的自然进程是很困难的。在这些情况下，采用一些替代指标可以辅助判断某一治疗方法的安全性和有效性。这些指标可能与治疗过程有关，包括手术时间、失血量、伤口感染、非计划再次手术与假关节形成（融合是否成功是一项重要评估指标）。目前，这些替代指标可能与患者客观的治疗结果直接相关，例如患者的身体机能；或与主观评价有关，如使用公认的调查问卷来评估患者对生活质量的主观感受。现有两种常用于评估治疗效果的验证实验设计：相对新兴的随机对照试验和相对经典的观察性研究试验。随机对照试验被公认是更好的验证方法。该方法的一个突出特点是患者和评估人员均不知晓患者接受了何种治疗，称为盲法。盲法研究难度较大，在药物研究中通常可行，但在治疗方法学研究中常常无法实现。这是由于治疗方法学中包括研究人群招募、患者意向、术者个人倾向和治疗费用等一系列问题。由于上述原因，治疗方法学的验证常通过观察性研究进行，即给予患有同一疾病的不同群体以不同治疗，然后观察、对比治疗效果，进而得出结论。

The principal criticism of observational studies is that they tend to overestimate the treatment effect, although this has been called into question recently[3]. Just like the randomized, all observational studies are not created equal. Ideal studies include case series enrolled prospectively and treated concurrently by the same treatment team or teams. In actual practice, concurrent enrollment is frequently difficult because of the evolutionary nature of surgical therapeutic methodology innovation. In reality many observational studies were and still are based on historical, retrospective data for either one or both study groups. This was the design of the 1941 AOA "End-Result Study of the Treatment of Idiopathic Scoliosis". It resulted in two clear messages: "69 percent of the cases at the end result were rated fair or poor" and "correction by the turnbuckle cast and subsequent fusion has yielded better results in this series than have other types of treatment."[4] They provided a beacon for treatment improvement for the next two decades.

对观察性研究的主要批评是它们倾向于高估治疗效果，这也是该观点近期被质疑[3]的原因。就像随机对照研究一样，所有观察性研究的情况也不尽相同。在理想的病例系列中，应前瞻性纳入患者，由相同的一个或多个治疗小组同时治疗。但在实际实践中，由于外科治疗方法常在创新中逐渐进化，通常很难控制患者同时入组。在实际研究中，许多观察性研究至今仍会纳入一组历史回顾性数据进行对照研究，或直接分析两组回顾性数据。这是 1941 年美国骨科学会“特发性脊柱侧凸治疗的最终结果研究”的设计，它产生了两个明确的信息：“最终结果中 69%的病例被认为治疗效果一般或较差”和“采用铰链石膏矫正后进行脊柱融合治疗的病例组相较于采用其他病例组，获得了更好的疗效。”[4]它们为未来二十年的治疗改进指引了方向。

In November 1962 Harrington read his second spine instrumentation paper, "The Management of Scoliosis by Spine Instrumentation: An Evaluation of More Than 200 Cases," before the Section on Orthopedic and Traumatic Surgery at the Southern Medical Association's 56th annual meeting in Miami Beach. His full paper, along with the comments of the assigned discussant, was published in December 1963.[5] An abbreviated version, presented to the Texas Orthopaedics Association in late April 1963 in Dallas, was published later that year,[6] and an even more abbreviated work was the last entry in *Scoliosis 1963*.[7] Harrington began his Miami Beach presentation with a list of questions raised by the study of his first 129 patients: (1) will spine instrumentation function to maintain correction; (2) is spinal fusion mandatory; (3) what is the importance of postoperative management; (4) how is loss of correction explained; and (5) is loss of correction inevitable.[8,9] On the basis of the first report he had concluded that spine instrumentation was biologically well tolerated, spine fusion was indicated in most cases, and fusion was more assured if the patient was immobilized in a molded body cast "for a minimum of six weeks and then allowed gradual mobilization." But problems had persisted, and he discussed them under the headings of instrument problems and spine fusion problems. Instrument problems he largely attributed to variation in surgical technique. Spine fusion problems he was more fatalistic about, stating, "It is quite apparent to the orthopedic world that no procedure of spinal fusion assures one a final result." He believed that "part of the answer to the problem of a total fusion mass lies in the postoperative management of the patient."

1962年11月，美国南方医学学会第五十六届年会在迈阿密海滩举行，哈灵顿在骨科和创伤外科分会前宣读了他的第二篇脊柱内固定论文《脊柱内固定治疗脊柱侧凸：对200多例病例的评估》。他的完整论文连同特邀讨论者的评论于1963年12月发表。[5] 1963年4月下旬，哈灵顿在达拉斯向得克萨斯骨科学会提交了缩略版的论文，并于当年晚些时候发表，[6]更为缩略的版本发表于《脊柱侧凸1963》的最后一章。[7]迈阿密海滩演讲开始时，哈灵顿以他对前129名患者的研究提出了一系列问题：(1) 脊柱内固定能否帮助维持矫正效果；(2) 脊柱融合术是否必须进行；(3) 术后管理为何重要；(4) 如何解释矫正丢失的发生；(5) 矫正丢失是否不可避免。[8,9]在第一份报告的基础上，他得出的结论是脊柱内固定在生物学上具有良好的相容性；在大多数案例下均会施行脊柱融合术，且在定制石膏模具中固定"至少六个星期，然后允许逐步活动"的患者，脊柱融合效果更为稳定。但由于问题一直存在，他分别就内固定和脊柱融合这两大类问题进行了讨论。他主要将内固定问题归因于手术技术的差异。对于脊柱融合问题，他更倾向于宿命论，他说："对于骨科界来说，很明显没有哪种脊柱融合手术可以保证完全达到预期效果。"他认为，"关于最终融合效果的问题，有部分的决定因素存在于患者的术后管理中。"

In "More Than 200 Cases" the one postoperative management variable he focused on was "down time," meaning logrolling in bed only. The constants were "(1) adequate instrumentation, (2) total subperiosteal exposure of the fusion site, (3) Moe technique of fusion on the concave side, (4) decortication of remaining posterior elements with overlap of the fragments obtained by decortication, not unlike the Hibbs procedure,

(5) pressure dressing, (6) molded Plaster of Paris cast from sternal notch to the symphysis when the wound was healed, and (7) no force of gravity loading of the spine until a specified time." He did not indicate whether he was or was not adding bone graft, so it seems likely he did not (later writings would show that he did not).[10] His case series was 208 patients, who were operated on during an unspecified time interval. Of these, 182 had scoliosis, 106 of them with idiopathic scoliosis, 53 with post-polio, and 23 with other. Analysis was limited to 143 patients from the scoliosis group; the other 39 scoliosis patients were operated on as demonstration cases elsewhere in the United States, Canada, and Mexico. Operation details probably don't represent all 143 patients as blood loss was reported for only 72 patients and ranged from 74 mL to 2,300 mL (less than 1,000 mL in 58). The average operating time was 94 minutes (range, 58 to 172 minutes), and the number of vertebrae instrumented was 9.5 (range, 6 to 18 vertebrae). Operative complications reported were infection in six (4.2%), dural tear in three, paraplegia in one, radiculitis in two, and death in one. The patient with paraplegia had a 70% recovery. As described in more detail previously, the death was due to pyelonephritis seven weeks postoperatively. The follow-up interval for the series of 143 patients wasn't given. Instrumentation complications occurred in 19 of 143 patients (13.2%). The breakdown of the nineteen by complication was instrument fracture in 48%, instrument disengagement in 24%, instrument erosion in 18%, intolerance to metal in 5%, and not provided in 5%. Pseudarthrosis occurred in 15 (10.5%) of the 143 patients with 14 related to instrument complications and one to infection.

在对“200 多例病例的评估”报告中，“卧床时间”是他关注的一个术后管理变量，即仅允许在床上翻身活动的时间。常量为“（1）足够时间的内固定，（2）融合部位骨膜下的充分暴露，（3）凹侧采用莫的融合技术，（4）去除剩余脊柱后部骨块，与剥脱获得的骨块混合，与希伯斯手术类似，（5）加压敷料，（6）刀口愈合后由胸骨切迹至耻骨联合部位采用成形石膏矫形，以及（7）在特定时间之前脊柱不承受重力载荷”。他没有说明他在术中是否进行了骨移植，而后来的著作也表明他没有添加骨移植物。[10]他的病例系列共有 208 名患者，他们在非指定的时间段内接受了手术。在这些病人中脊柱侧凸患者 182 名，其中特发性脊柱侧凸 106 例，脊髓灰质炎后脊柱侧凸 53 例，其他 23 例。仅对脊柱侧凸组中的 143 名患者进行分析；其余 39 名脊柱侧凸患者分别在美国、加拿大和墨西哥的其他地方作为手术示范病例。术中细节可能无法代表纳入分析范畴的 143 名患者，因为仅对 72 名患者术中失血情况做了报告，范围从 74 毫升到 2 300 毫升（共 58

名患者少于 1 000 毫升)。平均手术时间为 94 分钟(范围 58~172 分钟),平均固定节段数为 9.5 个(范围为 6~18 个节段)。报告的手术并发症中感染 6 例(4.2%),硬膜撕裂 3 例,截瘫 1 例,神经根炎 2 例,死亡 1 例。截瘫病人最终恢复了 70%。如前所述,患者的死亡是术后 7 周发生的肾盂肾炎导致的。研究未给出 143 名患者的随访间隔。在 143 名患者中有 19 名(13.2%)发生内固定相关并发症。19 名患者中,48%的患者内固定断裂,24%内固定移位,18%内固定腐蚀,5%对金属不耐受,5%原因不明。143 名患者中有 15 名(10.5%)有假关节形成,其中 14 名与内固定并发症相关,1 名与感染相关。

The principal outcome measured was curve correction loss versus "down time, non-gravity" (i.e., bed rest) before a uniform mobilization program. Results were based on patients with one year or more follow-up; absolute Cobb measurements were not given for any time interval. Curve correction loss was reported as the percent loss from the total correction obtained. For example, a correction from 60° to 20° equaled a 40° correction and a loss of 8° to 32° correction equaled a 20% correction loss. In the eight-week down group 50% lost more than 50% of their correction, in the ten-week group 40% lost less than 20%, in the twelve-week group 50% lost less than 20% and 72% lost less than 30%, and in the fourteen-week group 82% lost less than 20%. Based on these findings, Harrington concluded that the non-gravity downtime must be a minimum of three months in a teenager and five months in an adult. Drawing on his accumulated experience, he offered the following observations and recommendations. The instruments could not function in the "mobile axial skeleton" without erosion, disengagement, or fracture. Fusion was mandatory. A bone block was recommended for the concave facets and decortication with supplementary bone either autogenous or homogenous, added to the fusion mass especially in the lower thoracic and lumbar segments. Harrington closed with his plan for the future: "The next 200 cases will be used to establish the effectiveness of a new spinal fusion technique and test the worth of three instrument design changes."

在统一开始下床活动之前,测量的结果主要是用于衡量侧凸矫正丢失与"无重力卧床时间"(即卧床休息)之间的关系。结果基于随访一年或以上的患者数据;没有给出任何时间间隔的绝对柯布测量值。角度校正损失以所获得的总校正的损失百分比来展现。例如,从 60°到 20°共计获得 40°的矫正中,若矫正丢失 8°,最终矫正度数 32°,称为矫正丢失 20%。在一个为期 8 周的随访组中,50%的人矫正丢失超过 50%,在为期 10 周的随访组中,40%的人矫正丢失小于 20%,在 12

周的随访组中，50%的人矫正丢失小于20%，72%的人矫正丢失小于30%，而在14周的随访组中，82%的患者矫正丢失低于20%。基于这些发现，哈灵顿得出了结论，青少年的无重力卧床时间至少为3个月，成人为5个月。他根据自己积累的经验，提出了以下建议：内固定在没有侵蚀、移位或断裂时，无法发挥“移动轴向骨架”作用。脊柱融合术是必要的。对于凹面和剥离处，尤其是在下胸椎和腰椎节段，建议使用骨块填充融合，并用自体骨或同种辅助骨添加到融合块中。哈灵顿总结了他对未来的计划：“接下来的200例病例将用于验证新型脊柱融合技术的有效性，并评估三种内固定设计变化的价值。”

Frank H. Stelling, who was five years younger than Harrington, was the assigned discussant of his presentation. He began by noting that while he had an active scoliosis practice he had never used Harrington Spine Instrumentation, although he had observed Harrington do two surgeries. Stelling noted that fixation of bone by metals had initially been resisted, but after investigation and experience involving numerous complications and fixation types, many good fixations had evolved. He acknowledged the general need for a better method of scoliosis treatment and reviewed some of the shortcomings of the present methods. Stelling credited Harrington's dedication to his work, but commented, "He is endeavoring to do something that nearly every orthopedic surgeon can prove to him is fraught with danger and is probably an impossible situation." After reviewing many of the problems Harrington had covered in his paper, Stelling focused on the technical difficulty of performing both instrumentation and a good surgical fusion. He praised Harrington for accepting that permanent control of the curve required a secure fusion while criticizing Harrington's continuing procedural changes and lack of adequate follow-up. In closing, Stelling encouraged Harrington to continue his studies, but for the time being the procedure was not "ready for any and all to go ahead with. I doubt seriously if this will be the accepted method for the treatment of scoliosis." At the time of Stelling's discussion he had been chief surgeon of the Shriners Hospital in Greenville, South Carolina, for thirteen years. Thus, his views were acknowledged to be those of a well-established orthopaedic educator.

弗兰克·H. 施特林是哈灵顿演讲的特邀讨论者，他比哈灵顿年轻五岁。他首先指出，尽管他观摩过哈灵顿的两次手术，但他在脊柱侧凸治疗从未使用过哈灵顿脊柱内固定器械。施特林指出，金属固定骨骼的方法最初受到了抵制，但这种方法经过涉及众多并发症和固定类型的调查和经验，许多良好的固定方式已经发展起来。他承认对于一种更好的脊柱侧凸治疗方法的需求，并回顾了目前采用的方法的一些缺点。施特林赞扬了哈灵顿对工作的献身精神，但评论："他正在努力做一些几乎所有骨科医生都可以向他证明的事情，这充满了危险，而且可能是无法实现的。"在回顾了哈灵顿论文中提到的许多问题之后，施特林重点关注了同时进行内固定置入和达到良好脊柱融合的技术难度。他赞扬了哈灵顿对于长期控制侧凸需要确切的脊柱融合这一观点的接受，同时批评哈灵顿持续的操作变化和缺乏足够的后续随访的做法。最后，施特林鼓励哈灵顿继续他的研究，但目前该手术方式"还不具备让任何人继续与他一起做的条件。我严重怀疑这是否能成为治疗脊柱侧凸的普适方法"。在施特林应邀进行讨论时，他已经在南卡罗来纳州格林维尔的施赖・纳斯医院担任了 13 年的首席外科医生。因此，他的观点被公认是一位知名的骨科教育家的观点。

As incomplete as the data Harrington provided were, there was still enough to allow a comparison with Moe's 1958 report.[11] In Moe's series, data were reported separately for 130 idiopathic and 136 paralytic (post-polio) scoliosis patients, who were operated on consecutively between 1947 and 1956. One patient was lost to follow-up, and most were followed two to eight years with a few fourteen to eighteen months. In Harrington's series, statistical data were reported for 143 patients with scoliosis operated on in Houston. The exact number with idiopathic scoliosis wasn't given, but appeared to have been about 60% to 70% with most of the rest having paralytic scoliosis. They seemed to have been operated on consecutively and probably from sometime in 1960 to sometime in 1961. The number lost to follow-up was not given nor was the length of follow-up provided beyond the statement that the loss of correction was determined on patients with one year or more follow-up. The one outcome variable that could be compared was pseudarthrosis. In Harrington's patients the prevalence was 10.5%, 15 of 143 patients, 14 of whom were related to instrument complications and 1 to infection. In Moe's series, which Harrington did not cite, considering only his latest evolved articular facet fusion technique with addition of autograft, it was 7% for idiopathic and 14% for the paralytic scoliosis patients.[12] Based on this, the results appear to be similar and provide the earliest, objective validation that Harrington's results were equal to but not better than the best results being reported in a peer-reviewed series. However, Harrington's report was weakened by not documenting the length of follow-up and number of followed-up patients. The critical reader would likely be left with the impression that some patients had not been followed a year and that no patients were followed more than a year. These reporting weaknesses made it likely that the prevalence of pseudarthrosis would increase, invalidating the comparison to the Moe study. It is worth noting that a later analysis of a subgroup of Harrington's patients operated on at about this same time revealed a pseudarthrosis prevalence of 23% at three years' follow-up.[13]

尽管哈灵顿提供的数据不完整，但仍然足以与莫 1958 年的报告进行比较。[11] 在莫的病例系列中，分别报告了 130 名特发性和 136 名麻痹性（脊髓灰质炎后）脊柱侧凸患者的数据，这些患者在 1947 年至 1956 年间接受了手术。一名患者失访，大多数患者随访 2~8 年，部分患者只随访 14~18 个月。在哈灵顿的病例系列中，共报告了 143 名在休斯敦接受手术的脊柱侧凸患者的统计数据。特发性脊柱侧凸病例的确切数字没有给出，但占比约 60%~70%，其余大部分为麻痹性脊柱侧凸。手术可能是在 1960 年到 1961 年期间连续进行。随访的人数没有给出，也没有提供随访的时间长度，只是声明矫正丢失现象仅发生在随访一年或更长时间的患者中。假关节形成是可以比较的一个结果变量。在哈灵顿的患者中，假关节形成的发生率为 10.5%，在 143 名患者中有 15 名，其中 14 名与内固定并发症有关，1 名与感染有关。在莫的病例系列里，仅考虑他采用最新发明的应用自体移植物的关节面融合技术进行治疗的患者，其中特发性脊柱侧凸患者假关节形成率为 7%，麻痹性脊柱侧凸患者假关节形成率为 14%。[12]哈灵顿未引用该结果。两个研究的结果是相似的，哈灵顿的结果等效但不优于同行报告的最佳结果，这是最早且客观的一次验证。然而，哈灵顿的报告因没有记录随访时间和随访患者人数而被诟病。挑剔的读者可能会留下所有患者随访均未满一年的印象。这些缺陷可能使得患者假关节的发生率被低估，因而无法与莫的研究进行比较。值得一提的是，后来对大约在同一时间接受手术的哈灵顿病例系列的患者进行亚组分析显示，在三年的随访中，假关节的发生率为 23%。[13]

Moe's 1958 article had provided a strong endorsement for autograft. Considering only his latest fusion technique, the comparison of no added graft, bone-bank (homolo gous) graft, and autograft (apparently iliac crest) showed that the pseudarthrosis rates were 29%, 13%, and 7%, respectively, for idiopathic patients and 42%, 28%, and 14% for paralytic. It would be reasonable to conclude that Moe had settled the issue of the superiority of autograft and was on the road to permanently minimizing the risk of pseudarthrosis.[14] The first in-depth report on Moe's results since his 1958 article was presented at the AAOS annual meeting in Miami Beach in January 1963 and was published in 1964.[15] Included were private patients operated on by Moe between 1948 and 1960. Of 203 eligible patients, 196 (97%) had a minimum follow-up of 12 months, and most had much longer. Of this group, 100 had idiopathic, 78 paralytic, and 18 congenital scoliosis. With few exceptions they had facet block fusions and Risser localizer casts. They were kept in bed for five and a half months, followed by ambulation in a new Risser localizer cast for three months and later by a simple body cast for two months. Autograft was added in most patients fused below T12. Several intraoperative process details were provided for the 203 patients. Fifty had planned two-stage and 4 had three-stage procedures, totaling 261 operations. The average blood loss per operation was 1,800 mL (range, 300 to 5,300 mL). The average blood replacement was 2,091 mL, the average number of vertebrae fused was 9 per operation, and the average operating time was 3 hours 48 minutes.

莫发表于1958年的文章为自体骨移植提供了强有力的支持。使用他最新融合技术治疗的患者中，特发性侧凸患者采用不添加移植物、骨库（同种）移植物和自体移植物（髂嵴）治疗后假关节形成率分别为29%、13%和7%，麻痹型侧凸患者中假关节形成率分别为42%、28%和14%。可以合理地认为莫已经验证自体骨移植的优越性，即可以永久性地降低假关节形成的风险。[14]基于莫1958年文章的第一份深入报告于1963年1月在迈阿密海滩举行的美国骨科医师学会年会上首次呈现，后于1964年发表。[15]其中记录了1948年至1960年间由莫进行手术的私人患者。在203名符合条件的患者中，196名患者（97%）的随访时间至少为12个月，大多数患者的随访时间更长。在该组患者中，100人患有特发性脊柱侧凸，78人患有麻痹性脊柱侧凸，18人患有先天性脊柱侧凸。除少数病例外，他们均进行了脊柱融合，使用了里泽局部定位矫形石膏。病人遵医嘱卧床五个半月，随后在新的里泽定位矫形石膏固定下锻炼行走三个月，然后维持身体石膏固定两个月。大多数融合节段位于T12以下的患者添加使用了自体移植物。研究记录了203名患者的几个术中指标。其中50名患者进行了二期手术，4名进行了三期手术，共计进行了261例手术。每次手术的平均失血量为1 800毫升（范围为300至5 300毫升）。平均换血量为2 091毫升，每次手术平均融合9个节段，平均手术时间为3小时48分。

The most frequent early complications were accumulations of seroma or hematoma in the wound (12 of 203, 6%) and pressure sores (11 of 203, 5%). Two patients included in the follow-up died. One, an eleven-year-old girl with congenital heart disease and chronic otitis media, died of bronchopneumonia and septicemia six months after surgery. Her fusion was solid at autopsy. The other, who died of massive gastrointestinal hemorrhage one year after operation, showed a solid fusion on a radiograph taken three weeks before death. Pseudarthrosis was still the most frequent late complication, occurring in 38 patients 19% overall. Of these, 13 were diagnosed as idiopathie scoliosis (13 of 100, 13%), 22 were paralytic (22 of 78, 28%), and 3 were congenital (3 of 18, 17%). Autograft was used selectively, mainly for fusions extending below T12, so the value of autograft addition could not be assessed.

最常见的早期并发症是伤口积液或血肿（203 名患者中有 12 名，占 6%）与压疮（203 名中有 11 名，占 5%）。随访中的两名患者死亡。一名为 11 岁女孩，患有先天性心脏病和慢性中耳炎，术后 6 个月死于支气管肺炎和败血症。尸检时发现她的融合节段依然稳固。另一名患者在手术一年后死于胃肠道大出血，在死前三周拍摄的 X 光片上显示脊柱融合牢固。假关节形成仍然是术后最常见的晚期并发症，在 38 名患者中出现（占总数的 19%）。其中 13 名被诊断为特发性脊柱侧凸（100 名中有 13 名，占 13%），22 名为麻痹性侧凸（78 名中有 22 名，28%），3 名为先天性侧凸（18 名中有 3 名，占 17%）。自体骨移植物主要选择性地应用于延伸至 T12 节段以下的融合，因此无法评估添加自体骨移植物的价值。

From the inception of the scoliosis service at Gillette State Hospital for Crippled Children in 1948, Moe had pushed the existing methods of scoliosis treatment to their limits. Because of the center's focus, a large spine deformity practice had developed providing the number of patients necessary for case series. For many reasons the frequency of pseudarthrosis was easily underestimated. It was not always symptomatic, was difficult to diagnosis on X-ray, and was not always associated with convincing curve correction loss. Furthermore, it was unpleasant to the patient as it usually meant starting over (surgery, cast, and bed confinement), unpleasant to the surgeon because it represented failure, and easy to rationalize on any one clinic visit. This happened because scoliosis surgery patients were often treated by a team, diffusing responsibility and magnifying differences in X-ray measurement technique. As a result a pseudarthrosis might not become apparent for a year or more after surgery. In spite of his efforts to apply and improve existing fusion and cast techniques as well as to boldly face the realities of pseudarthrosis, Moe had been unable to reduce its frequency to desirable levels, which were probably 5% or less.

自 1948 年吉列州立残疾儿童医院开始提供脊柱侧凸医疗服务以来，莫就将现有脊柱侧凸治疗方法的应用推向了极限。由于中心吸引效应，一个大型脊柱畸形治疗中心已经发展起来，为病例系列的建立提供了充足的患者数量。由于多种原因，假关节形成的发生率很容易被低估。因为它并不总是有症状的，通过 X 线检查很难诊断，且并不总是与确切的侧凸矫正丢失相关。此外，患者不易接受假关节形成的诊断，因为它通常意味着治疗的重新开始（手术、石膏和卧床限制）；对外科医生来说同样不好接受，因为它代表手术失败。并且，它在任何一次门诊就诊时都容易合理推脱责任，发生这种情况是因为脊柱侧凸手术患者通常由一个团队治疗，分散了个人责任，并加大了 X 线测量技术的误差。因此，假关节形成现象可能在手术后一年或更长时间内均不易被发现。尽管莫努力应用和改进现有的融合和石膏固定技术，并勇敢面对假关节形成的现实，但他仍无法将其发生率降低到理想水平，即 5%或更低。

At the January 1963 AAOS meeting Harrington enjoyed some social time with his mentors, Frank Dickson and Rex Diveley[16] *See figure 7.1*. But his main mission was education, and Moe and Harrington repeated their instructional course lecture, of which Harrington bound his portion into his *Scoliosis 1963*.[17] Although it was a clear and comprehensive description of his technique, he did not address placement of the lower distraction hook, which had been problematic. He reviewed the results of "More Than 200 Cases," but provided no additional insight into the number of patients followed or the length of patient follow-up. He recommended bone grafting even though he was not using it at that point. Even if he did not hear Moe's paper presented, Harrington was almost certainly aware of Moe's latest findings that cast doubt on the effectiveness of autograft. Nor did Harrington provide any insight into the "new spinal fusion technique" that he had been increasingly been alluding to. He did introduce a highly structured postoperative activity and follow-up program that evolved over the next ten years into a "Blue Book," a sort of operator's manual with room for individualized patient instructions depending on their unique recovery and rehabilitation needs.[18]

在 1963 年 1 月的美国骨科医师学会会议上，哈灵顿与他的导师弗兰克·迪克森、雷克斯·戴夫利共度了一段社交时光。[16]（图 7.1）但他的主要任务是教育，莫和哈灵顿重复了他们的教学课程讲座，其中哈灵顿将他的部分教学内容结合到他当年的专著《脊柱侧凸 1963》中。[17]虽然这是对他的技术的一次清晰且全面的介绍，但他没有解决下部撑开钩的放置这一重要问题。哈灵顿回顾了“200 多例病例的评估”的结果，但没有提供更多关于随访患者数量或随访时间的信息。他建议植骨，即使他当时没有使用该技术。虽然他没有看到莫的论文，哈灵顿依然了解莫的最新发现，并对自体骨移植的有效性产生了怀疑。哈灵顿也没有进一步解释他屡次提到的“新脊柱融合技术”。他介绍了一个计划完整的术后随访项目活动，该活动在接下来的十年里演变成了一本“蓝皮书”，一本根据患者个体化的恢复和康复需求，为患者提供个性化指导的操作手册。[18]

Figure 7.1 ***Harrington seated on the divan with mentors Frank Dickson and Rex Diveley at the 1963 AAOS meeting in Chicago. (Harrington Archives)***
图 7.1　1963 年在芝加哥举行的美国骨科医师学会会议上，哈灵顿与导师弗兰克·迪克森、雷克斯·戴夫利坐在长沙发上（哈灵顿档案馆）

In February 1963 Harrington's paper, "Scoliosis in the Growing Spine," focusing on patient evaluation and management, appeared in *Pediatric Clinics of North America*.[19] In it he observed that the male/female incidence of scoliosis was nearly equal in patients with post-polio scoliosis, which differed greatly from adolescent idiopathic scoliosis where it was predominantly seen in females. He noted that there were "some 31 etiologic factors," emphasized the many different diagnostic categories of scoliosis, ex-tended the well-known relationship between growth remaining and curve progression, and expressed his belief that adolescent idiopathic scoliosis was a "dysfunction in the pre-collagen matrix of the columnar zone of the ossification zone" of the growth plate. He offered no new insights into the evolution of his surgical techniques and emphasized that spine fusion always accompanied instrumentation and that a cast always followed instrumentation.

1963 年 2 月，哈灵顿的论文《脊柱生长中的脊柱侧凸》发表在《北美儿科临床》杂志上，重点关注了患者评估和管理。[19]在文中，他观察到在存在脊髓灰质炎后遗症的患者中，脊柱侧凸的男性/女性发病率几乎相等。脊髓灰质炎脊柱侧凸与多发于女性的青少年特发性脊柱侧凸有很大不同。他指出，有“大约 31 种病因”，强调了脊柱侧凸的不同诊断类别，扩展了脊柱生长发育与脊柱侧凸进展之间这一为人熟知的联系，并表示他认为青少年特发性脊柱侧凸是因为生长板“骨化区柱状区前胶原基质功能障碍”。他没有对他手术技术的演变提出新的见解，但强调脊柱融合总是伴随着内固定置入，而后才是石膏固定的治疗思路。

For some time Harrington had been coyly hinting at a new fusion technique, and he chose back-to-back presentations on April 4 and 5, 1963, at the University of Arkansas and the Orthopedic Section of the Tennessee State Medical Society to unveil his dowel fusion technique involving a distraction outrigger. His presentation, “Spinal Fusion in the Idiopathic Adolescent Scoliotic,” was the second entry in *Scoliosis 1963*[20] and was the basis of a paper, “Spinal Fusion in the Treatment of Idiopathic Adolescent Scoliosis,” published in the December 1963 issue of the *Journal of the Tennessee Medical Association*.[21] These were his first descriptions of the Harrington dowel fusion technique, which he illustrated, and the distraction outrigger, which he did not illustrate although he indicated he had been using for six months to a year.

一段时间以来，哈灵顿一直含糊其词地暗示一种新的融合技术。1963 年 4 月 4 日至 5 日，在阿肯色大学和田纳西州医学会骨科分会上，哈灵顿连续地演讲了他应用外撑开器的骨栓融合技术。他的演讲“特发性青少年脊柱侧凸的脊柱融合术”，是《脊柱侧凸 1963》[20]中的第二篇文章，并且是发表在 1963 年 12 月的《田纳西州医学会杂志》[21]上的一篇论文《脊柱融合术治疗特发性青少年脊柱侧凸》的基础。这是哈灵顿对骨栓融合技术的首次描述，但他并未描述外撑开器，尽管他表示他已经使用该器械六个月到一年。

His new fusion technique was designed “to utilize the principles of compression bone healing, as established by Charnley[22] and Eggers,[23] best done by precision fitting of the bone mass into the inter-segmental soft-tissue contact points.”[24] Thus, he placed a structural graft to mechanically block the concave thoracic facet joints into their corrected position. *See figure 7.2*. The operation began with a thorough subperiosteal exposure, obtaining near maximum correction with an outrigger, applying the compression rod, cutting a #3 dowel from the concave facet with an oscillating saw, turning the doweled facet fragments laterally to a position between the adjacent transverse processes, cutting the next size larger #4 dowel from the exposed ilium, inserting the dowel cortex side down, and replacing the distraction outrigger with the distraction rod. The fusion operation was completed by decorticating the exposed bone on the concave side of the curve and at both ends and adding supplemental autogenous iliac crest bone graft. This appears to have been the first time he had used autogenous iliac bone graft, although he had been recommending it for some time. His preliminary assessment was that "from our observation of six months to a year, over 80% have shown no loss of correction and no evidence of pseudarthrosis."

他的新融合技术旨在“利用由查恩利[22]和埃格斯[23]建立的加压骨愈合原理，在理想状态下可精确嵌合骨块至节段间软组织接触点”[24]。因此，他放置了一个移植结构，以机械方式将胸椎凹侧关节面固定到正确的位置。(图 7.2) 手术开始时充分暴露至骨膜下，用外撑开器获得最大的矫正，应用压缩棒，使用摆动锯从凹侧小关节上切下#3 骨栓，将骨栓带有毛刺的一面向外转动到相邻横突之间的位置，从暴露的髂骨上切割下一个更大尺寸的#4 骨栓，将其皮质面朝下插入，并用撑开棒代替外撑开器。对弯曲处凹侧及两端的显露的骨皮质去皮质，并加入辅助的自体髂嵴移植骨，完成融合手术。尽管他已经推荐使用自体髂骨移植物一段时间，但这似乎是他第一次实际应用。他的初步评估是，“从我们六个月到一年的随访观察来看，超过 80%的患者没有矫正度数丢失，也没有假关节形成”。

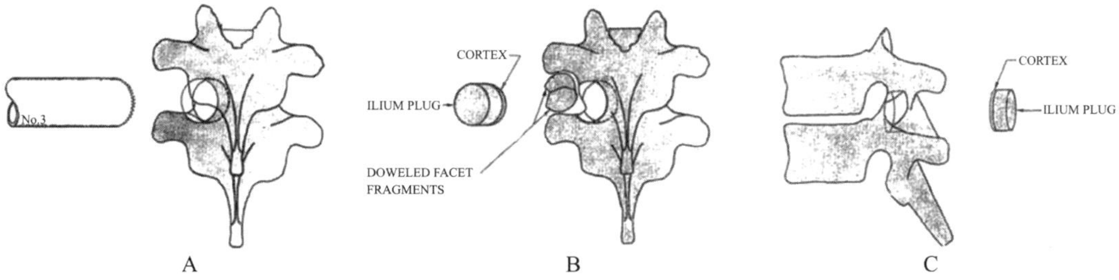

Figure 7.2 ***Concave thoracic facet dowel arthrodesis.*** (***Harrington Archives***)
图 7.2　凹侧胸椎小关节面骨栓融合术(哈灵顿档案馆)

Harrington detailed his beliefs about the spine fusion development timetable. He believed in the importance of removing the cortex and stress trabeculations on the concave side so that trabecular bone could "form in the mass without the barrier of lamellar bone between the bone mass and the attaching surface of each segment." He envisioned that an osteoid mass formed in three weeks a fibrous bone mass in the next six weeks, and fibrous bone with trabeculae and beginning "laminar cortical structure" by the twelfth week in the adolescent. Gradual gravitational loading over the next six weeks would result in stress-oriented trabecular bone, and at that point the cast could be removed (i.e., about four to four and a half months postoperative). He speculated that a totally adequate fusion mass was achieved in nine to twelve months. In neither of his April 1963 presentations nor his December 1963 publication of this manuscript was there an indication of the origin of his speculation.

哈灵顿详细阐述了他对脊柱融合技术发展史的看法。他深知在凹面去除皮质和骨小梁形成应力的重要性，这样骨小梁就可以“在移植骨块内形成，而在移植骨块和每个节段的附着面之间没有皮质骨屏障”。他设想在青少年的患者中，移植骨内在3周内形成一种类骨质，并在接下来的6周内形成纤维骨块，在第12周内形成带有骨小梁的纤维骨，并开始形成“层状皮质结构”。在接下来的6周内逐渐施加重力会使应力导向骨小梁，此时可以移除石膏（即术后大约4到4.5个月）。他推测在9~12个月内可以达到完全足够的融合强度。但在他1963年4月的演讲和1963年12月出版的手稿中，都没有阐述他的推测依据。

The clue to his heightened interest in the biology of bone grafting almost certainly traced to John F. LeCocq, who had been working to develop heterograft, specifically calf bone, as an acceptable supplemental bone graft material in humans. How LeCocq and Harrington first met is not known. But in a November 3, 1961, letter to James A. Dingwall at the Squibb Institute for Medical Researeh[25] Harrington mentioned spending time with LeCocq and becoming intensely interested in his work. Harrington wanted to begin using the product in 1962 provided that it was feasible from Squibb's standpoint and the product had no antigenic potential. Eighteen months later in May 1963 Dingwall and Squibb were able to provide Harrington with the heterograft in the five-inch rib "matchsticks" that he had requested.[26] Presumably the delay was to allow additional research and development of the product. Three months earlier Harrington had started collaborating with one of LeCocq's younger associates, Kirk J. Anderson,[27] who was collecting samples of prior bone-grafted sites as they became available in the ongoing care of the patient. His goal was to better understand the histologic record of bone-graft behavior, which was a neglected area of study. Anderson had already published several articles related to the biology of bone grafting. By April Harrington had sent ten specimens, and Anderson had prepared a manuscript based on these and twenty-seven others. The bone graft origin of the studied samples was sixteen autograft, three homograft, and eighteen processed heterograft. The bone graft types were cancellous, cortical, and corticocancellous. The interval to biopsy ranged from one month to thirteen years. The resulting paper, "End-Point Results of Processed Heterogenous, Autogenous and Homogenous Bone Transplants in the Human: A Histologic Study," was presented at the Western Orthopedic Association's annual meeting in Seattle in September 1963 and published in 1964.[28]

他对骨移植生物学的浓厚兴趣几乎可以确切地追溯到与约翰·F. 勒柯克的接触。约翰一直致力于开发异种骨移植物，特别是作为人类可能的补充骨移植材料的小腿骨。勒柯克和哈灵顿是如何相识的还不得而知。但在1961年11月3日写给斯奎布医学研究所的詹姆斯·A. 丁沃尔[25]的一封信中，哈灵顿提到与勒柯克共度的时光，并对他的工作产生了浓厚的兴趣。哈灵顿想在1962年开始使用该产品，但前提是在斯奎布医学研究所的评估中证实该移植物是可行的且没有抗原潜能。1963年5月，丁沃尔和斯奎布医学研究所终于给哈灵顿提供了他想要的"火柴棍"——5英寸肋骨异种移植物。[26]据推测，延迟供货是为了对该产品进行额外的研究和开发。在此之前的3个月，哈灵顿开始与勒柯克的一位年轻同事柯克·J. 安德森[27]合作，安德森正在收集先前患者骨移植部位的样本，因为这些样本能够从正在接受治疗的患者那里获得。安德森的目标是更好地了解骨移植后的组织学特征，这是一个曾被忽视的研究领域。安德森已经发表了几篇与骨移植生物学相关的文章。到4月，哈灵顿已经寄来了10个样本，安德森根据这些样本和其他27个样本各准备了一篇文章。研究样本的骨移植物来源于16个自体移植物、3个同种移植物和18个加工异种移植物。骨移植物类型为松质骨、皮质骨和皮质松质混合骨。活检的间隔从移植后1个月到13年不等。1963年9月在西雅图举行的西方骨科学会年会上，这篇名为《人体异种骨、自体骨和同种骨移植的最终结果：一项组织学研究》进行了展示，并于1964年发表。[28]

The findings did not reflect the orderly maturation process Harrington envisioned. "Residual portions of... cancellous autograft and homograft remained several years after bone-grafting. Cortical autograft and homograft bone did not advance beyond the end-point of incorporation or partial substitution as long as 13 years after grafting. The cancellous heterograft reached an end-point of incomplete remodeling by 1 year, while the cortical heterograft showed variable amounts of substitution at 1 year and thereafter." These findings were not reassuring, certainly in retrospect, but by then Harrington was deeply involved in developing his heterograft series.

研究结果与哈灵顿设想中的有序成熟的过程有所差异。"骨移植数年后，……自体松质骨移植物和同种异体移植物的残余部分仍然存在。自体皮质移植骨和同种异体移植骨在移植后长达 13 年的时间里，都没有超过或部分替代移植边界。异种松质骨移植物在 1 年时达到不完全重塑的终点，而异种皮质骨移植物在 1 年及之后显示出不同程度的替换。"这些回顾性发现令人不安，但那时哈灵顿已经沉浸于他的异种骨移植病例系列的开发。

Meanwhile, an important milestone in the life of Harrington Spine Instrumentation was passed on June 24, 1963, with the presentation of its first true validation study. The occasion was the annual meeting of the AOA held in Hot Springs, Virginia. The study from Moe's center was titled "Harrington Instrumentation in Correction of Scoliosis: A Comparison with Cast Correction."[29] The authors reviewed the four known efforts to correct scoliosis with instrumentation, all of which proved to be unsuccessful. They defined their experimental design, a prospective series with Harrington Instrumentation, and two historical control series operated on by Moe and his associates. The Harrington series was begun in 1960, and 66 patients had a minimum one-year follow-up. One of the historical control series had been operated on at Gillette State Hospital for Crippled Children (Gillette series) and included 86 patients operated on after July 1956 and before February 1960. The second series was from Moe's private patients (private series) and included 169 patients operated on between 1948 and 1960.

与此同时，1963 年 6 月 24 日，哈灵顿脊柱器械迎来了一个重要里程碑，在这天首次迎来了真正的验证研究。在弗吉尼亚州温泉城举行的美国骨科学会年会上，莫领衔的脊柱研究中心发布了一篇名为《哈灵顿器械矫正脊柱侧凸：与石膏固定治疗的比较研究》的文章。[29]作者回顾了四项已知的器械矫正脊柱侧凸尝试，这些均被证明是不成功的。他们展示了他们的实验设计，由一个应用哈灵顿器械的前瞻性病例系列，与两个由莫和他的同事完成的历史对照病例系列进行对照。哈灵顿的病例系列始于 1960 年，对 66 名患者进行了至少一年的随访。第一个历史对照系列为在吉列州立残疾儿童医院接受过手术的患者（吉列系列），包括 86 名 1956 年 7 月至 1960 年 2 月之间接受手术的患者。第二个历史对照系列来自莫的私人患者（私人系列），包括 169 名在 1948 年至 1960 年间接受手术的患者。

All three study series included patients with scoliosis of different types although the exact numbers were provided only for the Harrington series, which included 45 patients with idiopathic, 14 with paralytic, and 7 with congenital scoliosis. Children younger than ten years were not included, but adults were, with eight in the Harrington series being over twenty years of age. The average age in the three-study series was 14.2 years in private, 14.2 years in Gillette, and 16.8 years in Harrington. Their average Cobb preoperative measurement was 64°, 64°, and 74°, respectively. The Gillette and private series had Risser localizer cast correction before surgery, operation in cast, and continuation of the cast postoperative. The Harrington series had a Risser cast placed at ten to fourteen days postoperative without the localizer but with the neck extension. The fusion technique in all was the modified Hibbs technique, which included the facet joints, and a Moe type facet-block fusion. All Harrington operations were done in one procedure while multi-stage fusions were done in 23% of the private series and 66% in the Gillette. Comparing the private, Gillette, and Harrington series, the average operating blood loss (1,800, 1,800, and 1,900 mL, respectively), average operating time (3.8, 3.4, and 4.0 hours), and average vertebral segments fused (9, 6, and 10) were similar. Autograft was added in twenty-six and homograft in five of the Harrington patients, especially in those with arthrodesis extending into the lumbar spine. This fact was not provided for the comparison series, but based on prior reports it was probably about the same. All patients were followed for at least a year.

所有三个病例系列均包括不同类型的脊柱侧凸患者，其中只有哈灵顿病例系列提供了各类型的确切数字，他的整个病例系列包括45名特发性脊柱侧凸患者、14名麻痹性脊柱侧凸患者和7名先天性脊柱侧凸患者。病例系列中排除了10岁以下的儿童，但纳入了成人。哈灵顿病例系列中有8名患者年龄超过20岁。三个研究系列的平均年龄分别为：私人病例系列14.2岁，吉列病例系列14.2岁，哈灵顿病例系列16.8岁。他们的术前平均柯布角测量值分别为64°、64°和74°。吉列和私人系列在术前、术中石膏矫正和术后石膏固定中均采用了里泽局部定位石膏。哈灵顿病例系列在术后10~14天放置了里泽石膏，没有局部定位，但石膏伸展至颈部。总的来说，哈灵顿融合技术是希伯斯技术的改进，其中包括小关节面和莫型关节融合。所有哈灵顿病例系列的手术均在同期完成，而23%的私人病例系列与66%的吉列病例系列采用分期手术完成。哈灵顿病例系列与私人系列、吉列系列相比，平均手术失血量（分别为1 800、1 800和1 900毫升）、平均手术时间（分别为3.8、3.4和4.0小时）和平均融合节段（分别为9、6和10个）相似。哈灵顿系列患者中有26名加入了自体移植物，5名加入了同种移植物，尤其是那些固定术延伸至腰椎的患者。移植物放置情况没有纳入比较，但根据之前的报告，情况可能大致相同。所有患者至少随访一年。

Results were determined by curve correction and correction loss; times for Risser cast, recumbent, ambulatory, and total; and complications. Private, Gillette, and Harrington series postoperative correction (37°, 32°, and 41°, respectively) and correction loss (6°, 6°, and 10°) were similar. Comparative times of recumbent, ambulatory, and total Risser cast immobilization were private 5.5+5 = 10.5 months, Gillette 6.7+4.2 = 10.9, and Harrington 2.5+2.0=4.5. Thus, the Harrington patients spent less than half as long as those in the Risser cast. The private, Gillette, and Harrington series were compared for complications. The number and percent of deep wound infections were 2 (0.9%), 2 (2.3%), and 7 (11%), respectively. The number and percent with pseudarthrosis were 38 (19%), 24 (28%), and 6 (9%). The number and percent of necessary reoperations were 61 (31%), 32 (37%), and 16 (24%). Further immobilization required after reoperation and the resulting percentage of patients were 62 (34%), 26 (30%), and 6 (9%). Except for deep wound infections, the Harrington series clearly fared better. Three of their seven infections had occurred in the first six patients, during which time there had been a heavy traffic flow in the operating room because of the increased interest in the new operation. One patient was cured with debridement and antibiotics. The other six required instrumentation removal as part of their treatment. Aided by Risser cast correction, solid fusion and healed wounds were achieved in all. The authors commented that infection "seemed to be becoming less of a problem."

最终效果由弯曲矫正和矫正丢失情况确定。对三个病例系列的里泽石膏固定时间、卧床时间、门诊和治疗总计的时间、并发症情况均进行了比较，私人系列、吉列系列和哈灵顿病例系列术后矫正度数（分别为37°、32°和41°）和矫正丢失情况（6°、6°和10°）相似。卧床、门诊和里泽石膏固定的总时长分别为：私人系列5.5+5=10.5个月，吉列系列6.7+4.2=10.9个月，哈灵顿系列2.5+2.0=4.5个月。因此，哈灵顿病例系列中，患者花费的时间不到里泽石膏固定治疗组的一半。研究同时比较了私人、吉列和哈灵顿病例系列的并发症情况。深度伤口感染的数量和百分比分别为2（0.9%）、2（2.3%）和7（11%）。假关节形成的数量和百分比分别为38（19%）、24（28%）和6（9%）。二次手术的数量和百分比分别为61（31%）、32（37%）和16（24%）。再次手术后需要进一步固定的患者数量和百分比分别为62（34%）、26（30%）和6（9%）。除了深度伤口感染情况，哈灵顿病例系列在其他方面表现明显更好。他们的 7 例感染中有 3 例发生在前 6 名患者身上，因为在此期间，出于对新手术方式的兴趣，手术室里人流量很大。一名患者通过施行清创术和使用抗生素被治愈。其他 6 名患者需要去除内固定。在里泽石膏矫正的帮助下，所有患者实现了牢固的脊柱融合和良好的伤口愈合。作者评论说，感染“似乎不再是一个问题”。

The pseudarthrosis and requirement for cast immobilization after reoperation rates were all dramatically lower in the Harrington series. Although fewer in the Harrington, the reoperation rates were more nearly the same in all three. In the private and Gillette series almost all reoperations were due to pseudarthrosis. The pre-Harrington Instrumentation series had repeatedly shown 10%–50% or higher pseudarthrosis rates, which it should be noted were achieved in operations done by the thought leaders of orthopedic surgery.[30] In the Harrington series almost all sixteen reoperations were directly or indirectly instrumentation related. Five were for infection alone, two for a combination of infection and pseudarthrosis, three for pseudarthrosis alone, one for a combination of late operative site pain associated with metal corrosion and unsuspected pseudarthrosis, one for late operative site pain alone, one for removal of a broken rod, two for reseating the lower distraction hook, and one for repair of a pleural tear. These problems were all solved with reoperation.

在哈灵顿病例系列中，假关节形成和再次手术后对石膏固定的要求都显著降低。尽管哈灵顿病例系列中的手术数量较少，但三个病例系列的二次手术率几乎相同。在私人和吉列系列中，几乎所有二次手术都是由于假关节形成。哈灵顿器械之前病例系列显示 10%~50%或更高的假关节形成率，应该注意的是，这还是在骨科手术顶尖医师亲自主刀的情况下。[30]在哈灵顿系列中，16 次二次手术几乎所有都直接或间接地与内固定器械相关。5 例为单发感染，2 例为并发感染和假关节，3 例为单发的假关节形成，1 例为晚期与金属腐蚀相关的手术部位疼痛和意料之外的假关节形成，1 例为晚期手术部位疼痛，1 例为去除断棒，2 例为重新安装下部撑开钩，1 例为胸膜撕裂修复。这些问题都通过二次手术解决了。

The most common instrumentation-related problem was lower distraction hook position loss in nine patients, all of which occurred early in the series during the postoperative months while they were recumbent in their casts. Only two required reoperation, and in both the original correction was regained. In these two, the hook was found embedded in fibrous tissue, and in the other seven this, plus the support of the Risser cast and bed rest, "gave enough stability to prevent major loss of correction in many instances." As a result of this experience Moe had initiated one of the earliest modifications to Harrington Instrumentation, the addition of a central vertical keel to the blade of the distraction hook. This modified hook could be used at either end of the distraction rod. However, the authors reported, "by placing the lower hook directly into the lumbar lamina, rather than the joint, the hook can be locked more securely into place." With this placement the keel hook was not needed. Two distraction rods broke. In one case it was removed, and the fusion was found to be solid. The other patient was asymptomatic, had no further loss of correction, and the rod was left in. Two patients developed severe pain in the fusion area many months after operation. At exploration in one a pseudarthrosis and "a great deal of metal corrosion with discoloration of the tissues" were found. The instruments were replaced, the pseudarthrosis was repaired, and the pain disappeared. In the other patient the graft was solid, and there was no gross evidence of corrosion; the pain disappeared when the instruments were removed. Cast pressure sores were the second most common complication in the Gillette series, occurring in 9% (8 of 86). Their frequency was not listed for the private series, and none was reported in the Harrington. The authors emphasized their belief that external support with a full Risser cast incorporating the neck was essential for the successful use of the instrumentation. With experience, their number of complications appeared to be decreasing. They concluded that "with proper use and in experienced hands Harrington rods are a safe and effective addition to the surgical treatment of scoliosis."

最常见的内固定器械相关问题是9名患者的下部撑开钩移位，都发生于术后几个月，此时患者仍处于石膏固定状态。仅两名患者需要再次手术，并且都恢复了原来的矫正。在这两个病例中，撑开钩嵌在纤维组织中，而在其他七个病例中，加上里泽石膏支撑和卧床休息的辅助，"在许多情况下提供了足够的稳定性，阻止了矫正的大量丢失。"根据这些经验，莫对哈灵顿内固定系统进行了最早的一处修改，即在撑开钩的钩身部增加了一个中央垂直龙骨。这种改进的钩可以用在撑开棒的两端。然而，作者表示，"将下部钩直接固定于腰椎椎板，而不是小关节，撑开钩可以更牢固地锁定到位。"应用这种放置方法，就不需要改龙骨钩。两个病例出现撑开棒断裂的情况。在一个病例中，撑开杆被去除，脊柱融合依然稳固。另一名患者因没有症状，同时没有进一步矫正丢失情况，选择将棒留在了体内。两名患者在手术后数月出现融合区剧烈疼痛。探查发现，一名患者出现了假关节和“大量金属腐蚀并伴有组织变色”。在更换内固定器械、修复假关节后，患者疼痛消失。另一名患者的移植物是牢固的，并且没有明显的金属腐蚀迹象；取出内固定后疼痛消失了。石膏压疮是吉列系列中第二常见的并发症，发生率为9%（86例中出现8例）。私人系列中没有列出石膏压疮的发生率，哈灵顿系列中也没有报告。作者强调他们相信内固定器械成功的关键是延伸至颈部的完整的里泽石膏外固定装置。随着经验的积累，并发症的数量似乎在减少。他们得出的结论是：“通过正确使用和经验的累积，哈灵顿器械是一种安全有效的脊柱侧凸手术治疗方式。”

There were two assigned discussants, both experienced and highly respected scoliosis experts. The first, Albert C. Schmidt of Milwaukee, highlighted Moe's status as a very skillful surgeon with the opportunity to operate on a large number of scoliosis patients in a relatively short time. He expressed the view that time differences of post-operative immobilization should not be an important factor in choosing treatment. Nor did he think adding a second stage should be a deciding factor. He didn't comment on possible patient preferences. Schmidt wondered if the decrease in the pseudarthrosis rate in the Harrington series might be due to continued improvement in the author's fusion technique. This valid criticism of the experimental design was somewhat offset by the fact that the historical control patients had been operated on by Moe and his assistants. In addition, the Gillette series had been collected after July 1956, two years after Moe had arrived at his facet fusion technique.[31] Schmidt commented on surgical skill and experience: "One should be aware that catastrophic complications have occurred in patients whose curves were corrected with Harrington rods by other surgeons." The second discussant was John R. Cobb of New York who underscored the danger of too rapid correction of large deformities with this story. When I showed a colleague a curve of 96 degrees that I had reduced slowly over a period of weeks to about 30 degrees, he told me of a patient with a similar reduction at one operation with the rods in whom the renal artery ruptured. The result was a better roentgenogram and a dead patient. "He reminded the audience that Harrington had made many modifications to his procedure and that many surgeons were probably several modifications behind. He recommended that Harrington be allowed to complete his design and that he and a few other well-qualified surgeons determine the indications, contraindications, and precautions for using this procedure for the open reduction and internal fixation of scoliosis. In closing, he took the opportunity to say of Harrington, Dr. Harrington is a good man with a good idea. It would be too bad to have the poor results of people who shouldn't use this method be bad for a good man and his good idea."

两名特邀讨论者都是经验丰富且备受尊敬的脊柱侧凸治疗专家。第一位是密尔沃基的阿尔伯特·C. 施密特，他强调了莫是一名非常娴熟的外科医生，他有机会在相对较短的时间内为大量脊柱侧凸患者进行手术。施密特认为术后制动的时间差异不应成为选择治疗方式的重要因素。他也不认为增加第二阶段治疗应该是一个决定性因素。他没有评论不同医生间可能存在的患者选择偏好。施密特想知道哈灵顿系列中假关节形成率的降低是否因为术者融合技术不断改进。这种对实验设计的有效批评，在一定程度上，被莫和他的助手为历史对照系列中的患者进行过手术这一事实所抵消。此外，吉列系列是在1956年7月之后收集的，也就是莫掌握了他的小关节融合技术两年后。[31]施密特评论手术技巧和经验："人们应该意识到，其他医生在使用哈灵顿棒矫正患者弯曲时，发生了灾难性的并发症。"第二位讨论者是纽约的约翰·R. 柯布，他用这样一个故事强调快速矫正严重的脊柱畸形的危险。"当我向一位同事展示了一名侧凸患者时，我讲述了在数周内缓慢将其弯曲由96度减小到大约30度，他告诉我有一位患者采用哈灵顿器械手术获得了同样的矫形效果，但发生了肾动脉破裂，结果就是造成（虽然）X光片令人满意但病人死亡的情况。"他提醒听众，哈灵顿对他的手术过程进行了很多的改进，但许多外科医生可能还没有了解到这些改进。他建议让哈灵顿完成他的设计，并由他和其他几位权威的外科医生确定适应证和禁忌证，以及使用此术式进行脊柱侧凸切开复位内固定的注意事项。最后，他借机评价哈灵顿，"哈灵顿医生智者出高见。如果有不该采用本术式治疗的患者使用了该方法治疗，最终导致成效欠佳，这对于哈灵顿和他的手术方法会造成不该有的负面影响。"

For the future of spine instrumentation this day could be thought of as similar to April 12, 1955, when epidemiologist Thomas Francis presented the results of the Salk vaccine trial in "An Evaluation of the 1954 Poliomyelitis Vaccine Trials."[32] This Level of Evidence Ⅰ randomized, blinded trial had proved the Salk vaccine safe and effective. Moe and his colleagues had just presented what would now be labeled a Level of Evidence Ⅲ clinical study[33] supporting the use of Harrington Instrumentation in the surgical treatment of scoliosis of a variety of causes. This is the highest Level of Evidence an observational research protocol can attain. Moe and his co-authors emphasized that these results had been obtained "in experienced hands," and the discussants repeatedly urged restraint until the instruments and technique had further matured. The full-length paper and the comments of the discussants were published in March 1964.[34] There is no record that Harrington was at the 1963 AOA annual meeting. It was unlikely that he did attend because he was not a member of the organization and attendance of non-members was governed by invitation. He may not have even known about the presentation, and if he had a reaction to the report, it wasn't documented.

对于脊柱器械的未来，这一天与 1955 年 4 月 12 日同样重要，当时流行病学家托马斯·弗朗西斯在《对 1954 年脊髓灰质炎疫苗试验的评估》中介绍了索尔克疫苗试验的结果。[32]这一随机、盲法试验的证据等级Ⅰ级的临床研究已证明索尔克疫苗安全有效。莫和他的同事刚刚提出了现在被标记为证据等级Ⅲ级的临床研究[33]，支持在各种原因引起的脊柱侧凸手术治疗中使用哈灵顿器械。这是观察性研究设计可以获得的最高级别证据。莫和他的合著者强调，这些结果是“有经验的人”获得的，讨论者一再敦促在器械和技术进一步成熟之前保持克制。论文全文和讨论者的评论发表于 1964 年 3 月。[34]没有记录表明哈灵顿出席了 1963 年的美国骨科学会年会。事实上，他不太可能参加，因为他不是该组织的会员，非会员的出席是受制约的。他可能甚至不知道这次演讲，即使他对该报告有所反应，也没有记录在案。

On June 23, 1963, the day before Moe's paper was presented, Harrington's other major innovative effort came to fruition: the christening of his new boat, the *Twin Star*.[35] *See figure 7.3.* Harrington had designed, commissioned, and overseen the building of this 50 foot-long, twin-hulled, motor and sail-powered cruising catamaran. In the christening booklet he recounted the long journey to that June day. He recalled making sketches of a sailing catamaran while an intern in Charleston, South Carolina, having "built several conventional and unconventional monohull designs while completing his medical specialty training," and sharing the activity with Mary Alice, who cut and sewed the sails. Because of his lifelong fascination with watercraft, he had chosen to establish bis medical practice in Houston because of the potential of the Texas Medical Center and its proximity to open water. By about 1954 or 1955 he had become well enough established medically that he could again renew his lifelong love affair with boats. He began working on "many models and some model testing." His decision on a symmetrical rather than an asymmetrical hull design for the *Twin Star* was influenced by his research on the structure of human bone, which had impressed him with its strength and efficiency. Initially, he designed for a laminated plywood and fiberglass structure, but weight would have been a problem. A chance meeting with William Mason resulted in an offer to build the *Twin Star* of aluminum in Mason's Houston sheet metal shop, Belmas. While aluminum offered the advantages of strength, noncorrosiveness, and lightness, there was the disadvantage of contouring. Although originally designed to be primarily a sailboat, it gradually morphed into a motorsailer.

1963 年 6 月 23 日，即莫的论文发表的前一天，哈灵顿的另一项重大创新努力取得了成果：他的新船被命名为双星号。[35]（图 7.3）哈灵顿亲自设计、委托并监督建造了这艘长 50 英尺、双体和机帆混合动力的巡航双体船。在船只洗礼小册子中，他讲述了六月的一次漫长旅程。他回忆起在南卡罗来纳州查尔斯顿实习时画的双体帆船的草图，“在完成他的医学专业培训的同时，也完成了几个传统和非常规的单体船设计”，并与剪裁和缝制船帆的玛丽·艾丽斯分享了这些设计。由于他毕生对船只的迷恋，他选择在休斯敦开展医疗实践，一方面是因为得克萨斯医疗中心的潜力，另一方面是因为这里靠近开阔水域。到大约 1954 年或 1955 年，他在医学上已经足够成熟，可以再次抽出时间延续他毕生对船只的热爱。他着手“许多模型构建和一些模型测试”，对人体骨骼的研究给他留下了强度和效率的深刻印象，受此影响，他最终决定采用对称船体来设计双星号。最初，他设计了层压胶合板和玻璃纤维结构，但船只总重是个问题。一次与威廉·梅森的偶然会面，促成了双星号最终于休斯敦贝尔玛斯的梅森钣金车间被建造为铝制船体。虽然铝材具有强度高、耐腐蚀和重量轻等优点，但也有轮廓不佳的缺点。虽然最初设计的主要是一艘帆船，但它逐渐建造成了一艘机动帆船。

Figure 7.3 ***Twin Star.*** **(*Harrington Archives*)**
图 7.3　双星号(哈灵顿档案馆)

The *Twin Star* was big, weighing approximately sixteen tons, which was five tons heavier than Harrington had originally envisioned. She had twenty-five bulkheads, eighteen partial and seven total. Her internal design was described as "honeycombed with tangential and longitudinal structural members underneath a multi-contoured skin. In a general description I call her 'skin tension,' designed not unlike the structure of a human vertebra." The *Twin Star* had many safety features, including over twenty-five tons of water displacement flotation fixed on board. There were no explosives or inflammables. A diesel-powered generator supplied electricity for cooking, lighting, and air conditioning, and two GM diesel 120-horsepower engines provided propulsion power. Fuel tanks were in the far aft of the boat wing section between the hulls and separated from the rest of the boat by a bulkhead. Storage capacity was 395 gallons. The *Twin Star* had several unique features. The water system was gravity fed from an 80-gallon tank in the ceiling of the port and starboard salons. Harrington wrote, "All naval architects shun this idea and most say that you cannot do this, but the fact remains it has been done. If they would only figure the change in the center of gravity and the metacentric point of a structure functioning in a liquid media on two wide spaced hulls, they would find that the center of gravity and metacentric points are stable." The acoustics were so quiet that an extensive intercommunication system was installed. The insulation was so complete that the three-ton air conditioner could maintain a 70° temperature. For both comfort and security the nylon carpets were placed over a half-inch rubberlike mat of chemical-, fire-, and water-resistant EnsoLite. Each hull had six staterooms with eight feet of headroom and bunks that were six feet ten inches long. Storage spaces were ample, and the doors closed by slides to gravity, eliminating protruding hinges and handles. The decor included beautiful Lamin-Art and Formica woods and decorative vinyl. For relaxation the boat offered fishing, a bar, and an organ.

双星号很大，重约 16 吨，比哈灵顿预想中的还要重 5 吨。她有 25 个舱壁、18 个部分舱壁和 7 个全舱壁。她的内部设计被描述为“在多轮廓表皮下具有切向和纵向结构的蜂窝状结构。在一般描述中，我称她的设计拥有‘表皮张力’，与人类椎体结构相似”。双星号具有许多安全功能，包括固定在船上的超过 25 吨的排水浮力。船上没有易燃易爆物。一台柴油发电机为烹饪、照明和空调提供电力，两台 GM 120 马力柴油发动机提供推进力。油箱位于双船体之间船翼部分的最后端，与其余部分以舱壁分开。油箱存储容量为 395 加仑①。双星有几个独特

① 依美制，1 加仑约等于 3.785 412 升。

的功能。供水系统来自左舷和右舷沙龙天花板上的80加仑水箱，通过重力供水运行。哈灵顿写道，“所有船只建筑师都不赞同这个想法，大多数人说你不能这样做，但事实是它可以完成。如果他们只计算两个宽间距船体上的液体介质重心和结构的质心，他们会发现重心和质心是稳定的。”船体音响效果非常好，因此安装了广泛的内部通信系统。船体密封绝缘非常完整，3吨重的空调可以保持船体内部70华氏度。为了舒适和安全，在半英寸耐化学、防火和防水的英索利特橡胶状垫子上还放置了尼龙地毯。每个船体有6个特等舱，房间净高度为8英尺，铺位长度为6英尺10英寸。存储空间充足，门通过船体倾斜时的重力关闭，消除了突出的铰链和把手。装潢包括美丽的薄片艺术、富美家木材和装饰性乙烯基油漆。为了放松，船上提供钓鱼台、酒吧和风琴室。

The christening apparently went off without a hitch, but that was immediately followed by trouble. "After she was put in the channel, she struck a submerged log which knocked off both props, but we will have her operating again shortly, I hope."[36] The christening pamphlet didn't suggest any specific purpose for the boat. A newspaper article later in the year provided the answer or at least a hint Harrington was planning "to hold small medical meetings on the *Twin Star*."[37] He expressed the "opinion that the sea has definite advantages over the land when it comes both to concentration and to relaxation." And, "he thought the soothing sea setting would even tend to ease personal differences." That Harrington was ever able to use the *Twin Star* for continuing medical education meetings isn't documented. There were many opportunities to fulfill this purpose since so many surgeons came to see him operate with his instrumentation. But since he was in fulltime private practice and traveled extensively, it seems unlikely there was much time available for educational excursions on the catamaran. In fact, he sold the *Twin Star* to Houston oilman Franklin Beard sometime before June 1966.[38]

船只洗礼仪式顺利进行，但是麻烦紧随其后。“在她被放入航道后，她撞到了一根淹没的木头上，被撞掉了两根支柱，但我希望我们很快就会让她再次行动。”[36]洗礼小册子没有暗示这艘船有任何具体用途。当年晚些时候的一篇报纸文章提供了答案，或者至少暗示了哈灵顿计划“在双星号上举行小型医疗会议”。[37]他解释道：“海上环境明显优于陆地，能使人专注和放松。”并且他认为“平静的大海能抹去个体间的差异”。关于哈灵顿是否曾使用双星号进行医学继续教育会议，这一点没有记录在案。有很多机会实现这一目标，因为有很多外科医生来参观他的器械手术。但由于他从事全职私人执业医师并且经常出差，因此似乎不太可能有太多时间在这艘双体船上进行教育旅行。事实上，他在1966年6月之前的某个时候将双星号卖给了休斯敦石油商富兰克林·比尔德。[38]

The Harrington-Zimmer correspondence for 1963 continued to reflect a mutual effort to address issues as they came up and to explore possibilities to improve the instrumentation and technique. Once again Jim Hite, the company's chief engineer, was his principal contact person. Some less pressing issues included the availability of his latest movie, *Scoliosis Ⅲ*, that was devoted to total concept of care, which he felt some doctors would want to see. Zimmer reported the progress on the Harrington modification of the Cobb protractor.[39,40] Harrington asked for help in tracing the Harrington Instruments a prominent French scoliosis surgeon, Claude Regis Michel of Lyon, had ordered and not received.[41] Weightier topics were the possibility of a major change to the ratchet rod and development of an outrigger distraction apparatus. Zimmer had postponed work on the outrigger because of the possibility of a major rod and or hook design change.[42] The impetus behind this effort appeared to have been to simplify manufacturing and increase strength. Three alternative rod styles were drawn up.[43] Style 1 had the current ratchet design. Style 2 replaced the ratchet with threads of 1/4" inner, 5/16" outer diameters. Style 3 had circumferential grooves 1/4" apart over the entire length of a 5/16" outer diameter rod. Harrington signaled his willingness to consider styles two and three.[44] Four months after the three rod styles had been sent for mechanical testing, Hite reported the results that "Style 1 or a slight enlargement of your current design is superior."[45] However, in the process of producing the test specimens, Zimmer had "discovered a simplified method of attaching the hook to the lower end of the distraction rod. Rather than the two piece construction of the rod and stop collar we merely put a blind hole in the hook." Since the distraction rod was now the full 1/4" diameter to the end, a new hook, slightly larger than any current hook, was necessary. Hite sent a preliminary model. He closed with the comment that Zimmer had a sizable stock of rods and it would be impossible to make an immediate change.

1963年，哈灵顿和捷迈公司的持续合作反映出他们在共同努力解决出现的问题，并探索改进器械和内固定技术的可能性。公司的总工程师吉姆·海特再次成为他的主要联系人。与此同时他还处理了一些不太紧迫的问题，包括他最新的视频《脊柱侧凸Ⅲ》的可行性，这部视频致力于阐释全面的治疗概念，他认为有些医生会希望看到这部视频。捷迈披露了哈灵顿对于柯布量角器改良的一些进展。[39,40]哈灵顿请求查明一位著名的法国脊柱侧凸外科医生，里昂的克劳德·里吉斯·米歇尔在购买哈灵顿内固定器械后，未收到器械的原因。[41]此时更重要的事情是探讨对棘齿棒进行重大更改的可能性，以及开发外撑开器的可能性。由于棒和/或钩设计可能发生重大变化，捷迈推迟了和改进外撑开器相关的工作。[42]这些努力背后的动力似乎是为了简化制造工艺和增加器械强度。共有三种可供选择的改良样式。[43]样式 1 保留了当前的棘齿设计。样式 2 用内径 1/4 英寸、外径 5/16 英寸的螺纹代替了棘齿。样式 3 采用外径为 5/16 英寸的棒、通体具有间隔为 1/4 英寸的圆周槽。哈灵顿表示他倾向于样式 2 和 3。[44]在将三种改良样式送去进行机械力学测试的四个月后，海特提供了结果并表示“或许样式 1 在您当前设计的基础上，略微增大尺寸后效果更好”[45]。然而，在生产测试样本的过程中，捷迈“发现了一种简化生产工艺的方法。将钩连接到撑开棒下端的，并不是采用棒和止动环的两件式结构，只是在钩上做的一个盲孔”。由于撑开棒当前的直径是 1/4 英寸，因此这种改动需要一个稍大尺寸的新钩。海特完成了一个初步模型。他最后评论说捷迈库存了大量原尺寸的撑开棒，不可能立即做出改变。

Harrington signaled a willingness to try out this possible design change, but he agreed with Hite that no immediate design change should be made. He queried, “How are the instruments going? I get a little inkling from the relative checks to Baylor University College of Medicine, but this is no reflection of some of the complaints you may be getting on the side.”[46] Hite gave the question to Alvin D. Brallier, Zimmer sales manager, who responded, “As far as any complaints reaching the Sales Department, we can say that they are very, very few. In fact, in discussing this with Jim Hite, I told him that actually I knew of none to register with you. It also seems quite satisfactory as far as complete new sets of instruments are concerned. The orders seem to be arriving quite regularly.”[47] Not only did this end any discussion of rod design change, but it also ended the Zimmer correspondence for 1963!

哈灵顿表示愿意尝试这种可行的设计变更，但他同意海特的观点，即不应立即进行设计变更。他问道：“器械怎么样了？我从贝勒大学医学院的相关支票中略知一二，但这并不能反映您可能会收到的一些投诉。”[46]海特将这些问题交由捷迈销售经理阿尔文·D. 博拉利埃处理，阿尔文回答说：“就销售部收到的投诉而言，可以说是非常少。事实上，在与吉姆·海特讨论这个问题时，我告诉他实际上我没有接到投诉。就完整的新器械而言，它似乎很令人满意，订单似乎也定期到来。”[47]这段对话不仅结束了哈灵顿关于器械设计更改的讨论，而且还结束了

1963年他与捷迈的继续通信！

Harrington's professional travel schedule for the first half of 1963 had been packed. He had been away a total of 40 days on 6 separate trips with stops in 11 different cities. Although he was performing fewer demonstration surgeries, he was doing more consultations on patients of surgeons already using his instrumentation.[48,49] In the second half of 1963 Harrington made 4 professional trips lasting 36 days.[50] He visited six cities doing consultations, podium presentations, and three demonstration surgeries. One of the trips was to Vienna to attend the Triennial Congress of the SICOT on August 30 to September 16. It was his first trip overseas since Harrington Instrumentation had become available and represented a substantial amount of his limited and valuable time. Because of the logistical problems associated with staging such a diverse meeting, only general titles without assigned presentation times were listed as placeholders in the preliminary program. Harrington was listed as speaking on "Spine Instrumentation and Scoliosis." However, he used this opportunity to introduce a new topic, "Adult Paraplegia." It was his first presentation of a new use for Harrington Instrumentation, that of reduction and stabilization of thoracolumbar spine fractures. Spencer had presented the rehabilitation considerations at a meeting in Dallas.

1963年上半年，哈灵顿的出差日程安排得很满。他总共离开了40天，进行了6次旅行，在11个不同的城市停留。尽管他进行的演示手术较少，但他对采用哈灵顿器械治疗的患者进行了更多咨询。[48,49] 1963年下半年，哈灵顿进行了4次持续36天的出差访问。[50]他到访了6个城市，进行咨询、演讲，并进行了三台示范手术。其中一次旅行是去维也纳参加在8月30日至9月16日举行的国际矫形与创伤外科学会三年一度的大会。这是他自哈灵顿内固定器械问世以来的第一次海外旅行，占用了他有限而宝贵的时间。由于参加的会议众多，他在会议初步计划中仅将他演讲的概况列出，未提供对应的各项演讲时间。哈灵顿被指定在“脊柱器械和脊柱侧凸”主题会议上发表演讲。不过，他借此机会引入了一个新话题，“成人截瘫”。这是他首次介绍哈灵顿内固定的新用途，即减少和稳定胸腰椎骨折。斯宾塞在达拉斯的一次会议上对此提出了康复方面的考虑。

The cases of two patients, who were injured in 1961, were presented. A 24-year-old male and a 42-year-old female each had exploding fractures of L2 and incomplete paraplegia (the female's was about 90%).[51] (*See figure 6.9*) Both had received emergency laminectomy, further destabilizing their spines. Harrington was consulted after both had been referred to TIRR for rehabilitation. Instrumentation and fusion were performed in the male six months after injury and in the female two months. In the meager notes that remain he did not describe his rationale beyond that of providing immobilization. Distraction instrumentation was used, and three-point loads were not mentioned. Both patients had substantial neurologic recovery with the man having one short leg brace and the woman using no braces for ambulation! The surgical treatment of thoracolumbar spine fractures was out of favor at that time because long-term instability had been shown to be rare and laminectomy to improve the chance of neurological recovery had been found useless except in a few instances, particularly progression of neurological function loss.[52] Although it would be ten years before Harrington published a detailed explanation of his method of treating these fractures, he had awakened the possibility of surgical treatment.

演讲中呈现了在1961年受伤的两名患者的病例。一名24岁男性和一名42岁女性，均有L2节段爆裂骨折和不完全性截瘫（女性约90%瘫痪）。[51]（图6.9）两人都接受了急诊椎板切除术，这进一步破坏了他们脊柱的稳定性。在两人都被转介到得克萨斯州康复与研究中心进行康复治疗后，哈灵顿接受了患者的咨询。男性患者与女性患者分别于受伤后六个月、两个月接受了内固定器械置入和脊柱融合治疗。在仅存的少量笔记中，除了提供固定，他没有描述这样治疗的原因。治疗中使用了撑开器械，但没有提到三点载荷。两名患者的神经系统都得到了显著恢复，男性患者可以借助支具行走，而女性患者在没有支具时也可以行走！胸腰椎骨折的手术治疗在当时并不受欢迎，因为骨折引起的脊柱长期不稳定的情况很少见，且椎板切除术对于加快神经功能恢复的帮助不大，特别是无法使神经功能丧失的进展放缓。[52]尽管哈灵顿在十年后才发表了他治疗这些骨折的方法介绍，但他已经证明了手术治疗的可能性。

On his trip home Harrington stopped in Lyon on September 12 – 15.[53] Why he stopped is not known, but the first article in his *Scoliosis 1966* was an English translation of Stagnara's 1963 book, *Lateral Deviations of the Spine*. Harrington noted that in 1963 he had had the privilege of visiting Stagnara, the leading French scoliosis expert, in Lyon.[54] Stagnara and his publisher had granted permission for this translation and printing. One reason the contact between these internationally respected surgeons is so interesting is that Stagnara had been using heterograft (veal or colt bone) since 1950, which could only have reinforced Harrington's commitment to bovine heterograft. However, Stagnara described using it differently.[55] "Following Cauchoix, we make use of a compact transplant between the extreme spinous processes and we use an abundant graft of autoplastic bone of the iliac crest." Earlier Stagnara had written that "Moe (Minneapolis), Cauchoix, Cotrel (Berk-Plage) frequently use the two iliac crests in their poster aspects." Stagnara did not mention the facet joints so whether or not he did facet arthrodesis can't be determined from this publication. In describing Stagnara's posterior arthrodesis technique, Harrington later noted that the facets were partially destroyed in his technique.[56]

9 月 12 日到 15 日[53]，哈灵顿回家途中在里昂停留。他停留的原因还不得而知，但他在《脊柱侧凸 1966》中的第一篇文章是斯塔尼亚拉 1963 年出版的书《脊柱侧向偏移》的英文译本。哈灵顿指出，1963 年他有幸在里昂拜访了法国著名的脊柱侧凸专家斯塔格纳拉。[54]斯塔格纳拉和他的出版商同意出版本次英文译本。这些国际知名外科医生之间的接触如此有趣的原因之一是斯塔尼亚拉自 1950 年以来一直在使用异种移植骨（小牛骨或小马驹骨），这会加强哈灵顿对牛异种移植骨的信心。然而，斯塔格纳拉描述了异种移植骨不同的用法。[55]"在科舒瓦之后，我们在棘突末端之间使用了紧凑的移植物，并且我们使用了丰富的髂嵴自生骨移植物。"早些时候斯塔格纳拉写道："莫（来自美国明尼阿波利斯）、科舒瓦和科特雷尔（来自法国贝尔克普拉日）在他们的宣传中经常使用两个髂嵴。"斯塔格纳拉没有提到关节突关节，因此无法从该出版物中确定他是否进行了关节突融合术。后来在描述斯塔尼亚拉的后路融合技术时，哈灵顿指出，他的技术在操作过程中会部分破坏小关节。[56]

Scoliosis 1963 included an unpublished manuscript describing the technical details necessary to obtain optimal spine deformity radiographs.[57] Presented to the Missouri State Society of X-ray Technieians in May, it described how to take standing anteroposterior radiographs of the spine on a 36"-long film at a 72" tube-to-film distance. Until the time Harrington became active in scoliosis management, radiographs were taken on 14"×17" films, which meant that only in young children could the full length of the spine be visualized. Also, in *Scoliosis 1963* Harrington and Carlos Valbona presented their preliminary findings titled "Evaluation of Respiratory Function in Scoliosis: The Effect of Spinal Instrumentation."[58] They had studied 34 scoliotic patients whose median age was 12.5 years (range, 5 to 22 years), 29 of whom had post-poliomyelitis scoliosis. Twenty-eight had preoperative and follow-up studies done a median of one year (range, 3 months to three years) postoperative. Vital capacity was unchanged or changes were attributable to growth in thirteen, and it increased beyond that predicted from increase in height in ten. Vital capacity decreased in five. This appeared to be a clear improvement compared to a report on ten patients (six idiopathic and four post-poliomyelitis) studied preoperative and at an average of eighteen months (range, seven to twenty-five months) postoperative arthrodesis and turnbuckle cast immobilization in which average vital capacity decreased from −29% to −36%.[59]

《脊柱侧凸 1963》中包括一份未发表的手稿，描述了获得最佳脊柱畸形 X 光片所需的技术细节。[57]它描述了如何在距胶片 72 英寸的位置上，采用 36 英寸的 X 光胶片拍摄脊柱站立位前后位像，于 5 月提交给密苏里州 X 射线技师学会。在哈灵顿积极参与脊柱侧凸处理之前，X 光片是在 14 英寸×17 英寸的胶片上拍摄的，这意味着只能看到幼儿的脊柱全长片。此外，在《脊柱侧凸 1963》中，哈灵顿和卡洛斯·瓦尔博纳展示了他们的初步发现，题为《脊柱侧凸呼吸功能的评估：脊柱器械的影响》。[58]他们研究了 34 名脊柱侧凸患者，中位年龄为 12.5 岁（范围为 5 至 22 岁），其中 29 人为脊髓灰质炎后脊柱侧凸。28 名患者进行了术前和术后中位随访时间一年（范围 3 个月至 3 年）的研究。13 名患者肺活量未发生变化，或出现年龄增长导致的变化，10 名患者肺活量增加超过通过身高增长的预测值。5 名患者肺活量下降。相比于一项与对 10 名通过融合和石膏固定治疗的患者（6 名特发性脊柱侧凸患者和 4 名脊髓灰质炎后患者）进行的术前研究，和平均 18 个月（范围 7 至 25 个月）术后的随访研究结果相比，这似乎是一个明显的改善。另一项研究中患者平均肺活量从−29%下降到−36%。[59]

Other than royalties, it does not appear that the Harrington Surgical Research Fund had any important income. In October Harrington contributed a $100 honorarium received from the University of Texas, Galveston Branch for presenting a lecture and performing a demonstration operation.[60] In December a $100 reimbursement check from the AAOS for a copy of Harrington's scoliosis film was deposited.

除了版税，哈灵顿外科研究基金似乎没有任何主要收入。10 月，哈灵顿捐赠了在得克萨斯大学加尔维斯顿分校发表演讲和进行示范手术获得的 100 美元酬金。[60] 12 月，美国骨科医师学会存入了一张 100 美元的哈灵顿脊柱侧凸教学视频的报销支票。

By the dawn of 1964 Harrington Spine Instrumentation had attracted so much popular acceptance that it had taken on a life of its own. It was not that everyone had been won over, but the ranks of the holdouts were thinning. The initial calls for modifications had apparently been satisfied, and ongoing mechanical testing supported the ratchet rod design. The response of the Zimmer sales manager to Harrington's inquiry about complaints bears repeating: "complaints reaching the Sales Department are very, very few. In fact... I know of none to register with you."[61] Nonetheless, Harrington didn't decrease his teaching and learning schedule. During 1964 he made 9 trips, visiting 12 cities and taking him away from Houston for 50 days.[62] As reflected in his Bound Travel Arrangements, Harrington's lodging and airfare were now usually, if not always, paid by his hosts. Often an honorarium was provided, and sometimes he received a surgical fee for patients operated on. He appeared to have paid his expenses to the meetings of professional associations of which he was a member. As usual the orthopaedic surgeon's academic year began with the annual meeting of the AAOS, which took place this year in January in Chicago. Harrington displayed his new technique movie, exhibited the standing bed, and teamed with John Moe to present Instructional Course Lecture#75, "Scoliosis." It also gave him an opportunity to perform a few patient consultations and network with colleagues.

到 1964 年年初，哈灵顿脊柱内固定器械已经获得了广泛的认可，以至于它有了自己体系。但并不是每个人都被说服了，只是保守派人数减少了。最初的修改要求已经得到满足，当前正在进行机械测试以支持棘齿棒设计。捷迈销售经理对哈灵顿询问投诉情况的回应值得重提："销售部门接到的投诉非常非常少。事实上……我没有什么可向您汇报的。"[61]尽管如此，哈灵顿并没有改变他的教学和学习计划。在 1964 年期间，他进行了 9 次旅行，访问了 12 个城市，耗时 50 天。[62]正如他的"出境旅行安排"所反映的那样，哈灵顿的住宿和机票通常由东道主支付，通常主办方也会提供酬金，有时他还会收到病人的手术费。他似乎已经支付了他所属的专业学会会议的费用。与往常一样，骨科医生一年的学术活动始于每年的美国骨科医师学会年会，那年的年会于 1 月在芝加哥举行。哈灵顿展示了关于他的新技术的视频，展示了站立床，并与约翰·莫合作进行教学课程讲座#75——"脊柱侧凸"。这也让他有机会进行一些患者咨询，并与同事建立联系。

On Saturday and Sunday, March 14 and 15, he was on the guest faculty of a contiming medical education course, "Techniques in Surgery of the Spine," presented by the UCLA Center for the Health Sciences. The morning sessions were didactic, and the afternoon sessions were demonstration surgeries by the morning's speakers using closed circuit television. The first morning began with the presentation of "Technique of Interbody Fusion of the Lumbar Spine" by Paul H. Harmon, who was a prominent practitioner. This was the same Harmon who while in Chicago had helped refocus the Yale Poliomyelitis Study Group on the oral-fecal transmission of poliovirus. The remaining one hour and forty-five minutes of the morning were devoted to Harrington's presentation, "Surgery for Scoliosis of the Spine." This lengthy program was to become the draft from which Harrington and Zimmer developed the Harrington Spine Instrumentation technique manual. The following day's faculty members were all prominent surgeons, as were many of the more than 120 attendees, who came from 23 states and Canada.[64]

在3月14日和15日（星期六与星期日），他作为客座教授参加了由加利福尼亚大学洛杉矶分校健康科学中心举办的医学教育系列课程“脊柱手术技术”。上午的课程是口头授课，下午的课程由当日上午的演讲者使用闭路电视演示手术。第一天上午由杰出的执业医师保罗·H. 哈蒙介绍了“腰椎椎间融合技术”。他就是在芝加哥帮助耶鲁脊髓灰质炎研究小组重新关注脊髓灰质炎病毒的粪口传播的哈蒙。上午剩下的1小时45分钟由哈灵顿讲解“脊柱侧凸手术”。这个冗长的课程将成为哈灵顿和捷迈制订哈灵顿脊柱内固定器械技术手册的草稿。第二天的教员和来自全国23个州和加拿大的120多名听众都是著名的外科医生。[64]

This visit to UCLA also provided some insights into Harrington's efforts to de crease the financial burden of his many trips made for the purpose of providing medical education. He was to be paid a $300 honorarium with no additional allowance for travel expenses by the UCLA Center for the Health Sciences. In addition, Harrington had agreed to perform surgery on two patients (twelve- and fifteen-year-old sisters) two days before the course. The prearranged fee for this was $1,200 (whether the fee was per patient or for both isn't clear). His case log listed these operations and another on the day before the course at a hospital in northern California as having been performed.[65] No additional monetary information was provided, including whether or not he deposited the honorarium in the Harrington Surgical Research Fund, as he sometimes did.

我们通过哈灵顿对加利福尼亚大学洛杉矶分校的这次访问，也对他为减轻多次医学教育旅行产生的经济负担所做的努力有了一些了解。加利福尼亚大学洛杉矶分校健康科学中心将向他支付300美元的酬金，不提供额外的差旅费津贴。此外，哈灵顿已经同意在课程开始的前两天为两名患者（12 岁和 15 岁的一对姐妹）进行手术。手术预先收取费用 1 200 美元（尚不清楚是每位患者还是两位患者所交费用）。他的病例日志列出了这些手术，以及课程前一天在北加利福尼亚一家医院进行的另一次手术。[65]但没有记载额外的收支信息，包括他是否将酬金存入哈灵顿外科研究基金，因为他有时会这样做。

At the invitation of John Hall, Harrington attended the fourth combined meeting of the American, British, and Canadian orthopaedic associations with the orthopaedic associations of South Africa, New Zealand, Australia, and France on June 13–19. These combined meetings offered more social opportunities than usual, and Mrs. Harrington accompanied her husband to Vancouver. Hall's paper entitled "Congenita Scoliosis Treated by Harrington Instrumentation and Spinal Fusion" had been accepted for podium presentation, and Hall had invited Harrington to present the formal discussion.[66] Before the meeting the Harringtons had stopped in Seattle to visit Jim Tupper and possibly John LeCocq and Kirk Anderson, who was involved with the development of the heterograft bone Harrington was using.[67]

应约翰·霍尔的邀请，哈灵顿于 6 月 13 日至 19 日参加了美国、英国、加拿大、南非、新西兰、澳大利亚和法国骨科学会的第四次联合会议。这些联合会议提供了比平时更多的社交机会，哈灵顿的夫人陪他去了温哥华。霍尔已就他题为《采用哈灵顿内固定器械与脊柱融合治疗先天性脊柱侧凸》的论文进行了登台演讲，霍尔邀请哈灵顿进行正式讨论。[66]在会议之前，哈灵顿夫妇在西雅图停留时拜访了吉姆·塔珀，可能还有约翰·勒柯克和柯克·安德森，科克参与了哈灵顿使用异种移植骨的研发工作。[67]

About the time of this meeting in Vancouver several issues with Zimmer were being addressed. Hite broached the subject in this way: "My real reason in writing is to seek further information on the outrigger distraction device which I keep hearing about from various doctors in the field. Quite frankly I am asked to supply the gadget which some one saw you demonstrate in a previous surgical procedure. I believe the last time you and I discussed this you were still evaluating it and perhaps wishing to make additional refinements and modifications. I believe the last time you and I discussed this you were still evaluating it and perhaps wishing to make additional refinements and modifications. If you are interested in us producing and marketing such an instrument we probably should get started on the final design and preparations for production... and since it will take a rather lengthy period to integrate this into our flow of production we probably should get started."[68] Harrington promptly replied, sending the drawing of the outrigger device. "This is the final design and it works. I have used it on over one-hundred cases. Thorkild Engen, our orthotic man, has made a couple dozen of these and sells them but I have not pushed the sale of these. This is to supply a demand which I have kept to a minimum intentionally. I am sure there will be more demand for these in the future and if you would like to go into production let me know. This should be added to my royalty because I have spent money to develop it. It also occurs to me that there is a necessity, and pretty quick too, to have a little better functional description of the instrumentation including the outrigger, which would have Zimmer's name on it. I feel that now is the time to do this. What do you think?"[69] Hite responded favorably on all counts, but he did not address the royalty inquiry.[70]

在温哥华召开的会议中，参会者讨论了与捷迈有关的几个问题。海特谈到这件事的时候这么说："我这么写的真实原因是为了进一步了解这个业界不同医生持续讨论的外撑开器的更多信息。老实说，是有人看见您在之前的外科手术中使用了这个器械，所以希望我能够提供这个器械。我相信，上次我们交流时，您仍然在对它进行评估，以求进行修改和完善。如果您同意我们生产和销售该器械，我们可能应该着手最终设计并准备投入生产。而且，由于将其整合到我们的生产线中也需要很长一段时间，我们现在就应该着手准备。"[68]哈灵顿立即给出了回复，并寄出了外撑开器的图纸。"这是最终的设计，效果很好。我已经在100多个病例上使用了这个器械。我们的矫形器械师托基尔·恩金已经制作了几十个这样的产品并出售，但我没有推动它们的销售。我不得不尽可能地控制它的需求量，这样我们的供应才能跟得上。我相信未来会有更多需求，如果您想投入生产，请务必告知我。因为这个产品是我花钱开发的，所以我需要收取版税。我还想到，我们有必要尽快制作一份包含外撑开器等器械的使用说明书，其中应该写上捷迈的名字。我觉得是时候做这件事了。您觉得呢?"[69]海特在所有问题上都表示赞同，但他没有回应版税问题。[70]

Following the meeting, Harrington wrote Hite a lengthy letter, to which Hite promptly responded. Regarding the outrigger he wrote, "There was considerable discussion at the Vancouver meeting relative to the outrigger being a real neat device and you may be getting more requests for these. If the brochure I send you does not describe the outrigger sufficiently, we might add to it."[71] Hite indicated that they had three outriggers nearly completed and would soon send him one to evaluate.[72] Harrington also expressed the need for an illustrated technique brochure, and with this in mind he enclosed a copy of the paper he had presented at UCLA that might serve as a beginning. He was already having an artist work on illustrations, but wrote, "If they [Zimmer's advertising department] have a lot of money and can help me pay for the artist's sketches, I wouldn't mind that either." Hite's response was positive but suggested that the text be "summarized into less reading as a published technique." The outrigger provided temporary corrective distraction and either facilitated or did not interfere with subsequent steps in the operation. It was the catalyst for codifying and illustrating the steps of the operation and also was a testament to the advantages of having the surgeon innovator and the instrument innovator working independently but in the same setting.[73] *See figure 7.4.* In 1964 Harrington was at the midpoint in his commitment to Boplant®.

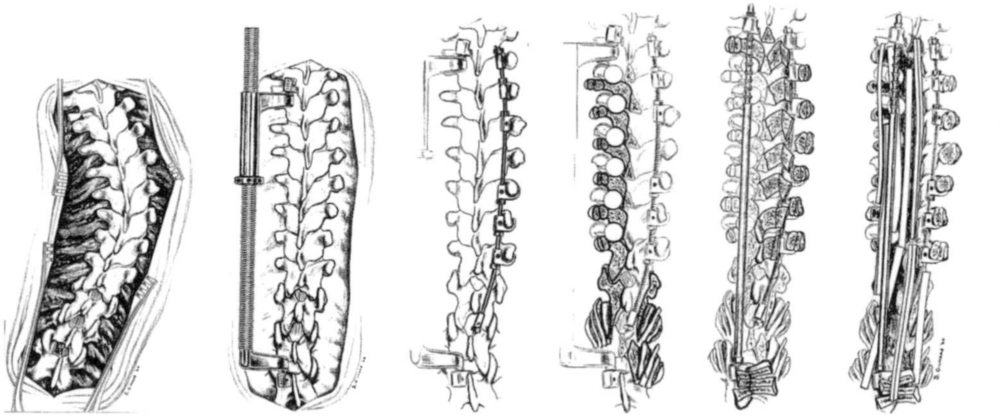

Figure 7.4 ***Instrumentation and arthrodesis steps for a typical right thoracic scoliosis. A. Exposure and distraction hook site preparation with a supralaminar distal distraction hook site. B. Application of the outrigger to gain preliminary concave distraction, stabilization during arthrodesis, and unobstructed access to the operating field. C. The convex compression instrumentation was inserted adding stability, limiting further lengthening of the spine, and adding a small amount of angular correction. D. Concave thoracic facet and lumbar facet fusions were done. E. The outrigger was replaced with the distraction rod and the exposed convex extraarticular decortication. F. Supplemental bone graft, in this illustration Boplant® heterograft, was added. (Harrington Archives)***

图 7.4　典型右胸椎侧凸的内固定器械融合术步骤:A. 显露和椎板上缘远端撑开钩位置准备。B. 应用外撑开器获得初步凹侧撑开,在融合术过程中保持稳定,并畅通无阻地进入手术区。C. 安装凸侧压缩棒增加稳定性,限制了脊柱的进一步延长,并提供了少量的角状矫正。D. 做凹侧胸和腰椎小关节融合术。E. 用撑开棒替换外撑开器,显露的凸侧小关节外去皮质。F. 辅助性植骨,在此插图中为 Boplant®异种骨(哈灵顿档案馆)

会后，哈灵顿写了一封很长的信给海特，海特立即回复了。关于外撑开器，他写道：“在温哥华会议上，大家热烈讨论了外撑开器是否为一种实用、灵巧的器械，该器械的需求量可能会增加。如果我寄给您的小册子对外撑开器的描述不够充分，我们可以进行补充说明。”[71]海特表示，他们已经有三个外撑开器即将完工，马上送哈灵顿一个让他进行评估。[72]哈灵顿还表示需要一本图文并茂的技术手册，考虑到这一点，他附上了一份在加利福尼亚大学洛杉矶分校提交的论文的副本，可以作为手册制作的基础。他已经请了一位美工在绘制插图，但他写道："如果他们（捷迈的广告部门）有很多钱，能帮我支付美工的插图费用，我也不会介意。”海特对此积极回应，但建议将这篇文章“精简为一篇字数较少的手术技术讲解稿来进行出版”。外撑开器提供了暂时的矫正性撑开，有助于，或者说不干扰后续手术步骤。这有利于手术流程的整理记录和说明，也证明了外科手术创新者和器械创新者既各自独立又在同一环境下工作的优势。[73]（图 7.4）1964 年，距离哈灵顿对 Boplant®承诺的期限只剩一半时间。

Harrington commented on four other less pressing issues. He was looking forward to the plastic protractors and commented that “personal contacts are improved by using a gimmick as a gift and I think we could use about one-hundred-fifty per year.” He mentioned again their ongoing work with developing shock-loaded hooks using Silastic (Dow Corning) as an interface. Hite commented that Zimmer was very interested in the shock-loaded design and pledged their help if needed. At that point Harrington was planning to visit Oswaldo Campos in Brazil in November for the purpose of designing instruments for use in small children with tuberculosis of the spine. He promised to keep Zimmer posted, but the trip was postponed to the following year. Harrington also wrote of the tendency of the hook holders to lose their efficiency, to which Hite responded, “The #1266-01 Harrington Hook Holders are subject to considerable rework because of the smallness or shortness of the little protruding bosses. This is easily done; I prefer to do it here at our plant and we do occasionally receive them back for repair.”

哈灵顿对其他四个不那么紧迫的问题发表了评论。他期待着塑料量角器的问世，并评论道：“通过将它作为公关礼物，可以改善人际关系，我认为我们每年可以使用大约 150 个。”他再次提到他们正在开发硅橡胶（道康宁公司生产）材质的减震载荷钩，让它作为一种缓冲。海特评论说，捷迈对减震载荷设计非常感兴趣，并承诺在需要时可以提供帮助。当时，哈灵顿正计划于 11 月访问身在巴西的奥斯瓦尔多·坎波斯，打算设计用于脊柱结核儿童患者的器械。他承诺会与捷迈保持联系，但行程被推迟到第二年。哈灵顿还写道，持钩器不好用，对此，海特回应说：“#1266-01 哈灵顿持钩器由于突出的小凸起很小或很短，所以要进行大量的返工。这很容易解决，我更喜欢在自己的工厂进行生产，很少有需要返修的。”

In addition to the several technical issues, Harrington mentioned an organizational discussion. “At the Vancouver meeting we came to the conclusion it was time to report instrumentation from a national standpoint. Doctors John Moe, Vernon Nickel, John LeCocq, Kirk Anderson, John Hall, Bob Keiser, Ed McDonnell and myself form this nucleus.” The possibility of national reporting on spine instrumentation use was thought provoking. Harrington reacted by posing this question to Hite: “Of course I have close contact with many doctors using this technique, but wonder if your sales department could furnish me a list of all the doctors' names and addresses that are using the instrumentation. I will treat this list with utmost integrity for I would like to broaden my correspondence with those interested in scoliosis.” Hite responded, “Our sales department will compile a list in the near future of at least the repeat users of the Harrington Instrumentation. This is quite a project and will require some time to compile.”

除了几个技术问题，哈灵顿还提到了一次组织讨论。“在温哥华会议上，我们得出了结论，是时候从全国性的角度报告这个器械了。约翰·莫、弗农·尼克尔、约翰·勒柯克、柯克·安德森、约翰·霍尔、鲍勃·凯泽、埃德·麦克唐纳和我组成了核心团队。”关于脊柱器械在全国范围内推广使用的可能性报告令人深思。哈灵顿向海特提出了这个问题：“当然，我与许多使用这个器械的医生都有着密切的联系，但不知道你们的销售部门能否向我提供一份表格，汇总使用该器械的所有医生的姓名和地址。我将严格遵守职业操守来对待这份名单，只用于跟这些同样有志于脊柱侧凸的医生多加联系。”海特回应：“我们的销售部门将尽快汇编一份名单，至少列出多次使用哈灵顿内固定器械的用户。这是一个大工程，需要一些时间来汇编。”

On July 20 Hite announced the shipping of “one (1) rather rough crude model of the Harrington Outrigger Distraction Unit. We merely attempted to build a usable unit following the drawings which you so graciously submitted. Since you have been using this particular design, I can only assume it is satisfactory. I think I would like to suggest some possible changes in the method of manufacturing, not in the design specifically. We wish you would take this one and give it a thorough workout and offer your constructive criticism for its improvement. In the meantime, I intend to attempt another model to produce the same end results but somewhat easier for us to produce.”[74] Hite had already planned to be in Texas in August and wanted to schedule a meeting with Harrington. During the rest of 1964 there were only seven more Harrington-Zimmer letters, which addressed diverse issues, such as an instrument order for George Bedbrook in Perth, Australia,[75] the scheduling of a consultation opportunity at the 1965 AAOS annual meeting, and the arrival of the protractors. The protractors were produced and just missed perfection as the lower end vertebra was not identified as transitional![76] *See figure 7.5.* The scheduling of the consultation opportunity was cleared with the AAOS in order to avoid any interference with their activities. The one time available was Monday, January 11, from 4:30 to 6:30 p.m.[77]

7 月 20 日，海特宣布“一个略显粗糙的哈灵顿外撑开器组套发货了。我们只是按照您慷慨提供的图纸来制造一个可用的组套。既然您一直在使用这种特定的设计，想必它是令人满意的。相较于具体设计，我更希望在制作工艺上做一些可能的改变。我们希望您能同意，并在完全使用这个组套后提出建设性的改进建议。与此同时，我打算尝试另一种模式，生产出的产品和之前一样，但生产起来更加容易”。[74]海特已经计划在 8 月份到得克萨斯州，并希望安排与哈灵顿会面。在 1964 年剩下的时间里，哈灵顿和捷迈只互通了 7 封信，其中涉及各种问题，如为澳大利亚珀斯的乔治·贝德布鲁克订购器械[75]，1965 年美国骨科医师学会年会讨论会的安排，以及量角器的问世。量角器被制作出来了，但由于下端椎体没有被确定为过渡性椎体，所以与完美只有一步之遥![76]（图 7.5）为了避免和美国骨科医师学会的活动冲突，已经就讨论会的安排与美国骨科医师学会进行了沟通。一个可行的时间是 1 月 11 日星期一下午的 4:30 至 6:30。[77]

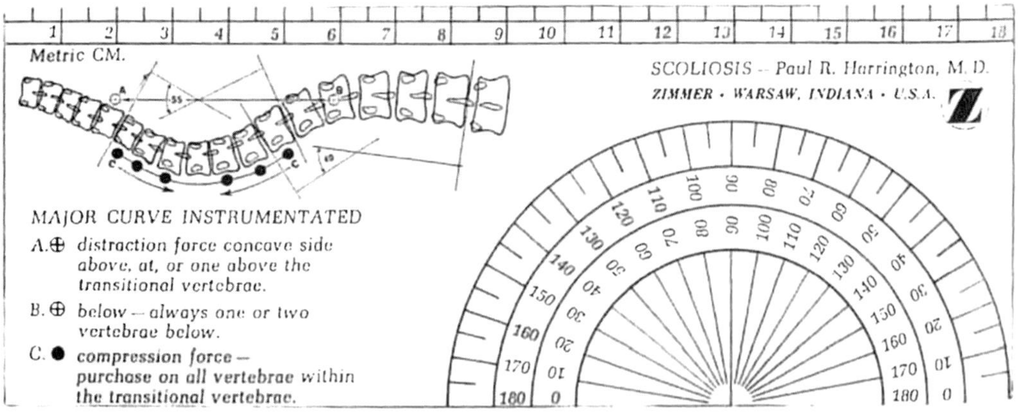

Figure 7.5 ***Pocket protractor.*** (***Harrington Archives***)
图 7.5　便携式量角器(哈灵顿档案馆)

Harrington's travel schedule finally let up in the last half of 1964. On July 16 he and John Moe were the guests of Charles Gregory at the Southwestern Medical School in Dallas.[78] In the afternoon they conducted a consultation clinic and, in the evening, made short presentations. From September 24 – 26 he attended the annual meeting of the Clinical Orthopaedic Society as a new member. This was their centennial meeting, and it convened at the Mayo Clinic in Rochester. The last trip of the year was probably the most fateful as it marked the occasion when the desire for a scoliosis society was born. The meeting, a continuation course in orthopaedic surgery organized by John Moe, was presented at the University of Minnesota by their Center for Continuation Study in Minneapolis on November 12 – 14.[79] This course, which focused on scoliosis and other spine deformities, was well attended and included some of North America's leading scoliosis physicians and surgeons on the faculty.

1964 年下半年，哈灵顿的旅行终于结束了。7 月 16 日，他和约翰·莫受查尔斯·格雷戈里邀请前往达拉斯西南医学院。[78]下午，他们进行了临床讨论会，晚上作了简短的汇报。9 月 24 日至 26 日，他以新会员的身份参加了临床骨科学会的年会。这是他们的百年纪念会议，在罗切斯特的梅奥诊所召开。这一年的最后一次旅行可能是最关键的，因为它标志人们产生了对脊柱侧凸研究学会的渴望。这次会议是由约翰·莫组织的骨科手术继续教育课程，于 11 月 12 日到 14 日在明尼阿波利斯的明尼苏达大学由他们的继续教育研究中心授课。[79]这门课程的重点是脊柱侧凸和其他脊柱畸形，参加人数很多，其中讲师包括一些北美顶尖的脊柱侧凸内外科医生。

During the year Harrington published "The Spine in the Handicapped Child."[80] He used it to illustrate the usefulness of his instrumentation in the treatment of scoliosis resulting from a variety of childhood diseases, including myelomeningocele, tumor irradiation, Friedrich's ataxia, and amyotonia congenita. The articles featured in his *Scoliosis 1964* included "Scoliosis," his AAOS Instructional Course Lecture presented in Chicago,[81] and the "Spine Instrumentation and Fusion Technique" lecture presented at UCLA's continuing education course, which was submitted to Zimmer as the guide for creating a technique brochure.[82] In both he mentioned the use of heterograft from calves marketed by Squibb. They were described as lead-pencil-size pieces prepared from calf ribs in the former and as concave facet dowels in the latter. The other two articles featured in *Scoliosis 1964* were of historical interest. One was an 1893 article by Reginald H. Sayre that was chosen because of the author's sound concepts and struggle using the limited methodology available.[83] The second was a translation from German into English of Wolff's classic article, "The Law of Transformation of Bone."[84]

在这一年里，哈灵顿出版了《残疾儿童的脊柱》。[80]他在书中阐述了他的器械在治疗由各种儿童疾病引起的脊柱侧凸中的有效性，这些疾病包括脊髓脊膜膨出、肿瘤扩散、弗里德赖希共济失调和先天性肌强直。他在《脊柱侧凸 1964》中提到：在芝加哥举办的美国骨科医师学会教学课程讲座"脊柱侧凸"[81]，以及在加利福尼亚州大学洛杉矶分校继续教育课程上开展的"脊柱内固定器械和融合技术"讲座材料，均已提交给捷迈，作为编写技术手册的指南。[82]在这两次讲座中，他都提到了使用斯奎布销售的取材自牛犊的异种移植骨。在第一个讲座中，异种移植骨被形容为铅笔芯大小的骨粒，在第二个讲座中，则被形容为凹侧的骨栓。《脊柱侧凸 1964》另外两篇文章是有历史价值的文章。其中一篇是雷金纳德·H. 塞尔于 1893 年撰写的一篇文章，这篇文章之所以被选中，是因为作者有合理的概念，并用有限的能获得的方法进行努力。[83]第二篇是将沃尔夫的经典文章《骨转化规律》从德语翻译成英语的文章。[84]

Not surprisingly, 1965 was another year of extensive travel with 8 trips and teaching activities in at least 14 cities that kept him away from his practice in Houston for 73 days. A trip to Australia and another to Brazil and Peru each lasted more than twenty days.[85,86]

1965 年，意料之中，他又进行了 8 次旅行和教学活动，去了至少 14 个城市，这让他有 73 天没有在休斯敦执业。一次澳大利亚之旅，一次巴西和秘鲁之旅，每次都持续了 20 多天。[85,86]

For the first time in seven years the AAOS annual meeting was held in New York City.[87] During the January 8-14 meeting Moe and Harrington presented their Instructional Course Lecture titled "Scoliosis" for the fourth consecutive year. Unlike the three preceding years, Harrington's presentation was not preserved. On the day before the meeting began Harrington did a demonstration operation at an Einstein College of Medicine affiliated hospital. During the meeting he consulted on at least ten patients, one of whom was a surgical follow-up. A month later he joined with Moe and Darius Flinchum of Atlanta, a proponent of concave rib resection as part of the surgical treatment of scoliosis,[88] in presenting a symposium on scoliosis at a sectional meeting of the American

College of Surgeons in Philadelphia.[89] The meeting was chaired by John Royal Moore, one of the leading academic orthopaedic surgeons of the time. Harrington's topic was "Spine Instrumentation in the Management of Scoliosis."

7 年来，美国骨科医师学会年会首次在纽约市举行。[87]在 1 月 8 日至 14 日的会议上，莫和哈灵顿连续第四年举办了题为"脊柱侧凸"的教学课程讲座。与前三年不同的是哈灵顿没有进行演讲。在会议开始前一天，哈灵顿在爱因斯坦医学院附属医院做了示范手术。在会议期间，他会诊了至少 10 名患者，其中一人是手术随访。一个月后，他与莫以及亚特兰大的达赖厄斯·弗林奇姆一起，在费城美国外科医师学会分会上开展了关于脊柱侧凸的研讨会。[88]弗林奇姆是凹侧肋骨切除术的倡导者，凹侧肋骨切除术是脊柱侧凸外科治疗的一部分。[89]会议由约翰·罗伊·穆尔主持，他在当时是骨科学界领头人之一。哈灵顿的演讲主题是"脊柱内固定器械在脊柱侧凸治疗中的应用"。

In early April he made a West Coast swing that began with an overnight visit with his psychiatrist cousin, George Leonard Harrington Ⅱ, a 1941 graduate of the University of Kansas School of Medicine who lived in Pacific Palisades.[90,91] After that he traveled to Portland, Oregon, where his hosts were Eldon G. Chuinard and his associates, particularly Lawrence Noall, who was the research fellow/co-author of the classic 1941 AOA-commissioned "End-Result Study."[92] While in Portland, Harrington lectured and operated on at least two patients at the Shriners Hospital for Crippled Children. In follow-up, chief surgeon Chuinard wrote, "I hasten to formally express our sincere gratitude and admiration for all of us who attended your lecture and operating clinic. It was one of the most stimulating things that has happened to orthopedics in Portland. There is just no doubt that you have made one of the monumental contributions to the treatment of scoliosis. It was a great pleasure and thrill to all of us to become more acquainted with you personally. There is no surgical contribution without the man-and knowing him adds to the great value."[93] Many have summed up Harrington's efforts as well, but none better than Chuinard. He wound this trip up with a visit to Seattle to operate and do consultations with Jim Tupper.

4 月初，他开始了在西海岸的一次旅行，首先是去拜访他住在太平洋帕利塞茨的堂兄，精神病医生乔治·伦纳德·哈灵顿二世，他 1941 年毕业于堪萨斯大学医学院。[90,91]之后，他前往俄勒冈州的波特兰，接待他的是埃尔登·G. 乔伊纳德和他的同事们，主要是劳伦斯·努尔，他是 1941 年美国骨科学会委托撰写的经典著作《最终结果研究》的研究员兼合著者。[92]在波特兰期间，哈灵顿在圣地兄弟会残疾儿童医院做了报告，并为至少两名患者进行了手术。之后，首席外科医生乔伊纳德写道："我真诚地向所有参加您讲座和手术的人表示感谢和钦佩。这是波特兰骨科发生的最激动人心的事情之一。毫无疑问，您为脊柱侧凸的治疗做出了不朽的贡献。对我们所有人来说，更多地了解您本人是一件非常愉快和令人激动的事情。没有您就没有外科手术的贡献——认识您会增加巨大的价值。"[93]许多人也总结了哈灵顿的努力，但没有人总结得比乔伊纳德更好。他结束旅行后来到了西雅图，在这里为病人进行了手术，并与吉姆·塔珀一起进行医疗咨询。

During springtime the focus of Harrington's presentations shifted from instrumentation technique to arthrodesis. The first presentation was simply titled "Arthrodesis of the Scoliotic Spines," which he presented to the Pan American Medical Association meeting in Miami in late April and to the Southwest Surgical Congress in Hot Springs, Arkansas, in May.[94] This was a concept presentation in which his stated goal was to make the complex simple. Although many etiologies of scoliosis and hyperkyphosis had been identified, the basic mechanism was either in bone formation or the kinetic force control of the growing, developing spine. Arthrodesis had been established by Hibbs in 1924 as the common denominator of successful surgical treatment. Since then deformity correction had been added, and various methods were used to accomplish fusion. Harrington's concept was that normal function of the vertebrae and facet joint growth centers required the force release supplied by the reciprocal motion resulting from symmetrical structure. Asymmetrical structure and continued growth acting together caused increasing deformity. As a simple method of determining how much asymmetry was self-perpetuating, he proposed the Harrington factor. He considered curve progression inevitable when the Harrington factor was 5 or more with growth remaining and that correction and arthrodesis were indicated. He noted that compensations resulted in secondary curves and that they corrected in direct proportion to the major curve correction. He thought that no functional motion occurred when the static loaded position between adjacent vertebrae angled 3° or more and that in the growing child treatment to reduce the factor to below 3 was indicated.[95] He reviewed the various methods of arthrodesis, emphasizing that a posterior arthrodesis was only a partial arthrodesis, leaving the curve subject to progression in spite of successful posterior arthrodesis in young patients. He listed a number of criteria for obtaining a successful arthrodesis but spent no time discussing the bone graft except to state that for nine years Stagnara had used prepared calf bone as his graft. He did not mention that Stagnara also used "an abundant graft of autoplastic bone of the iliac crest."[96] The manuscript left the impression that he was having difficulty reconciling arthrodesis with his concepts of the mechanical function of normal and deformed human spines.

这一年春季，哈灵顿演讲的重点从内固定器械转向融合。第一个演讲的标题很简单，就是“脊柱侧凸的融合术”，4月下旬在迈阿密举行的全美医学会会议，以及5月在阿肯色州温泉市举行的西南外科大会上，他都发表了这篇演讲。[94]这是一个对概念的演讲，他宣称自己的目标是让复杂的东西变得简单。虽然脊柱侧凸和后凸畸形的病因有很多，但其基本机制要么是骨骼形成异常，要么是生长发育中脊柱各个力的相互作用出现问题。融合术是希伯斯于1924年确立的，是手术成功的通用标准。从那时起，手术增加了畸形矫正，并使用了各种方法来完成融合。哈灵顿的概念是，椎体和小关节生长中心的正常功能需要由对称结构产生的往复运动提供力量来进行支持。不对称的结构和持续的生长共同作用导致畸形增加。为了用一个简单的方法来确定不对称程度有多大，他提出了哈灵顿系数。他认为，当哈灵顿系数大于等于5且仍在生长发育时，弯曲进展是不可避免的，需要进行矫正和融合手术。他指出，躯体代偿产生了继发弯，它们与主弯矫正程度成正比。他认为，当相邻椎体之间的静态载荷位置成3°或更大角度时，不会发生功能性活动，对于正在发育的儿童患者，应将该系数降至3以下。[95]他回顾了融合术的各种方法，强调后路融合术只是融合术的一种，尽管年轻患者成功地进行了后路融合术，但弯曲仍容易进展。他罗列了许多成功的融合术的标准，但没有花时间讨论骨移植，只是说斯塔格纳拉9年来一直使用事先准备的牛骨作为他的移植骨。他没有提到斯塔尼亚拉还使用了“大量的自体髂骨移植”[96]。这份手稿给人的印象是，他很难将关节融合术与他对正常和畸形人体脊柱的机械功能的概念相协调。

Harrington had become a member of the Canadian Orthopaedic Association after participating as the guest of John Hall in 1964 and attended the 1965 annual meeting held in Halifax on June 20–24.[97] He presented "One-year Follow-up of Cases Managed by Harrington Instrumentation and Fusion." He was followed on the program by J.R. Froggatt and G. Dean MacEwen's presentation with the very interesting title of "Surgical Treatment of Scoliosis: Comparative Study of Risser Jacket, Turnbuckle Jacket and Harrington Instrumentation." Unfortunately, no further details such as those found in abstracts, manuscripts, discussions, or letters have been preserved in the Harrington Archives.

1964 年，哈灵顿作为约翰·霍尔的嘉宾加入了加拿大骨科学会，并参加了 1965 年 6 月 20 日到 24 日在哈利法克斯市举行的年会。[97]他介绍了“应用哈灵顿内固定器械和融合病例的一年随访”。紧随其后的是 J. R. 弗罗迦特和 G. 迪恩·麦克尤恩的演讲，题目非常有趣：《脊柱侧凸的外科治疗：里泽背心，铰链背心和哈灵顿内固定器械的比较研究》。遗憾的是，哈灵顿档案馆没有保存相关的摘要、手稿、讨论或信件等材料来提供更多的细节。

In 1965 the Harrington-Zimmer communication slowed considerably. The focus for the first half of the year was developing the technique manual, which by late June was reportedly nearly ready for Harrington's evaluation.[98] Then on August 10 Harrington sent the company a list of questions.[99] First, he was getting calls about how to obtain the outrigger as it wasn't in the catalog. Second, he informed Hite that the TIRR computer department was working on developing a mathematical model of the spine and that work was progressing on measuring strain in the outrigger and the rod. Harrington asked if Zimmer would help them develop a distraction rod with a strain gauge that would allow direct load measurements not only at surgery but also for three weeks afterward. Third, he was supporting this research with royalty money. It had been used up, and the check for the last quarter had not yet arrived. Fourth, he wanted to take two outriggers with him to Australia in September and felt he could sell them there. Hite responded positively to these questions in fewer than ten days.[100] The outrigger was already available as catalog # 1248 and would continue to be in the new catalog due out in early 1966. The strain gauge project "is most intriguing and you can be assured of our complete cooperation." Hite assured him that the royalty check had been mailed early in the week. Two outriggers would be sent in time for him to take to Australia. Hite included instructions for their billing. He also wrote that he had had the pleasure of having John Moe spend a day at the plant just during the past week and that not surprisingly they had talked about scoliosis correction!

1965 年，哈灵顿和捷迈的交流大大减少。上半年的重点是编写技术手册，到 6 月下旬，手册已基本完善，等待哈灵顿对其进行评估。[98] 8 月 10 日，哈灵顿向该公司发送了一份问题清单。[99]第一，捷迈需要提供购买外撑开器的联系电话，这在目录中并未提到。第二，他告诉海特，得克萨斯州康复与研究中心计算机部门正在开发脊柱的数学模型，并且正在进行外撑开器和棒应力的测量。哈灵顿问捷迈能否帮助他们，开发一种带有压力计的撑开棒，可以在术中和术后3周内直接测量载荷。第三，他是用版税用来支持这项研究的，但已经花光了，而最后一个季度的支票还没送到。第四，他想在9月份带着两个外撑开器去澳大利亚，觉得可以在那里卖出去。海特在10天内积极回应了这些问题。[100]外撑开器已经作为目录#1248提供，并将继续存在于1966年初出版的新目录中。压力计项目“非常有趣，您可以放心与我们开展全面合作”。海特总结了他们的账单并向他保证，版税支票已经在本周初寄出。两个外撑开器也会及时发往澳大利亚。他还写道，就在上周，他有幸让约翰·莫在工厂待了一天，意料之中的是，他们谈论了脊柱侧凸的矫形！

Harrington completed his 1965 travels with two major overseas trips. The first was to Australia as the guest speaker at the annual general meeting of the Australian Orthopaedic Association in Sydney. Mary Alice accompanied him on this trip, which lasted from September 23 to October 17 and included a three-day stopover in Honolulu en route. Pre-trip arrangements provided this time for work at the Shriners Hospital in Hawaii with Don Jones. The second trip was in November to Rio de Janeiro to work with Oswaldo Campos. He continued to Lima, Peru, where he was the guest speaker for the Sociedad Latino-Americana de Orthopedia y Traumatologia during its annual meeting and returned through Gainesville, Florida, where he spent a day with Bill Enneking reviewing the status of their adolescent idiopathic scoliosis apex facet-histopathology project. The title he chose for his presentation at each of these meetings was “The Sixty-degree Idiopathic Scoliotic Patient.” In it he addressed “idiopathic scoliosis-from the mechanical point of view which I have developed over the past years.”[101]

1965年，哈灵顿进行了两次重要的海外旅行。第一次旅行是因为澳大利亚骨科学会在悉尼举办了年会，特别邀请他前往澳大利亚发表演讲。从9月23日到10月17日，玛丽·艾丽斯一直陪同他，他们还在火奴鲁鲁停留了三天。在旅行前，他还安排了与唐·琼斯在夏威夷圣地兄弟会医院一起工作的时间。第二次旅行是在11月，与奥斯瓦尔多·坎波斯一起前往里约热内卢。他作为拉丁美洲-美洲骨科和创伤学会年会的特邀讲者，继续前往秘鲁利马，并经佛罗里达州的盖恩斯维尔返回，在那里他与比尔·恩内金花了一天的时间考察他们的青少年特发性脊柱侧凸顶椎关节面-组织病理学项目的情况。他在这几次会议上的演讲题目都是“60度的特发性脊柱侧凸患者”。演讲中，他谈到，“我近年来发现，可从力学角度来看特发性脊柱侧凸。”[101]

Harrington viewed the human spine as having the physical and mechanical properties of elasticity and plasticity. Elasticity was possible because of the alternation of rigid elements (bone) with elastic elements (intervertebral disk, cartilage, and ligaments). Motion between vertebral bodies, vertical translation, tilt (coronal plane and presumably sagittal plane as well), and torque (vertical plane angulation) were each unrestricted for about 1.5° and then progressively damped to 5° beyond which point failure occurred. This provided a column that functioned on the principle of small angle deviations. Maintaining balance during gait with its alternating pelvic tilt and torque compensated for by counter-tilts and -torques in the spinal column was based on this principle. Plasticity was of two types: growth remodeling and internal (bone) remodeling. Growth remodeling occurred at the vertebral and facet endochondral growth centers as the result of physiological and pathological loads. This was commonly known as the Hueter-Volkmann principle, named for the two original observers.[102,103] Internal remodeling occurred in the bone, responded to Wolff's Law, and resulted in the bone structure most suited to resist the normal or abnormal forces acting on it.[104] In surgeon Julius Wolff's words, "Bone forms are determined solely by the statical stresses for which the bone is destined, as can be proved with the same security just as well from mathematical as from anatomical and clinical sources."[105]

哈灵顿认为人类的脊柱具有弹性和塑性等物理和机械特性。脊柱可能具有弹性是由于其存在刚性元素（骨）和弹性元素（椎间盘、软骨和韧带）的交替结构。椎体之间的运动、垂直平移、倾斜（冠状面和矢状面均有）和扭转（垂直平面角度在1.5°内都可自由活动，当度数逐渐进展，超过5°时便无法自由活动。这提供了一个根据小角度偏差原则运作的思路。在步态中保持平衡就是基于这一原则——通过脊柱的反倾斜和扭转来补偿交替的骨盆倾斜和扭转。弹性有两种类型：生长重塑和内部（骨）重塑。生理和病理载荷导致椎体和小关节软骨内生长中心发生生长重塑。这通常被称为许特-福尔克曼原理，以最先发现该原理的人的名字命名。[102,103]骨的内部重塑发生在骨中，符合沃尔夫定律，使骨结构可以以最好的方式抵抗作用于其上的正常或异常的应力。[104]用外科医生朱利叶斯·沃尔夫的话说，“骨骼的形状完全由骨骼所承受的静态应力决定，这一点可以从数学、解剖学和临床中得到同样可靠的证明。”[105]

Harrington concluded the fundamental portion of his presentation with the idea that spine instrumentation was based on the concept of applying normal spine function to the treatment and evaluation of results. For example, to obtain an excellent result, the curve magnitude had to be reduced and stabilized to the point that "reciprocal motion can take place to some degree in the secondary curves." Before proceeding to illustrate his points with clinical examples, he went on record as believing that "a five to ten year evaluation is mandatory for sound evaluation of results." He seemed to be increasingly able to link his physical view of spine function and malfunction with its effect on the function of the underlying biological structures.

哈灵顿总结了他演讲中的基础部分，认为脊柱内固定器械基于将正常的脊柱功能应用于治疗和结果评估的理念。例如，为了获得满意的疗效，弯曲角度的大小必须减小并稳定到“继发弯可以进行一定程度的往复运动”的程度。在用临床病例证明他的观点正确之前，他公开发表观点，认为“为了合理评估疗效，5~10年的随访必不可少”。他似乎越来越能够更好地将脊柱功能和功能障碍的物理概念与它对实际生物结构功能的影响联系起来。

Soon after returning home, Harrington wrote Hite that while in Rio de Janeiro he had operated on two young children having spinal tuberculosis with Campos and had found the Harrington Instruments to be helpful but too big and in need of a broader surface to purchase. He observed and listed twelve typical characteristics of tubercular kyphosis in young patients and sketched the hooks he thought might be helpful.[106] One was designed for the thoracic and one for the lumbar spine. He envisioned one segment hooks with bilateral hook anchors engaging the transverse processes in the thoracic spine and the inferior lamina in the lumbar spine. The hooks were to be connected by 18-gauge wires that were passed through holes in the bodies of the hooks to apply compression. *See figure 7.6.* Harrington enclosed his notes and drawings, asked for Hite's thoughts, and expressed some urgency as Campos planned to attend the 1966 annual AAOS meeting in Chicago. Harrington and Hite must have discussed the issue of implants for tubercular spine infection in young children by phone as there is no follow-up correspondence. Before closing, Harrington touched on a variety of topics. He asked for more protractors to give to visitors, inquired about the surgical brochure, and advised that he had the surgical technique translated into Spanish and offered it to Zimmer. In Lima over 300 orthopaedic surgeons had been present for his presentations, and Harrington noted they were enthusiastic about the procedure. Finally, he reminded Hite that John Moe was going to Sao Paulo for a month, which would really get the instrumentation going there.

回家不久后，哈灵顿写信告诉海特，在里约热内卢期间，他与坎波斯给两名患有脊柱结核的儿童做了手术，发现哈灵顿内固定器械很有帮助，但它太大了，需要更广阔的表面来放置。他观察和罗列了年轻患者中12个结核性后凸畸形的典型特征，并画了他认为有用的钩子的草图。[106]一个是为胸椎设计的，另一个是为腰椎设计的。他构思了一个带有双侧钩锚的节段钩，连接胸椎的横突和腰椎的下椎板。钩子将由18号钢丝连接，这些钢丝穿过钩主体上的孔，从而施加压力。(图7.6）哈灵顿附上了他的笔记和图画，询问海特的想法，并表示时间紧迫，因为坎波斯计划参加1966年在芝加哥举行的美国骨科医师学会年会。由于没有后续通信，哈灵顿和海特肯定通过电话讨论了采用内植物治疗幼儿结核脊柱感染的问题。在结束之前，哈灵顿谈到了各种话题。他要求给参会者更多的量角器，他还询问了手术手册的情况，并说他可以将手术技术翻译成西班牙语，并发给捷迈。在利马，300多名骨科医生出席了他的演讲，哈灵顿赞扬他们对手术充满热情。最后，他提醒海特，约翰·莫要去圣保罗一个月，将真正把内固定器械推广到那里。

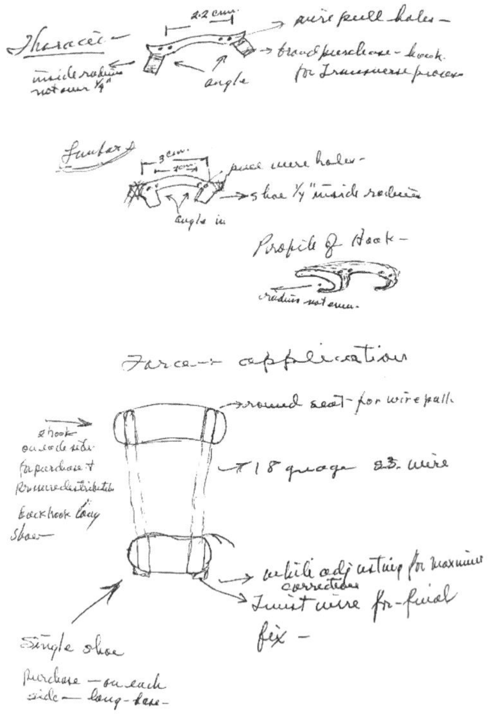

Figure 7.6　Sketches of a thoracic and a lumbar hook through which to apply a bilateral, posterior compressive load in a young child with tuberculous spondylitis (Pott's disease). (Harrington Archives)

图7.6　胸椎和腰椎钩的草图，通过胸椎和腰椎钩对患有结核性脊柱炎(波特病)的幼童施加双侧后方压力载荷。(哈灵顿档案馆)

Harrington's year-end publication, *Scoliosis 1965*, had four entries. The first three were unpublished manuscripts that he had presented on several occasions and were titled "Biomechanics of the Spine,"[107] "Arthrodesis of the Scoliotic Spines,"[108] and "Sixty-degree Idiopathic Scoliotic Patient."[109] They presented a maturation of his concept of mechanical deformity on underlying spinal biology, including both the major and the secondary curves. The fourth entry, "Scoliosis Abstracts," was a series of structured annotations of 95 of the most important scoliosis-related publications from Hibbs' classic 1924 paper to Harrington's last publication of 1964.[110] It was compiled by Stanley Hoppenfeld, senior advanced clinical trainee from July 1, 1964, to February 2, 1965.

哈灵顿的年终出版物《脊柱侧凸 1965》有四个部分。前三部分是他在多个场合演讲但未发表的手稿，题目分别是《脊柱生物力学》[107]《脊柱侧凸融合术》[108]《60 度的特发性脊柱侧凸患者》[109]。这些文章展示了他在脊柱生物学基础上关于机械畸形概念的逐渐成熟过程，包括主弯和继发弯等概念。第四个部分是《脊柱侧凸摘要》，是哈灵顿出版物的一系列整编好的注释，包括了从希伯斯 1924 年的经典论文到哈灵顿 1964 年的与最新、最重要的与脊柱侧凸相关的 95 篇出版物。[110]这部分是由斯坦利・霍本菲尔德汇编而成，他在 1964 年 7 月 1 日至 1965 年 2 月 2 日期间担任高级临床规培生。

During 1963—65 Harrington and Arthur Hodgson, founding professor and chair of the Department of Orthopaedic Surgery at Hong Kong Univerity, carried on a correspondence, which viewed through the dimension of time fits neatly into the innovative process that led to the first successful anterior spine instrumentation. It began with a March 7, 1963, letter written on Hodgson's behalf by his gifted young associate, Arthur Yau.[111] He indicated that Hodgson's had been quite interested in Harrington's "co-apters" (compression rod and hooks) for some time. Recently Hodgson had assisted Louis Goldstein, a leading scoliosis expert at the University of Rochester in New York, with a case in which the co-apters had been used. He "was greatly impressed" and felt the instrument would be ideal for the co-aption of spinal osteotomies. He asked how he could acquire a set of the instruments. Harrington promptly responded, recalled fondly having briefly met Hodgson earlier, indicated the instruments could be obtained from Zimmer, and offered his further assistance.[112] Their correspondence languished for fourteen months, but the silence was broken when Hodgson sent details, including photographs, of a case of a right thoracic scoliosis he had operated on anteriorly, providing concave distraction with a strut graft.[113] It was apparent that he had not been able to obtain the Harrington Instrumentation. This stimulated some detailed, lengthy letters about possible joint research, and Harrington bypassed Zimmer by mailing Hodgson the two sizes of compression rods and hooks and the instruments required to use them.[114] In October 1965 at a meeting in Sydney, they met for a second time and obviously enjoyed their conversations. The following month Hodgson sent the pre- and postoperative photographs illustrating usage of the compression rods and hooks Harrington had sent, but lamented that he was still having trouble getting the instrumentation from Zimmer.[115] *See figure 7.7.* Harrington responded that he would treasure the photographs. He sent two dozen hooks with rods and made some design suggestions to improve the compression instrumentation for anterior use.[116] This rich innovative vein spanning almost three years ended with Hodgson's thanks for the hooks and rods, the news that his schedule in 1966 would not allow their working together in Hong Kong as they had planned, and some musing about a possible redesign.[117] The third of the four steps—concept, approach, bone and joint technique, and purpose-specific design—that led to the first successful anterior spine instrumentation had been taken.

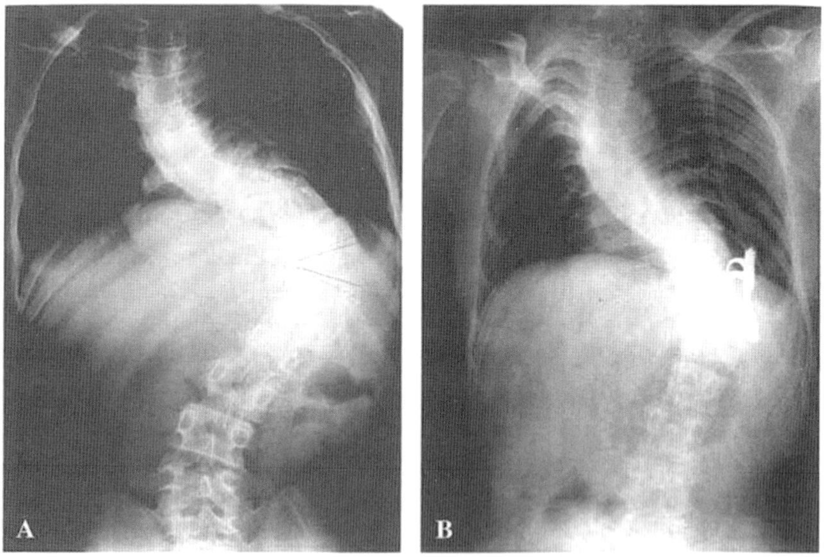

Figure 7.7 ***Coronal plane radiographs viewed posteriorto anterior of a thirteen-year-old female patient of Arthur Hodgson before (A) and after (B) anterior vertebral wedge resection and wedge closure with compression across the vertebral bodies with Harrington compression rods and hooks. ca. August-October 1965.*** **(*Harrington Archives*)**

图 7.7　阿瑟·霍奇森的 13 岁女性患者术前(A)和术后(B)后前位冠状面放射线照片。患者行前路椎体楔形切除,用哈灵顿压缩棒和钩通过椎体压缩楔形闭合。1965 年 8 月到 10 月(哈灵顿档案馆)

1963 年到 1965 年间，哈灵顿和香港大学骨科创始教授兼主任阿瑟·霍奇森写信交流，从时间维度来看，这一通信刚好可能促进第一个创新性前路脊柱内固定器械的成功。它始于 1963 年 3 月 7 日的一封信，这封信是由霍奇森才华横溢的年轻同事丘亚瑟代表霍奇森写的。[111]他表示，霍奇森对哈灵顿的“联合器械”（压缩棒和钩）感兴趣很久了。最近，霍奇森协助纽约罗切斯特大学的脊柱侧凸专家路易斯·戈尔茨坦处理了一个使用联合器械的病例。他“印象非常深刻”，并认为该器械将是配合脊柱截骨手术的理想选择。霍奇森问哈灵顿怎样才能买到一套器械。哈灵顿立即回复，深情地回忆起曾经与霍奇森短暂会面的情景，表示可以从捷迈那里买到器械，并向他提供进一步的帮助。[112]他们 14 个月没再联系过，直到霍奇森发来手术细节的照片，打破了两人之间的沉默。这是霍奇森手术过的一例右胸椎侧凸病例，通过支撑植骨提供了凹陷的撑开。[113]很明显，他没能得到哈灵顿器械。这促使哈灵顿写一封翔实而冗长的信，讨论联合研究，他绕过了捷迈，给霍奇森邮寄了两种尺寸的压缩棒和钩以及配套的器械。[114] 1965 年 10 月，在一次悉尼的会议上，他们第二次见面，两人相谈甚欢。一个月后，霍奇森寄出了使用哈灵顿寄来的压缩棒和钩的术前和术后照片，但遗憾的是，他仍然难以从捷迈那里获得器械。[115]（图 7.7）哈灵顿回应说，他会珍惜这些照片。他给霍奇森寄去了 24 个带棒的钩，并提出了一些设计建议，以改进压缩器械，供前路使用。[116]这条丰富多彩的创新之路跨越了三个年头，以霍奇森对钩棒的感谢结尾。1966 年哈灵顿的日程安排使他们无法按原计划在中国香港进行合作，以及本来计划的一些关于重新设计内固定器械的想法也无法实施了。另外还有一些人思考重新设计一个可行的器械。[117]四个步骤中的第三个步骤（四个步骤包括概念、入路、骨和关节技术以及特定目的的设计）造就了前路脊柱内固定器械的首次成功。

The years 1963 through 1965 might be characterized as years of validation and consolidation. Zimmer received very few complaints, and the system's usage was steadily growing. The only major additions to the set were the center hook for the 1/4” strut bar (requested by Moe to limit lateral displacement of the lower/lumbar distraction hook), the implant storage rack, and the outrigger. A technique manual and movie had been made. Harrington and Hite continued to work together closely. The major issue of concern as 1965 ended was serving the international users. Although Moe's Level of Evidence III study had validated the safety and efficacy of Harrington Spine Instrumentation and arthrodesis, the case series were small with 66 in the Harrington series, small enough to miss or at least obscure rare but devastating complications. The full story had not yet emerged.

可以说，1963—1965 年为验证和巩固该器械使用的年份。在此期间，捷迈很少收到差评，该器械系统的使用量也在稳步增长。唯一增加的主要是 1/4 英寸支撑杆的中心钩（应莫的要求，用以限制下/腰部撑开钩的侧方移位）、内植物器械盒和外撑开器。他们还制作了一份技术手册和一个视频。哈灵顿和海特继续密切合作。1965 年之后，他们关注的主要问题是为国际用户提供服务。尽管莫的Ⅲ级证据研究已经证实了哈灵顿脊柱内固定器械和融合术的安全性和有效性，但该病例系列的病例数太少，哈灵顿病例系列只有66 例，小到足以遗漏或至少掩盖罕见但惊人的并发症，给人一种“事情的全貌尚未浮出水面”的感觉。

（孙端 李章富 译　海涌 杨操 审校）

8 SCOLIOSIS RESEARCH SOCIETY (1966)

Having introduced an effective method of treating scoliosis, he stimulated great interest among surgeons who were confronted by spinal deformities. I believe this interest led directly to the formation of the Scoliosis Research Society.[1]

脊柱侧凸研究学会 (1966)

在介绍了一种治疗脊柱侧凸的有效方法后，他激发了脊柱畸形领域的外科医生的极大兴趣。我相信这种兴趣直接导致了脊柱侧凸研究学会的成立。[1]

Spinal arthrodesis with body cast correction and immobilization had moved scoliosis treatment out of the dark age when nothing could be done to interrupt the severity of its course. But it was not a panacea; sometimes the treatment was actually worse than the condition. No matter what, it always proved to be a major inconvenience. Months of confinement prevented attending school, playing with friends, and enjoying everyday activities. And lurking throughout treatment and recovery was the possibility of pseudarthrosis, the failure of the operation to result in fusion. This usually resulted in the patient starting the process all over again or just deciding to accept deformity and/or pain.

用躯体石膏固定和制动的脊柱关节融合术使脊柱侧凸治疗走出了当时无法采取任何措施来阻断其恶化过程的黑暗时代。但那不是灵丹妙药，实际上有时候治疗比病情本身更糟糕。无论如何，该技术已被证明会给生活造成很大的不便。数月的石膏固定阻止了上学、和朋友玩耍以及享受日常活动。在整个治疗和康复过程中，潜伏着脊柱融合术后假关节形成的风险。这通常会导致患者再次重复这个治疗过程，或者只能接受或畸形和/或疼痛。

To understand the origins of the Scoliosis Research Society (SRS), it is necessary to backtrack several years to 1957 when John Moe became clinical professor and director of the Division of Orthopedic Surgery at the University of Minnesota. One of his leadership initiatives was to create what would become an annual symposium on orthopedic surgery. This occurred the same year that the AAOS Committee on Scoliosis was disbanded because members could not bury their differences and work together to expand scoliosis knowledge and promote education.[2] As Moe's stature as a leading (some would argue the leading) expert on scoliosis grew, the symposium courses became increasingly devoted to scoliosis, filing the academic void left by the AAOS.[3] Ten years earlier in 1947 Moe had accepted the challenge to do better for patients when he established the scoliosis service at the Gillette State Hospital for Crippled Children in Minneapolis. By working tirelessly to perfect posterior arthrodesis and casting techniques, focusing his large practice on scoliosis, and carefully documenting his results, he was able to validate progress or its lack. His results showed improvement up to a point- and that point was about 1956.

为了了解脊柱侧凸研究学会的起源，有必要追溯到 1957 年。当时约翰·莫成为明尼苏达大学临床教授兼骨科主任。他的领导计划之一是创建一个关于骨科手术的年度研讨会。这发生在美国骨科医师学会脊柱侧凸委员会废止的同年，因为成员们无法解决彼此的分歧，而无法共同努力科普脊柱侧凸知识并促进教育。随着莫作为脊柱侧凸的引领者（有些人会质疑是否为引领者）地位的提高，研讨会课程变得越来越专注于脊柱侧凸，填补了美国骨科医师学会留下的学术空白。十年前的 1947 年，莫在明尼阿波利斯吉列州立残疾儿童医院开始脊柱侧凸临床工作时，就接受了为患者做得更好这个挑战。通过孜孜不倦地完善后路融合和石膏技术，他集中精力治疗脊柱侧凸，并仔细记录临床结果，他能够证实该技术的进步或缺陷。其结果显示，直到 1956 年前后，脊柱侧凸治疗效果才有明显改善。

There are many criteria by which one might judge the success of surgery for scoliosis, but the prevalence of pseudarthrosis was among the most important. In 1958 Moe reported his surgical results for 266 patients operated on at Gillette State Hospital for

Crippled Children between 1947 and 1956.[4] In 1964 he did the same for 196 patients operated on at Fairview Hospital and the University of Minnesota Hospitals between 1948 and 1960.[5] While it is true that there were many variables within and between the two series, the most important constant was Moe and his insistence on delivering the best possible treatment to each patient. He worked unremittingly toward the improvement of arthrodesis techniques and gave particular attention to careful application of a turnbuckle cast, localizer cast, or Milwaukee brace. A patient was prescribed bed rest for five or usually six months, followed by ambulation in a fresh, full localizer cast or Milwaukee brace for three months and body cast for an additional two months. In his 1947 to 1956 operated series Moe had decreased his pseudarthrosis prevalence for patients with idiopathic scoliosis from 56% with the early fusion technique to 15% with his facet fusion technique and down to 7% with the addition of autograft.[6] However, in his 1948 to 1960 series the pseudarthrosis prevalence was 13% with the facet fusion technique but increased to 15% with the addition of autograft. Moe and his colleagues opined that these results were not comparable because autograft was mainly used in longer fusions extending into the lumbar spine, which were thus at greater risk for developing pseudarthrosis.

人们可以根据许多标准来判断脊柱侧凸手术成功与否，但假关节发生率是最重要的一个标准。1958 年莫披露了他在 1947 年至 1956 年在吉列州立残疾儿童医院手术的 266 名患者的手术结果。1964 年，他对在 1948 年至 1960 年为费尔维尤医院和明尼苏达大学医院的 196 名患者的手术结果也做了同样的总结。虽然两个系列的内部和他们之间确实有很多变量，但最重要的相同之处是莫坚持尽可能为每个患者提供最好的治疗。他坚持不懈地改进融合技术，并特别注意仔细应用铰链石膏、局部定位矫形石膏或密尔沃基支具。患者通常被要求卧床 5~6 个月，然后在新的局部定位矫形石膏或密尔沃基支具保护下可下地行走 3 个月，再使用躯体石膏保护两个月。在 1947 年至 1956 年的手术系列中，莫将特发性脊柱侧凸患者的假关节发生率从早期使用融合技术的 56%降至使用关节突融合技术后的 15%和增加自体骨移植后的 7%。然而，在他的 1948 年至 1960 年的手术系列中，使用关节突融合技术，假关节的发生率为 13%，但随着自体骨移植的加入，假关节的发生率增加到 15%。莫和他的同事认为，这些结果并不具有可比性，因为自体骨移植主要用于向腰椎延伸的较长节段融合，因此假关节形成的风险更大。

As would be expected, Moe's 1947 to 1956 results were not as good for paralytic patients, who had a pseudarthrosis prevalence of 65% with the early fusion technique and

30% with the facet fusion technique. Considering only those operated on with his facet fusion technique and grafted with autologous bone, the prevalence further dropped to 14%. In his 1948 to 1960 operated group the pseudarthrosis prevalence in paralytics was 28% with the facet fusion technique and 22% when autograft was added. Moe again cautioned about the use of autograft mainly in fusions extending into the lumbar spine. These results are shown in *Table 8.1*.

Table 8.1　Pseudarthrosis Prevalence Related to Arthrodesis and Graft Technique (Percent rounded to unit)

Series Years Operated	Early/Non-Facet	Facet+No, Bank, or Autograft	Facet+Autograft
Idiopathic			
MOE 1947-56	56%	15%	7%
MOE & GUSTILO 1948-60	Not done	13%	15%*
Paralytic			
MOE 1947-56	65%	30%	14%
MOE & GUSTILO 1948-60	Not done	28%	22%*

* *Autograft used in a disproportionate number of long fusions into the lumbar spine.*

不出所料，莫 1947 年至 1956 年做的手术的结果对麻痹患者而言并没有那么好，他们在早期融合技术下假关节的发生率为 65%，在关节突融合技术下，假关节的发生率降为 30%。使用莫的关节突融合技术并加用自体骨移植的人，假关节发生率进一步降至 14%。在他 1948 年至 1960 年的手术系列中，麻痹患者的假关节发生率在关节突融合技术下为 28%，添加自体骨移植后为 22%。莫再次提醒大家，自体骨移植应主要用于延伸到腰椎的融合。这些结果如表 8.1 所示。

表 8.1　与融合术和骨移植技术相关的假关节发生率(百分比四舍五入到整数)

手术系列年代	早期/无小关节融合	小关节突融合+无/库存的异体骨/自体骨移植	小关节突融合+自体骨移植
特发性			
莫　1947—1956	56%	15%	7%
莫 & 古斯蒂洛　1948—1960	未做	13%	15%
麻痹性			
莫　1947—1956	65%	30%	14%
莫 & 古斯蒂洛　1948—1960	未做	28%	22%

注：自体骨移植在腰椎长节段融合中使用的比例较高。

In summary, even though in Moe's skilled hands the pseudarthrosis rate had been substantially lowered, it had stabilized at a pretty high level, which he almost certainly had observed anecdotally as the series evolved. In addition, Moe would have been very aware of the pseudarthrosis prevalence reported by other leading surgeons. *See Table 8.2.*

Table 8.2 Comparison of the Prevalence of Pseudarthrosis in Prominent Scoliosis Series Published in the US from 1950 to 1964

(Adapted and updated from Moe and Gustilo, 1964. Percent rounded to unit.)

Study	n	Scoliosis Type	Pseudarthrosis		Follow-up*
			n	%	
Ponseti & Friedman[7], 1950	117	51 idiopathic 43 paralytic 23 congenital	80	68	8+0
Cobb[8], 1952	363	Unclassified	15	4	not given
Gucker[9], 1956	78	Paralytic	44	56	4+1
Blount & associates[10], 1958	87	37 idiopathic 33 paralytic 17 miscellaneous	11 18 5	33 49 29	4+2
Risser & Norquist[11], 1958	242	167 metabolic 75 paralytic	31 23	19 31	6+0
Moe**[12], 1958	266	130 idiopathic 136 paralytic	30 56	23 41	14M-8Y
Goldstein[13], 1959	51	31 idiopathic 20 paralytic	3 2	10 10	18M-7Y
Moe & Gustilo***[14], 1964	196	100 idiopathic 78 paralytic 18 congenital	13 22 3	13 28 17	4+1

* *Follow-up in average years and months (Y+M) or range (_M-_Y).*

** *Not subdivided by arthrodesis or graft technique.*

*** *Not subdivided by graft technique.*

总之，尽管在莫熟练的手术操作中，假关节发生率已经大幅降低，但它依然稳定在相当高的水平上，随着该手术系列的演变，莫几乎可以肯定地观察到了这一点。此外，他也非常了解其他一流外科医生报告的假关节发生率。(表 8.2)

表 8.2 1950 年到 1964 年在美国发表的重要脊柱侧凸系列中假关节发生率的比较
（改编自莫和古斯蒂洛，1964 年。百分比四舍五入到整数。）

研究	n	侧凸类型	假关节数量 n	假关节发生率%	随访时间*
庞塞蒂 & 弗里德曼[7]，1950	117	51 特发性 43 麻痹性 23 先天性	80	68	8+0
柯布[8]，1952	363	未分类	15	4	未写
古克[9]，1956	78	麻痹性	44	56	4+1
布朗特和助手[10]，1958	87	37 特发性 33 麻痹性 17 多因素	11 18 5	33 49 29	4+2
里泽 & 诺奎斯特[11]，1958	242	167 代谢性 75 麻痹性	31 23	19 31	6+0
莫**[12]，1958	266	130 特发性 136 麻痹性	30 56	23 41	14 个月 ~8 年
戈尔茨坦[13]，1959	51	31 特发性 20 麻痹性	3 2	10 10	18 个月 ~7 年
莫 & 古斯蒂洛***[14]，1964	196	100 特发型 78 麻痹性 18 先天性	13 22 3	13 28 17	4+1

* 随访时间表示为平均年月（年+月）或范围（月–年）。
** 没有根据融合术或植骨技术进一步分组。
*** 没有根据植骨技术进一步分组。

Only the reports by John Cobb and Louis Goldstein appear to have been better than Moe's. However, neither was published in a peer-reviewed journal, and both require further comments. Cobb's report was published in 1952 as part of an instructional course lecture[15]. The patients were operated on from March 1935 through December 1951, a variety of bone graft types were used, and the patients were kept in bed in a turnbuckle cast for six to seven months. The follow-up interval was not reported. Pseudarthrosis diagnosis was based on its radiographic appearance. His reported pseudarthrosis prevalence of 4.1% (15 of 363) was dramatically lower than that reported by his contemporaries, and so it is placed in the outlier category. It was not a case series study but rather an expert opinion report, which has to be discounted. Unfortunately, more detailed outcome reports were never published from this pioneer's series.

只有约翰·柯布和路易斯·戈尔茨坦的报告结果似乎比莫的报告结果更好。然而，两者都没有发表在同行评审的期刊上，都需要进一步的讨论。柯布的报告于1952年作为教学课程讲座的一部分发表。[15]患者在1935年3月到1951年12月进行了手术，用了各种骨移植材料，并且戴上铰链石膏后卧床6~7个月，没有记录随访时间。假关节形成的诊断是基于其X光片表现。柯布报告的假关节发生率为4.1%（363人中的15人），大大低于同时代人的报告水平，并且因此被归入异常值类别。这不是一系列案例研究，而是一份专家意见报告，因此并不可信。遗憾的是，这个先驱者研究系列中从未发布过更详细的有关结果的报告。

Goldstein's report was more credible, even though it was published in 1959 as a small book and thus not peer reviewed.[16] His series began in 1939 and included 65 consecutive patients. The report was based on 54 consecutively operated on patients with follow-up ranging from 18 months to 7 years, 8 months. All were treated for six months in a turnbuckle cast, two months in bed in a fresh, bent cast that included a single shoulder strap and one thigh, and two months in an ambulatory cast with one shoulder strap. His pseudarthrosis prevalence was 13% (7 of 54). In 1952 Goldstein began using fresh autogenous iliac bone graft almost exclusively. To determine the effect of graft type, he focused on the 31 patients with idiopathic and 20 patients with paralytic scoliosis, eliminating the 3 patients with congenital scoliosis. The pseudarthrosis prevalence in patients receiving fresh iliac bone graft was 4% (1 of 25) compared to 15% (4 of 26) in patients receiving tibial osteoperiosteal autograft or banked bone chips. Goldstein's patients clearly had the lowest pseudarthrosis prevalence of any patient group when fresh autogenous iliac bone graft was used in every case, not just in those with fusion into the lumbar spine. However, his results were not totally convincing as the effect could have been an artifact of small numbers, operative sequence (the fresh autogenous iliac crest graft group was operated on last), or both. Thus, in the late 1950s the surgical treatment of scoliosis based on posterior arthrodesis and turnbuckle or localizer cast correction and immobilization seemed stalled at a pseudarthrosis prevalence of 10% to 20%.

戈尔茨坦的报告更可信，由于它于1959年作为小册子出版，因此没有同行评审。[16]他的系列始于1939年，包括65名持续接受治疗的患者。该报告基于54例连续手术病例，随访范围从18个月到7年8个月不等。所有人都使用铰链石膏治疗了6个月，再用重塑弯曲石膏进行了2个月的卧床治疗，最后在可行走的固定到一侧肩膀和大腿的石膏中接受了2个月的治疗。戈尔茨坦报告的假关节发生率为

13%（7/54）。1952 年，戈尔茨坦几乎只使用新鲜的自体髂骨移植。为了确定移植物类型的影响，他重点关注 31 名特发性脊柱侧凸患者和 20 名麻痹性脊柱侧凸患者，排除了 3 名先天性脊柱侧凸患者。接受新鲜髂骨移植的患者的假关节发生率为 4%（1/25），而接受胫骨自体移植或冷冻骨片的患者的假关节发生率为 15%（4/26）。每次使用新鲜的自体髂骨移植时，戈尔茨坦的病人的假关节发病率总是最低，也包括融合到腰椎的病例。然而，他的结果并不完全令人信服，可能因为病例数少、手术顺序不是很科学（新鲜的自体髂骨移植组患者是最后进行手术的），或两者兼而有之对结果都有影响。因此，在 20 世纪 50 年代末，基于后路融合术加铰链或局部固定石膏矫正和制动的脊柱侧凸手术的假关节发生率为 10%～20%。

In late 1958 an episode occurred, the report of which added fresh commentary and color to the North American scoliosis management scene.[17] A 33-year-old French scoliosis physician and surgeon named Yves Cotrel spent the last half of the year visiting major scoliosis centers in the United States and Canada, courtesy of a fellowship provided by Mr. and Mrs. Richard Eaton of New York City. Their devotion to France came through Mr. Eaton's parents and their connection with the French medical corps during and after World War II. Cotrel spent his first month with John Cobb. When he told Cobb about his planned trip across the United States to visit centers that had been recommended to him, Cobb's response was dismissive. "He told me he could not see the interest of such a trip and that it would be very tiring and a waste of time and I could learn everything in his department!" Cobb dissuaded him from stopping in Houston. "There's nothing of interest there. A surgeon from Houston presented a strange paper during the last meeting of the American Academy of Orthopedic Surgeons (A. A. O. S). He had this weird idea of inserting a metal rod in the spine to straighten it. It was completely crazy!" Cotrel continued, "I left town. I didn't stop in Houston. I would go there later. The name of the surgeon of whom Cobb spoke was Paul Harrington."

1958 年年底发生了另一件事，这一事件的报道为北美脊柱侧凸的治疗增添了新的讨论和色彩。[17]一位名叫伊夫 · 科特雷尔的 33 岁的法国脊柱侧凸外科医生凭借纽约市的理查德 · 伊顿夫妇提供的资金，在当年的下半年访问了美国和加拿大主流的脊柱侧凸中心。他们对法国的贡献来源于伊顿先生的父母以及他们在第二次世界大战期间和之后与法国红军团的联系。科特雷尔和约翰 · 柯布一起度过了第一个月。当他告诉柯布他计划穿越美国去访问被推荐给他的脊柱侧凸中心时，柯布的反应是不屑一顾的。“他告诉我，他看不到这种旅行的益处，这将是非常累人的，且浪费时间……我可以在他的部门里学到一切！”柯布劝阻他不要在休斯敦停留。“那里没有什么有趣的东西。有个休斯敦医生上次在美国骨科医师学会会议上提交了一篇奇怪的论文。他有一个怪异的想法，想在脊柱上插入一根金属棒来进行矫正。这完全疯了！”科特雷尔继续说，“我离开了小镇。我没有在休斯敦停留。我稍后会去那里。柯布提到的外科医生的名字是保罗·哈灵顿。”

The 1958 annual meeting of the AAOS had already been held in New York on February 1–6. There is no evidence in his archives or in the published proceedings of the meeting that Harrington had made either a podium or an exhibit presentation,[18] but it should be noted that John Hall also remembered Harrington presenting there.[19] However, this period of time did coincide with Harrington's increasing efforts to develop a rod within a sleeve instrumentation and nonfusion technique, as documented in his correspondence with Zimmer.[20] It is entirely possible that Harrington and Cobb spoke at the meeting, and if so, Harrington would almost certainly have explained his new direction, which might have led to Cobb's caustic opinion in 1958, which he later recanted when he favorably recognized Harrington's idea.[21]

1958 年美国骨科医师学会年会于 2 月 1 日至 6 日在纽约举行。在哈灵顿的档案或会议记录中，没有证据表明他做了演讲或展览演示，[18]但应该指出的是，约翰·霍尔也记得哈灵顿在那里演讲。[19]尽管如此，正如他与捷迈的通信中所记载的，这段时间确实与哈灵顿努力开发套管器械棒和非融合技术的时间相吻合。[20]哈灵顿和柯布完全有可能在会议上发言，如果是这样，哈灵顿肯定会解释他研究的新方向，这可能会导致柯布在 1958 年发表的苛刻批评，但后来当他认可了哈灵顿的想法，他就收回了原来的评论。[21]

Cotrel had many other interesting encounters during his fellowship, but three seem particularly pertinent to this story. In Pasadena he extended his stay beyond the month allotted because Joe Risser had so much scoliosis knowledge and experience to offer and was so willing to share it. During his stay, Risser excused himself near the end of a week as his daughter was marrying Eduardo Luque, a young Mexican orthopedic surgeon he described as a “ tall, nice man.” This would not be the last time Cotrel would hear about Luque. Cotrel had many interactions with Risser, a man of numerous talents and strong convictions, whom he considered to be “quite a character.” In Iowa City, Cotrel encountered Risser's antithesis when he was introduced to Arthur Steindler, the renowned professor and much-respected teacher. The elderly man had published many papers on the spine, and "the results of his work on scoliosis had been terribly disappointing." When Steindler learned Corel intended to dedicate himself to scoliosis treatment, his advice was. "Youngman, if I have any advice to give, do not do what I did. Don't waste your time. Study something else." Steindler died the following year. It is a shame that Cotrel wasn't able to see him during his prime. While in the upper Midwest, Cotrel visited Moe in Minneapolis and Blount in Milwaukee. Cotrel had these recollections of Moe. "I was immediately captivated by this large smiling giant. He wasn't dogmatic about his ideas and readily accepted those of others with curiosity, consideration and interest—even those of a young surgeon from another country who was just passing through. I had rarely encountered such an open mind in my earlier experiences." Just as he had with Risser, Cotrel extended his stay in Minneapolis. He was impressed with the thoroughness of Moe's fusion technique and learned from him "what was and what was not to be done." They developed a lasting friendship. Of Blount, the codeveloper of the Milwaukee brace, Cotrel wrote that he "was impressed with his personality" and noted that he continued to be an important contributor in spite of his Parkinson's disease.

科特雷尔在进修期间还有很多其他有趣的邂逅，但有三个经历似乎与这个故事特别相关。在帕萨迪纳，他逗留许久，超过了此前预计的一个月，因为里泽提供了丰富的脊柱侧凸知识和经验，并愿意和他分享。在他逗留期间，里泽还有一次在临近周末时请了假，因为他的女儿要嫁给年轻的墨西哥骨科医生爱德华多·卢克，他形容他是一个“高大、善良的男人”。这不是科特雷尔最后一次听到卢克这个名字。科特雷尔与里泽有很多互动，他认为里泽是一位才华横溢、信念感很强的人，并具有“相当特别的性格”。在艾奥瓦城，科特雷尔在与著名的教授、备受尊敬的老师亚瑟·斯坦德勒见面时，他发现这位老人站在里泽的对立面，这位老人发表了许多关于脊柱的论文，但“他在脊柱侧凸方面的研究结果非常令人失望。”当斯坦德勒得知科特雷尔打算致力于脊柱侧凸治疗时，他的建议是：“年轻人，如果我有任何建议，请不要做我做过的事。不要浪费你的时间。去学习别的东西。”斯坦德勒在第二年去世了。很遗憾，科特雷尔没能在斯坦德勒的全盛时期见到他。在中西部上游时，科特雷尔访问了在明尼阿波利斯的莫和在密尔沃基的布朗特。科特雷尔回忆起莫时，这样说道：“我立刻被这个微笑的大巨人迷住了。他的想法并不教条，并带着好奇心、体贴和兴趣欣然接受其他人的想法——即使是一个刚从另一个国家到来的年轻外科医生刚刚冒出来的想法。在我以前的经历中，我很少遇到如此开放的思想。”就像在帕萨迪纳一样，科特雷尔延长了他在明尼阿波利斯的逗留时间。莫的融合技术的彻底性给他留下了深刻的印象，并从他那里学到了“过去应该和不该做的事”。他们建立了持久的友谊。对于密尔沃基支具的联合研发者布朗特，科特雷尔写道，他“对他的个性印象深刻”，并指出，尽管他患有帕金森氏症，但他仍然是重要的贡献者。

In a short six months Cotrel had experienced the full spectrum of established scoliosis management practices in the United States. Because of this valuable knowledge, he must not have been surprised that Moe had already begun to claim his eventual place as the thought leader. As a result of Cobb's advice about the Houston surgeon with crazy ideas, however, Cotrel had almost missed the major breakthrough that was about to occur, but he compensated fast.

在短短的6个月里，科特雷尔便全面体验了美国公认的脊柱侧凸治疗方法。因为这些宝贵的知识，他一定不会惊讶莫已经开始宣称他作为思想领导者的最终地位。由于柯布对他提出的不要去拜访有疯狂想法的休斯敦医生的建议，科特雷尔差点儿就错过了即将取得的重大突破，但他很快便弥补了。

Exactly when the Moe-Harrington connection began is not documented with certainty although it was probably during a visit to Houston in 1959, the same year that Canadians John Hall and Jack Kennedy travelled together to see Harrington.[22] The following year Moe and Hall began using Harrington Instrumentation. Although Kennedy stayed involved with scoliosis practice for a while, he eventually went in a different direction and became a famous knee surgeon. Hall credited Moe with persuading Harrington to perform a meticulous arthrodesis and utilize his instrumentation as a method of correcting and holding correction until fusion occurred.[23, 24] An important indicator of the growing acceptance of Harrington Instrumentation was Harrington's inclusion on the faculty of Moe's 1960 edition of his annual symposium on orthopedic surgery that was held in December. Moe's 1964 annual symposium, A Continuation Course in Children's Orthopedics, was held November 12-14 and was largely devoted to scoliosis problems. His faculty included Walter Blount, Ignacio Ponseti, Vernon Nickel, Harrington, and Robert Winter, all established or emerging scoliosis surgery thought leaders.[25] One of the attendees was David B. Levine, a senior orthopedic resident at the Hospital for Special Surgery where John Cobb practiced. The hospital had sponsored Levine to the symposium because he was about to begin a fellowship in scoliosis at Rancho Los Amigos Hospital that would be directed by Vern Nickel and Jacquelin Perry. Levine had the following recollection: "During my residency I was always startled by Dr. John Cobb's comments about how he and Dr. Joseph Riser barely communicated. I thought communication in scoliosis was much needed and that a scoliosis society should be established for that purpose. I discussed this with Nickel who thought it was a great idea and encouraged me to propose it the next day during the meeting. He said he would support me. The next afternoon I was sitting in the back of a large auditorium and Nickel was sitting up front on the other side. He looked back at me and with his hand encouraged me to stand up with my proposal. So, I raised my hand, stood and proposed that we establish a national scoliosis society. Moe thought it was a great idea. Immediately, Harrington pledged $1,000 to start the society."

莫和哈灵顿何时开始联系的并没有明确的记录，但很有可能是在1959年访问休斯敦期间，这一年加拿大人约翰·霍尔和杰克·肯尼迪也一同到休斯敦面见了哈灵顿。[22]第二年莫和霍尔开始使用哈灵顿内固定器械。尽管肯尼迪随后研究了一段时间的脊柱侧凸，但他最终选择了不同的方向，并成了一位著名的膝关节外科医生。霍尔称赞莫说服了哈灵顿进行了细致的融合术，并将对他的内固定器械的应用作为一种矫形和维持矫形直到发生最终融合的方法。[23,24]哈灵顿内固定器械越来越被接受的一个重要标志是在1960年12月召开的骨科手术年度研讨会中，哈灵顿被莫列入了教员名单。莫1964年度的研讨会，主题为儿童骨科的延续课程，在11月12到14日召开，重点关注脊柱侧凸问题。教员包括沃尔特·布朗特、伊格纳西奥·庞塞蒂、弗农·尼克尔、哈灵顿和罗伯特·温特，所有人都是公认的脊柱侧凸手术的领导者或新星。[25]戴维·B. 莱文是参加者之一，他是特种外科医院的一位资深骨科住院医师，约翰·柯布曾在那里工作过。医院资助莱文参加研讨会，是因为他即将去兰乔洛杉米戈斯医院进修脊柱侧凸，弗农·尼克尔和杰奎琳·佩里将是他的导师。莱文后来回忆："在住院医师训练期间，我对约翰·柯布所说的他和约瑟夫·里泽几乎没有交流过这件事感到震惊。我认为在脊柱侧凸方面亟须交流，因此需要成立脊柱侧凸学会。我和尼克尔讨论了这件事，他认为这是一个极好的想法，并鼓励我在会议的第二天提出，并说他会支持我。第二天下午，我坐在巨大听众席的后排，尼克尔坐在另一侧的前排。他向后看我，并招手示意我站起来表达我的提议。所以，我举起手，并站起来提出了建立国家性脊柱侧凸学会的提议。莫认为这是极好的想法。哈灵顿随即拿出1 000美金作为学会的启动资金。"

Moe took charge and in February 1965 began an informal survey of interest in the orthopedic community. The responses were reassuring, and the first organizational meeting was scheduled during the time of the 1966 annual meeting of the AAOS, which was to be held in Chicago in late January. Moe asked Levine to draw up bylaws for the organization. Levine recalled that "after I returned to New York I discussed the proposal with my chairman, Philip D. Wilson, who suggested we call the organization the 'Scoliosis Club' and keep it small and informal."[26] In response, Levine promptly prepared a constitution of the club, and in their correspondence Levine congratulated Moe on his "tremendous success" in setting it up.[27] Moe also sought additional financial help for the prospective Scoliosis Club by enlisting the help of his former colleague and longtime friend, Claude Lambert of Chicago. Lambert had contacted Arthur Lesser, MD, the director of the Division of Health Services at the Department of Health, Education and Welfare in Washington, D.C. Lambert believed that Lesser had intimated that there might be $15,000 for such a program.[28] So Moe wrote to Lesser, noted the growing interest in childhood deformities, and mentioned "one of the prime purposes of this organization would be to correlate the advances that have been made to arrive at a universal decision as to what the form of treatment should be in any given case." End results of treatment and work on the etiology of idiopathic scoliosis were the two other purposes cited.[29] The organizational goal was to set up a central office with secretarial help, which in turn made it possible to consider an organizational meeting in the spring or summer. Lesser's response was negative, but it did leave the door open to an application for a grant to maintain a register or clearinghouse of information and research about scoliosis.[30] This ended the first effort to obtain grant support for the Scoliosis Club as well as any planning for a spring or summer organizational meeting in 1965.

莫着手负责这件事，并在1965年2月在骨科学界开展了一项非正式问卷调查。结果是让人满意的，于是第一次组织会议被安排在1966年1月下旬在芝加哥举办的美国骨科医师学会的年度会议期间举行。莫让莱文为组织起草章程。莱文回忆："在我回到纽约后，我和我们的主任菲利普·D. 威尔逊讨论了我的提议，他建议我将这一组织命名为'脊柱侧凸俱乐部'，并将其保持为小规模的和非正式的。"[26]作为回应，莱文迅速地为俱乐部制定了章程，并在与莫的通信中，对莫在俱乐部成立过程中所取得的"巨大成功"表示了祝贺。[27]莫也通过向其先前的同事以及长期的伙伴芝加哥的克劳德·兰伯特寻求帮助，来为未来的脊柱侧凸俱乐部寻求其他的经费来源。兰伯特联系了亚瑟·莱塞博士，他是华盛顿卫生、教育和福利部卫生服务部门的主任。莱塞暗示可能会资助该项目15 000美金。[28] 所以莫写信给莱塞，提到了大家对儿童脊柱畸形患病人数日益增长的关注，并提及“这个组织首要的目的之一便是将已经取得的研究进展综合起来，从而得出一个统一的结论，即对某一特定病例，治疗方式应该是一致的”。特发性脊柱侧凸治疗的最终结果和病因研究是该组织成立的另外两个目的。[29] 筹备目标是在秘书的帮助下建立中心办公室，以便在春季或夏季举行组织会议。莱塞并没有批准，但他保留了对脊柱侧凸俱乐部信息登记、交换以及相关研究资助的申请可能。[30] 就这样，第一次为脊柱侧凸俱乐部成立争取资助，使其在1965年春季或夏季举行一场组织会议的努力画上了句号。

In spite of the turndown from Lesser, enthusiasm for the Scoliosis Club was very favorable. So, as originally planned, the organizational meeting for the club was scheduled for 10:00 a.m. on Saturday, January 22, 1966, during the 33rd annual meeting of the AAOS at the Palmer House in Chicago.[31] This was one of the huge annual meetings that were often used by smaller professional associations to conduct their own business meetings. The Scoliosis Club originators made every effort to avoid interference with AAOS events. There were seventeen leading scoliosis physicians and surgeons on the list of attendees at the organizational meeting. *See Table 8.3.* Harrington's name is noticeable by its absence. It is documented that on Friday, January 21, he had stopped in Kansas City to see a patient he had operated on the year before and was en route to Chicago the next day when the organizational meeting was being held.[32] Since he had received and brought with him a copy of the proposed constitution of the Scoliosis Club, it is likely that he had been invited to the meeting. Whether others had been asked to attend is unknown.

尽管未得到莱塞支持，但大家对于脊柱侧凸俱乐部的热情仍然十分高涨。所以，按照原计划，俱乐部的筹备会议定于1966年1月22日周六上午的10点，在芝加哥帕尔默家园酒店举办第三十三届美国骨科医师学会年会期间召开。[31] 更小规模的专业学会经常在大规模年会期间举办自身工作会议，美国骨科医师学会年会就是这样的大规模年会之一。脊柱侧凸俱乐部的发起者们竭尽全力避免对美国骨科医师学会会议的干扰。在筹备会议的参加者中，17位脊柱侧凸领域的著名内外科医生名列其中。（表8.3）由于哈灵顿的缺席，他的名字更显眼。据记录，1月21日也就是周五，他去堪萨斯城看一年前接受他手术的患者，当先期筹备的会议召开时，他正在去芝加哥的路上。[32] 由于他已经收到并携带了一份脊柱侧凸俱乐部草拟章程的复印件，他有可能已经被邀请参会。其他人是否被邀请参会尚不可知。

Table 8.3 Attendees of the Organizational Meeting Leading to the Scoliosis Research Society

Gordon Armstrong *Ottawa, Ontario, Canada*	John E. Hall *Toronto, Ontario, Canada*	W. B. MacKinnon *Winnipeg, Manitoba, Canada*
William H. Bickel *Rochester, Minnesota*	J. William Hillman *Nashville, Tennessee*	John H. Moe *Minneapolis, Minnesota*
Walter P. Blount *Milwaukee, Wisconsin*	William J. Kane *Minneapolis, Minnesota*	Marr P. Mullen *Seattle, Washington*
John H. Doherty *New York, New York*	Robert P. Keiser *Coral Gables, Florida*	Vernon L. Nickel *Downey, California*
William F. Donaldson *Pittsburgh, Pennsylvania*	David B. Levine *New York, New York*	Jacquelin Perry *Downey, California*
Louis A. Goldstein *Rochester, New York*	Wood W. Lovell *Atlanta, Georgia*	

表 8.3 发起脊柱侧凸研究学会组织会议参与者

戈登·阿姆斯特朗 *渥太华,安大略省,加拿大*	约翰·E. 霍尔 *多伦多,安大略省,加拿大*	W. B. 麦金农 *温尼伯,马尼托巴省,加拿大*
威廉·H. 比克尔 *罗切斯特,明尼苏达州*	J. 威廉·希尔曼 *纳什维尔,田纳西州*	约翰·H. 莫 *明尼阿波利斯,明尼苏达州*
沃尔特·P. 布朗特 *密尔沃基,威斯康星州*	威廉·J. 凯恩 *明尼阿波利斯,明尼苏达州*	马尔·P. 马伦 *西雅图,华盛顿州*
约翰·H. 多尔蒂 *纽约,纽约州*	罗伯特·P. 凯泽 *科勒尔盖布尔斯,佛罗里达州*	弗农·L. 尼克尔 *唐尼,加利福尼亚州*
威廉·F. 唐纳森 *匹兹堡,宾夕法尼亚州*	戴维·B. 莱文 *纽约,纽约州*	杰奎琳·佩里 *唐尼,加利福尼亚州*
路易斯· A. 戈尔茨坦 *罗切斯特,纽约州*	伍德·W. 洛弗尔 *亚特兰大,佐治亚州*	

Moe presided at the organizational session and shared his thoughts about a society to promote the treatment of scoliosis by meeting to exchange ideas, standardize terminology, register clinical results, and disseminate information about scoliosis. He turned the podium over to Levine for a discussion of his draft of a constitution for the club.[33] The group expressed the opinion that the preferred name for the organization would be the North American Scoliosis Association. Blount suggested that further discussion of the constitution be postponed until after preliminary work was completed by an appropriate committee. The advisability of incorporation was discussed, and it was decided that consultation about this with John Hart of the AAOS was to be sought. The prospect of such an affiliation was discussed without final resolution. Regular meetings at a time and place other than those of existing societies were strongly endorsed. Discussion of membership categories was postponed and referred to the constitutional committee.

莫主持了筹备会议并分享了他的一些想法，学会可通过召开会议来交流想法、规范标准化术语、登记临床结果以及传播脊柱侧凸相关知识来促进脊柱侧凸的治疗。随后他让莱文上台介绍其为俱乐部起草的章程草案。[33]团体表达了组织名称更倾向于“北美脊柱侧凸学会”的意见。布朗特建议等组建一个恰当的委员会，在完成基本工作之后再进行章程的进一步讨论。会议讨论了并入美国骨科医师学会的可行性，并决定就此征求美国骨科医师学会主席约翰·哈特的意见。有关这种从属关系的前景的讨论没有得出最终的结论，但在现有学会举办的时间和地点以外的时间和地点举行定期会议得到了大力支持。此外，推迟了对会员类别的讨论，并将其提交到了章程起草委员会。

Moe was selected as president, Hall as vice-president, and Kane, a young member of Moe's staff, appointed secretary at Moe's suggestion. Moe's office at the University of Minnesota became the office of the new society. The members-at-large selected were Donaldson, Goldstein, Harrington, Levine, and Perry. Of the group, six were thought leaders and two, Kane and Levine, were just getting started, thus giving youth a voice from the beginning. A meeting of the executive committee was scheduled for the following morning at which time the constitution was to be discussed. Those attending the session enthusiastically discussed several spontaneously presented ideas for possible investigation, a few of which are of interest. Hillman, Hall, and Nickel suggested assessing scoliosis using perimetry. Nickel noted the possibility of a relationship between the apparent lack of elderly people with scoliosis and the development of "eddy currents" at the site of vascular turnings resulting in local atheromatous changes. Several thought the secretary's office could be used to disseminate materials of interest, such as the conference proceedings of British pulmonologist Phillip Zorab. When Levine mentioned the need for translation services, Bickel offered to help by utilizing the skills of the foreign-born Mayo Clinic fellows. Goldstein believed other specialists and scientists should be encouraged to contribute to the store of scoliosis knowledge, and Doherty cited the possibilities of studying twins.

莫当选为主席，霍尔为副主席，莫所在医院的年轻医生凯恩在莫的建议下被任命为秘书。莫在明尼苏达大学的办公室成为新学会的办公室。选定的主要委员有唐纳森、戈尔茨坦、哈灵顿、莱文和佩里。团体中的6位被认为是领导者，凯恩和莱文刚刚起步，但学会从一开始便给年轻人发声的机会。此外，学会确定于第二天早上召开执行会议讨论章程。参加会议的人进行了热烈的讨论，同时也提出了进行可能研究的想法，其中一些很有意思。希尔曼、霍尔和尼克尔建议应用视野检查法评估脊柱侧凸。尼克尔注意到老年脊柱侧凸患者数量的匮乏与血管转折处“湍流”的发展导致的局部动脉粥样硬化之间可能存在关系。一些人认为可用秘书办公室来传送一些有意思的资料，如英国肺科医生菲利普·佐拉布的会议记录。当莱文提及翻译服务的需要时，比克尔答应可以利用国外出生的梅奥医院同事的技能给予帮助。戈尔茨坦建议其他学科专家和科学家应加入进来以丰富脊柱侧凸知识的储备，多尔蒂提出了研究双胞胎侧凸的可能性。

The executive committee convened the following day to consider the proposed constitution.[34] Moe, Hall, Kane, Donaldson, Goldstein, Harrington, Levine, and Perry were present at the meeting and arrived at four decisions. The first was to change the name of the society to the Scoliosis Research Society. This was done "in order to promote the image of a productive organization and to discourage membership by individuals who will not actively further the aims and goals of the organization." The second was that "the Executive Committee will elect a President and Vice-President to serve one-year terms and a Secretary to serve a four-year term." The third decision was that "the Constitution shall be ratified by two-thirds of those members present at the first annual meeting of the Society." Finally, it was to be decided by postcard survey if the first annual meeting would be held June 10 and 11 or June 17 and 18, 1966.

第二天召开的执行委员会会议讨论了拟议章程。[34]莫、霍尔、凯恩、唐纳森、戈尔茨坦、哈灵顿、莱文和佩里出席了会议并达成了四项决议。第一项是将学会的名称更改为脊柱侧凸研究学会。这样做“是为了提升一个富有成效的组织的形象，并阻止那些不积极推动组织主旨和目标的个人加入”。第二项是“执行委员会将选举产生主席和副主席，任期一年，秘书任期四年”。第三项是“章程应由出席学会第一次年会的三分之二的会员审批通过”。最后一项为，通过回邮卡调查决定第一次年会是在1966年6月10日到11日召开还是6月17日到18日召开。

Figure 8.1 ***Harrington's draft of the SRS logo. (SRS Archives)***
图 8.1 哈灵顿绘制的脊柱侧凸研究学会标志草图(脊柱侧凸研究学会档案馆)

Kane remembered Harrington's contributions to the formation of the Scoliosis Research Society (SRS) as many and substantial. At the first meeting of the SRS executive committee, Harrington "spoke convincingly of the need to emphasize research by including the word in the name of the group." He "also offered to design a symbol for the organization and it was he who directed its creation, incorporating the lamp of knowledge, the staff of Æsculapius, and Andry's scoliotic sapling being straightened via a stake."[35] *See figure 8.1.* Kane also recalled that "one of Paul's most important judgments dealt with the character of the society as manifested in its membership requirements. Some of the group believed a club-like atmosphere made up of very select applicants who had been personally endorsed by existing members would best serve the desired candor and transparency required for the presentation of complications, errors, and missteps in an open and honest fashion. Paul and others pushed for appropriate prerequisites in terms of training and accreditation but also wanted to encourage a more robust and vigorous organization which would thrive by serving as a forum for professional education and networking between experienced seniors and educable younger doctors. The fine line of the latter approach became the blueprint for the growth and vitality of the S.R.S." On February 4 Kane mailed the executive committee members the minutes of the organizational and executive committee meetings.[36] He also enclosed an edited version of the constitution, which established the new name, Scoliosis Research Society, and a list of 68 proposed members. He requested that the executive committee members supply as much contact information for the proposed members as possible and any suggestions about their appropriate membership status, be it active, honorary, associate, or delayed.

凯恩一直记得哈灵顿对建立脊柱侧凸研究学会所做出的巨大贡献。在学会第一次执行委员会上，哈灵顿“令人信服地谈到需要通过在团体名称中加入‘研究’这个词来强调研究”。他“也答应为学会设计组织标志。正是他将知识之灯、阿斯克勒皮俄斯手杖以及通过木桩变直的安德里的侧弯树融合为组织标志”[35]。(图 8.1) 凯恩还回忆：“保罗涉及学会性质最重要的决定体现在对会员资格的要求上。团体中的一些人认为学会应该由非常优秀的申请者组成，俱乐部般的氛围将最有助于达到组织学会的目的，即以公开和真实的方式展现并发症、错误和失误。保罗和其他人在培训和认证方面提出了适当的先决条件，但也希望激励一个更强大、更有活力的组织，通过一个专业教育的论坛，在经验丰富的资深医生和可教育的年轻医生之间建立网络，并使其蓬勃发展。后一种方法的细微差别成为脊柱侧凸研究学会发展和保持活力的蓝图。”2月4日，凯恩将组织委员会和执行委员会的会议记录邮寄给执行委员会成员。他还附上了一份经过编辑的章程，其中为学会确立了新的名称——脊柱侧凸研究学会，以及一份包含68名被提名成员的名单。他要求执行委员会成员尽可能多地提供被提名的会员的联系信息，以及关于他们会员身份的任何建议，无论是活跃会员、荣誉会员、准会员，还是候补会员。

The SRS made it clear from the beginning that it was an orthopedic organization, reflecting the specialty's eighteenth-century origin as the entity devoted to the treatment of structural deformities of the body. Article I of the constitution read, "The Scoliosis Research Society shall consist of orthopedic surgeons, physicians, and scientists in other fields who have a special interest in furthering knowledge of the etiology, diagnosis, treatment and prevention of scoliosis." While the need for collaboration was recognized, the membership categories in Article III projected a hierarchical structure: "Active membership shall be limited to those orthopedic surgeons of the United States and Canada who devote a significant portion of their time to scoliosis and submit a written interest in joining the Scoliosis Research Society. Associate membership shall be limited to those orthopedic surgeons of other countries, and physicians and scientists in other fields who have demonstrated an interest in scoliosis and who submit a written interest in joining the Scoliosis Research Society." Honorary membership was provided for pioneers in the field. The executive committee was authorized to approve membership, terminate membership "if a member shows no active participation in the activities of the Society for two consecutive years," and determine membership dues. There were four purposes of the society listed in Article II: "1. To promote an exchange of ideas in the field of scoliosis by means of presentations and discussions, 2. to stimulate interest in the field of scoliosis in the medical profession, 3. to standardize terminology in scoliosis, and 4. to establish a Foundation for clinical and investigational research in the field of scoliosis."

脊柱侧凸研究学会从一开始就明确指出，它是一个起源于18世纪、致力于治疗身体结构性畸形的实体骨科组织。章程的第一条写道：“脊柱侧凸研究学会应由有志于促进脊柱侧凸的病因、诊断、治疗和预防研究的骨科医生、内科医生和其他领域的科学家组成。”虽然已经认识到合作的必要性，但在第三条中的成员类别中还是规划了一个层次结构："活跃会员资格仅限于在脊柱侧凸领域投入大量时间并提交加入脊柱侧凸研究学会意向书的美国和加拿大的骨科医生。助理会员仅限于其他国家的骨科医生，以及对脊柱侧凸表现出兴趣并提交加入脊柱侧凸研究学会书面意向的其他领域的医生和科学家。"荣誉会员的头衔则颁布给该领域的先驱。成员"如果连续两年没有积极参与学会活动"，执行委员会有权终止其会员资格。此外，第三条还确定了会费。第二条中列出了学会的四个宗旨："（1）通过介绍和讨论促进脊柱侧凸领域的学术交流；（2）激发医学界对脊柱侧凸领域的兴趣；（3）规范脊柱侧凸的术语；（4）建立脊柱侧凸领域的临床和调查研究基金会。"

The executive committee was defined in Article IV. There were to be eight members, each with a four-year term, and no member was eligible to serve more than two consecutive terms. Two new members were to be elected each year with a few shorter terms during the society's start-up years. The committee elected a chairman and a vice-chairman to serve one-year terms and a secretary-treasurer to serve a four-year term. The nominating committee was defined in Article V as having three active members appointed by the chairman prior to the annual meeting. Article VI charged the executive committee to determine the location of the regular meetings and provided that a member could bring a guest by registering the person with the secretary prior to the meeting. Article VII empowered the executive committee to "adopt such rules and regulations as may be necessary for the proper conduct of the work of the Scoliosis Research Society," and Article Ⅷ explained the rules for ratification. The dates selected for the first annual meeting of the SRS were Friday and Saturday, June 10 and 11, 1966, at the University of Minnesota campus in Minneapolis. The invitation letter was posted April 18, 1966, to approximately 68 prospective members, including the 8 executive committee members.

执行委员会的定义见第四条：执行委员会由 8 名成员组成，每人任期为四年。委员不得连任超过两届。在学会成立初期，每年将选出两名任期较短的新委员。委员会选出一名主席和一名副主席，任期一年；秘书一名，任期四年。第五条规定，提名委员会有 3 名活跃会员，由主席在年会前任命。第六条规定，执行委员会决定定期会议的地点，并规定会员可以在会议前通过秘书登记的方式带一名嘉宾参会。第七条授权执行委员会通过了脊柱侧凸研究学会正常开展工作所需的规则和条例，第八条解释了批准的规则。脊柱侧凸研究学会第一次年会的日期选定为 1966 年 6 月 10 日和 11 日，在明尼阿波利斯的明尼苏达大学校区举行。邀请函于 1966 年 4 月 18 日发送给大约 68 名拟任成员，其中包括 8 名执行委员会成员。

Moe eventually shared with Owen H. Wangensteen, the widely known and respected professor and chairman of the Department of Surgery at the University of Minnesota, his correspondence with Arthur Lesser at the Department of Health, Education and Welfare. He chose to wait until after the January 22 and 23 organizational meetings had been held. Wangensteen felt that the proposal needed sharper focus and that the monies asked for were not enough "to give the project real impetus."[38] He recommended bringing two fellows or residents into the project on a half-time basis and adding some medical student time. He also urged the writing of a "short historical sketch of the problem, with a short paragraph on each method of management." He suggested identifying what the nature of the problem really was and how it was proposed to dissect the problem. In the end he came up with about the same budget: $15,000. He also provided the name of an in-house resource that could provide additional advice for preparing a proposal that would interest the National Institutes of Health, which was not the agency Lambert had guided Moe to.

莫最终与明尼苏达大学广为人知且受人尊敬的教授兼外科系主任欧文·H.旺根施泰因分享了这一信息。他选择等到1月22日和23日的组织会议召开之后，与旺根施泰因分享了之前他与卫生、教育和福利部的亚瑟·莱塞的通信。旺根施泰因认为提案需要更明确的重点，所要求的资金也不足以给项目带来真正的支持。[38]他建议让两名专科培训医生或住院医生以兼职的方式参与该项目，并让一些医学生参与进来帮忙。他还敦促写一篇关于这个问题的简短的历史背景介绍，及每个问题的相应管理方法。他建议弄清楚问题的实质，以及确定解决问题的具体措施。最后，他得出了大约相同的预算：15 000 美元。他还提供了一个内部机构的名称，该机构可以提供额外的建议，以准备一份能够引起美国国家卫生研究院兴趣的提案，而这并不是兰伯特给莫建议的机构。

The executive committee, with all members present, met on Thursday evening, June 9 at 8 p.m.[39] They began by reviewing the final program of the meeting, scheduled for 8 a.m. to 5 p.m. on Friday and 8 a.m. to 3:30 p.m. on Saturday.[40] By far the most time was allotted to terminology and evaluation with four concurrent panels of two hours on Friday and a two-hour general meeting on Saturday. This reflected the committee members' belief "that the major effort at the first annual meeting should be directed toward the codification of an acceptable terminology." They also discussed the feedback they had received about the proposed constitution, and it became apparent that the document was subject to considerable revision. Of particular concern were the articles regarding the election, term length, and function of the officers and the executive committee. They again had allowed ample time in the program to address these and any other constitutional issues before ratification could be accomplished. Membership issues were discussed, and it was estimated there would be about 60 active and 6 honorary members. Honorary membership status was extended to John R. Cobb, William H. von Lackum, Joseph C. Risser, George J. Garceau, Albert Ferguson Sr., and Claude N. Lambert. Upcoming meeting sites were set with Minneapolis scheduled for the organization's second annual meeting in 1967, Houston in 1968, and Los Angeles in 1969. The suggestion of didactic presentations followed by a discussant was reviewed, and the recommendation made that a panel of discussants be used to avoid the time being monopolized by one discussant. The current officers were nominated to continue in their positions and were approved by the executive committee: Moe as president, Hall as president-elect, and Kane as secretary-treasurer. An important change had occurred during the executive committee meetings as the office of vice-president became that of president-elect, thus eliminating a largely ceremonial position and providing continuity of leadership. It was also decided that legal counsel would be solicited to prevent complications related to incorporation of the society.

执行委员会所有成员于6月9日星期四晚上8点出席了会议。[39]他们首先审查了会议的最后议程，主要议程时间为周五上午8点到下午5点，周六上午8点到下午3点30分。[40]到目前为止，术语和评估方面花费的时间最多，周五有四个并行小组会进行两小时的讨论，周六有一个两小时的全体会议。这反映了委员会成员的决心，即第一次年会的主要工作应该是编写可接受的术语。他们还讨论了收到的关于拟议章程的反馈，显然该文件需要进行相当大的修改。特别令人关切的是关于选举的条款、任期、官员和执行委员会的职能。他们再次在计划中留出了充足的时间，以保证在得到批准之前解决这些和任何其他的章程问题。接着，他们进行了会员身份问题的讨论，估计将有大约60名活跃会员和6名荣誉会员。荣誉会员分别是约翰·柯布、威廉·H. 冯·拉库姆、约瑟夫·R. 里泽、乔治·J. 加索、阿尔伯特·弗格森和克劳德·N. 兰伯特。即将召开的会议分别是1967年在明尼阿波利斯举行的第二届年会、1968年在休斯敦举行的第三届年会、1969年在洛杉矶举行的第四届年会。会议审查了由讨论者进行教学演讲的建议，并决定成立一个专家讨论小组来避免讨论时间被一个讨论者用完。目前的领导层成员被提名继续留任，并由执行委员会批准：莫为主席，霍尔为候任主席，凯恩为秘书兼财务主管。在执行委员会会议期间制订了一个重要制度，即将副主席头衔改为候任主席，从而避免了副主席这样一个作为礼仪性职务的称呼，并保持了领导层面的连续性。还决定设立法律顾问，以处理与学会运行相关的一些争执和其他情况。

Kane, who kept detailed minutes of the first annual meeting of the SRS, opened the first session by addressing logistical issues.[41] Moe took the podium to review the origins and organizational steps taken up to that time and then introduced Levine, who chaired the first constitutional session. This time for evaluation and discussion was entered into "quite enthusiastically and resulted in many valuable additions and deletions" that were to be incorporated into a form that could be voted on the following day. The second session of the morning was devoted to an in-depth discussion of terminology and evaluation by four panels of approximately ten each, meeting in separate rooms under the leadership of two members of the executive committee. These were described as "lively and fertile discussions... including such basic problems as the definition of scoliosis and the distinctions necessary between structural and non-structural scoliosis. Studies of scoliosis and the measurement of deviation from the true were also discussed as well as evaluation criteria which included onset and recognition, the curve pattern, the rib deformity, pulmonary function studies, decompensation, rotation and cosmetic appearance, and treatment results."

凯恩保留了第一届脊柱侧凸研究学会年会的记录，他在第一次会议的开幕式上谈到了后勤问题。[41]莫在讲台上回顾了会议的起源和组织步骤，然后介绍了主持第一次会议的莱文。这次大家评估和讨论的热情很高，产生了许多有价值的、可供增补和删减的内容，这些内容将被纳入第二天可以进行投票的表格中。上午的第二阶段会议专门由四个小组深入讨论术语和评估内容与方法，每个小组大约10人。在两名执行委员会成员的领导下，在不同的房间举行了讨论。会议的讨论气氛活跃，话题丰富，包括脊柱侧凸的定义、结构性和非结构性脊柱侧凸的关键区别等基本问题。会议还讨论了脊柱侧凸研究和测量的偏差，以及对发病机制和识别、弯曲类型、肋骨畸形、肺功能、失代偿、旋转和美容外观以及治疗结果在内的评估标准。

Following lunch, the third session convened, which was devoted to didactic presentations and discussions. It varied slightly from the preliminary program in that Hillman did not present on perimetry in scoliosis. The first presentation was given by Harrington on the topic of "Scoliosis Data Selection, Storage and Retrieval." Using slides and brochures created specifically for this meeting, he described the electronic data storage, processing, and retrieval program developed at the Texas Institute for Rehabilitation and Research over the prior seven years. He indicated that over a million and a half bits of information on his patients were carried on 30 feet of electronic tape.[42] If the SRS were to begin an electronic data processing program, he urged the need for internal stability at the involved institution and the availability of a mature and experienced programmer. The second paper, presented by Robert Winter and co-authored by John Moe and Vincent E. Eilers, was a retrospective review of over 250 cases of congenital scoliosis with a focus on progression with or without treatment. While some types were less dangerous, "a major portion of the scoliotics with congenital deformities of the spine will have a very malignant progression if it is not checked by bracing or surgery."[43] Moe addressed the special problems of congenital kyphosis. The third paper, authored by James Valuska and Moe, was titled "Evaluation of Treatment of Scoliosis by Harrington Instrumentation."[44] It had been presented a month earlier at the annual meeting of the AOA, and a lengthy abstract was published.[45] Unlike Moe's validation study[46] this was limited to patients with idiopathic scoliosis, which had increased from 45 to 131. The 100 Risser cast correction patients had been part of the authors' mixed pathology group published in 1964.[47] All studied patients had a minimum follow-up of eighteen months. The averages of a number of process variables for the two series are shown in Table 8.4.

Table 8.4 Average of a Number of Process Variables for the Harrington and Risser Series

Measurement	Harrington	Risser
Patients	131	100
Age	16.5 years	13.8 years
Preoperation curve	67°	61°
Maximally corrected curve	26°(61%)	28°(54°)
Final curve	37°(45%)	35°(42°)
Curve correction loss	11°(16%)	7°(12°)
Time in Risser cast	7 months	10.5 months
Time before ambulation	2.5 months	5.5 months
Pseudarthrosis by X-ray	22(17%)	13(13%)
Reoperation for Pseudarthrosis	8(6%)	13(13%)
Wound infection, immediate and delayed	7°	1.7°
Hook displacement	20(15%)	NA
Distraction rod breakage	6	NA
Removal of instrumentation	20	NA

午餐后，召开了专门用来教学演讲和讨论的第三节会议。它与初步计划略有不同，因为希尔曼没有介绍关于脊柱侧凸的视野检查法。哈灵顿做了第一个报告，主题是“脊柱侧凸数据选择、存储和检索”。通过使用专门为这次会议制作的幻灯片和手册，他描述了得克萨斯康复与研究中心在过去7年中开发的电子数据存储、处理和检索计划。他表示，超过150万比特的患者信息被存储在30英尺长的电子磁带上。[42]如果脊柱侧凸研究学会准备开始使用电子数据处理程序，他会敦促相关机构保持内部的稳定，并提供一名有经验的程序员。第二篇论文由罗伯特·温特报告，共同作者是约翰·莫和文森特·E. 艾勒斯。这篇论文回顾了250多名先天性脊柱侧凸患者，重点关注治疗或不治疗的侧凸进展。尽管某些类型的恶化风险较小，但对大多数先天性脊柱畸形的患者来说，如果没有支具和手术的干预，病情将会有非常严重的恶化。[43]莫对先天性脊柱后凸相关的一些特殊问题进行了讲解。第三篇论文是由詹姆斯·瓦勒斯卡和莫共同撰写，题为《哈灵顿器械治疗脊柱侧凸的疗效评价》。[44]这篇论文在一个月前美国骨科学会年会上已经交流过，并且摘要已经发表。[45]与莫的验证研究不同，[46]这篇研究仅限于特发性脊柱侧凸患者，并且患者人数已从45人增加到131人。100例接受里泽石膏矫正的病例，是作者于1964年发表的论文中的混合病因组的一部分。[47]所有研究患者的随访时间至少为18个月。表8.4显示了两个研究的变量平均值。

表8.4　哈灵顿和里泽研究的变量平均值

测量变量	哈灵顿	里泽
患者数量	131	100
年龄	16.5岁	13.8岁
术前弯曲度	67°	61°
最大矫正的弯曲度	26°(61%)	28°(54%)
最终弯曲度	37°(45%)	35°(42%)
矫正丢失	11°(16%)	7°(12%)
Risser石膏佩戴时间	7个月	10.5个月
恢复行走时间	2.5个月	5.5个月
假关节形成—X光片	22*(17%)	13*(13%)
假关节引起的二次手术	8*(6%)	13*(13%)
急性和迟发伤口感染	7%	1.7%
钩移位	20*(15%)	没用
断棒	6*	没用
内固定取出	20*	没用

*均指患者数量。

The authors concluded that Harrington Instrumentation as an adjunct to the treatment of scoliosis offered a number of advantages. A more severe curve in an older patient could be given better correction than with cast alone, and, in general, older patients were more tolerant of the treatment. They determined that final correction was improved because initial correction was better using the instrumentation and the total period of cast immobilization was less. Earlier ambulation with acceptable loss of correction was also possible. The advantages were somewhat offset by a larger number of complications, including infection, instrument displacement or breakage, and pseudarthrosis. The latter, shown only by X-ray, often disappeared with the passage of time. The authors expressed the opinion that the "incidence of pseudarthrosis can be lessened by the routine addition of generous amounts of autogenous bone. No one should undertake the use of Harrington instruments without first learning well the principles of the surgical treatment of scoliosis." The study had made it clear that Harington Instrumentation was an adjunct, not a panacea, for the treatment of idiopathic scoliosis.

作者得出结论，哈灵顿器械作为脊柱侧凸治疗的辅助手段具有许多优势。与单独使用石膏相比，可以使年龄较大的患者更好地矫正更严重的畸形，并且一般来说，大龄患者对这种治疗更为耐受。他们的最终矫正得到了改善，因为使用器械进行初始矫正效果更好，石膏固定的总时间更短。早期下床行走并出现可接受的矫正丢失也是可能的。但这些优势在一定程度上会被更多的并发症抵消，包括感染、器械移位或断裂、假关节等。而假关节仅在 X 光片上能够显示，往往随时间推移而消失。作者表示，“假关节的发生率可以通过常规添加大量自体骨来降低。在没有充分了解脊柱侧凸手术治疗原则的情况下，任何人都不应使用哈灵顿器械。”该研究已经明确表示，哈灵顿器械是治疗特发性脊柱侧凸的辅助手段，而非灵丹妙药。

The fourth and final presentation, given by Allan McKelvie, was on barium swallow studies in patients with scoliosis. An abstract was later published from his presentation at the British Orthopedic Association.[48] He had found that about 80% of patients with idiopathic scoliosis had hiatal hernia, although only about 5% to 10% were symptomatic. He included clinical findings and a discussion of spine and gut embryology. After the four presentations, the evening social hour and meal took place at the Town and Country Club of St Paul. As the minutes showed, "Following dinner, an informal discussion on the role of American Medicine towards the medicine of the underdeveloped nations of the world was undertaken. This informal forum gave rise to many interesting and provocative opinions."

第四个也是最后一个报告是由艾伦·麦凯尔维演讲的关于脊柱侧凸患者的钡餐研究。后来他在英国骨科学会发表演讲并发表了摘要。[48]他发现约80%的特发性脊柱侧凸患者有食管裂孔疝，虽然只有大约5%~10%是有症状的。报告还提及了临床发现，讨论了脊柱和肠道胚胎学。在四个报告之后，晚上的社交活动和晚餐在圣保罗的乡村俱乐部举行。如会议记录所示，"晚餐后，就美国医学对世界欠发达国家医学的作用进行了非正式讨论。这次非正式讨论产生了许多有趣和具有争议性的意见。"

The first session on Saturday began with a discussion of the constitution as amended and updated in Friday's constitutional session. The wording of the fourth purpose, "to establish a Foundation for clinical and investigational research," was changed to "to foster clinical and basic research in the field of scoliosis." Voting and holding office were specifically limited to active members. Honorary members were not subject to dues. The selection of the nominating committee was democratized by providing that two of the three members were to be elected from the floor. Executive committee officers were to be elected by the membership, not just by the committee itself. This committee's membership terms were limited to six consecutive years rather than eight, and its at-large members were elected annually for a period of one rather than four years. The provision that this committee should adopt such rules and regulations as might be necessary for the proper conduct of the work of the SRS was expanded with the caveat that "such rules and regulations will be subject to the majority approval of the active membership present at the next annual meeting." Presidents would be elected to a six-year cycle, including two years each as president-elect, president, and past president. The one guest per meeting rule was affirmed. With these matters decided upon, the vote for the constitution was unanimously in favor. The officers nominated and unanimously elected were John Moe as president, John Hall as president-elect, and Bill Kane as secretary-treasurer. Although apparently not voted on, the at-large members of the executive committee continued for the coming year. It was suggested that members attending this first annual meeting be classified as founding members.

周六的第一节会议首先讨论了在周五的会议上修改和更新的章程。将第四个目的的措辞"建立脊柱侧凸领域的临床和调查研究基金会"改为"促进脊柱侧凸领域临床和基础研究”。仅限于活跃会员拥有投票权并可以担任职务。名誉会员不需要缴纳会费。提名委员会的成员选择是民主化的，规定三名成员中的两名从全体会员中选举产生。执行委员会委员由会员选举产生，而不仅仅是由委员会本身决定。该委员会的成员任期限制为连续六年而不是八年，其委员每年选举一次，任期为一年而不是四年。放宽了该委员会应采用正确开展脊柱侧凸研究学会工作所需的规则和条例的规定，但警告说“此类规则和条例的实施必须得到出席下届年会的多数活跃会员的同意”。主席的选举周期为六年，包括候任主席、主席和前任主席各两年。确立了每次会议会员只能带一位嘉宾的规则。决定了这些事项后，关于章程，会员一致投票赞成。约翰·莫担任主席，约翰·霍尔担任候任主席，比尔·凯恩担任秘书兼财务主管。虽然没有进行投票选举，但执行委员会的委员在来年继续任职。有人建议将参加第一次年会的会员列为创始会员。

In the time remaining for the business meeting, the membership was informed of the upcoming meeting sites. The secretary-treasurer was directed to notify several professional societies and government branches about the foundation of the SRS, including the AOA, AAOS, Orthopaedic Research and Education Foundation, Orthopaedic Research Society, Department of Health, Education of Welfare, AMA, Internal Revenue Service, and SICOT. The discussion turned to federal involvement in research. Allan McKelvie, who practiced in Washington, D.C, led the discourse and urged the society to work toward establishing an Institute for Orthopedic Surgery at the National Institutes of Health. He suggested that annual meetings feature a symposium regarding allied problems, which would provide the opportunity to discuss scoliosis problems with pulmonary and cardiac specialists on a regular basis. If this suggestion generated much discussion, it wasn't recorded.

在会议剩余的时间里，会员被告知下次的会议地点。财务主管负责通知另外几个专业学会和政府部门脊柱侧凸研究学会成立的消息，包括美国骨科学会、美国骨科医师学会、骨科研究和教育基金会（OREF）、骨科研究学会（ORS）、卫生、教育和福利部、美国医学会（AMA）、国税局和国际骨科和创伤外科学会。之后，讨论转向了参加联邦政府研究的部分。执业于华盛顿特区的艾伦·麦凯尔维发表了演讲并建议学会共同努力，争取在美国国家卫生研究院成立骨科研究院。他建议在年会中为“联合”问题专门设置一个研讨会，这样可以提供一个机会让呼吸科、心脏科专家定期讨论脊柱侧凸问题。关于该建议是否引起过多讨论，并没有相关记录。

The results of the four panels' recommendations on terminology held the first day were discussed. "Considerable agreement" was reached on some points, such as exclusive use of the Cobb measurement to determine curve size. Also, the desirability of 36"-long standing radiographs was recognized. However, there was still confusion and disagreement on other terms. Moe took this opportunity to form a nomenclature committee to be chaired by Goldstein with Harrington, Hall, Schimidt, and Stelling as its members. These conversations on terminology and evaluation continued the rest of the morning. Following lunch, two movies were shown. One was by Blount and the other by Cotrel, who was not at the meeting. Both movies emphasized the benefits of active and passive exercises in the treatment of scoliosis. After they concluded, the first annual meeting of the SRS was adjourned at 3:00 p.m., Saturday, June 11, 1966. During the meeting a group picture was taken, which presumably included all attendants. There were 35, and they became known as the founding members. *See figure 8.2*. At some point two others were added to this list. William H. Bickel of Rochester, Minnesota, and Charles H. Herndon of Cleveland, Ohio, increasing the number of founding members to 37. Whether these two missed the meeting or were there but missed the photography session isn't known. Two founding members soon withdrew: Daniel Riordan, whose focus was hand surgery, and William Bickel for reasons undocumented.[49] Really glaring in its absence in any documentation was discussion of finances. For instance, room rentals at the Palmer House for the organizational meeting and the first executive committee meeting were not brought up. Time to talk about the costs of correspondence, photos, meals, registration fees, dues, and all the myriad of expenses associated with the first annual meeting was not found. In an unidentified draft of the SRS's early history Harrington's donation is credited with funding the society's infancy[50]. It also seems likely that Moe's office absorbed additional expenses during this time.

四个小组在第一天进行讨论以达成术语共识。在某些要点上达成了"一致同意"，例如，专门应用柯布测量角度来定义弯曲度大小。同时，认识到迫切需要36英尺长的站立位影像。然而，在其他的一些事项上仍存在混淆与争论。莫借此机会成立了命名委员会，戈尔茨坦作为主席，哈灵顿、霍尔、施密特和施特林作为委员。关于术语及评估的讨论持续了整个上午。午饭后展示了两个视频，一个来自布朗特，另一个来自科特雷尔，他们均未能参会。他们的视频中均强调了主动与被动训练对于治疗脊柱侧凸的益处。在学者们总结后，第一届脊柱侧凸研究学会年会在1966年6月11日周六下午3:00闭幕。会议中拍摄了合影，大约包括了所有的参会者，共计35人，他们也被认定为是创始会员。（图8.2）后来，另两位会员加入创始会员中，他们是明尼苏达州罗切斯特大学的威廉·H. 比克尔和俄亥俄州克利夫兰的查尔斯·H. 赫恩登。关于这两位会员是错过了整个会议还是错过了拍合照环节不得而知。后来有两位创始会员退出：丹尼尔·赖尔登，后来因转向手外科而退出；威廉·比克尔，其退出原因未记载。[49]难以忽略的是，关于财政方面的讨论并未记载在任何文书上。例如，组委会及第一次执行大会在帕尔默家园酒店的场地租赁费用并未被提及，关于第一次年会相关的通信、相片、餐饮、注册费、会费等繁杂的费用的讨论也没有被记录。在未经证实的记录脊柱侧凸研究学会早期历史的手稿中，哈灵顿的捐赠对于该学会的孕育有着重要功绩。[50]同时，莫的团队似乎在这段时间里也得到了额外的资金支持。

Figure 8.2 ***SRS founding members.*** **(*SRS Archives*)**
图8.2　脊柱侧凸研究学会创始会员(脊柱侧凸研究学会档案馆)

The fact that the SRS came into existence with no apparent turmoil seems remarkable given the prior difficulties of the AAOS in even maintaining a committee on scoliosis. As Moe's data so clear showed, the advancement of scoliosis treatment had hit a plateau that was far short of ideal. Scoliosis surgeons were ready for a new way forward. Hall remembered Harrington's contribution: "Having introduced an effective method of treating scoliosis, he stimulated a great interest among surgeons who were confronted by spinal deformities. I believe this interest led directly to the formation of the Scoliosis Research Society".[51] And the SRS found itself in the vanguard of orthopaedic clinical subspecialty professional associations, the first of many that were about to form.[52]

事实上，考虑到之前美国骨科医师学会在维持脊柱侧凸分会的基本运作时所面临的困难，脊柱侧凸研究学会能顺利地成立，而没有遇到较大的阻碍还是相当了不起的。正如莫的数据清楚显示的那样，当时脊柱侧凸治疗面临瓶颈，距离理想目标还很遥远。脊柱侧凸的外科医生需要开辟一条新的道路。霍尔记得哈灵顿的贡献："在介绍了一种治疗脊柱侧凸的有效方法后，他激发了脊柱畸形领域的外科医生的极大兴趣，我相信这种兴趣直接导致了脊柱侧凸研究学会的成立。"[51] 脊柱侧凸研究学会本身也作为骨科临床亚专业学会的先锋，成为未来将要组建的众多亚专业学会的领头羊。[52]

There were certainly other factors that, in retrospect, suggest the time was right for the creation of the SRS. One reason was that the previous generation's leaders were facing the harsh realities of aging. Risser was 74, and Cobb, who had uncontrollable hypertension, had suffered a debilitating stoke in 1965 and died in 1967 at the age of 64 years.[53] In their place, Moe, who was 60 years old, had risen as the master of existing methods of scoliosis evaluation and management. With his annual orthopaedic postgraduate course he had become the leading scoliosis educator in North America. As Cotrel had found out, he was gentle, open-minded giant who sought perfection.

回过头来看，还有一些其他因素也显示出脊柱侧凸研究学会的成立正合时宜。其中一个原因是老一辈的专家面临着严峻的年龄问题。那时里泽已经 74 岁，柯布患有难以控制的高血压，他在 1965 年经历了严重的中风，并在 1967 年逝去，享年 64 岁。[53]在他们那一代的专家中，莫刚满 60 岁，成了当时掌握所有脊柱侧凸评估及治疗方法的大师。凭借着每年的骨科研究生教育课程，他成了北美顶尖的脊柱侧凸教育专家。正如科特雷尔所了解的那样，他是一个儒雅、思想开明、追求完美的巨人。

But the commitment to change probably burned brightest in the young Canadian, John Hall, who remembered his early years with scoliosis as follows.[54] "In London, J.I.P. James was the guru of scoliosis and in 1954, the year I joined him as a registrar, he published a paper classifying 0-69° as mild, 70-99° as severe, and 100° + as very severe scoliosis. Just to show you what kind of patients he was working with, most of his patients was classified as severe. The Royal National Orthopaedic Hospital had a country branch with 480 orthopedic beds, of which approximately 200 were reserved for polio patients, 100 for those with tuberculosis, 50 for those with scoliosis (because patients stayed in the hospital for 1 year), and 20 for those with osteomyelitis. Two operating rooms served this unit. In the town branch, there were 100 beds for acutely affected patients with one operating room. Scoliosis patients at that time could expect to spend 1 year in a cast in the hospital. A 50% pseudarthrosis rate, 35% deep infection rate, and zero maintenance of correction was the unfortunate outcome. While sailing back to Canada [in 1957] with my wife after that experience, I told her that I did not know what I would do when I grew up, but I could tell her that it certainly would not be treating scoliosis. When I joined the staff of the Hospital for Sick Children in Toronto, my chief, Dr. Salter, informed me that I would have the opportunity to manage the patients with scoliosis. The method in use at the Hospital for Sick Children in Toronto at that time had been developed by Arthur LeMesurier in the 1940's. The patients was hung from the ceiling in a fishnet with the concave side of the curve down and was encased in plaster from head to toe. The operation was performed through a window in the back of the cast. It is easy to see why I was so receptive to Paul Harrington's method."

但改变的决心可能在这位年轻的加拿大人约翰·霍尔的身上表现得最为强烈，他回忆早年作为脊柱侧凸治疗追随者时的情形。[54] “在伦敦，J. I. P. 詹姆斯是脊柱侧凸领域的大师，1954 年，我加入他的团队，他发表的文章按照弯曲度的不同对脊柱侧凸进行分类，0~69°为轻度、70°~99°为重度，100°以上则是极重度。从他的分类就可看出他当时治疗的脊柱侧凸有多严重，其中大多数被划分为重度的脊柱侧凸。国立皇家骨科医院在郊区的院区有 480 张骨科病床，其中大约 200 张是为脊髓灰质炎患者准备的，100 张是为结核病患者准备的，50 张是为侧凸的患者准备的（因为这类患者需要住院 1 年以上），20 张是为骨髓炎患者准备的。院区内一共有两个手术间。在市中心院区有 100 张床和一个手术间。脊柱侧凸患者在那个时期需要在医院内接受约 1 年的石膏治疗。但不幸的结果是 50%的假关节形成率、35%的深层感染率及零矫形维持率。在完成学习回加拿大的途中（1957 年），我对妻子说，我不知道我执业后会专攻哪个方向，但让我肯定的是绝不治疗脊柱侧凸。当我入职多伦多病童医院后，我的主任，索尔特博士，告知我有机会去治疗脊柱侧凸患者。在那个时期，医院里采用的治疗方法仍是 1940 年左右由阿瑟·勒梅热勒提出的。将患者放在一个悬吊于天花板上的网袋中，侧凸凹侧朝向下方，然后用石膏从头到脚进行包裹。手术通过在石膏后方开的窗进行。这就很容易看出为什么我对保罗·哈灵顿的方法如此推崇了！”

John Hall's election, at the young age of 41 years, to become the second president of the Scoliosis Research Society validated the stature he had already achieved and foretold a larger legacy.

约翰·霍尔在41岁的时候，被选举为第二任脊柱侧凸研究学会主席，这肯定了他已经取得的成就，也预示着他将留下更大的遗产。

(赵钇伟 译　仉建国 审校)

9 AN IMPORTANT LAST DESIGN (1966-67)

"Can you accommodate me with this little research project?"[1]

最后一个重要的设计（1966—1967）

"你能协助我做这个小型研究项目吗?"[1]

The formation of the Scoliosis Research Society (SRS) would come to overshadow most other events of 1966, but Harrington began the year with the same demanding activities. His time was filled with Zimmer collaborations, lectures, consultations, demonstration surgeries, and professional travel. Increasingly he journeyed overseas. In 1966 his total days spent on trips peaked at 76, 51 of which were international. Mary Alice sometimes accompanied him, and occasionally they incorporated a day or more of sightseeing. But these were days lost from his private practice in Houston. In retrospect, it isn't surprising that the first faint hint of mortality appeared during that year.

1966年脊柱侧凸研究学会的成立使其他众多事件都黯然失色，但哈灵顿并未受此影响，仍以众多费时费力的行程开启了这一年。他的日程表上写满了与捷迈公司有关的合作、演讲、咨询、示范手术和专业会议。他开始更频繁地出席国际活动。1966年，他的出差天数高达76天，其中51天是国际行程。有时玛丽·艾丽斯会陪着他，偶尔他们会花一天左右的时间游玩。但是他在休斯敦私人诊所的工作暂停过一段时日。回想起来，不出意料的话，在这一年他可能第一次出现了危及生命的迹象。

The annual meeting of the AAOS took place in Chicago on January 22 – 27. In addition to being elected to and attending the first SRS executive committee meeting on January 23, Harrington presented a three-hour Instructional Course Lecture, "Scoliosis and Instrumentation," on January 25. It was his fifth consecutive year to present in this format, and he had asked that Zimmer have 100 to 150 copies of the new "Spine Instrumentation and Fusion Technique" brochure available. The brochure, which credited his presentation at the UCLA extension course as its source, was distributed to his lecture audience. He later asked Zimmer to amend it in the next printing in order to establish that the Texas Institute for Rehabilitation and Research (TIRR) in Houston, Texas, was the site of the work.[2] His notes indicated that he attended an Instructional Course Lecture the preceding day titled "Structure and Organization of Bone Part II Collagen and Apatite Crystals: The Mechanism of Calcification" presented by Melvin Glimcher. On his way home from the AAOS meeting Harrington went out of his way to visit William Enneking in Gainesville, Florida, to check on their facet histology study.

美国骨科医师学会年会于1月22日至27日在芝加哥举行。哈灵顿当选第一届脊柱侧凸研究学会执行委员会委员，并参加了1月23日的委员会会议。1月25日，他发表了一个时长3小时的教学课程讲座，题目是“脊柱侧凸与器械”。这是他连续五年以这种形式演讲，他要求捷迈提供100到150份新的《脊柱器械和融合技术》手册，以便分发给听众。该手册来源于他在加利福尼亚大学洛杉矶分校系列课程上的演讲，后来，他要求捷迈在下次印刷时修订，明确该工作的地点位于得克萨斯州康复与研究中心。[2]他的笔记显示，此前他参加了由梅尔文·格利姆彻主讲的题为“骨骼的结构和组织（第二部分）胶原蛋白和磷灰石晶体：钙化的机制”的教学课程讲座。在他从美国骨科医师学会会议返回的路上，哈灵顿特地去拜访了佛罗里达州盖恩斯维尔市的威廉·恩内金，以讨论小关节关节面组织学的研究。

His correspondence with Zimmer continued on a regular basis. The discussions about the instruments included fine-tuning of existing ones, critiquing of new ideas, and occasionally approving a new instrument, such as the outrigger. There were right-handed and left-handed versions, and he commented that the right-handed was the one most needed. He also approved the three versions with different length arms. Once more he inquired about royalties on the instrument. "Can you tell me Zimmer's attitude about putting this item on the royalty list?"[3] Four months later he was rewarded with news from Hite that four outriggers had been sold in 1965 and twenty-eight in 1966. He also learned that Zimmer President James Hartle was "establishing a suggested payment for this and I'm sure he will be in touch with you soon."[4] This was the last remaining correspondence on this topic. Other instrument topics were a minor modification of the #1252 keel hook and a gentle Harrington inquiry about progress on the "specially designed hook combination," presumably the result of his visit to Campos.

哈灵顿与捷迈保持着定期交流。他们的讨论包括对现有器械进行微调和对新想法的评判，偶尔还会批准一种新的器械，比如外撑开器。该器械分右利手和左利手两个版本，他认为右利手版本是最为需要的。他还批准了三个不同臂长的版本。他又一次询问了器械的版税问题。"你能告诉我捷迈对于把这个项目放进版税清单名单持什么态度吗？"[3] 4 个月后，他得到了来自海特的好消息：1965 年卖出了 4 个外撑开器，1966 年卖出了 28 个。他还了解到捷迈总裁詹姆斯·哈特尔正"为此事制订一个建议款项，我相信他很快会与您联系"。[4]这是关于此话题的最后一封通信。其他的器械相关话题是对 1252 号龙骨钩的一个小修改，以及哈灵顿对"特殊设计的钩组合"进展的简单询问，这大概是他访问坎普斯的结果。

Some of the Zimmer correspondence related to his international commitments. In February Harrington wrote that a group of people in Sydney, Australia, had accumulated enough money to send a patient to Houston for surgery. He had replied to them that when his regular fee was paid, he would donate instruments of an equal value to the Royal Prince Alfred Hospital's orthopedic service.[5] Zimmer asked him to submit an order for the desired equipment, designate to whom it was to be mailed, and indicate whether the bill was to be submitted to him or the TIRR.[6] Whether this donation occurred isn't documented. In March he had several contacts about his scheduled October trip to South Africa. He declined to open up a direct line of communication with the local representatives, noting that he would be in South Africa for over three weeks, would contact almost every orthopedic surgeon in the country, and would be happy to talk to the representatives along the way.[7] In May he received a letter from Zimmer's Hartle that included a program from a meeting held in Paris in November 1965 listing a film presentation by C.R. Michel of Lyon, France, titled "The Surgical Treatment of Scoliosis by the Harrington Technique." The letter also contained newspaper clippings about a patient who had the Harrington technique performed in Johannesburg, South Africa.[8]

和捷迈的部分通信与哈灵顿的国际事务有关。在通信中，哈灵顿提到，2 月，一群人为了把一个病人送到休斯敦做手术而筹集了足够的资金。他回复这些人说，在他的常规费用被支付后，他将向阿尔弗雷德王子皇家医院的骨科部门捐赠同等价值的器械。[5]捷迈请他提交一份所需设备的订单，指定邮寄对象，并说明账单是提交给他还是提交给得克萨斯州康复与研究中心。[6]同年 3 月，他为计划在 10 月进行的南非之行进行了几次接洽。他拒绝与当地代理商直接沟通，并指出他将在南非待三周多，会联系该国几乎所有的骨科医生，并很乐意在途中与当地代理商交谈。[7] 5 月，他收到了捷迈公司的哈特尔的来信，信中有一份 1965 年 11 月在巴黎举行的会议议程，其中列出了来自法国里昂的 C. R. 米歇尔的题为"应用哈灵顿技术的脊柱侧凸外科治疗"的视频演讲。信中还包括一名在南非约翰内斯堡接受哈灵顿技术进行治疗的病人的剪报。[8]

One hotly debated topic in scoliosis surgery of great interest to Harrington was the relative merit of different bone grafts. Fresh autograft bone from the patient's own body resulted in an additional operation site and occasionally in permanent morbidity, the most common of which was persistent donor site pain of varying though usually mild amounts. There wasn't definitive evidence that fresh autograft was superior to stored homograft (sourced from another person) with the exception of Goldstein's work that convincingly showed the importance of the type of autograft; he found the corticocancellous iliac crest autograft superior to tibial autograft as well as homograft.[9] It is clear that Harrington resisted using fresh autograft, just as he had earlier resisted using arthrodesis in conjunction with his instrumentation. His attention was drawn to preserved bovine calf bone, which was a heterograft (sourced from a different animal). After careful consideration, he arranged for the grafts to be prepared in such a way as to reduce surface exposure on the theory this would reduce immunological problems. He did six trial cases in 1962, and feeling reassured about their safety and efficacy, he began routinely using Squibb Boplant® (bovine calf bone) in June 1963. By the latter half of 1965, as the scientific programs were being prepared for the coming spring and summer, he had accumulated a series and had a fellow available to review it. Harrington must have considered the results promising as different versions of the study were submitted and accepted for presentation at the Texas Orthopaedic Association meeting in April and the Canadian Orthopaedic Association meeting in June. At the Texas meeting the title in the program was "Boplant® Calf Bone and Iliac Autogenous Bone: Comparison in Spine Fusion."[10] His abstract cited 73 patients followed for a year or more compared with patients receiving fresh autogenous iliac bone. The evaluation was to include correction obtained, correction maintained, and complications, but a manuscript has not survived.

在哈灵顿非常感兴趣的脊柱侧凸手术中，采用不同来源骨进行移植的优劣性是一个热议话题。患者自身的新鲜自体骨移植会额外增加手术部位，偶尔会导致永久性并发症。其中最常见的是持续的供体部位疼痛，疼痛程度不一，但通常是轻微的疼痛。戈尔茨坦的研究证实了自体骨移植的重要性，他发现了髂骨自体移植物优于胫骨自体移植物和异体骨移植物。[9]除此之外，没有明确的证据表明新鲜自体骨移植优于贮存的同种异体骨（来源于其他人）。很明显哈灵顿拒绝使用新鲜的自体移植物，就像过去他拒绝将他的器械用于融合术中。他开始关注一种贮存的小牛骨和某种异种移植物（来自不同的动物）。深思熟虑后，他开发了一种新的方式来制备移植物，通过减少表面的暴露来减少免疫排斥反应。1962 年，他做了六个案例试验，才确保了它们的安全性和有效性。1963 年 6 月，他开始定期使用 Squibb Boplant®（小牛骨）。到 1965 年下半年，在为即将到来的春夏准备学术项目时，他已经积累了一系列案例，并交给了一个同行审查。哈灵顿一定认为这个结果很有希望，因为他提交的不同版本的研究都被接收了，并分别在 4 月的得克萨斯州医学会会议和 6 月的加拿大医学会会议上做了陈述报告。在得克萨斯州的会议上，他演讲的标题是"Boplant®小牛骨和自体髂骨：脊柱融合疗效的比较"。[10]他的摘要收录了 73 名接受小牛骨或者新鲜自体髂骨移植的患者，在随访一年或更长时间后比较疗效。评估内容包括已改善的和维持的矫正程度以及并发症，但有关该项目的文章并未被保存下来。

The paper submitted to the Canadian Orthopaedic Association was co-authored with his fellow, Stanley Hoppenfeld, and titled "Boplant® Calf Bone and Iliac Autogenous Bone: Comparison in Spine Fusion."[11] The manuscript as presented was titled "Heterogenous Bone Implants in Scoliosis Fusions" and was authored by Harrington, who credited Hoppenfeld with developing "much of the historical content of this article."[12] The study reported that for the 304 cases "not one rejection or systemic reaction took place." Fifty-seven cases (19%) were reoperated for various reasons. Four patients bad prior grafting with Boplant® and none of them had shown a suggestion of sensitization. While he did not report the prevalence of pseudarthrosis, he made the reassuring statement that "specimens from the operative site, in a few cases, showed complete reorganization and incorporation of the original implant." Sometimes in medical science and practice, experimental results were anticipated. One factor causing this was the call for abstracts for scientific meetings, which encouraged authors to anticipate results in order to improve the competitiveness of their submissions. Although details were not documented, these results must have been discouraging, and Harrington stopped using Boplant® late in 1966 and no extra bone after that date.[13]

这篇提交给加拿大骨科学会的论文是哈灵顿与他的同事斯坦利·霍本菲尔德共同撰写的，题为“Boplant®小牛骨和自体髂骨：脊柱融合疗效的比较”。[11]另一份手稿的标题为“脊柱侧凸融合中的异体骨移植”，作者是哈灵顿，他称赞霍本菲尔德详细阐述了“这篇文章的大部分历史内容”。[12]该研究报告称，在304例病例中，“没有一例排斥反应或全身反应发生”。57名患者（19%）因各种原因再次手术。四个病人使用了Boplant®且均未见致敏迹象。虽然他没有报告假关节的情况发生，但他做出了有保障的声明，“在一些病例中，手术部位的标本显示出与原始内植物完全重组和结合的现象”。有时在医学科学和实践中，实验结果往往是符合预期的。造成这一现象的一个因素是学术会议对摘要的征稿要求，他们鼓励作者通过预测结果来提高稿子的竞争力。虽然没有详细的记录，但疗效对比的结果肯定是令人沮丧的，所以哈灵顿在1966年底停用了Boplant®，此后再也没有使用其他的骨移植材料。[13]

The Canadian Orthopaedic Association annual meeting held special significance to Harrington. Since Canadian scoliosis surgeons, beginning with John Hall, had been early supporters of his work, he showed his appreciation by accepting their invitation to join the Canadian Orthopaedic Association and by regularly attending and participating in their annual meetings. While there, he presented his assigned discussion of the paper by Dean MacEwen, which was titled "Congenital Scoliosis with Unilateral Bar."[14] In it MacEwen credited Blount with recognizing and reporting on this problematic patient category. Of 86 patients seen from 1940 through 1965, ten (12%) had a unilateral bar, and all had progressed or were progressing.

加拿大骨科学会年会对哈灵顿有着特殊的意义。从约翰·霍尔开始，加拿大脊柱侧凸外科医生都是他早期工作的支持者，所以他接受了邀请，加入了加拿大骨科学会，并定期参加年会以表示感谢。在那里，他参加了迪恩·麦克尤恩题为“伴单侧分节障碍的先天性脊柱侧凸”的报告的专题讨论。[14]在这个报告中，麦克尤恩称赞布朗特认识到并报告了有此问题的患者分类。从1940年到1965年的86

名患者中，10 名患者（12%）有单侧分节障碍，所有患者的病情都有进展或正在进展。

Harrington returned home for a period of relative calm before he and Mary Alice embarked on an aggressive fall travel schedule. During this lull, he and Zimmer corresponded on the naming of the ends of the #1250 distraction rod. Zimmer marketing had chosen the words notched end and collar end. Harrington disagreed and succeeded in having notched end replaced with ratchet end. The collar end designation stayed. Arrangements were made to have adequate quantities of educational materials as well as instrumentation parts available at the major stops on his upcoming international trips. He did take a three-day trip to Fort Worth to operate and made the observation that just 250 miles from home they were using an outdated technique manual. This prompted him to request that educational materials be made more widely available.

哈灵顿回到家里度过了一段相对平静的时间，然后他和玛丽·艾丽斯开始计划一个积极的秋季旅行。在这段时间里，他和捷迈回应了#1250 撑开棒两端的命名问题。捷迈市场部门选择了缺口端和轴环端这两个词。哈灵顿不同意，并成功地将缺口端替换为棘齿端，而轴环端的命名被保留了下来。在他即将进行的国际旅行的主要地点，都备好了足够数量的教学材料和器械。他花了三天的时间去沃思堡做手术，发现在这一离家仅 250 英里的地方，他们使用的是一本过时的技术手册，使他提出要更广泛地提供教学材料。

On September 3 the Harringtons departed Houston on a twelve-day trip that began in Paris with participation in the tenth congress of the Societe Internationale de Chirurg Orthopaedic et de Traumatologie (SICOT).[15] During the September 4–9 meeting he took part in the spine symposium titled "The Results at the End of Growth of the Treatment of Idiopathic Scoliosis." In addition to panel director John Moe, the panel members were Harrington, Adam Gruca from Poland, M.C. Manning from Great Britain, Yves Cotrel from France, and Pierre Stagnara from Fracce, all of whom were leaders in scoliosis management. It is worth noting that Gruca had developed his own instrumentation system, was President William T. Green's guest speaker at the 1957 annual meeting of the AAOS, and published a detailed report in 1958, four years before Harrington.[16] However, Gruca's instrumentation had never been accepted or validated. Each panel member was allotted fifteen minutes, although some time trading eventually occurred. In preparation for the meeting, Moe and Harrington had a cordial and substantive letter exchange. Moe intended to present the end result comparison of idiopathic scoliosis patients treated by Risser cast and Harrington Instrumentation that he and Jim Valuska had presented at the AOA in May and the SRS in June. It compared 131 Harrington Instrumentation 100 Risser localizer cast patients with a minimum of 18 months' follow-up.[17] Harrington Instrumentation provided both advantages and disadvantages, but the former outweighed the latter.[18] Harrington responded that he did not have the information to satisfy the title of the symposium.[19] He noted that he had just begun a five-year study on the 668 cases he had operated on from January 1961 to December 1965, but lacked sufficient data to draw any conclusions so he could merely provide impressions. He complimented Moe and criticized himself. "The work that you have done with instrumentation has certainly set the pattern of what can be done, but of course, I have many beautiful results, some rather mediocre and a few that are not so good." Harrington looked to future studies: "I believe that as time passes, we can establish by histological study and by re-operating the problems that have occurred and correlate these, that we can make statements with a reasonable amount of security."

9 月 3 日，哈灵顿夫妇从休斯敦出发，开始了为期 12 天的旅行，从巴黎开始，参加了法国国际矫形与创伤外科学会的第十届年会。[15]在 9 月 4 日至 9 月 9 日的会议上，他参加了题为“生长结束期特发性脊柱侧凸治疗的结果”的脊柱研讨会。除了专家小组主席约翰·莫，其他小组成员有哈灵顿、波兰的亚当·格鲁卡、英国的 M. C. 曼宁、法国的伊夫斯·科特雷尔和皮埃尔·斯塔格纳拉，他们都是脊柱侧凸治疗的领导者。值得注意的是，格鲁卡已经研发了自己的器械系统，并在 1957 年美国骨科医师学会年会上作为主席威廉·T. 格林的特邀演讲者。他在 1958 年，比哈灵顿提前 4 年发表了一份详细的报告。[16]然而，格鲁卡的器械从未被接受或验证过。每个专家成员都有 15 分钟的发言时间，不过最终还是有一些时间上的调整。在会议的准备工作中，莫和哈灵顿进行了一次真诚、务实的信件交流，莫打算介绍自己和吉姆·瓦卢斯卡在 5 月美国骨科学会会议和 6 月脊柱侧凸研究学会会议上展示过的用里泽局部矫形石膏和哈灵顿器械治疗特发性脊柱侧凸患者的最终结果比较。研究比较了 131 名使用哈灵顿器械的病人和 100 名使用里泽局部石膏矫形的病人，随访时间至少 18 个月。[17]哈灵顿器械既有优点也有缺点，但优势显著高于劣势。[18]但哈灵顿回应说，他没有资料来满足研讨会的题目需求。[19]他指出，自己刚刚开始对 1961 年 1 月至 1965 年 12 月期间他做过手术的 668 例病例进行为期 5 年的研究，缺乏足够的数据来得出任何结论，因此他只能提供一些感想。他一边称赞莫，一边反思自己。“你用器械所做的工作肯定为所有力所能及的事情树立了榜样，当然我也有很多满意的结果，不过有些则相当平庸，甚至还有差强人意的。”哈灵顿也展望了未来的研究：“我相信，随着时间的推移，我们可以通过组织学研究，重新处理现有的问题，并将它们联系起来，以做出合理的安全声明。”

In addition to the symposium, there were important submitted papers, roundtable presentations, and discussions involving leading scoliosis and spine deformity surgeons from around the world. Among them were Walter Blount (United States), Jean Cauchoix (France), AL. Fernandez (Spain), Arthur Hodgson (Hong Kong), Anders Langenskiold (Sweden), Joseph Risser (United States), and Robert Roaf (Great Britain).

除研讨会外，还有重要的投稿论文、圆桌会议和来自世界各地的引领脊柱侧凸和脊柱畸形领域的外科医生参与的讨论，其中包括沃尔特·布朗特（美国）、让·考乔伊斯（法国）、AL. 费尔南德斯（西班牙）、阿瑟·霍奇森（中国香港）、安德斯·朗根斯基奥尔德（瑞典）、约瑟夫·里泽（美国）和罗伯特·罗夫（英国）。

Although there is no specific evidence, it is possible that Harrington either learned or became more aware of screw placement into the pedicle at this meeting. Parisian Raymond Roy-Camille, whose focus was on trauma and tumor surgery, had been using pedicle screws for about four years.[20] The co-author of a paper on "Pseudarthrosis of the Femoral Neck in Young Patients," he was probably at the meeting, and Harrington might have seen some of his work with the pedicle screws at a scientific or commercial exhibit. A revelation that did occur at the SICOT was for the first time Harrington seeing copies of his instrument being marketed. This would have required his prompt attention because his license agreement with Zimmer stipulated that if "other parties offer for sale spine instrumentation of similar design using the names of Paul R. Harrington, M.D., and/ or Department of Rehabilitation, Baylor University ... we would expect Doctor Harrington and ... Baylor University ... to take proper steps to stop this practice."[21] The ensuing correspondence about copying lasted four months, and the continuity and pace of correspondence were impeded by his long, upcoming trip. It apparently began when someone, possibly Harrington or more likely one of his office staff since he was still in

Europe, wrote one of the copiers, Lépine of Lyon, France, asking for details of the Harrington Instrumentation equipment. Lépine's generic response, dated September 26, was cordial.[22] "Monsieur, in answer to your letter of September 12 we are enclosing the details of the Harrington instrumentation equipment. We remain at your disposal for all comp. information which you need to have. With sincere regards." The details were on two enclosed Lépine letterhead pages, each referring to Instrumentation d' Harrington. One page had pictures of three purported Harrington implants (distraction rod with the collar end modified by decreasing the diameter of the short protruding end to engage a hook, a smaller hook to engage the rod end opposite the ratchet end, and a ratchet hook) and three purported Harrington instruments (hook driver, hook holder, and distractor). The other page was a price list.

虽然缺乏明确的证据，但这次会议或使哈灵顿了解并加深了对椎弓根螺钉置入的认知。巴黎的雷蒙德·罗伊-卡米尔的主要方向是创伤和肿瘤外科，他已经使用椎弓根螺钉四年了。[20]作为文章《年轻患者股骨颈骨折假关节》的共同作者，他可能也参加了会议，哈灵顿可能在一些学术日程或者商业展览上看过一些他用椎弓根螺钉进行的工作。在国际矫形与创伤外科学会会议上，哈灵顿第一次看到哈灵顿器械的仿制品被销售，这立刻引起了他的注意。因为他与捷迈的许可协议规定，如果"其他以保罗·哈灵顿医学博士或/和贝勒大学医学院康复科的名义销售类似设计的脊柱器械，我们期望哈灵顿医生和……贝勒大学……联合采取必要的措施阻止这种行为"[21]。他和捷迈关于仿制器械的通信持续了四个月，通信的连续性和速度都因他即将进行的长途旅行而受到了影响。通信始于哈灵顿，或更可能是他办公室的同事，因为那时他还在欧洲。信是写给仿制者之一（法国里昂的勒平公司）的，询问哈灵顿器械的详细信息。勒平公司在9月26日的回复十分亲切[22]："先生，回复您9月12日的来信，现随函附上哈灵顿器械的详细资料。我们随时为您提供您所需要的公司所有信息。致以诚挚的问候。"详细信息写在信封里两页抬头为勒平的信纸上，每一页都提到了哈灵顿器械。其中一页有三个自称哈灵顿内植物（改良撑开棒轴环端，通过减小短的突出端直径来连接钩，一个更小的接连棒棘齿端另一端的钩，以及一个棘齿钩），和三个自称哈灵顿器械（钩推进器，持钩器和撑开器）的图片。另一页是价目表。

In a letter dated September 22, Harrington first reported his SICOT revelation to Hite.[23] "Dear Jim, Instrumentation is going continental fast and furious. In Paris, at the Zimmer Ltd. Company, I saw a set of my instruments on display. The Rockwell of their instrumentation must have been between ten and fifteen, and many small features were absolutely wrong. In going up the ladder of their company to let them know not to use my name on such instruments, I pointed out at least seven deficits in their reproduction of the instruments, all of which were serious mistakes, which brings to mind the point that we are going to get more and more of this problem. The demand for instruments on the continent and over the world is going to increase without question. One way to combat this is for Zimmer of Indiana to offer exceptional service and to come out with a statement saying that any variation in the intricate design of the instruments alters their efficiency and results in failure. Some statement similar to this would put other companies on the spot. We have no protection from the standpoint of patent, and I am sure there will be inquiries as to the design and specifications. In Paris, your representative from the Minnesota area and John Moe and myself discussed these general ideas, as well as the instrumentation cataloging in your brochure."

在一封日期为 9 月 22 日的信中，哈灵顿首先向海特报告了他在国际矫形与创伤外科学会会议上获得的启发。[23] "亲爱的吉姆，器械正在迅速地发展。在巴黎的捷迈公司，我看到我的一套器械被展出。它们的洛氏硬度肯定在 10 到 15 之间，许多小的特征是完全错误的。为了让他们公司知道不要在这些器械上使用我的名字，我指出他们的器械复制品上至少有 7 个缺陷，这些缺陷都是严重的错误，这让我想到我们可能会面临越来越多的这类问题。毫无疑问，欧洲大陆和世界各地对医疗器械的需求将会增加。对于印第安纳州的捷迈来说，阻止这个问题的方法之一是提供卓越的服务，并发表声明，表明器械复杂精细设计中的任何变化都会改变它们的有效性并导致失败。类似的声明会让其他公司望而却步。从专利的角度来看，我们没有受到保护，我相信会有人询问关于设计和产品规格的问题。在巴黎，你们来自明尼苏达地区的代理、约翰·莫与我本人讨论了这些大致的想法，以及你提供的宣传册中的器械目录。"

Further correspondence about the instrument copying issue was interrupted by his worldwide odyssey. Following the SICOT meeting, the Harrington had a few days to travel for pleasure before returning to Houston on September 15. Five days later they left on an extended trip to Honolulu, Sydney, Johannesburg, and other stops in South Africa. Their itinerary was anchored by two large medical meetings, the triennial meeting of the Pan-Pacific Surgical Association in Honolulu on September 20-28 and the biennial Orthopaedic Congress of South Africa in Durban on October 12-15, 1966. In between these meetings arrangements were made for consultations and surgeries in Sydney. Days were also scheduled for travel and sightseeing. They left Houston on September 20 and returned on October 27, meaning that they were absent from home and his practice for 38 days.

关于仿制器械问题的进一步通信被他的环球旅行打断了。国际矫形与创伤外科学会会议结束后，因为他们9月15日才返回休斯敦，哈灵顿夫妇得以有几天的时间去旅行。5天后，他们出发前往火奴鲁鲁、悉尼、约翰内斯堡和南非的其他地方。他们这次的行程包括参加两个大型医学会议，9月20日至28日在火奴鲁鲁举行的三年一次的泛太平洋外科学会会议，以及1966年10月12日至15日在德班举行的两年一次的南非骨科大会。在两个会议之间，哈灵顿在悉尼的医院进行了会诊和手术，还安排了旅游和观光。他们于9月20日离开休斯敦，10月27日才返回，这意味着他们已经离开家和他的诊所38天。

The triennial meeting of the Pan-Pacific Surgical Association promised to be a well-attended meeting since the previous one had drawn 1,400 doctors from 30 countries.[24] The orthopedic program chairman, Ivar Larsen, assembled a panel on scoliosis with H. Relton McCanoll Jr. as moderator, Moe as presenter of "The Treatment of Scoliosis by Non-operative Means with the Milwaukee Brace," Harrington as presenter of "The Surgical Management of Scoliosis by Instrumentation," and Risser as presenter of "The Clinical Management of Scoliosis." Each of the three speakers was allotted twenty minutes for his presentation, which left twenty minutes for discussion.[25] Invited speakers were warned upfront that funds were not available to cover their expenses, but they would receive an enrollment fee reduction. The men were urged to become members for $25, which Harrington did.

由于上届会议吸引了来自30个国家的1 400名医生参加，因此这次三年一度的泛太平洋外科学会会议有望成为一场与会人数众多的会议。[24]骨科项目主席伊瓦尔·拉森召集了一个关于脊柱侧凸的小组专家讨论会，由小H. 里尔顿·麦卡诺尔作为主持人，莫是“密尔沃基支具非手术方法治疗脊柱侧凸”的主讲人，哈灵顿是“应用器械手术治疗脊柱侧凸”的主讲人，里泽则是“脊柱侧凸的临床治疗”的主讲人。三位主讲人每人有20分钟的时间做报告，剩下的20分钟用于讨论。[25] 25名受邀演讲者事先被告知他们的报告是无偿的，但他们的注册费将获得减免。此外要求他们缴纳25美元成为会员，哈灵顿照做了。

Harrington preserved a copy of his notes titled "Treatment of Idiopathic Scoliosis."[26] He briefly reviewed the stages of Harrington Spine Instrumentation development and described the 5-year follow-up study he was conducting on 668 cases that he hoped would be complete in 1970. He postulated that this would help identify the most important of about twelve independent variables affecting results. These variables included length of body cast wear, duration of activity restriction, bone graft supplement used and type of fusion technique. His firm impression was that "partial posterior fusion of the scoliotic spine several years before maturity will lose correction as the vertebral column (bodies) grows to maturity," about 10° per growing year. He estimated his pseudarthrosis rate as greater than 10% and removal of instruments at 5%. He emphasized his belief that 98% of all idiopathic scoliotic patients progressed during growth.

哈灵顿保存了一份题为"特发性脊柱侧凸治疗"的笔记副本。[26]他简要地回顾了哈灵顿脊柱器械的研发历程，并描述了他对668名患者进行的5年随访研究，他希望这些研究能在1970年完成。他认为这将有助于确定影响结果的12个变量中最重要的一个。这些变量包括所穿戴躯体石膏的时长、限制活动时长、骨移植物的使用以及融合技术的类型。他印象深刻的是"在脊柱成熟前的几年，侧凸的脊柱部分后路融合将随着脊柱（躯体）的成熟造成矫正丢失"，每年大约有10°的矫正丢失。他估计假关节发生率大于10%，器械移位的发生率为5%。他强调他认为所有特发性脊柱侧凸患者中有98%的患者病情在成长过程中会发生进展。

From Hawaii the Harringtons traveled to Sydney where they were to stay in a VIP flat at the Royal Prince Alfred Hospital. But his hosts remembered that Harrington had been a bit slow navigating the several flights of stairs to the flat during his last visit in October 1965, and in deference to his physical abilities they offered a stay at a downtown hotel.[27] However, Hugh and Mary Barry insisted the American couple stay in their home, which they did.[28] Plans were scheduled for several clinics and surgeries, but no records detail what clinical work was accomplished.

哈灵顿一家从夏威夷来到悉尼，在悉尼他们住在阿尔弗雷德王子皇家医院的贵宾公寓里。但东道主记得哈灵顿在1965年10月最后一次访问时，走楼梯到公寓的速度有点慢，考虑到他的身体状况，他们建议他住在市中心的一家酒店。[27]然而，休和玛丽·巴里坚持要这对美国夫妇住在他们家里，他们也照做了。[28]这次行程计划中安排了几个门诊和手术，但没有详细记录哈灵顿完成了哪些临床工作。

The Harrington left Sydney on October 5 for the long flight to South Africa where he actively participated in the biennial Orthopaedic Congress of South Africa in Durban. He and Jean Cauchoix presented a symposium on scoliosis, and his movie, One Year Follow-up of Over 100 Cases, was played. Harrington also gave a new presentation, "Treatment of the Unstable Spine Other than Scoliosis." In it he described three patients with thoracolumbar spine fractures and incomplete paraplegia, whose unstable spines were stabilized with dual distraction rods and arthrodesis, and one three-year-old patient with tuberculosis of the spine, whose 90° thoracic kyphosis was reduced to 40° with two compression rods. At the conclusion of the congress the Harrington spent time in Cape Town, Johannesburg, and Pretoria. Consultations and surgeries had been planned but were not recorded. One of the Harrington's hosts was Professor W. D. Graham at the University of the Witwatersrand in Johannesburg, for whom Harrington was preparing a chapter for a book that Graham was editing.

哈灵顿一家于 10 月 5 日离开悉尼飞往南非，在那里他积极参加在德班举行的两年一度的南非骨科大会。他和让·考乔伊斯举办了一个关于脊柱侧凸的研讨会，并播放了他的视频《超过 100 例病例的 1 年随访》。哈灵顿还做了一个新的报告“除脊柱侧凸外的不稳定脊柱的治疗”。在这个报告中，他描述了三名胸腰椎骨折和不完全截瘫患者，其不稳定的脊柱通过双撑开棒和融合术得到了稳定，一名 3 岁的脊柱结核患者，其 90°胸椎后凸通过两根压缩棒减少到 40°。大会结束后，哈灵顿在开普敦、约翰内斯堡和比勒陀利亚度过了一段时间。咨询和手术是计划好的，但没有记录。其中一位东道主是约翰内斯堡威特沃特斯兰德大学的 W. D. 格雷厄姆教授，哈灵顿正在为一本格雷厄姆编写的书撰写一个章节的内容。

The Harringtons arrived home on October 27, and soon after he wrote Hite concerning Zimmer's international service.[29] "In my travels, I made a lot of contacts and heard several criticisms of the service rendered internationally: quoting various doctors in Australia and South Africa, 'the service stinks.' I inquired further and to be more specific, there is no supply in these countries for quick delivery. When orders are received and cannot be filled, they are back ordered and then forgotten until they are reminded, weeks or months later. Another feature is that there is nothing in the catalogue about a zero rod, one with no length to the shank. None of the catalogues have the outrigger listed and the local distributors are not acquainted with the instruments enough to talk intelligently. This could be helped by sending the operative procedure and its techniques which you have, to the distributors and to everyone who orders instruments. Everyone is sold the nuts and gadgets that hook onto the sacral bar, none of which I use. These are somebody else's ideas, and it doesn't sit too well when I say that I never use them, nor have I designed them. In Africa, I saw two of the old temporary hook clamping devices sold as new equipment. This is absurd. That was a temporary by-pass for lack of supply, and should not be sold as Harrington equipment. You might pass the above words to somebody who can do something about it." Uncharacteristically, no proof exists in the Harrington Archives that either Hite or anyone else at Zimmer responded to this strongly worded letter. Hite probably passed the letter to J. Alan Morgan, vice president of marketing, and discussed the matter with Harrington by phone. Morgan initiated the correspondence addressing unauthorized copying of Harrington Spine Instrumentation on November 7.[30] He was aware of the involvement of two companies: Zimmer Orthopaedic Limited in London, England, and Lépine in Lyon, France. He wrote to Harrington, "As a first step possibly you could write them. I would suggest asking them to cease using your name on unapproved instruments. If this does not work, ask them to let you approve the design, quality and materials. We will do what we can to help although Zimmer is not in favor of releasing its specifications. Perhaps you have other ideas about this situation." The wording suggested that the Zimmer had limited leverage.

哈灵顿夫妇于 10 月 27 日回到家中，不久他就写信给海特询问捷迈的国际服务。[29]“在旅行过程中，我接触了很多人，听到了一些对捷迈在国际上提供的服务的批评，以下为引用澳大利亚和南非的各种医生的话，‘这项服务太糟糕了’。我进一步询问，更具体地说，这些国家没有完善的快递物流。当收到订单却无法交货时，订单就会被退回，然后就不了了之，直到几周或几个月后才会收到提醒。此外，在目录中没有关于零位棒（一个没有长度的柄）的介绍。另一个问题是，没有一个目录列出了外撑开器，当地经销商对这些器械不够熟悉，无法进行有效沟通。这可以通过将已有的手术步骤及其技术材料发送给经销商来解决。挂在骶骨棒上的螺母和小配件售卖给了每个人，但这些我都没用过，这些都是别人的想法。当我说我从未使用过或设计过它们时，这让人不太舒服。在非洲，我看到两个旧的临时钩装置被作为新器械出售，这是荒谬的。这只是一个临时的备选方案，不应该被作为哈灵顿器械出售。你可以把上面的话告诉那些能做点什么事的人。”一反常态的是，哈灵顿的档案中没有证据表明海特或捷迈公司的其他人对这封措辞强硬的信做出回应。海特可能把信交给了营销副总裁 J. 阿兰·摩根，并与哈灵顿通过电话讨论了此事。摩根于 11 月 7 日发起了针对未经授权仿制哈灵顿脊柱器械公司的信函。[30]他知道有两家公司参与了此事：英国伦敦的捷迈骨科和法国里昂的勒平公司。他在给哈灵顿的信中写道："首先您尽可能写信给他们，建议他们停止在未经批准的器械上使用您的名字。如果这行不通，要求他们让您批准设计、质量和材料。尽管捷迈不赞成公布其规格，我们将尽我们所能提供帮助。也许您对这种情况有其他想法。"措辞表明捷迈的影响力有限。

Zimmer Orthopaedic Limited, a separate company from Zimmer in the United States, had already written a letter to Harrington on October 14, one which he received after his October 27 return to Houston.[31] They expressed pleasure in meeting him at the recent SICOT meeting and let him know that requests for Harrington Rods were coming from England and around the world. They appreciated the research and development that had gone into his complex equipment and assured him that they had the facilities to make products exactly to his specifications. Zimmer Orthopaedic offered a royalty of 5% of the net sales price. Harrington decided not to answer the letter and sent a copy of it to Hite, in which he noted that this company had an exhibit in Paris that displayed many defects in their reproduction of the Harrington Instrumentation.[32] There is no record that Harrington ever replied to Zimmer Orthopaedic Ltd. as Morgan had suggested he should.

捷迈骨科有限公司是美国捷迈的一家独立分公司，该公司于 10 月 14 日给哈灵顿写了一封信，他于 10 月 27 日返回休斯敦后收到。[31]该公司表示很高兴在最近的国际矫形与创伤外科学会会议上见到他，并让他知道英国和世界其他地方对哈灵顿棒的需求。他们对他为复杂器械所做的研究和研发工作表示欣赏，并向他保证，他们有能力完全按照他的规格制造产品。捷迈骨科提供了净销售价格 5%的特许权使用费。哈灵顿决定不回这封信，并寄了一份副本给海特。他注意到这家公司在巴黎有一个展示会，显示他们仿制的哈灵顿器械有许多缺陷。[32]没有记录表明哈灵顿曾像摩根建议的那样给捷迈骨科回信。

Harrington did promptly write Lépine.[33] "I have received a copy of a brochure showing instruments that bear my name, used in surgery for the correction of scoliosis. No one from your company has ever approached me for information as to the specifications as to the metal or design, including size and dimensions of the instruments themselves. This is an unusual and erroneous way to approach a situation. The fact that you use my name in connection with the instruments places me in the position of demanding that you reproduce the instruments to my specification and that you distribute literature showing how to use them. I suggest that if you continue to associate my name with your instruments that you must proceed ethically and properly meet my specifications in reproducing those instruments sold under my name."

哈灵顿确实曾立即致信勒平。[33]“我收到一份手册复印件，上面印着用于矫正脊柱侧凸手术的器械，还有我的名字。你们公司从来没有人向我询问过关于金属或设计的规格信息，包括器械本身的尺寸和规格。这是一种罕见的、错误的做事方式。你们在这些器械上使用我的名字，这一事实使我不得不要求你们按照我的规格重新制作这些器械，并分发说明书指导如何使用它们。我建议，如果要继续用我的名字冠名你们的器械，就必须合乎伦理，按照我的规范要求重新生产那些以我的名义销售的器械。”

Lépine replied, "Your letter of November 18th has been brought to our attention. We are sorry that you feel that your instruments have been incorrectly reproduced without your approval. We have never been aware of your feelings about this before we received your letter. Your colleague, Dr. Stagnara, had the occasion of meeting with you at Lyon and was very desirous of using your technique for scoliosis surgery. For one year he tried, without success, to procure your material, but the import of American material was regulated (by law prohibitive). At that time, he asked if we could make the instruments. We have in all good faith, believed that this had your approval. It is unhappy that this mutual understanding was—from your view—originally our mistake. We think all the same to reassure you that we have been manufacturing surgical instruments for a number of years. We have created models to meet the demand of the surgeons throughout Lyons: Ollier, LeRiche, Santy, Trillot, etc. The instruments have been reproduced by other establishments, which in our pinion are more censurable—if the name of the author is to be respected. It is in this spirit, and believing that you were in agreement, that we undertook to manufacture the rods and hooks that you invented. Be it well understood that we manufactured the rods with steel recommended by the Societe Francaise d'Orthopedie—steel that corresponds to the American Grade #316 L, in which the strength is the same as your rods. If we permitted ourselves to enlarge a bit the diameter of the rods, it was to adapt the diameter that would correspond to the metric system in effect throughout Europe. If you think that this small increase in diameter is the obstacle that prevents you from wanting your name on the instruments—we are ready to accept and modify the design. It is understood that we have not given to the surgeons buying this material a booklet concerning the technique, because we are not competent to do this. Surgeons do not buy material upon looking at our catalog, but after having seen the operation by a colleague or the technical publications in which the surgeons do part of the work. We hope that you understand our position and we are sorry if we have caused you any difficulty. With our best regards, Lépine Manufacturers."[34]

勒平公司回复："我们注意到您 11 月 18 日的来信。我们很抱歉，您认为您的器械在未经您同意的情况下被错误地仿制了。在收到您的来信之前，我们从未意识到您对此的感受。您的同事斯塔格纳拉医生曾在里昂与您见过面，非常希望使用您的技术进行脊柱侧凸手术。一年来，他试图采购你们的材料，均未成功，进口美国材料受到了限制（被法律禁止）。那时，他问我们是否可以做这些器械。我们真诚地相信这已得到您的批准。遗憾的是，在您看来，这种我们认为的互相理解其实是错误的。尽管如此，我们还是向您保证，我们已经生产手术器械很多年了。我们已经创建了模具，以满足整个里昂外科医生的需求：奥利尔、李黎世、桑蒂、特里洛等。这些器械也已被其他机构仿制。在我们看来，这些机构更应受到谴责——如果要尊重作者署名权的话。正是本着这种精神，所以也相信您会同意我们开始生产您发明的钩棒器械。众所周知，我们是用法国骨科学会推荐的钢材手工制造的，这种钢相当于美国 316 L 等级，其强度与你们的钢管相同。我们自行扩大一点棒的直径，是为了与全欧洲实行的公制的直径相适应。如果您认为直径的小幅度增加导致您不想让自己的名字出现在器械上，我们已经准备好接受和修改设计。可以理解的是，我们没有给购买这种材料的外科医生一本相关的技术手册，因为我们没有能力这样做。骨科医生不会看过我们的目录就购买器材，而是在看到同事做过这类手术或看到技术出版物提及外科医生做过的相关手术后才会购买。我们希望您能理解我们的立场，如果给您造成了任何困扰，我们很抱歉。我们向您致以最诚挚的问候——勒平生产商。"[34]

Harrington responded, "Gentlemen: Appreciate your prompt reply to my letter of November 18th. I can well understand your view, and have no criticisms of your approach. It is my intention to produce a general transcript of specifications of the instruments and why these specifications are critical. When this is available, I will see that it arrives in your hands. I am taking the liberty of sending a copy of your letter to Zimmer Manufacturing Company of Warsaw, Indiana, for I think your remarks are quiet [quite] pertinent. My primary purpose in meeting specifications is basically twofold; 1) to keep dissimilar metals under as firm a control as possible in order to reduce electrolysis, and 2) the Rockwell of the instruments should be in the neighborhood of 35. Other specifications that require consideration will be forthcoming in the above mentioned communication, which is in preparation. For the moment, your increase in the diameter of the rod is not a critical element. I do think that the electro-polishing is important. Your comment about surgeons buying material after seeing the surgery demonstrated is well founded. I would do my best, if I were you, to keep it that way. Again, appreciate your prompt response, and hope that international standardization of the instruments can be accomplished."[35] Harrington sent copies of these communications with Lépine to Morgan at Zimmer. This was apparently the last communication between Harrington and Lépine, and it is unknown if there was any communication between Zimmer and Lépine.

哈灵顿回复："先生们，感谢你们对我11月18日来信的及时回复。我很理解你们的观点，对你们的做法没有什么意见。我的目的是制作一个器械规格的记录本，并说明这些规格的重要性。有了这个，我会送到你们手里的。我已将你们的信寄给印第安纳州华沙的捷迈制造公司，因为我认为你们的话非常中肯。我要求满足规范的基本目的有两个：(1) 尽量严格控制不同金属，以减少电解；(2) 器械的洛氏硬度应在35左右。需要考虑的其他规格将在这封信函中提出。就目前而言，棒直径的增加并不是一个关键因素。我确实认为电抛光很重要。你们关于外科医生在看过手术演示后才购买材料的判断是有根据的。如果我是你们，我会尽我所能保持这种状态。再次感谢你们的及时回复，并希望该器械的国际标准化能够实现。"[35]哈灵顿将这些与勒平的通信副本寄给了捷迈的摩根。这显然是哈灵顿和勒平之间的最后一次交流，而勒平和捷迈之间是否有过沟通则不得而知。

At this point, the contact with the other instrument copier, Zimmer Orthopaedics Limited, had been limited to their post-SICOT meeting letter of October 14. On January 13, D. Douglas Davidson, managing director of Zimmer Orthopaedic Limited, wrote Harrington again to inquire about arranging a meeting at the 1967 AAOS annual meeting in San Francisco that began the next day. Davidson's goal was "to proceed with the manufacture of the Harrington Rods in the United Kingdom. We are continually receiving requests for this equipment from all over the world and we would like very much to be able to offer these Rods. I was very disturbed to see the other day a set of 'Harrington' rods made up in Titanium, and although we believe firmly in the values of Titanium as an implant material, it is quite unsatisfactory for a Harrington Rod, as the tensile strength is no more than 43 tons per sq. in. (approximately 86,000 lb. per sq. in.) Unfortunately, this kind of thing will continue to increase unless your equipment is made available in Europe and other parts of the world from one of the well-known companies like ourselves, and we trust it will be possible for you to allow us to manufacture these Rods in accordance with your exacting specifications."[36] Since Davidson's letter was dated just one day before the meeting, Harrington responded to him that he had not received the letter until returning home, and "Not being aware of your interest as expressed in your letter of January 13th, I never had the privilege of talking with you. It is still my intention to get together all information on all of my instruments, relative to their design, quality and demands of the metal requirements for tensile strength, into article form. This article is in the process of compilation, and when completed, will be available to everyone in the world. I talked to your chief engineer in Paris, whose name I have forgotten for the moment, and we discussed the possibility of the instruments being made of an alloy of stainless steel that would meet the requirements of a Rockwell from 32 to 35, which puts the tensile strength requirements between 130,000 p.s.i. and 145,000 p.s.i. I certainly agree, on the spur of the moment, that titanium is not acceptable. I have also documented the effect of electrolysis on similar metals including dissimilarities that occur in manufacturing. All of these specifications will appear in the article. I hope the situation you mention can be corrected with time."[37]

此时，与另一家器械仿制商捷迈骨科的联系仅限于他们在 10 月 14 日的国际矫形与创伤外科学会会议后发来的信件。1 月 13 日，捷迈骨科的总经理 D. 道格拉斯·戴维森再次写信给哈灵顿，询问是否可以第二天在圣弗朗西斯科举行的 1967 年美国骨科医师学会年会上安排一次会面。戴维森的目的是“继续在英国制造哈灵顿棒。我们不断收到来自世界各地对这种器械的请求，我们非常希望能够提供这些棒。前几天，我看到一组由钛制成的哈灵顿棒，感到非常不安。尽管我们坚信钛作为植入材料的价值，但对于哈灵顿棒来说，因钛的抗拉强度低于每平方英尺①43 吨（每平方英尺约为 8.6 万磅），并不能让人满意。不幸的是，此类事情将持续增多，除非你们的器械从像我们这样的知名公司提供到欧洲和世界其他地方，我们相信你们会允许我们按照你们严格的规格制造这些棒。”[36]由于戴维森来信的日期就在会面前一天，哈灵顿回复他说，他回家后才收到这封信，而且“由于不知道你在 1 月 13 日的信中所表达的兴趣，我一直没有机会与你交谈。我的目的仍然是收集所有关于我的器械的信息，有关它们的设计、质量和金属要求

① 1 平方英尺=0. 092 903 平方米。

的抗拉强度，最后整理成文章的形式。这篇文章正在撰写中，完成后，全世界的人都可以看到。我和你们在巴黎的总工程师谈过，他的名字我暂时忘记了，我们讨论了用不锈钢合金制造器械的可能性，它能满足洛氏硬度在32~35的要求，也就是说，抗拉强度要求在130 000到145 000磅/平方英尺之间。我当然立刻同意，钛是不可接受的。我还记录了电解对类似金属的影响，包括在制造过程中发生的不同反应。所有这些规范都将出现在这篇文章中。我希望你提到的情况能随着时间的推移得到纠正。”[37]

Harrington sent copies of these letters to Hite with further added comments. “It will take from one to five years for the article mentioned in my answer to get into the literature, and you had previous correspondence that I had with this company that they do not have my permission to reproduce my equipment without meeting our specifications. This would give us time to develop international contacts and supply that would make their production useless, I hope. This is the only way I know of to handle the situation.”[38] The previous correspondence Harrington referred to in this letter is not in the Harrington Archives.

哈灵顿将这些信件的副本寄给了海特，并进一步补充了评论。“我在回答中提到的文章需要一到五年的时间整理发表，你有我与这家公司之前的通信，他们并未获得我的许可，在不符合我们规格的情况下仿制我的器械。我希望这一到五年是给我们发展国与国之间联系和供应产品的时间，以让他们的产品变得无用。这是我所知道的处理这种情况的唯一办法。”[38]这封信中哈灵顿提及的之前的通信并未出现在其档案里。

This whole communication sequence about instrumentation copying and name usage was brought to a close by Morgan’s January 23, 1967, letter to Harrington. “I have read a copy of your letter to Jim Hite regarding the manufacture of Harrington Instrumentation by Zimmer [Orthopaedics], Ltd. in England. I think, under the circumstances, you have done about all you can do. The Harrington Instrumentation is available throughout the world and I think what these people have told you may have led you to believe that it isn’t. We have representatives and dealers located in all major countries excluding the Communist satellite block. The major objection to our instrumentation has been price and in this relation there is nothing we can do. There is no doubt that European manufacturers can undercut us by at least 50%. We shall continue to promote Harrington

Instrumentation throughout the world as best we can. I am sure that this is all you can expect of us."[39] Harrington promptly replied that he had "received your January 23 communication and agree that we have done about all we can do. Appreciate your cooperation on this ticklish subject."[40]

整个关于仿制器械和名称使用的通信在1967年1月23日摩根和哈灵顿的信中结束了。"我已经读了你写给吉姆·海特的信，知道了关于英国捷迈骨科生产哈灵顿器械的事。我认为，在这种情况下，你已经尽力了。哈灵顿器械全球可见，我认为这些人告诉你的可能会让你不相信这是事实。我们在所有主要资本主义国家都有代表和经销商。对我们器械的主要反对意见一直是价格过高，而这方面我们也无能为力。毫无疑问，欧洲制造商至少能比我们便宜50%。我们将继续尽我们所能在全世界推广哈灵顿器械。我相信这是你对我们的全部期望。"[39]哈灵顿立即回复说，他已"收到您1月23日的来函，并认可我们已竭尽全力。感谢你们帮助解决这个棘手的问题"[40]。

Although somewhat tedious, this sequence of correspondence resulting from Harrington's first exposure to copies of his instrumentation at the SICOT meeting touched on many important realities of the surgeon innovator and medical manufacturer interface. Without patent protection there was no leverage to prevent copying. Zimmer made it clear they would resist releasing specifications, but whether they could be forced to disclose them wasn't addressed. Harrington appeared to leave the door open to the possibility of using his brand name if the instrumentation was produced according to his specifications. But he made it obvious that he would decide when and where to publish them. Zimmer accepted Harrington's responses as having lived up to their agreement for brand name protection, although his correspondence with the copiers seemed more focused on specifications than name. The correspondence exposed the reality that neither Zimmer nor Harrington had much legal leverage to prevent others copying the instrumentation or using his name. The value of a patent in preventing the copying of Harrington Spine Instrumentation will never be known.

尽管有些乏味，但哈灵顿在国际矫形与创伤外科学会会议上第一次接触到他的仿制器械所产生的这一系列通信，触及了外科医生创新者和医疗制造商之间许多重要的现实问题。没有专利保护，就没有防止抄袭的手段。捷迈明确表示，他们将拒绝公布规格，但他们没有提及是否会被迫披露这些规格。如果器械按照他的规格生产，哈灵顿似乎为使用他的品牌名称的可能性敞开了大门。但是，他明确表示，他将自行决定何时何地发表这一声明。捷迈接受了哈灵顿的回答，认为他遵守了他们关于品牌名称保护的协议，尽管他与仿制厂商的交流似乎更关注规格而不是名称。这些信件暴露了一个事实，即捷迈和哈灵顿都没有多少法律手段来防止其他人仿制器械或使用他的名字。永远无人知晓专利在防止哈灵顿脊柱器械被抄袭仿制方面的价值。

Harrington closed out the year with his private publication, *Scoliosis 1966*, the fifth in his series. It featured the translation of a recent, extensive four-part treatise published in 1963 by Pierre Stagnara titled "Lateral Deviations of the Spine." Its four parts were "Examination of Scoliotics," "Postural Scoliosis," "Structural Scoliosis," and "Treatment of Scoliosis."[41] Harrington must have felt Stagnara's grafting practices vindicated his own use of heterograft. If so, he was hearing only part of Stagnara's message. Stagnara wrote "Important progress has been made in the preparation of homoplastic bone (Hyatt) and heteroplastic bone (Bassett) thanks to the process of lyophilization or dry freezing (drying in a vacuum at very low temperature). Following Cauchoix, we make use of a compact transplant placed between the extreme spinous processes and we make use of abundant graft of autoplastic bone of the iliac crest." He used the compact heterograft to maintain the deformity reduction. Stagnara continued, "The autoplastic bone, which is assimilated very rapidly, also has an induction effect. It produces the transformation of young connective tissue into osteoid tissue and into bone tissue." *Scoliosis 1966* also featured translations of the works of Hueter (1863) and Volkmann (1862) that led to their description of the effect of load on epiphyseal growth.[42,43]

哈灵顿以他的私人出版物《脊柱侧凸 1966》结束了这一年，这是他私人出版系列中的第五本。其特色是对皮埃尔·斯塔格纳拉发表于 1963 年题为《脊柱的横向偏差》的最新翻译。论文四部分分别是"脊柱侧凸的检查""姿势性脊柱侧凸""结构性脊柱侧凸""脊柱侧凸的治疗"。[41]哈灵顿一定觉得斯塔格纳拉的实践证明了他自己使用异种骨是正确的。如果是这样，他听到的只是斯塔格纳拉的部分见解。斯塔格纳拉写道："由于冷冻干燥或冻干（在真空中非常低的温度下干燥）的处理，同种异体骨和异种骨的制备方面取得了重大进展。在考乔伊斯之后，我们使用了位于极端棘突之间的紧密植骨和大量的自体髂骨移植。"他使用紧密异种骨移植来减少畸形。斯塔格纳拉继续说道："自体骨被迅速同化，有诱导作用。它使年轻结缔组织转变为类骨组织和骨组织。"《脊柱侧凸 1966》也翻译

了许特（1863 年）和福尔克曼（1862 年）的著作中有关载荷影响骨骺生长的描述。[42,43]

At the 1967 AAOS annual meeting Harrington attended the SRS executive committee meeting on Sunday morning, January 15.[44] This was the second midwinter meeting of the committee, coming just one year after the founding meeting in Chicago. Again all eight members were present, and Kane recorded the minutes.[45] With no outstanding debts or accounts receivable, there were assets of $192.43. Annual dues were levied for the first time: $10 for active and associate members. All members and guests attending the annual meeting would be charged a registration fee based on a reasonable projection of costs. Minneapolis had previously been chosen as the next meeting site, but for convenience's sake it was decided to move the meeting from the university campus to a downtown hotel. September 7-9 were the dates chosen: all day Thursday and Friday with just the morning on Saturday. A social program, including informal activities for those staying the weekend, was planned.

在 1967 年美国骨科医师学会年会上，哈灵顿参加了脊柱侧凸研究学会执行委员会于 1 月 15 日星期日上午召开的会议，这是该委员会的第二次冬季会议，距芝加哥成立大会仅一年。[44] 8 名成员都再次出席，凯恩做了会议记录。[45]由于没有未清偿债务或应收账款，资产为 192.43 美元。此次会议首次征收了年费：活跃会员和准会员每人 10 美元。出席年会的全体会员及嘉宾将根据合理的费用预估收取注册费。明尼阿波利斯市曾被选为下一次会议地点，但为了方便起见，决定把会议从大学校园转移到市中心的一家宾馆。选定的日期是 9 月 7 日至 9 日：周四和周五全天及周六上午。此前已经计划好，将一个社交活动项目，包括那些非正式的活动安排在周末。

Organizational issues were briefly addressed. "Since no vacancies will occur in the Executive Committee there was no necessity for the creation of a Nominating Committee." No discussion of this decision was recorded, but this was inconsistent with Article IV of their constitution that specified that the president and president-elect would each serve for a term of two years. Article V specified that executive committee "members at large will be elected annually for a period of one year." Membership requirements were probably the most important issue facing the executive committee and consumed most of their discussion time. The secretary had received many inquiries from individuals who could not apparently qualify, making it necessary that the membership requirements in Article III of the constitution be fleshed out. There was general agreement in the principle of quality over quantity. As active membership was limited to orthopedic surgeons in the United States and Canada, membership in the AAOS or the Royal College of Surgeons was considered a reasonable minimum requirement. The sensitive issue of experience was addressed in this way: "In addition to completion of the membership application form, the applicant shall also include 25 surgical case reports and/or any significant scientific paper pertinent to the problem of scoliosis." Attendance as a guest to one meeting prior to membership was required. It was realized that special circumstances, such as military deployment and service to small populations, might require closer examination. It was felt that the associate membership category was satisfactory for orthopedists from other countries or physicians and scientists in other fields. Concerning possibly overlooked older major contributors, the "Secretary was directed to contact a number of distinguished orthopedists who had devoted a considerable portion of their talents and time to the problem of scoliosis, and to offer them honorary membership in the Society."[46]

他们简要讨论了组织架构问题。"由于执行委员会不会出现空缺，因此没有必要设立提名委员会。"关于这一决定的讨论没有被记录下来，但这与他们组织章程的第四条不一致，章程规定主席和候任主席各任期两年。第五条规定，执行委员会"委员每年选举一次，任期一年"。会员资格可能是执行委员会面临的最重要的问题，消耗了他们大部分的讨论时间。秘书收到许多不符合条件的人的询问，因此有必要补充第三条关于会员资格的要求。人们普遍同意质量重于数量的原则。在美国和加拿大，正式会员仅限于外科医生，成为美国骨科医师学会或皇家外科医学院的会员被认为是合理的最低要求。执业经验的问题较为敏感，委员会是这样处理的："除了完成会员申请表，申请人还应提交包括25个手术病例报告和/或任何与脊柱侧凸问题有关的重要科学论文。"在成为会员之前，必须以参会者身份出席一次会议。会议明确了诸如军事部署和为少数人口服务等特殊情况可能需要更仔细地审查。会议认为，对来自其他国家的骨科医生或其他领域的医生和科学家来说，准会员类别是可行的。关于可能被忽视的年长的主要贡献者，"指定秘书联系一些杰出的骨科医生，他们在脊柱侧凸问题上投入了许多精力和时间，应授予他们荣誉会员资格。"[46]

Two days later Harrington presented a three-hour AAOS Instructional Course Lecture #74, "Scoliosis and Instrumentation," and the next afternoon he was invited to discuss the second showing of Moe's movie, *Halo Femoral Distraction as an Adjunct to Surgical Treatment of Severe Scoliosis*. He would not have been difficult for Zimmer Ltd. representatives to locate if they had tried.

两天后，哈灵顿做了一场3小时的美国骨科医师学会教学课程讲座#74，题为"脊柱侧凸和器械"，第二天下午，他被邀请去参加莫第二场视频的讨论，项目名称《halo股骨牵引作为治疗严重脊柱侧凸的辅助手段》。对于捷迈的代理商来说，只要他们尝试过，找到他并不困难。

To present Harrington's next major contribution to spine instrumentation, it is necessary to backtrack slightly to November 21, 1966, when he authored a new application for Harrington Spine Instrumentation that would result in two major new implant designs. His letter to Hite began, "For a number of years, I have been discussing with colleagues and toying with an approach to the management of a condition known as spondylolisthesis. I have a case with this condition, and he is willing and would like to approach it with this new thought, using instrumentation. To manage the condition completely, I need lag screws."[47] Spondylolisthesis is the forward displacement of the vertebra above on the vertebra below, usually occurring at LS on S1. The severity of the slip is commonly expressed as a grade that is based on the percent of forward displacement: grade Ⅰ, 0-25%; grade Ⅱ, 25%-50%; grade Ⅲ, 50%-75%; grade Ⅳ, 75% - 100%; and grade Ⅴ, displacement off the top of the vertebra below or spondylolisthesis. Severity is generally related to the cause: grade Ⅰ and Ⅱ are usually due to stress fracture of the pars interarticularis and grade Ⅲ, Ⅳ, and Ⅴ to dysplasia of L5. Harrington was specifically referring to grades Ⅲ and Ⅳ. He cited two enclosed sketches, one of the lag screws and the other of the construct it would be used with. *See figure 9.1.* He continued, "The lag screws would be used to purchase through the pedicles of the vertebra into the body and then manually be pulled back into anatomical by pulling toward an instrumented spine from the sacral bar to L3." Harrington thought that heavy 3/16" diameter threaded rods (#1257) would be adequate so the only special items he needed were lag screws, #18 gauge moderately flexible stainless-steel wire, and four 3/16"... Diameter rod compatible hooks (#1256) modified by adding an inner ridge (like the #1252 hook) to prevent slipping on the threaded sacral bar. He detailed the specifications for the lag screws. "I would need lag screws with an eye in the base and a screw driver head as shown. The diameter should not be over 1/4" overall, and the length of three sizes: 1", 1-1/2" and 2". I would like two of each of these sizes. The thread of the lag screw can vary to a size you are machined to. The drawing is just to give you an idea. Can you accommodate me with this little research project in the production of the 1256 hook variation and the lag screw?" Years later this line would turn out to be haunting as the FDA initially used it to eliminate Harrington's work as validating pedicle screw use prior to the 1976 Medical Device Amendments to the Food, Drug and Cosmetic Act.

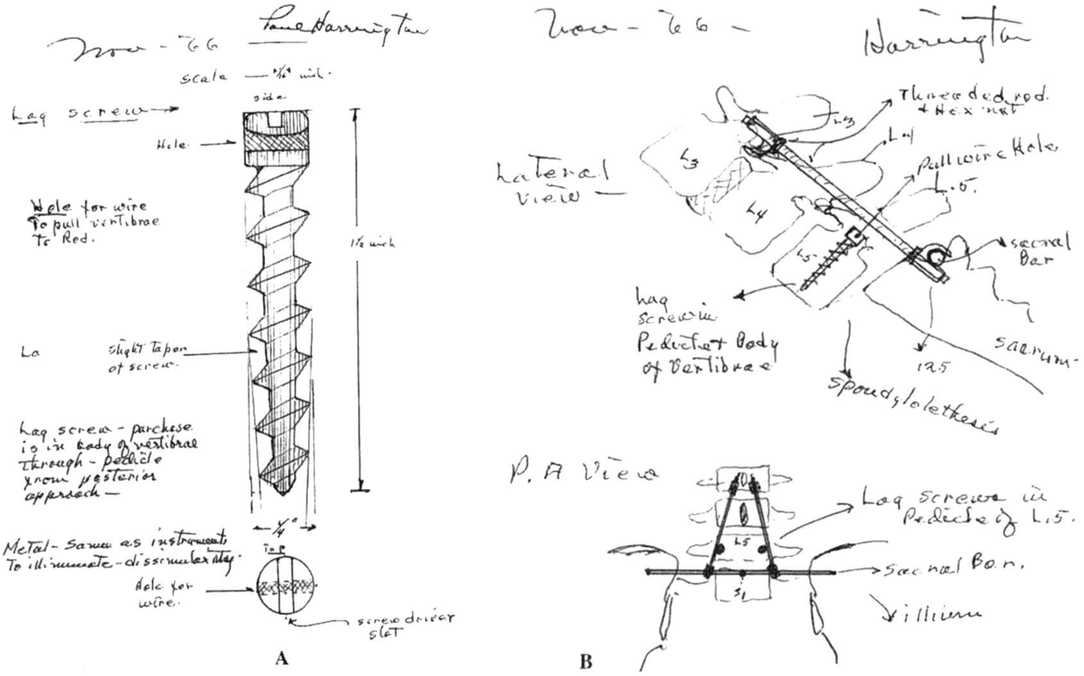

Figure 9.1 ***Drawings of (A) L5 lag screw and (B) high-grade spondylolisthesis reduction construct. (Harrington Archives)***
图 9.1 (A)L5 拉力螺钉和(B)高度脊柱滑脱复位结构的图纸(哈灵顿档案馆)

为了介绍哈灵顿对脊柱器械的下一个主要贡献，有必要稍微回溯到 1966 年 11 月 21 日，当时他为哈灵顿脊柱器械撰写了一份新的申请，从而产出了两种主要的新内植物设计。他给海特的信是这样开头的：“多年来，我一直在和同事们讨论一种治疗脊柱滑脱的方法。我有一个这种情况的病例，他愿意并且想要尝试这种新思路，即通过器械来处理。为了彻底处理病情，我需要拉力螺钉。”脊柱滑脱是指上位椎体较下位椎体向前滑移，通常发生在 L5—S1 节段。滑脱的严重程度通常表示为基于向前位移百分比：Ⅰ度 0~25%；Ⅱ度 25%~50%；Ⅲ度 50%~75%；Ⅳ度 75%~100%；Ⅴ度，完全脱位或椎体下垂。严重性一般与病因相关：Ⅰ度和Ⅱ度通常是由峡部裂所导致；Ⅲ度、Ⅳ度和Ⅴ度是由 L5 发育不良所导致。

哈灵顿特别提到了Ⅲ度和Ⅳ度。他引用了附件中的两张草图，一张是L5拉力螺钉，另一张是与之相配套使用的组合器械。(图9.1) 他继续说："拉力螺钉用来通过椎弓根进入椎体，然后手动拉回完成解剖复位，从骶骨岬拉到L3。"哈灵顿认为沉重的直径3/16英寸的螺纹棒（#1257）就足够了，所以他唯一需要的特殊物品是拉力螺钉、#18规格适度灵活的不锈钢丝和四个直径3/16英寸的兼容钩(#1256)。通过添加一个内部的脊（#1252钩子）改良，以防止在螺纹骶骨棒上滑动。他详细说明了拉力螺钉的规格。"我需要一个底部有一个孔和一个如图所示的螺钉驱动头的拉力螺钉。直径总体不应超过1/4英寸，长度有三个尺寸：1英寸、(1+1/2) 英寸和2英寸。每种尺寸我都要两件。拉力螺钉的螺纹可以根据加工的尺寸而变化。这幅图只是给你们一个构思。你能协助我一起完成这个1256号钩和拉力螺钉生产的小研究项目吗?"多年后，这段话被证明是令人难以忘怀的。在1976年《食品、药物和化妆品法案》医疗设备修正案之前，美国食品药品监督管理局最初用它来把哈灵顿的工作排除在外，以验证椎弓根螺钉的使用。

Before leaving for the AAOS annual meeting, Hanrrington had reminded Hite about the lag screw request and promised to mention it again in San Francisco.[48] Persistence paid off as Hite received the following letter, dated February 16, 1967. "Received your invoice #5093 dated January 24, 1967, which was a special order of three different lengths in lag screws (two 1", two 1 1/2" and two 2") and there were also four modified hooks. This design and equipment has been used and worked very nicely. I would like to have you give these a catalogue or order number so that they can be purchased. Also, I would like to have a copy of your drawings of the modified hook and the lag screws, as well as four more of the modified hooks and two 1" lag screws as soon as you can get them to me. I have another case to do. P.S. Jim, as an afterthought, these lag screws and hooks will be used with my basic instruments, therefore the Rockwell has to be the same to eliminate the effects of dissimilar metals. PRH."[49] The prompt and satisfactory response by Zimmer in producing these new instruments illustrated that even after all these years the cooperation between Harrington and Zimmer was still strong.

在动身去参加美国骨科医师学会年会之前，哈灵顿曾提醒海特自己关于拉力螺钉的要求，并承诺在圣弗朗西斯科再次提醒他。[48]他坚持不懈的努力终于获得了回报，海特收到了下面这封日期为1967年2月16日的信："收到您1967年1月24日的5093号单据，这是一个特殊订单，有三种不同长度的螺钉（两个1英寸、两个1-1/2英寸和两个2英寸），还有四个改良的钩。这种设计和器械已经被使用，并且效果良好。我希望您能提供给我一份产品目录或订货号以便购买。另外，希望您能尽快给我改良后的钩和拉力螺钉的图纸，以及另外四个改良后的钩和两个 1 英寸拉力螺钉的图纸副本。我还有另一项事务要办。除此之外，吉姆，经过反复思考，我想将这些拉力螺钉和钩与我的基础器械一起使用，因此它们的洛氏硬度必须一致，以消除不同金属间的影响。保罗 · R. 哈灵顿。”[49]捷迈公司在生产新器械时始终保持高水准，这也表明为什么即便过了这么多年，哈灵顿和捷迈公司之间的合作关系仍然牢不可破。

In the first quarter of 1967 Harrington operated on two thirteen-year-old patients, a female and a male. They were later reported on in both Italian[50] and English.[51] The female was asymptomatic except for progressive deformity of her low back and an unusual gait and posture. She had no back or leg pain. The male had suffered a fall four years earlier, sustained a low back injury, and had weak right foot dorsiflexion and a "sensory defect over the anterior lateral aspect of the leg." Standing lateral lumbosacral radiographs showed Grade Ⅲ/Ⅳ anterior displacement of L5 on the sacrum and reversal of the normal lumbosacral junction lordosis into kyphosis. The operation was performed through a posterior midline approach from L1 to "well down on the sacrum." The sacral bar was inserted from iliac wing to iliac wing. The loose neural arch of L5 was removed, and in both patients it was noted that a spina bifida occulta was present in the upper sacral segments. Blunt #1253 distraction hooks were placed under each side of the L1 lamina, and Moe keel hooks #1252 were reversed and placed as far laterally as possible on the sacral bar. Bilateral threaded rods with two nuts on either end were placed to join the upper to the lower hooks. Harrington described these as 1/8"-diameter rods, but they almost certainly were 3/16"-diameter, as Harrington had specified in his initial request to Hite. He also did not mention use of a 3/16" threaded rod compatible hook (#1256) to which a keel had been added. Distraction was applied, and a very gratifying reduction of L5 posteriorly occurred, providing good visualization for drilling the L5 pedicles with a 1/8"-diameter drill followed by placement of a lag screw. A #18 gauge stainless steel wire was used to secure the screw to the rod, a bilateral posterior lateral arthrodesis of L4 to S1 performed, and the incision closed. He did not specify if any supplemental bone graft was used. He also did not elaborate any plan for the future management of the instrumented but unfused spine from L1 to L4.[52] *See figure 9.2.*

1967 年第一季度，哈灵顿为两名 13 岁的患者做了手术，一男一女。相关工作在意大利语文献[50]和英语文献[51]中都有报道。该女性患者，除了腰部进行性畸形和异常步态和姿势外，没有任何症状，也没有背部或腿部疼痛。而这名男性患者在四年前摔倒，背部受伤，右脚背屈乏力，“腿前外侧有感觉缺失”，站立侧位腰骶 X 光片显示：L5 前滑脱Ⅲ/Ⅳ度，正常腰骶连接处由前凸变为后凸。手术的方式是通过后正中入路，从 L1 至“骶骨上方”进行。骶骨棒从一侧髂翼向另一侧髂翼插入。切除 L5 松弛的神经弓，两例患者骶骨上段均出现隐性脊柱裂。钝性 1253 号撑开钩放置在 L1 椎板的两侧下方，1252 号莫氏龙骨钩反向放置，并尽可能远地向外放置在骶骨棒上。放置两端有两个螺母的双螺纹棒，用以连接上钩和下钩。哈灵顿将其描述为直径 1/8 英寸的棒，但几乎可以肯定它们的直径是 3/16 英寸，因为这是哈灵顿最初向海特提出的要求。他也没有提到使用直径 3/16 英寸的螺纹棒兼容钩（#1256），而是在术中添加了龙骨。应用撑开力后，L5 的向后复位令人满意，并为使用直径 1/8 英寸的钻头钻孔 L5 椎弓根提供了良好的手术视野，随后放入拉力螺钉，并采用 18 号不锈钢丝将螺钉固定在棒上，行 L4 至 S1 双侧后外侧融合术，闭合切口。他没有具体说明是否使用了植骨材料，也没有详细说明固定但未融合的 L1 至 L4 脊柱未来的处理方案。[52]（图 9.2）。

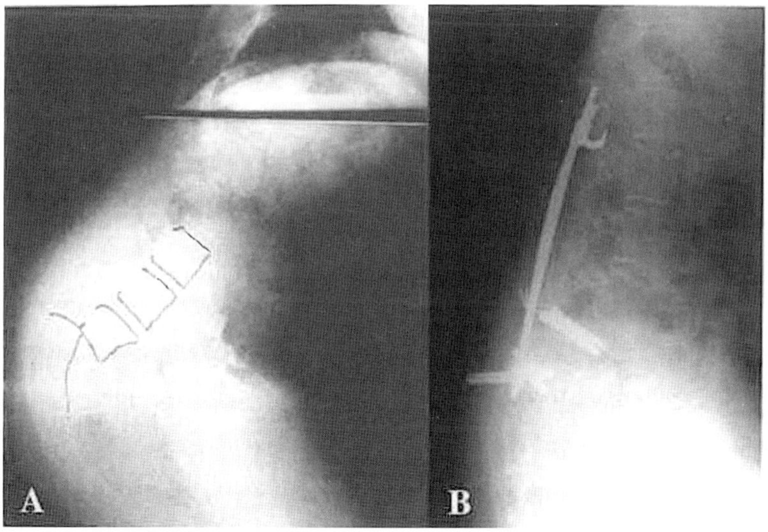

Figure 9.2 *Lateral spine radiographs showing (A) a severe L5 on Sl forward slip preoperative and (B) postoperative with near total stip reduction. Of note is the increase in trunk length. (Harrington Archives)*

图 9.2　脊柱 X 光侧位片显示　A. 术前 S1 上 L5 严重的前滑脱，B. 术后滑脱几乎完全恢复。值得注意的是躯干长度的增加（哈灵顿档案馆）

In the female patient “definite symptoms of a cauda equina syndrome appeared on the 3rd to 4th day, including diminished sensation over the left side of the perineum, loss of bulbocavemous reflex and reflex neurogenic bladder confirmed by cystometrogram." She was discharged to home bed rest on the fourteenth postoperative day and with a Foley catheter in place. Her neurological deficit had mostly resolved by one month postoperative and completely by six months, when she was last seen. The male patient had no complications and was discharged in a bilateral short leg spica cast. At six months, X-ray "suggested a developing fusion," the cast was removed and ambulation was begun. When last seen at eight months postoperative, he was asymptomatic. Nearly complete reduction of the spondylolisthesis had been achieved in both patients. The female had gained four centimeters of spine length, the male two centimeters. This elongation was considered to have possibly caused her cauda equina syndrome; another possibility was postoperative edema that caused compression of the cauda equina by the sacral bar.

女性患者在第 3 天至第 4 天出现了明确的马尾综合征症状，包括会阴左侧感觉减退、球海绵体反射消失，膀胱造影也证实反射性神经源性膀胱。术后第 14 天，患者留置导尿管，出院并在家卧床休息。术后 1 个月时，她的神经功能障碍已基本消除。术后 6 个月，最后一次随访时，她的神经功能障碍已完全消除。男性患者无术后并发症，予以双侧短腿髋人字石膏固定后出院。6 个月时，X 光片显示："正在发生融合"，患者拆除石膏并开始下床活动。术后 8 个月最后一次随访时，他仍然没有症状。两例患者脊柱滑脱几乎完全复位。女性病人的脊柱长度增加了 4 厘米，男性病人的脊柱长度增加了 2 厘米。脊柱的长度变化可能是导致她马尾综合征的原因；另一种可能是术后水肿导致骶骨棒压迫马尾神经。

The dual publication of a scientific paper is frowned on so it is fair to ask what special circumstances warranted that happening in the report of these two cases. Harrington had a visitor, Professor Dott Fiorenzo Travaglini of Florence, Italy, at the time the patients were operated on. These two cases were worked into a scientific presentation that Travaglini made at the LII Congresso della Societa Italiana di Ortopedia e Traumatologia held October 13-15, 1967, in Rome. A few days after the meeting, Travaglini wrote Harrington that the paper had been very well received and enclosed a translated copy of his paper, "fully adapted to our scientific customs." He asked Harrington, "before submitting it for publication, I would like you to go through it and check that everything is as we discussed in Houston."[53] Harrington promptly wrote back: "In my inadequate way, I have reviewed your Italian interpretation, and agree with your fine additions—particularly your completion of the bibliography—and you therefore have my permission to proceed."[54]

一篇科学论文的重复发表是不受欢迎的。所以我们有必要问一下，是什么特殊情况使得这个病例被用两种语言报道。意大利佛罗伦萨的多特·菲奥伦佐·特拉瓦吉尼教授访问哈灵顿时，正逢他给这两位患者手术。1967 年 10 月 13 日至 15 日，特拉瓦吉尼在罗马举行的意大利骨科和创伤学会学术会议上，将这两个病例纳入了科学报告。会议结束后几天，特拉瓦吉尼给哈灵顿写信说这个报告反响很好，并附上了一份他的论文的意大利语译文，"完全符合我们的学术规范"。他问哈灵顿："在提交出版之前，我希望您把它检查一遍，确保一切都和我们在休斯敦讨论的一样。"[53]哈灵顿立即回信说："我重新阅读了您的意大利语译本，提出一些拙见，并同意您的补充意见，特别是您完善了参考文献，因此我允许您继续发表。"[54]

In May 1967, five months before the Italian's presentation, Harrington had submitted this two-case study for presentation at the section on orthopedic and traumatic surgery of the Southern Medical Association's 61st annual meeting on November 13–16, 1967. Presented by the second author, Hugh Tullos, on November 15, it was essentially the same paper Travaglini had delivered. The submitted manuscript encountered many editorial snags which prompted Harrington in September 1968 to offer " my sincere apologies for the mess that was sent to you... i e. the manuscript of ' Reduction of Severe Spondylolisthesis in Children.' You may rest assured that we will straighten out all of the items concerned... It appears that a drastic change in personnel seems to be partly responsible."[55] The paper was finally published in the *Southern Medical Journal* in January 1969.[56]

1967 年 5 月，即在意大利学术报告的 5 个月前，哈灵顿提交了这两个病例报告，并准备在 1967 年 11 月 13—16 日举办的南方医学会第六十一届年会的骨科和创伤外科分会场作报告。由第二作者休·图洛斯于 11 月 15 日提交的这篇论文，实际上与特拉瓦吉尼已提交的论文相同。提交的手稿遇到了许多编辑上的问题，这促使哈灵顿在 1968 年 9 月写信给图洛斯："对儿童严重'滑脱的复位'手稿给您造成的混乱局面表示真诚的歉意……您尽可放心，我们会把所有有关的事项都弄清楚的……看来人事上的重大变动是部分原因。"[55]这篇论文最终于 1969 年 1 月发表在《南方医学杂志》上。[56]

An English translation of the Italian version is unavailable. However, comparing the illustrations of the printed versions of the papers shows both to have nineteen illustrations, of which seven are different. One intraoperative lateral X-ray included only in the Italian version is particularly interesting as it shows the same amount of reduction with distraction alone as with distraction after adding the lag screws and wires. The Italian version had twenty-nine references and the English version eighteen (to stay under the limit of twenty). In summary, the Italian version was published as part of a congress, the papers were similar but not identical, and there was no suggestion of any ulterior motive by either Harrington or the Italians.

意大利版本的英文翻译无法得到。然而，比较两篇论文印刷版的插图，发现两篇论文都有19幅插图，其中7幅不同。只有意大利版本有术中侧位X光片。这一点特别有趣，因为它显示了单独撑开与添加拉力螺钉和钢丝后撑开的复位量相同。意大利版本有29条参考文献，英语版本有18条（为保持在20条以内）。总之，意大利版本是作为大会的一部分发表的，两个版本的文章内容相似，但不完全相同，而且无论是哈灵顿还是意大利人都不像是有意为之的。

The Harrington-Zimmer correspondence continued to increase through 1966, but it decreased after that. This was actually a good sign and could have been predicted from Hite's positive comment to Harrington after the 1967 AAOS annual meeting: "It was a pleasure chatting with you once again... I think our problems were fewer this year than at any previous time."[57] Hite did go on to mention three items. He had just sent one each of the 2" through 12" #1250 distraction rods to Harrington for testing. Additionally, the minor changes Harrington had suggested for the #1272 periosteal elevator were being made. Furthermore, since Zimmer had received many questions about the use of the #1248 outrigger, Hite requested some illustrations that could be worked into an instruction brochure. Also, Advertising Manager Hamm had asked for copies of the supplemental technique manual Harrington had passed out at his instructional course lecture so they could be duplicated and distributed.[58] All these requests were fulfilled. However, while testing outriggers with longer arms, metallic wear dust at the junction of the nut and thread was noted. This led to a curious communication. Harrington apparently sent a technology clipping about a new stainless steel that had increased stress-corrosion resistance. Vernon R. Scott, chief of medical research, responded that in some acid solutions this new USS 18-18-2 stainless steel had significantly greater susceptibility to pitting and corrosion than the 316 stainless steel they were using.[59] This was the last correspondence on this issue and the last available Zimmer correspondence for ten months, the longest interlude to date.

哈灵顿和捷迈公司之间的通信在1966年持续增多，但在那之后就减少了。这实际上是一个好迹象，从海特在1967年美国骨科医师学会年会后对哈灵顿的积极评价中就可以预测到："很高兴再次与你聊天……我认为我们今年的问题比以往任何时候都要少。"[57]海特接着提到了三件事。他刚刚把2英寸到12英寸的1250号撑开棒都送给哈灵顿进行测试。哈灵顿建议的对#1272骨膜剥离器的小改动正在修改中。此外，由于捷迈公司收到了许多关于使用#1248外撑开器的问题，海特要求提供一些可以放在说明书中的插图。广告经理哈姆还要了哈灵顿在其教学课程讲座上分发的补充技术手册的副本，以便复制分发。[58]所有这些要求都得到了满足。然而，在测试长臂外撑开器时，螺母和螺纹连接处被发现有金属磨损的粉尘。这引发了一场不寻常的交流。显然，哈灵顿发来了一份关于一种新型不锈钢的技术简报，这种不锈钢具有更强的抗应力和抗腐蚀的能力。医学研究主任弗农·R. 斯科特回应说，在某些酸性溶液中，这种新型USS 18-18-2不锈钢明显比他们使用的316不锈钢更容易发生点蚀和腐蚀。[59]这是关于这个问题的最后一次通信，也是长达十个月的间隔之后，最后一次可获得的捷迈与哈灵顿的通信。

Harrington's time spent away from Houston changed during 1967. His 64 travel days were fewer than the year before, were restricted to North America, and did not include surgery.[60] In February he spent four days in St. Petersburg and Gainesville, Florida. The trip to the latter continued his research collaboration with Enneking. In April he had two days in San Antonio as a consultant to Brooke Army Medical Center and Wilford Hall USAF Hospital where he was confronted with the problem of lower mandible flattening and loss of cortex associated with Milwaukee brace wear. Dentists at the University of Texas Dental Branch in Houston had started speaking out about this problem and in 1965 had developed a soft bite appliance to better distribute and absorb the loads on the mandible.[61] By 1966 the problem was so frequent that they declared it "is impossible to take care of any new patients at the University of Texas Medical Branch." They had prepared a four-page information and instruction handout, "Management of Dental Problems during Milwaukee Brace Therapy," for inquiring dentists.[62] About this time Blount, the Milwaukee brace developer, and Moe were discovering that passive distraction with the mandible pad was not necessary and lowering it or, even better, replacing it with a throat mold eliminated this complication.[63] From San Antonio

Harrington went to the Southwestern Surgical Congress in Phoenix where apparently he did not participate in the scientific program, but likely did play in the golf tournament. In May he attended the Texas Orthopaedic Association meeting in Dallas and presented his study of the "Non-operative Treatment of Scoliosis."

哈灵顿离开休斯敦的时间在1967年发生了变化。他的差旅天数比前一年少，只有64天，目的地仅限于北美，且外出事项不包括手术。[60] 1967年2月，他在圣彼得堡和佛罗里达州的盖恩斯维尔待了四天。后者之行使他保持了与恩内金的研究合作。4月，他花了两天的时间，在圣安东尼奥担任布鲁克陆军医疗中心和威尔福德·霍尔美国空军医院的顾问，在那里他遇到了与密尔沃基支架磨损相关的下颌骨扁平和皮层丧失的问题。得克萨斯大学休斯敦牙科分校的牙医们已经开始公开谈论这个问题，并在1965年就已经开发了一种软咬合装置，以更好地分散和吸收下颌骨上的载荷。[61]到1966年，这个问题频繁出现，以至于他们宣称"得克萨斯大学医学部已不能再接受任何新病人"。他们准备了一份四页的信息和指导手册——《密尔沃基矫形支具治疗期间牙齿问题的处理》，供咨询的牙医使用。[62]大约在这个时候，密尔沃基矫形支具的研发者布朗特和莫发现，用下颌骨垫进行撑开是没有必要的。应该减少使用下颌骨垫，或者更好的选择是用咽喉模具代替它，以消除这种并发症。[63]哈灵顿从圣安东尼奥来到凤凰城的西南外科大会，据说在那里他没有参加科学会议议程，但可能参加了高尔夫比赛。5月，他参加了在达拉斯举行的得克萨斯州骨科学会会议，并报告了他关于"脊柱侧凸的非手术治疗"的研究。

By far the longest trip of the year lasted from June 18 to July 6. He attended the annual meeting of the Canadian Orthopaedic Association in Montreal where one paper was titled "Problems—Technique de Harrington" by Pierre Labelle and others with the discussion led by John Hall. No further details survived, but the problems likely included infection, implant dislodgement, pseudarthrosis, and rod breakage. This may have been the first presentation specifically focused on Harrington Instrumentation problems. After this meeting, Harrington briefly visited Philadelphia, Toledo, New York, and Baltimore to see patients in consultation or follow-up. The last stop on this multicity trip was Washington, D.C. where arrangements had been made for the SRS executive committee to meet on July 6 with Arthur J. Lesser, who was the director of the division of health services of the Department of Health, Education and Welfare. On March 16 Secretary Bill Kane and founding member and Washington, D.C. resident Allan McKelvie met with

Lesser, and Kane presented the aims of the SRS as follows: "I outlined the background of the founding of the society and presented the goals which the Society had set for itself. These included the institution of Fellowships for personnel at the senior and post-residency levels, the investigation of possible retrospective and prospective studies which might utilize computer techniques with the correlation and compilation of information available for various scoliosis centers in the country, the development of regional centers at first and ultimately a central research center, and finally, the incorporation of various other fields of clinical and basic research which should be involved in the over-all study of the scoliosis problem."[64] Lesser responded to Kane and McKelvie by describing the activities of the Children's Bureau, which was under his management. Included were fellowships aimed at care improvement of mentally defective children, regional programs for pediatric amputees, evaluation of new devices, development of clinical centers of increased competence for treatment of difficult problems, and preference for prospective studies. Lesser hinted at support for a pilot prospective study and the possibility of fellowship funding. He also suggested contacting Ross Laboratories, which had funded several multidiscipline pediatric conferences. Lesser arranged for Kane and McKelvie to meet five high ranking leaders in either the Department of Health, Education and Welfare or the National Institutes of Health (NIH). Their visit concluded with a roundtable meeting the following day.

1967 年 6 月 18 日到 7 月 6 日，哈灵顿一直在外出差，这是他这一年中最长时间的出差。他参加了加拿大骨科学会在蒙特利尔举行的年度会议，其中皮埃尔·拉贝尔等人一篇题为《哈灵顿技术—问题》的论文，由约翰·霍尔主持讨论。虽然细节未知，但问题大致包括感染、内植物移位、假关节和断棒。这可能是第一次专门针对哈灵顿器械问题的演讲。在这次会议之后，哈灵顿短暂地访问了宾夕法尼亚、托莱多、纽约和巴尔的摩，以会诊或随访患者。这次包括诸多城市的旅途的最后一站是华盛顿特区。在那里，脊柱侧凸研究学会执行委员会安排他于 7 月 6 日与卫生、教育和福利部卫生服务部门的主任亚瑟·J. 莱塞会面。3 月 16 日，学会秘书比尔·凯恩和创会会员、华盛顿特区居民艾伦·麦凯尔维会见莱塞，凯恩介绍脊柱侧凸研究学会的目标："我概述了学会成立的背景，并介绍了学会为自己设定的目标。其中包括为高年制医师和完成住院医师培训的人员设立专科培训项目；调查可能的回顾性和前瞻性研究，这些研究可利用计算机技术对国内各脊柱侧凸中心可用的信息进行关联和汇编；建立区域中心，最终发展成一个中央研究中心；在脊柱侧凸问题的全面研究中，应结合临床和基础研究等其他各个领域。"[64]莱塞在回答凯恩和麦凯尔维的问题时，描述了由他管理的儿童局的活动，其中包括旨在治疗改善智力缺陷儿童的培训项目、针对儿童截肢者的区域项目、新设备的评估项目、临床中心的发展、提高治疗疑难杂症的能力，并优先进行前瞻性研究。莱塞暗示他可以支持一项前瞻性试点研究，并可能提供培训项目基金。他还建议联系罗斯实验室，该实验室曾多次资助了儿科多学科会议。莱塞安排凯恩和麦凯尔维会见了卫生、教育和福利部（美国国家卫生研究所）的五位高级领导人。他们的访问以第二天的圆桌会议结束。

The meetings and roundtables had generated much enthusiasm, and the government representatives suggested a meeting of the SRS executive committee with representatives of the NIH, Vocational Rehabilitation Administration, and the Children's Bureau so July 6 at 1:00 p.m. was scheduled.[65] Pre-meeting communication with Merrill Read, director of the growth and development program, was designed to provide focus for the two-hour meeting, the purpose of which was to discuss the scope of the scoliosis problem in the United States, the diverse factors affecting it, and SRS's proposals for addressing the problem.[66] The anticipated attendance was fifteen, including the SRS representatives. Moe, Kane, Levine, Donaldson, Harrington, and Goldstein, who were six of the eight SRS executive committee members, were to be joined by McKelvie. Each made a five-minute presentation on a specific aspect of scoliosis. For example, Levine had reviewed the literature on "Cardio-Pulmonary Failure Caused by Scoliosis" and reported that we did not know "the number of premature deaths arising from scoliosis in this country annually."[67] He added that while severe scoliosis was known to cause early death, it was not known how severe the scoliosis must be and the English literature was "almost completely void on the subject." No post-meeting summaries or correspondence can be found in the Harrington and SRS archives, suggesting the meeting had been at least a temporary disappointment for the SRS.

会面与圆桌会议激发了与会者很大的热情，政府代表建议脊柱侧凸研究学会执行委员会与美国国家卫生研究所、职业康复管理局和儿童局的代表举行会议，并定于7月6日下午1点举行。[65]哈灵顿与成长与发育项目主任梅里尔·里德的会前沟通，旨在为两个小时的会议提供重点，其目的是讨论美国脊柱侧凸问题的范围、影响因素，以及脊柱侧凸研究学会解决问题的建议。[66]预计出席人数为15人，包括脊柱侧凸研究学会的代表。莫、凯恩、莱文、唐纳森、哈灵顿和戈尔茨坦是脊柱侧凸研究学会执行委员会8位成员中的6位，麦凯尔维将加入他们的行列。

每个人就脊柱侧凸的一个具体方面做了五分钟的报告。例如，莱文回顾了关于“脊柱侧凸导致心肺衰竭”的文献，并报告说他们不知道“在这个国家每年因脊柱侧凸引起的过早死亡人数”。[67]他补充说，虽然已知严重的脊柱侧凸会导致过早死亡，但尚不清楚脊柱侧凸的严重程度，英文文献的报道“在这方面几乎完全空白”。在哈灵顿和脊柱侧凸研究学会的档案中没有发现会议后的总结或通信，这表明至少对脊柱侧凸研究学会来说，这次会议是暂时让人失望的，并没有取得良好的效果。

In July 1967 one of the most important events in Harrington's professional life occurred: the recruitment of Jesse Hamilton Dickson to staff the TIRR Scoliosis Clinic for one day each week. *See figure 9.3*. This hiring was almost certainly related to Harrington's appointment as chief of surgical services at TIRR.[68] A Houston native, Dickson had just completed his education and training and was returning home to practice at the Kelsey Seybold Clinic. Medical practice was well understood in his family as his father and great-uncle were specialists in otorhinolaryngology.[69] Dickson had graduated from the Southwestern Medical School in Dallas in 1959, interned at Oklahoma University in 1959–60, completed the Baylor orthopedic residency in 1964, served in the US Air Force Medical Corps until 1966, and completed New York City's Hospital for Special Surgery Hip Fellowship in 1967. By the time he became a resident at Baylor, orthopedic residents were rotating with Harrington, so the two men had worked together before his hiring.

Figure 9.3 ***Jesse H. Dickson, ca late 1960s.*** (***SRS Archives***)
图 9.3　杰西 · H. 迪克森，20 世纪 60 年代末（脊柱侧凸研究学会档案馆）

1967 年 7 月，哈灵顿职业生涯中最重要的事件之一发生了：招聘杰西 · 汉密尔顿 · 迪克森为得克萨斯州康复与研究中心脊柱侧凸门诊的工作人员，每周工作一天。（图 9.3）这一招聘几乎可以肯定与哈灵顿被任命为得克萨斯州康复与研究中心外科主任有关。[68]迪克森是休斯敦人，刚刚完成了他的学业和规范化培训，正准备返回家乡，在凯尔西 · 西博尔德诊所工作。他的父亲和叔公都是耳鼻喉科的专家，所以他的家庭对医生这个行业很熟悉。[69]迪克森1959年毕业于达拉斯西南医学院，1959到1960年在俄克拉何马大学实习，1964年完成贝勒骨科住院医师培训，在美国空军医疗队服役到1966年，1967年完成纽约市特种外科医院髋关节专科培训。当他在贝勒大学做住院医生时，轮值时是以骨科住院医师身份跟着哈灵顿，所以在哈灵顿聘请他之前，他们两人就一起工作过。

The second annual meeting of the SRS was held in Minneapolis on September 7-9, 1967. Eighty-two were in the group picture, more than twice the number appearing in the first year's photograph. Fourteen scientific papers and seven cases were presented. An hour was allotted to discussing and clarifying the latest terminology document. There was a guest speaker for each of the two dinners. On Thursday John T. Robinson of Madison, Wisconsin, presented "Fossils in the Emergence of Man," and on Friday Yves Cotrel of Berk-Plage, France, spoke on "Urinary Hydroxyprolines in Scoliosis."[70] Abstracts of the fourteen scientific papers (three addressing pulmonary function, one biomechanics, two nonoperative treatments, and eight surgery or surgery-related topics) were published.[71]

脊柱侧凸研究学会的第二届年会于1967年9月7日至9日在明尼阿波利斯举行。这组照片中有82人，是第一届与会人数的两倍多。会议报告了14篇学术论文和7个病例，并且安排了一个小时用来讨论，以及规范的最新术语文件。会议的两场晚宴各有一位特邀演讲者，周四的演讲者是来自威斯康星州麦迪逊的约翰·T. 罗宾逊，其演讲主题为“化石与人类的出现”；周五的演讲者是来自法国贝尔克普拉日的伊夫斯·科特雷尔，其演讲主题为“脊柱侧凸患者尿中的羟脯氨酸”。[70]会议共计发表了14篇学术论文的摘要（3篇涉及肺功能，1篇生物力学，2篇非手术治疗，8篇手术或与手术相关的主题）。[71]

Improving or at least preserving pulmonary function was a major goal of scoliosis treatment as pulmonary failure was the cause of death in severe thoracic scoliosis, and scoliosis most commonly affected the thoracic spine. While the first two studies included patients with mixed pathologies, the third had only patients with idiopathic scoliosis. Lung volumes, vital capacity, and maximum breathing capacity were generally reduced as the scoliosis increased.[72,73] Ventilation/perfusion studies showed low ratios on the convex side from poorly ventilated but well-perfused areas and loss of preferential perfusion in the lower lobe. The concave side displayed low ratios from increased perfusion without an equal increase in ventilation.[74] Lung volumes were decreased in over 50% of patients after application of the preoperative corrective device, but not with the halo corrective device.[75] The effect of surgery on pulmonary function was inconsistent. In one study of post-polio and idiopathic patients, there was no improvement in pulmonary function at an average of twenty-four months after spine fusion with an average curve correction of 40%. However, in the study limited to patients with idiopathic scoliosis, 60% of those with one to four year follow-up after correction from 62° to 21° had stable or improved pulmonary function.[76]

改善或至少维持肺功能是脊柱侧凸治疗的主要目标，因为肺衰竭是严重胸椎侧凸死亡的原因，而脊柱侧凸最易影响胸椎。前两项研究包括混合病理的患者，而第三项研究只包括特发性脊柱侧凸患者。肺容量、肺活量和最大呼吸容量通常随着脊柱侧凸的增加而降低。[72,73]通气/灌注研究显示，凸侧通气不良但灌注良好区域的比例较低，且下叶失去优先灌注。凹面则显示灌注增加而没有相等通气增加的比率较低。[74]应用术前矫正器后，超过50%的患者肺容量下降，但halo矫正器并不会影响。[75]手术对肺功能的影响不一致。在一项针对脊髓灰质炎后和特发性脊柱侧凸患者的研究中，脊柱融合术后平均24个月，肺功能没有改善，平均弯曲矫正率为40%。然而，在一项仅限于特发性脊柱侧凸患者的研究中，从62°到21°矫正后随访1到4年的患者中，60%的患者肺功能稳定或改善。[76]

The biomechanics presentation, the first on this topic, attempted to explain scoliosis development through analysis of the force systems capable of initiating a lateral-rotatory displacement of the vertebral column. The importance of ribs in providing lateral stability to the thoracic spine was emphasized.[77] The focus of nonoperative treatment studies was the Milwaukee brace. Harrington presented his experience with 133 patients, 117 of whom were idiopathic, to describe his concept of nonoperative treatment and concluded that the brace was most effective for curves ranging from 20° to 45°.[78] Moe and Lai, analyzed the treatment course of 83 (71 adolescent and 12 juvenile) idiopathic scoliosis patients.[79] Brace wear for an average of three and a half years resulted in satisfactory or excellent results in 85% (60 of 71) of patients with adolescent idiopathic scoliosis with 64% (7 of 11) of the poor results having surgery. The brace was not satisfactory in maintaining correction after maximum cast correction of larger curves. Malocclusion occurred in 20% and pressure sores in 18%, but most were easily managed with brace alterations.

生物力学报告这一主题在会议上首次亮相，本研究试图通过分析能够启动椎体侧方旋转移位的力学系统来解释脊柱侧凸的发展。研究强调肋骨在提供胸椎侧方稳定性方面的重要性。[77]非手术治疗研究的重点是密尔沃基支具。哈灵顿介绍了他治疗 133 名患者的经验，其中 117 名患者为特发性脊柱侧凸，他描述了非手术治疗的概念，并得出了结论：支具对 20°至 45°弯曲最有效。[78]莫和赖分析了 83 名特发性脊柱侧凸患者（71 名青年，12 名少儿）的治疗过程。[79]青少年特发性脊柱侧凸患者中，85%（60/71）的患者佩戴支具平均三年半后，获得了满意或良好的治疗效果，64%（7/11）治疗效果较差的患者接受了手术治疗。当脊柱侧凸角度较大的患者获得最大限度的石膏矫正后，支具维持矫正效果并不满意。20%的患者发生咬合错位，18%的患者发生压疮，但大多数问题可以在更换支具后很明显地得到解决。

Three of the surgical studies were case series in which Harrington Spine Instrumentation had been used. In two, idiopathic scoliosis patients predominated.[80,81] In one, which had been presented the year before, only idiopathic scoliosis patients were included.[82] They were relatively large single surgeon series that ranged from 100 to 157 patients. Although complications and problems still occurred, the authors agreed that Harrington Instrumentation was a positive development in the treatment of scoliosis because it provided better lasting scoliosis correction, a satisfactory option for older patients as well as those with neuromuscular and congenital conditions, and decreased postoperative recumbent and total cast time. Uses without fusion were recommended against and were seldom used in the young child.[83] All authors noted that Harrington Instrumentation made it difficult to detect pseudarthrosis and sometimes allowed early incomplete fusion to progress to fusion. In one of the series, addition of fresh autogenous iliac crest corticocancellous bone graft in the 71 idiopathic scoliosis patients was associated with no pseudarthrosis 2 to 7 years postoperative.[84] The extent and duration of postoperative immobilization varied, but trended toward including a neck extension with a Risser localizer cast, body cast with addition of the Milwaukee brace chin and occiput portion, or Milwaukee brace.[85,86]

三项手术研究为使用哈灵顿脊柱内固定器械的系列病例报道。其中两项研究中特发性脊柱侧凸患者居多。[80,81]一项研究是在一年前公布的，只纳入了特发性脊柱侧凸患者。[82]他们都是相对较大的单一外科医生的系列病例报道，纳入患者从 100 名到 157 名不等。尽管并发症和问题仍然存在，但作者一致认为哈灵顿器械在脊柱侧凸治疗中是一个积极的发展，因为它提供了更好的、持久的脊柱侧凸矫正，对于大龄以及神经肌肉和先天性患者来说是一个令人满意的选择，并且减少了术后卧床和总的支具佩戴时间。虽然该器械不建议使用非融合的方法，并且很少应用于幼儿。[83]所有作者都注意到哈灵顿器械难以发现假关节，有时会导致早期不完全融合发展为融合。在其中一个报道中，71 名特发性脊柱侧凸患者，行新鲜的自体髂骨骨移植术后二至七年无假关节发生。[84]术后固定的程度和持续时间各不相同，但趋向于包括颈部延伸联合里泽局部定位矫形石膏固定，躯体石膏联合密尔沃基支具固定下颏和枕部，或单纯使用密尔沃基支具。[85,86]

Two studies focused on routine exploration for pseudarthrosis following surgery, one at one to two years postoperative[87] and the other at six months.[88] One or more pseudarthroses were found in 56% (25 of 45) and 53% (28 of 53), respectively. Harrington Instrumentation was used in the first study but not specified and probably not used in the second. The effect of additional unspecified bone graft usage was addressed in the first study. The incidence of pseudarthrosis was 78% (14 of 18) without and 38% (10 of 26) with. The author of the first paper concluded that Harrington Instrumentation itself did not lower the incidence of graft failure.

两项研究聚焦于术后假关节的常规探查，一项研究在术后 1 到 2 年,[87]另一项研究于术后 6 个月。[88]两项研究分别在 56%（25/45）和 53%（28/53）的患者中发现一个或多个假关节。在第一项研究中使用了哈灵顿器械，第二项研究中没有具体说明使用的器械，可能并没有使用。在第一项研究中讨论了增加植骨的影响，使用植骨技术的假性关节的发生率为 78%（14/18），而未使用植骨的发生率为 38%（10/26）。第一篇论文的作者得出结论，哈灵顿器械本身并不会降低植骨失败的发生率。

Finally, there were three unrelated surgical papers. Vern Nickel, Jacquelin Perry, and Malcolm Heppenstall presented their ten-year experience with "The Halo: An Analysis of Its Use on 174 Patients."[89] The average patient age was fifteen years, and the indications for usage were unstable cervical spines, extensive fusions for severe scoliosis, and revision of extensive fusions. Twelve patients had manageable complications. Four recommendations emerged: placement of anterior pins below the frontal protuberance, no routine tightening of pins, necessity of keeping pin sites clean, and gradual application of longitudinal traction and repeated checking of peripheral nerve function. Simmons presented his "Observations on the Technique and Indications for Wedge Resection of the

Spine," which was based on fourteen patients treated over ten years.[90] The indications for it were severe deformity with hyperlordosis, prior fusion with deformity, and hemivertebra. An anterior retroperitoneal approach with a combined or staged posterior approach, sometimes with posterior instrumentation, was usually required to perform the wedge resection. The deformity was better in all but one, in whom it was unchanged. There were no deaths or persistent morbidities. Moe and Bruce Sundberg studied the effect of posterior fusion on 42 out of 79 children from 1 to 10 years of age for a variety of indications in "Spine Fusions in the Scoliotic Growing Child."[91] Over an average of 48.6 months, there was no change in fusion length in 20, a 7 mm increase in one, and no change greater than 5 mm in the rest. Mild lordosis was found in 25% and severe in 4%. Sitting and standing heights continued to increase. "The authors concluded that failure of the fusion to elongate and risk of progressive lordosis are not absolute contraindications to early fusion in the growing scoliotic spine. However, they recommended that all possible methods of non-operative correction or prevention of progression be used before fusion is done." The Milwaukee brace seemed to provide the method.

最后，还有三篇其他的外科论文。弗农·尼克尔、杰奎琳·佩里和马尔科姆·赫本斯托尔以“halo：174 名患者的应用分析”为主题，展示了他们十年的经验。[89]患者平均年龄 15 岁，应用适应证为颈椎不稳定、重度脊柱侧凸广泛融合以及广泛融合后修复。12 名患者有可处理的并发症。他们提出了四个建议：前方针放置在额突以下，不需要常规拧紧针，必须保持进针点清洁，逐步应用纵向牵引力并反复检查周围神经功能。西蒙斯发表了他的“脊柱楔形切除术技术和适应证的观察”，这是基于十多年来治疗的 14 名患者的经验。[90]它的适应证是过度前凸的严重畸形，既往施行融合术之后的畸形和半椎体。通常需要腹膜后前路联合或分期应用后路进行楔形切除术，有时需要后路内固定。除了一例畸形状况没有改善，其余的畸形都有较好的改善，且无死亡或永久并发症发生。莫和布鲁斯·桑德伯格在“生长期儿童脊柱侧凸的脊柱融合”中，研究了在 79 名 1~10 岁儿童中，42 名患者的后路融合术效果。[91]术后平均随访 48.6 个月，20 名患者融合长度无变化，1 名患者增加 7 mm，其余患者变化不大于 5 mm；患者轻度前凸占 25%，重度前凸占 4%；患者的坐高和站高持续增加。“作者得出了结论，在脊柱侧凸生长期的儿童患者中，融合后不能生长和进行性前凸的风险并不是早期融合的绝对禁忌证。然而，他们建议在融合前，使用所有可能有效的非手术方式矫正或阻止侧凸进展。”密尔沃基支具似乎是一种选择。

In just two years the SRS had been able to bring together the major North American participants in scoliosis care, create international interest, and establish itself as the forum for the airing and exchange of knowledge about scoliosis. While continued success was not inevitable, all involved in the care of scoliosis patients ignored the SRS at their own peril. Unfortunately, there are no records of the executive committee or membership meetings from this second annual meeting so insights into the administrative deliberations and organization growth are limited to occasional correspondence and the increasingly detailed annual programs.

在短短两年时间里，脊柱侧凸研究学会已经能够将北美脊柱侧凸治疗的主要参与者聚集在一起，引发了国际关注，并将自己确立为传播和交流脊柱侧凸知识的论坛。尽管脊柱侧凸研究学会并不一定会一直成功，但所有参与脊柱侧凸患者治疗的人若忽视脊柱侧凸研究学会，则对自己不利。不幸的是，本届年会并没有执行委员会或会员会议的记录，因此对行政审议和组织发展的了解仅限于偶然的通信和日益详细的年度项目。

During the remainder of 1967 Harrington made four short trips. On September 18 he was the guest speaker at a meeting of the orthopedic section of the Nassau Academy of Medicine in Garden City, New York. His expenses were paid, and he received an honorarium of $100.[92] From October 11 to 13 he attended the Clinical Orthopaedic Society annual meeting in Columbus, Ohio, where he moderated a symposium on low back fusion featuring four presenters, whose topics were "The Distraction Rods," "Intervertebral (Dowel) Fusion," "The Wilson Plates," and "Transverse Process Fusion."[93] At its 1966 meeting in Chicago, the guest speaker had been Gale Sayers, football star at the University of Kansas and the Chicago Bears, who had received an honorarium of $50! On November 13 - 16 Harrington attended the annual meeting of the Southern Medical Association in Miami Beach where his co-author Hugh Tullos presented their paper titled "Reduction of Severe Spondylolisthesis in Children."[94] Harrington spent December 6-14 in New York City.[95] He made a two-hour presentation on "Scoliosis" and participated on a panel at "A 2 - 1/2 Day Institute on the Principles of Bracing," sponsored by Albert Einstein College of Medicine and the Montefiore Hospital's Department and Division of Rehabilitation Medicine. Four days later John Moe and he spoke at an evening program at the New York Academy of Medicine. Harrington discussed "Spine Instrumentation in the Management of Scoliosis: Surgical Technique and Case

Presentation." Moe's topic was "Methods of Treatment of Unusual Scoliosis Problems." David Levine, Ted Waugh, and Jacob Graham joined the discussion panel. While in New York, Harrington also saw a few consults and attended the New York Jets-Kansas City Chiefs football game.

在1967年剩下的时间里，哈灵顿进行了四次短途旅行。9月18日，他在纽约花园城拿索医学院骨科会议上做了特邀演讲。会议报销了他的费用，并给了100美元的酬金。[92] 10月11日至13日，他参加了在俄亥俄州哥伦布市举行的临床骨科学会年会，主持了一场关于腰椎融合术的研讨会。会上有四位演讲者，他们的主题分别是"撑开棒""椎间骨栓融合术""威尔逊钢板""横突融合术"。[93] 1966年在芝加哥举行的会议上，特邀演讲者是堪萨斯大学和芝加哥熊队的足球明星盖尔·塞耶斯，他还获得了50美元的酬金！11月13日至16日，哈灵顿参加了在迈阿密海滩举办的南方医学会年会，他的合著者休·图洛斯介绍了他们题为《儿童严重脊柱滑脱复位》的论文。[94] 12月6日至14日，哈灵顿在纽约度过。[95]他以"脊柱侧凸"为主题，做了两个小时的报告，并参加了由阿尔伯特·爱因斯坦医学院和蒙特菲奥里医院康复医学部主办的"为期两天半的支具原理学术研究"的专题讨论会。四天后，他和约翰·莫一道在纽约医学院的一个晚间节目上发表了讲话。哈灵顿详述了"脊柱侧凸治疗中脊柱内固定器械：外科技术和病例介绍"。莫的演讲主题是"罕见的脊柱侧凸问题的治疗方法"。戴维·莱文，泰德·沃和雅各布·格雷厄姆加入了讨论。在纽约期间，哈灵顿还进行了几次会诊，并观看了纽约喷气机队对堪萨斯城酋长队的橄榄球比赛。

After a hiatus of two years, Harrington published four papers in 1967. The Italian conference version of the "Reduction of Severe Spondylolisthesis in Children" was the first.[96] "Instrumentation in Spine Instability Other Than Scoliosis," given in South Africa in 1966, raised the possibility of using Harrington Instrumentation in the treatment of spine instabilities other than scoliosis (e.g., trauma and tuberculosis).[97] "Decisions in Scoliosis" outlined a conservative philosophy of care under the categories of diagnosis, severity, progression risk, and treatment selection.[98]

两年之后，哈灵顿于1967年发表四篇论文。第一篇是意大利会议版本的"儿童重度脊柱滑脱的复位"。[96]第二篇是1966年在南非发表的"脊柱侧凸以外脊柱不稳定的内固定器械"，提出了使用哈灵顿内固定器械治疗除脊柱侧凸以外的脊柱不稳定（如创伤和结核）的可能性。[97]第三篇"脊柱侧凸的决策"概述了诊断、严重程度、进展风险和治疗选择等类别下保守治疗的理念。[98]

The fourth paper, "Instrumentation in Structural Scoliosis," was the book chapter he had prepared for Professor Graham. It was a thorough, if somewhat delayed, statement of his surgical philosophy and techniques, which thus warrants further attention.[99] For the first time he illustrated the stable zone, which he defined as the coronal plane interval between vertical lines raised through the centers of the sacral facets. His theory was that if the centroid of the lower instrumented vertebra, represented by the location of the lower distraction hook, lay within the stable zone, no supplemental distal support was necessary. However, if the lower instrumented vertebra was not in the stable zone, supplemental support utilizing a sacral bar or dollar sign distraction force was needed. *See figure 9.4*. Experience would show that such supplemental support was virtually never indicated in idiopathic scoliosis deformities.

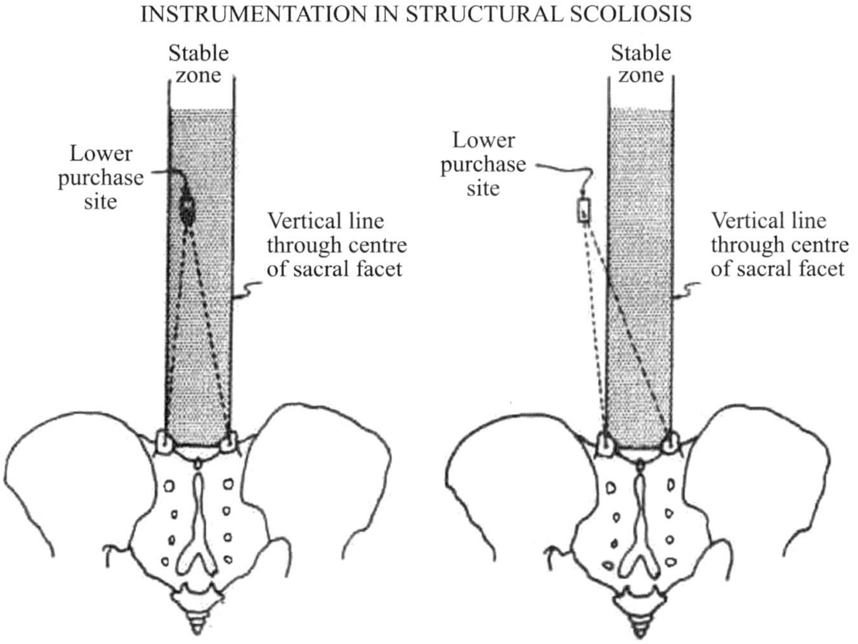

Figure 9.4 ***Harringtons concept of the stable zone, the space between vertical uprights through the center of the each sacral facet.* (*Harrington Archives*)**
图 9.4 **哈灵顿的"稳定区"概念,指的是通过骶骨小关节面中心的垂线之间的冠状面间隔(哈灵顿档案馆)**

第四篇论文《结构性脊柱侧凸的内固定器械治疗》是他为格雷厄姆教授撰写的书中准备的一个章节。这是对他外科理念和技术的一个完整的阐述，尽管时效性稍差，但仍然值得进一步关注。[99]他首次提出并阐释了“稳定区”这一概念，他将其定义为穿过骶骨小关节面中心的垂线之间的冠状面间隔。他的理论是，如果下器械固定椎的矩心（下撑开钩位置代表）位于稳定区域内，则不需要辅助远端支撑。然而，如果下固定椎的矩心不在稳定区域，则需要使用骶骨棒或钱字号撑开力进行辅助支撑。(图 9.4) 经验表明，特发性脊柱侧凸畸形中几乎从未应用过这种辅助支撑。

Another technical point that he enlarged upon in this book chapter was the placement of the lower distraction hook, acknowledged in his original paper as "the weakest feature of the whole procedure."[100] In that paper he limited placement to lumbar vertebra and described and illustrated this hook placement as a notch "through the lamina where it meets the base of the inferior articular process." It seemed he was trying to avoid placing the hook blade into the spinal canal and so minimize the risk to the spinal cord. He did offer an alternative site over the supralaminar ridge of the lower instrumented vertebra, but he severely restricted its usage. "A hook is never placed in a lamina directly over the spinal canal except below the level of the second lumbar vertebra because of the risk of penetration of the dura in the region of the caudal extremity of the spinal cord." With experience, Harrington had become comfortable with the small amount of lower distraction hook presence in the spinal canal as it hugged the underside of the lamina. His description of this hook site preparation, paraphrased and condensed somewhat, was a good example of economy of motion, for which he was known. "The inferior facet tip of the vertebra above the purchase site is removed by an osteotome. As it is removed, the rest of the inferior capsule of the facet will lift out, leaving the ligamenta flava in view. The ligamenta flava is stripped away from its insertion into the laminar ridge of the intended purchase site; it is not removed but reflected superiorly. A Kerrison punch is placed over the superior laminar ridge and a notch made in the ridge. The dura must be avoided as a notch the width of the hook is prepared. The posterior interior venous plexus may be annoying and can be managed by clipping or gently packing with Gelfoam® and a cottonoid."[101] Harrington also utilized this book chapter to publish the series of technique drawings carefully illustrating the sequence of steps in his operation of a typical right thoracic scoliosis. *See figure 7.4.* His instrumentation technique was mature at this point, but his supplemental bone graft technique was not since he had stopped using heterograft in late 1966. Inclusion of this step in this article illustrated the lag time between an article's acceptance and its publication.

他在这篇文章中详述的另一个技术要点是下端撑开钩放置，在他的原著中被认为是“整个操作过程中最薄弱的部分”。[100]在那篇论文中，他将撑开钩的放置位置限制在腰椎，并描述和说明了这种钩的放置为一个技术缺口，“穿过椎板，在那里它与下关节突的基底部相遇”。他似乎是在试图避免将钩尖端插入椎管，从而将对脊髓损伤的风险降至最低。他确实提供了下固定椎的椎板上缘的另一个位置，但他严格限制了它的使用。“除非在第二腰椎的水平以下，否则撑开钩永远不会直接放置在椎管上方的椎板上缘，因为存在穿透脊髓尾端硬膜的风险。”随着经验的积累，哈灵顿已习惯了允许少量下撑开钩被放置在椎管内，因为它扣紧了椎板的下方。经过稍加解释和浓缩，他对这个钩位置的尝试性描述是一个很好的减少手术步骤的例子，他也因此而闻名。“用骨凿去除上方抓牢部位椎体下关节突尖端之后，翻开小关节面的下方关节囊的其余部分，可见黄韧带；剥离预定手术部位的椎板缘附着的黄韧带；它不是被去除，而是向上翻。放置一个克里森咬骨钳在椎板缘，并在上缘咬一个缺口。钩子宽度应适应缺口，而且避免损伤硬脊膜。后方内静脉丛可能会很麻烦，可通过结扎或用吸收性明胶海绵和棉片轻压来处理。”[101]哈灵顿还利用这本书的这个章节出版了一系列技术示意图，仔细说明了他在进行典型的右胸脊柱侧凸手术的步骤顺序。（第 7 章的图 7.4）在这一点上，他的器械内固定术已经非常成熟，然而他在 1966 年年底已经停止使用异种骨移植，所以填充植骨术还未成熟。本文中仍然包含这一步骤，解释了文章从被收稿到发表之间的时间差。

He closed with a discussion of complications. At this point Harrington had operated on over 900 patients, and the information was based on a survey, which could be considered indicative but not definitive. A sampling of the findings follows: “There were no deaths, either in the operating room or within one hour after the operation, but there were seven deaths in the series: one of these cases had a malignant laryngeal spasm two hours after surgery; another had hydronephrosis and uremia eight weeks after surgery; and the remaining five were salvage cases.” One patient developed paraplegia with “partial recovery,” and eight developed radiculitis but recovered. Early instrumentation complications included infection (7 cases with one death from septicemia), graft rejection in 3 of 422 patients in whom Boplant® had been used, metal idiosyncrasy in 3, instrumentation cut-out (rare in the last 500 cases), and infrequent hematomas. Late instrumentation complications included rod fracture (20% after 18 months), erosion of purchase site (rare and dependent on surgical technique and postoperative management), early rod breakage (rare), and bursitis over the instruments (1–2%). However, the two most persistent late complications appeared to be pseud arthrosis, estimated at 20% early in the series and less than 5% in the last 500 cases, and what he described as "growth effect on progression of curve measurement with arthrodesis." He noted this as being frequent when over, two years of spine growth remained. At least as early as 1922, Robert Lovett in the pre-instrumentation, arthrodesis, and cast correction era described the phenomenon of this effect of curve progression following posterior fusion as follows: "The objection to the operation is that it is not effective on the bodies, but on the laminae or spinous processes and this leaves the bodies free to rotate as the patient grows while the posterior part of the spinal column is held stiffly by the ankylosis."[102] More recently this has been termed the crankshaft phenomenon.[103]

他最后讨论了一些并发症。此时，哈灵顿已经为900多名患者做了手术。这些信息是基于一项调查，可以被认为是参考性的，但不是确定的。调查的抽样结果如下："术中或手术后一小时内都无人死亡，但在这个系列病例中有7人死亡：其中一个病例在手术后两小时出现恶性喉痉挛；1例术后8周出现肾积水和尿毒症；剩下的5个是抢救性手术病人。" 1名患者出现截瘫，但"部分恢复"，8名患者出现神经根炎，但已康复。早期器械并发症包括感染（7例，1例死于败血症），422名使用Boplant®的患者中3名发生移植物排斥反应，3名发生金属变异，器械引发的皮肤损伤（最近500名患者中罕见）和罕见血肿。晚期器械并发症包括断棒（18个月后20%）、抱钩侵蚀（罕见，取决于手术技术和术后处理）、早期断棒（罕见）和内植物上的滑囊炎（1%~2%）。然而，两种最持久的晚期并发症似乎是假关节，在该病例系列早期估计为20%，在最近500名患者中不到5%，以及他所描述的"生长对融合术弯曲测量进展的影响"。他注意到这种情况经常发生，超过两年脊柱生长仍然存在。至少早在1922年，罗伯特·洛维特在用内固定器械前、融合术和石膏矫正时代就描述了在后路融合术后脊柱弯曲进展的现象："反对手术的理由是它对椎体无效，但对椎板或棘突有效，这使得身体随着患者的成长而自由旋转，而脊柱后部被强直僵硬地固定。"[102]后来，这种现象被称为曲轴现象。[103]

Harrington's year-end publication, *Scoliosis 1967*, had five entries. The first was an unpublished manuscript titled "Evaluation of Skeletal Maturity in Scoliosis," prepared by Thomas I. Lowry while a senior clinical fellow as an assistant to the TIRR scoliosis division under the Social and Rehabilitation Service and Training grant. The purpose of the study was to more clearly define the indicators of skeletal maturity, particularly those visible on a standing 36" erect spine X-ray. Study of 78 females with adolescent idiopathic scoliosis confirmed that both chronological age and skeletal age determined by hand-wrist X-ray had a variability of about 4 years and 2 years, respectively, when compared to the iliac apophyses, so neither was of added help in determining skeletal maturity. A helpful observation was that if a greater trochanter epiphysis was visible and the iliac apophyses were not visible, the iliac apophyses had not yet appeared.

哈灵顿本年的年终出版物《脊柱侧凸 1967》包含五篇文章。第一篇是一份未发表的手稿，题为“脊柱侧凸患者骨骼成熟度的评估”，由托马斯·I. 劳里撰写，当时他是得克萨斯州康复与研究中心脊柱侧凸部门的资深临床专科培训医生，在社会与康复服务和培训基金的资助下担任助理。这项研究的目的是明确定义骨骼成熟的指标，尤其是在 36 英寸直立脊柱 X 光片上的可见参数。对 78 名女性青少年特发性脊柱侧凸患者的研究证实，与髂骨骨骺相比，手腕 X 线测定的实足年龄和骨骼年龄分别有大约 4 岁和 2 岁的变异度，因此两者对于确定骨骼成熟度都没有帮助。一个有用的观察结果是，如果大转子骨骺可见而髂骨骨骺不可见，则说明髂骨骨骺尚未出现。

The second entry was “Familial (Idiopathic) Scoliosis: A Family Survey,” included with permission of the author, Ruth Wynne-Davies, and published the following year.[104] The inclusion of what became a landmark in its field undoubtedly reflected Harrington's growing fascination with the search for the etiology of idiopathic scoliosis. One of her summary points figured in his future research: “the age of the mother of the adolescent patients is significantly raised by comparison with the expected figure in the normal population.” The third entry was his “Reduction of Severe Spondylolisthesis in Children,” co-authored with Hugh Tullos. In introducing the paper, Harrington commented that “although it may be a publication in the future, it is believed to be of timely interest and for that reason is included at this time.”

第二篇收录的作品是“家族性（特发性）脊柱侧凸：一项家系调查”，经作者露丝·韦恩-戴维斯的允许收录，并于次年出版。[104]本文的收录是其领域的一个里程碑，反映了哈灵顿对特发性脊柱侧凸病因学研究日益增长的兴趣。露丝总结的观点之一在她未来的研究中得到了体现：“青少年患者母亲的实际年龄显著高于正常人群的预期数字。”第三篇文章是哈灵顿与休·图洛斯合著的“儿童重度脊柱滑脱复位”。在介绍这篇论文时，哈灵顿评论说：“虽然它可能会在未来出版，但此时此刻它应该是被及时关注的，因此现在被收录在内。”

The fourth entry had two parts, both dealing with the management of the large amount of data that would need to be gathered for registries and prospective studies. "Data Processing Procedure for Scoliosis" was prepared by William O. Reese Jr., program director of scoliosis projects at the TIRR scoliosis laboratory. Reese detailed the steps, which began in 1961, taken to develop an electronic data processing program for scoliosis research. The programs were written for the IBM 1410, which became available at Baylor University College of Medicine in 1962. The first application was to determine the optimum postoperative immobilization and cast times. However, when statistical analysis was attempted, it was discovered that the data-recording format was inadequate. With the help of a systems analyst, the program was thoroughly upgraded and enlarged, and by 1965 the data of over 950 patients had been entered. The information entered for each patient averaged 250 recorded or calculated items. It was estimated that 20% of the patients moved each year, so they added a program to keep track of patients on a semiannual basis. The magnitude of the program was apparent. The second portion of Reese's entry was "A Method for Recording Consecutive Spine Roentgenogram Measurements for Analysis." After many preliminary studies, measurement criteria were settled on in 1964. Approximately 100 drawings and measurements of 20 operated patients were made, and following their study, additions and deletions were made. The main addition was a coordinate system. They had measured 330 X-rays, and a comprehensive computer analysis was planned. The last entry in *Scoliosis 1967* was "Radiography in Scoliosis," a lecture Harrington had presented in 1963.

第四篇纳入的条目有两部分，两者都涉及大量数据的管理，这些数据是出于登记和前瞻性研究的需要进行收集的。“脊柱侧凸的数据处理流程”由小威廉·O. 里斯编写，他是得克萨斯州康复与研究中心脊柱侧凸实验室脊柱侧凸项目的项目主管。首先，里斯详细介绍了从1961年开始为脊柱侧凸研究开发电子数据处理程序所采取的步骤。这些程序是为IBM 1410编写的，贝勒大学医学院于1962年开始使用。第一个应用是确定最佳的术后固定和石膏固定时间。但是，当进行统计分析时，发现数据记录格式不充分。在一名系统分析师的帮助下，该程序进行了全面升级和扩大。到1965年，已有950多名患者的数据被输入。为每位患者输入的信息平均为250个记录或计算项目。据估计，每年有20%的病人搬家，所以他们增加了一个程序，每半年跟踪一次病人。该计划的重要性是显而易见的。里斯阐释的第二部分是“一种记录连续脊柱X光片测量以供分析的方法”。经过大量初步研究，测量标准于1964年确定。研究对20名手术患者进行了约100张的图示和测量，并在研究后进行了增删。主要增加的是一个坐标系统。他们检测了

330 张 X 光片，并计划进行全面的计算机分析。《脊柱侧凸 1967》的最后一篇文章是《脊柱侧凸的放射学》，这是哈灵顿在 1963 年做的一次演讲。

For Harrington, 1966 and 1967 were remarkable years. Even as use of his instrumentation had become more widespread, complaints about it had diminished. Accordingly, his correspondence with Zimmer had slowed and was now mostly involved with developing the needed educational material. He was fully engaged with the formation of the SRS, and his counsel was sought, respected, and often followed. His international travel peaked in the second half of 1966, beginning with the trip to the SICOT meeting in Paris. Although there was no documentation that he was exposed to pedicle screws while there, it was certainly possible. But what was well documented was apparently his first exposure to copies of his instrumentation. The correspondence that followed illustrated the helplessness of not having patent protection even though a patent might have done more to stimulate competition or might not have been worth the price of defense. At any rate, the productive ten-year relationship between Harrington and Zimmer stood the test of time and emerged as strong as ever. In November 1966 Harrington had the idea of a lag screw into the pedicle of L5 as an aid in the surgical treatment of severe spondylolisthesis, and Hite was able to produce them in slightly over a month, just in time for two landmark surgeries. But the two biggest events were almost unnoticeable. The importance of Harrington's recruitment of Jesse Dickson to staff the TIRR Scoliosis Clinic one day a week could not have been imagined unless one had known the ominous implications of Harrington's loss of physical stamina climbing stairs in Australia.

对哈灵顿来说，1966 年和 1967 年是非凡的。尽管他的器械应用越来越广泛，但相关投诉减少了。因此，他和捷迈公司的通信频次减少了，现在主要是开发所需的教育材料。他全身心投入于脊柱侧凸研究中心的成立，他的建议被人们追捧、尊重并遵循。他在 1966 年下半年的首趟差旅是前往巴黎参加国际矫形与创伤外科学会会议，他的国际差旅次数达到了顶峰。虽然没有文件表明他在那里接触了椎弓根螺钉，但这是非常有可能的。有记载表明，他显然是第一次接触他的器械仿制品。接下来的通信说明了没有专利保护的无助，即使一项专利可能更能刺激竞争，或者可能不值得付出为其辩护的代价。无论如何，哈灵顿和捷迈公司之间富有成效的十年关系经受住了时间的考验，并一如既往地牢固。1966 年 11 月，哈灵顿有了在 L5 椎弓根内植入一枚拉力螺钉的想法，以辅助重度脊柱滑脱的手术治疗。捷迈公司在一个多月的时间里就制造出了这种螺钉，正好赶上了两个具有里程碑意义的手术。但这两大事件几乎未曾引起关注。哈灵顿还聘请了杰西·迪克森加入得克萨斯州康复与研究中心进行脊柱侧凸临床工作，每周工作一天。只有人们了解到哈灵顿在澳大利亚爬楼梯时身体耐力下降的不祥迹象，才能领悟哈灵顿这一举措带来的无法想象的重要性。

（葛隽 张一健 沈怀霜 译　杨惠林 审校）

10 HEARTBREAK AND GODSEND (1968–72)

I want you to take my practice over, and the only thing I ask of you is that you maintain it.[1]

心碎与天赐之物 (1968—1972)

我希望你能接替我的工作，而我对你唯一的要求就是持之以恒。[1]

Nineteen sixty-eight was a pivotal year in Harrington's life. Looking back, there were forebodings, most prominently the total absence of correspondence between him and Zimmer during the last seven months of 1967. This trend continued in 1968 with just five letters exchanged during the year. His travel schedule also saw a marked shift in frequency and destination. He did not go overseas in 1967, and for the first time in seven years his 1968 travel documents were not bound into a volume. Something dramatic must have happened during the year to cause these changes.

1968 年是哈灵顿一生中至关重要的一年。现在回首，这是有些预兆的，其中最突出的是在 1967 年的最后七个月里他和捷迈公司之间完全没有通信。这种情况一直持续到了 1968 年，在这一年中他们只交换了五封信件。他的旅行频率和目的地也都发生了巨大的变化。1967 年他没有出国，他 1968 年的旅行文件没有装订成册，这是七年来的第一次。在这一年里肯定发生了一些重大的事情才导致了他的这些改变。

In 1968 Harrington was voted into membership in the American Orthopaedic Association (AOA), an important milestone indicating the acceptance of the man and his contributions.[2] "Spine Analysis,"[3] his thesis fulfilling a membership requirement at that time, was a project initiated in 1963 "in the hope of developing a more comprehensive series of quantitative spine measurements." He explained the background as follows: "As early as 1949 my interest in spinal curvature led to the conclusion that the whole axial skeleton should be considered for clinical evaluation of the deformed spine. This belief prompted the use of the 36" roentgenogram, which included not only the entire spine but the pelvis as well. Over the intervening years of practice, standing, lying, sitting, and bending 36" films were taken. Evaluation of these clinical observations indicated that the standing position was most representative of the total axial skeleton. For this reason, the standing anteroposterior 36" roentgenogram taken at a distance of 72" was established as standard procedure for all patients." He envisioned the project as involving four phases. In phase one he identified thirteen historically important radiographic landmarks. In phase two he prospectively modified the reference points and developed a data recording format.

He observed that "while the etiologies of other conditions causing scoliosis did not present similar structural mechanics, the geometric configurations of the idiopathic curve seemed to offer somewhat more reliable patterns." So in the third phase he limited patients to females with idiopathic scoliosis. To reduce measurement error, a 36" view box was equipped with a fixed parallel straight edge on one side and an adjustable protractor triangle to make all angular measurements. From seventeen identifiable landmarks, twenty-seven translational and angular measurements were made in the coronal plane. *See figure 10.1.* In phase four he tested measurement validity, using four measurements that should not change over time in adults with solid fusions, and found the measurements averaged 3% variability with the maximum being 7%. Test-retest reliability was excellent at 97%. At the time "Spine Analysis" was written, 500 X-rays of 100 patients with postoperative follow-up of 1 to 6 years had been analyzed. Some observations based on the findings were that the spinous process of S1 was a reliable landmark on which to base the other translational and angular measurements, the curves' inflection points appeared to be in the intervertebral disc space and not the vertebral body, and hook erosion measurements could not be made with the required degree of accuracy.

1968 年哈灵顿被评选为美国骨科学会会员，以表示对他本人及其贡献的认可，这对于哈灵顿而言是具有里程碑意义的。[2]他的论文《脊柱分析》[3]是 1963 年发起的一个项目，“旨在开发一套更全面的且定量的脊柱测量工具”，这也使他满足了入会的要求。他这样解释这篇文章的研究背景：“早在 1949 年，我对脊柱侧凸的关注使我认为在对脊柱畸形的临床评估中应当考虑整个中轴骨的改变。这种信念促使我使用 36 英寸 X 光片，而在 36 英寸 X 光片中不仅能看到整个脊柱，还能看到骨盆。在其间多年的实践中，拍摄了包括站立位、卧位、坐位、侧曲位等不同体位的 36 英寸 X 光片。从这些临床观察的评估中发现，站立位片最能代表中轴骨的情况。出于这个原因，在距离 72 英寸处采用前后位拍摄 36 英寸 X 光片是为所有患者设立的标准流程。”按照他的设想，该项目分为四个阶段。在第一阶段，他确定了 13 个具有历史意义的重要的 X 线定位标志。在第二阶段，他前瞻性地修改了参考点，并开发了一个病例数据的记录格式。他观察到“虽然其他病理原因导致的脊柱侧凸并没有出现相似的结构力学变化，但是特发性脊柱侧凸的几何布局似乎提供了更可靠的模式”。因此在第三阶段他将患者限定为患有特发性脊柱侧凸的女性。为了减少测量误差，他使用了一个长边为 36 英寸的投影箱，其中一侧配备了一个固定的平行直边，另一侧配备了一个可调节的量角器，以进行所有角度测量。根据 17 个可辨别的标志，在冠状位进行了 27 个平移和角度的测量。(图 10.1) 在第四阶段，他使用了四个测量值来测试测量的有效性，这些测量值在骨性融合的成年人中并不会随着时间的推移而改变，测量发现测量值的平均变异度为 3%，最大变异度为 7%，再测可信度高达到 97%。在撰写《脊柱分析》这篇文章时，哈灵顿已经分析了 100 名术后随访 1~6 年患者的 500 张 X 光片。基于这些 X 光片的一些观察结果表明，S1 的棘突是一个

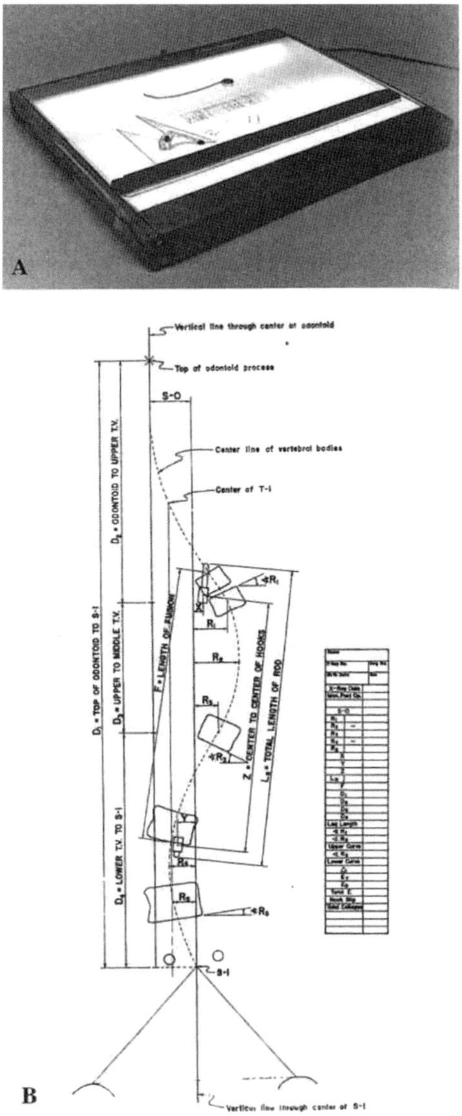

Figure 10.1 *A. View box equipped to make roentfenogram tracings. B. Measurements made. (Harrington Archives)*
图 10.1　A. 可进行 X 光片追踪的观察箱。B. 测量完成(哈灵顿档案馆)

可靠的标志，可以以此为基点进行其他平移和角度的测量；弯曲的拐点应当是椎间盘间隙而不是椎体；吊钩测量法并不能达到所需要的精度。

Harrington had high hopes that this systematic and quantified analysis would provide "a new dimension in accessing the scoliotic problem" and envisioned ten studies he intended to pursue. To what extent these studies further informed his practice isn't clear, and none resulted in a peer-reviewed publication. But his line of reasoning certainly resulted in his development of the stable zone concept (e.g., the recommendation that the lower distraction hook be located between vertical lines through the center of each sacral facet).[4] This, coupled with the flexibility radiographs of which he had been dismissive, eventually found practical application by Moe and his colleagues in identifying compensatory lumbar curves that could be selectively saved from instrumentation and arthrodesis.[5]

哈灵顿对这套测量方法寄予了厚望，希望这种系统性的量化分析方法能够提供“解决脊柱侧凸问题的新维度、新方向”，并设想了要继续进行深入探讨的十项研究。由于没有一项研究发表在同行评议的论文中，因此这些研究在多大程度上进一步影响了他的实践，目前尚不清楚。但他的论证思路无疑促使他形成并发展了他提出的稳定区概念。(即建议将下方撑开钩放在两侧腰骶小关节的垂直线之间)[4]。这一观点结合了他过去对灵活性 X 光片的不重视，最终由莫和他的同事在识别可以选择性避免植入和融合的代偿性腰弯方面找到了实际运用。[5]

Travel in 1968 appears to have been limited to three or possibly four trips. The first was early in the year to the 35th annual meeting of the AAOS that was held in Chicago where he delivered a "Treatment of Scoliosis" Instructional Course Lecture for the seventh consecutive year. The second was in April to the tenth National Congress of Orthopedics and Traumatology in Mexico City where he presented "Spondylolisthesis in the Growing Child."[6] The third was June 7–29 to the annual meeting of the South African Orthopaedic Association in Pretoria[7] where his primary presentation was a condensed version of his AOA "Spine Analysis" thesis that was titled "Spine Analysis of the Idiopathic Curve."[8] He also traveled to Johannesburg, Durban, and Cape Town where smaller meetings were held. In these cities Harrington lectured, showed, and commented on his technique movie. In addition, he evaluated patients and in one instance operated.

1968 年，哈灵顿仅仅安排了三或四次旅行。第一次旅行是年初前往在芝加哥举办的美国骨科医师学会第三十五届年会，他做了连续七年与“脊柱侧凸治疗”相关的教学课程讲座。第二次旅行是在 4 月前往于墨西哥城举办的第十届全国骨科与创伤学术会议上，他发表了“生长中儿童的脊柱滑脱”的演讲。[6]第三次旅行是 6 月 7 日至 29 日在比勒陀利亚[7]举行的南非骨科学会年会，他演讲的主题是他的美国骨科学会《脊柱分析》论文的浓缩版，题为“特发性脊柱侧凸的脊柱分析”[8]。他还前往约翰内斯堡、德班和开普敦，在那里举行了小型会议。在这些城市中，哈灵顿借助他的技术视频进行演讲、演示并且讨论。除此之外，他还亲自对患者进行了评估，并为其中一名患者实施了手术。

Whether Harrington made a fourth trip for the year is not clear. He was scheduled to speak at the annual meeting of the Western Orthopaedic Association in October, but it is possible that co-author William O. Reese Jr. substituted for him. The study was another offshoot of “Spine Analysis” titled “The Mechanics of the Idiopathic Scoliotic Curve.”[9] It was a geometric analysis of this curve with the primary goal of determining the amount of spine length lost due to scoliosis, which in turn would allow the more accurate determination of a patient’s true pulmonary function. The Cobb method was used because it was based on calculus. A formula for determining rotation from the Cobb was developed and validated. Likewise a formula for determining the true length of the scoliotic curve knowing the Cobb and the apex rotation angle was developed. This method of determining nondeformed height was never widely adopted, probably because an easier approach based on arm span was being developed.[10] Another goal of the “Spine Analysis” project was to develop formulas for converting scoliosis curve measurement from Cobb to Ferguson and vice versa, thereby allowing comparison of different patient series. They found that the Cobb angle could not be determined from the Ferguson but that the Ferguson could from the Cobb: Ferguson equaling Cobb + rotation divided by two. Again, this was not of practical importance as by then the Ferguson measurement method had fallen from use, no doubt at least partially the result of the SRS terminology committee’s early adoption of the Cobb measurement.

哈灵顿在同年是否进行了第四次旅行尚不清楚。他原定于 10 月在西部骨科学会年会上发言，但是共同作者小威廉·里斯可能代替他进行了发言。该研究是《脊柱分析》的另一个分支方向，标题为“特发性脊柱侧凸弯曲的力学研究”。[9]这是对脊柱侧凸所做的几何分析，其主要目的是确定由脊柱侧凸所导致的脊柱长度的缩短，相应地也会更准确地检测患者的真实肺功能。采用柯布测量法的原因是它基于微积分，之后通过柯布测量法得到的用于确定旋转度的公式被研究并验证出来。同样，通过已知柯布角和顶椎旋转度测量脊柱侧凸真实弯曲长度的公式也被研究出来。这种确定非畸形长度的方法并未被广泛采用，可能是因为之后一个基于臂展长度的更简单的测量方法被研究出来。[10]《脊柱分析》的另一个目的是开发一个公式，用于测量脊柱侧凸角度：柯布测量法和弗格森测量法之间能够进行相互转化，从而比较不同类型的患者。他们发现柯布角并不能通过弗格森测量法获得，但弗格森角可以通过柯布测量法获得：弗格森角等于柯布角加旋转度除以2。然而，由于脊柱侧凸研究学会术语委员会更早接纳并采用柯布测量法进行测量的缘故，弗格森测量法很少被人使用，于是这种换算公式就失去了实际意义。

The first Zimmer correspondence exchange of 1968 began with a March 27 letter to Jim Hite announcing that he had again started using the heavy threaded rods (3/16"-diameter) and its compatible hook (#1256) but that Methodist Hospital was getting no response when ordering them. He also asked that the flat side be taken off the sacral bar.[11] Hite promptly responded.[12] "The heavy threaded rods for use with #1256 Hooks can be ordered by #1257 as they were originally designated. We still have some customers using this 3/16" diameter rod and have always kept a supply available. They are not in the current catalogue because you had requested they be deleted. The last production run of #1261 Sacral Bars were left fully round following our conversation at the recent AAOS meeting last January. Thanks for your suggestions; both can be complied with immediately."

1968 年哈灵顿与捷迈的第一次通信交流始于 3 月 27 日他给吉姆·海特的一封信件，声称他将再次开始使用重型螺纹棒（直径 3/16 英寸）及与其配对的钩(#1256)，但是休斯敦卫理公会医院并没有订购到相应的器械。随后哈灵顿在信件中还要求去除在骶骨处使用的螺纹棒的扁平面。[11]海特很快回复[12]："与重型螺纹棒配套使用的#1256 钩可以替换成#1257 钩，因为这是原先指定好的。我们仍有一些客户还在使用直径 3/16 英寸的螺纹棒，因此供应量是充足的。它们并不在当前的目录中，是因为你曾经要求删除它们。在一月份美国骨科医师学会会议之后，根据我们的商议，#1261 骶骨螺纹棒已经去除了扁平面呈圆弧形。感谢您的建议，您的两个建议马上都会被采纳。"

The third annual meeting of the SRS, hosted by Paul and Mary Alice Harrington. was held in Houston all day Thursday and Friday September 5 and 6, 1968, followed by a

Saturday morning session.[13] There were approximately 100 registrants, nearly all of whom were in the group photograph. *See figure 10.2*. Twenty-four spouses attended the social program. Four half-day meetings were devoted to scientific sessions held at the Warwick Hotel and a fifth to visit the TIRR. The social program included a Thursday evening dinner featuring a speech by Alf Nachemson. The scientific program, for which outgoing President Moe credited Secretary Kane for its excellent organization, included twenty-three papers and two committee reports in addition to the guest lecture. They can be categorized into eight as diagnosis and evaluation, four as nonsurgical, ten as surgical, and one as laboratory research. Summaries of most of them were published.[14] For the first time the presentations and discussions were audio recorded and transcribed.[15] A sampling of them reflected the evolution of scoliosis management in general and spine instrumentation in particular. Nachemson's guest lecture, "A Long-term Follow-up of Non-treated Scoliosis," was the study of 117 of 130 (90%) patients seen in Gothenburg, Sweden, from 1927 to 1936.[16] Twenty had died compared to a predicted ten in the general population; the majority had died from the cardiac and pulmonary effects of their scoliosis. Based on other studies, Nachemson reported that patients with 60° or more thoracic scoliosis had 50% reduction in vital capacity, reduced working capacity, and increased mortality of more than 100%. He had found a great difference in prognosis based on diagnosis, but did not further elaborate on this. He "concluded that we should increase our efforts to prevent curves from progressing."

1968 年 9 月 5 日至 7 日，为期两天半的第三届脊柱侧凸研究学会年会在休斯敦举行，此次年会是由哈灵顿夫妇主办的。会议大约有 100 人参加，几乎所有人都在合影中，（图 10.2）并有 24 位会员的配偶参加了社交活动。[13]四个为期半天的学术研讨会在沃里克酒店举行，而在周六早上，所有人则是去参观了得克萨斯州康复与研究中心。社交活动包括周四晚上的晚宴，阿尔夫·纳切姆森在晚宴上致辞。即将卸任大会主席的莫称赞了凯恩秘书出色的组织能力，学术交流活动除了特邀演讲，还有关于 23 篇论文的交流讨论和两份委员会报告。论文内容包括 8 个诊断与评估类、4 个非手术类、10 个手术类和 1 个实验研究类。其中大部分的摘要均已发表。[14]此次会议第一次将演讲与讨论用音频的方式记录了下来。[15]其中部分论文反映了脊柱侧凸发展的总体情况，尤其脊柱器械的发展。纳切姆森的特邀演讲“未接受治疗的脊柱侧凸患者的长期随访”是一项针对 130 名脊柱侧凸患者中的 117 名（90%）进行随访调查的研究，这些患者是从 1927 年到 1936 年之间从瑞典哥德堡收集来的病例。[16]在随访期间有 20 名患者死亡，其中大部分患者的死因都是由脊柱侧凸导致的心肺功能障碍。综合其他研究发现，胸椎侧凸大于等于60°的患者肺活量将下降50%，肺的工作能力也会大幅下降，死亡率也会上升超过100%。另外纳切姆森也发现根据诊断进行预后评估存在很大的偏差，但没有进一步详细说明。他得出的结论是“我们应该努力阻止脊柱侧凸弯曲角度的继续恶化”。

1968
THE SCOLIOSIS RESEARCH SOCIETY
HOUSTON, TEXAS

First Row: Harrington, Kane, Goldstein, Donaldson, Hall, Moe, MacEwen, Levine, Edmonson, Kilfoyle, Tupper
Second Row: Thompson, Lagaard, Gustafson, Leatherman, Zuege, Velis, Larson, vonLackum, Lambert, Nachemson, Doherty, Badger, Lawson
Third Row: Nadel, Olsen, Valderama, Jonas, Curtis, McDonnell, Keiser, Bianco, Robinson
Fourth Row: Brennan, Stone, Leidholt, Levison, Hollenberg, Brooks, Murray, Welply
Fifth Row: Mullen, Hardy, Isaacson, Keever, Schultz, Galante, Finerman, Glock, Ashley, Peterson, Segovia
Sixth Row: Patterson, Haugh, Spiegel, Urbaniak, Graham, Cochran, Evarts, Devanny, Harrison, Lowry, Kettleson
Seventh Row: Adler, Holmblad, Fontanetta, Salanova, Waugh, Schmidt, Bruce, Rapp, Deyerle, Nash
Eighth Row: Dewald, Baker, Edholm, Liggett, Collis, Winter, Nelson, Hannon, Hoffer, Westphal, Slager
Ninth Row: Sobel, Flatley, Godfrey, Foley, Zadek, Wallace, Lowell, Thompson, W., Armstrong, Wright, Strayer, Dickson

Figure 10.2 ***Attendees at the third annual meeting of the SRS held in 1968 in Houston. Jon Moe, president, and Paul Harrington, local host.*** **(*SRS Archives*)**
图 10.2　1968 年在休斯敦举行的第三届脊柱侧凸研究学会年会的与会者。主席约翰·莫和主办者保罗·哈灵顿(脊柱侧凸研究学会档案馆)

The Milwaukee brace, at that time the only means of preventing mild and moderate curve progression, had recently been found to cause mandible deformities. This prompted two studies of forces in the brace. In each, the forces were small, approximately 5 pounds. In one study it was found that lowering the chin rest and replacing it with a throat mold decreased the traction forces without lowering the forces on or effectiveness of the thoracic pads.[17] In the other study the authors concluded that the low forces reflected the dynamic concept of the brace.[18] Two encouraging Milwaukee brace treatment series were presented. In one, only 2 of 39 patients who had completed treatment progressed to require surgery, and only 1 of 41 patients still under treatment had progressed.[19] In the other, of 185 patients who had completed wear or were in the weaning phase, net corrections of 20% to 50% were achieved with loss of less than 2% of the correction after the brace was discontinued in over 55%.[20] The average brace-wearing time was 36 months.

最近有研究发现作为当时唯一能够预防轻度和中度脊柱侧凸进展的密尔沃基支具会导致下颌骨畸形。这促使了两项针对支具力学方面的研究。在密尔沃基支具中，每个点的力量都大概只有5磅。其中一项研究表明，降低下巴固定架的位置，并用颌托代替固定，可以在不减少作用在胸垫上的力和有效性的前提下降低支具对下颌的牵引力。[17]另一项研究发现低作用力反映了支具的动态观。[18]随后，基于这两项研究制订出了两套使用密尔沃基支具进行脊柱侧凸矫正的治疗方案。在结束第一套治疗方案的39名患者中，只有2名患者的脊柱侧凸进展到需要手术的程度，而在41名正在执行治疗方案的患者中，也只有1名出现了脊柱侧凸。[19]另外，在使用了第二套治疗方案的185名患者中，无论他们是已经结束了矫正疗程或是还戴着支具，净矫正率都达到了20%~50%，而超过55%的患者在停用支具后矫正丢失小于2%。[20]患者平均佩戴支具的时间为36个月。

Immediately after the midafternoon coffee break on Thursday the morbidity and mortality committee was scheduled to make its first report. Chaired by Dean MacEwen, it was the result of discussions about neurological morbidity at the last annual meeting. After its conclusion, he had solicited the membership for information about patients who had "died within a year following surgery and patients with neurological complications with and without surgery and whether they were partial or complete."[21] Requested material was to be sent to MacEwen, who had promised to maintain the strictest confidence. The mortality portion of the report could not be given at the Houston meeting because data on the twenty to twenty-five deaths reported were with committee co-chair Wood Lovell and had not been analyzed. The very preliminary morbidity report that was presented reflected MacEwen's work only since the committee had not studied the material.[22] Nineteen cases with some amount of neurological morbidity had been reported. Of the fourteen with complete deficits three had full recovery, and of the five with incomplete neurological deficits one had full recovery. Of the nineteen, Harrington Spine Instrumentation had been used in fourteen, seven of whom had preliminary halo-femoral traction. Five of them had some neurological symptoms while in traction, and two had none. Seven of these fourteen patients with Harrington Instrumentation did not have preoperative halo-femoral traction, and of them four were idiopathic and considered perfectly normal and three had more complicated deformities. Thus, of the fourteen with Harrington Instrumentation, eight had preoperative findings that suggested they might be at risk, leaving six in whom Harrington Instrumentation was principally implicated.

按照计划，周四下午茶歇过后，并发症发生率和死亡率委员会计划立即发布第一份报告。这份报告是上次年会上关于神经系统发生率的讨论结果，报告发布会由迪恩·麦克尤恩主持。在报告结束后，他向参会会员征求了有关“术后一年内死亡患者以及术前或术后合并有神经系统并发症的患者，无论资料是否完整”的信息。[21]很快麦克尤恩就收到了所需要的资料，并保证对患者资料进行保密。报告中的20到25人死亡的相关数据是由委员会联合主席伍德·洛弗尔提供的，还未进行分析，因此这份报告中部分死亡率的数据无法在休斯敦会议上公布。麦克尤恩的工作仅初步反映了死亡和并发症的发生率，因为委员会尚未对所收集的资料进行研究。[22]据报道，有19名患者具有一定程度的神经系统功能障碍，在14名出现完全神经功能缺失的患者中，已有3人完全康复；而在5名有不完全性神经功能障碍的患者中，已有1人完全康复。在这19名患者中有14名接受了哈灵顿脊柱器械矫形，这14名患者中有7人在术前接受了初步的halo股骨牵引。而其中5名患者在牵引时就出现了一些神经系统症状。另外7位未进行halo股骨牵引的患者中，有4人是比较常见的特发性脊柱侧凸，另外3人均为复杂脊柱畸形。因此，在使用了哈灵顿矫形器械的14名患者中，8名患者在术前检查中就发现可能存在神经系统并发症的风险，而剩余6人的神经系统症状可能主要是由哈灵顿器械引起的。

Since the vascular supply of the spinal cord was incriminated in some of the notes, MacEwen studied the available knowledge in this area. This led to two insights. First, the spinal cord did not have a strong intercommunicating blood supply that could readily make up for missing segmental supply. Second, it spurred a greater awareness of the artery of Adamkiewicz, a long, small artery usually arising from an intercostal or vertebral vessel on the left side between T8 and L3 or L4. It entered the spinal canal through an intervertebral foramen, first coursing proximally before making a sharp turn to travel distally as the anterior spinal artery. The artery was thought to be vulnerable to injury by stretching that occurred during scoliosis correction. Harrington posed the first question of the discussion that followed. "The survey represents approximately how many cases that were done ... that you got this many catastrophes?" MacEwen responded, "This is one thing that we'll have to get back to the people for. I tried to keep this as simple as possible to get a foot in the door so to speak ... to just get the cases ... and then we will come back to you for more information." The questions voiced by some and likely foremost on all minds were how to avoid neurological injuries and how to treat them. MacEwen responded, "at the moment I have no idea." He repeatedly solicited more information from his listeners.

由于在一些记录中记载了脊髓的血管供应在手术中会受到牵连的问题，因此麦克尤恩研究了相关领域的知识。这就带来了两方面的问题。首先，脊髓并没有可以迅速补充血液供应缺失节段的强大的血管交通支。其次，一条长而小的动脉——阿达姆凯威斯动脉引起了大家的关注，这条动脉通常发自 T8 和 L3 或 L4 之间左侧的肋间动脉或椎动脉。它穿过椎间孔进入椎管，一开始向近端移动，然后急转弯向远端脊髓前动脉移动。在脊柱侧凸矫正术中，动脉容易受到牵拉损伤。哈灵顿对此提出了第一个问题："这项调查大概反映了多少已经完成的病例的情况……你遇到过这么多棘手的情况吗?"麦克尤恩回应道："(您提出的问题)是我们必须向大家反馈的事。在这项研究中，我尽可能简单地对此进行表述，可以这么说，我们刚拿到这些病历资料，在之后我们会反馈给您更多的信息。"有一些人提出的问题可能也是所有人最关心的问题，那就是如何避免神经损伤以及如何治疗神经损伤。麦克尤恩回答说："目前我还不知道。"他反复向台下与会人员征求更多的病人信息。

The morbidity and mortality data gathering and analyzing effort brought real meaning to the words *research society*. It cemented self-criticism and the pooling of experience as SRS principles. President Moe had appointed Mackwen to lead the effort, and many society members had responded with trust and submitted their nightmare cases. Less noticed was the case report of a postoperative cast syndrome in a thirteen-year-old girl with Harrington distraction instrumentation while in her preoperatively applied Risser localizer cast.[23] She recovered, and the presentation of her case resulted in a collaboration of three major centers that later bore fruit. Overall, the scientific program reflected the breadth of the scoliosis problem. The session devoted to lumbosacral scoliosis seemed to leave as many questions as answers. The list of causative diseases meriting either series or case reports because of their special management considerations continued to grow (e.g.,

Marfan's syndrome, neurofibromatosis, familial dysautonomia, and lymphangiectasia). The desire to understand the cause of the most common spine deformity, idiopathic scoliosis, had yielded negative findings in a clinical muscle study and led to another attempt to produce an animal model. Growth, pulmonary function, and treatment complications, pseudarthrosis in particular, received attention.

并发症发生率和死亡率数据的收集与分析工作给“研究学会”这一名称赋予了真正的意义。它使得自我检讨和经验汇总化作了脊柱侧凸研究学会的原则。主席莫随后任命麦克尤恩主导这项工作，很多会员非常信任地将自己手中棘手的病例资料交予麦克尤恩。在这些病例中，有一例并不起眼的病例，一名13岁的女孩在术前使用了里泽局部定位矫形石膏，并在术后出现了石膏综合征。[23]对这一病例的讨论促成了三个中心的合作，这些中心随后也取得了相应的成果。总的来说，科学计划反映了脊柱侧凸问题的广泛性。有关腰骶脊柱侧凸的专题会议在解决问题的同时也带来了新的问题。出于对一些病因明确的疾病（例如，马方综合征、神经纤维瘤病、家族性自主神经功能障碍和淋巴管扩张症）特殊治疗方式的思考，此类疾病的病例报告数量也在持续增加。由于在一项临床肌肉研究中并没有得到想要的结果，为了研究最常见的脊柱畸形特发性脊柱侧凸的病因，开始尝试构建一种脊柱侧凸的动物模型。生长、肺功能、并发症和假关节等方面的研究也受到了人们的关注。

During the last session, two papers of particular importance to Harrington Instrumentation focused on long-term follow-up and stiff curves. Since its introduction eight years earlier, the instruments had progressively replaced the Risser turnbuckle and localizer casts as the most used method of curve correction and immobilization. There were several short-term advantages, but questions remained about long-term benefits. Responding to repeated requests for long-term follow-up on the patients operated on by Hibbs and his colleagues at New York Orthopaedic Hospital, Strayer, Risser, and Waugh investigated.[24] Of 837 patients operated on for scoliosis from 1914 to 1940, only 58 (6 males and 52 females, 7%) patients with curves "of varied but representative etiologies" could be located and evaluated at an average of 34 years postoperative. An average of 15° (11° in the first five years) correction had been lost to follow-up. Pseudarthroses had been repaired in 24%, and nine additional patients (15%) were found to have one or more pseudarthroses at follow-up. They were doing well clinically and had "a striking lack of low-back symptoms." But, such a small sample could not have been considered representative of the whole group. The study illustrated the difficulty of obtaining statistically meaningful long-term follow-up in the highly mobile population of the United States.

在会议最后一部分，有两篇对哈灵顿器械特别重要的论文分别聚焦于长期随访和僵硬性侧弯上。自 8 年前问世至今，这些器械已经逐渐取代里泽铰链和局部矫形石膏，成为最普遍的侧凸矫正和固定方法。这些器械是具有短期优势的，但关于其带来的长期效益仍有待挖掘。为了回应希伯斯及其在纽约骨科医院的同事对他们手术患者进行长期随访的请求，斯特雷耶、里泽和沃对这些患者进行了研究调查。[24] 1914 年到 1940 年接受脊柱侧凸手术的 837 名患者中，只有 58 名（6 名男性、52 名女性，7%）患有“不同但具代表性病因”的脊柱侧凸的患者可以在平均术后 34 年内被找到并进行评估，接受随访时平均有 15°的（前五年为 11°）丢失。24%的假关节得到了修复，另外有 9 名患者（15%）在随访中出现了一处或多处假关节。他们在临床上表现良好，并且“没有明显腰痛的症状”。但是，如此小的样本量并不能代表整个群体。该研究说明了在美国高度流动的人口中难以获得具有统计学意义的长期随访数据。

Management of stiff curves had been made possible or at least greatly facilitated by the use of Harrington Instrumentation to restabilize a surgically destabilized spine. The year before Simmons had presented a series of mostly adult patients, and this time Leatherman presented "Resection of Vertebral Bodies," a study done mostly in children.[25] Loss of correction after his first attempt in 1957 had caused him to abandon the procedure until the accomplishments of Hodgson and the advent of Harrington Instrumentation had renewed his interest. His technique was anterior vertebral resection followed by staged posterior surgery a few days later that included compression and distraction Harrington Instrumentation. Twenty-four patients, fourteen with congenital scoliosis and ten with tuberculosis, had been operated on with only one major complication, a temporary paralysis that fully recovered following surgical revision. The author offered some precautions. "In resecting the vertebral bodies, extreme care is required to protect the spinal cord from trauma. Resection must also be limited to avoid jeopardizing the circulation of the spinal cord."

通过使用哈灵顿脊柱器械重新稳定手术过程中不稳定的椎体，僵硬性侧弯的矫正变得可能，或者至少大大方便了。在西蒙斯撰写的一系列大部分针对成年患者的研究发表的前一年，莱瑟曼发表了《椎体切除术》，这是一项主要针对儿童患者的研究。[25]由于在 1957 年第一次尝试后发生了矫正丢失，他放弃了手术，直到霍奇森的成就和哈灵顿器械的问世重新唤起了他的兴趣。他所运用的技术是前路椎体切除术，并在几天后分期进行后路手术（包括使用哈灵顿压缩和撑开器械）。在接受手术治疗的 24 名患者中，14 名患有先天性脊柱侧凸，10 名是结核性的脊柱侧凸，在术后他们仅有一例大的并发症：暂时性截瘫，但在手术修复后完全恢复。为此作者提供了一些预防措施。“在切除椎体时，需要格外小心，以保护脊髓免受损伤。同时，必须限制切除术的范围，以避免危及脊髓的血液循环。”

Two business meetings were scheduled, but minutes were apparently not made or kept. Subsequent records show that the new executive committee consisted of John Hall, president; Bill Kane, secretary-treasurer; and John Moe, immediate past-president. The newly elected members of that committee were President-elect Dean MacEwen and at-large members Allen Edmonson, Dick Kilfoyle, and Jim Tupper. Jacquelin Perry was elected to another at-large member term.[26] Harrington or Goldstein would have seemed to be at the front of the line to become president-elect, but they were not chosen. Why MacEwen was is probably best left as a mystery, although it is tempting to contemplate the sobering effect the first morbidity and mortality committee report may have had. It must have caused at least a temporary reflection on the safety of the direction that scoliosis surgery was taking and the man who was leading the way.

此次年会安排了两次会员商务会议，但是显然没有制订或保留会议记录。随后的记录显示，新的执行委员会成员包括现任主席约翰·霍尔、秘书兼财务主管比尔·凯恩以及即将卸任的前任主席约翰·莫。该委员会的新当选成员是候任主席迪恩·麦克尤恩和委员艾伦·德蒙森、迪克·基尔福伊尔和吉姆·塔珀。杰奎琳·佩里则继续委员的另一个任期。[26]哈灵顿或是戈尔茨坦似乎都是候任主席的有力竞争者，但是他们都没有最终被选中。麦克尤恩最终当选候任主席的原因依旧是个谜题，虽然人们很容易联想到是因为第一份并发症发生率和死亡率委员会报告所产生的引人深思的效果，事实上，这份报告确实至少在一定程度上引起了该领域带头人对于脊柱侧凸手术术中安全性的思考。

The second and last surviving 1968 letter exchange with Zimmer occurred in October and November and was again initiated by Harrington, who wrote to Robin Pemberthy, the export manager.[27] Harrington referred to enclosed copies of correspondence with Zimmer about setting up a research project with Oswaldo Campos of Rio de Janeiro for the application of instruments to tuberculosis of the spine in small children. Harrington noted that he had been the originator of the project and the one who had made the initial drawings sent to Zimmer three years before. He emphasized that the experimental instruments were to be sent to Campos but not billed. If expense was a problem, Harrington should be contacted. Pemberthy responded apologizing "for the poor handling of this order" and that "no order for the instruments was given to our specials department."[28] He continued that he had informed Campos in May that the hook and rod prices were \$7.50 each, and he had yet to receive a reply. Pemberthy said that even though Zimmer had not budgeted for Harrington Instrumentation research for the year, they were in error in not notifying Harrington and that no charge would be made. A priority was placed on fulfilling the order.

1968 年，哈灵顿与捷迈公司的第二次也是最后一次的信件交流发生在 10 月与 11 月，这次信件往来还是由哈灵顿发起的。[27]哈灵顿写信给出口部经理罗宾·彭伯蒂想要查阅随信所附的与捷迈公司的通信副本，内容涉及与里约热内卢的奥斯瓦尔多·坎波斯合作建立一个研究项目，将器械应用于小儿脊柱结核的治疗。哈灵顿表明他是该项目的发起人，也是三年前将原始图纸交给捷迈公司的人。同时他也强调，试验性器械将被送给坎波斯，但是并不会开具账单。如果费用方面存在任何问题，请联系哈灵顿。彭伯蒂随后出于“对这个订单的不当处理”而表示歉意，并且表示“没有向我们的特殊部门下订单”[28]。哈灵顿继续说道，他已经在五月份告知坎波斯钩和棒的价格是每个 7.5 美元，但是他还没有收到回复。彭伯蒂说，即使捷迈公司没有为哈灵顿器械研究保留预算，他们没有通知哈灵顿的行为也是错误的，所以他们不会收取任何费用，并答应将优先考虑完成这个订单。

What happened shortly after that was recalled by Jesse Dickson nearly thirty years later.[29] "I came in one day to the hospital, and one of the operating room nurses came out and said, 'Dr. Harrington's had a heart attack. He's in the intensive care unit and he wants to see you.'" On entering Harrington's room, Dickson remembered him as "sitting up, a little groggy but not too bad." Harrington said, "I don't know what's going to happen to me, but I'm telling you now that I want you to take my practice over, and the only thing I ask of you is that you maintain it." That was their arrangement, one based on trust. Suddenly, Dickson had four responsibilities: his private practice at the Kelsey Seybold Clinic, the TIRR scoliosis clinic, the hip clinic at the Houston Shriners

Hospital, and Harrington's private practice.[30] In time it would be proved that he not only carried on Harrington's practice but he also maintained his mentor's teaching load and improved his clinical research. For example, at the time of his heart attack Harrington still was not routinely using fresh autologous iliac crest bone graft, a practice that Dickson soon changed.[31] Harrington had made an excellent decision the year before by bringing Dickson into the TIRR scoliosis clinic and in doing so had found the perfect person to carry on his practice. Harrington had had one prior practice associate, a man who had trained at Children's Hospital in Boston. In 1954 Harrington had included him as a participant on his grant application to the NFIP.[32] As Dickson remembered, "Six months later the people in Boston told this guy that he shouldn't be associated with that crazy doctor. So the recent Boston trainee left Harrington's practice."[33] When Dickson was in his residency from 1960 to 1964, he had some opportunity to work with Harrington, which was a reflection of his future mentor's growing acceptance. In contrast, when Hall had first visited Harrington in 1959, residents were still not allowed to work with him.[34] The only other associate Harrington had had was in about 1966 when Page Nelson had apparently helped in the TIRR scoliosis clinic.

在将近三十年后，杰西·迪克森仍能回忆起在此之后不久发生的事情。[29]“有一天，我来到医院，手术室的一位护士出来和我说‘哈灵顿医生心脏病发作了。他现在在重症监护室，他想见你’”。在进入哈灵顿的病房后，迪克森记得他“坐起来，有点昏昏沉沉，但情况不算太糟”。哈灵顿说：“我不知道我的病情将如何变化，但是我现在想告诉你的是我希望你能接替我的工作，而我对你唯一的要求就是持之以恒。”这是他们两个人之间基于信任达成的约定。忽然之间，迪克森肩负了四项职责：“他在凯尔西·西博尔德的私人诊所的工作、得克萨斯州康复与研究中心脊柱侧凸诊所的工作、位于休斯敦圣地兄弟会医院髋关节诊所的工作和哈灵顿的私人诊所的工作。”[30]最终事实证明他不仅继续了哈灵顿的工作，而且还兼顾了哈灵顿的教学任务，并改善了他的临床研究。例如，在哈灵顿心脏病发作期间，他所做的手术仍然不经常使用自体髂骨移植物，迪克森很快改变了这种做法。[31]一年前哈灵顿做出了一个极佳的决定，那就是将迪克森带入了得克萨斯州康复与研究中心脊柱侧凸诊所，就此找到了继承他工作的最佳人选。哈灵顿之前有一位实习助理，他曾在波士顿儿童医院接受培训。在 1954 年，哈灵顿将他列为国家小儿麻痹基金会拨款申请的参与者。[32]正如迪克森回忆的那样，“六个月后，波士顿的医生告诉那位实习助理，让他不要和那个疯狂的医生（哈灵顿）联系。所以最后的一名实习助理就这样离开了哈灵顿。”[33] 1960 年至 1964 年，迪克森担任住院医师，因而有机会和哈灵顿一起共事，这也从侧面表现出了他的导师越来越被大众接受。相比之下，当霍尔于1959年第一次拜访哈灵顿时，住院医师还不被允许与他一起工作。[34]哈灵顿唯一的助理是佩奇·纳尔逊，1966年左右，他在得克萨斯州康复与研究中心脊柱侧凸诊所协助哈灵顿工作。

Soon after his hospitalization for his heart attack Harrington wrote a 1968 year-end letter simply addressed "To My Friends." He told them that he had suffered a heart attack in November, was progressing well, but was scheduled for major abdominal surgery when his cardiac recovery was complete. He was sure everyone would understand "that it would be some time before I will be able to continue my work." In announcing that Jesse Dickson would be carrying on his work, he endorsed him unreservedly. To add a little seasonal cheer, he enclosed a copy of a proposed activity program submitted by one of his patients in Philadelphia that was a parody of the detailed and precise activity programs Harrington was well known for providing his patients. For instance, his patient wrote: "Three months and you can start your activity program. This consists primarily of holding your golf clubs to check your grip."

心脏病发作住院后不久，哈灵顿在1968年年底写了一封标题为"我的朋友"的信。他告诉朋友们他在11月心脏病发作，目前情况稳定，但他计划在心脏完全恢复后进行腹部手术。他相信每个人都能理解"我还需要一段时间才能继续开展我的工作"。在宣布杰西·迪克森将接任他的工作时，他毫无保留地支持了他。为了增加一点圣诞节的气氛，他附上了计划的活动项目清单，这些项目是由他的一名在宾夕法尼亚州的患者提供的，他模仿了哈灵顿为他的病人所准备的详细而精准的活动项目。例如，他的病人这样写道："三个月后你就可以开始你的活动计划了。这其中主要包括去打你喜欢的高尔夫。"

Harrington would never fully recover his health.[36] After his heart attack and while still in intensive care, he was found to have an abdominal aneurysm, which was resected in the spring of 1969. Before the operation he had had trouble with hypertension and at surgery was found to have four renal arteries, two of them involved in the aneurysm itself. After the resection his blood pressure dropped to normal, which caused dizziness. What followed was a hard recovery when he was diagnosed with carotid artery disease. In the latter part of 1969 or early 1970 he had carotid surgery during which his transverse aorta was found to be so plaque filled that it was difficult to find a place to make the anastomosis. Again, recovery was prolonged, and the prognosis for Harrington ever returning to practice became more improbable. Why did Harrington, an athletic and physically aware person, have so much atherosclerosis? The answer would likely be cigarette smoking. He had become a heavy smoker probably during World War II, when the marketing for cigarettes was so intense and the smoking habit so prevalent. After years of study on its usage and results, in 1964 the causative evidence linking smoking to lung cancer was conclusive and that to atherosclerosis was probable. That year US Surgeon General Luther Terry began a vigorous anti-smoking campaign.[37]

哈灵顿再也没能完全恢复健康。[36]在他心脏病发作仍在重症监护室的时候，他被发现患有腹部动脉瘤，并在1969年春天进行了切除手术。在手术之前他就一直患有高血压，在术中发现4条肾动脉中的2条参与了动脉瘤的形成。在切除动脉瘤之后他的血压恢复到了正常水平，但这也导致了他出现眩晕的症状。当被诊断出患有颈动脉疾病之后，他经历了艰难的恢复过程。在1969年下半年或1970年年初，他接受了颈动脉手术，术中发现他的横主动脉内满是斑块，已经很难找到吻合的部位。在经过又一次的手术之后，他身体能够完全恢复的时间又延长了，他能回到临床的可能性也越来越小。为什么哈灵顿这样一个健壮的、平时对自己身体也非常重视的人会有如此多动脉硬化斑块呢？有可能是因为哈灵顿喜欢抽雪茄。他在第二次世界大战期间成了一名重度烟民，因为当时香烟的营销非常火爆，吸烟也非常普遍。1964年，经过多年对吸烟及其引发结果的研究，有关吸烟会引发肺癌的病因学证据已经十分确凿，并且可能会导致动脉粥样硬化。因此当年美国卫生局局长卢瑟·泰瑞发起了轰轰烈烈的禁烟运动。[37]

In 1968 Harrington published one paper, "Nonoperative Treatment of Scoliosis." which he described as being based in a force-over-time factor, with the goal of reducing this factor in smaller curves by frequent rest periods and in larger curves with the addition of a Milwaukee brace.[38] His study was based on 94 patients, 82 (87%) with idiopathic scoliosis, whose treatment began in 1963 and 1964 and continued for an average of 29.5 months. Only four had received surgery during this time. Resulting mandibular problems were just beginning to be recognized, and Harrington attributed them to habitual resting of the chin on the chin piece.

1968年，哈灵顿发表了一篇名为《脊柱侧凸的非手术治疗》的论文，他称这种治疗手段是基于"随时间而变化的力学因素"，在侧凸较小的患者中通过频繁的休息；在侧凸较大的患者中通过外加密尔沃基支具以达到减轻力学因素的目的。[38]他研究的对象是94名脊柱侧凸患者，其中有82名（87%）为特发性脊柱侧凸的患者，他们的治疗始于1963年和1964年，平均疗程为29.5个月。在此期间，只有4人接受了手术治疗。而非手术治疗所产生的下颌畸形问题才刚刚开始被意识到。哈灵顿将其归因为下巴习惯性地靠在下颌垫上。

Had there ever been any doubt about Harrington's total commitment to his work. *Scoliosis 1968*, the seventh annual private volume of his personal intellectual odyssey, would have removed it.[39] In Section I, "Principles of Scoliosis," he summarized his theory on the pathogenesis of scoliosis as "the breakdown or collapse of the complex dynamics of axial skeletal function." While this had been his theme from the beginning. he added a lengthy discussion of the molecular structure of the collagen and mineral components of skeletal tissues, which was knowledge that was rapidly increasing at the time. In Section II, Harrington provided the "Design and Specifications of Instruments, Recommended Operative Technique and a Terminology Glossary."[40] Here he listed the metal specifications and drawings with the dimensions necessary to duplicate his instrumentation components except for the 3/16"-diameter threaded rod and hooks. This article could have landed in the hands of implant copiers since he sent soft-bound books of each year's edition to a limited number of his colleagues.

如果有人对哈灵顿对待工作的完全投入有任何怀疑，那么他的第七本年度私人出版物《脊柱侧凸1968》就不会发表了。[39]在第一章“脊柱侧凸的原理”中，他将脊柱侧凸发病机制的理论总结为“中轴骨功能的复杂动力学的失衡或塌陷”。虽然这是他最初的理论，但是在这之后他对骨骼系统的胶原蛋白和矿物质成分的分子结构进行了长篇的讨论，有关这些方面的理论知识得到了极大的丰富。在第二章中，哈灵顿提供了“器械的设计与规格、推荐的手术技术和术语表”。[40]在这一章节中，他还列出了除直径3/16英寸的螺纹棒和钩以外复制其器械部件所需要的金属规格和图纸尺寸。他将每一年的文章装订成册，且仅分给极少的同事，因此他所撰写的文章可能已经流传到做器械内植物的医生手中。

In this article Harrington provided five insights into his early 1950s design thinking that are critical to understanding how his instrumentation came about. First, he wrote about spine fixation sites: "Quite early in the study, it was determined the force required to correct a deformed spine should be applied directly to the posterior elements; i.e. lateral tilt would be corrected and some derotation would take place, particularly if compression and distraction or a combination of forces could be applied at the same time." Second, he described the basic shape of the implants: "It should be noted that each hook is in a different plane around the central axis of the compression rod. This was considered fundamental to the original design of the instruments since it was realized that no two levels of vertebral segments were in the same plane. Purchase sites, therefore, vary in their position relative to a common force. This idea was incorporated into the basic design of the distraction rod as well. The purchasing hooks are never in the same planes; therefore, the whole system (both the compression and distraction systems) had to be designed around a circular, tubular or rod-like mechanism." Third, he addressed mechanical properties: "There had to be a slight give and take since the mechanism could not be extremely rigid and devoid of elastic properties. Elastic modules [modulus] of the instruments had to have an operational range within certain given specifications in order to be tolerated by living bone and not cause an extreme condition such as erosion of the purchase sites." Fourth, he mentioned the dimensions of the distraction hook: "The dimensions of the radius of this purchasing shoe, its angle, and the proper length for the extension were determined over a period of time by trial, error and observation." Fifth, he discussed instrument connections: "In the original design of the instruments, it was realized that a loose fit would be necessary to facilitate ease of introduction and also adjustment of forces, yet the fit would have to be secure enough so that slipping would not occur when the shifting demands of body movement took place."

在这篇文章中，哈灵顿对他早期在20世纪50年代所提出的设计思想提供了五条见解，这对于了解他如何设计出哈灵顿器械至关重要。第一，他写了有关脊柱固定位点："在这个研究的最早期，矫正脊柱畸形所需要的力应当直接施加到后部结构，这点是确定的；即当压缩和撑开或是所有的力均能在同一时间施加，那么躯干倾斜就会被矫正，同时会有一些去旋转的效果。"第二，他这样描述他的内植物的基本形状："值得注意的是，每一个钩都应该位于压缩棒中心轴周围的不同平面上。这被认作是器械初始设计的基础，因为人们意识到没有两个椎体节段是在同一平面上的。"因此，让钩固定牢固的位置应当根据作用力的位置而作出相应的改变。这个想法也被纳入了压缩棒的基本设计中。钩固定的位置永远不会在同一平面，因此，整个器械系统（压缩和撑开系统）必须设计成圆形、管状或棒状。第三，他设法解决了器械的机械性能："因为这套器械并不能只充满刚性而缺乏弹性，因此在这一方面必须有所改进。器械的弹性模量必须在某些已经确定的规格内，以便既被自体骨组织所耐受，又不会造成固定点被腐蚀等极端情况。”第四，他提到了撑开钩的尺寸：“这款固定系统的尺寸半径、角度和其延伸的合适距离都是经过一段时间反复的试验、试错和观察后确定的。”第五，他讨论了器械的连接问题：“在器械最初的设计中发现，器械之间的松动连接对于引入和调整力量大小是必要的，但是这种连接又必须足够牢固，这样才能在身体运动时不发生滑动。”

The metal was a stainless steel alloy, designated Uniloy 316-L, which contained a small amount of molybdenum (2.21 %) to increase resistance to pitting corrosion. Its mechanical properties were hardness, Rockwell 30/30.5; yield point within 0.2% of 133,500 pounds per square inch (psi); and tensile strength of 146,200 psi. The #1250 distraction rod, the #1251 distraction hook, and their ratchet interconnection were undoubtedly the most difficult to get right. Because the ratchets obviously weakened the rod, the key to strengthening the rod was to minimize the detrimental effect of the ratchets. This was achieved by leaving fillets of graduated, slightly increasing radii at the six notches beginning at the solid portion of the rod. The goal was a distraction construct that would withstand at least one year's loading, which was estimated to be 3,650,000 cycles, based on an estimated 10,000 motion and respiration movements a day. The rod's fatigue strength was tested on a testing machine in Harrington's laboratory. *See figure 10.3.* A rod tested at 150 pounds loading lasted 3,876,810 cycles before fatigue failure, and the one tested in a similar manner at 100 pounds had not fatigue fractured at 7 million cycles, or the equivalent of two years. Harrington did not specify the length of rod tested, but the ratchet engaged was the sixth from the end. He concluded that the distraction rod had a margin of strength safety of 1.6 to 1.8, 60% to 80%. The #1258 small (1/8"-diameter) compression rod was also strengthened by using "a fillet construction and reduction of the depth of the valley of the thread."

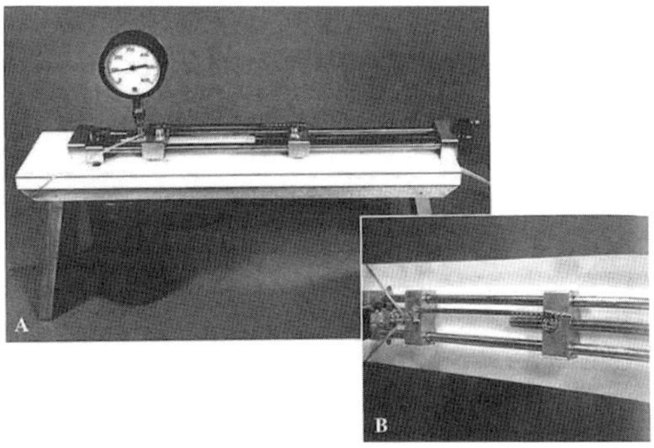

Figure 10.3 ***Machine designed to determine the fatigue strength of the Harrington distraction rod. A. Full side view. B. Detail top-profile view.*** (***Harrington Archives***)

图 10.3 确定哈灵顿撑开棒疲劳强度的机械设计机器。A.完整的侧视图。B.细节俯视图(哈灵顿档案馆)

该金属是一种不锈钢合金，被命名为尤尼洛依不锈镍铬钢 316-L，其中还有少量的钼（2.21%），以提高对腐蚀的抵抗力。材料的硬度是洛氏30/30.5，屈服点在133 500磅/平方英寸①的0.2%以内；抗拉强度为146 200磅/平方英寸。#1250撑开棒、#1251撑开钩和它们对应的棘轮相互连接毫无疑问是最难搞定的。因为棘齿会明显削弱棒的作用，而加固棒的关键则是尽量减少棘齿的不良影响。这是通过从棒的固态部分开始数起的六个凹口处留下标有刻度的、半径轻微增加的圆角来实现的。其目的是使得撑开组合可以承受至少一年的载荷，按照每天有10 000次运动和呼吸活动的频次，估计一年的载荷量约在3 650 000次循环。棒的疲劳强度是在哈灵顿实验室的测试机上进行的测试。(图10.3) 在150磅的载荷下测试的棒在疲劳断裂之前持续了3 876 810次循环，而以类似方式在100磅下测试的棒在7 000 000次循环（或相当于两年的载荷量）下并没有出现疲劳性断裂。哈灵顿没有具体说明测试棒的长度，但啮合的棘齿是从末端算起的第六个。他得出的结论是撑开棒的强度安全边界为1.6至1.8，即60%至80%。#1258小压缩棒（直径1/8英寸）的强度也通过使用“圆角结构和减少螺纹深度”得到了增强。

Section III of *Scoliosis 1968* consisted of three parts, each concerning mechanical studies stimulated by Harrington's collaborations at Rice University and the University of Houston. In Part 1, Rice Professor James R. Sims explained and illustrated the differences between pure axial column loading and eccentric column loading.[41] During laboratory testing he had noted high friction between the hook and rod during lengthening, so that at no time did spines receive the full distraction load applied. He also predicted that the loads carried by the distraction rod would remain at peak only a short time. Part 2 was the master's thesis of one of Sims' students.[42,43] The purpose was to develop a mathematical analogy of the spine in order to analyze the effect of applied loads on the column. Having done this, the need was for a Harrington distraction rod with an implantable load cell to gain accurate loading information. Part 3 was the master's thesis, completed in August 1965, of a student of Professor Ardis White at the University of Houston.[44,45] A strain-gauge-fitted outrigger was used to measure the loads being applied during surgery. The maximum load ranged from 63 to 140 pounds with a loss of 9% to 40% while in place. During loosening, the load decreased more rapidly than during insertion. This study also ended with investigation into the possibility of an implantable strain gauge. There was a third Harrington-stimulated biomechanical study in 1968, a

① 1平方英寸=6.451 6平方厘米。

project by two University of Houston engineering students.[46] Their purpose was to compare theoretical with actual midpoint deflections of progressively eccentrically loaded Harrington distraction rods of varying length, each with the mobile distraction hook seated on the third shoulder from the rod's end. The predicted and actual deflections were close.

《脊柱侧凸 1968》的第三章由三部分组成，每个部分都涉及哈灵顿在与莱斯大学和休斯敦大学的合作过程中所进行的力学研究。在第一部分，莱斯大学教授詹姆斯・R. 西姆斯解释并说明了纯轴向柱和偏心柱载荷之间的差异。[41]在实验室测试期间，他注意到在拉长过程中钩子与棒之间的摩擦力很大，因此脊柱在任何时候都不会承受施加的全部撑开载荷。他还预测说，撑开棒承载的载荷只会在短时间内保持在峰值水平。第二部分是西蒙斯的一名学生的硕士论文。[42,43]他的研究方向是开发脊柱的数学模拟，以分析在柱上施加载荷的影响。在完成数学模拟分析后，需要带有植入式称重传感器的哈灵顿撑开棒来获得准确的载荷情况信息。第三部分是休斯敦大学阿迪丝・怀特教授的学生于 1965 年 8 月完成的一篇硕士论文。[44,45]一个装有应变计的外撑开器用于测量手术过程中所施加的荷。最大载荷范围为 63~140 磅，当施加到具体部位时会有 9%~40%的减少。在松动期间，载荷比插入期间减少得更快。该研究还以植入式应变计的可行性分析结束。1968 年第三个由哈灵顿棒激发的生物力学研究，是休斯敦大学工程系两名学生的一项研究。[46]这项研究的目的是比较逐步增大偏心载荷时不同长度的哈灵顿撑开棒的理论和实际中心偏转的差距，每个撑开棒在从棒底数起的第三个肩部都装有移动分离钩。预测的偏转和实际的偏转非常接近。

The January-February 1969 issue of *Clinical Orthopaedics and Related Research* featured the index report on Dwyer Instrumentation, which quickly became the second successful spine instrumentation as well as the first successful anterior spine instrumentation.[47] Dwyer's friend and colleague John Stephen provided this profile. "Alan Dwyer was born in 1920, the son of a general practitioner. He graduated in medicine in 1942 and served in Borneo in the later war years. Returning to Sydney and St. Vincent's Hospital, he moved into orthopaedics. His interest in the spine was fostered by a visit to Arthur Hodgson in Hong Kong in about 1960.... He conceived the idea of excising the discs as multiple wedges to obtain correction and, together with an engineer, Arthur Sherwood in 1963, developed and inserted a system of titanium screws and cable, with approximation of the screws by means of a tensioning device and crimping of the screw heads.... He applied the technique to the thoracic, thoracolumbar and lumbar spine.

Some cases were massive and extended over 10 or 12 segments and many hours of operation. He was determined, meticulous and inexhaustible."[48] Dwyer published another article in 1973.[49] Sadly, he died too early, at age 55 of cancer of the esophagus in 1975.

1969 年 1 月至 2 月的《临床骨科与相关研究》刊登了关于德怀尔内固定器械的报告，德怀尔器械迅速成为第二个成功的脊柱器械，也是第一个成功的前路脊柱器械。[47]德怀尔的朋友和同事约翰·斯蒂芬提供了德怀尔的相关介绍。“艾伦·德怀尔出生于 1920 年，是一位全科医生的儿子。他于 1942 年毕业于医学专业，并在战争尾声在婆罗洲服役。回到悉尼和圣文森特医院后，他转入骨科。1960 年拜访过中国香港的阿瑟·霍奇森之后，他对脊柱领域的兴趣被激发了起来……他构想出了将椎间盘切除，以形成多个楔形来进行矫形的想法，并和另一位工程师亚瑟·舍伍德在 1963 年研发并插入了一套钛螺丝钉和钢索系统，通过张力装置及卷曲的螺钉头来构造螺丝类似物。他将该技术应用于胸椎、胸腰椎和腰椎。在一些病例中涉及的节段比较多，有的长达 10 或 12 个节段，手术时长也会相应地延长。他意志坚定，一丝不苟，不知疲倦。”[48]德怀尔在 1973 年发表了另一篇文章。[49]遗憾的是，他英年早逝，于 1975 年死于食管癌，享年 55 岁。

Nineteen sixty-nine was an extremely difficult year for Harrington medically, and for the first time in seven years he did not give an instructional course lecture at the annual meeting of the AAOS. But he was far from inactive academically as three publications appeared in the first two months of the year. In January the "Pathological Changes in Scoliosis" study he had been conducting with Enneking appeared in print.[50] This study had been progressing for several years was very important to Harrington's concepts of scoliosis initiation and progression, and requires detailed consideration. It was "a histological study of the changes in the joints between the articular processes of the vertebrae in normal and scoliotic children to see if the changes would support the hypothesis that asymmetrical growth causes the deformity of the posterior elements in idiopathic scoliosis." At the time of surgery for scoliosis, the inferior articular processes from the convex and concave sides of the apical vertebra of the primary curve were obtained for study in 171 patients. To understand the normal development and age-matched structure of these processes and to provide control groups for comparison, autopsy material from persons with normal spines were obtained. The development group included specimens from fifteen children ranging in age from fetus to ten years. The control group consisted of autopsy specimens of T9 obtained from twenty-six similarly aged (thirteen to twenty years) females with normal spines at the time of death.

1969 年对于哈灵顿而言，是极其艰难的一年，七年来他第一次没有在美国骨科医师学会年会上进行教学课程讲座。但他在学术上并非不活跃，在这年的头两个月，他发表了三篇论文。一月，他与恩内金一起撰写的《脊柱侧凸的病理学改变》出版了。[50]这项研究已经进行了数年，是一项需要仔细考虑的、对哈灵顿的脊柱侧凸发病与进展的理念非常重要的研究。同时，这项研究是对“正常儿童和脊柱侧凸儿童脊椎骨关节突之间关节变化的组织学研究，以了解这些变化是否支持以下假设：不对称的生长会导致特发性脊柱侧凸患者后部结构畸形”。在进行脊柱侧凸手术时，从 171 名患者主弯顶椎的凸侧和凹侧获取下关节突进行研究。为了了解这些关节突的正常发育和对应年龄的正常结构，并且为了给研究提供对照组进行对比分析，这些正常的关节突都是从脊柱正常的尸检标本中获得的。发育组中包含了 15 个从胎儿到 10 岁年龄的儿童标本。对照组中包含了从 26 名年龄相仿（13 岁到 20 岁）的女性尸体上获得的正常脊柱 T9 节段尸检标本。

Carefully oriented histological sections perpendicular to the articular surface were prepared and examined for chondrogenesis, enchondral ossification, subchondral bone formation, and degenerative cartilage changes. Enneking, who was the examiner in all cases, worked without knowledge of clinical information. Two sections from each control and scoliotic specimen were graded for each of the four variables on a scale of two to eight. “Two represented the normal picture in a growing female child; eight represented the most severe change observed.” The scores from the four variables were added, resulting in a composite score ranging from 8 (best) to 32 (worst). After three months Enneking repeated the grading process. Any case in which either the section or the repeat grades differed by more than one point was excluded. Specimens from 59 scoliosis patients eventually met all the stringent requirements for study: females between the ages of 13 and 20, idiopathic scoliosis, curve apex between the eighth and tenth vertebrae, and adequate roentgenograms and specimens.

他们准备了精准垂直于关节表面的组织切片，并检查了切片的软骨形成、软骨内骨化、软骨下骨形成和退行性软骨改变。恩内金是所有病人的检查者，他在不了解临床信息的情况下工作。每组对照和脊柱侧凸标本的两个切片会按照上述四个变量进行等级 2 到 8 的分级。“2 代表发育中女孩的正常生理情况；8 则代表所观察到的最严重的病理改变。”将四个变量的分数相加，从而得到由 8（最好）至 32（最差）的综合分数。三个月后，恩内金重复了分级的过程。任何部分评分或重复计算的评分相差超过一分的情况最终都会被排除在外。从 59 名脊柱侧凸患者那里获得的标本最终满足了研究的所有严格要求：年龄 13 至 20 岁的女性，特发性脊柱侧凸，侧凸顶椎位于第八和第十椎体之间以及足够的 X 光片和标本。

The results showed that the histological grades of the scoliosis patients were significantly higher than the control group and that this increase was not related to curve severity, as judged by the Harrington factor. At all stages of maturity the histological grades were significantly greater for the convex than the concave specimens. This was also true for each of the four components of the histological grade. Bone density of the convex and concave specimens was similar at all levels of skeletal maturity and similar to the control at all levels of skeletal maturity. The authors concluded that, "Histological evidence, correlated with clinical observation, is presented which suggests that a portion of the deformity seen in idiopathic scoliosis is not due to asymmetrical enchondral growth. Analysis of the data further suggests that the deformity is produced by an extra-osseous cause and that the changes in bone and cartilage are secondary adaptations. There is no clear answer as to whether this adaptation is biological, physical, or a combination of the two. Finally, if a metabolic error is primary, it most likely should be sought for in extraosseous tissue." These findings clearly did not support the hypothesis that "asymmetrical growth causes the deformity of the posterior elements in idiopathic scoliosis." To explain the gross deformity of the posterior elements, the authors speculated that they might be the result of physical molding over a long period of time. Their study can be criticized by what seems to be a mislabeling of convex and concave sides in the introductory figures. But its design and thoroughness seems to have forever ended consideration of asymmetrical growth of facet joints as the, or even a, cause of idiopathic scoliosis.

最终结果表明按照哈灵顿系数来分析，脊柱侧凸患者的组织学评分明显高于对照组，并且这种增加与侧凸弯曲的严重程度无关。在整个成熟的阶段中，凸侧标本的组织学评分明显高于凹侧标本，同时四个变量的评分都呈现了同样的趋势。凹侧和凸侧标本的骨密度在各级骨骼成熟度上相似，同时也与对照组的各级骨骼成熟度相似。作者的结论是“组织学证据和临床所观察到的现象相结合，表明特发性脊柱侧凸的部分畸形不是由于不对称的软骨生长。这些数据的分析报告进一步表明，畸形是骨骼之外的原因引起的，骨骼和软骨的变化是继发性适应的结果。而对于这种继发性适应是生物学上的、物理学上的还是两者共同作用的结果，目前还没有明确的答案。最后，如果代谢紊乱是原发性的，那么原因需要从骨外组织中寻找。”这些发现显然不支持“不对称生长导致特发性脊柱侧凸后部结构畸形”的假设。为了解释后部结构的显而易见的畸形，作者推测它们可能是长时间物理成形的结果。他们的研究可能会因为在介绍性图片中对凹侧和凸侧的错误标记而受到批评。但这个研究的全面性及其设计已经永远终结了将小关节不对称发育作为特发性脊柱侧凸病因或是病因之一的考量。

Harrington had two more publications in 1969. “Reduction of Severe Spondylolisthesis in Children” introduced his operative technique for partial reduction and stabilization of grades III and IV spondylolisthesis.[51] His third publication of the year, “Pitfalls in the Interpretation of Pulmonary Function Studies in Scoliotic Patients,” with Carlos Vallbona listed as first author, reported the preoperative and one-year postoperative evaluation of twenty-two patients with post-polio scoliosis and twelve patients with idiopathic scoliosis.[52] The post-polio patients' curves averaged 100° before and 77° after surgery, a 23% correction, and their vital capacities were 1.19 liters and 1.22 liters. The idiopathic scoliosis patients' curves averaged 74° before and 46° after surgery, a 37% correction, and their vital capacities were 2.09 liters and 2.27 liters. Corrected height was determined by the method the group had developed to include vertebral rotation in the formula. Vital capacity, a measure of restrictive impairment and functional reserve capacity related to rib cage deformity, improved after surgery for idiopathic scoliosis both in liters and in liters per uncorrected or corrected height. Only the vital capacity in liters improved in the post-polio patients, and then just slightly. The authors concluded that use of corrected height reflected more serious pulmonary involvement than the uncorrected height. This was particularly true for the post-polio patients' preoperative functional residual capacity where the differences were 10% to 15% greater loss of pulmonary function when using corrected height.

同年，哈灵顿又发表了两篇文章。《儿童严重椎体滑脱的复位》介绍了他对Ⅲ度和Ⅳ度椎体滑脱进行部分复位和稳定的手术方法。[51]这年他发表的第三篇文章《脊柱侧凸患者肺功能研究的认知误区》，他与卡洛斯·瓦尔博纳并列为第一作者，该研究报道了对22名患有脊髓灰质炎后脊柱侧凸患者和12名特发性脊柱侧凸患者进行的术前及术后一年的相关评估。[52]脊髓灰质炎后脊柱侧凸患者的弯曲角度在术前平均为100°，术后平均为77°，矫正率为23%，他们的肺活量分别为1.19升和1.22升。特发性脊柱侧凸患者术前弯曲角度平均为74°，术后平均为

46°，矫正率为37%，他们的肺活量分别为2.09升和2.27升。矫正后身高是通过该小组开发的包含椎体旋转度等因素在内的公式计算得出的。肺活量是衡量因肋骨畸形所引起的限制性通气功能障碍以及功能残气量的指标。在特发性脊柱侧凸术后，肺活量（无论术后是否矫正身高）都会有所改善。而在脊髓灰质炎后脊柱侧凸术后患者中的肺活量仅以升为单位有所改善，且改善程度不大。之后作者得出了结论，与未矫正身高相比，使用矫正后身高可以反映出更严重的肺部受累。尤其是针对脊髓灰质炎后脊柱侧凸患者的术前功能残气量检查时，使用矫正后身高进行计算得到的肺功能，相比使用非矫正身高计算得到的肺功能会有10%~15%的降低。

In 1969 the study of pulmonary function became a major topic in scoliosis. In fact, the first six papers of the fourth annual meeting of the SRS, held September 4-6 in Anaheim, California, under the presidency of John Hall, were devoted to pulmonary function. These presentations and the entire meeting were well documented in the program,[53] recorded and transcribed proceedings,[54] and published paper summaries[55]. This marked the peak in pulmonary function study reporting. The first paper found that using measured height of the trunk-shortened scoliosis patient to calculate predicted pulmonary function underestimated the pulmonary deficit. Arm span, an easily obtained measure, had been found to correlate well with nondeformed height; the relationship was arm span/1.03 ±.02 = nondeformed height.[56] Patients with thoracic curves of 60° or more had arm span/height ratios greater than 1.05, which was the abnormal threshold. The second paper reported that pulmonary function deteriorated for about a year after surgery and then stabilized in adolescent patients with scoliosis (apparently of mixed cause) who received preoperative correction and in most cases Harrington Instrumentation.[57] The third paper found that vascular perfusion of the lungs was altered by scoliosis with diminished basilar perfusion and zones of abnormal perfusion on the concave side.[58] These perfusion abnormalities were diminished in the supine position, where the curve was smaller, thus supporting orthopedic stabilization and correction of severe scoliosis.

1969年，有关肺功能的研究成为脊柱侧凸领域的主要话题之一。实际上，9月4日至6日在加利福尼亚州阿纳海姆召开的由约翰·霍尔主办的第四届脊柱侧凸研究学会年会的前六篇论文都是关于肺功能的。这些汇报和整个会议流程[53]和抄录的会议议程[54]及发表的论文摘要[55]中都被详细地记录在案。这届会议标志着有关肺功能的研究进入了高峰期。第一篇论文发现，使用躯干短缩的脊柱侧凸患者的身高来计算患者的预计肺功能会低估患者的肺功能缺损度。臂展作为一种比较容易获得的测量方法，被发现与未变形的身高密切相关，它们之间的关系是：臂展/1.03±0.02=未变形的身高。[56]胸椎侧弯度数60度或以上的患者臂展/身高比大于1.05，这是异常阈值。第二篇论文报道说，在接受术前矫正并且在术中使用哈灵顿器械进行矫正之后脊柱侧凸青少年患者（显然是多重原因造成的脊柱侧凸）的肺功能在术后一年会持续恶化，然后稳定下来。[57]第三篇论文发现，肺部血管灌注因脊柱侧凸而改变，并伴有肺底灌注减少和凹侧异常灌注。[58]这些灌注异常在仰卧位时减少，因为处于仰卧位时弯曲角度会减小，从而支持严重脊柱侧凸的骨科稳定和矫形。

In the fourth paper devoted to this topic, study of the effects of scoliosis therapies on pulmonary function revealed that properly fitted Milwaukee braces usually did not improve lung function or ventilation/perfusion ratios but that these were sometimes decreased by a poorly fitted brace.[59] Patients with severe curves and right heart and respiratory failure, who were improved in halo-femoral traction, benefitted from scoliosis surgery. Those who were not improved could be expected to worsen. Five years after Harrington Instrumentation and fusion, lung volumes and pulmonary reserve were not improved but ventilation/perfusion ratios were. Long-term intermittent positive pressure breathing was not helpful. In the fifth paper, a post-poliomyelitis scoliosis case series of 111 patients treated with spine fusion from 1955 through 1968 found that vital capacity improved an average of 1% per year for at least 10 years postoperative.[60] In the sixth, 50 patients aged 11 to 78 years with nontreated idiopathic scoliosis were studied with a focus on the 40 with thoracic curves.[61] All lung volumes decreased with increasing scoliosis. Airway and perfusion studies revealed early airway closure and shifting of lung perfusion from the basal to the apical parts of the lungs, correlating with curve severity and demonstrating partial atelectasis in living patients with severe 90°+ curves.

在专门讨论肺功能的第四篇论文中，针对脊柱侧凸治疗对于肺功能影响的研究表明，正确佩戴密尔沃基支具通常不会改善肺功能或通气/灌注比值，但肺功能有时会因支具的不当佩戴而减弱。[59]通过halo股骨牵引改善右心衰竭和呼吸衰竭的严重侧凸患者可以通过脊柱侧凸矫形手术获益。而那些心肺功能不能通过halo股骨牵引改善的患者的病情可能会恶化。在接受哈灵顿器械矫形和融合手术的五年后，患者的肺容积和肺储备功能并没有改善，但是通气血流比值得到了改善，长期间歇性正压呼吸对患者并没有帮助。在第五篇论文中，从1955年到1968年接受脊柱融合治疗的111名脊髓灰质炎后脊柱侧凸患者中，发现在至少术后10年肺活量平均每年会提高1%。[60]第六项研究在50名11岁至78岁未接受治疗的特发性脊柱侧凸患者中进行，重点关注了其中40名胸椎侧凸的患者。[61]随着脊柱侧凸弯曲角度的增大，所有肺容量都会减少。气道和灌注研究显示，早期气道关闭和肺灌注从肺底部转移至肺尖部的改变与侧凸严重程度相关，并表明侧凸角度大于90°的患者存在部分肺不张。

Thanks to the recorded and transcribed proceedings, the presentations and lively discussions of these papers were preserved.[62] For example, one premise of scoliosis treatment, especially regarding the larger curves for which surgery was used, was that pulmonary function would be improved. In fact, pulmonary function was usually very little changed. It was recognized that pulmonary volume studies, such as vital capacity, had their limitations and that a 20% change was required for significance. Ventilation/perfusion studies, such as with Xenon-131, were believed to be more promising. Thoracic curves, either single or part of a double curve, were responsible for the decrease in pulmonary function. Physical therapy had not been shown to increase pulmonary function. Winter cited an exception to this finding. Yves Cotrel in France had reported a 30% to even 50% improvement—but it should be noted that these patients had been under supervised, in-hospital therapy for eighteen months and over a period of time about half of the improvement was said to have been lost. Winter also pointed out the serious effect lordosis had on pulmonary function and emphasized the importance of trying to prevent incorporation of the ribs in the fusion mass.

得益于记录和转录的会议记录，有关这些论文的汇报和热烈的讨论得以保存。[62]例如，脊柱侧凸治疗的一个前提是患者的肺功能能够得到改善，这是侧凸角度较大的患者手术前尤其需要解决的问题。事实上，肺功能通常改善得很少。人们意识到，肺容量研究（例如肺活量）是有局限性的，超过20%的改变才具有显著性。使用像氙-131这种类型的通气血流比值研究被认为是更有前景的。胸椎侧凸无论是单弯还是双弯都是导致肺功能下降的部分原因。没有证据证实物理疗法可以改善肺功能。但是温特提到一个例外。法国的伊夫斯·科特雷尔称物理疗法对于肺功能有30%甚至50%的改善，但值得注意的是，这些患者一直处于监护状态下，并经历了18个月的住院治疗。又经过一段时间后，据说此前已改善的肺功能减弱了一半。温特还指出脊柱前凸对肺功能的严重影响，并强调了融合时避免波及肋骨的重要性。

During this SRS annual meeting at least 7 of the 32 papers presented involved Harrington Instrumentation in some manner. Three were of particular interest. Moe's group reported on the successful management of postoperative wound infections with closed suction irrigation.[63] With this technique he had been able to avoid removal of Harrington Instrumentation. Pierre Stagnara reported on the incorporation of Harrington Instrumentation into his scoliosis treatment program that included a perfected preoperative distraction cast to aid in the correction of the many patients with severe scoliosis who were referred to him.[64] President Hall presented a masterful summation of the many factors involved in "The Management of Scoliosis."[65] When surgical management was indicated, he made it clear "that Harrington Instrumentation and spine fusion with autogenous iliac-crest bone was the treatment of choice." His presentation was followed by an uninstrumented case series, "Second Look Spinal Exploration for Scoliosis," reporting pseudarthrosis rates of 58% (29 of 52) for idiopathic and 68% (23 of 34) for paralytic patients operated on between 1956 and 1966 whose fusions were routinely explored at 5 months postoperative.[66] The arthrodesis was of the Hibbs type as modified by Moe, thus including the facet joints with placement of bone graft into the cut-out articular facets. Most patients had autogenous graft although some had bank bone, and the surgery was done by residents with staff supervision. A Milwaukee brace or occasionally a Risser cast and bed confinement were used for postoperative correction and immobilization.

在这次脊柱侧凸研究学会年会期间，提交的32篇论文中至少有7篇在某些方面涉及哈灵顿器械，其中3篇更是对其特别感兴趣。莫的小组汇报了闭式引流冲洗方式在处理术后伤口感染上的成功应用。[63]使用闭式引流冲洗的手段能够避免去除哈灵顿器械。皮埃尔·斯塔格纳拉将哈灵顿器械加入他的脊柱侧凸治疗项目当中，其中包括一个性能良好的术前撑开性石膏，以对严重脊柱侧凸患者的矫形手术起到作用。[64]主席霍尔对"脊柱侧凸的治疗"中所涉及的诸多因素进行了技术性总结。[65]当需要进行手术治疗时，他明确表示"哈灵顿器械和应用自体髂骨进行脊柱融合固定手术是可供选择的治疗方案"。在他的汇报之后是一组未使用器械固定的病例汇报——"脊柱侧凸的二次脊柱探查"，报告称在1956年至1966年接受手术治疗的患者在术后五个月的例行融合情况随访中，特发性脊柱侧凸患者假关节的发生率为58%（29/52），麻痹性脊柱侧凸患者假关节的发生率为68%（23/34）。[66]采用的融合术是经过莫改良的希伯斯法，因此其中包括将骨移植物放置到切除关节面的椎间小关节处。大部分患者采用自体骨移植，有些患者也会采用骨库骨移植，手术是由住院医生在主治医师的指导下完成的。术后的矫形和固定通常会用到密尔沃基支具，有时候也会使用里泽石膏和限制床。

Discussion of these papers quickly focused on pseudarthrosis, the bane of scoliosis and other spine deformity surgery since the beginning of spine arthrodesis surgery in 1911. The panel was chaired by William Donaldson with Louis Goldstein and Harrington as members. That day at least Goldstein had the last word. "In some 180 consecutive patients in whom instrumentation was used, I consider the Harrington instruments just a minor adjunct in the treatment program. If you consider it a major part of treatment, you are going to have problems. You are going to have complications. The rods are going to break, the hooks are going to slip out, you are going to lose correction and have trouble with your fusion. We have not altered our treatment program one bit since using the instrumentation except in ambulating a little earlier. Otherwise, the meticulous fusion going in before instrumentation, bone added, and the postoperative immobilization with & well molded localizer cast applied under corrective forces have allowed us to maintain correction and the rod gives you fine internal fixation for a temporary period, for exactly how long I don't know. I would be hesitant to rely upon the compression system as John Hall does to decide whether you need external support or not but I think that if one uses adequate external immobilization it will maintain correction until the fusion is quite well organized and incorporated, then the rod is fixed within the fusion mass and it probably still gives you some supporting function. I have not had one rod break in patients with idiopathic scoliosis that have now gone over a period of eight years. We have removed only two rods in the idiopathic cases and one was in a patient who was infected and after two and one-half years of an intermittent draining sinus, he did have a pseudarthrosis to begin with, he healed his pseudarthrosis, he did have some 26% loss of correction or so."[67]

自 1911 年脊柱融合术开展以来，这些研究的讨论很快就都集中在脊柱侧凸手术和其他脊柱畸形手术导致的假关节形成的问题上。由威廉·唐纳森担任这方面的专家组主席，路易斯·戈尔茨坦和哈灵顿是专家组成员。那天戈尔茨坦最后发言，"在大约 180 名应用器械治疗的患者中，我认为哈灵顿器械只是治疗计划中的一个次要辅助工具。如果你将器械作为治疗计划中的主要部分，你就会遇到并发症、断棒、脱钩、矫正丢失，同时融合困难等问题。自从使用器械以来，我们并没有改变我们的治疗计划，只是会稍微早一点让患者进行自体活动。另外，在植入器械之前进行细致的融合、骨骼的填充以及在矫正力作用下应用成型良好的局部定位石膏，使得我们可以维持矫形效果。棒在短暂的一段时间内可以给予你们一个良好的内固定，至于具体可以维持多长时间我不知道。我会犹豫是否像约翰·霍尔那样依赖压缩系统来决定是否需要外固定协助支持，但我认为，如果使用足够的外固定手段，外固定可以维持矫正效果直到融合，随后棒可以固定在融合块中，这时它可能会起到一些支撑功能。我到现在为止八年多的时间里没有在一个特发性脊柱侧凸患者身上发生过断棒的情况。在特发性脊柱侧凸的患者中我们也仅去除过两根棒，其中之一是因为患者发生了感染，并且经过两年半间歇性的窦口引流处理，他开始有假关节形成，之后他的假关节治愈了，他确实丢失了大约26%的矫正度。”[67]

Goldstein had the stature and statistics to support his scold. In March he had published his report on 80 consecutive idiopathic scoliosis patients with 90 curves whose treatment included Harrington Instrumentation in addition to arthrodesis and fresh autogenous iliac bone grafts followed by a Riser localizer cast and bed immobilization for an average of 3. 5 months.[68] Plaster-cast immobilization lasted a total of 7. 8 months (range, 5 to 12 months). Acute wound infection had occurred in one spine incision and two iliac crest graft donor site incisions. One patient had a partial brachial plexus palsy that completely resolved. At a minimum follow-up of 18 months, 76 patients (95%) with 86 curves had solid fusions, an average maintained curve correction of 60% (67° pre-operative to 27° at follow-up), and an average curve correction loss of only 2.7°. Four patients (5%) with four curves had a pseudarthrosis with an average 13.3° loss of curve correction.

戈尔茨坦有足够的地位和统计数据来支持他的言论。3月，他发表了关于80名特发性脊柱侧凸患者的90处弯曲的研究，这些患者接受了哈灵顿器械矫形固定融合术，进行了自体骨移植，并在术后接受了里泽定位矫形石膏和平均时长3.5个月的床上制动。[68]石膏固定总共持续了7.8个月（样本时间跨度为5~12个月）。总共有一处脊柱切口和两处髂骨移植供区发生了急性伤口感染。一名患者的部分臂丛神经麻痹完全消失。在为期至少18个月的随访中，76名患者（95%）的86处弯曲实现了牢固融合，平均维持的矫正率为60%（术前67°，随访时27°），平均侧凸矫正度丢失仅为2.7°。有假关节形成的4名患者（5%）平均矫正度丢失为13.3°。

One of the half-day scientific sessions was held at Rancho Los Amigos Hospital where an anterior spine surgery seminar moderated by Jacquelin Perry featured presentations by Robert Winter on anterior approach[69] and Edward Simmons on biomechanics and Dwyer Instrumentation.[70] Other highlights of this SRS meeting included Wood Lovell's report of the morbidity and mortality committee's mortality data.[71] Thirty-seven cases had been submitted, and of the 34 with known causes of death, 17 (50%) were pulmonary system related. MacEwen reported on the twenty-two neurologically normal patients who had a neurological complication. Analyzed by paralysis extent, sixteen had complete paraplegia, three had partial paraplegia, and three had other neurological complications. Seven (44%) of the complete paraplegias had 50% to 100% recovery and nine (56%) had no recovery. Analyzed by treatment, nine of them had received posterior instrumentation and arthrodesis. Six of the nine had complete paraplegia, all at the T5-T8 level, and none had complete recovery. The other three had partial paraplegia and all recovered. Ten patients had been treated with preoperative halo-femoral traction, leaving three in a miscellaneous category. Analysis by diagnosis wasn't reported. Two neurological complication risk factors were noted: "significant" preoperative kyphosis and neurological changes in halo-femoral traction. Fewer than twenty members submitted mortality and/or morbidity data, and the denominator, the size of the pool of patients the morbidity and mortality numbers had come from, was unknown. Thus, the incidence could not be determined. Nickel reported that Tetsuya Tamaki, a Rancho fellow from Japan, and Leon Brooks were working on the possibility of spinal cord monitoring. Ron DeWald presented the development of a halo-hoop apparatus.[72] Blount reported on the sequence leading to the throat mold and ending iatrogenic mandible changes from the Milwaukee brace chin rest.[73] Elected to the executive committee were Dave Levine as secretary-treasurer-elect and at-large directors Bob Zuege from Milwaukee, Ted Waugh from Orange, California, and Bob Keiser from Coral Gables, Florida. Harrington's design of the SRS emblem was accepted. *See figure 10.4.*

Figure 10.4 ***Final SRS emblem.*** (***SRS Archives***)
图 10.4　最终的脊柱侧凸研究学会会徽(脊柱侧凸研究学会档案馆)

其中半天的学术交流环节——前路脊柱外科专题在兰乔洛杉米戈斯医院举行，由杰奎琳·佩里主持，在这次研讨会上主要是以罗伯特·温特前入路术式[69]的汇报以及爱德华·西蒙斯生物力学和德怀尔内固定器械[70]的汇报为主。此次脊柱侧凸研究学会会议的其他亮点包括伍德·洛弗尔有关发生率和死亡率委员会的死亡率数据汇报。[71]总共提交了37例病例，在已知死因的34例中，17例（50%）与呼吸系统有关。麦克尤恩汇报了22名神经系统正常但出现神经系统并发症的患者。按瘫痪程度来分析，16名为完全性截瘫，3名为部分截瘫，3名为其他神经系统并发症。7名完全性截瘫（44%）恢复了50%~100%，9名（56%）没有恢复。通过对他们的治疗手段进行分析，其中9人接受了后路器械矫形固定融合术。9人中有6人完全截瘫，均为T5-T8水平，没有人完全恢复。其余3人为部分截瘫，均已恢复。没有患者接受术前halo股骨牵引治疗，剩下3名属于其他类别。通过诊断进行的分析并没有在会上进行汇报。两大神经系统并发症的风险因素被着重强调出来：术前“显著”的脊柱后凸畸形和halo股骨牵引中神经症状变化。不到20名会员提交了发生率和死亡率的相关数据资料，并且计算发生率和死亡率的分母，也就是患者的规模，他们并不清楚，因此无法确定发生率。尼克尔报道说一位来自日本的专科医生田崎也和利昂·布鲁克斯正在研究脊髓监测的可能性。罗恩·德沃尔德介绍了halo环装置的发展。[72]布朗特汇报了使用密尔沃基支具下颌托导致的喉咙不适以及最终导致医源性下颌骨改变的一系列事件。[73]作为秘书兼财务主管候选人的戴夫·莱文、来自密尔沃基的名誉主任鲍勃·祖格、来自加利福尼亚州橘郡的泰德·沃和来自佛罗里达州科勒尔盖布尔斯的鲍勃·凯泽被选为执行委员会委员。哈灵顿设计的脊柱侧凸研究学会会徽被采纳了。（图10.4）

In 1969 the first Harrington-Zimmer correspondence of consequence was not exchanged until November when he requested right- and left-hand nonratchet hooks, initially with a #1251 hook body (1/4"-diameter rod compatible) and later with #1256 (3/16"-diameter rod compatible) and #1259 (1/8"-diameter rod compatible) hook bodies.[74,75] The important problems he saw in need of addressing were "spine fractures as well as for the spina bifida field Which is growing greater and greater in demand."

1969年，哈灵顿和捷迈公司之间的第一次通信直到11月才开始，当时他要求左侧和右侧的非棘齿钩，最初使用#1251钩体（兼容直径为1/4英寸的棒）后来使用#1256钩体（兼容直径为3/16英寸的棒）和#1259钩体（兼容直径为1/8英寸的棒）。[74,75]他认为需要解决的重要问题是“（器械）在脊柱骨折以及脊柱裂领域的需求越来越大”。

Scoliosis 1969, the eighth annual issue of his academic pursuits, opened with quotations from Lent C. Johnson's "Physiological Response of Bone and Cartilage to

Stress."[76] His thesis considered bone as a complex organ rather than a tissue or material and that its biological function as a storehouse of calcium for homeostatic mechanisms had taken precedence over its mechanical function. Bone in its organismal context he saw as part of the mesodermal continuum dependent upon an extensive blood and nerve supply subject to local control. He related his viewpoint to skeletal growth, decay, and myeloproliferative disease.

《脊柱侧凸1969》，是哈灵顿学术研究的第八本年度出版物，开篇引用了伦特·C. 约翰逊的“骨与软骨对压力的生理反应。”[76]在他的论文中，他认为骨骼是一个复杂的器官，而不是组织或材料，并且其生物学功能（作为自动稳态机制的钙库）优先于其机械功能。他认为骨骼在其组织环境中是部分中胚层的延续体，有广泛的血液和神经分布，并受局部因素调控。他将他的观点与骨骼发育、衰老以及骨髓增生性疾病联系在了一起。

Harrington followed with a discussion of "Pathological Response of Bone to Instrumentation."[77] The issues covered were electrolysis, infection, erosion, hook dislocation, rod fracture, hook cutout, and pseudarthrosis. Corroded implants from a patient were studied, and the conclusion drawn was that "mechanical breakdown, creating a dissimilarity in metals, sets up the electrolytic process." Infection had occurred in 6 of approximately 1,100 cases. In five of them it did not appear to impair healing, and the implants were removed to eliminate drainage. The sixth case ended in tragedy. A sixteen-year-old girl with idiopathic scoliosis had an unremarkable hospital course. About four days after discharge she developed a high fever, was hospitalized, her cast removed revealing a normal incision, and antibiotics were started. Within the next twenty-four hours a small, fluctuant area developed in the wound from which a few drops of pus were aspirated. From that point she deteriorated and died a day later of extensive staphylococcus septicemia. It was felt that prophylactic antibiotics prior to surgery and for the first five postoperative days had given a false sense of security.

哈灵顿随后讨论了“骨对内植物器械的病理反应”。[77]所涵盖的问题包括电解、感染、侵蚀、脱钩、断棒、钩断裂和假关节形成。他研究了从一名患者身上获得的腐蚀内植物，得出的结论是“力学损坏会导致金属间的差异，从而建立电解过程”。大约1 100例病例中有6例发生感染。其中5例似乎并没有引起伤口难愈，内植物被去除以终止伤口引流。第六例发生感染的患者最终遗憾去世。一名患有特发性脊柱侧凸的16岁女孩在住院期间并无大碍，但大约在出院后第四天，发高烧并住院治疗，去除她的石膏后发现切口正常，于是开始使用抗生素治疗。在接下来的24小时内，刀口处出现了一个小的、具有波动感的区域，从中吸出了几滴脓液。从那时起，她的病情开始恶化，并在一天后死于广泛的葡萄球菌败血症。术前预防性应用抗生素和术后连续5天使用抗生素给人一种虚假的安全感。

Hook erosion into the bone sites had been a concern from their first use in about 1951. However, it had been minimized by postoperative immobilization in a molded body cast for five to six months and the addition of an arthrodesis. Hook dislocation had been prevented by placing the lower distraction hook over the superior border of the lower instrumented vertebra and by placing the Moe keel hook #1252 into a notch cut into the inferior facet of the upper instrumented vertebra. On the compression side the end hooks had a tendency to slip laterally. This could have been counteracted by leaving the costotransverse ligament intact at the upper end and by placing the lower hook into the lamina of T12 or L1. Hook cutout was mainly related to technique deficiencies. Interestingly, if the compression system had to be abandoned, he recommended protection of the distraction rod with a Risser localizer cast or Milwaukee brace for six to nine months. Rod fractures earlier than eighteen months postoperative had become rare as the result of rod design strengthening and the addition of arthrodesis. Although he did not mention casting, he offered the view that "when fracture occurs eighteen months or more after surgery, there is no detrimental effect in 98% of these cases." If a broken rod was to be removed, he left the hooks unless the patient requested their removal. Harrington addressed pseudarthrosis last and repeated his reservations about the capacity of a posterior fusion to control the ongoing anterior column growth as well as the underlying scoliosis process. He commented that "an interbody fusion is almost mandatory at the apex of severe curves and particularly so to supplement instrumentation in severe salvage operations." He did not mention fresh autogenous iliac grafts or grafts of any type.

在大约1951年钩被首次使用之后，植入钩的部位的骨骼腐蚀一直是一个问题。但是，通过术后使用躯体石膏进行5~6个月的固定并附加融合术可以大大减少这种情况的发生。通过将下撑开钩放置在下固定椎的上缘并将#1252莫氏翻转钩放置在上位固定椎的下关节面的凹口处，以防止脱钩。压缩侧的端钩有侧方滑动的趋势。这可以通过在上端保留完整的肋横突韧带，并将下撑开钩放置在T12或L1的椎板中来抵消。钩断裂主要与技术欠缺有关。有趣的是，如果不得已放弃压缩系统，哈灵顿建议用里泽局部定位石膏或密尔沃基支具保护撑开棒6~9个月。因为棒自身的强度提升同时外加术中应用融合术，术后18个月内发生断棒的情况十分少见。虽然他没有提到石膏，但是他提出了“当断棒发生在手术后18个月或更长时间时，98%的病例都不会有不利影响”。如果需要去除断裂的棒，除非患者本人要求去除钩，否则他不会连同钩一起去除。哈灵顿在最后谈及假关节，并重申他对用后路融合术来控制脊柱前柱生长和潜在脊柱侧凸进程的保留意见。他评论道：“椎体融合对于严重侧凸的顶椎来说是必要的。特别在严重脊柱侧凸的治疗方案中，器械辅助支持也是必要的。”他并没有提及新鲜自体髂骨移植或其他方式的骨移植。

In the last section of *Scoliosis 1969* Harrington provided a comprehensive and detailed description of his approach to the scoliotic problem.[78] Two important features of this lengthy section warrant further detail. First, patients with post-polio trunk muscle weakness and the resulting scoliosis had decreased pulmonary function. In addition, surgery temporarily decreased pulmonary function by about 50%. As a result, quite specific pulmonary function parameters were established for stratifying the extent of pulmonary preparation a patient should have prior to scoliosis surgery and the postoperative regimen.[79] For example, patients with 50% or less predicted normal vital capacity usually had elevated hemoglobin and electrocardiogram changes indicating chronic hypoxia. Preoperative preparation involved two months or more of increasing acclimation to an iron lung. Progress was measured by the decrease in hemoglobin levels, an improved vital capacity, and electrocardiograms. Postoperative care included respiratory support with the iron lung, aerosol mist, frequent supervised coughing, and turning. Second, he provided a detailed description of his dissection technique exposing the spine for instrumentation and arthrodesis. This phase of the operation had not been included in his earlier writings about his instrumentation and arthrodesis techniques.[80]

在《脊柱侧凸1969》的最后一章中，哈灵顿对他治疗脊柱侧凸的手段进行了全面而详细的描述。在冗长的描述过程中，有两个重要特点需要进一步说明。[78]第一，脊髓灰质炎后躯干肌肉无力导致的脊柱侧凸患者肺功能会下降。此外，手术使肺功能暂时性降低约50%。因此，设立了非常具体的肺功能参数，用于给病人在术前和术后方案中进行肺功能程度分级。[79]例如，预测正常肺活量为50%及以下的患者，通常有血红蛋白升高和心电图的改变，表明其存在慢性缺氧。术前准备包括两个月或两个月以上对呼吸机的适应时间。呼吸机的作用是通过血红蛋白水平的降低、肺活量的改善和心电图的改善来衡量的。术后处理包括呼吸机辅助通气、雾化剂雾化、时常监督患者咳嗽咳痰并翻身。第二，他提供了在进行器械植入和融合时脊柱显露技术的详细步骤。他之前发表的刊物都没有包含他的器械植入和融合技术这一手术过程。[80]

Nineteen seventy had a promising start for Harrington because he again gave his instructional course lecture at the AAOS annual meeting held that year in January in Chicago. He also apparently discussed three issues with Zimmer. He asked them to prepare a display board of his instrumentation that included a force indicating distractor. The subject of child-sized implants was also mentioned. Follow-up correspondence from James F. Bennett at Zimmer arrived soon afterwards.[81] He asked if the force indicating distractor recently described by Nachemson and Elfstrom[82] was the type of measuring device he wanted illustrated on the display board, and Harrington replied that it was. He also stated that the child-sized instruments he had referred to were already being made by Zimmer and that Oswaldo Campos was using them, implying that Bennett needed to check within the company.[83] The Zimmer marketing committee approved the display board, and the fine details were worked out in three letter exchanges. The finished display board was delivered to Harrington in October 1970.[84] In June 1971 he wrote, "We have used the demonstration exhibit that you had made for me extensively and it has proved quite an asset in teaching visiting physicians."[85]

1970 年对哈灵顿而言有一个充满希望的开端，因为他在当年 1 月于芝加哥举行的美国骨科医师学会年会上再次进行了教学课程讲座。他甚至还与捷迈讨论了三个议题。他要求他们为他的器械准备一个展示板，其中包括一个显示撑开力的指示器。其间还提到了儿童内植物的尺寸问题。捷迈公司詹姆斯·F. 班尼特的跟踪信件很快就收到了。[81]捷迈询问哈灵顿，纳切姆森和埃尔夫斯特龙[82]最近所描述的作用力指示器是不是他想要在展示板展示的测量设备，哈灵顿给予了肯定的回复。哈灵顿还表示，他所提到的符合儿童尺寸的器械已经由捷迈制造完成，奥斯瓦尔多·坎波斯正在使用它们，这意味着班尼特需要在公司内部进行检查。[83]捷迈营销委员会批准了展示板的请求，并在三封信件往来后制订了细节。完成的展示板于 1970 年 10 月交付给了哈灵顿。[84] 1971 年 6 月，他写道："我们广泛使用了您为我们制作的演示展品，事实证明它对于教授来访的医生很有帮助。"[85]

Harrington had not practiced since his heart attack in November 1968, and the prospects for returning to it must have seemed dim. Thus, in March 1970 he wrote

Zimmer asking that all future royalty checks, beginning with the first quarter of 1970, be sent directly to him at his home address,[86] a request supported by Spencer.[87] By June 1970 Harrington wrote Hite, "We are still feeling better and better." He had three things on his mind.[88] First, he inquired about the small offset experimental hooks he had ordered in November 1969 (1/4"-diameter compatible) and December (3/16"- and 1/8"-diameter compatible). Second, he told Hite that the nuts for the 3/16"-diameter threaded compression rod (#1257) were not big enough to prevent recess of the rod into the 1/4"-diameter rod compatible distraction hook with the keel (#1252) as was being used for high-grade spondylolisthesis reduction. Third, Harrington announced his intent to start a research project involving distraction rod placement in baboons and shared his thoughts about downsizing the implants for the experiments. Hite responded that the request for offset hooks had gotten misplaced, "perhaps because of passing through too many hands."[89] Zimmer's special production director had assured Hite that the twenty-four hooks and twelve nuts would be made and promptly shipped.

哈灵顿自 1968 年 11 月心脏病发作后便没有进行过临床工作，重返手术台的希望渺茫。因此，在 1970 年 3 月，他写信给捷迈，要求从 1970 年第一季度开始，将之后所有的版税支票直接寄到他的家庭住址，[86]斯宾塞也支持哈灵顿的这一要求。[87]到 1970 年 6 月，哈灵顿写信给海特："我们仍然感觉越来越好。"他心里一直想着三件事情。[88]首先，他询问了他在 1969 年 11 月（兼容直径 1/4 英寸）和 12 月（兼容直径 3/16 英寸和直径 1/8 英寸）订购的小曲柄试验钩。其次，他告诉海特，用于直径 3/16 英寸螺纹压缩棒（#1257）的螺母不够大，无法防止棒嵌入于直径 1/4 英寸撑开钩内，而撑开钩是在严重椎体滑脱复位中使用到的，与龙骨（#1252）兼容。最后，哈灵顿宣布他打算开始一项在狒狒体内放置撑开棒的研究项目，并分享了他有关缩小实验内植物尺寸的想法。海特回应："也许是因为这个需求经过了太多人的手，因此对曲柄钩的要求被随意搁置了。"[89]捷迈的特别生产总监向海特保证，24 个钩和 12 个螺母将立刻制造完毕并及时发货。

Harrington's professional travel dramatically increased in 1970, up to five from his sole trip in 1969. In addition to the January trip to Chicago, he presented a talk on high-grade spondylolisthesis at the Texas Orthopedic Association meeting at Salado Springs in September and the following month one on "Variations in the Flexibility of the Idiopathic Scoliotic Curve" at the Western Orthopedic Association meeting in Port-land, Oregon. The real increase, however, came in overseas travel, with attendance at the Fifth

Combined Meeting of Orthopedic Associations in Sydney, Australia, April 11 - 17.[90] There he was the assigned discussant of Alan Dwyer's report on "Anterior Instrumentation in Scoliosis." Based on 70 patients Dwyer claimed the advantages of his procedure as rapid convalescence, fusion of fewer spinal segments, and avoidance of spinal cord stretching. He also noted that the blood supply to the cord did not appear to be at risk. Dwyer reported that the twenty-seventh patient operated on had permanent paraplegia from a misdirected screw. One other patient had temporary paraplegia. Harrington raised the possibility of increased complications from the anterior approach, particularly if relatively bulky metal devices were near vital structures.[91] The trip lasted from April 1 to May 7 and included pre-meetings in Auckland, New Zealand, and post-meetings in Melbourne, Brisbane, Singapore, Kuala Lumpur, and Hong Kong. Harrington took part in the scientific sessions of these meetings. The trip ended with three days in Japan. Harringtons expenses for the 37-day tip were $1,106, of which 51,000 came from the Harrington Surgical Royalty Fund and the remainder from his pocket.[92] In November he traveled to the United Kingdom and contributed an unusual case report of resolving scoliosis, which was published the following year. But, his most important meeting of 1970 was that of the Scoliosis Research Society.

1970 年，哈灵顿的职业旅行次数显著增加，从 1969 年的唯一一次旅行增加到了五次。除了 1 月份的芝加哥之行，他还于 9 月在萨拉多斯普林斯举行的得克萨斯骨科学会会议上发表了关于严重脊柱滑脱的演讲，随后的一个月在俄勒冈州波特兰举行的西部骨科学会会议上，他还发表了“特发性脊柱侧凸弯曲的柔韧性变化”的演讲。然而，职业旅行次数真正的增长来自海外旅行，他出席了 4 月 11 日至 17 日在澳大利亚悉尼举行的第五届骨科学会联合会议。[90]在那里，他被委派讨论艾伦·德怀尔关于“脊柱侧凸前路器械”的汇报。基于对 70 名患者的分析，德怀尔声称他的手术具有恢复迅速、脊柱融合节段更少和避免脊髓牵拉的优点。他还指出，脊髓的血液供应似乎并没有被危及。德怀尔还说，第 27 名接受手术的患者因螺钉使用不当造成永久性截瘫。另一名患者出现暂时性截瘫。哈灵顿提出进行前路手术术后并发症会增加的可能性，特别是如果相对笨重的金属装置靠近重要器官结构。[91]这次旅程从 4 月 1 日持续到 5 月 7 日，包括在新西兰奥克兰的会前会议和在墨尔本、布里斯班、新加坡、吉隆坡和香港的会后会议。哈灵顿参加了这些会议的学术讨论环节。在日本三天后这次旅程告一段落。哈灵顿 37 天的旅行费用为 1 106 美元，其中 1 000 美元来自哈灵顿的手术版税基金，其余部分由他本人垫付。[92] 11 月，他前往英国并提交了一份罕见的脊柱侧凸治疗的病例报告，该报告于次年发表。但是，他在 1970 年最重要的会议是脊柱侧凸研究学会的年会。

The annual meeting of the SRS had rapidly become the premier gathering of the year for the scoliosis management community. Its fifth meeting was held on September 10-12, 1970, in Toronto under the presidency of John Hall.[93] In addition to published abstracts,[94] audio recordings of the meeting were made, transcribed, and preserved as the proceedings.[95] Because of cost, this third year of the recordings was also the last. Attendance set a new record with 147 registered for the scientific program, a total swelling to 190 with spouses. The meeting had evolved to two and a half days long with about an hour each for two business sessions where most committee reports were given. The remaining fifteen hours were devoted to scientific papers and discussions. Instructional lectures and technical demonstrations were not usually part of the program since those in attendance were generally the thought and practice leaders and those who weren't were expected to utilize visitations and other means to increase their knowledge and skill if they planned to continue treating scoliosis and other spine deformities. One or two dinners brought everyone together socially. The general themes of the meeting were disease, deformity, and therapy. The subthemes were disease cause and natural history; deformity type, severity, and natural history; and therapy indications and contraindications, complications, and outcomes. Each subtheme had many different knowledge deficiencies, resulting in an almost limitless number of topics worthy of study. Harrington Spine Instrumentation may have been the immediate impetus for the formation of the SRS, but it was the breadth and depth of spine deformities in particular and spine disorders in general that caused it to flourish. Harrington Instrumentation had opened a Pandora's box.

脊柱侧凸研究学会年会已迅速成为脊柱侧凸治疗界一年中最重要的聚会。1970 年 9 月 10 到 12 日，第五届年会在多伦多举行，约翰·霍尔作为主席出席。[93] 除了已公布的摘要，[94]会议还进行了录音、转述，并作为会议记录保存下来。[95]由于成本问题，第三年的录音记录也成了最后一次。出席会议的人数创造了新的纪录，有 147 人登记参加，连同与会人员的配偶，总人数达到了 190 人。会议持续了两天半，举行了两个大约一小时的会员商务会议，大部分委员会报告都在会议上发表。剩下的 15 个小时专门用于分享学术论文和交流讨论，教学课程讲座和技术演示通常不包括在内。因为出席的人一般都是思想和实践的领导者，而那些没有出席的人如果打算继续从事脊柱侧凸和其他脊柱畸形的治疗，则应利用访问进修和其他方式来增加他们的知识，提高他们的技能。一两顿晚餐可以让大家聚在一起进行社交活动。会议的总主题是疾病、畸形和治疗。子主题有病因和自然史；畸形类型、严重程度和自然史；治疗的适应证、禁忌证、并发症和疗效。每个子主题都存在许多不同的尚未明确的知识领域，因此几乎有无限的主题值得研究。哈灵顿脊柱内固定器械可能是脊柱侧凸研究学会成立的直接动力，但正是脊柱疾病，特别是脊柱畸形的广度和深度，才使其蓬勃发展，就像是哈灵顿脊柱内固定器械打开了潘多拉魔盒。

The meeting opened with a business session during which Secretary-treasurer Kane reported that the SRS was on sound financial footing with a year-round treasury balance of about $1,000. Arrangements had been made for the Orthopedic Research and Education Foundation to accept and earmark donations for SRS use. The long-term goal of two traveling fellows during the year had been realized, although financing them had been a strain. Prospects for affiliation with the much larger American Academy of Orthopedic Surgeons (AAOS) were moving forward, a devclopment that would greatly increase the SRS's educational opportunities. The dilemma about the proper size of the organization was briefly described: small enough for frank, candid discussions and large enough to educate as many people as possible about scoliosis. Member participation in the society was expected, and later in the meeting the first effort to create a data base, utilizing punch cards, was introduced. Member participation was considered compulsory, based on Article Ill, item 7 of the constitution as it was originally adopted: "Membership may be terminated by the Executive Committee if the member shows no active participation in the activities of the Society for two consecutive years."[96]

会议以商务会议开始，秘书兼财务主管凯恩报告说，脊柱侧凸研究中心的财务状况良好，全年的财政盈余约为 1 000 美元。骨科研究和教育基金会已经设立，并接受捐款以用于脊柱侧凸研究学会。在这一年中，两名访问学者的长期目标已经实现，尽管为他们提供资金仍较困难。加入更大的机构——美国骨科医师学会的目标正在推进，这将大大增加脊柱侧凸研究中心的教育机会。会议简要介绍了关于确定组织规模的难题：小到可以进行坦诚的讨论，大到可以影响尽可能多的人了解脊柱侧凸。会议期望会员能积极参与到学会的活动中来，并在会议后期首次利用打孔卡片建立会员数据库。根据最初通过的章程第三条第七项，会员的参与被认为是强制性的："如果会员连续两年没有积极参加学会的活动，执行委员会可以取消其会员资格”。[96]

A nominating committee was formed to propose a slate of president-elect and four executive committee members. The terminology committee had no new activity to re-port, but it anticipated cooperating with the AAOS's larger terminology standardization effort. The morbidity and mortality committee was organizing a data gathering and analyzing effort based on the Keysort Card System. This committee had still not functioned as such because up to this point there hadn't been enough material to consider. The co-chairs, Lovell for mortality and MacEwen for morbidity, had continued to gather data and reported it. Sixty percent (45 of 75) active members had submitted mortality data, and the rate turned out to be about 1% (54 of 5,500). The most common causes of death were pulmonary infection or failure in fifteen, other pulmonary-related problems in eight, and cardiac arrest in eleven. The mortality rate was highest in patients with a neuropathic scoliosis, principally post-polio scoliosis. The morbidity data were still limited to neurological changes. Twenty-two members had submitted data on 3,000 cases with a neurological complication incidence of 0.7%. The report was still very preliminary, and not all of the case material had been analyzed. However, patients with a congenital etiology, especially with kyphoscoliosis, were especially at risk, and for patients having distraction instrumentation, it seemed reasonable to immediately remove the rod and hooks.

会议同时成立一个提名委员会，提出候任主席和四名执行委员会成员名单。术语委员会没有新的活动要报告，但预计将与美国骨科医师学会的大型术语标准化工作进行合作。发生率和死亡率委员会正在组织一项基于键控卡片系统的数据收集和分析工作。这个委员会仍然没有发挥其作用，因为到目前为止，还没有足够的材料可以参考。两名联合主席，洛弗尔负责死亡率，麦克尤恩负责发生率，他们继续收集数据并进行报告。60%（45/75）的活跃会员提交了死亡数据，死亡率约为1%（54/5 500）。最常见的死亡原因是肺部感染或衰竭（15例），其他肺部相关问题（8例），心搏骤停（11例）。神经源性脊柱侧凸患者的死亡率最高，主要是脊髓灰质炎后的脊柱侧凸。发生率数据仍局限于神经源性脊柱侧凸。22个成员提交了3 000例病例的数据，神经系统并发症的发生率为0.7%。该报告仍然是非常初步的，因为它并没有对所有的病例资料进行分析。然而，有先天性病因的患者，特别是脊柱侧后凸的患者，出现这些并发症的风险尤其大，对于应用撑开器械的患者，立即去除棒和钩似乎是合理的。

The scientific program featured 32 presentations (the same number as the year before) that could be broadly categorized as fifteen evaluative, three nonsurgical, twelve surgical, and two laboratory research. The biomechanics of Harrington Instrumentation was the subject of the first three presentations. Based on clinical usage, the most vulnerable part of the construct initially was the lower distraction hook-bone interface. This had been solved in January 1962 by moving the hook to a supralaminar position.[97] This moved the most vulnerable site to the upper distraction hook fixation to the relatively weak thoracic facet/lamina bone interface where hook dislodgement and cutout were the most common modes of failure.

科学项目共有32个报告（与前一年相同），可大致分为15个评估性报告、3个非手术性报告、12个手术性报告和2个实验室研究报告。哈灵顿内固定器械的生物力学研究是前三个报告的主题。根据临床应用情况，最初该结构最脆弱的部分是下撑开钩—骨界面。1962年1月，通过将钩子移到椎板上缘位置，这个问题得到了解决。[97]这把上部撑开钩固定最脆弱的部位移到了相对较弱的胸椎小关节/椎板骨界面，而钩子脱落和切割成为最常见的失败的内固定形式。

The first study presented was designed to better understand the variable loads on the rod and the possibilities for controlling them. "Intravital Wireless Telemetry of Axial Forces on Harrington Distraction Rods" had been performed in four teenage females with idiopathic scoliosis.[98,99] Twenty to 40 kiloponds of force were applied at the time of surgery.[100] Immediately after surgery, lifting and turning as well as coughing increased the load on the rod, putting the upper hook-bone junction at risk of failure. The load on the rod decreased fairly rapidly over the first hour and then more slowly, stabilizing at about one-third of the force applied at surgery. The load on the rod was decreased by both the Risser cast and even more by the Milwaukee brace with a decrease in both the standing and walking positions of about 5 kiloponds. About half of the relief was contributed by the two side straps. This reinforced the importance of the lateral force provided by the Milwaukee brace thoracic pad, which lowered the load on the mandible and occiput by about 1.86 kilograms (approximately 4 kiloponds).[101,102] The telemetry rod was replaced with a standard Harrington distraction rod at a second operation two to three weeks later, at which time the arthrodesis was done.

第一项研究的设计者是为了更好地了解棒上的可变载荷和更好地调节载荷的可能性。对4名患有特发性脊柱侧凸的女孩进行了“哈灵顿撑开棒活体内轴向力的无线遥测”。[98,99]结果显示在手术时施加了20~40千克的力。[100]棒上的载荷在第一个小时内下降得相当快，然后变得相对缓慢，最后稳定在手术时施力的三分之一左右。通过里泽石膏和密尔沃基支具的使用，棒上的载荷都有所下降，在患者处于站立和行走体位时都下降了约5千克力。约有一半的缓解是由两边的带子促成的。这支持了密尔沃基支具胸垫提供的侧向力的重要性，它将下颌骨和枕骨的载荷降低了大约1.86千克（大约4磅）。[101,102]在2到3周后的第二次融合术时，遥测杆被替换为标准的哈灵顿撑开棒。

The third study was focused on the upper distraction hook-bone interface.[103] The author first studied the distraction load to lamina failure of autopsy specimens. He found that children's posterior elements were weaker than adults, strength was gained as they aged to maturity, lumbar lamina were stronger than thoracic, and strength was related to the surface area of the attachment. After proving that methyl methacrylate polymerized in situ with specific precautions to decrease heat from the methyl methacrylate did not cause any adverse effects in experimental animals, the author had proceeded to successful clinical use. Work to design thoracic laminar hooks with greater bone contact surface area was progressing.

第三项研究的重点是上撑开钩—骨界面。[103]作者首先在椎板消失的情况下研究了尸检标本的撑开载荷。他发现，儿童的后柱结构比成人弱，随着年龄增长到成熟期，强度会增加，腰椎板强度比胸椎大，而强度与接触的表面积有关。在证明甲基丙烯酸甲酯在原位聚合并通过采取特定的预防措施，减少甲基丙烯酸甲酯的热量，不会对实验动物造成任何不良影响后，作者成功地进行了临床应用。设计具有更大骨接触面积的胸椎椎板钩的工作正在进行。

The middle paper in this session was a report on a serious attempt to modify and improve the basic Harrington design.[104] The authors had noted that it was possible to obtain further correction with Harrington Spine Instrumentation if a corrective lateral force was applied to the compression rod. To permit this, the authors had increased the distraction rod diameter from 1/4" to 5/16" and machined the connections to the end hooks to prevent rotation. A transverse loading tool was added to translate the convex compression rod toward the distraction rod. In the very lively discussion that followed, Harrington congratulated the authors on their excellent studies and presentations before reiterating the simplicity of his instrumentation and explaining most of the problems discussed as technique failings. He emphasized the correction and stability advantages of adding the compression instrumentation, which many surgeons did not do. His experience was that the compression added an average of 16% to the scoliosis correction. During the discussion, the possible dangers of overcorrection were mentioned but not further developed.

关于哈灵顿内固定术生物力学的第二篇论文是尝试改进哈灵顿基本设计的报告。[104]作者注意到，如果在压缩棒上施加一个矫正侧向力，就有可能用哈灵顿脊柱内固定器械获得进一步的矫正。为了做到这一点，作者将撑开棒的直径从1/4英寸增加到5/16英寸，并改良了与钩末端的连接，以防止旋转。增加了一个横向载荷工具，使凸形压缩杆向撑开棒方向移动。在随后非常热烈的讨论中，哈灵顿对作者出色的研究和演讲表示祝贺，并重申他的器械的简单性，解释所讨论的大多数问题是因为技术上的缺陷。他强调了增加压缩器械有矫形和稳定的优点，而许多外科医生并没有这样做。他的经验是，加压使得脊柱侧凸矫正率平均增加了16%。在讨论中还提到了过度矫正可能带来的危险，但没有进一步展开。

At least seven papers presented later in the meeting had direct bearing on the results and discussions of these first three presentations. One was Bob Gillespie's presentation of John Hall's case series of 220 patients with idiopathic scoliosis treated by Harrington Instrumentation and spine fusion.[105] The series, which included some young adults, had been operated on from 1961 to 1967 and followed a minimum of two years. Hall's operation included "a very thorough dissection of the spine, radical excision of the joints and a large quantity of autogenous bone." Follow-up care was a body cast and bed rest for three months, followed by ambulation in a body cast for three more months. Three patients (less than 2%) developed a pseudarthrosis, and all three had been fused to the sacrum. Thirteen patients (6%, 13 of 220) were considered to have an unsatisfactory result most often caused by too short instrumentation and fusion. Three patients had an unsatisfactory result because of infection. This relatively complication-free series substantiated Harrington's view that most problems were technique related. Further bolstering Harrington's comment was the presentation of Ron De Wald and Merle Schrodt titled "Errors in Judgment in the Treatment of Scoliosis."[106] This qualitative analysis of personal and referred patients revealed judgment errors that were assigned to seven groups, which were based on failure to do the following: fuse the correct curve, fuse at the correct level, make the correct diagnosis, recognize the late progression of secondary curves, stabilize the spine after laminectomy, manage conservatively, and observe. The presentation by Ed Simmons' group on "Biomechanical Studies with a Scoliosis Simulator" provided experimental support for the use of the compression rod.[107] In this simulated scoliosis model utilizing a calf spine, all correction obtained by a distraction rod was lost under compression loading to 66 pounds. Addition of a compression rod prevented all or most of the correction loss. These results were nearly as good as the more complicated and slightly larger Armstrong modification and considerably better than the anterior Dwyer Instrumentation.

在会议的后期，至少有7篇论文对前三个报告的结果和讨论有导向性作用。其中一篇是鲍勃·吉莱斯皮对约翰·霍尔通过哈灵顿器械和融合术治疗220名特发性脊柱侧凸患者的病例系列的介绍。[105]该病例系列包括一些年轻的成年人，他们在1961年到1967年进行了手术，且至少随访了两年。霍尔的手术包括“完全的脊柱切开分离，彻底的小关节切除，大量的自体骨移植”。后续处理方法是躯体石膏和卧床休息3个月，然后3个月活动佩戴躯体石膏。3名患者（不到2%）出现了假关节，这3名患者融合到骶骨。13名患者（6%，220名中的13名）效果不理想，最常见的原因是内固定和融合节段太短。3名患者因感染而导致不满意的结果。这个并发症相对少的研究报告证实了哈灵顿的观点，即大多数问题都与技术有关。罗恩·德·瓦尔德和梅尔·施罗德题为“脊柱侧凸治疗中的判断错误”的报告进一步支持了哈灵顿的观点。[106]对个人和转诊病人的定性分析显示，判断错误被分为七组，其依据是未能做到以下几点：融合正确的弯曲、在正确的节段融合、作出正确的诊断、认识到继发性弯曲的后期进展、稳定椎板切除术后的脊柱、保守治疗和观察。爱德华·西蒙斯团队关于“脊柱侧凸模拟器的生物力学研究”的报告为加压棒的使用提供了实验支持。[107]在这个利用小牛脊柱的模拟脊柱侧凸模型中，在压缩载荷为66磅的情况下，通过撑开棒获得的所有矫正都会丧失。增加一个压缩棒可以防止所有或大部分的矫正丢失。这些结果与更复杂、体积稍大的阿姆斯特朗改良方案一样好，并大大优于德怀尔内固定器械。

Fusion to the sacrum was emerging as a problem as shown in all three of Hall's patients with pseudarthrosis that had fusion attempt to the sacrum. This had been recognized by the Rancho Los Amigos group's series of 53 patients, most with an underlying neurological or muscular disease, whose long arthrodesis to the sacrum was immobilized with a halo-bilateral hip spica cast for six months.[108] This resulted in 30% serious hip problems, and the authors retreated to a postoperative halo-body cast. This solved the hip problems, but the rate of pseudarthrosis, which probably was not known at that point, was not commented on.

是否需要融合到骶骨是一个新出现的问题，霍尔的3名患者都在试图融合到骶骨的过程中出现了假关节。兰乔洛杉米戈斯团队的53名患者也出现这种情况，这些患者大多有潜在的神经或肌肉疾病，在骶骨融合术后用halo双侧髋人字石膏固定了半年。[108]这导致30%的患者髋关节出现了严重问题，作者退而求其次，采用术后的halo躯体石膏。这解决了髋关节的问题，但是没有人对假关节的发生率发表意见，因为假关节在当时可能并不为人所知。

The hazards of trunk elongation that the morbidity and mortality committee had identified continued to receive attention. The possibility of identifying patients at risk from vascular stretch was studied in a series of 45 patients who had preoperative thoracic angiograms.[109] In two patients the vascular pattern was so poor that scoliosis surgery was cancelled and conservative care was pursued in spite of the large curves. Of course, the actual extent of risk from surgery could not be determined. Also, a trunk elongation hazard of a different kind that had been briefly presented as a case report two years earlier was further delineated.[110] The complication had been around for a while and was known as the cast syndrome. In addition to traction, there was some suggestion this could have resulted from lumbar hyperlordosis, although that was disputed. The principal symptom was increasing vomiting, and the cause was high abdominal obstruction. It was seen infrequently and recognized to be associated with body casts. With the advent of Harrington Instrumentation, the complication became more frequent, and it became apparent that a body cast was not the principal cause. To better describe the condition, the authors titled their paper "The Spinal-Traction Syndrome-Arteriomesenteric Duodenal Obstruction Associated with Correction of Spinal Curvature: With Report of Three Illustrative Cases." The obstruction occurred in the lower portion of the duodenum, which was located in a somewhat immobile position in the retroperitoneum and subject to compression if the already acute angle between the superior mesenteric artery and aorta was further narrowed by whatever mechanism. By the time the authors full-length paper was complete, they had identified seventeen cases reported in the literature from 1878—1970. They had added thirteen new cases, all associated with treatment for scoliosis, of whom eleven had Harrington Instrumentation.[111] One Harrington Instrumentation patient died. Treatment began with removal of a traction cast or Milwaukee brace, if present.

Otherwise, positioning in the left lateral decubitus position or prone, nasogastric suction, and hydration were recommended. If this failed, surgical decompression was performed. If it appeared that the ligament of Treitz was holding the fourth portion of the duodenum in the arterial angle, division of the ligament could be tried. If this didn't adequately remove the obstruction, bypassing it with a duodenojejunostomy was recommended.

发生率和死亡率委员会发现的躯干延长的危险持续受到关注。在45名有术前胸腔血管造影的病人中，研究识别有血管拉长风险的病人的可能性。[109]有两名患者的血管情况非常差，以至于脊柱侧凸手术被取消，尽管弯曲角度很大，但还是采取了保守治疗。当然，手术的实际风险无法确定。另外，也进一步解释了两年前曾作为病例报告简要介绍过另一种躯干延长的危险。[110]这种并发症已经存在了一段时间，被称为石膏综合征。除了牵引之外，还有人认为这可能是腰椎过度前凸造成的，尽管这一观点有争议。这种并发症的主要症状是呕吐加剧，原因是高位腹部梗阻。这种情况并不常见，被认为是与躯体石膏有关。随着哈灵顿内固定器械的出现，这种并发症变得更加频发，而且很明显躯体石膏并不是导致这种并发症的主要原因。为了更好地描述这种情况，作者将他们的论文命名为《脊柱牵引综合征——与脊柱弯曲矫正有关的动脉——肠道十二指肠梗阻：三个典型病例报告》。梗阻发生在十二指肠的下部，它在腹膜后的位置有些不固定，如果肠系膜上动脉和主动脉之间已经很小的角度由于任何机制发生进一步缩小，十二指肠就会受到压迫。当作者的长篇论文完成时，他们已经在1878—1970年的文献中发现17例病例。他们又增加了13例新病例，这些病例都与脊柱侧凸的治疗有关，其中11例进行了哈灵顿内固定器械矫形术。[111]一名经哈灵顿器械治疗后的病人出现死亡。治疗开始时，如果有牵引石膏或密尔沃基支具，则需要全部拆除。其他情况，建议采取左侧卧位或俯卧位、经鼻胃管抽吸和补液。如果失败，则进行手术减压。如果发现韧带将十二指肠的第四节段固定在动脉角，可以尝试分割韧带。如果仍不能充分消除梗阻，建议用十二指肠空肠造口吻合术绕过梗阻段。

Concern about the neurological and gastrointestinal complications associated with vertical distraction and the need for greater spine instrumentation stability were stimulating interest in alternative corrective loading possibilities. The Armstrong modification of Harrington Instrumentation had added transverse, horizontal translation to vertical translation. In the last session of the meeting an alternative surgical innovation was presented based purely on transverse loading. Professor Robert Roaf of Liverpool had carefully studied the pathologic anatomy of the scoliosis deformity and concluded that rotation（in the transverse plane）was a major part of the deformity and was due to asymmetrical growth of the posterior articulations（similar to Harrington's views）and unequal horizontal muscle forces.[112] After he had concluded that direct application of horizontal corrective forces was the best way to correct rotation, he devised a plate and hooks instrumentation to accomplish this. He was criticized for his too short instrumentation and fusion, leaving out vertebrae still in the curve.

对与纵向撑开相关的神经和胃肠道并发症的关注，以及对用更好的器械稳定脊柱的需要，激发了人们对改变矫正载荷可能性的兴趣。哈灵顿器械的阿姆斯特朗改良版在垂直平移的基础上增加了横向、水平平移。在会议的最后一节，有人提出了一种纯粹基于横向载荷的替代性手术创新。利物浦的罗伯特·罗夫教授仔细研究了脊柱侧凸畸形的病理解剖学，并得出了结论：旋转（横断面）是畸形的主要部分，是由于后方小关节的不对称生长（类似于哈灵顿的观点）和不均衡的水平肌肉力量造成的。[112]他得出了直接应用水平矫正力是矫正旋转的最佳方法的结论后，设计了一个有钢板和钩的器械来达到这个目的。他的这一设计被指责器械和融合节段太短，忽略了仍然在弯曲内的椎体。

There were several other important surgically oriented presentations. Ken Leatherman reported on "Neurological Problems in Kyphosis and Scoliosis" and emphasized the importance of anterior decompression.[113] Arthur Yau described "The Treatment of Scoliosis in Hong Kong," illustrating treatment of very severe deformities with the halo-hoop and Harrington and Dwyer instrumentations in a challenging climate.[114]

还有其他几个重要的以手术为导向的报告。肯·莱瑟曼报告了“脊柱后凸和脊柱侧凸的神经性问题”，并强调了前方减压的重要性。[113]邱亚瑟描述了“香港脊柱侧凸的治疗”，阐明了如何在一个充满挑战的环境中使用 halo 环牵引、哈灵顿及德怀尔内固定器械治疗非常严重的畸形。[114]

The second scientific session featured three evaluative studies on the effects of scoliosis and its treatment on pulmonary function. The importance of this topic had been again underscored by the results of the second（1970）mortality report that documented postoperative respiratory complications as the most common cause of death. In the first study the authors reported on the importance of preoperative pulmonary evaluation and postoperative respiratory management of patients with severe thoracic scoliosis.[115] Patients with vital capacity and maximum voluntary ventilation values below 40% often required assisted ventilation for a period postoperatively. The operability of the most compromised patients was helped by their response to halo-femoral traction, a positive response indicating operability and a negative one inoperability. The second pulmonary study addressed the "Ventilation Perfusion Relationships Following Correction of Kyphoscoliosis."[116] At one year postoperative, pulmonary function studies had not changed. However, ventilation-perfusion was improved as evidenced by increased arterial oxygen and decreased lung dead space. Distribution of ventilation and perfusion was found to be normal up to 65°, but above 70° the distribution of ventilation and perfusion was permanently altered. The authors recommended repair of scoliosis before it passed 65°. The third study focused on "Pulmonary Function in Scoliosis One Year after Surgical Correction."[117] One hundred of John Hall's patients with scoliosis of varying types and degrees were studied preoperatively and at one year postoperatively, one year after surgery, including Harrington Instrumentation, pulmonary function had not changed. The authors concluded that long-term study would be necessary to learn if surgical correction prevented progression of pulmonary dysfunction. This finding and prospect possibly added to the sense of urgency that would develop around the school screening movement.

学术分会第二部分介绍了三项关于脊柱侧凸及其治疗对肺功能影响的评估性研究。第二次（1970年）死亡率的报告结果再次强调了这一主题的重要性，该报告记录了术后呼吸系统并发症是最常见的死亡原因。在第一份研究中，作者报告了严重胸椎侧凸患者进行术前肺部评估和术后呼吸处理的重要性。[115]肺活量和最大自主通气量低于40%的患者在术后一段时间内往往需要辅助通气。最脆弱的病人是否能手术是由halo股骨牵引对他们是否有效来帮助评估的，有效表示可以，无效则不能。第二项肺部研究涉及"脊柱侧后凸矫正术后的通气和灌注的关系"。[116]术后一年，肺功能没有变化。然而，通气-血流比值得到了改善，表现为动脉血氧的增加和肺部无效腔的减少。侧凸65°以内通气和灌注的分布是正常的，但是一旦超过70°，通气和灌注的分布就会发生永久性的改变。作者建议在脊柱侧凸超过65°之前对其进行手术。第三项研究关注"脊柱侧凸矫形手术后一年的肺功能"。[117]约翰·霍尔对100名不同类型和度数的脊柱侧凸患者术前和术后一年的研究表明，术后一年，包括应用哈灵顿内固定器械术后，肺功能没有变化。作者总结说，有必要进行长期研究以了解手术矫正是否能阻止肺功能障碍的进展。这一发现和前景可能增加了学校筛查行动的紧迫感。

Probably the best evaluative paper was delivered by Winter, Moe, and Wang on "Congenital Kyphosis."[118] It demonstrated the power of pooling case material too unusual to be meaningful individually. From the 101 cases collected, they were able to identify three types: I, failure of formation; II, failure of segmentation; and III, combination. They also offered concrete recommendations for evaluation and management: (1) deformity progressed with growth, (2) Milwaukee brace treatment was of little or no benefit, (3) fusion was the treatment of choice, (4) ideal treatment was posterior fusion at a young age, (5) anterior and posterior fusion were recommended for bigger deformities, (6) paralysis was frequent, especially high thoracic deformity, (7) anterior decompression was indicated for paralysis, (8) posterior laminectomy was contraindicated, and (9) traction was highly dangerous.

可能最好的评估论文是由温特、莫和沃发表的《先天性脊柱后凸》。[118]这篇论文展示了汇集病例材料的力量，因为这些材料太少，单独使用没有意义。收集的101例病例分为以下三种类型：一、形成障碍；二、分节不良；三、混合型。他们还提出了评估和治疗的具体建议。(1) 畸形随着生长而进展，(2) 密尔沃基支具治疗很少或没有好处，(3) 融合是可选的治疗方法，(4) 理想的治疗是在年轻时进行后路融合，(5) 对于较严重的畸形建议采用前后路融合，(6) 截瘫痪经常发生，特别是高位胸椎畸形，(7) 前方减压适用于截瘫患者，(8) 后路椎板切除术是禁忌证，(9) 牵引是非常危险的。

At the second business meeting Harrington was nominated and elected president-elect. The four at-lark: executive committee members elected to serve with him were Charles Herndon, John Moe, Jack Kennedy, and Frank Wilson.[119] In addition to serving on a discussion panel and being elected president-elect, he presented a paper for the first time in three years. His study, utilizing three-dimensional photography, was inspired by the stereophotogrammetry techniques that were employed to explore the surface of heavenly bodies.[120] He and co-author Herron had studied twenty normal subjects and twenty patients. The method was presented as a no-radiation method of screening for and documenting change in trunk shape. The presentation did not generate much discussion. Nevertheless, this SRS meeting must have buoyed his spirits. The Canadians in general and John Hall in particular had been early and steadfast supporters, and Hall's clinical studies provided important validation of the usefulness of Harrington Instrumentation.

在第二次会员商务会议上，哈灵顿被提名并当选为主席。与他一起任职的四位执行委员会成员是查尔斯·赫恩顿、约翰·莫、杰克·肯尼迪和弗兰克·威尔逊。[119]除了担任专家讨论小组成员和当选为候任主席，他还在三年内首次提交了一篇论文。他受到了立体摄影测量技术的启发，在研究中采用了三维摄影技术。[120]他和共同作者赫伦研究了20名正常人和20名病人。该方法是一种用于筛查和记录躯干形状变化的无辐射方法。该报告没有引起很多讨论。尽管如此，这次脊柱侧凸研究学会的会议一定让他精神振奋。加拿大人，特别是约翰·霍尔，是他早期坚定的支持者，霍尔的临床研究为哈灵顿内固定器械的实用性提供了重要的验证。

Harrington arrived home to find that TIRR had received the twenty-four offset hooks and twelve wider nuts with a Zimmer invoice dated September 10, 1970, for \$532.19.[121] He wrote Hite on October 12, enclosing a copy of the invoice.[122] "This comes as quite a surprise. Would you please inform me if this procedure is correct and if we can expect a bill for all experimental designs? I had not been informed of this before." Bennett replied for Zimmer that an error had been made and the invoice would be cancelled.[123] He explained that the surgeon was not usually billed for experimental instrumentation and implants but was for instruments or implants which had to be specially modified. In the last Zimmer correspondence of the year, Bennett reported that the "right-handed" outrigger would be made available on a special order basis only and that the larger 3/8"-nut for the 3/16"-diameter threaded compression rod (#1257) would be added to the catalog.[124] This outrigger was needed for left apex thoracic curves and also for spondylolisthesis reduction.

哈灵顿到家后发现，得克萨斯州康复与研究中心收到了24个偏移钩和12个较宽的螺母以及一张日期为1970年9月10日的捷迈发票，金额为532.19美元。[121]他于10月12日写信给海特，附上了发票的副本。[122]“这相当让人惊讶。你能告诉我这个程序是否正确，我们是否可以期待所有实验设计的账单？我之前没有被告知此事。”班尼特代表捷迈回答，流程出现了错误，发票将被取消。[123]他解释说，外科医生通常不会为实验性器械和内植物开具账单，而是为必须进行特别改良的器械或内植物开具账单。在捷迈今年给哈灵顿的最后一封信中，班尼特说，“右利手”外撑开器将只在特殊订单的基础上提供，和直径3/16英寸的螺纹压缩杆（#1257）配套的更大的3/8英寸螺母将被添加到目录中。[124]这种外撑开器需要用于左侧胸弯顶椎，也需要用于脊柱滑脱复位。

Scoliosis 1970, Harrington's ninth annual edition of his research endeavors, had five entries. The first two, "Spine Analysis of the Idiopathic Curve" and "The Mechanics of the Idiopathic Curve," were condensed from his 1968 AOA thesis, "Spine Analysis," detailing his effort to develop a valid and reliable method of quantifying spine deformity using standing 36" anteroposterior X-rays of the spine.[125] The third entry, "Variations in the Flexibility of the Idiopathic Scoliotic Curve,": was conducted to determine the effect of patient age and curve magnitude on surgical correction.[126] Fifty female patients were studied preoperative with a prone lying posteroanterior radiographs and standing pre-and postoperative anteroposterior radiographs to compare percent curve flexibility and correction. The data permitted the limited conclusion that optimum surgical correction was obtained in curves less than 60° in patients fifteen to twenty years old. The fourth entry, "The Possible Etiology of Idiopathic Scoliosis: A Case Report," was inspired by an observation attributed to A.I. Kazmin that apical intervertebral disc changes with convex displacement of the nucleus may have been more important than bone changes in the production of idiopathic scoliosis.[127] Harrington would present this case report at the SRS's 1971 annual meeting. The fifth entry, "Three-Dimensional Photography in the Detection, Evaluation and Documentation of Structural Abnormalities," was the one he had presented at the annual meeting in 1970.[128] The following May he presented this paper to the orthopaedic division of the Texas Medical Association meeting held in Houston. It was not a technique that generated interest.

《脊柱侧凸 1970》是哈灵顿的第九本年度研究成果，共有五个条目。前两个条目，“特发性脊柱侧凸脊柱弯曲分析”和“特发性脊柱侧凸脊柱弯曲的力学”，是从他 1968 年的美国骨科学会论文《脊柱分析》中浓缩出来的，详细描述了他为开发一种有效和可靠的方法，利用站立位 36 英寸脊柱正位 X 光片对脊柱畸形进行量化付出的努力。[125]第三个条目，“特发性脊柱侧凸弯曲柔韧性变化”，是为了确定患者年龄和弯曲度大小对手术矫正的影响。[126]对 50 名女性患者进行术前俯卧后前位 X 光片和术前术后站立前后位 X 光片的研究，以比较弯曲柔韧性和矫正率。从这些数据可以得出有限的结论，即在 15 至 20 岁的病人中，小于 60°的弯曲可以获得最佳的手术矫正。第四个条目，“特发性脊柱侧凸的可能病因：一个病例报告”，灵感来自 A. I. 卡兹明的观察，即在特发性脊柱侧凸的产生中，顶椎椎间盘的变化和髓核的凸侧移位的影响可能比骨骼变化更大。[127]哈灵顿将在 1971 年的脊柱侧凸研究学会年会上提交这份病例报告。第五个条目是他在 1970 年年度会议上呈现的文章《三维摄影在结构异常的检测、评估和记录中的应用》。[128]第二年

5 月，他在休斯敦举行的得克萨斯医学会骨科分会上提交了这篇论文。但是这并不是一项能引起兴趣的技术。

Nineteen seventy-one seemed to get off to a slow start, probably because the annual meeting of the AAOS was held several weeks later than usual. Before leaving to participate, Harrington took care of some important business. For the last four quarters at his request he had personally received the royalty checks from Zimmer. Since there was no visible end to his disability in sight, Harrington took steps to receive the checks for as long as they lasted. On March 5 he wrote the "Royalties Division" at Zimmer to make this change permanent.[129] He noted that after his heart attack he could not return to private practice and needed royalties to bolster his reduced income. To close his royalty account at Baylor, he requested that Zimmer notify A.O. Johnson, treasurer of the Baylor College of Medicine, of the date the checks started coming directly to him. He also asked that a statement be made that Baylor's name would not be used in the future in connection with Harrington Instrumentation, while acknowledging that this had not been done in the past. He closed expressing his thanks and commenting that "the checks are indeed appreciated." Spencer wrote Johnson a note that he agreed and that the account should be closed then or when the funds were depleted.[130] Harrington must have begun wondering how long the checks could be expected to continue. There were no patents and no royalty duration stipulations in the 1960 agreement with Zimmer. It would be a while before he would know the company's attitude on the duration of his royalty payments.

1971 年似乎有一个缓慢的开始，可能是因为美国骨科医师学会的年会比往常晚了几个星期举行。在参加会议之前，哈灵顿处理了一些重要的事务。在过去的四个季度里，应他的要求，他在家中收到了捷迈的版税支票。由于他的症状没有好转，哈灵顿采取了措施，以确保他会一直收到这些支票。3 月 5 日，他写信给捷迈的"版税部门"，要求作出永久性改变。[129]他指出，心脏病发作后，他无法回到私人诊所，需要版税来支撑他减少的收入。为了关闭他在贝勒的版税账户，他要求捷迈公司通知贝勒医学院的财务主管 A. O. 约翰逊版税支票直接移交给他的日期。他还发表声明称今后在哈灵顿内固定器械方面不会使用贝勒的名字，同时承认过去没有这样做。他最后表示感谢并评论："确实很感谢这些支票。"斯宾塞给约翰逊写了一张纸条，表示他同意，并表示之后或当资金耗尽时会关闭该账户。[130]哈灵顿一定开始想，这些支票可以持续多久。在 1960 年与捷迈的协议中，没有专利费和独家使用费期限的规定。他还需要一段时间才能知道公司对他的专利费支付期限的态度。

Harrington's first documented trip in 1971 was March 6-11 to San Francisco for AAOS's annual meeting, where he presented Instructional Course Lecture #84 on the treatment of scoliosis. The interim meeting of the SRS executive committee was held on Sunday, March 7, from noon to 4:00 p.m. with all eight members (including Harrington) in attendance.[131] The minutes reflected orderly growth and management. Active and associate members numbered 106, and active members' dues were raised to $75. They decided that all members were exempt from annual meeting registration. It was announced that the AAOS committee on scoliosis, chaired by MacEwen, was scheduling a postgraduate course on scoliosis. On March 8 Harrington was scheduled to present a paper titled "Treatment by Harrington Instrumentation" to the younger, affiliated Orthopaedic Research Society (ORS), whose meetings overlapped with the AAOS and of which Harrington was a member.

1971 年，哈灵顿在 3 月 6 日至 11 日去圣弗朗西斯科参加美国骨科医师学会的年会，这是他在本年度第一次的参会记录，在那里他进行了关于脊柱侧凸治疗的教学课程讲座#84。脊柱侧凸研究学会执行委员会的临时会议于 3 月 7 日星期日中午至下午 4 点举行，所有 8 名成员（包括哈灵顿）出席了会议。[131]会议记录反映了学会有序的进步和管理。活跃会员和准会员人数为 106 人，活跃会员的会费被提高到 75 美元。他们决定所有的会员都不必进行年度会议注册。会议宣布，由麦克尤恩担任主席的美国骨科医师学会脊柱侧凸委员会正在安排脊柱侧凸的研究生教育课程。3 月 8 日，哈灵顿被安排向成立不久的附属骨科研究学会（ORS）提交一篇题为《使用哈灵顿内固定器械治疗》的论文，该学会会议与美国骨科医师学会年会的日期重叠，哈灵顿也是该学会的会员。

Zimmer correspondence for the rest of the year was limited to eight letters, the seminal one to Hite.[132] In it Harrington asked for the material specifications of the implant material used in the fabrication of his instrumentation. The reason for the request wasn't given, but he indicated he had a late July deadline to meet. The second issue was a request for help with educational audiovisual material. He announced that he had produced two audiovisual instructional courses for the AAOS and had received a proposal about doing a new instructional course on technique for which slides would be inadequate. To do this correctly he thought would require two films, one on surgical technique and the other on postoperative care. He estimated the cost of the technique movie to be $4,000-$6,000 and the postoperative movie to be $3,000-$5,000.

在这一年的其余时间里，捷迈的信件只有8封，其中有一封是写给海特的。[132]在信中，哈灵顿第一个问题是要求提供用于制造其内固定器械植入材料的材料规格。要求的原因没有给出，但他表示最后期限是7月下旬。第二个问题是要求提供教育性视听材料。他宣布，他已经为美国骨科医师学会制作了两套视听教学课程，并收到了一份关于制作新的技术教学课程的建议。他认为要正确地完成这项工作，仅幻灯片是不够的，需要两部视频，一部关于手术技术，另一部关于术后处理。他估计技术视频的成本为4 000~6 000美元，术后处理视频的成本为3 000~5 000美元。

Hite requested responses from the appropriate Zimmer operating units. The first to respond was Vernon Scott, research services director.[133] He stated that hooks and rods were made from 316L stainless steel alloy produced by consumable electrode vacuum melting. The chemical analysis was chromium 17.5%, nickel 13.5%, molybdenum 2.5%, manganese 2% maximum, silicon 0.5% maximum, carbon 0.03% maximum, phosphorous 0.03% maximum, sulfur 0.03% maximum, and the balance iron. Uniloy was simply a patented trade name of one of the steel mills, Universal Cyclops Steel Co., and didn't specifically identify the individual steels, which the numbering system did. The method of cold working was the same regardless of the mill this specific steel was purchased from. The steel was cold worked to a hardness of approximately 35 on the Rockwell "C" scale, giving it a tensile strength of 130,000 to 140,000 pounds per square inch. "The cold working consists of cold rolling between rolls and final finishing by cold drawing thru a series of dies down to the final dimensions desired. This cold drawn material is then machined to the hook and rod dimensions and contours."

海特要求捷迈的相关操作部门作出回应。[133]第一个回应的是研究部门主管弗农·斯科特。他说，钩和棒是用消耗性电极真空熔炼生产的316 L不锈钢合金制成的。化学成分分析包括铬17.5%、镍13.5%、钼2.5%、锰2%、硅0.5%、碳0.03%、磷0.03%、硫0.03%，其余为铁。尤尼洛依不锈镍铬钢只是其中一家钢铁厂赛克洛普斯钢铁公司的专利商品名，并没有像编号系统那样明确标识每种钢材。无论从哪个钢厂购买这种特定的钢材，其冷加工方法都是一样的。这种钢被冷加工到洛氏约35的“C”级硬度，使其抗拉强度达到每平方英寸130 000至140 000磅。“冷加工包括在轧辊之间进行冷轧，并通过一系列的模具进行冷拉伸，最终达到所需的尺寸。然后，这种材料被加工成钩和棒的尺寸和轮廓。”

Scott described the process that the hooks and rods passed through in a series of six treatments designed to make them as strong and inert as possible. First, they were mechanically polished using a series of successively finer mesh abrasives, the last being a very fine mesh aluminum oxide that was softer and finer than jeweler's rouge. Second, they were cleaned in a hot vapor solvent degreaser to remove the polishing compound and any oil that might have been on the surface. Third was stress relief treatment. a process in which they were placed in an electric furnace at 750° F for three hours. This assured the implants maximum condition of strength by removing machining and polishing stresses. Fourth, the implants were again cleaned. Fifth, they were electropolished to remove any remaining surface blemishes. Sixth, the implants were placed in nitric acid for a treatment known as passivation, which enhanced their natural inert surface, giving it maximum body compatibility. Harrington had also asked about the percent likelihood of a surface scratch to cause corrosion. Scott was unable to provide such a precise answer because of the varying severity of a scratch as well as differences in body response. Instead, he suggested that the importance of protecting the implants from nicks and scratches should be impressed on everyone concerned.

斯科特描述了钩和棒通过一系列六种处理的过程，旨在使它们尽可能坚固和具有惰性。第一，使用一系列更细的磨料对它们进行机械抛光，让它们变成一种非常细的氧化铝，比珠宝商的胭脂水粉更柔软、更精细。第二，它们在热蒸汽溶剂脱脂剂中被清洗，以去除抛光剂和任何可能存在于表面的油。第三，应力消除处理，将它们放在 750 华氏度的电炉中 3 小时。通过消除加工和抛光应力，确保内植物的最大强度状态。第四，再次对内植物进行清洗。第五，对它们进行电抛光，以去除任何剩余的表面瑕疵。第六，将内植物放入硝酸中，进行钝化处理，以增强其天然的惰性表面，使其具有最大的体内兼容性。哈灵顿还问到了表面划痕导致腐蚀的可能性。斯科特无法提供这样一个精确的答案，因为划痕的严重程度不同，身体的反应也不同。相反，他建议，应该让每个人都认识到保护内植物不被刮蹭的重要性。

Kenneth Johnson, director of marketing, answered Harrington about the cost of new movies.[134] He began by restating his interpretation of Harrington's request and acknowledging how well surgeons had received his past films. He followed with the news that Zimmer had recently assisted Ken Leatherman with a short film about the Harrington technique and continued with the news that he had met with both the Zimmer executive vice president and the president, who said they were already over their advertising and film budget for the year. However, they wanted to help and would be willing to cover the costs of the technique film. Harrington promptly responded with his thanks, stating a goal of keeping the cost of the film to around $5,000, for which Zimmer would not be billed until after January 1972.[135] In passing, he mentioned noticing that Zimmer had been purchased by a pharmaceutical house and wondered how that would affect their relationship and Zimmer's personnel. Johnson replied that Bristol-Myers and Zimmer had agreed in principle to merge prior to 1972 and that the plan was to continue to operate autonomously.[136] At that point they did not foresee any changes in their relationship or any dramatic changes in personnel.

营销总监肯尼斯·约翰逊回答了哈灵顿关于新视频成本的问题。[134]他首先重申了他对哈灵顿提出的要求的解释，并承认外科医生对他过去的视频反映良好。他接着说，捷迈最近协助肯·莱瑟曼制作了一部关于哈灵顿技术的短片，并继续说，他已经会见了捷迈的执行副总裁和总裁，他们说今年的广告和视频预算已经超标。然而，他们想要提供帮助，并愿意支付技术视频的费用。哈灵顿迅速进行了回复，对此表示感谢，并要把视频的成本控制在 5 000 美元左右，直到 1972 年 1 月以后才向捷迈开出账单。[135]他顺便提到，他注意到捷迈已被一家制药厂收购，想知道这将如何影响他们的关系和捷迈的工作人员。约翰逊回答说，勃列斯多·迈耶公司和捷迈公司在 1972 年之前已经原则上同意合并，计划是捷迈继续自主经营。[136]在那时，他们并未预见到彼此之间的任何关系变化或携迈公司人员上的重大变动。

The sixth annual meeting of the SRS was held under the presidency of Dean Mac Ewen in Hartford, Connecticut, on Wednesday morning to Friday noon, September 8–10, 1971. The entire scientific program on Thursday was conducted at Newington Children's Hospital. The two and a half day format had been established at the second annual meeting, however, the change from Thursday-Saturday to Wednesday-Friday was made necessary by the unavailability of hotel rooms. With the exception of Hong Kong in 1977, the Wednesday-Friday schedule was followed for the remainder of Harrington's life. Possibly this was done to accommodate the convention hotels or to gain better rates from them, but it meant another weekday, workday lost from practice or research.

第六届脊柱侧凸研究学会年会在迪恩·麦克尤恩的主持下，于 9 月 8 日至 10

日，星期三上午至星期五中午在康涅狄格州的哈特福德举行。周四的全部学术活动是在纽因顿儿童医院进行的。两天半时长的会议形式是在第二届年会时确定的，然而，由于无法提供酒店房间，会议时间从星期四到星期六被更改为星期三到星期五。除了 1977 年在香港举办的年会，在哈灵顿的余生中，脊柱侧凸研究学会年会一直沿用周三至周五的时间安排。这样做可能是为了迎合会议酒店的要求，或从他们那里获得更优惠的价格，但这意味着会议时长又多了一个工作日，失去了一天的实践或研究时间。

The meeting was well documented by the program,[137] minutes of the annual executive committee[138] and the membership business meetings,[139] and published paper summaries.[140] A number of important administrative initiatives came to fruition, including changing from a not-for-profit unincorporated association to an incorporated society in Illinois effective September 17, 1971, reclassifying active members to active fellows. discontinuing future traveling fellowships because of financial concerns, and expanding the bylaws, which included splitting the secretary-treasurer position into two. The SRS and AAOS were cooperating in planning future scoliosis postgraduate education courses with two already scheduled in the fall of 1972 and the spring of 1973. Total attendance at this meeting reached a new high of 208. The scientific program featured 36 presentations. another new high. Categorizing the papers by principal focus, there were nineteen evaluative, four nonsurgical treatment, ten surgical treatment, and four laboratory research. Of the 36 papers, 4 were focused principally on Harrington Instrumentation. One introduced the use of compression instrumentation for treatment of dorsal roundback.[141]

这次会议按计划被记录,[137]年度执行委员会[138]和会员商务会议[139]的记录以及发表的论文摘要[140]很好地将整个过程记录了下来。一些重要的行政举措取得了成果：包括从 1971 年 9 月 17 日起在伊利诺伊州将学会从非营利性的非法人学会转变为法人学会；将活跃会员重新分类，称为活跃研究员；由于财务问题而停止未来的交流访问学者项目；以及扩大章程，将秘书兼财务主管的职位分为两个。脊柱侧凸研究学会和美国骨科医师学会正在合作计划未来的脊柱侧凸研究生教育课程，其中两个课程已经被安排在 1972 年秋季和 1973 年春季。本次会议的总出席人数达到了 208 人，创历史新高。学术项目共有 36 个报告，又是一个新纪录。按主要重点对论文进行分类，有 19 篇评估性论文、4 篇非手术治疗论文、10 篇手术治疗论文、4 篇实验室研究论文。在这 36 篇论文中，有 4 篇的主题集中在哈灵顿内固定器械上。其中一篇介绍了使用加压内固定器械治疗圆背畸形。[141]

Undoubtedly the most important paper presented was "A Model for Electrical Monitoring of Spinal Cord Function in Scoliosis Patients Undergoing Correction" by Clyde Nash and neurosurgical colleagues Jerald Brodky and Tom Croft.[142] The authors noted that more effective techniques for the correction of scoliosis had increased the risk of spinal cord damage and to date there was no method of monitoring the anesthetized patient's spinal cord function. Beginning with anesthetized cats, spinal cord motor and sensory function had been monitored by recording the average evoked potentials transmitted across the spinal cord and monitored over the scalp. The effects of progressive. controlled, localized, and reversible spinal cord trauma were studied. A few patients had been monitored. This technology seemed to have the potential for providing early warning of overlengthening, the likely cause of the apparently increased risk of spinal cord damage from Harrington Instrumentation and other powerful lengthening techniques such as halo traction.

毫无疑问，最重要的论文是克莱德·纳什和神经外科同事杰拉尔德·布罗奇以及汤姆·克罗夫特发表的《脊柱侧凸患者矫形中脊髓功能电生理监测的模型》。[142]作者指出，更有效的脊柱侧凸矫形技术增加了脊髓损伤的风险，到目前为止，还没有监测麻醉病人脊髓功能的方法。从麻醉猫开始，通过记录经由脊髓和头皮传输的平均诱发电位来监测脊髓运动和感觉功能。监测一些病人，研究进展性的、控制性的、局部性的和可逆性的脊髓损伤的影响。这项技术似乎有可能提供过度延长的早期预警，过度延长很可能是哈灵顿内固定器械和其他强大的延长技术（如 halo 牵引）使脊髓损伤风险明显增加的原因。

At this point the Dwyer anterior spine instrumentation was the only competition for Harrington's. John Hall was probably best able to provide an independent assessment of this newer instrumentation. He reported on 32 patients operated on for idiopathic, congenital, myopathic, or neuropathic scoliosis and followed for 3 to 18 months.[143] No major problems had been encountered. He presented the limitations and pitfalls of the procedure and assessed the place of this operation in the treatment of scoliosis.

在这一点上，德怀尔前路脊柱内固定器械是哈灵顿唯一的竞争对手。约翰·霍尔可能是能够对这种较新的内固定术器械进行独立评估的最佳人选。他报告了因特发性、先天性、肌病性或神经源性脊柱侧凸而进行手术的患者，并对其进行了 3 至 18 个月的随访。[143]没有遇到过大的问题。他介绍了该手术的局限性和缺陷，并评估了该手术在脊柱侧凸治疗中的地位。

The scientific program was especially meaningful for Harrington for at least two reasons. First, new fellow Jesse Dickson presented his first study, which was titled "Preoperative and Postoperative Evaluation of Scoliotic Patients for Hiatal Hernia."[144] It had been inspired by the observation that 3% to 4% of patients having Harrington Instrumentation had unusually severe and prolonged upper gastrointestinal symptoms postoperatively and by an unconfirmed report that 85% of patients with scoliosis had hiatal hernia.[145] Dickson performed esophagograms on 60 consecutive patients operated on for scoliosis and found the incidence of hiatal hernia to be 6.2% pre- and 2.1% postoperatively in the idiopathic scoliosis group and none in patients with scoliosis of known cause. Three of the idiopathic patients had superior mesenteries artery syndrome, one requiring duodenojejunostomy. This occurrence was not accompanied by hiatal hernia. Second, Harrington demonstrated his abiding interest in the etiology of scoliosis with the presentation of an adolescent idiopathic scoliotic case in whom thoracic apex intervertebral discography, inspired by Kazmin, had demonstrated convex displacement of the nuclei.[146] This fit his observation that the scoliosis deformity seemed to begin in the disc(s) rather than the vertebral body or bodies.[147]

这次学术项目对哈灵顿来说特别有意义，至少有两个原因。首先，新会员杰西·迪克森介绍了他的第一项研究，题目是“脊柱侧凸患者食道疝的术前和术后评估”。[144]该研究的灵感来自这样的观察：3%~4%接受哈灵顿内固定器械治疗的患者，在术后有异常严重的且长时间的上消化道症状，以及一份未经证实的报告，即 85%的脊柱侧凸患者有食管裂孔疝。[145]迪克森对一批连续的脊柱侧凸手术患者进行了食管造影，发现特发性脊柱侧凸组的食管裂孔疝的发生率术前为 6.2%，术后为 2.1%，已知原因的脊柱侧凸患者组没有发生食管裂孔疝。3 名特发性患者有肠系膜上动脉综合征，其中一名需要做十二指肠空肠造口术。这种情况的发生并不伴有食管裂孔疝。其次，哈灵顿展示了他对脊柱侧凸病因学的持久兴趣，他介绍了一例青少年特发性脊柱侧凸病例，在卡兹明的启发下，该病例的胸椎顶椎椎间盘造影显示了髓核向凸侧移位。[146]这符合他的观察，即脊柱侧凸畸形似乎开始于椎间盘，而不是椎体。[147]

The presidential guest speaker for the sixth annual meeting of the SRS was Phillip A.

Zorab, whose topic was "A Physician's Role in Scoliosis Research." Zorab was a pulmonologist and had been a pioneer in patient evaluation and management during and after the post-World-War-Il polio epidemics in the United Kingdom. This inspired him to organize a symposium on scoliosis that was held at the Institute of Diseases of the Chest at The Brompton Hospital, London, on July 5-6, 1965.[148] Its success caused him to organize additional symposia.

第六届脊柱侧凸研究学会年会的主席特邀演讲者是菲利普·A. 佐拉布，他的主题是“内科医生在脊柱侧凸研究中的作用”。佐拉布是一名肺科医生，在第二次世界大战后英国的脊髓质炎流行前后，他一直是进行病人评估和治疗的先驱。这促使他组织了一次关于脊柱侧凸的研讨会，该研讨会于1965年7月5日到6日在伦敦布朗普顿医院的胸部疾病研究所举行。[148]这次研讨会的成功促使他组织了更多的研讨会。

Harrington published two papers in 1971, one of which had been presented at Zorab's third symposium held on November 13, 1970. The symposium was also convened at The Brompton Hospital and resulted in a small book, *Scoliosis and Growth*, that was published in 1971. Harrington was listed as one of the participants, and his presentation was titled "The Missing Link (A Case Report)."[149] The case was a girl born with an eventration, or missing abdominal wall on one side only (the side was never specified). She was also "diagnosed as being hemiplegic, of low mentality and having torticollis." The eventration repair had been done immediately after birth. "The diaphragm was tethered but the repair was so bad that that they did not think it would survive a good cough. But she survived and at age two and a half years was referred to Harrington to manage her 75° left thoracolumbar scoliosis. She did not have pelvic obliquity or a compensatory thoracic scoliosis of any consequence. The vertebrae of the thoracolumbar scoliosis were mildly rotated toward the convexity. She was treated with a Denis Browne bucket and standing bed with a footboard. Eighteen months later her scoliosis had improved, although her balance was still poor. The same treatment was continued for two and a half more years, and four years after first being seen for scoliosis, she was independently standing and her scoliosis had further improved. A year later, when she was seven and a half years old, there was still a little hemiatrophy of the right lower extremity musculature without limb length inequality, but her balance function was good and her scoliosis hac further improved. At age nine her scoliosis had resolved. Harrington summarized, "This infant had been permitted two years of gravity-loading of the spine before the spine righting reflexes were developed, and as a consequence deformity resulted. The 'hemiplegic' diagnosis was more apparent than real. Initial total restriction of the patient's gravity-loading, controlled until she established her righting reflexes and then continued control of gravity-loading of the spine over the next four years, resulted in the gradual restoration of a dynamic spine, normal in both contour and function. This, in my estimation, proves the statement I made years ago, that the human spine will develop its inherent form if dynamic balance can be established."

哈灵顿在1971年发表了两篇论文，其中一篇曾在1970年11月13日举行的佐拉布的第三次研讨会上发表。该研讨会也是在布朗普顿医院召开的，研讨会内容形成了一本小书《脊柱侧凸与生长》，于1971年出版。哈灵顿是与会者之一，他的演讲题目是“缺失的环节（一个病例报告）”。[149]该病例为一名出生时腹部隆起的女孩，或仅在一侧腹壁缺失（未指明是哪一侧）。她还被“诊断为半身不遂，心智低下，并有斜颈”。腹壁修复是在出生后立即进行的。“横膈膜被系上了，但修复得太糟糕了，他们认为它不能忍受剧烈咳嗽带来的压力。”但是她活了下来，并在两岁半时被转诊给哈灵顿，治疗她的75°左胸腰弯。她没有骨盆偏斜或代偿性胸弯。胸腰弯的椎体向凸侧轻度旋转。她接受了丹尼斯·布朗氏桶和带脚板的站立床治疗。18个月后，她的脊柱侧凸得到了改善，尽管她的平衡能力仍然很差。同样的治疗又持续了两年半，在第一次因脊柱侧凸就诊的四年后，她已经能够独立站立，脊柱侧凸也进一步改善。一年后，当她7岁半时，右下肢肌肉仍有少许偏瘫，无下肢不等长，但平衡功能良好，脊柱侧凸进一步改善。9岁时，她的脊柱侧凸已经解决。哈灵顿总结：“这个婴儿在脊柱翻正反射形成之前对脊柱进行了两年的重力加载，因此导致了畸形。‘偏瘫’的诊断很明显。最初完全限制病人的重力载荷，控制到她建立翻正反射，在接下来的四年里继续控制脊柱的重力载荷，结果逐渐恢复了脊柱活动，轮廓和功能都正常了。据我估计，这证明了我多年前的说法，即如果能够建立动态平衡，人类脊柱将按照固有的形式发育。”

Harrington published one other paper in 1971, and the topic was quite different. "Spondylolisthesis Children: Observations and Surgical Treatment" was a continuation of his work on high-grade spondylolisthesis that had begun with his custom implant design conceived and ordered in late 1966 and first used in early 1967.[150] His 1969 publication had been based on the first two patients, and he later added seven more. During this

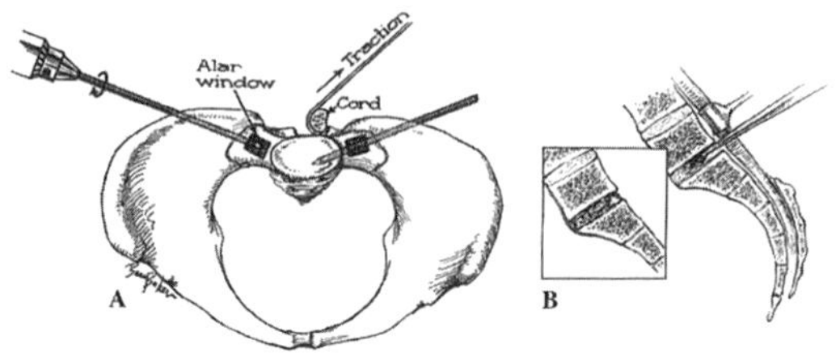

Figure 10. 5 ***A. Illisacral anchor. B. Posterior interbody fusion of L5-S1.*** ***(Harrington Archives)***
图 10. 5　A. 骶髂骨锚。B. L5-S1 后路椎体间融合术(哈灵顿档案馆)

series he had made several substantial changes in technique. First, hypoplasia of the posterior pelvic ring had often made it difficult, if not impossible, to pass the iliac to iliac threaded sacral bar. The solution involved using two separate short threaded bars for placement through the ilium and into the S1 body, giving rise to the iliosacral anchor. *See figure 10.5A*. To aid anchor placement and accommodate the reversed hooks, windows were cut into the top of the sacral ala. Second, the lag screw wires passing over the rods did not break, indicating that the L5 lag screws were probably not necessary. Third, a L5-S1 posterior interbody fusion had been added to address the tendency to lose reduction during follow-up. *See figure 10. 5B*. Although not completely documented, it appears that Harrington operated on all nine patients between early 1967 and November 1968 when he had his heart attack.

1971 年，哈灵顿发表了另一篇主题完全不同的论文《儿童脊柱滑脱：观察和手术治疗》，这是他在重度脊柱滑脱方面工作的延续。该工作始于 1966 年年底构思和订购的定制内植物设计，1967 年年初首次进入实践。[150] 1966 年他的发表基于一开始的两名病人，之后他又增加了七人。在这个系列中，他对技术进行了一些实质性的改变。第一，骨盆后环的发育不良常常使髂骨与髂骨螺纹骶骨的连接变得困难，甚至不可连接。解决办法是使用两根单独的短螺纹棒，通过髂骨并进入 S1 椎体，从而产生了髂骶骨锚。（图 10. 5A）为了帮助锚的放置和适应反转的钩子，在骶骨的顶部开了窗。第二，穿过棒的拉力螺钉钢丝没有断裂，表明 L5 拉力螺钉可能是不必要的。第三，增加了 L5 - S1 后路椎体间融合术，以解决随访期间复位丢失的趋势。（图 10. 5B）虽然没有完整的文件记录，但哈灵顿似乎是在 1967 年年初至 1968 年 11 月自己心脏病发作期间对所有 9 名患者进行的手术。

Harrington's year-end publication of academic activities, *Scoliosis 1971*, featured four studies. Ken Roth wrote "Spinal Deformities in Myelomeningocele: A Radiological Assessment" that was based on the X-rays of 149 patients whose age averaged 4.5 years when first seen and whose follow-up averaged 2.75 years.[151] Criteria for deformity were scoliosis greater than 40°, kyphosis greater than 45°, and lordosis if the sacrum was horizontal to the floor when in the standing position. Spine deformity was found in 50% (74 of 149). The prevalence and type of spine deformity at T12 and above were 81% (38 of 47) and kyphosis 82% (31 of 38). For those with paralysis at the L3-4 level the prevalence was 45% (22 of 49), and the deformity types were scoliosis 68% (15 of 22) and lordosis 32% (7 of 22). Kyphosis was usually a progressive deformity and required treatment. The exception was the patient with a narrow interpedicular distance. Eighty-three percent of scoliosis deformities required surgical correction. Lordosis was infrequent but could develop in older, higher functioning patients, and if it "becomes ap-parent, treatment should be undertaken at once." The second and third entries in *Scoliosis 1971* were published in *Clinical Orthopaedics and Related Research* in 1973 in relation to the Nicholas Andry Award.

哈灵顿本年度的年终学术出版物《脊柱侧凸 1971》，介绍了四项研究。肯·罗斯撰写了“脊髓脊膜膨出患者中的脊柱畸形：放射学评估”，该报告基于 149 名患者的 X 光片，这些患者首次就诊时平均年龄为 4.5 岁，随访平均时长 2.75 年。[151]畸形标准为脊柱侧凸大于 40°，后凸大于 45°，前凸站立时骶骨与地面水平。50%的病人（74/149）发现脊柱畸形。T12 及以上部位脊柱畸形的发生率和类型为 81%（38/47），脊柱后凸占 82%（31/38）。对于 L3-4 水平瘫痪的患者，畸形患病率为 45%（22/49），畸形类型为脊柱侧凸 68%（15/22）和前凸 32%（7/22）。后凸通常是一种进行性畸形，需要治疗。唯一的例外是椎弓根间距较窄的患者。83%的脊柱侧凸畸形需要进行手术矫正。脊柱前凸并不常见，但在年龄较大、功能较强的患者中可能会出现，如果它“变得很明显，应立即进行治疗”。《脊柱侧凸 1971》的第二和第三篇文章发表在 1973 年的《临床骨科和相关研究》上，与尼古拉斯·安德利奖有关。

The fourth entry in *Scoliosis 1971* was "Observations of Spinal Maturity in Adolescent Idiopathic Scoliosis" by Allen Barber, which was done when he was a senior medical student at the Baylor College of Medicine.[152] Thirty-eight adolescent girls had serial anteroposterior scoliosis radiographs from which T1-S1 length and iliac apophysis status were determined. Thirty-one of them had serial wrist (presumably including the hand) radiographs. The findings confirmed that chronological and skeletal age did not usefully correlate and affirmed that the more available iliac apophysis maturation was as accurate an indicator of spine maturity as skeletal age determined from a wrist X-ray using the Greulich-Pyle atlas. Additional helpful findings were that a grade O iliac apophysis implied a skeletal age of less than fourteen years and a grade 4 implied fifteen years or older, menarche usually occurred within four months of the iliac apophysis appearance, and after menarche or the appearance of the iliac apophysis, the T1-S1 length increased an average of 2.2 cm. The study further validated the iliac apophysis as a guide to maturity and remaining growth. In closing *Scoliosis 1971*, Harrington reiterated the importance of following and appropriately managing scoliosis patients with grey zone curves until they were skeletally mature.

《脊柱侧凸 1971》的第四项研究是艾伦·巴伯的“青少年特发性脊柱侧凸的脊柱成熟度观察”，这是他在贝勒医学院高年级时做的。[152]他对38名年轻女性进行了连续的前后位脊柱侧凸X光片检查，从中确定了T1-S1的长度和髂棘骨骺的状态。其中31人进行了连续的腕部（大概包括手）X光片。研究结果证实，年龄和骨骼年龄并不存在有用的关联，并肯定了更大的髂棘骨骺成熟度与使用骨龄图谱从手腕X光片上确定的骨骼年龄一样，是反映脊柱成熟度的准确指标。其他有用的发现是，0级髂棘骨骺意味着骨骼年龄小于14岁，4级意味着15岁或更大，月经通常在髂棘骨骺出现后四个月内发生，在月经或髂棘骨骺出现后，T1-S1长度平均增加2.2厘米。该研究进一步验证了髂棘骨骺作为脊柱成熟度和剩余生长情况的指南。在《脊柱侧凸 1971》的结束语中，哈灵顿重申随访和适当处理具有进展性弯曲的脊柱侧凸患者，直到他们骨骼发育成熟的重要性。

The 1972 AAOS annual meeting took place in Washington, D.C., and Harrington presented his instructional course lecture focused on the treatment of scoliosis for the last time. It had been a good run, nine lectures in ten years. Thanks to his breakthrough and the interest it helped generate, there were now younger members who could deliver the message well. On January 30 he was also able to attend SRS's semiannual meeting of its board of directors. All eight members were there as were all eight committee chairmen and Alf Nachemson, local host for the 1973 meeting in Gothenburg, Sweden.[153] There were several important developments. First, Ted Riseborough, chairman of the data retrieval committee, reported that the present data cards were insufficient for documenting the course of a patient and the actual results. Secretary Levine reported that the cards were being widely used and were not designed to evaluate progress and results. Solutions were discussed, and the decision was made to continue for another year and add patient identification, if possible. Second, Ed Simmons, chairman of the research committee, reported that the morbidity and mortality collection effort had been assigned to the research committee. Third, Ted Waugh, terminology committee chairman, reported that an inclinometer for clinical quantification of the paravertebral asymmetry had been developed at the University of California, Irvine and had been field-tested.

1972 年美国骨科医师学会年会在华盛顿特区举行，哈灵顿最后一次发表了以脊柱侧凸治疗为主题的教学课程讲座。这是一个运转良好的长期项目，在十年中哈灵顿做了 9 次演讲。由于他的技术突破和它所引起的对脊柱侧凸治疗的兴趣，现在有更年轻的会员加入进来，可以很好地传授知识。1 月 30 日，他还能参加脊柱侧凸研究学会半年一次的委员会会议。所有 8 个成员全部到场，还有所有 8 个委员会主席和 1973 年在瑞典哥德堡举行会议的当地主办人阿尔夫·纳切姆森。[153] 当时有几个重要的进展。首先，数据检索委员会主席泰德·里斯伯勒报告说，目前的数据卡不足以记录病人的病程和实际治疗结果。秘书莱文报告说，这些卡片正在被广泛使用，但并不是为了评估进展和结果。他们讨论了解决方案，并决定继续沿用一年，如果可能的话，增加患者身份识别信息。其次，研究委员会主席爱德华·西蒙斯报告称发生率和死亡率的收集工作已分配给研究委员会。第三，术语委员会主席泰德·沃报告说，加州大学欧文分校已经开发出一种用于临床量化椎旁不对称的倾斜仪，并已进行了实地测试。

Harrington-Zimmer correspondence in 1972 began in anticipation of the annual meeting of the AAOS with a January 17 letter to Hite in which Harrington had two requests.[154] The first was the design of the split sacral bar for unilateral iliosacral anchorage for the purpose of high-grade spondylolisthesis reduction. He had described and illustrated the idea a year earlier.[155] His request was for an additional sacral bar in two lengths, 1-3/8" and 1-7/8" overall, with a driving end fitting like the Zimmer screw head (#126-04) that a Stryker holding screwdriver (#264-01) could grasp. The other request was for the threads on the 1/8"-diameter compression rod to be slightly overcut to avoid binding when the rod was bent as necessary for the compression device. The 1/8"-diameter rod-nut binding issue was referred to Robert E. Beam, Zimmer's engineering director, whose mid-February reply came after the AAOS meeting.[156] Beam replied that current tolerances allowed the 1/8"-diameter rod to be bent to a radius of $7^{1/4}$" before the nut bound on the rod. He suggested the possibility that out-of-tolerance situations in manufacturing might have accounted for the problems Harrington was experiencing, but added that this did not appear to have been the case on inventory parts he had tested. Harrington immediately responded, "I just did an operation and spent forty minutes on a nut that would not turn on a threaded rod. Your specification and tolerance between the nut and threaded rod has to be changed."[157] Harrington continued that his scrub nurse said sometimes the nuts bound on a straight rod. "This has to be corrected." Harrington offered to check all of their 1/8"-diameter rods (#1258), raised the question of slight burrs, and closed asking how he could help answer the problems. This was the last correspondence about this issue, and it left Harrington's problem unresolved.

1972 年，哈灵顿和捷迈的通信预期开始于美国骨科医师学会年会期间。1 月 17 日，哈灵顿在给海特的信中提出了两个要求。[154]首先是设计用于单侧骶髂固定的分体式骶骨杆，以达到复位重度脊柱滑脱的目的。他在一年前就描述并说明了这个想法。[155]他要求增加两种长度的骶骨棒，（1+3/8）英寸和（1+7/8）英寸，其驱动端与捷迈螺丝钉头（#126-04）相配，斯特赖克的螺丝刀（#264-01）可以与之匹配。另一个要求是 1/8 英寸直径压缩棒上的螺纹稍微过切，以避免在压缩装置需要弯曲棒时被绑定。提交直径 1/8 英寸的棒-螺母结合问题给捷迈公司的工程总监罗伯特 · E. 比姆，他在 2 月中旬的美国骨科医师学会会议后作出了答复。[156]比姆回答说，目前的耐受力允许直径为 1/8 英寸的棒在螺母束缚在杆上之前被弯曲到 $7^{1/4}$ 英寸的半径。他认为，制造过程中出现的过度耐受力情况可能是哈灵顿遇到问题的原因，但他补充，在他测试过的库存零件中似乎没有出现这种情况。哈灵顿立即回复："我刚刚做了一台手术，花了 40 分钟来处理一个在螺纹棒上无法转动的螺母。你必须改变螺母和螺纹棒的规格以及他们之间的耐受力。"哈灵顿接着说，他的护士说有时螺母会绑在直棒上。"这必须得到纠正。"[157]哈灵顿提出了检查他们所有直径 1/8 英寸的棒（#1258），提出了轻微毛刺的问题，并询问他如何帮助解决这些问题。这是关于这件事的最后一封信，哈灵顿提出的问题最终也没有得到解决。

Harrington's problem with the compression rod assembly may have been related to technique and his statement, "I just did an operation." Dickson recalled that by 1972 Harrington had medically recovered as much as he was going to and sometime during the year progressed from seeing a few patients to working full-time. If Harrington did do the surgery, Dickson had done the exposure and Harrington the rest. However, Harrington had recurrent dizzy episodes, and one day walked out of the operating room saying, "Jesse, I can't do this operation as well as I used to, even though I can probably still do it better than anybody else in the world. But it's not up to par for me, so I quit."[158] Dickson's recollection was that Harrington's return to practice lasted approximately nine months and that he "quit" in the early part of 1973. Harrington listed the date of his retirement from practice in his curriculum vitae as April 1973.[159]

哈灵顿的压缩棒组件问题可能与技术和他的声明有关，"我刚做了一台手术"。迪克森回忆说，到 1972 年，哈灵顿的身体已经恢复到他预期恢复的程度，在那一年的某个时候，他从为几个病人看病恢复到全职工作。如果哈灵顿真要做手术，也是迪克森主刀，将手术部位显露出来，其余的由哈灵顿来做。然而，哈灵顿的头晕症状反复发作，有一天他走出手术室说："杰西，我不能像以前那样做这个手术了，尽管我可能仍然比世界上任何其他人做得更好。"[158]根据迪克森的回忆，哈灵顿恢复后大约持续工作了 9 个月，但他在 1973 年年初"离开工作岗位"。哈灵顿在他的简历中列出的他退休的日期是 1973 年 4 月。[159]

After a slight delay, the iliosacral bars Harrington had requested in his January 17 letter were prepared as special order sacral rods 1-3/8" and 1-7/8" long. Zimmer's Lyle Johnston succinctly described them as rods that would be identical to the #1261 sacral rod, except they would be considerably shorter and have a screwdriver slot in the blunt end that would accept Zimmer's #264-01 Stryker screwdriver.[160] Six of each length were shipped on May 9, 1972, and were marked no charge.[161]

稍过了一段时间后，哈灵顿在 1 月 17 日的信中要求的骶髂杆被准备为特别订购的骶骨棒，长（1+3/8）英寸和（1+7/8）英寸。捷迈公司的莱尔·约翰斯顿简明扼要地将其描述为与#1261 骶骨棒相同的棒，只是它们会短得多，并且在钝端有一个螺丝刀槽，可以兼容捷迈公司的#264-01 斯特赖克螺丝刀。[160] 1972 年 5 月 9 日，每种长度各六根的骶骨棒被运走，并标明不收费。[161]

Nineteen seventy-two must have been somewhat bittersweet for Harrington. On the sweet side he was experiencing practice for the first and only time after his heart attack. And it gave him an opportunity to see on a day-to-day basis just how capable Dickson was. On the bitter side he must have been gradually realizing that he wouldn't be able to continue practicing. For instance, in early March 1972 he participated in the Brook General Hospital Symposium in San Antonio with a new presentation, "The Development and Further Prospects of Internal Fixation of the Spine." But, in October the paper was given not by him but by Louis Goldstein at the SICOT meeting in Tel Aviv.[162] Furthermore, a July letter to Zimmer about the new technique movie suggested that even with return to what must have been a curtailed practice, cash flow was a concern.[163] "I have a bit of a personal problem: my office has been paying bills as they have come in on this production. The usual arrangement… is 1/3 of the estimate at the beginning, 1/3 at completion of final production and 1/3 at final delivery. We are now 80% of the way through the second third. Would it be possible to acquire one-third to two-thirds of the amount we discussed ($5,000 to $6,000) and the rest when we send your copy of the final production?"

对哈灵顿来说，1972年一定是有些苦乐参半的。让他感到甜蜜的一面是，他在心脏病发作后第一次也是唯一一次的工作，让他有机会每天都能看到迪克森的能力。而让他痛苦的一面在于，他一定逐渐意识到了他将无法继续工作。例如，1972年3月初，他参加了在圣安东尼奥举行的布鲁克综合医院研讨会，发表了一篇新的演讲，"脊柱内固定的发展和进一步展望"。但是，10月份，在特拉维夫举行的国际矫形与创伤外科学会会议上，这篇文章不是由他报告的，而是路易斯·戈尔茨坦。[162]此外，他在7月写给捷迈的一封关于新技术视频的信表明，即使采取了缩减支出的做法，现金流也是一个问题。[163]"我有一个小小的个人问题：我的办公室一直在支付这次制作的账单。通常的安排……是在开始时支付估算的1/3，在最后生产完成时支付1/3，在最后交付时支付1/3。我们现在已经完成了第二个1/3的80%。是否有可能先获得我们讨论的金额的1/3到2/3（5 000至6 000美元），其余的在我们寄给你的最终制作的副本时获得?"

In March 1972 his only publication of the year, "Technical Details in Relation to the Successful Use of Instrumentation in Scoliosis" appeared. It was the clearest, most detailed description of scoliosis patient care utilizing Harrington Instrumentation that would probably ever be written[164] and had been presented in December 1971 at the postgraduate course on the management and care of the scoliosis patient sponsored by the New York Orthopaedic Hospital.[165] It included the manufacturer's specifications of the metal used and the methods of implant fabrication, for which he gave due credit to V.R. Scott. Harrington plainly listed the principles he had followed in hook design: (1) accommodation of the multicontoured posterior elements of the spine, (2) hook purchase areas amenable to varying force, (3) uniform hook aperture allowing a common purpose rod to be as close as possible to the hook thereby minimizing the undesirable effects of eccentric loading, and (4) self-centering, loosely fitted hook-rod interfaces to decrease bone-metal contact force and thus limit erosion. In "Technical Details" Harrington definitively illustrated the proper placement of the lower distraction hook as over the "superior laminar border of the purchasing [lower instrumented] vertebra." He stated that the L5 level should never be instrumented because the lordotic position of the L5 lamina limited the security provided at more proximal levels by the hook's long shoe. The upper distraction hook site was prepared by cutting a notch in the facet and driving the hook into the pedicle at the proper angle. Hook stability could be increased by using a #1252 keel hook or, as Hall routinely did, by moving the hook medially into the intervertebral canal next to the dura mater. This placed the hook shoe medial to the pedicle, which would prevent lateral displacement of the hook, a not too uncommon problem. Harrington attributed some of the late rod breakage to "the fact that the upper purchase hook is not included in the fusion mass."

1972 年 3 月，他发表了当年唯一的出版物《成功使用脊柱侧凸内固定器械的技术细节》。这可能是有史以来对使用哈灵顿内固定器械进行脊柱侧凸患者治疗的最清晰、最详细的描述，[164]并于 1971 年 12 月在纽约骨科医院主办的脊柱侧凸患者处理和治疗毕业后课程上发表演讲。[165]它包括制造商对所使用的金属的规格和内植物的制造方法，为此他给予了 V. R. 斯科特应有的赞扬。哈灵顿清楚地列出了他在钩设计中所遵循的原则：(1) 适应脊柱的多面体后部结构；(2) 钩的抓牢区域可承受不同的力；(3) 统一的钩孔径，使通用棒尽可能靠近钩子，从而将偏心载荷的不良影响降到最低；以及 (4) 自定中心，松散地安装钩棒接口，以减少骨-金属接触力，从而限制侵蚀的程度。在"技术细节"中，哈灵顿明确说明了下部撑开钩的正确位置是在"紧贴 [下部内固定器械] 椎体的椎板上缘"。他说，L5 水平不应该放置内固定器械，因为 L5 椎板的前凸位置限制了钩子的长轴在更近端水平上提供的安全性。通过在小关节上切开一个缺口，并以适当的角度将钩插入椎弓根，来准备上部撑开钩的位置。使用#1252 龙骨钩或按照霍尔的常规方法，将钩向内侧移动至硬膜旁的椎管内，可提高钩的稳定性。这样就把钩的长轴放在椎弓根的内侧，从而防止钩向侧方移位，这是一个常见的问题。哈灵顿将一些棒的后期断裂归因于"上方抓牢的钩没有和融合块融为一体"。

The seventh annual meeting of the SRS was held in Wilmington, Delaware, on Wednesday, September 13, through noon on Friday, September 15, 1972.[166] Dean MacEwen, the local host, was completing the second year of his presidential term. The total attendance was 206, comprising 80 members, 80 guests, 40 spouses, and 6 staff. This total was two less than had attended the 1971 annual meeting and was the first time that attendance had not grown. During the annual meeting there were two board of directors meetings[167] and two membership business meetings[168] where information was shared and decisions made that determined the society's future. It was of great importance that plans for the next meeting were progressing well because it annually put the society's financial survival on the line. This was especially true for the upcoming 1973 meeting, when Harrington would be president, because it would be the first overseas meeting. Scheduled for Gothenburg, Sweden, a post-meeting was also being planned for Lyon, France. The reports of their local hosts, Alf Nachemson in Sweden and Pierre Stagnara in France, were detailed and no doubt reassuring to the SRS leadership. The 1974 meeting had tentatively been scheduled as a return to Houston, however with Harrington's approval it was changed to San Francisco. The reason was not given, but was likely partly due to protecting Harrington from the considerable added strain of hosting the meeting.

第七届脊柱侧凸研究学会年会于1972年9月13日星期三至9月15日星期五中午在特拉华州的威尔明顿举行。[166]当地的主办者迪恩·麦克尤恩正处在其主席任期的第二年。出席会议的总人数为206人，包括80名会员、80名嘉宾、40名配偶和6名工作人员。这个总数比参加1971年年会的人数少了两人，也是第一次出现出席人数没有增长的情况。在年会期间，有两次委员会会议[167]和两次会员商务会议[168]，会上分享了信息并做出了影响学会未来的决定。下一届年会的顺利进行是非常重要的，因为每年学会的财政生存都会被放在第一位。对于即将到来的1973年年会，尤其如此，因为这将是第一次海外会议，届时哈灵顿将担任主席。会议预定在瑞典哥德堡举行，还计划在法国里昂继续举行会后会议。瑞典的阿尔夫·纳切姆森和法国的皮埃尔·斯塔格纳拉是东道主，他们的报告很详细，无疑让脊柱侧凸研究学会的领导层感到放心。1974年的会议原定在休斯敦举行，但经哈灵顿同意后改为在圣弗朗西斯科举行。原因没有说明，但可能部分是为了保护哈灵顿免受主办会议的巨大压力的影响。

Under MacEwen's leadership a number of milestones in the maturation of SRS had occurred. The society, now incorporated, had completed its application for affiliate status with the AAOS. Its application for tax-exempt status had been approved by the Internal Revenue Service. Also, effective May 1972 the society was covered for the first time by comprehensive general liability insurance, workmen's compensation, and fire and theft insurance. An important decision made at the meeting was to reduce the president's term from two years to one year, a major change that was approved unanimously by the membership. This was undoubtedly part of the application process to become an affiliate of the AAOS, which had one-year presidential terms. The change most directly affected Harrington, who had been elected to a two-year term. There is nothing to suggest he was upset with the decision.

在麦克尤恩的领导下，脊柱侧凸研究学会逐渐成熟，过程中出现了许多里程碑事件。该学会现在已经注册成立，已经完成了成为美国骨科医师学会附属机构的申请。脊柱侧凸研究学会免税情况的申请已被国内税务局批准。另外，从1972年5月起，该学会首次获得了全面的保险，包括一般责任保险、工伤赔偿、火灾和盗窃保险。会上做出的一个重要决定是将主席的任期从两年缩短为一年，这一重大变化得到了会员的一致认可。这项改动无疑是申请成为美国骨科医师学会附属学会的过程中的一部分，因为美国骨科医师学会的主席任期也是一年。这一变化直接影响到哈灵顿，因为他已被选为两年任期，但没有任何证据表明他对此决定感到不高兴。

Much of the society's work was done by its eight committees, each of which was expected to submit and defend a written report. Some committees had encountered headwinds. For instance, the education committee had tried to persuade the press to run stories about scoliosis but had accomplished little because the topic was viewed as being of little interest to the average reader. This had not stopped the committee from making two informational films, an exhibit for the public and for schools, a sound-slide program for nurses, and the beginning of a school screening for scoliosis in New Jersey. The data retrieval committee again expressed concern about potential and future problems of the punch card system. The membership committee had recommended three applicants for membership; and the board accepted them. However, the membership chairman had requested a meeting between the committee and the president and/or his designee. This may well have been because the committee was overwhelmed with twenty-four applications in various stages of completion, an additional twenty-five forms that had been distributed but not yet returned, and seven corresponding member applications in varying stages of completion. It was clear the SRS membership process was under strain as Harrington assumed the presidency.

该学会的大部分工作是由8个委员会完成的，每个委员会都要提交书面报告并进行答辩。一些委员会遇到了阻力。例如，教育委员会曾试图说服媒体刊登有关脊柱侧凸的报道，但收效甚微，因为人们认为普通读者对这个话题不感兴趣。但这并没有阻止委员会制作了两部宣传片，为公众和学校举办了展览，为护士制作了有声幻灯片，以及在新泽西州开始进行脊柱侧凸的学校普查。数据检索委员会再次对建档卡系统的潜在问题表示关注。会员委员会推荐了三名申请者成为会员，委员会接受了他们。然而，会员主席要求会员候选人与主席和/或主席指定的人会面。这很可能是因为委员会被24份处于不同完成阶段的申请书压得喘不过气来，另外还有25份已经分发但尚未返回的表格，以及7份处于不同完成阶段的相应会员申请。很明显，在哈灵顿担任主席期间，脊柱侧凸研究学会的会员申请程序承受了很大的压力。

The research coordinating committee had been particularly active compiling lists of research works and facilities with the intent of encouraging collaboration. The morbidity and mortality reporting efforts, just recently assigned to the research coordinating committee, had been continued. The morbidity report was based on information provided by 46 of 90 members (51%), less than the 65% needed for statistics from such surveys to be considered valid. Because the total number of patients operated on was not collected, the incidence of complications could not be determined. The morbidity report detailed nine neurological, eight instrumentation, four traction, and four intrasurgical cardiac arrest complications. Only one of the nine neurological complications was secondary to Harrington distraction instrumentation. This twenty-two-year-old male had previously undergone repair of a congenital heart defect (tetralogy of Fallot) and had double curves of 138° and 105°. He received preoperative halo-femoral traction, apparently without incident. At operation, two overlapping Harrington distraction rods were inserted without incident. Five hours postoperative the patient suddenly became paraplegic, and the rods, were immediately removed. Four months postoperative the return of motor power in the legs was almost complete, although bladder control had not returned. The mortality report was based on five deaths, all in patients with complex and complicated scoliosis problems.

研究协调委员会一直在特别积极地汇编研究成果和设施的清单，目的是鼓励合作。最近刚刚分配给研究协调委员会的发生率和死亡率报告工作也在继续。发生率报告是基于90个成员中的46人（51%）提供的信息，低于此类调查所需的65%的统计数据被认为有效。由于没有收集接受手术的病人的总数，因此无法确定并发症的发生率。发生率详述报告了9例神经系统并发症、8例内固定并发症、4例牵引并发症和4例术中心搏骤停并发症。9例神经系统并发症中只有一例是使用哈灵顿撑开内固定器械后继发的。这名22岁的男性曾接受过先天性心脏缺陷

（法洛四联症）的修复，有 138°和 105°的双弯。他在术前接受了 halo 股骨牵引，显然没有发生问题。手术时，置入两根重叠的哈灵顿撑开棒，没有发生意外。术后 5 小时，病人突然发生截瘫，术者立即取出棒。术后 4 个月，腿部运动能力几乎完全恢复，但膀胱控制能力尚未恢复。死亡率报告基于 5 例死亡、都有复杂的脊柱侧凸问题的患者。

The terminology committee reported their progress in developing an inclinometer to allow quantification of the rotational deformity of the thoracic apex. They also had been working to define key terms and had designated 57. The majority of the committee thought that the term *structural* curve should be used to replace *primary* and *major*. They also proposed that *compensatory* curve should be used to replace secondary and minor. Furthermore, *double structural* curve should be used to replace the terms *double primary* and *double major*.

术语委员会报告了他们在研发倾斜仪方面的进展，以便对胸椎顶椎的旋转畸形进行量化。他们也一直在努力定义关键术语，并已制订了 57 个术语。委员会的大多数成员认为应该用“结构性弯”这一术语来代替“原发弯”和“主弯”。他们还建议用“代偿性弯”来代替“次弯”和“小弯”。此外，应使用“双结构性弯”来取代“双原发弯”和“双主弯”这两个术语。

New officers nominated and elected during the meeting were Robert B. Winter as president-elect and Gordon Armstrong as at-large member.[169] Officers continuing were Dean MacEwen who moved to past-president, Paul Harrington who moved to president, David Levine as secretary, James Hardy as treasurer, and at-large members Ken Leatherman and Lawrence Noall. The last action of the meeting was approval of Harrington's standing and ad hoc committee appointments for the coming year. They, just like the board, were solid members of the SRS, and he could expect their support.

会议期间提名并选出新的领导者，罗伯特·B. 温特当选候任主席，戈登·阿姆斯特朗为委员。[169]迪恩·麦克尤恩转任前任主席，保罗·哈灵顿为主席，戴维·莱文担任秘书，詹姆斯·哈迪担任财务主管，还有委员肯·莱瑟曼和劳伦斯·诺尔。会议的最后一项任务是批准哈灵顿提出的来年的常设和特设委员会的任命。他们就像其他的几个委员会一样，成员都是脊柱侧凸研究学会可靠的会员，他期待获得他们的支持。

There were two presidential guest speakers: Alfred R. Shands, whose topic was "History of Scoliosis," and George Dommisse, who presented his original and seminal research on the "Blood Supply to the Spinal Cord and Spine." The program featured 40 presentations including 19 evaluative, 7 nonsurgical, 11 surgical, and 3 laboratory research. Seven of the 40 mentioned a major use of Harrington Instrumentation although the focus of the paper might have been evaluative (e.g., pulmonary studies. The paper that most influenced Harrington Instrumentation and its evolution was "Complications of Fusion in Lumbar Scoliosis" that was presented by John H. Doherty.[170] He "described a postural complication observed in patients with thoracolumbar scoliosis treated by Harrington Instrumentation and spine fusion with resultant loss of lumbar lordosis. The postural defect was characterized by a fixed forward inclination of the trunk and inability to stand erect except by flexing the knees. In one patient the inclination was so severe that bilateral pelvic osteotomy (Salter procedure) had been required to restore upright posture." The effect of Doherty's insight on Harrington Instrumentation was swift and sustained. The sagittal plane had been mentioned several years before in relation to problems instrumenting in the presence of increased thoracic kyphosis, but the need had not taken on urgency. Loss of normal lumbar lordosis would quickly prove to be a bigger and less easily ignored problem.

会上有两位主席特邀演讲：阿尔弗雷德·R. 尚兹，他的主题是“脊柱侧凸的历史”，以及乔治·多米斯，他介绍了他对“脊髓和脊柱的血液供应”的原创和开创性研究。这次学术项目有40个演讲，包括19个评估性的、7个非手术性的、11个手术性的和3个实验室研究。在这40个报告中，有7个提到主要应用哈灵顿内固定器械，尽管论文的重点可能是评估性的（例如，肺部研究）。对哈灵顿内固定器械影响最大的论文是约翰·H. 多尔蒂发表的《腰椎侧凸融合的并发症》。[170]他“描述了在接受哈灵顿内固定器械治疗和脊柱融合的胸腰椎侧凸患者中观察到腰椎前凸的丧失导致的姿势缺陷并发症。这种姿势缺陷的特点是躯干固定向前倾斜，除非屈膝，否则无法直立。在一个病人中，倾斜是如此严重，以至于需要进行双侧骨盆截骨术（索尔特手术）来恢复直立的姿势”。多尔蒂的见解对哈灵顿内固定器械的影响是迅速而持续的。几年前在胸椎后凸增加情况下的内固定器械治疗问题时已经提及矢状面，但这种需求并没有变得紧迫。很快正常腰椎前凸的丧失被证明是一个更大的、不容易被忽视的问题。

Two papers addressed the rapidly evolving field of spinal cord function monitoring during surgery. Les Nash and his colleagues had continued their laboratory and clinical studies on cord sensory function using cortical evoked potentials produced in the dorsal columns by stimulation of the sciatic nerve. Using a cat model, they had found that lowering the blood pressure decreased the amount of weight applied to the exposed spinal cord necessary to abolish the cortical evoked potential and that raising the blood pressure restored the evoked potential. Clinically, two patients with cord compression had improved after elevation of their blood pressure. "The authors suggested that ischemia may play a role in the loss of cord function following corrective surgery on the spine and noted that the blood pressure should be maintained during spinal surgery and that the cortical evoked potential might be useful to monitor patients undergoing surgery of this type."[171] These results lent living support for one of George Dommisse's principal findings from his painstaking microdissection of the spinal cord blood supply in fetal, neonatal, and postnatal cadavers of various ages: the blood supply to the spinal cord in the region of T4-9, the level of the distraction paraplegia, was normally decreased. His beautiful illustrations have been preserved in a thesis completed in 1972[172] and a book published in 1975.[173]

有两篇论文论述了迅速发展的术中脊髓功能监测领域。莱斯·纳什和他的同事们继续在实验室和临床上研究脊髓感觉功能，刺激坐骨神经而在背柱产生皮层诱发电位。他们使用猫的模型，发现降低血压可以减少施加在暴露的脊髓上的重量，这对消除皮层诱发电位是必要的，而提高血压则可以恢复诱发电位。在临床上，两名脊髓受压的病人在血压升高后有了改善。"作者认为，缺血可能在脊柱矫形手术后的脊髓功能丧失中起作用，并指出在脊柱手术期间应保持血压平稳，皮层诱发电位可能有助于监测接受这种类型手术的病人。"[171]这些结果为乔治·多米斯从他对胎儿、新生儿和出生后不同年龄的尸体的脊髓血液供应的艰苦显微解剖中得出的主要结论之一提供了明确的证据支持：T4-9 区域，即撑开性截瘫的水平，脊髓的血液供应通常减少。他的精美插图被保存在 1972 年完成的一篇论文[172]和 1975 年出版的一本书中[173]。

The second paper addressing spinal cord function was based on motor function and did not involve any new technology.[174] Pierre Stagnara and his colleagues acknowledged that there was always a slight but real risk of paraplegia with Harrington distraction instrumentation. The monitoring approach they used was based on partially awakening the patient during surgery while maintaining dissociation of pain and consciousness.

Endotracheal anesthesia was used, and during the partial awakening nitrous oxide was replaced with oxygen and air. If needed, retesting could be done to adjust the amount of distraction that could be tolerated. The technique had been used in 124 operations, many in adults with severe kyphoscoliosis and diminished vital capacity. Stagnara's presentation was not listed in the program, but his abstract was published with the others.[175]

第二篇论述脊髓功能的论文基于运动功能，不涉及任何新技术。[174]皮埃尔·斯塔格纳拉和他的同事们承认，使用哈灵顿撑开内固定器械总是有轻微但真实的截瘫风险。他们采用的监测方法是在手术中部分唤醒病人，让他们保持疼痛和意识的分离。使用气管内麻醉，在部分唤醒过程中，用氧气和空气代替氧化亚氮。如果需要，可以进行重新测试，以调整可以容忍的分散注意力的量。该技术已被用于124次手术，其中许多次是用在患有严重脊柱侧凸和生命力很弱的成人身上。斯塔格纳拉的演讲没有被列入会议日程，但他的摘要与其他演讲者的一起发表。[175]

Scoliosis surgery in adults was starting to attract attention. Harrington participated with Moe in a scheduled discussion session on this subject. In a scientific session Edgar Dawson presented the Moe group's experience with a series of 82 consecutive patients, aged 20 to 65 years.[176] At an average 3.5 years' follow-up only 40% of those operated on for cardiovascular compromise were improved whereas 77% to 80% were improved if the indication was pain, cosmetic, or both. Twenty-seven percent developed pseudarthrosis and 21% infection until prophylactic antibiotics lowered this to 2% to 3%. When prophylactic antibiotics became the norm is difficult to pinpoint, but it seems to have been around this time.

成人的脊柱侧凸手术开始引起了人们的注意。哈灵顿和莫一起参加了关于这个主题的预定讨论会议。在学术分会上，埃德加·道森介绍了莫的小组对82名年龄在20~65岁之间的病人进行治疗的经验。[176]在平均3.5年的随访中，只有40%因心血管疾病而接受手术的病人得到了改善，而77%~80%的患者的脊柱疼痛程度、美观度或两者均得到了改善。27%的人出现了假关节，21%的人出现了感染，直到预防性抗生素将这一比例降低到2%~3%。预防性抗生素的使用何时成为常规很难准确确定，但似乎就是在这个时候。

The last paper selected for discussion as related to Harrington Instrumentation was the "Present Status of the Transverse Loading System (Modified Harrington Instrumentation)" by Gordon Armstrong.[177] Results of ten patients were presented, including photogrammetry studies showing "no significant adverse effects of this device on the rotation of the spine." For right thoracic apex flexible curves of 65° or less, the instrumentation was probably a slight improvement of Harrington Instrumentation. But, the transverse loading system was not versatile enough to really be competitive. However, it did introduce the idea of transverse connection, a concept that lasted.

最后一篇被选中讨论的且与哈灵顿内固定器械有关的论文是戈登·阿姆斯特朗撰写的《横向加载系统的现状（改良型哈灵顿内固定器械）》。[177]论文介绍了10名患者的结果，包括摄影测量学研究显示“该装置对脊柱的旋转没有明显的不利影响”。对于65°或更小的右胸弯顶椎柔韧性好的弯曲，该内固定器械可能是对哈灵顿内固定的轻微改善。但是，横向加载系统的用途不够广泛，无法真正具有竞争力。然而，它确实引入了横向连接的概念，最终，这一概念持续了下来。

Very vital to the history of Harrington Instrumentation was the rapid development of Jesse Dickson as Harrington's worthy successor. In less than four years he had not only maintained his mentor's practice, but he had also become a member of the SRS as an active fellow and become a member of the new data retrieval committee, on which he would serve seven of the next eight years. Dickson was a reliable and able stand-in teacher of Harrington's concepts and practice. He was also a contributor to the science of scoliosis. For the second year in a row he presented a scientific study at the annual SRS meeting. "Growth Arrest in Tall Scoliotic Girls" was the study of nine adolescent girls with scoliosis and projected height of 175 cm (5'9") who were treated with the Milwaukee brace and high doses of estrogens.[178] In all of them, height increased a further 19 mm or less, response to the brace was as anticipated, and the time in brace was considerably reduced.

对哈灵顿内固定器械的历史非常重要的是，杰西·迪克森作为哈灵顿当之无愧的继承人迅速进步。在不到4年的时间里，他不仅坚持了他的导师的做法，而且还成了脊柱侧凸研究学会的活跃研究员，成了新的数据检索委员会的委员，在接下来的8年里，他将在该委员会任职7年。迪克森是哈灵顿的概念和实践的一个可靠和干练的完美践行者。他也是脊柱侧凸科学领域的一个贡献者。他连续2年在脊柱侧凸研究学会年会上提交了一份科学研究报告。“患有脊柱侧凸的高挑女孩的生长阻滞”是对9名患有脊柱侧凸、预计身高为175厘米的青春期女孩的研究，她们接受了密尔沃基支具和大剂量的雌激素的治疗。[178]所有这些人，身高增加了19毫米或更少，对支具的反应与预期的一样，而且支具的使用时间大幅缩短。

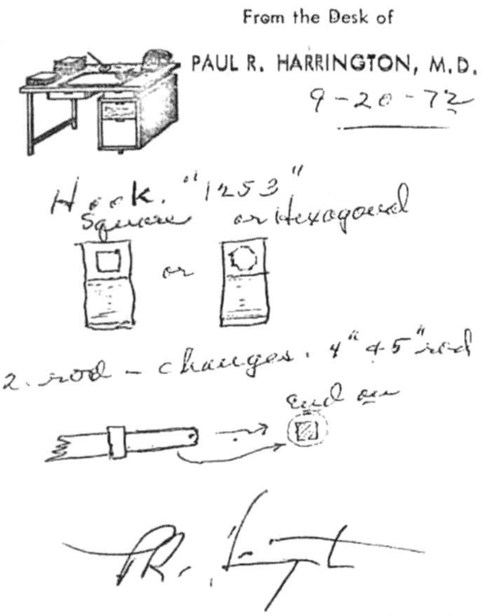

Figure 10.6 ***Harrington's sketches of the square shoulder hook and rod designed to prevent rod rotation as suggested by John Moe. (Harrington Archives)***

图 10.6　哈灵顿设计的方形肩钩和棒的草图,以防止棒旋转,由约翰·莫建议(哈灵顿档案馆)

The 1972 SRS annual meeting further impressed on Harrington the need for child-sized instruments. But this old need was eclipsed by the new problem of loss of lumbar lordosis. Accordingly, on September 20, just five days after the last day of the meeting, Harrington wrote James F. Bennett at Zimmer, zeroing in on the lumbar lordosis issue. "I have a request from Moe to make available to him, only, an experimental redesign of the larger distraction hook, the 1253 (large hook with the blunt end). Enclosed is a sketch of what he would like." *See figure 10.6.* "His objective is to bend the distraction rod and purchase on the lower hook in the same plane and the fixation to the hook as is obvious by this drawing will keep the rod from rotating. Making a hook available with a square or hexagonal purchase hole has a definite indication in some cases and eventually may become part of the total instrumentation."[179] Harrington went on to say that Moe wanted only the 4"- and 5"-rod end modified as smaller or greater lengths would seldom be necessary. He finished with some thoughts about the square shouldered clearance, leaving the decision to Bennett.

1972 年的脊柱侧凸研究学会年会使哈灵顿进一步认识到适合儿童的器械的需求。但是这个旧的需求被腰椎前凸丧失的新问题所掩盖。因此，9 月 20 日，哈灵顿写信给捷迈公司的詹姆斯·F. 班尼特，将腰椎前凸问题作为重点。"我有一个来自莫的请求，希望能向他提供一个较大的经过实验性再设计的撑开钩，即 1253 号钩（带钝头的大钩）。"（图 10.6）"他的目标是折弯撑开棒，并在同一平面的下端钩上抓牢，并且从这张图中可以明显看出，固定在钩上将防止撑开棒旋转。在一些病例中，提供带有方形或六边形孔的钩有肯定的适应证，最终可能成为整套器械的一部分。"[179]哈灵顿接着说，莫希望只修改 4 英寸和 5 英寸棒的一端，因为很少需要更小或更大的长度。他最后谈到了关于方肩间隙的一些想法，把决定权留给了班尼特。

In this same letter Harrington also mentioned that he had several requests for the child-sized compression book. Harrington referred back to a letter from Zimmer dated January 27, 1970,[180] U and his reply on February 2, 1970,[181] addressing the needs of Oswaldo Campos of Rio de Janeiro in treating young children with tuberculosis of the spine. It seemed Harrington felt the need to reacquaint himself with the outcome of this correspondence and to better serve the requests for small implants as he requested a copy of the drawing he had made for Campos. He closed this part of the correspondence with the observation that the requests for a child-sized hook were going to increase as a use had been found "in treating early congenital curves of the spine." Zimmer's L. J. Dietrich promptly responded to this letter.[182] Enclosed were copies of the prints of the instruments designed for Campos based on Harrington's sketches. Dietrich quickly moved to the square or hexagonal purchase for the nonrotation issue, and he indicated that he was meeting with Moe the following day. Finally, Dietrich introduced a third subject, the blunt-tipped version of the strut bar hook with the midline fin, or keel, that currently was only being manufactured as a special item for Moe. He asked Harrington's permission to add this hook to the Harrington Instrumentation set based on the demand for it from surgeons. Harrington replied that adding the blunt hook as requested was fine.[183] The experimental number on this book was #99-6524, and it became #1262 in the catalog, fitting in well with its sharp, chiseled tip version's #1252.

在这封信中，哈灵顿还提到他有几个关于适用于儿童的尺寸的压缩钩的要求。哈灵顿提到捷迈公司 1970 年 1 月 27 日的一封信,[180]以及他在 1970 年 2 月 2 日的回信,[181]谈到里约热内卢的奥斯瓦尔多·坎波斯在治疗婴幼儿脊柱结核时的需求。哈灵顿觉得有必要重新了解这次通信的结果，并更好地满足对小型内植物的要求，因为他要求提供一份他为坎波斯绘制的图纸的副本。他在结束这部分交流时说，对儿童大小的钩的需求将会增加，因为已经发现“在治疗脊柱的早期先天性脊柱侧凸方面”的用途。捷迈公司的 L. J. 迪特里希及时地回复了这封信。[182]随函附上了根据哈灵顿的草图为坎波斯设计的器械的副本。迪特里希很快就谈到了通过加固方形或六边形来解决不旋转的问题，他表示第二天要和莫见面。最后，迪特里希介绍了第三个主题，即带有中线鳍或龙骨的钝头版支撑棒钩，目前只作为提供给莫的特殊产品在生产。他请求哈灵顿允许根据外科医生的需求，将这种钩加入哈灵顿内固定套装。哈灵顿回答，按照要求增加钝钩很好。[183]这个钩的实验编号是#99-6524，在目录中变成了#1262，与它的尖凿形钩尖版本的#1252 很相称。

Figure 10.7 ***Reduced throat height, from 3/8" (9.5 mm) to 1/4" (6.35 mm), 3/16" threaded rod copatible hook for pediatric use. (Harrington Archives)***
图 10.7　降低喉部高度，从 3/8 英寸(9.5 mm)到 1/4 英寸(6.35 mm)，3/16 英寸螺纹棒配合钩在儿科使用(哈灵顿档案馆)

Most of Harrington's reply related to the small hooks that could be used to apply either distraction or compression in small children, items he reported receiving more and more requests for. Actually, Zimmer had just sent one 6"-long, 1/8"-diameter threaded rod, two hex nuts for it, and two child-sized hooks. With one exception the hook was the same as the 1/8"-diameter threaded rod compatible hook #1259. The one difference was that the throat height had been decreased from 3/8" (9.5 mm) to 1/4"(6.35 mm). Harrington commented that the smaller 1/8"-diameter threaded rod (#1258) would not in its current form withstand the expected compression forces when used as a distraction rod. So the first choice Harrington offered was to produce a pediatric hook for the larger 3/16"-diameter threaded rod (#1257), which he thought would withstand any needed compression force. In simplest terms this would mean reducing the height of the hook opening of the 3/16"-diameter rod compatible hook (#1256, sharp, or #1254, blunt) from 3/8" to 1/4", respectively. The second choice Harrington offered was to strengthen the 1/8"-diameter rod (#1258) by cutting shallower threads. He closed by recommending Ken Leatherman of Louisville, Kentucky, the largest potential user of small hooks in the country, as the one to best pass judgment on the two choices. Harrington again requested that catalog item #1263, a sacral rod eyelet, be removed. "This is a poor item and should not be part of Harrington Instrumentation." The 3/16"-diameter threaded rod compatible pediatric hook was eventually chosen. *See figure 10.7.*

哈灵顿的大部分回复都与小钩有关，这些小钩在小孩子中可以用来撑开或加压，他报告说，越来越多的人要求使用这些小钩。实际上，捷迈只是寄来了一根 6 英寸长、直径 1/8 英寸的螺纹棒，两个六边形螺母，以及两个儿童尺寸大小的钩子。除了一个例外，该钩与直径为 1/8 英寸的螺纹棒兼容钩#1259 相同。唯一的区别是，喉部高度从 3/8 英寸（9.5 mm）降至 1/4 英寸（6.35 mm）。哈灵顿评论，目前来看，较小的直径 1/8 英寸的螺纹棒（#1258），在作为撑开棒使用时，无法承受预期的压缩力。因此，哈灵顿提供的第一个选择是为较大的直径 3/16 英寸的螺纹棒（#1257）生产一个适用于儿童的钩，他认为这可以承受任何需要的压缩力。简单来说，这意味着将直径为3/16英寸的棒兼容钩（#1256，尖的，或#1254，钝的）的钩口高度分别从3/8英寸降低到1/4英寸。哈灵顿提供的第二个选择是通过切割更浅的螺纹来加强直径1/8英寸的棒（#1258）。他最后推荐肯塔基州路易斯维尔的肯·莱瑟曼，他是该县小钩的最大潜在用户，是对这两种选择作出判断的最佳人选。哈灵顿再次要求删除目录中的#1263条目，即骶骨棒眼。“这是一个糟糕的项目，不应该是哈灵顿内固定器械的一部分。”最终，哈灵顿选择了直径为3/16英寸的螺纹棒兼容适用于儿童的钩。(图10.7)

The last Zimmer correspondence for 1972 was somewhat trivial but nevertheless illustrates the conflict of interest practices of the time. Harrington had solicited financial support from a local representative of Zimmer for refreshments at an October golf outing during the annual meeting of the Western Orthopedic Association in Houston. Support of no more than $200 was pledged. About 50 golfers participated, and the final refreshment bill was $155.12. In his thank-you letter to Zimmer, Harrington reported that several golf carts roamed the course displaying a sign reading, "With compliments of Zimmer, Warsaw, USA." Harrington added that the course was too wet for the carts so participants had to carry their bags in the 87° temperature and 94% humidity.

1972年的最后一封来自捷迈的信件有些微不足道，但还是说明了当时的利益冲突。哈灵顿曾向捷迈公司的一位当地代理寻求资金支持，以便在10月休斯敦西部骨科学会年会期间的一次高尔夫郊游中提供茶点。承诺的支持不超过200美元。大约有50名高尔夫球员参加，最后的茶点费用为155.12美元。在写给捷迈的感谢信中，哈灵顿称几辆高尔夫球车在球场上荡游，上面写着“来自美国华沙的捷迈公司的问候”。哈灵顿补充说，球场太湿，无法使用手推车，因此参赛者不得不在87°的温度和94%的湿度下背起他们的高尔夫球包。

Harrington wrapped up his academic year with *Scoliosis 1972*.[184] This twelfth and last edition of his annual academic pursuits contained a brief summary of each of the 38 entries. These included a few related extramural articles, some translations, and classics of historical interest, which reflected the range and depth of Harrington's knowledge of and interest in scoliosis. In closing the series, he acknowledged his indebtedness to his young associate. "Dr. Dickson has taken over my work with extraordinary efficiency and dedication following an extensive series of cardiovascular incidents necessitated my retirement from medicine. Observing his outstanding ability and pleasant personality in the continuation of my practice gives me untold satisfaction." [185]

哈灵顿以《脊柱侧凸 1972》结束了他的学术生涯。[184]他的第十二本，也是最后一本的年度学术出版物，包含了 38 个项目中每个项目的简短摘要。还有一些相关的课外文章、一些翻译作品和具有历史价值的经典著作，反映了哈灵顿对脊柱侧凸相关知识和兴趣的广度和深度。在结束这一系列文章时，他承认他对他的年轻助手的感激之情。"在我因一系列严重心血管疾病而不得不退休后，迪克森医生以非凡的效率和奉献精神接替了我的工作，能在他接替我工作的过程中了解到他杰出的能力和善良的品行，我感到无比的欣慰。" [185]

There was no doubt that Paul Harrington was an expansive person and that 1968 through 1972 were years of contraction for him. His heart attack in November 1968 when he was 57 years old left him physically disabled to a degree that only slowly became clear to him. But his actions and activities suggest that he bore the burden with grace and dignity and that he maintained an undiminished passion for understanding scoliosis. Harrington was fortunate to have a loving family. He was also fortunate that Jesse Dickson was willing to carry on his practice and in doing so took it to a new level of excellence. During these four years Harrington was able to actively participate in scoliosis research and teaching, missing very few opportunities in spite of having at least two major surgeries during this time.

毫无疑问，保罗·哈灵顿是一个胸襟开阔的人，1968 年到 1972 年对他来说是处在低谷的几年。他在 1968 年 11 月，自己 57 岁时心脏病发作，从此，他的身体处于残疾状态，这种残疾的程度只有他自己清楚。但他的行动和活动表明，他优雅而有尊严地承受了这一负担，而且他对探索脊柱侧凸保持着不灭的热情。哈灵顿很幸运地拥有一个充满爱的家庭。他也很幸运，因为杰西·迪克森愿意继承他的事业，并在此过程中把他的事业推向了一个新的高度。在这四年中，哈灵顿能够积极参与脊柱侧凸的研究和教学，尽管在此期间他至少经历了两次大手术，但他很少错过这种机会。

Harrington Spine Instrumentation was still very much in its growth phase, which began in earnest with the SRS's formation in 1966. It was a powerful new therapeutic methodology that was changing scoliosis practice by providing the spine deformity surgeon with some direct control of spine position and stability for the first time. But initially the distraction hook sites, both distally and proximally, were unstable. To be successful, a good fusion had to occur, and Harrington Instrumentation alone did not improve its likelihood. Even excellent arthrodesis technique was not enough to reliably obtain fusion. Two things were required: fresh autogenous iliac crest bone graft, which surgeons seemed reluctant to use probably because of the frequent, though usually slight, morbidity, and full-time external immobilization with a cast or brace for a minimum of six months.

随着1966年脊柱侧凸研究学会的成立而真正开始发展的哈灵顿脊柱内固定器械仍处于成长阶段，这是一种强大的新的治疗方法，首次为脊柱畸形外科医生提供了对脊柱位置和稳定性的直接控制，从而改变了脊柱侧凸方面的医学实践。但最初的撑开钩，无论是远端还是近端，都是不稳定的。要获得成功，必须进行良好的融合，而仅靠哈灵顿内固定器械并不能提高融合的可能性。即使是优秀的融合技术，也不足以可靠地获得融合。还需要做两件事：新鲜的自体髂骨移植（外科医生似乎不愿意使用这种移植，可能是因为它经常发生并发症，尽管通常是轻微的），以及用石膏或支具进行至少六个月的外固定。

Just as parents are taught by their children, Harrington Instrumentation was now being taught by the SRS. By forming a community for gathering information, rare events were brought into focus, for instance, the rare case of paraplegia from the forceful elongation of the spine by distraction. Pooling of experiences was needed to uncover this catastrophic complication. Awareness and understanding of the relationship between the less rare but potentially fatal complication of duodenal obstruction and its relationship to distraction elongation of the spine began with a case report. How ironic that these potentially catastrophic complications were first aired at the SRS meeting hosted by Harrington in Houston in September 1968. Did they delay his rise to the SRS presidency? We'll never know. Much more importantly, whether his instrumentation sequence mitigated the neurological risk, as was his experience, was never tested. Research leading to intraoperative neurological monitoring was launched, and four years later methods of the early recognition necessary for prevention were becoming increasingly available. The duodenal obstruction complication was unraveled in 1972 by the pooling of experience at three large centers resulting in a clear understanding of the pathophysiology and effective treatment recommendations. But by then there was another teachable moment when the complication of loss of lumbar lordosis in patients with distraction instrumentation of thoracolumbar scoliosis was aired and the evolution of posterior spine instrumentation started to accelerate.

就像父母被他们的孩子教导一样，哈灵顿内固定器械现在也被脊柱侧凸研究中心“教导”。通过形成一个收集信息的行业，罕见的事件成为焦点，例如，通过撑开力拉长脊柱导致截瘫的罕见案例，需要汇集经验来发现这种灾难性的并发症。对十二指肠梗阻这种不太罕见但有可能致命的并发症及其与撑开拉长脊柱之间关系的认识和理解，始于一份病例报告。具有讽刺意味的是，这些潜在的灾难性并发症是在 1968 年 9 月由哈灵顿在休斯敦主办的脊柱侧凸研究学会年会上首次公布的。这些事情是否推迟他成为脊柱侧凸研究学会主席的时间我们将永远不会知道。更重要的是，正如他的经验，他的内固定器械是否能降低神经系统的风险这一点从未被验证过。术中神经监护的研究已开始推进，四年后已有可能做到早期识别预防。1972 年，三个大的研究中心汇集经验解开了十二指肠梗阻并发症的谜团，从而对病理生理学和有效的治疗建议有了清晰的认识。但当时另一个值得教导的时刻出现了，即公开发表了胸腰弯撑开内固定器械治疗患者的腰椎前凸丧失的并发症，脊柱后路内固定的发展开始加速。

（姜横 陈建 译　周许辉 殷国勇 郝定均 审校）

11 RECOGNITION (1973–75)

the capacity to look at a problem in an entirely original way that is a great gift[1]

表彰 (1973—1975)

以一种完全独到的方式看待问题的能力是一种伟大的天赋[1]

Even though Harrington's limited physical stamina would soon cut short his return to practice, he was still very actively engrossed in work. His new movie on surgical technique was nearly ready to send to Zimmer. Also, in early January the company's representatives traveled to Houston to continue work on the design of the child-size implants.[2] He recognized the need for a smaller distraction rod sized between the 1/8" (0.125") and 3/16" (0.188") diameter threaded compression rods, and after some discussion the odd size of 21/128" (0.164") diameter was settled on. They decided that following fatigue testing, three carefully selected surgeons would field-test it.

尽管哈灵顿的体力有限，可能不会再重返工作岗位，但他仍然非常积极地专注于工作。他已经准备好将关于手术技术新的操作视频交付给捷迈公司。此外，在1月初，该公司的代表前往休斯敦继续设计符合儿童尺寸的植入物。[2]他意识到需要一种直径介于1/8英寸（0.125英寸）和3/16英寸（0.18英寸）之间的较小的撑开棒放置在螺纹加压棒之间，经过讨论，最终确定棒的直径为21/128英寸（0.164英寸）。他们决定在经过疲劳测试后，由3名精心挑选的外科医生进行实地测试。

On February 1, 1973, Harrington presided at the SRS's semiannual board of directors meeting in Las Vegas held during the annual meeting of the AAOS, with which the SRS was now formally affiliated.[3] Some of the issues that were discussed provide a flavor of the meeting and the future of the organization. The first overseas annual meeting of the SRS was high on the agenda. Plans for convening it in Gothenburg, Sweden, were carefully reviewed with Alf Nachemson, who was in attendance and would serve as its local host. A post-meeting after Gothenburg was being planned for Lyon, France, where President-elect Robert Winter would soon visit and meet with local host Pierre Stagnara. The glossary that the SRS had been working on from its founding received final approval and was published during the year.[4] Managing the contentious issues of SRS size and membership qualifications was passed to Winter, who was directed to chair an ad hoc committee on review and revision of membership qualifications.

1973年2月1日，在美国骨科医师学会年会期间，哈灵顿在拉斯维加斯主持了脊柱侧凸研究学会的半年度委员会会议，此时脊柱侧凸研究学会已正式加入美国骨科医师学会。[3]会议上讨论的一些问题为会议的风格和组织的未来奠定了基调。脊柱侧凸研究学会的第一次海外年会是会议议程上的重点。阿尔夫·纳切姆森仔细陈述了在瑞典哥德堡召开会议的计划，并将作为东道主承办会议。而在哥德堡之后，会议计划在法国里昂举行，届时候任主席罗伯特·温特将会与东道主皮埃尔·斯塔格纳拉进行会面。脊柱侧凸研究学会自成立以来一直在编写的术语表获得了最终批准，并于当年发布。[4]脊柱侧凸研究学会规模和会员资格等有争议的问题的处理交给了温特，他担任着审查和修订会员资格的特设委员会的主席。

While at the AAOS annual meeting Harrington got together with Dane Miller, Zimmer development engineering director. This appears to have been the first time the two had met, and Harrington later told Hite that he had spent several hours with Miller discussing possible Harrington Spine Instrumentation redesign and cataloging changes to reflect the growing use of the instruments in treating other pathologies.[5] But follow-up from Miller apparently lagged.

在美国骨科医师学会年会上，哈灵顿与捷迈公司的研发工程总监戴恩·米勒会面。这似乎是两人第一次见面，哈灵顿后来告诉海特，他和米勒花了几个小时讨论了手册目录变化的可能性和对哈灵顿脊柱器械的重新构思，以适应该器械在治疗其他疾病中日益广泛的应用。[5]但米勒的后续跟进工作显然滞后了。

In his communications Harrington did not dwell on his health, but it was clearly impeding his ability to participate in various activities. In late March he was alerted that a lawsuit against Zimmer based on a broken Harrington Rod was being scheduled for trial, but his secretary replied on the same day the letter arrived that he had been admitted to the hospital, was scheduled for surgery, and could not serve as a defense witness.[6] Additionally, due to his physical condition, arrangements had to be made for a substitute, probably Houston neurosurgeon James Greenwood, to fulfill orthopedic surgeon Harrington's invitation to present his work on spine fracture management at the annual meeting of the Harvey Cushing Society of the American Academy of Neurological Surgeons meeting in Los Angeles on April 8-11.[7,8] Greenwood was a past president of the Cushing Society. Harrington later described his health problem as being vertebral artery occlusion causing "a posterior artery syndrome and I could not walk for a while."[9] He considered April 1973 to be the end of his practice.[10]

在交流中，哈灵顿没有很在意自己的健康状况，但不良的身体状况显然妨碍了他出席多项活动。3 月下旬，他被告知捷迈因一桩哈灵顿棒断棒事故而被起诉，诉讼即将开庭，但他的秘书在信件送达的同一天回复捷迈公司，哈灵顿已入院并计划接受手术，不能作为辩护证人。[6]此外，原本哈灵顿被邀请在 4 月 8 日至 11 日于洛杉矶举行的美国神经外科学会哈维·库兴分会年会上介绍他在脊柱骨折治疗方面的工作，但由于他的身体状况，不得不安排他人代为出席，代为出席的人很可能是休斯敦神经外科医生詹姆斯·格林伍德——库兴学会的前任主席。[7,8]哈灵顿后来将自己的健康问题描述为椎动脉闭塞导致“后动脉综合征，我一时无法行走”[9]。他经过慎重考虑，决定在 1973 年 4 月终止行医。[10]

An important recognition in Harrington's life played out at nearly the same time. In late winter 1972 he was invited to submit a manuscript for publication in *Clinical Orthopaedics and Related Research* and also for consideration for a Nicolas Andry Award from the Association of Bone and Joint Surgeons (ABJS). The suggested topic was "a long term follow-up report on the evolution and results of the Harrington Operation for scoliosis."[11] Harrington accepted the challenge, and on January 5, 1973, he and co-author Jesse Dickson submitted the manuscript that they titled "An Eleven-year Clinical Investigation of Harrington Instrumentation."[12] Barely mentioned was a short companion paper, "The History and Development of Harrington Instrumentation." On March 19 Harrington was notified that he had won the prestigious award, and arrangements were also made for him to present his study at ABJS's annual meeting scheduled for May 2-6 on Sea Island, Georgia.[13] When his condition worsened and it became apparent that he could not honor this commitment, Dickson was asked to deliver the speech. Afterwards, Harrington wrote his thanks to the ABJS for their "exceptional recognition of my work."[14] He also happily reported that he could walk without a cane and had better balance each day. ABJS President Nordby promptly replied, conveying "real pleasure in recognizing you for your excellent work over these years."[15] Nordby continued, "I had meant to write you sooner, complimenting Doctor Jesse H. Dickson on the excellent manner of his presentation of the paper and his fielding questions in a most forthrightand satisfactory way."

在同一时间哈灵顿也收到了人生中一次重要的嘉奖。1972年晚冬，他接到了《临床骨科和相关研究》杂志的约稿，并被考虑提名骨与关节外科医师学会（ABJS）颁发的尼古拉斯·安德利奖。受邀投稿的主题是“关于哈灵顿手术治疗脊柱侧凸的演变和结果的长期随访报告”。[11]哈灵顿接受了邀约，并在1973年1月5日和杰西·迪克森提交了他们的题目为《哈灵顿器械11年临床研究》的文章。[12]还有一篇同时发表的很少提到的简短论文《哈灵顿器械的历史和发展》。3月19日，哈灵顿被告知他获得了这一享有盛名的奖项，并被安排5月2日到6日在佐治亚州海岛举行的骨与关节外科医师学会年会上发表自己的研究成果。[13]当时他的病情恶化，很明显他无法赶赴会场，迪克森被邀请替其发表演讲。之后，哈灵顿写信感谢骨与关节外科医师学会“对我的工作特别认可”。[14]他还高兴地说，他可以不用拐杖行走，每天保持平衡的能力也更好了。骨与关节外科医师学会主席诺德比立即回复：“很荣幸能表彰您这些年来的出色工作。”[15]并接着说，“我本来想会后早点写信给您的，杰西·H. 迪克森医生在会上演讲的论文报告非常出色，回答问题也非常坦率直接，令人满意。”

Based on his correspondence, Harrington must have been feeling better by April 20 for despite the lack of any follow-up from his extended conversation with Miller at the AAOS meeting, Harrington wrote to him, signaling his enthusiasm for progress with the instrumentation."I am writing to you in reference to our conversation in Las Vegas earlier this year regarding beginning work on a whole new set of instruments. As you know, I am very interested in getting started on plans to introduce these new instruments which would be considerably streamlined and refined with excellence in every detail. Please let me know of any progress that you have made and any ideas that you might have along this line. I will be waiting to hear from you."[16] A handwritten note near the right lower margin of the office copy reads: "Conference Mr. Miller and Dr. H. Thursday, May 10 completed. Mr. Engen is to come up with a price on his outriggers—this should be made known to Mr. Miller—he may buy them." It is unknown whether Miller and Engen met or a purchase was made.

根据哈灵顿的信件，到4月20日，他的身体状况有所好转，因为虽然他在美国骨科医师学会会议上与米勒的长谈没有任何后续，但哈灵顿仍然写信给他，表明自己对器械研发的热情。"我写信给你是关于今年早些时候我们在拉斯维加斯关于开始一套全新的器械的研究的谈话。如你所知，我对开始计划介绍这些新器械很感兴趣，这些器械在每个细节上都相当精简和完善。请让我了解你在这项研究工作中已经取得的任何进展和想法。我会等你的消息。"[16]在信的副本的右下角有一张手写的便条，上面写着："米勒先生和哈灵顿博士的会议于5月10日星期四结束。恩金先生要给他的外撑开器出个价——这事要告诉米勒先生——他可能会买。" 目前还不清楚米勒和恩金是否见过面或进行了购买。

Two weeks later Harrington had several matters to discuss with Zimmer so he wrote Hite, his most durable contact at the company.[17] The first issue was that Dr. Marion Weiss of Warsaw, Poland, had readapted Gruca's spring technique for the treatment of spine fractures. Harrington seemed to be letting Zimmer know that he was aware of Weiss's US lecture tour and that several surgeons had asked Zimmer to produce the implants. He offered no judgment on the worth of the procedure. His second point was a reminder of his AAOS contact with Miller and the needs of Harrington Instrumentation. He also informed Hite that the new surgical technique movie had been completed and would be mailed in a few weeks. He suggested the need for a meeting, asking how best to schedule one since he preferred not to travel because of his recent rather serious illness. Harrington closed, "I realize a lot of this is outside of your realm of function, but I have no one else to turn to get the job done." Hite took care of business, and on May 25 Miller wrote Harrington to "explain the current status of the modification and improvement of Harrington Instrumentation," adding that "there is considerable activity in the Research and Development Department associated with your instrumentation."[18] The fatigue resistance of the smaller diameter rod (presumably the 0.164" diameter) was "somewhat limited" in compression. Methods of increasing the fatigue life being considered were increasing the radius in the thread root and grit blasting or shot peening the machined threaded surface to "impart a compressive stress on the surface." The marketing department had been charged with developing additions to the catalog for spondylolisthesis, fracture, and salvage surgery. Miller reported that the 3" and 4" long iliosacral rods had been increased from the 1-3/8" and 1-7/8" lengths Harrington had originally requested and received[19,20] and that they would be ready in a week or two. Finally, the 3/16"-rod diameter compatible #1254 hook was receiving the pediatric shoe modification that Harrington had recommended.

两周后，哈灵顿写信给他在捷迈公司里最熟悉的联系人海特，因为有几件事要和捷迈讨论。[17]第一个问题是波兰华沙的马里恩·韦斯重新应用了格鲁卡的弹簧技术治疗脊柱骨折。哈灵顿似乎是想让捷迈知道，他知道韦斯在美国的巡回演讲，还有几位外科医生要求捷迈制作内植物。他没有对这一手术的价值作出判断。信中第二点提到了他在美国骨科医师学会与米勒的联系以及对哈灵顿器械的需求。他还告诉海特，外科新技术的操作视频已经完成，将在几周内邮寄。他建议有必要召开一次会议，并询问怎样才是最好的安排，因为他最近患了相当严重的疾病，所以他不想出行。哈灵顿最后说道："我知道很多事情都超出了你的职责范围，但没有其他人可以帮我完成这项工作。"海特完成了哈灵顿的嘱托，5 月 25 日，米勒写信给哈灵顿，"解释哈灵顿器械的修改和改进的现状"，并补充道，"研发部门与您的器械相关的活动相当多"。[18]直径较小的棒（推测直径为 0.164 英寸）的抗疲劳性能在压缩时"有些受限"。提高疲劳寿命的方法是增加螺纹根部的半径，以及对加工过的螺纹表面进行砂喷或喷丸强化，以"在表面实施加压应力"。市场部负责在脊柱滑脱、骨折和急救手术的目录下方增加新的内容。米勒说，3 英寸和 4 英寸髂骶棒的长度相较于哈灵顿最初要求和收到的（1+3/8）英寸和(1+7/8) 英寸的长度已经有所增加，他们将在一到两周内准备好。[19,20]最后，根据哈灵顿的建议，为了适用于儿童，将直径 3/16 英寸的棒进行修改，以兼容 #1254 的钩。

Zimmer had received the new technique movie and judged it well made and very educational.[21] The only real quibble was the mention of another trade name, for which Harrington apologized. Zimmer intended to buy three copies from the Houston audiovisual company and make them available on a no-cost basis to any surgeon who wanted to view the surgical demonstration. Zimmer noted that they had already paid $3,000 toward the expense, reminded Harrington that his original estimate had been $4,000 to $6,000, and inquired about other additional charges. Harrington responded that all bills were not yet in, but when they were, he would update them as soon as possible.[22]

捷迈收到了这部新技术视频短片，认为它制作精良，很有教育意义。[21]唯一一个小瑕疵是提到了另一个商品名称，哈灵顿为此道了歉。捷迈打算从休斯敦视听公司购买三份副本，并免费提供给任何想要观看手术演示的外科医生。捷迈指出，他们已经支付了 3 000 美元的费用，并提醒哈灵顿，他最初的预算是 4 000~6 000 美元，并询问了其他额外费用。哈灵顿回应，所有的账单还没有出来，一旦出来了，他会尽快更新。[22]

Six weeks later on July 17 Miller wrote again providing more insight into the long discussion the two had had at the AAOS meeting. The focus was an alternative implant material Titanium 6 Aluminum 4 Vanadium, "Tivanium."[23] Miller wrote, "We here at Zimmer are very enthusiastic about its introduction in several carefully selected implant applications. Although there is only a small amount of data available thus far on the distraction rod study the fatigue testing program is proceeding with satisfactory progress." Miller explained the basis of their enthusiasm and enclosed copies of three published papers supporting these points. First, compared to 316 LVM stainless steel, Tivanium was less stiff, which should reduce stresses around the implant.[24] "One should expect, therefore, increased fusion rate due to higher stresses carried by the fusion."[25] Second, titanium and its alloys had been shown to have better biocompatibility, resulting in better fatigue and fatigue corrosion resistance.[26,27] Finally, to bring the Miller and Harrington communication up-to-date, three each of the sacral rods and four of the modified 1254 hooks were shipped on July 17.[28]

6 周后的 7 月 17 日，米勒再次回信，就两人在美国骨科医师学会会议上进行的长时间讨论提出了更多见解。重点是另一种替代植入材料钛 6 铝 4 钒，即"钛"。[23]米勒写道："我们捷迈公司非常热衷于将其引入几个精心挑选的内植物应用中。虽然到目前为止，关于撑开棒研究的数据很少，但疲劳测试项目取得了令人满意的进展。"米勒解释了他们为何如此积极，并附上了支持这些观点的三篇已发表论文的副本。首先，与 316 LVM 不锈钢相比，钛的硬度较低，这可以降低内植物周围的应力。[24]"因此，可以预期，融合所承载的更高应力会使融合率提高。"[25]其次，钛及其合金已被证明具有更好的生物相容性，从而具有更好的抗疲劳和疲劳腐蚀性能。[26,27]最后，为了尽快更新米勒和哈灵顿的交流成果，三根骶骨棒和四个改良的 1254 钩于 7 月 17 日被分别装运。[28]

By now the eighth annual meeting of the SRS in Gothenburg, Sweden, followed by the post-meeting in Lyon, France, was only two months away. Given Harrington's recent medical history, some hesitancy about making such an ambitious trip could have been expected, but he seemed to be eagerly anticipating it. His defense witness role in the broken Harrington Rod case was taken care of by deposition, for which he charged $250, thus eliminating the stress and strain a personal appearance would have caused. Presiding over the upcoming meetings and renewing his attachments to Europe must have been powerful motivators for him to travel. But before embarking, he had two career milestones to celebrate at home. On July 3 Joe W. King, head of Baylor College of Medicine's Division of Orthopedic Surgery, and William A. Spencer wrote Associate Dean Hebbel Hoff nominating Harrington for promotion from associate professor to professor.[29] In a three-plus page letter the men reviewed Harrington's many contributions to the college community since becoming a member in 1947. Their request was approved by the executive faculty committee on August 20. His promotion was not marked by any large ceremony.

此时距在瑞典哥德堡举行的第八届脊柱侧凸研究学会年会以及在法国里昂举行的后续会议已经只有两个月了。考虑到哈灵顿的病情，可以预料到他对这样一次长时间的行程是有些犹豫的，但他似乎也非常期待。在哈灵顿棒断棒案件中，他以笔录的形式完成了辩护证人的证词，为此他收取了 250 美元，从而消除了个人出庭可能带来的压力和紧张情绪。他此次旅行的强大动力是主办即将到来的会议和重塑与欧洲的联系。但在出发之前，他有两个职业里程碑要在家里庆祝。第一个里程碑是 7 月 3 日，贝勒医学院骨科主任乔 · W. 金和威廉 · A. 斯宾塞写信给副院长赫布尔 · 霍夫，提名哈灵顿从副教授晋升为教授。[29]在一封三页多的信中，他们回顾了哈灵顿自 1947 年成为学院一员以来对学院的诸多贡献。他们的请求在 8 月 20 日得到了执行教员委员会的批准。哈灵顿的晋升没有举行任何盛大的仪式。

The other recognition did involve ceremony. On August 10, 1973, Harrington received the Cora and Webb Mading Medal for his "Major World Wide Contributions to the Management of Scoliosis and to Rehabilitation Medicine."[30] The entire six pages of the August 1973 issue of the *Promethean*, the official publication of the Texas Institute for Rehabilitation and Research (TIRR), was devoted to his career and character. Included was a memory from the late 1940s. "In those early days, his qualities of leadership became apparent. A very personable and dynamic man with great warmth and humanity, he was able to stimulate his staff, motivate his patients and influence others. He became known as a demanding physician with a high standard of excellence who never leaves a doubt that his first interest is his patients. He has a unique understanding of the trauma of his patients and their families; they feel this and respond to it." After citing Harrington's global influence, Arthur Hodgson of Hong Kong wrote the following: "You have also stimulated Orthopaedic Surgeons to think, to think about other methods of correction of spinal deformities; and in this you have been an outstanding leader in the orthopaedic world."

相反，另一项嘉奖举行了仪式。1973 年 8 月 10 日，哈灵顿获得了科拉和韦布·马丁奖章，以表彰他“对脊柱侧凸治疗和康复医学的重大贡献”。[30]得克萨斯康复与研究中心的官方出版物《普罗米修斯》1973 年 8 月刊的整整六页都是关于他职业生涯和个性的介绍。其中包括一段 20 世纪 40 年代末的回忆，“他的领导才能在很早就显现了出来。他是一个非常有风度和活力的人，充满热情和仁慈，他能够激励他的员工，激励他的病人，并影响其他人。人们认为他是一位要求严格、精益求精的医生，并且从不怀疑他首要关注的是他的病人。他对病人及其家属的创伤有着独特的理解；他们能感受到并做出回应。”在列举哈灵顿的全球影响力后，中国香港的阿瑟·霍奇森写道：“你也激发了骨科医生去思考，思考其他矫正脊柱畸形的方法；在这方面，你一直是骨科界的杰出领导者。”

Years later, when giving the annual Hixon Hour Lecture at Harrington's alma mater, Jesse Dickson remembered that Harrington, in accepting this prestigious medal, dedicated it to his first nineteen patients.[31] During Dickson's speech about Harrington's life and work he added this insight: "Paul, as you can see, accomplished a great deal during his life. But to me, what was important about Paul was the fact that he was truly, really a very nice person. He had the welfare of mankind at heart. Not merely in a very vague way, but in a very personal sense. He was really concerned about the good of his family, his patients, his friends, and you and me as individuals. I doubt if anyone who ever knew Paul came away with a negative feeling."

多年以后，杰西·迪克森还记得在哈灵顿的母校做一年一度的“希克森时刻”演讲时，提及在接受这一久负盛名的奖章时，哈灵顿将它献给他最初的 19 位病人。[31]在迪克森关于哈灵顿的生活和工作的演讲中，他补充了这样的见解：“正如你所看到的，保罗在他的一生中取得了很大的成就。但对我来说，保罗最值得称道的是他真的是一个非常好的人。他把人类的福祉放在心上。不仅仅是以一种非常模糊的方式来表现，而是以一种非常个人的形式。他真的很关心他的家人、他的病人、他的朋友，以及你我个人的福祉。我觉得任何认识保罗的人在离开他时都不会有消极的感觉。”

Dane Miller had come to the Mading Medal ceremony prepared to present Harrington with an appreciation plaque from Zimmer. A few days after the event Harrington's secretary, Jeri Bone, wrote Mr. Miller.[32] "On behalf of Dr. Harrington I would like to thank you for the lovely plaque which was given to Dr. Harrington from Zimmer. I am only sorry that you were unable to make the presentation during the ceremony, but I understand that there was a mix-up in the program and it was overlooked. Dr. Harrington sincerely appreciated the plaque and the good wishes that came with it and it will hang on his office wall as a reminder of the happy occasion of August 10, 1973."

戴恩·米勒来到马丁勋章的颁奖典礼上，准备向哈灵顿赠送捷迈的感谢牌匾。活动结束几天后，哈灵顿的秘书杰里·博恩给米勒先生写了一封信，[32]“我谨代表哈灵顿医生感谢捷迈公司送给哈灵顿医生的令人愉快的牌匾。我很抱歉您不能在典礼上颁奖，但我知道这是安排上的混乱导致它被忽视了。哈灵顿医生非常感谢这枚牌匾以及伴随而来的美好祝愿，它将被挂在他办公室的墙上，作为对1973 年 8 月 10 日这一快乐时刻的回忆。”

September 1973 brought the long-awaited SRS meeting in Gothenburg, which ran from the seventeenth through the twenty-first with the follow-up meeting in Lyon on the twenty-sixth and twenty-seventh. Both meetings represented years of planning, and Harrington cast aside all doubts that he would be able to attend them and complete his presidential of office. The local host in Sweden was Alf Nachemson, and the program chairman was Ted Waugh, who had once been Nachemson's research fellow. The French scoliosis community had strong leaders and a long record of excellence. Harrington had been instrumental in helping Nachemson and the French scoliosis community to agree on plans for these historic meetings.

1973 年 9 月，人们期待已久的脊柱侧凸研究学会会议在哥德堡召开，会议从 17 日持续到 21 日，26 日和 27 日在里昂举行了后续会议。这两次会议都经过了多年的筹划，哈灵顿打消了他能否出席会议并完成主席任期的所有疑虑。瑞典当地的主办人是阿尔夫·纳切姆森，学术议程主席是泰德·沃，他曾经是纳切姆森的研究员。法国脊柱侧凸界有强有力的领导者和长期辉煌的纪录。哈灵顿在帮助纳切姆森和法国脊柱侧凸界就这些历史性会议的计划达成一致方面发挥了重要作用。

Indeed, the meeting in Gothenburg had been worth working and waiting for. It drew the largest total number of attendees (257, including spouses), the largest number of papers presented at an annual meeting (49, a record not passed for six years), and the most new members in a year since the founding year (20 new active fellows, 10 new corresponding members [8 in 1972 and 2 in 1973], and one new associate member).[33,34] The difficult issue of membership qualification was confined to board of directors' deliberations, where the ad hoc committee charged with addressing this question proposed a program designed to limit the annual increase in the number of active fellows to 5% yearly. The dialogue was to be continued. At the first membership meeting President Harrington presented certificates to the new members.[35] George Dommisse, who was from Pretoria, South Africa, and had been last year's presidential guest speaker, presented President Harrington a copy of his thesis, *The Blood Supply of the Human Spinal Cord at Birth*, for the Scoliosis Research Society. In accepting the gift, Harrington announced Dommisse's election to honorary membership and presented a certificate to him.

事实上，哥德堡会议是值得付出和期待的。它吸引了最多的与会者（257 人，包括会员配偶），最多的年会发表论文（49 篇，此纪录在 6 年内未被打破），以及自成立以来最多的新成员［20 名新活跃研究员，10 名新通讯成员（1972 年 8 名，1973 年 2 名）以及 1 名准新成员］。[33,34]会员资格这一棘手问题受限于委员会的审议，负责解决这一问题的特设委员会提出了一个计划，旨在将活跃研究员人数的年增长限制在每年 5%。对话将继续进行。在第一次会员大会上，主席哈灵顿向新会员颁发了证书。[35]来自南非比勒陀利亚的乔治·多米斯是去年的主席特邀演讲者，他向主席哈灵顿赠送了一份他为脊柱侧凸研究学会撰写的论文《出生时人类脊髓的血液供应》的副本。在接受礼物时，哈灵顿宣布多米斯当选为荣誉会员，并向他颁发了证书。

Included in the business meetings were several committee reports. Dickson was the chair of the data retrieval committee and reported difficulties in retrieval due to incomplete input. The plan was to stick with the current commitment to the pilot computer study while continuing with the data retrieval punch cards. The research committee reported that the latest operative mortality rate was 0.56% (14 of 2,500) and neurologic morbidity was six paraplegias with no information about the size of the patient pool from which they were drawn. Calendar-year reporting was planned for the future. The second business meeting began with officer election, which saw Ken Leatherman of Louisville, Kentucky, chosen as president-elect. Committee reports continued with the liaison chair announcing that representatives of about twenty nations had met with selected board of director members regarding the possible formation of an International Society of Scoliosis. Following discussion, no one was in favor of forming such a group or of allying with SICOT. At the concluding business meeting Hall's motion that the board of directors explore the possibility of granting active fellowship to Nachemson passed unanimously. There was an international desire for more involvement than corresponding membership. Sometime during the meeting a group picture was taken to document the historic occasion of the first overseas meeting of the SRS. *See figure 11.1.*

1. Alf Nachemson
2. David B. Levine
3. G. Dean MacEwen
4. Kenton D. Leatherman
5. John H. Moe
6. Robert B. Winter
7. Paul R. Harrington
8. James H. Hardy
9. Gordon W. D. Armstrong
10. John D. Leidholt
11. R. Kirklin Ashley
12. Jacob J. Graham
13. Michael Fontanetta
14. Dennis Paterson
15. S. Henry LaRocca
16. Jorge O. Galante
17. Ivan Ferraretto
18. Thomas T. Laughlin, Jr.
19. Marr P. Mullen
20. John H. Hurley
21. Robert W. Florence
22. Edward H. Simmons
23. John P. Kostuik
24. John H. Doherty
25. Ronald L. DeWald
26. Allan M. McKelvie
27.
28. Bob Keiser
29. Alvin S. Isaacson
30. Gordon Robin
31. John E. Hall
32. James W. Tupper
33. Philip A. Zorab
34. Sidney L. Wallace
35. Glenn Edwards
36. Alberto Ponte
37. Andrew W. Lawrence
38. Wilton H. Bunch
39. Thomas I. Lowery
40. Walter P. Blount
41. Robert Rolf
42. Robert C. Zuege
43. Robert B. Keller
44. Hamlet A. Peterson
45. Worth Miller Gross
46. Edmond J. McDonnell
47. Charles I. Nadel
48. Charles Manning
49. Horton L. Murray
50.
51. Alexander M. Wright
52. Hugo A. Keim
53. Anders F. Langenskiold
54. Walter P. Bobechko
55. George F. Dommisse
56. Jean Pierre Lebard
57. Vernon L. Nickel
58. William F. Donaldson
59. Jean Dubousset
60. Randolph B. Cockrell
61. Wood W. Lovell
62. Basil M. Boyd
63. Claude Regis Michel
64.
65.
66. Allen S. Edmonson
67. Page W. Nelson
68. Stanley Hoppenfeld
69. Charles F. Heinig
70. Theodore R. Waugh
71. Clyde Lester Nash, Jr.
72. Richard F. Slager
73. Gordon L. Engler
74. Allan Dwyer
75. Keith D. Vanden Brink
76.
77. Jose Valderama
78. David S. Bradford
79. Gijs Slot
80. James E. Holmblad
81. George Jonas
82. André Vincent
83. Richard M. Kilfoyle
84. Howard H. Steele
85. Luther M. Strayer
86. Kenneth M. Hannon
87. Jesse H. Dickson
88. Ben E. Veraart
89.
90. Arthur Liggett

Figure 11.1 ***Picture and roster of attendees at the eighth annual meeting of the SRS held in Gothenburg, Sweden. Paul Harrington, president, and Alf Nachemson, local host.*** (***SRS Archives***)

图 11.1 在瑞典哥德堡举行的第八届脊柱侧凸研究学会年会的与会者名单和照片。主席保罗·哈灵顿和当地主办者阿尔夫·纳切姆森(脊柱侧凸研究学会档案馆)

会员商务会议讨论了几份委员会报告。迪克森是数据检索委员会的主席，他报告了由于输入数据不完整而导致的检索困难的问题，他们的计划是在继续研究数据检索收集的同时，继续进行目前的计算机试点研究。研究委员会报告称，最新的手术死亡率为0.56%（14/2 500），神经系统发病情况为6例截瘫，但没有关于病人总数的信息。今后计划采用年度报告的形式。第二次会员商务会议以领导者选举开始，肯塔基州路易斯维尔的肯·莱瑟曼被选为候任主席。委员会的报告继续进行，联络主席宣布大约20个国家的代表已经与选定的委员会成员会面，讨论成立国际脊柱侧凸学会的可能性。经过讨论，没有人赞成组建这样一个组织，也没有人赞成与国际矫形与创伤外科学会结盟。在最后的会员商务会议上，霍尔提出的委员会共同商讨授予纳切姆森活跃研究员称号的议案获得了一致通过。委员会希望脊柱侧凸研究学会能吸引更多的国际参与者加入研究，而不是仅仅单纯授予通信会员资格。会议期间合影留念，记录了脊柱侧凸研究学会首次海外会议的历史性时刻。(图 11.1)

The crown jewel of the SRS lay in the scientific sessions of its annual meetings where problems were shared and the search for solutions encouraged. Paper summaries of this portion of the meeting were published early the following year.[36] The problems drawing attention in 1973 were distraction (longitudinal translation) paraplegia, seemingly an annual topic; thoracic lordosis in three related papers; lateral translation correction loads in two related papers; and vertebral body resection for tumor. Distraction paraplegia was by then recognized as an occasional complication. Unknown was the margin of safety in day-to-day practice. Ponte's experience suggested that the safety margin was narrow, given that 6 of 182 patients (3.3%) developed paraplegia after Harrington Instrumentation augmented with costotransversotomy, which allowed greater correction.[37] In all of them paralysis was at the T8 level, and fortunately in all, recovery had occurred either by raising a low blood pressure to above normal or by removal of the rod. Whether or not Harrington's operative sequence, involving placement of compression instrumentation between initial and final distraction, was followed was not mentioned in the abstract.

学术环节是脊柱侧凸研究学会年度会议皇冠上的明珠，在会议上分享问题并鼓励寻找解决方案。这部分会议的书面摘要在次年年初发表。[36] 1973 年引起关注的问题是撑开性（纵向平移）截瘫，这似乎在每年都是年度话题；胸椎前凸相关文献三篇；两篇论文与侧方平移矫正载荷相关；一篇内容是椎体肿瘤切除。撑开性截瘫当时被认为是一种偶然的并发症。在日常实践中，安全边际是未知的。庞特的经验表明安全边际较窄，182 名病人接受哈灵顿器械加肋横突切除术，以便达到更大的矫正，有 6 例（3.3%）出现截瘫。[37]所有病人的瘫痪都在 T8 水平，幸运的是，所有病人都通过将低水平血压提高到正常水平以上或去除哈灵顿棒而恢复。在摘要中没有提及手术是否遵循哈灵顿的操作顺序，包括在初始和最终撑开之间放置压缩器械。

The problem that received the most attention (in three papers) was diminished or even negative sagittal plane kyphosis. Nash and Nevins made two related observations: first that scoliosis corrections of as much as 60% did not usually improve pulmonary function and second that scoliosis patients tended to have reduced anterior-posterior chest diameters.[38] They determined the anterior-posterior/lateral chest diameter ratio from standard radiographs, which was lower in children with thoracic scoliosis than controls, and found that postoperative pulmonary function was lower in patients with lower anterior-posterior/lateral chest diameter ratios. This suggested that changes in pulmonary function were better correlated with thoracic roundness than lateral curvature. Following the same theme, Winter reported on four patients with "malignant idiopathic lordoscoliosis" ranging from −6° to −40°.[39] Following Harrington Instrumentation and fusion, two patients with significant decrease in their lordosis had marked improvement in vital capacity while the other two had no improvement in either lordosis or vital capacity. Finally, Brown and Perry reported on nine post-polio patients with progressive scoliosis who had long (cervical spine to the sacrum) posterior fusions at an average age of eight and one-half years.[40] At the end of growth they had handicapping lordosis. The need to counteract thoracic lordosis and produce thoracic kyphosis exposed a weakness in Harrington Instrumentation. It lacked the capacity to produce positive posterior angulation of the thoracic spine, requiring a posterior translation of the thoracic spine apex.

在三篇论文中，最受关注的问题是矢状面后凸的减少甚至负矢状面后凸。纳什和内文斯进行了两个相关的观察：第一，高达 60%的侧凸矫正通常不能改善肺功能，第二，脊柱侧凸病人的前后胸径往往呈缩小的趋势。[38]他们通过标准 X 光片确定了胸椎前后径/侧径比值，胸椎侧凸患者的这一比值低于对照组，并发现胸椎前后径/侧径比值较低的病人术后肺功能较差。这表明肺功能的变化与胸部圆度的相关性高于侧方弯曲度。温特报告了 4 例“恶性特发性前侧凸”病例，范围为-6°至-40°。[39]经哈灵顿器械内固定融合术治疗后，2 例前凸角明显减小的病例肺活量明显改善，另2例前凸角和肺活量均无改善。最后，布朗和佩里报告了9例患有进行性脊柱侧凸的脊髓灰质炎病例，他们在平均年龄8岁半时进行了长节段（颈椎至骶骨）的后路融合。[40]在生长末期，他们出现了阻碍性前凸。而消除胸椎前凸并形成胸椎后凸的需求，暴露了哈灵顿器械的缺点。它缺乏使胸椎向后正向成角的能力，需要将胸椎顶点向后平移。

Two other papers focused on the need for direct lateral translation for smaller lateral curves. Study of idiopathic scoliosis models led Schultz to conclude that "disk-stiffness reduction should allow large increases in immediate lateral correction with the application of lateral forces."[41] Just as he had three years earlier, Roaf made the case for horizontally (laterally) applied forces to correct lateral curves of less than 45° as well as the accompanying transverse plane rotation deformity, using posterior spine implants he had designed.[42] In addition to distraction paraplegia and transverse plane translational instrumentation needs, increasingly extensive spine resection was addressed by guest speaker Bertil Stener in "Resection of the Spine for Tumors."[43] These large operations sometimes included the sacrum and left the spine with varying amounts of instability, up to and including total instability. Currently available spine instrumentation could not completely compensate for the increasing amounts of spine instability sometimes resulting from increasingly complex spine surgeries.

另外两篇论文关注的是对于较小的侧方弯曲需要直接的横向平移。对特发性脊柱侧凸模型的研究使舒尔茨得出了结论："椎间盘刚度的降低应允许在施加侧方力的情况下即刻进行侧方矫正。"[41]像三年前一样，罗夫使用他设计的脊柱后路内植物，水平（侧方）施加力量来矫正小于45°的侧凸以及伴随的水平面旋转畸形。[42]除了撑开性截瘫和横向平移器械这些议题，特邀演讲者伯蒂尔·斯坦纳做了题目为"脊柱肿瘤切除术"的演讲，他提到了运用越来越广泛的脊柱切除术。[43]这些大手术有时涉及骶骨，使脊柱出现不同程度的不稳定，甚至完全不稳定。目前可用的脊柱内固定器械不能完全弥补越来越多的脊柱失稳（有时是由日益复杂的脊柱手术所导致的）。

Sometime during the meeting President Harrington presented "A Written Presidential Welcome," in which he offered the "opinion that we have an armamentarium for treating scoliosis which is almost complete."[44] He listed fifteen present and future projects of the SRS, abbreviated as follows: federal support, international communication and interaction, modification and improvement of data retrieval, creation of specific problem study groups, announcement of postgraduate fellowships in scoliosis, continued morbidity and mortality analyses, refinement of terminology, establishment of a program for school screening, education of school officials and general doctors, lay public education, expectation of total member participation and answers to the international membership problem, public relations, establishment of a basic research award, encouragement of non-orthopedist participation, and expansion of interest in related spinal deformities.

会议期间，主席哈灵顿发表了“主席欢迎致辞”，其中他提出了“我们有一套几乎完整的治疗脊柱侧凸的医疗配备”。[44]他列举了脊柱侧凸研究学会目前和未来的15个项目，简称如下：联邦支持、国际交流和互动、数据检索的修改和完善、创建特定问题研究小组、脊柱侧凸研究生专科培训公告、并发症发生率和死亡率的继续分析、术语精练、建立学校筛查项目、学校职能人员和普通医生的教育、公众教育、对全体会员参与的期望和对国际会员问题的解答、公共关系、设立基础研究奖、鼓励非骨科医生参与和提升对扩大脊柱畸形相关的研究兴趣。

Many conferees reconvened September 25 – 27 in Lyon for the Tuesday through Thursday meeting of the “Groupe d'Etude de la Scoliose.”[45] The first day featured a choice of three tours. The Wednesday-Thursday scientific program included a tour of the Centre de Readaptation Fonctionnelle des Massues, presentations about plaster casts, braces, and traction-suspension, and focused scientific exhibit presentations followed by comments. Twenty-two presentations were made by current and future leaders of the French scoliosis community, many of whom were or would become internationally known for the thoughtfulness, quality, and originality of their work. More detail about the meeting in the form of abstracts or proceedings was apparently not made or kept.

许多与会者于9月25日至27日在里昂再次召开了周二至周四的“脊柱侧凸练习组”会议。[45]第一天有三种参观学习方式可供选择。周三至周四的学术活动包括参观马苏埃基金中心，介绍石膏、支具和牵引—悬吊，以及重点的学术展示和评论。法国脊柱侧凸界现任和未来的领军学者做了22场演讲，他们中许多人已经或将要以其工作的思想性、高品质和原创性而享誉国际。但是，此次会议没有以摘要或会议记录的形式提供或保存更多细节。

The trip to Sweden alone would have to have been physically difficult for Harrington. Whether or not he made the post-SRS meeting trip to Lyon isn't clear although there are a couple of suggestions that he did not. Minutes of the SRS board of directors' meeting immediately after the last scientific program, which he would have been expected to attend as the immediate past-president, did not list him as being present. Several months later he wrote Dommisse that he "had to have his carotids done on my return from Sweden" and that he continued to plod along with his basal artery syndrome.[46]

就哈灵顿的身体状况而言，完成瑞典之行就已经相当困难了。目前尚不清楚他是否参加了脊柱侧凸研究学会会议后的里昂之行，尽管有一些迹象表明他没有参加。在最后一个学术日程结束后的脊柱侧凸研究学会委员会会议记录中，他本应以刚卸任的主席身份出席，但没有记录表明他在场。几个月后，他写信给多米斯说，"我从瑞典回来后就需要做颈动脉手术"，他还得继续忍受基底动脉综合征的折磨。[46]

The Harrington-Zimmer correspondence slowed to a trickle for the remainder of 1973. The only implant design change was to decrease the hook tip thickness of the #1253 and # 1254 hooks by 1/64", from 1/16" to 3/64".[47] Instrumentation sets for spondylolisthesis, fractures, and salvage operations were being prepared. Harrington commented that these were the only changes he intended to make at the moment.[48] He inquired, "Have you heard from Leatherman on his critique of the children's implant? I talked with him at length during a recent European meeting and I would like to work closely with him on any suggestions he might have. He is willing to add this to the Harrington Instrumentation. "Another correspondence was also probably a byproduct of the Gothenburg meeting. Harrington asked J. Alan Morgan, Zimmer's president at the time, to donate a set of Harrington instruments to Dr. Balu Sankaran, FRCs, director professor at the Central Institute of Orthopaedics in New Delhi. India.[49] Morgan had responded favorably and had a package of twenty-three instruments worth $575. 15 prepared for overseas shipment and sent to Harrington for mailing. Harrington also requested and received an instrumentation rack from Zimmer and arranged for Methodist Hospital, Houston and TIRR to fill it with Harrington Instrumentation. Harrington contributed a movie and some technique information, and he arranged for these valuable gifts to be sent through diplomatic channels.[50] Whether they were received is not known.

在 1973 年剩下的时间里，哈灵顿和捷迈之间的通信变得越来越少。通信中对内固定器械唯一的改变是将#1253 和#1254 钩的钩尖厚度从 1/16 英寸减少到 3/64 英寸，减少了 1/64 英寸。[47]腰椎滑脱、骨折和挽救性手术的器械正在制备中。哈灵顿表示这是他目前唯一打算做出的改变。[48]他询问："你有没有听过莱瑟曼对儿童内植物的批评？在最近的一次欧洲会议上，我与他进行了详细的交谈，我愿意就他可能提出的任何建议与他密切合作。他愿意将此建议添加到哈灵顿器械中。"另一份通信可能也是哥德堡会议的"副产品"。哈灵顿要求捷迈当时的总裁 J. 艾伦·摩根捐赠一套哈灵顿器械给印度新德里中央骨科研究所的主任教授巴卢·桑卡兰博士。[49]摩根做出了积极回应，他准备了一套价值 575.15 美元的器械，共 23 件，准备运往海外，交给哈灵顿去邮寄。哈灵顿还从捷迈那里申请并收到了一个器械盒，并安排休斯敦卫理公会医院和得克萨斯州康复与研究中心用器械盒放置哈灵顿器械。哈灵顿还提供了一部手术操作视频和一些技术资料，他安排通过外交渠道寄送这些珍贵的礼物。[50]然而，这些物品是否被顺利接收不得而知。

Of Harrington's 38 total lifetime academic publications, 6 appeared in 1973, making this by far his most productive year. Five were coauthored with Jesse Dickson, another indication of Harrington's good fortune that Dickson answered his call after his heart attack in November 1968. The six published papers that follow are ordered by the year they were first presented and are accompanied by a brief summary. "The Evolution of the Harrington Instrumentation Technique in Scoliosis" study revealed that while idiopathic scoliosis postoperative curve corection had been stable at 64% to 66% over the eight years of the study (1961–68), correction maintenance at three years' follow-up had improved from 24% to 51%.[51] The four major technique changes credited with this improvement were moving the lumbar distraction hook from the articular facet to the lamina, increasing cast and immobilization time, and adding a dowel fusion in the thoracic spine and a posterior-lateral fusion in the lumbar spine.

在哈灵顿一生发表的 38 篇学术论文中，有 6 篇发表于 1973 年，这是他迄今为止最多产的一年。其中 5 篇是与杰西·迪克森合著的。迪克森可以算是哈灵顿运气很好的明显例证：1968 年 11 月，哈灵顿心脏病发作后，迪克森接受了他的招聘（哈灵顿的事业后继有人）。接下来发表的 6 篇论文按它们首次发表的年份排序，并附有一个简短的摘要。《哈灵顿脊柱侧凸器械技术的演变》中的研究表明，虽然特发性脊柱侧凸术后弯曲矫正在 8 年的研究中（1961—1968 年）稳定在 64%~66%，但在 3 年的随访中，矫正维持率从 24%提高到 51%。[51]与此相关的四个主要技术变化如下：将腰椎撑开钩从关节突移至椎板，增加石膏和制动时间，在胸椎中增加榫钉（骨栓）式融合和在腰椎中增加后外侧融合。

The "Pre- and Postoperative Evaluation of Scoliotic Patients for Hiatal Hernia" study revealed the incidence was 6.2% and 2.1%, respectively, in idiopathic scoliosis and zero in scoliosis of known cause, results much lower than in a previous study.[52,53] It ended hiatal hernia as a likely cause of serious gastrointestinal dysfunction in patients with scoliosis. Reporting these findings, Dickson made his first presentation at an SRS annual meeting and the same year became a fellow. This was at the society's sixth meeting, which was held in Hartford, Connecticut, in 1971. In "The Development and Further Prospects of Internal Fixation of the Spine" the four categories in which spine instrumentation could be helpful were discussed: scoliosis, fractures below T1 with or without paraplegia, grades III and IV spondylolisthesis, and salvage of the "lumbar spine syndrome."[54] "Harrington Instrumentation in the Fractured, Unstable Thoracic and Lumbar Spine" described usage in twenty-nine patients operated on since January 1, 1960.[55] Distraction instrumentation utilized the almost always intact anterior longitudinal ligament to gain realignment and stabilization. Three cases were presented, and the authors' impression was that the procedure speeded rehabilitation and might result in more neurological recovery, although at that point there were too few cases to be sure.

《脊柱侧凸病人食管裂孔疝术前和术后评估》一文的研究显示，在特发性脊柱侧凸中，食管裂孔疝的发生率分别为6.2%和2.1%，在已知原因的脊柱侧凸中为0，这一结果远低于之前的研究。[52,53]它终结了食管裂孔疝作为脊柱侧凸病人严重胃肠功能障碍的可能原因的观点。迪克森在脊柱侧凸研究学会年会上以此观点作了他的第一次报告，并在同年成为一名会员。这是该学会的第六次会议，于1971年在康涅狄格州哈特福德举行。《脊柱内固定的发展和进一步展望》一文讨论了可能受益于脊柱内固定的四类疾病：脊柱侧凸、伴或不伴截瘫的T1以下骨折、Ⅲ及Ⅳ度脊柱滑脱以及"腰椎综合征"。[54]《哈灵顿器械在不稳定胸腰椎骨折中的应用》一文描述了自1960年1月1日以来29名病人的应用情况。[55]撑开器械几乎总是利用完整的前纵韧带来获得脊柱的重新排列和稳定。作者展示了三个病例，并认为该手术加速了病人脊柱的康复，且可能获得更多的神经功能的恢复，但是当时病例数过少，结果难以确定。

"The History and Development of Harrington Instrumentation" was Harrington's recollection of history prepared to accompany "An Eleven-year Clinical Investigation" for receipt of the 1973 Nicolas Andry Award.[56] In "An Eleven-year Clinical Investigation of Harrington Instrumentation: A Preliminary Report of 578 Cases" patients were studied who had idiopathic scoliosis (curves between 30° and 90°), were aged eleven through twenty years, had no prior spine surgery, and were operated on by Harrington or Dickson at Methodist Hospital, Houston. They were divided into eight chronological study groups (Ⅰ–Ⅷ) to determine which "type of fusion, fusion supplementation, post-operative casts, and postoperative mobilization" gave the optimal long-term result. Although the statistics cited were still evolving after the technique change or changes had been made, observations as the current group progressed suggested what, if any, change was needed for the next group. The three-year follow-up of patients in the first four groups was 85% (327 of 384).

《哈灵顿器械的历史和发展》是哈灵顿为接受 1973 年获得的尼古拉斯·安德利奖而准备的历史回顾。[56]在《哈灵顿器械 11 年的临床研究：578 例病例的初步报告》中，他研究了 11~20 岁的特发性脊柱侧凸（角度在 30°~90°之间）病人，这些病人没有脊柱手术史，在休斯敦卫理公会医院由哈灵顿或迪克森完成手术。他们按时间顺序被分为八个研究组（Ⅰ–Ⅷ），以确定哪种"融合类型、辅助融合、术后石膏固定和术后活动"具有最佳的长期疗效。虽然所引用的统计数据在技术变更后仍在不断变化，但随着当前组的进展，观察结果会提示下一组需要什么变化（如果有的话）。前四组病人 3 年随访率为 85%（327/384）。

In this report the high prevalence of pseudarthrosis (23%, 7 of 31), hook dislocation (35%, 11 of 31), and change in instrument position (32%, 10 of 31), as well as the loss of correction obtained (eventually 43%, 67% to 24%, $n = 28$ at three years) in Group Ⅰ (January 1961 to January 1962) resulted in moving the lumbar distraction hook to the lumbar lamina, adding a Moe-type concave facet fusion in the thoracic spine, and increasing the recumbent cast time from one to three months and the total cast time from two to four and a half months. In Group Ⅱ (January 1962 to mid-1963) the prevalence of pseudarthrosis (6%, 3 of 53) and hook dislocation (2%, 1 of 53) was greatly improved, but the change in implant position (43%, 23 of 53) rate was still high. For Group Ⅲ (mid-1963 to late 1966) a dowel concave facet fusion was done, experimental calf bone graft (Boplant) added, and cast time further increased to three months recumbent and six months total. Pseudarthrosis prevalence further improved (1%, 2 of 168) and no hook dislocations occurred, but changes in instrument position (23%, 39 of 168) and the three-year loss of correction obtained (eventually 28%, 65% to 37%, $n = 144$) remained high. By radiographic and direct observation on reoperated patients the heterogenic bone graft (Boplant) was found unsatisfactory because of poor incorporation into the fusion mass and the appearance of blocking transformation of the fusion mass. Although no wound infections had been encountered in groups Ⅰ and Ⅱ, prophylactic antibiotics were "used and carried throughout the hospitalization period" in Group Ⅲ. Two infections developed, one resulting in death due to a deep abscess and septicemia occurring after discharge. Also, genitourinary infections peaked at 6% (10 of 168) in Group Ⅲ. Prophylactic antibiotics were discontinued for the remainder of the study, and the wound infection rate was 0.6% (2 of 326) from that point on. The major change in Group Ⅳ (late 1966 through 1968), in addition to stopping use of Boplant, was the addition of a bilateral lateral gutter fusion from T11 down to the lower end of the fusion site although no extra bone was added. This "dramatically improved the maintenance of correction," the three-year loss of correction obtained being reduced to 14% (64% to 50%, $n = 109$), although the "fusion mass was still felt to be only reasonable."

在本研究中，第一组（1961 年 1 月至 1962 年 1 月）假关节（23%，7/31）、脱钩（35%，11/31）、器械移位（32%，10/31）以及矫正丢失（最终 43%，67% 至 24%，3 年 $n=28$）的发生率较高，致使腰椎撑开钩移至腰椎椎板，在胸椎增加了一个莫的凹侧小关节进行融合，并将卧位石膏时间从 1 个月增加到 3 个月，总石膏固定时间从 2 个月增加到 4.5 个月。第二组（1962 年 1 月至 1963 年中期）假关节（6%，3/53）和脱钩（2%，1/53）的发生率明显改善，但内植物移位（43%，23/53）仍然很高。第三组（1963 年中期至 1966 年后期）采用凹侧关节突融合术，增加了实验性牛犊骨植骨（Boplant®），石膏固定时间进一步延长至卧位 3 个月，共 6 个月。假关节发生率进一步改善（1%，2/168），无脱钩发生，但内植物移位（23%，39/168）和 3 年矫正丢失（最终 28%，65%～37%，$n=144$）仍然很高。通过对再次手术病人的 X 光片和直接观察，发现异种骨移植效果并不令人满意，因为融合块整合不良，转化受阻。尽管第一组和第二组没有出现伤口感染，但第三组“在整个住院期间全程预防性使用抗生素”，还是出现两例感染，其中一例出院后因深部脓肿和败血症而死亡。此外，第三组泌尿生殖系统感染率最高，达 6%（168 例中的 10 例）。在剩余的研究中停止使用预防性抗生素，从那时起，伤口感染率为 0.6%（326 例中的 2 例）。第四组（1966 年末至 1968 年）的主要变化是，除了停止使用异种骨，增加了从 T11 到融合部位下端的双侧后外侧融合术，并且没有增加额外的植骨。这“极大地改善了矫形的维持率”，3 年矫正丢失率减少到 14%（64%～50%，$n=109$），尽管“感觉融合块只能算得上是差强人意”。

Harrington's 1968 heart attack meant that he operated on almost all the patients in groups Ⅰ through Ⅳ and Dickson operated on almost all in groups Ⅴ through Ⅷ. In Group Ⅴ (January through December 1969) autogenous iliac bone was added to supplement the fusion. The compression assembly was omitted as others reported comparable results with distraction only. The result was 10% less postoperative correction. In groups Ⅵ (January through December 1970), Ⅶ (January through December 1971), and Ⅷ (January through July 1, 1972) the compression assembly and autogenous iliac crest bone graft were used, and the only change was postoperative immobilization. In all three groups the total cast time was nine months, but more activity was gradually permitted. In groups Ⅵ and Ⅶ a Milwaukee occiput-chin extension was added for the first six months, but the fusion mass suggested that a body cast high in the front and back would be satisfactory.

1968 年，哈灵顿心脏病发作，这意味着他几乎为所有第一组至第四组的病人做了手术，而迪克森几乎为所有第五组至第八组的病人做了手术。第五组（1969 年 1 月至 12 月）采用自体髂骨辅助融合。去掉压缩棒，因为其他人的报告与仅使用撑开棒的结果差不多。结果是术后矫正减少了 10%。第六组（1970 年 1 月至 12 月）、第七组（1971 年 1 月至 12 月）和第八组（1972 年 1 月至 7 月 1 日）使用了压缩棒和自体髂骨植骨，唯一的变化是术后制动。在这三组中，石膏总使用时间均为 9 个月，但逐渐允许病人有更多活动。在第六组和第七组中，前 6 个月增加密尔沃基枕—颏扩展固定，但融合块提示躯体前、后高位石膏固定的结果是令人满意的。

From the beginning Harrington considered minimizing operative time and blood loss important to the safety and success of the surgery. He achieved his operative time and blood loss goal with an average operating time of 116 minutes, a blood loss of 748 cc, and blood replacement of 629 cc. For comparison, two contemporary series reported from major scoliosis centers reported an average operative time of 240 minutes, with the average blood loss in one of 1,900 cc[58] and the average blood replacement in the other of 5.3 units (approximately 2,500 cc)[59]. Harrington passed his attention to time and blood loss on to Dickson, who had the capacity to meet his mentor's standards. Comparing Harrington (groups Ⅰ-Ⅳ) and Dickson (groups Ⅴ-Ⅷ), the average operating time was 106 minutes for the former and 127 minutes for the latter, blood loss was 618 cc and 878 cc, and blood replacement was 575 cc and 683 cc. The differences could largely be attributed to obtaining the autogenous iliac crest bone graft, something Harrington did not do and Dickson did. Any effect this small difference in time and blood loss may have had on the safety and success of the procedure was overshadowed by the high frequency of hook dislocation and changes in instrument position in the first four groups.

哈灵顿从一开始就认为减少手术时间和出血量对手术的安全和成功很重要。他达到了控制手术时间和出血量，平均手术时间为 116 min，平均失血量为 748 cc，平均输血量为 629 cc。相比而言，来自主要脊柱侧凸中心的两项同期系列报告的平均手术时间为 240 min，平均失血量为 1 900 cc,[58]输血量为 5.3 个单位（约 2 500 cc）。[59]哈灵顿把他对时间和失血量的关注传授给了迪克森，后者有能力达到他的标准。哈灵顿第一组～第四组和迪克森第五组～第八组的平均手术时间分别为 106 min 和 127 min，术中出血量分别为 618 cc 和 878 cc，输血量分别为 575 cc 和 683 cc。这种差异很大程度上是由于迪克森进行了自体取髂骨移植，而哈灵顿没有。这些在时间和出血量方面的微小差异对手术的安全性和成功率可能产生的影响被前四组中脱钩和内植物移位的高发生率所掩盖。

Nineteen seventy-three must have been both bitter and sweet for Harrington. In April, at the age of 61, it became clear that poor health would prevent him from ever practicing again. But that did not stop him from contributing to the clinical science he loved. With the invaluable collaboration of Jesse Dickson they had completed a major clinical study, "Eleven-year Clinical Investigation," which provided a remarkably detailed picture of the evolution of their surgical technique. It had also been a year of recognition. Harrington had been able to successfully complete his term as president of the SRS, leading the society during its first overseas annual meeting. Additionally, he was honored by his peers in the Houston Orthopaedic Club in 1973 (and would receive a similar recognition from the Houston Surgical Society the following year).[60] But, there was a sense of change emerging as some presentations had begun to identify the need for a wider spectrum of instrumentation corrective load applications.

1973 年对哈灵顿来说一定是喜忧参半。这一年 4 月，61 岁的他很明显因为身体状况不佳而无法再次行医。但这并没有阻止他为自己热爱的临床科学做出贡献。在杰西·迪克森的鼎力相助下，他们完成了一项重要的临床研究——“11 年临床研究”，该研究为他们的外科技术的演变提供了非常详细的说明。这也是他被认可的一年。哈灵顿顺利结束了他作为脊柱侧凸研究学会主席的任期，并领导该学会第一次在海外举行年会。此外，他于 1973 年在休斯敦骨科俱乐部获得了同行的赞誉（并于次年获得了休斯敦外科学会的类似表彰）。但是，他在进行一些演讲时意识到了器械矫正载荷需要得到更广泛的应用，于是出现了做出改变的想法。

The 1974 annual meeting of the AAOS was held in Dallas, approximately 250 miles from Houston. For some undocumented reason Harrington, the immediate past president, did not attend the semiannual meeting of the SRS board of directors on January 20. The themes were expansion of educational activities and membership criteria. AAOS counsel had advised SRS that there was no pathway for Nachemson to become an active member without changing the bylaws. He was elected to honorary membership in the SRS and thus was precluded from elected leadership positions, which were reserved for active fellows.

1974 年的美国骨科医师学会年会在距离休斯敦大约 250 英里的达拉斯举行。由于一些未被说明的原因，前任主席哈灵顿没有出席于 1 月 20 日举行的每半年召开一次的脊柱侧凸研究学会委员会会议。会议主题是扩大教育活动和放宽会员标准。美国骨科医师学会曾建议脊柱侧凸研究学会如果不改变章程，纳切姆森就无法成为一名活跃会员。他被选为脊柱侧凸研究学会的荣誉会员，因此被排除在领导职位的选举之外，因为这些职位是仅留给活跃研究员的。

Harrington did meet with Dane Miller, and a vigorous correspondence lasting through March ensued. Miller summed up Zimmer's activity on behalf of Harrington Instrumentation in a follow-up letter.[61] First, he had initiated a manufacturing order for a set of Tivanium hooks and rods, which were to have a "gold colored nitride surface to avoid any possibility of mix up in the operating room." At this stage mixing of implants was not recommended. Second, he was also working to arrange a meeting in Louisville with Leatherman at his earliest convenience to complete the "infant Harrington instrument design." Final designs would be sent to Harrington for his approval. And third, in a follow-up to their meeting with Ken Johnson in marketing, the request for updating the marketing information on Harrington Instrumentation had been re-initiated. Although not his responsibility, Miller took responsibility for reporting any progress in the marketing division to Houston. Harrington appreciated this update, but asked for more information about Tivanium, "its use and tolerance in vivo and also need a reaction evaluation in tissue."[62]

哈灵顿确实会见了戴恩·米勒，随后的通信一直持续到了3月。米勒在随后的一封信中总结了捷迈公司有关哈灵顿器械的工作。[61]第一，他发起了一套钛钩和棒的制造订单，这些器械要有一个“金色的氮化物表面，以避免在手术室中发生混淆”，在这个阶段，不建议混合内植物。第二，他还在努力安排与莱瑟曼在路易斯维尔见面，以便后者尽早完成“婴幼儿哈灵顿器械设计”。最终的设计将送交哈灵顿批准同意。第三，在他们与市场部的肯·约翰逊会面的后续谈话中，重新提出更新哈灵顿器械市场营销资料的请求。虽然这不是他的职责，但米勒还是承担了向休斯敦报告市场营销部门的所有工作的进展。哈灵顿对这些跟进工作表示赞赏，但也要求获得更多关于钛的信息，“它在体内的使用情况和耐受性，同时还需要一个在组织中的反应评估”。[62]

Soon Miller was able to report that he and Dan Page had met with Leatherman and found him very receptive to the design they had discussed earlier with Harrington. Leatherman had requested a supply of “a series of implants for use on infants.”[63] Miller added that they were trying to locate a ratcheting mechanism required for this implant system, a surprising comment as there is no evidence that a different ratcheting system was ever discussed with Harrington. In the same communication Harrington was alerted that a set of Tivanium Harrington Instruments would soon be sent for him “to examine or test in ways you see fit.” Also enclosed were a number of articles that addressed Harrington’s concerns about the in vivo tolerance of titanium.

很快米勒回复，他和丹·佩奇已经和莱瑟曼见过面，发现他非常乐于接受他们之前和哈灵顿讨论过的设计方案。莱瑟曼要求提供“一系列用于婴幼儿的内植物”。[63]米勒补充，他们正试图找到这种植入系统所需的棘齿机制，这很令人惊讶，因为没有证据表明他们曾经与哈灵顿讨论过不同的棘齿系统。在同一封信中，哈灵顿被告知很快就会收到一套钛金属制作的哈灵顿器械，“以你认为合适的方式进行检查或测试”。还附上了一些文章，解决了哈灵顿对钛在体内耐受性的担忧。

Initiating the updating of marketing information had fallen to development engineer Page, who exchanged letters with Harrington that were dedicated to identifying the specific Harrington Instrumentation components for each of three new sets.[64,65] In addition to the existing scoliosis set there would be sets for fracture of the thoracic and lumbar spine, spondylolisthesis, and salvage of lumbosacral syndrome. Distraction rod #1250 lengths in 1” intervals, hook selections, and sacral bars (3” and 4”) to be provided were the following: fractures were 3" to 6" rods and #1251 and #1253 hooks; spondylolisthesis 0" to 3" rods, #1252 hooks, and sacral bars; and salvage 2" to 5" rods, #1252 hooks, and sacral bars.[66] Each would have a short outrigger.

更新市场资料的重任落在了研发工程师佩奇肩上，他与哈灵顿互相通信，以确定三套新的哈灵顿器械的具体组件。[64,65]除了现有的脊柱侧凸器械，还有用于胸腰椎骨折、脊柱滑脱和腰骶综合征挽救性手术的器械。需提供规格长度为1英寸的#1250撑开棒、3英寸的钩和4英寸的骶骨棒：骨折采用3~6英寸的棒和#1251和#1253钩；脊柱滑脱用0~3英寸的棒，#1252钩和骶骨棒；挽救性手术用2~5英寸的棒，#1252钩和骶骨棒。[66]每个器械都会有一个短的外撑开器。

Two late March 1974 letters were especially insightful. One was from Harrington to Miller. "I have received the tivanium rods and have put both of them to the Harrington test with my bare hands. I have thrown them both off center when they are rolled. A plastic deformation develops under specification."[67] He commented that the design of the hooks was excellent, but asked for information about the rod malleability. "I am not intimating that these rods are extremely inferior, they are not. I do not believe, however, that they would stand 200 lbs. eccentric loading over seven million times." Harrington closed with the reiteration of a recent complaint about a spring calibrated spreader prototype he had received, and been billed for, that wasn't even close to being properly calibrated.[68] The Tivanium Harrington Instrumentation project had obviously hit a major obstacle, and related correspondence stopped for the next six months. Soon after it appears that Harrington visited the Zimmer plant in Warsaw, Indiana, and the focus of their work was on completing the instruments and instrument sets for other uses as well as the accompanying educational material.[69,70]

1974年3月底的两封信意义重大。一封是哈灵顿写给米勒的。"我已经收到了钛棒，并徒手对它们进行了力学测试。折弯时它们发生了偏心形变。可以根据需要进行塑形。"[67]他评价说，钩子的设计非常出色，但他询问了有关棒的延展性的信息。"我并不是说这些钛棒是极差的。然而，我不相信它们能承受200磅偏心载荷并承受载荷超过700万次。"哈灵顿在结束时重申了他最近的投诉，是关于他收到的一款附带账单的弹簧校准吊具的原型机，但这款吊具甚至没有正确校准。[68]钛制哈灵顿器械项目显然遇到了重大障碍，相关的通信在接下来的六个月里中断了。不久之后，哈灵顿参观了捷迈在印第安纳州华沙的工厂，他们的工作重点是完成其他用途的器械和相关组件，以及配套的教学材料。[69,70]

The second insightful March 1974 letter came from David O. Warner, Zimmer finance director, confirming a recent telephone conversation that "Zimmer will continue to pay the royalties, as described in Mr. Hartle's letter of October 27, 1960, for your lifetime or through July 1977, whichever should be the longer period."[71] Warner continued that "Zimmer will pay these royalties to you or to any person or foundation that you may wish to designate in writing." At this point Harrington was working to establish his legacy and identify resources to fund it. This letter from Warner must have reassured him about his livelihood, and on July 2, 1974, the Mary Alice and Paul R. Harrington, M.D. Distinguished Professor of Bio-Physical-Chemistry was established at the University of Kansas in Lawrence. He chose his alma mater because of his immense gratitude for the quality education he had received in the state's public school system. Establishing this professorship was a financial reach for the couple as at that time $250,000 was the minimum required, an amount that had to be realized through added installments. The title of the professorship was chosen due to Harrington's growing conviction that solving the secrets of spine disease would progressively move from morphological to molecular study. He had begun to detail this conviction in a book-writing project, "The Human Spine."

1974 年 3 月，捷迈的财务总监戴维·O. 沃纳发出了第二封有重要意义的信，确认最近的一次电话交谈"正如哈特尔先生 1960 年 10 月 27 日的信中所描述的那样，捷迈将向您终身支付版税（专利）或继续支付到 1977 年 7 月，以较长的时间为准"[71]。沃纳继续表示，"捷迈将向您或您以书面形式指定的任何个人或基金会支付这些税款。"这时，哈灵顿正在处理善后事宜，并确定资金来源。沃纳的这封信肯定让他对自己的生活感到安心，1974 年 7 月 2 日，玛丽·艾丽斯和保罗·R. 哈灵顿生物–物理–化学杰出教授职位在堪萨斯大学劳伦斯校区成立。他选择母校是因为他非常感激他在该州公立学校系统中接受的优质教育。对这对夫妇来说，设立这一教授职位是一项经济负担，因为当时最低要求是 25 万美元，这一数额必须通过额外的分期付款来实现。之所以选择上述学科的教授职位头衔，是因为哈灵顿越来越相信，解决脊柱疾病的秘密将逐步从形态学研究转向分子研究。他开始计划在正在编写的一本书《人类脊柱》中详细表述这一观点。

Harrington also established Harrington Spine Foundation accounts, one each at Baylor College of Medicine and the Methodist Hospital, Houston.[72] These funds, which were never large, appear to have been used to support his academic activities. Nearly five years later in April 1979 he directed that the majority of the balance in the account at Methodist Hospital be used to establish an endowed annual Orthopedic Resident Scientific Paper Award. According to his curriculum vitae, a Paul R. Harrington Archives and Library was also established at TIRR.[73]

哈灵顿还在贝勒医学院和休斯敦卫理公会医院设立了哈灵顿脊柱基金。[72]这些资金并不多，用来支持他的学术活动。大约五年后，1979 年 4 月，他指示将卫理公会医院账户余额的大部分用于设立一个年度骨科住院医师学术论文奖。根据他的生平，保罗·R. 哈灵顿档案馆和资料室也在得克萨斯州康复与研究中心建立起来。[73]

The ninth annual meeting of the SRS was held at the St. Francis Hotel in San Francisco on September 11 – 13 1974. The first meeting of the board of directors took place in the late afternoon of the tenth, the last one Harrington was eligible to attend, and he was there.[74] He and Jack Kennedy, of London, Ontario, Canada, who was becoming a prominent knee surgeon, were elected to honorary membership. President Winter had organized a subscription dinner on the tenth to pay tribute to Harrington and had used the dinner invitation to solicit funds for a Harrington Library for scoliosis and spine information.[75] A sum of $22,000 had been raised.[76] The dinner, co-hosted by Bob Winter and John Moe, was well attended. The principal tribute was billed as "Reminiscences of the Early Days of Dr. Harrington's Work in Scoliosis" and was delivered by Vern Nickel of Rancho Los Amigos Hospital in Downey, California.[77] He reviewed the history of the epidemic polio years of the late 1940s and 1950s from the vantage point of respiratory polio and post-polio scoliosis, adding some firsthand and behind-the-scenes insights. He noted that the survival of patients with respiratory paralysis was greatly improved with the liberal use of tracheostomy to provide an adequate airway and allow suction of secretions, and respirators. However, subacute and chronic care, in addition to rehabilitation, had not kept pace, resulting in large numbers of patients requiring expensive, continuing custodial care.

第九届脊柱侧凸研究学会年会于 1974 年 9 月 11 日至 13 日在圣弗朗西斯科的圣弗朗西斯酒店举行。第一次委员会会议于 10 日下午晚些时候举行，哈灵顿也出席了会议，这是他有资格参加的最后一次会议。[74]他和来自加拿大安大略省伦敦市的杰克·肯尼迪被选为荣誉会员，后者后来成了一名著名的膝关节外科医生。温特主席在 10 日组织了一场向哈灵顿致敬的募捐晚宴，并利用晚宴为哈灵顿资料室募集资金，用于脊柱侧凸和脊柱资料的收集，[75]共筹集到 22 000 美元。[76]晚宴由鲍勃·温特和约翰·莫共同主持，出席人数众多。最主要的致辞来自加利福尼亚州唐尼兰乔洛杉米戈斯医院的弗农·尼克尔，他声明是为了“回忆哈灵顿医生在脊柱侧凸方面的早期工作”。[77]他从呼吸道脊髓灰质炎和脊髓灰质炎后脊柱侧凸的角度，回顾了20世纪40年代末和50年代流行的脊髓灰质炎的历史，并增加了一些第一手的和幕后的资料。他指出，随着气管切开术和呼吸机的广泛使用，呼吸麻痹病人的生存率大大提高，气管切开术提供充足的气道，并允许吸出分泌物。然而，除康复外，亚急性和慢性治疗没有跟上步伐，导致大量病人需要昂贵的持续监护处理。

From the beginning the NFIP's policy was that no poliomyelitis patient would be denied care. This was "eating up the funds of the Foundation" even as they were spending ever more on basic research. Nickel credited Basil O'Connor with the foresight to select Ken Landauer, medical director of the New York State Rehabilitation Hospital, "to develop new concepts of care in respiratory polio. His new concept was to treat this group of patients as a categorical disease and organize a group of specialists to develop new approaches for improved care and reduced costs." Several respiratory care centers resulted, the first in Houston in 1950 and not far behind the biggest at Rancho Los Amigos Hospital in 1952.[78] Nickel became chief orthopedist at Rancho in 1953, succeeding Vernon Thompson.[79] By then ill with cancer, Thompson had been an innovator developing the Thompson nail for hip fracture treatment in the 1930s. He was aware of Harrington and his then fledgling work, believed he was on the right track, and encouraged Nickel to support him. Nickel and Harrington first met in 1956 at a meeting of respiratory centers in Houston. "During the visit I was asked to speak to the Houston Orthopedic Association and after a few brief remarks on scoliosis collapsing spines and poliomyelitis I realized from the atmosphere that this was not a subject that was openly discussed in Houston. I quickly changed the thrust of my talk to the severely paralyzed hand in patients with respiratory polio and was received with much more warmth." It was at that meeting, while enjoying refreshments together, that Harrington insisted on introducing Nickel to Fred Bloom, M.D. and the halo Bloom was using for maxilla-facial problems. This marked the birth of halo traction for spine deformity.[80]

从一开始，国家小儿麻痹基金会的政策就是不拒绝治疗任何脊髓灰质炎病人。即使他们在基础研究上投入了更多的资金，但这也“消耗了基金会的资金”。尼克尔称赞巴兹尔·奥康纳有远见，选择纽约州康复医院的医疗主任肯·兰道尔

"来发展呼吸道脊髓灰质炎治疗的新概念。他的新概念是将这类病症作为一种分类疾病来对待，并组织一组专家来开发改善治疗和降低成本的新方法"。于是几家呼吸治疗中心应运而生，1950 年在休斯敦成立了第一家，紧随其后于 1952 年在兰乔洛杉米戈斯医院成立了最大的一家。[78]尼克尔于 1953 年接替弗农·汤普森，成为兰乔医院的首席骨科医生。[79] 20 世纪 30 年代，当时身患癌症的汤普森发明了治疗髋部骨折的汤普森钉。他知道哈灵顿和他当时刚刚起步的工作，相信他的方向是正确的，并鼓励尼克尔支持他。尼克尔和哈灵顿第一次见面是在 1956 年休斯敦的一次呼吸中心的会议上。"在访问期间，我被邀请到休斯敦骨科学会发表演讲，在简短地谈论了几句脊柱侧凸、脊柱塌陷和脊髓灰质炎之后，我从气氛中意识到，这不是一个能在休斯敦公开讨论的话题。我很快把演讲的重点转向了呼吸性脊髓灰质炎病人的严重瘫痪上来，现场氛围得到了缓和。"就在那次会议的茶歇时，哈灵顿坚定地把尼克尔介绍给弗雷德·布卢姆博士，还介绍了布卢姆治疗上颌骨面部问题的头环牵引架。这标志着 halo 牵引术治疗脊柱畸形的诞生。[80]

In his tribute, Nickel noted that the NFIP had awarded and in 1955 funded Harrington's two research grant proposals, one involving inducing and reversing scoliosis in mice and the other involving clinical application of instrumentation. The original opposition to his clinical research proposal "by a large number of distinguished orthopedic surgeons that were active as medical advisors to the NFIP" had never abated, and the foundation remained "under great pressure to discontinue support for his work." Nickel recounted the pressure the NFIP placed on Rancho to provide a formal meeting for Harrington to present his work. Thompson chaired the meeting, and Harrington presented his case clearly and honestly, including some tremendous problems he had encountered. Some of the younger orthopedists realized Harrington's approach was "a dramatic change with potential far beyond anything we had seen." The road ahead was still long but now at least it was open.

在他的致敬中，尼克尔指出，国家小儿麻痹基金会在 1955 年赞赏并资助了哈灵顿的两项研究提案，一项是诱导和逆转小鼠脊柱侧凸，另一项是器械的临床应用。"许多作为国家小儿麻痹基金会医学顾问的著名骨科医生"最初对他的临床研究提议的反对声从未减弱，基金会仍然"承受着停止支持他工作的巨大压力"。尼克尔讲述了国家小儿麻痹基金会对兰乔施加压力，要求他们为哈灵顿提供一次正式会议，以展示他的工作。会议由汤普森主持，哈灵顿清楚而真诚地陈述了他的病例，包括他遇到的一些重大问题。一些年轻的骨科医生意识到哈灵顿的方法是“一个巨大的变革，其潜力远远超过我们所见过的任何事物”。前面的路还很漫长，但至少现在它变得开阔了。

Figure 11.2 ***Harrington tribute dinner, September 10, 1974. Left to right: Bob Winter, Paul and Mary Alice Harrington, Joln Moe, and Vern Nickel. (Harrington Archives)***

图 11.2 哈灵顿致敬晚宴，1974 年 9 月 10 日。从左到右：鲍勃·温特、保罗和玛丽·艾丽斯·哈灵顿、约翰·莫，还有弗农·尼克尔(哈灵顿档案馆)

Nickel described Harrington's "personality as one of dogged persistence. He was certain he had an idea with merit and he had the guts and temerity to stick with it. His interest in scoliosis, probably more than anything else, focused interest on this problem. He was also one of the first to really apply modern principles of engineering to the development of instrumentation development of materials, and determination of stresses." For emphasis, Nickel coined a spoonerism, *orthoneering engipedics*. He also credited Harrington as having the great gift "to look at a problem in an entirely original way." Nickel's presentation was well received by the large number of attendees. *See figure 11.2*. Several others, including Moe, offered their remarks, and many letters of tribute were received from those who had not been able to attend. The tribute letter from Houston heart surgeon Denton Cooley provided some idea of the obstacles Harrington must have had to overcome in his home medical community. "I have known no more remarkable and sincere person in my entire professional career. His contributions to orthopedic surgery have been outstanding. When he began his work on scoliosis most people in this locale thought he was doing a monstrous thing. His perseverance and ultimate success in this field is well justified and testimony to the type of man he is."[81]

尼克尔形容哈灵顿“具有顽强的个性。他确信他的想法是富有价值的，且他有勇气和胆量坚持下去。他对脊柱侧凸的兴趣，可能比其他任何东西都更浓。他也是首批真正将现代工程学原理应用于器械开发、材料研发和应力测定的人之一”。为了强调这一点，尼克尔使用首音互换创造了新词，*orthoneering engipedics*(骨科工程学工程科医生)。他还称赞哈灵顿具有“以一种完全独到的方式看待问题”的伟大天赋。尼克尔的演讲受到了众多与会者的好评。(图 11.2) 包括莫在内的其他几个人也发表了讲话，许多未能出席的人也写了致敬信件。休斯敦心脏外科医生丹顿·库利的祝贺信让我们了解到哈灵顿在他的家乡医疗社区对于必须克服的障碍的一些想法。“在我的整个职业生涯中，我没见过比他更杰出、更真诚的人了。他对骨科的贡献是杰出的。当他开始研究脊柱侧凸时，当地的大多数人都认为他在做一件可怕的事情。他在这一领域的坚持不懈和最终的成功证明了他是一个怎样的人。”[81]

For the first time the SRS program booklet[82] was accompanied by a separate companion booklet with abstracts of the papers to be presented,[83] which would no longer be published in a later issue of the *Journal of Bone and Joint Surgery*. The ninth annual meeting of the SRS in 1974 included the presidential guest speaker, corresponding member Waldemar Carvahlo Pinto from Sao Paulo, Brazil, whose topic was “The Role of Traction in Pre-operative Correction of Scoliosis.”[84] For his presidential address President Winter had chosen “The Third Era” as his title.[85] He opened by crediting Harrington for proposing that treatment was available for any curve and the new need was for colleague education about the optimal time for referral. This stimulated Winter's vision of the four eras in the field of spine deformity. The first era was the dark ages when there was no effective treatment. This era ended in 1911 with the advent of spinal arthrodesis. The second era was ending in 1974 with effective treatment methods (arthrodesis and Milwaukee brace) having been developed. The third era was dawning with the effort to treat before the deformity progressed too far, and the fourth era would begin when the mystery of why spines got crooked could be answered. He listed six specific proposals to address the current problems of unawareness and the need for education: set specific and achievable goals, educate at every level, attack the problem of unawareness at high government levels, attack the basic unawareness of scoliosis, provide international leadership, and address quality of care.

脊柱侧凸研究学会[82]第一次配备了单独的日程小册子，其中有将要展示的论文摘要，[83]这些论文将不再发表在新一期的《骨与关节外科杂志》上。1974 年第九届脊柱侧凸研究学会年会邀请了来自巴西圣保罗的通讯会员，主席特邀演讲者瓦尔德玛·卡瓦罗·平托，他的主题是“牵引在脊柱侧凸术前矫正中的作用”。[84]温特主席的演讲题目是“第三时代”。[85]他首先赞扬了哈灵顿提出的任何畸形都可以得到治疗的建议和对同行进行关于最佳转诊时间的宣教的需求。这激发了温特对脊柱畸形领域四个时代的见解。第一个时代是没有有效治疗方法的黑暗时代，这个时代在 1911 年随着脊柱融合术的出现而结束。第二个时代在 1974 年随着有效的治疗方法（脊柱融合术和密尔沃基支具）的出现而结束。第三个时代开始于人们努力在畸形症状发展之前进行治疗。第四个时代即将开始，那时脊柱畸形的奥秘将得到解答。他列出了六项具体建议，以解决当前意识缺乏的问题和教育需求：制订具体并可实现的目标，在各级进行教育，让政府高层意识到相关问题，加深对脊柱侧凸的认识，提高国际领导力和解决治疗质量问题。

Winter's main focus, which was the third era, was aimed at overcoming public and professional unawareness and ignorance of the problems associated with scoliosis and other spine deformities. It was based on the premise that effective treatment was available. The hoped-for result was earlier referral, the opportunity to treat those needing treatment at a more opportune time, and prevention of unmanageable problems. Education at every level was the method to achieve the aim of this era. To accomplish these goals, the SRS needed to broadcast its message. One long sought step on this path was affiliation with the AAOS, a much larger organization with an extensive educational program. Success had been achieved and for the second year was noted on the SRS annual meeting program cover: "An Affiliate of the American Academy of Orthopaedic Surgeons." Inside the program was the AAOS "official recommendation to any program of routine examination of school children for detection of scoliosis and other crippling spine deformities." The AAOS likewise gained from this affiliation because of SRS members' contributions to its educational programming.

温特的主要关注点是第三个时代，旨在解决公众和专业人士对脊柱侧凸和其他脊柱畸形相关问题的忽视和不了解。这是以有效的治疗手段为前提的。为了实现这个目标，所期望的结果是更早地转诊，有机会在更合适的时间治疗那些需要治疗的人，并预防无法控制的问题。对各级医师宣教是实现这个时代目标的手段。为了实现这些目标，脊柱侧凸研究学会需要传播相关信息。在这条道路上，一个长期寻求的目标是加入美国骨科医师学会，一个更大的、具有众多的教育项目的组织。这个目标取得了成功，第二年脊柱侧凸研究学会年会的封面上写着："美国骨科医师学会附属机构。"该年会包含美国骨科医师学会"对任何常规检查项目的学校儿童脊柱侧凸和其他致残性脊柱畸形的检测的官方建议"。美国骨科医师学会同样也得益于脊柱侧凸研究学会会员对其教育项目的贡献。

Harrington Spine Instrumentation continued to be widely used with generally satisfactory results. However, two studies of patients with neuromuscular disease-related deformities reported from top North American centers suggested that the surgical treatment armamentarium was not yet complete. Willard Hull reported on a series of patients with spine deformity of various types associated with myelomeningocele that had been operated on by Moe's group.[86] Harrington Instrumentation was used in 50% (18 of 36). Forty-three percent (16 of 37) had a major wound infection, and 76% (27 of 37) developed a pseudarthrosis. Bob Gillespie and John Wedge reviewed the results of surgery in twenty paraplegic children.[87] The surgeries included both Harrington and Dwyer instrumentations and spinal osteotomy. All patients were wheelchair bound and had complete sensory loss in the buttocks area along with varying degrees of bladder and bowel dysfunction. The results were found to be "extremely poor with a high incidence of pseudarthrosis, wound infection, and instrument failure." Residual pelvic obliquity was the main factor contributing to these poor results. Lumbosacral fixation problems were being called out again as the Rancho group had at the 1970 annual meeting when they reported the 30% (16 of 53) incidence of unacceptable hip problems in paralytic patients immobilized for six months in a halo-bilateral hip spica cast in an attempt to obtain lumbosacral fusion.[88] Harrington and Dickson's series of operated-on adult idiopathic scoliosis patients was presented. Of the 139 patients, the most common complications were urinary tract infection early and pseudarthrosis late. Only one patient was dissatisfied with the outcome.

哈灵顿脊柱器械持续得到了广泛使用，总体效果令人满意。然而，来自北美顶级中心的两项关于神经肌肉性脊柱畸形病人的研究报告表明，外科治疗器械还欠缺完善。威拉德·赫尔报道了一系列由莫的小组手术治疗的与脊髓脊膜膨出相关的各种类型脊柱畸形的病人。[86] 50%（36 人中有 18 人）使用了哈灵顿器械。43%（37 人中有 16 人）有严重的伤口感染，76%（37 人中有 27 人）出现假关节。鲍勃·吉莱斯皮和约翰·韦奇回顾了 20 名麻痹性儿童的手术结果。[87]手术包括应用哈灵顿棒和德怀尔内固定器械和脊柱截骨。所有病人均需坐轮椅，臀部感觉完全丧失，并有不同程度的膀胱和肠道功能障碍。结果发现“假关节、伤口感染和内固定失败的发生率极高”。残余骨盆倾斜度是导致这些不良结果的主要因素。当兰乔小组在 1970 年的年会上报告称麻痹性病人中 30%（53 人中的 16 人）发生了不可接受的髋关节问题时，腰骶部固定问题再次被提出，他们在尝试采用 halo 双侧髋关节石膏固定 6 个月以获得腰骶部融合。[88]会议介绍了哈灵顿和迪克森的一组成人特发性脊柱侧凸手术病例。在 139 名病人中，最常见的并发症是早期尿路感染和晚期假关节形成。只有一名病人对治疗结果不满意。

The 1974 annual meeting ended with the second meeting of SRS board of directors, convened by its new president, Ken Leatherman. One of the issues addressed was concern about the conduct of the subscription dinner honoring Harrington, as expressed by Walter Blount, who questioned bundling fund-raising with recognition and characterizing Harrington as having requested that the library's location be at Fairview Hospital in Minneapolis.[89] The board thought a fitting tribute was desirable, but believed that alternatives other than a library should be considered. President Leatherman appointed an ad hoc committee to study the matter and make recommendations to the board.[90] The committee consisted of Robert Winter, Clyde Nash, Edward Simmons, and Jesse Dickson as chair. The committee met in Chicago on November 18, 1974, and their principal recommendation was that the money should be used to establish "The Harrington Guest Lectureship, a fund used to bring prominent physicians and researchers in the field of scoliosis to speak at the annual SRS meetings."[91] They also concluded "that in as much as the above-stated objectives are not those originally used to solicit the funds, all donors should be given the opportunity to have their contributions returned." Other recommendations concerned the administration of the funds. A follow-up letter in February 1975 indicated that all previous donors had been given the option of having their money returned, but that few had chosen to do so as the balance in the Harrington Guest Lectureship Fund was $21,800.[92] Thus, the Harrington Guest Lectureship was born.

1974 年年会以脊柱侧凸研究学会委员会的第二次会议结束，会议由新任主席肯·莱瑟曼召集。其中一个问题是对为致敬哈灵顿而举办的晚宴感到担忧，沃尔特·布朗特表示，他质疑将筹款与嘉奖捆绑在一起，并指出哈灵顿曾要求将资料室设在明尼阿波利斯的费尔尤维医院。[89]委员会认为适当的致敬是可以的，但也认为应该考虑除资料室之外的其他选择。莱瑟曼主席任命了一个特别委员会来研究此事，并向委员会提出了建议。[90]委员会由罗伯特·温特、克莱德·纳什、爱德华·西蒙斯组成，杰西·迪克森担任主席。委员会于 1974 年 11 月 18 日在芝加哥开会，他们的建议是，这笔钱应该用于建立“哈灵顿特邀演讲席位，该基金用于邀请脊柱侧凸领域的杰出医生和研究人员在脊柱侧凸研究学会年度会议上发言”。[91]他们还总结说“鉴于上述目标并非最初用于募集资金的目的，所有捐助者都应有机会收回其捐款”。其他建议涉及对基金的管理。1975 年 2 月后续的一封信表明，之前所有的捐赠者都可以选择退还他们的捐款，但很少有人选择这样做。因为哈灵顿特邀演讲席位基金的余额是 21 800 美元。[92]哈灵顿特邀演讲席位诞生了。

About a month after returning home from the 1974 SRS annual meeting, Harrington received what was to be his last letter from Dane Miller.[93] Miller had been at the honorary dinner and commented that “based on the comments by the various speakers at the dinner I suspect you can probably leap tall buildings at a single bound.” He also expressed satisfaction that the special set projects were progressing well. But the major message in his letter was as follows: “I hope you have been able to read the reports I transmitted to you in San Francisco. Based on the column loading analysis of the Harrington Instrumentation, it does not appear that this is an ideal application for ‘Tivanium.’ I'm sorry we were not able to discuss the details of these papers in person. In short, the tivanium rod that Harrington had been able to bend by hand was not strong or durable enough to replace the Harrington Rod made of 316 LVM stainless steel. Harrington did not document his reaction to this seeming setback. From September to early December he and Zimmer engineer George Shen exchanged seven letters devoted to the details of the special implant sets they were developing, principally the short sacral rod and the yoke connector to go with it.[94,95] Their letters' tones were optimistic, a good note on which to finish such a productive eighteen-year (June 1955 to December 1974) correspondence, during which over 350 letters and uncounted drawings were exchanged by Harrington and his Zimmer collaborators. Today they reside in the Harrington Archives.

从1974年脊柱侧凸研究学会年会上回来大约一个月后，哈灵顿收到了戴恩·米勒的最后一封信。[93]米勒出席了这次荣誉晚宴，他评论：“根据晚宴上不同演讲者的评论，我认为你离成功咫尺之遥。”他还对特别项目进展顺利表示满意。他信中的主要信息如下：“我想你已经阅读了我在圣弗朗西斯科转交给你的报告。根据哈灵顿器械的脊柱载荷分析，似乎应用‘钛’不理想。很抱歉我们没能当面讨论这些文件的细节。”简而言之，哈灵顿用手就可以折弯的钛棒不够坚固，也不够耐用，无法取代由316 LVM不锈钢制成的哈灵顿棒。哈灵顿没有记录他对这一挫折的反应。从9月到12月初，他和捷迈公司的工程师乔治·沈互通了7次信，专门讨论他们正在开发的特殊内植物的细节，主要是短骶骨棒和与之配套的轭式连接器。[94,95]他们书信中的语气是乐观的，这对结束如此卓有成效的18年（1955年6月至1974年12月）通信做了一个很好的注解，在此期间，哈灵顿和捷迈公司的合作者互通了350多封信和无数的图纸。今天，它们都被保存在哈灵顿档案馆。

In many ways 1974 was a liberating year for Harrington. His frequent instrument design input was over, as was his leadership role in the SRS. Dickson had proven himself capable of practicing and teaching on par with his mentor. Although Harrington had no publications during the year, several were in progress. But, Harrington Spine Instrumentation would now be pretty much on its own as time had caught up with its creator.

从很多方面来讲，1974 年对哈灵顿来说都是自由的一年。他结束了频繁的器械设计，他在脊柱侧凸研究学会中的领导任期也结束了。迪克森已经证明自己在工作和教学方面的能力与他的老师相当。虽然哈灵顿在这一年中没有发表任何文章，但有几篇文章正在写。但是，哈灵顿脊柱器械只能自求多福了，因为它的创造者已经敌不过时间的裹挟。

As he entered 1975, Harrington received word that the University of Kansas had chosen him for two honors. Notification first came from Dr. S. Dwight Woods, president of the University of Kansas Medical Alumni Association, located on the medical center's campus in Kansas City, Kansas, that he had been chosen the association's Alumnus of the Year.[96] With that came the invitation to present the Peter T. Bohan Lecture, a 30-minute presentation of his own choosing to be given at the 1975 annual banquet on Friday, May 16. An honorarium of $250 was provided for the lecture. Harrington readily accepted, and he indicated that his lecture topic would be "Instrumentation of the Human Spine" and that he would like to present the check to a worthy cause.[97] In his acceptance letter Harrington had also inquired about a patient who he believed was Woods' son. Indeed, this was the case since in 1969 after Harrington's heart attack Dickson had operated on him for spondylolisthesis using Harrington's operation.[98] Woods felt his son was "doing reasonably well and has achieved a satisfactory result… still has rather odd posture on standing… and… has not had any more difficulty with the nerve root pain which had been so troublesome prior to the operation."[99] Woods closed by suggesting the Distinguished Medical Teacher Fund as a worthy cause to receive his honorarium. Harrington agreed and made this donation.[100]

1975 年，哈灵顿收到了消息，堪萨斯大学授予他两项荣誉。最先通知他的是在堪萨斯州堪萨斯城医学中心的堪萨斯大学医学校友会主席 S. 德怀特 · 伍兹博士，他被选为校友会的年度校友。[96]随后，他应彼得 · T. 博安讲座邀请于 1975 年 5 月 16 日星期五，在年度晚宴上进行了演讲。因为有 250 美元的酬金，所以哈灵顿欣然接受邀请并进行了一场 30 分钟的演讲。他的演讲主题是“人类脊柱器械”，并表示他愿意把这张支票捐给一项有价值的事业。[97]在他的受邀信中，哈灵顿还询问了一个他认为是伍兹儿子的病人。事实上，这是一例在 1969 年哈灵顿心脏病发作后，迪克森用哈灵顿器械做的脊柱滑脱的病例。[98]伍兹认为他的儿子“手术做得相当好，取得了令人满意的结果，就是站立姿势有点奇怪，手术前一直困扰着的神经根疼痛都已经缓解了”。[99]伍兹最后建议杰出医学教师基金会将接受哈灵顿的酬金作为一项有价值的事业。哈灵顿同意并进行了捐赠。[100]

The notification for the second award came from the University of Kansas Alumni Association, located on the main campus in Lawrence, informing Harrington that he was one of five chosen to receive a Citation for Distinguished Service.[101] This highest honor given at the University of Kansas was a joint presentation of the Alumni Association and the university. The citation would be presented during commencement exercises in Memorial Stadium on Monday evening, May 19. In his letter acknowledging Harrington's acceptance, Chancellor Archie Dykes succinctly stated the Harrington case.[102] "We know of no one more deserving by reason of service to humanity, continued interest in the University, and the personal qualities we would hope all Kansas alumni would exemplify."

第二个奖项的通知来自位于劳伦斯主校区的堪萨斯大学校友会，通知哈灵顿他是五位被选为杰出服务奖的人之一。[101]这一堪萨斯大学的最高荣誉是校友会和大学共同颁发的。颁奖典礼将于5月19日星期一晚上在纪念体育场举行的毕业典礼上进行。在感谢哈灵顿出席的信中，校长阿奇·戴克斯简要地陈述了哈灵顿获奖的原因。[102]“我们认为，您致力于人类服务，持续关注母校，个人品质更是堪为全体校友楷模，如此种种，无人可以比肩。”

Harrington's Bohan Lecture title expanded slightly during the writing to "Harrington Instrumentation for Treatment of Unstable Deformities of the Human Spine."[103] He set the tone in the opening remarks. "To return home is always ajoy. To receive the University of Kansas Medical Alumni Association Award is indeed an honor. And, to have the privilege of presenting the Peter T. Bohan Lecture to my friends, colleagues, and the graduating class of 1975 is beyond my fondest dream. But such is fate and I humbly thank you. The clinical career of Dr. Bohan was a long and dedicated one. I was born one block from St. Margaret's Hospital, where Dr. Bohan was Physician-in-Chief and began his early teaching. As you can well imagine, it was a privilege to gain my medical education at Bell Memorial Hospital in Kansas City in the shadows of such men as Dr. Bohan, Professor Ralph H. Major, Professor Logan Clendening, Dean Wahl, and many others. As if that were not enough, I was on the K.U. campus at Lawrence with such aspiring young medical students as Dave Robinson, Frank Allbritten, Max Allen, Franklin Murphy, and many more. So you can see, returning to K.U. has brought back memories of many happy moments in the 1930's." After presenting an overview of his spine instrumentation contribution, he closed with this thought for the soon-to-be graduates. "You have chosen a profession dedicated to the relief of human suffering. How tall you stand in this profession is directly related to how effectively and compassionately you serve your fellow man."

哈灵顿在博安讲座上的演讲最终略微扩展成名为《哈灵顿器械治疗人类脊柱不稳定畸形》的文章。[103]他在开场白中就定下了基调。"回家总是一种快乐。获得堪萨斯大学医学校友会奖确实是一种荣誉。能够有幸向我的朋友、同事和1975届的毕业生们做彼得·T. 博安讲座的演讲，这是我做梦也想不到的事情。但这就是命运，我只能说感谢。博安博士的临床生涯是漫长而敬业的。我出生在距离圣玛格丽特医院一个街区的地方，博安医生是那里的首席内科医师，并在那里开始了他的早期教学。你们可以想象一下，在堪萨斯城的贝勒纪念医院，在博安医生、拉尔夫·H. 梅杰教授、罗根·克伦德宁教授、迪恩·瓦尔和许多其他名人的影响下，我接受了医学教育，这是一种多么大的荣幸。还有，我在堪萨斯大学劳伦斯校区与有抱负的年轻医学生戴夫·鲁宾逊、弗兰克·奥尔布里顿、马克斯·艾伦、富兰克林·墨菲等人在一起交流。所以你可以看到，回到堪萨斯大学让我想起了20世纪30年代的许多快乐时光。"在概述了他对脊柱内固定的贡献之后，他为即将毕业的学生总结了这样一句话，"你们选择了一个致力于减轻人类痛苦的职业。你们在这个行业的站位高度直接关系到你们如何有效和富有同情心地为病人服务。"

Figure 11. 3 ***Receiving the University of Kansas Distinguished Service Citation, the highest honor given by the university, from Chancellor Archie R. Dykes, May 19, 1975. (Harrington Archives)***

图11.3 1975年5月19日，收到校长阿奇·R. 戴克斯颁发的堪萨斯大学杰出服务奖，这是堪萨斯大学授予的最高荣誉（哈灵顿档案馆）

Three evenings later he received the Citation for Distinguished Service. *See figure 11.3*. Others honored that evening were Robert B. Docking, former governor of the State of Kansas, from Arkansas City, Kansas; Clarence M. Kelley, Director of the Federal Bureau of Investigation, from Washington, D. C.; Thomas B. Robinson, managing partner of Black and Veatch Consulting Engineers, in

Shawnee Mission, Kansas; and Lloyd H. Ruppenthal, attorney and well-known state leader, from McPherson, Kansas.[104]

3 天后，他获得了杰出服务奖。（图 11.3）当晚的其他获奖者还有来自堪萨斯州阿肯色市的前堪萨斯州州长罗伯特 · B. 多金；来自华盛顿特区的联邦调查局局长克拉伦斯 · M. 凯利；来自堪萨斯州肖尼米逊市的布莱克和韦奇咨询工程师公司的执行合伙人托马斯 · B. 鲁宾逊；来自堪萨斯州麦克弗森的律师和著名的州领袖劳埃德 · H. 罗森塔尔。[104]

The tenth annual meeting of the SRS convened under President Ken Leatherman in Louisville, Kentucky on September 10–12, 1975.[105] As shown in photographs, both Paul and Mary Alice Harrington attended. For the first time the program booklet included abstracts of the papers presented, a practice that is still continued. The first Harrington Guest Lecturer was Arthur Hodgson of Hong Kong, whose talk was "The Place of Anterior Spinal Surgery in the Management of Spinal Deformities." Leatherman presented his presidential address, "The Scoliosis Research Society, Past, Present and Future." Allen Edmonson presented the morbidity report. Since the surgical morbidity report had been reset to calendar years, in 1974 surgeons reported on 3,677 operations with the percentage of surgeons reporting probably an all-time high at 84% (115 of 137).[106] Complications were requested in five categories: neurologic, hematologic, infection, instrument failure, and genitourinary. Complications could be related to instrumentation type, but the total number of operations by instrumentation type or by disease/deformity category was not available. Overall neurological complications occurred in 39 of 3,677 operations (1%). Data involving 34 neurological complications were sufficient to allow detailed analysis. Harrington Instrumentation was associated with sixteen complications, fourteen at the spinal cord level. Six were reported as complete spinal cord lesions; four recovered and two did not. Eight were reported as incomplete spinal cord lesions; seven of them recovered, and the other had an incomplete recovery. Dwyer Instrumentation was associated with one neurological complication, an incomplete lesion at T12 with no recovery. Osteotomy or vertebral body resection was associated with eight neurological complications. All eight patients had congenital kyphosis, scoliosis, or both. Three were reported as complete spinal cord lesions; one recovered and two did not. These two had incomplete spinal cord lesions before surgery. Three had incomplete spinal cord lesions, and all recovered. Thus, four of the six with spinal cord level lesions recovered. The other two had postoperative urinary bladder paralysis and recovered within six months. Traction was associated with five neurological complications, two incomplete cord, one bulbar, and two brachial plexus. All five recovered when the traction was stopped. Four were associated with surgery in general that was not related to the specific procedure. None involved the spinal cord, and all four recovered. Of the 34 total patients, 23 (68%) had spinal cord level paralysis. Nine (not including the patient with traction bulbar paralysis) had complete spinal cord paralysis, and five (56%) recovered. Fourteen had incomplete spinal cord paralysis, and twelve of them (86%) recovered and one partially recovered. Except for the traction group, treatment details, such as instrumentation removal, were not provided.

1975 年 9 月 10 日至 12 日，在肯塔基州路易斯维尔召开了由肯·莱瑟曼主席主办的第十届脊柱侧凸研究学会年会。[105]保罗和玛丽·艾丽斯·哈灵顿都参加了。此次会议的日程手册刊印了参会论文的摘要，这一做法一直延续至今。第一位哈灵顿特邀演讲者是来自中国香港的阿瑟·霍奇森，他的演讲题目是“脊柱前路手术在脊柱畸形治疗中的地位”。莱瑟曼发表了他的主席演讲，“脊柱侧凸研究学会的过去、现在和未来。”艾伦·埃德蒙森提交了并发症发生率报告。由于手术并发症发生率报告重新要求按每年进行统计，1974 年外科医生报告了 3 677 例手术，外科医生提交报告的百分比可能是有史以来最高的 84%（137 人中有 115 人）。[106]并发症分为五个类别：神经系统、血液系统、感染、内固定失败和泌尿生殖系统。并发症可能与器械类型有关，但按器械类型或疾病/畸形类别划分的手术总数不详。3 677 例手术中有 39 例（1%）发生了神经系统并发症，涉及 34 例神经并发症的数据足以进行详细分析。哈灵顿器械有 16 例，14 例发生在脊髓水平，6 例为完全性脊髓损伤：4 人康复，2 人没有康复；8 例报告为不完全性脊髓损伤：其中 7 人康复，另 1 人不完全康复。德怀尔内固定器械有 1 例神经系统并发症，即 T12 处不完全损伤且未恢复。截骨术或椎体切除与 8 例神经系统并发症相关，所有 8 例病人均有先天性后凸、脊柱侧凸畸形或两者兼有。其中 3 例报告为完全性脊髓损伤：1 人康复，2 人没有康复，这 2 名病人术前均有不完全性脊髓损伤；3 例有不完全性脊髓损伤，最终全部康复。因此，6 名病人脊髓损伤病人中有 4 名病人恢复。另外还有 2 名病人术后发生了膀胱麻痹，于 6 个月内逐渐恢复。牵引相关的神经系统并发症有 5 例，2 例脊髓不完全性损伤，1 例在延髓，2 例为臂丛神经，牵引停止后，5 例都恢复了。4 例与一般手术有关，与具体手术操作无关，没有 1 例涉及脊髓，4 例都康复了。在 34 例病人中，23 例（68%）发生脊髓水平瘫痪。9 例（不包括牵引性延髓麻痹病人）发生完全脊髓麻痹，5 例（56%）康复。14例为不完全性脊髓麻痹，其中12例（86%）恢复，1例部分恢复。除牵引组外，未提供治疗细节，如是否取出内固定等。

In April 1975, just a few months before the annual meeting, MacEwen and his group published the neurological morbidity results they had gathered from 1965 to 1971, which had been periodically reported on since the 1968 annual meeting of the SRS.[107] Although both the 1965-71 and the 1974 studies had to struggle with a certain amount of incomplete data, they provided a wealth of helpful information. Comparing the 1965-71 to the 1974 study, the incidence (where the denominator was known) of neurological complications was 0.72% (57 of 7,885 patients) in the former and 1.06% (39 of 3,677 patients) in the latter. Complete or incomplete paraplegia occurred in 85% (74 of 87) and 68% (23 of 34), and Harrington Instrumentation was used in 57% (42 of 74) and 61% (14 of 23). Considering only those patients in whom Harrington Instrumentation was used, recovery from complete paraplegia occurred in 48% (10 of 21) in the 1965-71 study and 67% (4 of 6) in the 1974 study. Those with incomplete paraplegia had an excellent or good recovery in 67% (14 of 21) in the former and 88% in the latter (7 of 8, with one who had an incomplete recovery). In the 1965-71 series the rods were removed in 62% (26 of 42) of the patients, but no information was provided in the 1974 series.

1975年4月，就在年会的几个月前，麦克尤恩和他的团队发表了他们从1965年到1971年收集的神经系统并发症发生率结果，这些结果自1968年脊柱侧凸研究学会年会以来就被定期报告。[107]尽管1965年到1971年和1974年的研究数据有一些不完整，但它们仍提供了大量的有用信息。将1965年到1971年的研究与1974年的研究进行比较，前者神经并发症的发生率（分母已知）为0.72%（7 885例中有57例），后者为1.06%（3 677例中有39例）。完全性或不完全性截瘫发生率分别为85%（87例中有74例）和68%（34例中有23例），其中哈灵顿器械的使用率为57%（74例中有42例）和61%（23例中有14例）。仅考虑使用哈灵顿器械的病人，在1965年到1971年的研究中，完全截瘫的恢复率为48%（21例中有10例），而在1974年的研究中，完全截瘫的恢复率为67%（6例中有4例）。不完全截瘫病人中，前者有67%（21例中有14例）的病人恢复良好，后者为88%（8例中有7例，其中1例恢复不完全）。在1965年到1971年的系列研究中，62%的患者取出了哈灵顿棒，但在1974年的系列研究中没有提供任何相关信息。

The 1965-71 series addressed the question of rod removal and the timing of it on spinal cord function recovery. Including all complete and incomplete patients, Harrington Rod removal at less than three hours resulted in 75% (nine of twelve patients) recovering, at more than three hours 57% (eight of fourteen) recovering, and with no removal 31% (five of sixteen) recovering neurological function. The data supported MacEwen's principal conclusions, which were that "the Harrington Rod should be removed immediately postoperatively whenever a cord lesion has caused complete paralysis" and that it should "probably" be removed for incomplete lesions. The 1965-71 study group data also allowed MacEwen to list a number of risk factors, including congenital curves, kyphosis, pretreatment neurological deficit, and neurological change while in preoperative traction. What neither the 1965-71 nor the 1974 morbidity studies provided was any guidance about the Harrington Instrumentation configuration used. For years Harrington had taught that the compression rod should be placed before final distraction, protecting the spine and spinal cord from overdistraction. His only documented case of postoperative paraplegia was in an adult with a 160 right thoracic idiopathic curve.[108] Although the compression didn't totally protect this patient, her curve size made her an outlier. Distraction was let down two notches (1/4"), and at five years' follow-up she had incomplete but functional return.[109]

1965 年至 1971 年的系列报告讨论了内固定取出的问题以及取出时机对脊髓功能恢复的影响。在所有出现完全和不完全脊髓损伤的病人当中，在 3 小时内取出哈灵顿内固定器械的，有 75%（12 名病人中有 9 名）的患者脊髓神经功能恢复；在 3 小时以上取出的，57%（14 名病人中有 8 名）的患者功能恢复；未取出内固定器械的，有 31%（16 名病人中有 5 名）的患者功能恢复。这些数据支持了麦克尤恩的主要结论，即“当脊髓损伤导致完全瘫痪时，立即进行手术取出哈灵顿内固定器械”，并在不完全损伤时也应考虑取出内固定。麦克尤恩在 1965 年到 1971 年的研究数据中还列出了一些危险因素，包括先天性侧凸、脊柱后凸、治疗前神经功能缺失和术前牵引时发生的神经功能变化等。1965 年到 1971 年和 1974 年的并发症发生率研究都没有提供任何关于使用哈灵顿内固定器械的指导。多年来，哈灵顿一直主张在最后一次撑开前，应放置加压棒，以防止脊柱和脊髓过度牵引。他唯一记录在案的术后截瘫病例是一名特发性脊柱侧凸右胸弯 160°的成年患者。[108]虽然加压并没有完全保护这名患者，但她的侧弯角度使她成为一个特例。撑开降低了 2 个刻度（1/4 英寸），在 5 年的随访中，患者有不完全脊髓损伤但有部分功能恢复。[109]

The largest morbidity category in the 1974 report was instrument failure in 80 patients or 2.1%. Seventy-one were associated with Harrington Instrumentation, not surprising given its dominance in availability. Loss of hook fixation was most common, occurring in 43 patients. Twenty were found at the upper hook, nine at the lower hook, two at both hooks, and twelve involving both hooks and the rod. Breakage of the rod occurred in twenty-four and loss of distraction in four. Dwyer Instrumentation failed in six operations, five in the cable and one with loss of screw fixation. Three morbidity categories had low occurrence rates: hematologic (33, 0.8%), infection (46, 1.3%), and genitourinary (43, 1.1%). They were not related to the type of instrumentation used.

1974 年的报告中有 80 例病例发生了内固定失败，这是发生率最高的并发症，占比 2.1%。其中 71 例与哈灵顿器械在应用方面的主导地位有关。这并不奇怪，钩固定失败最为常见，共发生 43 例。上端钩有 20 例，下端钩有 9 例，两个钩都有问题的有 2 例，钩和棒都有问题的有 12 例。断棒有 24 例，撑开失败的有 4 例。应用德怀尔器械失败的有 6 例，5 例为缆绳问题，1 例为螺钉固定失败。血液系统（33，0.8%）、感染（46，1.3%）和泌尿生殖系统问题（43，1.1%）相关并发症的发生率较低，它们的发生与所使用的器械类型无关。

Even though it was not possible to relate the complications to the specific instrumentation used, this expanded morbidity report moved the focus from neurological complications to instrumentation failure. The 79% (eleven of fourteen) recovery of cord level paraplegia suggested that awareness and monitoring followed by action to diminish or remove distraction had been successful in making the operation safer. Instrumentation failure was vigorously discussed with Harrington placing the blame on technique and Hall making a strong case for placement of the upper distraction hook slightly more medial, under the thoracic lamina rather than under the facet.[110] However, the frequency of hook fixation loss discovered by the expanded morbidity reporting effort had exposed and focused attention on the intrinsic instability of the Harrington Instrumentation spine construct. The lack of disease, deformity, and instrumentation denominators prevented tighter focus on the most problematic uses. But several of the presentations during the meeting did.

尽管不可能将并发症与所使用的特定器械联系起来，但这份并发症发生率报告将关注重点从神经并发症转移到内固定失败上来。脊髓水平截瘫患者中有 79%（11/14）出现恢复，表明术中唤醒、神经监测和之后减少或去除撑开器械的措施使手术变得更加安全。与会者积极讨论了内固定失败的问题，哈灵顿将责任归咎于技术，霍尔则极力主张将上撑开钩置于更内侧的胸椎板下方，而非关节突下方。[110]然而，扩展的并发症发生率报道发现了钩固定失败的频率，它被曝光并将问题聚焦于哈灵顿脊柱内固定器械结构的内在不稳定性上。由于缺乏疾病、畸形和内固定的共性指标，无法对其最具争议性的用途进行更进一步的探讨，但会议上还是有几场演讲对其有所提及。

Pelvic fixation problems included inability to correct deformity and provide stability. In two studies of neuromuscular disease-related deformity from Rancho Los Amigos, sacral hooks, sometimes accompanied by anterior transverse process fusion, were showing promise.[111,112] As an indication of how desperate surgeons were to gain better pelvic fixation, Dwyer Instrumentation had been extended under the major vessels to the anterior sacrum in two patients with myelomeningocele.[113]

骨盆固定问题包括无法矫正畸形和不能提供稳定性。在兰乔洛杉米戈斯医院的两项神经肌肉性脊柱畸形研究中，骶骨钩（有时伴有前横突融合）显得未来可期。[111,112]在两名脊髓脊膜膨出的病人中，德怀尔内固定器械被放置在主要血管下方被延伸至骶骨前部，表明外科医生迫切地想要获得更好的骨盆固定。[113]

The restlessness in the spine deformity surgery community was illustrated by three reports of innovation. Hall used Dwyer staples modified to allow two screws per vertebral body.[114] Beginning at each end vertebra, he instrumented segmentally toward the apex and in this manner spread the load at each end over several levels. The apex vertebra and adjacent end plates were resected as were the posterior elements, through a posterior incision if necessary. The cables were used to close the resected area. Hall cautioned the operation could be safely done only in patients with no cord function. Finally, there were two reports of myelomeningocele kyphosis straightening by applying an anteriorly directed transverse apex load to a longitudinal instrumentation member, plate or rod, applied to the front of the spine.[115,116] The 1975 tenth annual meeting of the SRS had again clearly shown that there was ample room for spine instrumentation innovation.

三篇关于脊柱畸形外科创新的报道打破了脊柱畸形外科界的宁静。霍尔使用德怀尔钉，对其进行了改进，以允许每个椎体植入两枚螺钉。[114]从两侧端椎开始，他分段地向顶椎固定，并以这种方式将每一端的载荷分散到多个水平上。切除顶椎和相邻终板，必要时通过后部切口切除后部附件，缆绳用于闭合切除区域。霍尔警告说，只有在没有脊髓功能障碍的病人身上才能安全地进行手术。最后，有两篇关于脊髓脊膜膨出后凸矫正的报道，其方法是对脊柱前方的纵向内固定构件（板或棒）施加前向横向顶端加压。[115,116] 1975 年第十届脊柱侧凸研究学会年会再次明确表明，脊柱器械还有很大的创新空间。

This meeting was also probably the last time Harrington actively contributed to the discussions. He carried on an active correspondence with Dommisse, and before the 1976 meeting in Ottawa, Canada, he wrote that he was "quite limited in physical endurance, being dizzy most of the time. Due to the limitations, I cannot tolerate hour after hour activity so we just don't go to meetings; otherwise I am fortunate to feel fairly good."[117] A few months later, recalling an enjoyable trip together to Kruger Park, Harrington revealed that "I am advised not to travel out of the United States and jeopardize my fairly stable cardiac circumstances."[118]

这次会议也可能成为哈灵顿最后一次积极参与讨论的机会。他与多米斯保持着积极的通信，在 1976 年加拿大渥太华的会议之前，他写道，他"身体的耐力相当有限，大部分时间都感到头晕。由于身体状况的限制，我不能忍受长时间的活动，所以我们无法去参会；除此之外，我很幸运，感觉还不错"[117]。几个月后，在回忆起一起去克鲁格公园的愉快旅行时，哈灵顿说："有人建议我不要离开美国，以免危及我相当稳定的心脏状况。"[118]

From 1973 through 1975 Harrington continued to prove himself a leader and finally received the much-deserved recognition from his profession and his alma mater. Harrington Spine Instrumentation continued its dominance as Dwyer Instrumentation, the only other option, did not have the range of possible uses and had its own shortcomings. However, weaknesses continued to be uncovered in Harrington Instrumentation, often for uses for which it was not designed. In 1973 its inability to be used to address loss of thoracic kyphosis was established. In 1974 its shortcomings in patients with neuromuscular conditions requiring fixation to the pelvis or lacking posterior spinal elements were highlighted. In 1975 the SRS morbidity report uncovered the fact that distraction hook dislodgement was still a problem. The occurrence of traction paraplegia, brought to light in 1968, had not been eliminated, but simply decreased. Year by year Harrington Spine Instrumentation problems and shortcomings were beginning to accumulate, and it became inevitable that an alternative would be developed at some point. But until then, Harrington Spine Instrumentation continued to be helpful and widely used in the treatment of spine deformities of an increasingly wide variety.

从 1973 年到 1975 年，哈灵顿继续证明自己是一个领导者，并最终当之无愧地得到了业界同人和母校的认可。哈灵顿脊柱器械继续保持其主导地位，作为唯一可以替代哈灵顿器械的德怀尔内固定器械很少被应用，并且自身也存在一些局限性。然而，哈灵顿器械的不足之处也不断被发现，且常常是因为被用于非设计之初的用途。1973 年，它被确认不能用于解决胸椎后凸减少的问题。1974 年，在治疗需要骨盆固定的神经肌肉性脊柱畸形病人或脊柱后部结构缺失的病人时，器械的缺点就凸显了出来。1975 年，脊柱侧凸研究学会的并发症发生率报告揭示了一个事实，即撑开钩移位仍然是一个问题。1968 年发现的撑开性截瘫并没有完全消除，只是减少了。年复一年，哈灵顿脊柱器械的问题开始累积，不可避免地将在某个时候被一种新的方案替代。但在那之前，哈灵顿脊柱器械仍然发挥着重要作用，仍广泛应用于种类越来越多的脊柱畸形的治疗。

（王挽涛 马文政 译　郑召民 朱悦 赵杰 审校）

12 DOCUMENTATION—EVOLUTION (1976-80)

Nothing Endures But Change[1]

记录—变革 (1976—1980)

唯有变化乃为永恒[1]

Although not an abrupt demarcation point, the end of the Scoliosis Research Society's tenth annual meeting in Louisville in September 1975 could be said to mark the beginning of Harrington's final chapter on Earth. Despite his precarious health status he entered a phase of his life that turned out to be one of his most productive as he was free to spend his available energy organizing his files and completing his academic work, as best he could. Dickson's performance must have given him peace of mind about the future of his practice, clinical research, and status within the SRS. Whereas the connection between Harrington's activities and those of the SRS had proceeded in conjunction since the formation of the organization in 1966, their paths now diverged. Harrington concentrated on documentation and the SRS on evolution, particularly in relation to spinal instrumentation. Zimmer's assurance of royalties until he died not only helped make up for his shortened practice years but also provided the resource to fund his ongoing academic work.

1975 年 9 月，在路易斯维尔举行的脊柱侧凸研究学会第十届年会完美结束，尽管不能称它为一个突然的转折点，但可以说其标志着哈灵顿生命终章的开始。虽然他的健康状况已经岌岌可危，但他也进入了人生中最有收获的阶段之一，因为他可以竭尽所能，自由地将可用的精力花费在整理文件和完成学术工作上。迪克森的优异表现让哈灵顿对他在执业、临床研究和脊柱侧凸研究学会中的地位等都感到未来可期。虽然自1966年脊柱侧凸研究学会成立以来，哈灵顿一直与其同道而行，但现在两者的道路出现了分歧。哈灵顿专注于文献整理，而脊柱侧凸研究学会则专注于发展，特别是与脊柱内固定有关的。捷迈保证在哈灵顿去世前会一直支付版税费用，这不仅帮助补偿了哈灵顿缩短执业年限后的资金损失，还为他正在进行的学术工作提供了资金。

Sometime in 1974 Harrington had begun work on his most ambitious academic project, the synthesis of his thought and work into a book titled *The Human Spine-Yesterday, Today and Tomorrow*. In 1975 he began seeking a publisher, describing his book as having a "broad scope and extensive pictorial documentation... The spine and its function will be reviewed in terms of evolution, genetics, environment, physiology, chemistry, and physics. Most importantly, the book will be a documentation of an era in which man ceased to consider the spine simply in structural terms and began to regard it as a living, functional system susceptible to adaptation and transformation. Diseases of the spine will be discussed, not as pathological states but as malfunctions of the human body which eventually lead to malformation of the spine. In short, I hope to present a totally new approach to the study of the human spine."[2] Of the three parts, only a portion of the second, "Today," had current clinical relevance. Of the four publishers approached only C.V. Mosby expressed any interest, but a little over a year later it had waned.[3] The main reason given for this change was that there was not enough practical information in what would prove to be a very expensive book for them to produce. The Mosby editor rightly surmised that Harrington would proceed and wrongly concluded that he would publish it through TIRR.

1974年，哈灵顿着手进行他最具雄心的学术项目，将他的思想和实践凝练为一本名为《人类脊柱：历史、现状和未来》的书。1975年，他开始寻找出版商，并描述本书"范围广泛、图文并茂……我们将从进化、遗传学、环境、生理学、化学和物理学等方面对脊柱及其功能进行综述。最重要的是，这本书将是一个时代的记录，在这个时代，人们不再简单地从结构上去研究脊柱，而是开始将它视为一个生动的、易于适应和改变的功能系统。人们不应该把脊柱疾病当作病理状态来讨论，而是一类最终可导致脊柱畸形的人体功能障碍。简而言之，我希望提出一种全新的方法来研究人类脊柱。"[2]在历史、现状和未来这三个部分中，只有

第二部分“现状”目前具有临床意义。在联系的四家出版商中，只有C.V.莫斯比公司对此书抱有兴趣，但过了一年多，这家出版商的兴趣也减弱了。[3]这种改变的主要原因是，对他们来说，这是一本非常昂贵的书，而书中却没有足够多的实用资料。莫斯比的编辑猜测哈灵顿会继续寻求出版机会，但错误地以为他会通过得克萨斯州康复与研究中心出版这本书。

The manuscript was divided into five sections.[4] In the preface he acknowledged the creative process triggered by the 1950s polio epidemics. In the basic science section, he credited the influence of environment on the inherent potential of developing living systems (e.g., the Japanese bonsai tree). The pathogenesis of scoliosis section was the longest with the unifying focus being dynamic balance and structural equilibrium. It included his shot pellet (BB)-marked spine radiographic study suggesting T7 as the mechanical weak point of the human spine, a three-plane histological study showing extensive facet asymmetry and shape change implying shift of weight posteriorly and change from gliding to weight-bearing function, a mouse model of induced and resolving scoliosis, and his operated adolescent idiopathic facet pathology study with Enneking suggesting the changes seen were secondary adaptations. In addition, it described a well-documented case of resolving scoliosis coinciding with delayed neurological maturation and the possibility that asymmetrical mechanics began with eccentric intervertebral disc location. The instrumentation section detailed the development of Harrington Spine Instrumentation and stressed the importance of spinal balance and the stable zone. Finally, in the epilogue he stated his belief that a molecular deficiency would be found to explain idiopathic scoliosis and speculated on the importance of vitamin C, which had been the subject of his senior medical school thesis on collagen.

手稿分为五部分。[4]在序言中，他介绍了由20世纪50年代脊髓灰质炎疫情引发的创造过程。在基础科学部分，他认为环境对发展中的生物系统（如日本盆景树）有内在潜力的影响。脊柱侧凸发病机理部分的篇幅最长，集中阐述了动态平衡和结构平衡。其中包括标记为弹丸的脊柱射线照相研究，表明T7是人类脊柱的机械弱点。一项三平面组织学研究显示了T7广泛的小关节不对称性和形状变化，这意味着重心向后转移，从滑动到承重功能的变化。通过一个诱发和解决脊柱侧凸的小鼠模型，和一项他与恩内金进行的青少年特发性小关节病理学研究，他们发现，能看到的变化是继发性改变。此外，这本书还介绍了一例有完整资料记载的脊柱侧凸的病例，该病例与神经系统发育延迟有关，也可能与不对称力学开始于偏心椎间盘的位置有关。器械部分详细介绍了哈灵顿脊柱器械的发展，并强调了脊柱平衡和稳定区的重要性。最后，在结语中，他强调了自己的观点，即某种特定的分子层面的缺陷可以导致特发性脊柱侧凸，并推测维生素 C 在过程中起到重要作用，这是他在医学院时所写的关于胶原蛋白的论文的主题。

Over the course of four years Harrington employed from time to time at least three freelance writers, one freelance editor, an orthopaedic resident, and a senior medical student to help complete *The Human Spine*. In the summer of 1978 the medical student, Terry Clyburn, also helped Harrington organize his archives.[5] Because of this support activity, the manuscript was resubmitted to C.V Mosby in February 1978 with Dickson's strong commitment to see it to publication.[6] The next related correspondence was four months later when arrangements were being made for Eugenia Klein, an editor at Mosby, to meet with Harrington in July in Houston as an extension of an already planned trip.[7] Whether this meeting took place isn't documented. After a twelve-month silence Harrington submitted an extensive revision in June 1979,[8] and C.V. Mosby responded two months later with extensive editorial guidance and the suggestion that underwriting of the publication cost by the institute might be necessary.[9] By that time exhaustion and age seem to have taken their toll on Harrington, and efforts to publish ceased. The manuscript in its various versions eventually came to rest on somewhat more than six feet of shelf space filling ten legal and five letter-size archive boxes.[10] Harrington did continue writing the intended last chapter, which was printed in the form of a pamphlet that he sent to his friends in early 1980.

在四年的时间里，哈灵顿至少聘请了三名自由写作者，包括一名自由编辑、一名骨科住院医生和一名医学生来帮助完成《人类脊柱：历史、现状和未来》。1978 年夏天，医学生特里 · 克莱伯恩也帮助哈灵顿整理了他的手稿。[5]在这些人的支持下，该手稿于 1978 年 2 月重新提交给 C. V. 莫斯比公司，迪克森郑重承诺会看到它出版。[6]下一次相关的通信是在四个月后，当时安排了莫斯比的编辑尤金尼娅 · 克莱恩于 7 月在休斯敦与哈灵顿会面，作为已安排好的一次旅行的延伸。[7]这次会面是否举行并未记录在案。在失去音信一年之后，1979 年 6 月哈灵顿提交了一份全面修改的稿件，[8] C. V. 莫斯比公司在两个月后做出了回复，提供了全面的编辑指导，并建议可能需要研究所承担出版费用。[9]但那时，哈灵顿已经非常疲惫和年迈，书的出版不得不终止了。这份不同版本的手稿最终搁置在六英尺多一点的架子上，里面装满了 10 个法律文件和 5 个信纸大小的档案箱。[10]哈灵顿确实继续写了预定的最后一章，只不过是以小册子的形式印刷的，他在 1980 年年初将其寄给了他的朋友们。

In addition to working on *The Human Spine*, completion and initiation of studies for either possible presentation at professional association meetings or submission for publication or both were important to him because they were designed to provide continued improvement of patient care and foster professional advancement. In the six years from 1975 through 1980 Harrington, Dickson, and their colleagues published nine strong papers. This remarkable end of life academic output was greatly aided by, indeed heavily dependent upon, Dickson's comparable operative skill and his almost immediate adoption of autogenous iliac crest bone graft when he became responsible for the practice. Six of these nine publications were focused on scoliosis. The first four, presented in their chronological publication order, were clinical studies based on the large scoliosis surgical experience Harrington and Dickson had gained, and the two that follow reflected Harrington's efforts to understand the basic science of scoliosis.

除了《人类脊柱：历史、现状和未来》的撰写，学术研究的立项与完成，在专业学会会议上发表报告，以及专著的出版对他来说都非常重要，因为它们旨在持续改善患者治疗和促进本专业进步。从 1975 年到 1980 年的 6 年间，哈灵顿、迪克森和他们的同事发表了 9 篇很有说服力的论文。哈灵顿在生命末期的这一非凡的学术成果，实际上在很大程度上依赖迪克森当时高超的手术技巧，以及在开始负责手术时即采用自体髂骨移植术的选择，这些因素极大地促进了他们对学术成果的总结。这 9 份出版物中有 6 份是关于脊柱侧凸的。前 4 份（按出版时间顺序排列）是基于哈灵顿和迪克森大量脊柱侧凸手术经验的临床研究，随后的 2 份反映了哈灵顿对探索脊柱侧凸基础科学的努力。

"Results of Harrington Instrumentation and Fusion in the Adult Idiopathic Scoliosis Patient," presented to the SRS in 1974, was published in late 1975. It reported their 11 year (1961–72) experience based on 132 consecutive patients 20 years of age or older, of whom 113 (86%) had a minimum 2-year and an average 3.9-year follow-up.[11] Mechanical back pain or fatigue was the indication for surgery, and no patient was operated on solely for cosmetic reasons. The goal was spine stabilization with any correction being an added benefit. Preoperative traction was not used. The average preoperative curve was 72°, the operating time was 130 minutes (range, 73 to 235 minutes), the average blood loss was 874 milliliters (range, 214 to 2,480 mL), and the average curve correction was 48% (range, 19% to 83%). There were twenty-four early complications, including two deaths, one of which was due to a stroke. The other was a 22-year-old female with right thoracic idiopathic scoliosis of 170° corrected to 100° at 7 weeks postoperative from hydronephrosis caused by ureteral obstruction at the pelvic brim.[12] There were 52 late complications, the most common of which was documented or probable pseudarthrosis in 20 of the 113(18%) followed patients. When autogenous iliac crest bone graft was used, only one of 50 patients developed a pseudarthrosis. All but one of the 113 followed patients reported that their procedure was worthwhile.

1974 年提交给脊柱侧凸研究学会的《成人特发性脊柱侧凸患者的哈灵顿内固定融合效果》于 1975 年年底出版。该研究报告了他们 11 年（1961—1972 年）的经验，这些经验基于 132 名 20 岁或以上的患者，其中 113 人（86%）至少随访 2 年，平均随访 3.9 年。[11]手术的指征为机械性背痛或疲劳，没有一位患者单纯因为外观问题而接受手术。手术目标首先是稳定脊柱，其次是矫形。所有患者均未使用术前牵引。术前平均弯曲为 72°，平均手术时间为 130 分钟（73~235 分钟），平均失血量为 874 cc（214~2 480 cc），平均弯曲矫正率为 48%（19%~83%）。有 24 例早期并发症，包括两例死亡，其中一例死于中风。另一位是一名右侧胸椎特发性脊柱侧凸由 170°矫正至 100°的 22 岁女性，术后 7 周时因骨盆边缘输尿管梗阻导致肾积水而死亡。[12]有 52 例出现了晚期并发症，其中记录在案中最常见或者最可能发生的是假关节形成，在 113 例随访病例中有 20 例（18%）。当使用自体髂骨移植时，50 例病例中只有 1 例出现假关节。113 名随访患者中，除 1 人外，其余患者均表示手术是值得的。

"Result of Early Ambulation in the Surgical Treatment of Scoliosis" was presented at the annual meeting of the SRS in 1975 and published in 1976 under the title "The Postoperative Management of Scoliosis Patients Treated with Harrington Instrumentation and Fusion." It compared idiopathic scoliosis patients operated on without added bone graft and one body cast for three months recumbent and three months ambulatory to patients with autologous iliac bone grafting and ambulation in two body casts, the first for six months and the second for three.[13] Fewer patients developed pseudarthrosis (4% versus 0.6%) and correction loss was less (8.3° versus 4.3°) in the second group. Results of the second group compared favorably to patients ambulated in a full Risser cast, which included the neck.[14]

1975年，《脊柱侧凸手术治疗早期活动的效果》在脊柱侧凸研究学会年会上报道，并于1976年以《哈灵顿内固定和融合治疗脊柱侧凸患者的术后处理》为题发表。该研究将在不植骨、仅用一个躯体石膏的情况下，分别进行3个月的卧床或3个月行走的特发性脊柱侧凸患者，与两个自体髂骨移植加躯体石膏的患者进行了比较，这两组患者中一组在术后6个月开始行走，另一组在术后3个月开始行走。[13]第二组出现假关节的患者较少（4%对0.6%），矫正丢失较小（8.3°对4.3°）。第二组的结果与使用包括颈部在内的完整里泽石膏行走的患者相比，表现较为良好。[14]

"Results of Harrington Instrumentation in the Treatment for Severe Scoliosis" was presented at the eleventh annual meeting of the SRS in 1976 and published in 1979. The study group was patients with scoliosis greater than 90° operated on from July 1963 to December 1974.[15] Two hundred seven patients met these inclusion criteria, 37 having had one or more prior surgeries for their scoliosis. Eleven lacked long-term follow-up, leaving 196 patients (95% of the study group) eligible for follow-up study. Their diagnostic categories were idiopathic, post-polio, congenital, and other. Their mean age preoperatively was 19.9 years (range, 9 to 56 years), and their mean curve size was 107°. The goal of surgery was considered to be stabilization with any correction an added benefit. No patients were treated with preoperative traction or cast. The mean operating time was 2 hours 23 minutes, the mean blood loss 1,041 mL, and the mean blood replacement was 1,045 mL. The mean postoperative curve correction was 42%, and at two years it was 34%. Curve correction was most influenced by and indirectly related to patient age and curve size. Early complications occurred in 36 of the 207. There were five deaths at the time of or shortly after surgery: one of intraoperative cardiac arrest, one of postoperative pulmonary embolism, and three of respiratory or cardiac failure. Paraplegia developed in an 18-year-old man with a 180° scoliosis and 160° kyphosis of unstated cause, who had preoperative paraparesis with 80% loss of lower extremity function and loss of bowel and bladder control. The other 30 early complications all cleared, including the one deep wound infection. The most common late complication was pseudarthrosis: 14% (19 of 135) before and 8% (5 of 65) after autograft use. The results were comparable to cited series using preoperative traction or casting.

1976年在脊柱侧凸研究学会第十一届年会上，哈灵顿汇报了《哈灵顿器械治疗严重脊柱侧凸的结果》，并于1979年发表。研究组为1963年7月至1974年12

月手术的侧凸角度大于90°的患者。[15] 207 名患者符合这些入选标准，37 名患者曾接受过一次或多次脊柱侧凸手术。11 名患者缺乏长期随访，最终对 196 名符合要求的脊柱侧凸患者（研究组的95%）进行随访研究。诊断类别包括特发性、脊髓灰质炎后遗症、先天性和其他。术前平均年龄19.9 岁（范围9 岁到56 岁），平均弯曲角度 107°。手术的目标首要为稳定脊柱，其次是矫形。患者均未进行术前牵引或石膏治疗。平均手术时间为 2 小时 23 分钟，平均失血 1 041 cc，平均输血 1 045 cc。术后平均弯曲矫正率为 42%，两年时为 34%。弯曲矫正程度受患者年龄和弯曲大小影响最大，并与之间接相关。207 名患者中有 36 名出现早期并发症。术中和术后不久出现了 5 例死亡病例：1 例术中心搏骤停，1 例术后肺栓塞，3 例呼吸或心力衰竭。一例存在 180°脊柱侧凸和 160°脊柱后凸的 18 岁男子术后出现了截瘫，原因不明。但他在术前便存在 80%的下肢功能丧失，大小便失禁。其他 30 例早期并发症全部消失，包括一例深部伤口感染。最常见的晚期并发症是假关节形成：使用自体骨移植前发生率为 14%（19/135），使用自体骨移植后发生率为 8%（5/65）。结果与以往应用术前牵引或石膏的患者没有显著差异。

"Clinical Review of Patients with Broken Harrington Rods" was published in 1980. Patients with scoliosis of all causes operated on by the authors from 1961 through 1974 were included and divided by year of operation into Group A, those operated on from 1961 through 1968, and Group B, those operated on from 1969 through 1974. The dividing point was when fresh autogenous iliac crest bone graft began being used.[16] Comparing Group A to Group B, distraction rod breakage was 12.5% (141 of 1,128) versus 2.1% (19 of 888), reinstrumentation was required in 23 versus none, and compression rod fractures occurred in 3.5% versus 0.1%. The authors' conclusion was that "the clinical management of rod fractures must be individualized." They deemed the breakage in Group B as acceptable and added that "we see no need to change the basic design of the instruments unless newly developed metals or engineering capabilities offer improved endurance limits of the rods."

1980 年，《哈灵顿棒断裂患者的临床回顾》发表。作者于 1961 年至 1974 年间对各种原因的脊柱侧凸患者进行了手术，并按手术年份分为 A 组（1961—1968）和 B 组（1969—1974）。分界点是新鲜自体髂骨移植开始使用的时间。[16] A 组与 B 组相比，撑开棒断裂率为 12.5%（1 128 例中有 141 例）和 2.1%（888 例中有 19 例），A 组有 23 例需要重新置棒，而 B 组没有；压缩棒断裂发生率为 3.5%和 0.1%。作者的结论如下："撑开棒断裂的临床治疗必需个性化。"他们认为 B 组的断棒率是可以接受的，并补充道，“我们认为没有必要改变器械的基本设计，除非新开发的金属或工艺提高了棒的耐久极限。”

The two papers addressing the basic science of scoliosis were authored by Harrington alone. “Is Scoliosis Reversible? In Vivo Observations of Reversible Morphological Changes in the Production of Scoliosis in Mice” had been funded by the NFIP, completed approximately twenty years earlier, and bound in 1957.[17] With slight revision the report was published in 1976—that's dogged persistence indeed![18] Progressive thoracolumbar scoliosis resulted when the right elbow and knee of five-day-old inbred mice were tethered together with a suture through the joints. By 35 days 60° to 100° scoliosis had developed with facet (but not vertebral body) endochondral ossification asymmetry that resolved after the tether was released. Harrington interpreted this as showing the importance of normal function (reciprocal motion) to growth.

两篇关于脊柱侧凸基础科学的论文是由哈灵顿独自撰写的。《脊柱侧凸是可逆的吗？小鼠脊柱侧凸产生过程中可逆形态学变化的体内观察》由国家小儿麻痹基金会资助，在约 20 年前完成，最早可追溯到 1957 年。[17]该论文经过轻微修改于 1976 年发表，这的确是锲而不舍![18]将 5 天大的近交系小鼠的右肘和膝盖通过关节用缝合线拴在一起时，导致了进行性胸腰椎侧凸。到 35 天时，60°至 100°脊柱侧凸已发展为小关节（而非椎体）软骨内骨化不对称，在松脱系绳后该不对称性得以解决。哈灵顿解释，这表明了正常功能（往复运动）对生长的重要性。

“The Etiology of Idiopathic Scoliosis” was published in 1977 and reflected Harrington's decades-long thirst to understand the origin of this medical enigma.[19] Based on his studies and experience, he was convinced “that the genetic factor plays a part, but not a major role in the etiology of idiopathic scoliosis.” A mother-daughter pilot study had not shown that late pregnancy (35 years or older) contributed to idiopathic scoliosis etiology. He was drawn to the possibility that collagen was the target protein and vitamin C the lacking nutrient. Harrington's interest in this vitamin dated back at least as far as his senior medical school thesis, “The Therapeutic Value of Cevitamic Acid.[20] He added the following acknowledgment to the end of his “Etiology” paper: “To my friend and colleague, Dr. Moe—the Father of the Modern Treatment of Scoliosis. I would like to pass on this thought: ‘Tomorrow, when we can comprehend the molecular chemistry of the living process, can we then predict and perhaps prevent idiopathic scoliosis?’”

1977 年，《特发性脊柱侧凸的病因学》发表，反映了哈灵顿几十年来对探索这一医学谜团起源的渴望。[19]根据他的研究和经验，他确信“遗传因素在特发性脊柱侧凸的病因中起着部分作用，但不是主要作用”。一项母女家系研究没有显示晚期妊娠（35 岁或以上）会导致特发性脊柱侧凸。一种其他的病因的可能性引起了他的关注，即胶原蛋白是目标蛋白质，而维生素 C 是缺乏的营养素。哈灵顿对这种维生素的兴趣至少可以追溯到他的医学院论文《抗坏血酸的治疗价值》。[20]他在《特发性脊柱侧凸的病因学》的论文结尾处补充了以下几点致谢：“致我的朋友和同行，脊柱侧凸现代治疗之父莫医生。我想传递这样的想法：‘未来，当我们能够理解生命过程的分子化学时，我们能够预测并预防特发性脊柱侧凸吗?’”

The remaining three papers published from 1975 through 1980 addressed two new indications for Harrington Spine Instrumentation. Two papers focused on its use with unstable thoracic and lumbar spine fractures, a treatment that Harrington had reawakened. Distraction was used to restore spine height and pressure over the gibbus to reduce the sharp angular kyphosis. Overdistraction was prevented by the intact anterior longitudinal ligament. Permanent stability was provided by arthrodesis. The third paper was the culmination of his several years' work to develop an effective operation for high-grade spondylolisthesis, a low occurrence condition for which consensus about indications for treatment and treatment methodology was notably lacking.

1975—1980 年发表的其余三篇论文讨论了哈灵顿脊柱器械的两个新适应证。其中两篇论文集中讨论了它在不稳定胸椎和腰椎骨折中的应用。因为这种治疗方法，哈灵顿重新出现在人们的视野中。采用撑开法可以恢复脊柱高度和臂骨上方的压力，以减少锐性角状后凸。完整的前纵韧带防止了过度撑开。融合术提供了永久稳定性。第三篇论文是他这几年来致力于研发的一种有效手术治疗严重腰椎滑脱症的成果。严重腰椎滑脱症是一种发病率较低的疾病，在治疗适应证和治疗方法方面缺乏共识。

"Instrumentation of the Spine for Fracture Dislocations in Children," published in 1977, was notable for its neurosurgical origins and combined neurosurgical and orthopaedic surgery authorship.[21] It reported a series of thirteen children, aged eleven through sixteen years, who were treated with Harrington Instrumentation and fusion and were followed for two years. The three with incomplete paraplegia improved, and both the sagittal angular and translational deformity corrections of about 50% were maintained.

Use in this age group was supported."

1977 年出版的《儿童脊柱骨折脱位内固定》以其作者团体的强大阵容而闻名，由神经外科医生发起，并联合骨科医生一起撰写。[21]该研究报告了 13 名儿童，年龄从 11 岁到 16 岁，他们接受了哈灵顿内固定和融合治疗，随访两年。三位不完全截瘫患者情况有所改善，矢状角和侧方平移畸形矫正率均维持在 50%左右。结果支持此技术可在此年龄组使用。

"Results of Reduction and Stabilization of the Severely Fractured Thoracic and Lumbar Spine" was presented at the eleventh annual meeting of the SRS in 1976 and published in 1978. It analyzed 95 consecutive patients treated from 1962 to 1976 and followed a mean of 21 months.[22] Complications occurred in twenty-six patients (14%). The most common were error in placement of the instruments in seven patients and hook dislodgment in six. Two patients died, both of respiratory failure. Neurologic function improved one to three grades in thirteen patients, not better than reported for postural reduction and bed rest. "No patients lost neural function as a result of operative treatment." The average hospital stay, which included self-care rehabilitation, was 107 days.

1976 年在脊柱侧凸研究学会第十一届年会上，哈灵顿还汇报了《严重胸腰椎骨折复位和稳定的结果》，并于 1978 年发表。该研究分析了 1962—1976 年连续治疗的 95 名患者，平均随访 21 个月。[22] 26 名患者发生并发症（14%）。最常见的是器械放置错误，共 7 名患者，6 名患者的钩移位。2 名患者死亡，均为呼吸衰竭。13 名患者的神经功能改善了一到三级，但并不比已报道的体位复位和卧床休息效果好。"没有患者因手术治疗而丧失神经功能。"平均住院时间为 107 天，包括自我管理下的康复。

"Spinal Instrumentation in the Treatment of Severe Progressive Spondylolisthesis" was published in 1976. It described the origin and three-phase evolution of the operation Harrington developed to treat this condition over a period of eight years and twenty-four patients.[23] Reduction of the spondylolisthesis was accomplished with distraction. No specific provision was made for correction of lumbosacral kyphosis. Out of this process came the A-frame L1 to sacral bar structure, the short outrigger, iliosacral screw anchor and yoke connector, L3 to bilateral iliosacral bars, and L5-S1 posterior interbody fusion.

1976 年，《脊柱器械治疗严重进行性脊柱滑脱》发表。它描述了手术治疗的起源和三个阶段的演变，作者应用哈灵顿内固定器械在8年的时间里进行了24例手术。[23]腰椎滑脱的复位是通过撑开完成的。没有具体提及腰骶后凸的矫正。在这个过程中，出现了A型框架L1至骶骨棒结构、短的外撑开器、髂骶螺钉锚和轭连接件、L3至双侧髂骶棒以及L5-S1后路椎体间融合。

Paul Harrington was good company, shared his wisdom freely, and made lasting friends. There were still many who came to Houston to learn more about his practice that was being continued by Dickson, to dig deeper into his thought process, or both. A particularly noteworthy visit was that of John P. O'Brien, Director of the Department for Spinal Disorders at the Robert Jones and Agnes Hunt Orthopaedic Hospital in Oswestry, United Kingdom, and a protege and former colleague of Arthur Hodgson. O'Brien came prepared to interview Harrington, and an insightful twenty-two page transcript resulted from their August 23, 1976, session.[24] Harrington made clear that his interest in vitamin C was not a passing fancy. Beginning with his senior medical school thesis, his interest in the vitamin had been a fixture in his thought process. Based on his experience as a young intern and resident in South Carolina, he believed vitamin C deficiency in the poorly nourished population was associated with an increased hysterectomy incision dehiscence. In Houston he felt that he treated disc problems successfully with vitamin C, as did his neurosurgical colleague, James Greenwood. As his involvement with scoliosis grew, he became convinced of the importance of connective tissue health as well as the importance of vitamin C in its health. A question about a point of no return in a scoliosis curve gave Harrington the opening to discuss the Harrington factor. He expressed his conviction that idiopathic scoliosis was caused by the disc. He emphasized operating on smaller curves (40° to 60° or 70°) in order to avoid operating on bigger curves because he believed all the curves eventually worsened. Harrington held that rib surgery was unnecessary if curves were done when smaller.

保罗·哈灵顿是一位好同事，他毫无保留地分享自己的智慧，和许多人结成了长久的友谊。还有很多人来到休斯敦，想了解更多关于那些被迪克森继承的哈灵顿的技术实践，深入挖掘他的思想过程，或者两者兼而有之。一次特别值得注意的访问是英国奥斯沃斯特里的罗伯特·琼斯和阿格尼斯·亨特骨科医院脊柱外科主任约翰·P. 奥布赖恩，他是阿瑟·霍奇森的门生和前同事。奥布赖恩准备与哈灵顿面谈，1976年8月23日，他们的谈话被记录在一份22页的文件上。[24]哈灵顿明确表示，他对维生素C的兴趣并不是一时兴起的。从他撰写医学院毕业论文开始，就一直在思考维生素C的作用。根据他在南卡罗来纳州的实习生和住院医师的经验，他认为在营养不良人群中维生素C的缺乏与子宫切除术切口裂开发生率偏高有关。在休斯敦，他觉得他用维生素C成功地治疗了椎间盘问题，他的神经外科同事詹姆斯·格林伍德也是如此。随着他与脊柱侧凸的关系日益加深，他开始相信结缔组织健康的重要性以及维生素C对其健康的重要性。一个关于脊柱侧凸弯曲无法矫正的问题给了哈灵顿讨论哈灵顿系数的机会。他确信特发性脊柱侧凸是由椎间盘引起的。他强调对较小的弯曲（40°至60°或70°）应使其避免发展到较大弯曲后进行手术，因为他相信所有弯曲最终都会加大。哈灵顿认为，如果弯曲较小时进行手术，则不需要额外进行肋骨手术。

On the subject of Dwyer Instrumentation, Harrington was largely negative except in the spastic child with a lumbar or thoracolumbar curve where he thought it was unsurpassed. In discussing the complication of paraplegia, he explained again the rationale of applying compression force first to prevent overstretching. Concerning the low back syndrome, he believed the etiology was lordosis and that his instrumentation put the lumbar disc back into its vertical load position. As to the etiology of idiopathic scoliosis his thought was that as more was known about the genetic problem "we'll find it an infinitesimal part of the hereditary background of scoliosis." To wrap up the interview, O'Brien asked whether Harrington thought that in the next 25 to 50 years a space age strain-gauge (mechanical) or a molecular/biological approach would be more important. A single-spaced, narrow-margined, three-page rambling response followed. Harrington's answer was simple, molecular/biological, but his path to it was convoluted. Basically, his view was that the dynamics of life were more meaningful than statics. In a very small part of his long answer, he provided added insight into his life. "I was an athlete when I was a kid—in fact that's how I got through medicine in semi-pro ball—I hate to admit it, but we were poor people. Why was I a success? I had 4,000 polio patients in the acute epidemic—and do you know how I got'em? Because the National Foundation paid no doctor to take care of them. That's why I've got 300 triples and over 400 opponens transplants and that sort of thing. Even when we operated, we operated free. Muscular activity always fascinated me—not because I was an athlete—but in the efficiency in why one person could run faster than the other."

哈灵顿对“德怀尔内固定器械”基本上持否定态度，除了在伴有腰椎或胸腰椎侧弯的痉挛型儿童中德怀尔内固定器械效果超群。在讨论截瘫的并发症时，他再次解释了首先应用压缩力量以防止过度拉伸的原理。关于腰椎综合征，他认为病因是前凸，他的内固定器械使腰椎间盘回到其垂直载荷位置。关于特发性脊柱侧凸的病因，他的想法是，随着对遗传问题的了解越来越多，“我们会发现遗传只是发生脊柱侧凸的一小部分因素。”为了结束会谈，奥布赖恩问哈灵顿是否认为在未来25~50年内，宇宙空间时代，是机械应变仪重要还是分子/生物方法更为重要。(以后的医学发展是以机械为主还是以分子生物为主。)随后的回答被记录在三页间隔很短、边缘很窄且杂乱无章的纸上。哈灵顿的回答很简单，未来是分子/生物学的，但它的道路很曲折。基本上，他的观点是，生命的动态比静态更有意义。在他很长的回答的一小部分中，他对自己的人生有了更多的见解。“我小时候是一名运动员，事实上，我通过打半职业篮球赛才担负得起医学院的学费——我不愿意承认，但我们都是穷人。为什么我成功了？我有4 000名急性感染的脊髓灰质炎患者，你知道为什么他们会在我这里吗？因为国家基金会没有钱请医生来医治他们。这就是为什么我做了300例三头肌和400多例对掌肌移植之类的手术。即使我们做这类手术，我们也不会收一分钱。肌肉的活动总是让我着迷，这不是因为我是一名运动员，而是因为我想知道为什么一个人可以跑得比另一个人更快。”

O'Brien continued on to the SRS meeting in Ottawa and after returning home wrote Harrington. “I want to thank you very much for the wonderful hospitality I enjoyed in Houston. It was a great experience. It was marvelous talking with you and meeting Mary Alice.”[25] It was obvious that O'Brien and Harrington had connected.

奥布赖恩继续到渥太华参加脊柱侧凸研究学会会议，回国后写信给哈灵顿。“非常感谢你在休斯敦的盛情款待。这是一次很棒的经历。与你交谈并见到玛丽·艾丽斯真是太棒了。”[25]很明显，奥布赖恩和哈灵顿保持着联系。

The eleventh annual meeting of the SRS was held in Ottawa, Ontario, Canada, on September 4-6, 1976, under the presidency of Ed Simmons.[26] For the first-time extended abstracts were to be published in a companion publication of the Journal of Bone and Joint Surgery named *Orthopedic Transactions*.[27] It was the society's second gathering in Canada, and Simmons was the second Canadian president. This meeting, the 1973 meeting in Gothenburg, Sweden, the 1973 post-meeting in Lyon, France, and the 1977 meeting scheduled for Hong Kong with a pre-meeting in Japan were rapidly establishing the SRS as an internationally oriented professional association. The second Harrington Guest

Lecturer Was Yves Cotrel of Berk-Plage, France, who further burnished the global credentials of the SRS. Cotrel's presentation was titled "Spinal Fusion for Scoliosis by Tibial Autogenous Graft, Harrington Instrumentation, and Transverse Traction Device (G.T.+H+D.T.T.): Results of First 295 Operated Cases."

1976 年 9 月 4 日至 6 日，第十一届脊柱侧凸研究学会年会在加拿大安大略省的渥太华顺利召开，由爱德华·西蒙斯担任本次大会的主席。[26]此次会议首次将扩展摘要发表在《骨与关节外科杂志》的姊妹刊《骨科汇刊》上。[27]这是学会第二次在加拿大举办年会，西蒙斯也是第二任加拿大籍主席。本次会议，与 1973 年在瑞典哥德堡的会议、1973 年在法国里昂的会后会议以及 1977 年在中国香港的会议和在日本举行的会前会议，一同使脊柱侧凸研究学会迅速成为一个国际性的专业学会。第二位哈灵顿特邀演讲者是来自法国贝尔克普拉日的伊夫斯·科特雷尔，他进一步提高了脊柱侧凸研究学会的全球地位。他的报告题目是“通过胫骨自体骨移植，哈灵顿器械与横向牵引装置（G. T. +H+D. T. T）进行脊柱侧凸融合术：前 295 名手术患者的结果”。

The 1976 meeting featured nine presentations in which Harrington Instrumentation was extensively or exclusively used. Seven of the presentations reported positive experiences: three for fractures[28,29,30] and one each for adult scoliosis,[31] Scheuermann's kyphosis,[32] myelomeningocele,[33] and Duchenne's muscular dystrophy.[34] Two of the presentations reported negative experiences. One was a myelomeningocele series where the problem reported was a technical difficulty because of missing posterior spine elements.[35] The other was a complication of scoliosis surgery resulting in loss of lumbar lordosis with stooped posture and chronic muscle strain.[36] Neither was a new criticism.

在 1976 年的会议上，有 9 个报告中大量使用或仅使用了哈灵顿器械。7 个报告肯定了它的效果，包括 3 个骨折[28,29,30]、1 个成人脊柱侧凸[31]、1 个休门氏病后凸[32]、1 个脊髓脊膜膨出[33]和 1 个肌营养不良症。[34]另外两个为负面结果，1 个为脊髓脊膜膨出，由于脊柱后部结构缺失造成技术性困难；[35]另有 1 个的脊柱侧凸手术造成了腰椎前凸丢失的并发症，伴有前倾姿态和慢性肌肉劳损。[36]但是提出的这两点批评并不新鲜。

Dwyer Instrumentation, the only alternative, was designed for anterior use so it had limited adaptability, but was still viable as presented in two experimental studies.[37,38] A new alterative was Weiss springs, a posterior instrumentation for spine fracture treatment.

Two preliminary papers were presented on this topic; the second was moderately critical.[39,40] Weiss springs were actually not new but were an adaptation of the Gruca spring instrumentation of scoliosis, and neither became accepted.

德怀尔内固定器械是哈灵顿内固定器械唯一的替代品，但它是为前路手术而设计的，所以适应范围有限，不过仍然有两项实验性研究报道了它的可行性。[37,38]一种新的替代方法是韦斯弹簧，是一种用于脊柱骨折治疗的后路器械。有两篇初步研究对这个主题进行了报道，其中第二篇持批评态度。[39,40]韦斯弹簧实际上并不是一项新技术，而是格鲁克弹簧在脊柱侧凸治疗上的一种改进，但是两者均未被业界接受。

Among these presentations was an innovation that illustrated the possibilities of three-dimensional correction and internal stability. "Segmental Correction of Scoliosis with Rigid Internal Fixation" was based on bilateral, segmental sublaminar wire anchors connected to rods with a twist knot, and thus adjustable.[41] It allowed delivery of four of the degrees freedom of motion corrective loads (coronal and sagittal translation and angulation) to the spine. Vertical translation and to a lesser extent axial angulation loads and position were by products of direct loads. The result was internal stability (resistance to deforming loads), eliminating the need for postoperative mobilization without supplemental external immobilization with a cast or brace. This was something the one-degree freedom of motion (vertical translation) Harington Instrumentation could never achieve.

在所有的报告中，有一项创新展现了三维矫正和内部稳定的可能性。“刚性内固定脊柱侧凸节段性矫形”是一种基于双侧、节段性椎板下钢丝锚定连接到棒的技术，因而可调节棒带扭转结。[41]它可以向脊柱提供 4 个自由度的运动矫正载荷(冠状面和矢状面，平移和成角)。垂直平移和较小程度的轴向角度载荷和位置是直接载荷的副产物。从而实现了内部的稳定（抵抗变形载荷)，术后无需使用石膏或支具进行额外的外固定。这种垂直平移方向上的自由度是哈灵顿内固定器械无法实现的。

Two events on the program could not have been better timed symbolically.[42] On the morning of the meeting's second day Simmons presented his presidential address titled "New Frontiers." On the morning of the third day and as part of the coffee break after the scientific session that included "Segmental Correction," 30 minutes were allowed to observe the changing of the guard outside Canada's Parliament Hall. The guard was changing in scoliosis and spine deformity surgery as well, but the pace would prove to be slower!

大会上有两项议程的时间安排得非常合适。[42]会议第二天上午，西蒙斯发表了题为“新前沿”的主席演讲。第三天上午，在包括“节段性矫正”等专题会议结束后，作为茶歇的一部分，有30分钟的时间供与会者观看加拿大议会大厅外面卫兵的换岗仪式。脊柱侧凸和脊柱畸形手术中的“卫兵”也在改变，但是将以较为缓慢的步调进行。

"Segmental Correction" was the brainchild of Eduardo Luque, whose instrumentation became known as Luque Rod Instrumentation (LRI) or Segmental Spinal Instrumentation (SSI). Probably the only factor that prevented this new surgical innovation from completely taking over the spine instrumentation market was that it required multiple entries into the posterior spinal canal, thus repeatedly exposing the spinal cord to direct trauma. Regardless of the fate of his technique, the concepts of multi-planar correction and no postoperative external immobilization were revolutionary for the scoliosis and other spinal deformities professional community. SSI would come to be considered as ushering in the second generation of spine instrumentation; Harrington Instrumentation was the first. Eduardo Roberto Luque Rebollar (1931－2001) was of Spanish-Mexican heritage and received his undergraduate and medical degrees at Stanford, where he was a runner on the track team.[43] After interning at McGill and receiving plastic surgery training in Mexico and orthopedic training in Devon, England, he completed his residency under the tutelage of Joe Risser at the Los Angeles Orthopedic Hospital. He met his future wife, Katherine Risser, when she accompanied her parents to an orthopedic convention in Mexico City where Luque served as the interpreter. The origin of Luque's breakthrough is well described by his obituarist, Albert E. Sanders, M.D. "In addition to his private practice he, with the help of Walt Disney whom he had met as a resident, developed the Dr. German Diaz Lombardo Orthopedic Hospital for indigent children and adults. Eduardo cared for a large number of young people with scoliosis at this facility and also at the Shrine, where he directed the scoliosis program. Many of his patients lived in shanties a long way from Mexico City and tolerated poorly the postoperative casts used in the Risser or Harrington techniques. A neurosurgical colleague taught him to pass sublaminar wires for fixation of cervical injuries and he combined this with the Harrington system. He came to realize that the hooks were not necessary, that the system using two smooth rods was strong enough so that no cast was needed and that it was possible to control sagittal alignment as well." In his closing Sanders drew a compelling picture of his friend: "Luque's creativity, enthusiasm for living, and compassion for others won him many close friends both in and outside the medical community."

"节段矫正"最先由爱德华多·卢克提出，因此其内固定装置被命名为卢克棒（LRI）或节段性脊柱器械（SSI）。阻碍这种新技术完全占领脊柱器械市场的唯一因素可能是它需要多次从后路进入椎管，从而使脊髓反复暴露于直接损伤的风险中。不管该项技术的命运如何，多平面矫正和术后无需外固定的概念对脊柱侧凸和其他脊柱畸形专业领域来讲都是革命性的。节段性脊柱器械被认为引领了第二代脊柱器械的发展；哈灵顿器械则是第一代。爱德华多·罗伯托·卢克·雷博拉尔（1931—2001）是西班牙裔墨西哥人，在斯坦福大学获得了医学学士学位，并曾是田径队的一员。[43]结束在麦吉尔大学的实习之后，卢克又在墨西哥接受了整形外科的培训，以及在英国德文郡的骨科培训，最终在约瑟夫·里泽指导下于洛杉矶骨科医院完成了他的住院医师培训。在那里，他结识了未来的妻子凯瑟琳·里泽：当时凯瑟琳正陪父母参加墨西哥城的一个骨科会议，而担任翻译的正是卢克。卢克的讣告作者阿尔伯特·E. 桑德斯博士对卢克棒这项突破性技术的源头有着很好的描述，"除了他的私人诊所，他还在自己担任住院医师时期认识的沃尔特·迪斯尼的帮助下，为贫困儿童和成人建立了德尔曼·迪亚斯·隆巴多博士骨科医院。卢克在这个医院治疗了很多患有脊柱侧凸的年轻人，在他主持脊柱侧凸项目的圣地医院也做了同样的事情。他的许多患者住在离墨西哥城很远的棚户区，因此对里泽或哈灵顿技术的术后石膏外固定耐受性很差。一位神经外科的同事教他通过椎板下的钢丝固定颈椎损伤，于是卢克将其与哈灵顿系统结合起来，并意识到钩子并不是必要的：使用两根光滑内固定棒的系统足够坚固，所以也不需要术后石膏，而且双棒系统还可以维持矢状位序列。"在结语中，桑德斯为他的朋友勾勒了一个有目共睹的形象："卢克的创造力、对生活的热情和对他人的同情使他收获了许多医学界内外的亲密朋友。"

One of the podium presentations was the "Morbidity Report, Scoliosis Research Society, 1975" presented by John Kostuik.[44] One hundred twenty-one of approximately 170 surgeon members (71%) had provided information on 4,439 patients, an average of 37 patients per respondent. Harrington Instrumentation was used in 77% of the patients,

Dwyer Instrumentation in 4.5%, and "other fusions" in about 16%. The questionnaire was extensive, and with only a few exceptions past data had provided sufficient insight into surgical morbidity. Notable exceptions were the occurrence of pressure sores in 1.6% (72 patients), deep wound infection in only 1% (42 patients), and some form of instrument failure in 2.5% (111 patients), which were 90% related to distraction hook problems. Because of their gravity, most of the presentation was focused on neurological complications, which occurred in 1.1% (49 of 4,439 patients). Cord lesions and complete or incomplete paraplegia occurred in 53% (26 of 49 patients), peripheral nerve root or brachial plexus problems in 45% (22 of 49 patients), and cranial nerve problems in 2% (1 of 49 patients). Older patients with larger curves and those with curves due to congenital, postirradiation, or neurofibromatosis conditions appeared to be at greater risk. A surgeon's caseload was not definitively related to neurological complications, although the impression was that busier surgeons had fewer. The principal surgery or treatment most commonly associated with neurological complications was, in decreasing order of frequency, Harrington Instrumentation in seventeen patients (ten with concurrent procedures associated with neurological complications), traction in ten patients, vertebral body resection in nine patients, and other in thirteen patients (divided into seven possible causation categories). The only denominator provided was for vertebral body resection, revealing an incidence of 12% (9 of 74 patients).

约翰·科斯图克发表了一篇题为“脊柱侧凸研究学会 1975 年并发症发生率报告”的大会演讲。[44]大约 170 名外科医生中有 121 名（71%）提供了共 4 439 名患者的资料，平均每位受访医生提供了 37 名患者的资料。有 77%的患者使用了哈灵顿内固定器械，有 4.5%的患者使用了德怀尔内固定器械，另有大约 16%的患者采用了其他融合技术。问卷内容广泛，既往数据中除少数据外，均对了解手术相关并发症发生率提供了充分的帮助。值得注意的是，1.6%（72 名患者）发生了压疮，仅 1%（42 名患者）深部伤口感染，2.5%（111 名患者）内固定失败，而内固定失败 90%与撑开钩相关。由于严重性的原因，大部分报告集中在神经系统并发症，发生率为 1.1%（49 名患者）。其中，有 53%（26/49）的患者出现了脊髓病变和完全性或不完全性截瘫，另有 45%（22/49）的患者出现了周围神经根或臂丛问题，其余 2%（1/49）的患者出现颅神经问题。侧凸较严重的大龄患者以及先天性、射线照射后或神经纤维瘤病导致的脊柱侧凸患者发生神经系统并发症的风险似乎较大。尽管在人们印象中经验越丰富的外科医生越不容易导致病人发生神经系统并发症，而结果显示外科医生的诊治数量与神经系统并发症之间并无明确相关性。与神经系统并发症相关的主要手术或治疗方式按发生频率由高到低依次为：哈灵顿内固定术 17 例（有 10 例同时伴有可能造成神经系统并发症的其他手术或操作）、牵引 10 例、椎体切除术 9 例和其他手术 13 例（其中又可分为 7 类）。唯一提供的一项统计基准是关于椎体切除的，其术后并发症的发生率为 12%（9/74）。

Of the twenty-six patients with paraplegia, twelve (46%) were complete. Full recovery occurred in 50% (six of twelve patients) with incomplete recovery in 25% (three of twelve) and no recovery in 25% (three of twelve). Fourteen of the twenty-six (54%) had incomplete paraplegia; seven of the fourteen had full and seven had incomplete recovery (50%). Harrington Rod removal was done within six hours in eight patients, four with complete and four with incomplete paraplegia. Full recovery occurred in 75% (six of eight patients); three of the six had complete and three had incomplete paraplegia. The Stagnara wake-up test was specifically helpful in three patients in whom the rods were removed before closure. There was complete recovery from postoperative complete paraplegia in two of them and incomplete recovery in the other. Kostuik closed his report with this thought: "Through constant observation, discussion, and experience it is hoped that the already low incidence of neurological problems will continually be decreased by members of the Scoliosis Research Society."

在 26 名截瘫患者中，12 名（46%）为完全性截瘫。有 50% 的瘫痪患者（6/12）最终完全恢复，而 25%的患者（3/12）为不完全恢复，另有 25%的患者（3/12）完全未恢复。26 名截瘫患者中剩余 14 名患者（54%）为不完全性截瘫：7 名患者完全恢复，7 名患者不完全恢复（50%）。共计 8 名（4 名完全性瘫痪和 4 名不完全性瘫痪）患者在发生截瘫后的 6 小时内便取出了哈灵顿内固定器械。最终有 75%的患者完全康复（6/8），其中 3 名为完全性截瘫，3 名为不完全性截瘫。有 3 名最终需要取出哈灵顿棒的患者在关闭手术切口前进行了唤醒试验，对于做出取出哈灵顿棒的决定起到了很重要的作用。这 3 名截瘫患者中有 2 名术后完全恢复，1 名不完全恢复。科斯图克是这样结束自己报告的："通过不断的探究、讨论和总结经验，脊柱侧凸研究学会的会员们有望让本就较低的神经系统并发症的发生率进一步降低。"

Finally, some seemingly unrelated program entries deserve mention. There were two 90-minute sessions for seven concurrent research coordinating committee workshops.

Based on their titles, workshop one, Instrumentation and Implants, and workshop six, Studies on Three-Dimensional Recording of the Spine, were directly related to Luque's breakthrough. Based on the workshop reports, there was no direct interaction between these two workshops.[45] In the scientific program the first presentation was devoted to the new imaging method, computerized axial tomography, and how it might affect spine deformity analysis.[46] In a departure from the recent past there was not one study of spinal cord monitoring presented.

最后，一些看似无关紧要的项目也有必要在这里进行提及。统筹委员会举办的 7 次研讨会中，有两个 90 分钟的会议值得关注。从它们的题目来看，研讨会一:《器械和内植物》；以及研讨会六:《脊柱三维构建的研究》，都与卢克技术的进展直接相关。从两个研讨会报告的内容来看，二者之间没有直接的联系。[45]第一个报告聚焦于新的影像方法，如轴位 CT，以及它如何影响脊柱畸形的分析。[46]但与最近研究不同的是当时的研讨会中并没有任何关于脊髓监测的研究报告。

During the 1976 meeting President-elect Louis Goldstein became president, and R. Kirklin Ashley of San Francisco was elected president-elect. In the months that followed Goldstein began to have doubts that he had the physical stamina to lead the society during the upcoming trip to Japan and Hong Kong for the 1977 combined pre-meeting and annual meeting. He opted to resign, and the much younger Ashley finished Goldstein's term before serving his own. Also, during the 1976 meeting Dickson was elected to a one-year term on the board of directors, an indication of his growing stature within the SRS. He was also enjoying success in developing presentations of high-quality clinical studies that were later published. In the previous three years he and his colleagues had presented four papers, all of which were published.

在 1976 年的会议当中，候任主席路易斯·戈尔茨坦当选了学会主席，来自圣弗朗西斯科的 R. 柯克林·阿什利则当选候任主席。但在当选之后的几个月里，戈尔茨坦逐渐担心自己是否有足够的体力领导脊柱侧凸研究学会来举办 1997 年在日本的年会前会议和中国香港的脊柱侧凸研究学会年会。于是他选择辞去职位，由更为年轻的阿什利代为完成任期，然后再开始阿什利自己的任期。在 1976 年的会议上，迪克森也当选为委员会成员，任期一年，这表明了他在脊柱侧凸研究学会的地位不断提高。他还借助高质量研究成功进行了多次报告，后续都得以发表。在过去的三年里，他和他的同事有四篇论文在大会上进行演讲，这些论文也成功发表。

In brief, the 1976 SRS meeting witnessed a breakthrough innovation with Luque's SSI. It was inspired by need, amplified by volume, and made possible by a unique person in a unique surrounding, which, of course, were similar to those elements accompanying Harrington's breakthrough two decades earlier. Planned interaction between three-dimensional analysis and spine instrument development did not seem to occur. Harrington Spine Instrumentation remained unchallenged for instrumentation leadership, but problems presented by limited spine fixation sites, flattening of lumbar lordosis, and limits on freedom of motion load application were becoming more apparent.

简而言之，1976年脊柱侧凸研究学会会议见证了卢克在节段性脊柱内固定方面的突破性创新，它的灵感来自临床需求，先在论文中进行阐述，并最终由不可替代的卢克在特定的条件下将其变为现实，犹如二十年前哈灵顿突破时所具备的条件。但预想中的脊柱三维分析和手术器械发展之间的交互作用似乎并没有发生。哈灵顿器械在内固定方面的领导地位仍未受到挑战，但其展现出来的脊柱固定部位有限、腰椎前凸消失和载荷器械活动受限等问题越来越明显。

Although generally out of the SRS loop, Harrington kept up an active and interesting correspondence, some of it in relation to his book-writing effort. One frequent correspondent was John O'Brien. In response to a question from Harrington about his position at Oswestry, O'Brien replied that as director of the new Department of Spinal Disorders he was dealing fulltime with all aspects of spine disorders. He described it as a fascinating and unique position to see the disparities between areas of spine care where expertise and technology had been developed to a high point, such as scoliosis, and those where it had not, such as low back pain. His conclusion was that "instrumentation in the field of low back pain is very primitive and requires a long, hard, critical look."[47] The growing success of spine instrumentations in the treatment of scoliosis was resulting in their appropriation for the treatment of the low back pain problem. O'Brien was very well prepared and situated to see the problems and/or follies of applying a treatment before understanding the condition. This conundrum would be evolving for years.

尽管哈灵顿基本上不再参加脊柱侧凸研究学会的活动，但他一直与学会维持着积极而有趣的通信往来，其中一些与他的专著写作有关。约翰·奥布赖恩就是其中一位主要的作者。在回答哈灵顿关于他在奥斯沃斯特里的职位问题时，奥布赖恩回答，作为新的脊柱疾病部门的主任，他要全职处理涉及脊柱疾病各个方面的事情。哈灵顿认为这是一个有趣而独特的职位，能够看到脊柱治疗各领域之间的差异：部分领域，如脊柱侧凸，专业知识和技术已经发展到一个很高的高度；而部分领域，如腰痛，其发展则远不及前者。他总结道："腰痛领域的手术器械仍非常原始，需要长时间、严谨、批判性的研究。"[47]脊柱器械在脊柱侧凸治疗中的日益成功使其被用于治疗腰痛。奥布赖恩充分意识到这些问题，但在了解病情之前盲目地应用一种治疗方式是愚蠢的。而这个难题将会持续困扰人们多年。

The twelfth annual meeting of the SRS was held in Hong Kong, October 24–27, 1977, under the presidency of Kirklin Ashley.[48] It was preceded by a joint meeting of Japanese (led by President Kengo Yamada) and North American scoliosis societies in Kyoto on October 20 and 21.[49] During these 8 days of meetings, attendees heard 63 scientific presentations and participated in workshops, discussion sessions, business meetings, and cultural and social events. Of great significance was that acquaintances were made and friendships formed and strengthened. It is important to understand that most presentations at SRS meetings were not directly related to spine instrumentation research, development, and use. Because of its status as an enigma and the largest scoliosis diagnostic category, idiopathic scoliosis etiology and pathogenesis-related research possibilities generated many studies, most of them resulting in negative findings. Early detection methods, patient evaluation (including all manner of diagnostic, imaging, and physical performance studies), and nonoperative management and treatment likewise provided an almost endless array of possibilities for study and presentation. However, despite years of meetings the economics of treatment had not been addressed, but that changed during the pre-meeting of the Japanese Scoliosis Society.

1977年10月24日至27日，第十二届脊柱侧凸研究学会年会于在中国香港举行，柯克林·阿什利担任会议主席。[48]在此之前的10月20日和21日，日本脊柱侧凸学会（主席为山田健吾）和北美脊柱侧凸学会在京都举办了联合会议。[49]在6天的会议中，参会者听取了63个学术报告，并参加了研讨会、讨论会议、会员会议以及文化和社会活动。重要的是参会者们相互结识，加深了友谊。有一点值得注意，本次脊柱侧凸研究学会会议上的大多数报告与脊柱器械的研究、发展和使用并没有直接联系。由于特发性脊柱侧凸对众多研究者来说仍然是一个谜题，作为占比最多的脊柱侧凸类型，其病因和发病机制的研究潜力催生了一大批相关研究，但多数研究均未取得有意义的成果。早期检测手段、患者评估（包括各种诊断、影像学和身体形态研究）以及非手术处理和治疗也为研究和报告提供了几乎无限的可能性。然而，虽然既往多年会议未曾讨论过治疗的经济问题，但在日本脊柱侧凸学会的会前会议上，这种情况发生了改变。

Alf Nachemson and Lars Dahlberg addressed the cost-benefit question in their study, "The Economic Aspects of Scoliosis Treatment,"[50] which was limited to thoracic scoliosis patients only. Actual costs were determined for Milwaukee brace treatment and Harrington Instrumentation and fusion. Actual results were determined for the surgical patients, and an experience- and literature-based assumption was made that a 30° scoliosis could be prevented from progressing by bracing. The effect of non-treatment was based on the 145 patients with single thoracic curves receiving disability pensions in Sweden in 1971, most of whom had been unable to work since the age of 50 years because of their scoliosis. The diagnostic category of these patients was not documented. Progression of curves at maturity was based on 228 patients with curves of varying size diagnosed at different ages up to maturity. The analysis showed that for Milwaukee brace treatment started at age 11 years for a 30° thoracic scoliosis the benefit was 90 times the cost and for operative treatment in an 11-year-old child with a 50° thoracic curve the benefit was 30 times the cost.

阿尔夫·纳切姆森和拉斯·达尔伯格在他们的研究“脊柱侧凸治疗的经济问题”中阐述了脊柱侧凸治疗的成本—效益问题,[50]但该研究仅限于胸椎侧凸的患者。密尔沃基支具和使用哈灵顿器械进行融合的实际费用是可以确定的。对于手术患者来讲，手术实际效果也是可以确定的，并且基于经验和文献可以做出推测，即30°以下的脊柱侧凸可以通过支具阻止病情进展。另外，通过对1971年瑞典接受残疾抚恤金的145名单胸弯脊柱侧凸患者进行研究，人们得出了未行治疗的后果——其中大多数患者在50岁以后就因脊柱侧凸而无法再工作了。但这些患者的诊断类别并没有被记录。基于228名在发育成熟前不同年龄诊断为不同程度脊柱侧凸的患者，人们对发育成熟后侧凸的进展进行了研究。分析显示，30°胸椎侧凸患儿若从11岁开始进行密尔沃基支具治疗，则获益是花费的90倍，11岁的50°胸椎侧凸患儿手术治疗的获益是花费的30倍。

The SRS program included two lectures. The third Harrington Guest Lecture, "Nothing Endures But Change," delivered by Peter F. Williams of Melbourne, Australia, interpreted current change as away from mechanical skills and toward causal research. The presidential lecture was written by Louis A. Goldstein, who had stepped aside from his office because of health concerns, and was delivered by his associate,

Peter William Haake. Its title was "The Surgical Treatment of Scoliosis, A Forty-Year Personal Experience."[51] Goldstein's odyssey had begun in 1937 when disagreements between and among scoliosis experts nearly led to blows, resulting in his establishment of the scoliosis service at the University of Rochester (New York). It was the epitome of a thoughtful scoliosis service implementation. For example, there was not a single fatality in his first 351 consecutive cases, which began when open drop ether was the principal, if not only, anesthetic option. But it was his May 1952 decision to only use fresh autogenous iliac crest bone grafts that more than anything else secured his legacy since his very low pseudarthrosis rate was remarkable. His decision was the result of the opportunity provided by staged arthrodesis operations to observe the striking difference in early graft incorporation between allograft and autograft. Until 1960 Moe had used autograft mainly for long fusions extending into the lumbar spine, but not thoracic fusions. After visiting Rochester to prepare for their AAOS instructional course presentation and seeing the massive fusions, Moe commented that he would also start including iliac crest in his thoracic fusions.

脊柱侧凸研究学会学术议程中包括了两个演讲。第一个演讲是由澳大利亚墨尔本的彼得·F. 威廉姆斯主讲的第三次哈灵顿特邀演讲“唯有变化乃为永恒”。他将当前的变化解读为从机械技术转向病因学研究。主席演讲则是由路易斯·A. 戈尔茨坦撰写的，但其因健康问题而无法亲自演讲，由他的助手彼得·威廉·哈克代为演讲。其题目是“脊柱侧凸的外科治疗，四十年的个人经验”。[51] 1937 年，戈尔茨坦开始了漫长的探索，当时脊柱侧凸专家之间的分歧几乎导致学界分崩离析，于是他便在罗切斯特大学（纽约）建立了脊柱侧凸治疗中心。这是当时建立脊柱侧凸治疗系统的一个典型代表。在他的前 351 例连续病例中，没有一例死亡，这些病例最早开始于开放滴注乙醚即使不是唯一但仍是主要麻醉方式的年代。但 1952 年 5 月，他决定只使用新鲜的自体髂骨进行骨移植，这比任何其他方面都更能奠定他的传奇地位，因为他手术的病人假关节的发生率非常低。他的决定来自分期融合术，他观察到同种异体移植物和自体移植物在早期移植物融合方面有显著差异。1960 年，莫开始将自体骨移植主要用于涉及腰椎的长节段融合术，并没有用于胸椎融合术。在参观罗切斯特的同时来准备他们的美国骨科医师学会教学课程演讲的过程中，他们看到大量融合的病人，莫表示他也将开始在胸椎融合术中使用自体髂骨移植。

Surprisingly, Luque Instrumentation, last year's star, was not represented in the scientific program in 1977. Harrington Instrumentation was still by far the most commonly used, and there did not appear to be any major negative comments about it. Nor did there appear to be any evolution of his instrumentation, but there was an important evolution in technique. The new method, "End-fusions in the Treatment of Some Progressing or Severe Scoliosis in Childhood or Early Adolescence," was presented by Pier Marchetti and introduced the technique of "fusing pairs of vertebrae at the ends of the curve."[52] Five or six months following that, Harrington Instrumentation was performed, and serial lengthening was carried out during growth. "The spine is protected with a Milwaukee brace during this period. When bone development is mature, a standard fusion of the whole curve can be carried out." Fourteen patients had been treated. On the surface this sounds like a return to Harrington's original concept. However, this was not a reintroduction of instrumentation without arthrodesis, but rather instrumentation with postponed fusion to provide time for growth. Harrington had posited that once straightened and stabilized the spine would grow straight, bringing the rod along with it. As reintroduced, the rod was used to provide serial lengthenings to mechanically elongate the spine. This technique would become widely used.

但令人惊讶的是，1976 年的热点——卢克器械并没有出现在 1977 年会议的各个学术议程中。到目前为止，哈灵顿器械仍然是最常用的，而且似乎没有太大的负面评价。尽管哈灵顿器械在器械方面似乎没有任何发展，但在技术上有一个重要的进展。皮耶尔·马尔凯蒂提出了“端椎融合治疗儿童或青少年早期进展性或严重脊柱侧凸”的新方法，并介绍了“端椎成对融合”技术。[52]施行此技术后 5 到 6 个月，再行哈灵顿器械矫形术，并在生长过程中进行一系列延长操作。“在此期间，使用密尔沃基支具来保护脊柱。当骨骼发育成熟时，就可以对整个弯曲范围实施标准的融合手术了。”有 14 名患者采取了此种技术方案。从表面上看这像是回到了哈灵顿最初的概念。然而，这并不是在未行融合的情况下再次进行内固定，而是内固定后延迟融合，给予患者的脊柱继续生长的时间。哈灵顿曾经假定，一旦脊柱变直并稳定下来，它就会带着内固定棒以直的姿态继续生长。再次行内固定手术时，该棒也应该被延长，从而机械性地拉长脊柱。这项技术将被广泛应用。

It was Dwyer Instrumentation's turn to take the spotlight again, but this time as the starting point for evolution. Dwyer Instrumentation had three main shortcomings: production of unphysiological thoracolumbar kyphosis, instability related to the flexible cable, and lack of repeated adjustability. Klaus Zielke addressed these by developing screws with top or side open heads to receive "a threaded rod like a Harrington compression rod with nuts."[53] The nuts had a domed protrusion on one side and nuts facing each other nested in matching screw head recesses completing the connection. This allowed adjustment throughout the procedure. The system featured a rotation instrument based on three-point force application that could be used to deliver corrective angular loads in the coronal, transverse, and sagittal planes with the corrected positions being maintained by the stiff threaded rod. The authors reported on use in 56 patients. Zielke Instrumentation became known as VDS, Ventral Derotation Spondylodesis Instrumentation, and it replaced the Dwyer as the anterior instrumentation of choice. Alan Dwyer did not live to see his instrumentation eclipsed because he died in 1975 at age 50 of esophageal carcinoma.[54]

这次的焦点变成了德怀尔内固定器械，但这一次是作为促使演变的开始。德怀尔内固定存在三个主要缺点：会产生非生理性的胸腰椎后凸畸形、有与柔性缆线相关的不稳定性及不可重复进行调节。克劳斯·齐尔克通过开发顶部或侧面开口的螺钉来解决这些问题，这种螺钉可以适配“带有螺母的哈灵顿棒那样的螺纹棒”。[53]螺母的一侧有一个穹隆突起，螺母相对嵌套在相匹配的螺钉头凹槽中，完成连接。这允许在整个操作过程中进行调整。该系统具有一个基于三点受力的旋转装置，可用于在冠状面、横断面和矢状面提供矫正的角度载荷，并通过刚性的螺纹棒维持矫正好的位置。作者报告了56名患者的使用情况。泽尔克内固定被称为VDS，即腹侧去旋转脊柱融合内固定，它取代了德怀尔内固定成为前路内固定的一种选择。因为年仅50岁的艾伦·德怀尔死于食管癌，所以他并没有看到自己的内固定器械逐渐退出历史舞台的过程。[54]

In the presentation that immediately followed, Lyle Micheli and John Hall illustrated their method of addressing the Dwyer shortcomings by replacing the cable with a solid titanium rod.[55] They also connected Hall's earlier work evolving the Dwyer staple, which accommodated one screw anchor per vertebral body, to a double screw staple.[56] They suggested the possibility of using these components to stabilize the spine following trauma, pointing the way forward for other innovators.

在随后的报告中，莱尔·米切利和约翰·霍尔阐述了用坚实钛棒替换线缆来解决德怀尔内固定缺陷的方法。[55]他们还利用霍尔早前的成果完善和推进了德怀尔置钉技术——建议将每个椎体锚定一颗螺钉改为双螺钉共同固定同一椎体。[56]他们提出了使用这些组件在创伤后稳定脊柱的可能性，为其他创新者指明了前进的方向。

The growing variety of spine implants available andbroad spectrum of spine pathologies seemed to invite innovation, both in instrumentation use and surgical approach. Posterior placement of Dwyer Instrumentation with two-screw-hole staple fixation was presented.[57] The indication for its use was spine stabilization after resection of fixed, congenital lumbar kyphosis in patients with high-level myelomeningocele paraplegia. Staged and sequential anterior and posterior approaches were commonplace, but simultaneous approaches were newer.[58]

脊柱内植物种类的增加和脊柱疾病的广泛发展似乎促进了手术器械和手术方式两方面的创新。[57]当时出现了采用双钉道的后路德怀尔内固定器械，用于高位脊髓脊膜膨出性截瘫的僵硬性先天性腰椎后凸患者在截骨后的脊柱固定。分期和分步的前后入路较为常见，但前后路一期完成则是创新的地方。[58]

Death andspinal cord level paralysis were (and are) the most feared complications associated with spine deformity surgery. But, of the two, spinal cord level paralysis was less understood, as deaths were nearly always associated with an already severely ill patient. The incidence of death and neurological injury of any type was for each around 1%, with spinal cord level paralysis of any extent representing about 60% (0.6% overall) of the neurological injuries with about 50% (0.3% overall) of these having functional or better recovery. Distraction paraplegia, brought to awareness by the SRS morbidity effort in 1968, was the most common type of spinal cord injury and had stimulated development of spinal cord function monitoring. Three reports that represented the current state of such monitoring were presented. Two recorded sensory (distal to proximal) transmission.[59,60] The other recorded motor (proximal to distal) transmission.[61] Both techniques depended on the long tracts in the white matter of the spinal cord. Neither provided deeper insight into spinal cord structure.

死亡和截瘫在过去和现在都是脊柱矫形手术最严重的后果。但是，在这两者中，人们对脊髓瘫痪知之甚少，因为死亡几乎总是见于此前病情严重的患者。不同类型的死亡和神经损伤的发生率均在1%左右，不同程度的脊髓瘫痪则约占神经损伤患者的60%（占患者总体并发症的0.6%），其中约50%的患者（总体0.3%）恢复了功能性的或较好的恢复。撑开性截瘫是最常见的脊髓损伤类型，1968年脊柱侧凸研究学会对其发生率的研究引起了人们的注意，并促进了脊髓功能监测的发展。有三份相关的研究报告阐述了脊髓监测的现状。其中两项是关于感觉传导（远端到近端），[59,60]另外一项关于运动传导（近端到远端）。[61]两种技术都基于脊髓白质中的长束。但两者都没有对脊髓结构有更深入的见解。

A spinal cord structure and function correlative study was presented by George Dommisse that was titled "Experimental Paraplegia in the Sub-Human Primate, The Baboon 'PappioUrsinus.'" Two minutes of spinal cord compression resulted in paraplegia with recovery over three months.[62] Pathologic studies initially revealed a local spinal cord infarct and "micro anatomical changes throughout almost the entire length of the cord." In spite of recovery "there was no effective regeneration of neural tissues. Recovery of function is attributed to selective sparing of fiber tracts within the white matter and has been observed in the presence of extensive central and post-central necrosis." The opinion was offered that these findings might have "a possible bearing on the etiology of some neuromuscular diseases and perhaps also of scoliosis."

乔治·多米斯提出了一项脊髓结构和功能相关的研究，题为“亚人类灵长类动物的实验性截瘫——狒狒的截瘫”。研究结果显示脊髓受压超过2分钟便可以导致截瘫，需要超过3个月的时间恢复。[62]病理学研究最初揭示了局部脊髓梗死和“几乎贯穿整个脊髓长度的微观解剖变化”。尽管存在恢复，但不存在神经组织的有效再生。功能的恢复归功于白质内纤维束的选择性保留，这一点可在出现广泛的中枢和中枢后坏死时观察到。有观点认为，这些发现可能“与某些神经肌肉疾病的病因有关，也可能与脊柱侧凸有关”。

The thirteenth annual meeting of the SRS was held in Cambridge, Massachusetts, on September 13–15, 1978, under the continuing presidency of Kirklin Ashley.[63] Pierre Stagnara was the fourth Harrington Guest Lecturer, and his topic, "The Surgical Treatment of Kyphosing Scoliosis in Adult Patients," was consistent with the growing attention to scoliosis and spine deformity problems in adults. Paul and Mary Alice Harrington attended the meeting.[64]

1978年9月13日至15日，第十三届脊柱侧凸研究学会年会于在马萨诸塞州的剑桥举行，由柯克林·阿什利继续担任主席。[63]皮埃尔·斯塔格纳拉是第四位哈灵顿特邀演讲者，他的主题“成人脊柱后凸和侧凸的外科治疗”，与人们对成人脊柱侧凸和脊柱畸形问题的日益关注相一致。保罗·哈灵顿和玛丽·艾丽斯·哈灵顿一同出席了此次会议。[64]

For the second straight year after its introduction there were no papers on Luque Instrumentation, and the evolutionary insights it offered seemed to have fallen on deaf ears. Harrington Instrumentation continued to receive the vast majority of attention. "Biomechanical Aspects of Harrington Spinal Instrumentation," given by Zimmer engineer George Shen, addressed the specifications, design, and static and dynamic test findings gathered over the years.[65] The adequacy of design was later confirmed clinically by Wendell Erwin, Dickson, and Harrington's study of 888 consecutive patients receiving autogenous iliac crest bone graft and early ambulation with body cast external immobilization for nine months. Follow-up averaged 5.4 years. Broken distraction rods occurred in nineteen (2.1%) patients, and a compression rod broke in one patient. Distraction rod breakage came at an average of 2.6 years postoperative, and no patient required reinstrumentation or rod removal.[66]

在卢克内固定器械推出后的第二年，没有一篇相关的论文发表，它提供的发展性的见解似乎被学界完全忽略了，受到绝大多数关注的还是哈灵顿内固定器械。捷迈公司的工程师乔治·沈做了"哈灵顿脊柱器械的生物力学"的报告，阐述了多年来收集到的哈灵顿内固定器械相关的规格、设计和动静态测试结果。[65]后来，温德尔·埃尔文、迪克森和哈灵顿对888名患者连续进行了9个月的自体髂骨植骨和躯体石膏外固定早期活动的研究，从临床上证实了这项设计的正确性。经过平均5.4年的随访，其中19名（2.1%）患者发生了撑开棒的断裂，1名患者发生了压缩棒的断裂。撑开棒断裂发生在术后平均2.6年，且没有患者需要再行固定或去除内固定棒。[66]

Distraction paraplegia continued to be a concern and the evolving risk a continuing a stimulus to develop reliable, continuous monitoring. Ensor Transfeldt and Ed Simmons performed animal experiments to correlate the pathophysiology of the spinal cord under stretch.[67] Spinal-evoked response correlated with loss of neurological function and, very importantly, with the amount and duration of distraction. Recovery following release of stretch correlated with neurological function return. "No pathological lesions were noted in spinal cords with a recoverable response. Vascular impairment was thought to contribute to the early changes in the evoked response." Mechanical disruption of the fiber tracts correlated with no return of spinal-evoked response. The spinal-evoked changes could be classified into immediate, early, and late with both diagnostic and prognostic value. This study would have removed any doubt that spinal cord stretch was the cause of distraction paraplegia and would have explained the variability in time and extent of paraplegia.

撑开性截瘫仍是一个令人担忧的问题，而不断发展的风险刺激着我们不断研发可靠且持续的监测。恩索尔·传斯菲尔德和爱德华·西蒙斯进行了动物实验，以探究脊髓在拉伸下的病理生理学。[67]脊髓诱发反应与神经功能的丧失相关，而且非常重要的是，与撑开的次数和持续时间相关。撑开解除后的恢复情况与神经功能恢复相关。“在反应恢复的脊髓中未观察到病理改变，认为血管损伤是诱发反应早期改变的原因。”纤维束的机械性破坏与脊髓诱发反应没有恢复相关。脊髓诱发反应的改变可分为即刻、早期和晚期，具有诊断和预后价值。本研究消除了关于脊髓牵拉是否是撑开性截瘫原因的疑问，并解释了截瘫时间和程度的差异性。

A Harrington Instrumentation technique modification was included in Moe's presentation, "Harrington Instrumentation without Fusion Combined with the Milwaukee Brace for Difficult Scoliosis Problems in Young Children" case series of three.[68] Beginning in 1973, he used the fully threaded rod, which had at least two drawbacks: scars grew into the threads making rod exchange more difficult and the addition of physiological sagittal plane bends weakened the rod. The solution was a rod with a smooth central portion and threaded ends. This was the second year in a row the concept of instrumentation without fusion followed by periodic lengthening in young children with severe curves had been presented.

莫的题为“不伴融合哈灵顿内固定联合密尔沃基支具治疗儿童重度脊柱侧凸”的病案报告（3 名患者）中包含了关于哈灵顿内固定器械技术改良的内容。[68]从 1973 年开始，莫开始使用全螺纹内固定棒，这种方法至少有两个缺点：首先，螺纹处会长入瘢痕组织，使内固定棒的更换变得更加困难；其次，矢状面上的生理弯曲会削弱内固定棒的牢固性。解决办法是使用中间光滑而两端带有螺纹的内固定棒。这是连续第二年有报告提出了不融合情况下施行内固定和周期性延长来治疗幼儿重度脊柱侧凸的概念。

New anterior spine instrumentation was presented in 1978 by Harold Dunn.[69] It appeared to evolve from the Dwyer innovation and the two screws per vertebral body evolution that followed. It was designed to provide six-degree freedom-of-motion stability. In addition to two screws per body, it featured thicker staples that prevented screw toggle and two longitudinal rods. It was mainly designed for anterior two motion segment stabilization following spine fracture. This initial report involved sixteen patients.

1978 年，哈罗德·邓恩提出了一项新的脊柱前路内固定方式。[69]它似乎是改进自德怀尔，每个椎体使用两枚螺钉固定。它的设计提供了六个自由度的活动稳定性。除每个椎体打入两枚螺钉外，它使用了两个纵向内固定棒以及更厚的 U 型钉，以防止螺钉弯曲。它主要用于脊柱骨折后的双活动节段的前路稳定。该初步报告包含了 16 名患者。

There were several trends that emerged from the program. One was increasing interest in adult scoliosis. Susan Swank presented the Moe group experience with 194 patients operated on from 1961 to July 1976.[70] The average age at surgery was 30 years with the oldest patient aged 65 years. Complications occurred in 52%, including ten minimum of wound infections, one paraplegia, and two deaths. Patients were followed a one year (average, 3.4 years). Pulmonary function had "changed very little' at an average of two years' follow-up. Seventeen (9%) developed a pseudarthrosis. These results were similar to those reported earlier from Harrington and Dickson's series with two exceptions. Moe's patients appeared to be older, and 47 had staged surgery, whereas none of Harrington and Dickson's did.[71] Another emerging trend was concern about long-term low back pain after scoliosis fusion. The two papers that addressed this issue came to said it had opposite conclusions. One posited that pain had increased[72] while the other said it had not.[73] However, these conclusions were based on small follow-ups of 46% and 55%, respectively. Finally, three-dimensional spine deformity analyses got some attention with the study by Bob Gillespie's group titled "Computerized Spatial Analysis of the Spine in Idiopathic Scoliosis."[74] This was followed by Gus White's paper, "A Systematic Approach to the Problem of Clinical Stability in the Thoracic Spine."[75] The program committee was doing its part to link form and function.

本次会议中出现了几个趋势。一个是人们对成人脊柱侧凸的兴趣明显增加。苏珊·斯沃克介绍了 1961 年 7 月至 1976 年 7 月由莫团队进行手术的 194 名患者。[70]手术患者平均年龄为 30 岁，最大年龄为 65 岁。并发症发生率为 52%，包括 10 例伤口感染、1 例截瘫、2 例死亡。所有患者均最少随访 1 年（平均 3.4 年）。在平均两年的随访中，肺功能“变化很小”。17 名患者（9%）发生了假关节。这些结果与哈灵顿和迪克森早期报道的结果相似，但有两个例外。莫团队中的患者似乎年龄较大，47 名患者接受了分期手术，而哈灵顿和迪克森的患者均未接受分期手术。[71]另一个新趋势是对脊柱侧凸融合术后长期腰痛的担忧。研究这个问题的两篇论文得出了相反的结论。一项研究认为术后腰痛逐渐加重，[72]而另一项研究则持相反意见。[73]这些结论分别基于46%和55%的小规模随访。最后，鲍勃·吉莱斯皮的小组的一项题为“特发性脊柱侧凸的脊柱计算机空间分析”的研究使得人们开始关注脊柱畸形的三维分析。[74]其次是格斯·怀特的论文《胸椎稳定性临床问题的系统方法》。[75]学会会员正在尽其所能地将脊柱畸形的形态与机能联系起来。

The fourteenth annual SRS meeting was held in Seattle on September 11–14, 1979, under the presidency of David B. Levine,[76] and expanded abstracts were published the following year.[77] Paul and Mary Alice Harrington attended the meeting.[78] The guest speaker was Ruth Wynne-Davies of the United Kingdom, the world's leading expert some unknown reason was billed as the Presidential Guest Speaker rather than the Harrington Guest Lecturer. The meeting did the genetics of idiopathic scoliosis, who for not reveal any new spine instrumentation innovations, but did feature several first-time presentations to the SRS of evolutionary applications and several ongoing studies of new or modified instruments. Possibly the most original was titled "Contoured Double Distraction Rods for Correction of Spinal Deformity" by Nobumasa Suzuki and Gordon Armstrong.[79] The use was devised "for relatively mild single and double curve patterns which are sufficiently flexible so that virtually complete straightening can be achieved." They had used contoured square-ended Harrington distraction rods "to apply a significant derotational force. This is achieved by contouring the rod so that the convex force is applied at the level of maximal rotation." The second rod added stability. Surface (Moire) topography was used to document the deformity improvement. The technique, mainly applicable to lumbar and thoracolumbar curves, optimized delivery of corrective translational and angular loads to the scoliosis apex and minimized end vertebrae translational/distraction loading.

1979年9月的11日到14日，第十四届脊柱侧凸研究学会年会在西雅图召开，由戴维·B. 莱文[76]担任主席，并于次年将扩展的会议摘要进行了发表。[77]保罗·哈灵顿和玛丽·艾丽斯·哈灵顿出席了会议。[78]特邀演讲者是英国的鲁思·温–戴维斯，不知什么原因，这位特发性脊柱畸形基因方面的世界权威专家被邀请为主席特邀演讲者，而不是作为哈灵顿特邀演讲者。这次会议没有出现任何脊柱器械创新，但在脊柱侧凸研究学会上首次展示了一些逐渐发展的应用，以及一些正在进行的或全新的或改良的器械的研究。可能最原创的一项报告是铃木信政和戈登阿姆斯特朗的“预弯的双撑开棒矫正脊柱畸形”。[79]它的主要用途为“相对较轻的单弯和双弯类型，具有足够的柔韧性，从而可以几乎完全矫正”。他们使用了预弯方形末端的哈灵顿撑开棒来“沿着哈灵顿棒的轮廓线施加一个显著的去旋转力，让凸侧的力施加在旋转最大的节段上”。第二根棒增加了稳定性。采用体表形态影像学记录畸形改善情况。该技术主要适用于腰弯和胸腰弯，优化了矫正的平移和成角载荷向顶椎的传递，并将端椎的平移/撑开载荷最小化。

The second evolution involved Luque Instrumentation, but was probably a reflection of Luque's earlier thinking as he developed his innovative instrumentation. Presented by John Herring, the study was titled "Segmental Wiring of the Spine with Harrington Instrumentation and Spine Fusion—A Report of Twenty-One Consecutive Cases."[80] As Luque developed his technique, he had discarded the Harrington hooks and thus direct vertical translation as a corrective and stabilizing load.

第二个演变涉及了卢克内固定器械，但这可能体现了卢克研发创新器械时的早期想法。约翰·赫林进行了一项题目为“利用哈灵顿器械进行脊柱节段钢丝固定和脊柱融合术——21 例连续病例”的报告。[80]随着卢克技术的发展，他舍弃了哈灵顿钩，而将直接纵向平移作为矫正和稳定脊柱的载荷。

For the fourth annual meeting in a row, instrumentation without fusion was a program topic. But this year there were three studies! In "Segmental Spinal Instrumentation in Growing Children" Luque and Cardoso presented a 5-year follow-up of (apparently) 38 paralytic patients treated without fusion or external support.[81] Their average age at first surgery was 7.2 years, the average scoliosis was 73° preoperative and 30° at follow-up, the average area of immobilization 8 interspaces, and the average growth over the area of fixation 4.9 centimeters. Complications related to the operated and instrumented area occurred in 67% of patients, the most frequent being fractured Harrington Rods. The authors concluded that subperiosteal dissection did not lead to arthrodesis and that some growth potential remained in the instrumented area, Harrington Rods were inadequate for SSI without arthrodesis and casting, and the area of instrumentation that would be long enough for a fusion was often too short. This was not a report to inspire confidence in the procedure.

在接下来的第四届年会将非融合内固定作为一个议程话题。而今年更是有三个研究亮相。卢克和卡多索在“生长期儿童的节段性脊柱内固定”中报道了 38 名未行融合或外固定支具的麻痹性患者的 5 年随访结果。[81]这些患者初次手术平均年龄为7.2岁，术前平均脊柱侧凸柯布角为73°，随访时平均为30°，固定范围平均为8个节段，内固定区域平均增长4.9 cm。67%的患者发生了与手术和内固定相关的并发症，最常见的是哈灵顿棒断裂。作者的结论如下：骨膜表面分离并未导致融合，并且固定区域仍有一定的生长潜能；对于没有融合和石膏固定的节段脊柱内固定患者，单纯使用哈灵顿棒是不够的，另外对于融合来讲足够长的节段范围对于内固定范围而言则往往太短了。这份报告并没有建立起人们对于这一手术技术的信心。

The other two reports were from the Gillespie team at the Hospital for Sick Kids in Toronto. "Rod Design Criteria for Instrumentation without Fusion" was a report from their grant-funded, five-year interdisciplinary team effort to "provide an effective approach to non-fusion stabilization."[82] Fatigue studies were reported for Harrington Rods, continuous carbon fiber reinforced rods, and some new stainless-steel designs. Even though the continuous carbon fiber reinforced rods were stronger than Harington's, they failed with explosive fracture. One stainless steel design for children older than seven years "comprises a distraction tube guided by a continuously threaded rod and lock-nut arrangement. Two had been used clinically. The other stainless steel design features were simply a rod with 30% to 50% greater load carrying capacity than a Harrington a Rod that could be cut to proper length during surgery. "Instrumentation without Fusion—A Clinical Experience of Sixteen Cases" was the other report by the Gillespie team.[83] After reciting the problems with fusion of the immature spine, the authors committed to "a re-application of Paul Harrington's original concept of instrumentation without fusion." The report was preliminary with only a few facts provided. The patients' ages at surgery ranged from 3-1/2 to 13 years, and the follow-up lasted from 6 months to 4 years. The scoliosis averaged 70° preoperative and 35° postoperative. Problems with this procedure included hook cutout and rod fracture.

另外的两份报告来自多伦多病童医院的吉莱斯皮团队。有一份报告题为“不伴融合内固定棒设计标准”，由医院基金会赞助，经过跨学科团队耗时5年完成，旨在“提供一种不进行融合的有效稳定脊柱的方法”。[82]团队对哈灵顿棒、连续碳纤维增强棒和一些新的不锈钢器械进行了疲劳测试，结果显示尽管连续碳纤维增强棒比哈灵顿棒的刚性更强，但它们还是出现了断裂的情况。一种不锈钢材质的“包括一个由连续螺纹杆和锁紧螺母引导的撑开装置”被设计出来用于7岁以上儿童的手术。临床上已有2名患者使用了这项设计。其他不锈钢装置仅仅是一根比哈灵顿棒承载能力强 30%～50%的内固定棒，可以在手术中裁成合适的长度。吉莱斯皮团队另有一篇“未融合的内固定——16 名患者的临床经验”的报告，[83] 在回顾了未成熟脊柱融合的问题后，作者致力于回归保罗·哈灵顿的最初设想——不伴融合的内固定。这是一份初步报告，只提供了一部分结果。患者手术年龄自 3 岁零 6 个月至 13 岁不等，随访时间 6 个月至 4 年。术前脊柱侧凸平均为 70°，术后平均为 35°。这一手术方法同样出现脱钩和断棒等问题。

After introducing his anterior fixation device the year before, Dunn returned with "A Comparison of Spinal Bending Stability with Posterior and Anterior Fixation Device[s]."[84] The testing apparatus allowed gross bending motion of a cadaver spine in a 360° range about the spinal axis. The bending pattern pre-fracture after simulated injury of T12 and after a series of instrumentations was determined for six spines. Weiss springs posteriorly and one anterior or two unlinked anterior rods spanning one vertebral body above and one below the injury site did not provide adequate stability. The optimum configuration was the two linked anterior rods spanning one level above and one below the injury site, although the stability provided by the dual Harrington Rods posteriorly and the one anterior rod spanning two vertebral segments above and two below the injury site were not significantly different. How the rods were anchored to the vertebral bodies was not explained in the abstract.

邓恩在一年前的脊柱侧凸研究学会年会上介绍了他的前路固定装置，今年他又带来了“前后路固定装置对脊柱弯曲稳定性的比较”[84]的报告。报告中的研究使用了能够允许尸体脊柱围绕脊柱轴心进行 360°范围内的大幅度弯曲活动的测试设备。邓恩对 6 具尸体的脊柱模拟了 T12 损伤以及后续的一系列内固定操作，并对相关的弯曲模式进行了测定。报告认为后方韦斯弹簧、一根或两根未连接的前路棒跨越损伤部位上下各一个椎体并不能提供足够的稳定性。尽管跨越损伤节段的上下两个椎体节段后方的双哈灵顿棒和前方单棒提供的稳定性没有显著差异，但是最合适的配置是在损伤节段上下各一个节段放置两根连接的前路棒。但邓恩的摘要中并没有讲解如何将这些棒锚定到椎体上。

Scoliosis and spine deformity surgery, usually done in patients during their first two decades of life, was almost entirely concerned with spine stabilization and alignment, occasionally with spinal canal decompression, though seldom with radiculopathy. In this regard the Ed Simmons and Roger Jackson presentation of a series of 31 adult scoliosis patients with painful idiopathic lumbar or thoracolumbar scoliosis and associated radicular symptoms was futuristic.[85] The involved root was almost always in the concavity of the compensatory lumbosacral curve or at the apex of the major curve. The authors found that straightening of the major curve was usually effective in relieving the nerve compression and that Dwyer Instrumentation and fusion of the major curve were the best means to achieve this.

脊柱侧凸和脊柱畸形手术通常在患者20岁之前进行，这关乎患者脊柱后续的稳定和协调。脊柱侧凸患者偶尔需要进行椎管减压术，但很少出现神经根病变。在这方面，爱德华·西蒙斯和罗杰·杰克逊对31名伴有疼痛的特发性腰椎或胸腰段脊柱侧凸和相关神经根症状的成人脊柱侧凸患者进行了一次前瞻性报告。[85]报告内容显示累及的神经根几乎全部位于代偿腰骶弯的凹侧或主弯顶椎区域，作者认为主弯变直后通常能有效解除神经根压迫，而德怀尔内固定器械和主弯融合是达到这一目的的最佳方案。

The 1979 annual meeting also featured an innovative surgical technique, "Free Anterior Vascular Pedicle Bone Grafting for the Treatment of Kyphosis."[86] After noting his experience of a 20% fracture occurrence in free fibula or rib anterior strut grafting, David Bradford described this new technique in which the rib with the intercostal artery and vein was preserved and used as a strut graft.

1979年的年会中有人提出了一项创新性的手术技术，"游离血管蒂前路植骨治疗脊柱后凸"。[86]大卫·布拉德福德注意到使用游离腓骨或肋骨作为既往的支撑性植骨材料有20%的骨折发生率，于是提出了将这一保护肋间动静脉的肋骨用作支撑性植骨的新技术。

The surgical treatment of high-grade spondylolisthesis, which was known to be difficult, was the topic of three sequential presentations. The first reported on seven patients with slips greater than 50 % treated with Harrington Instrumentation and reversed alar hook placement to facilitate reduction of the lumbosacral kyphosis.[87,88] At an average of 2.2 years postoperative the L5-S1 slips had been reduced an average of 19% (range, 13% to 38%. Sagittal decompensation was improved in six of the seven patients. The second presentation, which Dickson was assigned to discuss, involved seventeen patients treated with L1-S1 Harrington Instrumentation and fusion followed by staged anterior L5-S1 interbody fusion in fifteen.[89,90] Slip reduction ranged from 75% to 100% and was maintained in patients with (but not those without) anterior interbody fusion. Two patients developed a cauda equina syndrome, and the rods had to be removed. Both recovered and had in situ fusions. The third speaker described a new operation sequence based on the principle that the deformity was a kyphosis and required realignment and anterior stabilization.[91] The treatment sequence was posterior decompression, skeletal traction, and anterior reduction and interbody fusion. The first ten patients had been followed a minimum of nine months. The average anterior L5 slippage was greater than 95% preoperative and 33% postoperative while the L5-S1 kyphosis was 70° preoperative and postoperative was completely corrected in all but one patient. Six patients had complications that were believed to be avoidable.[92] The recognition of high-grade L5-S1 spondylolisthesis as a localized kyphosis probably doomed usage of distraction as the principal corrective load.

众所周知，严重的脊柱滑脱的手术治疗较为困难，因此连着有三项报告将其作为演讲的主题。第一项报告报道了 7 名 II 度及以上的滑脱患者，采用了哈灵顿内固定器械并放置反向鼻翼钩来促进腰骶部后凸的复位。[87,88]术后平均 2.2 年的随访结果显示，L5-S1 滑脱平均减少了 19%（13%~38%）。7 名患者中 6 名矢状面失代偿得到了改善。第二项报告是迪克森的命题报告，涉及 17 名接受 L1-S1 哈灵顿内固定和融合术的患者，其中有 15 名施行分期前路 L5-S1 椎间融合术。[89,90]滑脱复位效果为 75%~100%，并且在前路椎间融合的患者中得以维持。术后两名患者出现了马尾综合征，需要将棒取出。两者症状均得到了改善并进行了原位融合。第三位讲者描述了一种新的手术顺序，对于脊柱后凸的患者，需要恢复序列和实现前路稳定。[91]他提出的治疗顺序为后路减压、骨牵引、前路松解复位、椎间融合。对前 10 名患者进行了至少 9 个月的随访后发现，L5 前滑脱患者牵引后较术前得到了超过 95%的改善，较术后则是超过了 33%；L5-S1 后凸畸形患者术前后凸角平均 70°，术后除 1 名患者外均得到了完全矫正。6 名患者出现了被认为是可以避免的并发症。[92]报告中将 L5-S1 重度滑脱看作一种局限性后凸，可能需要把使用撑开器作为主要的矫正操作。

Perhaps the most consequential development at the 1979 meeting was interest in treatment of radicular symptoms.[93] The focus of the SRS founders was on spine deformity, principally in the first two decades of life when radicular symptoms were uncommon. However, as patients aged and radicular symptoms became more common, the question of who would meet their challenge was becoming increasingly asked. Would this be accomplished by expanding the focus of the SRS from patients with deformity in the first two or three decades of life or by leaving adult and complex spine problems to other spine specialists?

1979 年会议上取得的最重要的进展很可能是对神经根症状治疗的兴趣。[93]尽管脊柱侧凸研究学会在最初创办时的重点在于脊柱畸形，主要关注的是 20 岁之前的患者，此时神经根性症状并不常见。然而，随着患者年龄的增长和神经根性症状的增加，越来越多的人开始产生了疑问：谁来应对这些挑战？是通过将脊柱侧凸研究学会的重点从 20 岁或 30 岁之前的畸形患者扩展开来，还是将成人和复杂的脊柱问题留给其他脊柱专家？哪条路径可以实现上述目标？

In the interval between the 1979 and 1980 SRS meetings Harrington worked to complete his remaining tasks. Plans had long been in progress to provide him an opportunity to lecture at his medical school alma mater, which he had never done (his 1975 Bohan lecture had taken place at a convention hotel). What emerged was a one-day program on December 10 titled "Scoliosis and Related Spine Deformities."[94] Its secondary title was "A Workshop for Nurses and Other Screening Personnel" since voluntary school screening for scoliosis had been done for several years and was well received by Kansas school and public health nurses. An excellent turnout heard the star himself present "Scoliosis: The Problem, The Difficulties, The Solution." Much of the program was devoted to a live clinic for presentation of children and adolescents with known false positive physical findings or mild to moderate scoliosis. This provided an ample opportunity for open discussion, an intermingling of speakers, attendees, and patients and their parents. By the meeting's end it was apparent the program had been a success.

在 1979 年和 1980 年脊柱侧凸研究学会会议期间，哈灵顿完成了他剩下的工作任务。很长一段时间以来他一直计划着能够在自己母校的医学院进行一次演讲，但一直没有实现（1975 年的博安演讲是在一个会议酒店进行的）。最终决定在 12 月 10 日举办一场为期一天的“脊柱侧凸和相关脊柱畸形”会议。[94]由于进行脊柱侧凸筛查的私立学校已经发展了几年，并受到了堪萨斯州的学校和公共卫生护士的一致好评，因此这个会议的次标题是“护士和其他筛查人员讲习班”。他亲自主持了“脊柱侧凸：问题、困难和解决方案”这一环节，内容主要是现场诊疗，为假阳性体征或轻、中度脊柱侧凸的儿童和青少年提供就诊。这为发言者、参会者与患者及其父母之间的相互交流提供了充足的便利。到会议结束时，这个项目取得了明显的成功。

Although Harrington's book writing project, *The Human Spine*, had come to an end, he reworked its final chapter into a booklet titled "A Story and A Viewpoint."[95] It repeated the medical school origin of his interest in adrenal cortex atrophy as observed at the time of autopsy on a severely burned patient. This led to his interest in vitamin C and the apparently successful use of megadoses (i. e., one to three grams/day taken in divided doses every six hours) in the management of low back syndrome. This booklet, completed in 1980, was the final summation of his views about the physical and biological universe, the universal importance of collagen that was described as the greatest building block of the body, and the importance of vitamin C to collagen metabolism. Harrington sent copies to many of his friends and acquaintances, which seemed to bring his writing to a close. After receiving his copy, Linus Pauling, winner of two Nobel Prizes (chemistry in 1954 and peace in 1962) and vitamin C enthusiast, called him, and they enjoyed a cordial fifteen-minute conversation.[96]

尽管哈灵顿的《人类脊柱：过去、现状和未来》写作计划已经接近尾声，但他将书稿的最后一章重新编写成了一本小册子《一个故事和一个观点》，[95]再次讲述了他对严重烧伤患者尸检时观察到了肾上腺皮质萎缩的故事，这也是他与医学院的渊源。这次的尸检结果使他对维生素 C 产生了兴趣，他成功将大剂量维生素 C（即 1~3 g/d，每 6 小时分次服用）应用到对腰椎综合征患者的治疗当中。这本完成于 1980 年的小册子，包括了他对人体和生物系统最后的观点总结，比如组成人体各处结构的胶原蛋白的重要性，以及维生素 C 对胶原蛋白代谢的重要性。哈灵顿给他的许多朋友和熟人寄去了这些小册子，这似乎是为他的写作生涯拉上了帷幕。两次诺贝尔奖得主（1954 年诺贝尔化学奖和 1962 年诺贝尔和平奖）、维生素 C 的忠实拥趸莱纳斯·鲍林收到小册子后便给哈灵顿打去了电话，两人在电话里进行了 15 分钟的亲切交谈。[96]

Another matter that received his attention was the Mary Alice and Paul R. Harrington, M.D. Distinguished Professor of Bio-Physical-Chemistry at the University of Kansas in Lawrence.[97] The fund had been established a little over five years before and was designated to help fund the research of Professor Takeru Higuchi. However, the fund principal was not yet large enough to provide meaningful research support. Another complication was that Harrington was so identified with medicine that the fund seemed misplaced in Lawrence. Higuchi and the Harringtons agreed, and in February 1980 the letter of gift was amended, moving the fund to the university's medical campus in Kansas

City, Kansas. The goal, as stated in the amending letter, was to support "research in the area of orthopaedics with emphasis on molecular medicine." An unstated goal was to increase the fund through solicitations.

另一件值得铭记的事情是堪萨斯大学劳伦斯校区成立了玛丽·艾丽斯和保罗·R. 哈灵顿医学博士生物-物理-化学杰出教授基金。[97]尽管5年前学校成立了一项用于资助樋口建教授研究的基金，但是基金的规模尚不足以提供有意义的研究支持。另一个难题是，哈灵顿在医学界有如此高的声望，以至于该项基金似乎不适合再由劳伦斯校区进行管理。樋口教授和哈灵顿夫妇达成了统一意见，并在1980年2月修改了基金捐赠文书，将基金转移到位于堪萨斯州堪萨斯城的大学医学院。修改后的基金捐赠文件中写道，本项基金的目的是支持"以分子医学为重点的骨科领域研究"。还有一个未进行说明的目标是通过募捐来扩大基金规模。

On April 24-26 Dickson was the guest speaker at "An Instructional Course in Spinal Deformities," organized by Harrington's friend John O'Brien at the Robert Jones and Agnes Hunt Orthopaedic Hospital in Oswestry, U.K. Over a hundred attended from western Europe, Israel, Australia, and the United States. One of Dickson's presentations was an oration titled "The Concepts and Contributions of Paul Harrington." O'Brien reported to Harrington that the audience "sat spell bound... because very few people really had the opportunity to know you. At its completion he received a standing ovation which I have never seen given at Oswestry."[98]

4月24日至26日，迪克森担任了"脊柱畸形教学课程"的特邀演讲者，此课程由哈灵顿的朋友约翰·奥布赖恩在英国奥斯沃斯特里的罗伯特·琼斯和阿格尼斯·亨特骨科医院组织进行。一百多名来自西欧、以色列、澳大利亚和美国的学员参加了该项课程。迪克森也进行了一项题目为"保罗·哈灵顿的概念和贡献"的演讲。奥布赖斯是这样对哈灵顿描述当时的场景的：观众"被迷住了……因为很少有人真正有机会去了解你。演讲结束时，全场听众起立鼓掌，我从未在奥斯沃斯特里见过这样的场景"[98]。

The SRS was the first purely orthopaedic subspecialty to organize as a separate professional association.[99] Since its beginning the SRS had strived to preserve its history, so on May 21, 1980, the organization's historian and seasoned interviewer, Robert B. Keller, and Jesse Dickson sat down with Harrington to record his oral history.[100] At this point Harrington Spine Instrumentation still maintained nearly complete dominance in the practice it had pioneered twenty years earlier. Using artifacts from the research and development steps and the advantage of their thirteen-year association, Dickson was able to amplify key aspects of this creative process. The evolution of the hook openings from arc to extended semicircle, the increase in hook-bone surface contact, the perfection of the ratchet mechanism to accommodate varying transverse plane hook-to-rod orientation, the 1/8" rather than 1/4" stepwise lengthening. And the overarching effort to keep it simple were never made clearer. The personal cost in time, focus, and dollars was likewise discussed. These and other exchanges provided additional insights into Harrington's life and creative process.

脊柱侧凸研究学会是第一个单独由骨科亚专业组织起来的独立的专业学会。[99]自成立以来，脊柱侧凸研究学会一直努力记录它的历史，因此在 1980 年 5 月 21 日，该组织史学工作者和经验丰富的访谈人罗伯特 · B. 凯勒同杰西 · 迪克森、哈灵顿一道进行了座谈，对哈灵顿的口述进行了记录。[100]在当时，哈灵顿脊柱内固定器械在临床实践中仍然保持着绝对的主导地位，尽管它作为先驱于 20 年前发明。利用来自后续研发的器械和改善的手术技术，再加上与哈灵顿长达 13 年的合作关系，杰西 · 迪克森得以将这一天才设计的一些关键点和优势更好地发挥出来。钩的开口由弧发展成半圆；钩与椎体接触面积的增加；棘齿的完善以适应变化的横向平面钩—杆方向；以 1/8 英寸而不是 1/4 英寸为延长单位。但我们没能更清楚地了解使其简化的所有努力。访谈还讨论了个人在时间、精力和金钱方面的投入。这些以及其他各个方面的交流让我们能够更深刻地理解哈灵顿的生活和创作过程。

Whatever negative feelings that had existed between Harrington and Engen appeared to have faded with time. *See figure 12.1.* No documentation of any dispute has been found. Engen's recollection of the slow trial, error, and observation research process they followed is instructive. The hooks and whole set of instrumentation hadn't just evolved overnight. "It was like you went from one stepping stone to another. You had to earn the right to move to the next step. Once

Figure 12.1 ***Harrington and Engen. July 1980.*** **(*Harrington Archines*)**
图 12.1　哈灵顿和恩金。1980 年 7 月(哈灵顿档案馆)

you had done that, you then created a large foundation and you moved to an even larger one. You earned the right to go through all these processes."[101]

随着时光的推移，哈灵顿和恩金之间过往的所有恩怨似乎都已经慢慢消退，（图 12.1）也没有发现任何记录过二人存在争执的资料。恩金对他们所遵循的缓慢试验、发现错误和观察研究的科研流程的回顾很有启发意义。正如罗马不是一天建成的，钩和整套器械也不是一夜发展成的。“就像你从一块垫脚石走到另一块。你必须为自己赢得迈出下一步的权利。你只有这样做了，才能创造一个坚实的基础，然后通往另一个更广阔的天地。你需要为自己赢得经历所有这些过程的权利。”[101]

Since at least the early 1970s the Harringtons annually visited his older sister, Verna Tate, and her retired railroad engineer husband in early summer.[102] Beginning in 1974 he began to spend a day at his alma mater for the purpose of reconnecting with his memories and connecting with the current academic climate. The time was spent discussing scoliosis, research, and the news of the day: in other words, it was a mixed social and professional visit. Harrington was introduced to and became acquainted with several faculty members, including bone researcher H. Clark Anderson and medical historian Robert P. Hudson. What was not known until later was his growing desire to have his professional materials archived at the University of Kansas Medical Center. The 1980 visit to Kansas City was especially poignant because it was apparent that his health was failing fast and it might be his last trip home. Yet he exuded an air of calm, which he attributed to the peace of mind afforded by his belief that he had found a proper home for the professorship. Arriving at his sister and brother-in-law's high-rise apartment building overlooking the Missouri River, he remarked that "I'm not sure it was worth it, the Rods I mean." He cited various interests that he and a number of others had sacrificed because of the intensity required to create the Harrington Spine Instrumentation. And even that accomplishment left him with some sense of failure as it had required fusion to make his instrumentation work.

至少从 20 世纪 70 年代初开始，哈灵顿夫妇每年都会在初夏拜访他的姐姐韦尔娜·泰特和她退休的铁路工程师丈夫。[102]从 1974 年开始，他开始每年花一天的时间去拜访他的母校，以重拾他的记忆和接触当前最新的学术氛围。这一天的时间被用来讨论脊柱侧凸、研究和最新时事，换句话说，这是一次社交和学术的混合性访问。哈灵顿被介绍给了几位教职工，包括骨骼研究员 H. 克拉克·安德森和医学史专家罗伯特·P. 赫德森。直到后来才知道，他越来越想把他的专业资料存放在堪萨斯大学医学中心。1980 年的堪萨斯城之行则尤其令人心酸，因为很明显哈灵顿的健康状况每况愈下，这可能是他最后一次回到母校。然而，他却流露出一种平静的神情，因为他认为教授这一职位是他最合适的归宿，因而心情平静。当他在姐姐和姐夫的高层公寓中俯瞰密苏里河时，他感慨道："我不确定这是否值得，我指的是发明脊柱内固定器械系统（棒）。"他谈到因为需要高强度的工作来创造哈灵顿脊柱内固定器械，从而他和其他很多人不得不舍弃很多其他爱好。即使取得了这样的成就，他仍然会感到些许挫败感，因为他的内固定方式仍然无法避免融合。

The fifteenth annual SRS meeting convened in Chicago on September 17-19, 1980. The president was William J. Kane and the Presidential Guest Speaker was J. R. Pincott, FRCS from London, whose topic was "Histological Studies in Idiopathic and Experimental Scoliosis."[103] From 1981 on the billing reverted back to Harington Guest Lecturer.[104]

第十五届脊柱侧凸研究学会年会于 1980 年 9 月 17 日到 19 日在芝加哥召开。主席为威廉·J. 凯恩，主席特邀演讲者是来自伦敦的皇家外科医师学会会员 J. R. 平科特，他演讲的主题是"特发性和实验性脊柱侧凸的组织学研究"。[103]从 1981 年开始特邀演讲嘉宾重新被叫作哈灵顿特邀演讲者。[104]

The first eight papers of the program were studies of spine instrumentation, five of them devoted to Luque's SSI! In the four years since he had introduced his instrumentation only two papers, including one of his, had made it through the competitive process to the program. In 1980 two of the five were Luque's work. In "Kyphosis and Lordosis, Correction and Production" he presented the evidence that SSI was effective in increasing or decreasing kyphosis or lordosis to normal "within the limits of the corresponding contractures and soft tissue releases undertaken or the osseous osteotomies done." Paired 3/16" or 1/4" rods were bent to the anatomical lordosis and kyphosis, and, using bilateral sublaminar wires, transverse loads were used to approximate the spine to the rods. Luque considered the fixation provided to be rigid, which encouraged rapid arthrodesis and did not require external immobilization.

此次会议项目中的前 8 篇报告均关于脊柱内固定，其中 5 篇聚焦卢克的节段性脊柱器械。自卢克首次介绍他的器械以来，四年间总共只有两篇论文通过筛选在大会上进行报告，其中还包括卢克本人的那篇。1980 年的大会中，相关的 5 篇论文中有 2 篇是卢克本人的研究。在《后凸和前凸，矫正和结果》一文中，他给出了证据，当完成相应范围内的挛缩和软组织松解以及骨性截骨的所有限制后，节段性脊柱内固定手术能够有效地增加或减少脊柱后凸和前凸到正常。配对的直径为 3/16 英寸或 1/4 英寸棒被弯成脊柱解剖上的生理前凸和后凸，并用双侧椎板下钢丝固定，使用横向载荷使脊柱贴向内固定棒。卢克认为提供的固定是刚性的，这促进了快速融合，术后不需要进行外部制动。

The harmful effects of the loss of physiological lumbar lordosis with posterior distraction had been identified by Doherty at the 1972 meeting[105] and by Denis and Moe at the 1976 meeting.[106] At the 1980 meeting posture and gait analysis studies were presented that had been a suggested by observation of a patient with mild hip and knee extension weakness following spinal cord injury.[107] After Harrington distraction instrumentation and fusion with loss of some lumbar lordosis he was "forced to rely on crutches to walk, as he lacked the range for hip hyperextension and the quadriceps strength for a crouch." This stimulated the study of nine patients (sex distribution unspecified) with idiopathic scoliosis that had successful Harrington Instrumentation and fusion. All of these still young patients were asymptomatic except that three of the females could not wear high heels. By X-ray more lumbar lordosis than thoracic kyphosis had been lost following surgery. Posture and gait analysis showed excessive hip extension in five and crouch posture in three. Avoidance of unnecessary fusion of lumbar curves was one way to limit the problems with lumbar curve fusion and had been a long-term goal of Moe.[108] In the "Selection of Fusion Levels in Thoracic Idiopathic Scoliosis" Howard King and others analyzed their 29-year experience with 455 patients operated on for major thoracic and double thoracic and lumbar idiopathic curves. Inclusion of the lumbar curve was necessary in only 13.9% of the patients. The full-length publication became a classic.[109]

1972 年会议上的多尔蒂[105]以及 1976 年会议上的丹尼斯和莫，[106]均认为后路撑开导致的生理腰椎前凸丢失会产生有害后果。在 1980 年的会议上，有专家通过观察一名脊髓损伤后髋和膝关节轻度伸展无力的患者，做了姿势和步态分析研究。[107]该患者在施行哈灵顿撑开内固定和融合术后，腰椎前凸部分丧失，“被迫依靠拐杖行走，因为他无法完成髋关节的过伸以及屈膝时股四头肌力量不足”。这促使专家对 9 名已经成功实施哈灵顿内固定融合的特发性脊柱侧凸患者（性别分布未明确）进行研究。除 3 名女性患者不能穿高跟鞋外，其余患者均未出现临床症状。X光片显示，术后腰椎前凸的丢失多于胸椎后凸角的纠正。姿势步态分析显示5名患者出现髋关节过伸，3名患者维持蹲伏姿态。避免不必要的腰椎侧凸融合是减少融合出现问题的一种方法，也是莫的长期目标。[108]在题为“胸椎特发性脊柱侧凸融合节段的选择”的报告中，霍华德·金等人分析了他们29年来455名主胸弯、胸腰双主弯的特发性脊柱侧凸患者的手术经验。只有13.9%的患者需要纳入腰椎弯曲。这个报告完整版发表后也成了经典。[109]

When the scoliosis or kyphosis was large and usually stiff, mechanical straightening of the spine was not possible or advisable because of the danger of stretching the spinal cord. Luque presented his approach to this problem in "Two Stage Vertebrectomy in Severe Deformities of the Spine," which was based on seven patients.[110] The anterior approach to remove the vertebral body and adjacent discs was done first, followed by a posterior approach to remove the posterior vertebral elements and instrument the spine. Illustrations in his other presentation suggested that he formed proximal and distal cantilever foundations to apply coronal and sagittal angular corrective loads. One patient required supplemental external immobilization. Luque reported that a solid posterior arthrodesis was present after six months and that interbody fusion at the vertebrectomy site occurred in all.

如果脊柱侧凸或后凸较为严重且通常为僵硬型，脊柱的机械性矫直是不现实的或者说是不可取的，因为会存在脊髓受到牵拉的风险。卢克针对这一问题提出了解决方法，并在包含7名患者的“重度脊柱畸形中两期椎体切除术”的报告中进行了介绍。[110]首先进行前路手术切除椎体和邻近椎间盘，然后进行后路手术切除椎体后方结构并完成脊柱内固定。他利用另一份报告中的插图解释，他在近端和远端构造了悬臂梁，借此施加冠状和矢状方向的成角矫正载荷。1名患者术后需要辅助外固定。卢克在报告中提到，患者6个月后实现了坚实的后路融合，所有椎体切除部位均发生了椎间融合。

Two of the SSI papers reported biomechanical testing. In the study by Dennis Wenger's group, four calf spine constructs were tested in vitro to failure in four load modes: longitudinal compressive, rotation, forward bending, and side bending.[111] The single Harrington distraction rod faired the poorest, and the other three constructs (the Harrington distraction and compression transversely connected, the Harrington distraction rod and sublaminar wires, and the Luque double L-rods and sublaminar wires) were fairly equivalent except in forward- and side-bending where constructs with sublaminar wires did somewhat better. A unique advantage of the Luque construct was the avoidance of hook site stress. The second biomechanical study, produced by Zimmer, was based on mathematical modeling that compared the effectiveness of the Milwaukee brace, SSI, and Harrington Instrumentation (not stated but apparently distraction only).[112] The study concluded that "Segmental Spinal Instrumentation is powerful in the correction of spinal deformities."

有关节段性脊柱内固定的两篇论文报道了生物力学测试。丹尼斯·温格的研究小组利用四头小牛的脊柱构建在四种载荷模式下（纵向压缩、旋转、前屈和侧屈）进行了体外测试。[111]结果显示单一的哈灵顿撑开棒效果最差，其他三种构件(利用横联连接的哈灵顿撑开和压缩棒、哈灵顿撑开棒联合椎板下钢丝，以及卢克双L棒联合椎板下钢丝）中除在前屈和侧屈模式下椎板下钢丝的效果稍好外，其他情况下各个结构之间效果基本相同。卢克构件独有的一个优势是避免了钩部位的应力。第二项生物力学研究是由捷迈进行的，该研究基于数学模型，比较了密尔沃基支具、节段性脊柱内固定和哈灵顿内固定的效果（虽然并未说明，但显然只使用了哈灵顿撑开棒)。[112]该研究得出以下结论："节段性脊柱器械在矫正脊柱畸形方面具有强大的效果。"

Luque's multi-degrees freedom of motion instrumentation and surgical techniques were expanding the reach of spine deformity surgery. But the expansion was happening slowly, and the "Segmental Spinal Instrumentation by Laminar Wiring" study presented by Andy Sullivan was the first SRS clinical SSI presentation not made by Luque."[113] Twenty patients in whom Harrington Instrumentation could not be used or in whom it was felt that SSI advantages outweighed disadvantages were selected for study. All had difficult spine deformities, and none had idiopathic scoliosis. Based on the series, the SSI advantages cited were rigid internal fixation, adaptability and simplicity, no instrumentation failure to date, and minimal external immobilization necessary. The disadvantages were a large implant mass in a small child, increased fixation site preparation time, difficulty predicting correction, and wide decortication impossible but maybe unnecessary. Unanswered questions remaining were the ease of implant removal, growth if facetectomy was not done, and the extent of postoperative casting necessary. The possibility of neurological injury was not experienced or discussed.

卢克保留多方位运动自由度的内固定器械和手术技术扩大了对脊柱畸形手术

的适应范围。但它的推广是缓慢的，安迪·沙利文的“使用椎板线缆的节段性脊柱内固定”是脊柱侧凸研究学会会议上第一个非卢克本人展示的与节段性脊柱内固定相关的研究报告。[113]该研究选择了 20 名不能实行哈灵顿内固定或认为在他们身上节段性脊柱内固定手术优点大于缺点的患者。所有患者均有复杂的脊柱畸形，无特发性脊柱侧凸。通过对这部分患者的研究，安迪·沙利文认为节段性脊柱内固定的优点包括内固定牢靠、适应性强、操作简单、未出现内固定失败的案例，以及术后仅需要最低程度的外固定。缺点是对儿童而言，植入物体积较大，增加了固定部位的准备时间，难以预测矫正效果，没办法进行大范围去除骨皮质(但是可能也没必要)。节段性脊柱内固定仍存在一些有待观察的问题，比如植入物取出的难易程度、无用关节突切除的生长情况以及术后石膏外固定的必要程度。另外，神经损伤的风险也没有太多经验可以借鉴和讨论。

There were two new evolutions from Harrington Instrumentation presented. In “A New Instrumentation System for Fracture-Dislocation of the Dorso-Lumbar Spine” Rae Jacobs explained the rationale for changing the correction and stabilizing load from vertical translation to sagittal angulation produced by four-point bending.[114] The resulting instrumentation had unique features, including a 7-mm diameter smooth rod threaded at either end with locking nuts, washers keyed to the rod, and hooks fixed to the Washers by meshing radial grooves. The entire device was inserted as a single assembly, the connection mechanism facilitating insertion by “separating rod contouring and hook rotation positioning into two operations. The upper hook has in addition a sliding cover that locks in the lamina avoiding excessive distraction of the injured spine. The inferior hook is inserted first and is locked by the proximity of the lamina.” Mechanical testing in four-point bending over seven cadaver vertebral segments showed the experimental device to have “nearly three times the strength, one third the deformation, and twice the energy absorption of the Harrington distraction rods.” A multicenter clinical trial was underway.

哈灵顿内固定出现了两项新的改进技术。在“腰椎骨折脱位的新型内固定系统”的报告中，雷·雅各布斯讲解了将矫正和稳定载荷从纵向平移改为四点弯曲产生的矢状成角的根本原因。[114]由此形成的内固定系统有着独有的特点，包括一个直径为 7 mm 的光滑杆，其两端有锁紧螺母的螺纹，锁定在杆上的垫圈，以及通过径向槽啮合固定在垫圈上的挂钩。整个装置作为单个组件进行置入，并将联结装置通过“预弯棒和旋转固定挂钩”两个步骤来完成置入。头端的钩上还有一个滑动的盖子，可以锁在椎板上，避免过度撑开损伤脊柱。首先插入尾端钩，并通过邻近椎板进行锁定。雷·雅各布斯等人在7具尸体的椎体上进行了四点弯曲力学测试，结果表明实验器械的“强度是哈灵顿撑开棒的近三倍，形变是三分之一，能量吸收是哈灵顿撑开棒的两倍”。一项多中心的临床试验也正在进行。

In "Studies in Compression Instrumentation" Denis Drummond presented the design rationale for modifying Harrington compression hooks by placing a posterior slot in the hook body so that the rod could be placed into preplaced hooks.[115] Referred to as the Wisconsin compression system, the modification consisted of a bushing and opposing nuts to complete the connection. Mechanical testing in tension revealed Harrington compression to be 18% stronger than the Wisconsin system, but both were much stronger than the bony fixation site. The Wisconsin system required 2.5 times longer to fail, suggesting it absorbed more energy. Results of clinical use were in the early stages.

在“压缩内固定器械的研究”的报告中，丹尼斯·德拉蒙德介绍了改良型哈灵顿压缩钩的设计原理，通过在钩体中放置一个后槽，使内固定棒可以放置在预先放置的钩中。[115]该系统被称为威斯康星压缩系统，由一个套管和对置螺母组成，以完成连接。力学测试显示哈灵顿压缩系统比威斯康星系统强18%，但两者都比骨性固定部位强得多。威斯康星系统失效所需要的时间是哈灵顿系统的2.5倍，表明它可以吸收更多的能量。临床应用结果尚处于早期阶段。

Harold Dunn presented the clinical extension of his work on "Anterior Spine Stabilization-An Implant System."[116] Thirty patients had been operated on and followed one to six years. Four had one-rod fixation one vertebra above and below the site of injury, and two of them had failed. Thirteen had one-rod fixation two or more levels above and below the site of injury, and two of them had failed. Eight had undergone fixation one level above and below the site of injury with an implant "rigidly linking two rods together and affixing them to the vertebral bodies at two points at least 80° apart on the vertebral body circumference." None had failed, but the follow-up was only for one to two years. None of the four earlier failures had been early or catastrophic. Twenty-four of the 30 patients had incomplete paralysis, all were decompressed, and 18 improved. The course of the other six isn't clear. Six of the 30 patients had complete paralysis below the injury, and none improved.

哈罗德·邓恩介绍了他的“脊柱前路稳定——一项内植物系统”的临床推广工作。[116]包括30名手术患者，并进行了1~6年的随访。4名患者施行单棒固定，范围包括伤椎上下各1个椎体，其中2名患者发生了内固定失败；13名患者同样进行了单棒固定，但是固定范围包括伤椎上下至少各两个椎体，同样有2名患者发生内固定失败。8名患者在损伤部位上下各1个椎体处进行了水平双棒固定，并通过内植物“将两根棒牢固地连接在一起，并将它们固定在椎体周长上至少成80°角的两点上”，经过1~2年的随访后，无手术失败病例。研究中出现的4名患者的内固定失败都不是早期发生的或灾难性的。30名患者中有24名为不完全瘫痪，均予以减压，18名发生好转，另外6名患者情况不明。30名患者中，有6名发生创伤部位以下的完全瘫痪，术后均未发生改善。

At the 1980 annual meeting of the SRS spinal instrumentation innovations and their mechanical testing reached new levels of sophistication, but the highlight was a technique that only advanced instrumentation techniques would allow, namely vertebrectomy and spine shortening.[117] Contrasted with what could be done was the meeting's other highlight—what should be done. By following the rules Moe had carefully worked out over almost 30 years, it was possible to avoid long fusions into the lumbar spine in most patients with adolescent idiopathic scoliosis.[118]

在1980年的脊柱侧凸研究学会脊柱内固定创新年会上，相关的力学测试研究在精密方面达到了新的高度，但全场的焦点只属于一种在先进内固定技术下才能实现的手术——椎体切除和脊柱缩短术。[117]会议的另一个亮点是讨论了对于脊柱畸形患者，我们应该做什么，与之前的能够做什么形成了对比。通过遵循莫近30年来精心制订的规则，大多数青少年特发性脊柱侧凸患者可以避免涉及腰椎的长节段融合。[118]

Two months after the fifteenth annual meeting of the Scoliosis Research Society, Paul Randall Harrington died. The date was November 29, 1980, slightly more than 69 years after his birth on September 27, 1911. Though the cause was not given in his obituaries, he had suffered the effects of atherosclerosis, which first became apparent at the time of his heart attack in November 1968.

脊柱侧凸研究学会第十五次年会的两个月后，1980年11月29日，保罗·兰德尔·哈灵顿与世长辞，享年69岁（哈灵顿出生于1911年9月27日）。尽管在他的讣告中没有说明去世原因，但他实际早已患有冠状动脉粥样硬化，在1968年11月的心脏病发作时首次被注意到。

At Harrington's funeral William A. Spencer, his one-time recruit, his chairman, and his all-time champion, delivered the eulogy.[119] It contained firsthand observations and insights that could only have emerged from the trial-by-fire, 30-year colleagueship of kindred spirits. The eulogy was long but paraphrasing it would risk losing nuance in translation. The first two paragraphs convey the message.

在哈灵顿的葬礼上，威廉·A. 斯宾塞——他的伯乐、他的主任和他永远的支持者——致了悼词。[119]文字中包含了斯宾塞对于哈灵顿的亲身观察和理解，只有经过30年的患难与共后才能写出这样的悼词。悼词洋洋洒洒，情真意切，任何转述都不能表现出字里行间细微的情感流露。因此这里摘录了悼词的前两段。

> He was a giant in orthopedic surgery. He aggressively treated severe curvature of the spine for which there was little possible in advanced stages. He showed how one could succeed in recognizing and treating this deformity of the spine and paralysis and handicap comprehensively, first from polio and then from many other causes. He had immense imagination and unbounded creativity. He matched it with unbelievable tenacity and great skill of mind and hand. He tackled insurmountable problems and failed, but tried again and again. He had to overcome criticism of a new procedure. He pressured us all relentlessly. He expected us to be more responsive to the needs of our patients and his efforts with the same restless drive and enthusiasm he had. He got intensive medical pre-operative and post-operative support from Gunyon Harrison and Carlos Vallbona for his most devastated patients with great risks of pulmonary and circulatory complications. He developed research in scoliosis. He sought out anyone who could contribute what he did not know in order to understand why and how. He developed and tested completely different ideas of its cause and progression. What he developed worked! He enlisted his colleagues like Thorkild Engen to develop Proper implanted instruments and surgical tools for his procedures.
>
> 他是骨科界的巨人，将重度脊柱畸形的晚期治疗由不可能变为可能。他向我们展示了如何成功、全面地诊治脊柱畸形，以及畸形带来的瘫痪和残疾，最初为脊髓灰质炎后的脊柱畸形，然后再扩展至其他各种类型的脊柱畸形。他有天马行空的想象力和无限的创造力，并匹配以难以置信的坚韧和绝佳的工作能力。他试图去解决那不可逾越的难题，虽

然失败了但仍一次次地发起挑战。他必须去克服伴随新技术而来的批评。他无情地鞭策我们，并希望我们能像他一样，对患者更加负责以及有着永不停歇的动力和热情。在术前术后，他得到了加尼恩·哈里森和卡洛斯·巴利沃纳的大力支持，他们帮助他治疗那些最严重的、有肺部和循环系统并发症风险的病人。他发展了脊柱侧凸的研究，并始终对新鲜事物保持好奇，并刨根问底，以便了解其背后的原因和方法。他发展并检验了很多完全不相关的观点的成因和进展。他大力发展的事情终于取得了成效！同时，他也招募了像托基尔·恩金这样的同事来为他的手术研发合适的植入器械和手术工具。

He had humility in his empathetic and always helpful relation to other persons but not in the energetic devotion to his work. Most of all, those persons we call patients appreciated him. He maintained this equanimity in the operating theater as well as the bedside. His patients and families' appreciation for this attitude even exceeded their gratitude for his Success and offset his rare failures.

他总是谦卑、善解人意、乐于助人，并且在工作方面永葆热情，精力充沛。最重要的是，那些患者们都对他十分推崇。无论是在手术室还是在病房，哈灵顿都保持着一种沉着从容的气质。病人们及家属对他这种为人处世的态度的赞赏甚至超过了手术成功后对他的感激，自然也忽略了他某些微不足道的小缺点。

For months Mary Alice received condolence letters from near and far, from patients and colleagues, all conveying the common themes of gratitude for her husband's humanism and sorrow for the family's loss of such a great man. The president of the SRS wrote that "He made the greatest single contribution to the treatment of spinal disorders in the history of surgery."[120] A leading scoliosis surgeon on the East Coast wrote, "His innovative medical ability and skill first attracted me. His genuine goodness, honesty, and innate compassion were the traits that made the bond permanent."[121] A patient, who had three of his pioneering surgeries after having polio at the age of seven years, wrote Mary Alice, "Please know at this time of your sorrow that those of us whose lives he helped save grieve at our loss, too."[122] Parents, who felt he had saved their daughter's life when she contracted polio in the early 1950s and later operated on her five times to control her scoliosis, wrote, "Words cannot express how much we cared for your husband."[123] Jesse Dickson, the man with the capacity and will to carry on Harrington's practice when he no longer was physically able, was in a position to know him very well. In the obituary he wrote for his mentor, Dickson recounted Harrington's achievements and closed with this thought, "Paul will be remembered, not only for the development of the Harrington instruments, but also for his straightforward frankness, his bowties, his par golf, his smile, his trumpet, and above all for being a nice person."[124]

几个月来，玛丽·艾丽斯收到了来自四面八方的吊唁信，纷纷对她丈夫的人道主义精神表示感激，以及对她的家庭失去这样一位伟大的人而感到悲伤。脊柱侧凸研究学会的主席写道："在外科手术史上，他对脊柱疾病的治疗做出了最大的贡献。"[120]美国东海岸一位卓越的脊柱侧凸外科医生写道："最开始吸引我的是他的创新医疗能力和手术技术，而让这份友谊保持下去的是他的善良、诚实和与生俱来的同情心。"[121]一位7岁的患者因脊髓灰质炎曾接受过3次哈灵顿开创性的手术，他在写给玛丽·艾丽斯的信中写道："当你悲伤的时候，请不要忘记那些被他拯救的生命同样也在哀悼他的离去。"[122]一位患者的父母认为是哈灵顿救了他们女儿的命，当他们的女儿在20世纪50年代初感染了脊髓灰质炎之后，哈灵顿为她前后做了5次手术以控制她的脊柱侧凸的进展。这对父母在信中写道："言语无法表达我们对你丈夫的怀念。"[123]杰西·迪克森，这个有能力也愿意在哈灵顿体力不支的时候继续他的事业的人，对哈灵顿有着深入的了解。在他写给导师的讣告中，迪克森讲述了哈灵顿的成就，并深情结尾："保罗将被世人铭记，不单是由于他对哈灵顿内固定器械研发的卓越贡献，还有他的坦率、他的领结、他的高尔夫、他的笑容、他的小号，以及最重要的——他的高尚品格。"[124]

（李章富 王建强 译　海涌 钱邦平 审校）

Epilogue
后 记

In *Dogged Persistence* the elements of the lifelong process that led to the creation of the first successful spine instrumentation system have been dissected and can be broadly categorized as problem, person, and situation. The problem that launched this story was post-polio scoliosis, a collapsing spine deformity beginning in childhood or adolescence for which the existing treatment was marginally better than the condition itself. Its prevalence was low and, because of the epidemic occurrence of polio, erratic. The sustained North American polio epidemics following World War II had the important effect of magnifying the problem, calling attention to people suffering from this sometimes deadly deformity. This in turn brought greater professional and popular awareness of scoliosis of all causes and spine deformities in general. The curve patterns of adolescent idiopathic scoliosis, the most common scoliosis, resembled post-polio scoliosis closely enough to make the instrumentation potentially interchangeable. This coincidence helped to sustain the development of the instrumentation despite the impending elimination of post-polio scoliosis after the introduction of the successful polio vaccination in 1955.

《锲而不舍》讲述了第一个取得成功的脊柱内固定系统的诞生过程，其成功的要素可以大致归纳为三个方面：问题、人物和处境。引发这段历史的问题是脊髓灰质炎后脊柱侧凸，一种始于儿童或青少年时期的脊柱塌陷畸形。当时的治疗方法效果欠佳，无法逆转疾病的自然病程。因为脊髓灰质炎的流行具有不稳定性，这种侧凸的整体发病率不高。然而第二次世界大战后，北美脊髓灰质炎的持续流行和恶化放大了这个问题，引起了人们对这种有时可致命的脊柱畸形的关注，同时提高了专业人员和公众对脊柱畸形，特别是由其他原因引起的脊柱侧凸的认识。青少年特发性脊柱侧凸作为最常见的脊柱侧凸，其脊柱弯曲特点与脊髓灰质炎后脊柱侧凸非常相似，因此，脊柱内固定系统具有在这两种疾病中通用的可能。尽管1955年成功引入脊髓灰质炎疫苗后，脊髓灰质炎后脊柱侧凸逐渐消失，但这种可通用的巧合维持了脊柱内固定系统的持续发展。

The *person*, Paul Randall Harrington, was later described as having the great gift of being able "to look at a problem in an entirely original way." His concept was that scoliosis resulted from asymmetrical spine loading which caused asymmetrical spine growth. The corollary was that removal of the asymmetrical load would restore symmetrical growth, thus making arthrodesis/fusion unnecessary. Although his concept was eventually disproved, its pursuit sustained his intense curiosity. Many rightly described Harrington as being a natural leader who was both inquisitive and persistent with the rare combination of being both an iconoclast and a perfectionist, as well as, above all else, self-assured. He needed each of these traits because his radical departure from the established orthopedic practice not only exposed his patients to unknown risks but also himself to the possible loss of reputation and livelihood.

人物：保罗·兰德尔·哈灵顿后来被描述为具有“以全新的方式看待问题”的伟大天赋。他认为脊柱侧凸是脊柱由于不对称的载荷而导致生长不对称；其推论是，去除不对称载荷可恢复对称生长，因此无须进行脊柱融合术。尽管他的理念最终被推翻，但对这一理念的追求使他保持了强烈的好奇心。许多人描述哈灵顿是一个天生的领导者，他既好奇又执着，是一个罕见的突破传统者和完美主义者的结合体，而且最重要的是，他很自信。这些性格特点都是他所需要的，因为他彻底背离了当时的骨科实践理念，不仅使他的病人面临未知的风险，他自己也可能失去名誉，变得穷困潦倒。

The *situation* was the sustained polio epidemics in Houston from 1948 to 1955, the time and place where Harrington began his medical and surgical practice. At the age of 37, Harrington still had the energy and idealism of youth. Heading up the Houston unit of the National Foundation for Infantile Paralysis (NFIP) when the epidemic began, he immediately became involved in the diagnosis and acute care of polio patients. He was able to make time for this added work because his private practice was less than two years old and still building. As a solo practitioner he was not answerable to associates, who would almost certainly have been very critical of the time he was devoting to the NFIP unit. He also brought an unspoiled mind to the problem of post-polio scoliosis since he had virtually no exposure to it during his orthopedic residency. Houston, with its just forming Texas Medical Center and recently relocated Baylor College of Medicine along with nearby Rice Institute (which became Rice University in 1960), placed him in the midst of a professional environment conducive to his creative work. But, his quest was long and difficult. As Vern Nickel observed, "he was right on the nip and tuck of being totally washed out of the system." By using the word *system*, Nickel was referring to the orthopedic hierarchy within the medical community. The precariousness of Harrington's position was illustrated by his long hiatus between board certification in orthopaedic surgery and acceptance into a most important professional association: an interval of eleven years rather than the usual three. The coming together of the elements of *problem*, *person*, and *situation* explains why the quest for successful spine instrumentation was so long and difficult.

处境：1948 年至 1955 年，脊髓灰质炎在休斯敦持续流行，此时哈灵顿正在此处开始其医疗和外科实践。37 岁的他，仍具有年轻人的精力和理想主义。他领导着国家小儿麻痹基金会的休斯敦分部，在疫情初始便迅速投身于脊髓灰质炎患者的诊断和急性期治疗。他之所以能够胜任这些额外的工作，是因为他的私人诊所成立不到两年，且还在建设中。作为一名个体医生，他不需要对同事负责。如果他在医院工作，同事们无疑会对他长时间投入国家小儿麻痹基金会的工作感到不满。由于他在当骨科住院医师期间从未遇到脊髓灰质炎后脊柱侧凸的问题，他对该疾病的认识并未囿于成见。当时休斯敦刚拥有新成立的得克萨斯医学中心和近期搬入的贝勒医学院及在附近的莱斯研究所（1960 年成为莱斯大学），这使哈灵顿处于对创造性工作有利的专业环境之中。然而，他的探索道路漫长而艰难。正如弗农·尼克尔所言，“他正处于被体制彻底淘汰的边缘”。尼克尔所说的“体制”即医学界中骨科的等级制度。哈灵顿的学术地位岌岌可危，从其取得骨科医师资格到被一个最重要的专业学会接纳，间隔了整整 11 年之久（通常是 3 年）。问题、人物和处境三个因素结合，解释了对成功的脊柱内固定系统的探索为何如此漫长而艰难。

Five collaborations proved to be critical to Harrington's creative process. The first was with Bill Spencer, who in 1950 assumed leadership of the Houston response to the polio epidemics, thus freeing Harrington from that duty and allowing him to concentrate on the orthopedic aspects of patient care. As chair of rehabilitation medicine, Spencer was Harrington's administrative leader and unfailing advocate, affording him the support and protection needed in that bureaucratic environment. Spencer's excellent management of the NFIP's response to the polio epidemics lent mainstream credibility to Harrington's work.

有五段合作关系对哈灵顿的创造过程至关重要。第一个是与比尔·斯宾塞的合作，他在1950年承接了休斯敦应对脊髓灰质炎疫情的领导工作，从而将哈灵顿从该职责中解放出来，使他能够专注于骨科患者的治疗。作为康复医学部门的主任，斯宾塞是哈灵顿的行政领导和不折不扣的拥护者，为他提供了在官僚主义环境下所需的支持和保护。斯宾塞领导国家小儿麻痹基金会应对脊髓灰质炎疫情的出色表现使哈灵顿的工作获得了主流的认可。

The second important collaborator was Tork Engen, recruited by Spencer from the Georgia Warm Springs NFIP unit in 1954 to establish and develop the orthotics department at the newly established Southwestern Poliomyelitis Respiratory Care Center. He aided Harrington in developing his spine instrumentation system, and there is no question that Engen made important design and prototype contributions to the work. Harrington often credited him for this input, but their relationship cooled, probably because of Engen's unrealized expectations of participation in the manufacture of the instruments. In reality Engen was not equipped for medical implant manufacturing. Since most of the creativity and virtually all of the risk were Harrington's, he needed to maintain control of the instrument research and development. With time the friendship between the two men appeared repaired.

第二个重要的合作者是托基尔·恩金，他是斯宾塞1954年从佐治亚州沃姆斯普林斯国家小儿麻痹基金会招聘的，以在新成立的西南脊髓灰质炎呼吸中心建立和发展矫形科。他帮助哈灵顿开发了脊柱内固定系统，毋庸置疑他对这一器械的设计和原型做出了重要贡献。哈灵顿时常将贡献归功于他，但他们的关系逐渐冷淡下来，这可能是由于恩金没有参与制造脊柱器械的愿望。实际上，恩金并不具备制造医疗内植物的资质。因其大部分的创造灵感来源于哈灵顿，且几乎所有的风险都由哈灵顿承担，同时，哈灵顿还需要始终保持对脊柱器械研发的管控。所幸随着时间的推移，两人的友谊也逐渐修复了。

Harrington's third collaboration was with the NFIP, which in 1955 awarded two research grants to support his work, their first ever to develop a surgical procedure. In 1959 the NFIP pressured the Rancho Los Amigos NFIP unit in Downey, California, to provide Harrington a platform on which to present his work at a time when other opportunities were not available.

哈灵顿的第三个合作是和国家小儿麻痹基金会进行的。1955 年，国家小儿麻痹基金会给予哈灵顿两项研究经费以支持他的工作和他们开创的新术式。1959 年，国家小儿麻痹基金会要求位于加利福尼亚州唐尼的兰乔洛杉米戈斯国家小儿麻痹基金会分部为哈灵顿提供一个平台，让他能够在没有其他机会的情况下展示自己的成果。

Professor James R. Sims of Rice University, the fourth and least visible of the collaborators, seems to have been the one who provided Harrington with the engineering mentoring he needed to address the mechanics of his pursuit.

莱斯大学的詹姆斯·R. 西姆斯教授是哈灵顿的第四个合作者。他们之间的合作看似最不起眼，但他为哈灵顿提供了脊柱内固定器械的机械问题所需的工程指导。

Harrington's fifth collaboration, which began in the spring of 1955, was with Zimmer Manufacturing Company. Of the many contacts he had with Zimmer personnel over the years that with Chief Engineer Jim Hite was the longest and most productive. Beginning in December 1958, Hite pushed Harrington to complete the design, continued pushing him to develop educational materials, and was able to address most of the questions and suggestions he received from new users following the spine instrumentation's launch in 1960. The interaction between Harrington and Zimmer, spanning nearly twenty years, proved to be a model of the productive medical-industrial collaboration necessary to address an unmet clinical need. There is nothing to suggest that either Harrington or Zimmer mismanaged their conflicts of interest.

哈灵顿第五个合作的对象是捷迈生产制造公司，他们的合作开始于 1955 年春天。多年来，哈灵顿与捷迈的众多员工都有往来，但与首席工程师吉姆·海特的交往时间最长、最有成效。1958 年 12 月，海特敦促哈灵顿完成设计并继续开发教具。海特解决了自 1960 年脊柱器械推出以来新用户提出的大部分问题和建议。哈灵顿和捷迈合作近二十年，无疑是解决临床需求中遇到的问题所必需且富有成效的医工合作典范，而且哈灵顿与捷迈之间不存在处理不当的利益冲突。

Harrington and his collaborators made good use of the ten-year gestation period, from 1949 through 1959 of Harrington Spine Instrumentation. Its twenty-five-year dominance of the market it created is a testament to the thoroughness of this extended period of trial and error. The system was never patented and was so well designed and engineered that there was no need to redesign it. Its introduction was supported by an intense educational effort, which helped stimulate orthopedic surgeons into serious study of scoliosis and other spine deformities. This led to the formation of the Scoliosis Research Society (SRS) in 1966. Just two years later when he was 57, a myocardial infarction left Harrington permanently physically disabled, a burden he bore with dignity and grace. This occurred about seventeen months after he had found the perfect heir to his practice and clinical research. Jesse H. Dickson not only filled these roles but also became a regular contributor to the peer-reviewed SRS annual meeting scientific programs and the orthopedic literature. Dickson served as the SRS president in 1990.

哈灵顿和他的合作者成功把握了哈灵顿脊柱器械从 1949 年到 1959 年的 10 年酝酿期。该产品随后在自己创造的脊柱器械市场上占据了 25 年的统治地位，反映出在这段漫长时期不断试错与调整完善的缜密态度。该内固定系统从未申请过专利，其设计和组装完备，甚至没有重新设计的必要。由于它的推出同时伴随着有力的教育支持，促使骨科医生认真投入对脊柱侧凸和其他脊柱畸形的研究。这也促成了脊柱侧凸研究学会于 1966 年成立。遗憾的是，仅仅两年后，一场心肌梗死导致 57 岁的哈灵顿再也不能彻底回到自己的工作岗位上。虽然经受如此苦难，他仍保全了自己的尊严和体面。约 17 个月以后，哈灵顿找到继续践行他的实践理念和临床研究的完美继承人——杰西 · H. 迪克森。迪克森成功肩负起这些责任，成为脊柱侧凸研究学会年度会议学术项目和同行评议的骨科文献的定期贡献者，并于 1990 年担任脊柱侧凸研究学会主席。

But, Harrington Spine Instrumentation had its design limitations, providing some direct position and stability control principally in the coronal plane, making supplemental stability control by postoperative casting necessary. Beginning with the third annual meeting of the SRS in 1968, a growing list of problems was identified. The first and most serious was distraction paraplegia associated with Harrington Instrumentation, the overall incidence of which eventually proved to be approximately 0.5%, accounting for roughly half of the neurological complications reported. This stimulated the development of spinal cord monitoring designed to alert the surgeon to impending loss of neurological function. Another distraction pathology was obstruction of the retroperitoneal portion of the duodenum, previously attributed to body casting. Soon loss of lumbar lordosis (1972), inability to correct thoracic lordosis (1973), inadequacy of pelvic fixation (1974), and low frequency but persistent distraction hook fixation loss (1975) were also reported.

然而，哈灵顿脊柱器械设计上有一定的不足：它仅对脊柱冠状面的位置和稳定性提供直接的固定，以致术后必须进行额外的石膏固定来弥补其他方向上稳定性不足的问题。自1968年第三届脊柱侧凸研究学会年会开始，越来越多的副作用与并发症问题逐渐浮现。首个也是最严重的问题是与哈灵顿器械有关的撑开性截瘫，最终统计其总发生率约为0.5%，约占报告的神经系统并发症的一半。这促使了脊髓监测器的研发，旨在提醒外科医生即将发生的神经系统功能丧失。另一个撑开引发的并发症是十二指肠腹膜后部分的梗阻，以往将其归因于躯体石膏。此外，腰椎前凸丧失（1972年），无法纠正胸椎前凸（1973年），骨盆固定不足（1974年），以及发生率低但持续存在的脱钩（1975年）等问题也有报道。

These Harrington Spine Instrumentation deficiencies signaled the opportunity for innovation. The first came in 1969 when Australian Alan Dwyer introduced anterior instrumentation. Dwyer Instrumentation provided two-dimensional position and stability control in the coronal and transverse planes, but supplemental stability control by postoperative casting was still necessary. The second and more serious challenge to the supremacy of Harrington Spine Instrumentation usage was introduced in 1976 by Mexican surgeon Eduardo Luque. It featured segmental anchorage of rods to the spine with sublaminar wires. Luque Instrumentation provided two-dimensional position and stability control in the coronal and sagittal planes. Although weak in vertical translation and transverse rotation control, it approached three-dimensional position and stability control closely enough to make postoperative casting unnecessary. However, passage of multiple sublaminar wires at least theoretically exposed the patient to increased risk of neurological injury, thus limiting its acceptance. Because of these reasons, Harrington Spine Instrumentation continued to be the most widely used spine instrumentation, even after Harrington's death.

哈灵顿脊柱器械的这些不足意味着存在继续创新的机遇。第一个是1969年由澳大利亚人艾伦·德怀尔引入的前路固定器械。尽管术后仍需石膏固定，德怀尔内固定器械能提供冠状面和横断面的二维稳定性。第二个是1976年墨西哥外科医生爱德华多·卢克开发的脊柱器械，对哈灵顿脊柱器械的市场主导地位提出了更加严峻的挑战。它的特点是用椎板下钢丝将棒节段性锚定在脊柱上。卢克脊柱器械在冠状面和矢状面上维持了脊柱的稳定性，虽然对垂直平移和横向旋转的控制能力较弱，但已基本维持三维稳定，无需术后石膏固定。然而，多个椎板下钢丝穿过椎管至少在理论上增加了患者神经损伤的风险，从而限制了其接受程度。由于这些原因，即使在哈灵顿去世后，哈灵顿脊柱器械仍然是使用最广泛的脊柱器械。

It was Cotrel-Dubousset Instrumentation (CD), introduced in North America in 1984, that surpassed Harrington Instrumentation's leadership position.[1] CD forever changed spine instrumentation surgery by addressing deformities in three dimensions, providing a construct stable and strong enough to eliminate the postoperative cast, and increasing the monetary value of the spine instrumentation market.[2] At that time the price for a typical right thoracic scoliosis Harrington construct was approximately $300 while that for a CD was about $3,000.[3] Some of the price difference between these two constructs was offset by CD's eliminating the cast and shortening hospital stays. But, Cotrel-Dubousset's technological breakthrough and price margins, even though associated with a learning curve increase in complications, further stimulated the already increasing pace of spine instrumentation innovation. A multi-billion dollar industry was born.

1984 年在北美推出的科特雷尔–杜布塞特器械则超越了哈灵顿器械的领导地位。[1]科特雷尔–杜布塞特器械永远地改变了脊柱器械手术的方式，它解决了三维畸形，能为脊柱提供足够牢固的结构支撑而无须术后石膏固定，同时科特雷尔–杜布塞特器械提高了脊柱器械市场的货币价值。[2]当时，典型的右胸脊柱侧凸哈灵顿器械的价格约为 300 美元，而科特雷尔–杜布塞特器械的价格约为 3 000 美元。[3]因为无需石膏固定且住院时间较短，这两种器械之间的部分价格差异被科特雷尔–杜布塞特器械的优势抵消。此外，尽管科特雷尔–杜布塞特器械的技术突破和丰厚利润与并发症的曲线增长有关，它进一步促进了不断加速的脊柱器械创新的步伐。一个价值数十亿美元的产业由此诞生。

Poliomyelitis, the *problem* at the root of this story, is down but not out. Thanks to vaccinations it was eliminated from North America during Harrington's lifetime. However, in the early 1980s many of the 20- to 30-year survivors experienced increasing muscle weakness. This could not be attributed to a reactivated polio infection or death of the spinal cords anterior horn cells, as in amyotrophic lateral sclerosis (ALS). Rather it was traced to "death of individual nerve terminals in motor units that remain after polio" and was labeled post-poliomyelitis muscular atrophy (PPMA).[4] Progression of muscle weakness was about 1% per year, which could be problematic for survivors with severe disability and limited muscle reserves. In 1988 the World Health Assembly developed the

Global Polio Eradication Initiative to rid the world of polio. Due to this effort, the 350,000 new cases a year were reduced 99%, and endemic disease in 125 countries shrank to just 3. Worldwide polio elimination is elusive for technical and cultural reasons, but still possible.[5]

脊髓灰质炎是这个故事的根源性问题，它虽已被控制却没有完全消失。幸亏有疫苗的接种，北美的脊髓灰质炎在哈灵顿在世时已被消灭。然而在20世纪80年代初，许多20至30岁的幸存患者出现了日益严重的肌无力症状。其病因并非重新激活的脊髓灰质炎病毒或脊髓前角细胞的死亡，如肌萎缩型脊髓侧索硬化症（ALS）。相反，它是由于“脊髓灰质炎残余运动单元中个别神经末梢的死亡”，并被命名为脊髓灰质炎后肌肉萎缩症（PPMA）。[4] 1988年，世界卫生大会制定了《全球消除脊髓灰质炎倡议》，以彻底消除脊髓灰质炎。这项努力使得每年35万例的新发病例减少了99%，出现新发病例的国家由125个减少到仅3个。由于技术和文化原因，尽管实现在全球范围内消除脊髓灰质炎的目标困难重重，但仍有可能。[5]

In the past fifty years the SRS has grown into an international leader in spine deformity research, education, and outreach. It has over 1,500 members from nearly every country in the world. Its annual meeting is held in the early fall, and its scientific sessions are packed with knowledge seekers, adolescent idoopathic scoliosis with its unknown etiology still commands their attention. However, the focus has shifted toward evaluation and management of spine deformities associated with aging, early onset spine deformities, and previously inoperable deformities. Because of increasingly challenging deformities and heightened patient and surgeon expectations, spine instrumentation evolution moved toward the pedicle screw as the bone anchor of choice. This began gradually in the 1980s as surgeons realized that the pedicle screw provided the most complete direct control of spine position and stability. As the transition gathered momentum, a major regulatory obstacle was encountered in the 1990s when the Food and Drug Administration refused to license the pedicle screw for labeling and marketing as a device that preceded the Medical Device Amendments of 1976 to the Food, Drug and Cosmetic Act. Off-label use increased, and some patients, mainly adults with back and leg pain problems that were unhappy with their outcomes, sought relief through legal action. This resulted in a multidistrict litigation with companies, surgeons, and professional associations, including the SRS, as defendants. Resolution of the impasse began in January 1995 when the FDA approved pedicle screws for labeling and marketing through the FDA 510K regulatory process for the narrow indication of high-grade spondylolisthesis. This breakthrough was based on Harrington's work with pedicle screws beginning in late 1966, as is documented by materials in the Harrington Archives.[6] More recently, Harrington Archives material has provided the FDA with the support it needed in 2013 to approve non-fusion devices for labeling and marketing based on the 510K regulatory process.[7] It would have been impossible in the 1970s to foresee the importance of Harrington's legacy to these future pedicle screw and non-fusion device regulatory stories. Maybe the great pains he took to see that his materials were preserved was another manifestation of his special genius, that is, seeing what others failed to see.

在过去的50年里，脊柱侧凸研究学会已发展成为脊柱畸形研究、教育和拓展方面的国际领导者。它拥有来自世界上几乎所有国家的1 500多名会员。年会在初秋举行，学术会议上挤满了前来求知的学者，青少年特发性脊柱侧凸及其未知的病因仍然是他们关注的焦点。然而，目前重点已经转移到与老化有关的（退变性）脊柱畸形、早发性脊柱畸形和对以前无法手术的畸形的评估和治疗。由于面临更具难度和挑战性的脊柱畸形，同时病人和外科医生的期望值也越来越高，脊柱器械已将椎弓根螺钉作为内固定的首选。这始于20世纪80年代，此时外科医生意识到椎弓根螺钉能最完全地直接控制脊柱的位置和稳定性。然而，转型的势头却在20世纪90年代遇到了一个重要的监管障碍：当时美国食品药物监督管理局拒绝将椎弓根螺钉作为《联邦食品、药品和化妆品法案》1976年医疗器械修正案之前的设备进行商标注册和销售。超适应证的使用增加使得一些主要是腰腿痛问题的成年患者对治疗效果不满，他们通过法律诉讼索赔。由此引发了一场由公司、外科医生和专业学会（包括脊柱侧凸研究学会）作为被告的多地区诉讼。1995年1月，美国食品药品监督管理局通过510K监管流程批准了椎弓根螺钉的商标和销售，以适用于治疗重度脊柱滑脱症，这一僵局才逐渐被打破。这一突破也是基于1966年底哈灵顿开展的椎弓根螺钉研究工作，这项工作在哈灵顿档案中有记载。[6]最近，哈灵顿档案馆在2013年为美国食品药品监督管理局提供了依据510K监管流程批准非融合器械商标和销售所需的支持。[7]在20世纪70年代，人们不可能预见到哈灵顿的遗产对未来椎弓根螺钉和非融合器械监管的重要性。也许哈灵顿为保存自己的材料而付出巨大努力是他特殊天赋的另一种表现，即看到别人看不到的东西。

Study of the Harrington Archives leaves no doubt about his devotion to his Kansas roots and explains why he entrusted them to the University of Kansas Medical Center

Archives. A number of Harrington legacy developments have occurred at his alma mater in the 35 years since his death. The Mary Alice and Paul R. Harrington Distinguished Professor of Orthopedic Surgery is now in its second generation as H. Clarke Anderson, MD (1990–2011) has been succeeded by Jinxi Wang, MD, PhD (2011–present). *See figure 1*. The laboratory's name, Harrington Laboratory for Molecular Orthopedics, reflects the couple's wish for its focus. The Harrington Archives displays, which opened in 1986, have welcomed over 1,000 visitors. Retired Zimmer Chief Engineer Jim Hite, who was so vital to the instrumentation system, visited in 1994. *See figure 2*. In 2005 the Harrington Spine Symposium commemorating the twenty-fifth anniversary of his death was attended by over 100 registrants from 17 countries.[8] Best presentation awards were presented to John Fowles, Canada, Humanities; Alain Moreau, Canada, Basic Science; Jack CY Cheng, Hong Kong, Clinical Science; and Hans Möller, Sweden, Clinical Practice.

哈灵顿档案毫无疑问地表明了他对故乡堪萨斯州的热爱，并解释了他将这些档案材料委托给堪萨斯大学医学中心档案馆的缘由。在他去世后的35年里，他的母校见证了许多哈灵顿遗产的发展。玛丽·艾丽斯和保罗·R. 哈灵顿骨科杰出教授现已延续到第二代，H. 克拉克·安德森医学博士（1990—2011）已由王金熙博士（2011年至今）接任。（图1）实验室的名称“哈灵顿分子骨科实验室”反映了哈灵顿夫妇对实验室研究重点的期望。1986年开放的哈灵顿陈列馆已经接待了超过1 000名参观者。对脊柱器械研发至关重要的捷迈公司退休总工程师吉姆·海特于1994年来访。（图2）2005年，来自17个国家的100多名注册者参加为纪念哈灵顿逝世25周年而举办的哈灵顿脊柱研讨会。[8]最佳演讲奖颁发给了加拿大的约翰·福尔斯（人文）和阿兰·莫罗（基础科学），以及中国香港的郑振耀（临床科学）和瑞典的汉斯·莫勒（临床实践）。

Figure 1 ***Harrington Distinguished professors A. H Clarke Anderson, MD; B. Jinxi Wang, MD PhD.*** (***Harrington Archives***)

图1 哈灵顿杰出教授。A. H. 克拉克·安德森，医学博士；B. 王金熙，医学博士，哲学博士（哈灵顿档案馆）

Figure 2 ***Zimmer Chief Engineer Jim Hite.*** (***Harrington Archives***)

图2 捷迈公司总工程师吉姆·海特（哈灵顿档案馆）

If Harrington were alive today, he would be pleased with the advances being made in growth modulation by mechanical means, both delayed fusion and especially non-fusion techniques. He would probably be disappointed though not surprised that no one had yet connected the pieces of the idiopathic scoliosis puzzle that fascinated him. His mouse experiment suggested that large postural scoliosis would resolve if the cause of the scoliosis, tethering of the fore and hind limb of the same side, was removed, and growth remained. His "Missing Link" case report suggested the same for structural scoliosis, the scoliosis cause being asymmetrically delayed neurological development. His collaboration with Enneking suggested "that the deformity is produced by an extra-osseous cause and that the changes in bone and cartilage are secondary adaptations." Someday the idiopathic scoliosis problem and the right person will be in the situation to finally fit together the pieces of the idiopathic scoliosis puzzle.

如果哈灵顿今天还活着，他会为力学手段对生长调控技术发展的作用感到高兴，这包括延迟融合技术，特别是非融合技术。但是也有可能让他感到失望，这也不足为奇，因为还没有人把令他着迷的特发性脊柱侧凸的方方面面研究透彻。他的小鼠实验表明，如果脊柱侧凸的原因是同侧前肢和后肢的栓系，栓系被解除，小鼠可以继续生长，那么即使较大的姿势性脊柱侧凸也能得到恢复。他的“缺失环节”案例报告认为结构性脊柱侧凸的原因也是不对称的神经发育迟缓。他与恩内金的合作表明，“畸形是由骨外原因造成的，骨骼和软骨的变化只是二次适应”。终有一天，特发性脊柱侧凸的谜题将会被合适的人于某种特定情况下解决。

Vem Nickel had a way with words, and people too for that matter. He had a lot of fun with orthoneering engipedics, as he tried to increase interest in orthopedic engineering. So it is probably safe to assume that he at least smiled, if not whooped, when he came up with dogged persistence to describe Paul Harrington's personality. How right can you get!

弗农·尼克尔巧于言辞，善于交际。当他试图增加人们对矫形外科工程的兴趣时，他同样从矫形工程中的工程矫形学获得了很多乐趣。因此，当他用锲而不舍来描述保罗·哈灵顿的个性时，可以肯定地说，如果哈灵顿没有欢呼的话，至少会笑着说：“你说得太对了！”

（朱剑 译　郑召民 邝冠明 刘辉 审校）

NOTES
注 释

The Paul R. Harrington Archives (HA), located in the University of Kansas Medical Center Archives, houses many of the primary resources and unpublished works cited in *Dogged Persistence*. For these materials, additional location information is included in the footnotes as a suffix.

位于堪萨斯大学医学中心档案馆的保罗·R. 哈灵顿档案馆（HA）收藏了许多在《锲而不舍》中引用的主要资源和未发表的作品。对于这些材料，额外的位置信息作为后缀包括在脚注中。

Boxed materials are cited as HA#: Folder #; Page # (e.g., HA 124: 1; 5-7).

方框中的材料引用为 HA#：文件夹#；页号（例如，HA 124：1；5-7）。

More than one box under the same number is cited as HA #/# (e.g., HA 144/2: 5; 3,9).

相同数字下的多个方框被引用为 HA#/#（例如，HA 144/2：5；3、9）。

Added folders are identified by a lower case letter (e.g., HA 106: 4a; 5-7). Page numbers are only provided if necessary to find the sources.

添加的文件夹用小写字母标识（例如 HA 106：4a；5-7）。页码只在必要时提供，以查找来源。

The HA contains a number of privately bound volumes (BV), including two yearly series: *Scoliosis* followed by the year (*1962* through *1972*) and "Bound Travel Arrangements" (BTA) followed by the year (*1961* through *1967*). These volumes and their contents are cited in the unpublished category, and if additional information is needed to locate the source, the order of suffix is HA: BV or BTA; page or other description as needed (e.g., HA: BV; Chapter 3, 10-12 or HA: BV; *Scoliosis 1966*, section 2, or HA: BTA; 1961).

哈灵顿档案包含了一些私人装订的卷（BV），包括两个年度系列：脊柱侧凸之后的年份（1962 年至 1972 年）和“绑定旅行安排”（BT）之后的年份（1961 年至 1967 年）。这些卷及其内容被引用在未发表的类别中，如果需要额外的信息来定位来源，后缀的顺序是 HA：BV 或 BTA；页或其他需要的描述（例如，HA：BV；第 3 章，10—12 或 HA：BV；脊柱侧凸 1966，第 2 节，或 HA：BTA；1961）。

Unpublished materials in loose-leaf notebooks (LLNB) are cited as HA: LLNB; page (eg, HA: LLNB; 3).

活页笔记本（LLN）中未发表的材料被引用为 HA：LLNB；页（例如，HA：LLNB；3）.

The Collected Writings of Paul Randall Harrington (CW) was published in 1992 and contains 35 of his 38 publications. For the out-of-print or difficult to find, a suffix has been added to the footnote as CW: PRH; page.

《保罗·兰德尔·哈灵顿文集》（CW）出版于 1992 年，收录了他 38 部著作中的 35 部。对于绝版或难以找到的，脚注已加后缀为 CW：PRH；页。

The Harrington Spine Symposium (HSS) is cited as HSS: LLNB; page.

哈灵顿脊柱研讨会（HSS）被引用为 HSS：LLNB；页。

Harrington Research Notebooks are cited as HRN: volume; page.

哈灵顿研究笔记本被引用为 HRN：卷；页。

The Scoliosis Research Society (SRS) Archives are located in the University of Kansas Medical Center Archives. References to the SRS Archives are cited as SRS: folder; page. Larger materials are located as box SRS: tub (e.g., SRS 33: 3).

脊柱侧凸研究学会档案馆位于堪萨斯大学医学中心档案馆。脊柱侧凸研究学会档案的参考文献被引用为 SRS：文件夹；页。较大的材料位于箱 SRS：桶（例如，SRS 33：3）。

Many important SRS annual meeting presentations were never published as full length scientific papers, but these sources are available: (1) Abstracts of all the annual meetings except the first in 1976, although it is well documented by Secretary William J. Kane's minutes (e.g., SRS 1:1). Abstracts for the second through eighth meetings, 1967-73, were published in the following year in *JBJS Am*. From 1974 on the abstracts were printed with the annual program. From 1977 through 1999, beginning with the 1976 meetings, extended abstracts were published by *JBJS Am* as separate volumes titled *Orthopedic Transactions*. (2) Transcribed recordings of the third through fifth meetings in 1968-70. Unbound copies are located in the SRS Archives and bound copies in the Harrington Archives. These are rich sources of additional information and dialogue that for the sake of brevity are not always cited in the footnotes. When they are, the suffix guide to this material in general is SRS Proceedings: 1968, 69, or 70; location.

许多重要的脊柱侧凸研究学会年会报告从未作为完整的科学论文发表，但这些来源是可用的：(1) 除了 1976 年的第一次，所有年会的摘要都被威廉·J. 凯恩秘书很好地记录了下来（例如，SRS 1：1）。1967 年到 1973 年第二次到第八次会议的摘要在第二年发表在《骨与关节外科杂志》（美国卷）上。从 1974 年起，摘要与年度计划一起印刷。1977 年到 1999 年，从 1976 年会议开始，《骨与关节外科杂志》（美国卷）将扩展的摘要作为单独的卷出版，名为《骨科汇刊》。(2) 1968—1970 年第三至第五次会议的笔录。未装订的副本存放在脊柱侧凸研究学会档案馆，装订的副本存放在哈灵顿档案馆。这些都是补充信息和对话的丰富来源，为了简洁起见，脚注中并不总是引用这些信息和对话。如果是，该材料的后缀指向通常是脊柱侧凸研究学会会议记录：1968，69 或 70；位置。

（朱剑 陈凡 译　郑召民 刘宏建 朱泽章 审校）

References
参考文献

PREFACE

1. Barbara W. Tuchman, *Practicing History* (New York: Alfred A. Knopf, 1981), 9.

2. Paul R. Haringion, "The Human Spine" (unpublished material, 1975 – 1980). HA 47: Preface.

CHAPTER 1

1. Paul R. Harington, " Harington Instrumentation for Treatment of Unslable Deformities of the Human Spine" (paper presented at Peter T. Bohan Lecture, Kansas Ciy, MO, May 10, 1975).HA 101: 23; 1. HA: BV.

2. Joseph H. McDowell, *Building a City: A Detailed History of Kansas Ciy, Kansas* (Kansas City, KS: Kasis Ciry Kansan, 1969), 10. HA 122/3: 12.

3. "Missouri River," accessed June 5, 2013, Wikipedia, http://en.wikipedia.org/wiki/Missouri_river.

4."Kansas River," aeeessed June 5, 2013, Wikipedia, http://en.wikipedia. org/wiki/Kansas_River.

5. "Lewis and Clark Expedition," accessed June 5, 2013, Wikipedia, http://en.wikipedia. org/wiki/Lewis_and_Clark_expedition.

6. " Louisiana Purchase," accessed September 18, 2013, Wikipedia, http//en.wikipedia.org/wiki/Louisiana_Purchase.

7. " Arabia Steamboat Museum," accessed May 24, 2013, Wikipedia, http//en.wikipedia.org/wiki/Arabia Steamboat.

8. Grant W. Harrington, *Historic Spots or Mile-Stones in the Progress of Wyandotte Couny, Kansas* (Merriam. KS: The Mission Press. 1935), 138.

9. "Kansas River."

10. "History of the Kansas City Metropolitan Area," accessed June 3, 2013, Wikipedia, http://cn.wikipedia.org/wiki/ History_of Kansns_City.

11. Harrington, *Historic Spots in Wyandotte County*, 113–14.

12. McDowell, *Building a Ciy*, 1.

13. Harrington, *Historic Spots in Wyandotte County*, 105, 133–44.

14. lbid., 238.

15. Nicole Elcheson, *Bleeding Kansas: Contested Liberty in the Civil War Era* (Lawrence. KS: University Press of Kansas, 2004), 89.

16. Harrington, *Historic Spots in Wyandotte County*, 182,191.

17. Charles P. Deatherage, *Early History of Greater Kansas Ciy Misouri and Kansas; The Prophetic City at the Mouth of the Kaw*, vol. 1 (Kansas City, MO: Charles P. Deatherage, 1928), 697.

18. Harrington, *Historic Spots in Wyandotte County*, 238–40.

19. Eicheson, *Bleeding Kansas*, 205–06.

20. "American Civil War," accessed November 27, 2013, Wikipedia. http://en.wikipedia.org/wiki/American_Civil_War.

21. Eicheson, *Beeding Kausas*, 219–45.

22. McDowell, *Building a City*, 2.

23. Ibid., 7.

24. Ibid., 18–19.

25. Joe H. Vaughan, *Kansas City: Kansas* (Charleston, SC: Areadia Puhlishing, 2012), 11.

26. McDowell, *Building a City*, 9.

27. "Gustavus Franklin Swift," accessed May 21, 2013, Wikipedia, http://en.wikipedia.org/wiki/Gustavus_Franklin_Swift.

28. McDowell, *Building a Ciy*, 9.

29. "How K C Became 1 of the Great Stock Markets of World," accessed June 3, 2013, http:/kckl. ent. sirsi. net/custom/web/content/kscollection/kckthenandnow/howkcbecane. pdf.

30. Eicheson, *Beeding Kausas*, 249–53.

31. Harrington, *Historic Spots in Wyandotte County*, 237–47.

32. "History of the Kansas City Metropolitan Area."

33. Laura H. Haringion, "Recollections of Laura Harrington" (unpublished

material, 1933-39). HA 122/2: 3.

34. "Harrington Genealogy" (unpublished material, 1911-80). HA 103: 5 and 6.

35. One guinea equals one pound and one shilling.

36. Harington, "Recollections L. H." HA 122/12: 3; 34-35.

37. Ibid.

38. "Harrington Genealogy," HA 102: 5; 1.

39. Ibid., 8.

40. Harrington, "Recollections L. H." HA 122/2: 3; 2.33

41. "Harrington Genealogy," HA 102: 5; 2-3.

42. Ms, Ray Lloyd, "Feture Story About Mrs. Laura H. Harington," *The Journal of the Kansas City Stoke*, February. 1938. HA 102: 7.

43. Harrington, "Recollections L. H." HA 122/2: 3; 2.

44. Ibid.

45. Ibid., 34.

46. Laura died of heart failure as age 59 or 60. Additional information is nat available. 47. Harrington, "Recollections L. H." HA 122/2: 3; 4.

48. "Romance in Old School," Kansas City Star, May 19, 1921. HA 102: 7.

49. Harrington, "Recollections L. H." HA 122/2: 3; 4.

50. Ibid., 24.

51. Lloyd, "Mrs. Laura H. Harington." HA 102:7.

52. Ibid.

53. Harrington, "Recollections L. H." HA 122/72: 3; 29.

54. "Harrington Genealogy," HA 102: 5; 9.

55. Harrington, "Recollections L. H." HA 1222: 3; 5.

56. Ibid., 5, 7.

57. Ibid., 6.

58. "Harrington Genealogy," HA 102: 5; 1.

59. Harrington, "Recollections L. H." HA 122/2: 3; 5-6.

60. Ibid., 28-29.

61. Marjorie Sollee, "A History of Wyandotte High School," aceessed June 7, 2013, http://www.kckps.org/disthistory/pdf%20files/wy_hs_history_msallee.pdf. HA 122/3: 12; 1.

62. Ibid., 1-3.

63. Ibid., 3,6-8,10.

64. "Plessy v. Ferguson" accesed June 7, 2013, wikipedia. http://en.wikipedia.org/wiki/Plessy_v_Ferguson.

65. DavidJ. Peavler, "Drawing the Color Line in Kansas Ciy: The Creation of Sumner High School," *Kansas History: A Journal of the Central Plains* 27 (Autumn 2005). HA 122/3: 12.

66. Ibid.

67. Ralph H. Major, *An Account of the University of Kansas School of Medicine* (Kansas City. KS: Univarsity of Kansas Medical Alumni Association, 1968), 1.

CHAPTER 2

1. Laurm H. Harrington, "Recollections of Laura Harrington" (unpublished material, 1933-39). HA 122/2: 3; 47. Junior high track coach's opinion of Paul's importance, ca. 1924.

2. Theodore Don Carlos Fowler, oral history to Eugene W. I. Pearce, August 7, 1997, HA 144/2: 2; 8.

3. Harrington, "Recollections L. H." HA 122/2: 3; 1-51.

4. Ibid., 12.

5. Ibid., 36.

6. lbid., 36-37.

7. Ibid., 43-45.

8. Ibid., 43.

9. Ibid., 38.

10. Ibid., 37.

11. "Miscellaneous Biographical Material" (unpublished material, 1911-80). HA 149: 1; 2.

12. Harrington, "Recollections L. H." HA 122: 3; 8.

13. Ibid., 21-24, 28, 30.

14. Ibid., 46.

15. lbid., 7-8.

16. Ibid., 43.

17. Ibid., 45-46.

18. "Miscellaneous Biographical Material." HA 149: l; 3-4.

19. Harrington, "Recollections L. H." HA 122/2: 3; 38.

20. Ibid., 39-40.

21. "Miscellaneous Biographical Material." HA 149: 1; 5-8.

22. Ibid., 10.

23. Ibid.

24. Harrington, "Recollections L. H." HA 122/2: 3; 40.

25. Ibid., 47.

26. "Teacher's Removal Is Again Prolested & Fire on School Board," *Kansas City Star*, ca. 1927. HA 102: 7.

27. Morjorie Sallec, "A History of Wyandote High School." aecessed Junc 7, 2013, http://www.kckps.org /disthistory/pdf%20fledwy_hs_history_msallee pdf. HA 122/3: 12;1.

28. Patricia Adams, "The History of Our Public Schools: Wyandotte County, Kansas (1844—2012)," accessed May 23, 2013, Kansas City Kansas Public Schools, http://www. kckps.org/dischistory/.

29. "Miscellaneous Biographical Material." HA 149: 1; 13.

30. Ibid. HA 140: 2; 4.

31. Ibid., 6-8.

32. Ibid., 2.

33. Harrington, "Recollections L. H." HA 122/2: 3; 38.

34. Ibid., 46.

35. Ibid., 46-47.

36. Ibid., 42.

37. "Miscellaneous Biographical Material." HA 149: 2; 3, 13.

38. Ibid. HA 149: 1; 12, 14.

39. Bess Helwig, letter to Laura Harrington. 1930. HA 122/2: 3; 9-10.

40. "Miscellaneous Biographical Material." HA 149: 2; 22.

41. Ibid., 10.

42. Ibid. HA 149: 1; 13.

43. Ibid. HA 149: 2; 22.

44. Helwig, 1930.

45. "Miscellaneous Biographical Material." HA 149: 2; 14.

46. Ibid., 22.

47. Ibid., 4.

48. Ibid., 20.

49. Ibid., 18-19.

50. Harrington, "Recollections L. H." HA 122/2: 3; 45.

51. Helwig, 1930.

52. "Miscellaneous Biographical Material." HA 149: 2; 23.

53. Ibid., 17.

54. Ibid., 22.

55. Ibid., 25-26.

56. Harrington, "Recollections L. H." HA 122/2: 3; 41.

57. "Miscellaneous Biographical Material." HA 149: 2; 12.

58. Harrington, "Recollections L. H." HA 122/2: 3; 44.

59. Ibid., 42.

60. "Miscellaneous Biographical Material." HA 149: 2; 22.

61. Representative U. S. Guyer, letter to Paul R. Harrington in re Annapolis application. September 27, 1929. HA 149: 1; 16.

62. "Miscellaneous Biographical Material." HA 149: 1; 19.

63. Don Pierce, *Basketball at the University of Kansas*. 1956-57 (Lawrence, KS: University of Kansas. 1956). HA 122/3: 15; 4.

64. "Miscellaneous Biographical Material." HA 149: 4; 4.

65. Ibid., 3.

66. Ibid., 14.

67. Ibid., 18.

68. Ibid., 19.

69. Ibid., 18

70. Ibid. HA 149: 5; 16.

71. Unknown, "Thy Rod anl Thy Staff" (unpublished material. later 1960s). HA 102: 1; 5.

72. "Miscellaneous Biographical Material." HA 149: 1; 19.

73. Ibid. HA 149: 6; 17.

74. Ibid. HA 149: 5; 8.

75. Ibid., 7.

76. Ibid., 3.

77. Ibid., 16.
78. Ibid. HA 149: 4; 19.
79. Ibid. HA 149: 5; 4–5.
80. Ibid.
81. Ibid., 16.
82. Ibid. HA 149: 6; 9.
83. Ibid.
84. Ibid.
85. Ibid.
86. Ibid., 15.
87. Ibid. HA 149: 7; 24.
88. Ibid. HA 149: 6; 19.
89. Ibid., 26.
90. Ibid., 29.
91. Ibid., 18.
92. Harrington, "Recollections L. H." HA 122/2: 3; 13.
93. Ibid., 15–16.

CHAPTER 3

1. Max Allen, *Medicine under Canvas: The 77th Evacuation Hospital* (Kansas City, MO: The Sosland Press, Inc., 1949), 168–69. Characteristics of the United States Army's 750 bed/cot 77th Evacuation Hospital. European Theater of Operations, 5 August 1942–June 1945.

2. Stanley R. Friesen and Robert P. Hudson, *The Kansas School of Medicine: Eyewitness Reflections on Its Formative Years* (Kansas City, KS: University of Kansas School of Medicine, 1996), 1–2.

3. Helen M. Sims, *Simeon Bishop Bell, M.D.* (Kansas City, KS: University of Kansas Medical Center, 1979). HA 122/3: 14; 1–5.

4. Margaret Landis, *The Winding Valley and the Craggy Hillside: A History of the City of Rosedale, Kansas* (Kansas City, KS: Landis, 1976).

5. Sims, *Simeon Bell, M.D.*, 5–8.

6. Ralph H. Major, *An Account of the University of Kansas School of Medicine* (Kansas City. KS: University of Kansas Medical Alumni Association, 1963), 2–3.

7. Sims, *Simeon Bell, M.D.*, 9.

8. Friesen, *Kansas School of Medicine*, 3–6.

9. Sims, *Simeon Bell, M.D*, 9–2.

10. Friesen, *Kansas School of Medicine*, 6–8.

11. Major, *An Account*, 85–91.

12. "Bachelor of Arts" (diploma, University of Kansas, 1935). HA 116.

13. Jesse H. Dickson, "Paul Randall Harrington: His Life and Work" (paper presented at Hixon Hour, video recorded and transcribed lecture, Kansas City, KS, January 15, 1998). HA 146: 2; 6.

14. Harold L. Patterson and Alice Patterson, letter to Mary Alice Harrington. May 29, 1991. HA 122/3: 3.

15. "Miscellaneous Biographical Material." HA 149: 8; 2.

16. Paul R. Harrington, oral history to Robert B. Keller and Jesse H. Dickson, May 21, 1980. HA 144/1: 17; 6.

17. Ibid., 9.

18. Major, *An Account*, 64–65.

19. Paul R. Harrington, "The Adrenal Cortex" (junior medical school thesis, University of Kansas, 1937). HA 101: 7.

20. Paul R. Harrington, "The Therapeutic Value of Cevitamic Acid" (senior medical school thesis, University of Kansas 1938). HA 101: 7.

21. "Ascorbic Acid," accessed July 24, 2014, Wikipedia, http://en.wikipedia.org/wiki/Ascorbic_acid.

22. "Doctor of Medicine" (diploma, University of Kansas, 1938). HA 116.

23. Frederick E. Reed, Jr., letter with enclosures to Marc A. Asher, January 16, 1997. HA 144/1: 13.

24. "Charleston, South Carolina Years" (unpublished material, 1938–40). HA 101: 14.

25. Ibid.

26. Reed, January 16, 1997. HA 144/1: 13.

27. "Charleston Years."

28. Paul R. Harrington, letter to Mrs. Laura Harrington, 1938–39. HA 122/1: 17.

29. Laura Harrington, "My Garden" (unpublished material, 1939). HA 122/1: 17.

30. Paul R. Harrington, letter to Laura Harrington, June 3, 1939. HA 122/1: 17.

31. Unknown, "Thy Rod and Thy Staff." HA 102: 1.

32. Paul R. Harrington, "Reaction to Laura Harrington's Death" (unpublished material, 1939). HA 122/2: 3A; 53.

33. Harrington, "Recollections L.H." 21–25.

34. Harrington, "Reaction to L. H. Death," 54.

35. Ibid.

36. "Marriage License and Endorsement" (State of Kansas, 1939). HA 102: 5; 12.

37. "Harrington Genealogy" (unpublished material, 1911–80). HA 102: 5; 6.

38. Harrington, "Reaction to L. H. Death," 57.

39. Rex L. Diveley, letter to Paul R. Harrington, January 29, 1940. HA 101: 5.

40. Paul R. Harrington, "Diary of Paul Harrington" (unpublished material, 1940–74). HA 122/2: 4; 1.

41. Ibid., 3.

42. Ibid., 3–4.

43. Ibid., 5.

44. Ibid., 7–10.

45. Ibid., 12–13.

46. Ibid., 11.

47. Ibid., 16, 18, 21.

48. Ibid., 17.

49. Ibid., 16.

50. Ibid., 22.

51. *Encyclopaedia Britannica*, 15th ed. s.v. "World War II."

52. Harrington, "Diary of Paul Harrington." HA 122/2: 4; 23.

53. Ibid., 22.

54. Ibid.

55. Ibid., 24.

56. There are two, completely unrelated men with the last name Dickson important to this story. Frank Dickson played an earlier role and Jesse Dickson a later role with no overlap between the two. If there is any possibility of confusing the two, the first name initial will be added.

57. Rex L. Diveley, "Obituary: Frank D. Dickson 1882—1964," *J Bone Joint Surg Am* 46 (1964). HA 103/2: 2a.

58. "Dr. Frank Dickson Dies at Age of 81," *Kansas City Star*. January 19, 1964. HA 103/2: 2a.

59. "Rex L. Diveley, M.D.," *AAOS Bulletin*, September 1978. HA 103/2: 2b.

60. Mervin T. Sudler, nomination for faculty appointment of Frank D. Dickson to Kansas University Chancellor, July 17, 1917.

61. "Rex L. Diveley. M.D."

62. Richard H. Kiene, "Obituary: Rex L. Diveley, M.D. (1892—1980)," *Greater Kansas City Med Bull* 76 (1981). HA 103/2: 2b.

63. Rex L. Diveley, "Anterior Poliomyelitis: A Study of the Acute Stage with Special Reference to the Early Diagnosis and Treatment," *J Bone Joint Surg* 11 (1929).

64. Trend analysis using the multiple linear regression technique by Sue Min Lai. PhD. p=0.0281.

65. JamesJ. Hamilton, "History of the Dickson-Diveley Clinic" (unpublished material. 2012). HA 103/2: 3.

66. Thornton Brown, *The American Orthopaedic Association: A Centennial History* (Chicago: AOA, 1987), 31.

67. Frank D. Dickson, "Presidential Address: American Academy of Orthopaedic Surgeons," *J Bone Joint Surg* 18(1936).

68. Frank D. Dickson, "Presidential Address: American Orthopaedic Association," *J Bone Joint Surg* 22 (1940).

69. Kiene, "Obituary: Rex L. Diveley. M.D. (1892—1980)."

70. Harrington, "Diary of Paul Harrington." HA 122/2: 4; 24.

71. Ibid., 24-25.

72. Ibid., 28.

73. Ibid., 16.

74. "Sulfonamide (Medicine)," accessed March 15, 2014, Wikipedia, http://en.wikipedia.org/wiki/Sulfonamide_%28medicine%29.

75. Carol Ballentine, "Taste of Raspberries, Taste of Death: The 1937 Elixir Sulfanilamide Incident," accessed July 31, 2014, U.S. Food and Drug Administration, http://www. fda. gov/AboutFDA/WhatWeDo/History/ProductRegulation/SulfanilamideDisaster/default.htm.

76. J. Albert Key, Charles J. Frankel, and Thomas H. Burford, "The Local Use of Sulfanilamide in Various Tissues," *J Bone Joint Surg* 22 (1940). HA 103/5.

77. Willis C. Campbell and Hugh Smith, "Sulfanilamide and Internal Fixation in the Treatment of Compound Fractures," *J Bone Joint Surg* 22 (1940). HA 103/5.

78. Richard A. Brand, "The Use of Sulfathiazole in the Treatment of Subacute and Chronic Osteomyelitis: Frank 4. Dickson MD (1882—1964), Rex L. Diveley MD, Richard Kiene MD. The4th President of the AAOS 1935 (FDD)," *Clin Orthop Relat Res* 466 (2008). HA 103/5.

79. Frank D. Dickson, Rex L. Diveley, and Richard Kiene, "The Use of Sulfathiazole in the Treatment of Subacute and Chronic Osteomyelitis." *J Bone Joint Surg Am* 22(1941). HA 117: 1.

80. Rex L. Diveley and Paul R. Harrington, "Chemotherapy in Infections of the Bones and Soft Tissues," *JAMA* 117(1941), HA 108: 2.

81. Charles S. Venable and Walter G. Stuck, *Internal Fixation of Fractures* (Springfield. IL: Charles C. Thomas. 1947), 54-58.

82. Harrington, "Diary of Paul Harrington." HA 122/2: 4; 30-31.

83. Ibid., 280.

84. EllaIrene Miller (Buhler), oral history to Eugene W. J. Pearce, August 14, 1997. HA 144/2: 4.

85. Paul R. Harrington, "Curriculum Vitae" (unpublished material, 1974). HA 101: 2.

86. *Encyclopaedia Britannica*, 15th ed., s.v. "World War II."

87. Allen, *Medicine under Canvas*, 9-10.

88. Ibid., 1.

89. Ibid.

90. Oscar P. Hampton, Wounds of the Extremities in Military Surgery (S1. Louis: C. V. Mosby, 1951), 21-48.

91. Zachary B. Friedenberg, *Hospital at War: The 95th Evacuation Hospital in World War-ll* (College Station, TX: Texas A&M University Press, 2004), 20.

92. Allen, Medicine under Canvas, 1.

93. Ibid., 15-16.

94. Ibid., 25.

95. *Encyclopaedia Britannica*, 15th ed., s.v. "World War II."

96. Ibid.

97. Allen, *Medicine under Canvas*, 26.

98. Ibid., 29–30.

99. Ibid., 32.

100. Ibid., 33–34.

101. Paul R. Harrington, "World War II Patient Documentation" (unpublished material. 1942–44). HA 101:10.

102. Allen, *Medicine under Canvas*, 34–36.

103. Ibid., 36–38.

104. *Encyclopaedia Britannica*, 15th ed., s.v. "World War II."

105. Harrington, "Curriculum Vitae." HA 101:2.

106. Harrington, "Patient Documentation." HA 101:10.

107. Allen, *Medicine under Canvas*, 44.

108. Ibid., 44–56.

109. Ibid., 56–58.

110. Ibid., 58–63.

111. Harrington, "Patient Documentation." HA 10l: 10.

112. *Encyclopaedia Britannica*, 15th ed., s.v. "World War II."

113. Allen, *Medicine under Canvas*, 63–64.

114. Harrington, "Patient Documentation." HA 10l: 10.

115. Allen, *Medicine under Canvas*, 65.

116. Ibid., 62–63.

117. Ibid., 66, 68–69.

118. Harrington, "Patient Documentation." HA 101: 10.

119. Allen, *Medicine under Canvas*, 70–71.

120. Ibid., 71–74, 99–101.

121. *Encyclopaedia Britannica*, 15th ed., s.v. "World War II."

122. Allen, *Medicine under Canvas*, 74.

123. Ibid., 75.

124. Ibid., 81.

125. Ibid., 85.

126. Ibid., 86–88.

127. *Encyclopaedia Britannica*, 15th ed., s.v. "World War II."

128. Allen, *Medicine under Canvas*, 89.

129. Ibid., 90–92.

130. Ibid., 93.

131. Ibid., 94–99.

132. Ibid., 99–101.

133. Paul R. Harrington, "Orthopedic Surgery in an Evacuation Hospital: Lecture Manuscript" (unpublished material, 1944). HA 101: 10.

134. Rex L. Diveley, letter to Paul R. Harrington, February 24, 1944. HA 101: 10.

135. Paul R. Harrington, letter to Rex L. Diveley, February 26, 1944.

136. Hampton, *Military Surgery*, 94–101.

137. William Waugh, *John Charnley: The Man and the Hip* (London: Springer-Verlag, 1990),21–25.

138. John Charnley, "Fractures of the Femoral Shaft: Mechanics of Reduction and Fixation." Lancet 1 (1944).

139. *Encyclopaedia Britannica*, 15th ed., s.v. "World War II."

140. Harrington, February 26, 1944.

141. Hampton, *Military Surgery*, 94–101.

142. Allen, *Medicine under Canvas*, 101–04.

143. Ibid., 104–05.

144. Ibid., 105–06.

145. Ibid., 124. This seems illogical as the total tonnage of the two options is very different, 300 versus 750. But the citation is correct.

146. Ibid., 111–15.

147. Ibid., 117–18.

148. Ibid., 121.

149. Ibid., 122–23.

150. Ibid., 126.

151. Ibid., 135.

152. Ibid., 139.

153. Ibid., 141.

154. Ibid., 142–43.

155. Ibid., 146–47.

156. Ibid., 143.

157. "Malmedy Massacre," accessed September 17, 2014, Wikipedia, http://en.wikipedia.org/wiki/Malmedy_massacre.

158. Allen, *Medicine under Canvas*, 141-48.

150. Ibid., 153.

160. Ibid., 156.

161. Ibid., 151-53.

162. Ibid., 159-60.

163. Ibid., 160-63.

164. Ibid., 164. Credited to Snow Job, the newspaper of the 610th Ordnance.

165. Ibid., 166-67.

166. Harrington, May 21.1980. HA 144/1: 17; 11.

167. Allen, *Medicine under Canvas*, 170.

168. Ibid.

169. Ibid.

170. Ibid., 168-69.

171. John R. Paul, "Poliomyelitis Attack Rates in American Troops (1940—1948)," *Amer J Hyg* 50 (1949).

172. William M. Kirby, "U. S. Army Separation Qualification Record" (unpublished material, 1945). HA 102: 10.

173. Hamilton, "Dickson-Diveley Clinic," HA 103/2: 3; 1.

174. Harrington, "Curriculum Vitae." HA 101: 2; 1.

175. Paul R. Harrington, "Early Beginnings of the Harrington Spinal Instrumentation" (unpublished material, 1977). HA: BV: 2.

CHAPTER 4

1. John R. Paul, *A History of Poliomyelitis* (Hartford, CT: Yale University, 1971), 158. Statement attributed to Professor C-E. A. Winslow of Yale University questioning Flexner's theory that polio is "a respiratory disease.

2. Russell A. Hibbs, "The Treatment of Deformities of the Spine Caused by Poliomyelitis: A Report of Eight Cases in Which Fusion Operations Were Performed," *JAMA* 69 (1917).

3. Robert W. Lovett, *Lateral Curvature of the Spine and Round Shoulders*

(Philadelphia: P. Blakiston's Son & Co., 1907).

4. Joseph C. Risser, "Scoliosis-Before Hibbs ond After" (paper presented at Post-graduate Course on the Management and Care of the Scoliosis Patient New York October 2-4. 1969).

5. Thomas M. Daniel, "The History of Tuberculosis," *Respir Med* 100 (2006).

6. Micheal Underwood, *A Treatise on the Diseases of Children with General Directions for the Management of Infants from the Birth*, 2nd ed. (London: Mathews, 1789).

7. Paul, *Poliomyelitis*, 20-25.

8. John Shaw, *On the Nature and Treatment of the Distortions to Which the Spine and the Bones of the Chest Are Subject* (London: Longman, Hurst, Rees, Orme. Brown, and Green, 1823). 30-47.

9. John Shaw, *Engravings, Illustrative of a Wonk on the Nature and Treatment of the Distortions to Which the Spine and the Bones of the Chest Are Subject* (London; Longman, Hurst, Rees, Orme Brown, and Green.1824), Plate IV.

10. Paul, *Poliomyelitis*, 30.

11. Ibid., 33.

12. Ibid., 54-55

13. Ibid., 30.

14. Ibid., 60.

15. Ibid., 64.

16. Ibid., 69.

17. Ibid., 38.

18. Ibid., 41, 43.

19. Frederick A. Packard, "Acute Anterior Poliomyelitis Occurring Simultaneously in a Brother and Sister; with Remarks Upon Its Etiology." *J Nerv Ment Dis* 26 (1879).

20. Paul, *Poliomyelitis*, 65, 72.

21. Karl Oskar Medin, "Ueber Eine Epidemie Von Spinaler Kinkerlahmung" (paper presented at Verh. X Internat. med. Kongr., Berlin.1890). As cited by John R. Paul, *A History of Poliomyelitis*, 74.

22. Paul, *Poliomyelitis*, 75-78.

23. Ibid., 58.

24. Charles S. Caverly, "Notes of an Epidemic of Acute Anterior Poliomyelitis," *JAMA* 26 (1896).

25. Paul, *Poliomyelitis*, 79-86.

26. Ivar Wickman, *Beitrage Zur Kenntnis Der Heine-MecdinschenKrankheit* (*Poliomyelitis Acuta Und Verwandrer Erkrankungen*) (Berlin: Karger, 1907). As cited by John R. Paul, *A History of Poliomyelitis*, 89.

27. Paul, *Poliomyelitis*, 88-97.

28. Karl Landsteiner and Erwin Poppet, "Mikroscopische Praparate Von Einem Menschlichen Und Zwei Affenruckenmarken," *Wien klin*, *Wschr*: 21 (1908).As cited by John R. Paul, *A History of Poliomyelitis*, 98.

29. Paul, *Poliomyelitis*, 93-103.

30. Ibid., 104-05.

31. Ibid., 107-25.

32. Ibid., 126-36.

33. Ibid., 243-45.

34. Ibid., 251.

35. Claude H. Lavinder, Allen W. Freeman, and Wade H. Frost, "Epidemiologic Studies of Poliomyelitis in New York City and the Northeastern United States During the Year 1916." *Publ Hlth Bull* (Wash) 91 (July 1918): 209-11.

36. Paul, *Poliomyelitis*, 150-53.

37. Lavinder, "Epidemiologic Studies," 214.

38. Paul, *Poliomyelitis*, 212.

39. Ibid., 212-24.

40. Ibid., 190-99.

41. Paul A. Offit, *The Cutter Incident*: *How America's Firsr Polio Vaccine Led to the Growing Vaccine Crisis* (New Haven, CT: Yale University Press, 2005), 14-18.

42. Paul, *Poliomyelitis*, 300-23.

43. Zachary B. Friedenberg, "Franklin D. Roosevelt: His Poliomyelitis and Orthopaedies," *J Bone Joint Surg Am* 91 (2009).

44. Paul, *Poliomyelitis*, 308-09.

45. David M. Oshinsky, *Polio*, *an American Story* (New York: Oxford University Press, 2005), 34-35.

46. Offit, *Cutter*, 19-20.

47. Ibid., 20.

48. Ibid., 24.

49. Oshinsky, *Polio, an American Story*, 58–60.

50. Philip Drinker and Louis A.Shaw, "Apparatus for Prolonged Administration of Artificial Respiration; Design for Adults and Children," *J Clin Invest* 7 (1929).

51. Paul, *Poliomyelitis*, 326.

52. John B. West, "The Physiological Challanges of the 1952 Copenhagen Poliomyelitis Epidemic and a Renaissance in Clinical Respiratory Physiology," *J Appl Physiol* 99 (2005).

53. David Bodian, "The Virus. the Nerve Coll. and Paralysis. A Study of Experimental Poliomyelitis in the Spinal Cord." *Bull Johns Hopkins Hospital* 83 (1948).

54. NFIP, *Poliomyelitis: Annual Statistical Review* (New York: NFIP, 1958). HA 122/4: 16. Graph and statistical analysis by Dr. Sue Min Lai.

55. Oshinsky, *Polio, an American Story*, 61–64.

56. Kenneth Kingery, *As I Live and Breathe* (New York: Grosset & Dunlap. 1966).

57. Kathryn Black, *In the Shadow of Polio* (Cambridge, MA: Perseus, 1996).

58. William J. Kane, *Let Yourself Be Loved: The Life and Letters of Will Jenks* (Saint Paul, MN: Syren Book Company, 2004).

59. Daniel J. Wilson, *Living with Polio: The Epidemic and Its Survivors* (Chicago: University of Chicago Press, 2005), 162–68.

60. Paul, *Poliomyelitis*. 60.

61. Paul H. Harmon, letter to the editor, *JAMA* 109 (1937): 1061.

62. Paul, *Poliomyelitis*. 280.

63. Ibid., 250.

64. Ibid., 157–58.

65. Joseph C Risser, "Important Practical Facts in the Treatment of Scoliosis," in *Instructional Course Lectures*, *AAOS* (Ann Arbor. MI: J. W. Edwards.1948).

66. Percivall Pott, "Remarks on That Kind of Palsy Frequently Found to Accompany Curvature of the Spine, and Is Supposed to Be Caused by It. Together with Its Method of Cure, 1779," in *Medical Classics*, vol. 1. no. 4. Emerson Crosby Kelly (Baltimore: Williams & Wilkins, 1936).

67. Robert B. Duthie and Albert B. Ferguson. Jr., *Mercer's Orthopedic Surgery*, 7th ed. (Baltimore: Williams and Wilkins, 1973). 565–69.

68. Fred H. Albee, "Transplantation of a Portion of the Tibia into the Spine for Pott's Disease," *JAMA* 57 (1911).

69. Russell A. Hibbs, "An Operation for Progressive Spinal Deformity. A Preliminary Report of Three Cases from the Service of the Orthopaedic Hospital" *N Y Med J* 93 (1911).

70. Ibid.

71. Albee, "Transplantation of a Portion of the Tibia."

72. Fritz Lange, "Support for the Spondylitic Spine by Means of Buried Steel Bars, Attached to the Vertebrae," *Am J Orthop Surg* 8 (1910).

73. Leon L. Wiltse, "The History of Spinal Disorders," in *The Adult Spine: Principles and Practice*, 2nd ed., ed. John W. Frymoyer (Philadelphia: Lippincott-Raven, 1997), 29.

74. Russell A. Hibbs, "Treatment of Vertebral Tuberculosis by Fusion Operation," *JAMA* 71 (1918).

75. Alan DeForest Smith, "Study of Autopsy Specimens of Fused Spines and of Cases Subjected to Secondary Operation," *J Bone Joint Surg* 5 (1923).

76. Russell A. Hibbs and Joseph C. Risser, "Treatment of Vertebral Tuberculosis by the Spine Fusion Operation: A Report of Two Hundred and Eighty-Six Cases: A Second Series." *J Bone Joint Surg* 10 (1928).

77. Fred H. Albee, "The Bone-Graft Operation for Tuberculosis of the Spine: Twenty Years' Experience," *JAMA* 94 (1930).

78. G. K. McKee, "Comparison of the Results of Spinal Fixation Operations and Non-Operative Treatment in Pott's Disease in Adults," *Br J Surg* 24 (1937).

79. PaulP. Swett, George E. Bennett, and Dang M. Street, "Pott's Disease: The Initial Lesion, the Relative Infrequency of Extension by Contiguity. the Nature and Type of Healing, the Role of the Abscess, and the Merits of Operative and Non-Operative Treatment," *J Bone Joint Surg* 22 (1940).

80. "Streptomycin," accessed November 24, 2014, Wikipedia, http://en.wikipedia.org/wiki/Streptomycin.

81. Gregory L. Armstrong, Laura A. Conn, and Robert W. Pinner, "Trends in Infectious Disease Mortality in the United States During the 20th Century," *JAMA* 281 (1999).

82, Paul, *Poliomyelitis*, 10, 79, 148.

83. Herbert P. H. Galloway, "The Treatment of Paralytic Scoliosis by Bone-Grafting," *Am J Ortho Surg* 212 (1914).

84. Herbert P. H. Galloway, "Discussion of A. Mackenzie Forbes," *J Bone Joint Surg* 2 (1920).

85. Hibbs, "Treatment of Deformities of the Spine."

86. Russell A. Hibbs, "A. Report of Fifty-Nine Cases of Scoliosis Tented by the Fusion Operation," *J Bone Joint Surg* 6 (1924).

87. Joseph C. Risser, interview by Robert B. Keller and B. Randolph Cockrell, May 23, 1980, videotape, SRS Archives.

88. Russell A. Hibbs, Joseph C. Risser, and Albert B. Ferguson, Scoliosis Treated by the Fusion Operation: An End-Result Study of Three Hundred and Sixty Cases," *J Bone Joint Surg* 13 (1931).

89. Alan Deforest Smith, Felix L. Butte. and Albert B. Ferguson, "Treatment of Scoliosis by the Wedging Jacket and Spine Fusion: A Review of 265 Cases," *J Bone Joint Surg* 20 (1938).

90. Joseph C. Risser et al, "Three Types of Body Casts," in Instructional Course Lectures. *AAOS* (Ann Arbor, MI: J. W. Edwards. 1953). Figure II.

91. Hibbs, "Scoliosis Treated by the Fusion Operation."

92. Joseph C. Risser and Albert B. Ferguson, "Scoliosis: Its Prognosis," *J Bone Joint Surg* 18 (1936).

93. Felix L. Butte, "Scoliosis Treated by the Wedging Jacket: Selection of the Area to Be Fused," *J Bone Joint Surg* 20 (1938).

94. Smith, "Wedging Jacket and Spine Fusion."

95. Alfred R. Shands, Jr. et al., "End-Result Study of the Treatment ofIdiopathic Scoliosis," *J Bone Joint Surg* 23 (1941).

96. Reginald H. Sayre, "The Treatment of Neglected Cases of Rotary Lateral Curvature of the Spine," *Trans N Y Med Assn* 9 (1892). HA: BV; Scoliosis 1964.

97. Henry Albert Reeves, *Bodily Deformities and Their Treatment: A Handbook of Practical Orthopaedics* (Philadelphia: P. Blakiston's Son & Co., 1885), 30.

98. Samuel Kleinberg, "The Operative Treatment of Scoliosis," *Arch Surg* 5 (1922).

99. Samuel Kleinberg, "The Results of Spine Fusion for Scoliosis," *J Bone Joint Surg* 11 (1929).

100. John R. Cobb, "Outline for the Study of Scoliosis," in *Instructional Course Lectures*, AAOS (Ann Arbor, M1: J. W. Edwards, 1948).

101. Shands, "End-Result Study."

CHAPTER 5

1. *A Very Special Place* (Houston, TX: TIRR, 1979). HA 122/7: 12; 5. Twentieth anniversary edition with Dean Emeritus Stanley Olson's recollection of the mood toward severe disability in 1950.

2. Vernon L. Nickel, oral history to Marc A. Asher, June 11, 1991. HA 144/1: 6; 14. Nickel recalling Harrington's position in the ortheopaedic hierarchy in the 1950s.

3. Edwin T. Smith, *History of Orthopaedic Surgery in Houston* (Austin, TX: Eakin Publications, 1983), 7-9.

4. Patrica L. Jakobi, "Foster, Joseph Beverly," accessed June 13, 2012, Texas State Historical Association, http://www.ishaonline.org/handbook/online/articles/ffo-44.

5. Paul R. Harrington, "Early History of Practice in Houston (Polio)" (unpublished material. 1974). HA 101: 40; 1.

6. *Poliomyelitis*, *Annual Statistical Review*, 1958. HA 122/4:16.

7. Sue Harrington Price, Randall Harrington, and Richard Harrington, "After Dinner Remarks for the Family" (paper presented at Harrington Spine Symposium, Kansas City, KS, July 30, 2005), HSS: LLNB; 122A.

8. Offit, *Cutter*, 54.

9. Harrington, "Early History of Practice in Houston." HA 101: 40;1.

10. William A. Spencer and Linda Pickle, "Paul R. Harrington, M.D., Recipient of the Cora and Webb Mading Medal," *The Promethean*, *August*, 1973. HA 101: 21.

11. Harrington, "Early Beginnings of the Harrington Spiral Instrumentation." HA: BV; 2.

12. Harrington, "Early History of Practice in Houston." HA 101: 40; 2.

13. Ibid., 2.

14. Ibid., 2-3.

15. M. Sanders, Y. Subbarow, and R. C. Alexander, "Effective Antiviral Synthetic," *Tex Rep Biol Med* 6 (1948).

16. Paul R. Harrington, "Chemotherapy and Poliomyelitis: The Use of Darvisul on Human Subjects," *Tex State J Med* 45 (1949).

17. Dickson, "Paul Randall Harrington: His Life and Work," 12.

18. Oshinsky, *Polio, an American Story*, 94.

19. Ibid., 112–15.

20. Ibid., 114–21.

21. Albert B. Sabin and Peter K. Olitsky, “Cultivation of Poliovirus in Vitro in Human Embryonic Tissue,” *Proc Soc Exp Biol Med* 34 (1936).

22. JohnF. Enders, Thomas H. Weller. and Frederick C.Robbins, “Cultivation of the Lansing Strain of Poliomyelitis Virus in Cultures of Various Human Tissues,” *Science* 109(1949).

23. Oshinsky, *Polio, an American Story*, 122.

24. Ibid., 124–25.

25. Ibid., 126.

26. Dorothy M. Horstmann, “Poliomyelitis in the Blood of Orally Infected Monkeys and Chimpanzees,”*Proc Soc Exp Biol Med* 79 (1952).

27. Dorothy M. Horstmann, R. W. McCollum, and A. D. Mascola, “Viremia in Human Poliomyelitis,” *J Exp Med* 99 (1954).

28. Offit, *Cutter*.

29. Harrington, “Curriculum Vitae,” 11.

30. Paul R. Harrington, “Standing Bed in Poliomyelitis,” *Phys Ther Rev* 32 (1952).

31. Paul R.Harrington, “Research Notebooks” (unpublished material, 1942–60). HRN: 1; 20–27.

32. Paul R. Harrington, “Bracing the Child’s Paralytic Foot,” *Southwest Med* 40 (1959).

33. Harrington, “Early History of Practice in Houston,” 3.

34. Harrington, May 21, 1980. HA 144/1: 17; 14.

35. Harrington, Early History of Practicen Houston,” 4.

36. Thomas Gucker III, “Changes in Respiratory Function with Scoliosis.” Abstract. *J Bone Joint Surg Am* 40 (1958).

37. C. D. Cook et al., “Pulmonary Physiology in Children: III. Lung Volumes, Mechanies of Respirtion and Respiratory Muscle Strength in Scoliosis,” *Pediatries* 25 (1960).

38. Harrington, May 21, 1980. HA 144/1:17;14.

39. Paul R. Harrington, “Well Documented Failure of Observarion”(unpublished

material, 1963). HA 130: 4a.

40. Harrington, "Research Notebooks." HRN :1; 28–32.

41. Harrington, "Early History of Practice in Houston," 4.

42. Harrington, "Early Beginnings of the Harrington Spinal Instrumentation," 10.

43. Harington, "Early History of Practice in Houston," 3–4.

44. Ibid., 4.

45. Harrington, "Research Notebooks." HRN: 1; 102.

46. Paul R. Harrington, "Treatment of Scoliosis: Correction and Internal Fixation by Spine Instrumentation," *J Bone Joint Surg Am* 44 (1962)

47. Don King, "Internal Fixation for Lumbosacral Fusion," *J Bone Joint Surg Am* 30 (1948).

48. Spencer, "Mading Medal," 2.

49. Vemon L. Nickel, "Reminiscences of Early Days of Dr Harrington's Work in Scoliosis" (unpublished material, 1974). HA 101: 22: 7.

50. Paul, *Poliomyelitis*, 331.

51. Harrington, "Early Beginnings of the Harrington Spinal Instrumentation," 5.

52. *Very Special Place*, 5.

53. Ibid.

54. Ruth SoRelle, "Dr. William Spencer: A Firm Believer That Medicine Can Rehabilitate," Houston Chronicle, September 14, 1987. HA 122/7: 11.

55. *Very Special Place*, 5.

56. Spencer, "Mading Medal," 2.

57. Ibid., 4.

58. L. K. Smith et al., "Muscle Testing: Part 1. Description of a Numerical Index for Clinical Research," *Phys Ther Rev* 41 (1961).

59. Harrington, "Early History of Practice in Houston," 5.

60. Harrington, "Research Notebooks." HRN: 1; 34–37.

61. Harrington, "Early Beginnings of the Harrington Spinal Instrumentation," 10.

62. Harrington, "Research Notebooks." HRN: I; 38–49.

63. Harrington, "Early History of Practice in Houston," 6.

64. Harrington, "Research Notebooks." HRN: 1; 52–53.

65. Ibid., 70–74.

66. Harrington, "Early History of Practice in Houston," 7.

67. Harrington, "Research Notebooks." HRN: 1; 89.

68. Ibid., 90-91.

69. Ibid., 93, 103.

70. Harringon, "Early History of Practice in Houston," 8.

71. James R. Sims, " Section III, Part 1: Structural Mechanics of Spine Instrumentation," *Scollosis* (unpublished materal, 1968).

72. Paul R. Harrington, " The History and Development of Harrington Instrumentation," *Clin Orthop Relat Res* 93(1973).

73. Nickel, "Reminiscences," 12.

74. Ibid., 8.

75. *Dorland's Illustrated Medical Dictionary*, 28th ed., s.v. "orthosis."

76. Thorkild Jensen Enge, oral history to Eugene W. J. Pearce, October 16, 1996. HA 144/1: 14; 1-3.

77. Ibid., 4.

78. Ibid., 5-7.

79. Rachel Kelley, "Thorkild Engen Remembered," Orthotics and Prosthetics Business News,May 15, 2006. HA 103/2: 8.

80. Engen, October 16, 1996, 8-9.

81. Ibid., 9-10.

82. Ibid., 10-12.

83. Ibid.,13.

84. Ibid., 13-14.

85. Kelley, "Obituary: Engen."

86. Engen, October 16, 1996, 14-15.

87. Ibid., 15-16.

88. Ibid., 17.

89. Harrington, "Research Notebooks." HRN: 2; 41.

90. Harrington, "Early History of Practice in Houston," 7, 9.

91. Harrington, "History and Development of Harrington Instrumentation."

92. Harrington, "Treatment of Scoliosis."

93. Dickson, "Paul Randall Harrington: His Life and Work." HA 146: 2; 11.

94. Harrington, "Research Notebooks." HRN: 1; 102-117.

95. Marc A. Asher, Robert B. Keller, and Nancy J. Hulston, "The Moe-Harrington

Connection" (unpublished material, 1991). HA: Permanent Exhibit.

96. Harrington, "Research Notebooks." HRN: 1; 118.

97. Ibid., 119-22.

98. Harrington, "Early History of Practice in Houston." HA 101: 40; 9.

99. Paul R. Harrington, *Walking Lock Rod for Strut Fixation of Spine and Self Locking Spinal Hook*, 1955. Signed original drawings. HA 113: 1.

100. Harrington, "Early History of Practice in Houston," 8.

101. Ibid.

102. Harrington, "Research Notebooks." HRN: 2; 7.

103. Ibid., 2.

104. Harrington, "Early History of Practice in Houston," 7.

105. Paul R. Harrington, "An Experimental Study of Scoliosis" (unpublished material, 1957). HA: BV.

106. Harrington, "Research Notebooks." HRN: 2; 5-7, 9, 12-34, 42-80.

107. Harrington, "An Experimental Study of Scoliosis."

108. Equivalent metric dimensions rounded to tenths are 1/8" = 3.2 mm, 3/16" = 4.7 mm, and 1/4" = 6.4 mm.

109. Forrest Perkins, letter to Paul R. Harrington, June 16, 1955. HA 124: 1.

110. Paul R. Harringrton, letter to Forrest Perkins, June 21, 1955.

111. Harrington, "Research Notebooks." HRN: 1; 38-39, 54, 59.

112. Ibid., 35, 50.

113. Paul R. Harrington, letter to Zimmer, April 9, 1956. HA 124: 2.

114. Harrington, "Early History of Practice in Houston," 9.

115. Don L. Eyler, "Legacy of Heroes," accessed July 12, 2012, AAOS, http://www6.AAOS.org/About/Heroes/transeripts/eyler.cfm.

116. Don L. Eyler, letter to Robert H. Fain, May 24, 1973. HA 122/3:1.

117. Nickel, "Reminiscences." HA 101: 22.

118. Don L. Eyler, reminiscences to Harrington Archives, August 18, 1997. HA 144/1: 38.

119. Nickel, June 11, 1991. HA 144/1: 6; 8-9.

120. Jacquelin Perry and Vernon L. Nickel, "Total Cervical—Spine Fusion for Neck Paralysis," *J Bone Joint Surg Am* 41(1959).

121. Vermon L. Nickel et al., "The Halo: A Spinal Skeletal Traction Fixation

Device," *J Bone Joint Surg Am* 50 (1968).

122. Charles Bonnett et al., "Evolution of Treatment of Paralytic Scoliosis at Rancho Los Amigos Hospital," *J Bone Joint Surg Am* 57 (1975).

123. Patrick W. O'Donnell et al., "The History of the Halo Skeletal Fixator," *Spine* 34 (2009).

124. Eyler, August 18, 1997.

125. Dickson, "Paul Randall Harrington: His Life and Work." HA 146: 2; 23.

126. R. E. Delp, letter to Paul R. Harrington, October 10, 1956. HA 124: 3.

127. Paul R. Harrington, letter to R. E. Delp. October 19, 1956.

128. James P. Keeton, letter to Paul R.Harrington, December 5, 1956.

129. Paul R. Harrington, letter to James P. Keeton, December 26, 1957.

130. James P Keeton, letter to Paul R. Harrington, December 19, 1956.

131. James P. Keeton, letter to Paul R. Harrington, January 10, 1957. HA 124: 4.

132. Paul R. Harrington, letter to James P. Keeton, January 17, 1957.

133. James P. Keeton, letter to Paul R. Harrington, January 22, 1957.

134. Paul R. Harrington, letter to James P. Keeton, February 5, 1957.

135. Paul R. Harrington, letter to James P. Keeton, February 13, 1957.

136. James P. Keeton, letter to Paul R. Harrington, February 18, 1957.

137. "Polio V-Day," *Houston Post*, April 1, 1957. HA 101: 17.

138. Dickson, "Paul Randall Harrington: His Life and Work." HA 146: 2; 12-13.

139. Price, "After Dinner Remarks."

140. Paul R. Harrington, letter to James P. Keeton, May 14, 1957. HA 124: 4.

141. Harrington, December 13, 1956. HA 124: 3.

142. Harrington, May 14, 1957. HA 124: 4.

143. James P. Keeton, letter to Paul R. Harrington, May 17, 1957.

144. Paul R. Harrington, letter to James P. Keeton, May 24, 1957.

145. Paul R. Harrington, "5/16 Inch Ratchet Rod" (unpublished material, June 1957). HA 135: 8.

146. Paul R. Harrington, letter to James P. Keet, May 30, 1957.

147. Harrington, "An Experimental Stdy of Scoliosis."

148. Paul R. Harrington, "Is Scoliosis Reversible? In Vivo Observations of Reversible Morphologieal Changes in the Production of Scoliosis in Mice," *Clin Orthop Relat Res* 116 (1976).

149. Harrington, "History and Development of Instrumentation."

150. Harrington, "The Human Spine." HA 47: Book 1; Preface page 3.

151. Harrington, May 30, 1957. HA 124:4.

152. Paul R. Harrington, letter to Jim Hite, June 11,1959. HA 124: 6.

153. J. F. Hartle, letter to Paul R. Harringon, July 1, 1957. HA 124: 4.

154. James P. Keeton, letter to Paul R. Harringon, July 2, 1957.

155. Paul R. Harrington, "Discussion of Carlos E. Ottolenghi's Presentation: Surgical Methods of Improving Scoliosis in Poliomyeliti Patients," *Fouth International Poliomyelitis Conference* (Geneva, Switzerland, NFIP, July 12, 1957).

156. Harrington, "Curriculum Vitae." HA 101: 2; 3.

157. Nickel, June 11, 1991. HA 144/1: 6; 13.

158. Eyler, August 18, 1997. HA 144/1: 18; 3.

159. Paul R. Harrington, letter to James P. Keeton, September 12, 1957. HA 124: 4.

160. James P. Keeton, letter to Paul R. Harrington, September 26, 1957.

161. Paul R. Harrington, letter to James P. Keeton, November 8, 1957.

162. Ibid., 163.

163. James P. Keeton, letter to Paul R. Harrington, November 18, 1957.

164. "Proceedings of the 1958 Meeting of the American Academy of Orthopaedic Surgeons," *J Bone Joint Surg Am* 40 (1958): 715-42.

165. Yves P. Cotrel, *In the Sands of Berck: The Unexpected Journey of a Physician from Brittany* (Paris, France: Fondation Yves Cotrel, 2004), 70.

166. John E. Hall, "Spinal Surgery Before and After Paul Harrington," *Spine* 23 (1998):1356.

167. Paul R. Harringron, letter to James P. Keeton, April 17, 1958. HA 124: 5.

168. Keeton, November 18, 1957. HA 124: 4.

169. Harrington, April 17, 1958. HA 124: 5.

170. James P. Keeton, letter to Paul R. Harringron, May 8, 1958.

171. Paul R. Harrington, letter to James P. Keeton, May 20, 1958.

172. Paul R. Harrington, letter to James P. Keeton, May 16, 1958.

173. James P. Keeton, letter to Paul R. Harrington, May 23, 1958.

174. Paul R. Harrington,letter to James P. Keeton, July 25, 1958.

175. Zimmer, sales order to Paul R. Harrington, August 5, 1958.

176. James P. Keeton, letter to Paul R. Harrington, August 8, 1958.

177. Paul R. Harrington, letter to James P. Keeton, October 15, 1958.

178. James P. Keeton, letter to Paul R. Harrington, October 21, 1958.

179. Jim Hite, letter to Paul R. Harrington, December 12, 1958.

180. Paul R. Harrington, letter to Jim Hite, December 29, 1958.

181. Paul R. Harrington, *Self-Adjusting Strut Bar*, 1958. Signed original drawing. HA 113: 2.

182. Harrington, December 29, 1958. HA 124: 5.

183. Jim Hite, letter to Paul R. Harrington, January 6, 1959. HA 124: 6.

184. Paul R. Harrington, letter to Jim Hite, January 8, 1959.

185. Paul R. Harrington, "In Recognition of the Scientific Exhibit Shown at the Twenty-Sixth Annual Meeting of the Academy" (award, AAOS, 1959). HA 116.

186. Paul R. Harrington, letter to Jim Hite, April 28, 1959. HA 124: 6.

187. Jim Hite, lelter to Paul R. Harrington. April 30, 1959.

188. Harrington, June 11, 1959.

189. Ibid.

190. Jim Hite, letter to Paul R. Harrington, September 14, 1959.

191. Paul R. Harrington, letter to Jim Hite, June 1, 1959.

192. Paul Vermilion, laboratory report on a broken strut, June 23, 1959.

193. Paul R. Harrington, letter to Jim Hite, June 22, 1959.

194. Jim Hite, letter to Paul R. Harrington, June 28, 1959.

195. Harrington, December 13, 1956. HA 124: 3.

196. Ketton, January 22, 1957. HA 124: 4.

197. Jim Hite, letter to Paul R. Harrington, July 9, 1959. HA 124: 6.

198. Zimmer, *Strut Bar with Full* 1/4" Diameter Shank, 1959. Blueprint. HA 113: 5.

190. Harrington, June 22, 1959. HA 124: 6.

200. Hite, June 28, 1959.

201. Paul R. Harrington, letter to Jim Hite, July 1, 1959.

202. Paul R. Harrington, letter to Jim Hite, July 13, 1959.

203. Paul R. Harrington, letter to Jim Hite, August 14, 1959.

204. Paul R. Harrington, letter to Jim Hite, August 26, 1959.

205. Paul R. Harrington, letter to Jim Hite, September 24, 1959.

206. Paul R. Harrington, letter to Jim Hite, November 17, 1959.

207. Jim Hite, letter to Paul R. Harrington, December 2, 1959.

208. Paul R. Harrington, letter to Jim Hite, December 10, 1959.

209. Author's recollection.

210. Harrington, June 22, 1959. HA 124: 6.

211. Zimmer, *Universal Swivel Hook*, 1959. Drawing. HA 113:4.

212. Hite, September 14, 1959. HA 124: 6.

213. Harrington, September 24, 1959.

214. Harrington, November 17, 1959.

215. Paul R. Harrington, letter to Jim Hite, August 30, 1960. HA 124: 7.

216. Paul R. Harrington, letter to Jim Hite, July 15, 1959. HA 124: 6.

217. Harrington, August 14, 1959.

218. Harrington, February 13, 1957. HA 124: 4.

219. PaulR. Harrington, letter to Jim Hite, October 27, 1959. HA 124: 6.

220. Harrington, April 17, 1958. HA 124: 5.

221. Hite, July 9, 1959. HA 124: 6.

222. Harrington, July 13, 1959.

223. John H. Moe, "38 Years' Experience in Scoliosis Treatment," in *Selected Writings*; *John H. Moe*, *M.D.*, K. B. Wood (Minneapolis, MN: Twin Cities Scoliosis Spine Center, 1993), 518–27.

224. Joseph C. Risser, "Scoliosis Treated by Cast Correction and Spine Fusion: A Long Term Follow-up Study," *Clin Orthop Relat Res* 116 (1976).

225. Walter P. Blountet al., "The Milwaukee Brace in the Operative Treatment of Scoliosis," *J Bone Joint Surg Am* 49 (1958).

226. Walter P. Blount and John H. Moe, *The Milwaukee Brace*, 2nd ed. (Baltimore: Williams & Wilkins, 1980).

227. John H. Moe, "A Critical Analysis of Methods of Fusion for Scoliosis: An Evaluation in Two Hundred and Sixty-Six Patients," *J Bone Joint Surg Am* 40 (1958).

228. Francis G. Alan, "Scoliosis: Operative Correction of Fixed Curves," *J Bone Joint Surg Br* 37 (1955).

229. "Proceedings of the Sixth Congress of the International Society of Orthopaedic Surgery and Traumatology," *J Bone Joint Surg Br* 36 (1954).

230. H. Leslie Wenger, *The Spine Jack Operation for Scoliosis* (New York: Dr. H.

Leslie Wenger, 1957).

231. H. Leslie Wenger, "Spine Jack Operation in the Correction of Scoliotic Deformity. A Direct Intrathoracic Attack to Straighten the Laterally Bent Spine: Preliminary Report," *Arch Surg* 83 (1961).

232. F. W. Holdsworth and A. Hardy, "Early Treatment of Paraplegia from Fractures of the Thoraco-Lumbar Spine," *J Bone Joint Surg Br* 35 (1953).

233. Philip D. Wilson andL. Ramsay Straub, "Lumbosacral Fusion with Metallic-Plate Fixation," in *Instructional Course Lectures*, Charles N. Pease (Ann Arbor, MI: J. W. Edwards, 1952).

234. Arthur R. Hodgson and Francis E. Stock, "Anterior Spinal Fusion A Preliminary Communication on the Radical Treatment of Pott's Disease and Pott's Paraplegia," *Br J Surg* 44 (1956).

235. Hiromu Ito, Junichi Tsuchiya, and Goichi Asami, "A New Radical Operation for Pott's Disease: Report of Ten Cases," *J Bone Joint Surg* 16 (1934).

236. Nickel, June11, 1991. HA 122/1: 6; 14.

237. Ibid., 4-6.

238. Asher, "Moe-Harrington Connection."

239. Hall, "Spinal Surgery Before and After."

240. Paul R. Harrington, "Geographical List of All Operated Patients" (unpublished material, 1951-63). HA: LLNB.

241. Marc A. Asher and Christopher Crenner, eds. "Final Program, "*Harrington Spine Symposium* (Kansas City, KS, Harrington Archives, July 28-30, 2005). HSS: LLNB; 133-4.

242. Jim Hite, letter to Paul R. Harrington, October 22, 1959. HA 124: 6.

243. Harrington, December 10, 1959.

CHAPTER 6

1. Jim Hite, letter to Paul R. Harrington, June 30, 1960. HA 124: 7.

2. Harrington, "Treatment of Scoliosis."

3. Paul R. Harrington, "Certificate of Fellowship" (AAOS, 1960). HA 116.

4. Paul R. Harrington, "Certificate" (American Board of Orthopaedic Surgery, 1949). HA 116.

5. Charles V. Heck, *Fifty Years of Progress* (Chicago: AAOS, 1983), 152-54.

6. Jim Hite, letter to Paul R. Harrington, February 4, 1960. HA 124: 7.

7. Jim Hite, letter to Paul R. Harrington, February 10, 1960.

8. Jim Hite, letter to Paul R. Harrington, April 20, 1960.

9. Paul R. Harrington, letter to Jim Hite, April 25, 1960.

10. Paul R. Harrington, letter to Jim Hite, July 7, 1960.

11. Jim Hite, letter to Paul R. Harrington, July 12, 1960.

12. Jim Hite, letter to Paul R. Harrington, May 9, 1960.

13. Paul R. Harrington, letter to Jim Hite, May 11, 1960.

14. Engen, October 16, 1996. HA 144/1: 14; 19-20.

15. Paul R. Harrington, letter to Jim Hite, May 27, 1960. HA 124: 7.

16. Jim Hite, letter to Paul R. Harrington, June 7, 1960.

17. Brown, *The American Orthopaedic Association*, 1,8-10.

18. Paul R. Harrington, "Surgical Instrumentation for Management of Scoliosis" (paper presented at annual meeting of AOA, Hot Springs, VA, May 30-June 2, 1960). HA 106: 4a.

19. Paul R. Harrington, "Surgical Instrumentation for Management of Scoliosis." Abstract. *J Bone Joint Surg* Am 42 (1960): 1448.

20. Paul R. Harrington, "Surgical Instrumentation for Managementof Scoliosis" (paper presented at Continuation Course for Orthopaedic Surgeons and General Physicians at the Minnesota Center for Continuation Study, Minneapolis, December, 1960). Figures 1A and B.

21. Nickel, June 11, 1991. HA 144/1: 6; 10.

22. Harrington, August 14, 1959. HA 124: 6.

23. Harrington, September 24, 1959.

24. Harrington, "Surgical Instrumentation for Management of Scoliosis." Minneapolis, 1960. Figures 2A and B.

25. Brown, *The American Orthopaedic Association*. 135.

26. John R.Cobb, "The Problem of the Primary Curve," *J Bone Joint Surg Am* 42 (1960).

27. Hite, June 30, 1960. HA 124: 7.

28. Harrington, "History and Development of Harrington Instrumentation."

29. Paul R. Harrington, letter to Jim Hite, June 14, 1960. HA 124: 7.

30. Harrington, April 17, 1958. HA 124: 5.

31. Jim Hite, letter to Paul R. Harrington, July 22, 1960. HA 124: 7.

32. Paul R. Harrington, letter to Jim Hite, August 11, 1960.

33. Harrington, "Treatment of Scoliosis," 604.

34. Harrington, "Geographical List of Patients." HA: LLNB.

35. Harrington, August 30, 1960. HA 124: 7.

36. Jim Hite, letter to Paul R. Harrington, September 9, 1960.

37. William A. Spencer, memorandum to Stanley W. Olson, September 8, 1960. HA 124: 8.

38. Paul R. Harrington, letter to J. F. Hartle, September 21, 1960.

39. J. F. Hartle, License/Royalty Agreement to Paul R. Harrington, October 27, 1960. A minor mistake in the agreement that appears three times is reference to the Baylor University Department of Medicine, rather than Baylor University College of Medicine. HA 124: 8.

40. Jim Hite, letter to Paul R. Harrington, Decembar 21, 1959. HA 124: 6.

41. Harrington, June 14, 1960. HA 124; 7.

42. Paul R. Harrington, letter to Jim Hite, December 18, 1962. HA 124: 10.

43. Zimmer, "Harrington Instrumentation Product Information" (unpublished material, ca.1960). HA 125: 1.

44. Paul R. Harrington, letter to Jim Hite, January 30, 1961. HA 124: 9.

45. J. F. Hartle, letter to Paul R. Harrington, October 28, 1960. HA 124: 8.

46. *Very Special Place*. HA 122/7: 12; 5.

47. Nickel, "Reminiscences," HA 101: 22; 8-9.

48. Hall, "Spinal Surgery Before and After," 1356.

49. Jane S. Smith, *Patenting the Sun* (New York: Anchor, 1991). Epigraph.

50. Ibid., 338.

51. Paul R. Harrington, letter to A. O. Johnson, May 9, 1962. HA 124: 8.

52. Paul R. Harrington, letter to A. O. Johnson, May 15, 1962.

53. Harrington, "History and Development of Harrington Instrumentation," 112.

54. Jim Hite, letter to Paul R. Harrington, October 4, 1960. HA 124: 7.

55. Paul R. Harrington, letter to Jim Hite, October 7, 1960.

56. Paul R, Harrington, letter to Jim Hite, October 26, 1960.

57. Paul R, Harrington, letter to James R. Sims, November 8, 1960.

58. Jim Hite, letter in Paul R. Harrington, November 3, 1960.

59. Taussig Associates, mechanical test results to Jim Hite, November 15, 1960.

60. WalterIsaaeson, *Steve Jobs* (New York: Simon & Schuster, 2011), 343-4.

61. Paul R. Harrington, letter to Jim Hite, November 22, 1960. HA 124: 7.

62. "Spines of Steel," *Time*, November 14, 1960, 56.

63. Harrington, "Treatment of Scoliosis," 593.

64. Paul R. Harrington, "Spine Instrumentation in the Management of Spine Deformity and Instability" (thesis, AOA. 1961). HA: BV; Figure 29 caption.

65. Paul R. Harrington, "The Management of Scoliosis by Spine Instrumentation; An Evaluation of More Than 200 Cases," *South Med J* 56 (1963).

66. Harrington, "Surgical Instrumentation for Management Of Scoliosis." Abstract, *J Bone Joint Surg Am* 42 (1960): 1448.There are three differing versions of the same paper and discussing their nuances is important.

67. Paul R. Harrington, "Time Article-Patient Inquiries" (unpublished material, 1960-65). HA: BV.

68. Harrington, "Geographical List of Patients."

69. Asher, "Final Program," 134.

70. Harrington, "Surgical Instrumentation for Managementof Scoliosis." HA: BV.

71. Ibid. Figure 5.

72. Jim Hite,letter to Paul R. Harrington, December 29, 1960. HA 124: 7.

73. Paul R. Harrington, "Bound Travel Arrangements, 1961-67." HA: BTA.

74. Paul R. Harrington, letter to Jim Hite, January 4, 1961. HA 124: 9.

75. J.F. Hartle,letter to Paul R. Harrington, January 16, 1961.

76. Naomi Rogers, "Silence Has Its Own Stories': Elizabeth Kenny, Polio and the Culture of Medicine," *Soc Hist Med* 21 (2008): 156.

77. Paul R, Harrington, *Scoliosis: Harrington Spine Instrumentation in the Management of Scoliosis* (Houston: Texas Industrial Film Company, 1960), 16-mm film. HA 122/4: 4.

78. Paul R. Harrington, letter to J. F. Hartle, February 8, 1961. HA 124: 9.

79. Paul R. Harrington, letter to J. F. Hartle, January 23, 1961.

80. Jim Hite, letter to Paul R. Harrington, January 25, 1961.

81. Harrington, January 30, 1961.

82. "TIRR Travel Fund" (unpublished material, 1960-65). HA 122/7: 20.

83. Harrington, May 9, 1962. HA 124: 8.

84. "TIRR Travel Fund."

85. Paul R. Harrington, "Biomechanics of the Spine, 1961" (unpublished material, 1961). HA 106: 6.

86. Paul R. Harrington, "Biomechanics of the Spine, 1965," *Scoliosis* (unpublished material, 1965). HA: BV.

87. Harrington, "The Human Spine." HA 47; Preface: 3.

88. Harrington, "1961 AOA Thesis." Figure 9.

89. Harrington, "Biomechanics of the Spine, 1965." Figure 49.

90. Harrington, "Geographical List of Patients."

91. Ibid.

92. Harrington, "Bound Travel Arrangements."

93. Asher, "Final Program," 135.

94. "TIRR Travel Fund."

95. Harrington, "Bound Travel Arrangements."

96. Ibid.

97. Asher, "Final Program," 141.

98. James W. Tupper, "The Influence Paul Harrington Had on My Professional Life" (paper presented at Harrington Spine Symposium, Kansas City, KS, July 28-30, 2005). HSS: LLNB: 20.

99. Paul R. Harrington, letter to Jim Hite, May 6, 1960. HA 124: 7.

100. Jim Hite, letter to Paul R. Harrington, June 9, 1961. HA 124: 9.

101. Paul R. Harrington, letter to Jim Hite, June 23, 1961.

102. Joseph M. Tambornino, Earl N. Armbrust, and John H. Moe, "Harrington Instrumentation in Correction of Scoliosis: A Comparison with Cast Correction," *J Bone Joint Surg Am* 46 (1964).

103. Hite, June 9, 1961. HA 124: 9.

104. Harrington, June 23, 1961.

105. JimHite, letter to Paul R. Harrington, September 19, 1961.

106. Paul R. Harrington, letter to Jim Hite, September 29, 1961.

107. *Zimmer*, *Standard Set of Harrington Spine Instrumentation* (Warsaw. IN: Zimmer Manufacturing Company, ca.1961). HA 125: 1.

108. William A. Spencer et al., "Rehabilitation in Concept and in Practice," *South Med J* 55 (1962).

109. Sir William Osler, "Medicine in the Nineteenth Century," *in Acquanimitas and Other Addresses to Medical Students, Nurses and Practitioners of Medicine*, 3rd ed. (Philadelphia: The Blakiston Company, 1932).

110. *Webster's New Collegiate Dictionary*, 9th ed., s.v. "Promethean."

111. Alvin D. Brallier, letter to Paul R. Harrington, December 19, 1961. HA 124: 9.

112. Paul R. Harrington, letter to Alvin D. Brallier, December 22, 1961.

113. Harrington, "Surgical Instrumentation for Management of Scoliosis." Abstract. *J Bone Joint Surg Am* 42 (1960): 1448.

114. Mark B. Coventry, letter to Paul R. Harrington, July 31, 1962. HA: BV. Pasted inside front cover of 1 of 4 copies. The thesis was returned with complimentary comments but AOA membership would have to wait.

115. Harrington, "1961 AOA Thesis." HA: BV.

116. Nickel, "Reminiscences." HA 101: 22; 10.

117. Harrington, May 21, 1980. HA 144/1: 17; 38.

118. Harrington, "Treatment of Scoliosis."

119. Harrington, "The Human Spine." HA 47: Preface; 3.

120. Kelly A. Lefaivre, Babak Shadgan. and Peter J. O'Brien, "100 Most Cited Articles in Orthopaedic Surgery," *Clin Orhop Relat Res* 469 (2011).

121. Joseph C. Risser and Donald M. Norquist, "A Follow-up Study of the Treatment of Scoliosis," *J Bone Joint Surg Am* 40 (1958).

122. Moe, "Critical Analysis of Fusion."

123. Harrington, "1961 AOA Thesis," 4.

124. Paul C. Colonna and Frederick Vom Saal, "A Study of Paralytic Scoliosis Based on Five Hundred Cases of Poliomyelitis," *J Bone Joint Surg* 23 (1941).

125. Harrington, "Bound Travel Arrangements."

126. Harrington, "Curriculum Vitae." HA 101: 2; 5-6.

127. William A. Spencer, letter to Stanley W. Olson, December 29, 1961. HA 101: 3. Spencer must have meant Harrington was limiting his private practice to scoliosis.

128. William A. Spencer, letter to Michael E. DeBakey, January 4, 1962. HA 101: 3.

129. Stanley W. Olson, memorandum to Paul R. Harrington, July 1, 1959.

130. Hebbel E. Hoff, letter to Paul R. Harrington, July 8, 1969.

131. Jim Hite, letter to Paul R. Harrington, April 13, 1962. HA 124: 10.

132. Paul R. Harrington, letter to Jim Hite, April 1962.

133. Jim Hite, letter to Paul R. Harrington, July 19, 1962.

134. Paul R. Harrington, letter to Jim Hite, July 26, 1962.

135. Jim Hite, letter to Paul R. Harrington, October 18, 1962.

136. Paul R. Harrington, letter to Jim Hite, October 25, 1962.

137. Harrington, December 18, 1962.

138. Paul R. Harrington, "Spine Instrumentation in the Management of Spine Deformity and Instability: AAOS; I.C.L. #44," *Scoliosis* (unpublished material, 1962). HA: BV.

139. Paul R. Harrington, "Scoliosis in the Growing Spine," *Pediatr Clin North Am* (1963).

140. Harrington, "Treatment of Scoliosis."

141. Harrington, "More Than 200 Cases."

142. Paul R. Harrington, interview by John P. O'Brien, August 23, 1976. HA 101: 26; 14.

143. Paul R. Harrington, "Principles of Scoliosis: Concept," *Scoliosis* (unpublished material, 1962). HA: BV.

144. Harrington, "Scoliosis in the Growing Spine." CW: PRH; 65-85.

145. Harrington, "1961 AOA Thesis," 26-27.

146. Harrington, "History and Developments of Harrington Instrumentation."

CHAPTER 7

1. John R. Cobb, "Discussion of Tambornino, Armbrust and Moe," *J Bone Joint Surg Am* 46 (1964): 322-23.

2. Ira Rutkow, *Seeking the Cure: A History of Medicine in America* (New York: Scribner, 2010), 35-39, 44.

3. Kjell Benson and Arthur J. Hartz, "A Comparison of Observational Studies and Randomized, Controlled Trials," *N Engl J Med* 342 (2000).

4. Shands, "End-Result Study."

5. Harrington, "More Than 200 Cases." CW: PRH; 54-64.

6. Paul R. Harrington, "Present Status of Spine Instrumentation in Scoliosis," *Am J Orthop* August (1963). CW: PRH; 96-99.

7. Paul R. Harrington, "Present Status of Spine Instrumentation in Scoliosis," *Scoliosis* (unpublished malarial, 1963).

8. Harrington, "Treatment of Scoliosis," *J Bone Joint Surg Am* 44 (1962): 591-611.

9. Harrington, "More Than 200 Cases."

10. Paul R. Harrington and Jesse H. Dickson, "An Eleven-Year Clinical Investigation of Harrington Instrumentation: A Preliminary Report of 578 Cases," *Clin Orthop Relat Res* 93 (1973).

11. Moe, "Critical Analysis of Fusion."

12. Ibid.

13. Harrington, "Eleven-Year Investigation."

14. Moe, "Critical Analysis of Fusion."

15. John H. Moe and Ramon B. Gustilo, "Treatment of Scoliosis: Results in 196 Patients Treated by Cast Correction and Fusion," *J Bone Joint Surg Am* 46 (1964).

16. "Picture, left to right. Drs. Paul Meyers, Frank Dickson, Rex Diveley. Harrington and Richard Kiene" (unpublished material, 1963). HA 134: 1.

17. Paul R. Harrington, "Scoliosis: AAOS; I.C.L. #41," *Scoliosis* (unpublished material, 1963).

18. Paul R. Harrington and Jesse H. Dickson, The Blue Book (Houston: Harrington and Dickson, 1972). HA 110.

19. Harrington, "Scoliosis in the Growing Spine."

20. Paul R. Harrington, "Spinal Fusion in the Idiopathic Adolescent Scoliotic," *Scoliosis* (unpublished material. 1963).

21. Paul R. Harrington, "Spinal Fusion in the Treatment of Idiopathic Adolescent Scoliosis," *J Tenn Med Assoc* 56 (1963). CW: PRH; 86-95.

22. John Charnley, "Positive Pressure in Arthrodesis of the Knee Joint," *J Bone Joint Surg Br* 30 (1948).

23. George W. N. Eggers, "The Influence of the Contact-Compression Factor an Osteogenesis in Surgical Fractures," *J Bone Joint Surg Am* 31 (1949).

24. Harrington, "Spine Fusion in the Treatment of Idiopathic Adolescent Scoliosis."

25. Paul R. Harrington, letter to James A. Dingwell, November 3, 1961. HA 122/5: 16.

26. James A. Dingwall, letter to Paul R. Harrington, May 17, 1963.

27. Kirk J, Anderson and Paul R. Harrington, correspondence, 1963 – 66, HA 122/5: 13.

28. Kirk J. Andersonet al., "End-Point Results of Processed Heterogenous, Autogenous and Homogenous Bone Transplants in the Human; A Histologic Study," *Clin Orthop Relat Res* 33 (1964).

29. Tambornino, "Harrington Instrumentation in Correction of Scoliosis."

30. Moe, "Treatment of Scoliosis."

31. Moe, "Critical Analysis of Fusion."

32. Smith, Patenting the Sun, 311–12.

33. *Journal of Bone and Joint Surgery*, "Instructions for Authors," accessed March 21, 2013, http://jbjs.org/public/instructionsauthors.aspx.

34. Tambornino, "Harrington Instrumentation in Correction of Scoliosis."

35. Paul R. Harrington, *Twin Star Christening* (La Porte, TX: Houston Yacht Club, 1963). HA 101: 16.

36. Paul R. Harrington, letter to Kirk J. Anderson, July 3, 1963. HA 122/5: 13.

37. Miriam Kass, "M.D. Hopes to Hold Meetings," *Houston Chronicle*, 1963. EA 10l: 16.

38. "The 'Twin Star' Is an Eyecatcher," *Pasadena Post*, Thursday, June 30, 1966. Oversize personal scrapbook.

39. Paul R. Harrington, letter to R. E. Hamm, February 20, 1963. HA 124: 11.

40. Jim Hite, letter to Paul R. Harrington, April 8, 1963.

41. Paul R. Harrington, letter to Zimmer Sales Department, February 20, 1963.

42. Jim Hite, letter to Paul R. Harrington, March 7, 1963.

43. Zimmer, "Three Alternate Harrington Distraction Rod Designs" (unpublished material, 1963).

44. Paul R. Harrington, letter to Jim Hite, March 23, 1963.

45. Jim Hite, letter to Paul R. Harrington, July 8, 1963.

46. Paul R. Harrington, letter to Jim Hite, July 11, 1963.

47. Alvin D. Brallier, letter lo Paul R. Harrington, July 18, 1963.

48. Harrington, "Bound Travel Arrangements."

49. Asher, "Final Program," 137.

50. Harrington, "Bound Travel Arrangements."

51. Paul R. Harrington, "Adult Paraplegia" (unpublished material, 1963). HA

106: 10.

52. Ludwig Guttmann, "Surgical Aspects of the Treatment of Traumatic Paraplegia," *J Bone Joint Surg Br* 31 (1949).

53. Harrington, "Bound Travel Arrangements."

54. Pierre Stagnara, "Lateral Deviations of the Spine." Translated from French by Carlos Vallbona, MD. HA: BV; *Scoliosis* 1966.

55. Pierre Stagnara, "Lateral Deviations of the Spine; Treatments of Scoliosis." Translated from French by Carlos Vallbona. MD. HA: BV; Scoliosis 1966, 24-25.

56. Paul R. Harrington, "Arthrodesis of the Scoliotic Spines," *Scoliosis* (unpublished material, 1965). 15.

57. Paul R. Harrington, "Radiography in Scoliosis," *Scoliosis* (unpublished material, 1963).

58. Paul R. Harrington and Carlos Vallbona, "Evaluation of Respiratory Function in Scoliosis; The Effects of Spinal Instrumentation," *Scoliosis* (unpublished material, 1963).

59. Cook, "Pulmonary Physiology."

60. E. Burke Evans, letter to Baylor University College of Medicine, October 24, 1963. HA 124: 8.

61. Brallier, July 18, 1963. HA 124: 11.

62. Harrington, "Bound Travel Arrangements."

63. Paul H. Harmon, "The Use of Chemicals as Nasal Sprays in the Prophylaxis of Poliomyelitis in Man," *JAMA* 109 (1937): 1061.

64. Paul R. Harrington, "Surgery for Scoliosis of the Spine" (paper presented at Techniques in Surgery of the Spine, Los Angeles, March 14-15, 1964). HA 106:12.

65. Harrington, "Geographical List of Patients" HA: LLNB.

66. John E. Hall, "Congenital Scoliosis Treated by Harrington instrumentation and Spinal Fusion" (paper presented at Fourth Combined Meeting of the Orthopaedic Asociations, Vancouver, B. C., Canada, 1964). HA 105: 2; 43.

67. Paul R. Harrington, letter to James W. Tupper, June 3, 1964. BTA.

68. Jim Hite, letter to Paul R. Harrington, May 18, 1964. HA 124: 12.

69. Paul R. Harrington, letter to Jim Hite, June 3, 1964.

70. Jim Hite, letter to Paul R. Harrington, June 16, 1964.

71. Paul R. Harrington, letter to Jim Hite, June 24, 1964.

72. Jim Hite, letter to Paul R. Harrington, July 3, 1964.

73. Paul R. Harrington, "Instrumentation in Structural Scoliosis," *Mod Trends Orthop* (1967). CW: PRH; 109-37.

74. Jim Hite, letter to Paul R. Harrington, July 20, 1964.

75. Paul R. Harrington, letter to Zimmer Sales Department, September 17, 1964.

76. Paul R. Harrington, letter to R. E. Hamm, December 24, 1964.

77. David L. Evens, letter to Paul R. Harrington, November 2, 1964.

78. Harrington, "Bound Travel Arrangements."

79. *Continuation Course in Orthopedic Surgery* (Minneapolis. University of Minnesota, November 12-14, 1964). BTA.

80. Paul R. Harrington, "The Spine in the Handicapped Child," *Am J Orthop* (June-July 1964). CW: PRH; 100-08.

81. Paul R. Harrington, "Scoliosis: AAOS; I.C.L. #75," *Scoliosis* (unpublished material, 1964).

82. Paul R. Harrington, "Spine Instrumentation and Fusion Technique," *Scoliosis* (unpublished material, 1964).

83. Sayre, "Treatment of Neglected Cases." HA: BV; *Scoliosis 1964*, section 2.

84. Julius Wolff, *The Law of Transformation of Bone*. Translated from German by Dr. Jurg U. Baumann. HA: BV; Scoliosis 1964, section 4.

85. Harrington, "Bound Travel Arrangements,"

86. Asher, "Final Program." HA: LLNB; 139.

87. Harrington, "Bound Travel Arrangements."

88. Darius Flinchum, "Rib Resection in the Treatment of Scoliosis," *South Med J* 56 (1963).

89. Harrington, "Bound Travel Arrangements."

90. Ibid.

91. "Harrington Genealogy," HA 102:6.

92. Shands, "End-Result Study."

93. Eldon G. Chuinard, letter to Paul R. Harrington, April 20, 1965. HA: BTA.

94. Harrington, "Arthrodesis of the Scoliotic Spices."

95. Harrington, "Scoliosis in the Growing Spine."

96. Stagnara, "Lateral Deviations of the Spine."

97. "Preliminary Scientific Program," *Annual Meeting of the Canadian Orthopaedic*

Association (Halifax, Nova Scotia, Canada, Canadian Orthopaedic Association, June 20–24, 1965). HA: BTA.

98. R. E. Hamm, letter to Paul R. Harrington, June 28, 1965. HA 124; 13.

99. Paul R. Harrington, letter to Jim Hite, August 10, 1965.

100. Jim Hite, letter to Paul R. Harrington, August 19, 1965.

101. Paul R. Harrington, "The Sixty-Degree Idiopathic Scoliotic Patient," *Scoliosis* (unpublished material, 1965).

102. C. Hueter, "Anatomical Studies on the Joints of the Extremities in Newborns and Adults." Translated from German by Dr. Jurg U. Baumann. HA: BV; *Scoliosis 1966*.

103. R. Volkmann, "Surgical Studies on Bone Deformation and Bone Growth." Translated from Germanby Dr. Jurg U. Baumann. HA: BV; *Scoliosis 1966*.

104. *Dorland's Illustrated Medical Dictionary*, 28th ed., s.v. "Wolff's Law."

105. Wolff, *Transformation of Bone*, 144.

106. Paul R. Harrington, letter to Jim Hite, December 17, 1965. HA 124: 13.

107. Harrington, "Biomechanics of the Spine, 1965."

108. Harrington, "Arthrodesis of the Scoliotic Spines."

109. Harrington, "The Sixty-Degree Idiopathic Scoliotic Patient."

110. Stanley Hoppenfeld, "Scoliosis Abstracts, 1924–64," *Scoliosis* (unpublished material, 1965).

111. Arthur Yau, letter to Paul R. Harrington, March 7, 1963. HA 122/1: 14.

112. Paul R. Harrington, letter to Arthur Yau, March 22, 1963.

113. Arthur R.Hodgson, letter to Paul R. Harrington, May 20, 1964.

114. Paul R. Harrington, letter to Arthur R. Hodgson, September 2, 1964.

115. Arthur R. Hodgson, letter to Paul R. Harrington, November 9, 1965.

116. Paul R. Harrington, letter to Arthur R. Hodgson, December 15, 1965.

117. Arthur R. Hodgson, letter to Paul R. Harrington, December 21, 1965.

CHAPTER 8

1. Hall, "Spinal Surgery Before and After."

2. Heck, *Fifty Years of Progress*, 110–12.

3. "Dr. John H. Moe Exhibit," accessed July 24, 2013, Twin Cities Spine Center, http://www.tcspine.com/about-us/dr-john-h-moe-exhibit.

4. Moe, "Critical Analysis of Fusion."

5. Moe, "Treatment of Scoliosis."

6. Moe, "Critical Analysis of Fusion."

7. Ignacio V. Ponseti and Barry Friedman, "Changes in the Scoliotic Spine after Fusion," *J Bone Joint Surg Am* 32 (1950).

8. John R. Cobb, "Technique, After-treatment, and Results of Spine Fusion for Scoliosis," in *Instructional Course Lectures*, *AAOS*, ed. Charles N. Pease (Ann Arbor, MI: J. W. Edwards. 1952).

9. Thomas G. Gucker, III, "Experiences with Poliomyelitic Scoliosis after Fusion and Correetion," *J Bone Joint Surg Am* 38 (1956).

10. Blount, "Milwaukee Brace in Operative Treatment."

11. Risser, "Treatment of Scoliosis."

12. Moe, "Critical Analysis of Fusion."

13. Louis A. Goldstein, The Surgical Treatment of Scoliosis. ed. C. W. Goff. American Lectures in Orthopaedic Surgery (Springfield, IL: Charles C. Thomas. 1959).

14. Moe, "Treatment of Scoliosis."

15. Cobb, "Treatment and Results."

16. Goldstein, *Surgical Treatment of Scoliosis.*

17. Cotrel, *In the Sands of Berck*, 58–88.

18. "Proceedings 1958 AAOS Annual Meeting."

19. Hall, "Spinal Surgery Before and After."

20. Harrington, November 8, 1957. HA 124: 6.

21. Cobb, "Discussion of Tambornino, Armbrust and Moe."

22. Hall, "Spinal Surgery Before and After."

23. Ibid.

24. John H. Moe et al., *Scoliosis and Other Deformities* (Philadelphia: W. B. Sounders, 1978). 4.

25. "Dr. John H. Moe Exhibit."

26. David B. Levine, letter to John H. Moe, December 7, 1972, SRS 1:1.

27. David B. Levine, letter to John H. Moe, February 9, 1965.

28. Claude L. Lambert, letter to John H. Moe, January 19, 1965, SRS 1: la.

29. John H. Moe, letter to Arthur J. Lesser, February 16, 1965.

30. Arthur J. Lesser, letter to John H. Moe, March 2, 1965.

31. William J. Kane, "Minutes of the Organizational Meeting Leading to the

Formation of the Scoliosis Research Society" (unpublished material, January 22, 1966). SRS 1:1.

32. Harrington, "Bound Travel Arrangements."

33. David B. Levine, "Constitution of the Scoliosis Club" (unpublished material, 1965). SRS 1: 1.

34. William J. Kane, "Minutes of the Fist Executive Committee Meeting Leading to the Formation of the Scoliosis Research Society" (unpublished material, January 23, 1966). SRS 1: 1.

35. WilliamJ. Kane, "Paul R. Harrington's Seminal Influence on the Scoliosis Research Society" (paper presented at Harington Spine Symposium, Kansas City, KS. July 28-30,2005). HSS: LLNB: 12.

36. William J. Kane, letter with five enclosures to SRS executive committee members. February 4, 1966, SRS 1:1.

37. David B. Levine and SRS Founding Members, "Scoliosis Research Society Constitution: Three Edition Maturation" (unpublished material, 1965-66). SRS 1: 1.

38. Owen H. Wangensteen, letter to John H. Moe and William J. Kane, May 2, 1966. SRS 1: 1.

39. William J. Kane, "Minutes of the Executive Committee Meeting" (unpublished material, June 9, 1966). SRS 1: 1.

40. "Program," *First Annual Meeting of the Scoliosis Research Society* (Minneapolis. June 10-11, 1966). SRS 1: 2.

41. William J. Kane, "Minutes of the Fist Annual Meeting of the Scoliosis Research Society" (unpublished material. June 10-11, 1966), SRS 1: 1.

42. Paul R. Harrington, "Scoliosis Data Selection, Storage and Retrieval" (paper presented at First Annual Meeting of the SRS, Minneapolis, June 10-11, 1966).

43. Robert B. Winter, John H. Moe, and Vincent E. Eilers, "Congenital Scoliosis" (paper presented al First Annual Meeting of the SRS, Minneapolis, June 10-11, 1960).

44. James W. Valuska and John H. Moe, "Evaluation of Treatment of Scoliosis by Harrington Instrumentation" (paper presented at First Annual Meeting of the SRS, Minneapolis, June 10-11, 1966).

45. John H. Moe and J. W. Valuska, "Evaluation of Treatment of Scoliosis by Harrington Instrumentation." Abstract. *J Bone Joint Surg Am* 48 (1966): 1656-57.

46. Tambornino, "Harrington Instrumentation in Correction of Scoliosis."

47. Moe, "Treatment of Scoliosis."

48. Allan M. McKelvie, "The High Incidence of Hiatal Hernia in the Scoliosis of Childhood." Abstract. *J Bone Joint Surg Br* 49 (1967): 187.

49. "Scoliosis Research Society Membership Category List" (unpublished material, 1970). SRS 1: 1.

50. "History of the Scoliosis Research Society" (unpublished material, ca. 1970).

51. Hall, "Spinal Surgery Before and After."

52. Mark Wieting, letter to Marc A. Asher, March 20, 2008. HA 103/4: 20.

53. Philip D. Wilson, "Obituary: John Robert Cobb 1903—1967," *J Bone Joint Surg Am* 50 (1968).

54. Hall, "Spinal Surgery Before and After."

CHAPTER 9

1. Paul R. Harrington, letter to Jin Hite, November 21, 1966. HA 124: 14.

2. Paul R. Harrington, letter to Jim Hite, February 9, 1966.

3. Paul R. Harrington, letter to Jim Hite, February 7, 1966.

4. Jim Hite, letter to Paul R. Harington, June 28, 1966.

5. Harrington, February 9, 1966.

6. Jim Hite, letter to Paul R. Harrington, February 16, 1966.

7. Paul R. Harrington, letter to Alvin D. Brallier, March 29, 1966.

8. J. F. Hartle, letter lo Paul R. Harrington. May 4, 1966.

9. Goldstein, Surgical Treatmentof Scoliosis.

10. Harrington, "Bound Travel Arrangements."

11. J. P. Moreau, letter to Paul R. Harrington, January 28, 1966. HA 105: 4.

12. Paul R. Harrington, "Heterogenous Bone Implants in Scoliosis Fusions" (paper presented at Annual Meeting of the Canadian Orthopaedic Association, Calgary, June 4. 1966). HA 107: 1.

13. Harrington, "Eleven-Year Investigation."

14. Harrington, "Bound Travel Arrangements."

15. "Preliminary Program" (paper presented at Tenth Congress of the Societe Internationale de Chirurgie Orthopediqueet de Traumatologie [SICOT], Paris, France, September 4-9, 1966). HA: BTA.

16. Adam Gruca, "The Pathogenesis and Treatment of Idiopathic Scoliosis," *J Bone*

Joint Surg Am 40 (1958).

17. John H. Moe, letter to Paul R. Harrington, July 26, 1966. HA: BTA.

18. Moe, "Evaluation of Treatment of Scoliosis by Harrington Instrumentation."

19. Paul R. Harrington, letter to John H. Moe, August 13, 1966. HA: BTA.

20. Raymond Roy-Camille, Gerard Saillant, and Christian Mazel. "Internal Fixation of the Lumbar Spine with Pedicle Screw Plating," *Clin Orthop Relat Res* 203 (1986).

21. J. F. Hartle, License/Royalty Agreement to Paul R. Harrington, October 27, 1960.

22. Lepine, letter to Monsicur, September 26, 1966. HA 124: 14.

23. Paul R. Harington, letter to Jim Hite, September 22, 1966.

24. Ivar J. Larson, letter to Paul R. Harrington, September 25, 1964. HA: BTA; 1966.

25. H. Relton McCarroll, letter to Paul R. Harrington, John H. Moe, and Joseph C. Risser, November 9, 1965. HA: BTA; 1966.

26. Paul R. Harrington, "Treatment of Idiopathic Scoliosis" (paper presented at Pan-Pacific Surgical Association, Honolulu, September 20–28, 1966). HA 107: 2.

27. Harry Tyer, letter to Paul R. Harrington, September 5, 1966. HA: BTA.

28. Paul R. Harrington, letter to Harry Tyer, September 16, 1966.

29. Paul R. Harrington, letter to Jim Hite, November 2, 1966. HA 124: 14.

30. J. Alan Morgan, letter to Paul R. Harrington, November 7, 1966.

31. D. Douglas Davidson, letter to Paul R. Harrington, October 14, 1966.

32. Paul R. Harrington, letter to Jim Hite, November 7, 1966.

33. Paul R. Harrington, letter to Lepine, November 18, 1966.

34. Lepine, letter to Paul R. Harrington, December 14, 1966.

35. Paul R. Harrington, letter to Lepine, December 21, 1966.

36. D. Douglas Davidson, letter to Paul R. Harrington, January 13, 1967. HA 124: 15.

37. Paul R. Harrington, letter to D. Douglas Davidson, January 20, 1967.

38. Paul R. Harrington, letter to Jim Hite, January 20, 1967.

39. J. Alan Morgan, letter to Paul R. Harrington, January 23, 1967.

40. Paul R. Harington, letter to J. Alan Morgan, January 27, 1967.

41. Stagnara, "Lateral Deviations of the Spine."

42. Hueter, "Anatomical Studies on the Joints."

43. Volkmann, "Surgical Studies an Bone Deformation and Bone Growth."

44. Paul R. Harrington, "AAOS Annual Meeting Participation" (unpublished material, 1967). HA: BTA.

45. William J. Kane, "Minutes of the SRS executive committee meeting" (unpublished material, January 15, 1967).

46. Ibid.

41. Paul R. Harrington, letter to Jim Hite, November 21, 1966. HA 124: 14.

48. Paul R. Harrington, letter to Jim Hite, January 5, 1967. HA 124: 15.

49. Paul R. Harrington, letter to Jim Hite, February 16, 1967.

50. Paul R. Harrington, Hugh S. Tullos, and Fiorenzo H. Travaglini, "Trattamento Chirurgico Della Grave Spondilolistesi Nell infanzia" (paper presented at LII Congresso Della Societa Italiana Di Ortopedia E Traumatologia, Rome, October 13-15, 1967). HA 110: 4.

51. Paul R. Harrington and Hugh S. Tullos, "Reduclion of Severe Spondylolisthesis in Children," *South Med J* 62 (1969).

52. Paul R. Harrington, "High Grade Spondylolisthesis Reduction" (unpublished material, 1968). HA 110: 6.

53. Fiorenzo H. Travaglini, letter to Paul R. Harrington, October 20, 1967. HA 110: 4.

54. Paul R. Harrington, letter to Fiorenzo H. Travaglini, October 25, 1967.

55. Paul R. Harington, letter to Rudolph H. Kampmeier, September 19, 1968. HA 110: 6.

56. Harrington, "Reduction of Severe Spondylolisthesis."

57. Jim Hite, letter to Paul R. Harrington, January 25, 1967. HA 124: 15.

58. R. E. Hamm, letter to Paul R. Harrington, February 3, 1967.

59. Vernon R. Scott, letter to Paul R. Harington, May 1, 1967.

60. Harrington, "Bound Travel Arrangements."

61. J. Garland Watson Jr., letter to James O. Copper, June 23, 1965. HA 122/5: 1.

62. J. Garland Watson Jr., "Management of Dental Problems During Milwaukee Brace Therapy" (unpublished material, 1966).

63. Walter P. Blount, "The Specter of the Bite Deformity Can Now Be Laid" (paper presented at Fourth Annual Meeting of the SRS, Anaheim, September 4-6,

1969).

64. William J. Kane, letter to the SRS executive committee, March 21, 1967. SRS 1: 1a.

65. William J. Kane, letter to the SRS executive committee, May 9, 1967. SRS 1: 1a.

66. Merrill S. Read, letter to William J. Kane, April 26, 1967. SRS 1: 1a.

67. David B. Levine, "Cardio-Pulmonary Failure Caused by Scoliosis, NTH meeting" (unpublished material, July 6, 1967). SRS 1: 1a.

68. William A. Spencer, letter to Paul R. Harington, September 25, 1967. HA 101: 3.

69. Jesse H. Dickson, oral history to Eugene W. J. Pearce, October 16, 1996. HA 144/1: 10.

70. "Program," *Second Annual Meeting of the SRS* (Minneapolis, SRS, September 7-9, 1967). SRS 1: 3.

71. "Paper Summaries from the Second Annual Meeting of the Scoliosis Research Society; Minneapolis, September 7-9, 1967," *J Bone Joint Surg Am* 50 (1968): 845-50. SRS 1: 3.

72. John T. Makley et al., "Pulmonary Function in Scoliosis" (paper presented at Second Annual Meeting of the SRS, Minneapolis, September 7-9, 1967).

73. Hugh D. Westgate, "Hemi-Lung Ventilation and Perfusion Changes Secondary to Thoracic Scoliosis" (paper presented at Second Annual Meeting of the SRS, Minneapolis, September 7-9, 1967).

74. Ibid.

75. Makley, "Pulmonary Function in Scoliosis."

76. Kuddusi Gazioglu et al., "Study of Respiratory Function in Idiopathic Scoliosis: Comparative Evaluation Before and After Orthopaedic Correction of the Curvature" (paper presented at Second Annual Meeting of the SRS, Minneapolis, September 7-9, 1967).

77. Gerner A. Olsen and J. Hamilton Allan, "Lateral Stability of the Spine" (paper presented at Second Annual Meeting of the SRS, Minneapolis, September 7-9, 1967).

78. Paul R. Harrington, "Critical Observations of Idiopathic Scoliosis. Concept of Non-Operative Treatment" (paper presented at Second Annual Meeting of the SRS, Minneapolis, September 7-9, 1967).

79. John H. Moe and Charles C. Lai, "Non-Operative Treatment of Idiopathic Scoliosis with the Milwaukee Brace" (paper presented at Second Annual Meeting of the SRS, Minneapolis, September 7-9, 1967).

80. John E. Hall, "Harrington Instrumentation and Spine Fusion: Follow-up Study in 157 Patients" (paper presented at Second Annual Meeting of the SRS, Minneapolis, September 7-9, 1967).

81. Robert P. Keiser, "Surgical Treatment of Scoliosis by Harrington Instrumentation: A Report of One Hundred Consecutive Cases" (paper presented at Second Annual Meeting of the SRS, Minneapolis. September 7-9, 1967). HA: BTA; manuscript.

82. Moe, "Evaluation of Treatment of Scoliosis by Harington Instrumentation."

83. Ibid.

84. Hall, "Harrington Instrumentation and Spine Fusion."

85. Moe, "Evaluation of Treatment of Scoliosis by Hartington Instrumentation."

86. Keiser, "Surgical Treatment of Scoliosis by Harrington Instrumentation."

87. Jacob J. Graham, "Pseudarthrosis in Scoliosis: Routine Exploration of Forty-Five Operative Cases" (paper presented at Second Annual Meeting of the SRS, Minneapolis, September 7-9, 1967).

88. Virgil R May and William R. Mauck, "A Critical Analysis Of Exploration of the Spine Fusion in the Treatment of Scoliosis" (paper presented at Second Annual Meeting of the SRS, Minneapolis, September 7-9, 1967).

89. Vernon L. Nickel, Jacquelin Perry, and Malcolm Heppenstall, "The Halo: An Analysis of Its Use on 174 Patients" (paper presented at Second Annual Meeting of the SRS, Minneapolis, September 7-9, 1967).

90. Edward H. Simmons, "Observations on the Technique and Indications for Wedge Resection of the Spine" (paper presented at Second Annual Meeting of the SRS, Minneapolis, September 7-9, 1967).

91. John H. Moe and A. Bruce Sundberg, "Spine Fusions in the Scoliotic Growing Child" (paper presented at Second Annual Meeting of the SRS, Minneapolis, September 7-9, 1967).

92. Olga Tole, letter to Paul R. Harrington, September 25, 1967. HA: BTA; September 18-19 segment.

93. W. H. Blodgett, "Clinical Orhopaedic Society" (unpublished material, 1967). HA: BTA; October 11-14 Segment.

94. Harrington, "Reduction of Severe Spondylolisthesis."

95. Paul R. Harrington, "New York City, December 6 – 14" (unpublished material, 1967). HA: BTA.

96. Harrington, "Trattamento Chirurgico Della Grave Spondilolistesi Nell'infanzia."

97. Paul R. Harrington, "Instrumentation in Spine Instability Other Than Scoliosis," *Suid-Afrikaanse Tydskerif vir Chirurgie* 5 (1967), CW: PRH; 138-43.

98. P. W. Nelson and Paul R. Harrington, "Devisions in Scoliosis." South Med *J* 60 (1967).

99. Harrington, "Instrumentation in Structural Scoliosis." CW: PRH: 109-37.

100. Harrington, "Treatment of Scoliosis," 601-04.

101. Harrington, "Instrumentation in Structural Scoliosis."

102. Robert W. Lovett, *Lateral Curvature of the Spine and Round Shoulders*, 4th rev. ed. (Philadelphia: P Blakiston's Son &Co., 1922), 190.

103. Jean Dubousset, John A. Herring, and Harry L, Shufflebarger, "The Crankshaft Phenomenon," *J Pediatr Orthop* 9 (1989).

104. R. Wynne-Davies, "Familial (Idiopathic) Scoliosis; A Family Survey," *J Bone Joint Surg Br* 50 (1968).

CHAPTER 10

1. Dickson, October 16, 1996. HA 144/1: 9; 9. Paul Harrington's request of Jesse Dickson.

2. AOA, *Membership Directory* 2004—2005 (Rosemont, IL: AOA, 2004), 271.

3. Paul R. Harrington, "Spine Analysis" (thesis, AOA, 1968). HA: BV.

4. Harrington, "Instrumentation in Structural Scoliosis." CW: PRH; 109-37.

5. Howard A. King et al., "The Selection of Fusion Levels in Thoracic Idiopathic Scoliosis," *J Bone Joint Surg Am* 65 (1983).

6. Harrington, "Curriculum Vitae."

7. Paul R. Harrington, correspondence with South African colleagues, 1968. HA 122/6: 11.

8. Paul R. Harrington, "Spine Analysis of the Idiopathic Curve," *Scoliosis* (unpublished material, 1970). HA: BV; 1-24.

9. Paul R. Harrington and William O. Reese, Jr., "The Mechanics of the Idiopathic Scoliotic Curve." *Scoliosis* (unpublished material, 1970). HA: BV; 26-58.

10. Norman G. G. Hepper, Leo F. Black, and Wand S. Fowler, "Relationships of Lung Volume to Height and Arm Span in Normal Subjects and in Patients with Spinal Deformity," *Am Rev Resp Dis* 91 (1965).

11. Paul R. Harrington, letter to Jim Hite, March 27, 1968. HA 124: 16.

12. Jim Hite, letter to Paul R, Harrington, April 3, 1968.

13. "Program," *Third Annual Meetingofthe SRS* (Houston, SRS, September 5-7, 1968). SRS 1: 5.

14. "Paper Summaries from the Third Annual Meeting of the SRS, Houston, September 5-7, 1968," *J Bone Joint Surg Am* 51 (1969): 201-06, SRS 1: 4 and 5.

15. "Proceedings," *Third Annual Meeting of the SRS* (Houston, SRS, September 5-1, 1968). SRS 1: 4 and 5. HA: BV.

16. Alf Nachemson, "A Long-Term Follow-up Study of Nun-Treated Scoliosis" (paper presented at Third Annual Meeting of the SRS, Houston, September 5 - 7, 1968).

17. Jorge Galante, Albert B. Schulz, and Ronald DeWald, "Measurements of Forces During the Correction of Idiopathic Scoliosis with the Milwaukee Brace" (paper presented at Third Annual Meeting of the SRS, Houston, September 5-7, 1968).

18. George V. B. Cochran and Theodore R. Waugh, "The External Forces in Correction of Idiopathic Scoliosis" (paper presentedat Third Annual Meeting of the SRS, Houston, September 5-7, 1968).

19. Allen S. Edmonson, "Evaluation of Milwaukee Brace Treatment in Idiopathic Scoliosis" (paper presented at Third Annual Meeting of the SRS, Houston, September 5-7, 1968).

20. David N. Kettleson and John H. Moe, "Milwaukee Brace Treatment of Idiopathic Scoliosis" (paper presented at Third Annual Meeting of the SRS, Houston, September 5-7, 1968).

21. G. Dean MacEwen and Wood W. Lovell, morbidity and morality committee letter to SRS members, February 15, 1968. SRS 1: 5.

22. G. Dean MacEwen, "Neurological Morbidity Report 1968" (paper presented at Third Annual Meeting of the SRS, Houston, September 5-7, 1968). SRS Proceedings 1968: tape 2 side 2; 1-9.

23. Charles M. Evarts, "The Cast Syndrome. A Report of a Case Following Spine Fusion for Scoliosis" (paper presented at Third Annual Meeting of the SRS, Houston,

September 5–7, 1968).

24. Luther M. Strayer III, Joseph C. Risser, and Theodore R. Waugh, "Results of Spine Fusion for Scoliosis Twenty-Five Years or More after Surgery" (paper presented at Third Annual Meeting of the SRS, Houston, September 5–7, 1968).

25. Kenton D. Leatherman, "Resection of Vertebral Bodies" (paper presented at Third Annual Meeting of the SRS, Houston, September 5–7, 1968).

26. William J. Kane, "Minutes of the Executive Committee Meeting, January 18, 1969, New York," accessed October 10, 2014, http://archives srs. org/documents/minutes_bod_exec/1969%20January%2018%20Executive%20Committee%20Minutes.pdf.

27. Paul R. Harrington, letter to Robin Pemberthy, October 24, 1968. HA 124: 16.

28. Robin Pemberthy, letter to Paul R. Harrington, November 1, 1968.

29. Dickson, October 16, 1996. HA 144/1: 9; 9. Dickson recalled the month as October but Harrington's year-end letter referred to November.

30. Ibid., 10–11.

31. Ibid., 12.

32. Paul R. Harington, "NFIP Research Grant CTAE-133 (Clinical Scoliosis) and CTAE-134 (Experimental Scoliosis)" (unpublished material, 1959). HA 122/2: 8.

33. Dickson, October 16, 1996. HA 144/1: 9; 23.

34. Hall, "Spinal Surgery Before and After."

35. Paul R. Harington, letter to my friends, December 1968. HA 122/3: 4.

36. Dickson, October 16, 1996. 6–8.

37. "Luther Terry," accessed October 10, 2014, Wikipedia. http://en.Wikipedia.org/wiki/Luther_Terry.

38. Paul R. Harrington, "Nonoperative Treatment of Scoliosis," *Tex Med* 64 (1968).

39. Paul R. Harington, "Section I: Principles of Scoliosis," *Scoliosis* (unpublished material, 1968).

40. Paul R. Harrington, "Section II: Design and Specifications of Instruments. Recommended Operative Technique, and Terminology," *Scoliosis* (unpublished material, 1968).

41. Sims, "Structural Mechanics."

42. Carter D. Crawford, "Section III, Part 2: Spine Investigation: A Biomechanical Investigation," *Scoliosis* (unpublished material, 1968).

43. Carter D. Crawford, "Spine Investigation: A Biomechanical Investigation" (master's thesis, Rice University, 1964). HA 122/5: 15.

44. Polyvios G. Panayides, "Section III, Part 3: Measurement of Forces in Surgical Instruments and in Implants in the Human Body," *Scoliosis* (unpublished material, 1968).

45. Polyvios G. Panayides, "Measurement of Forces in Surgical Instruments and in Implants in the Human Body" (master's thesis, University at Houston, 1965). HA; BV.

46. Jim Stevens and Tim Willis, "Analysis of Deflection of Harington's Columns Subjected to Compressive Loading" (term project, University of Houston, 1968). HA 122/5: 18.

47. Alan F. Dwyer, N.C. Newton, and Arthur A. Sherwood, "An Anterior Approach to Scoliosis: APreliminary Report," *Clin Orthop Ralat Res* 62 (1969).

48. John Stephen, "Alan Dwyer-Man of Ingenuity, Integrity. and Determination" (paper presented at Harrington Spine Symposium, Kansas City, XS, July 28 – 30, 2005).

49. Alan E. Dwyer, "Experience of Anterior Correction of Scoliosis," *Clin Orthop Relat Res* 93 (1973).

50. William F. Enneking and Paul R. Harrington, "Pathological Changes in Scoliosis," *J Bone Joint Surg Am* 51 (1969).

51. Harrington, "Reduction of Severe Spondylolisthesis."

52. Carlos Vallbona et al., "Pitfalls in the Interpretation of Pulmonary Function Studies in Scoliotic Patients," *Arch Phys Med Rehabil* 50 (1969).

53. "Program," *Fourth Annual Meeting of the SRS* (Anaheim, September 4–6, 1969). SRS 1: 6.

54. "Proceedings," Fourth Annual Meeting of the SRS (Anaheim, September 4–6, 1969). SRS 1: 6. HA: BV.

55. "Paper Summaries from the Fourth Annual Meeting of theSRS, Anaheim, September 4–6, 1969, " *J Bone Joint Surg Am* 52 (1970): 399–409, SRS 1: 6.

56. Byron E. Johnson and Hugh D. Westgate, "Methods of Predicting Normal Lung Volumes in Scoliotic and Other Deformed Patients" (paper presented at Fourth Annual Meeting of the SRS, Anaheim, September 4–6, 1969).

57. Jacob J. Graham, Jerome A. Schack, and Arthur S. Liggett, "Cardiopulmonary Function in Scoliosis: A Preoperative and Postoperative Study" (paper presented at Fourth Annual Meeting of the SRS, Anaheim, September 4-6, 1969).

58. Edward J. Riseborough and Daniel Shannon, " The Effects of Scoliosis on Pulmonary Function as Determined by Studics with Xenon-l33" (paper presented at Fourth Annual Meeting of the SRS, Annual, September 4-6, 1969).

59. Hugh D. Westgate and Byron E. Johnson, "Effects of Scoliosis Therapy on Pulmonary Function"(paper presented at Fourth Annual Meeting of the SRS, Anaheim, September 4-6, 1969).

60. Richard A. Silver et al., "The Evaluation of Pulmonary Function in Patients with Scoliosis Due to Poliomyelitis Before and After Treatment" (paper presented at Fourth Annual Meeting of the SRS, Anaheim, September 4-6, 1969).

61. Alf Nachemson et al., " Clinical Follow-up and Regional Lung Studies in Patients with Non-Treated Idiopathic Scoliosis" (paper presented at Fourth Annual Meeting of the SRS, Anaheim, September 4-6, 1969).

62. "Proceedings," 52-66.

63. Donald L. Gaines, John H. Moe, and Joseph Bocklage, "Management of Wound Infections Following Harrington Instrumentation and Spine Fusion" (paper presented at Fourth Annual Meeting of the SRS, Anaheim, September 4-6, 1969).

64. Pierre Stagnara et al., "Distraction Cast for the Treatment of Scoliosis" (paper presented at Fourth Annual Meeting of the SRS, Anaheim, September 4-6, 1969).

65. John E. Hall, "The Management of Scoliosis" (paper presented at Fourth Annual Meeting of the SRS, Anaheim, September 4-6, 1969).

66. Robert S. Mathews and Frank H. Stelling. III, "Second Look Exploration for Scoliosis" (paper presented at Fourth Annual Meeting of the SRS, Anaheim, September 4-6, 1969).

67. "Proceedings," 256-57.

68. Louis A. Goldstein, " Treatment of Idiopathic Scoliosis by Harrington Instrumentation and Fusion with Fresh Autogenous Iliac Bone Grafts," *J Bone Joint Surg Am* 51(1969).

69. Robert B. Winter, John H. Moe, and Arnold Leonard, "The Anterior Approach for Deformities and Diseases of the Spine" (paper presented at Fourth Annual Meeting of the SRS, Anaheim, September 4-6, 1969).

70. Edward H. Simmons and H. Garside, "A Biomechanical and Clinical Study of Anterior Spinal Instrumentation" (paper presented at Fourth Annual Meeting of the SRS, Anaheim, September 4-6, 1969).

71. G. Dean MacEwen and Wood W. Lovell, "Morbidity and Mortality Committee Report 1969" (paper presented at Fourth Annual Meeting of the SRS, Anaheim, Septembcr 4-6, 1969). SRS Proceedings: 1969; reports 8-14, discussion 14-23.

72. Ronald L. DeWald, "Fixed Skeletal Traction for the Treatment of Severe Scoliosis" (paper presented at Fourth Annual Meeting of the SRS, Anaheim, September 4-6, 1969).

73. Blount, "The Specter of the Bite Deformity Can Now Be Laid."

74. Paul R. Harrington, letter to Jim Hite, November 6, 1969. HA 124: 17.

75. Paul R. Harrington, letter to L. Lyle Johnston, December 31, 1969.

76. Lent C. Johnson, "Physiological Response of Bone and Cartilage to Stress," *Scoliosis* (unpublished material,1969).

77. Paul R. Harrington, "Pathological Response of Bone to Instrumentation," *Scoliosis* (unpublished material, 1969).

78. Paul R. Harington, "General Approach to Scoliosis," *Scoliosis* (unpublished material, 1969).

79. This section provided by Dr. Guy M. Harrison.

80. Harrington, "Instrumentation in Structural Scoliosis."

81. James F. Bennett, letter to Paul R, Harrington, January 27, 1970. HA 124: 18.

82. Alf Nachemson and Gösta Elfström, "A Force-Indicating Distractor for the Harrington-Rod Procedure," *J Bone Joint Surg Am* 51 (1969).

83. Paul R. Harrington, letter to James F. Bennett, February 2, 1970.

84. James F. Bennett, letter to Paul R. Harrington, October 20, 1970.

85. Paul R. Harrington, letter to Jim Hite, June 29, 1971. HA 124: 20.

86. Paul R. Harrington, letter to Tom R. Hughes, March 23, 1970. HA 124: 18. Hughes (correct name. Thomas H. Hughes) wrote Harrington Zimmer's approval but soon wrote again requesting a supporting letter from Spencer.

87. William A. Spencer, letter to Thomas H. Hughes, May 15, 1970.

88. Paul R. Harrington, letter to Jim Hite, June 23, 1970.

89. Jim Hite, letter to Paul R. Harrington, July 17, 1970.

90. "Proceedings of the Fifth Combined Meeting of the Orthopaedic Associations, Sydney, Australia, April 13–17, 1970," *J Bone Joint Surg Br* 52 (1970). HA 122/1: 9.

91. Alan F. Dwyer, "Anterior Instrumentation in Scoliosis," Abstract. *J Bone Joint Surg Br* 52 (1970).

92. *Fifth Combined Orthopaedic Meeting* (Sydney, Australia, April 13–17, 1970). HA 122/1: 9.

93. "Program," *Fifth Annual Meeting of the SRS* (Toronto, September 10–12, 1970). SRS 2: 14.

94. "Paper Summaries from the Fifth Annual Meeting of the SRS, Toronto, September 10–12,1970," *J Bome Joint Surg Am* 53 (1971).

95. "Proccedings," *Fifth Annaal Mecting of the SRS* (Toronmo, September 10–12, 1970). SRS 2:2. HA:BV.

96. "Program," 2.

97. Harrington, "Eleven-Year Investigation."

98. Alf Nachemson and Gösta Elfström, "Intravital Wireles Telemetry of Axial Forces in Harington Distraction Rods" (paper presented at Fifth Annual Meeting of the SRS, Toronto, September 10–12, 1970).

99. Alf Nachemson and Gista Elfsrom, "Intravial Wirelest Telemetry of Axial Forces in Harrington Distraction Roxin Patients with Idioputhic Scoliosis," *J Bone Joint Surg Am* 53 (1971).

100. Augustus A. White and Manchar M. Panjabi, *Clinical Biomechanies of the Spine*, 2nd ed. (Philadelphia: J. B. Lippincott, 1990). Kilopond (kp) is a metric measure of force and 1 kp= 2.2 poundforce.

101. Galante, "Measurement of Forces During Correction."

102. Jorge Galante et al., "Forces Acting in the Milwaukee Brace on Patients Undergoing Treatment for ldiopathic Scoliosis," *J Bone Joint Surg Am* 52 (1970).

103. Theodore R. Waugh, "The Biomechanical Basis for the Utilizaion of Methy Methacrylate in the Treatmem of Scoliosis" (paper presented at Fifth Annual Meeting of the SRS, Toronto, September 10–12, 1970.

104. S. H. G. Connock and Gordon W. Armstrong, "A Transverse Loading System Applied to a Modified Harrington Instrumentation" (paper presented at Fifth Annual Meeting of the SRS, Toronto, September 10–12, 1970).

105. John E. Hall and Rohert Gillespie, "ldiopathic Scoliosis Treated by Harrington Instrumentation and Spine Fusion"(paper presented at Fifth Annual Meeting of the SRS, Toronto, September 10-12, 1970).

106. Ronald DeWald and Merle Schrodt, "Errors in Judgment in the Treatment of Scoliosis"(paper presented at Fifth Annual Meeting of the SRS, Toronto, September 10-12, 1970).

107. E. A. Sue-A-Quan, H. Garside, and Edward H. Simmons, "Biomechanical Stodies with a Scoliosis Simulator(paper presented at Fifth Annunl Meeting of the SRS, Toronto, September 10-12, 1970).

108. H. Leon Brooks, John C. Brown, and Charles A. Bonnelt, "Hip Function in Paralytic Scoliosis After Preoperative Halo-Femoral Traction, Spine Fusion, and Prolonged Casting" (paper presented at Fifth Annual Meeting of the SRS, Toronto, September 10-12, 1970).

109. Hugo A. Keim and Sadek K. Hilal, "Spinal Angiognaphy in Scoliosis Patients" (paper presented at Fifth Annual Meeting of the SRS, Toronto, September 10-12, 1970).

110. Charles M. Evars, Robert B. Winter, and John E. Hall, "The Spinal—Taction Syndrome: Arteriomesenteric-Duodenal Obstruction Associated with Corretion of Spinal Curvature.With Report of Three lllustrative Cases" (paper presented at Fifth Annual Meeting of the SRS, Toronto, September 10-12, 1970).

111. Charles M. Evarts, Rober B. Winter, and John E. Hall, "Vascular Compression of the Duodenum Associated with the Treatment of Scoliosis," *J Bone Joint Surg Am* 53 (1971).

112. Robern Roaf, "Rotation, Its Causes and Treatment of Scoliosis" (paper presented at Fifth Annual Meeting of the SRS, Toronto, September 10-12, 1970).

113. Kenton D. Leatherman, "Neurological Problems inKyphosis and Scoliosis" (paper presented at Fifth Annual Meeting of the SRS, Toronto, September 10-12, 1970).

114. Arthur Yau et al., "The Treatment of Scoliosis in Hong Kong" (paper presented at Fifth Annual Meeting of the SRS, Toronto, September 10-12, 1970).

115. Hugh D. Westgate and Byron E. Johnson, "Preoperative Pulmonary Evaluation and Postoperative Respiraton Management of Patients with Severe Thoracie Scoliosis (paper presented at Fifth Annual Meeting of the SRS, Toronto, September 10-12,

1970).

116. D. C. Shannon, Edward J. Riseborough, and H. Kazemi, "Ventilation Perfusion Relationships Following Correction of Kyphoscoliosis"(paper presented at Fith Annual Meeting of the SRS, Toronto, September 10–12, 1970).

117. André Lamarre et al., "Pulmonary Funetion in One Year After Surgical Corection"(paper presented at Fifth Annual Meeting of the SRS, Toronto, September 10–12, 1970).

118. Robert B. Winter, John H. Moe, and J. F. Wang, "Congenital Kyphosis"(paper presented at FiFth Annual Meeting of the SRS, Toronto, September 10–12, 1970).

119. "Proceedings,"150–55.

120. R. E. Heron and Paul R. Harington, "ThreeDimensional Photography in the Detection, Evaluationand Documenlation of Structural Abnormality"(paper presented at Fifth Annual Meeting of the SRS, Toronto, September 10–12, 1970).

121. Zimmer invoice to TIRR, September 10, 1970. HA 124: 18

122. Paul R. Harrington, letter to Jim Hite, Octoher 14, 1970.

123. James F. Bennelt, Ietter to Paul R. Harrington, October 20, 1970.

124. James E. Bennett, letter to Paul R. Harrington, December 22,1970. Bennett must have meant left-handed.

125. Harington, "Spine Analysis." HA: BV.

126. Paul R. Harrington, "Variations in the Flexibility ofthe Idiopathic Scoliotic Curve," *Scoliosis* (unpublished material, 1970).

127. Paul R. Harrington, "The Passible Etiology of Idiopathic Scoliosis: A Case Report," *Scoliosis* (unpublished material, 1970).

128. R. E. Heron, Paul R. Harrington, and J. E. Hugg, "Three-Dimensional Photography in the Detection, Evaluation and Documentation of Structural Abnormalities," *Scoliosis*(unpublished material, 1970).

129. Paul R. Harrington, letter to Zimmer, Royalies Division, March 5,1971. HA 124: 20.

130. William A. Spencer, memo to A. O. Johnson, March 5, 1971.

131. David B. Levine, "Minutes of the Executive Commitlet Meeting, March 7, 1971, San Francisco," accessed July 10, 2014, SRS Archives, http://archives.srs.org/documents/minutes_bod_exec/index.html.

132. Harrington, June 29, 1971.

133. Vemon R. Scott, letter to Paul R. Harrington, July 2, 1971.

134. Kenneth H. Johnson, letter to Paul R. Harington, Sepember 7, 1971.

135. Paul R. Harington, letter to Kenneth H. Johnson, September 15, 1971.

136. Kenneth H. Johnson, letter to Paul R. Harington, September 21, 1971.

137. "Program," *Sixth Annual Meeting of the SRS* (Hartford, CT, September 8-10, 1971). SRS 3: 3.

138. David B. Levine, "Minutes of the Sixth Annual SRS Executive Committee Meeting, Parts I and II, September 7 and 10, Hartford, CT" (unpublished material, 1971). SRS 3: 3.

139. David B. Levine, "Minutes of the Sixth Annual SRS Business Meetings, September 8 and 10, Hartford, CT(unpubished material, 1971).

140. "Paper Summaries from the Sixth Annual Meeting of the SRS, Hartfond, CT, September 8-10, 1971," *J Bone Joint Surg Am* 55 (1972).

141. Theodore A. Wangner, Marr P. Mullen, and James W. Tupper, "Operative Experienee with Increased Doral Kyphosis (Analysis of Eleven Cases with One to Eight Year Follow-up!" (paper presented at Sixth Annual Meeting of the SRS, Hartford, CT, September 8-10, 1971).

142. Clyde L. Nash, Jerald S. Brodky, and Thomas J. Croft, "A Model for Electrical Monitoring of Spinal Cord Function in Scoliosis Patients Undengoing Correction" (paper presented at Sixth Annual Meeting of the SRS, Hartfard, CT, September 8-10, 1971). SRS 3: 4; manuscript.

143. John E. Hall and Irvin S. Spira, "Dwyer Amterior Instrumentation and Interbody Fusion of the Spine in the Management of Scoliosis. Preliminary Report" (paper presented at Sixth Annual Meeting of the SRS, Hartfonrd, CT, September 8-10, 1971).

144. Jesse H. Dickson, "Preoperative and Postoperative Evaluation of Scoliotic Patients for Hiatal Hernia" (paper presented at Sixth Annual Meeting of the SRS, Hartford, CT, September 8-10, 1971).

145. Mckelvie, "The High Incidence of Hiatal Hernia."

146. Paul R. Harrington, "The Possible Etiology of Idiopathic Scoliosis, a Case Report" (paper presented at Sixth Ammual Meeting of the SRS, Hartford, CT, September 8-10, 1971).

147. Harrington probably attended a meeting in Nijmegen, Netherlands in 1970 or

1971 and met Kazmin.

148. Phillip A. Zorab, ed. "Proceedings," *Symposium on Scliosis* (London, UK, National Fund for Research into Poliomyelitis and Other Crippling Diseases, 1965).

149. Paul R. Harrington, "The Missing Link' (a Case Report)," in *Scoliosis and Growth*, ed. Phillip A. Zorab (Edinburgh: Churchill Livingstome, 1971), 105-07.

150. Paul R. Harrington and Hugh S. Tullos, "Spondylolisthesis in Children: Observations and Surgical Treatment," *Clin Orthop Relat Res* 79(1971).

151. Ken Roth, "Spinal Deformities in Myelomeningocele: A Radiological Assessment," *Scoliosis* (unpublished material, 1971), 1-29.

152. Allen Barber, "Observations of Spinal Maturity in Adolescent ldopathic Scoliosis," *Scoliosis* (unpublished material, 1971), 90-102.

153. David B. Levine, "Minutes of the Semi-Annual SRS Board of Diredors' Meeting, January 30, Washington, DC" (unpublished material, 1972).

154. Paul R. Harrington, letter to Jim Hite, January 17, 1972. HA 124: 21.

155. Harington, "Spondylolisthesis in Children."

156. Robent E. Beam, letter to Paul R. Harington, February 11, 1972. HA 124: 21.

157. Paul R. Harrington, letter to Roert E. Beam, February 18, 1972.

158. Dickson, October 16, 1996. HA 144/1:9; 8.

159. Harrington, "Curriculum Viac." HA 101: 2; 1.

160. Lyke Johnston, letter to Paul R. Harrington, May 1, 1972. HA 124: 21.

161. Zimmer, packing slip to Paul R. Harrington, May 9, 1972.

162. Harington, "Curriculum Vite," 10.

163. Paul R. Harrington, letter to Kenneth H. Johnon, July 25, 1972. HA 124: 21.

164. Paul R. Harrington, "Technical Details in Relation to the Successful Use of Instrumentation in Scoliosis," *Onthop Clin North Am* 3(1972).

165. Paul R. Harrington, "Instrumentation Techniques in Spin Surgery" (paper presented at Postgraduate Course on the Management and Care of the Scoliosis Patient, New York, December 1971), 50-58. Clendening Lihrary, Walter P. Blount Collection.

166. "Bogram," *Seventh Annual Meeing of the SRS* (Wilmington, DE, September 13-15, 1972). SRS 3:6.

167. David B. Levine, "Minutes of the Aanual SRS Board of Directors' Meeting, September 12 and 15, Wilmington, DE" (umpublished material, 1972).

168. David B. Levine, "Minutes of the Seventh Annual SRS Business Mectings, September 13 and 14, Wilmington, DE" (unpublished material, 1972).

169. Ibid.

170. John H. Doherty, "Complications of Fusion in Lumbar Scoliosis" (paper presented at Seventh Annual Meeting of the SRS, Wilmington, DE, September 13-15, 1972).

171. Russell W. Hardy, Jr., Clyde L. Nash, Jr, and Jerald S. Brodkey, "Folllow-up Report, Experimental and Clinical Studies in Spinal Cord Monitoring: The Effect of Pressure, Anoxia and Ischemia on Spinal-Cord Function" (paper presented at Seventh Annual Meeting of the SRS, Wilmington, DE, September 13-15, 1972). SRS 3: 6; manuscript.

172. George F. Dommisse, "The Blood Supply of the Human Spinal Cord at Birth. A Report on a Micro-Dissection Study of 27 Foetal and Neonate Cadavers" (Maser of Surgery thesis, University of Cape Town, South Africa, 1972). Clendening Library, SRS Collection.

173. George F. Dommisse, *The Arteries and Veins of the Human Spinal Cord from Birth* (Edinburgh: Churchill Livingstone, 1975). Clendening Library, SRS Collection.

174. Catherine Vauzelle, Pierre Stagnara, and P. Jouvinroux, "Functional Monitoring of Spinal Cord Activity During Spinal Surgery" (paper presented at Seventh Annual Meeting of the SRS, Wilmington, DE, September 13-15, 1972).

175. "Paper Summaries from the Seventh Annual Meeting of the SRS, Wilmington, DE, September 13-15, 1972," *J Bone Joint Surg Am* 55 (1973).

176. Edgar G. Dawson, Aryton Caron, and John H. Moe, "Surgical Management of Scoliosis in the Adult" (paper presented at Seventh Annual Meeting of the SRS, Wilmington, DE, September 13-15, 1972).

177. Gordon W. D. Armstrong, S. H. G. Connock, and T. J. Blachut, "Present Status of the Transverse Loading System (Modified Harrington Instrumentation)" (paper presented at Seventh Annual Meeting of the SRS, Wilmington, DE, September 13-15, 1972).

178. Jesse H. Dickson, "Growth Arrest in Tall Scoliotic Girls" (paper presented at Seventh Annual Meeting of the SRS, Wilmington, DE, September 13-15, 1972).

179. Paul R. Harrington, letter to James F. Bennett, Scptember 20, 1972. HA 124: 21.

180. Bennett, January 27, 1970. HA 124: 18.

181. Harrington, February 2, 1970.

182. L. J. Diettrich, letter to Paul R. Harrington, September 27, 1972, HA 124: 21.

183. Paul R. Harrington, letter to L. J. Diettrich, October 4, 1972.

184. Paul R. Harrington, "Abstracts and Discussion of Scoliosis 1962 through 1971 Issues," *Scoliosis* (unpublished Material, 1972).

185. Ibid., 257.

CHAPTER 11

1. Nickel, "Reminiscences." HA 101: 22; 2.

2. L. J. Diettrich, letter to Paul R. Harrington, January 26, 1973. HA 124: 22.

3. David B. Levine, "Minutes of the Semi-Annual SRS Board of Directors Meeting, February 1, 1973, Las Vegas," accessed 2014, SRS Archives, http://archives.srs.org/documents/minutes_ bod_ exec/1973% 20February%201 % 20BOD% 20Semi-Annual% 20% 20BOD%20Meeting% 20Minutes.pdf.

4. Louis A. Goldstein and Theodore R. Waugh, "Classification and Terminology of Scoliosis," *Clin Orthop Relat Res* 93 (1973).

5. Paul R. Harrington, letter to Jim Hite, May 4, 1973. HA 124: 22.

6. Jeri Bone, letter to Vernon R. Scott, April 4, 1973.

7. Harrington, "Curriculum Vitae." HA 101: 2; 10. S. Harrington, August 23, 1976, HA 101: 26: 2.

9. Paul R. Harrington, May 9, 1973. HA 101: 20.

10. Harrington, "Curriculum Vitae." HA 101: 2; 1.

11. Marshall R. Urist, letter to Paul R. Harrington, March 17, 1972. HA 101: 20.

12. Paul R. Harrington, letter to Marshall R. Urist, January 5, 1973.

13. Eugene J. Nordby, letter to Paul R. Harrington, March 19, 1973.

14. Harrington, May 9, 1973.

15. Eugene J. Nordby, letter to Paul R. Harrington, May 15, 1973.

16. Paul R. Harrington, letter to Dane A. Miller, April 20, 1973. HA 124: 22.

17. Harrington, May 4, 1973.

18. Dane A. Miller, letter to Paul R. Harrington, May 25, 1973.

19. Harrington, January 17, 1972, HA 124: 21.

20. Johnston, May 1, 1972.

21. Kenneth H. Johnson, letter to Paul R. Harrington, May 22, 1973. HA 124: 22.

22. Paul R. Harrington, letter to Kenneth H. Johnson, May 30, 1973.

23. Dane A. Miller, letter to Paul R. Harrington, July 17, 1973.

24. Guenther H. Hille, "Titanium for Surgical Implants," *J Mater* 1 (1966).

25. Miller, July 17, 1973.

26. D. F. Williams, "A Combined Metallurgical and Histological Study of Tissue-Prosthesis Interactions in Orthopaedic Patients" (paper presented at Prostheses and Tissue: The Interface Problem, Clemson University, April 14-18, 1973).

27. Patrick G. Laing, "Compatability of Biomaterials," *Orthop Clin North Am* 4 (1973).

28. Dane A. Miller, shipping order to Paul R. Harrington, July 17, 1973.

29. Joe W. King and William A. Spencer, letter to Associate Dean Hebbel Hoff, July 3, 1973. HA 101: 4.

30. Spencer, "Mading Medal." HA 101: 21.

31. Dickson, "Paul Randall Harrington: His Life and Work," HA 146: 2; 11, 15.

32. Jeri Bone, letter to Dane A. Miller, August 13, 1973. HA 124: 22.

33. David B. Levine, "Minutes of the SRS Annual Board of Directors' Meetings, Parts I and II, September 17 and 21, 1973, Gothenburg, Sweden," accessed February, 2014, SRS Archives, http://archives. srs.org/documents/minutes_bod_ exec/1973%20September%2017%20BOD%20Meeting%20Minutes.pdf.

34. "Program," *Eighth Annual Meeting of the SRS* (Gothenburg. Sweden, SRS Archives, September 17-21, 1973). HA: SRS Programs.

35. David B. Levine, "Minutes of the SRS Annual Business Meetings, September 17-21. 1973, Gothenburg, Sweden." accessed 2014, SRS Archives, http://archives. srs.org/documents/minutes_ bod_ exec/1973%20September/2017%20BOD%20Meeting%20Minutes.pdf.

36. "Paper Summaries from the Eighth Annual Meeting of the SRS, Gothenburg, Sweden, September 17-21, 1973," *J Bone Joint Surg Am* 56 (1974).

37. Alberto Ponte, "Postoperative Paraplegia Due to Hypercorrection of Scoliosis and Drop in Blood Pressure" (paper presented at Eighth Annual Meeting of the SRS, Gothenburg, Sweden, September 17-21, 1973).

38. Clyde L. Nash and Kerry Nevins, "A Lateral Look at Pulmonary Function in

Scoliosis" (paper presented at Eighth Annual Meeting of the SRS, Gothenburg, Sweden. September 17-21, 1973).

39. Robert B. Winter, Wood W. Lovell, and John H. Moe, "Malignant Idiopathic Lordoscoliosis (paper presented at Eighth Annual Meeting of the SRS, Gothenburg, Sweden, September 17-21, 1973).

40. John C. Brown and Jaequelin Perry, "Thoracic Lordosis Following Long Posterior Spine Fusions for Paralytic Scoliosis (paper presented at Eighth Annual Meeting of the SRS, Gothenburg, Sweden, September 17-21, 1973).

41. Carl Hirsch and Albert Schultz, "Mechanical Analysis of Techniques for Improved Correction of Idiopathic Scoliosis (paper presented at Eighth Annual Meeting of the SRS, Gothenburg, Sweden, September 17-21, 1973).

42. Robert Roaf, "Horizontal Forces in the Correction of Scoliosis" (paper presented at Eighth Annual Meeting of the SRS, Gothenburg, Sweden, September 17-21, 1973).

43. Bertil Stener, "Resection of the Spine for Tumors" (paper presented at Eighth Annual Meeting of the SRS, Gothenburg, Sweden, September 17-21, 1973).

44. Paul R. Harrington, "A Written Presidential Welcome" (paper presented at Eighth Annual Meeting of the SRS, Gothenburg. Sweden, September 17-21, 1973). HA 145: 1.

45. "Post-Convention Meeting with Groupe d' Étude de la Scoliose," (Lyon, France, September 25-27, 1973). SRS 4:1.

46. Paul R. Harrington, letter to George F. Dommisse, January 23, 1974. SRS 4: 4.

47. Dan Page, letter to Paul R. Harrington, September 12, 1973. HA 124: 22, Measurements made years later suggest the hook tip thickness change was never activated.

48. Paul R. Harrington, letter to Dan Page, October 17, 1973.

49. J. Alan Morgan, letter to Paul R. Harrington, October 23, 1973.

50. Paul R, Harrington, letter to Dr. Balu Sankaran, December 10, 1973.

51. Jesse H. Dickson and Paul R. Harrington, "The Evolution of the Harrington Instrumentation Technique in Scoliosis," *J Bone Joint Surg Am* 55 (1973).

52. Jesse H. Dickson and Paul R. Harrington, "Pre-and Postoperative Evaluation of Scoliotic Patients for Hiatal Hernia," *South Med J* 66 (1973).

53. McKelvie, "The High Incidence of Hiatal Hernia."

54. Paul R. Harrington and Jesse H. Dickson, "The Development and Further Prospects of Internal Fixation of the Spine," *Isr J Med Sci* 9 (1973). CW: PRH; 259-64.

55. Jesse H. Dickson, Paul R. Harrington, and Wendell D, Erwin, "Harrington Instrumentation in the Fractured, Unstable Thoracic and Lumbar Spine," *Tex Med* 69 (1973).

56. Harrington, "History and Development of Harrington Instrumentation."

57. Harrington, "Eleven-Year Investigation."

58. Tambornino, "Harrington Instrumentation in Correction of Scoliosis."

59. Goldstein, "Treatment of Idiopathic Scoliosis by Harrington Instrumentation and Fusion with Fresh Autogenous Iliac Bone Grafts."

60. Paul R. Harrington, "Curriculum Vitae" (unpublished material, 1974). HA 101: 2: 12.

61. Dane A. Miller, letter to Paul R. Harrington, February 11, 1974. HA 124: 23.

62. Paul R. Harrington, letter to Dane A. Miller, February 14, 1974.

63. Dane A. Miller, letter to Paul R. Harrington, March 5, 1974.

64. Dan Page, letter to Paul R. Harrington, March 11, 1974.

65. Paul R. Harrington, letter to Dan Page, March 20, 1974.

66. Rod length refers to the full 1/4-diameter rod between the collar and the beginning of the ratchets.

67. Paul R. Harrington, letter to Dane A. Miller, March 27, 1974.

68. Paul R. Harrington, letter to Mike Hall, March 19, 1974.

69. Paul R. Harrington, letter to Ken Johnson, May 14, 1974.

70. George Shen, letter to Paul R. Harrington, July 8, 1974.

71. David O. Warner, letter to Paul R. Harrington, March 25, 1974.

72. "Harrington Spine Foundations" (unpublished material, 1974-79), HA 122/3: 5.

73. Harrington, "Curriculum Vitae." HA 102: 2.

74. Theodore R. Waugh, "Minutes of the SRS Annual Board of Directors and Member Meetings, September 10-13, 1974. San Francisco," accessed 2014, SRS Archives, http://archives.srs.org/documents/minutes_ bod_exec/1974%20September%20BOD%20Meeting%20Minutes.pdf.

75. Robert B. Winter, letter lo William J. Kane, August 7, 1974. SRS 4: 2.

76. Waugh,"Minutes."

77. Nickel,"Reminiscences." HA 101: 22.

78. Colleen A. Fliedner, G. Maureen Rodgers, and Thomas E, Hall. *Rancho Los Amigos Medical Center*: Centennial(1888—1988) (Downey, CA: Rancho Los Amigos Medical Center, 1990). 246.

79. Nickel, "Reminiscences."

80. Eyler, May 24, 1973. HA 122/3: 1.

81. Denton A. Cooley, letter to Robert B. Winter, August 27, 1974. HA 101: 22.

82. "Program," Ninth Annual Meeting of the SRS (San Francisco, September 11-13, 1974). SRS 4: 4.

83. " Abstracts of Papers Presented," *Ninth Annual Meeting of the SRS* (San Francisco, September 11-13, 1974).

84. Waldemar C. Pinto, "The Role of Traction in Pre-Operative Correction of Scoliosis" (paper presented at Ninth Annual Meeting of the SRS, San Francisco September 11-13, 1974).

85. Robert B. Winter,"The Third Era" (paper presented at Ninth Annual Meeting of the SRS, San Francisco, September 11-13, 1974). HA 145: 1.

86. Willard J. Hull et al.,"Spinal Deformity in Myclomeningocele: Natural History. Evaluation and Treatment (paper presented at Ninth Annual Meeting of the SRS, San Francisco, September 11-13, 1974).

87. Robert Gillespie and John H. Wedge,"The Problems of Scoliosis in Paraplegic Children" (paper presented at Ninth Annual Meeting of the SRS, San Francisco, September 11-13, 1974).

88. Brooks,"Hip Function in Paralytic Scoliosis After Preoperative Halo-Femoral Traction. Spine Fusion, and Prolonged Casting."

89. Walter P. Blount, letter to Robert B. Winter, August 23, 1974. SRS 4: 2.

90. Waugh,"Minutes."

91. Jesse H. Dickson et al., letter to Kenton D. Leatherman, November 18, 1974. SRS 4: 2.

92. Jesse H. Dickson, letter to SRS Board of Directors, February 20, 1975.

93. Dane A. Miller, letter to Paul R. Harrington, October 7, 1974. HA 124: 23.

94. George Shen, letters to Paul R. Harrington, September 13, October 3, November 5, November 22, 1974.

95. Paul R. Harrington, letters to George Shen, September 25, December 5, December 5, 1974.

96. S. Dwight Woods, letter to Paul R. Harrington, December 19, 1974. HA 101: 25.

97. Paul R. Harrington, letter to S. Dwight Woods, December 23, 1974.

98. S. Dwight Woods, letter to Paul R. Harrington, January 9, 1975.

99. The "odd posture on standing" was likely a result of loss of lumbar lordosis.

100. Helen M. Sims, letter to Paul R. Harrington, March 13, 1975.

101. Dwight D. Sutherland and Archie R. Dykes, letter to Paul R. Harrington, January 21, 1975. HA 101: 24.

102. Archie R. Dykes, letter to Paul R. Harrington, February 15, 1975.

103. Paul R. Harrington, "Harrington Instrumentation for Treatment of Unstable Deformities of the Human Spine" (paper presented at Peter T. Bohan Lecture, Kansas City, MO, May I6, 1975). HA: BV. HA 101: 23.

104. Sutherland, January 21, 1975.

105. "Program," *Tenth Annual Meeting of the SRS* (Louisville, September 10-12, 1975).

106. Allen S. Edmonson, "Morbidity Report. January through December 1974" (paper presented at Tenth Annual Meeting of the SRS. Louisville, September 10-12, 1975). SRS 4: 9.

107. G. Dean MacEwen, William P. Bunnell, and Krishnaswami Sriram, "Acute Neurological Complications in the Treatment of Scoliosis: A Report of the Scoliosis Research Society," *J Bone Joint Surg Am* 57 (1975).

108. Paul R. Harrington, "Unusual Case Presentations" (unpublished material. 1961). HA: BV; figure 17.

109. Harrington, August 23, 1976. HA 101: 26; 14.

110. Author's recollection.

111. Cameron Lindberg, John C. Brown, and Charles A. Bonnett, " The Surgical Treatment of Spinal Deformity in Myclodysplasia" (paper presented at Tenth Annual Meeting of the SRS, Louisville, September 10-12, 1975).

112. Matthew Malerich, John C. Brown, and Charles A. Bonnett, "Evaluation of the Large Sacral Alar Hook and Anterior Transverse Process Fusion in the Treatment of Paralytic Scoliosis (paper presented at Tenth Annual Meeting of the SRS, Louisville,

September 10-12, 1975).

113. C. Scott Harrison, "Use of the Dwyer Instrumentation to Fuse into the Sacrum" (paper presented at Tenth Annual Meeting of the SRS, Louisville, September 10-12, 1975).

114. John E. Hall, "Dwyer Instrumentation Plus Vertebral Body Resection in Paraplegic Scoliosis" (paper presented at Tenth Annual Meeting of the SRS, Louisville, September 10-12, 1975).

115. Douglas W. McKay, "The McKay Plate for Kyphosis of the Spine" (paper presented at Tenth Annual Meeting of the SRS, Louisville, September 10-12, 1975).

116. Jan W. Duncan et al., Surgical Treatment of Meningomyelocele," *Tenth Annual Meeting of the SRS* (Louisville, September 10-12, 1975).

117. Paul R. Harrington, letter to George F. Dommisse, July 30, 1976. SRS 5: 3.

118. Paul R. Harrington, letter lo George F. Dommisse, October 4, 1976.

CHAPTER 12

1. Peter F. Williams, "Nothing Endures but Change: Third Harrington Guest Lecture" (paper presented at Twelfth Annual Meeting of the SRS, Hong Kong, October 24-27, 1977). HA 145: manuscript.

2. Paul R. Harrington, letter to Eugenia A. Klein, August 29, 1975. HA 41:9.

3. Eugenia A. Klein, letter to Paul R. Harrington, October 26, 1976.

4. Marc A. Asher, "Harrington's The Human Spine," in *Pathogenesis of Idiopathic Scoliosis*, cd. Rae R. Jacobs (Chicago: SRS, 1984).

5. Terry A. Clyburn, oral history to Marc A. Asher, November 6, 2009. HA 144/1: 7.

6. Vicki L. Albright, letter to Eugenia Klein, February 6, 1978. HA 41:9.

7. Eugenia A. Klein, letter to Vicki L. Albright, June 6, 1978.

8. Vicki L Albright, letter to Eugenia A. Klein, June 26, 1979.

9. Eugenia A. Klein, letter lo Vicki L. Albright, August 13, 1979.

10. Harrington, "The Human Spine." HA 35-49.

11. R. Craig Ponder et al., "Results of Harrington Instrumentation and Fusion in the Adult Idiopathic Scoliosis Patient," *J Bone Joint Surg Am* 57 (1975).

12. Harrington, "Unusual Case Presentations." HA: BV: Figure 18.

13. Wendell D. Erwin, Jesse H. Dickson, and Paul R. Harrington, "The

Postoperative Management of Scoliosis Patients Treated with Harrington Instrumentation and Fusion," *J Bone Joint Surg Am* 58 (1976).

14. Lloyd L. Leider, John H. Moe, and Robert B. Winter, "Early Ambulation after the Surgical Treatment of Idiopathic Scoliosis," *J Bone Joint Surg Am* 55 (1973).

15. Richard S. Curtis et al., "Results of Harrington Instrumentation in the Treatment for Severe Scoliosis," *Clin Orthop Relat Res* 122(1979).

16. Wendell D. Erwin, Jesse H. Dickson, and Paul R. Harington, "Clinical Review of Patients with Broken Harrington Rods," *J Bone Joint Surg Am* 62 (1980).

17. Harrington, "An Experimental Study of Scoliosis."

18. Harrington, "Is Scoliosis Reversible? In Vivo Observations of Scoliosis in Mice."

19. Paul R. Harrington, "The Etiology of Idiopathic Scoliosis." *Clin Orthop Relat Res* 126 (1977).

20. Harrington, "The Therapeutic Value of Cevitamic Acid." HA 101: 7.

21. Benjamin Brenner et al., "Instrumentation of the Spine for Fracture Dislocations in Children," *Childs Brain* 3 (1977).

22. Jesse H. Dickson, Paul R. Harrington, and Wendell D. Erwin, "Results of Reduction and Stabilization of the Severely Fractured Thoracic and Lumbar Spine," *J Bone Joint Surg Am* 60 (1978).

23. Paul R. Harrington and Jesse H. Dickson, "Spinal Instrumentation in the Treatment of Severe Progressive Spondylolisthesis," *Clin Orthop Relat Res* 117(1976).

24. Hanrrington, August 23,1976. HA 101:26.

25. John P. O'Brien, letter to Paul R. Harrington, October 5, 1976

26. "Program," Eleventh Annual Meeting of the SRS (Ottawa, Ontario, Canada, SRS Archives, September 4-6, 1976).

27. "Transactions of the Eleventh Annual Meeting of the SRS. September 4-6, 1976, Ottawa, Ontario, Canada," *Orthop Trans* 1 (1977).

28. Jesse H. Dickson, Paul R. Harrington, and Wendell D. Erwin, "Reduction and Stabilization of the Severely Fractured Spine Using Harrington Instrumentation" (paper presented at Eleventh Annual Meeting of the SRS, Ottawa, Ontario, Canada, September 4-6, 1976).

29. Gordon W. L. Armstrong, Eric W. Peterson, and I. V. Adair, "Harrington Instrumentation for Spinal Fractures" (paper presented at Eleventh Annual Meeting of

the SRS, Ottawa, Ontario, Canada, September 4-6, 1976).

30. Gordon Robin, Zvi Yosipovitch, and Myer Makin, "Harrington Instrumentation in Thoraco-Lumbar Fracture Dislocation" (paper presented at Eleventh Annual Meeting of the SRS, Ottawa, Ontario, Canada, September 4-6, 1976).

31. Richard S. Curtis et al., "Results of Harrington Instrumentation in the Treatment of Severe Scoliosis" (paper presented at Eleventh Annual Metting of the SRS, Ottawa, Ontario, Canada, September 4-6, 1976).

32. Dennis Wenger et al., "Surgical Management of Scheuerman's Kyphosis" (paper presented at Eleventh Annual Meeting of the SRS, Ottawa, Ontario, Canada, September 4-6, 1976).

33. Kenton D. Leatherman, "Spinal Deformity in Myelodysplasia-Surgical Treatment" (paper presented at Eleventh Annual Meeting of the SRS, Ottawa, Ontario, Canada, September 4-6, 1976).

34. Dennis N. Sakai et al., "Spinal Collapse in Duchenne's Muscular Dystrophy" (paper presented at Eleventh Annual Meeting of the SRS, Ottawa, Ontario, Canada, September 4-6, 1976).

35. Dennis C. Patterson and Andrew D. Sutherland, "The Management of Spinal Deformity in Patients with Myelomeningocele" (paper presented at Eleventh Annual Meeting of the SRS, Ottawa, Ontario, Canada, September 4-6, 1976).

36. Francis Denis and John H. Moe, "The Iatrogenic Loss of Lumbar Lordosis" (paper presented at Eleventh Annual Meeting of the SRS, Ottawa, Ontario, Canada, September 4-6, 1976).

37. Anthony P. Dwyer et al., "Telemetric Monitoring of Cable Tensions Following Dwyer Spinal Instrumentations" (paper presented at Eleventh Annual Meeting of the SRS, Ottawa, Ontario, Canada, September 4-6, 1976).

38. Michael F. Schafer, Dan Page, and George Shen, "Mechanical Evaluation of the Dwyer Screw/Cable Attachment" (paper presented at Eleventh Annual Meeting of the SRS, Ottawa, Ontario, Canada, September 4-6, 1976).

39. Marr P. Mullen, Donald R. Gunn, and James W. Tupper, "Early Experience with Weiss Spinal Spring Instrumentation for Unstable Fractures and Other Spinal Deformities" (paper presented at Eleventh Annual Meeting of the SRS, Ottawa, Ontario, Canada, September 4-6, 1976).

40. Courtney W Brown et al., "Weiss Spring Instrumentation for Fracture

Dislocation of the Spine with Associated Neurological Deficit" (paper presented at Eleventh Annual Meeting of the SRS, Ottawa, Ontario, Canada, September 4 - 6, 1976).

41. Eduardo R Luque and Alfredo Cardoso, "Segmental Correction of Scoliosis with Rigid Internal Fixation" (paper presented al Eleventh Annual Meeting of the SRS Ottawa, Ontario, Canada, September 4-6, 1976).

42. "Program," 25, 33.

43. Albert E. Sanders, "Eduardo Luque (1931—2002)" (unpublished material, 2008). HA 103/4: 9.

44. John P. Kostuik, "Morbidity Report, Scoliosis Research Society, 1975," *Orthop Trans* 1 (1977): 141-42.

45. "Program," 18. SRS 5:3.

46. William P. Bunnell, Leo V. Gould, and Hansen A. Yuan, "Computerized Axial Tomography in the Study of Spinal Deformity" (paper presented at Eleventh Annual Meeting of the SRS, Ottawa, Ontario, Canada, September 4-6, 1976).

47. John P. O'Brien, letter to Paul R. Harrington. September 8, 1977. HA 101:26.

48. "Program," Twelfth Annual Meeting of the SRS (Hong Kong, October 24-27, 1977). SRS 5: 4.

49. "Program," Joint Meeting of Japanese and North American Scoliosis Society (Kyoto, Japan. Japanese Scoliosis Society, October 20-21, 1977). SRS 5: 4.

50. Alf Nachemson and Lars Dahlberg, "The Econoinic Aspects of Scoliosis Treatment" (paper presented at Joint Meeting of the Japanese and North American Scoliosis Societies, Kyoto, Japan, October 20-21, 1977).

51. Louis A. Goldstein, "The Surgical Management of Scoliosis: A Forty-Year Personal Experience" (paper presented at Twelfth Annual Meeting of the SRS, Hong Kong, October 24-27, 1977). Read by P. William Hanke. SRS 5:4. HA 145: 1; manuscript.

52. Pier Giorgio Marchetti and A. Faldini, "'End Fusions' in the Treatment of Some Progressing or Severe Scoliosis in Childhood or Early Adolescence" (paper presented at Twelfth Annual Meeting of the SRS, Hong Kong, October 24-27, 1977).

53. Klaus Zielke, R. Stunkat, and F. Beaujean, "Dcrotation and Fusion-Anterior Spinal Instrumentation" (paper presented at Twelfth Annual Meeting of the SRS, Hong Kong, October 24-27, 1977).

54. Stephen, "Alau Dwyer."

55. Lyle J. Micheli and John E. Hall, "The Use of Modified Dwyer Instrumentation in Anterior Stabilization of the Spine" (paper presented at Twelfth Annual Meeting of the SRS, Hong Kong, October 24-27,1977).

56. Hall, "Dwyer Instrumentation Plus Vertebral Body Resection in Paraplegic Scoliosis."

57. Hugh P. Brown, "Surgical Management of Congenital Lumbar Kyphosis in Myelomeningocele, A Preliminary Report of a New Procedure" (paper presented at Twelfth Annual Meeting of the SRS, Hong Kong, October 24-27, 1977).

58. David L. Spencer and Ronald L. DeWald, "Simultaneous Anterior and Posterior Spine Fusion: Indications and Techniques" (paper presented at Twelfth Annual Meeting of the SRS, Hong Kong, October 24-27, 1977).

59. Clyde L. Nash, "Spinal Cord Monitoring in Course of Spinal Surgery" (paper presented at Joint Meeting of Japanese and North American Scoliosis Societies, Kyoto, Japan, October 20-21, 1977).

60. Yoshio Harada et al., "Spinal Cord Monitoring Using Evoked Potentials" (paper presented at Twelfth Annual Meeting of the SRS, Hong Kong, October 24-27, 1977).

61. Tetsuya Tamaki et al., "Spinal Cord Monitoring Utilizing Evoked Potential in Course of Spinal Cord Surgery" (paper presented at Joint Meeting of Japanese and North American Scoliosis Societies, Kyoto, Japan, October 20-21, 1977).

62. George F. Dommisse, "Experimental Paraplegia in the Sub-Human Primate, the Baboon 'Papio Ursinus'" (paper presented at Twelfth Annual Meeting of the SRS, Hong Kong, October 24-27, 1977).

63. "Program," Thirteenth Annual Meeting of the SRS (Cambridge, MA, September 13-15, 1978).

64. Author's recollection.

65. George Shen et al., "Biomechanical Aspects of Harrington Spinal Instrumentation" (paper presented at Thirteenth Annual Meeting of the SRS, Cambridge, MA, September 13-15, 1978).

66. Erwin, "Broken Harrington Rods."

67. Ensor E. Transfeldt and Edward H. Simmons, "Spinal Cord Monitoring in Experimental Spinal Cord Distraction" (paper presented at Thirteenth Annual Meeting of

the SRS, Cambridge, MA, September 13-15. 1978).

68. John H. Moe et al., "Harrington Instrumentation without Fusion Combined with the Milwaukee Brace for Difficult Scoliosis Problems in Young Children" (paper presented at Thirteenth Annual Meeting of the SRS, Cambridge, MA, September 13-15, 1978).

69. Harold K. Dunn, "Internal Fixation of the Spine—A New Implant System" (paper presented at Thirteenth Annual Meeting of the SRS, Cambridge, MA, September 13-15, 1978).

70. Susan Swank et al., "Treatment of Scoliosis in the Adult" (paper presented at Thirteenth Annual Meeting of the SRS, Cambridge, MA, September 13-15, 1978).

71. Ponder, "Harrington in Adult Idiopathic Scoliosis."

72. Howard H. Ginsburg et al., "Back Pain in Post-Operative Idiopathic Scoliosis: Long Term Follow-up Study" (paper presented al Thirteenth Annual Meeting of the SRS, Cambridge, MA, September 13-15, 1978).

73. Alan Moskowitz et al., "Long Term Follow-up of Scoliosis Fusion, (paper presented at Thirteenth Annual Meeting of the SRS, Cambridge, MA, September 13-15, 1978).

74. Robert Gillespie, V. James Raso, and Gregory M. McNeice, "Computerized Spatial Analysis of the Spine in Idiopathic Scoliosis1' (paper presented at Thirteenth Annual Meeting of the SRS, Cambridge, MA, September 13-15. 1978).

75. Augustus A. White, Manohar Panjabi, and Jeffrey N Hausfeld, "A Systematic Approach lo Clinical Stability in the Thoracic Spine" (paper presented at Thirteenth Annual Meeting of the SRS, Cambridge, MA, September 13-15, 1978).

76. "Program," Fourteenth Annual of the SRS (Seattle, September 11-14, 1979). SRS 5: 6.

77. "Transactions of the Fourteenth Annual Meeting of the SRS, September 12-14. 1979, Seattle," *Orthop Trans* 4 (1980).

78. Author's recollection.

79. Nobumasa Suzuki and Gordon W. D. Armstrong, "Contoured Double Distraction Rods for Correction of Spinal Deformity" (paper presented at Fourteenth Annual Meeting of the SRS, Seattle, September 11-14, 1979).

80. John A. Herring, "Segmental Wiring of the Spine with Harrington Instrumentation and Spinal Fusion—A Report of Twenty-One Consecutive Cases" (paper

presented at Fourteenth Annual Meeting of the SRS, Seattle, September 11–14, 1979).

81. Eduardo R. Luque and Alfredo Cardoso, "Segmental Spinal Instrumentation-in Growing Children" (paper presented at Fourteenth Annual Meeting of the SRS, Seattle, September 11–14, 1979).

82. Gregory M. McNeice et al., "Rod Design Criteria for Instrumentation without Fusion" (paper presented at Fourteenth Annual Meeting of the SRS, Seattle, September 11–14, 1979).

83. James P. O'Brien et al., "Instrumentation without Fusion—A Clinical Experience of Sixteen Cases (paper presented al Fourteenth Annual Meeting of the SRS, Seattle, September 11–14, 1979).

84. Harold K. Dunn, A. U. Daniels, and E. Marlow Goble, "A Comparison of Spinal Bending Stability with Posterior and Anterior Fixation Device" (paper presented at Fourteenth Annual Meeting of the SRS, Seattle, September 11–14, 1979).

85. Edward H. Simmons and Roger P. Jackson, "The Management of Nerve Root Entrapment Syndromes Associated with Collapsing Scoliosis of Idiopathic Lumbar or Thoracolumbar Curves" (paper presented at Fourteenth Annual Meeting of the SRS, Seattle, September 11–14, 1979).

86. David S. Bradford, "Free Anterior Vascular Pedicle Bone Grafting for the Treatment of Kyphosis" (paper presented at Fourteenth Annual Meeting of the SRS, Seattle, September 11–14, 1979).

87. Lyle J. Micheli, John E. Hall, and Harold V. Reese, "Indications for Spinal Instrumentation in the Surgical Management of Spondylolisthesis" (paper presented at Fourteenth Annual Meeting of the SRS, Seattle, September 11–14, 1979).

88. Lyle J. Micheli, John E. Hall, and Henry V. Reese, "Indications for Spinal Instrumentation in the Surgical Management of Spondylolisthesis," *Orthop Trans* 4 (1980): 28.

89. Michael Neuwirth, Ronald L. DeWald, and Rudolph Taddonio, "Staged Reduction and Circumferential Fusion for Spondylolisthesis (paper presented al Fourteenth Annual Meeting of the SRS, Seattle, September 11–14, 1979).

90. Michael Neuwirth, Ronald L. DeWald and Rudolph Taddonio, "Reduction and Staged Circumferential Fusion for Severe Spondylolisthesis in Adolescents and Children," *Orthop Trans* 4 (1980).

91. David S Bradford, "Treatment of Severe Spondylolisthesis—A Combined

Approach for Reduction and Stabilization" (paper presented at Fourteenth Annual Meeting of the SRS, Seattle, September 11–14, 1979).

92. David S. Bradford, "Treatment of Severe Spondylolisthesis—A Combined Approach For Reduction and Stabilization," *Orthop Trans* 4 (1980): 29.

93. Simmons, "The Management of Nerve Root Entrapment Syndromes Associated with Collapsing Scoliosis of Idiopathic Lumbar or Thoracolumbar Curves."

94. University of Kansas, "Scoliosis and Related Spine Deformities Workshop" (unpublished material, 1979). HA 101: 29.

95. Paul R. Harrington, "A Story and a Viewpoint of Clinical Molecular Medicine" (unpublished material, 1980). HA 110: 14.

96. Clyburn, November 6, 2009.

97. "Harrington Distinguished Professorship Letters of Gift" (unpublished material, 1974. 1980), HA 101: 30.

98. John P. O'Brien, letter to Paul R. Harrington, April 30, 1980. HA 122/1: 15.

99. Wieting, March 20, 2008. HA 103/4: 20.

100. Harrington, May 21,1980. HA 144/1: 17.

101. Engen, October 16, 1996. HA 144/1: 14: 38–39.

102. This and the following paragraph are based on the author's recollections.

103. "Program," *Fifteenth Annual Meeting of the SRS* (Chicago, September 17–19, 1980). SRS 6:1.

104. "Program," *Sixteenth Annual Meeting of the SRS* (Montreal, Quebec, Canada. September 16–18, 1981). SRS 6: 2.

105. Doherty, "Complications of Fusion."

106. Denis, "Iatrogenic Loss of Lordosis."

107. M. J. Wasylenko, S. Skinner, and Jacquelin Perry, "Analysis of Posture and Gait Following Spine Fusion with Harrington Instrumentation" (paper presented at Fifteenth Annual Meeting of the SRS, Chicago, September 17–19, 1980).

108. Howard A. King et al., "Selection of Fusion Levels in Thoracic Idiopathic Scoliosis" (paper presented at Fifteenth Annual Meeting of the SRS, Chicago, September 17–19, 1980).

109. King, "The Selection of Fusion Levels in Thoracic Idiopathic Scoliosis."

110. Eduardo R Luque, "Two Stage Vertebrectomy in Severe Deformities of the Spine" (paper presented al Fifteenth Annual Meeting of the SRS, Chicago, September

17-19, 1980).

111. Dennis Wenger et al., "Comparative Mechanics of Segmental Spinal Instrumentation versus Traditional Harrington Instrumentation in Scoliosis Treatment-Laboratory Analysis" (paper presented at Fifteenth Annual Meeting of the SRS, Chicago, September 17-19, 1980).

112. G. Shen et al., "Segmental Spinal Instrumentation (SSI): Mathematical Analysis and Comparative Study" (paper presented at Fifteenth Annual Meeting of the SRS, Chicago, September 17-19, 1980)

113. J Andy Sullivan and Stephen Connor, "Segmental Spinal Instrumentation by Laminar Wires" (paper presented al Fifteenth Annual Meeting of the SRS, Chicago, September 17-19, 1980).

114. Rae R. Jacobs et al., "A New Instrumentation System for Fracturc-Dislocalion of the Dorso-Lumbar Spine" (paper presented at Fifteenth Annual Meeting of the SRS, Chicago, September 17-19, 1980).

115. Denis S Drummond, James S. Keene, and Rajesh G Narcehania, "Studies in Compression Instrumentation" (paper presented at Fifteenth Annual Meeting of the SRS, Chicago, September 17-19, 1980).

116. A. U Daniels and Harold K. Dunn, "Anterior Spine Stabilization-An Implant System" (paper presented at Fifteenth Annual Meeting of the SRS, Chicago, September 17-19, 1980).

117. Luque, "Two Stage Vertebrectomy in Severe Deformities of the Spine," 29.

118. King, "Selection of Fusion Levels in Thoracic Idiopathic Scoliosis," 51.

119. William A. Spencer, "Eulogy for Paul R. Harrington, M.D." (unpublished material, 1980). HA 104: 3,

120. Gordon W. D Armstrong, letter to Mary Alice Harrington, December 19, 1980. HA 104: 16.

121. Edmond J. McDonnell, letter to Mary Alice Harrington, December 7, 1980. HA 104: 16.

122. Sandra Wade Hogan, letter to Mary Alice Harrington, December 5, 1980. HA 104: 15.

123. Ruth and Art Quaintance, letter to Mary Alice Harrington, December 1980. HA 104: 15.

124. Jesse H. Dickson, "Obituary: Paul Randall Harrington. M. D. (1911—

1980)," *J Bone Joint Surg*: *Am* 63(1981). HA 102: 11.

EPILOGUE

1. Yves P. Cotrel and Jean Dubousset,"New Segmental Posterior Instrumentation of the Spine (paper presented at Nineteenth Annual Meeting of the SRS, Orlando. FL, September 19-22, 1984),

2. John P. Kostuik,"Current Concepts Review: Operative Treatment of Idiopathic Scoliosis," *J Bone Joint Surg Am* 72 (1990).

3. Author's recollection.

4. Marinos C. Dalakas et al., A Long-Term Follow-up Study of Patients with Post-poliomyelitis Neuromuscular Symptoms," *N Engl J Med* 314 (1986).

5. Ewen Callawaly,"Polio's Moving Target," *Nature* 496 (2013).

6. Bailey Lipscomb, letter lo Marc A. Asher, August 25, 2005. HA 103/3: 2.

7. Lee Grant, letter to Christopher Crenner, October 1, 2014. HA 103/3: 2.

8. Asher,"Final Program." HHS: LLNB; 123A, 185-200.

INDEX
索 引

(黄宇明 译　郑召民　李明　冯世庆 审校)

译者的话

新冠疫情改变了人们的出行和做事方式，奔忙于临床教学与科研一线的临床医生也悄然刹车，结束疲于奔命的学术交流，节省下大量时间用来休息和陪伴家人。但，对于一个临床医生来说，坚持在线上进行国内国际交流，和同道互相学习启迪的初心始终未变。闲暇之余，我查阅历史上大流行疾病资料，联想到第一个成功研发脊柱侧凸矫形器械的美国学者哈灵顿（1973 年任脊柱侧凸研究学会主席），他的器械研发动力源于第二次世界大战后对美国休斯敦脊髓灰质炎大流行后遗症——脊柱侧凸治疗的大量需求，尽管脊髓灰质炎疫苗的成功研发和接种使得该疾病目前已经基本消失，但当年的大流行及其后遗症给包括美国总统罗斯福等众多家庭造成了极大痛苦。深夜，我与远在美国堪萨斯大学医学中心的王金熙教授聊起脊柱外科的发展，隐约记得 2014 年访问堪萨斯大学医学中心时（图 1），脊柱外科马克·A. 阿舍教授（1997 年任脊柱侧凸研究学会主席）带我参观哈灵顿档案馆时提到在写一本有关哈灵顿的传记，了解到该书 2015 年已出版，随后王教授买了一本寄给我，出于一些原因，将近一个月才收到。通读一遍后，我觉得十分有趣且具有一定的价值，遂联系了国内对此感兴趣的几位脊柱侧凸和脊柱外

图 1　马克·A. 阿舍教授和郑召民教授，堪萨斯大学医学中心。

科同道商议将其译成中文，并尽快出版。杨惠林教授曾于2014年访问并参观哈灵顿档案馆，于是他当即联系了苏州大学出版社，出版社也欣然同意出版。

我们决定翻译本书，遂邀请国内志趣相投的同道组成一个强大的译校团队。王全熙教授十分高兴，帮助解决了本书的翻译合同和有关事宜，让本书能够以中英双语的方式出版。读完本书方知为什么哈灵顿把自己对脊柱侧凸器械的研发历程及脊柱和脊柱侧凸研究的宝贵原始材料给了母校堪萨斯大学医学中心医学历史与哲学系档案馆，而没有放在他工作的休斯敦贝勒医学院。王全熙作为第二任哈灵顿冠名的杰出教授，或许是受哈灵顿的影响，同样表达了对母校的感恩。

由于各种原因，正如本书第9章提到哈灵顿器械相当长一段时间仅在欧美、澳大利亚甚至南非和日本等国家应用，直到改革开放后北京协和医院吴之康教授向戈登·W. D. 阿姆斯特朗（1981年任脊柱侧凸研究学会主席）学习应用哈灵顿棒治疗脊柱侧凸后于1981年在国内率先使用哈灵顿棒，才开启了我国应用哈灵顿器械治疗脊柱侧凸的时代。之后，哈灵顿器械陆续应用于脊柱骨折、脊柱滑脱等脊柱疾病的治疗。见证我国应用哈灵顿内固定器械的一代代医生们已经退出或将要退出职场。1989年，我从河南医科大学（现郑州大学河南医学院）毕业留母校附属医院工作后开始接触哈灵顿器械，工作两年后于1991年跟随许振华教授攻读骨科硕士研究生，第二年跟随老师们进行临床学习。1992年，我主管过一例脊柱侧凸患儿，利用哈灵顿器械进行矫形手术，术后发生截瘫，连夜进入手术室取出哈灵顿棒，进行石膏固定。恩师许振华知道后一大早来病房体察病人、安抚家属，术后病人有发烧，但半年后完全恢复。其间听闻国内一知名教授也有一名术后截瘫未恢复的患者与其产生纠纷，让我对本书提及的“撑开性截瘫”记忆犹新，很长一段时间内，我对这个“魔棒”望而生畏，甚至不愿意涉足脊柱外科尤其脊柱侧凸领域。1994年我在苏州医学院（现苏州大学苏州医学院）攻读博士研究生期间，正值母校大量培训全国脊柱外科医生来推广应用椎弓根螺钉技术，这才再度激起了我对脊柱外科的兴趣。苏州大学苏州医学院是我国第一个介绍应用椎弓根螺钉技术治疗脊柱疾病的医学院，我的博士生导师，现已98岁高龄的董天华教授最早给国内骨科同道介绍“胸腰椎骨折治疗的新概念”时，首次提到椎弓根螺钉的应用，综述发表于《中华骨科杂志》（1987，7：72–74），唐天驷等老师对其进行国产化引进并消化改良，将其应用于脊柱骨折、脊柱滑脱等的治疗。那时唐老师和杨惠林教授像哈灵顿推广哈灵顿棒一样，应邀到全国各地推广椎弓根螺钉技术。2004年，杨惠林教授整理并牵头申报的椎弓根螺钉技术系列研究获得国家科技进步二等奖。1997年，我博士毕业答辩前夕，恰逢留学法国研修脊柱侧凸多年的邱勇教授回国开展工作，在他拜见导师唐天驷教授时，我在母校第一次见到邱勇教授。当时他谈到脊柱侧凸的复杂性和高风险性，让我深感难度之大，所以我毕业后未敢涉足相关领域。2000 年，我赴美国凤凰城跟随托尼·杨等人学习微创脊柱技术，回国后在中山大学附属第二医院工作，在唐老师的支持下，2001 年我翻译出版《微创脊柱外科技术》，开展经皮椎体强化技术（PVP，PKP）研究。2004 年与杨惠林教授翻译《经皮椎体成形术》，推广改进这一有较好临床效果的技术。2017 年，杨惠林教授和我联合，再次获得国家科技进步二等奖。

2003 年，由于前期与香港大学吕维嘉教授和梁智仁院士在合作研发含锶骨水泥通过经皮强化（PVP）治疗脊柱骨折的临床应用的过程中相处愉快，经吕教授推荐并亲自安排，我有机会于2004 年在香港大学跟随陆瓞骥和张文智教授（2017 年任脊柱侧凸研究学会主席）学习脊柱外科，重启了我对脊柱侧凸的兴趣。2005 年初我调入中山大学附属第一医院，这所让我终生难忘、永远感恩的广东乃至华南最好的治疗疑难杂症的医院给我提供了良好的平台。业内皆知脊柱侧凸矫形手术是脊柱手术皇冠上的明珠，而开展研究和手术治疗，需要一个团队，此时我意识到应该组建团队，于是有了动力赴美学习脊柱侧凸。2008 年，我赴美国做 AO 脊柱研修生，首次亲历贝鲁兹·A. 阿克巴尼亚（Behrooz A. Akbarnia）、彼得·牛顿（Peter Newton）、瑟琳娜·胡（Serena Hu）（分别在 2006 年、2019 年、2023 年任脊柱侧凸研究学会主席）等一批脊柱侧凸国际大师的手术。我与于滨生教授合作，进行脊柱骨盆固定研究。多棒内联生物力学和国人髂骨钉道解剖学的研究，于 2009 年获脊柱侧凸研究学会旅行奖学金（GOP Traveling Fellowship），这是中国学者首次获此殊荣，这使我在 2010 年初有机会赴美国特种外科医院（HSS）跟随时任脊柱侧凸研究学会主席的奥赫贝巴·鲍彻-阿德杰（Oheneba Boachie-Adjei）学习。2014 年和 2018 年先后两次受教育部高级访问学者项目资助赴美国参观学习拉里·伦克（Lawrence G. Lenke）（2011 年任脊柱侧凸研究学会主席）脊柱畸形手术。其间 2014 年赴美国迈阿密儿童医院参观哈利·L. 舒弗尔巴格（Harry L. Shufflebarger）（2000 年任脊柱侧凸研究学会主席）脊柱侧凸手术。2014 年也有幸赴堪萨斯大学医学中心参观哈灵顿和脊柱侧凸研究学会档案馆，有机会结识《锲而不舍》一书原著作者阿舍医生，因此今天有缘且有兴趣翻译该著作。

回首当初，难以想象我会对脊柱侧凸领域如此投入，历经十余年打造了一支好的脊柱侧凸治疗团队，作为我院脊柱侧凸多学科诊疗团队（MDT）的召集人和首席专家，先后与海涌、邱勇、吕国华、郝定军、仉建国和李明等教授组织翻译了《脊柱畸形的手术治疗》《儿童脊柱外科学》《脊柱畸形精要》《早发性脊柱侧凸》《脊柱矢状面平衡》《微创脊柱畸形外科学》等脊柱畸形书籍；并被推选为于 2021 年成立的粤港澳大湾区脊柱侧凸畸形联盟的理事长，2023 年当选中国医药教育协会骨科脊柱分会脊柱畸形工作组组长。

虽然1985年后哈灵顿矫形器械用于脊柱侧凸手术世界范围内逐渐被椎弓根螺钉取代，但其研发历程对我们今天脊柱和脊柱侧凸的治疗改进仍有现实意义。他的成功研发及改进临床应用持续近30年，是脊柱外科、骨科乃至医学史上医工结合、成果转化的成功典范。在我国当下鼓励创新、强调成果转化的今天，无疑有着十分重要的借鉴意义。在脊柱外科的发展中，探索脊柱疾病的发病机理，寻找有效的治疗方法，应该学习哈灵顿锲而不舍的精神，敢于试错纠错，实事求是。借鉴历史可以让我们更好地把握和预见未来，少走弯路，做到事半功倍。哈灵顿的成功和他的精神在当下和未来永远激励一代又一代的医务工作者在疾病治疗的创新和探索之路上不断奋进。

今朝的欣欣向荣才是我们需要把握的良辰美景，今天的脊柱外科医生生活在一个幸福的椎弓根钉时代。哈灵顿器械虽然不再应用，但哈灵顿成功研发这一器械的历程和他对临床研究的严谨态度值得借鉴和学习，这也是我们组织国内同道翻译本书的初心和目的。值此第39个教师节来临之际，我将本书献给母校河南医科大学和苏州医学院，也献给已故恩师许振华教授，以及两位90多岁高龄的恩师董天华和唐天驷教授，感恩你们的培养！

郑召民　2023年，广州

THE AUTHOR: MARC A. ASHER, M. D.
原著作者马克·A. 阿舍医学博士简介

Figure 1 ***Marc A. Asher, M. D.***
图1 马克·A. 阿舍，医学博士

Marc Addason Asher, M. D. (Figure 1), the author of "Dogged Persistence", was born on August 15, 1936 to St. John, Kansas (KS) farmer James Manley Asher and high school mathematics teacher Lucile Turner Asher. He graduated from St. John High School in 1954 (Figure 2A), Kansas State University B.S. in 1958, and Kansas University (KU) M.D. in 1962 (Figure 2B). He then served in the United States Public Health Service as a General Medical Officer in KS for two years. He worked as an assistant resident in Surgery at Baltimore City Hospital and then completed his Harvard Combined Orthopaedic Surgery Residency as well as a Research Fellowship at Harvard. His first post in orthopedics was as an Assistant Professor of Orthopedic Surgery at the University of Texas in San Antonio in 1970-71. In 1972 he returned to his alma mater starting as a general orthopedist then sub-specialized in pediatric orthopedics and spine deformity (Figure 2C), rising from Assistant Professor to full professor (1979). In 2003 he was further promoted to University Distinguished Professor, the first surgeon to receive this title in the history of KU. Marc A. Asher, M.D. died February 1, 2019 of heart failure. He willed his body to the Department of Anatomy at the University of Kansas School of Medicine.

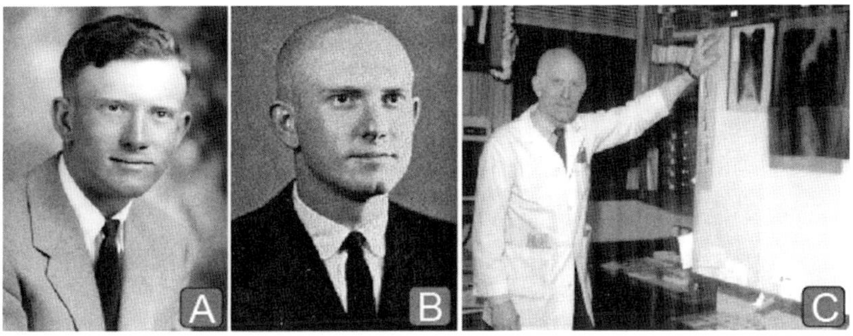

Figure 2 ***A. High school graduation.*** ***B. Medical school graduation.*** ***C. Spine Surgeon at KU Medical Center.***
图 2 A. 高中毕业 B. 医学院毕业 C. 在堪萨斯大学医学中心脊柱外科

《锲而不舍》的作者马克·阿达森·阿舍医学博士（图 1）于 1936 年 8 月 15 日出生在美国堪萨斯州圣约翰市。他的父亲詹姆斯·曼利·阿舍是农场主，母亲露西尔·特纳·阿舍是高中数学老师。他 1954 年毕业于堪萨斯州圣约翰高中（图 2A），1958 年毕业于堪萨斯州立大学，获学士学位，1962 年毕业于堪萨斯大学，获医学博士学位（图 2B）。他在堪萨斯州做了两年的美国公共卫生局医学官员，随后在巴尔的摩市医院做外科助理住院医师，继而在哈佛大学附属医院完成了联合骨外科住院医师临床规范化训练和博士后实验研究。1970—1971 年，他在位于圣安东尼奥的德克萨斯大学骨科任助理教授。1972 年，阿舍博士回到母校堪萨斯大学医学中心骨科工作，从普骨科逐渐专攻小儿骨科和脊柱畸形专科，并从助理教授逐级晋升，于 1979 成为正教授。他于 2003 年晋升为大学杰出教授，是堪萨斯大学建校后第一位获得此职称的外科医生(图 2C)。马克·A. 阿舍医学博士于 2019 年 2 月 1 日逝于心力衰竭。按照他的遗嘱，他的遗体被捐赠给了堪萨斯大学医学院的解剖学系。

In clinical practice, Dr. Asher not only provided high quality care to his patients at KU Medical Center but also established a network of clinics across the state, bringing specialized orthopedic care to children in far rural areas of Kansas. To recognize his outstanding contributions, the State of Kansas honored him with the Distinguished Kansan of the Year in 2007 and KU Hospital established the Marc A. Asher, MD, Comprehensive Spine Center in 2008. Dr. Asher edited the first edition of Orthopaedic Knowledge Update for the American Academy of Orthopaedic Surgeons (AAOS) and participated in the development of the Isola Spinal Instrumentation System, which was available from 1989 through 2011 as one of the world's leading spine implant systems. He was the 28th president of the Scoliosis Research Society (SRS) in 1997 and received the

Lifetime Achievement Award from the Pediatric Orthopaedic Society of North America in 2004 and from the SRS in 2009.

在临床工作中，阿舍博士不仅在堪萨斯大学医疗中心为患者提供高质量的医疗服务，而且还在全州建立了诊所网络，为堪萨斯州偏僻地区的儿童提供骨病专科服务。为了表彰他的杰出贡献，堪萨斯州政府在2007年授予他年度杰出堪萨斯人奖，堪萨斯大学医院2008年创建了马克·A·阿舍医学博士综合脊柱中心。阿舍博士为美国骨科医师学会主编了第一版《骨科知识更新》并参与开发Isola脊柱器械系统，该系统在1989年至2011年期间是世界领先的脊柱内固定系统之一。他于1997年担任脊柱侧凸研究学会第二十八任主席，并获得北美小儿骨科学会(2004年)和脊柱侧凸研究学会(2009年)颁发的终身成就奖。

In 1971 Dr. Asher met Dr. Paul Harrington, a Kansas native, KU graduate, and originator of the world's first successful spinal implant system. Their close relationship remained until Harrington's death in 1980. Dr. Harrington created the Mary Alice and Paul R. Harrington, M. D., Distinguished Professorship at KU and willed his archives to KU Medical Center. Dr Asher worked diligently and persistently with the Archives' administrators for development of the Harrington Archives (opened in 1986) and on fundraising for the Harrington Professorship, leading to the investiture of H. Clarke Anderson, MD, Professor of Bone Pathology and Chairman of the Pathology Department at KU Medical Center as the first Harrington Distinguished Professor in 1990.

1971年，阿舍博士首次与他的堪萨斯同乡，堪萨斯大学校友及世界首位脊柱内固定系统的奠基者哈灵顿博士会面，此后一直保持密切关系，直至哈灵顿于1980年逝世。哈灵顿博士在堪萨斯大学设立了玛丽·艾丽斯和保罗·哈灵顿杰出教授职位并将自己的技术资料留给了堪萨斯大学医学中心的档案馆。阿舍博士与档案馆的管理者一起辛勤筹备，使哈灵顿档案馆于1986年正式开放。他坚持不懈地为哈灵顿冠名教授职位募集资金，获得充足资金后于1990年任命堪萨斯大学医学中心骨病理学教授兼病理科主任、H. 克拉克·安德森医学博士为首任哈灵顿杰出教授。

In early 2005 I was recruited as the designated heir of the Harrington Distinguished Professor (official investiture in 2011). My major mission for the first year was to work with Dr. Asher and establish a new research laboratory named "Harrington Laboratory for Molecular Orthopedics" to reflect Dr. and Mrs. Harrington's wish. Dr. Asher was so excited about the new lab. In March 2005, a moving truck carrying research instruments from my previous lab at Harvard arrived at KU Medical Center one day following his neck surgery. Surprisingly, he appeared in the new lab with a wound drain in his neck and a draining bag in his hand while we transferred research instruments from the moving boxes to the benches. My colleagues and I were moved to tears, but no one was able to persuade him to go back to his hospital bed until the work was done. He said, "I wanted to witness this exciting event that I had waited on for so many years." He joined lab meetings whenever available, donated his subscriptions of Science, Nature, and New England Journal of Medicine to the lab, and brought many visitors to the lab, including Professor Jesse Dickson who was Dr. Paul Harington's successor and SRS 1990 President (Figure 3).

Figure 3 ***Left*: *Jinxi Wang*, *Middle*: *Jesse Dickson*, *Right*: *Marc Asher*, *at the Harrington Laboratory.***
图 3　左：王金熙，中：杰西·迪克森，右：马克·阿舍在哈灵顿实验室

2005 年初，我被聘为哈灵顿杰出教授的指定继承人（2011 年正式就职）。我第一年的主要任务是与阿舍博士合作建立一个新的实验室，命名为"哈灵顿分子骨科实验室"，以表达哈灵顿夫妇的愿望。阿舍博士对新实验室充满了期待。2005 年 3 月，在他接受颈部手术后的第一天，从我之前在哈佛大学附属医院的实验室运送仪器设备的搬运卡车抵达了堪萨斯大学医学中心。出乎意料的是，当我们把研究仪器从搬运箱转移到实验室工作台上时，他脖子上插着伤口引流管，手里拿着引流袋，出现在新实验室里。大家感动得热泪盈眶，但没有人能够说服他回到病床上，直到工作结束。他说："我想见证这一等待了很多年的激动人心的事件。"他只要有空就参加实验室的会议，把自己订阅的《科学》《自然》和《新英格兰医学杂志》捐给实验室，还把许多来访者带到实验室，其中包括保罗·哈灵顿博士的继任者杰西·迪克森教授（1990 年任脊柱侧凸研究学会主席）（图 3）。

Following his retirement in 2008, Dr. Asher continued to publish research papers, deliver academic lectures (Figure 4) as a University Distinguished Professorship Emeritus, and participate in philanthropic activities as a Life Trustee of the KU Endowment Association (KUEA). He was on the top Roll of Honor of the 2013 KUEA Annual Report for cumulative giving of $5 million or more. He published Dr. Harrington's biography "Dogged Persistence" in 2015. He enthusiastically helped the expansion of the Harrington Laboratory from 3 sections to 5 sections and supported the development of the KU Musculoskeletal Research Institute. He continued to attend KU Musculoskeletal Seminar Series despite his weakening health condition in 2018. Dr. Marc Asher has proven to have as much "dogged persistence" as Dr. Paul Harrington. His lifelong selfless devotion to orthopedic surgery and research will be remembered forever.

Figure 4 ***Marc Asher, MD, delivering research lecture.***
图 4　马克·阿舍医学博士在发表学术演讲

2008 年退休后，阿舍博士作为荣休大学杰出教授继续发表研究论文和学术演讲（图 4），并作为堪萨斯大学基金会（KUEA）的终身受托人继续参与慈善捐赠活动。在 2013 年堪萨斯大学基金会年度报告中，他因累计捐赠超过 500 万美元而荣登最高荣誉榜。他于 2015 年出版了哈灵顿博士的传记《锲而不舍》。他热情帮助哈灵顿实验室的扩建（从 3 个组扩大到 5 个组）和支持堪萨斯大学肌肉骨骼研究所的发展。2018 年，尽管他的身体日渐衰弱，但他仍继续参加堪萨斯大学肌肉骨骼系列讲座。马克·阿舍博士与保罗·哈灵顿博士一样具有“锲而不舍”的精神。他毕生对骨科临床工作和研究的无私奉献将被永远铭记。

Acknowledgments: I thank Elinor Asher (Dr. Asher's wife), Janet Asher Vreeland (Dr. Asher's daughter), Douglas Burton, MD (Professor of KU Orthopedics), and Nell Lucas (KU Endowment Association) for providing Dr. Asher's personal information and reviewing this document.

答谢:感谢阿舍博士的夫人埃莉·阿舍和他的女儿珍妮特·阿舍·弗里兰,道格拉斯·伯顿医学博士(堪萨斯大学骨科教授),以及莽尔·卢克斯(堪萨斯大学捐赠基金会)提供阿舍博士的个人资料并审阅本文。

Jinxi Wang, MD, PhD
王金熙,医学博士,哲学博士
Harrington Distinguished Professor of Orthopedic Surgery, University of Kansas School of Medicine
堪萨斯大学医学院骨科哈灵顿杰出教授
September 2023, Kansas City
2023 年 9 月于堪萨斯城